The United States and Morocco 1776-1956

by

Luella J. Hall

The Scarecrow Press, Inc.
Metuchen, N. J. 1971

ISBN 0-8108-0338-0
Library of Congress Catalog Card Number: 71-142233

To My Mother

Preface

Almost a thousand years elapsed after the founding of the small independent tribal state of Morocco by the Idrisid dynasty in 788 before the nascent republic of the United States contemplated entering into self-protecting treaty relations with the (now decadent) Sherifian Empire in 1776. During the intervening ten centuries, Morocco had twice expanded into large empires, including at her greatest extent most of the Iberian peninsula and all of North Africa to the western border of Egypt. She had achieved and was maintaining a high level of civilization during the period when most of western Europe was suffering the blight known as the Dark Ages. These years of glorious achievement were followed by internal disintegration, invasions from Arabia and Europe, and continuous decay. Morocco had maintained her entity, but at the expense of degradation to the status of a pirate state, the least powerful of the North African Barbary States.

The practice of piracy brought the far distant United States into the arena with European countries in opposition to the Barbary States. From 1776 until Morocco's escape from European imperialism and attainment of independence in 1956, the United States was intimately associated with the powers of Europe contending for hegemony over Morocco. Consistently and firmly, the United States used treaty rights obtained in 1787, in 1880, and at Algeciras in 1907 to brake the onward course of European conquest.

It is surprising that the part played by the United States in Morocco since 1776 has been almost entirely neglected in both American history and in the innumerable volumes written by English, German, French, Spanish, and other European historians. No study has hitherto been made of American-Moroccan relations as a whole, although some episodes have been publicized. As a domestic problem, the unpublished consular dispatches in the National Archives reveal a sordid story of the inefficiency, ignorance, corruption, and immoral conduct of many of the American consuls serving before and during the 20th century. This record is not redeemed by that of the State Department, whose actions during that time may be characterized as inefficient, negligent and frequently parsimonious.

In foreign affairs, it is probable that the United States has had more important relations with Morocco than with any other minor country. Morocco has been a proving ground for what used to be the two major American foreign policies, the Monroe Doctrine and the Open Door. In Morocco the inherited Anglo-American antagonism manifested itself. The Moroccan problem has engaged the study of some of the greatest American statesmen, including Washington, Jefferson, Franklin, John Adams, John Quincy Adams, Seward, Lincoln, and the two Roosevelts. It was in relation to Morocco that Theodore Roosevelt first declared and implemented his second corollary to the Monroe Doctrine. Franklin Roosevelt used Morocco as his locale for the defeat of the Nazi-Pétain stranglehold on France. In Morocco the United States fought unceasingly for the Open Door from her first treaty in 1787 until she gave up that treaty in 1956 to aid the newly independent country.

Finally, in relation to Moroccan diplomatic history in general, the role of the United States needs to be revealed in its true perspective vis-à-vis that of the European powers, without either over-emphasis or diminution of its importance. This book aims to begin that task of historiography. The still existing need for this is illustrated by a book written by a noted British expert on North African affairs and published in 1966. That book has three index references to the United States for the period of this study, containing a total of 121 words. In addition, his list of countries attending the Algeciras Conference omits even the name of the United States!

For the writing of this book I wish to acknowledge many helpful services from the librarians of Stanford University and of the Hoover Institution on War, Revolution, and Peace, where both primary and secondary materials were extensively used. To the staffs of the Department of State Annex, the National Archives, and the Library of Congress I am grateful for courtesy and helpfulness far beyond the call of duty. I owe a special debt to several people in Washington, D. C. for their personal interest and help in solving my problems: the late Dr. E. T. Parks, Head of the Historical Division of the Department of State and his successor, Dr. Arthur G. Kogan; the late Dr. Carl L. Lokke, Chief of the Foreign Affairs Branch of the National Archives; and Mrs. Judy Carroll, head of his office staff. In Palo Alto, California, two personal friends have aided my project from its inception. Mr. Bruce Bliven has offered unfailing encouragement and general information and advice and I am especially grateful to Dr. Graham H. Stuart, Professor Emeritus of Stanford University and a well-known writer on Moroccan subjects, for his reading of the entire manuscript and his many suggestions and criticisms.

Luella J. Hall

Seal Beach, California
December 31, 1969

Contents

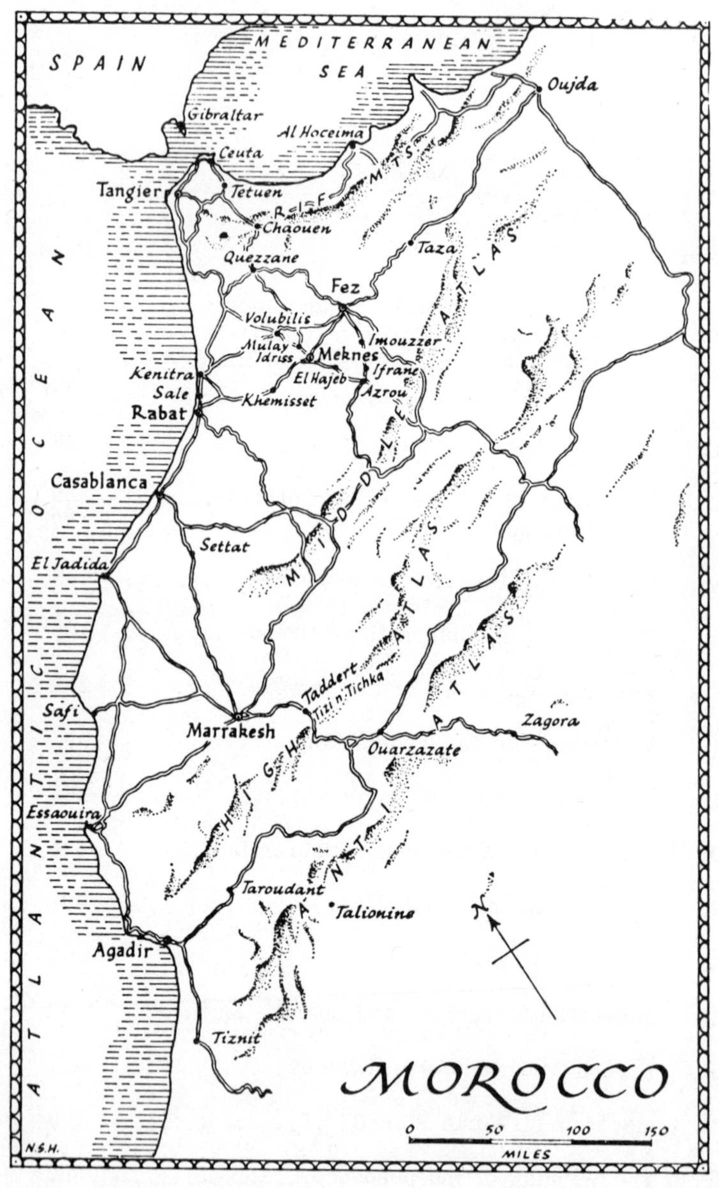

From Robin Bryans, Morocco, Land of the Farthest West, first published by Faber and Faber, London, (1965).

Chapter I

The Evolution of the Sherifian Empire (788-1790)

Northwest Africa includes the trio of modern states known as Morocco, Algeria, and Tunisia. In ancient and medieval times these countries were not clearly differentiated, for their boundaries were shifting and undefined. The Arabs called the whole area Djerira-al-Maghreb, or "Island of the West," commonly shortened to the Maghreb. Morocco was appropriately designated Maghreb-al-Aksa, or the "Farthest West." Europeans sometimes referred to the entire region as Africa Minor. As Roman provinces, the western Mediterranean shoreline controlled by the legions was named Mauritania Tingitana, with Tingis (Tangier) as its capital. The area approximating the present Tunisia was Africa, or Ifriqiya in Arabic. During the period of pirate hegemony, the littoral from Salé to eastern Libya was called the Barbary Coast, and the Barbary States included Tripoli, which was a base of the sea rovers. The southern boundary of the Maghreb has been both variable and indefinite, but most of the Sahara should be embraced in the Maghreb, for the Saharan peoples are similar in race, language, religion, and way of life to the desert dwellers north of them.

By location and history Northwest Africa belongs to three continents--Europe and Asia as well as Africa. The Mediterranean both separates and unites Africa and Europe. All the Maghreb has been subject to European commerce and conquest during most of its history. Morocco, however, has been aptly described as "an unattached fragment of the European continent," for it has had particularly close historical relations with Gibraltar and Spain, and is geographically part of the Atlantic community. Morocco is relatively isolated by the Atlas Mountains and the desert from her sister states, and until the fifth century A. D. had European affiliations only with Rome. During the eighteenth and nineteenth centuries, Morocco stayed aloof from the economic and political progress of Western Europe and remained medieval in economy and feudal in government. The Maghreb has had many connections with Asia, such as colonization by

Phoenicians, conquest by Arabic population and culture, inclusion in the original Islamic Empire, and, excepting Morocco, membership in the Ottoman Empire. All Northwest Africa is predominantly Muslim, but Morocco adhered to the Islamic Empire centered in the Near East for only one generation, and thereafter, under every dynasty, sought to create and maintain a "Western Islam."

The earliest known inhabitants of the Maghreb, the Berbers, are usually classified with the Egyptians as Hamites. There are several theories about their racial background, but they were probably a mixture of the aboriginal Gaetulians and Libyans with the Indo-European Medes, Persians, and Armenians who migrated to North Africa from Europe. The Berbers are of Caucasian stock, as are also the principal invaders of the region, the Arabs. Unlike many aborigines, the Berbers were neither exterminated[1] nor assimilated, and they remain today the major ingredient of the North African peoples. When the great waves of invading Arabs poured into the Maghreb, their numbers declined as they pushed westward, and consequently Morocco has the largest proportion of Berbers. Throughout history, the Moroccans have manifested most strongly the characteristic Berber traits--individualism, aggressiveness, isolationism, and opposition to authority.

Several other elements have entered into the composition of the Moroccan people. In ancient times Morocco underwent successive invasions by Phoenicians, Romans, Vandals, and Byzantines. More numerous and more permanent contributions to the population were made in the medieval period by the Arabs and in the modern era by the Portuguese, Spanish, French, Italians, and Maltese. The predominant ethnological strain has remained Caucasian--the Berbers (Hamites), the Arabs and Jews (Semites), and the Europeans. There has been, however, some mingling of racial strains, especially between Arabs and Berbers and between Moroccans and Negroes (both Berbers and Arabs imported Negro slaves from south of the Sahara). Little inclination to combine with groups outside their own has been shown by the Jews and the Europeans. The latter, of several nationalities, were brought in as captured Christian slaves during pirate days, but from the fifteenth century onward they entered as invaders and colonizers. 1

Of this mixed population, chiefly Berber, the large majority now speak Arabic, the official language of Morocco.

Next in number are those who speak only various Berber dialects. There are but three main divisions of Berbers--the Mamsuda (including the Chomara), the Zenata, and the Sanhaja--but there are numerous sub-tribes. The Berber dialects are oral only; there is no written Berber language.

With the Arab invasion, the Berbers retired or were driven into southern Morocco, the Sus, and into the Atlas Mountain valleys and the deserts south of them. The Arabs, Jews, and Europeans settled chiefly in the coastal towns and the adjacent lowlands, but many Arabs and some Jews were to be found in rural districts of the interior.

Before the French occupation in the twentieth century, Morocco was divided politically into two parts, the _blad al maghzen_, near the towns, whose inhabitants acknowledged the central authority, and the _blad es siba_, the territory of the rebellious tribes.

The Arab-Berber division extends to both religion and government. Nominally, the Berbers are Muslims, and their present-day religion shows no traces of early Jewish and Christian conversions. But the Berbers retain much of their primitive paganism and superstitions and maintain many pristine social customs at variance with Muslim practices.[2] In government the Berbers tended toward democracy in their tribal assemblies. Both Arab and Berber rulers of Morocco, however, strove to impose autocracy upon both the democratic Berbers and the Arabs, who honored as an aristocracy the sherifs, alleged descendants of the Prophet.

In the Maghreb, Morocco is the most fortunate country. It has the most strategic location and most fertile soil; it enjoys an abundance of natural resources and the best of climates. The country comprises about 172,104 square miles, and lies wholly within the temperate zone between 28 and 36 degrees north latitude and 2 to 11 degrees west longitude. Shaped like an irregular quadrilaterial, it measures 620 miles on the Atlantic coast, 290 miles along the Strait of Gibraltar and the Mediterranean, 310 miles on the Algerian frontier, and 680 miles on the Sahara border. There are no natural boundaries, and the political boundaries have varied greatly under the several dynasties and are still unsatisfactory to contemporary expansionists.[3]

Physically, Morocco resembles California in many respects; they have been called "Geographic Look-Alikes."[4] While the latter, with an area of 158,693 square miles, is smaller than Morocco, its rapidly growing population surpasses that of Morocco, which the census of 1960 reported to be 11,598,070.[5] California is farther north, extending from approximately 33 degrees to 42 degrees north latitude. If the map of Morocco is placed so that the Atlantic-Mediterranean coastline forms a western boundary, there is a marked likeness to the Pacific coast of California. The three Atlas ranges are analogous to the Sierra Nevada range of California, and in both regions the mountain chains form a barrier against the hot winds and storms from the deserts farther east. Approaching close to the coast, the mountains and rugged hills of Mediterranean Morocco are much like the Coast Ranges of northern California. The Moroccan mountains contribute to the isolation and impregnability of their valley dwellers; the Sierra Nevada range was for a long period a formidable barrier to migration from east to west. Morocco lacks topographical features comparable to the Great Central Valley of California and to the Coast Ranges from south of San Francisco to the Mexican border. Noted alike for a pleasant sub-tropical climate, both California and Morocco suffer from extremes of winter cold in the north and in the mountains and of summer heat in the southern plains and the eastern deserts. In both places strong ocean gales occur. Morocco has no harbor comparable to those of San Francisco and San Diego, but aside from these, California as well as Morocco has a scarcity of good natural harbors. Both regions have fertile soil in valleys and coastal plains productive of many varieties of vegetables, grains, and fruits, and grazing lands unexcelled for raising cattle, sheep, and horses-- and in Morocco, goats, donkeys, and camels also. Mineral resources are abundant, although those of Morocco are but slightly developed--there having been no Gold Rush in the Atlas ranges --and the oil wells in Algeria are located to the east. Another parallel is seasonal precipitation; winter is the period for rain and snow. Both regions suffer from periodical drouths which cause especially great losses in the less developed Morocco.[6] Earthquakes have been more frequent in California, but in that state there has not yet been one as destructive as that in Agadir. Finally, the Far West of the United States and of Africa are meccas for tourists because of their scenery and climate.

Into this favorable environment enjoyed by the indigenous Berbers came the pioneer colonizers, the Phoenicians, establishing trading posts along the western coasts of the Mediterranean. After the conquest of Phoenicia by Assyria, the migrating Phoenicians established their new capital at Carthage, which became the center of a wealthy and powerful commercial empire. The Carthaginians were sailors, merchants, and miners, not settlers, and they made profitable use of the native wealth of the Maghreb by peaceable trade with the natives. They founded trading settlements along the Barbary Coast and in Spain; among the most important ones were Tangier (about 579 B. C.), Malaga, Cartagena, and Barcelona. They conquered Sardinia, Malta, and Corsica and enlisted the famous native slingers of the Balearic Isles in their army. Their galleys explored the African coast to Guinea, and they probably engaged in tin commerce with Britain, as the earlier Phoenicians had done. Carthage checked the expansion of the Greek city states in Sicily, but was vanquished in the Punic Wars (264 to 146 B. C.) by a more powerful rival, Rome. The Berber population probably absorbed the Carthaginians remaining in the Maghreb. Punic civilization had been naturalized in the more developed Berber territory, and the Punic language survived in some parts among the upper classes for 600 years after Roman rule began. As near to Arabic as Spanish is to French, the Punic language may have paved the way for the later triumph of Arabic culture in the Maghreb.[7]

During the six centuries of Roman occupation, the Maghreb, as well as Cyrenaica and Egypt, shared in the material and intellectual civilization promoted by the Roman administration. Only the narrow seacoast area along the Mediterranean and the peninsula abutting on the Strait of Gibraltar were included in Roman territory, however, for, like the Carthaginians, the Roman did not penetrate far into the interior. About 42 A. D., the Emperor Claudius established Mauretania Tingitana as a colony with a southern boundary passing a few kilometers south of Rabat and a little to the south of Meknes and Fez. Tangier was the administrative capital and chief site of export for supplies to Rome. From Tangier the Romans built excellent roads to Salé along the coast and to Volubilis in the interior. A new Carthage was built upon the site of the one destroyed in 146 B. C., but it was a city of Romans. Throughout the Roman period and the following two centuries under Byzantine and Vandal rule, the center of power remained in the revived city of Carthage. The Romans renamed this province in the eastern Maghreb "North Africa," or Ifriqiya in Arabic. Mauretania, on the western periphery of the empire, was much less important but it shared in the general progress.

Today travelers admire and marvel at the magnificent remains of Roman cities from Cyrene in Libya to Volubilis in Morocco and the nearby roads, dams, and country houses, all constructed by the master builders and engineers of Rome. The Romans also greatly improved agriculture and forestry, already highly developed under Carthaginian auspices.

Emperor Diocletian evacuated the southern portion of Mauretania in 285 A. D. and made the rest a part of the Spanish diocese. Christianity was introduced into the Maghreb in the third century A. D., and four bishoprics were later established there. St. Augustine, Bishop of Hippo, was one of the great Church Fathers. His opponents described him as "Punic," and it is noteworthy that Septimus Severus, born near Leptis Magna in 146 A. D., was probably of Punic descent. Although there were some native leaders, there is no clear evidence of the extent to which the Berbers assimilated Roman culture. Many authorities believe, however, that the Berber masses in the Roman era were Christianized.[8]

After the Roman legions withdrew from the Maghreb to fight the German tribes invading from the north, there was an interlude of two centuries of little significance in North Africa. Leading the Vandals across the Strait of Gibraltar in 429, Gaiseric devastated the whole coast of the Maghreb and set up a kingdom in the former center of the Carthaginian Empire, ceded to him by the Roman Emperor in 439. This conquest was made by about 80,000 warriors, whose chief exploits were the capture of the capital and naval base in 439 and the sack of Rome in 455. The Vandals struck a fatal blow to the declining economy of Rome by pirating her ships, raiding the Mediterranean coast cities, and withholding taxes and grain of North

Africa. In 534, Belisarius, the great Byzantine general, conquered the Vandal kingdom, but he was unable to put down the ensuing Berber revolt until 548. The Vandals disappeared from history, to be replaced by a number of Christian Berber kingdoms in the Maghreb. Belisarius controlled effectively only eastern Algeria, but Byzantine commerce and culture extended as far south as Volubilis. Eventually Byzantine rule was confined to Ceuta. At this time probably only a majority of the natives of the Maghreb had adopted Judaism or Christianity.[9]

Before the end of the eighth century Morocco was developing a personality distinct from the rest of the Maghreb, which has been maintained to the present, although during the intervening centuries two Moroccan empires included large areas in Northwest Africa and Spain. Beginning in the seventh century, the first Arab invasion brought all northern Africa, from Egypt to the Atlantic coast, into the Muslim Empire, which was founded by the successors of Muhammad under the Omayyad Caliphate reigning at Damascus (661-750). Despite strong resistance to the new imperialism, the Berbers eventually had to submit to the Arabs and accept the dominance of Islam and the Arabic language. During the eleven and a half centuries since the state of Morocco was founded, the Berber-Arabic rivalry has continued. Of the six dynasties ruling since the Arab conquest, three of the most powerful have been Berber, the founders of which, paradoxically, usurped and wielded power as fanatical champions of their last adopted faith.

In 682 the Arab general, Okba ben Nafi, captured Ceuta. He then pushed southward into the Sus. Okba and his army came primarily as missionaries for Islam, which made rapid progress among the Berbers. But when the Arab hordes returned in 707 under Mousa ben Noceir, all of Morocco was subjected to both military and religious conquest. From the northern shore the invaders proceeded victoriously through the Sus, the Draa, and Tafilalt, receiving the submission of the great Berber tribes. From Tangier, taken in 710, and also from Tetuan and Arzila, most of the Christians fled into Spain. Of Tangier, then the most important town in the west, the Arab historian Al Makkari, writes: "They say that Tangier had never been taken by an enemy before the days of Mousa, and, once in the hands of the Muslims, it became one of their strongest citadels."[10]

Led by Tarik ibn Zaid en-Nafisi, the Muslims soon achieved a much greater triumph. With one hundred horsemen and the same number of footsoldiers (Muslimized Berbers), he crossed the Straits in 710, overran Visigothic Spain, and returned laden with spoils. This easy victory was possible because the Visigothic kingdom was rent by dissension among the nobles, estrangement of the persecuted Jews, and indiffierence of the enslaved lower classes. This exploit is commemorated by the names of the rocks bordering the Strait--Jabel Tarik (Gibraltar) near Algeciras and Jebel Mousa on the Moroccan coast. In 711 Tarik returned with a large army, and in 712 Mousa followed with another, both containing a majority of Berber soldiers. The Muslim forces conquered the whole Iberian Peninsula, except the mountains of the Asturias, and invaded France as far as Tours, where they were halted by Charles Martel in 732. It was not until 759, however, that the Muslims were expelled entirely from France.[11]

At first the Iberian Peninsula was combined with Morocco in the province of Maghreb, with the capital at Qairawan. The Omyyad Caliph was represented by a governor, and the peninsula was under a sub-prefect. Gradually the propaganda for Islam won over many Christians, who converted their churches into mosques. This religious conversion continued under the next Islamic dynasty, the Abbasid Caliphate (750-1259), but this government never controlled either Spain or Morocco politically.[12]

Both in Spain and in Morocco the Berbers rebelled against their Arab overlords. The Spanish Arabs required large reinforcements from Syria and Egypt to put down the uprising. The Berbers in the peninsula retained a jealous hatred of the Arabs because of the latter's appropriation of most of the booty, the government, and the fertile lands. The conquest of Morocco was achieved only after seventy years of murderous warfare, after which the Berbers submitted under a pledge of brotherhood-which the Arabs did not keep. The Arab-Berber enmity lasted in Spain until the eleventh century.[13]

Tunisia had withdrawn from the declining Omyyad Caliphate in 745, and Spain became the second part to secede from the vast Islamic empire. Under independent Muslim rulers, Spain enjoyed the Golden Age of her history. The founder of the new government was Abd er-Rahman. Escaping from the general massacre of the Omyyad house, he made his way across North Africa from Egypt, and, after wandering five years among the Berbers, he finally reached Morocco. Crossing over the Strait to Spain--the Arabic Andalus, hence Andalusia--he made himself head of the amirate of Cordova in 756. Before his death in 788, Abd er-Rahman had laid a strong foundation upon which his successors built the most glorious civilization of the medieval era. He curbed the unruly Arab chieftains, suppressed disorders, tolerated Jews and Christians, and adorned his capital city. Although there were lapses from his able and benevolent rule, the amirate of Cordova became an "enlightened, erudite, and knightly kingdom at a time when the Christian peoples of the West were little better than ignorant and boorish savages."

The height of power and magnificence was attained by Cordova under Abd er-Rahman III (912-961). All Andalusia enjoyed the beauty, learning, peace, and prosperity of his reign. Agriculture and industry were highly developed. The craftsmen were world-famous, and distinguished scholars, historians, doctors, astronomers, and artists flocked to Cordova. To protect this idyllic existence, Abd er-Rahman found it necessary to maintain a large fleet and efficient army, composed chiefly of foreign mercenaries.[14] In the last years of the Caliphate the Moroccan rulers owed allegiance to Cordova, and the influx of Andalusian culture to Morocco began, to be accelerated later. Another current of Muslim culture flowed northward into the Christian kingdoms expanding in power and territory southward from the Asturias. The Arabized Christians introduced the Arabic language and Muslim science and learning which were thereafter available to European scholars.[15]

The merging Christian states in the north of the Iberian Peninsula attacked Andalusia relentlessly, and the last Muslim rulers were puppets unable to cope with rival factions and rebellious mercenaries. After the sack of Cordova by Berbers in 1010, Muslim rule in Andalusia rapidly declined. The Caliphate of Cordova was divided into many small kingdoms and independent cities, and half the Muslim princes in Andalusia paid tribute to the ruler of Christian Castile-Leon.[16] The time was propitious for a second invasion of the peninsula by Moroccan Berbers.

Coincidentally with the rise of the Amirates of Cordova, Morocco had been attaining independence. Its founder was Mulai Idris ben Abdallah, a descendant of the Prophet's daughter, Fatima, and hence a sherif. Defeated in a battle with the Abbasid Caliph, he too wandered across North Africa as a fugitive, arriving finally at Volubilis. Honoring his ancestry, the Muslims there made him their ruler in 788. The neighboring Berber tribes supported him also, even though most of them were not Muslims. Thus the Berbers gained the moral advantage of acknowledging Muhammad's direct descendant as a legitimate caliph. Henceforth, Morocco was actually independent of the Abbasid Caliphate.

The original Morocco extended only to what was later known as the Kingdom of Fez, although Tlemcen was included temporarily. In a jahad, or holy war, several more provinces were annexed, including the city of Salé. After a reign of only three years Idris was poisoned, supposedly by an emissary of the Abbasid Caliph, Harun er-Rashid. His son, Mulai Idris II, founded Fez, the future dynastic capital, and extended his dominion over Berber tribes in the north. The Idrisids ruled until 985, and were followed by the insignificant Miknasa and Magwara lines. Because of dynastic dissensions, sectional rule of the disintegrating kingdom, a severe attack by the Abbasid Caliph, and the invasion of the destructive Hilali, the rulers after the first two Idrisids were without distinction. Aside from the establishment of independence, the chief contributions of the Idrisid dynasty were the founding of Fez, later the intellectual and commercial center of Morocco, and the founder's tomb at Mulai Idris, a shrine for Muslim pilgrims to the present day.[17]

The Arabs in Morocco remained a small minority until the middle of the eleventh century, when tribes began entering from the east. This great migration consisted of from 150,000 to 200,000 Arabs, the Beni Hilali and the

Beni Soleim. Expelled from Arabia into upper Egypt, they had been encouraged by the Fatamid Caliph of Egypt to go to the west, which he presented to them. These tribes settled in the plains, where they remained, pushing most of the Berbers into the foothills and mountain valleys. The Berber word Tahilalt, or "the place of the Hilali," has been corrupted to Tafilalt. The new immigrants were Bedouins, marauding nomads, who systematically pillaged every village and destroyed the buildings, aqueducts, dams, cisterns, and bridges built by the Romans. Lands formerly irrigated returned to the desert, and the water problem was aggravated by the destruction of great expanses of forest. Thus Morocco suffered a devastation from which she has never fully recovered.[18]

The anarchy and disintegration of Morocco afforded the opportunity for the establishment of the first Berber dynasty, the Almoravids or Murabtis (1061-1149).[19] Two powerful Berber clans were rivals for control over the decadent kingdom. The Zenata, driven by their opponents, invaded Morocco by the Taza corridor, but they succeeded only in founding a number of principalities. The other tribe, the Sanhaja, true nomads from the western Sahara, was destined to consolidate Morocco. Converted in the ninth century by a religious zealot to the austere Islamic cult of Malikism, and inspired by religious fantaticism and a lust for booty, they swept from their fortified convents across the desert and occupied the Draa, the Tafilalt, the Sus, and the Tadla regions between 1055 and 1059. Usurping the place of the original leader, Youssef ben Tashfin (1061-1106) set up the new dynasty. He is noted as the founder of Marrakesh and the builder of a mosque at Sur al Khair. After two attempts, he took over Fez with great slaughter, but he later built up and improved the city. The capture of Tangier and Ceuta completed his conquest of Morocco. By the addition of Algeria and Oran he expanded his domain almost to Algiers and made Morocco a true empire.[20]

The second conquest of the Iberian Peninsula was made by the Almoravids. They came by invitation of the Muslim amirs of Andalusia, who summoned them to aid against the growing power of King Alfonso VI of Leon. Youssef led his fierce Berber army to complete victory over the Christian ruler in 1087, killing thousands of Christians. Another expedition to the Iberian Peninsula in 1088 was unsuccessful, but after two years of preparation, a third invasion resulted in Youssef's subjugation of Arabs, Berbers, and Christians alike. Before the end of the eleventh century the Moors lost most of Portugal, but eventually the Almoravids were masters of the rest of the Iberian Peninsula. Youssef tacitly acknowledged the Abbasid Caliphate at Bagdad, but he was actually independent and was addressed as Amir al Mumnin--a title of the Caliphs.[21] Of the five Almoravid monarchs, only the first was an eminent ruler. The successors of Youssef encountered rebellions in both Andalusia and Morocco. In the former, the Iberian Crusades by Christian knights against the Muslims weakened Muslim power.[22]

The prime importance of the Almoravid period is that Morocco became a bridge between eastern and western Islam. From the East came scholars, merchants, and craftsmen, while from the Iberian Peninsula there was a steady migration of political and religious refugees and fugitives from justice, including both agriculturists and scholars. Fez, for example, received from Qairawan and Andalusia thousands of families whose descendants formed the most intellectual class in Morocco. Under this dynasty also, Morocco gained great wealth by trade with the kingdom of Ghana (Guinea), whereby salt was exchanged at Tafilalt for the gold of the Sudan. The ruler Ali ben Youssef in the twelfth century erected in Marrakesh, Fez, and other cities many great structures in the Andalusian style.

When the widespread Almoravid Empire began to fall apart, the task of reuniting and extending the empire was undertaken by a second Berber dynasty, the Almohades or Muwahhadi (1149-1269). Like its predecessor, this dynasty was founded by a religious fanatic. Claiming to be a sherif, Muhammad ibn Tumart was really a Masmuda Berber from the Sus. Expounding his doctrine of puritanical unitarianism, he was proclaimed to be the mahdi foretold by the Prophet.[24] After being expelled from Mecca, Egypt, and Tunisia, Muhammad received asylum among the superstitious Berbers of the High Atlas, where his alleged miracles won their allegiance. With a force from seven leading Masmuda tribes, he overpowered neighboring Berbers and impressed them into his service. In the Atlas he organized a state with revenues from taxation and a powerful army of religious warriors. At his death, his martial disciple, Abd al Mumin, was prepared to expand this territory.

Abd al Mumin (1130-1165) brought all of Morocco under his control and then conquered Muslim Spain, again split into numerous small states. By capturing the chief cities of Algeria, Tunisia, and Libya, he expanded the Moroccan Empire to its farthest limits, to the western border of Egypt. "Prayers were said in his name in all the mosques from Tripoli to Cordova." His reign is rated one of the greatest in Moroccan history. He not only organized this vast country with sound administrative, economic, and social institutions, but also he won the respect and affection of his subjects. Among his important enterprises were the building of the castle and windmill at Gibraltar, the rebuilding of Tlemcen and Meknes, and the construction of the aqueduct at Salé. He ordered all the mosques, walls, and fortresses throughout the empire to be repaired. The roads between Barka and Wad Nun were made safe for travel and trade. He assembled a large fleet of four hundred vessels furnished by Ceuta, the Riff ports, and Oran, and eighty from the Iberian Peninsula, with which he made expeditions to Spain and Tunisia. Spreading throughout his empire the Andalusian culture, he founded schools and universities. It was he who began using the customary letter salutation, "Praise be to the only God." Abd al Mumin's successors continued his great work. Famous Almohade monuments are the Tower of Hassan and the Oudaiyah fortress at Rabat (the capital of this dynasty), the Giralda Tower at Seville, and the Koutoubiya Mosque at Marrakesh.[25]

From 1213 to 1269 the Almohade Empire disintegrated. The nine amirs of this period were of inferior character and ability and their short reigns were marked by several violent deaths. The Iberian Peninsula, except Granada, freed itself from their grasp; Tunisia and Tlemcen set up independent governments; and the Beni Marin maintained rulers in the parts of the empire which they were gradually conquering.[26] Thus the largest and greatest empire of Morocco came to an end.

The Beni Marin or the Marinids (1215-1258) presided over the contraction of the empire. "Like the locusts for number," this Berber horde, which belonged to the Zenata tribe, poured through the Atlas valleys from their desert home east of Tafilalt. They had been accustomed to use pastures in the north every year, and in 1185 they had furnished troops to the Almohades in a battle in the peninsula. But in 1212, observing the weakness and chaos in the empire, they came as invaders. Under their leader, Abd al Hakk, famous for piety and miraculous powers, they defeated the Almohade army in the Riff (1216). The next year an army of Almohade Arabs was vanquished after slaying they leader of the Marinids. Two sons of Abd al Hakk carried on the war, a typical nomad invasion, for twenty-seven years.

Eventually the eastern part of Morocco fell to the Marinids, and elsewhere the Almohades had jurisdiction only over the towns. At first the Beni Marin gave allegiance to the caliph of the recently independent Tunisia (1230) who threatened to subjugate all of Morocco, for he had seized not only Tlemcen, but also Seville, Valencia, and Murcia in Spain and was proclaimed leader in Tangier, Ceuta, Alcazar, Meknes, and Tafilalt. Later the Beni Marin maintained their independence of both Marrakesh and the again independent Tlemcen (1235). Under Abu Bakr, third son of Abd al Hakk, the Marinids conquered all the strategic cities of western Morocco, the Tafilalt, and the Draa. The Tunisian Caliphate soon ceased its attacks on the reunited Morocco. In 1226 the last Almohade ruler ended his reign at Marrakesh.

Until 1359 the Beni Marin amirs carried on valiant wars in vain efforts to restore the former Moroccan suzerainty over Algeria, Tunisia, and Spain. They also had to quell several revolts in Morocco. The last large migration of Arabs, the Masqil, reached Morocco in the thirteenth century. They were Bedouins from southern Arabia. Subduing the Berber nomads, they passed through the Moroccan steppes and occupied the area from north of the Draa to the Moulaya. As the Marinids weakened, the Arabs crossed over the Atlas passes and traveled westward until the vanguard arrived near Rabat. This incursion increased Arab population and influence in the rural districts.

The Marinids are remembered less for their military prowess than for their patronage of the arts and construction of beautiful public buildings. Most famous is Abu al Hassan (1341-1349), who employed skillful architects, engineers, and craftsmen to build artistic baths, fountains, hostels, aqueducts, bridges, walls, and fortifications. The era of the Marinids was for North Africa what the contemporary Gothic period was for Europe. Yakub II (1258-1286) was renowned for his just government, interest in philosophy, and establishment of refuges for the sick, blind, insane, and lepers. Religion and learning were fostered by founding New Fez, with its great mosque, and by the establishment of medersas, or colleges, in Fez, Meknes, Salé, Marrakesh, and Ceuta. However, religion was degraded by the rise of a great number of "holy men," or marabouts, and many religious fraternities, both indigenous and imported from the East. From Spain, as a war indemnity, Yakub II obtained for his college in Fez thirteen loads of Arabian manuscripts on theology, jurisprudence, and literature. This dynasty was notable also for carrying on an extensive trade with Europe and combatting the piracy which threatened it.[27]

As in previous dynasties, the first strong rulers were followed by weak and incompetent ones, and from 1361 to 1471 the country was divided and ravaged by civil war. In 1471 the Beni Marin line ended, and the period was concluded by two rulers from the Wattasi, a related Zenata tribe (1471-1524). Thus passed away the last dynasty of the Berbers, who had been in power for more than four and a half centuries.[28]

During the fifteenth century began the long series of invasions from Europe which were to be an important factor in Moroccan history until 1956. It seemed probable at first that Morocco would be divided between Spain and Portugal. In 1415, by their capture of Ceuta, the Portuguese initiated their colonization project. By 1515 they had seized Alcazar, Casablanca, Arzila, Tangier, Safi, and Azemour and had founded Mazagan and Agadir. In less than a century they dominated the Atlantic coast of Morocco. Meanwhile, Spain had achieved political union through the marriage of the monarchs of Castile and Aragon, and by the conquest of Granada from the Moroccans in 1492. Spain was soon to become the most powerful and extensive empire in the world;

she had taken the first step toward expansion by her American adventure of 1492. But Spain still lagged behind her small Iberian neighbor in colonizing Morocco, for she had annexed only Melilla in 1497 and Penon de Valez in 1508. However, following the extinction of Muslim rule in Granada, Ferdinand and Isabella entered upon a crusade against the Islamic world. They expelled the Moors and Jews from Spain with great cruelty. During the next Moroccan dynasty the refugees from Spain fought the Spanish from Morocco and Spain warred with all the Barbary states.

At the accession of the second sherifian dynasty (the Saadians, 1549-1654), Morocco did not deserve the name of empire. In the central Maghreb was rising the state of Algeria, which would soon annex Tlemcen. The Kingdom of Fez, with Marrakesh as a vassal, was the sole remnant of the gigantic Almohade Empire. Safi had formed a "republic;" Portugal controlled the other Atlantic ports. Both Spain and Portugal were threatening conquest of the country, and expansion of the now diminutive Morocco was possible only toward the south.

In this time of troubles, the principal chiefs and religious leaders of Morocco elected as their leader Muhammad Al Kaim bi Amr Illah, a sherif of high repute in the Draa. An ancestor of his had imported from near Medina in order to assure good date crops. After occupying the Sus, the chosen ruler built up a strong military force. His successors gradually took over the estranged parts of Morocco and won great prestige by driving the Portuguese out of all their purloined ports, except Mazagan, by 1578. They also assisted in checking the Turks, who designated as their viceroys the Dey of Algeria (1570) and the Bey of Tunisia (1571).[29] But the greatest military event of the Saadian period was the battle of Alcazar in 1578, which had momentous results. Both the Moroccan and the Portuguese rulers were killed, leaving the latter's throne to the Spanish monarchy until 1640, and Portugal had to abandon all ambition to expand into Morocco.

The most illustrious member of the Saadian dynasty was Ahmed V (1578-1603), self-styled al Mansour, "The Victorious." After reorganizing his army on the Turkish model, he prepared to extend his realm southward. A strong military expedition crossed the Shara and conquered the highly advanced Negro kingdoms of Timbuktu and Gao.[30] It returned to Morocco in 1591, laden with a tremendous booty of gold, ivory, ebony, slaves, eunuchs, concubines, horses, and other valuables. Another great source of Moroccan revenue was the large ransoms paid by Europeans for Christian slaves. With his great military prestige and wealth, "The Golden," as he was now called, was able to enter into amicable and profitable relations with several European countries, including England and Spain, which became his ally against Turkey. With Queen Elizabeth I The Golden carried on a secret traffic supplying him with munitions, ship-building materials, and marine gear needed in the then flourishing industry of the corsairs. Many foreign mercantile establishments, chiefly English, French, and Dutch, located in the former Portuguese ports and conducted a brisk trade with their homelands. Captain John Smith, later of Virginia fame, reported from his observations in Morocco that the magnificent buildings erected with the Sudan gold, mostly in Marrakesh, were fabricated by English goldsmiths, plumbers, carvers, stone polishers, and watchmakers, who were well paid in money and goods. Al Mansour was noted not only for his appreciation of skilled craftmanship and patronage of the arts, but also for an interest in science, the construction of military bastions, and the development of a very lucrative sugar industry. Withal, he was widely read, wrote prayers and a treatise on politics, and was a skilled calligraphist.[31]

After the death of this eminent monarch, Moroccan history repeated itself. Then came the customary scrambles for succession, the series of feeble rulers, and the establishment of small states, some of them under control of marabouts.[32] In addition, the collapse of the Saadian dynasty was hastened by the Moriscos expelled from Spain in 1606, who had created a corsair "republic" at Rabat and Salé.[33]

Before its extinction, the Saadian dynasty introduced an important political innovation under Muhammad XIII (1637-1654). The title of <u>amir</u>, hitherto used by Moroccan rulers, was changed to <u>sultan</u>, and until the time of Muhammad V, Morocco was officially a sultanate. The title emperor was used interchangeably with that of sultan, however, and Morocco was usually known as the Sherifian Empire. "The titles of the Moorish ruler were "as elastic as the ingenuity of the scribe addressing him."[34]

The stage was set for the appearance of the third sherifian and the sixth line of rulers--the Alouite or Filali dynasty, which came to power in 1659 and is still ruling. The Alouite family, descended like the Saadians from Ali, Muhammad's son-in-law, had been invited to the Tafilalt region. Summoned by the Arabs of Fez to rule them, the first Alouite began in 1659 a precarious rule which lasted until he was superseded by his brother Er-Rasheed II (1664-1672). The latter is regarded as the real founder of the dynasty. During his reign Er-Rasheed completed the conquest of the petty states formed before his accession and once more unified the country. Unfortunately, he set the precedent for bloodshed and tyranny followed by others of his line.[35]

Among all the rulers of Morocco, probably none is more outstanding--or more notorious--than Mulai Ismail (1672-1727). He was a contemporary of those infamous tyrants, Louis XIV, whom he emulated, and Peter the Great, whom he surpassed in cruelty. His English slave, Pellow, described him thus: "voluptuous, covetous, passionate, treacherous, more than a tyrant, he tamed the natural savageness of his subjects by showing himself still more savage than they." Yet, though universally feared during his lifetime, he has been honored and revered after his passing, not only for his strength, but also for his piety, as demonstrated by meticulous observance of outward forms and his frequent public prostrations at praying places. A copy of the Koran was always borne before him, and he committed his murders mostly on Fridays, thus making them religious rites. He aspired to social and political equality with the leading monarchs of Europe, even seeking to add to his harem an illegitimate daughter of Louis XIV. His individual murders and wholesale butcheries, often performed with tortures of incredible brutality, promoted obedience and order. There is no census of his harem and children, but one estimate is that he had three hundred wives at one time, nine hundred sons, and two hundred daughters. Many of the daughters were slain at birth.

Made formidable by his efficient administration and large, well trained armies, as well as by his corsair fleet, Ismail secured respect from European rulers. The armies were composed of Arab tribesmen, European renegades, and hereditary Negro troops.[36] Larache was taken from Spain, and Tangier, ceded by Portugal to England, was abandoned to Ismail in 1684. One instance of enlightened foreign policy is to be noted. In return for arms and ammunition for his siege of Ceuta and an exchange of prisoners with a bonus of ransom from the English, Ismail granted to England a treaty recognizing the right of protection for her subjects and their interests in Morocco.

Ismail had a mania for building. In his newly founded capital of Meknes and elsewhere, he erected walls, kasbahs, barracks, palaces, stables, and colleges. It was an economical hobby, for he requisitioned the materials without remuneration and employed slave labor of Moorish prisoners and Christian captives.[37]

After Ismail came the deluge--anarchy, brigandage, atrocities, oppression, and civil war. The former guardians of law and order, the black troops, used their power to enthrone and overthrow no less than seven of Ismail's sons, ending with Abd Allah V, who was occupying the throne for the sixth time when he passed away in 1757. He had inherited his father's appetite for slaughter.[38]

Sidi Muhammad XVI (1757-1790) restored goodness and wisdom as royal virtues. His first objective was to clean up the mess in Morocco. He dispersed an insurgent Arab army and brought the Negro troops under control. Oppressive governors were impoverished and imprisoned; fortifications were rebuilt; Salé and Rabat, now possessing only one pirate ship, lost their independence. In 1760, Mogador and Fedala were built, and the French failed to capture Salé and Larache. To revive education, Ismail's library of 12,000 volumes was divided among the leading mosques.

Muhammad's foreign policy was one of friendship and cooperation with Europe and even with Turkey. In 1768 the latter sent him a shipload of military supplies, used by him the next year to recover Mazagan from Portugal. The sultanate entered upon an era of treaty-making. Pacts were signed with England in 1760 and 1783; with France in 1767; with Spain in 1767, 1780, and 1785; with Denmark in 1767; with Tuscany in 1778; and with the infant republic of the United States in 1787. Moorish embassies visited London, Vienna, Paris, Lisbon, Madrid, the Hague, and Malta.

To terminate this unwanted and unwonted peace, the black troops at Meknes rebelled. Sent to put down the uprising, the Sultan's son, al Yazid, was induced instead to allow the rebels to proclaim him sultan. With difficulty Muhammad suppressed the Negro troops with Udaia and Berber contingents. In sanctuary at Zarhon, al Yazid was pardoned by his benevolent father. Muhammad was lenient with the Negro soldiers also, scattering them around the country as garrisons. This action only served as a deployment, for they staged other revolts later.

To rebellion were added the problems of drouth and famine (1776 and 1782), which the Sultan tried to alleviate by granting large sums of money. But the populace hailed a new leader, a mahdi especially favored by the Berbers, whose adherents were routed by Muhammad's forces. A continued vexation was the conduct of al Yazid. He committed robbery while on a pilgrimage to Mecca and was subsequently disowned and cursed by his father. The unrepentant son took refuge in a sanctuary, where he planned another rebellion. While on the way to chastise his son, Muhammad died (1790). Again Morocco was ravaged by an orgy of bloodshed reminiscent of the days of Ismail.[39]

Thus passed from the Moroccan scene after a reign of thirty-three years one of the most enlightened and benevolent rulers of Morocco. He had released many prisoners "on the principle of making peace with heaven."[40] During his reign the United States had entered into relations with Morocco, the development of which is correlated with the careers of the eleven succeeding sultans, all of the Alouite dynasty. It was very fortunate that the first American treaty with Morocco was obtained while Sidi Muhammad XVI was in office, as otherwise it would have been difficult to make one with his successors.

The Peoples of Morocco

I. Caucasian

Berbers

Gaetulians and Libyans: Aborigines
Medes)
Persians) Immigrants from the Near East
Armenians)

Arabs

First invasion, 7th century A. D.
Conquest and annexation of the Iberian Peninsula, 712-
Great Arabic invasion, the Beni Hilali and Beni Soleim, middle of eleventh century
Third Arabic invasion, the Masqil, thirteenth century

Jews

Refugees after the Diaspora
Refugees from the Iberian Peninsula, after 1492

Mediterranean Invaders (ancient and medieval periods)

Phoenicians
Romans
Vandals
Byzantines

European Invaders (modern period)

Portuguese
Spanish
French
Italians
Maltese
English

II. Negroid

Tribes from the Sahara Desert and southward

Dynastic Periods of Moroccan History (788-1790)

Dynasties	Eminent Monarchs
I. Idrisid Dynasty (788-1061) Arabic--Sherifian	Idris ben Abdallah (788-791) Founder of Morocco Idris II Founder of Fez
II. Almoravide Dynasty (1061-1149) Berber	Youssef ben Tashfin (1061-1106) Founder of Marrakesh Capture of Tangier and Ceuta Conquest of Algeria and Oran; Morocco a true empire Conquest of most of Iberian Peninsula
III. Almohade Dynasty (1149-1269) Berber	Abd al Mumin (1150-1165) Conquest of all Morocco Conquest of Muslim Spain Expansion of Morocco to western border of Egypt Establishment of administrative, social, and economic institutions Buildings, navy, schools, colleges
IV. Merinid Dynasty (1213-1524) Berber	Abd al Hassan (1341-1349) Builder of baths, hostels, aqueducts, walls, forts Yakub II (1258-1286) Interest in philosophy Just government Religion and learning Trade with Europe; combatting of piracy European invasions, 1415-

V. Saadian Dynasty (1524-1659) Arabic--Sherifian	Ahmed V (al Mansour, "The Golden (1578-1603) Subjugation of Negro kingdoms of Gao and Timbuktu Great wealth from Sahara and ransom of Christian slaves Piracy developed; corsair republic of Rabat and Salé Interest in crafts, arts, science
	Muhammad XIII (1637-1654) Morocco a sultanate
VI. Alouite Dynasty (1659--	Al Rashid II (1664-1672) Real founder of the dynasty Unification of the country
	Mulai Ismail (1672-1727) Most notorious tyrant, infamous for incredible cruelty, but honored for piety Enormous harem and progeny Efficient administrator Large armies, including one of Negroes, corsair fleet Social and diplomatic relations with Europe Founder of Meknes Builder of walls, kasbahs, barracks, palaces, stables, colleges Unification and pacification of entire realm by force and fear
	Muhammad XVI (1757-1790) Enlightened and benevolent ruler Negro troops controlled Rebellions of his son Conquest of Salé and Rabat

Revival of education
Policy of friendship and
and cooperation with
Europe and Turkey
Era of treaty-making
First American-Moroccan
treaty made, 1786

Notes

1. More detailed accounts of the land and peoples of Morocco are given in the following: Nevill Barbour, editor, A Survey of North West Africa (The Maghreb) (hereafter cited as Barbour, North West Africa), 1-2; Lorna Hahn, North Africa; Nationalism to Nationhood (hereafter cited as Hahn, North Africa), 55; John Gunther, Inside Africa (hereafter cited as Gunther, Inside Africa), 7, 39-40, 42, 67; Augustus Henry Keane, Africa, I, North Africa, Second Edition, Revised (hereafter cited as Keane, North Africa), 28-29. 72-86; Budgett Meakin, The Moors: A Comprehensive Description (hereafter cited as Meakin, The Moors), 2-4, 6-7; Graham H. Stuart, The International City of Tangier, Second Edition (hereafter cited as Stuart, Tangier), 2.

2. Gunther, Inside Africa, 42-43, 65-67; Walter Burton Harris, France, Spain, and the Rif (hereafter cited as W. B. Harris, France, Spain and the Rif), 23-33; Meakin, The Moors, 1-3.

3. Barbour, North West Africa, 75.

4. "Geographical Look-Alikes," National Geographic School Bulletin, XLII (March 23, 1963), 354-359, with maps and illustrations. Another comparison of California and Morocco is in Melvin M. Knight, Morocco as a French Economic Venture (hereafter cited as Knight, Morocco as a French Economic Venture), 14-15.

5. "Morocco Population Up," Washington Post and Times-Herald, Sept. 25, 1960, 11A.

6. Barbour, North West Africa, 75-79; Norman Dwight Harris, Intervention and Colonization in Africa (hereafter cited as N. D. Harris, Colonization in Africa), 243-245; Gunther, Inside Africa, 42; Norman Dwight Harris, Europe and Africa (hereafter cited as N. D. Harris, Europe and Africa), 279-280.

7. Barbour, North West Africa, 9-10, 12-14; Sheridan H. Garth, The Pageant of the Mediterranean (hereafter cited as Garth, Pageant of the Mediterranean), 205-208.

8. Ibid. 208; Barbour, North West Africa, 82; Stuart, Tangier, 2-3.

9. Barbour, North West Africa, 208; Wallace E. Ferguson and Geoffrey Brunn, A Survey of European Civilization, Second Edition, (hereafter cited as Ferguson and Brunn, European Civilization), 130-131-

10. Ministry of Foreign Affairs, A Glimpse into Morocco's History (hereafter cited as Glimpse into Morocco's History), 5; Budgett Meakin, The Moorish Empire: A Historical Epitome (hereafter cited as Meakin, Moorish Empire), 23-25.

11. Ibid., 24-31; Francis Horace Mellor, Morocco Awakes (hereafter cited as Mellor, Morocco Awakes), 1-3; Bertram Thomas, The Arabs: The Life History of A People Who Have Left Their Deep Impress on the World (hereafter cited as Thomas, The Arabs), 96-98.

12. Ibid., 102-103.

13. Meakin, Moorish Empire, 31.

14. Mellor, Morocco Awakes, 3-13.

15. Barbour, North West Africa, 25-26.

16. Mellor, Morocco Awakes, 12-13.

17. Ibid., 6, 18; Meakin, Moorish Empire, 36-47.

18. Ibid., 32-33; E. W. Bovill, The Golden Trade of the Moors (hereafter cited as Bovill, Golden Trade of the Moors), 4-5, 58-59.

19. The name Almoravids is derived from the Arabic Al Morabitum, meaning "members of the Ribat or military convents."

20. Bovill, Golden Trade of the Moors, 70-78; Glimpse Into Morocco's History, 8-9; Barbour, North West Africa, 83-84; Meakin, Moorish Empire, 49-54.

21. Ibid., 56-59; Bovill, Golden Trade of the Moors, 76-77.

22. Meakin, Moorish Empire, 60-63.

23. Bovill, Golden Trade of the Moors, 66-68; Glimpse Into Morocco's History, 9.

24. Almohades means "those who proclaim the oneness of God." A Mahdi is an expected spiritual and temporal ruler destined to establish the reign of righteousness throughout the world-analogous to the Jewish messiah.

25. Meakin, Moorish Empire, 65-83; Glimpse Into Morocco's History, 10-11.

26. Meakin, Moorish Empire, 84-87; Mellor, Morocco Awakes, 13-14; Henri Terrasse, History of Morocco, translated by Hilary Tee (hereafter cited as Terrasse, History of Morocco, 229-230.

27. Barbour, North West Africa, 85; Meakin, Moorish Empire, 89-109; Glimpse Into Morocco's History, 12-13.

28. Meakin, Moorish Empire, 109-111.

29. The sea power of the Ottoman Turks in the western Mediterranean was destroyed by the Battle of Lepanto in 1571. Led by Don John of Austria, natural brother of Philip II, and allied with a Papal and a Venetian fleet, the Spanish navy inflicted a tremendous defeat on the Turkish navy.

30. The Moroccan army was composed chiefly of Spanish and Portuguese renegades. The Negro culture was destroyed. The conquered kingdoms became the prey of rival Moorish pashas who won independence from Morocco in 1620 and continued to rule at Timbuktu until 1780. William L. Langer, editor and compiler, An Encyclopedia of World History, rev. ed. (hereafter cited as Encyclopedia of World History), 524.

31. Meakin, Moorish Empire, 115-129; Bovill, Golden Trade of the Moors, 135-139, 147-182; Barbour, North West Africa, 85-86; Glimpse Into Morocco's History, 14-15.

32. The prominent place of the marabouts and religious fraternities in Moroccan history is discussed by Eugene Aubin, in Morocco of Today, translated from the French (hereafter cited as Aubin, Morocco of Today), 375.

33. Meakin, Moorish Empire, 129-135; Barbour, North West Africa, 86.

34. Ibid., 199. The most common salutation from the people was Maulàna (Our Lord), incorrectly but commonly pronounced Mulai for the singular form Maulai (My Lord); this was the form of address for all of sherifian descent. Sultans named Muhammad were titled Seyyidi, vulgarly Sidi (Mr.) or Sidna (Our Master).

35. Ibid., 136-138.

36. Negroes of both sexes, imported from the Sudan and collected from all parts of Morocco, were settled in huge camps, where Ismail himself supervised their training and propagation. Said to number 100,000 at their master's death, these troops became powerful enough to install and depose sultans, until they were dispersed in various parts of Morocco by Sidi Muhammad XVI. Ibid., 155-156. Mulai Ismail was known as the "Black Sultan," not on account of his deeds, but because of his skin. Although a sherif, he had a Negro slave for a mother.

37. Ibid., 139-159; Bovill, Golden Trade of the Moors, 176.

38. Meakin, Moorish Empire, 163-166.

39. Ibid., 166-169.

40. Ray Watkins Irwin, The Diplomatic Relations of the United States With the Barbary Powers, 1776-1816 (hereafter cited as Irwin, Diplomatic Relations of the United States with the Barbary Powers), 6.

Chapter II

The Problem of Piracy

The first problem leading to diplomatic relations between Morocco and the United States was piracy. In the Mediterranean, as on many other highways of commerce, piracy was an ancient, though hardly an honorable, occupation. The sea robbers dared to challenge even Roman hegemony over that vast land-locked sea. During the Early Middle Ages, the period of many invasions, migrations, and wars all around the perimeters of the Mediterranean, many champions of both Cross[1] and Crescent became pirates and preyed upon each other's ships and shores. The enslavement of captives was practiced by both parties in the "Holy War," and galley slaves furnished the motive power for many vessels of all types. Reports of the atrocities suffered by Christian slaves in Barbary aroused great sympathy for them in Europe, and in 1199 the "Order of the Holy Trinity and Redemption of Captives" was founded in Paris. Its members, known as Mathurins, devoted their lives to ransoming captives and ameliorating their condition while imprisoned.

In the later medieval period, there developed an extensive exchange of goods, protected by commercial treaties between the Barbary rulers and the great trading cities of southern Europe. "Christian shipping lay in every African port from Tripoli to Agadir, discharging hardware, cloth, Venetian beads, and other manufactured goods, and loading slaves, eunuchs, gold, ivory, ebony, ostrich feathers, and skins." Many Europeans adventured into the Maghreb, either as commercial agents, civilian employees, or mercenaries in every Muslim army.[2]

At the opening of the fifteenth century, the close ties between the Iberian Peninsula and the Maghreb prevailing under the Almoravid and Almohade dynasties had been broken (only Granada remained under independent

Muslim rule after 1285), and the Christian Crusade against Islam was about to proceed into Morocco. The subsequent success of Portugal in occupying Moroccan ports and of Spain in eliminating the last vestige of Muslim rule from Granada stimulated a rapid resurgence of piratical warfare. The Muslim refugees driven from Spain into Morocco were impelled by hope of revenge and by economic necessity to attack Spanish shipping and towns, while Moroccans opposed Spain's evident ambition to annex their Mediterranean ports. The fanatical intolerance and bigotry of the Spanish monarchs in persecuting the non-Christians who remained in their country and the fantastic project of Cardinal Ximenes to Christianize North Africa by force provoked a natural reaction in Morocco, where piracy was again elevated to the status of a Holy War.[3]

A former enemy of Morocco, Turkey now became an ally in the Muslim front against Europe. During the sixteenth century, after expanding westward over all northern Africa except Morocco, the Ottoman Empire launched a determined drive to make the Mediterranean a Turkish lake.[4] Aligned with the Holy Roman Empire under Charles V (1519-1556), Spain led the offensive against advancing Islam, but had only temporary success in her seizure of Ceuta, Oran, and Algiers. The first agents of the Sublime Porte were two brothers, Arouj and Khaired-Din, who, operating from Algeria, inaugurated the piratical warfare which was to plague the Mediterranean for almost three and a half centuries. They had many able, but none so talented, successors in their vocation.[5]

The crushing defeat of their navy at Lepanto in 1571 barred the Turks from the Western Mediterranean, but Constantinople continued to control the central and eastern Maghreb by means of Turkish officials originally known as admirals and pashas.[6] After 1587, piracy became a capitalist enterprise, with the owners of pirate cruisers paying tithes from their earnings to the representatives of the Turkish sultan. The slave trade became the most lucrative business in Algeria, Tunisia, and Tripoli, for Christian slaves were in great demand for the manual labor which the martial-minded natives disdained.[7] Although Turkish power in North Africa continued to decline, the Bashaw of Tripoli, the Bey of Tunis, and the Dey of

Algeria remained nominally feudal lords under the Ottoman sultan. Practically, they were independent of him and received their power from the soldiers who elected them. In all these states administration was extremely inefficient and corrupt, and the revenues of the rulers consisted largely of the spoils brought in by the pirates. On the land, robbery was the best paying occupation, and the prevalence of brigands made life and property unsafe and prevented the normal development of industry and commerce.[8]

However decadent they might have been internally, the predatory states were gaining in international prestige. After 1570, European powers began to recognize and treat with the corsairs on equal terms, sending consuls, missions, and royal letters, and making treaties which were repeatedly broken by Barbary. Although piracy had once rated as patriotism in European wars--as, for instance, in the well-known case of the Elizabethan Seadogs--it was then outlawed among the Christian nations. Privateering, or the licensing of privately owned ships by governments to supplement or substitute for navies, was recognized in European relations. However, the Barbary states made their own system of international law for intercourse with Europe. By this system, war was declared to be the normal relationship between Muslim and Christian peoples, unless specific peace treaties were made. The Ottoman sultan and his satellites claimed the Mediterranean as their _mare clausam_; other countries could use the sea only by paying tribute as a sort of rental. According to these principles, piracy became legitimized as privateering, and captured seamen were prisoners of war. The Barbary rulers exploited their theory by their repeated use of petty pretexts to emphasize the existence of war and thus to extort money from the enemy either by blackmail or by robbery.[9]

The seventeenth century was one of prosperity for the pirates. The strength and audacity of the corsairs were augmented in 1609 by the expulsion of the Moriscos[10] from Spain. They not only operated on the seas, but also invaded the coasts and inland districts of Italy, Spain, and the Mediterranean islands on robbing and kidnapping expeditions. Finally they ventured to attack the coasts of England, Ireland, and Iceland. The Moroccan pirates frequented the Atlantic. Their chief port, Salé, had a shallow harbor, so they were forced to use lighter and smaller vessels than were employed by the other Barbary powers.[11]

The subservience of the great powers of western Europe to the gangsters of Barbary has been ascribed to cowardice, mutual jealousy, and shortsighted self-seeking. In retrospect, it seems incredible that nations actively engaged in building world empires--England, France, Spain, and the Netherlands--should have submitted to the losses occasioned by capture of valuable ships and cargoes, the mounting increases in insurance rates, and the enslavement of their citizens. There are explanations, if not excuses, for the pusillanimity of Europeans. Each of the most advanced powers was concentrating its resources and manpower on two objectives--establishing its claim to as large areas as possible in Europe, in the Orient, and in the Americas, and fighting its rivals in these areas. As examples of these religious-imperialist wars, which occupied so much of the seventeenth and eighteenth centuries, may be cited the Dutch wars of independence, the Hapsburg-Bourbon conflicts, the Thirty Years' War, and the Second Hundred Years' War--that series of Franco-British conflicts between 1689 and 1815. Both in war and in peace, a large part of international commerce was carried on by neutrals, who were obliged to take the risks of piracy. Moreover, despite many experiences to the contrary, the stronger European countries, especially France and England, were confident that they could do business with Barbary to the detriment of their rivals, and of each other. The minor powers were reduced to ineffectual bribery of the pirate powers.[12]

However, the European attitude toward the Barbary states was not always one of obsequious submission. During the seventeenth century Dutch and French attacks on the pirates inflicted punishment and released captives, and English expeditions against Algiers and Salé liberated a number of slaves. England's position toward piracy was somewhat anomalous, for many Englishmen were employed as mercenaries in Moorish armies. One of these mercenaries, Captain John Smith, returned from Morocco in disgust at the "bloody murthers rather than warre," and even asserted that British pirates taught their trade to the Moors.[13] Yet England made the most aggressive attacks on piracy, not only in Barbary but also in the West Indies. Many vessels and captives from the Atlantic coast colonies in America were rescued in the Mediterranean. Finding many treaties of immunity with the countries of the Maghreb worthless, England was constrained to keep a permanent naval force in the Mediterranean and to supply convoys for merchant vessels. By repeated expeditions, bombardment of towns, and naval engagements, England finally taught the Barbary pirates to have some respect for her flag. Passes issued to ships from the British colonies in America enabled their fish, tobacco, and sugar to reach Mediterranean markets in comparative safety. Unfortunately, England had abandoned a position potentially able to control the western Mediterranean when she returned Tangier to Mulai Ismail in 1684. She had received the city from Portugal in 1661.[14]

During the eighteenth century, Spain had several conflicts with Morocco and Algeria; she made treaties with both and also with Tunisia. Great Britain received the strategic post of Gibraltar from Spain in 1713.[15] Nevertheless, an audit of the books recording the tributes paid to the Barbary powers would have shown a booming business. Regular tributes first assessed by Mulai Ismail were being paid to Morocco by the Netherlands, Venice, Sweden-Norway, Austria, Denmark, and Sardinia. The other Barbary states were also exacting large payments[16] in the eighteenth century.[17]

Under Sidi Muhammad XVI (1757-1790), Morocco was gaining in political stability and international prestige, and during his reign the definite decline of piracy became evident. The increasing technical superiority of European fleets made them less vulnerable to attacks from pirate vessels. In the sixteenth and seventeenth centuries, the "Sally Rovers," crusaders against the infidels, had dispatched ships as far as Devon and Cornwall. Varying greatly in numbers, sizes, and types of vessels, their fleets had been the only organized navy ever possessed by Morocco and had paid shares of their profits to the sultan in return for his subsidies. A depression in the national industry after 1700 was followed by an unsuccessful attempt to promote the renaissance of piracy in the second half of the century. Sidi Muhammad XVI repulsed French attacks on Salé and Larache and expelled Portugal from Mazagan. His resort to extensive treaty-making indicated the decadence of Morocco's most ancient and profitable institution. In 1773 a single Tuscan frigate destroyed three of five Moorish vessels. Sidi Muhammad had only twenty corsairs with from eighteen to fifty guns apiece, eleven of them frigates.[18]

As captures by piracy decreased, another opportunity arose to secure Christian slaves. Reviving trade with Europe brought to Moroccan shores, especially in the south, many shipwrecked sailors, overventuresome traders, and explorers. These intruders were captured and held for ransom.[19] Christian slaves were said to be better treated in Morocco than in any other Barbary state,[20] but this did not make the existence of slavery a less serious problem.

England made some amends for her error of withdrawing from Tangier in 1684 by cultivating the friendship of Morocco and securing substantial assistance against France in the Anglo-French wars (1689-1763). The Moors aided in the capture of Gibraltar in 1704, and a profitable commerce developed between Gibraltar and Morocco.[21] The possession of this strategic stronghold enabled England to build up amity and commerce with Morocco and to protect the sultan from attacks. England shared control over the Straits of Gibraltar with no European power, and she furthered her commercial interests in the Mediterranean by tolerating the Moorish pirates.

Very great benefits were bestowed upon the British colonies in America by the peace purchased by England from the Barbary powers. Jefferson estimated that one-sixth of the wheat and flour exported from the Thirteen Colonies, one-fourth in value of the dried and pickled fish, and some rice found markets in Mediterranean countries. This export commerce employed annually from eighty to one hundred ships, of 20,000 tons, navigated by 1200 seamen.[22] Other American exports to southern Europe and Africa were rum, rice, pine, oak and cedar lumber, beeswax, and onions. From these regions the colonies imported goods officially valued, in 1769, at Ł228,682, consisting mostly of wines, salt, oil, and Morocco leather. In 1779 the value of American exports to the Mediterranean areas was £707,000.[23] Equipped with admiralty passes, the colonial vessels were usually safe, but there were occasional encounters with pirates in spite of the immunity promised by treaties and enforced by the patrol of armed English ships in the Mediterranean.

As one means of coercion, Great Britain withdrew these passes from the colonists when they revolted.[24] Two weeks after the Declaration of Independence, a committee of the Continental Congress reported to that body a plan to combat the menace to American commerce from the discovery that the vessels from across the Atlantic were no longer protected. The plan of the committee was to include in the proposed treaty with France a pledge that her monarch would protect, defend, and secure the people and property of the United States from the plunderings of the Barbary powers as effectually and fully as His British Majesty had previously done.[25] By this obscure entry of July 18, 1776, the Moroccan problem was first recorded in the annals of the United States.

It was natural that Congress should hope to find a new protector in the arch-enemy of the former mother country. The prestige of France in Morocco was probably second only to that of Great Britain. In 1577 France had been the first European nation to establish a consulate in Morocco, and in 1767 she had obtained diplomatic and consular protection by a treaty which later served as a model for other powers.[26] However, the French king's promise in the treaty of 1778 to "employ his good offices and interposition" with the Barbary states "for the benefit, convenience, and safety" of his American ally[27] did not prove to be of much value. In August, 1778, the American commissioners to France, Benjamin Franklin, John Adams, and Arthur Lee, requested the aid of France for American vessels held in Italian ports by fear of corsairs. Mention was made also of Italian merchants who were cut off from American commerce because of the risks attending piracy.[28] The French Minister of Foreign Affairs, Comte de Vergennes, and the Minister of Marine, M. de Sartine, pointed out that French intervention could not secure respect for the American flag or freedom for American commerce. However, the French government offered assistance in negotiating treaties between its ally and the Barbary states.[29]

The commissioners asked Congress for authority to negotiate and for funds to purchase gifts for the Barbary rulers, but although Congress referred the matter to a committee, no further action was taken at that time.[30]

The United States then turned to the Netherlands for support. A letter from the American commissioner to Vienna and Berlin, read in Congress on February 22, 1779, proposed that in a treaty of commerce the Netherlands should agree to employ good offices and interposition against all attacks or depredations aimed against the United States by any Barbary state.[31] In the treaty obtained by John Adams in 1782 it was promised that in any American negotiation with a Barbary power for Mediterranean passports "their High Mightinesses" would "second such negotiations in the most favorable manner, by means of their consuls, residing near the said King, Emperor, and Regencies."[32]

A third attempt to obtain effective European aid in Moroccan relations also failed. On June 1, 1783, the American commissioners negotiating a definitive peace treaty with Great Britain asked to have included a provision that His Britannic Majesty would offer aid to the United States by good offices and interposition against all attacks by Barbary powers.[33] The British Cabinet refused to make this concession. Its chief motive was probably the traditional British policy of crippling prospective commercial rivals. A bill for free trade between the United States and Great Britain, introduced by Pitt in 1783, was likewise defeated. In the debates on this bill Lord Sheffield frankly expressed the British attitude:

> It is not probable the American States will have a very free trade in the Mediterranean; it will not be to the interests of any of the great maritime powers to protect them there from the Barbary States. If they know their interests, they will not encourage the Americans to be carriers--that the Barbary States are advantageous to the maritime powers is obvious... The Americans cannot protect themselves... They cannot pretend to a navy.[34]

While vainly soliciting European support, the United States had been neglecting opportunities to deal directly with Morocco. In what was virtually a recognition of the independence of the United States, Sultan Sidi Muhammad XVI issued a declaration[35] on February 20, 1778, notifying all consuls and Christian merchants in Tangier, Salé, and Mogador that henceforth all vessels flying the American flag might freely enter Moroccan ports. There they would be permitted to "take refreshments, and enjoy in them the same privileges and immunities with those of the other nations with whom His Imperial Majesty maintains peace."[36]

It was more than a year later that the American commissioners began to investigate the possibility of direct contact with Morocco. Thereafter, negotiations were conducted for seven years under the aegis of Franklin, Adams, Jay, and Jefferson, until eventually the American objective of an equitable treaty was attained. To account for this prolonged negotiation, one can cite the slow and uncertain trans-Atlantic communication of that time, the inexperience of the desultory Congress, and the variations of policy advocated by the American commissioners, as well as the unorthodox methods of approach used by the Moroccan sultan.

Receiving no acknowledgment of his gesture of good will in 1778, the Sultan made another attempt to establish relations with the United States through M. Stephen d'Audibert Caille, a French merchant of Salé.[37] On May 26, 1779, Franklin wrote to the Committee of Foreign Affairs that he had received two letters from a Frenchman offering to act as minister for the United States and remarking that His Imperial Majesty "wondered we had never sent to thank him for being the first power on this side of the Atlantic that had acknowledged our independence." Franklin had not answered the letters because he had been warned by French officials that his correspondent was an unsafe person with whom to deal. The American commissioners were still awaiting instructions from Congress about negotiating with Morocco through the good offices of France.[38] Caille then wrote to John Jay, American representative at Madrid, on April 21, 1780, soliciting his aid in conveying the message to Congress and enclosing a copy of his commission from the Sultan to act as consul for all nations which had none in Morocco. Jay belatedly forwarded this letter to Congress on November 30, 1780.[39]

On November 28, 1780, Congress directed Franklin, if he had no objection, to assure Caille in terms most respectful to the Emperor that it sincerely wanted to cultivate the most perfect friendship with him, desired a treaty of commerce, and would find a favorable opportunity to make its wishes known formally.[40] Although Congress informed Sidi Muhammad in December[41] of its intention to appoint an envoy to negotiate the treaty, no action was taken.[42]

More than two years later, Robert Montgomery, an American merchant at Alicante, Spain, made the next move in the diplomatic game. Ostensibly acting for the United States he proposed, on January 4, 1783, that the Emperor send a representative to Paris to make a treaty with an envoy from Congress. Designated as the Moroccan peace envoy at Montgomery's suggestion, Giacomo Francisco Crocco addressed letters to Franklin in July and November of 1783. Indicating his readiness for his appointed role, Crocco requested $15,000 for traveling expenses, an amount, he noted, far less than usually paid to Moroccan representatives by European nations. He warned Franklin that treaty making frequently required several years and that failure to accept the Sultan's offer might "forever indispose him against the United Provinces."[43]

Franklin, Adams, and Jay referred Crocco's proposal to Congress, pointing out the urgency of obtaining a treaty with Morocco.[44] The only reply that Franklin could make to Crocco was that Montgomery had probably acted without authority from Congress and that when conditions were more settled the latter would undoubtedly take the proper steps to secure the friendship of a monarch whose character they had long esteemed and respected.[45] Suspicious of the status and good faith of Crocco, as he had been of Caille, Franklin wrote to William Carmichael, United States consul at Madrid, trying to obtain information about Crocco.[46]

Congress did not appreciate the officiousness of Montgomery. A committee of that body reported on March 16, 1784, that it was not in the interest of the United States to have non-citizens in diplomatic or consular posts and that Franklin, Jay, and Adams be instructed to investigate the circumstances under which Montgomery had communicated with the Sultan in the name of the United States.[47]

Another free lance diplomat for the United States was reported to John Jay by Thomas Barclay, American consul at L'Orient, France. Barclay had met an unnamed man from Meknes, bearing a character testimonial from the Emperor of Morocco, who volunteered to go either alone or with an American to the Court of Morocco to negotiate a treaty. He would do this service for only 2,000 pounds sterling. Barclay also recommended that none but Americans take part in such negotiations.[48]

Meanwhile, although much occupied in making peace with Great Britain, Adams and Franklin were keeping Robert Livingston, in charge of American foreign affairs, informed of their views on the Barbary situation. They agreed in blaming Great Britain for the perpetuation of piracy.[49] A year later, on July 10, 1784, Franklin recorded in his diary an interesting conversation with d'Audibert Caille. The latter proposed two methods of enforcing peace on the pirate states--either the refusal of all commercial intercourse or the forcible suppression of piracy by France.[50]

Fortunately, after 1783 there were no more volunteers interfering in American-Moroccan relations. But Congress was still dilatory, however; it had taken no action on various committee reports on the Barbary problem. These reports had recommended either that treaties be negotiated with all the Barbary powers or that passes be secured, with the aid of the Netherlands and France, if necessary.[51] It had been reported that Algerine cruisers lay in wait for the new flag. On October 1, 1783, Sidi Muhammad signified the exhaustion of his patience by seizing an American ship, the Betsey, and holding her as a hostage at Tangier.[52]

Finally Congress was compelled to take some action. It was evident the aggressive Algerines might totally destroy American commerce in the Mediterranean. The closing of the British, French, and Spanish West Indies to American ships made the situation even more desperate.[53] The United States had treaties of commerce with only three European states--France, the Netherlands, and Sweden.[54] On May 7, 1784, Congress appointed Jefferson to assist Adams and Franklin in negotiating treaties of commerce with Russia,

Austria, Prussia, Denmark, Saxony, Hamburg, Great Britain, Spain, Portugal, Genoa, Tuscany, Rome, Naples, Venice, Sardinia, and the Ottoman Porte, as well as all the Barbary States. Treaties of amity and commerce with the last were to be for ten years or for as much longer as could be arranged. Congress also expressed appreciation for the amicable disposition of the Emperor of Morocco and regret that the late war had delayed a response to his advances.[55] Five days later commissions were given to the three men, or a majority of them, to negotiate the treaties, and David Humphreys was appointed secretary to the commission.[56]

The first task confronting the commissioners was the rescue of the *Betsey* and her crew. In this and in all later dealings with Sidi Muhammad, William Carmichael was an invaluable assistant.[57] From November, 1784 to September, 1789, he carried on an extensive correspondence with Jefferson on Barbary affairs. He solicited the aid of the governments of France, the Netherlands, Sweden, and Denmark in effecting the release of the *Betsey*. However, it was to none of these, but to Spain, that the United States was indebted for the surrender of the ship and sailors on July 9, 1785.[58] Jefferson regarded the good treatment of the prisoners as another evidence of Sidi Muhammad's desire of "receiving us into the number of his tributaries."[59]

In July, 1785, the capture of two American ships and the enslavement of their crews by the Algerines[60] emphasized the importance of becoming friends with the one Barbary power which had shown a conciliatory attitude. It initiated also the problem of the Algerine captives, which was to plague the American government and people for thirty years.

After their first meeting at Passy on August 30, 1784, Adams, Franklin, and Jefferson studied their problem intensively. Many of their communications were written, for Adams was appointed minister to Great Britain on March 14, 1785.[61] Between November 11, 1784, and October 11, 1785, the commission sent nine reports to Congress on their progress with various treaties. In relation to Barbary, they gave the results of their investigations and asked for funds and further instructions.[62] On

February 14, 1785, Congress appropriated a sum not to exceed $80,000 from money borrowed in the Netherlands, or from any American funds in Europe, to be used in making the four treaties with Barbary. The commissioners were empowered to appoint agents to negotiate the agreements.[63] On March 11, 1785, the Secretary for Foreign Affairs submitted to Congress the commission for appointment of these delegates, with instructions for the approval of any treaties made by them.[64]

From the beginning, in letters to his friends, Jefferson urged a consistent policy. He advocated relentless war if the pirates would not accept an "equal treaty." He insisted that the United States should not pay tribute, because it was too expensive, frequently ineffective, and derogatory to the national honor. Repeatedly he emphasized the necessity of establishing a navy to protect American commerce.[65] Evidently this aggressive policy did not appeal to Congress, for on June 3, 1785, that body ordered the sale of the few armed vessels owned by the United States at the end of the Revolution.[66]

The views of Adams did not accord with those of Jefferson. Adams considered the Mediterranean trade sufficiently valuable to preserve at any cost except war, which would increase insurance rates on all commerce. The United States was not strong enough to wage war alone, for

> As long as France, England, Holland, the Empire, etc., will submit to be tributary to these robbers, and even encourage them, to what purpose should we make war upon them? The resolution might be heroic, but would not be wise. The contest would be unequal. They can injure us very sensibly, but we cannot hurt them in the smallest degree... Unless it were possible, then, to persuade the great maritime powers of Europe to unite in the suppression of these piracies, it would be very imprudent for us to entertain any thoughts of contending with them.[67]

When Adams consulted Vergennes on March 20, 1785, he asked advice about the means of negotiating, since the commission originally had no power to delegate its work. The French foreign minister suggested that negotiations be carried on in Morocco instead of in France. He thought that peace would be costly, but if Algeria and Morocco would take the lead, the other Barbary states would follow at less expense. Although the French government asserted its desire to be of service, the tone of the declaration permitted no doubt that the United States must rely upon her own initiative.[68]

When Franklin left Paris on July 12, 1785, to return to America,[69] Jefferson succeeded him as minister to France. Thereafter the treaty negotiations were conducted jointly by Jefferson at Paris and by Adams at London. Congress recognized this separation as a handicap and sent a special agent, John Lamb, formerly a trader in Algeria, with instructions and a plan for a treaty with Morocco.[70] Greatly worried by the long delay in Lamb's arrival, on August 14 Jefferson suggested the selection of another agent.[71] Adams finally agreed, and Jefferson drafted a treaty, based partly on a plan of Franklin's, and appointed Thomas Barclay, consul general of the United States at Paris, to go to Morocco. One half of the $80,000 was to be reserved for Algeria, and $20,000, or a little more if demanded, was to be used for the treaty with Morocco.[72] Lamb finally arrived before Barclay's departure, bringing a treaty plan so similar to Jefferson's that few changes were necessary. Both Jefferson and Adams distrusted Lamb. They decided, however, to send him to Algeria and Barclay to Morocco, as originally planned. Commissions were issued accordingly on October 5, 1785.[73]

The apprehension concerning Lamb's unreliability proved to be well founded. He failed utterly in his mission, and the problem of Algerian relations remained to be solved. With the assistance of Col. William Franks, who accompanied him, Barclay achieved a diplomatic triumph, however.

Delayed by the settling of accounts with M. de Beaumarchais, Barclay left Paris on January 15, 1786.[74] Again Adams and Jefferson sought the aid of France, asking the King to use his influence through his consuls and referring to Article VIII of the treaty of 1778.[75] As before, the monarch replied amicably; he had expressly recommended the American envoys to the French representatives in Morocco, but the Americans had to comply with the conditions demanded.[76]

Once more it was Spain, and not the American ally, which furnished real and substantial support. Barclay and Franks spent two and a half months in Madrid, where Carmichael secured the backing of the King and the Prime Minister, Count de Florida Blanca. With letters from the latter to the Emperor of Morocco and to the Spanish officials in Andalusia and Morocco and a Mathurin at Meknes, the Americans left Cadiz on May 27, 1786, and arrived at Mogador five days later.[77]

Jefferson and Adams had provided Barclay with the draft of the proposed treaty, a letter to the Emperor, and detailed instructions.[78] Included in the last was the assignment to make as thorough a study as possible of the commerce, ports, naval forces, language, government, religion, prisoners, and captures of Morocco. Barclay's expenditures were limited to $20,000.

Barclay arrived at Morocco City (Marrakesh) on June 19, 1786. He had a cordial reception, although he declined a ceremonious one, and he was honored by two audiences with Sidi Muhammad.[79] The emperor suggested that his treaty with Spain be used as a model for the one with the United States. Since a copy was not at hand, Barclay used the opportunity to submit instead the draft he had brought. Several articles met with opposition, but the form finally accepted contained in substance all of Barclay's proposals. The Emperor accepted even Barclay's declaration that the United States would offer for the treaty no tribute but friendship. When offered a favor, Barclay accepted none except the ruler's promise to send letters to Constantinople, Tunisia, Tripoli, and Algeria, recommending their alliance with the United States.[80]

Except for a supplementary article added later, the treaty was completed by July 15, 1786. Barclay had reason to feel that "the King, throughout the whole, has acted in the most gracious and condescending manner; and I really believe that the Americans possess as much of his respect and regard as does any Christian nation whatsoever." The Emperor, Barclay added, was now at peace with all the world except Russia, Malta, Hamburg, and Danzig, although he was complaining much about his treatment by England.[81]

Subject to confirmation by Congress, Francisco, Joseph, and Girolamo Chiappi were appointed by Barclay as consular agents for the United States at Marrakesh, Mogador, and Tangier respectively.[82] He also rendered a full account of his mission, with documents. His total expenses for travel and presents[83] were about L3,966.[84]

A document of great interest is Barclay's report on conditions in Morocco. Of special significance are his views on the commercial value of the treaty:[85]

> It will appear that few of the articles produced in Morocco are wanted in our parts of America, nor could anything manufactured here find a sale there, except a little Morocco leather, which is very fine and good... Still this country holds out objects to the Americans sufficient to make a treaty of peace and commerce a matter of consequence. Our trade to the Mediterranean is rendered the securer for it, and it affords us ports where our ships can refit, if we should be engaged in a European war, or in one with the other Barbary states. Our vessels will certainly become the carriers of wheat from Morocco to Spain, Portugal, and Italy, and may find employment at times when the navigation of our country is stopped by the winter season; and we shall resume our old mule trade from Barbary to Surinam and possibly to some of the West India islands.[86]

Although he did not think that Sidi Muhammad would break the treaty deliberately, Barclay predicted a period of contention after the Sultan's death, when treaties would avail little. He considered the present emperor to be just, courageous, liberal, stern, and a lover of his people. He was on the most cordial and friendly footing with Spain, but there was no other nation of which he had so bad an opinion as of the English.[87]

The treaty was accompanied to the United States by a friendly letter from the Emperor to the President of Congress and another from the Moorish Minister, Sidi Fennish, which was highly commendatory of Barclay.[88] Adams recommended Barclay for the approbation of Congress,[89] which was duly voted to him on July 23, 1787, when Congress also replied most cordially to Sidi Muhammad and resolved to convey thanks to the King of Spain for his services.[90] The treaty was formally ratified by Congress on July 18, 1787.[91] It was not until November 2, 1788, however, that Carmichael received from Francisco Chiappi the Emperor's ratification of the treaty and the long promised letters commending the United States to the favor of the rulers of Tunisia and Tripoli. Sidi Muhammad had been delayed by campaigns against rebellious tribes and by rumored plans to declare war against Great Britain and Denmark.[92]

Neither the Emperor's letters nor the mediation with Algeria promised by Spain as soon as she had made peace with that leading pirate state proved fruitful of results.[93] The failure of Lamb's negotiations with Algeria[94] and the Dey's exorbitant demands for ransom convinced Jefferson that war was the only road to peace.[95] His plan was to form a league of European nations with the United States to carry on concerted action against Barbary, beginning with Algeria. A naval force, raised by quota among league members, was to cruise continuously in the pirate-infested regions until peace without price was achieved.[96] The plan failed because of the lack of enthusiasm among the European powers[97] and of the inability of Congress to provide funds for its quota. Several attempts to obtain the release of American prisoners from Algeria were also unsuccessful.[98]

Following the departure of Barclay from Morocco, leaving the three Chiappi brothers to represent American interests under the recently made treaty, there was a period of tension. Francisco Chiappi was playing the ambivalent role of chief agent for the United States and secretary of the foreign department of Morocco. The chief service of the Chiappis was to reveal the restiveness of Sidi Muhammad under his experimental foreign relations. Joseph Chiappi reported the Emperor's dissatisfaction over the poor response from some nations to his offers of peace and friendship. The Netherlands was facing an attack from five Moroccan frigates if she did not soon make peace. The treaty with the United States might be used to justify transporting Dutch prizes to United States ports. Jefferson told Jay that "it seems to depend on the Dutch whether the Barbary powers shall learn the way to our coast."[99] The much prized treaty with Morocco was seen to have some dangerous implications.

Acting as an imperial official, Francisco Chiappi notified all European consuls in Tangier that Morocco's peace with all nations would last only until 1789. Thereafter, every nation must safeguard its shipping in the Mediterranean by a new peace agreement.[100] Morocco wanted peace, but would send "ten galliots and eight galleys" into the Straits of Gibraltar to close it to any nation showing hostility to the Emperor. Moroccan cruisers at Algeciras, Tangier, and Tetuan could control the Straits. Ships of enemies would be burned and their crews would be imprisoned. And, finally, the involvement of the United States was again threatened:

> His imperial majesty will also send his frigates to America, provided with European pilots, and if they make any prizes, they shall be dealt with as above mentioned, as his imperial majesty stands in no want of money, or any worldly effects; and he trusts that God will make him conqueror.[101]

This apparently complete reversal of Sidi Muhammad's attitude and policy in foreign relations was caused by determined opposition from the powerful governors of his ports, who demanded that pirates should resume bringing booty to Salé, Rabat, and Tangier. Another source of pressure on the Emperor was the large number of his subjects still thirsting for revenge against Christian nations for the expulsion of the Moors from Spain. To maintain the peace which he really desired, the Emperor hoped to placate his war-seeking subjects by offering them the gifts, envoys, and beneficial commercial treaties to be obtained as a substitute for piratical war.

The American commissioners in Europe expressed to their home government their apprehension that the United States itself might not be safe from Moroccan raiders. The American republic was in a dangerous situation at this time for the Continental Congress was rapidly disintegrating and correspondence with Morocco was broken off.[102]

With the inauguration of George Washington as

president on April 30, 1789, the United States government attained a higher status in stability and responsibility. The new executive was aware of the importance of maintaining good relations with Morocco, and Jefferson, now Secretary of State, was in an advantageous position to work for peace with all of Barbary. On December 1, 1789, Washington addressed a letter to his "great and magnanimous friend," Sidi Muhammad, informing him of the recently reorganized American government and apologizing for the lack of attention to Morocco during the transitional period. Washington also thanked the Sultan for the letters mediating for the United States which he had sent to the rulers of Tunisia and Tripoli and promised continued effort to promote friendship and harmony between Morocco and the United States.[103]

In 1791, while still confronted with the serious Algerian problem, the United States had to reconsider the Moroccan situation. For four years American-Moroccan relations, though precarious, had remained peaceful. Jefferson's anxiety about possible American entanglement in Moroccan hostilities with the Netherlands and Great Britain had proved to be unnecessary.[104] When the *Polly* of Salem was captured by Moorish cruisers, the vessel was released by the Emperor with liberal supplies.[105] When Sidi Muhammad XVI died in April, 1790, however, Morocco was again plunged into civil war in the traditional contest over succession to the throne.

The imperial umbrella was first seized by Muhammad's outcast son, al-Yazid. Surnamed "The Bloodthirsty," his reign of terror, although lasting less than two years (1790-1792) made him a rival of Mulai Ismail in infamy. This reign could only have ended in a violent death for al-Yazid. Al-Yazid selected Great Britain as his favorite friend, excluding this country alone from his general declaration of war, while he displayed a special hatred for Spain.[106]

Both Jefferson and Washington urged upon Congress the prime necessity of restoring peace with Morocco.[107] Congress promptly appropriated $20,000 on March 3, 1791, to repurchase the peace treaty.[108] On May 13 Barclay was appointed to negotiate with al-Yazid,[109] receiving a commission making him the first American consul to

Morocco. Col. David Humphreys, the minister resident of the United States to Portugal, was named the dispenser of the funds--not over $10,000 for presents and an annual salary of $2,000, with sea expenses, for Barclay. But because of the civil war which raged even after the slaying of al-Yazid, Barclay decided to observe events from Lisbon, Cadiz, and Gibraltar until peace could make his mission fruitful.[110]

Meanwhile, Washington had appointed Admiral John Paul Jones consul to Algeria to make peace and to ransom American captives. Since there had been no reply from Jones, who, in fact, had been ill (he passed away on July 18, 1872), Barclay was instructed on June 11, 1792, to take his place as soon as his task in Morocco was completed. Without waiting for the cessation of the war in Morocco, Barclay was about to depart for Algeria when he became ill. He died at Lisbon on January 19, 1793.[111]

On March 21, 1793, Col. Humphreys was directed to replace Barclay. He reported to Jefferson on October 8 that a year's truce had been concluded between Algeria and Portugal. Since Algeria was now at peace with all states except the Hanseatic cities and the United States, the Dey began to send frigates into the Atlantic. Dynastic conflict continued in Morocco and the decayed Moorish vessels were not a serious menace to American shipping. Resenting British interference in the making of the Algerian truce, Portugal was furnishing a convoy to protect ships of the two remaining enemies of Algeria.[112]

Al Hisham, one of the four rival emperors reigning in various parts of Morocco, held the primacy at Marrakesh (1792-1795), but his brother Soliman II finally gained control over the whole country. Early in 1795 he gave notice that he would seize the vessels of any country which did not send envoys to him.[113] Jefferson instructed Col. Humphreys on March 28, 1795, to obtain the recognition of the treaty of 1786 from the new emperor at a maximum cost of $25,000. As his agent, Humphreys appointed James Simpson, American consul at Gibraltar, on May 21, 1795.[114]

During July and August of 1795, Simpson negotiated

with Mulai Soliman in Rabat. As presents he had selected chiefly field pieces, small arms, and gunpowder. Mulai Soliman was not satisfied with presents alone, but inquired what annual tribute the United States would pay. To Simpson's reply that his government would pay none, the Emperor countered with the refusal of any treaty. Simpson was advised to return whence he came, but later he was permitted to remain in Morocco until Col. Humphreys could be consulted about the tribute demanded. Before departing to put down a new rebellion, however, Soliman declared publicly that since the Americans were the Christians most esteemed by his father, he would be the same with them as his father was.[115] Instead of a formal endorsement of Sidi Muhammad's treaty, he gave Simpson a letter from himself to the "President of America, a Prince, and to all the States," which concluded thus: "And we are at peace, tranquillity, and friendship with you, in the same manner as you were with our father, who is in glory. Peace."[116]

However, this easily won peace was threatened with rapid destruction. Soliman was still fighting the insurrection around Marrakesh, and the rebels there were obtaining strategic materials from American merchants supplying them at Mazagan and Safi from vessels of the United States. Emperor Soliman threatened war if the United States did not stop this illegal trade.[117] Humphreys found it difficult to explain to a Muslim despot that the free enterprise of American citizens could be curbed only by a law of Congress, requiring considerable time for passage. Fortunately, when the rebels were defeated, Soliman's estrangement from the United States ended.

While peace was being reaffirmed with Morocco, the first treaties of peace and friendship with other Barbary powers were being made--with Algeria on September 5, 1795, and with Tripoli on November 4, 1796.[118] Their conclusion put a temporary halt to the building of the United States navy, which had been inspired chiefly by the Algerine attacks on American ships and citizens. Jefferson's report of December 28, 1790[119] had laid before Congress the alternatives of war, tribute, or ransom. On February 22, 1792, the Senate advised Washington of the desirability of a navy as soon as finances would permit;

meanwhile, funds for tribute and ransom were recommended. From February 6 to March 10, 1794, there were heated debates in Congress over the bill to establish a navy. The opposition feared that a navy would involve the United States in European conflicts and would destroy American liberty. The law passed on March 17, 1794, provided for the building of six frigates, with suspension of construction if peace were made meantime with Barbary. The three vessels under way when the treaty with Algeria was made were completed, forming a navy nucleus of the Constitution, the United States, and the Constellation; the materials for the other frigates were sold, except those needed to build the frigate presented to Algeria.[120]

In his message to Congress on December 7, 1796, Washington declared his adherence to the policy advocated by Jefferson since the latter's first contact with the problem of piracy:

> To an active external commerce, the protection of a naval force is indispensable. This is manifest with regard to wars in which the State itself is a party. But... to secure respect to a neutral flag requires a naval force, organized and ready to vindicate it from insult or aggression... From the best information I have been able to obtain, it would seem as if our trade in the Mediterranean, without a protecting force, will always be insecure, and our citizens exposed to the calamities from which numbers of them have just been relieved. These considerations invite the United States to look to the means, and to set about the gradual creation of a navy.[121]

Washington's warning was well founded. Apparently the treaty made with Tunisia in August, 1797,[122] had completed the pacification of Barbary. But scarcely had Jefferson become president when his familiar problem returned to plague him. Envious because of richer gifts received by Tunisia, Tripoli declared war on the United States in 1801. Unfortunately, the foundation of the navy, which had been strengthened during the undeclared war against France under President John Adams, had been weakened later by Adams and Jefferson.[123] But Jefferson was able to send a small squadron to blockade the coasts of Tripoli and to protect American commerce. Successive reinforcements were necessary to achieve satisfactory results.[124] It was not until June 4, 1805, that Tripoli agreed to a treaty pledging peace without tribute or captivity for Americans.[125]

Meanwhile, the United States had established a permanent consulate in Morocco. When negotiating the confirmation of the Treaty of 1786, Simpson had been advised by the Sultan that the United States should appoint a resident consul for the greater protection of her vessels. Washington had already anticipated this need by requesting funds for this purpose in his message to Congress dated March 2, 1795. Landing at Tangier on December 7, 1797, Simpson was cordially received as the "Consul General" of the United States. Thus he was at hand to prevent the war with Tripoli from involving Morocco to the point of destroying the reforged bonds of peace with the United States.[126]

Mulai Soliman had misjudged the Tripolitan War as a favorable time for attacking the audacious nation which had refused him tribute. In January, 1801, he had not even one vessel afloat, but he was building two frigates. In February, 1802, he wanted to send wheat to Tripoli, and he also demanded the release of a Tripolitan cruiser blockaded at Tangier. Backed by Commodores Dale and Morris of the American squadron, Simpson refused assent to Soliman's desires. Then Soliman declared war. Simpson crossed over to Gibraltar, but later the Emperor invited him to return to Morocco. Soliman next asked for annual gifts, but Simpson proved the untruth of his assertion that these had been stipulated in the Treaty of 1786.

Next the Emperor tried to claim as his own property the blockaded Tripolitan ship, the Mashuda, and sent thirty Moors from Tetuan to take the vessel when Simpson refused it a passport. Soliman was partially conciliated by Jefferson's promise of a present of one hundred gun carriages. War with Morocco could be more serious than with Tripoli, for the Atlantic coast ports could not be effectively blockaded, and the Madeira and Atlantic coast commerce of the United States would be endangered as well as the Mediterranean trade.[127]

On August 16, 1801, Simpson informed Commodore

Morris that peace had been restored. Thereafter Morris gave up the blockade of Tripoli, permitting passports to send Moroccan wheat there, both because he wished to avoid war with Morocco and also because the domestic supply of grain in Tripoli was said to be abundant.[128] As late as March 22, 1803, however, Jefferson was trying to maintain peace by sending money and stores to Morocco and Algeria.[129]

Later in 1803 hostilities with Morocco were resumed. In July two Moroccan cruisers sailed to search for American prey. One of these was taken into custody by Commodore Bainbridge after it had captured an American brig. The other was boarded and taken over by Commodore Preble. When the commodores went to Tangier with their frigates to interview Soliman, he was reported to be disavowing all hostile acts. On October 10 he gave an audience to Preble and Tobias Lear during which he capitulated without conditions. He recognized the blockade of Tripoli and agreed to release an American ship held at Mogador and to dismiss the governor of Tangier, whom he blamed for the unfriendly acts against the United States. He ratified the Treaty of 1786 again and sent abundant provisions to the American war vessels. In return his two offending cruisers were returned to him.[130]

Jefferson informed Congress on December 5, 1803, of the amicable adjustment of all difficulties with Morocco and of the reconfirmation of the Treaty of 1786. He also commended the energy and initiative of the American naval officers[131] and advocated that Congress indemnify the captors of the returned Moorish vessels.[132]

As reinsurance against Moroccan backsliding, Simpson employed the potent persuasion of the American Mediterranean Squadron. Apparently Soliman intended to intervene for Tripoli again, since he was fitting out cruisers and had requested a passport to send a cargo of provisions there. Commodore Barron, now commander of the squadron, refused to raise the blockade of Tripoli and sent the frigates *Congress* and *Essex* to Tangier, where they patrolled the Moroccan coast to Salé before returning to Gibralter.

Simpson was not engaged in the completion of the Tripolitan War. Victory was achieved by the United States after a strong offensive by the squadron under Commodore Barron and a spectacular land campaign planned and led by William Eaton, American consul at Tripoli.[133] Unfortunately, the treaty negotiated by Tobias Lear and signed on June 4, 1805, did not adequately reflect the American exploits. It did, however, provide for peace without tribute, although ransom for the captured American officers and crews was set at $60,000 and presents were to be given by each new consul from the United States.[134]

The year 1803, therefore, is a milestone in American-Moroccan relations. The treaty of 1786 had been the first between a Christian power and a Barbary state that did not provide for tribute, but not until 1803 was Morocco's ruler finally resigned to being deprived of both tribute and ransom. Hereafter, no officially inspired attacks were made by Morocco upon American vessels. There were a few cases of so-called piracy, really plundering of stranded vessels, on the coasts of the Sus and the Riff, and the instance of the *Ann Lucy* at Mazagan.[135] Under later rulers there were some revivals of piracy by rebellious tribes, but Mulai Soliman signified his final loyalty to the Treaty of 1786 by several acts implementing it. In 1814 he formally abolished Christian slavery.[136] Four years later he officially ended the practice of commissioning vessels to prey on European ships, and the British did not blame this mild-tempered ruler for the occasional attacks on their ships, for they realized that his control over many of his subjects was merely nominal.[137] Undoubtedly he was within his rights when, in 1820, he dispatched his vessels to capture European ships carrying on contraband trade in animals and grain along the Riff coast.

Although the United States practically solved her part of the piracy problem between 1786 and 1803, it would be an error to conclude that any such definite dates can be set for the termination of Moroccan piracy on other Christian ships. The institution died out slowly in all the Barbary states. It had begun to decline by 1750 and was greatly weakended by an attack from Tuscany in 1773; Sidi Muhammad's inclination toward peace treaties was probably a necessity transformed into a virtue. During the reign of Emperor Abd er-Rahman (1822-1859), piracy had become practically extinct, but in 1828 it was decided to revive the "Holy War by Sea." The capture of two Austrian merchantmen caused a conflict lasting several years. The searching of British ships in the Atlantic was stopped only after the blockade of Tangier by a British squadron.[138]

In 1836, learning that Morocco was planning to send out a new armed cruiser, probably to attack the merchant ships of the smaller states, Foreign Minister Palmerston instructed John Hay, the British consul general at Tangier, to register a protest. The Moors found the handling of this vessel so difficult that they gave up the plan. More serious was the fitting out of two war vessels at Larache in 1841, admittedly with the design of capturing the ships of all countries which had no treaties or diplomatic relations with Morocco. Vigorous British protests were effectively reinforced by a Spanish frigate arriving at Tangier to liberate a Spanish ship. In 1840 the governments of Denmark and Sweden-Norway failed to gain the Sultan's consent to terminate their annual tributes. Four years later, when threatened with war by both France and Spain, Abd er-Rahman yielded after stubborn resistance to the mediation of France and Great Britain. The resulting agreement of April, 1845, provided that no future payments of tribute would be required if arrears were paid up.[139]

Piracy by the Riffian tribes along the Mediterranean coast was virtually an independent enterprise. In 1831 reports were made to the British government that ships cast ashore were plundered and that their crews were maltreated or murdered. After especially pernicious activities of the Riffian and other pirates on the Atlantic in 1834 and 1835 had been followed by stern warnings and threats from Great Britain, the depredations became less frequent. The Riffs destroyed a British brig in 1846. The Sultan professed inability to control them, but the governor of the Riff succeeded in punishing the guilty. To carry out the warning that another act of piracy would result in reprisals by British forces, a British fleet was sent in 1848 under Sir Charles Napier to avenge a new attack. Through the influence of the French government, which feared that Great Britain might occupy Moroccan territory, and of Gibralter merchants, who feared loss of trade, Napier withdrew without a definite settlement. Nevertheless, the demonstration was effective for several years. The period 1852-1856 was marked by unprecedented activity of the Riffians against British, Spanish, and French nationals. After many conflicting plans had been abandoned, the personal intervention of John Hay with the Riffian chiefs secured results. The pirate tribes were so terribly punished by troops of the Sultan and of the Beni Snassen that this last stronghold of piracy was finally destroyed permanently. In the British-Moroccan treaty of 1856 the Sultan of Morocco was bound to repress and punish piracy and to aid the British government in doing the same.[140] This may be regarded as the last word on the subject of Moroccan piracy as it relates to European countries.

The principles repudiating tribute and ransom were not finally accepted by the other Barbary states until thirty years after Morocco first set the example. Despite her treaty and her tribute, Algeria, always the most aggressively hostile of them all, did not accept the American policy on piracy until 1816. After the war of 1812, the United States was free for a final and effective chastisement of the Algerian corsairs who had committed outrages during that conflict. Then the squadrons led by Decatur and Bainbridge forced new treaties from Algeria, Tripoli, and Tunisia.[141] The Dey's clumsy attempt to falsify the Shaler-Decatur treaty of June 6, 1815, was foiled by Commodores Shaler and Chauncy in August, 1816. On December 23, 1816, Algeria formally agreed to the abolition of her chief industry.[142] Thus Madison finished the work with which his colleague Jefferson had struggled throughout his entire career as peace commissioner, secretary of state, and president.[143]

After 1816, the United States was no longer harassed by piracy, but her victories did not make the world safe from the scourge. At the Congress of Vienna, Tsar Alexander proposed an international squadron in the Mediterranean to abolish piracy. Great Britain refused to agree to any plan which would admit Russian warships into the Mediterranean.[144] It was feared that Russia was merely seeking a pretext to secure naval bases there from which to attack Turkey and Buenos Aires.[145] In the characteristic family manner, John Quincy Adams expressed his ideas on the significance of the American achievement in 1815:

> If it be discovered that the American commerce can be freely carried on in the Mediterranean without being subject to the tax of tribute to the pirates, a sudden spasm of philanthropy will immediately seize the British bosom for imparting the same benefits to itself and perhaps even to the traders of other nations. Let us then hold the Bashaws and the Divans, the Beys and the Deys, stubbornly to the execution of their treaties, and let us hear no more of tribute in any shape. But it is sufficient for us to exempt ourselves from these humiliations, and to leave the commerce of Europe to the protection and policy of its own governments.[146]

A French historian quotes Lord Castlereagh to the effect that "the destruction of the Regencies... would inevitably result in the creation upon the coast of Africa of states united to France, which would destroy our influence in the Mediterranean, and in consequence ruin our commerce."[147] In 1816, however, a combined English and Dutch fleet under Lord Exmouth bombared Algiers and dictated a treaty abolishing slavery for prisoners of war. At this time 1,642 captives were liberated. Tunisia and Tripoli were also compelled to renounce enslavement of Christians.[148] Yet in 1817 Tunisian pirates dared to cruise in the English Channel and the North Sea, where they captured vessels from Hamburg and other Hanse cities. As late as 1825, Sweden, Denmark, Portugal, and Naples were still paying tribute.[149] The $26,000 paid to Algeria in 1812 was the last acknowledged tribute paid by the United States to any Barbary power, although for some years afterwards large sums went to finance "intercourse," chiefly for gifts. France, Sardinia, and the Netherlands made treaties with Algeria similar to that imposed by the United States,[150] but Algerian performance often failed to square with promises. Eventually, France, to whom the United States had first applied for aid in 1778, became the heir to the estates of three of the pirate dynasties which had mocked and ravaged the Christian powers for centuries.

The American-Moroccan treaty of 1786 is significant for several reasons, both related and unrelated to piracy.

As the first treaty omitting tribute, its moderate cost distinguishes it from the first agreements with the other Barbary states. To the original expenditure by Barclay of about 3,966 pounds of sterling[151] need be added only the $13,000 spent by Simpson to obtain the confirmation of the treaty.[152] The first payment to Tripoli of $56,000 was not supplemented by annuities, for only Algeria secured regular tribute. But there was some expense for ceremonial presents, and by the exchange of prisoners after the war of 1805 Tripoli received $60,000 as ransom for the excess number of Americans. The treaty of 1797 with Tunisia, negotiated by Barlow, cost $107,000.[153] Peace with Algeria cost almost a million dollars in 1795. A report of Timothy Pickering, laid before Congress on January 6, 1797, gave $642,500 as the amount paid for ransom, tribute, and presents to Algerian officials. In addition, the United States agreed to build a frigate and supply naval stores, which brought the total original cost up to $992,463.25. The annual tribute in naval stores was estimated as $144,246.63 for the first two years.[154] Between March 4, 1789, and September 30, 1801, the Dey of Algeria was paid $258,846.58.[155] And even after tribute ceased in 1812, annual appropriations of several thousand dollars were made for presents until the mid-century.[156]

The first American-Moroccan treaty deserves careful study not only because it established a durable basis for relationships between its makers, but also because it set forth principles later incorporated into the foreign policy of the United States. Yet it is a simple document containing but twenty-five brief articles, the first one merely an introductory statement of agreement between the parties. The last article provides that "this treaty shall continue in full force, with the help of God, for fifty years."[157]

Designed originally to end piracy and enslavement of captives, the treaty has seven articles and a supplementary article much like an amendment, added as a special testimonial of the Emperor's good will, which dealt with the abolition of these evils in very specific terms.[158] American citizens brought to the Emperor or into his ports by Muslims,[159] whether natives of Morocco or not, were to be released with their goods. Vessels of either country could put into the ports of the other for provisions and supplies. Protection, assistance, and non-payment of duty were granted to American ships seeking repairs or driven by disaster into the ports of Morocco or onto the coast of Wadnun. By the supplementary article, protection was promised to any American vessel in the Emperor's ports or within gunshot of his forts, and neither Muslim nor Christian power at war with the United States would be allowed to follow or engage such an American ship. No American ship of war putting into Moroccan ports would be examined for fugitive slaves. In case of war between the United States and Morocco, the captives were not to be enslaved, but were to be exchanged, rank for rank, and a deficiency in matching numbers was to be made up by paying one hundred Mexican dollars for each person lacking. Prisoners were to be exchanged within twelve months after capture.

Another group of provisions regulated the conduct of the two countries during war.[160] Signals or passes were to be used to identify all vessels. Neither party was to take a commission from any country with which the other was at war. If a prize ship taken from a country at war with either party should contain subjects or goods of the other party, the said subjects and goods should be unmolested. Also, goods belonging to a nation at war with either party, if on the vessels of the other party, should pass freely. This is a clear statement of the "free ships, free goods" doctrine so consistently championed by the United States in later years. Vessels of either party fighting with vessels of any Christian power within gunshot of the forts of the other were to be defended by the latter. Reciprocal salutes of warships were stipulated. If Moroccan vessels warring with a Christian power should sail from American ports, or if American vessels in conflict with either Muslim or Christian peoples should sail from Moroccan ports, no enemy vessel would be permitted to follow for twenty-four hours. Since the most probable wars would be between the United States and the other Barbary powers, these provisions were largely to the advantage of the United States. Finally, if disagreements should arise over any infringement of the treaty, peace was to be kept until a friendly application could be made for an arrangement. There was to be no appeal to arms unless such an application were rejected. If war did ensue, nine months were to be allowed for subjects of either party to dispose of their effects or retire with their property.

Equally enlightened and progressive were the principles of commercial intercourse. Merchants of both countries were guaranteed freedom in the selection of employees and interpreters and in the purchase and sale of goods. Captains of vessels were not to be detained in port or to suffer from interference with cargoes and freight rates. If contraband goods were discovered on a vessel, punishment was to be imposed only upon the person who had brought it upon the ship.[161]

Most important of all the commercial provisions were the following, which the United States claimed as the basis for her policy of "equality of economic opportunity" in Morocco:

> The commerce of the United States shall be on the same footing as is the commerce with Spain or as that with the most favored nation for the time being, and their citizens shall be respected and esteemed and have full liberty to pass and repass our country and seaports whenever they please without interruption...
>
> Whatever indulgences in trade or otherwise shall be granted to any of the Christian powers, the citizens of the United States shall be equally entitled to them.[162]

The remaining sections of the document deal with the establishment of the consular system of the United States in Morocco, with its correlative institutions of extraterritoriality and protection.[163] American consuls were permitted to reside in any seaport of Morocco, to enjoy all privileges granted to consuls of any other nation, and to be free from responsibility for debts of fellow nationals. They were given authority to settle disputes between American citizens "or any persons under their protection" and to assist at murder or assault trials in which both Americans and Muslims were involved. If an American citizen should die intestate in Morocco, the consul or some person worthy of trust was to take charge of his effects until an heir could arrive. If the heir were present, he would be assigned the property of the deceased forthwith.

The consul was to be the judge of the validity of any alleged will.[164]

In its development the Moroccan problem of piracy is seen to be of considerable significance in American history. No diplomatic question gave a better demonstration of the constructive statesmanship of Franklin, Adams, and Jefferson--particularly of the last. The practical executive ability of Barclay and Simpson is almost unknown, while the public holds in high honor the exploits of the naval commanders, Preble, Barron, Bainbridge, and Decatur, worthy heirs to the tradition founded by John Paul Jones.[165] The glory of the spectacular naval victories against Tripoli and Algeria has obscured the sober triumphs of diplomacy which removed the centuries-old curse of piracy in Morocco. Occasionally critics unfriendly to Jefferson censure without warrant his alleged timidity or parsimony. Very rarely are the achievements of the navy depreciated.[166] But appreciation of the real nature and worth of the work of Jefferson, his colleagues, and his lieutenants grows as the facts become known.[167]

The first American-Moroccan treaty occupies a place in the story of American contributions to the development of international law. It gave recognition to the later American principles of belligerent and neutral rights and the policy of the most favored nation and the Open Door. It was not unique among American treaties in this; these principles were embodied in all of the treaties made by the Continental Congress between 1778 and 1788.[168] The achievement of American diplomacy in obtaining such liberal commercial provisions in the treaty with Morocco is not greatly lessened by the fact that they were the "result of an evolution of four and a half centuries of commercial intercourse with Europe."[169]

During the nineteenth century the growth of foreign interests and influence in Morocco was rapid, and international rivalry and protection made Morocco a problem again. In these developments the United States played an active and influential part.

Notes

1. The Christian pirates were chiefly Greeks, Sardinians, Maltese, and Genoese.

2. Gardner Weld Allen, Our Navy and the Barbary Corsairs (hereafter cited as Allen, Barbary Corsairs), 2-3; Stanley Lane-Poole, The Story of the Barbary Corsairs (hereafter cited as Lane-Poole, Barbary Corsairs), Fourth Edition, 23-25, 28; Bovill, Golden Trade of the Moors, 111.

3. Ibid., 204-205; Lane-Poole, Barbary Corsairs, 26-27.

4. It was in this Turkish period of rule, dating from early in the 16th century, that the eastern and central Maghreb were first divided into three distinct areas: Tripolitania, Tunisia, and Algeria, with approximately the same frontiers that exist today. Algeria was most important at this time because it was the headquarters of the Barbarossas, who added the former territories of Tlemcen, Bougie, and Constantine to their domain. Barbour, North West Africa, 32.

5. David Hannay, "Barbary Pirates," Encyclopedia Britannica, Eleventh Edition (hereafter cited as Hannay, "Barbary Pirates," E.B.), III 383; Allen, Barbary Corsairs, 3-5; Juan Cabal, Piracy and Pirates, A History (hereafter cited as Cabal, Piracy and Pirates), 69-80.

6. Ibid., 113-114; Encyclopedia of World History, 389.

7. Lane-Poole, Barbary Corsairs, 186-187; 256-260; Barbour, North West Africa, 30-31; William Ray Manning, "Diplomatic Relations with the Barbary Powers," Cyclopedia of American Government, 3 vols., I, 121-122.

8. N. D. Harris, Colonization in Africa, 214-215.

9. Barbour, North West Africa, 36-37.

10. The Moriscos were Muslims supposedly converted to Christianity but suspected by the Spanish of secretly retaining their original faith.

11. Allen, *Barbary Corsairs,* 6-7; Hannay, "Barbary Pirates," *E. B.*, III, 383; Augustin Bernard, *Le Maroc,* Sixth Edition (hereafter cited as Bernard, *Le Maroc*), 289; Lane-Poole, *Barbary Corsairs,* 188.

12. Ibid., 256-257; Irwin, *Diplomatic Relations of the United States with the Barbary Powers,* 15-16.

13. Smith was evidently ignorant of the history of piracy, for the Barbary pirates had had many instructors from Genoa, Sicily, Greece, Catalonia, and Pisa long before the advent of the English pirates. Meakin, *Moorish Empire,* 243, 254, 256.

14. George Louis Beer, *The Old Colonial System,* 1660-1754, 2 vols. (hereafter cited as Beer, *Old Colonial System*), I, 121-127; Stuart, *Tangier,* 7-9; Allen, *Barbary Corsairs,* 8.

15. Salvador de Madariaga, *Spain* (hereafter cited as Madariaga, *Spain*), 337.

16. It was not until 1845, after the Battle of Isly, that the last of these tributes to Morocco was tendered. Bernard, Le Maroc, 290; Francis Rosebro Flournoy, *British Policy Toward Morocco in the Age of Palmerston* (1830-1865) (hereafter cited as Flournoy, *British Policy Toward Morocco*), 105-107.

17. Meakin, *Moorish Empire,* 290; Lane-Poole, *Barbary Corsairs,* 258.

18. Barbour, *North West Africa,* 36; Lane-Poole, *Barbary Corsairs,* 188-191; Meakin, *Moorish Empire,* 262; Budgett Meakin and Kate A. Meakin, "Morocco," *E. B.*, XVIII, 857.

19. Meakin, *Moorish Empire,* 303.

20. Lane-Poole, *Barbary Corsairs,* 242; quoting Capt. John Braithwaite, *History of the Revolutions in Morocco,* 345ff.

21. Francis R. Flournoy, "Political Relations of Great Britain with Morocco from 1830 to 1841," (hereafter cited as Flournoy, "Political Relations of Great Britain with Morocco"), Political Science Quarterly, XLVII (March, 1932), 28.

22. American State Papers, Class I, Foreign Relations, 6 vols. (hereafter cited as A. S. P., F. R.), I, 104.

23. Irwin, Diplomatic Relations of the United States with the Barbary Powers, 18. The statistics are quoted from David McPherson, Annals of Commerce, Manufactures, Fisheries, and Navigation, 4 vols., III, 572-573 and are based upon offical English records.

24. Committee of Secret Correspondence to Franklin, Dean, and A. Lee, December 21, 1776; Revolutionary Diplomatic Correspondence of the United States, edited by Francis Wharton, 6 vols. (hereafter cited as Wharton), II, 230.

25. Journals of the Continental Congress, 1774-1789, edited by Worthington C. Ford and others, 32 vols. to 1787 (hereafter cited as W. C. Ford, Journals), V, 578.

26. Stuart, Tangier, 38; Bernard, Le Maroc, 290.

27. W. C. Ford, Journals, XI, 426-427.

28. Franklin, Lee, and Adams to Vergennes, Aug. 28, 1778. Wharton, II, 698.

29. Sartine to Vergennes, Sept. 21, 1778. Ibid., II, 731; Vergennes to the Commissioners at Paris, Sept. 27, 1778. Ibid., II, 746-747.

30. Proceedings relative to Barbary, Feb. 24, 1779. Ibid., III, 61-62.

31. W. C. Ford, Journals, XIII, 219, 223-224.

32. Malloy, Treaties, II, 1240.

33. Wharton, VI, 471.

34. Allen, Barbary Corsairs, 26-27; Irwin, Diplomatic Relations of the United States with the Barbary States, 23-25.

35. The declaration pertained also to vessels under Russian, German, Prussian, Hungarian, Neapolitan, Sardinian, Tuscanian, Genoese, and Maltese flags--all banners of minor countries hitherto paying frequently ineffectual tribute to Morocco.

36. Wharton, IV, 172-173.

37. An account of the dealings of d'Audibert Caille with countries other than the United States is given by Francis Torrance Williamson in Germany and Morocco before 1905 (the Johns Hopkins University Studies in Historical and Political Science, Series LV, No. 1) (hereafter cited as Williamson, Germany and Morocco before 1905), 101-102.

38. Albert Henry Smythe, editor, The Writings of Benjamin Franklin, 10 vols. (hereafter cited as Smythe, Franklin), VII, 328; Franklin to the Committee of Foreign Affairs, May 26, 1779, Wharton, III, 192-193.

39. Caille to Jay, April 21, 1780; Jay to Congress, Nov. 30, 1780, Wharton, IV, 169-174.

40. Instructions from Congress to Franklin, Nov. 28, 1780, Ibid., IV, 164; W. C. Ford, Journals, XVIII, 1104.

41. The first official communication of the United States government to the ruler of Morocco read as follows:

The Congress of the 13 United States of North America to the high, potent, and most noble prince, the King and Emperor of Morocco.

Most Noble and Puissant Prince:

We the Congress of the 13 United States of North America, have been informed of your majesty's favourable regard to the interests of the people we represent, which has been communicated by Monsieur Etienne d'Audibert Caille of Salé, consul of foreign nations unrepresented in your majesty's states. We assure you of our earnest desire to cultivate a sincere and firm peace and friendship with your majesty and to make it lasting to all posterity... Should any of the subjects of our states come within the ports of your majesty's territories, we flatter ourselves they will receive the benefit of your protection and benevolence. You may assure yourself of every protection and assistance to your subjects from the people of these states whenever and wherever they may have it in their power. We pray your majesty may enjoy long life and uninterrupted prosperity.

December 1780 (no day), and our independence 5.

42. Secret Journals of the Acts and Proceedings of Congress, from the first meeting thereof to the dissolution of the confederation by the adoption of the Constitution of the United States, 4 vols. (hereafter cited as Secret Journals), III, 543-544.

43. Crocco to Franklin, Nov. 25, 1783, Wharton, VI, 734.

44. Adams, Franklin, and Jay to Congress, Sept. 10, 1783; Adams to Congress, Sept. 10, 1783; Franklin to Congress, Sept. 13, 1783; Wharton, VI, 690-692, 697-698.

45. Franklin to Crocco, Passy, Dec. 15, 1783, Diplomatic Correspondence of the United States of America, from the signing of the definitive treaty of peace, 10th September, 1783, to the adoption of the Constitution, March 4, 1789, Second Edition, 3 vols. (hereafter cited as D. C. of the U. S.), I, 373-374.

46. Franklin to Carmichael, Passy, Dec. 15, 1783, Ibid., I, 374-375; Smythe, Franklin, IX, 126-127.

47. W. C. Ford, *Journals*, XXVI, 143-144.

48. Barclay to Jay, Nov. 14, 1783, *D. C. of the U. S.*, I, 68.

49. Adams to Livingston, July 3, 1783 and July 12, 1783, Wharton, VI, 513, 538; Franklin to Livingston, July 25, 1783, Smythe, *Franklin*, IX, 71.

50. Excerpt from Franklin's Diary, July 10, 1784, *Ibid.*, X, 352-354.

51. Committee reports to Congress, W. C. Ford, *Journals*, XXIV, 404; XXV, 531, 821, 824-825.

52. Samuel Gwynn Coe, *The Mission of William Carmichael to Spain* (hereafter cited as Coe, *Carmichael*), 57.

53. Emory Richard Johnson and others, *A History of the Domestic and Foreign Commerce of the United States*, 2 vols. (hereafter cited as Johnson, *Commerce of the United States*), I, 160.

54. *Register of the Department of State, in Four Parts, Corrected to March 1, 1874* (hereafter cited as *D. S. Register, 1874*), 128-129.

55. Resolution of Congress, *D. C. of the U. S.*, I, 80-83; W. C. Ford, *Journals*, XXVI, 360-362.

56. *D. C. of the U. S.*, I, 501; *Secret Journals*, III, 536; Wharton, VI, 804.

57. Carmichael was charge d'affaires in Madrid from June, 1782 to September 29, 1789 and from April 20, 1790 to September 5, 1794. *D. S. Register, 1874*, 58, 98. For his services from March to June, 1785 see Coe, *Carmichael*, 62-63.

58. Coe, *Carmichael*, 57, 59, 61-62; Carmichael to Franklin, Feb. 27, 1784. *D. C. of the U. S.*, III, 285-287; Goublot to Carmichael, Sale, June 25, 1785, *Ibid.*, I, 634; Carmichael to Jefferson, July 19, 1785, *Ibid.*, I, 633; Florida Blanca to Carmichael, July 24, 1785, *Ibid.*, I, 301.

59. Jefferson to Madison, Sept. 1, 1785, Andrew Adgate Lipscomb, editor, *The Writings of Thomas Jefferson,* Montecello Edition, 20 vols. (hereafter cited as Lipscomb, *Jefferson*), V, 107-108.

60. Allen, *Barbary Corsairs,* 13-14.

61. *D. S. Register, 1874,* 58.

62. Reports of the Joint Commissioners and Ministers Plenipotentiary for the formation of treaties of amity and commerce with foreign powers to Congress; Nov. 11, 1784, 534-540; Dec. 15, 1784, 544-545, Feb., 1785, 551-552; March 18, 1785, 562-564; April 13, 1785, 576-577; May 11, 1785, 581-582; June 18, 1785, 592-593; Aug. 14, 1785, 597-598; Oct. 2 and 11, 1785, 600; *D. C. of the U. S.*, I.

63. W. C. Ford, *Journals,* XXVIII, 65-66.

64. *Ibid.*, 140-148.

65. Paul Leicester Ford, editor, *The Writings of Thomas Jefferson,* 10 vols. (hereafter cited as P. L. Ford, *Jefferson*), IV: Jefferson to Monroe, Nov. 11, 1784, 10-11; Jefferson to Horatio Gates, Dec. 13, 1784, 24; Jefferson to Monroe, Feb., 1785, 31-34.

66. Johnson, *Commerce of the United States*, II, 17.

67. Adams to Jay, Dec. 15, 1784, *D. C. of the U. S.*, I, 471.

68. Adams to Jefferson and Franklin, March 20, 1785, *Ibid.*, II, 566-568; the Commissioners to Vergennes, March 28, 1785, *Ibid.*, 568-569; Vergennes to the Commissioners, April 28, 1785, *Ibid.*, 572-574.

69. Allen, *Barbary Corsairs,* 28.

70. William Kirk Woolery, *The Relations of Thomas Jefferson to American Foreign Policy, 1783-1793* (Johns Hopkins University Studies in Historical and Political Science), IX (hereafter cited as Woolery, *Thomas Jefferson*), 21-22.

71. Jefferson to Jay, Aug. 14, 1785 and Aug. 30, 1785, D. C. of the U. S., I, 598 and 642.

72. Ibid., II, 331-332.

73. Jefferson to Adams, Sept. 24, 1785, Ibid., II, 16-17; Adams to Jay, Feb. 16, 1786, Ibid., 565-566 and Ibid., I, 657.

74. Jefferson to Jay, Jan. 27, 1786, Ibid., 713-714.

75. The Commissioners to Vergennes, March 28, 1786, Ibid., 568-569.

76. M. Marshal de Castries to M. de la Foret, Jan. 22, 1786, Ibid., 235.

77. Woolery, Thomas Jefferson, 25. For evidence of the important influence exerted by Spain on American-Moroccan relations, see the following: Coe, Carmichael, 63-66, 70; Carmichael to Jefferson, Aug. 17, 1786, D. C. of the U. S., I, 817-818; Jefferson to Jay, Dec. 31, 1786, Ibid., II, 13; the Emperor of Morocco to the King of Spain, June 28, 1786, Ibid., 699; Lasby Effendi to Don Salmon, Ibid., III, 313-314; Don Salmon to Count de Greppi, June 25, 1786, Ibid., 315-316; Carmichael to Jay, Sept. 2, 1786, Ibid., 319-320.

78. Jefferson and Adams to the Emperor of Morocco, D. C. of the U. S., I, 663-664; draft of treaty, Ibid., 666-673; instructions, Ibid., 658-662. Irwin, Diplomatic Relations of the United States with the Barbary States, 30.

79. Barclay to Adams and Jefferson, June 10, 1788, D. C. of the U. S., III, 29 and Sept. 13, 1786, Ibid., II, 720-721.

80. Barclay to Adams and Jefferson, Sept. 18, 1786, Ibid., 721-725.

81. Barclay to Adams and Jefferson, July 16, 1786, Ibid., III, 33-34; supplementary article, signed by Barclay at Madrid, Dec. 4, 1786, Ibid., II.

82. Commissions of agents, July 15, 1786, Ibid., 725.

83. Characteristically, the New Englander Adams complained that Barclay had exceeded his allowance and that he had to go to Holland to borrow more money to pay the interest on former loans. Adams had already notified Jay in January, 1787, of his intention to resign his ministry in Great Britain and return to America. On October 5, 1787, Congress passed a resolution accepting his resignation with a vote of thanks. It was to be effective on February 24, 1788. Adams confided to Jay shortly before he left England that he had been "personally treated with the same uniform tenor of dry decency and cold civility which appeared to have been the premeditated plan from the beginning." Adams to Jay, May 23, 1787 and Jan. 24, 1787, 751 and 692-693; resolution of Congress, Oct. 5, 1787, 798; Adams to Jay, Feb. 14, 1788, 826-827; Ibid., II.

84. Barclay to Adams and Jefferson, July 13, 1787 and Oct. 2, 1786, Ibid., 76 and 694-695.

85. The situation in Barbary was a vital factor in the commercial depression in 1786 which gave so powerful an impetus toward the constitutional convention of 1787. The merchants of the country declared that the British trade restrictions, the Barbary piracies, New Jersey's refusal to pay her quota of requisitions, and New York's taxing of products from neighboring states would abolish American government and commerce alike. John Bach McMaster, A History of the People of the United States from the Revolution to the Civil War, 7 vols. (hereafter cited as McMaster, History), I, 361-364, 405.

86. Barclay to Adams and Jefferson, Nov. 10, 1786, D. C. of the U. S., II, 701-705.

87. Ibid., Sept. 13, 1786, 716-720.

88. The Emperor of Morocco to the President of Congress, June 28, 1786, Ibid., 698-699; Sidi Fennish to Adams and Jefferson, June 28, 1786, Ibid., 700.

89. Adams to Jay, Jan. 27, 1787, Ibid., 693-694.

90. Secret Journals, IV, 365-370.

91. W. C. Ford, Journals, XXXII, 355-364.

92. Carmichael to Jay, Nov. 5, 1788, D. C. of the U. S., III, 370-371.

93. Carmichael to Adams and Jefferson, Feb. 3, 1786, Ibid., I; Carmichael to Jay, Sept. 2, 1786, Ibid., III, 319-320.

94. Coe, Carmichael, 71-72.

95. Elated over his success in Morocco, Barclay offered to go to Tunisia, Tripoli, and Algeria to secure similar treaties. Jefferson declined his offer (Sept. 22, 1786) because of Spanish and French advice to make a treaty with Turkey first and because of the objection of Adams to treating with Algeria. Ibid., 70.

96. Allen, Barbary Corsairs, 40-41; Jefferson to Monroe, Aug. 11, 1786, P.L. Ford, Jefferson, IV, 265; Ibid., I, 91-94.

97. Vergennes put an end to planning by Jefferson and Lafayette for international action. He commanded the latter to desist, saying that neither Great Britain nor France would permit such an enterprise, because "both these governments profitied by the piratical system." Beckles Willson, America's Ambassadors to France (1777-1927). A Narrative of Franco-American Diplomatic Relations (hereafter cited as Willson, America's Ambassadors to France), 27. For current ransom prices in Barbary, see Meakin, Moorish Empire, 287. According to Meakin (p. 305), "in 1790 there were so few prisoners in Morocco that the Sultan tried to purchase all of them in Algeria to exchange them for Moorish prisoners in Europe."

98. Woolery, Thomas Jefferson, 30-35.

99. Jefferson to Jay, May 4, 1788, D. C. of the U. S., II, 148-149.

100. Letter from Emperor of Morocco to all Foreign Consuls, Tangier, May 7, 1788, Naval Documents Related to the United States's Wars with the Barbary Powers (hereafter cited as N. D. of U. S.), III, 17.

101. Letter from Francisco Chiappi to all Foreign Consuls, Tangier, May 9, 1788, Ibid., III, 18.

102. The activities of the Chiappis are detailed by Robert Henry Bahnsen, in Diplomatic Relations of the United States and Morocco (Doctoral Dissertation, College of the Pacific, Stockton, California, June, 1958), 79-85.

103. The text of this letter is cited in full in Landau, Moroccan Drama, 184-185.

104. Jefferson to Jay, May 4, 1788, Lipscomb, Jefferson, VII, 3; Jefferson to Jay, May 23, 1788, Ibid., 20.

105. Coe, Carmichael, 80.

106. Meakin, Moorish Empire, 169-171.

107. Jefferson to Congress, Dec. 28, 1790, N. D. of U. S., I, 23; Washington to the Senate, Feb. 22, 1791, State Papers and Publick Documents of the United States, Second Edition, X, 101.

108. The American government was never under the illusion that the mission of annual tribute from the treaty provisions obviated the necessity of presents on appropriate occasions, such as the accession of a new ruler.

109. On March 31, 1791, Washington addressed a letter to his "Great and Magnanimous Friend," al-Yazid on the loss of his father. The President also spoke of his satisfaction at the accession of so worthy a

successor to the throne of Morocco. He felt confident that the treaty made by al-Yazid's father to continue for fifty years would meet with the royal patronage of the son. Jared Sparks, editor, The Writings of George Washington, X, 144-146.

110. Henry Merritt Wriston, Executive Agents in American Foreign Relations (hereafter cited as Wriston, Executive Agents), 621; Secretary of State to the President, transmitted to Congress on Dec. 16, 1793, A. S. P., F. R., I, 288-290; Lipscomb, Jefferson, VIII, 199-202.

111. A. S. P., F. R., I, 292-293.

112. Ibid., 244-299.

113. Irwin, Diplomatic Relations of the United States with the Barbary Powers, 82.

114. A. S. P., F. R., I, 525-526.

115. Simpson to Sec. of State, Aug. 18, 1795, Ibid., 526.

116. Simpson to Sec. of State, Sept. 14, 1795, Ibid., 526-527.

117. Humphreys to Sec. of State Pickering, Dec. 16, 1796, N. D. of U. S., I, 148.

118. Charles Oscar Paullin, Diplomatic Negotiations of American Naval Officers, 1778-1883 (hereafter cited as Paullin, Diplomatic Negotiations of American Naval Officers), 56.

119. Lipscomb, Jefferson, III, 94-111.

120. Henry James Ford, Washington and His Colleagues, A Chronicle of the Rise and Fall of Federalism: Chronicles of America, 50 vols., XIV, 106-113; McMaster, History, II, 170-171; Samuel Flagg Bemis, editor, The American Secretaries of State and Their Diplomacy, 10 vols. (hereafter cited as Bemis, American Secretaries of State), II, 89-92, 126, 209.

121. A. S. P., F. R., I, 30-31.

122. William M. Malloy, compiler and editor, Treaties, Conventions, International Acts, Protocols, and Agreements between the United States of America and Other Powers, 1776-1909, 2 vols. (hereafter cited as Malloy, Treaties), II, 1794-1800.

123. On March 3, 1801, Adams signed the act to reduce the navy, at the presidential discretion, to a stated number of vessels and personnel. In pursuit of economy, Jefferson began the execution of this law before the need for a strong force in the Mediterranean became evident. Edward Channing, A History of the United States, 6 vols. (hereafter cited as Channing, History), IV, 264.

124. Messages of Jefferson to Congress, A. S. P., F. R., I, 58, 61-63.

125. For the text of the treaty see Malloy, Treaties, II, 1788-1783. Some American accounts of the Tripolitan War are in McMaster, History, III, 200-204; Edward Channing, The Jeffersonian System, 1801-1811, The American Nation, 28 vols., XII, 36-46; Paullin, Diplomatic Negotiations of American Naval Officers, 58-87; Francis Rennell Rodd, General William Eaton, the Failure of An Idea; Irwin, Diplomatic Relations of the United States with the Barbary Powers, 106-160; Louis B. Wright and Julia H. Macleod, The First Americans in North Africa, 76-183.

126. Jefferson to Gallatin, Aug. 9, 1802, and Gallatin to Jefferson, Aug. 16, 1802, in The Writings of Albert Gallatin, edited by Henry Adams, 3 vols. (hereafter cited as Adams, Gallatin), I, 83-84, 87.

127. Gallatin to Jefferson, Aug. 20, 1802, Ibid., 90-91; Jefferson to Gallatin, Sept. 8, 1802, Ibid., 96; Henry Adams, History of the United States during the Administrations of Jefferson and Madison, 4 vols. (hereafter cited as Adams, Jefferson and Madison), I, Book 2, 138.

128. For the events of 1801-1802, see A. S. P., F. R., II, 466-469; Irwin, Diplomatic Relations of the United States with the Barbary Powers, 114-116.

129. Jefferson to Madison, March 22, 1803, P. L. Ford, Jefferson, VIII, 221.

130. American State Papers, Class VI, Naval Affairs, 1794-1836, 4 vols. (hereafter cited as A. S. P., N. A.), I, 115-117; III, 124; and A. S. P., F. R., II, 591-592.

131. John Quincy Adams did not join in the general chorus of eulogy for the administration. Writing under the pseudonym of "Publius Valerius" in The Reportory on Oct. 30, 1804, he said: "When the disposition of our naval force and the Barbary War are held up as objects of glory to our general government... we struggle to applaud in vain... What can be meant by the assertion that we have dictated terms of peace to some of the Barbary powers, and rendered harmless the hostility of others?... The simple fact is that the people of the United States have paid many thousand dollars and restored two armed ships; for what? Why, for the Emperor of Morocco to disavow the violation of his treaty with us. Is this dictating terms of peace?" Worthington Chauncey Ford, editor, The Writings of John Quincy Adams, 7 vols. (hereafter cited as W. C. Ford, John Quincy Adams), III, 57-58.

132. A. S. P., F. R., II., 592.

133. William Harlan Hale, "'General' Eaton and His Improbable Legion," American Heritage, XI (Feb., 1960), 26-33, 104-106; Samuel Flagg Bemis, A Diplomatic History of the United States (hereafter cited as Bemis, Diplomatic History of the United States), 177.

134. Ibid., 178.

135. Meakin, Moorish Empire, 271.

136. Ibid., 290.

137. Flournoy, "Political Relations of Great Britain with Morocco," 30.

138. Meakin, Moorish Empire, 270-271.

139. Flournoy, British Policy Towards Morocco, 51-52, 77, 79, 80-85, 97, 106-107.

140. Ibid., 40, 45-46, 122-124, 153-165; Sir John Drummond Hay, "How Piracy Was Stopped in Morocco," Living Age, CLXXV (Dec., 1887), 551-557; Alice Drummond Hay and Mrs. L. A. E. Brooks, A Memoir of Sir John Drummond Hay, Sometime Minister at the Court of Morocco, Based on His Journals and Correspondence (hereafter cited as Sir John Drummond Hay), 144-158, 183.

141. A. S. P., N. A., I, 396-399.

142. For the text of the treaties see Malloy, Treaties, I, 6-17. For the events see Paullin, Diplomatic Negotiations of American Naval Officers, 114-120; McMaster, History, IV, 352, 355; Wriston, Executive Agents, 625-626; Thomas Hart Benton, editor, Abridgement of the Debates of Congress, from 1789 to 1856, 16 vols. (hereafter cited as Benton, Debates of Congress), I, 475-479.

143. James Parton, Life of Thomas Jefferson, Third President of the United States (hereafter cited as Parton, Jefferson), 296-301, 636-640; Bemis, American Secretaries of State, II, 1-93.

144. Sir Adolphus William Ward, Sir G. W. Prothero, and Stanley Leathes, editors, Cambridge Modern History, 14 vols. (hereafter cited as Cambridge Modern History), X, 19-20.

145. Sir Adolphus William Ward and George Peabody Gooch, editors, Cambridge History of British Foreign Policy, 1783-1919, 3 vols. (hereafter cited as British Foreign Policy), II, 7, 13.

146. W. C. Ford, John Quincy Adams, V, 428.

147. Jean Darcy, France et Angleterre. Cent Années de Rivalité Coloniale, 43-47; quoted by Leonard Sidney Woolf, Empire and Commerce in Africa; A Study in Economic Imperialism (hereafter cited as Woolf, Empire and Commerce in Africa), 73.

148. Lane-Poole, Barbary Corsairs, 293-294, 296, 298; Sir Harry Hamilton Johnston, The Opening Up of Africa, 200; Alfred T. Mahan, "Admiral Lord Exmouth," Atlantic Monthly, LXXII (July, 1893), 27-41.

149. Allen, Barbary Corsairs, 11-12.

150. Eugene Schuyler, American Diplomacy and the Furtherance of Commerce, 231-232.

151. Barclay to Adams and Jefferson, July 13, 1787, D. C. of the U. S., II, 76.

152. A. S. P., F. R., II, 372.

153. Rodd, General William Eaton, 34; John Bassett Moore, A Digest of International Law, 8 vols. (hereafter cited as Moore, Digest), V, 396.

154. Bemis, American Secretaries of State, II, 209; Allen, Barbary Corsairs, 56-57; Parton, Jefferson, 637.

155. A. S. P., F. R., II, 372.

156. Manning, "Diplomatic Relations with the Barbary Powers," 122.

157. Hunter Miller, editor, Treaties and Other International Acts of the United States of America, 4 vols. to 1935 (hereafter cited as Miller, Treaties), II, 185-226 contains the Arabic text, the original English translation, and a revised English translation and notes.

158. Articles 6-10, 12, 16 and supplementary article, Ibid., 213-215.

159. The word "Moor" used in the original English translation obviously means Muslim or Mohammedan--hence, any subject of a Barbary state, and has been so interpreted.

160. Articles 2-5, 10-11, 13, 24; Miller, _Treaties,_ II.

161. Articles 14-15, 17-9; _Ibid._, 215-216.

162. Articles 14, 24; _Ibid._, 215-217.

163. "In the making of these early (Barbary) treaties the feature of extraterritoriality appears not to have been thought important. The treaties resemble those of England, France, and Holland of the seventeenth century, which were published previous to the American negotiations in Dumont, _Corps universal diplomatique du droit des gens_, Amsterdam, 1776 and later, in Wenck, _Codes juris gentium_, Leipsic, 1781 and later." Frank E. Hinckley, _American Consular Jurisdiction in the Orient,_ 19.

164. Articles 20-23; Miller, _Treaties,_ II, 216-217.

165. "The American Navy, four thousand miles from its base, starved by a niggardly Congress and an economizing Treasury, operated under most difficult conditions. The Barbary coast, a lee shore during the winter months, could not be properly blockaded. Yet officers and men showed a gallantry and resourcefulness that earned them the esteem of the British service, and the hospitality of Malta and Gibraltar; American traders were able to go their way unmolested, and the final treaty with Tripoli was more honorable and less expensive than any European power had previously extorted." Samuel Eliot Morison, _The Oxford History of the United States,_ 1783-1917, 2 vols. (hereafter cited as Morison, Oxford History), I, 237.

166. Editorial, "The United States and the Barbary States," _Atlantic Monthly_, VI (Dec., 1860), 641-657.

167. The briefest and probably the most inaccurate account of the abolition of Moroccan piracy is that given by Fred Warren, in "Morocco," Fortnightly Review, XXXVI N. S. (Aug., 1884), 191: "On the conclusion of the great war in 1815 nations had time to turn their attention to the suppression of Moorish piracy, and the bombardment of Algiers by Lord Exmouth crushed it forever."

168. The treaties were made with France, the Netherlands, Sweden, Prussia, and Morocco. James B. Angell, "Diplomacy of the United States, 1789-1850," in Narrative and Critical History of America, edited by Justin Winsor, 8 vols., VII, 461.

169. "The earliest extant commercial treaty with Majorca in 1339 quaranteed entire freedom of persons, goods, and ships involved in commerce with Morocco by sea or land. A treaty of 1358 with Pisa provided for extraterritorial jurisdiction for consuls... The treaty of 1631 with France confirmed the right to appoint consuls in all parts where French interests existed, with reciprocal extraterritorial jurisdiction. In 1684 Mulai Ismail accepted responsibility for payments of debts due from Moors to foreigners. British treaties of 1721 and 1728 stipulated that disputes between the English and Moors should be settled by the governor and consuls, and native servants of British subjects should be free from all taxation." Meakin, Moorish Empire, 167, 380-384.

Chapter III

Chronicles of the American Consuls (1795-1873)

The five-year interlude occupied by al-Yazeed's savage rule and the subsequent civil war of succession had threatened to undo the achievements of the beneficient and progressive rule of Sidi Mohammed XVI, but the latter's efforts to strengthen Morocco and to modernize her economic and political relationships with Europe and the United States were continued by the next three occupants of the Sherifian throne--Mulai Soliman (1795-1822), Mulai Abd er-Rahman (1822-1859), and Sidi Muhammed XVII (1859-1873). However, they were unable to halt the accelerating internal decline of their realm, to extend imperial control over the expanding blad-es-siba, or to offer successful resistance to the persistent encroachment of European powers, both by the peaceful penetration of commerce with its correlative institution of protection and by military intervention. There were unsuccessful palace revolutions, and non-imperial pretenders to the throne (known as roguis) occasionally meanced the dynasty also. Throughout the nineteenth century the name "Moorish Empire" was merely a diplomatic fiction; like the Holy Roman Empire, it was "a generic term, chosen for its convenience to designate a multitude of contradictions, a confused medley which knew neither organization nor spontaneity."[1] In theory absolute rulers of both church and state, the sultans continued to have their power restricted by tradition and by pressures from the non-dynastic sherifian families, the tribal chiefs, the saints, the Ulema, the secret religious confraternities, and their own appointees and harem inmates. The medieval maghzen, lacking any systematic plan of administration and governing chiefly by corruption, intrigue, and occasional displays of force and cruelty, effectually prevented any well-meaning ruler from introducing reforms necessary to save Morocco from European aggression.

In this confused and chaotic environment the American consular service might have exerted an appreciable influence for order and progress. The objective of the American representatives--peace and commerce--were implicit in the Treaty of 1786. The first aim was achieved by several renewals and steadfast maintenance of the treaty, together with a constant supervision of the extirpation of piracy. The second task of the consuls was never satisfactorily accomplished; American merchants were unable to meet European competition. Although the American consuls did not participate in the great rivalry for territory and control which dominated European relations with Morocco, especially after 1830, their awareness of it is evident in their reports to the State Department.

The consular dispatches from Tangier to Washington reveal several reasons for the failure of American representatives to pull their weight in the diplomatic councils of Morocco. The Americans were unsophisticated in the ways of either European or Muslim courts, and they usually found language barriers difficult to surmount. Generally speaking, they were political appointees, untrained in diplomatic theory or practice, and occasionally they embraced the abundant opportunities offered in the corruption of the protection system. The home government frequently treated its deputies with indifference and neglect, as is attested by the many complaints by consuls about unanswered dispatches. The consuls reiterated their concern about establishing the prestige and dignity of the new nation at the Moorish Court and in the Consular Corps at Tangier, which was particularly difficult because of the lower salaries and inferior housing provided by the United States. But on all occasions the champions of the Republic proudly waved the Star-Spangled Banner to assert the superiority of their form of government over the effete monarchies of Europe and Morocco.

Another basis for the inferior status of the American representatives was their short tenure of office. During the seventy-eight years comprising the reigns of the three sultans (1795-1873), there were two acting consuls and thirteen counsuls, two of whom had served at two different times, and a third (Felix Mathews) who had begun his second term in 1870--a total of eighteen different consulships.

Since James Simpson, the first American consul in Morocco,[2] was in service from December 6, 1797, until his death on March 8, 1820, over twenty-two years, the brevity of the terms of his successors is evident. In striking contrast to this American record in personnel and tenure is that of the protagonists on the consular stage, the British representatives, father and son--Edward Drummond Hay and John Drummond Hay. The latter was preeminently the ideal professional diplomat; he served in Morocco forty-one years after succeeding his father in 1845.

During his long tenure of office, James Simpson's correspondence with six secretaries of state[3] dealt chiefly with the following themes: the consul's appraisal of the character of Mulai Soliman and his personal relations with that monarch, the relations of the Barbary states to Morocco and to the United States, the policy and practices of Mulai Soliman regarding piracy and ransom, European-Moroccan relations, American-Moroccan commerce, such internal problems of Morocco as plagues and rebellions, and the domestic problems of Simpson, chiefly salary and housing.[4]

Simpson's initial estimate of Mulai Soliman was very high; he hoped that the tranquility of the country would continue under a sovereign of such "innate good qualities, as a blessing to his people and a comfort to Christians they have for some years back been strangers to." Four years later, however, he wrote that the Emperor lacked able and honest ministers and this his current advisers acted on no principle but that of amassing treasure for him, regardless of consequences; in the corn trade they had found means of gratifying their master's ruling passion.[5] Simpson believed, however, that the Emperor's friendship for the United States must be sincere, for he had received the American gifts most graciously, although they consisted only of "very fine flowered muslins, Holland, damasks, cloth, tea, sugar, and some plate." Moreover, Mulai Soliman displayed more amity toward the United States than he did toward the givers of really rich presents, such as the Portuguese, who renewed their treaty with 160 mules and 50 camels, and the Danes, who presented 140 mules, or the Spanish who found their gift, worth over $300,000, ineffectual in securing the ascendancy over Soliman which they had enjoyed over his father.[6] However, Simpson prudently nourished this apparent friendship by modest gifts to the Emperor and his entourage on appropriate occasions. But ever after the unpleasantness over Tripoli resulting in the War of 1801-1803, the American consul maintained an attitude of watchfulness over Mulai Soliman.

Simpson's first services to his country were obtaining the confirmation of the Treaty of 1786 and helping to shorten the later conflict with Morocco. Naturally, Simpson was gratified that, aside from the great aberration of the war of 1801-1803, the Emperor continued to abjure piracy and ransom in relation to Americans. The sporadic pillaging of wrecked American vessels by tribesmen in southern Morocco[7] was beyond the effective control[8] of Mulai Soliman. Nevertheless, the Emperor was able to obtain the release by ransom of the crew of an American vessel. He also succeeded in having brought to him at Marrakesh eleven Christian slaves, including five Americans, whom he redeemed and turned over to their respective consuls.[9] The rescue of other American captives was effected by Simpson at a considerable cost to the United States Treasury, giving rise to the grave problem of inflationary ransom prices. Between 1799 and 1816 Simpson reported the capture by the Emperor's frigates of vessels from Prussia, Hamburg, Bremen, Lubeck, and Greece. However, the Emperor refused Tunisian corsairs the privilege of using Tangier harbor as a sanctuary for their captures.[10]

During the consulship of Simpson, the United States achieved the final solution of her longstanding problem of Barbary piracy. The prolonged controversy with Great Britain and France over neutral rights and impressment and the ensuing War of 1812 compelled the United States to withdraw her squadron from the Mediterranean. A precarious peace continued with Tripoli and Tunisia but Algeria at once began to capture American vessels and to demand more gifts. Not until after the War of 1812 was the United States able to retaliate against Algerian attacks. Then a squadron under Commodore Decatur reinforced Consul William Shaler and Captain Bainbridge in dictating a peace treaty to the Dey of Algeria. The treaty of 1815, revised in 1816, put an end to tribute and ransom, gave the United States most-favored-nation status, and even forced Algeria to pay a nominal reparation of $10,000. Restive and dissatisfied with this ignominious defeat, the Dey unwisely attempted reprisals upon Great Britain; thereupon, a large British and Dutch fleet under Lord Exmouth bombarded Algiers and destroyed the pirate fleet.[11]

Even this severe chastisement, however, failed to reform the Dey of Algeria; various European countries continued to suffer from insults and exactions until the French conquest of Algeria ended her independence.[12]

Between 1806 and 1816 Simpson relayed to Washington reports of affairs in Algeria and other Barbary states.[13] He kept a watchful eye on reactions of Morocco to these events, giving the prudent advice that

> There can be no doubt that they (United States ships) will ... meet a friendly reception in the Ports of this Empire; it will be well, however, should the squadron capture any vessel under the Barbary colors, that the Captains avoid as much as may be sending such here, as notwithstanding whatever professions may be made, such events are looked upon, in all these Governments as participating of a common injury amongst the Family.[14]

A large part of Simpson's correspondence with the State Department pertained to the relations of Morocco with various European countries. On December 24, 1802, he submitted a detailed analysis of their political and commercial dealings. Russia had never had any intercourse with Morocco; Prussia, Germany, Italy, Naples, Sardinia, Malta, and all other independent islands in the Mediterranean had never had treaties. France and England had never paid tribute, but had made infrequent presents; both these countries, as well as Spain, formerly so influential, were on bad terms with the Emperor. The thrifty Dutch had hitherto paid no tribute and were stingy with gifts; they, too, were in disfavor. The amounts and kinds of tributes and gifts paid by other countries were noted.[15]

Later dispatches recorded a number of tributes paid in cash and goods, the rivalry between Great Britain and France for supplies for their war against each other, the

Emperor's unpopular restrictions on the export of wheat and cattle, and the favors shown to Great Britain in return for war supplies, as well as the long continued hostility to Spain shown by Mulai Soliman. Frequently Simpson called attention to the paucity of American contributions to the Emperor's store of gifts; finally he was spared further embarrassment by the arrival of the long promised one hundred gun carriages. In general, Simpson did not consider the Emperor's policy in international relations productive of good will. On March 8, 1814, he reported that commerce had been greatly limited by prohibition of the exportation of all staple commodities such as grains and pulse, wool, oil, soap, linen and leather manufactures, sheep, and poultry and the closing of all ports except Mogador, Salé, Larache, Tangier, and Tetuan.[16] Another unfavorable criticism made on May 18, 1819, referred to Mulai Soliman's autocratic handling of foreigners:

> In the course of my residence, we have seen a variety of instances of merchants, and, including myself, five consuls removed at the will of the sovereign. Such events may be dreaded in the most despotic government on earth.[17]

Regarding the prospects for lucrative American-Moroccan commerce, Simpson was not optimistic. On March 2, 1804, he ventured the opinion that "in all times ... we shall only see occasional speculations take place as ... a regular commercial intercourse between the countries cannot be hoped for on a grand scale." During 1805 only one American merchant ship arrived at Tangier. Since Mogador was thought likely to be the chief port of call, on May 7, 1807, when five American ships were in the harbor, the flag of the United States was first displayed there on the house of Mr. Renshaw, a recently appointed vice consul. The Emperor, visiting the city on that occasion, honored Mr. Renshaw with a private audience and assured him of protection. Simpson pointed out that the Emperor's restrictions on exports in 1814 would seriously limit all commerce. In 1818, because of the scarcity and high price of grain, Indian corn from the United States was first resorted to for the relief of the inhabitants of Tangier and the vicinity.[18]

Simpson's reports[19] include frequent references to the plagues which recurrently ravished Morocco until recent times. These epidemics were often accompanied by famines caused by drouth and locusts. A very serious outbreak traveled over the country for three years (1799-1801). During part of 1799 the consuls and their families took refuge in Tariffa.[20] In Simpson's last dispatches is a series of reports on a plague with high mortality rates which raged over Morocco from June, 1818, to February, 1820.[21]

Political plagues devastated Morocco also--traditional rebellions against the reigning emperor. In 1802 Mulai Soliman easily put down a tribal revolt near Fez. Two roguis threatened his throne briefly. In 1805 Mohamet Derhazy from Wazan, talented in legerdemain, won fame and a following as one of supernatural powers. He announced his ordination by the Prophet at God's command to free the Muslims of the West from the tyranny of the descendants of Mulai Ismail and those of Algeria from the dominion of the Turks. In 1809 an army sent to Tedla punished the adherents of the son of a sherif there who had declared his sovereignty over an independent country. In 1810, 1811, and 1912 armies were sent successively to subdue rebellious tribes in the Sus, in the northeastern provinces, and in the Riff. The next imperial punitive expedition was directed against the rich agricultural provinces of Shawia, Dequella, and Abda, which had been insubordinate for several years against the Emperor's policy of prohibiting the export of grain. The most serious rebellion of the reign, however, was that of the Berbers of the Middle Atlas (1819-1820). The death of the heir apparent, Mulai Ibrahim, on June 12, 1819, during an unsuccessful attack on the Berbers was regarded by Simpson as a very serious misfortune for Morocco. The provinces surrounding Meknes did not rally to his support, and, at Simpson's last report, the Emperor remained penned up in that city.[22]

Jealous of the prerogatives and dignity of his position, like most later American consuls, Simpson had three personal problems which he placed before the State Department. The first, of relatively short duration, concerned his independence as consul. On September 24, 1816, Simpson reported to Secretary of State Monroe that a letter of July 21 indicated that Consul General Shaler thought that the consulate of Morocco had been placed under his jurisdiction and that thereafter Simpson was to make reports to him by every conveyance, as well as to Washington. Simpson hoped that this was not so; he had replied to Shaler only that as the rate of exchange operated very disadvantageously against the negotiation of bills in Washington, he hoped that Shaler would furnish him with money from bankers at London when necessary.[23] Madison had invited William Shaler to serve as a civilian on the peace commission to secure a satisfactory treaty from Algeria and then to remain there as consul general for all the Barbary states. Shaler had accepted the offer. He actually made but one visit to each of his subordinate consulates, to Morocco in October 1816 and to Tunisia and Tripoli in September 1817. Since his inspections convinced him that there was no reason why the other Barbary consulates should be dependent upon that of Algeria, he recommended that the independence of each should be restored, and his recommendation was later accepted by Monroe.[24] On July 22, 1817, Simpson objected to "a circumstance unprecedented in this empire"--the alleged appointment of Mr. John O'Sullivan of New York as an independent consul at Mogador.[25]

Of prime importance to Simpson was having a residence and consular quarters fit for a Christian to live in and for the consul of the United States to work in. He made several attempts to rent or purchase a suitable edifice or to purchase a lot for the later building of adequate quarters, but on April 30, 1802, he was informed that the President did not choose that a consular house should be built at the public charge. On July 1, 1816, Simpson protested to Alexander J. Dallas, Secretary of the Treasury, that he had charged the house rent of sixteen dollars monthly from October 1, 1800, to June 30, 1810, to his expense account, but on May 15, 1810, the Secretary of State informed him that house rent was no longer chargeable to the government. Simpson was accordingly drawing on the treasury for the house rent he had paid during the last six years, a total of $1,152, for no other nation required its consuls to provide their quarters at personal expense. A few days later Simpson wrote Monroe of a suitable residence for sale; he hoped that the government would take action to relieve him of the privations and inconvenience he had experienced during his entire consulship.[26] But Simpson was doomed to frustration on his housing problem as he was on his larger one on salary, which was closely associated with it.

The story revealed by Simpson's voluminous correspondence concerning salary[27] is one of incredible negligence and irresponsibility of the United States Government and of lack of economic sense in Simpson.

Simpson's service in Moroccan affairs extended longer than his formal occupancy of the consulship, beginning on his arrival at Tangier on December 7, 1797. Early in 1793 after Barclay's death, at the request of Col. David Humphreys, he had taken over supervision of affairs in both Morocco and Algeria. In May 1795 he had been deputized by Humphreys to go to Mulai Soliman's court, where he obtained the recognition of the Treaty of 1786. As early as January 3, 1795, Simpson had written Humphreys, then in the United States, that he could not think of relinquishing his position at Gibraltar for one in Barbary for the salary of $2,000 a year provided for the latter. He had accepted the appointment at Tangier in full confidence that his salary would be equal to that of other consuls in Morocco and to the unavoidable expenses there. He had always stipulated that $4,000 was the minimum salary required, and for the first year and a half after arrival he drew his salary for that amount, and his bills were paid without question. No consul in Tangier at the head of his department received less than this sum and some were paid considerably more. In spite of "humble representations ... in continuation made on this subject," however, for almost eight years after receiving a promise of consideration, on December 26, 1803, Simpson had received no reply whatever to his pleas for an adequate compensation. Meanwhile, he had received no payment for any of his services between 1793 and 1797.[28]

An act of Congress in May, 1810, fixing the compensation of public ministers and consuls in Barbary was very unsatisfactory to Simpson. There was no allotment for a secretary, which every consulate in Morocco had except the American and the Dutch. House rent was no longer allowed, and contingent expenses without previous authorization by the President were limited to $3,000 per annum for each consul. The salary of the consul at Morocco was continued at $2,000, although his colleague in Algeria was awarded $4,000. Simpson had never charged or allowed any agent to take consulage, but had paid each assistant for his services. If this low salary continued, Simpson would be driven from the service.[29]

On February 21, 1811, Simpson took the positive step of sending Secretary Robert Smith a statement of the salary to which he considered himself entitled, with the request that this be laid before Congress for his relief at the next session. According to Simpson's figures, for salary for the thirteen years from August 17, 1797, to August 16, 1810, at $4,000 annually, his salary would have been $52,000, which when added to the one year's salary promised him for an outfit, would make a total of $56,000 due him. Since he had drawn $34,000 for salary, the government still owed him $22,000. Simpson expressed gratification to Monroe on April 3, 1813, that at that session of Congress arrangements would be made for consuls to Morocco which would relieve him from his distress. The promise was never fulfilled, and an appended pencilled memorandum on Simpson's statement revised Simpson's account to grant him salary for thirteen years at $2,000, or $26,000 with a $2,000 allowance for outfit--a total of $28,000. Rejecting the two last bills for salary drawn by Simpson for $4,000, he was charged with having received $30,000 in salary, which left him with an adverse balance of $2,000.[30] However, Simpson's financial situation was somewhat improved by a statement of account two years later, crediting him with 15 years' salary at $30,000, to which were added $2,000 for the outfit, $3,000 for house rent, and $750 for stationery, etc., making a total of $35,750. Since the consul had now had bills of $34,000 honored, he had $1,750 still due him from the government.[31]

Simpson persisted, however, in his appeal to Congress, appointing an agent, Mr. James Riley, to represent him and soliciting the backing of Col. Humphreys and Secretary of State John Quincy Adams. Adams transmitted a strong recommendation of Simpson's petition to Congress to the Chairman of the Committee on Foreign Relations, Nathaniel Bacon, together with the letter to Col. Humphreys, now deceased. Adams declared that the opinion that Simpson's services had been faithful, diligent, and highly useful to the United States had been entertained by all presidents of the United States and was evidenced by the records of every secretary of state. If not increased, as recommended by Shaler, to an equality with that of the consul of Algeria, it would be useful to raise the salaries of the other Barbary consuls to at least $3,000.[32]

As volunteer acting consul, on March 15, 1820, John Simpson penned his first dispatch to J. Q. Adams. He reported that his father James Simpson had passed away on the 8th from a sudden attack of apoplexy and that, as the eldest son and only person on the spot who could take charge of the affairs of the consulate, he would do so until arrangements of the government could be known. He humbly entreated that in consideration of his father's long and faithful services he might himself be honored with appointment to the position. In a dispatch dated April 18, 1820, he again solicited the recommendation of Adams for the office.[33]

The dispatches of John Simpson continued for a year. A gracious personal message to him from the Emperor was sent to Adams to show that "the affairs and flag of the United States continue to be respected." Simpson gave brief accounts of the plague still prevalent in many regions and of the continuation of the serious rebellion against Mulai Soliman. The revolt was intensified by the defection of the Black Troops to the mountaineers. Soliman's chances of retaining his throne seemed so small that the consul advised that his successor should await the outcome of the contest and not waste a present on one who might be deposed. When Mulai Ibrahim Ben Yazid, son of the infamous Yazid, already proclaimed emperor at Fez, was acknowledged also at Tangier (February 1821), Simpson joined the other consuls in presenting gifts to him. But the death of Ibrahim on March 15, followed by Mulai Soliman's offensive against another pretender, Mulai Said, inspired Simpson to draw upon the government for $2,000 to acknowledge the prospective return of the former ruler.[34]

The successor to the Simpsons, John Mullowny from Pottsgrove, Pennsylvania, did not hasten to his position. He had received his commission and instructions on June 20, 1820, but did not reach Gibraltar until September 25 and Tangier until June 17, 1821. In the meantime he had appointed vice consuls at Mogador and Tetuan, and, while waiting out the plague and insurrection in Morocco, had shopped in Marseilles for a suitable gift for the winning emperor. Arriving on the U. S. S. Ontario, Mullowny enjoyed agreeable attentions to his person. He forwarded a letter from Mulai Soliman to the President.[35]

A first order of business reported by Mullowny was the financial problem left by James Simpson, whose son John prepared his accounts up to 1819 for transmissal by Mullowny to the State Department. John Simpson addressed to J. Q. Adams[36] on July 20, 1821, a letter with a memorial to accompany these accounts and to reinforce the previous petition to Congress to pay Simpson the back salary he had claimed, or at least $4,000 a year up to the time of the law in 1810. James Simpson had died, his son wrote, after a service of nearly twenty-four years in "a most barbarous country, almost totally excluded from civilized society," in debt to nearly $7,000, and leaving his youngest son and daughter penniless. Adams was asked to present this memorial to the proper ones to secure equity and justice from the State.[37]

Mullowny suggested that to add dignity or respect to the nation or flag it would be well to have ships of war passing near Tangier appear in the offing and show the flag. In view of the civil war still continuing between Mulai Soliman and his nephew, this was probably sound advice. The consul sent several dispatches concerning the campaigns and their outcome, not forgetting to mention the atrocious treatment accorded to bodies of slain enemies.[38]

Mullowny was well pleased over his status in consular and imperial circles. Prince Mulai Ali, the Emperor's second son, showed him marked attention, and the Consular Corps elected him president. In gift-giving he quickly developed much skill; the presence of Mulai Soliman with his retinue and adherents at Tangier increased expenses, but Mullowny had made it clearly understood that he had gone as far in presents as his government would permit. Prince Mulai Ali, Governor of Tangier, returned presents from the Spanish and French consuls, but he kept Mullowny's, although it was far inferior to theirs. To the Emperor, Mullowny had given two presents within six months; to hold his friendship and that of his officers and also to economize was difficult; yet, he said, "I should not fear to place my influence in opposition to any individual, though much weightier presents are put in the scale against me." Mullowny used very modern propaganda methods in the entertainment which he gave at his house to the Moorish notables. He displayed "different actions, such as the *Constitution* and *Guerriere*, the *United States* and *Macedonian*, ... the fleets on Lake Erie, McDonough's victory, and the defeat of the British at New Orleans .... When explained they were much astonished to find the Americans on the footing they are among the Christian nations. My personal attention to them and free converse about our country made me agreeable to them, and this became a substitute for what was more expensive." Perhaps there was just a hint of superiority in Mullowny's reporting the summary expulsion from Tangier, with their families and effects of the Swedish consul and of John J. Simpson, recently appointed consul from Sardinia.[39]

The most important evidence of imperial favor, however, was that Mulai Soliman promised a house for Mullowny and any future American consul, free of rent, thus putting the United States on the same footing as all other Christian powers, for whom he had already provided either a house or the ground for one. This house the consul was free to repair or to enlarge with his own money.[40]

Early in his term of office, Mullowny showed a forward-looking attitude on American commerce with Morocco. In advancing this enterprise he had the backing of Mulai Soliman, who wrote him:

> I order and permit a free trade with all Americans in any part of my Empire, the Americans are more to me than any other nation, and whatever footing the most-favored-nation is on, they are to be favored more than any other.

The present situation was not encouraging, however; "no vessel of the United States has been in the empire, till December last when one arrived at Mogador from Boston ... her cargo, dry goods, provisions, rum, brandy, cordage, and copper, sailed without effecting sales for the Cape Verde Islands."

In another phase of commerce, however, Mullowny was disinterested. The Emperor had complimented the consuls with the care of the quarantine regulations and had issued an order placing all vessels under their direction. But though Mullowny joined the members of the Consular Corps in consultation on public health, he considered those concerns too partial and his country too distant to receive any benefit or effect.[41]

Mullowny's appreciation of Morocco as a bridge to American commerce in the Mediterranean was manifested in his advocacy of a lighthouse on Cape Spartel:

> A lighthouse on Cape Spartel ... appears to me to be a great and essential point to be gained, by all the maritime nations ... We stand foremost in promoting the good of the Christian part of the world, and particularly in the Mediterranean, though the most distant from it. This will be an additional attention to our noble and hardy tars .... Though perhaps too flattering, I indulge in believing we (the consuls here) could induce the Emperor to give permission to build it and to give sufficient ground for it in such a way as to secure it to be a permanent and peaceful possession.[42]

The Emperor Mulai Soliman passed away on November 28, 1822, at Marrakesh.[43] He had just reasserted his power after the revolts raised successively by his nephews, Ibrahim and Said, the sons of al Yazid, supported by the Sherif of Wazan, had made them masters of the northern kingdom in 1821.[44] With but an inconsequential opposition from Mulai Said, another nephew of the late Emperor, Abd er-Rahman, was proclaimed sovereign.[45]

During his long reign (1822-1859) Abd er-Rahman, a pacific, frugal person desirous of continuing the policy of his predecessor, encountered not only domestic, economic, and political problems impossible to solve, but also inimical relations with several foreign countries, leading to actual war with France. He is credited, however, with making a large contribution to the abolition of piracy from which Great Britain, Spain, Prussia, and Austria continued to suffer.[46]

The new ruler had promptly advised the consuls of all the countries with which he was at peace--Great Britain, France, Spain, Portugal, Sweden, Denmark, the United States, and Sardinia--that this peace and the treaties made with Soliman would be maintained.[47] But, true to traditional Moorish custom, this promise required ratification by presents from the benefitted parties.

Abd er-Rahman appointed as his "ambassador and consul to all Europe" a Jew, Meier Macnin, with exclusive control over duties and rules for exportation of Moroccan produce from four ports. Mullowny doubted whether this plan would raise the revenues much needed by the Emperor, because the large treasure left by Soliman in Meknes was still in possession of the Black Troops, who were squandering it. Mullowny tactfully informed Abd er-Rahman that Macnin's request for an ambassador was unnecessary, since the treaty with the United States, confirmed by the Emperor's own declaration, was to run for fifty years. Mullowny thwarted the request for an ambassador because he knew it was only the means of securing an extravagant present; he told Macnin that if an American ambassador were required, it was probable that the United States would wish to have her envoy meet one from Morocco in some third country. Shortly afterwards, the Emperor admonished Mullowny that since the hundred gun carriages annually promised by the American-Moroccan treaty had not been delivered for many years, he should inform His Majesty how many were now due and when and where he would deliver them. The consul replied that although Mulai Soliman had once purchased one hundred gun carriages from the United States, there was no mention in the treaty of any gun-carriages due as gifts. Mullowny's statement was accepted. The instigator of this mischief, Mullowny thought, was Hadj Hashhash, who had caused trouble in 1803. It had been intimated to Mullowny that his present, worth about $2,000, was insufficient, and he heard of a plan to request two thousand gun barrels in addition. To the one who made this observation Mullowny asserted that the United States never intended giving gifts to enrich any person; she would return favors, but would buy kindness from none. In contrast to the American attitude about gifts, Mullowny listed the valuable offerings being made by Great Britain (about $18,000) and France, as well as the presents sure to be made by Sweden and Denmark in addition to their annual tributes. However, when transmitting the accounts of the consulate for the last two years, Mullowny regretted that his expenses had been increased by unexpected demands, when "reasoning, producing the treaties, or remonstrating against such incorrectness" were unavailing. Such methods were repugnant, but necessary to preserve the peace. Mullowny reported on May 16, 1824, that since December of 1822 only one American vessel had been in Morocco.[48]

Mullowny was the first of several consuls to have the unpleasant duty of informing the State Department of the embarrassing situation created by the debts of his predecessor. On February 7, 1824, he wrote that reports were in circulation that the United States was indebted to Simpson's estate. The late consul's affairs were involved in both Morocco and Gibraltar, and a Jew presenting Simpson's note for $3,000 had been surprised at Mullowny's refusal to aid in getting it paid. Simpson's real estate might be sold for $1,500, but his debts probably exceeded $7,000.[49]

Mullowny also inherited his predecessor's problems regarding housing and salary. He presented a lengthy exposition of the reasons why American consuls deserved as "respectful" a residence as those of other nations. But on their low salaries the Americans could afford only a consular house "pointed out as an existing proof of the poverty" of their country. Mullowny had been obliged to build a house for himself, which he offered for sale to the United States government. A consular house must provide quarters for all Americans visiting in Tangier, for, if respectable, there were no comfortable accommodations for them elsewhere, and, if men of inconsiderate habits, their conduct might result in the punishment of loathsome confinement. Mullowny wanted to avoid the "melancholy experiment" tried on Simpson, who had died in debt, leaving his daughter to the charity and protection of friends. Although Simpson had drawn a salary of $4,000 for three years, Mullowny was being expected, with higher living costs, to render the same services for $3,000 all expenses included.[50]

Mullowny continued to adhere to his principle of gift-giving--"Americans may compensate for favors, but they never buy or beg for them." While deploring the national custom of demanding presents, he insisted that American failure to observe such a longstanding and universally accepted custom would result only in a loss of good will, prestige, and profit for the United States. He regretted that the Secretary of State saw fit to question the amounts he had spent for largess; "I regret to think that I am considered prodigal at home, here I am said to be scanty-handed and marked as penurious; it is difficult to avoid both."[51]

Mullowny was not a friendly colleague of the French consul. The latter was stigmatized as a malevolent meddler and mischief maker, who had removed by artifice and pen three consuls--Grober, John Simpson, and the Spanish consul--and who devoted himself to the suppression of republicanism. However, Mullowny was well situated in that he had well tried friends near the person of the King; these had been secured at his private expense, not appearing in public accounts, since his gifts of wine and cordials had been bestowed in confidential secrecy.[52]

Abd er-Rahman made a good impression on the American consul. Late in 1824 Mullowny described him as mild, though decisive, planning his operations to prevent the shedding of blood. With peace and plenty general over the empire, the people were cheerful, happy, and not overworked. In 1827 the consul reported that since his recent defeat of the rebels, the Emperor was in perfect peace and power and reigned with good temper, mercy, and justice. The Emperor's good reputation was enhanced by many evidences of friendship for the United States, for whom he manifested benevolent treatment of shipwrecked crews not shown to sailors of other countries.[53]

In striking contrast to his amicable attitude toward

the United States, Abd er-Rahman had antagonistic relations with representatives of Sardinia, Great Britain, Spain, France, and Austria. From time to time Mullowny had observed evidences of attempts to rebuild a Moroccan navy. His final conclusion was that there was no fear of a renaissance of Moorish sea power:

> Five gunboats are slowly being built in Tangier. They prove the art of naval architecture is lost in this empire ... Such is the decayed power now at war with Austria, which lacks in management to annoy a weak and futile enemy. Here they have but two men (one aged) as commanders ... As to sailors, there are none ... They are unfortunate in a belief they are formidable in war and terrific to their enemies. They will remain so till force destroys their erroneous opinions. They will with these boats perplex the Christian world by depredations on their commerce. They think five boats equal to subdue the largest frigate of any nation.[54]

Mullowny made few references to American-Moroccan commerce. In reporting an imperial edict opening the port of Mazagan to foreign trade, Mullowny expressed the opinion that this would be of small advantage to Americans. The poor harbor and anchorage, the slowness of transactions, and the lack of common language would discourage even the most enterprising American traders. Some years before there had been through the harbor of Mogador a considerable exchange of rice, indigo, tobacco, cotton, and Indian and Chinese goods from the United States for hides, goat skins, gums, and other goods from Morocco. But for the last five years nothing had been done in that region. However, under William Willshire, who was consular agent for both Great Britain and the United States at Mogador, there was considerable commerce with Great Britain. Only two American merchantmen had entered Moroccan ports between November 9, 1824, and May 27, 1826.[55]

On May 12, 1826, Mullowny addressed directly to recently inaugurated President Andrew Jackson a comprehensive proposal for the complete abolition of piracy, tribute, and gift-giving, principally directed against Algiers,

Tunisia, and Tripoli, but also against Morocco. He suggested a convention of representatives of all commercial nations to form an alliance for carrying out a program of sanctions binding upon both Christian and Muslim powers to prohibit the evils which had marked their intercourse for centuries. In the proportionment of vessels to execute this mandate the United States, France, and Russia had equal forces, exceeded only by Great Britain. The necessity for international action seemed urgent, for

> France is now engaged in war with Algiers for outrages committed, Austria with this power, England also very lately, the Sicilies are in perplexities here, Hamburg and Hanseatic towns are considered at war, Sweden and Denmark pay tribute to all, Portugal and others to some, and all acquiesce in the habit of presents, vieing with one another who will be most humble in those shameful practices.

As a postscript to his grand design, Mullowny urged again the construction of a lighthouse on Cape Spartel--a project later carried out, but not on American initiative. Like earlier American plans for international cooperation against the Barbary states, Mullowny's scheme was preserved in State Department archives.[56]

Of great interest to Mullowny was the relationship to be established between Morocco and the recently liberated South American republics, whose independence was not yet recognized by Spain. On July 22, 1826, Mullowny noted that the Emperor had instructed the Bashaw of Tangier to give good treatment to any South American vessels touching that port and had stated his willingness to make treaties with the new states. A year later the Spanish consul, attempting to prevent the landing of a Colombian brig at Tangier, "was told to keep his mouth shut about what vessels should enter His Majesty's harbors," and the ship's captain received from the Emperor freedom of the harbor and a request for a consul from his country to make a treaty. The Emperor further directed the Spanish consul not to trouble him in future about the South American states, for since the United States had acknowledged them to be independent, they could use Moroccan ports until they could send a consul. Mullowny asked His Majesty's minister whether Morocco would claim tribute from South American countries; the reply was that tribute would be exacted from them "and all that should desire to form a treaty in the future." This policy was, of course, of prime interest to the United States, because her treaty would require renewal in 1836. Mullowny thought that Morocco was anxious to keep Sweden and Denmark paying tribute as a precedent for tributes to be demanded from others. The Austrians alone would humble their views, but more speedily should they unite with other powers.[57]

Numerous references are found in Mullowny's dispatches to the prolonged antagonism between the British Consul and Abd er-Rahman and his influential officers, especially the Bashaw of Tangier. The Bashaw, of high prestige since conquering a castle in rebellion against the former and present ruler for thirty years, was prepared to force the issue against the British. The seizure and temporary detention of two British ships by a Moorish vessel in August 1828 led to the appearance at Tangier of two British sloops of war to demand damages. Mullowny's diary gives a long account of the subsequent British blockade of Tangier, beginning on November 22, 1828, and terminated on January 20, 1829, after a reduction of the damages asked by the British. During this incident Mullowny denied the current rumor, said to be firmly believed by the British consul general, that he corresponded with the Emperor and that his influence and advice governed all imperial actions.[58]

While the Austrians continued their feeble attacks on Moroccan ports and the Moors were building their five-vessel navy, a new era in British-Moroccan relations was beginning. On July 24, 1829, the unpopular British representative finally departed and was succeeded by Sir Edward Drummond Hay, soon to become the leader of the consular corps. The early contacts between Hay and Mullowny augured well for later British-American cooperation in Morocco. When Mullowny, at Tangier nine years without a vacation, asked for six months' leave starting in May, 1830, he reported that Hay had politely offered to take charge of American affairs for that period at no expense to the American Consulate.[59]

In his last dispatch, dated June 30, 1830, Mullowny offered with pride the evidence of the sustained prestige of the United States in Morocco. An American vessel wrecked on the Moroccan shore of the Straits of Gibraltar had its cargo saved and its crew assisted and courteously treated by the Moors; this was quite different from the recent plundering of two British and one French ships recently wrecked in that vicinity. His conclusion seemed justified that "this instance adds to the repeated respect our Flag has met with in this Empire."[60]

As successor to John Mullowny, G. A. Porter served briefly as acting consul. He advised the State Department that his replacement, Samuel Carr, should arrive in a vessel of war, since, whatever the flag, the appearance of a warship in a Moorish port always tended to lessen the habitual arrogance of the natives. Porter added that no American vessel had visited Morocco during his residence there.[61]

Though serving only a short time in 1832, Samuel J. Carr became the first consul to blacken the image of the United States in Morocco. On July 25, 1832, Carr had written to the Secretary of State, Edward Livingston, most enthusiastically about his forthcoming mission to Marrakesh to present the customary gift to the Emperor. He was proud to be the first American consul to penetrate to this capital and the "first to hoist there the Stars and Stripes of our dear country over the habitation of its representative to those degenerate descendants of a once powerful people." His journey was planned to be an ambitious scientific project, also; "it is my intention to examine minutely the geological character of the country and every object that would ten to illustrate either its present condition or past history." He predicted that an American brig recently arrived at Mogador was the harbinger of a considerable commerce for the United States. But Carr's dispatch of October 8, 1832, was a complaint at his removal from office after "little more than three months;" he had contracted "pecuniary engagements" and could not leave until his debts were paid. He begged Secretary Livingston, "For God's sake, Sir, ask the President who has been the means of placing me in this unhappy situation in this barbarous country to do all that he can to take me out of it, for my family are perfectly miserable at my situation."[62]

Strangely enough, James R. Leib had been appointed to succeed Samuel Carr on June 21, 1832, before the latter had started his disastrous career, and had arrived at his post by October 4. The events of Carr's consulate are known through Leib's accounting of them in a series of dispatches from October 4, 1832, to September 1, 1834. Leib first reported that Carr had been in a street brawl with some natives, in which he had brandished a pistol and narrowly escaped with his life, and that he had contracted large debts in Gibraltar and Tangier. A month later Leib convened the Consular Corps as a court of inquiry concerning charges against Carr and by Carr against the Moors. Carr's debts, contracted in the name of the United States government, were about $1,000 in Gibraltar and $2,500 in Morocco. Leib could find in the consulate no copy of the treaty of 1786 and no government property except some badly designed seals. Later Leib designated Carr as either a villain or a madman who had tried to assassinate his successor. Leib said there was no suitable place of confinement for Carr at Tangier, and bills for the latter's unpaid debts came to both Livingston and Leib.[63]

When Edward Drummond Hay accused Leib of improper treatment of Carr, such as binding of his hands and feet and poor food and housing, the American consul indignantly denied the right of the Consular Corps to intervene. If the Corps should interfere in a domestic matter, Leib declared, he would separate himself from it publicly, for "the Star-Spangled Banner can stand alone." After an investigation by American naval officers, Leib was exonerated from Hay's charges. Leib made several reports on the case and the "intrigues" of the Consular Corps, alleging that the affidavits of the renegade British were inspired by Moors and Jews who feared that if Carr died his debts would not be paid. In his sole attempt at self-defense, Carr made no complaint against Leib but attributed his misfortunes to illness and debts incurred in anticipation of a longer term of office. Carr was on his way to the United States before May 16, 1833, and a month later Leib reported $2,358.91 paid on his debts. As late as September 1, 1834, the consul was still petitioning the American government to pay the rest of Carr's debts and thus ended an affair which was "a sort of standing reproach to our Government."[64]

Early in his mission Leib stated two objectives for the United States in pursuing a positive policy of friendship with the Emperor and his court officials. The first was to insure good treatment for Americans cast upon the coasts or otherwise falling into the hands of the Moors. The second was to cooperate with the rest of the civilized world in the commercial development of Morocco in which the British and the French were already leaders.[65]

In his lengthy account of his mission to Fez, beginning on September 26, 1833, Leib described the "extraordinary honors" paid to his party and the elaborate ceremonial attending his reception by the Emperor. Abd er-Rahman assured him that whatever he desired in Morocco was already granted,[66] for "we esteem your nation above every other on the earth." Leib returned thanks "for the respect and consideration in which our flag has ever been held within this empire," and said that the honors paid to him would be considered entirely as offered to the flag. Commerce could not be established by treaty, Leib reminded the State Department, but only by attracting the Emperor's favor by gifts and by the personal influence of the consul. In regard to his own contribution toward the betterment of American-Moroccan relations, Leib was very complacent:

> I have the best reason for believing that I have placed the Consulate on a footing which it has never enjoyed before; and that I am the very first American who has carried the star-spangled banner, which has floated so proudly in nearly every other quarter of the world, into the heart of the Empire of Morocco.

But despite his short experience with Morocco's international policy, Leib was not naïvely unaware of the motivation underlying it. He commented on it realistically:

> It may be inferred that the flag of the United States is duly respected by the Moors; and, it is to be hoped, feared .... However, ... the Moors ... are, after all, but a half-civilized people .... In their political intercourse with us, not the slightest reliance is to be placed on anything they say .... Whatever advantages we may hope to obtain must be achieved by the judicious

application of liberality and the timely exhibition of force.[67]

However stoutly he defended the necessity and expediency of presenting gifts to the Moroccan ruler and officials, Leib was decidedly nonplused by having to accept some in return. As a special mark of favor while at Fez the consul received from the Emperor an enormous lion and two fine horses. The "Sultan of Beasts" was an especially difficult problem because of the expense of his transportation, "nouriture," and keepers, and the necessary confinement in the consulate's restricted quarters. Finally Secretary of State Forsyth was convinced, after an extensive correspondence, that "the refusal of a present is ever an acknowledged symptom of hostility--a sort of moral outrage"--and that sale of the animals could be concealed best in the far distant United States. Eventually the animals were disposed of at "upwards of $6,000," and Leib expressed dissatisfaction that it was necessary for him to draw upon the American consul at Gibraltar for $4,000 to pay part of the balance due him for their care and other expenses of his mission.[68] Already Leib was beset by financial problems familiar to all his predecessors.

The problem of a consular residence remained; unless the government would provide one, each consul must build one for himself, "with ruinous financial results." Leib was occupying the house built by the late consul Mullowny, whose heirs now desired a settlement of his estate. Other suggestions for improving the American consulate were a reference library, for which a minimum list was presented, and five items requiring increased expenditures for support of the personnel. Leib's requests for the last seem modest: raising the salary of the consul, more liberal provision for contingent expenses, organization of a corps of young men to serve as interpreters at Muslim courts, increasing the salary of interpreter Peter Boyn (now $15.00 per month), and appointment as Arabic secretary of John F. Mullowny, now acting vice consul, at $600 per year.[69]

Another familiar topic in Leib's reports was that of an epidemic of Asiatic cholera causing dreadful ravages throughout Morocco. In this matter Leib did not cooperate with his consular colleagues in the international body for control of health and sanitation, which had been developing in Tangier since 1792 and which had been joined by the United States in 1797. This body had been permitted by the emperors to make regulations for maritime quarantine of the plagues and for sanitation in Tangier.[70] While recovering from a severe attack of the plague himself, Leib had protested to the president of the board of health that cholera was a disease essentially founded in the imagination and caused by want and fear, since it was not at all contagious, infectious, or communicable, a quarantine would have only fatal and mischievous consequences and was a relic of barbarism.[71]

In more vital matters, also, Leib was at odds with some of his colleagues. During 1836 he was deeply involved in the game of power politics played by the British and the French. He had an important role to play in obtaining the renewal of the American-Moroccan treaty of 1786. But ironically he followed the example of Samuel Carr, whom he had criticized so severely for disgracing the name of American consuls in Morocco.

When Thomas N. Carr, the next American consul, reached Gibraltar on August 27, 1838, he found that Leib had left Tangier for Cadiz as a drunken maniac, threatening the life of his successor. Several later dispatches described the deplorable conditions in the consulate. The archives were scattered about from Tangier to Cadiz, no records had been kept by Leib, the storeroom keys were missing, and claims were being made daily by Leib's creditors. Reports were that Leib had been really insane for the last two years. Presents promised to the Sultan, many of them damaged, were still in the storeroom of the consulate. Roofs of several rooms were tumbling down.

More serious than material damages were those to the prestige of the United States, which had ranked in respect with France and Great Britain before the coming of Samuel Carr. Leib's conduct had still further lowered the reputation of the United States, for he had been offensive and disagreeable to both Moors and his fellow consuls. During the preceding winter, Leib's madness had manifested itself in scenes such as this:

> Wrapped up in the American flag, he would spend whole nights upon the terrace, making signals, by running lanterns up and down the flag staff, to the fleet which he had ordered from the Mediterranean for the purpose of battering the town; at the same time uttering the most discordant sounds, and alarming all the inhabitants. The Moors, like the other Mahometans, have great respect for an insane person, but the immediate causes of the insanity in this case are too well known, and, even by an insane person, it was not very agreeable to the Moorish authorities to have it demonstrated that there was an American line of battle ship, the Pennsylvania, which could knock down all the walls and batteries of Tangier in fifteen minutes, and to be assured that she was coming in a short time to do so.

Leib's extravagances in Tangier and "all the ports of Spain from Cadiz to Malaga, made this consulate the most notorious in this quarter of the world." Finally the Sultan directed Leib to remain in the consulate in the custody of his dragoman. Since leaving Tangier, Leib had continued his irresponsible conduct and contraction of debts. Using Leib's liabilities as a text, Carr preached to the American government an impassioned, if not eloquent, sermon on the penurious treatment of its representatives in Morocco, where most of the other consuls were receiving from three to five times the salary of their American colleague.[72] Carr requested a letter of thanks from the President for the vice-consul of Sweden and Norway, who had taken charge of the American consulate for long periods during the frequent and prolonged absences of Leib.

To rehabilitate the reputation of the United States, Carr recommended suitable presents for the Sultan and his entourage. He asked permission and funds for a mission to Fez to present the additional gifts promised when the treaty of 1836 was made. The mission was authorized and in June 1839 was carried out by John F. Mullowny, who reported that the Emperor greatly appreciated the two field pieces and ammunition among his gifts, since he was then suppressing one of the perennial tribal revolts. In his letter of thanks to Carr, Abd er-Rahman said, "I believe you are the only nation that likes me. You have always been friendly toward me, and yours is a nation that

I should like to serve." But Carr was deeply embarrased by the Sultan's gift--this time it consisted of two lions! He had tried in vain to reject them, for he had to keep them in a room of his residence. In April 1840 he complained because he had to draw a draft on the State Department to pay for their keep.[73]

Carr was harassed by financial problems. He was annoyed by the creditors of former consuls, found his salary and contingent fund inadequate, and could borrow money only in small sums at fifty per cent interest. He urged that the United States purchase and repair Mullowny's property and complete payment of Leib's debts. Convinced that the American stake in Morocco was valuable because trade prospects were improving there and that there were opportunities for commerce between Fez and the Negro nations south of the Sahara, he urged the State Department to restore the prestige and influence of the American consulate.[74]

During 1840 and 1841 Carr sent several reports of the Emperor's activity in combatting tribal rebellions. He also made many observations on the current war by France against Algeria and Abd er-Rahman's involvement in it. The consuls speculated about the purpose of the Emperor's unconcealed preparations of his small navy for war and his collection of military supplies. Sir Edward Drummond Hay informed Carr that the Bashaw at Larache admitted that Morocco was intending to seize vessels of nations without treaties and consuls in Morocco. Hay was instructed by his government to warn the Emperor that Great Britain would resist any attempt to revive piracy and plunder against any nation. However, Carr voiced the traditional American distrust of British motives in Barbary:

> Notwithstanding this apparently disinterested decision of Great Britain, it is plain to see that her own interest is consulted in the movement--it is part of a system she has established to keep the Emperor at peace, so long as peace suits her purpose, and a rupture at this moment, which the execution of the Sultan's orders could not fail to produce, would be greatly injurious, if not destructive, to the important benefits desired by Great Britain at this time from this country.[75]

On December 29, 1841, Secretary of State Daniel Webster notified Thomas Carr of his removal from office. Like his two predecessors, Carr left his position without honor for himself or his country. As he was departing from Tangier on March 25, 1842, he was forcibly detained by the Bashaw of the province. This incident came near rupturing American-Moroccan relations. It occasioned a congressional investigation and a prolonged and acrimonious controversy carried on in diplomatic dispatches and in American and foreign newspapers.

Critics of Carr, including his successor, John F. Mullowny, said that the insult had been provoked by Carr's neglect to present his farewell letter from the Sultan to the Bashaw of Tangier. Carr denied that this was customary. When finally permitted to depart, he struck his flag staff at Tangier, thus formally suspending the functions of the consulate. Commodore Charles W. Morgan, commander of the American naval forces in the Mediterranean, was summoned by Carr to enforce respect for the American flag. The assault on himself was not a personal matter, Carr declared. He cited instances of outrages committed by Moors on citizens of Portugal, Spain, Great Britain, France, and Naples, as well as the annual tribute still collected from Sweden and Denmark. Letters of the Sultan, publicly read at various seaports, referred to the American people in most disparaging terms. The consular corps at Tangier protested against the treatment of Carr, and Hay sent Carr a personal letter advocating a united front of all Christian powers to repress "this spirit of ultra Barbarity." But Commodore Morgan did not arrive at Tangier for over two months, and then he proceeded in a manner showing his profound ignorance of the country. Consul Mullowny, long delayed from taking his post, was finally able to terminate the "diplomatizing and humbuggings," as Carr called the protracted negotiations. The lieutenant governor of Tangier was removed from office, the offence was publicly disavowed, it was agreed that Carr would hold no other government office, and the flag of the United States was again hoisted at Tangier with a salute of twenty-one guns from the Moorish batteries.[77]

In a review of the affair in the New York _Daily Plebeian_ of May 8, 1843, Carr defended himself from charges in a newspaper article inspired by Morgan. Carr criticized Morgan's conduct as deserving of court martial and accused Secretary of State Webster of withholding significant documents from the congressional inquiry held.[78] The Commodore blamed his "little delay" upon the British consul, saying that Hay had supported the Moorish authorities until the Webster-Ashburton treaty was safely concluded. In one respect only did Carr agree with Morgan--Carr asserted that "the Empire of Morocco is as much under British control ... as the Rock of Gibraltar." Mullowny, Carr charged, was a protégé of the British Consul, and therefore should not represent the United States at Tangier. Carr concluded indignantly:

> The Moor has insulted our flag with impunity .... Our gallant little navy in the wars with Algiers, Tunis and Tripoli had won for itself a name that insured honor and respect to the American flag; but this has been wantonly sacrificed by the recent proceedings at Tangier.[79]

Thus John F. Mullowny, son of Thomas Carr's predecessor, began his term inauspiciously. He had been informed of his appointment on March 16, 1842,[80] and had arrived at Gibraltar on June 12, but his formal landing at Tangier and acceptance by the Emperor[81] were not accomplished until March 18 of the next year. From him, also, Commodore Morgan received severe criticism because the promised vessel of war was not sent for the consul's ceremonial entry into Tangier. Not until the visit of the U. S. S. Preble to Tangier on June 12, 1843, was the "amicable arrangement of the late unfortunate difficulty ... finally confirmed."[82]

Mullowny's dispatches were concerned chiefly with Abd er-Rahman's numerous conflicts with Spain and France and with the determined efforts of Sweden and Denmark to put an end to tribute-paying--an objective finally reached. The Emperor's growing apprehension over the menace of the protection system to his sovereignty was indicated by a decree that none of his Jewish or Moorish subjects was henceforth to act as a consular agent in any port of the empire.[83]

The concluding chapter of the story of the Carr-Mullowny feud was a long one. On June 28, 1845, Mullowny acknowledged the receipt of the notice of his dismissal and replacement by Carr. He warned the State Department that this would offend the Sultan. Since his father's death, Mullowny recalled, only one American consul had been satisfactory to the Moorish government. In his campaign for reappointment, Carr alleged that his former assistant had betrayed all secrets of the American consulate to Edward Drummond Hay. Moreover, Carr had been obliged to pay many of Mullowny's debts. As Carr described him, Mullowny was uneducated, of loose habits, and unrespected by either the consular corps or the Moroccan officials. Already the American commerce nourished by Carr had disappeared because of Mullowny's "British predilections and utter neglect and incompetency." Denying that he was under British influence, Mullowny asserted that Hay was only a personal friend. None of the American consuls before himself, except Leib, had spoken any language but English, but Mullowny had devoted his lifetime to studying Arabic and European languages. His removal, Mullowny pleaded, would leave him destitute and unfit for any other position.[84] But the State Department was convinced of its duty to redress the alleged injustice done by Carr's removal in 1842.

During the eleven months after his return to Gibraltar to resume his position, Carr corresponded with Secretary of State Buchanan about a suitable naval escort to Tangier, the intrigues of the British and French consuls with the perfidious and corrupt Mullowny to bar his return, and the steps taken to secure the Sultan's eventual acceptance of him. Mullowny's incompetence was exposed by the absence of consular records, an unrepaired and leaking consulate with broken and useless furniture, and his debt of $1,479 to the interpreter.[85]

During his second consulship, Carr became even more antagonistic toward the British representative in Tangier. An active assistant to his father in saving Morocco from disintegration in 1844-45, John Drummond Hay succeeded to the office of British consul general in 1845. He was a master of Turkish, Italian, Spanish, French, and Arabic. After diplomatic experience in both Turkey and Egypt, he was well fitted for another post in a Muslim country. He soon demonstrated fairness, honesty, tact, and common sense in dealing with Moorish chicanery. During his subsequent career of forty years, he surpassed even his father in prestige and became famed as the most influential man in Morocco. At times he represented Denmark, the Netherlands, and Austria-Hungary as well as his own country.[86] From Carr, however, Hay obtained neither sympathy nor cooperation in his efforts to curb French and Spanish aggression against Morocco.

Although Carr had expressed great contempt for France's diplomacy during her conflict with Morocco, he hailed with patriotic fervor the Second French Republic. He was incensed because at Tangier "on this occasion--the birth of a New Nation--the Flag staffs were left naked!" He continued:

> The American flag was at once given to the breeze, and by the side of it floats the flag of the New Republic .... The Institutions, and forms of Government of the United States, have too long been made an object of contumely, and misrepresentation, by the Monarchical Representatives at this place; and in many instances to the injury of our national interest. The day of detraction has now passed away; the attention of all Europe and a part of Africa, at this moment, is directed with wonder and admiration to the Great Republic of the West.[87]

Evidently Carr congratulated himself on having restored the prestige of his country in Morocco. In 1847 he induced Abd er-Rahman to issue a declaration of piracy against Spanish privateers supposed to be operating under Mexican license against American vessels near Morocco and legalized the Emperor's seizure and confiscation of any privateer which might enter Moroccan ports. However, when three vessels, possibly American, were reported stranded on the Wadnun coast, the Emperor refused to investigate or assume any responsibility for any deeds of the Sheik of Wadnun. Appearance of the U. S. S. Princeton at Tangier had some effect, Carr thought, both upon the Moors and upon some of the consuls, "who would have been too happy to know that our war with Mexico had consumed all our strength and neutralized all our energies." Carr accused Hay of keeping information on this matter secret.[88]

In two lengthy dispatches Carr made recommendations for improvement of American commerce with Morocco. From 1810 to 1830, Carr declared, when both depended upon native agents, the United States and Great Britain had had nearly equal trade with Morocco. Since 1830, while American trade had almost ceased, with the employment of paid English agents and "deception of forging the American Stamp" on certain goods, the value of British commerce had increased to $8,000,000. Carr's last official act was to prepare for President Polk a long argument favoring the establishment by treaty of direct trade with the Sheik of Wadnun. The main port of Wadnun, he said, gave entry to "the southern and eastern parts of Africa and the vast interior countries" and would be an ideal naval base for American vessels.[89]

For the second time Carr suffered the ordeal of an ignominious dismissal.[90] Up to May 5, 1847, he had received no acknowledgment of his dispatches to the State Department. No investigation was held to sift the charges and countercharges. Secretary of State Buchanan claimed that Carr was recalled because letters from the Sultan and other Moroccan officials declared him to be persona non grata. Carr attributed his removal, this time as before, to the intrigues of John F. Mullowny with the British and the French representatives in both Tangier and Washington. Carr remained in office until July 19, 1848, when he made way for T. Hart Hyatt.[91]

During his short period of service, Hyatt had few incidents of a novel or spectacular nature to report. He was permitted to repair the consulate, found almost in ruins and with but one habitable room. For this purpose there was allotted the $1,000 originally earmarked for a gift to the Sultan when he had been expected to visit Tangier. Hyatt requested a further appropriation of $1,550 to pay a note given by Mullowny to the interpreter of the consulate. Carrying out the investigation proposed by Carr, Hyatt found no evidence that the wrecked ships in Wadnun had been American. He suggested that American commerce might be stimulated by publicizing recent reductions in duties announced by the Sultan.[93]

The strained relations between Morocco and both Great Britain and France during 1848 and 1849 were the topic of several dispatches by Hyatt. He was gratified to be able to report that by letters and by conversation the Moroccan minister of foreign affairs revealed the most friendly feeling toward the American government and nation. Hyatt thus explained this cordiality toward the United States:

> This Empire is so constantly embroiled in petty difficulties with almost every country with which it has intercourse, that it seems to look upon the United States as about the only nation that attends to its own business and that acts upon just and liberal principles.

He urged, though, that American war vessels pay longer and more frequent visits to Morocco, especially at Tangier.[94]

On February 25, 1850, Hyatt transmitted to the Secretary of State a document of historical interest. It was a letter from Guiseppe Garibaldi, a refugee since the overthrow of the Roman Republic which he had established, who had been living for three months in Tangier with the Sardinian consul general. Garibaldi begged permission to command a merchant ship under the protection of the North American flag. Hyatt explained that to qualify for such protection, a ship must be owned by an American citizen, registered from an American port, and have at least some American seamen on board. Nevertheless, since it was the spirit of the American people to succor and protect the "victims of tyranny and martyrs to Freedom," he submitted the petition to his government for consideration.[95]

Following the precedent set by former consuls, Hyatt left office in frustration and disgrace. He had been embarrassed by the failure of the State Department to reply to his dispatches for the last year and a quarter. His last communication told of the theft of his personal property and the two copies of the treaty with Morocco; this occurred during his absence in Gibraltar. George V. Brown, the next consul, told of Hyatt's departure on July 1, 1850. The latter was commended for leaving a comfortable consular house, unsurpassed by any in Tangier. However, Brown condemned Hyatt for causing the arrest of a Moroccan, Hamet, for the robbery of the consulate, when all evidence pointed to an Englishman, the husband of Hyatt's paramour, with whom he had been traveling in Spain. Brown secured Hamet's release and made other restitution for an act bringing upon Hyatt "the merited contempt of the entire consular corps."[96]

As an introduction to consular life, Brown clashed with the French charge over the latter's employment of one Joseph Shirqui, discharged interpreter of the American consulate. Shirqui was a contrabandist and grafter who had defrauded both the American and Moorish authorities. Shirqui announced his intention to erect a dwelling in the yard of the American consulate on ground which he claimed he had purchased from John F. Mullowny some years before. Twice Brown asked the State Department to back him in protesting the hiring of Shirqui by the French. The Sultan showed his good will by refusing to recognize the man as a French employe.[97]

Endorsing a project of the consular corps, Brown asked for one hundred thirty Spanish dollars to help build a brick wall around the Christian cemetery to prevent its being outraged by the Moors. He requested also an additional sum to repair James Simpson's grave, now a mass of rubbish.[98]

The still serious problem of piracy appeared early in Brown's dispatches. He reported engagements of both British and Spanish vessels with the Kabyles, carrying on their traditional occupation near the Spanish prison colonies of Melilla and Ceuta. Hearing that Americans taken prisoner in Cuba might be in these prisons, Brown asked for funds and authority to ransom them and also other Americans who might be captured by pirates.[99]

From no previous consul had the State Department received so many statistics, bits of advice, and arguments designed to revive the moribund American commerce with Morocco. The Sultan had granted privileges making the United States a favorite nation--permitting, without a present, the hoisting of the American flag over the vice-consulate at Tetuan and waiving all charges on American ships calling at Tangier. Brown appointed vice-consuls in several ports, none of them American citizens. He prepared detailed information on shipping, tariff, imports, exports, commercial regulations, and land transportation.[100] Although the direct commerce between Morocco and the United States was insignificant, indirectly, via Gibraltar and Marseilles, Brown observed, there was an extensive exchange of products. The "coarse domestic," a cotton textile introduced by Americans and now the principal import of Morocco, had been imitated and monopolized by Manchester manufacturers. If the United States would abolish or reduce its tariff on wool, hides, and skins, it could become a formidable competitor of Great Britain in Moroccan trade.[101]

Boasting that he was the Sultan's favorite consul, Brown cited many instances of imperial courtesy. The information on commerce, he said, would have been unobtainable without the cooperation of Moorish officials. For months he made confidential reports to the Sultan on the progress of the Crimean War, which the latter valued highly because since the United States was the only important neutral power represented in Morocco, he could better depend on intelligence received from her agent. By the Sultan's orders, the Bashaw of Tangier was constrained to permit Brown to attend official receptions in civilian dress.[102]

Brown's relations with his fellow consuls were less cordial than with the Moorish Sultan and his officials. Although he had always hoisted the American flag for all sorts of European events, "even the death of the wife of the Spanish vice consul, of tainted reputation, poisoned by her husband," Brown was insulted by the Consul-General of Sweden-Norway. The latter refused to fly his flag to honor the late vice-president, W. R. King. However, Sweden's flag was conspicuous in a violent rain storm on Queen Victoria's birthday! Brown recalled the earlier experience of Hyatt, when the consular corps, headed by Hay, had declined to raise their flags to do homage to Washington. Brown expressed the righteous wrath of a republican:

> It is not to be denied that there is a very great

> reluctance, on the part of foreign representatives residing in Tangier, to admit the United States to an equal footing with the governments they represent. I question whether on the face of the globe, there can be found a spot where republicans and republican forms of government are held in such utter detestation as in this place.[103]

Throughout his tenure of office, Brown wrote of himself as intimately acquainted with diplomatic intriques and rivalries, especially those of France and Great Britain. Because of his vaunted activity and intimacy with men of importance, it must have been a great blow to learn of his release from duty. On October 31, 1854, Samuel P. Collings was notified of his appointment as consul to Morocco. He arrived in Tangier on January 2, 1855, to begin a term of little more than six months, which was marked by pettiness and futility. Annoyed at the delay of forty days before he received the Sultan's permission to disembark, Brown protested to the Secretary of State that this "absurd relic of barbarian custom" should no longer be countenanced. During this enforced stay, however, Brown embraced the opportunity to educate Collings for his position. Assuring the newcomer that his suspicion of surveillance in Gibraltar was well founded, Brown warned Collings that "an active system of most ferocious and wanton persecution" had begun to prevent his acceptance by the Sultan. Collings was informed that the French and the British had absolute control, not only of the consular corps, but also of the foreign policy of the empire. However, the Sultan finally received Collings graciously.[104]

The first item on the agenda of Collings was an indictment of Brown's conduct:

> At the time of communicating the conspiracies formed against me, he declared the entire diplomatic corpse (sic.) to be the most infamous and abandoned scoundrels and prostitutes on the face of the earth, engaged only in the indulgence of evil habits and bad passions and eager as hornets in cider time to involve all who came within their influence in the same fatal folds of demoralization and ruin. At the same time ... and even before my arrival here, he was in constant ...

> communication with these very people, assuring them of the utter infamy of my character, of the utter impossibility of their associating with me, of my revolutionary and ferocious disposition and principles, calumniating my family more wickedly than words can express, soliciting and urgeing (sic.) their active cooperation ... in keeping me out of the country, and if I should get in to drive me out of it.

Collings charged further that Brown spread slanders among the Moors and Jews and tried to "trap" Dr. W. W. Bidlack, who accompanied Collings, at Gibraltar. To Joseph Eshrieky, who had paid a large price for Brown's furniture, Brown delivered the yard and stables of the consulate with permission to wall up all outlets on the yard, making the consulate uninhabitable. Furthermore, Brown had pocketed money granted from United States funds for rent of the land claimed by Eshrieky. Collings removed the obstructions from the doors and windows and claimed the entire premises for the United States. Later Collings forwarded documents to prove that Brown accepted presents from foreigners and sold commercial agencies, vice consulates, and protection. Brown even took every useful book from the consulate. Such actions, Collings warned, "rendered the foreign service, or the United States, the mockery and scorn of the representatives of all other countries."[105]

Collings made one essay at promoting American-Moroccan commerce. Noticing a proposal in Congress to purchase beasts of burden for army use on the western frontiers, he recommended camels, which could be secured most conveniently from Morocco.[106]

Like his predecessors, Collings expressed distrust of the motives and activities of John Drummond Hay, especially in relation to the latter's persistent attempts to obtain from Abd er-Rahman a more liberal treaty of commerce and reforms in Moroccan government. Hay, he remarked, was "more than half a Moore (sic.), looks like one, and the Moores (sic.) rarely tell the truth, when its opposite will answer their purpose equally as well."[107]

Unfortunately, Collings did not have an opportunity to see the vindication of Hay's integrity. On June 16, 1855,

Moses Pariente informed Secretary Marcy of the death of Collings after a short illness. Here the "half-Moore" Hay came forward like a Christian gentleman. He put Pariente in charge of the American consulate and placed a guard over the property. He made funeral arrangements, and loaned money to both Mrs. Collings and Pariente. Again the State Department was guilty of negligence. Pariente complained of not receiving replies to his dispatches and asked for remuneration for his services and for money advanced by him for contingent expenses. Up to June 24, 1856, he had not been paid. Twice before that date, George V. Brown--for it was he who succeeded his former detractor--requested the State Department to reimburse Hay and Pariente.[108]

Although reappointed on January 29, 1856, Brown did not return to Tangier until April 1, 1856. One of his first acts was to refute the charges against him made by Collings, who, he said, had been a "mere dupe of a wretched vagabond," Bidlack. An investigation was made by two visiting Americans, strangers to Brown. According to their report, the Jews who had made affidavits against Brown now confessed to perjury under coercion and were to be dismissed from their posts. Later Brown presented to the State Department an extensive review of the legal question involved in Sherqui's claim to owning part of the American consulate grounds. The conclusion was that the land in dispute had originally been sold illegally by Thomas Carr and that no further claim would be made on the consulate premises.[109]

While continuing reports on the recurrent French and British controversies with Morocco, Brown devoted several dispatches to the topic so much emphasized during his first term as consul. He outlined the benefits of the recently concluded British-Moroccan treaty of commerce, and, ignoring the most-favored-nation provision of the American-Moroccan treaty of 1836, he urged that the United States make a new treaty with Morocco similar to the one just made with Great Britain. In his statistics of commerce for 1854 and 1855 he noted a big increase in the number of ships and tonnage, chiefly for the British. He advised that American merchants be informed of recent more liberal commercial regulations issued by the Sultan.

Announcing a plan to make a similar study of each province, he prepared a comprehensive report on the province of Tangier, including historical, geographic, social, and economic data. When asked to explain why his report bore such a striking resemblance to that presented by the British vice consul to Parliament, Brown replied that for the past seven years all tables for the British consulate's reports had been prepared by Moses Pariente, the interpreter of the American consulate.[110]

Passing away on September 3, 1859, Sultan Abd er-Rahman did not live long enough to learn whether his new treaties of 1856 with Great Britain would be, as Hay had assured him, the most direct route to the regeneration of Morocco. His death greatly alarmed both Europeans and Jews, and many fled to ships or to other countires. At first many tribes rejected the new ruler, Sidi Muhammad XVII, eldest son of the former sultan. Raids by Kabyles were threatened, and extensive war preparations by Spain were evident. By September 12, however, Brown was able to record the proclamation of Sidi Muhammad in the principal cities and the subsidence of the panic.[111]

Between March 4, 1859 and June 19, 1860, Brown sent to Washington a number of accounts of the background and events of the Spanish-Moroccan War. This conflict furnished another occasion to indict the United States government of niggardliness. Brown pointed out that every country, except the United States, had made liberal allowances to compensate their agents for expenses incurred in Gibraltar during the wartime exodus there. Brown, the only consul to venture back to Tangier during the war, lost all his furniture when the ship carrying it sank. His wife died from a derangement due to the terrors of the situation. On March 6, 1861, Brown begged for a three months' leave of absence to repair his physical and mental health. But on May 10, when he learned of the outbreak of the Civil War, he decided that it would be cowardly and disloyal to abandon his post. He wanted to use his influence with the Moorish government to secure protection for American vessels in Moroccan ports and to arrest and detain there ships of the revolting states, and, conversely, to prevent privateers from making arrangements for disposal of their prizes in Tangier. Brown thought that Spain's anxiety to end her war against Morocco had been caused by her designs on Mexico while the United States was involved in civil conflict.[112]

James De Long, appointed to replace Brown on September 18, 1861, began his work on November 30, and the two men met with the lack of amenity customary at the change of American consuls. Brown called the attention of the State Department to the "wretched orthography" in De Long's copying of the oath of office administered to him. It was not difficult to interpret Brown's intimations that it was important for the United States to be represented at Tangier by a man of ability, discretion, social position, temperate habits, and the breeding requisite for associating with men of science, superior accomplishments, and polished manners. In turn, De Long complained of Brown's retention of the office for twenty days after his arrival and gave the usual unfavorable report of the condition of the consular property. The dispatch and letter books had been mutilated; the consular house was delapidated, leaking, and in bad repair generally; the furniture was broken and nearly worthless; most of the books were rotted; and many documents were mildewed and eaten by mice.[113]

During his short tenure of office, De Long was known chiefly because of a notorious incident involving Morocco in the American Civil War. Originally he had assured Seward that federal men-of-war could obtain all their supplies in any Moroccan port, but that Confederate privateers would be treated as pirates in these ports. However, in practice this principle resulted in an international crisis of some magnitude. The officers of the Confederate commerce raider Sumter, which had sunk two Union ships in the Mediterranean, stopped off at Tangier. They were en route from Gibraltar to Cadiz on a French vessel to purchase coal for their ship. At Tangier they were arrested by De Long, aided by the Moorish police. Later the Moroccan minister asked for their release, but De Long refused to consider them political prisoners. To De Long's inquiry, "Shall seventy-six years of uninterrupted friendship ... between your government and that of the United States be brought to an end for the sake of pirates?" the Moroccan minister could only give assurance of continued cooperation. Assisted by Moroccan troops, American marines dispersed a European mob attempting to release the Confederates. De Long had the captives conveyed in irons to an American ship-of-war, which he had summoned, and taken to the United States. Support of the European mob was denied by all the consuls in Tangier, who offered judicial investigation of any persons under their jurisdiction accused of participating in the demonstration.

The matter now became an international incident. The French foreign minister, M. Thouvenal, became angry at an impolitic note sent by De Long to his consular colleagues, reprimanding them for their alleged lack of support. Thouvenal declared that the taking of these men from a French ship was analogous to the Martin Koszta case of a few years before. The question was debated in the British Parliament, where the incident was considered an abuse of consular jurisdiction by extending it to "alleged political offenses." Since the Moorish government was said to have yielded to De Long only at the threat of war, the question was put "whether the British Government will take means to protect our faithful ally from such infringement of its independence." The Under-Secretary of Foreign Affairs hoped that the President[114] would release the men "for the sake of justice, of humanity, and of the sacred right of affording asylum to persons accused of political offences." The matter was settled eventually because of the firmness and logical arguments of Secretary of State Seward, who denied that the French government, had any right to protect the men. Seward asserted that they were not political refugees from a recognized government but were subject to the American consul, since they were captured in an act of war against their lawful government.[115]

De Long resented his government's "reward" for his patriotic efforts; on March 19, 1862, three letters from Brown reached different persons in Tangier saying that the Senate had not confirmed De Long's appointment and that a man named McMath would shortly become consul. De Long feared that his removal would be interpreted throughout Europe as a reprimand for arresting the Confederate agents and would have an adverse effect upon the attitude of the Moorish authorities. He sent Seward a letter from the Viceroy Prince Mulai Abbas to refute the charges in the British Parliament that the Moroccan authorities had supported De Long under a threat of war. In his last dispatch, dated June 10, 1862, De Long reported the arrival of McMath and his own impending departure.[116]

Jesse H. McMath began his service under potentially unpleasant circumstances, but he was received in a friendly way by the Moroccan authorities and people and by his consular colleagues in Tangier. It was a significant symbol of amity that on July 4, 1862, the flags of all consulates in Tangier were raised.[117]

As instructed, McMath initiated cordial relations with the Moroccan government by thanking Prince Mulai Abbas for his assistance to De Long and his expression of friendship for the United States and hope for her success in the war against the rebels. In April, 1863, the Moorish Minister for Foreign Affairs assured McMath that his country, being a sincere friend of the "American nation" would never aid or give countenance to the insurgents, and would expect like conduct from the United States in case of a rebellion in Morocco. He also said that France did not act as a friend of the United States in proposing mediation and thereby encouraging the rebels. Later, however, McMath had some difficulty in obtaining an imperial edict that any vessel sailing under the Confederate flag would enter any Moroccan port only on pain of seizure. McMath thought he had foiled a plan to have five guns from the *Sumter*, stored in Gibraltar Bay, purchased for the Emperor and delivered at Mogador.[118]

McMath reiterated the arguments of his predecessors that the American representatives should have the financial backing and official rank to place them on a par with their European colleagues. He won an initial victory in his campaign by obtaining $950 to rehabilitate the consular house and make it compare favorably with any in Tangier. In May, 1863, he commented on the international rivalry over rank. Both Spanish and French representatives had been promoted recently to ministers to make them equal in rank to the British envoy. Two years later McMath confessed that he had been calling himself a consul general instead of a consul, because both the arms and seal of the consulate were for the higher rank and also because no other nation sent to Morocco such a low-ranking representative as a consul. The Moorish authorities paid great deference to rank, and there was a distinct cleavage between ministers and those of inferior grade. Since the United States was one of the six first class powers in the world, and had recently vindicated her honor and dignity, would it not be appropriate to show appreciation to Morocco for its long friendship, so particularly manifested during the last four years, by naming the American representative there a minister resident? In June, 1866, McMath urged this action even more cogently by pointing out that of twelve countries represented in Morocco the United States gave its representative the lowest rank and compensation, and yet the Americans were expected to live as well and to entertain as liberally as their fellows, many of whom received double and some triple their salary.

It was probably in despair at receiving no reply to his plea that McMath sent Seward a "private and non-official" communication on October 1, 1866. Since in President Lincoln's message to Congress in December, 1863, among five consulates singled out for special mention, McMath's had been placed first for good administration, he ventured to ask for a position as minister resident in Europe, Central or South America, Hayti, or Santo Domingo. Like other American consuls, McMath presented a dismal view of his environment:

> Here we are cut off from all the advantages of European society and enclosed in a city but little better than a prison. To Europeans and Americans it is one of the most unattractive and dismal places for two thirds of the year, during the rainy season, that can be found anywhere. There are no amusements, no public walks, in fact nothing but very narrow dirty streets, Moors, Jews, and dogs, the scavangers of the city, to be seen during a great part of the year ... I can hardly imagine a city possessing fewer attractions for foreign agents than this does ... and I do most earnestly beg the President to transfer me to another post ... in any legation anywhere on the continents or islands named.[119]

But, although he regretted on February 15, 1867, that his suggestion about raising the rank of American representatives had not merited a reply from the State Department, McMath stayed on. He endorsed the request of his interpreter, Moses Pariente, for an increase in salary; after being in United States service over sixteen years, Pariente was receiving only half the salary paid other interpreters. In one other respect McMath thought the United States government was careless of its prestige--almost three years had passed since the customary salutes had been given and received by an American vessel in the port of Tangier. A steamer visiting there the preceding month was not a saluting ship. The consul begged for the largest and best ship of the European squadron to visit Tangier soon and for another with a saluting battery to visit and display the flag at Rabat, Casablanca, Mazagan, Safi, and Mogador. Two years later after giving a detailed account of the failure of the Moorish Minister of Foreign Affairs to give a satisfactory decision in the case of a Moor who had defrauded the American vice consul, McMath explained that it was Moroccan custom to present large claims directly to the Sultan's government, and that a payment of such claims usually followed promptly after the appearance of a war vessel from the country concerned.[120]

The plague was still a problem for the Board of Health in Tangier. The Asiatic cholera appearing in July, 1865 at Gibraltar disrupted supply lines for beef from Morocco and caused some dissension among the members of the board. Again in 1868 crop failure, famine, and cholera drove crowds of starving refugees into Tangier, where they besieged the consulates for food. McMath asked for a contribution for relief of these miserable people.[121]

McMath made few communications on the subject of commerce, which was not of great interest to the United States during and after the Civil War. For 1863 he reported that the foreign commerce of Morocco, at all times insignificant, was not likely to be materially increased. There was no direct commerce with the United States, but coarse wool from the interior was reshipped in large quantities to America from Gibraltar, London, and Marseilles. Export duties were fixed by the new Spanish-Moroccan treaty, but there were many special regulations. Of great interest to the southern United States was the news that the Sultan in 1863 had sponsored the raising of cotton on large tracts of crown land and that it was successfully cultivated. The Sultan had decreed this industry to be a state monopoly. In 1864 the Sultan removed the prohibition which he had formerly imposed on merchants going into the interior to obtain wool and cereals. The crop failure of 1866 caused the suspension of the exportation of grain after the six months' notice required by treaty. There were no American merchants in the empire and no American establishments on the coast.[122]

In three of the projects sponsored by foreign powers for the progress of Morocco, McMath was a participant. They were the reformation of the protection system, the Jewish problem, and the establishment of the Cape Spartel Lighthouse under international management.

The protection of native Moors and Jews by consuls of foreign countries represented in Tangier resulted in a steadily worsening situation which became the main topic of an international conference in 1880. In August, 1863, the French and Spanish representatives had made two written agreements with the Moroccan government designed to limit and regularize protection. All other representatives at Tangier later adhered to these agreements, without previously submitting them to their governments for approval; thus McMath committed the United States in this matter.[123]

The Jewish problem was of great interest to the American consul. The traditional Moorish antagonism toward the Hebrews, prevalent among the masses, was exacerbated at this time by their extensive purchase of protection and by their use of foreign influence to enforce unjust claims and to imprison their debtors. By usury, moreover, many Jews oppressed both Moors and their co-religionists. In 1863 two Jews were tortured and executed without trial for the alleged murder, by poisoning, of the Spanish receiver in the customs house in Safi. This crime provoked protests to the Moroccan government from Tangier and foreign Jewish societies. Before the arrival of McMath's account of this crime, it had been called to the attention of the State Department by the Board of

Delegates of American Israelites in New York. McMath was instructed to "exert all proper influence to prevent a repetition of the barbarous cruelties to which Israelites in the Moorish Empire have, on account of their religion, been subjected." Secretary Seward was certain that a similar course would be followed by representatives of all Christian powers in Tangier. McMath had already reported privately to Washington, however, that the Spanish Minister and all his staff showed great hostility to Jews and were continually inciting Moorish officials to cruel and unjust punishments. The Sultan, he said, was a friend of the Jews, but he had to yield to misrepresentations from his officials or demands from Spanish officials for beatings and decapitations. McMath could recall no other instance in modern history where subjects of a semi-civilized power pled for protection against the agent of a civilized power.[124]

In 1864 a British subject, Sir Moses Montefiore, went on a mission to the Moorish court as a delegate of the Jewish societies of Europe. He obtained an imperial edict to Moorish officials, directing that Jews be granted full legal equality and protection of person and property. However, this edict caused great displeasure among the Moorish masses, and numerous instances of further outrages against Jews were reported.[125]

Several accounts were sent to Seward concerning the progress of the establishment of the Cape Spartel Lighthouse, first advocated by John Mullowny in 1821 and considered by the consular corps as a joint venture in 1852. Begun in 1861, the structure was completed in 1864. The Sultan granted the perpetual neutrality of the lighthouse on condition that the ten powers represented at Tangier[126] would supervise and maintain it. Each country agreed to pay an annual contribution of $285. This financial arrangement was approved for the United States by Secretary of the Treasury Chase. Although McMath had negotiated the convention for his government, he expressed to Seward his disapproval of such extravagance:

> I confess myself unable to discover upon what principle my government, having no commerical interest in this country, ought to contribute to the perpetual maintenance of a lighthouse on this coast any more than the

South American republics and other nations that have no trade with Morocco.

Although the lighthouse was first illuminated on October 15, 1864, the international convention was not signed until May 31, 1865. It was to run for ten years, with an annual extension thereafter until renounced by any of the signers. On October 15, 1864, the consular corps at Tangier assumed control of the lighthouse, and on July 11, 1865, regulations were promulgated controlling their functions as the International Commission of Cape Spartel. After repeated prodding by McMath, the treaty was ratified by President Johnson on July 14, 1866, and proclaimed on March 12, 1867. Thus Jesse McMath has the distinction of being the first American agent to take part in making and enforcing an international convention pertaining to Morocco.[127]

McMath was notified on June 9, 1869, that his place would be taken by Felix A. Mathews. Letters from Muhammad Bargash and the Sultan favoring the retention of McMath proved to no avail. The exchange of charges made indicates that the reputation of the American consulate was still vulnerable. McMath protested to Secretary Fish against the appointment to Tangier of "a person of the lowest birth and character," who would make the consular "mansion" the rendezvous of the Spanish relatives and former acquaintances of Mathews, of the "lowest class of the foreign people of this city." Sir John Hay said that Felix Mateos[128] had been a British protégé in his youth at Tangier; because of his antecedents he was unfit to represent a great and respectable nation.[129] Mathews accused McMath of slandering and misrepresenting him to his future colleagues and the Moroccan authorities and trying to buy certificates against his character. McMath's purpose, Mathews thought, had been to keep out one who, knowing all the languages spoken in Tangier and the customs of the populace, would soon discover all the unlawful doings at the consulate for the past seven years. Mathews urged an investigation, not only of the conduct of McMath, but also of several of his predecessors who were said to have made money in the protection racket; it was high "time to stop further abuse committeed under shelter of our flag and to show this people that our banner does not float here to shield corrupt doings but to protect lawfully American interest."[130]

As a result of the movement against him in Tangier, Mathews was removed on November 23, 1869. By some vagary, extreme even for the State Department, his successor, John T. Robeson, was recalled on July 29, 1870, and Mathews was reinstated, resuming his work at Tangier on October 1, 1870.[131] During the seventeen years that he occupied his position Mathews continued to be a controversial character, as well as an active one in many important affairs.

Mathews soon joined in the battle of the American consuls for rank, prestige, and salary comparable to those of their colleagues. Again he declared the consular house to be dangerious to live in and urged its proper repair.[132] He challenged the State Department's contention that American consuls had no diplomatic character. He emphasized that only the American representative still held the humblest rank of consul, placing him in the lowest position on all ceremonial occasions and causing the Moroccans to regard this as evidence of weakness in the American nation. Secretary Fish was obdurate, however, and it was not until December 18, 1883, that Secretary Frelinghuysen raised the Tangier office to the status of a diplomatic agency and consulate general with an increased salary of $3,000.[133]

Contrasting statistics on commerce for 1870 and 1872, Mathews said that the former year's record, with a heavy decline because of the war in France, was greatly improved in 1872. In the latter year, in spite of the Sultan's restrictive policies, exportation was the largest known and the total for imports was greater than for the four preceding years. The imports were chiefly from Great Britain, and as before there was no direct American trade with Morocco.[134]

The unfriendly relations between the British and American representatives continued. They first disputed about the jurisdiction over the American consulate's interpreter and dragoman, who was Scottish. (Robeson had dismissed Moses Pariente, who was immediately employed by Hay.) Hay and his government persisted in claiming both civil and criminal jurisdiction over Peter Scott.[135]

A second cause of dissension between Mathews and Hay pertained to the former's conviction that the British minister had great control over Sidi Muhammed XVII, which he was using effectively to secure preferential treatment for British claimants against the Moorish government. On the other hand, Mathews was unable to collect for Isaac Bencazar, American vice consul in Safi, a sum of $12,500 owed him by a Moorish governor. The case had been pending since the time of McMath, during which time the Sultan had used every device of procrastination and evasion to prevent a trial of the case on its merits. The recalcitrance of the Moorish government, Mathews charged, was due to the secret agreement with Sir John Hay to prevent subjects of other nations from having their claims paid if British claims were privately met. Hay was alleged also to have proposed to the Moorish government, as a trial court, a tribunal admitting only the testimony of Muslims, none of whom would testify against the Sultan's interests. Citing incidents given in dispatches of predecessors, Mathews drew a grave indictment against his British colleague:

> The consular and diplomatic career of Sir John Hay in this place for the last thirty years has been marked by a succession of intrigues in order to keep up his personal interest with the Moorish government, for which he has not spared the most audacious arts and contrivances, always taking the Moorish side in any dispute, whether right or wrong, when he thought that his private interests might be served. It is also asserted that his interference was the cause of the late war between Spain and Morocco .... He has mixed himself up in every foreign misunderstanding, always, however, in an underhanded manner.[136]

When he passed away on September 11, 1873, Sidi Muhammad XVII had been enjoying fourteen years "unmolested, except by customary foreign embassies and claims."[137] His successor, however, was to wage a losing fight to rescue his country from the decadence developing rapidly since the advent of Sir Edward Drummond Hay in

Sultans of Morocco	American Consuls and Consuls General	British Consuls General and Diplomatic Agents
Mulai Soliman (1795-1822)		
	James Simpson (1797-1820)	
	John Simpson * (1820)	
	John Mullowny (1820-1830)	
Abd er-Rahman (1822-1859)		
	G. A. Porter * (1830-1832)	Edward Drummond Hay (1829-1845)
	Samuel Carr (1832)	
	James R. Leib (1832-1838)	
	Thomas N. Carr (1838-1842)	
	John F. Mullowny (1842-1845)	
	Thomas N. Carr (1845-1848)	John Drummond Hay (1845-1886)
	T. Hart Hyatt (1848-1850)	
	George W. Brown (1850-1854)	
	Samuel Collings (1855)	
	George V. Brown (1856-1861)	

Sidi Muhammad XVII (1859-1873)		
	James De Long (1861-1862)	
	Jesse H. McMath (1862-1869)	
	Felix A. Mathews (1869)	
	John T. Robeson (1869-1870)	
	Felix A. Mathews (1870-1887)	
Mulai Hassan (1873-1894)		
	William Reed Lewis (1887-1889)	William Kirby Green (1886-1890)
	Robert Stalker * (1890)	
	Felix A. Mathews (1890-1893)	Charles Euan Smith (1891-1893)

*Acting officials

Morocco in 1829. In this period of Moroccan decay, the American consuls, avowedly non-mixers in foreign politics, had nevertheless a minor role to play.

Notes

1. Stephen H. Roberts, History of French Colonial Policy (1870-1925), 2 vols. (hereafter cited as Roberts, History of French Colonial Policy), II, 547.

2. Thomas Barclay, appointed as consul for the specific purpose of negotiating the renewal of the treaty in 1791, was never confirmed by the Senate and died before he could enter Morocco and carry out this mission.

3. Timothy Pickering (1795-1800), John Marshall (1800-1801), James Madison (1801-1809), Robert Smith (1809-1811), James Monroe (1811-1817), and John Quincy Adams (1817-1825).

4. The dispatches of Simpson, in manuscript form, are in the Department of State Archives, Consular Dispatches, Tangier, I-IV, in the National Archives, Washington, D. C. The dispatches of succeeding consuls are from later volumes of the same series. The consular dispatches are cited hereafter as C. D., Tangier.

5. Simpson to Sec. of State, No. 3, Dec. 16, 1797 and No. 35, Jan. 8, 1802, C. D., Tangier, I.

6. Simpson to Sec. of State, No. 9, July 17, 1798 and No. 12, Feb. 27, 1799, ibid.

7. "At the time the late Emperor Sidi Mohamet concluded the Treaty of 1786 with the United States, he wished the World to believe his dominion extended far beyond where in fact it reached. This gave rise to the second clause of the 10th Article, which certainly neither he or any of his Successors have had it in their power to fulfill. When Muley Soliman has been able to get any Christians out of the hands

of the Arabs, he has sent them to Tangier .... but to have reliance on him for the release of all would seriously hazard the loss of many." Simpson to Sec. of State, No. 108, 27, 1806, Ibid., IV.

8. Simpson to Sec. of State, No. 26, July 14, 1800, Ibid., I.

9. Simpson to Sec. of State, No. 138, April 14, 1808, Ibid., II.

10. Simpson to Sec. of State, No. 12, Feb. 27, 1799 and No. 28, Aug. 30, 1800, Ibid., I; No. 84, Oct. 6, 1804, Ibid., II; No. 85, Oct. 15, 1804, Ibid.; No. 101, Aug. 30, 1805, Ibid.; No. 108, March 27, 1806, Ibid.; No. 113, July 7, 1806, Ibid.; No. 114, Aug. 22, 1806, Ibid.; and No. 115, Sept. 16, 1806, Ibid.; No. 226, Sept. 24, 1816, Ibid., III.

11. Bemis, Diplomatic History of the United States, 178-179 and Bemis, American Secretaries of State, III, 276.

12. Lane-Poole, Barbary Corsairs, 296-300; Allen, Barbary Corsairs, 11-12.

13. Simpson to Sec. of State, No. 107, Feb. 17, 1806, C. D., Tangier, II; No. 136, Dec. 30, 1807, Ibid.; No. 188, July 7, 1813, Ibid., III; No. 197, July 11, 1814, Ibid.; No. 225, Sept. 10, 1816, Ibid.

14. Simpson to Monroe, No. 208, Aug. 22, 1815, Ibid.

15. Simpson to Sec. of State, No. 53, Dec. 24, 1802, Ibid., I.

16. Simpson to Sec. of State, No. 38, March 19, 1802, Ibid.; No. 40, June 5, 1802, Ibid.; No. 56, May 14, 1803, Ibid., II; No. 59, July 9, 1803, Ibid.; No. 68, Oct. 17, 1803, Ibid.; No. 73, Feb. 28, 1804, Ibid.; No. 89, April 2, 1805, Ibid.; No. 98, July 13, 1805, Ibid.; No. 104, Dec. 26, 1805, Ibid.; No. 105, Jan. 21, 1805, Ibid.; No. 112, May 26, 1806, Ibid.; No. 123, June 3, 1807, Ibid.; No. 128, Aug. 27,

1807, Ibid.; No. 139, April 26, 1808, Ibid.; No. 143, Sept. 24, 1808, Ibid.; No. 150, July 9, 1809, Ibid.; No. 166, Feb. 21, 1811, Ibid., III; No. 189, Aug. 20, 1813, Ibid.; No. 192, March 8, 1814, Ibid.; No. 275, May 18, 1819, Ibid., IV.

17. Simpson to Sec. of State, Ibid.

18. Simpson to Sec. of State, No. 74, March 2, 1804, Ibid., II; No. 107, Feb. 12, 1806, Ibid.; No. 124, June 12, 1907, Ibid.; No. 172, March 2, 1812, Ibid., III; No. 192, March 8, 1814, Ibid.; No. 257, March 30, 1818, Ibid.

19. Many of Simpson's dispatches are illegible because they were immersed in vinegar by the authorities at Gibraltar to disinfect them from the plague.

20. Simpson to Sec. of State, No. 15, April 30, 1799, C. D., Tangier, I; No. 16, June 8, 1799, Ibid.; No. 17, June 24, 1799, Ibid.; No. 19, July 30, 1799, Ibid.; No. 20, Aug. 17, 1799, Ibid.; No. 21, Nov. 23, 1799, Ibid.; No. 22, March 8, 1800, Ibid.; No. 23, May 14, 1800, Ibid.; No. 25, June 7, 1800, Ibid.; No. 26, July 14, 1800, Ibid.; No. 27, Aug. 15, 1800, Ibid.; No. 38, March 19, 1802, Ibid.

21. Simpson to Sec. of State, No. 271, Feb. 20, 1819, Ibid.; IV; No. 275, May 18, 1819, Ibid.; No. 276, June 14, 1819, Ibid.; No. 277, June 24, 1819, Ibid.; No. 281, Sept. 19, 1819, Ibid.; No. 283, Oct. 18, 1819, Ibid.; No. 285, Dec. 13, 1819, Ibid.; No. 287, Jan. 8, 1820, Ibid.; No. 289, Feb. 5, 1820, Ibid.

22. Simpson to Sec. of State, No. 39, May 13, 1802, Ibid., I; No. 102, Sept. 23, 1805, Ibid., II; No. 150, July 9, 1809, Ibid.; No. 165, Oct. 1, 1810, Ibid.; No. 168, April 13, 1811, Ibid., III; No. 179, July 6, 1812, Ibid.; No. 209, Oct. 12, 1815, Ibid.; No. 277, June 24, 1819, Ibid., IV; No. 281, Sept. 19, 1819, Ibid.; No. 283, Oct. 18, 1819, Ibid.; No. 285, Dec. 13, 1819, Ibid.; No. 287, Jan. 8, 1920, Ibid.; No. 289, Feb. 5, 1920, Ibid.

23. Simpson to Monroe, Sec. of State, No. 226, Sept. 24, 1816, Ibid., III.

24. Roy Franklin Nichols, Advance Agents of American Destiny (hereafter cited as Nichols, Advance Agents), 108, 121, 126.

25. Simpson to J. Q. Adams, No. 243, July 22, 1817 and No. 244, Aug. 11, 1817, C. D., Tangier, III.

26. Simpson to Sec. of State, No. 3, Dec. 16, 1797, Ibid., I; No. 12, Feb. 27, 1799, Ibid.; No. 14, March 11, 1799, Ibid.; No. 15, April 30, 1799, Ibid.; No. 32, Nov. 15, 1800, Ibid.; No. 35, Jan. 8, 1802, Ibid.; No. 38, March 19, 1802, Ibid.; No. 39, May 13, 1802, Ibid.; No. 53, Dec. 24, 1802, Ibid.; No. 71, Dec. 26, 1803, Ibid., II; No. 179, July 6, 1812, Ibid., III; and No. 218, July 30, 1816, Ibid. Simpson to Sec. of Treasury, No. 29, July 1, 1816, Ibid., III.

27. The correspondence continued from May 14, 1800, until Sept. 19, 1819, sometimes as whole letters devoted to the subject, but often only paragraphs in dispatches covering many other topics also.

28. Simpson to Sec. of State, No. 105, Jan. 21, 1806, C. D., Tangier, II; No. 118, Oct. 28, 1806, Ibid.; No. 156, Jan. 6, 1810, Ibid.; No number, Jan. 13, 1810, Ibid.; No. 168, April 13, 1811, Ibid., III.

29. Simpson to Robert Smith, No. 162, Aug. 18, 1810, Ibid., II.

30. The United States of America to James Simpson, Statement of Account, Aug. 16, 1810, Ibid., III; Simpson to Smith, No. 166, Feb. 21, 1811 and No. 172, March 2, 1812, Ibid.; Simpson to Monroe, No. 182, April 3, 1813, Ibid.

31. The United States of America to James Simpson, Statement of Account, Dec. 31, 1817, Ibid.

32. Simpson to J. Q. Adams, No. 243, July 22, 1817, Ibid.; Simpson to Col. David Humphreys, Aug. 20, 1818, Ibid.; J. Q. Adams to Nathaniel Bacon, Feb. 17, 1819, Ibid., IV.

33. John Simpson to Adams, No. 1, March 15, 1820; April 3, 1820; April 18, 1820, Ibid.

34. John Simpson to Adams, No. 2, March 15, 1820; July 9, 1820; July 10, 1820; March 6, 1821; March 19, 1821; March 27, 1821, Ibid.

35. John Mullowny to Adams, June 2, 1820; June 20, 1820; No. 3, Sept. 25, 1820; No. 6, Dec. 29, 1820; May 8, 1821; No. 8, June 26, 1821; Ibid.

36. John Simpson sent two later appeals to John Quincy Adams, one from Gibraltar on July 12, 1822, and the other from Lissa on January 24, 1824; C. D., Tangier, IV. In the second letter he stated that since he had received no contradictory answers to his repeated claims, and since he had so long ago remitted through John Mullowny all his father's vouchers and accounts, he hoped that Adams would allow him on this account at least the $2,000 for which he was about to draw upon Adams for 30 days order of Peter Pedersen, H. D. Majesty's Minister to the United States.

37. John Simpson to Adams, July 20, 1821, Ibid.; Petition of John Simpson to Government of the United States, July 20, 1821, Ibid.

38. Mullowny to Adams, No. 8, June 26, 1821; No. 10, Aug. 19, 1821; No. 11, Sept. 29, 1821; No. 13, Jan. 31, 1822; No. 15, May 15, 1822; Ibid.

39. Mullowny to Adams, No. 10, Aug. 19, 1821; No. 12, Jan. 1, 1822; No. 13, Jan. 30, 1822; No. 15, May 15, 1822, Ibid.

40. Mullowny to Adams, No. 12, Jan. 1, 1822, Ibid.

41. Mullowny to Adams, No. 10, Aug. 19, 1821; No. 12, Jan. 1, 1822; No. 15, May 15, 1822, Ibid.

42. Mullowny to Adams, No. 10, Aug. 19, 1821, *Ibid.*

43. Terrasse, in his *History of Morocco*, 145, says that Mulai Soliman died broken-hearted over the revival of revolts during the last part of his reign.

44. Meakin, *Moorish Empire*, 172.

45. Mullowny to Adams, No. 19, Dec. 19, 1822; No. 20, Dec. 23, 1822; No. 24, Aug. 30, 1823; *C. D., Tangier*, IV.

46. Meakin, *Moorish Empire*, 173-175.

47. Abd er-Rahman to Consuls in Tangier, Dec. 28, 1822, *C. D. Tangier*, IV.

48. Mullowny to Adams, No. 25, Nov. 22, 1823; No. 26, Dec. 15, 1823, No. 27, Feb. 7, 1824; No. 28, Feb. 20, 1824; No. 29, May 16, 1824; *Ibid.*

49. Mullowny to Adams, No. 27, Feb. 7, 1824, *Ibid.*

50. Mullowny to Henry Clay, No. 39, Sept. 7, 1825; No. 43, Feb. 15, 1826; No. 45, May 27, 1826; No. 48, May 22, 1827, *Ibid.*

51. Mullowny to Clay, No. 36, May 16, 1825; No. 43, Feb. 15, 1826; No. 56, Aug. 16, 1828, *Ibid.*

52. Mullowny to Adams, No. 30, Nov. 8, 1824; Mullowny to Clay, No. 51, Sept. 13, 1827; *Ibid.*

53. Mullowny to Adams, No. 30, Nov. 8, 1824; No. 34, March 25, 1825; No. 35, April 2, 1825. Mullowny to Clay, No. 36, May 16, 1825; No. 49, June 11, 1827; *Ibid.*

54. Mullowny to Adams, No. 31, Oct. 27, 1824; No. 46, July 22, 1826. Mullowny to Clay, No. 48, May 22, 1827; No. 51, Sept. 13, 1827; No. 57, Nov. 7, 1828; No. 58, No.v 28, 1828; No. 59, Jan. 1, 1829. Mullowny to Van Buren, No. 62, June 30, 1829; No. 64, July 24, 1829; No. 65, Oct. 15, 1829; No. 66, March 10, 1830; *Ibid.*

55. Mullowny to Clay, No. 37, Sept., 1825; Mullowny to Sec. of Treasury, Rush, No. 3, May 27, 1826, Ibid.

56. Mullowny to Andrew Jackson, May 12, 1829, Ibid.

57. Mullowny to Clay, No. 46, July 22, 1826; No. 50, June 26, 1827; No. 51, Sept. 13, 1827. Mullowny to Van Buren, No. 62, June 30, 1829; Ibid.

58. Mullowny to Clay, No. 57, Nov. 7, 1828; No. 58, Nov. 28, 1828; No. 59, Jan. 21, 1829, Ibid.

59. Mullowny to Van Buren, No. 64, July 24, 1829; No. 65, Oct. 15, 1829, Ibid.

60. Mullowny to Van Buren, No. 69, June 30, 1830, Ibid.

61. Porter to Livingston, May 25, 1832, Ibid., V.

62. Samuel Carr to Livingston, July 25, 1832, 56-58; Oct. 8, 1832, 69-70; Ibid.

63. Leib to Livingston, Oct. 4, 1832, 67-68; Nov. 6, 1832, 71-74; Dec. 26, 1832, 75; Dec. 28, 1832, 79. Robert Bright to Leib, Gibraltar, Dec. 10, 1832, 80. Bright to Livingston, Gibraltar, Dec. 10, 1832, 81. Bill from Robert Bright, Aug. 8, 1832, 82, Ibid.

64. Deposition of Edward William Auriol Drummond Hay, Jan. 18, 1833, 85-88; Leib to Consular Corps in Tangier, Jan. 20, 1833, and Feb., 1833, 96-98. James Renshaw, U. S. Frigate *Brandywine*, to Leib. March 27, 1833, 101, Leib to Livingston, May 17, 1833, 107-110; June 14, 1833, 124-126. Samuel Carr to Sec. of State, July 8, 1833, 140-146; Leib to Livingston, May 16, 1833, 106; June 15, 1833, 131-136; Leib to Sec. of State, Sept. 1, 1834, 197-198; Ibid.

65. Leib to Livingston, Jan. 20, 1833, 83-84, Ibid.

66. The purpose of Leib's mission was to prepare the way for the renewal of the Treaty of 1786. The negotiations for this are discussed in Chapter IV.

67. Leib to Sec. of State McLane, Nov. 7, 1833, 160-163; Nov. 28, 1833, 166-167, 171; C. D., Tangier, V.

68. Leib to Sec. of State, Nov. 7, 1833, 163; March 1, 1834, 82; July 20, 1834, 188-189; July 27, 1834, 190-191; Aug. 4, 1834, No. 35, April 26, 1836, Ibid.

69. Leib to Sec. of State, April 15, 1834, 184-185; July 30, 1834, 193; No. 32, Feb. 17, 1836, Ibid.

70. Stuart, Tangier, 21-22.

71. Leib to John Forsyth, No. 24, Jan. 10, 1835, C. D., Tangier, V.

72. Thomas N. Carr to Forsyth, Gibraltar, Aug. 27, 1838; No. 1, Sept. 7, 1838; No. 2, Sept. 11, 1838; No. 3, Oct. 2, 1838; No. 4, Jan. 22, 1839, Ibid., VI.

73. Carr to Forsyth, No. 6, June 14, 1839; June 17, 1839; No. 7, Sept. 3, 1839; No. 11, April 17, 1840. Mullowny to Carr, June 10, 1839, Ibid.

74. Carr to Forsyth, No. 11, April 17, 1840, Ibid.

75. Carr to Forsyth, No. 15, June 23, 1840; No. 20, Feb. 28, 1841. Carr to Webster, No. 26, Aug. 24, 1841; No. 27, Sept. 11, 1841; No. 28, Oct. 8, 1841; Ibid.

76. Department of State, Instructions, Barbary Powers, (hereafter cited as D. S., Instructions, Barbary Powers), XIV, 25.

77. Carr to Morgan No. 1, April 7, 1842. Hay to Carr, April 28, 1842. Carr to Webster, May 19, 1842; May 26, 1842; May 30, 1842. Mullowny to Webster, No. 3, June 15, 1842; No. 5, Dec. 25, 1842; No. 6, March 7, 1843; No. 7, April 15, 1843. Mullowny to Upshur, No. 8, Oct. 3, 1843; Ibid.

78. Morgan to Upshur, Oct. 26, 1842, United States, 27th Congress, 3rd Session, 1842-1843, Executive

Documents, II, Doc. 22, Ser. No. 419, 1-5; Webster to House of Representatives, Feb. 18, 1843, Ibid., V, Doc. 165, Ser. No. 422, 1-7. In the Report of the Secretary of the Navy, Dec., 1842, A. P. Upshur commended Morgan for his "skill and address" in "asserting with proper firmness the respect due to our flag." United States, 27th Congress, 3rd session, 1842-1843, Senate Documents, I, Ser. No. 413, 536-537.

79. Carr, "Review of Our Relations with Morocco," New York Daily Plebeian, May 8, 1843, 2.

80. Webster to Mullowny, March 16, 1842, D. S. Instructions, Barbary Powers, XIV, No. 1, 25-27.

81. An important instruction from Secretary of State Daniel Webster was that no more presents were to be given to rulers of Barbary Powers.

82. Mullowny to Webster, No. 6, March 7, 1842; No. 7, April 15, 1843. Mullowny to Upshur, No. 8, Oct. 3, 1943, C. D., Tangier, VI.

83. Mullowny to Upshur, No. 9, received April 11, 1844; Mullowny to Calhoun, Feb. 9, 1845 and July 1, 1844; Ibid.

84. Mullowny to Buchanan, No. 17, June 28, 1845; No. 18, July 10, 1845; July 27, 1845; Sept. 10, 1845; Oct. 1, 1845; Ibid. Carr to William L. Marcy, Washington, March 18, 1845, Papers of Thomas N. Carr, in National Archives, Washington, D. C.

85. Carr to Buchanan, Sept. 30, 1845; No. 1, Oct. 17, 1845; No. 2, Oct. 20, 1845; No. 3, Oct. 27, 1845; No. 4, Nov. 2, 1845. Carr to Polk, July 15, 1846, C. D., Tangier, VI.

86. His career is described in A Memoir of Sir John Drummond Hay, edited by Mrs. L. A. E. Brooks and Alice Drummond Hay.

87. Carr to Buchanan, No. 25, April 13, 1848, C. D., Tangier, VI.

88. Carr to Buchanan, No. 10, Feb. 3, 1847; No. 12, May 5, 1847; No. 13, June 22, 1847; No. 16, July 28, 1847; No. 17, Aug. 23, 1847; No. 18, Aug. 30, 1847, Ibid.

89. Carr to Buchanan, No. 26, May 5, 1848; Carr to Polk, Oct. 29, 1848, Ibid.

90. Apparently Carr had an insatiable desire, either for service in Morocco, or for vindication of his record. On March 4, 1853, he again applied for the office of consul there. Carr to Franklin Pierce, New York, March 19, 1853, Papers of Thomas N. Carr, National Archives.

91. Carr to Buchanan, May 5, 1847; No. 15, June 28, 1847; No. 20, Sept. 30, 1847; No. 24, March 1, 1848; No. 27, June 12, 1848; No. 29, July 19, 1848; Nov. 21, 1848; C. D., Tangier, VI; Sec. of State to Carr, No. 12, Nov. 18, 1848, D. S., Instructions, Barbary Powers, XIV, 77-86.

92. Hyatt's last dispatch is dated from Tangier on June 18, 1850.

93. Hyatt to Buchanan, No. 2, July 28, 1848; No. 3, Aug. 12, 1848; No. 5, Sept. 29, 1848; No. 8, Dec. 8, 1848; Hyatt to John M. Clayton, No. 13, June 6, 1849; C. D., Tangier, VII. Buchanan to Hyatt, Feb. 9, 1849, D. S., Instructions, Barbary Powers, XIV, 87-89.

94. Hyatt to Clayton, Oct. 12, 1849, C. D., Tangier, VII.

95. Garibaldi to Hyatt, Feb. 22, 1850; Hyatt to Garibaldi, Feb. 23, 1850; Hyatt to Clayton, No. 20, Feb. 25, 1850, Ibid.

96. Hyatt to Clayton, No. 22, May 23, 1850, and No. 23, June 18, 1850; George V. Brown to Clayton, No. 2, July 15, 1850; Brown to Webster, No. 4, Aug. 30, 1850; Ibid.

97. Brown to Webster, No. 7, April 22, 1851; No. 9, June 1, 1851; Aug. 15, 1851; Ibid.

98. Brown to Webster, No. 8, May 26, 1851, Ibid.

99. Brown to Webster, No. 13, Oct. 30, 1851: No. 14, Nov. 7, 1851; Ibid.

100. Thomas N. Carr remained on the job of scouting out commercial opportunities for the United States in Morocco. On May 5, 1851, he sent Daniel Webster a long letter urging the United States to open negotiations for a trade agreement with the Sheik of Wad-Nun. This ruler was really wholly independent of the Sultan of Morocco and there were great riches to be acquired through trade with his realm. Carr offered to interest American capitalists in this commerce, and two letters, evidently inspired by Carr, reached Webster just before Carr's letter, inquiring about business prospects in Wad-Nun. Carr to Daniel Webster, May 5, 1851, Consular Letters, Zanzibar and Muscat, III (evidently misfiled; belonging to Morocco material).

101. Brown to Webster, No. 5, Jan. 15, 1851; No. 11, Aug. 15, 1851; No. 12, Oct. 25, 1851; No. 16, Jan. 30, 1852; No. 19, July 9, 1852; No. 22, Oct. 3, 1852. Brown to Everett, No. 24, Nov. 27, 1852. Brown to Marcy, No. 26, July 9, 1853; No. 29, Jan. 2, 1854; No. 31, Jan. 5, 1854; No. 32, Feb.25, 1854; No. 33, March 10, 1854; No. 35, July 13, 1854; C. D., Tangier, VII.

102. Brown to Marcy, No. 36, July 14, 1854; Ibid.

103. Brown to Marcy, No. 24, May 24, 1853; Ibid.

104. Brown to Marcy, No. 37, Feb. 15, 1855; Collings to Marcy, No. 1, Jan. 3, 1855; No. 2, Jan. 5, 1855; Feb. 13, 1855; Ibid.

105. Collings to Marcy, Feb. 20, 1855; May 25, 1855; Ibid.

106. Collings to Marcy, March 27, 1855; Ibid.

107. Collings to Marcy, April 25, 1855, Ibid.

108. Pariente to Marcy, June 16, 1855; Nov. 13, 1855; Dec. 31, 1855; Elizabeth Collings to Marcy, June 28, 1855; Brown to Marcy, No. 2, April 15, 1856; No. 3, April 17, 1856, No. 6, June 24, 1856; Ibid.

109. Brown to Marcy, No. 3, April 17, 1856; No. 8, July 21, 1856. Brown to Lewis Cass, No. 16, April 28, 1857; Ibid.

110. Brown to Marcy, No. 9, July 24, 1856; No. 10, Aug. 26, 1856. Brown to Cass, No. 15, April 10, 1857; No. 18, July 25, 1857. Brown to Appleton (Ass't. Sec.), No. 6, Oct. 3, 1858; Ibid.

111. Brown to Cass, No. 4, Sept. 7, 1859; No. 5, Sept. 9, 1859; No. 6, Sept. 12, 1859; Ibid.

112. Brown to Cass, No. 15, Jan. 7, 1861. Brown to William H. Seward, No. 16, March 6, 1861; No. 17, May 10, 1861; Ibid., VII; No. 18, June 6, 1861; No. 19, Nov. 5, 1861; Ibid., VIII.

113. De Long to Seward, Sept. 18, 1861; No. 1, Jan. 20, 1862. Brown to Seward, No. 18, Nov. 17, 1861; No. 20, Nov. 30, 1861; Ibid.

114. The attitude of Lincoln in this affair is of interest. The State Department had debated whether the Moroccans should have aided the American consul, since the United States did not allow the Maghzen to interfere with her citizens. Seward notified De Long that Lincoln was disturbed because apparently the United States had been assuming authority in Morocco obviously detrimental to the Sultan's sovereignty. Referring to American extraterritoriality in Morocco, the President was prepared to place Morocco on the same treaty footing as any other nation enjoyed with the United States. Seemingly Lincoln was not acquainted with the historical record and ramifications of the protection system in Morocco. Bahnsen, Diplomatic Relations of the United States and Morocco, 145-146.

115. De Long to Seward, No. 2, Feb. 14, 1862; Feb. 20, 1862; No. 5, Feb. 27, 1862. De Long to Consuls in Tangier and their replies, March 1, 1862; C. D., Tangier, VIII. United States, 37th Congress, 3rd Session, House Executive Documents, Messages and Documents of the State Department, Doc. No. 1, 413-417, 859-880. Hansard, Parliamentary Debates, Third Series, CLXV, Feb. 6, 1862-March 24, 1862, 914, 1230-1231, 1594-1597. Seward to McMath, April 28, 1862, D. S. Instructions, Barbary Powers, XIV, No. 2, 245-254.

116. De Long to Seward, No. 7, March 20, 1862; No. 9, May 23, 1862, C. D., Tangier, VIII.

117. De Long to Seward, June 10, 1862; McMath to Seward, No. 4, July 14, 1862; No. 5, July 22, 1862; Ibid.

118. F. W. Seward (Acting Sec.) to McMath, July 1, 1862, D. S., Instructions, Barbary Powers, XIV, 258. McMath to Seward, No. 6, Nov. 19, 1862; No. 9, April 12, 1863; No. 13, Sept. 30, 1863; No. 21, April 21, 1864; C. D., Tangier, VIII.

119. McMath to Seward, No. 8, March 2, 1863; No. 10, May 29, 1863; No. 29, June 2, 1865; No. 38, June 18, 1866; Oct. 1, 1866; Ibid.

120. McMath to Seward, No. 32, Feb. 2, 1866; No. 42, Feb. 15, 1867; No. 46, Aug. 6, 1867, Ibid.; No. 51, Feb. 3, 1868, Ibid., IX.

121. McMath to Seward, No. 31, Oct. 7, 1865; No. 37, May 30, 1866, Ibid., VIII; No. 51, Feb. 3, 1868, Ibid., IX.

122. McMath to Seward, No. 20, April 2, 1864; No. 41, Jan. 16, 1867, Ibid., VIII.

123. Earl Fee Cruickshank, Morocco at the Parting of the Ways, The Story of Native Protection to 1885 (hereafter cited as Cruickshank, Morocco at the Parting of the Ways), 17.

124. Meakin, The Moors, 460; McMath to Seward, No. 12, Sept. 24, 1863; No. 15, Nov. 5, 1863; No. 16, Jan. 12, 1864; No. 22, July 1, 1864; C. D., Tangier, VIII. Seward to McMath, Dec. 9, 1863, D. S., Instructions, Barbary Powers, XIV, 275-276.

125. Cruickshank, Morocco at the Parting of the Ways, 23-25; Flournoy, British Policy Towards Morocco, 245-247.

126. The ten powers were Austria, Belgium, France, Great Britain, Italy, The Netherlands, Portugal, Spain, Sweden-Norway, and the United States. Germany, unrepresented in Morocco until 1873, adhered to the agreement on March 4, 1878. See Stuart, Tangier, 26-34, for a detailed account of the establishment and maintenance of the lighthouse.

127. Graham H. Stuart, "The International Lighthouse at Cape Spartel," American Journal of International Law (hereafter cited as Stuart, "International Lighthouse"), XXIV, No. 4, 770-776. McMath to Seward, No. 19, March 26, 1864; No. 29, June 2, 1865; No. 33, March 8, 1866; No. 35, May 4, 1866; No. 39, Sept. 20, 1866; No. 42, Feb. 15, 1867; C. D., Tangier, VIII. Seward to McMath, June 27, 1864; Chase to Seward, June 11, 1864; McMath to Seward, March 26, 1864; Hunter to McMath, Nov. 7, 1864; Department of State, Messages and Documents, Papers Relating to Foreign Affairs (hereafter cited as Foreign Affairs), Part IV (1864-65), 413-414, 428.

128. Mathews (original name, Mateos), the natural son of a Gibraltar women and a Spanish refugee doctor, was born and spent his boyhood at Tangier. When about eighteen years old he shipped as a steward on the U. S. S. Constitution and later lived in the United States. When appointed consul to Morocco, he was residing at Martinez, California. McMath to Fish, Aug. 5, 1869, C. D., Tangier, IX.

129. McMath to Fish, Aug. 1869, with enclosure of letter from the Sultan to President Grant; Aug. 5, 1869,

with enclosures relating to Mathews, Ibid. Hamilton Fish to McMath, No. 42, June 9, 1869, D. S., Instructions, Barbary Powers, XV, 267.

130. Davis to Mathews, April 29, 1869; Mathews to Fish, No. 7, Oct. 30, 1869, C. D., Tangier, IX.

131. Davis to Robeson, Nov. 19, 1869; Fish to Robeson, No. 1, Nov. 23, 1869; Fish to Mathews, No. 2, Nov. 23, 1869; July 14, 1870; July 21, 1870. Davis to Robeson, July 29, 1870. D. S., Instructions, Barbary Powers, XV, 271-273, 277-279.

132. Mathews to Fish, No. 15, Dec. 28, 1870; No. 34, July 21, 1871, C. D., Tangier, IX and No. 65, Feb. 14, 1872, Ibid., X.

133. Mathews to Fish, No. 51, Dec. 8, 1871, Ibid. Fish to Mathews, Jan. 16, 1872, D. S., Instructions, Barbary Powers, XV; Frelinghuysen to Mathews, Dec. 18, 1883; Ibid., XVI.

134. Mathews to Fish, No. 26, April 21, 1871, C. D., Tangier, IX and No. 103, April 20, 1873, Ibid., X.

135. Mathews to Fish, No. 41, Sept. 23, 1871 and No. 46, Oct. 25, 1871, Ibid., IX. Mathews to Fish, No. 50, Dec. 7, 1871; No. 52, Dec. 8, 1871; No. 70, April 16, 1872; Ibid., X.

136. Mathews to Fish, No. 60, Jan. 1872; No. 62, Feb. 9, 1872; No. 63, Feb. 11, 1872; Ibid.

137. Meakin, Moorish Empire, 178-179.

Chapter IV

The Monroe Doctrine in Morocco (1830 - 1873)

In 1815, when Mulai Soliman and James Simpson were still laying the foundations for American-Moroccan relations, the battle of Waterloo concluded the first chapter of modern European imperialism. In this era, extending over exactly four centuries, the nations of Europe emerging from the disintegrated Roman Empire had contended for control over Africa, the Americas, Asia, and Australia. The smaller countries, Portugal and the Netherlands, had first fallen behind in the race for colonies, leaving the contest for hegemony to Spain, France, and England. The series of conflicts known as the Second Hundred Years' War (1689-1815) had resulted in Napoleon's failure to unite continental Europe and in the loss of most of France's first empire. Great Britain, however, had greatly enlarged her empire and had achieved hegemony of the sea. The triumph of Great Britain was not complete, for she had lost her thirteen Atlantic Coast colonies, which established the first independent nation in America. Shortly thereafter, the successful revolts of the Spanish and Portuguese colonies in the Americas produced a number of new American nations, and the major part of the two continents was free from the dominion of Europe.

Africa, the continent nearest to Europe, whose Mediterranean coast had been incorporated into the Roman Empire, had few European outposts in 1815. Morocco, whose invasion by the Portuguese in 1415 reintroduced European imperialism there, had expelled the Portuguese from several ports and the British from Tangier by 1815 and had yielded to the Spanish only four minor posts along the Mediterranean coast. Cape Colony, conquered from the Dutch by the British, was the only important European possession in Africa. There were a number of small trading factories, forts, and spheres of interest along the Atlantic and eastern coasts of Africa, with undefined boundaries and claims, held chiefly by Great Britain, France, Portugal, and Spain. These footholds were valued chiefly as depots for the dying negro slave trade and as way stations to India.

However, France and Spain were not long reconciled to being deprived of the power, prestige, and potential wealth conferred by ownership of overseas empires. An opportunity to partially recoup their losses in the Americas was presented by the support of the Quadruple Alliance[1] under the aegis of Metternich, prime minister of Austria. Formed to maintain the treaty of Vienna, which distributed the territorial and dynastic spoils after Napoleon's defeat, the Quadruple Alliance suppressed the epidemics of revolutions of 1820 and 1821 in Spain, Portugal, Naples, and Greece. A congress planned for Paris was rumored to be aimed at dispatching an effective Franco-Spanish force to reconquer the Spanish-American republics.

Obviously, the British government had a compelling interest in forestalling such an intervention. Sated for the time being with territory, the British were determined to wage a winning war for trade, not only with their own colonies, but also with extra-European independent countries. Since Russia also decreed an extension of her colony of Alaska, there was only one ally, albeit a weak one, available for Great Britain--the United States. Accordingly, the new British foreign minister, George Canning, proposed to Richard Rush, the American minister in London, that joint action be taken in opposition to the reconquest of liberated American colonies.

Since the Thirteen Colonies and later the United States had been involved in every phase of the Second Hundred Years' War, the American government was fearfully impressed with the danger of being drawn again into the maelstrom of European conflict. Both Madison and Jefferson advised President Monroe to cooperate with Great Britain. But Secretary of State John Quincy Adams firmly opposed coming in "as a cock-boat in the wake of the British man-of-war." Adams was particularly averse to Canning's proposal that neither the United States nor Great Britain should appropriate any part of the former Spanish domain. He also had faith that Britain's sea power would be used if necessary to foil the plot of her rivals; hence the United States could assert her position independently without commitment to enforce it.

The views of Adams prevailed. His formula for the American policy, interspersed in President Monroe's message to Congress on December 2, 1823, consisted of four propositions for maintaining the status quo. For Russia, there was the warning that the American continents, because of their free and independent condition, were henceforth not to be considered subjects for future colonization by any European power. Another warning and two promises were addressed to the Quadruple Alliance. Since the political system of the allied powers was essentially different from that of republics, the United States would consider any attempt to extend it to any part of the American hemisphere as dangerous to her peace and safety, and any attempt by any European power to oppress or control the destiny of countries which had won their independence would be considered the manifestation of an unfriendly disposition toward the United States. Ignoring Florida, Monroe asserted that the United States had not interfered with any existing European colony and would pledge herself not to do so. Finally, the doctrine of two hemispheres was completed by the second promise, "Our policy in regard to Europe...remains the same, which is not to interfere in the internal concerns of any of its powers."

Thus was promulgated the foreign policy later named the Monroe Doctrine, which many Americans then and throughout the history of the United States have credited with preserving the Americas from foreign aggression. The Spanish American leaders were under no such illusion, however; they learned that on October 9, 1823, Canning had secured from the French ambassador, Polignac, a formal denial of France's intention to intervene in Spanish America. Canning publicized this diplomatic victory to his former allies also. In both Spanish America and Europe the protection of the former's independence was rightly credited to the British navy, not to Monroe's verbal challenge.[2]

Deflected from recovering their American colonies, France and Spain sought territorial possessions elsewhere.

Morocco, with which they had long had commercial associations, was a promising field for colonization. Great Britain, however, valued this independent country not only for the trade it afforded, but also for its strategic locations as the gateway to the Mediterranean route to India. British imperial policy could not tolerate the conquest of Morocco by any past or future rival for world power. Thus it happened, that although the political, social, and economic decadence of Morocco invited her exploitation and conquest, the mutual jealousies of the expectant heirs of the Sherifian Empire prolonged the years of the Sick Man of Africa, as they did later the life of his Ottoman cousin, until long after most of Africa had been earmarked for civilization.

The British theory that the introduction of commerce employed to introduce civilization would save Morocco from conquest did not seem overoptimistic. Foreign commerce appeared destined for steady expansion there. During the French Revolution and Napoleonic Wars the British had established mutually profitable trade with Morocco. In exchange for ordnance and munitions, Mulai Soliman had furnished enough fresh beef, grain, vegetables, mules, and horses to aid materially the success of the British garrison at Gibraltar, the British Navy in the Mediterranean, and the allied troops in Cadiz and Portugal.[3] Prospects for trade appeared even better under Sultan Abd er-Rahman (1822-1859), for he subdued rather quickly the customary accession revolts and was more eager for commerce than his two predecessors had been.[4]

The conflicting imperialistic ambitions began to clash in 1830, when the Bourbon monarchy started the second French empire by invading Algeria. This movement was neither popular nor consistent; it served the desires of politicians and dynasts grasping at glory and power.[5] But France was suspected of ultimate designs upon Morocco, and British diplomats set resolutely about the task of foiling her sinister aims. The Sultan Abd er-Rahman expressed great confidence in the friendship of Great Britain and received with unusual cordiality the British agent and consul general, Edward Drummond Hay. To Lord Palmerston, the British foreign minister from 1830 to 1841,[6] the French government was induced to give explicit assurances that the area of conquest would not extend to either Tunisia or Morocco. Palmerston also secured larger naval appropriations to counteract the forward policy of France in the Levant and in the Mediterranean.[7]

Thus Lord Palmerston established the bases of British policy on Morocco which were to be followed with fair consistency for the next sixty years. This policy was part of the general British policy of protecting "backward states" in order to defend and to expand opportunities for trade. But more important in Morocco were the safeguarding of the British food supply in the Mediterranean and the prevention of any other power's use of Morocco as a base to dominate Mediterranean and African sea routes to India. In the Mediterranean both France and Russia were dangerous antagonists. The Straits Convention of 1841 saved Constantinople from Russia and Alexandria from France. The Anglo-French rivalry in Tunisia, Morocco, and Egypt, however, continued for over six decades.[8]

British objectives in Morocco were threefold: to strengthen friendship with the rulers by sending capable representatives, to develop commerce by securing new concessions and privileges, and to maintain the independence and integrity of the country. The preservation of Morocco and Tunisia from conquest was not an isolated policy; it was analogous to the British attitude toward Portugal, Turkey, Switzerland, Belgium, and Luxemburg. Furthermore, it was similar to the American policy of the Monroe Doctrine, which the British government had instigated a few years earlier:

> Both were purely unilaterial; both were concerned with states sparsely populated and at a low stage of political and economic development; both were maintained over a long period of time with a large measure of success. Indeed, it would not be inaccurate to refer to Palmerston's Moroccan policy as a British Monroe Doctrine.[9]

Since the primary interest of both Great Britain and the United States was avowedly the extension of commerce in Morocco, the British government might have expected to receive there, as it had in Spanish America, the verbal if not the active support of the United States. To be sure, the two situations were not exactly parallel. In the

Americas, Great Britain had intervened to prevent the reconquest of colonies which had won independence by revolution; in Morocco, she offered resistance to the subjugation of a country independent for many centuries. In the Americas, the United States feared that the return of European powers as neighbors would be dangerous not only to her peace and safety, but also to her form of government; in Morocco, Great Britain feared the absorption of the country by European states would destroy both her commerce there and the lifeline to her Asiatic empire. In the Americas, republican states were supported; in Morocco, a despotic and decadent monarchy was upheld. However, Great Britain and her former colonies might have found a common basis for an actual, if unacknowledged, cooperation in Morocco as they had in America but for three circumstances. The Americans lost an active interest in Morocco because their anticipated trade failed to develop; they were absorbed in westward expansion to the Pacific and wanted no part in European quarrels over Africa; and after their two wars for independence they regarded Great Britain as their chief rival and foe not as a potential ally.

Consul John F. Mullowny aptly summed up British policy as "keeping Morocco at peace with Europe."[10] This task required two-edged diplomatic tools--one to warn away the would-be aggressor, the other to induce the sultans to give proper respect to the rights of foreign powers. Before the great scramble for Africa began in 1881, there were three powers against which the British representatives in Morocco exercised eternal vigilance--France, Spain, and the United States. The predatory purposes of the first two were overt from the first. That the United States was also an object of suspicion by Great Britain is still but little known.

French interests in Morocco were historical, economic, and strategic. To her priority in sending consuls and in treaty-making, France could add the prestige gained by the liberal privileges of the treaty of 1767 and the later agreements with Morocco. Economically, Morocco offered decided attractions in her alleged sub-soil riches and in her virgin market for European goods, as well as in her potential supply of food and raw materials. Finally, as a Mediterranean coast country, France was interested in the free passage of the Strait of Gibraltar. Actually, she was ambitious to dominate as long a shoreline as possible on the Mediterranean and to use this strategic position in rehabilitating her world empire. After the acquisition of Algeria, the doctrine of natural boundaries was formulated to extend it to the Atlantic, but "the law of geographical unity was invoked by the French only after the event and as an extra weapon in their armoury."[11]

With a Moroccan policy alternating between aggression and obstruction, Spain was determined in the nineteenth century to follow her obvious path to expansion. In the days of Charles V, Spain had thought of "nothing but the gold of America and the soul of the Netherlands;" now that the Canning-Monroe Doctrine had sealed the loss of her continental American territory, she returned to fulfill her manifest destiny in Morocco. Geographically, historically, and racially, no country could claim closer relations with Morocco than Spain did. Her exiled Jews and Moriscos "had spread a leaven of hispanification over all Morocco, so that ... the language of business and the coinage were Spanish .... But Gibraltar stood in the way, a wedge of foreign spirit drawn in between two peoples who, for centuries, had mingled together in peace and war.[12] And Spain alone retained bases for expansion into Morocco, although they were but garrisons and convict camps.[13] In the threefold program of Spain--recovery of Gibraltar, union with Portugal, and acquisition of Morocco--the last project had undoubted priority.[14]

Unlike France and Spain, the United States was playing an apparently disinterested role in Morocco. She was profiting by the policy of isolation declared in the Monroe Doctrine in pursuing her manifest destiny triumphantly to the Pacific, while interpreting her promise of non-intervention in European internal affairs as covering European rivalries in Africa. Clinging to the idea that here might develop a market worth preserving, the American government was determined to maintain the treaty relations established with Morocco in 1786. The American consuls chiefly concerned in the implementation of this policy were James Leib, Thomas Carr, John F. Mullowny, T. Hart Hyatt, George Brown, Samuel Collings, and Felix A. Mathews. All of them, except John F. Mullowny, were pleased to practice political non-cooperation with their British colleagues, Edward and John Drummond Hay.

Leib's mission to Fez in 1833 had the objective of applying for the renewal of the Treaty of 1786. Sultan Abd er-Rahman promised this renewal on condition of receiving a special letter from President Jackson or a special commission for negotiations. On July 4, 1835, Leib was empowered to negotiate a treaty of navigation and commerce.[15] William B. Hodgson came on the frigate Constitution bearing Leib's instructions and suitable presents for the Sultan and his officials. After some discussions with Moroccan officials, most of the negotiations were by correspondence and Leib did not see the Sultan personally. Acting under his power to appoint agents, on August 22, 1836, Leib sent from Tangier to the Sultan's court at Meknes the acting vice consul, John F. Mullowny, and the interpreter of the consulates, Peter Boyn. Leib reported their negotiations to the State Department on September 26, 1836. "The most remarkable feature in the negotiation of the present treaty," he wrote, "is the fact that it was sealed by the Emperor before giving him his present, and without stipulating to give him anything--a circumstance hitherto unknown in the history of Morocco."[16]

The treaty of 1836, with the original text in Arabic, was signed at Meknes on September 16, 1836, and endorsed by Leib at Tangier on October 1, 1836. Until its official proclamation on January 30, 1837, it went through the regular routine for treaty-making.[17] The document is an almost literal copy of the original treaty, except that the supplementary article of the latter was not repeated, and the new agreement adds to the provision for a fifty-year term the condition that the treaty shall continue thereafter unless and until twelve months' notice of denunciation is given by either party.[18]

There is no indication of illegitimate American ambitions regarding Morocco in the official record of the negotiations. However, the British and the French governments temporarily diverted their mutual rivalry toward the United States and acted together to defend the Sultan from the conqueror of Florida.

In a confidential dispatch, dated February 17, 1836, and addressed to Lord Glenelg, Secretary for War and Colonies, E. W. A. D. Hay[19] expressed grave suspicions of American intrigues to secure the island of Perejil, near Ceuta.[20] This information he had recently received from Sir Menander Woodford, the Governor of Gibraltar. Hay continued:

> The report is, I verily believe, too well founded. I have taken all means within my power to sift this business and I am strongly inclined to believe that long before the late misunderstanding between the United States and the French Government,[21] it was a closely cherished project of the North Americans to plant themselves upon this coast in some position they might hope to be advantageous both in a military and in a commercial light.
>
> Toura ("Perejil" of the Spaniards), as there is no water to be had on this little island, could hardly be viewed by the U. States Government as worth occupying by them, unless they had also some footing on the neighboring mainland or an understood prospect of lasting good fellowship with the Moors,--a hope upon which, all experience tells, no state the most powerful or however lavish in wooing the friendship of the faithless tyrants of Morocco can ever calculate.
>
> It has therefore appeared to myself that it is to Alcassor Grare--a ruined place upon a bay of the fine district Angera--exactly halfway between Tangier and Ceuta, to which the attention of the U. S. has been drawn; and if they are allowed to put into execution their rumored project of building a fort at Alcassor Grare, they would doubtless fortify Toura, which they might supply, and between this island and the main--distant I think about half-a-mile--some of their vessels certainly might take refuge where there is I believe fair anchorage and good shelter in about eight fathoms of water.

During March, 1836, Granville, the British Ambassador in Paris, made several reports to Palmerston on conversations on this subject with Thiers, the French Minister of Foreign Affairs. Thiers wanted to know whether

His Majesty's government proposed to take any step to counteract the success of the American negotiations, which would be against both French and British interests.[22] Thiers had received his information from the French consul at Tangier. The French government was planning to send four war vessels to Tangier to back up its protest against the aid recently given by Moroccan troops to Abd al-Kader. The French consul would be instructed to avail himself of the presence of this squadron to thwart the American plot, for after the conclusion of a treaty for the cession of a naval station, any attempt to dispossess the United States of it would entail war.[23] On March 14 it was reported that although Hodgson had left Tangier, the French consul believed he still hoped to attain the objectives of his government.[24]

On May 14, 1836, Hay's confidential report to Palmerston optimistically predicted the failure of the American negotiations. Hay revealed that the French diplomatic agent, Mechain, had warned the de facto minister of foreign affairs for Morocco that the cession of any Moroccan territory would be highly offensive to France, and that if any nation whatsoever presumed to put such a scheme into effect, a French force would drive out the intruders. The Moroccan official had denied that the American consul had made any such proposal. Mechain thought it possible that the consul was unaware of the curiously secret negotiations of Hodgson, lately chief interpreter of the United States mission in Constantinople, sent from Washington "expressly for this extraordinary negotiation." Mechain also ventured to inform the Moroccan minister that the French and the British governments in close alliance had guaranteed the integrity of the Ottoman Empire and would doubtless be equally united in the determination to prevent encroachment on Moroccan soil. His observations on the Americans' alleged project were not meant as a menace to Morocco, but as an assurance of British and French support. Hay had told Mechain, unofficially, that he could endorse the sentiments which the latter had expressed. However, since the American plot was probably foiled or at a deadlock, he would avoid mentioning the matter to the Moorish government, unless later instructed to do so.[25]

Leib was cognizant of the current rumors concerning

American designs. On August 26, 1836, he sent to the Secretary of State an extract from the Gibraltar Chronicle, quoting a Paris news item of July 18 from the Toulonnais, as follows:

> The conferences relating to the establishment of the Americans on the east coast of Morocco are only suspended. The demands of the Emperor are exorbitant, but the difficulties are to be removed by gold; and of this the Americans have plenty. The difficulty arises from the Emperor's requiring that the Americans should guarantee him against all armed opposition to their establishment from the European Powers, and the United States have not the means of furnishing this guarantee; they are therefore obliged to use diplomacy which will exhaust a great deal of time, but will end at last to the advantage of the Americans. Such, at least, is the general opinion here.

Leib's denial of the rumored American machinations was unequivocal:

> I send this Trifle merely as a sample of the many follies which have lately filled the European papers--in conjuncture of the probable objects of our existing negotiations. I should deem them unworthy of notice; but that they are not without a certain degree of influence here. The Department will readily believe that I have no agency in matters of this kind--and, observing a natural reserve in regard to the present posture of our affairs with Morocco, the speculations of the newspaper politicians of Europe exhaust themselves in idleness, similar to the enclosed.[26]

As a last bit of judicious counsel, Leib reminded his superior officer of American opportunities for extending the sphere of commercial connections in Morocco. On February 8, 1837, he wrote:

> The Emperor is merely intimidated by the vicinity of Gibraltar, and being hard pressed by the French, on the confines of his Empire, he would probably not be unwilling to make a powerful friend and mediator of a Nation which, from its isolated condition and known policy,

stands aloof from the domestic policy of Europe--from which he has nothing to fear, and with which a friendly intercourse could produce to him nothing but advantage.[27]

Evidently the American Congress did not regard the renewal of the treaty with Morocco as an important event. Several years after its conclusion, President Polk had to remind that body that "our treaties with the Sublime Porte, Tripoli, Tunis, Morocco, and Muscat also require the legislation of Congress to carry them into execution, though the necessity for immediate action may not be so urgent as in regard to China."[28] American business men were also indifferent to Moroccan opportunities.[29] A writer in a trade journal expressed his astonishment at their almost total neglect of the Moroccan market. He also pointed out prospects for trade beyond the imperial jurisdiction in "Suse" and "Wednoon," concluding, "We think a permanent establishment upon the coast is not by any means essential."[30]

In view of the chronic American lethargy concerning Moroccan affairs, it is difficult to understand how the British not only conceived the idea of American ambition for a territorial cession there but also recorded this unsubstantiated rumor as a fact in official and other publications. Two examples may be given of this strange aberration of British experts on Morocco. One of the best known bibliographies on Morocco in English is by Sir Robert Lambert Playfair and Dr. Robert Brown, entitled "A Bibliography of Morocco, from the Earliest Times to the end of 1891," in the Royal Geographical Society, Supplementary Papers, Vol. III, Part III, 203-476. On pages 440-441 are listed two items in a then unnumbered Foreign Office series. Item 2117, No. 1, to and from Consul General at Tangier, Mr. Drummond Hay, diplomatic and consular, January to June, 1836, is entitled: "The Government, U. S. A., contemplates occupying an island on the coast near the Straits of Gibraltar as a strategic position. Mr. Hodgson sent from America to negotiate." Item 2119, No. 3, Vice-consuls at Tangier and Mogadore, Bell and Wiltshire, foreign and domestic, various, January to December, 1836, tells of the "design of the American Government for acquiring a position on the Coast of Morocco discussed between England and France." Budgett Meakin accepts the charge of American conspiracy as a fact. In his article, "Yesterday and To-day in Morocco," in the Forum, XXX (November, 1900), 364-374, he says on page 368:

> The position and policy of "Uncle Sam" has till recently placed him beyond suspicion of designs upon this country, and he might have had a free hand in its regeneration. His only attempt to encroach upon its territories was the request made in 1836 for a coaling station on the Straits of Gibraltar, which was of course refused. His fifty-year treaty was then renewed by Leir (sic.), but from that time his changing office-bearers seem to have lost all interest in the country.

The Anglo-French entente to obstruct the United States was only a brief interlude in the persistent opposition of the British government to French expansion in North Africa. Palmerston had reluctantly acquiesced in the fait accompli of the invasion of Algeria. Even after menacing incidents in 1836, 1837, and 1838, he had perforce accepted French assurances that they would commit no aggression upon either Morocco or Tunisia.[31] But the forced cession of Tlemcen to France in 1834 and the use of Moroccan border regions as bases for Abd al-Kader to attack French armies in Algeria involved Abd er-Rahman in the Franco-Algerian War.[32]

A third party who saw the possibility of interesting the United States in North African affairs was Abd al-Kader, proclaimed Amir of Mascara in 1832, who for ten years thereafter fought a winning war against the French. The future national hero of Algeria was a sherif--learned, devout, and a great soldier and leader. He was supported by all the tribes of western Algeria and had much active sympathy in Morocco--at first from Abd er-Rahman himself. But he met eventual defeat in 1847 because of an opponent of great military genius, Marshal Bugeaud, and the refusal of the Kabyles Berber mountain tribes to aid the Arabs against the French.[33] In 1836, however, the Algerian leader had fair prospects of success with British, Moroccan, and perchance American support. The Franco-Algerian-Moroccan conflict became an important topic in the dispatches of American consuls.

James Leib was the first consul to deal with the

Algerian situation. On April 30, 1836, he transmitted to the Secretary of State a letter in Arabic from Abd al-Kader. Learning of unfriendly relations between the United States and France, the Algerian amir offered to deliver to the Americans all of the Barbary coast between Algiers and Oran then held by the French; in this task his land forces would assist the American navy. In return, the United States was asked to become an ally of Algeria against France. Leib's reply was that since American-French relations were now amicably arranged, the United States could not accept Abd al-Kader's offer or encourage his hostilities against France. Leib suspected that the proposal was known to the Sultan, but the matter was being kept strictly secret in order not to embarrass American treaty negotiations then being carried on with Morocco.[34]

Abd al-Kader's next attempt to secure American support was made to Thomas N. Carr. An elderly Moor, claiming to come from Abd al-Kader, said:

> That the amir wished to open a communication with me, that he knew well the power and the generosity and the friendship for the Moors of the U. S. government, and, above all, that he knew it was uncomplicated in the relations with other Christian Powers, and could do as it pleased; and moreover, that it did not much like the French, and that not a great while ago it had come very near declaring war against France. I desired to know what was the object of this communication .... I could get only general and vague replies, such as that Abd Al-Kader wanted some one who could give him information upon which he could rely, and assistance, but without specifying what kind of assistance or information.

Carr replied that he could not recognize as an agent anyone without official credentials. He did not know whether to believe the alleged emissary's claims regarding Abd al-Kader's large resources in men and money. From many little circumstances Carr concluded that the chief Moroccan dignitaries, if not the Emperor himself, had been participating in Abd al-Kader's activities. It was reported that a sixth French mission was to be sent to demand that Abd er-Rahman break openly with the Algerian leader.[35]

In February, 1840, Carr reported that the amir was rumored to be receiving strong support from the Moorish tribesmen and direct assistance from the Sultan with arms, ammunition, and men. He refused to transmit to the President the request of the Bashaw of Tangier that the United States furnish his master with a few small field pieces. A personal letter from Abd al-Kader, received on October 15, 1840, asked Carr for a continuation of correspondence and friendship. The courier told Carr that the amir was so well supplied with men, money, and ammunition that he was confident of victory over the French. From this messenger Carr heard also the familiar rumor that for several years both the Sultan and his subjects had believed that the United States had contemplated establishing a depot for her Mediterranean fleet on some part of the African coast. Carr thought that the Moors were very anxious to learn the truth of this matter, and he knew that both British and French consuls had communicated on this topic with their respective governments.[36]

During 1840 and 1841 Carr made several reports on the Sultan's expeditions against rebellious subjects. He said that both the Sultan and the authorities at Gibraltar were supplying Abd al-Kader with money and military stores. Great Britain was represented as playing a double role, inciting the Sultan, yet holding him back from war with France "until such time as it can be made to favor her interest in other quarters." In September, 1841, Edward Drummond Hay protested against naval preparations being made which seemed to presage a revival of the old Moorish customs of piracy and plunder.[37]

The year 1844 was one of decision for Morocco, as 1846 was for the United States. But, unlike Polk, Abd er-Rahman was not decisive. John F. Mullowny's reports to Washington dealt chiefly with the Sultan's apparently persistent problem of survival. While he was occupied in trying to quell revolts by his nomadic tribesmen, probably inspired by Abd al-Kader, Sweden, Denmark, and Spain threatened war against him. Mullowny gave most attention, however, to the long anticipated Franco-Moroccan War. He admitted the Sultan's impotence to prevent forays of his troops into Algeria to harass the French armies; any attempt to stop this "holy war" and make peace with

France might enable Abd al-Kader to usurp the throne of Morocco. Mullowny predicted that a Franco-Moroccan war, if it began, would result in the partition of Morocco among the European powers, with Great Britain claiming her share bordering on the Straits of Gibraltar. Such a war would be an undisguised blessing for Morocco, however; "before six months we may probably see the great work commenced of civilizing Morocco, and the only way to do so is to conquer it."[38]

The French vanquished Morocco in three decisive campaigns--the bombardment of Tangier by the French fleet under the Prince de Joinville, the complete defeat of the Moroccan army near the river Isly by Marshal Bugeaud, and the bombardment and estruction of Mogador and occupation of Mogador Island by the French fleet. The attack on Tangier, city "protected by Allah," was witnessed by spectators on fifteen neutral vessels--a British and a Spanish squadron and one vessel each of the United States, Sweden, Denmark, and Sardinia. Tangier was pillaged by Moroccan mountaineers after the French assault. Edward Drummond Hay was the peacemaker, who, failing to prevent this war, persuaded France and Morocco to cease hostilities. He also postponed the imminent conflicts with Spain, Sweden, and Denmark. But his success in these tasks involved such great fatigue and hardships on a mission to the Sultan's court that after an illness of several months he passed away early in 1845.[35]

It was Hay's second son, John Drummond Hay, who came to Tangier in the summer of 1844 to complete the peace negotiations and who succeeded his father in 1845. After the victories of France, revolts against the vacillating Abd er-Rahman threatened the rapid disintegration of Morocco, and war fever was high in Great Britain over both France's annexation of Tahiti and the possibility of her conquest of Morocco. At the outset of his career in Morocco, John Drummond Hay won spectacular success in dealing with both Morocco and her European antagonists. The Spanish-Moroccan treaty disputes over the boundary of Ceuta and various mutual claims were settled virtually on British terms by the treaty of September 19, 1844, and a supplementary agreement in April, 1845. By the Treaty of Tangier in 1845 France obtained from Morocco practically the same terms as already conceded by the Sultan to Edward Drummond Hay. Abd er-Rahman agreed to cease aiding Abd al-Kader and to accept delimitation of the Algerian-Moroccan boundary. At first the French demanded the Moulaya river as a boundary, but the British protest forced them to compromise on an ill-defined line farther east. France was also granted the right of pursuit of Algerian troops entering Morocco. As co-mediator with a French representative, John Hay was influential in securing Swedish and Danish treaties with Morocco which, in April, 1845, finally terminated the centuries-old custom of paying tribute.[40]

However, Abd al-Kader had become more menacing to Morocco. Mullowny reported that he was now preaching a holy war against the Sultan for abandoning him to the Christians. On his second tour of duty in Morocco, Thomas N. Carr continued the narrative of the French-Algerian-Moroccan embroilment from both an anti-British and an anti-French viewpoint. He sympathized with the Sultan in his fear of the amir, whose operations were probably directed by the British and whose arms and ammunition were known by all the consuls to be furnished by the Gibraltar garrison. If France should fight both Algeria and Morocco, England would probably be urged by the Moors to accept Tangier for safe-keeping.[41]

Maintaining his base of operations in eastern Morocco, Abd al-Kader organized a formidable advance against the French, which was checked by Marshal Bugeaud only with great difficulty. In 1845 it was widely rumored in Morocco that France was about to assert her treaty right to attack the amir's Moroccan base. Carr informed the State Department on August 18, 1846, of an unofficial probing of American intentions if France were to resume her war on Morocco:

> A question twice put to me by the (French) Admiral ... (was) whether in the event of any European power seizing upon the territory of Morocco, say France, the U. States would be willing to accept and possess herself of a portion of the same if offered. I replied that our policy upon the question of territorial acquisitions was very generally known to the world at large; we did not desire foreign territory, the principle was in opposition to the spirit of our Institutions.[42]

Hay was alert to maintain the traditional British policy. In August he informed all his consular colleagues that since any French invasion of Morocco would threaten the unity of the country and the throne of her ruler, the British government would be obliged to intervene to prevent it. Knowing that Abd al-Kader still had prospects of usurping his throne, the Sultan displayed a willingness to cooperate with France against the amir. On November 17, 1846, Carr reported that the threatened French invasion had been replaced by a friendly mission bearing gifts of immense value to the Sultan's court. France's change of policy, Carr thought, was due to Great Britain's firm support of Abd er-Rahman and the daily increasing influence and power of Abd al-Kader throughout Morocco. Early in 1847 the Sultan joined the French in military operations.

In September Carr made dire predictions that the Sherifian throne would be won by Abd al-Kader. The amir, who had been in the Riff country for the last eighteen months, was said to have inflicted a decisive defeat on the Sultan's son in a battle near Fez, after which most of the Moroccan army had deserted to join the Algerian forces. Great Britain, Carr charged, had been covertly working for this denouement. French policy also had been devious; the French were now in friendly correspondence with the man whom their severities had driven out of Algiers, offering to make him Sultan of Morocco and head of the Barbary states:

> The diplomacy of France in this country is about as rational and reliable as our neighbors of Mexico. In point of sincerity it falls below the Mexican standard, and is only equalled by the diplomacy of Morocco.[43]

Carr proved to be a false prophet. By December 28, 1847, he was obliged to reverse his prediction and to report that a French steamer from Oran had brought news of Abd al-Kader's surrender to the French. A successful expedition against the Kabyles enabled France to claim completion of the conquest of Algeria by August, 1848. For years afterwards, however, the borderlands were the bases for desert corsairs, who served France well in later diplomatic controversies.[44]

France's policy of intimidation, to be adopted shortly by Spain also, was continued relentlessly after 1845. The conquest of Algeria increased the military prestige of France among all the Muslims on the Mediterranean. The French were not resting upon their arms, however; they employed many measures to increase their stature in the eyes of the Moors. In an enlarged consular establishment, the rank of the head of mission was raised to chargé d'affaires. The first chargé, Chasteau, was ably seconded by his son-in-law, Léon Roches, formerly secretary of Abd al-Kader and later chief interpreter to Marshal Bugeaud. Roches traveled to secure news and to make contacts with leading Moroccans. Several Moroccan officials were put on the French payroll. The French sought especially to gain the support of the Täibya, under the Grand Sherif of Wazan, and of other religious confraternities of great influence in both Algeria and Morocco. Both Hay and Carr observed the mounting success of the French propaganda. The Sultan no longer listened to British advice, but he showed great honor and respect for the French representatives. Bou Selham, the acting minister for foreign affairs in Morocco, consulted the French chargé constantly, as did other Moroccan officials. The honors paid to Chasteau on a court visit were said to be the greatest ever paid to a foreign representative in Morocco. An even more ominous portent of the collapse of British policy was Bou Selham's statement of his approval of a defensive and offensive Franco-Moroccan alliance, made to Chasteau in 1845. The Maghzen also welcomed French proposals of military instructors for the Moroccan army and of supervision of Moorish education. In 1846 the Sultan accepted the gift of an artillery battery, accompanied by French soldiers who remained in Morocco as instructors in its use.[45]

Paradoxically, the British, who had actually preserved the independence and dynasty of Morocco, were treated with ingratitude and contempt for their inability to prevent the Franco-Moroccan war altogether. As early as 1846, Hay found British influence and commerce declining rapidly, while illicit trade across the Algerian frontier was growing. The French were taking the initiative in developing the natural resources by obtaining concessions to exploit copper and antimony mines. Hay set to work to rebuild the economic foundations of British political ascendancy in Morocco. Of his many proposals to raise British prestige, a few were endorsed by his superiors. His official rank at Tangier was raised from diplomatic agent to chargé d'affaires, but the making of a new treaty was postponed. To erase the Moorish impression of British pusillanimity, Hay carried out his policy of making more authoritative demands for reforms and for more frequent visits of British warships to Moroccan ports. To save British commerce from extinction by monopolies held by the Sultan's favorites and by concessions granted to French firms, Hay began to work for a complete reformation of trading regulations. To counteract the vigorous "friendship crusade" of the French representatives, he relied upon continuing demonstration of the practical benefits of British protection of Morocco from all foreign aggression. But both the American and French representatives in Tangier predicted at various times from 1846 to 1848 that France would win this diplomatic game eventually.[46]

In 1846 Hay began a series of missions to the sherifian court, where he spoke fearlessly and frankly of the need for financial, political, and educational reforms and pleaded the cause of the Jews. In 1847 and 1848 he obtained some reductions of import and export duties favorable to British trade and prevented the increase of the cost of cattle purchased in Morocco for the Gibraltar garrison. All foreign commerce was benefited by British naval demonstrations in 1848 against the Riff pirates, whom the Sultan admitted inability to control. On this occasion, there was a curious reversal of roles--the French government intervened to see the controversy settled peacefully, expressing its disapproval of the occupation of any Moroccan territory by British forces. The visit of Sir Charles Napier's fleet to the Riffian shores was monitory, rather than punitive, but the policy of the "authoritative tone" increased Moorish respect for the British. To conciliate the Moroccans, the British used more than one opportunity to provide transportation for members of the Sultan's household.[47]

The February Revolution (1848), which caused revolts and turmoil in France until December, resulted in a rapid decline in French prestige in both Morocco and Algeria. Taking advantage of this situation, Spain seized the

Zaffarines,[48] islands which the French had previously tried to obtain from the Sultan for a naval station. This affront to France was aggravated by Spain's refusal to accept French mediation in the subsequent dispute. Contrary to his guiding principle, Palmerston declined to interfere, probably because he wanted the good will of Spain to counteract the power of France. The reduction of French forces in Algeria, recall of prominent army officers to France, and withdrawal of French warships from the Mediterranean further weakened the Moors' faith in the superior strength of France. Her Majesty's government did not neglect, however, to warn that they "would see with very great concern any new concession on the part of the Moorish government."[49]

During 1848, T. Hart Hyatt also discussed Anglo-Moroccan controversies in his dispatches. Two disputes, settled after the appearance of British war vessels, arose over the Sultan's revocation of exporting privileges of a British merchant and a piratical attack by Riffians on a British brig. The British experiences led Hyatt to advocate more frequent visits from American men of war. American vessels, he thought, might serve not only to protect American commerce but also to prevent the anticipated British seizure of Tangier.[50]

Attempting to restore their prestige in Morocco, French representatives twice brought their country to the brink of war. Pretexts were not hard to find. In 1849, among several alleged wrongs and insults to France the most serious were the arrest of a protégé and the imprisonment of a courier. In 1851 a French fleet bombarded Salé, nominally to exact reparation for a pillaged ship. During both these crises Hay was virtually the director of Morocco's foreign policy. Reinstated in his former position of authority, he alternately hectored and cajoled France and Morocco with his customary firmness and finesse. Again he gave France the solemn warning "that the occupation of any portion of the Moorish Coast by France could not fail to be viewed by Great Britain in a very serious light." Hay's efforts were aided by the withdrawal of Chasteau and Roches from Morocco and by the diplomatic duet performed by Palmerston and Louis Napoleon in opposition to Russia and Austria. Napoleon himself proposed a settlement on the basis of "forgive and forget," demanding only that in future the French chargé should have the right of corresponding directly with the Sultan. On Hay's advice, this privilege, really stipulated in all the treaties, was extended to all foreign representatives in Morocco. The second crisis ended by March, 1852. The Moors thought that they had won the victory, but large forces in Algeria still kept France in a position to win the admiration and respect of the Moors.[51]

During the crisis of 1849 Hyatt apparently had thought that he might exert some influence on events. Until Hyatt discovered his duplicity, the French chargé had enjoyed American cooperation, while secretly negotiating with Morocco through the Neapolitan consulate. Hyatt considered the English chargé very officious, as always, with the usual result of widening the breach and making adjustment more difficult. He regarded Hay's policy of combining an "authoritative tone" with conciliatory acts as very strange and anomalous, and he considered the Moors sagacious enough to discriminate between a selfish, time-serving policy and one based upon truth and justice. As evidence of the high status of Americans in Morocco, Hyatt cited to Secretary of State Clayton the proposal of the Moroccan minister of foreign affairs to submit the Franco-Moroccan disputes to Hyatt's arbitration.[52] France refused arbitration. The Moroccans hoped that strained Franco-American relations at this time might be of advantage to themselves, but, as Hyatt pointed out, they prevented him from being an impartial mediator. This offer, Hyatt observed, showed that Morocco looked upon the United States "as about the only nation that attends to its own business and that acts upon just and liberal principles." In case of an American rupture with France, Hyatt advised,

> It might be of much service to us to have as our friends, if not allies, a government holding so important a key to the entrace of the Mediterranean as this--and also to have a place for a foothold on the main land at a point so much more contiguous to France than any portion of our own territory.

In reporting the settlement of the Franco-Moroccan

quarrel, Hyatt expressed his belief that if he had had the requisite instructions, he could easily have concluded an American alliance with Morocco for mutual protection against French aggression.[53]

George Brown made the Anglo-French rivalry for the mastery of Morocco the main theme of his story about foreign affairs. He gave a vivid description of the background and events of the bombardment of Salé. Since the shore batteries of Salé and Rabat had inflicted more damage on the French ships than the latter had on the town, Brown thought that the retreat of the French would destroy their influence in Morocco. He advised that if the United States ever had hostilities with Morocco, the blockade of Tangier and Mogador would be an effective method of attack, but bombardment of towns did little damage. Although desiring peace between Morocco and all the rest of the world, Brown invariably gave his counsels only upon solicitation, and his policy had weight with the Moroccan government because he was viewed as the agent of a nation disposed to allow the Sultan to retain his own empire and to manage its internal affairs in accordance with his own judgment. Turning from this indirect to a direct criticism of Hay, Brown charged that in concluding peace, the Moorish government, instigated by the English chargé, had perpetrated a fraud upon the French government. The Moors had conceded the French demand for future direct communication with the Sultan. Actually, the French government had the expense of a courier to convey its letters to the Sultan, but the communications went first to the Moorish prime minister at Fez, then to the English chargé at Tangier. Hay then dictated the answers, the Sultan's seal was affixed by the Moorish prime minister, and finally the French courier returned from Fez to Tangier with the Sultan's replies. Brown had been asked by Hay to cooperate with this system, but after reading dispatches of British officials, he could not approve of intrigues so foreign to American policy. When the French representative proposed an international lighthouse at Cape Spartel, Brown was certain that the protection of shipping was not his chief objective. Hay said that the British government would cooperate to prevent France from obtaining exclusive jurisdiction over a work so near Gibraltar.[54]

During the Crimean War the Anglo-French alliance against Russia was extended to cooperation in Morocco, which could be useful as a benevolent neutral. British suspicion of an American plan to seize Perejil was reawakened in 1854;[55] this time Hay's action was unilateral. The Spanish fortress of Melilla was reputed to be under consideration as an alternative base. The British Foreign Office instructed Hay to exert every effort "to prevent the United States or any other government from getting a footing on Moorish territory." Accordingly, Hay served notice that "the British Government would never permit the temporary or permanent occupation of any port, or point, in the territory of Morocco by any foreign government."[56]

As in 1836, the American archives do not bear witness to any such scheme of the United States. Apparently, the only important communication by the American government to the Maghzen at this time was a proposal sent also to other neutral powers, relating to the protection of neutral trade and ships in the Crimean War. Brown declined to present this to the Moroccan authorities because he felt certain of its rejection. In his dispatch advising no attempt to get Morocco to join a treaty on neutral rights in which Russia was interested, Brown set forth frankly his opinion of both the Moroccan government and his British colleague. He described the Sultan as little better than an imbecile, so entirely devoted to his religion and his harem that he rarely heard of any events outside of his seraglio. The domestic affairs of Morocco were entrusted to the prime minister and the foreign affairs to Hadj Muhammad Lechteeb, residing at Tetuan. But the real foreign minister was the English chargé, who more than once had informed Brown that Great Britain claimed a protectorate over Morocco and would resist any interference with the Sultan's rights. All matters relating to foreign affairs were referred, often without breaking the seals, to John Drummond Hay. Brown had learned of this secret intrigue three years before, when he was asked to act as adviser to Lechteeb during Hay's leave of absence in England. As "adviser" Brown had virtually undertaken the entire management of the foreign affairs of the empire and dictated and sent off dispatches under the Moorish official seal. Since his return, Hay had remained really the Sultan of Morocco. Hence it would be highly impolitic to ask Hay's approval of a treaty which would make Morocco a party to a permanent treaty with Russia, with whom at this time Morocco had no treaty of peace and friendship. If Brown were to act again as Hay's substitute during his forthcoming absence in England, such a treaty might be arranged by Brown.[57]

Brown was undoubtedly right in thinking that any neutrality professed by Morocco in the Crimean War would be strictly benevolent toward the Anglo-French alliance. Hay persuaded the Sultan to exclude Russian privateers from Moroccan ports and to permit the shipping of beef and other food from Morocco for the use of allied naval forces near Gibraltar.[58]

Another invitation for the United States to intervene in Moroccan affairs came in 1855. The French and British governments, acting jointly, had succeeded in compelling the Sultan to sanction the execution of an insane sherif for the murder of Paul Rey, a French citizen. Collings asserted that the murderer, an Algerian Muslim, had been treated with great injustice by French officials in Morocco. When the French government made further demands for an indemnity for Rey's family, Collings declared this action to be "impudent, unreasonable, in violation of principles of comity and justice." Hay also refused his support, and the claim was finally dropped. While the matter was under discussion, Morocco proposed that the dispute be submitted to the arbitration of the United States. Furthermore, the American government was requested to direct its representative to "arbitrate or use its good offices in all affairs" in Morocco's international relations. Collings regarded this incident as an indication of France's aim to conquer Morocco and annex it to Algeria. He pointed out to the State Department that the maintenance of this Empire, in its present hands, was of importance to the safety and welfare of mankind and that the neutrality and friendship of Morocco would be of vast importance to the United States as affording shelter to and supplies for the navy in case of war with European powers. Hay saw in the Moroccan proposal the leaders' disappointment at the unusual Anglo-French accord, which impelled them to seek "another protector and adviser in the place of the British Government." To the Sultan's ministers Hay expressed his emphatic disapproval of their proposal, which could not be admitted for a moment.[59]

Accompanying Brown on his return to Tangier after the brief and unfortunate career of Collings was the belated reply of the State Department to the proposal for American arbitration forwarded by Collings. President Pierce wrote a letter to Abd er-Rahman, politely declining to act as umpire in a controversy between His Majesty and the Government of France. The President believed that "he could not accept His Majesty's invitation without deviating from the policy hitherto pursued by the Government under similar circumstances." On April 1, 1856, Brown informed Secretary Marcy that the difficulties between France and Morocco had been amicably arranged by the withdrawal of French pretensions to an indemnity and the sending of a more peaceably disposed French chargé to Tangier.[60]

During the eleven years that he had been fending off French, Spanish, and American threats to Morocco's independence, Hay had never relaxed his efforts to make Morocco safe for British merchants. Many reforms were needed to attain this objective. The regularization of extra-treaty practices in consular jurisdiction, permission for foreigners to travel in all parts of Morocco, removal of trade restrictions, and abolition of monopolies all required a new treaty.[61] When about to depart on a mission to Marrakesh, Hay had assured Collings that he would seek no exclusive advantage for the British subjects or government, but would try to open the door of Morocco to the commerce of all nations. His government, Hay said, viewed "with concern the decay and gradual dissolution of this Empire, as calculated to invite its absorption by France--a result to which his government never could or would consent, as giving to France the control of the commerce of the world." Collings was skeptical of Hay's professed altruistic aims.[62]

After many months of vexatious negotiations, begun during the mission to Marrakesh, Hay succeeded in the great achievement of making the British-Moroccan treaties of 1856, one a general treaty of peace and friendship, the other a convention of commerce and navigation.[63] His diplomatic skill and persistence had so completely won the respect of Abd er-Rahman that the Sultan offered him the post of foreign minister of Morocco. Despite Hay's long *sub rosa* experience in that office, as described by Brown, Great Britain was not prepared to assume so formally the protection of Morocco, and Hay declined the appointment.[64]

The commercial convention of 1856 abolished all monopolies on imported goods except tobacco, smoking pipes, opium, sulphur, powder, saltpeter, lead, arms, and ammunition. It limited export duties to a few specific articles. The import duties were fixed at a maximum of ten percent *ad valorem*, and a schedule of rates for export duties was fixed. The sultan retained the right to prohibit the export of any article, but not to change the conventional export duties. British vessels in Moroccan ports were to pay the same dues as national vessels, at rates fixed in the treaty.

The general treaty guaranteed freedom of travel and residence, religious liberty, security of persons and property, and freedom from taxation, forced loans, and arbitrary search and visit for British subjects and protégés. The number of protégés was somewhat limited, for while the British diplomatic agent at Tangier was not restricted, a consular officer was limited to four: an interpreter, a guard, and two domestic servants. Protection was granted to native Moors serving as British consular agents, with their families living in the same house, but they were not allowed to extend protection to others. This last provision was supplemented by Article IV of the treaty on commerce and navigation, which stated that natives employed by British subjects as brokers, factors, or agents (*semsars*) should be treated and regarded as other subjects of the Moorish Empire. Here was a definite statement that natives employed by non-official British subjects could not enjoy protection.

The year 1856 marked another notable service of Hay for the international relations of Morocco. The Riffian tribes near the Spanish outposts had persisted in piracy, and the Sultan had no power over them. Although acknowledging their nominal ruler as the Caliph of Allah, the wild Riffians allowed him no secular authority except the appointment of a Riffian governor who collected a small annual tribute of mules and honey for the imperial revenues. In August, 1856, both the British and the French made claims on the Sultan, the former for destruction of a vessel and cargo, the latter for return of a ransom paid the Riffs for captured seamen. The Sultan's refusal to assume responsibility for acts of the pirates gave the French license to prepare an invasion of the Riff. Hay then persuaded Abd er-Rahman to pay both claims and to promise a punitive force against the pirates. Hay admitted to Brown that the British would cooperate in any invasion to prevent the French occupation of territory. But no invasion occurred; a visitation to the Riffian chiefs by Hay, unarmed, and accompanied by only the captain of a British frigate, obtained a promise to abandon piracy which was kept by the Riffians. Hay had appealed to the Riffians of inland villages not to tolerate from the coast dwellers the un-Muslim conduct of attacking the English, their friends who had often conveyed their brethren to worship in Mecca. He had also warned that British forces would subdue whole tribes if any individuals committed another piracy. The Treaty of 1856 also bound the Sultan to suppress and punish piracy and to aid the British government to do this.[65]

Although only a few of the economic reforms provided for in the Treaty of 1856 were immediately inaugurated, there was a rapid upsurge of confidence among European traders. By 1858, there were three times as many of them in Morocco as before the treaties. The refusal of Abd er-Rahman to take many measures which would encourage the entrance of foreign merchants and capital was based on the rapid growth of protection of native semsars in the interior. Shortly before his death Abd er-Rahman threatened to close the western ports to commerce, saying that he would rather be a sovereign over a country without trade than a chief without the power of governing the subjects of his own empire.[66]

Abd er-Rahman did not live long enough to discover whether the effectuation of the British treaties would lead eventually, as Hay had assured him, to the regeneration of Morocco. For six months before his death on September 3, 1859, in reprisal for Riffian raids near Ceuta and Melilla, Spain had refused successively greater concessions in order to force war upon him. Fortunately, his successor, Sidi Muhammad XVII, quelled the accession revolts in a few days and then devoted his full attention to this latest foreign aggression.[67]

Spain officially declared war on October 22, 1859. Brown sent the State Department vivid and voluminous accounts of the diplomatic and military compaigns preceding and during the war. He denounced Spain's aggression and sympathized with the new ruler. Hay informed him that Her Majesty's government had warned the government of Spain that the United States might take the conduct of Spain toward Morocco as a precedent for future action in Cuba. Brown regretted that "for the past three years no American vessel of war has touched at a Moorish port." He surmised that with five aspirants for the throne, the Spanish had estimated Morocco to be ripe for revolution and conquest. Instead, the Holy war inspired by the Spanish attack completely disrupted the 59-day schedule for victory published in advance by the Spanish military leader.

In view of the many anti-Spanish activities of Hay, his "clever little colleague," Brown declared the British pretense of neutrality to be absurd. But Hay had not received adequate support from his government. If he were to advise the Moorish government, Brown said,

> I would point to Tunis and say, like her, throw off the British influence which only leads you into difficulties with other nations and then abandons you, and form a friendship with France, your neighbor, and from whom you have the most to fear. From Great Britain, who requires your supplies for Gibraltar, you have nothing to fear.[68]

Despite the valiant resistance of the Moors, Tetuan was captured by the Spanish troops. Thereupon, Hay was instructed to reaffirm the steadfastness of British policy regarding Morocco:

> Any occupation of the Coast of Morocco on the part of Spain could not be viewed otherwise than in a very serious light by Great Britain and could scarcely fail to lead to evils of great magnitude .... You will not conceal from the Spanish government that any attempted

landing of Spanish troops at Tangier, or the coast adjacent, would be resisted by Her Majesty's squadron.[69]

The overt intervention of Great Britain undoubtedly saved Morocco from the loss of both Tetuan and Tangier.[70] The principal terms of the peace treaty, signed on April 30, 1860, were the cession to Spain of a zone around Melilla, recognition of Spain's right to punish attacks by the Riffians, and acknowledgment of Spain's claim to an unidentified fishing village on the Sus coast, called Santa Cruz de Mar Pequeña.[71] Tetuan was retained as security for the payment to Spain of an indemnity of £4,000.000. Again Hay took a leading part in the difficult negotiations. The commercial treaty of 1861 was probably of greater value to Spain, for it extended protection somewhat, made Spain a most favored nation, and, like preceding agreements, authorized the establishment of Catholic missions in Morocco.[72] In general, the Spanish-Moroccan treaty of 1861 followed as a model the British commercial convention of 1856.

Great Britain, also, extended her control over Morocco as a result of the war. Even to release Tetuan from Spanish control, the British government was unwilling to guarantee the loan for the indemnity to Spain. When a private loan was raised in London, however, the British government made a treaty with Morocco to safeguard the interests of the British bondholders. To insure payment of bonds for L501,200, British consuls and consular agents in Morocco were appointed to receive half of the customs receipts for the British creditors, while Spanish commissioners similarly collected the other half to apply on the indemnity. The British loan was paid off by 1883 and the Spanish indemnity by 1887. Under the improved customs administration, receipts increased from L322,904 in 1862 to L1,639,748 in 1883. Supervision, fixed salaries, and changing of customs officials every three months, together with increased commerce, were responsible for this gain in revenue. Thus was given a practical demonstration of the efficiency of one reform which Hay had urged for years--the support of public officials by adequate salaries instead of extortion and bribery. Nevertheless, the new system, although retained for the customs service after 1883, was not extended to other officials.[73]

After 1861 both Spain and France abandoned frontal attacks on Morocco. It is true that France carried on minor military actions against frontier tribes in 1864 and 1870,[74] for which she might claim treaty sanction. Spain, however, seemed to acquiesce in the frustration of her forward policy by Great Britain. But the confidential dispatches of Señor Merry y Colon, the Spanish minister at Tangier from 1860 to 1874, to his chief reveal that Spain was only biding her time:

> Neither politically nor economically could Spain live if France or England should take possession of Morocco, Morocco must some day belong to Spain .... The Question of Morocco, with that of Portugal and Gibraltar, comprises the whole international policy of Spain.

When Señor Merry went on missions to the Moroccan court in 1863, 1864, and 1865, he was accompanied by general staff officers who prepared military maps and descriptions of the country for the Spanish minister of war. Spanish naval authorities made careful studies of all ports of the empire. Spain was doomed to impotence, however, by her revolutions of 1868-1875, followed by debt, civil war, and colonial revolt. By a policy of obstruction, however, she was able to block the granting of telegraph, railway, and commercial concessions which would have augmented the power of her chief rivals in Morocco.[75]

Early in his career as American consul, Jesse McMath became aware of the smouldering antagonism of the three rivals in Morocco. In a private letter to Secretary Seward, dealing chiefly with Spanish persecution of Moroccan Jews, he said:

> It is the daily boast of Spaniards that Spain will yet possess this country. Perhaps this may be the secret aim of her officials. There is one thing quite certain, a great rivalry exists between Spain, England, and France for power and influence in Morocco; each would like to hold the key to the Mediterranean to the exclusion of the others. And I believe that at no distant day the world will witness the armies of those Nations contending for the possession of Morocco.

France holds the balance of power between Spain and England.[76]

After the Spanish-Moroccan War, Sultan Muhammad XVII had two major causes for apprehension. One was the persistently hostile attitude of Spain toward Great Britain. In 1868 there was much discussion over the proposal of exchanging Gibraltar for Ceuta. Hay favored the plan because a British base at Ceuta would be an adequate peacetime coaling station and would be a center for safeguarding Morocco against any other power and for promoting the reform and development of Morocco. Furthermore, Spain might be conciliated by the return of Gibraltar to her. Since the idea received little public or official support in Great Britain, Hay was obliged to continue his fight for reform through the Moorish government.[77]

Because his second problem was the rapid expansion of foreign commerce after the commercial treaty of 1856, Sidi Muhammad was disinclined to establish European landed proprietors and to grant other economic concessions in Morocco. Great Britain in particular was profiting from her treaty. From 1861 to 1865 about three-fourths of the imports and over two-thirds of the exports were listed on British ledgers. McMath reported in 1864 that the Sultan had rescinded his regulation of 1862, which forbade merchants to go into the interior to buy wool and cereals, and that none but treaty restrictions were now in effect. The increase in British trade was especially noteworthy because the French government tried to divert Moroccan commerce through Algeria. In 1863 the French imposed only moderate duties on Moroccan and Tunisian products entering overland, and in 1867 they removed all duties from natural or manufactured products from Tunisia, Morocco, and south of Algeria.[78]

The attitude of Sidi Muhammad was not based, of course, upon the commercial development itself. It was caused by the great influx of Europeans after 1856. By 1865 there were forty British firms represented in Morocco, instead of the three or four operating nine years earlier. Casablanca was built up by European merchants from an insignificant fishing village to be the chief port of the country. In pursuit of commerce the immigrant merchants, backed by their official representatives, developed the system of protection, which the French in particular found to be a weapon as effective as war to undermine the sherifian government. The merchants were increasing the numbers of their brokers, largely Hebrews. Protection for their agents, as defined by treaty, meant tax exemption only, but gradually the consuls and other foreign agents had withdrawn the semsars from their native allegiance and were bringing them under the authority of the consular courts. The flight of so many subjects--and their taxes and military service--threatened to destroy the political and economic bases of the Moroccan state.[79] The opportunities for personal gain in the competitive marketing of illicit protection promoted a new type of rivalry among the foreign representatives. Abd er-Rahman had foreseen the grave dangers of protection. During the reign of Sidi Muhammad XVII the foreigners themselves attempted to regularize and control the practices of the protection system. However, their agreement of 1863 failed to solve the problem for them, and it remained a major preoccupation of the sultans.

In spite of continued efforts to induce Sidi Muhammad to reform his administration on the bases of honesty and efficiency, Hay found the Sultan impossible to convince. The ruler was not moved by Hay's arguments that his corrupt and venal officials were chiefly responsible for the growth of protection, the impoverishment of the masses, the perennial revolts, and the persecutions of the Jews in the interior, which were an international scandal.[80] Yet undoubtedly Sidi Muhammad realized that his sovereignty and the independence of his country were menaced by the state-within-a-state being created by protection. Hay had never hesitated to express his unfavorable criticisms directly to the Sultan, and he attributed his influence to this frankness:

> This government is the most miserable in the world, and with the exception of the Sultan himself, who is an honest man without energy, Aji, and one or two others, they are a corrupt and venal set .... Not only my Spanish colleagues, but I may say all in their turn, attribute the good favour in which I am held by the Sultan and his Myrmidons to my giving secret counsels

> in opposition to the demands of representatives of other foreign governments, and thus currying favour. They cannot and will not understand that I have managed to maintain a certain ascendancy over the mind of the Sultan, in questions with other foreign powers, from the very fact of my never having hesitated in speaking my mind and recommending the most unpalatable concessions. The late Sultan, as also the present, found that when they had not accepted my disinterested advice, troubles ensued and they paid dearly. I therefore still hold my ground at the court, although Morocco has found itself on more than one occasion, as in the last Spanish war, abandoned by England.[81]

Apparently despondent over his prodigious task and distrustful of even the self-chosen protector of his country, Sidi Muhammad sought a new savior. In June, 1871, Felix Mathews visited the Sultan at Fez. The recently arrived American consul, boasting of being the first to carry the American flag to this capital of Morocco, described his reception as one never before accorded to any representative of the most favored European state. At a private interview, the Sultan confessed his awareness that the integrity of his dominions was maintained solely by the mutual jealousies of the European powers. At any time that these powers could agree on their various portions, they would dismember Morocco. In that event, to anticipate an appeal to arms, he desired that America act as arbiter, and he would be willing to place his country under an American protectorate.[82] For the second time the United States declined to assume such a responsibility. The reply of the acting secretary of state, dated August 22, 1871, read as follows:

> While this Government would regret any attempt, on the part of foreign powers, at a dismemberment of the Empire of Morocco, and would consent to use its friendly offices to prevent such an act, it would nevertheless decline to accept any offer from His Majesty to confer upon the United States a protectorate over his dominions.[83]

It is not surprising that the country which had been so reluctant to acquire Alaska four years before was unwilling to rush into African adventures where even the most aggressive European powers feared to tread. The reports of Mathews during 1872 and 1873 must have confirmed the opinion of the State Department that Morocco was a problem to shun. His descriptions of the barbarous conditions of the people and government, the perfidious intrigues of Hay, and the economic backwardness of Morocco emphasized the unwisdom of accepting such a burdensome protectorate. There was no intimation that Mathews appreciated Hay's strenuous efforts to secure reforms.

As evidence of the low cultural level of the populace, Mathews cited that printing and real libraries were unknown, although a few Moors possessed the *Koran* and some other Muslim books. The largest collection of books in the Empire was undoubtedly that in the American consulate. The government was an arbitrary despotism, nominally guided by the precepts of the *Koran.* From the decrees of the Muslim courts there was an appeal only to the Sultan's edicts, and in the tribunals only the testimony of Muslims was admitted. Of Sidi Muhammad Mathews had a most unfavorable opinion:

> The history of Morocco is a chain of barbarous atrocities, the cruelty of the former Sultans being now exchanged for the avarice of the present .... The reigning Sultan through the dishonesty of his advisers added possibly to avaricious inclinations inherited from his father keeps not a single promise when its fulfilment would interfere with his interests, and the instances have been few in which he has fulfilled his promises to foreigners unless some display of armed force has been shown ... It will mostly be found .... that these unpleasant ruptures have been brought about by the intrigues or interference of the present British minister .... When by every kind of rapacity the Bashaw has amassed a large property it then becomes the business of the Sultan to divert these ill gotten gains into his own treasury .... The Bashaws .... gather their wealth directly from the Caids under them, the Caids obtain theirs from the Sheeks or heads of villages who in turn squeeze every cent from ... the poor inhabitants under their control .... No person who has accumulated wealth dares to show it.[84]

In stigmatizing the career of John Drummond Hay as a "succession of intrigues," in which he was "always taking the Moorish side," although he had caused the Spanish-Moroccan War, Mathews quoted the charges of former American consuls as evidence. His opinion might have been different if he could have read Hay's account of his last interview with Sidi Muhammad on April 23, 1872. Denouncing the Moroccan government as "the worst in the world," Hay had then proceeded to castigate it in terms far more scathing than those used by Mathews--and to the Sultan's face.[85]

The annual report on Moroccan commerce for 1872 and 1873 would also prove that American rejection of a protectorate was a wise decision:

> Morocco ... is still unfortunately as backwards as it was three or four centuries ago, there are no roads in the Empire, no newspapers, no telegraphs, no railroads, no vehicles of any description, and not even a wharf or jetty to land and ship merchandise, and ... articles of commerce ... are not allowed exportation .... The exportation of wheat and barley ... is still strictly prohibited, for fear that the farmers may sell all their harvest and cause a famine--an error that has actually brought famine at various epochs, as the farmers only plant sufficient seed for their use, and very little ever to sell for home consumption.

Mathews included statistics and information showing that production and trade for these years had been unusually good. More than one half of the tonnage was British and over two thirds of the remainder was French.[86]

When Sidi Muhammad died on September 11, 1873, an era of Moroccan history was passing away also. The problem of maintaining the independence of his realm, which had occupied most of his predecessor's reign and all of his, remained unsolved. For forty-three years Great Britain had endeavored to adapt and to implement for Morocco the Canning-Monroe Doctrine declared by the United States and enforced by Great Britain in support of the independence of Spanish America. But the United States had refused both cooperation with Great Britain in defending the Sherifian Empire from the aggressions of France and Spain and also independent action to arbitrate Morocco's disputes or to assume a protectorate over her. Furthermore, the attitude of the American representatives toward the Hays, father and son, had been consistently uncooperative and antagonistic, and for Morocco the Americans had looked upon European conquest and "civilization" as a foregone but too long delayed destiny.

Under Sidi Muhammad's successor, Mulai Hassan (1873-1894), the rivalry of national imperialisms to appropriate Morocco was to be gradually and temporarily replaced by an international imperialism nominally regulated by treaty. Under this new policy of the European powers the United States assumed briefly a greater interest in African affairs. However, the Monroe Doctrine remained an important issue in American-Moroccan affairs in relation to its negative principle of non-intervention in European concerns. Mathews and Hay continued as non-coperative and almost inimical colleagues until the latter's retirement in 1886; Mathew's second term of office ended a year later, but he came back for a third term from 1890 to 1893. Within ten years after the end of Mulai Hassan's reign, the British Monroe Doctrine for Morocco was finally abandoned by its sole defender.

Notes

1. The Quadruple Alliance, often erroneously called the Holy Alliance, was renewed in November, 1815, by the four allies which had defeated Napoleon--Austria, Prussia, Russia, and Great Britain. This became a Quintuple Alliance in 1818 by the admission of the defeated power, France. The alliance became a quadruple one again in 1822, when Great Britain refused to cooperate in its anti-revolutionary policy and withdrew. Four congresses were held between 1818 and 1822, at the last of which the British Foreign Minister George Canning, although unable to prevent intervention in the revolution in Spain, by his defection succeeded in destroying the congress system as an organization for international action.

2. For an account of the background, provisions, and significance of the Monroe Doctrine, see Thomas A. Bailey, A Diplomatic History of the American People, First Edition (hereafter cited as Bailey, Diplomatic History), 178-192.

3. Flournoy, "Political Relations of Great Britain with Morocco," 29.

4. Meakin, Moorish Empire, 173.

5. N. D. Harris, Europe and Africa, 13; Woolf, Empire and Commerce in Africa, 74-75.

6. Lord Palmerston occupied the following Cabinet offices: foreign minister, 1830-1841; foreign minister, 1846-1851; home secretary, 1852-1855; prime minister, 1855-1858 and 1859-1865. From 1830 to 1865 his influence in foreign affairs was very strong, whatever office he held. Encyclopedia Britannica, Edition of 1961, XVII 157-159.

7. Flournoy, "Political Relations of Great Britain with Morocco," 27, 30-36.

8. James Edgar Swain, The Struggle for the Control of the Mediterranean Prior to 1848; A Study in Anglo-French Relations (hereafter cited as Swain, Struggle for the Control of the Mediterranean), 46, 57-61, 63-66, 117.

9. Flournoy, "Political Relations of Great Britain with Morocco," 39-40, 54-55.

10. Mullowny to Calhoun, No. 11, July 1, 1844, C. D., Tangier, VI.

11. Roberts, History of French Colonial Policy, II, 547.

12. Salvador de Madariaga, Spain: A Modern History (hereafter cited as Madariaga, Spain: A Modern History), 262-264.

13. Melilla, Ceuta, Peñon de la Gomera, and Alhucemas.

14. Cruickshank, _Morocco at the Parting of the Ways_, xviii.

15. D. S., _Register, 1874,_ 87.

16. Miller, _Treaties,_ IV, 65-66.

17. The treaty was submitted to the Senate on Dec. 26, 1836 with President Jackson's message of Dec. 20, 1836; the Senate advised ratification on Jan. 17, 1837, and the treaty was ratified on Jan. 28, 1837. _Ibid._, 33.

18. _Ibid._, 60-64.

19. Hay to Gleneig, Feb. 17, 1836, _Foreign Office Documents in the British Record Office_ (hereafter cited as _F. O., Docs._), 52/40.

20. The location of the island is shown on the frontispiece map of Morocco in Walter Burton Harris, _The Land of an African Sultan: Travels in Morocco, 1887, 1888, and 1889_ (hereafter cited as W. B. Harris, _Land of an African Sultan._

21. Hay refers to the long protracted and acrimonious negotiations between France and the United States over the payment of the French spoliation claims--a dispute settled partly through the good offices of the British government.

22. Granville to Palmerston, March 4, 1836, _F. O., Docs._, 27/520.

23. Granville, Dispatch No. 102, March 11, 1836, _Ibid._

24. Granville, Dispatch No. 109, March 14, 1836, _Ibid._

25. Hay, Confidential to Palmerston, May 14, 1836, _F. O., Docs.,_ 52/40.

26. Leib to Sec. of State, No. 37, Aug. 26, 1836, _C. D., Tangier,_ V.

27. Leib to Sec. of State, No. 42, Feb. 8, 1837, _Ibid._

28. United States, 53rd Congress, 2nd Session, House Miscellaneous Documents, XXXVII, Messages and Papers of the Presidents, IV (1841-1849), 551.

29. In "Northwest Africa and Timbuctoo," Bulletin of the American Geographical Society," XIII (1881), 210-211, Felix A. Mathews gave this account of the decline of American commerce with Morocco: "Commerce between this country and the United States was carried on through this port of Mogador in Morocco since the year 1792; it was impeded by a dispute between Morocco and America in the year 1804 and 1805, which, however, was amicably adjusted, and the trade resumed in 1806. Vessels sailed from Salem, Boston, and other parts of the United States, with West Indian and American produce, called at Mogador and received in return the various articles of South Barbary produce, and by these means the agents of American merchants established at Mogador were enabled to undersell the British in all West India and American goods, and even in those of the East Indies. During the early trade of the United States with West Africa, the American brig 'Commerce' Capt. James Riley, was shipwrecked in August, 1815, when the captain and crew were made captives by the Arabs of Wadnoon, and released after much suffering and labor. Since, the American direct trade declined and at last ended at the beginning of the civil war."

30. Dr. W. S. Mayo, "Morocco and Its Facilities for American Commercial Enterprise," Hunt's Merchants' Magazine, V (Dec., 1841), 489-506.

31. Flournoy, British Policy Towards Morocco, 55-58.

32. Victor Piquet, Le Maroc, geographie, histoire (hereafter cited as Piquet, Le Maroc), 176-177.

33. Encyclopedia Britannica, edition of 1961, I, 28.

34. Leib to Sec. of State, Gibraltar, April 30, 1836, C. D., Tangier, V.

35. Carr to Forsyth, No. 9, Dec. 25, 1839, Ibid., VI.

36. Carr to Forsyth, No. 10, Feb. 12, 1840 and No. 18, Oct. 15, 1840; Ibid.

37. Carr to Forsyth, June 23, 1840; No. 17, Aug. 24, 1840; No. 20, Feb. 28, 1841. Carr to Webster, No. 26, Aug. 24, 1841; No. 27, Sept. 11, 1841; No. 28, Oct. 8, 1841; Ibid.

38. Mullowny to Calhoun, No. 10, April 8, 1844; No. 11, July 1, 1844; No. 12, July 24, 1844; No. 13, July 29, 1844; No. 14, Aug. 15, 1844; No. 16, Feb. 9, 1845; Ibid.

39. Mullowny to Calhoun, No. 12, July 24, 1844 and No. 14, Aug. 15, 1844; Ibid.; Flournoy, British Policy Towards Morocco, 92-96.

40. Ibid., 102-108; Sir John Drummond Hay, 66, 68-71; Mullowny, to Calhoun, No. 16, Feb. 9, 1845, C. D., Tangier, VI. The text of the treaty is given in Edgard Rouard de Card, Traités de la France avec les pays de l'Afrique du Nord, 334-338.

41. Mullowny to Calhoun, No. 16, Feb. 9, 1845; Carr to Buchanan, No. 5, Nov. 7, 1845; C. D., Tangier, VI.

42. Flournoy, British Policy Towards Morocco, 109-111; Carr to Buchanan, No. 7, Aug. 18, 1846; No. 8, Aug. 30, 1846; No. 9, Nov. 17, 1846; No. 19, Sept. 2, 1847; C. D., Tangier, VI.

43. Carr to Buchanan, No. 23, Dec. 28, 1847, Ibid.; Andre Maurois, Lyautey (hereafter cited as Maurois, Lyautey), 102-103; N. D. Harris, Europe and Africa, 251.

44. Flournoy, British Policy Towards Morocco, 112-119.

45. Ibid., 117-121.

46. Sir John Drummond Hay, 131-140, 238-239, 277-282.

47. Flournoy, British Policy Towards Morocco, 121-125.

48. According to Bernard, Le Maroc, page 307: "Spain occupied the Zaffarine Islands .... An attempt of Spain to occupy the island of Perejil was checked by England." Hyatt reported to Buchanan on Sept. 6, 1848, Spain's demand for reparations for the murder by Riffians of several Spanish smugglers marooned on Perejil Island; C. D., Tangier, VII.

49. Flournoy, British Policy Towards Morocco, 126-128, 130.

50. Hyatt to Buchanan, No. 6, Oct. 27, 1848; No. 7, Nov. 11, 1848; No. 8, Dec. 8, 1848; No. 10, Feb. 13, 1849; C. D., Tangier, VII.

51. Flournoy, British Policy Towards Morocco, 129-143.

52. The Gibraltar Chronicle and Commercial Intelligencer of Oct. 19, 1849, 3, commented on this proposal: "The willingness of the Moorish Government to submit their dispute to the decision of a disinterested and impartial umpire would seem to indicate fairness on their part." Enclosure with dispatch No. 17 of Hyatt to Clayton, Nov. 2, 1849, C. D., Tangier, VII.

53. Hyatt to Clayton, No. 12, April 14, 1849; No. 14, Oct. 12, 1849; No. 15, Oct. 17, 1849; No. 17, Nov. 2, 1849; No. 18, Nov. 9, 1849; Ibid.

54. Brown to Webster, No. 14, Dec. 4, 1851; No. 15, Dec. 9, 1851; No. 18, March 20, 1852; No. 21, Aug. 27, 1852, Ibid.

55. In the following dispatch from Hay to Salisbury, May 23, 1877, F. O. Docs., 99/177, Hay apparently confuses the episodes of 1836 and 1854: "The United States Govt. had many years ago put forward a secret proposal to purchase Parsley Island or Alcassor Graire on the Straits. I checked at once the negotiation. About two years ago there was a rumor that another foreign government had

put forward a similar proposal. I then advised the Moorish Govt., if this report was true, to reply that they could not listen to any proposition for the sale or cession of territory and with a view to checking further negotiations, to state that a similar request on the part of another powerful government had already been declined by the Sultan." The reference to Alcassor Graire points to the affair of 1836, when Hay's father indicated in a dispatch his intention to make no direct representation to the Moroccan government.

56. Hay to Claredon, May 1, 1854, F. O. Doc., 99/60; Jan. 4, 1855 and May 23, 1855, Ibid., 99/65; Clarendon to Hay, May 18, 1854, Ibid., 99/60; cited by Flournoy, British Policy Towards Morocco, 152.

57. Marcy to Brown, Sept. 8, 1854 and Brown to Marcy, No. 37, Oct. 28, 1854, C. D., Tangier, VII.

58. Flournoy, British Policy Towards Morocco, 152.

59. Ibid., 150-151; Collings to Marcy, April 25, 1855 and May 3, 1855; C. D., Tangier, VII.

60. Marcy to Brown, No. 2, Feb. 21, 1856, D. S., Instructions, Barbary Powers, XIV, 186; Brown to Marcy, No. 1, April 1, 1856, Ibid.

61. Great Britain, Sessional Papers, Commons, Feb. 3-March 21, 1857, XVI, Accounts and Papers, II, Paper 2201, 70-88; Sir John Drummond Hay, 167-168; Flournoy, British Policy Towards Morocco, 165-173.

62. Collings to Marcy, April 25, 1855, C. D. Tangier, VII.

63. For the text of the treaties see: Great Britain, Sessional Papers, Commons, Feb. 3-March 21, 1857, XVIII, Accounts and Papers, XI, Papers 2190 and 2191; British and Foreign State Papers, 1855-1856, XLVI, 176-187.

64. Flournoy, British Policy Towards Morocco, 170-179; Sir John Drummond Hay, 176-181.

65. Ibid., 144-158; 183; Hay, "How Piracy Was Stopped in Morocco," 551-557; Brown to Marcy, No. 11, Aug. 28, 1856; Oct. 3, 1856; C. D., Tangier, VII.

66. Flournoy, British Policy Towards Morocco, 233-234, 238.

67. Sir John Drummond Hay, 205-206; Brown to Cass, No. 1, March 4, 1859; No. 2, April 2, 1859; Sept. 7, 1859; Sept. 9, 1859; Sept. 12, 1859; No. 7, Oct. 5, 1859; No. 8, Oct. 19, 1859; No. 9, Oct. 25, 1859, C. D., Tangier, VII.

68. Brown to Cass, No. 10, Oct. 27, 1859; No. 10, Nov. 2, 1859; No. 11, Nov. 12, 1859; No. 12, Nov. 27, 1859; No. 13, Dec. 1, 1859; No. 14, Dec. 5, 1859; No. 15, Dec. 10, 1859; No. 16, Dec. 14, 1859; No. 17, Dec. 15, 1859; No. 18, Jan. 20, 1860; No. 19, Jan. 23, 1860; No. 3, Feb. 14, 1860; No. 4, Feb. 26, 1860; Nov. 6, March 8, 1860; No. 7, March 12, 1860; No. 8, March 19, 1860; No. 9, March 26, 1860; No. 10, March 27, 1860; No. 11, May 3, 1860; No. 12, June 3, 1860; No. 13, June 19, 1860; Ibid.

69. Archives of the British Legation of Tangier, F. O. Dispatch, March 12, 1859; cited by Stuart, Tangier, 12.

70. Sir John Drummond Hay, 205-207, 213. A detailed account of the British role in the war is given in Flournoy, British Policy Towards Morocco, 191-215.

71. This was reclaimed as a former pioneer colony of Spain. In 1878 Spain identified the place as Ifni.

72. Piquet, Le Maroc, 180; Meakin, Moorish Empire, 176-178.

73. Sir John Drummond Hay, 218-219; Flournoy, British Policy Towards Morocco, 241; Great Britain, Sessional Papers, Commons, Feb. 6-Aug. 7, 1862, LXIV, Accounts and Papers, XXXVI, Papers 2906 and 2916.

74. Piquet, Le Maroc, 179-180.

75. Merry to the Spanish Minister of State, July 1, 1869; cited by Cruickshank, Morocco at the Parting of the Ways, xxi-xxiv.

76. McMath to Seward, private letter, Nov. 5, 1863, C. D., Tangier, VIII.

77. Sir John Drummond Hay, 233-235.

78. Flournoy, British Policy Towards Morocco, 235-236; Foreign Affairs, Part IV, 1864-1865, 432; Arthur Girault, The Colonial Tariff Policy of France, 80.

79. Flournoy, British Policy Towards Morocco, 238; Hugo C. M. Wendel, "The Protégé System in Morocco," (hereafter cited as Wendel, "Protégé System in Morocco"), Journal of Modern History, II (March, 1930), 51-52.

80. Flournoy, British Policy Towards Morocco, 240-249.

81. Sir John Drummond Hay, 236.

82. The following highly fanciful version of this incident is of interest. "Fifteen years ago the Sultan of Morocco sent an embassy to the President of the United States, with a request that he should take them under his protection. This embassy was stopped by the Minister of the United States in Tangier as soon as they made known to him the object of their mission." Stephen Bonsal, Jr., Morocco As It is, With An Account of Sir Charles Euan Smith's Recent Mission to Fez (hereafter cited as Bonsal, Morocco As It Is), 32-33. See also Stuart, Tangier, 13.

83. Mathews to Fish, No. 29, June 29, 1871, C. D., Tangier, IX; Davis (Acting Sec. of State), to Mathews, No. 18, Aug. 22, 1871, D. S., Instructions, Barbary Powers, XV, 291.

84. Mathews to Fish, No. 61, Jan. 27, 1872 and No. 62, Feb. 9, 1872, C. D., Tangier, X.

85. Mathews to Fish, No. 63, Feb. 11, 1872, Ibid.; Sir John Drummond Hay, 277-282.

86. Mathews to Fish, April 20, 1873 and July 15, 1874; C. D., Tangier, X.

Chapter V

Morocco as an International Ward
(1792 - 1894)

The reign of Mulai Hassan III (1873-1894) was inaugurated by several months of hard fighting before the last of the imperial capitals, Fez, submitted to his authority. His accession was an augury for his career as sultan; the rest of his life was a succession of personally led expeditions against rebellious subjects in both urban and rural areas. Among foreigners his reputation was that of a bloodthirsty tyrant, but his own people viewed him more justly as a good, even a strong, ruler, forced into incessant warfare to preserve his heritage. The other major task that he essayed was to play off against each other the predatory foreign powers seeking to take advantage of the decadence and anarchy of his country. In diplomacy he failed, as he did also in his only significant experiment in social and economic reform. Like Peter the Great, he tried to modernize his realm by sending student missions to Europe, but they were unable to utilize their alien knowledge at home. In all aspects of her cultural life, Morocco remained fossilized, and her "absolute" monarch continued to be a puppet of the ultra-reactionary court officials, tribal chiefs, and religious leaders.[1]

However, at various times Mulai Hassan did show comity and a desire for rapprochement with his Christian enemies. An appropriate gesture to commemorate the centennial of both American independence and American-Moroccan relations was the sending of a Moorish villa and a large consignment of native manufactures to the Philadelphia exposition of 1876. Moorish envoys made return visits to England, France, and Italy, where they were received by Queen Victoria, saw troop reviews by President McMahon and King Victor Emmanuel, and made valuable gifts of horses and Moorish goods to their hosts. The Sultan presented an adjoining garden for the enlar of the Christian cemetery at Tangier, for which the European and American governments later built a wall and garden lodge. Acknowledging the naval supremacy of Great Britain, he ordered four war vessels constructed there. He paid tribute to the artistic preeminence of France by having his gold coinage minted in Paris. At the request of the British government, he donated a site for a Protestant church, to which Queen Victoria contributed $500. His toleration of the infidels' religion extended even to Protestant missions. The English North African Mission, organized in 1886, was represented in all North Africa from Morocco to Egypt. The women missionaries in Fez and Sefrou were welcomed in the harems for educational and medical services, but made no converts. Much less esteemed by the Moors were the members of the American Mission, supported by the Gospel Union of Kansas City. Interdicted by the Europeans from preaching in the streets of Larache and Meknes, the Americans met no success in their tours of rural districts. Perhaps the most striking evidence of the Sultan's amiability was his allowing the entry of newspapers into Morocco--the *Al-Maghreb Al-Aksa* and the *Réveil du Maroc* in 1883 and *The Times of Morocco* in 1884, all in Tangier.[2]

One of Mulai Hassan's ventures toward amity was rebuffed by the United States. On December 1, 1885, Mathews reported with pleasure that the Sultan intended sending an embassy of notables to Washington the next spring to report on American industries and to foster commerce. The consul informed Secretary Bayard that Moroccan embassies sent to several European countries had had all expenses for transportation and lavish entertainment paid by the countries visited, for which the Moors returned presents from the Sultan.[3] To a reminder from Mathews on April 29, 1886, that the Sultan's proposal was still unanswered, Bayard replied on June 10, 1886, that the President hesitated to risk a refusal of Congress to appropriate the necessary funds, which would appear like a discourteous rejection of friendly overtures. But the United States would be pleased to receive an envoy from Morocco and extend him every courtesy "within the power of the Executive to afford." In a letter addressed directly to President Cleveland on May 12, 1887, the Sultan again suggested an embassy to America "to renew and consolidate our good relations by God's consent." When Foreign Minister Torres repeated this proposal in November, 1888, the new Consul Lewis declined the honor on the ground that "our customs and ways are quite different from those of Europe, we do not receive or give presents, nor do we extend royal hospitality." Lewis thought that such a visit would be most inexpedient for the United States:

> The Moors have been accustomed when sending an Embassy to have it conveyed from Tangier and entertained till its return by the power to which it is accredited, this being quite foreign to our customs .... A government without a Court--without Ambassadors--a simple business institution, in short, will be to them incomprehensible.[4]

Accordingly, the United States remained a terra incognita to the Moroccans for several years longer.

From its beginning, neither Mathews nor Hay viewed the Hassan régime optimistically. From September, 1873 to August, 1875, the former kept Secretary of State Fish informed about the current plagues and rebellions and the pressure put upon the new ruler by the foreign representatives in Tangier to restore order. In June, 1874, the United States corvette Alaska came with British, Portuguese, Spanish, Italian, and French frigates to protect their nationals at Tangier. An American frigate, the Franklin, also visited this port in March, 1875.[5]

With dogged perserverance, Hay redirected his propaganda for reform toward Mulai Hassan. To a friend he wrote: "I suppose the young Sultan intends to tread in the footsteps of his ancestors and remain stagnant .... I have but faint hope of success, as the ministers and satellites of the Court are either rogues or fools." On an official mission to Fez in 1875, Hay met with a magnificent reception from both the Court and the populace. However, he made little progress toward securing the practical economic reforms which he advocated,[6] although most of them had been promised by Sidi Muhammad in 1873. In 1879 Hay wrote: "A vigorous tyrant would be preferable to our good, well-meaning sultan," whom he described as intelligent but stupidly avaricious.[7]

Mulai Hassan displayed greater faith in military preparedness than he did in economic reform. He would not promote commerce, but to resist both insurrection and foreign aggression he welcomed aid in building up his military strength. He sent a number of young Moors for military training to the British garrison in Gibraltar and took into his service British and French army officers.[8] He also purchased large quantities of modern arms and artillery and fortified Tangier.[9] Since Germany, too, appeared to be ambitious to establish in Morocco not only commercial firms but also military and naval strongholds, Hassan's strengthening of his defenses seems justifiable. Mathews duly reported to Washington the appearance of a German squadron of three vessels at Tangier on January 27, 1874,[10] and the exchange of salutes between them and the port battery; "on this occasion, the German flag was hoisted for the first time in Tangier."[11]

The one reform which received the enthusiastic and enduring support of Mulai Hassan was the reorganization of the system of protection. In this endeavor he was ably seconded by Hay. Their joint efforts to restore the independence of Morocco resulted instead in a brief interlude during which the rival national imperialisms were replaced by an international imperialism nominally regulated by treaty. Furthermore, there was an experimental, but brief, extension of the principle of international guardianship to other parts of Africa. Even the professedly isolationist United States participated in four international conferences during the nineteenth century and ratified three of the conventions made there--with the characteristic reservations absolving her from responsibility for helping to enforce them. The last three of these international pacts, accompanied and followed by a retrogression to the centuries-old national rivalry in the conquest of Morocco, were made during the reign of Mulai Hassan.

The movement toward international guardianship over Morocco had originated in 1792, when the consular corps in Tangier began to consider among its problems the public health of Tangier. In this as well as in later encroachments of the European representatives upon the sovereign powers of the Maghzen, foreign assistance was acknowledged by the sultans as a necessity for the continuance of Morocco's intercourse with other countries. The perennial plagues spread from Mecca by the thousands of Muslims making annual pilgrimages there induced the sultans to accept the aid of the Consular Corps in controlling these devastating scourges.

The original public health committee in Tangier included representatives of Portugal, Sweden, Great Britain, Venice, Denmark, and the Netherlands. Spain joined the group in 1793 and France and the United States in 1797. At first the consular corps made recommendations only, limited to maritime quarantine. Later its advisory powers were extended to towns and districts and to other infectious diseases besides the plagues. In 1805, the public health of Tangier was placed under consular supervision. In 1840 the Sultan promoted the diplomatic body to the rank of a Sanitary Council with power to make regulations to safeguard the health of the principal ports of the Empire.

The presidency of the Council rotated monthly (trimonthly after 1884) among the foreign representatives. To execute its orders, the Council had designated officials. A quarantine station established on Mogador Island in 1865 greatly facilitated the work of the Council. Imperial edicts in 1892 and 1893 made the Sanitary Council, renamed the Hygiene Commission, virtually the city council of Tangier. The membership of this body was now increased to twenty-six, selected as follows: ten by the legations, a Moroccan by the Sultan, a Jew by the chief rabbi of Tangier (never appointed), two Muslims by the local administration, and twelve members by an electorate composed of voluntary subscribers and foreign subjects. The funds to support this city government were the 15,000 pesetas contributed annually by Morocco, small grants by the participating foreign governments, voluntary contributions, and various small taxes and license fees. The great weakness of this commission was its inability to establish a native police force because of the contest for its control among the foreign powers.[12] When the reign of Mulai Hassan ended, the foundations were already laid for the later establishment of the international city of Tangier by the principal powers interested in Morocco.

The second project tending toward the internationalization of Morocco was the establishment of the lighthouse on Cape Spartel. This indispensable aid to navigation, advocated by John Mullowny as early as 1821, was discussed by the foreign representatives in Tangier as a joint enterprise in 1852. On May 31, 1865, the ten countries then represented at Tangier signed the convention providing that they would maintain and operate the lighthouse, sharing equally in the expense and respecting its neutrality even in case of war between any contracting parties or between any of them and Morocco. This delegation of adminstration and support was not to "import any encroachment on the rights, proprietary and of sovereignty, of the Sultan." The foreign representatives began control over the lighthouse on October 15, 1864, and their functions as the International Commission of Cape Spartel were defined in regulations promulgated on July 11, 1865. The treaty was to be in effect for ten years, with annual extensions until denounced by any one of the signatories and with annual rotation of the presidency among them.[13]

Under international auspices the Cape Spartel Lighthouse continued to operate without friction, causing the sultans no apprehension of possible undermining of their authority. Nevertheless, it was a second step in extending international supervision over legitimate functions of the Maghzen. For the United States, the Cape Spartel Lighthouse convention, the first international treaty to which this country was a party, was significant as a precedent for the future cooperation of the American Government in Moroccan and African guardianship.

During the nineteenth century the movement for international control over Morocco reached its culmination. Plague, piracy, and protection--for centuries these had been the features of the Moroccan image causing Morocco to be seen as a Bad Neighbor to the civilized nations of the West. These were considered matters of international import of rightful concern to the outside world. By the repeated application of force, diplomacy, and charity of foreign nations the first two had been ameliorated or abolished by the time of Mulai Hassan. There were other blemishes on the Moorish visage, such as slavery, famine, poverty, and oppression of both Moroccans and Jews. These internal ills also were frequent subjects of foreign protest and aid in times of stress. Associated with the abuses of protection, the Jewish problem became one for international intervention. It was the ancient system of protection, however, manipulated by the powers for the purpose of subverting the Moroccan state, which led to the third and final phase of the internationalization of the Sherifian Empire.

The system of protection, long applied to Moroccan notables to exempt them from extraordinary taxation, had been extended gradually to Christians and native Jews for judicial and commercial reasons after the sultans decided to make treaties with European countries and the United States. Conceding it as a necessary evil under their archaic government, the sultans sought to keep it under their control. During the reign of Hassan's two predecessors, however, two treaties permitted the rapid acceleration of protection. Abd er-Rahman had been alarmed at the results of the treaty made with Great Britain in 1856, by which British merchants (and also those of all other "most favored" nations) could appoint native brokers who were promised complete liberty in buying and selling and protection against any interference by the Sultan's officials.[14] This extension of protection to native agents became more serious, however, after the Spanish-Moroccan treaty of commerce in 1861. This provided that chargés d'affaires or consul generals might appoint as interpreters or servants either Moroccans or subjects of other countries, who would be exempt from all taxes. The same privileges were accorded to consuls, vice-consuls, and consular agents in Moroccan ports; however, Moroccans of the last two classes could give protection only to members of their families living at home.[15]

Quickly the "industry of extraterritoriality" became a protection racket through elastic definitions of the treaty terms "merchant," "broker," and "family." Particularly menacing to the economy of the state and the sovereignty of the Sultan was the diffusion of protection throughout the rural regions. Since land ownership was allowed only to natives, many Europeans bought wealthy Moorish landowners as protégés, who could then escape taxation and extortion from the Sultan's officials. Many Europeans also acquired native associates in raising cattle and sheep for their mutual advantage in evading Moroccan commercial restrictions and collecting damages, often on fraudulent claims, from the Moroccan government.[16]

Realizing and deploring the abuses following his treaty of 1856, Hay entered in 1859 upon a vigorous campaign to eliminate them. He exhorted his own subordinates throughout Morocco to observe the treaty provisions strictly and reported the worsening conditions to London. He also admonished his colleagues at Tangier to obey the rules. Always a champion of the Jews, Hay opposed the adoption by numerous wealthy ones of the role of protected brokers, knowing that their action would subject the poor and defenseless masses of the Hebrews to increased persecution from the fanatical Muslims. Aware that his rivals, especially the French and the Spanish, were misusing protection not only to diminish British trade, but also to destroy the Sultan's power over his subjects, Hay regarded the abolition of irregular protection as a necessity for the success of the British policy in Morocco. When on a mission to the Moorish Court in Marrakesh in 1863, Hay submitted to Sidi Muhammad a proposal that British subjects be permitted to rent land from either the Moroccan government or its subjects for cotton culture. The Sultan declined on the ground that all other foreign representatives in Tangier would be entitled to the same privilege, and there would be a great extension of the existing irregularities. He also declared his intention to have his foreign minister, Cid Muhammad Bargash, negotiate with the foreign representatives at Tangier on the problem of protection.[17]

While on this mission, Hay made a declaration of principles on protection which his government was willing to follow. Angered by this independent action, the Spanish and French representatives then negotiated jointly with the Sultan and succeeded in making an agreement with him. This agreement was in the form of identical notes addressed to the Sultan's commissioner and dated August 19 and 20, 1863. Apparently without instructions from their governments, the representatives of Belgium, Great Britain, Sardinia, Sweden-Norway, and the United States approved of the terms. Since the British assent was given by the chargé d'affaires during Hay's absence, Hay later asserted correctly that the British government had never sanctioned the arrangement.[18]

The identical notes of 1863 were essentially a "gentlemen's agreement," in no sense a convention as was later claimed by the French. It aimed to prevent the Jewish and Moroccan vice-consuls and consular agents from arrogating privileges given by treaty to foreign representatives of the first rank only.[19] Protection was made an individual privilege, limited to the time of actual service, and covering only the consular aide, his wife, and his minor children living with him. It was not hereditary, except for the Benchimol family, which had served the French government as interpreters for several generations. Protégés were divided into two classes. The first included natives actually employed in legations and consular offices. The second comprised the native brokers employed by foreign merchants in the wholesale importing and exporting business. Each merchant was limited to two brokers for each branch of his business in the various ports. Agricultural associates were not given full protection, for they were subject to taxation. But no judicial action could be taken involving them without notification of the consular authorities, who might be present to protect their interests. The consulates were required to furnish lists of their protégés to the local authorities and identification cards to their protégés. The regulations also exempted all fully protected persons from taxation and the jurisdiction of Moorish courts. The immediate reactions to the agreement were favorable. Both the Spanish and the British ministers gave their subordinates orders for its strict observance.[20]

For a time there was even a prospect for the amelioration of the situation of the Jews without their resorting to irregular protection. In 1863 the execution without trial of two Jews accused of murdering the Spanish receiver in the custom house at Safi instigated foreign intervention. Secretary Seward was inspired by the board of delegates of the American Israelites in New York to instruct Mathews to exert all proper influence to prevent another such outrage--a course certain to be followed by representatives of all Christian powers in Tangier.[21] In 1864 Sir Moses Montefiore, a British subject, was delegated by the Jewish societies of Europe to go on a mission to the Moroccan Court. He succeeded in obtaining an imperial edict to Moorish officials, ordering that Jews be treated with perfect equality in the adminstration of justice and in the protection of person and property. The Sultan's commands caused great displeasure among his subordinates, however, and within three months Havas was reporting new instances of oppressions.[22] Moorish antagonism toward the Jews[23] was caused not only by their extensive purchase of protection but also by their use of foreign influence to enforce unjust claims and to imprison their debtors. By usury, moreover, they oppressed both Moors and their poor co-religionists.[24] Every war of the nineteenth century between Morocco and a foreign power was made an occasion for Jewish pogroms, as was also any change of ruler, famine, fire, or epidemic.[25]

During the commercial expansion of the 70's, there was a great growth of regular protection and a revival of irregular protection. In the interior districts, both Jews and Moors served as semsars, but Hay charged that the French merchants usually selected wealthy Moroccan farmers as agents.[26] This practice interfered with the Sultan's claim on their militia or police service. The exemption of foreigners and their protégés from agricultural and gate taxes caused large losses to the Sultan's revenues. Some consular agents were guilty of officious meddling in Moroccan court proceedings. Probably no rank of foreign officials was entirely guiltless of extending irregular protection in some form. Regular protection was sometimes used to cover criminal or corrupt practices, and it was commonly granted for only nominal services. Natives employed as consular agents often evaded the regulation against protecting their fellow countrymen.[27]

Other serious abuses arose after the agreement of 1863. The number of semsars exceeded the limit agreed upon. "At every point of contact with the Europeans the authority of the Sultan receded." Some Moorish subjects, especially Jews, went abroad,[28] obtained naturalization papers, and returned to claim, as foreigners, exemption from taxation and jurisdiction of the Moorish government. The Sultan was unwilling to recognize as foreign subjects those natives who returned to remain permanent residents of Morocco, and the Spanish and the British governments took the same view.[29]

With the exception of Spain during her war with Morocco, political motives did not seem to be dominant in the extension of protection. More commonly the diplomatic and consular officials were actuated by commercial or personal gains for themselves. In 1877, Hay reported that the German and Belgian representatives were supporting his campaign against irregular protection. French and Spanish practices, also were generally legal, and after 1868, Italian customs improved. The extraordinary fact was that the most reprehensible offenders represented countries with little trade and very few residents in Morocco--namely, the Portuguese chargé d'affaires and the American consul, Felix Mathews.[30]

Before the advent of Mathews in Morocco in 1870, the State Department had received accusations of corrupt protection against various American consuls, but he was the first American representative to be charged officially with extensive abuse of this institution. From the beginning of his service, Mathews laid a foundation of evidence for his integrity. In his first report, dated June 27, 1871, Mathews listed 51 American protégés, including three granted "nominal protection ... for the purpose of introducing petroleum into the interior." From that time on, with monotonous repetition, every semiannual report until January 1, 1881, read: "No protection has been given to any person by this Consulate during the last preceding six months."[31] On August 31, 1876, Hay charged that Mathews "was selling protection like a tradesman sells his goods." In a confidential dispatch of March 23, 1877, Hay stated that since coming to Morocco Mathews was alleged to have protected upwards of 100 wealthy Moorish subjects engaged in mercantile or agricultural pursuits, "and yet the United States have no trade, and there is only one United States citizen resident in Morocco."[32]

Mathews had definite instructions from the State Department regarding the American policy on protection. In the case of a consular agent of the United States at Safi, Secretary Fish rejected the theory of Mathews that "by precedent any foreign representative can ... for the upholding of commerce and for considerations of humanity concede the protection of his flag to such of the subjects of Morocco as he may deem proper persons to extend this favour to." The protection of the United States was to be given to a consular agent only for the discharge of his official duties, and would not be granted for the business or safety of any alien in a foreign country.[33]

On March 10, 1877, Cid Muhammad Bargash conferred with the foreign representatives at his home in Tangier, at which he presented twenty proposals made by the Sultan to limit protection to the stipulations in the British and the Spanish treaties and the agreement of 1863. The representatives were requested to discuss the propositions among themselves and to draw up a written agreement to make its observance binding upon all alike. It was decided to hold a series of meetings for discussion. Meanwhile, Hay prepared for the forthcoming conference by working for a consensus among his colleagues. The British government approached all the governments represented at Tangier, receiving replies apparently favorable to the Moroccan proposals, although France made some reservations. At Lisbon and Washington the British officials preferred the charges made by Hay against the Portuguese and American representatives at Tangier. The Portuguese government responded immediately with a promise to avoid all abuses in the future.[34]

Acting Secretary Seward informed the British Embassy at Washington that the State Department would require an investigation of Hay's charges before issuing any instructions to Mathews; Hay had no right to dictate the number of American protégés. When asked to reply to the charges against him, and to discontinue at once any existent irregular protection, Mathews made a categorical denial of having protected over one hundred Moroccans. On the contrary, he said, in 1871 he had withdrawn protection granted to over forty Moorish subjects by his predecessors, retaining only a few individuals who seemed entitled to protection "according to treaty stipulations and the long established local precedents." His course had always been sanctioned and approved by the Moorish government.[35] Because of the "unrelenting oppression and most cruel extortions" of natives, especially Jews, it was difficult for any foreign representatives not able to divest themselves entirely of common humanity to refuse mediation with the numerous petty tyrants. For seven years, Mathews said, he had extended "protection" from his own resources to thousands of Moorish and other subjects to alleviate their illness and destitution. Hay was well known at the courts of Madrid, Rome, Lisbon, and Rio de Janeiro for his underhanded accusations against their consular officers. Although Hay himself was protecting whole villages of farmers, as well as two hundred beaters employed in his boar hunts, and many employees of the consulates of Austria, Denmark, and Holland under his charge, he was making false charges of irregular protection against other foreign representatives for the sole purpose of destroying all commerce except the British. Later Mathews sent to the State Department four letters from prominent Moroccans, including the Grand Vizier and the Sherif of Wazan, which he said should entirely clear him of Hay's charges.[36]

The official investigation of Mathews, conducted by the American consul at Gibraltar, resulted in the former's complete exoneration, expressed in terms greatly resembling Mathews' own words. However, Hay did not withdraw his charges. He asserted that Mathews had deceived the American government, and apparently proved his case by forwarding other letters to his own government from prominent Moroccans, including some of the original witnesses for Mathews, who admitted that the friendly conduct of the American consul toward the Moors included the granting of irregular protection. However, in a confidential report the State Department dismissed Hay's accusations as "wholly unsubstantiated" and "partial and disingenuous," as well as "eminently unfriendly to Mr. Mathews."[37]

But after this incident, the State Department issued more definite instructions to Mathews. Secretary Evarts directed him to make no official interpositions for Jews who were not American citizens, although he might use his personal influence to shield them from oppression. For Moors naturalized in the United States and returning to Morocco, Mathews was to claim the same privileges and immunities as might be enjoyed by Moors naturalized in other countries, unless their governments had special treaties of naturalization with Morocco, as the United States had not. At first Evarts decreed that American protection should not be given to Moorish commercial agents, because the United States statutes forbade the issuing of passports to any but American citizens, and a written protection from a consul would be virtually a passport. After Mathews had made detailed explanations of the perils and difficulties involved in carrying on commerce in the interior, the State Department conceded that Moorish agents employed by American citizens might receive American protection with safe-conducts for the discharge of their duties.[38]

Evidently Mathews continued to follow what he considered a higher law than treaties or directives of the State Department, as his subsequent career indicated. He was inspired by ideals of humanitarianism and progress in defending irregular protection. He could not allege its necessity to serve the commercial interests of the United States, for in his report for 1878-79 he admitted that

> It is to be regretted that Morocco ... offers so poor a market for many branches of American industry and trade, notwithstanding my efforts to introduce into use many of the products of our machinery, agricultural and otherwise. And the imports into ... Morocco from the United States ... were all conveyed in foreign vessels. Only one vessel bearing our flag brought into this port a cargo of flour and petroleum in the latter part of February.[39]

Meeting with Bargash on nine occasions from July 9 to August 10, 1877, the diplomatic corps was unable to reach a satisfactory solution for all the problems presented. The twenty demands of the Moorish minister were to be the basis for the agenda of the Tangier conference of 1879 and the Madrid conference of 1880 also. Bargash still wanted to confine protection to the limits of the British and the Spanish treaties of 1856 and 1861 and the agreement of 1863. Hay opposed the last arrangement; he advocated that native <u>semsars</u> should be unlimited in number, but should be under foreign protection only in matters pertaining to their employment. He thought also that foreigners and protégés should pay the agricultural taxes. Mathews was even more generous to the Sultan in suggesting that the gate tax also should be paid by everybody. The Sultan's demand that Moors naturalized abroad return to their original allegiance when returning to Morocco was opposed by the American, Portuguese, and French representatives. Various administrative details were discussed, and many principles were accepted. Finally, on August 10, the diplomatic corps sent a collective note to the Moroccan foreign minister informing him that a definitive agreement could be made only after securing the approval of their respective governments. On the whole, the attitude of most of the diplomatic corps had been very conciliatory, especially in the matter of taxation. The British, German, and Belgian representatives were prepared to accede to all of Mulai Hassan's requests. The Spanish minister alone remained obdurate;[40] he insisted upon yielding no treaty right without compensation.[41]

Conditions in Morocco during 1878, however, together with pressure from the British government, brought the Spanish government around entirely to Hay's viewpoint. In that year Morocco suffered from a terrible famine, followed in the autumn by a cholera epidemic which forced the quarantining of Gibraltar against all goods from Morocco. Large sums were raised in London and Tangier to aid the starving poor. Mathews reported in 1879 that the famine had wiped out whole districts and that it was estimated that en months of starvation and disease had reduced the population by at least one-fifth.[42] Spain was converted to the support of the Sultan because the threatened disintegration of Morocco would come at a time when Spain itself was too weak and disunited to seize the spoils. The new Spanish minister at Tangier, Diosdado, believed that the most effective way to sustain Morocco was to reduce protection.[43]

Beginning in February, 1879, the adjourned conferences of the diplomatic corps were continued in Tangier over a period of three months.[44] Cid Muhammad Bargash submitted certain old and some new demands to the foreign representatives. Each of the latter testified that he and his own country were guiltless of wrongdoing, but all conceded the existence of abuses requiring radical reform. The Italian minister had now become the irreconcilable element, expressing utter disbelief in any power of the Sherifian government to regenerate itself and demanding for Italian interests the preservation of all "customary" as well as all treaty rights of protection.[45]

The abuses of chief importance listed by Bargash were the dictatorial language of certain consular officials to Moorish officers, the refusal of returned naturalized Moors to submit to the taxation and laws of their native country, the buying of protection by political prisoners and even criminals, and the serious depletion of the Sultan's revenues by the withdrawal from taxation of wealthy agricultural associates and other groups. These conditions were promoting anarchy and tribal revolts and were leading to the eventual loss of the Sultan's sovereignty. Bargash offered the guarantee of his government that no injustice would be tolerated toward ex-protégés, and he demanded in return that all persons protected in violation of treaties and the agreement of 1863 should be removed forthwith from the lists. Hay urged that the renunciation of abuses by the foreign representatives would give them the influence and prestige needed to induce the Maghzen to carry through the fundamental reorganization admitted to be essential for the continued existence of Morocco as an independent state.[46]

The conference ended, as the earlier one had, without reaching an agreement. The Portuguese, American and French representatives held out against the Moroccan views on naturalization. The French and Italian ministers refused to surrender the right to choose commercial agents in the interior or to let them be arrested, even for murder, by the native authorities. The Italian minister, with his new claim for "customary" protection, also opposed the removal from protection of any of his protégés granted this status prior to 1871. Bargash was so exasperated by the demands relating to native brokers that he declared the closing of Morocco to all commerce might be the best solution of the problem of protection.[47]

On July 28, 1879, Hay proposed that Lord Salisbury sponsor an international commission meeting outside Morocco and composed of new delegates capable of approaching the question with open minds. During a visit to England in August, Hay repeated his suggestion for such a conference to be held at Madrid.[48] This proved to be the plan finally acceptable to all the powers--the forging of an instrument to save Morocco from herself[49] and from any individual foreign power by making it an international ward.

Preliminary arrangements for the proposed conference began on October 7, 1879, when the British Foreign Office circularized its diplomats in the capitals of all countries represented in Morocco, instructing them to ascertain the views of the interested countries regarding a conference on protection. All the countries addressed, except two, accepted Madrid as the locale and accepted to the proposed meeting without reservation or comment. The United States inquired the date and the nature of the business of the conference, and France reserved the question of the privileges of the semsars. By May 6, 1880, each of the powers had selected as its delegate its minister resident at Madrid, except Denmark, which was represented by the British delegate, Sackville West. Cid Muhammad Bargash acted for Morocco.[50]

An interesting debate occurred in the Spanish Chamber of Deputies in November, 1879, between Señor Carvajal of the opposition and the Duke of Tetuan, the foreign minister. The former demanded that Spain secure the support of her sister Latin states in order to pursue her true national objectives of union with Portugal, recovery of Gibraltar, and fulfillment of her destiny in Morocco. Protection should be extended in Morocco in order to facilitate Spanish colonization there, instead of in Algeria. The Duke of Tetuan upheld the policy of developing Morocco's confidence in Spain and abjuring permature adventures. When Señor Canovas del Castillo became minister of state in January, 1880, he also declared for a policy of close cooperation with Great Britain. Spain, he said, would strive to maintain her treaty rights and to preserve the independence of Morocco.[51]

Gratified at the selection of Madrid for the conference, the Spanish government issued the invitations. Besides the powers represented at Tangier, it was decided to bring in Russia, which chose, however, not to take part. Here was a recognition of the principle that henceforth any change in the status of Morocco would be considered by all world powers. The invitations, issued on April 10, 1880, were accepted by Austria-Hungary, Belgium, Denmark, France, Germany, Great Britain, Italy, Morocco, the Netherlands, Portugal, Sweden-Norway, Spain, and the United States. The date was set for May 15, 1880, and each country named its representative at Madrid[52] as its conference delegate.[53]

Señor Canovas del Castillo, later presiding officer of the conference, advised a previous entente between Great Britain and Spain. The latter wished to uphold the *status quo* under the British and Spanish treaties of 1856 and 1861 and favored limiting the discussions strictly to protection. As proof of her sincerity, Spain could offer her recent action in declining the request of certain Moorish tribes near Melilla to be received under Spanish protection. But at the same time Canovas was intimating discreetly to Admiral Jaurès that, although for the present the *status quo* seemed preferable, if ever the Empire of Morocco should collapse, it might be well for France and Spain to extend the boundaries of their respective possessions to the Moulaya River.[54]

Just before the conference the British elections brought into power the new Gladstone ministry. As a well-known champion of backward peoples, Gladstone chose to maintain the Salisbury-Hay policy and to continue the support already promised to Spain.[55]

To counterbalance the Anglo-Spanish entente, a Franco-German cooperation was promised. Both before and after the conference Bismarck assured the French government that he would support it in Morocco as he had done since the Congress of Berlin in Tunisia, Egypt, and Greece. He would give France proof of his benevolence in Morocco, where Germany did not possess any material interest. This cooperation was to contribute largely to the successful outcome of the conference for French interests.[56]

The Foreign Office instructed Admiral Jaurès not to surrender the protection of *censaux*--a right which France claimed to have exercised always with moderation and reserve. She would permit the levying of agricultural taxes on her brokers, but in return she would require the formal recognition of the right of ownership of immovable property in Morocco by foreigners. The basis of France's determination to concede no rights without compensation was the necessity felt at this time to use a strong hand on Morocco. France was preparing to secure a southern extension of the Algero-Moroccan boundary line into the western Sudan. Furthermore, French merchants demanded governmental support of the system of protected *censaux*, claiming that it was essential for competiton with British merchants.[57]

In the matter of protection, there was no chance of an Anglo-American rapprochement. Hay had derided the list of protégés furnished by Mathews for the conference of 1877. In his official report, Hay alleged that the list of protégés presented by Mathews to his colleagues did not correspond with that delivered by him to the local authorities.[58] In 1880, in a dispatch to Salisbury, Hay for the second time charged Mathews with falsifying his lists. "I shall not be surprised," he added, "to learn also that the lists, which may be presented by the other Representatives, now that it is known that they may be submitted to their respective governments, will also be greatly curtailed." Denying the countercharges by Mathews, Hay stated categorically to his own government that he protected no Moroccans not actually in the service of Great Britain or of the other governments that he represented. His list of protected personal servants included only two gardeners and his chief guard for expeditions into the interior. In his report to the State Department just before the conference, Mathews listed 28 persons, plus three families, all Moroccans or Jews except the American consular agent at Casablanca, John Cobb; all these protégés, Mathews asserted, paid taxes and were willing to pay any lawful tax.[59]

The instructions sent from the State Department to the American delegate, General Lucius Fairchild, reviewed the whole story of Hay's charges against Mathews, exonerating the latter. They stated that in principle the United States was cordially in favor of the adoption by common consent of an equitable rule to do away with the excessive and injurious exercise of the prerogatives of foreign protection for natives which had grown up under the shadow of treaty stipulations and usage. But regard must be had for the proper maintenance and security of consular establishments and the necessary employment of natives as guards, interpreters, and servants, and in agents in such capacities as might be essential to the proper representation and protection of foreign commercial interests. However, the American government could not see with complacent indifference any proceedings looking to an investigation of the past conduct of foreign representatives at Tangier or to sitting in *ex parte* judgment on their motives and morality.[60]

Instructed by the State Department to transmit any pertinent information to Fairchild, Mathews advised American opposition to the reform of protection:

> It is pretended in the name of the Moorish Government that the protection extended by foreign representatives is a growing evil and a detriment to the Moorish treasury, which is thus deprived of the taxes which are properly due from the protected persons .... This pretension ... is absurd, for it is well known that Morocco has no system of taxation, but only the arbitrary will of the Moorish officials, who deprive their subjects of all they possess. The Jews are the only subjects of Morocco who have a regular prescribed tribute or annual tax ... and indeed it is paid principally by those Jews who are naturalized citizens or protégés of foreign nations .... The laws of the country are obeyed by all, irrespective of nationality, religion, or protection.
>
> It is further stated ... that the system of protecting Moorish subjects is of great prejudice to the rights and independence of Morocco. Morocco has a population of 7,000,000; of these, 500 are those under foreign protection, and chiefly Israelites, who invariably pay their tribute and are the most submissive and inoffensive people .... The assertion that this insignificant number of quiet, peaceable people are of prejudice to the rights and independence of Morocco is well nigh baseless.
>
> It is further stated that there have been irregularities and even corruption in according protection .... Such has been the case in some instances, though it cannot be proved, there is undoubtedly a remedy ... and it is in the hands of the chiefs of missions and the Moorish minister of foreign affairs ... to investigate each case that comes within their notice .... It will be imprudent to abandon the only way of protecting the interests of our citizens or merchants having to deal in Barbary .... Unless the Moorish government moderates its morals and effects a complete change in the administration of justice, equalization of taxes, and payment of its officials with a regular salary, there will be no security for their persons or property.[61]

The early views of Fairchild seem to have been both sensible and fair:

> I am now inclined to the opinion that it is claiming altogether too much of any nation to demand that when its subjects go to a foreign country and there become naturalized they shall have the right to return to their native land to reside and be exempt from the payment of ordinary taxes and from the criminal and civil jurisdiction of the government. I am sure the United States would never for a moment allow such exemptions ....
>
> If Morocco is to be considered and treated as an independent nation, I now fail to see why foreign representatives should have the right in any way of protecting Moorish subjects, who are neither in their employ nor in the service of foreign merchants as agents or brokers. If one such Moor can be "protected" out from under the jurisdiction of his government and rendered independent of the laws of his country, then a hundred, a thousand, or a million, or any other number may, and the Emperor be relieved of all his subjects and of the trouble of governing them. True, the Emperor might be a happier man to be thus relieved, but why should that happiness be conferred on him, and his burden assumed by the representatives of other powers?[62]

Very soon, however, Fairchild seems to have been influenced by the anti-British bias of Mathews, who wrote:

> The Moorish government ... never ... thought of raising the question .... Sir John Hay ... is the moving soul and body of this uncalled for movement on protection .... We are their great rival in commerce, our commerce and manufacturers are rapidly wedging and turning aside the British everywhere and it is nothing but natural that they should resort to every device to maintain their supremacy ... in the most unsuspicious and indirect way.

In a memorandum on the conference, Fairchild noted:

> The B (British) are willing to perpetuate and increase their influence there to go almost any length in lessing (sic.) the guards which present treaties throw about commerce, knowing that the farther they go in that direction the better will M. (Morocco) be pleased, and feeling certain that their own people who reside or trade in Mo. (Morocco) will be fully protected on the personal demand of their minister.[63]

Apparently the Italian government had little at stake in Morocco. A member of the British Legation declared that Italy's trade with Morocco was practically nil, but that, although the legal number of her protégés would not exceed ten, on her lists and off them there was "an army of not less than one hundred." The presence of two Italian ironclads in the bay of Tangier during the conference presaged the important part which Italy aimed to play.[64] Before the conference the French and Italian governments discovered a community of views. The latter's representative at Tangier was accused by Hay of practicing irregular protection to enhance his personal prestige. Italy was prepared to sanction the protection of *semsars* and to put the burden of reform upon the Moorish government. In view of her ambitions in Tunisia at this time, it was good policy for Italy to demonstrate strength in dealing with North African affairs and also to offer conciliatory support to France at Madrid.[65]

While the two groups of great powers were lining up and negotiating to anticipate the results of the conference, international Jewry was laying down a diplomatic barrage designed to win the battle for equal rights for Jews in Morocco. The Sultan's firman of 1864, enjoining upon his officials the duty of securing justice and protection of person and property for Jews, had been ineffective in preventing many atrocities against them. The burning of a Jew just before the conference was exploited by the Jewish societies in their campaign. As one who had always acted effectively to assist Jews being mistreated, Hay thought the attitude of the Anglo-Jewish Association very ill-advised when it protested his advocacy of the abolition of irregular protection. This abolition would concern only about 1500 wealthy Jews and their families now protected by French, Italian, Portuguese, and American representatives, but would not affect the 200,000 unprotected Jews who suffered for the illegal acts of their protected brethren, especially for their practice of faking claims against unprotected Moors. Although Mulai Hassan was humane and just, he could not control his fanatical subjects if he were to attempt removing the disabilities of Jews sanctioned by centuries-old customs. The Sultan did exhort his lieutenant governor at Mazagan to cease his persecution of Jews. Moreover, when on a mission to the court in the spring of 1880,[66] Hay obtained the Sultan's promise of administrative reforms to promote justice for the Jews. Mulai Hassan also pledged himself to revise the British treaty of commerce in return for British support on protection. Hay also obtained at Fez the settlement of three cases of murdered Jews.[67] The Jewish socictics, however, were insistent that the conference itself should prescribe radical reforms, and they carried on propaganda to this end in the French and British press and in memorials to the French, British, Spanish, and American governments. Forgetting Hay's long record of friendship for the Moroccan Jews, the press articles severely criticized the British and Spanish ministers at Tangier for their wish to curtail protection. On the other hand, the Italian and American[68] representatives were eulogized as champions of the Jews.[69]

Before the conference met the alignment of the principal European powers was known to diplomats; with Morocco were Great Britain and Spain and against her were France, Italy, and Germany. Austria-Hungary wavered between the first group and Germany. Fairchild was soon disillusioned. He saw that the question was not likely to be answered on its merits, for it must be made to serve the ambitions of rival powers, and he had learned that:

> The Government of Morocco is so thoroughly bad and unreliable, except for mischief, that, if this conference should come to naught, it will go on in its persecutions and barbarous practices until the civilized world shall be disposed to join and send it to the wall, where sooner or later it ought to go, and the sooner the better, if it does not mend its ways.[70]

The first international conference on Morocco, under the presidency of Canovas del Castillo, held seventeen meetings between May 19 and July 3, 1880.[71] On June 12, in spite of Austrian and Italian efforts to offer satisfactory propositions, it appeared that the conference had already failed. Jaurès and Cid Muhammad Bargash had come to a deadlock because the Moroccan insisted that censaux should be selected only from town dwellers and should be under local authority, with protection only for foreign property in their charge.[72] Three days later, however, a compromise was reached, partly as a result of pressure put upon Bargash by Fairchild.[73] The Moorish delegate agreed to let the provision regarding brokers remain as stated in the agreement of 1863; in return, the powers conceded that foreigners and protégés should pay both agricultural and gate taxes. An additional advantage for the foreigners was the permission to purchase immovable property with the previous consent of the Sultan and in accordance with Moroccan law. A second time the conference was in danger of inglorious dissolution, when the Italian representative claimed for his country the right of "customary" protection in return for special services. This obstacle was overcome by the compromise limiting the number so protected to twelve for each country. Fairchild did not approve of this proposal, regarding it as "asking too much that Morocco shall reward services given to other states," but he voted for it for the sake of harmony.[74] Thus France won the first round of the contest, and Italy won the second.

The American delegate displayed interest chiefly in the discussions on naturalization. Well in advance of the conference, the Moroccan position on this had been announced. On February 18, Bargash stated that since the laws of Morocco did not permit either Muslim or Jewish subjects to transfer their allegiance, the Sultan could no longer permit naturalized Moors returning to Morocco to claim foreign citizenship. Although the governments of Great Britain, Germany, Austria-Hungary, Belgium, Denmark, Spain, and the Netherlands promptly acknowledged the legality of the Sultan's decision, Italy, Brazil, Portugal, France, and the United States would not accede.[75] On February 28, Mathews had denied the right of Morocco to take the contemplated action, because of Articles XIV, XX, and XXIV of the American-Moroccan treaty of 1836 and Articles V and XV of the Spanish-Moroccan treaty.[76] There were few Moorish subjects naturalized in the United States, he said, and all but two were Jews who had returned to Morocco to carry on business with the United States.[77]

In the conference discussions Fairchild declared that the United States had the right and duty of protecting completely, by all legitimate means her naturalized citizens, wherever they were. But he conceded that the subjects of no country ought to seek naturalization elsewhere with the sole aim of returning to their fatherland and thereby evading its laws. He would join the other foreign representatives to protect Morocco from such injustice and fraud. After some discussion, the delegates unanimously agreed to recognize fully the naturalization of all Moroccan natives then residing in Morocco. For the future, every Moroccan subject naturalized in a foreign land and then returning to Morocco must, after a sojourn equal to that which was necessary for him to regularly obtain naturalization, choose between his future submission to the laws of the Empire and the obligation to quit it, unless it could be proved that foreign naturalization had been obtained with the consent of the Moroccan government.[78]

The Jewish problem was prominent throughout the deliberations. Hay had not retreated from his earlier position that protection was no remedy for the Jews as a class, because it would not save any unprotected one from the persecutions incited by the arrogance and anti-social conduct of some of the protégés. When asked to cease opposing irregular protection, Hay urged a representative of the Anglo-Jewish Association to join him in abolishing the abuses of the protection system. Only if the sovereign rights of the Sultan were respected[79] would the foreign representatives find themselves morally strong enough to speak effectively for the abolition of cruelties toward Jew and Muslim alike. A premature removal of the social stigmas on Jews, if forced by foreign pressure, would result only in fanatical attacks on the Jews by the Moors.[80] Nevertheless, a Jewish alliance sent representatives to Madrid to urge action by the conference.[81]

The religious phase of the Jewish problem was eventually merged with a general movement for religious toleration initiated by the Vatican and sponsored before the conference by the envoy of Austria-Hungary. To avoid raising such a controversial matter at the conference, the Austrian delegate merely read a declaration in favor of religious liberty. This document, together with a letter from Mulai Hassan promising adherence to its principles, was included in the signed proces-verbal of the conference.[82]

To the American State Department the religious aspect of the conference seems to have been the most important. Fairchild was instructed to support the Austrian proposal. Secretary Evarts approved of the treaty as a whole, but "regretted that it contained no provision for liberty of conscience and worship, if not throughout the empire, then to protected persons."[83] In his message to Congress, President Hayes said that the United States had "lost no opportunity to urge upon the Emperor of Morocco the necessity of putting an end to the persecutions so prevalent in that country of persons of a faith other than the Moslem, and especially the Hebrew residents of Morocco."[84]

An American periodical considered the unprecedented participation of the United States in an international conference unworthy of mention. The Nation was curiously unaware of the centuries of historical development of the system of protection which formed the background of the conference. It spoke of the Treaty of Madrid as "the first successful attempt to bring Morocco into close and formal relations with the European Powers," which resembled "the capitulations with the Porte, having as its motive the establishment of consuls with regulated powers in the chief towns, because the English, Spanish, and French traders were eager to get at a country so very rich in natural resources."[85]

By May 1, 1881, a majority of the signatory powers had exchanged ratifications at Tangier. The Russian government signified its adherence to the convention on April 4, 1881. On May 5, 1881, the Senate of the United States unanimously advised and consented to the ratification of the convention, which was proclaimed on December 21, 1881.[86]

Admiral Jaurès had good cause to congratulate his government upon the success achieved by France through the consistent support of his German and Italian colleagues.[87]

France had won her fight to retain the provisions of the British treaty of 1856, the Spanish treaty of 1861, and the regulations of 1863 as the basic principles of protection. Moreover, the 1863 agreement had been elevated in rank from an exchange of notes between diplomats to an international treaty.

Hereafter there were to be three classes of protégés. The first class included the employees of chiefs of mission, unlimited in number; the employees of consuls, limited to one interpreter, one guard, and two servants; and a secretary for each consul, vice-consul, or consular agent. These protégés were exempt from all but the agricultural and gate taxes. Lists of this class were to be submitted annually to the Moroccan minister of foreign affairs. A consular agent who was a Moorish subject could have only one soldier-protégé. In the second class were the native brokers, of whom two were allowed for each main and branch establishment, with no restriction upon their place of residence--this was France's triumph. Even the servants of native protégés and foreigners enjoyed a kind of protection, for they could not be arrested without notification of the consular authorities responsible for their employers. The third class comprised the beneficiaries of the "customary" protection for which Italy had contended. This privilege was reserved for persons who had performed some signal service for a foreign power; it was limited to twelve persons for each power. Hereditary protection was allowed in only one case, for the Benchimol family, interpreters for France during several generations.

Other regulations were designed to eliminate abuses of the past. Except as guards, the foreign representatives could employ no sheiks or other Moroccan officials, and no protection could be given to any Moor under pursuit by the law. Moors naturalized abroad and returning to Morocco were required to choose, after residing in Morocco for as long a time as needed to make them naturalized citizens elsewhere, either to submit to Moorish laws or to leave the country, unless their naturalization had been permitted by the Sultan.

Aside from the regularization of protection, there were significant general principles embodied in the Madrid

Convention. The European representatives hailed the new right of foreign ownership of real estate in Morocco as a great victory, not realizing how restricted this right would be by the requirement of the previous consent of the sultan and regulation under Moroccan law. Of greater importance was the controversial Article XVII, providing most favored nation treatment for all the convention powers, which France, who first proposed this principle, later tried vainly to have limited to protection alone. Broadly interpreted, Article XVII "was to discourage any foreign intervention and safeguard the independence and territorial integrity of Morocco until the beginning of the 20th century."[88] The Germans envisaged the Morocco established by the Madrid Conference as "an independent state, in which an international guarantee granted economic liberty to foreign enterprise against any threat of unequal treatment, and whose independent status was a matter of international concern."[89] For many years they strove to maintain this viewpoint.

The divergent American and British estimates of the significance of the conference are of interest. General Fairchild was naïvely optimistic in reporting that "all the questions which have been at issue between Morocco and the powers ... have been happily settled, justly and fairly and to the reasonable satisfaction of all concerned." On the contrary, Hay had the acumen to foresee that the abuses retained in the treaty, such as the retention of protégés hitherto irregularly protected by Italy and other powers and the continuance of native semsars in the interior, would largely invalidate the reforms of the document. "The French policy," he wrote, "has been je veux, and the silly Italians, who really have no trade or interest in Morocco except to maintain its independence, backed the French." He was fearful that remonstraces to the Sultan on his misgovernment would no longer have any weight.[90]

Affording only a very brief interlude in the penetration of protection, the Madrid truce was followed by two almost simultaneous invasions of North Africa which ushered in the general grabbing of the continent by European powers. In April, 1881, acting upon the hint of Bismarck that it was time to pick the ripe Tunisian pear before it was spoiled or stolen by others, French troops entered Tunisia.[91] The conversion of the country into a French protectorate was justified by the well-publicized need of saving Algeria from raiding frontier tribes and by the less heralded objective of safeguarding investors in Tunisian bonds and business enterprises. Ungrateful public opinion forced the resignation of the aggressive foreign minister, Ferry.[92] His downfall probably caused the timidity of French diplomacy which resulted the following year in the establishment of Great Britain in Egypt.[93]

From 1876, when Disraeli had purchased from the bankrupt and incompetent ruler of Egypt the controlling shares in the Suez Canal, the fate of the country was predestined. The opportunity for obstruction offered by the Anglo-French financial condominium imposed upon the new viceroy in 1879 was lost by France in 1882 when she refused to assist in putting down the rebellion of Arabi Pasha. Repeatedly declaring her intervention to aim only at the restoration of order, Great Britain remained in control of military and financial affairs in her unacknowledged protectorate. Meanwhile, reiterated requests from France for a terminal date for the "temporary" occupation of Egypt proved embarrassing. Thus was forged a weapon ready for Bismarck to brandish over the heads of British diplomats when they tried to interfere in his newly adopted career of colonizer.[94]

The immediate reaction of Italy to the French seizure of Tunisia was an application for partnership with the recently formed Dual Alliance of Germany and Austria-Hungary. Bismarck was not eager to assist Italy in securing revenge for her frustrated ambition to annex Tunisia, for during the decade after 1875 he was pursuing with seeming success the policy of conciliating France. He saw in the Mediterranean a wide area where he could allow France a free hand, and he hoped to convince his late opponent that a friendly German Empire of 45,000,000 people was more valuable than a million Alsace-Lorrainers.[95] The Triple Alliance of Germany, Austria and Italy was a purely defensive one to protect its members from attacks by Russia or France; by Italy's desire, it contained a clause stating that it was in no case to be considered as directed against England. In fact, Bismarck rejected the inclusion of Great Britain in the pact only because he wished to avoid involvement in her wide-spread frictions with France and Russia.[96]

Following closely upon the conclusion of the Triple Alliance came the revival of a forward policy in Morocco by Spain, France, and Italy. King Alfonso XIII hoped to secure the support of the Triple Alliance in Morocco, and in 1883 he visited the Kaiser in Berlin.[97] Some success, of both an obstructive and constructive nature, attended Spanish schemes in 1883. Of the former sort was the defeat of a project sponsored by some British subjects, who formed a company capitalized at £1,000,000 to build railways, telegraph lines, and other public works in Morocco. Despite the powerful aid of Hay, the Spanish minister, Diasdado, was able to block the British enterprise.[98] "Every foreign enterprise of any importance would constitute here a state within a state ... since day by day it is becoming more difficult to uphold the fiction of the autonomy and independence of Morocco," Diasdado wrote his government. The constructive gain for Spain was the long-deferred cession of Ifni, designated by treaty as a fishing station, but intended by its new owners to become the commercial outlet for the products of the Sus, the Wad Nun, Timbuktu, and the Sudan.[99]

Italy also had hoped to utilize the Triple Alliance to achieve her newborn ambitions in Morocco. Because of his current policy on France, Bismarck was irritated by Italy's request for aid in 1884. When asked for protection against interference by France with Italy's interests in Morocco, he declared that Germany would not face the possibility of a great war "because of vague anxieties about Italy's interests which are not immediate, but which represent future hopes in regard to Morocco, or the Red Sea, or Tunis, or Egypt, or other parts of the world."[100]

While involvement in conflicting European imperialisms was propelling Morocco toward a threatened war with France in 1884, a survey of all aspects of the Moroccan problem supposedly soved at Madrid revealed the total failure of international diplomacy there. Hay reported in that year, "The Convention of Madrid has become a dead letter in every respect."[101] Certainly the failure of the treaty was evident in regard to the Jewish persecutions, the collection of the new taxes, and the reform of protection, while the Sultan refused to attempt any internal reforms. Moreover, the internationalization of the Sherifian Empire by guaranteeing every foreign nation most favored nation status in an independent country was being overtly undermined by France, who gave every evidence of intending to repeat her triumph in Tunisia.

The persecutions and murders of Jews increased after the Madrid convention, partly, Mathews thought, because a rumor was circulated that they were no longer under foreign protection. The State Department directed Mathews to cooperate with Levi A. Cohen, appointed by the Union of American Hebrew Congregations as their agent at Tangier. A protest made to the Sultan by the diplomatic corps at Tangier, calling attention to the non-punishment of offenders against the Jews, had only temporary results.[102] The crimes reached a horrible climax in Jewish massacres at Demnat in 1884 and 1885, which were followed by extensive emigration of Hebrews to the United States, Venezuela, and England.[103]

That fanaticism could not be exorcised by edict had long been Hay's conviction. Fairchild, who continued his interest in the Moroccan Jews, came to agree with Hay:

> It is to be hoped that the sultan of Morocco is not well informed of all that is taking place in Europe, for if he should learn of the anti-Jewish agitation which now exists in Germany ... he may feel encouraged to increase, rather than diminish, the oppressions of the same race in his dominions. We cannot expect to find a more enlightened liberality in Morocco than exists among the highly educated people of Europe.

After a visit to Tangier in March, 1881, Fairchild reported:

> The treatment of the Jews is not now in any perceptible degree better or more humane than it was before the writing of the letter of the sultan to the Madrid conference .... The Sultan dare not grant religious liberty to non-Moslems because of the danger of losing his throne .... European complications may arise which

> will be of vast benefit to Morocco, and I look forward with pleasure to the day ... when some one or more of the European nations will have gained such ascendancy over it as to be able to compel, by force if necessary, a more enlightened and liberal administration of affairs. Thus the people of Morocco can be relieved, and I see at present no other hope.[104]

Continuing to report atrocities against Jews, unpunished in spite of Mulai Hassan's many promises to take action, Mathews had described also the general deterioration of Moroccan government during 1879 and 1880. Crimes had increased in the proportion of one to twelve, and it was not Jews alone who were pillaged and massacred, for in the six months previous more than one hundred Muslims had been assassinated, although armed and in a position to defend themselves. The lives and property of Christians were also in jeopardy. During 1881 Mathews furnished evidence that the Sultan's edicts were being ignored or falsified by provincial governors. He also reviewed the traditional legal and social disabilities imposed on Jews, although they were the "mainstay of commerce and industry .... and the only link between civilization and barbarity." He made vigorous protests against the persecution of the Jews at Demnat.[105]

The Sultan was aggrieved because his expected revenues from the payment of agricultural and gate taxes by foreigners and protégés did not materialize. Because of protests from their nationals and consular officials the foreign representatives were unable to put into effect the regulations agreed upon with the Moroccan foreign minister. Commissions failed to settle disputes, and as late as 1884 no taxes had been collected. In retaliation, the Moroccan government refused to grant to any foreigner the right to acquire immovable property.[106]

The evils of protection were augmented after 1880 by the contest entered into by all foreign representatives--even the British, eventually--to secure equality in the number of commercial agents. Whereas before the Madrid conference only about a dozen <u>censaux</u> were from the rural districts, by April, 1881, the number was about 200. The foreign representatives were unable to agree in their interpretation of the terms relating to commercial agents, and each extended protection as he chose. The number of fraudulent and exorbitant claims presented by this class of protégés continued to grow and to menace the Moroccan treasury.[107]

It remained for France to demonstrate new possibilities in the protection system. Ordega, the French representative at Tangier since 1882, had boasted openly to his colleagues of his ambition to imitate his consular colleague in Tunisia. The close cooperation of Ferry[108] and Bismarck was no secret, and when France took under her protection early in 1884 the Sherif of Wazan, the other powers were prepared for any eventuality. The Sultan claimed this act to be illegal, because the Sherif had served him in settling tribal disputes, but France insisted on her right to reward the Sherif for similar special services in Algeria. Rumors were current that French protection would be extended to all the Sherif's officials and religious fathers, and regional disturbances tended to confirm reports that the Sherif planned to seize the throne and reign under French protection. War appeared inevitable for several months, and there is evidence that Ferry's scheme of a Franco-Spanish partition of Morocco was rejected by Spain. The Sherif of Wazan remained a French protégé, but Ordega was transferred to Bucharest, and Morocco remained intact.[109] Meanwhile, the French government was officially declaring its allegiance to the international pact guaranteeing the independence of Morocco.[110]

Although as late as the fall of 1884 there was talk of a Franco-German naval alliance, it failed to develop because of French suspicions of the German Machiavelli and fear of becoming involved with Great Britain.[111] The Franco-German cooperation continued only during 1885, and a forward policy in Morocco was not its objective in this year.

During 1884-1885 the interest of the great powers shifted suddenly from northern to central Africa. It had taken many years to convert Bismarck to the policy of adding colonies to the German Empire,[112] but the decision to raise the German flag over Angra Pequeña on April 24,

1884, marks the entrance of a new umpire on the diplomatic field. The great valley of the Congo, explored by an American, claimed by Portugal, coveted by France and Great Britain, and controlled by King Leopold I of Belgium, was masquerading by 1884 as an international state, the International Association of the Congo.[113] By an Anglo-Portuguese treaty of February, 1884, the hostility of the powers excluded from claims in the Congo was aroused. In cooperation with France, Bismarck adopted the Portuguese suggestion of an international conference and issued invitations to thirteen other countries[114] to meet at Berlin. The inclusion of the United States in the list was due mainly to the fact that she had been the only country to recognize the new Congo state and to send a consul there.[115] However, the American delegate did point out in an address to the conference that the first exploration of the Congo by Stanley, an American citizen, inspired his country to hope that this discovery might be utilized for civilization of the natives, abolition of the slave trade, and action to avoid international rivalry over special privileges.[116]

The Berlin Conference was in session from November 15, 1884 to February 26, 1885. In his opening address as chairman, Bismarck advocated the policy of transplanting the Open Door policy from Asiatic to African soil.[117] John A. Kasson, the American minister to Germany, attended as delegate for the United States, with instructions to work for unrestricted freedom of trade in a neutralized, international Free State of the Congo.[118] This was the first venture of the United States endeavoring to establish the policy of the Open Door by international agreement.

The conference was successful in formulating a General Act fulfilling the aims set forth in the agenda. It affirmed the principle of freedom of navigation and trade for all nations in the Congo and Niger basins, provided for the adoption of joint measures for the suppression of slavery and the slave trade, and made rules for the future acquisition of territory on the African coast.[119] By this concerted action Bismarck thought that he had broken the British hegemony in the colonial world.[120]

The American government, however, refused to ratify the convention signed by its representative. In the House of Representatives, without authority in this matter, several resolutions were introduced to the effect that "no commercial advantage warrants a departure from the traditional policy of this Government which forbids all entangling alliances with the nations of the Old World" or participation "in any political combination or movement outside the American continent."[121] The defeat of the treaty was insured by the attitude of incoming President Cleveland, who announced in his first message to Congress:

> Holding that an engagement to share in the obligation of enforcing neutrality in the remote valley of the Kongo would be an alliance[122] whose responsibilities we are not in a position to assume, I abstain from asking the sanction of the Senate to that general act.[123]

Although in his message of the following year Cleveland did declare a sort of moral protectorate over Liberia,[124] after he became president the United States discontinued abruptly the development of an African policy. After her participation in the Cape Spartel and Madrid conventions on Morocco and the Congo Conference, and after admitting an informal protectorate over Liberia, the United States might have become one of the major powers determining the fate of Africa. The Nation published several editorials pointing out the dangerous position from which the President had rescued the country:

> The appearance of our agents in such a Congress indicates nothing, therefore, but our willingness to become part of the 'European System,' to share in its deliberations ... and abide by its votes. That this position can be successfully defended while insisting on the absolute exclusion of Europe from all political influence on this continent is impossible .... We cannot maintain that our interest in the spread of civilization justifies us in joining Europe in settling the fate of Africa, when we deny that any interest in civilization would warrant Europe in settling the fate of Central and South America. Surely, if we admit that England, France, Germany, Italy, Austria, Russia, Belgium, and Portugal are not enough to manage the affairs of

> Central Africa, we cannot decently hold that the United States alone are competent to take charge of the American Continent from the Rio Grande to Cape Horn, covered as it is in great part either by pure savagery or by "rum, Romanism, and rebellion."[125]

While interest in Central Africa partially diverted European rivalries from Morocco, Hay continued his customary labors there. The last six years of his diplomatic career were spent in vain efforts to introduce reforms. So angered was Mulai Hassan at the results of the Madrid convention, that he persisted in his old policy of "promise, pause, postpone, and then leave the matter alone." In collaboration at times with the German, French, and Italian ministers, Hay carried on fruitless negotiations to secure a revision of the British commerce treaty of 1856. A severe drouth and famine in 1881 and the crisis of 1884 in Franco-Moroccan relations served as pretexts, among other incidents, for prolonged postponement so characteristically Moroccan, and a mission to Marrakesh in 1882 met with no success. Finally, early in 1887, the Sultan delivered the ultimatum that he would sign no new treaty until the abuses of protection were abolished. Hay lost also all his other campaigns--to abolish extortion by the trumped-up claims of protégés, to induce Mulai Hassan to cease his punitive expeditions for "eating up" his indigestible subjects, to institute among many prison reforms a restriction on the period of imprisonment for debt, and to secure the abolition of slavery. Slavery in Morocco Hay regarded as a rather benign institution, but there was a great deal of anti-slavery propaganda in British periodicals at this time. As throughout his whole residence in Morocco, Hay continued to be a champion of the Jews.[126]

When Hay retired in June, 1886[127] from sweeping the "Augean stable" kept by the "stupid and stagnant" government of Morocco, he was bitter over the noticeable waning of British influence. In apprehension over the growing power of France, he had suggested in the previous year a possible new policy to frustrate her:

> Germany apparently has an eye on the future .... If we can take no steps to check the aims of France to become the mistress of the Straits, and if it be found

> that Germany would be ready to confront France in her Algerine possessions by taking possession of this country, I should say that it would be far better that she should occupy the highway to the East and to India than France, which Power never ceases in all parts of the world to be the jealous and covert enemy of England.[128]

It was Spain, however, which made the next threatening gestures toward Morocco. In 1885 she revived old claims and raised her flag at an inlet called Rio de Oro where she declared a protectorate over a region of 270,000 square miles, extending to Cape Bojador. This area was not part of Morocco, but it was in close proximity along the Atlantic coast.[129] In November, 1887, she failed in her attempt to make an unobtrusive appropriation of Perejil Island.[130] Her proposal to summon another conference on Morocco in the same year was abandoned after a change of ministry.[131]

By 1887, however, Germany was becoming a power to be reckoned with in any calculations concerning the future of Morocco. Among several eminent European explorers of Morocco since 1850, was Dr. Gerhard Rohlfs, one of the greatest.[132] Diplomatic relations between Germany and Morocco were established in 1873. Following his early policy to let France find compensation for Alsace-Lorraine in Morocco, Bismarck refused the offer of a Moroccan port in 1878[133] and forbade German assistance to Abdal-Kader in 1883. There is no evidence that Bismarck endorsed popular writings urging the acquisition of a Germany colony in Morocco or that he stimulated the activity of the German consul in Tangier, who was charged by the French with fomenting pan-Islamic plots and schemes to divide Morocco between Spain and Turkey.

Although abstaining from territorial aggrandizement, the German government was fostering the establishment of economic interests under consular auspices. Between 1871 and 1886 sixteen business firms located in Morocco. To supplement official activities, there were numerous economic and scientific societies after 1880 which sponsored expeditions to Morocco (notably the one of 1886 led by Jannasch), issued serial publications, and carried on propaganda to encourage commerce with Morocco and other undeveloped areas.[134]

In Europe also Bismarck's diplomatic policy was being reorientated by 1887. Emerging out of a complicated background, in which British and German interests were ranged against those of France and Russia, were several pacts directly affecting Morocco. The first was an exchange of notes between the British and Italian governments on February 12, 1887, signed by Austria-Hungary also on March 24. The three powers agreed to uphold the status quo on the Mediterranean, Adriatic, Aegean, and Black Sea shores and to oppose all foreign invasion into these regions in a manner to be decided upon according to circumstances. In addition, Great Britain promised Italy support against a third power at "every other point whatsoever of the North African coast," and especially in Tripoli, in exchange for Italian support in Egypt. In order to induce Italy to renew the Triple Alliance, Bismarck inserted in the German-Italian treaty the pledge that Germany would fight with Italy against France, if the latter should extend her occupation, protectorate, or sovereignty in any form whatsoever in either Morocco or Tripoli. The renewal of the Triple Alliance on February 20 was followed on May 4 by a Spanish-Italian agreement, to which Austria-Hungary acceded, binding Spain not to make any political arrangement with France in regard to North Africa which was aimed against the interests of Italy, Germany, or Austria-Hungary. There was to be abstention from all unprovoked attack and provocation.[135] Thus Great Britain gained not only the aid of Germany against France, but also of Bismarck's Triple Alliance partners and of Spain as well.

The above agreements also contained clauses to checkmate Russian ambitions in the Balkans. The duplicity of Bismarck's diplomacy is shown by the three-year "reinsurance" treaty which he made with Russia on June 18, 1887. By this secret understanding each party was pledged to benevolent neutrality in case of a French attack on Germany or an Austrian advance on Russia.[136] Although the final strand in the net of entangling ententes broke in the spinning when Salisbury refused an Anglo-German alliance in 1889,[137] it seemed after 1887 that the German-led group would be able to dominate completely the future of North

Africa. Great Britain, outside the ring, was morally obligated to go to war if France should attack Morocco. But France refrained from attack. Throughout the 90's France adhered to the *status quo*, opposing equally the predominance of any power in Morocco or the latter's self-reformation. By preventing either individual of collective intervention, she hoped to preserve a future free for herself.[138] Events after 1895 helped to weaken, and eventually counter-diplomacy obliterated, the Moroccan stakes of all the entente-makers of 1887, except Germany. And in the meanwhile, the international settlement made at Madrid was giving cumulative proofs of its impotence.

In 1887 Mathews followed his arch-opponent Hay out of the diplomatic service in Morocco. Aside from his pro-Jewish activities, after 1880, Mathews had reported on the concerns and actions routine in his position. As usual, he had asked for funds (about $1500) to repair the badly damaged consular house, had pressed American protégés' claims against the Moroccan citizens and government, and had complained at length about the corrupt and inefficient Moorish government with its antiquated taxation system and extortion causing recurrent rebellions. He had lamented the fact that in spite of his unremitting efforts the United States did not raise its low rank in commerce.[139] During 1881 Mathews described the commercial field open to foreign nations, including the United States, in the area between Morocco and Timbuctoo and the regions of the Sus and Wadnoon. Here, in the *blad-es-siba*, an English company had established a trading post in 1878. To prevent the local natives from falling under European control, in 1882 the Sultan opened the port of Agadir. Later he warned foreign traders that they would trade elsewhere on the Wadnoon coast at their own peril.[140] Mathews had kept vigilant watch over the foreign relations of Morocco also. He narrated the disputes over tribal raids into Algeria and the protection of the Sherif of Wazan by France, as well as the conciliatory attitude of France after Ordega's transfer. He noted the more aggressive moves of Spain after the Madrid convention. There was no apparent neglect of official duty to cause his removal from the post where, in January, 1884, he had served fourteen years without a vacation.[141]

Moreover, there had been some evidence of State Department approval of the record of Mathews. At his request, his son Jasper had been appointed vice consul at Tangier, an unsalaried post, so that Mathews would not have to demean himself by transacting the business of the Cape Spartel Lighthouse and the Board of Health with the vice-consuls of the other countries. Of greater importance was the raising of the consulate to the grade of diplomatic agency and the consulate-general, with an increase of salary for the consul-general to $3,000.[142]

However, the State Department was at last convinced that Mathews was deeply involved in the progressive corruption of protection. At the beginning of 1881 Mathews transmitted to Washington a list of American protégés, a total of thirteen men, seven commercial and consular agents and six employees at the Tangier consulate.[143] During the next five years rumors persisted at Tangier that Mathews and his staff were guilty on two counts--selling irregular protection and harassing the Moroccan government with large, often fraudulent, claims made by American citizens and protégés, for which unprotected natives were often imprisoned and cruelly punished. Mathews became virtually ostracised by his fellow diplomats.[144] Early in 1886 the rumors became a public indictment when Ion Perdicaris, a Greek claiming American citizenship, appeared as a champion of the Moors and the nemesis of Mathews.[145]

The Mathews-Perdicaris feud started when the former protested the intervention of the French minister in the case of a Moor charged with murder, whom Perdicaris then repudiated as his protected _semsar._ Perdicaris accused Mathews of having foisted upon him in the protégé lists many wealthy Jews and Moors from whom only the consulate had received pecuniary rewards. Mathews then removed from his records all _semsars_ credited to Perdicaris. After Perdicaris had complained of Mathews in person at the State Department in Washington, an investigation of the charges was ordered. The investigation was conducted by Darius Ingraham, American consul at Cadiz. In his report of this inquiry, Mathews charged that Perdicaris aimed to replace Mathews and to force out as many foreign landholders from Tangier as possible in order to acquire their holdings cheaply. On March 25, 1886, Acting Secretary Porter informed Mathews that he had been completely vindicated by Ingraham's report.[146]

Although rebuffed in his first attack on Mathews, Perdicaris did not long remain silent. In a book published in London[147] he charged that he had discovered 142 natives, American protégés, who were pressing claims totalling $100,000 at a time when there were only three real American citizens in all Morocco.[148] Mathews reported to Washington that Perdicaris and Captain Rolleston, an English newspaper correspondent, interferred with American traders, circulated calumnious reports in Morocco, sent articles to European and American newspapers, and tried to bribe Moorish witnesses to testify against the United States consulate. Clippings enclosed with Mathews' dispatches showed that while the New York World, the London Times and Globe, and the Madrid Imparcial accepted the charges of Perdicaris, the three Moroccan papers, the Times, the Réveil du Maroc, and the Al-Maghreb Al-Aksa defended and praised the American consul. Perdicaris also sent further evidence to the State Department.[149]

The climax to this scandalous affair came when an ex-American protégé accused of several crimes and refused assistance by Mathews, escaped trial by a Moorish tribunal by taking refuge at the home of Perdicaris. Since Perdicaris refused to surrender the man and offered armed resistance by his servants to Moorish authorities, Mathews arrested Perdicaris for 24 hours and charged him a $50 fine and $6.50 costs for contempt of court, insubordination, and defiance of authority. The native aroused much sympathy among foreign residents of Tangier, to whom he alleged that he had been imprisoned by Jasper Mathews for refusing to pay a sum of $10,000 to the vice-consul. Perdicaris went to Washington to prefer charges against Mathews for "persecution" of his ex-protégé, and in the Trenton Daily True American of October 16, 1886, he published a detailed public indictment of Mathews. Mathews asserted that the imprisonment was wholly by orders of the Moroccan authorities, was caused by the prisoner's failure to provide bail, and had been prolonged only by the illness of the Moroccan Foreign Minister.[150]

Evidently the State Department was impressed by the evidence offered by Perdicaris, for after a third investigation of his conduct on protection, Mathews was found guilty of giving irregular protection to a large number of natives, was reprimanded, and was directed to conform to the Madrid convention. The foreign representatives at Tangier had a number of secret meetings to discuss the charges of extortion made by the imprisoned Moor against Mathews and his son.[151] Mathews again tried to defend himself, protesting against the State Department's order that he make reparation to Perdicaris by returning the $56.50 assessed against him and reviewing the grounds of the original action. Later he reported a total of 66 protégés of all classes in the Tangier district and denied that imprisoned debtors were subjected to whipping and that anyone except Perdicaris had ever been imprisoned by the American consulate. This last statement was corroborated by Muhammad ben El Arby Torres. But all the protestations of Mathews were in vain; in February, 1887, the State Department notified him that his successor had been appointed.[152] Writing from New York on May 11, 1887, Mathews requested from Porter "a word on the cause of my dismissal after thirty-seven years in national service in several departments." On May 20, 1887, the Department made the laconic reply that he had been recalled "for the promotion of public service."[153]

The exposé of Mathews was at least partly responsible for the proposal of a new conference at Madrid to reconsider protection problems. The other interested governments expressed their favorable attitude to the Spanish government. Disagreements arose, however, when the proposed agenda encountered varying views from the Sultan and the different governments. The conference project had to be abandoned,[154] and the Madrid Convention declined steadily in prestige and observance.

Appointed to clean up the mess made by Mathews, William Reed Lewis began work giving loyal lip service to reform. But in his short term of office, from March 14, 1887, to January 8, 1890, he brought the status of his office to a new low.

Lewis introduced very early the three topics customary for new consuls--the necessity for repair of the consular house, the absence or ambiguity of his predecessor's accounts, and the desirability of his promotion to rank of consul general and diplomatic agent.[155] The State Department could not reconcile the reported condition of the consulate with the expenditures vouched for by Mathews and admitted that the United States had no valid title to the property other than the will of the Sultan. Lewis recommended that the building be sold for business and a new one be acquired outside the town walls. Regarding accounts, Lewis asked whether consular fees should not have been included in financial reports to the State Department. His coming as a consul, Lewis said, caused the ignorant Moors to believe that Col. Mathews was still his superior officer.[156]

In an early account of the foreign relations of Morocco, Lewis described the crisis of October, 1887, when Mulai Hassan was reported dead from typhoid fever then epidemic in the interior. There were twenty known aspirants for his throne, and there was a swarming of warships to protect foreigners from an anticipated general revolution. At Tangier were naval vessels from France, Spain, Portugal, Great Britain, Italy, and Germany, but none from the United States, while Spanish troops were concentrated along the Mediterranean, especially near Ceuta. Lewis thought that at Tangier the greatest danger was from the large population of lawless but patriotic Spaniards. But the Sultan survived, and before the end of the year Feraud, the French minister, had made a successful mission to his court, whence he returned with a large indemnity for a murdered French officer and an arrangement for the continuance of a French mission in Meknes and French military attachés at the Sherifian court.[157]

Like all preceding consuls, Lewis felt obligated to make reports on the hypothetical American-Moroccan commerce. He stressed the large market open for American imports if there were any direct communication and pointed out that existing exports were not listed in the customs because of indirect shipping. In April, 1889, he boasted of a large increase in exports to the United States under his promotion, but complained that Moorish officials placed many obstacles in the way of American commerce.[158]

The major part of Lewis's correspondence with the State Department concerns his handling of the protection problem. He began this onerous task by obtaining the release of seventeen persons in prison for alleged debts to American protégés; this was accomplished by the aid of the British minister, W. Kirby Green, and in spite of the underhanded opposition of Sid Hadj Muhammad Torres, the Sultan's foreign minister at Tangier, who remained antagonistic to Lewis. Lewis was much inconvenienced from the beginning by the "abusive and untruthful" articles in the Moroccan press and in the London Times. Throughout his stay he was harassed by Levi Cohen, editor of Le Révilé du Maroc and professional partisan of "Barbary Jewry," whom Lewis accused of frustrating him in order to show the terrible loss Mathews had been to Morocco. Lewis asked to have a former State Department directive for consular aid to Cohen rescinded.[159]

A series of dispatches from Lewis pertained to inquiries regarding the cases of individuals listed as American protégés, many of them evidently through fraudulent naturalization or in violation of the Madrid treaty. John Cobb was replaced as consular agent at Casablanca by Joseph Roffe; both of these men were later enemies of Lewis. Lewis reduced the list of consular agents from over ninety to thirteen, declaring that there were no longer "unofficial" or unlisted American protégés in Morocco. Lewis was obliged to have a British vice consul because there were only three native Americans in Tangier. "Ion Perdicaris, who has left Morocco with his family to be absent at least eighteen months; the Rev. Baldwin, here only occasionally; and Jasper Mathews, whose connection with many gross outrages proves him to be a totally unfit man for any position under our government." Because of these innovations, John Cobb sent communications to Porter denouncing Lewis for being totally ignorant of the language, manners, and customs of the country, being surrounded by a pro-Perdicaris clique interpreters and advisers, and for busily selling off the minor consulates to the highest bidder. In his reply to this diatribe, Lewis ascribed Cobb's enmity to his friendship for Mathews and to Lewis's refusal to accept a bribe to reappoint Cobb as consular agent. Lewis categorically denied that he or his staff were in any way under the influence of Perdicaris, that he was neglecting

American business interests, or that he was selling consular agencies.[160]

By the end of 1887 Lewis reported great advances in his crusade to reform protection. Through the cooperation of Mulai Hassan, he had persuaded the governors of the various provinces to send all prisoners held on account of American claims to Tangier. By September 13 a total of 42 men, women, and children had been released, some by death. In his year-end report Lewis said that since March he had been able to entirely reorganize the American system of protection and to bring all its operations within the provisions of existing treaties. On his arrival he had found over 800 persons enjoying protection. Under Mathews, the names of the official protégés had been forwarded only in part to the Department and the class of unofficial protégés had been by far the larger. An example of the latter class was the inhabitants of a village near Tangier famed for boar hunts; about 300 employed as beaters had refused to pay taxes because their village was an American colony. Now all unofficial protection had been entirely abolished and all official protégés were named on the lists sent to Washington. On January 1, 188, there were 104 officially listed protégés under the United States consulate--29 employees of the consul and his subordinates, 26 semsars, and 49 American citizens residing in Morocco.[161]

In striking contrast to the foregoing indictment of Mathews' conduct was the judgment passed by Lewis just seven months later, in this comprehensive analysis of his predecessor's personality and career in Tangier:

> From the year 1870 until the 15th of March 1887, ... our country was represented in Morocco by Colonel Felix A. Mathews, a native of Tangier, and a man who, but for the abuses of the protégé system, would have been a Moorish subject; but who, the natural son of a British subject by a Spaniard, was taken under British protection about the year 1845 when nine years of age, his father, Dr. Gaspar M. Ximenes, a political refugee, having died.
>
> Colonel Mathews was reared in an atmosphere of political and domestic corruption such as was common here

forty or fifty years ago, he left here as a lad for America, and rose, as a man can ... in our country, from nothing, to the standing of an honorable citizen and soldier, and within a comparatively few years, was sent to represent the country of his adoption in that of his nativity. Col. Mathews was shrewd, clever, and personally agreeable; but a true oriental in the careless administration of his office, a carelessness, which, at last, brought him to trouble, and gave color to charges, for many of which, his subordinates were guilty, and which never, in a civilized land, could be proved against him.

I am personally familiar with all the charges that have been made against Col. Mathews, and there is not one of them that cannot be proved against every member of the Diplomatic Corps at Tangier today. The sale of protection and of Agencies can be proved by the simple purchase of oaths, which can be bought as easily as a bale of hides; for no native's oath is of the least value to any honest man. I am convinced that, while every charge against Col. Mathews could be proved by purchased evidence, none of a serious character would be proved honorably. I believe that his subordinates were corrupt, and further, that he had not, in anger, a nice enough perception of delicate points of justness and honor, perhaps by reason of his early education and surroundings here.

In regard to his abuses of the protégé system, he acted with all his colleagues without system, without care, but generally in a manner to alleviate the oppression of a race always persecuted here.

In regard to the imprisonment of debtors, he knew that imprisonment was the only method of collecting debts in Morocco, and with all his colleagues countenanced its use. Philanthropy, being more common among native born Americans than among the native born subjects of Barbary.

In regard to bribery, I believe that he was morally innocent of it, he accepted and gave presents right and left; as did his predecessors, and his colleagues; when

> he was asked a favor or a right a present was brought to him, and when he wanted either, he carried in his hand the same: in short, I believe that Col. Mathews is morally innocent of the charges made against him from time to time, though that under the quality of evidence to be purchased here, and unsparingly used against him, he could never have proved his innocence away from here, that he is, alone, to blame for a careless, and shiftless, administration of his office, due largely, if not entirely, to his nativity and early life.
>
> I have gone thus fully into the charges made against my predecessor ... because I am anxious that any impression which my early dispatches and letters may have given as to his character, may be further informed, by these remarks, indeed, a common act of justice to Col. Mathews.

As a means of enhancing the prestige and authority of the American representative, Lewis urged that the consul be given the title and prerogatives of a chargé d'affaires, on a par with his colleagues and that he be received with due ceremony on arrival from an American war vessel. Lewis did not ask this promotion for himself, as he would welcome a transfer soon to northern Europe, England, or Canada.[162]

Concerning the reconvening of the Madrid conference proposed for May, 1888, Lewis and Perdicaris had opposing opinions. Lewis suggested to the State Department that another international convention to abolish protection was unnecessary and undesirable. With two added provisions the Treaty of Madrid could be made effective. One was to guarantee the Sultan's revenues by requiring all foreign subjects and protégés to pay regular taxes, agreed upon by all the powers and collected by the consulates. The other was to have the Department of State regulate the granting of protection to native semsars only for exporting and importing with United States merchants. Spain's motives in urging the conference, Lewis asserted, were well known in Morocco; Spain had no commercial interests there, but was imbued with a desire for the expansion of territory and political power. If protection were abolished, merchants of other nations would be obliged to entrust their commercial interests either to the Spanish, the largest foreign element in Morocco, or to the Gibraltar British. By increasing the number of her nationals in Morocco, Spain could eventually take over Morocco, and "the ignorantly corrupt government of Morocco is preferable to that of Spain." Without protection, the Jews would be completely at the mercy of the Moors and Spaniards. Perdicaris was gratified that a new conference was in prospect. His plan for reform was a collective consular tribunal to try all cases of foreigners and to hear all claims against natives before presenting them to the Moorish authorities. Thus usury, forgery, and cruel imprisonment of debtors as well as extortion such as practiced by the American consulate in a notorious case could be eliminated. The Sultan should abolish economic restrictions, honor the right of foreigners to acquire land, and allow concessions for development of public works.[163] But there was no second Madrid conference, and the abuses of protection persisted.

When Lewis strayed from the path of virtue which he continued to map in his dispatches to Washington is not indicated in them. He had complained at the end of 1887 that the Moroccan foreign minister was systematically obstructing and delaying his reform efforts, because, on an annual salary of $300, Torres could not live if abuses of consular protection were ended.[164] From March to November of 1888 much of the official correspondence of Lewis related to his controversies with Sid Muhammad Torres over the latter's refusal to recognize certain protégés claimed by the American consulate, the ill-treatment of American protégés and denial of their claims by Moroccan authorities, and personal insults to Lewis. Lewis accused the Spanish minister of encouraging Torres, and his suspicion was publicized in the New York World. On April 7, 1888, Lewis introduced an innovation for resolving disputes in Morocco--arbitration was agreed upon to settle the claims against the Moorish government for its neglect or refusal to observe and enforce the treaty rights of American citizens and protégés. It was notable that both Hay's successor, Sir William Kirby, and the Italian minister urged the Sultan to accept this arbitration. When Mulai Hassan refused to accept the initial agreement, Mr. Strobel, the secretary of the United States Legation at Madrid, was directed on April 28, 1888, to go to Tangier to assist Lewis.

After negotiating from May 2 to May 8, with the aid of Commander Folger of the U. S. S. *Quinnebaug*, Lewis and Strobel completed a second arrangement. By this four matters were to be decided, with other claims eligible for presentation, by Lewis and two appointees of the Sultan. In case of the disagreement of this tribunal, one of the foreign representatives at Tangier might be named umpire. After Lewis had summoned a "naval show" to Tangier, an award was made on the four claims specifically enumerated on May 15, without the need of an umpire. Other private claims were submitted to a sub-committee. Ten days later the Sultan thanked Lewis for inaugurating the new system in Morocco.[165] After reforming the method of settling claims of foreigners and protégés, Lewis proceeded to settle the Jewish Problem in protection. To end the persecution of Jews by giving them really effective protection, he suggested placing the entire Hebrew population of Morocco under an international protectorate. This would replace the twelve often conflicting jurisdictions failing to safeguard the minority of protected Jews, chiefly the wealthy and predatory class. Under such a tribunal, taxes could be collected equitably from all Jews and foreign Jewish alliances would lose their opportunity to exploit those who reveled, for a price, in persecution.[166]

After a six month's trial of the arbitration system, however, Lewis pronounced it as "kept only outwardly" by the Moors. The total amount claimed was $440, 000, without interest, and only two of the cases had been settled. He declared that the inaction of the Moorish government was due to its belief that the State Department would not enforce settlement of private claims. The claims of all other countries had been collected from the Sultan, some during the presence of ironclads. In 1889 there were new disputes over recent claims. Lewis blamed Strobel's theory of diplomacy by arbitration, supported by Lewis's colleagues at Tangier, against which Lewis had argued in vain. He therefore urged the direct and forceful intervention of the State Department to compel Moroccan adherence to American treaty rights.[167]

Other difficulties plaguing Lewis in 1889 came to the attention of the State Department. A Jewish moneylender asked the latter to pay from Lewis's salary the loan made to the consul; Lewis paid the debt himself, alleging that this was an instance of supporters of Mathews trying to get him recalled. Joseph Roffe, whom Lewis had appointed vice-consul at Casablanca, resigned by request, to be replaced by John Cobb, and wrote several letters directly to the State Department charging Lewis with ignoring evidence of Cobb's extending and withdrawing protection for money and other irregularities, as well as refusing to pay the Sultan rent for property he had occupied for nine years. Roffe alleged also that Lewis and Cobb acted together to sell consular agencies. He furnished clippings from Moroccan newspapers detailing these corrupt practices of Lewis. Learning of Roffe's tattling, Lewis, in a rage, grossly insulted Roffe. Robert Stalker, acting consul during Lewis's absence, also forwarded to Washington a defamatory communication against Roffe from Cobb. Roffe seems to have had no response from Secretary Blaine to several cables during November and December, 1889, begging for an investigation.[168] However, the impact of charges against Lewis was finally forcing action by his superiors.

Accusations of official corruption were serious enough, but there was added to this the charge that Lewis was a wife-murderer. A private inquiry directed by United States Consul Folsom of Sheffield absolved him from the last charge. Lewis finally cabled Secretary Blaine that he preferred removal at request of the Moors to resignation, and he got his wish. Budgett Meakin has given this version of the incidents which ended the career of Lewis:

> Notwithstanding all the complaints that reached the State Department at Washington, no redress could be obtained, and only official white-washings resulted. At last Morocco reeked with charges and allegations against the United States consul, and the Moorish Government, unable to put up with him any longer telegraphed to President Harrison in 1889, demanding his recall. It is true that this request was at once acceded to, and the recall made by wire next morning; but the Moorish Government received no other answer than a visit from the consul at Gibraltar, who was sent to arrange for a temporary substitute. Nor was any

notice taken of its formal letter of complaint and explanation, of which the telegram was an epitome, penned by the writer. Such behavior on the part of the officials of the State Department was a grave political error.

A curious attempt at bluff was made by the consul ... when the Moors began to disregard his threats and to formulate their own complaints against him .... Sid Haj Muhammad Torres ... refused attention to certain claims made by the United States consul, on the ground that they were manifestly unjust. The consul thereupon threatened that if his demands were not attended to by a given date he would summon two vessels of war; and he later fixed the date on or about which they were to arrive, and, if need be, bombard the town .... It was pointed out that the local English paper had mentioned some weeks previously that two American training ships had sailed for the Old World, and that about the date mentioned they would be at Tangier.

.... The consul was promptly informed that he would no longer be permitted to extend the protection of the American flag to any one who could pay his price .., or to have Moorish subjects arrested and thrown into jail without trial ... and that if he continued to sell customs passes, intended to cover only his own personal effects and provisions, for the smuggling in of contraband goods, that privilege would be withdrawn from him and the cases in question searched .... When the next case of arms was taken from the bonded stores under his order, the customs administrators refused to pass it unopened. The consul ... arrived on the scene with the Stars and Stripes, supported by a posse .... But the lieutenant governor ... was there before him with the police, and the rash American had to content himself with wrapping the case in the flag and protesting against the insult. It was at this point that the Moorish patience gave out, and that afternoon his recall was demanded by wire.[169]

Robert Stalker, the former vice consul who served as acting consul from January 8 till May 1, 1890, was occupied chiefly with disposing of claims against Lewis for illegal imprisonment and trying in vain to have Sid Muhammad Torres recognize and protect semsars of an American firm of Philadelphia. He also forwarded to the State Department a lengthy statement by ex-consul Lewis from the Times of Morocco, repeating and editorializing on a New York Sun dispatch. Lewis alleged that the charges against him were the result of "tittle-tattle by the wife of the English representative and his recall was the work of an English editor in Tangier." Thus the Anglo-American feud in Morocco was being continued. Stalker also made a significant report that Count Tattenbach had left on April 12 with a large entourage of official, military, and civilian persons on a mission to the Sultan. Stalker declared it to be well known that Germany coveted a coaling station near the French frontier in Algeria as a base for future operations against either Algeria or Morocco, should another European war enable her to oust France from North Africa. It was also believed that Germany desired a protectorate over Morocco, to be acquired by persuading the Sultan that only Germany could be relied upon to be a disinterested and powerful protector.[170]

Mulai Hassan was indeed searching for a new patron after the departure of Sir John Drummond Hay in 1886. In 1888 he turned for succor, not to Washington, where his predecessor had failed, but to Rome. A Moroccan mission was sent on the advice of Spain and in a Spanish war vessel.[171] The naïvete of the Sultan in his apparent belief that the Pope was still ruling Christendom and would therefore be able and willing to save Morocco from his subject nations is perhaps understandable. The Spanish motives are not so easily comprehended.

Under the successors of Hay, British power and prestige were steadily declining. The first, Sir (then Mr.) William Kirby Green, former vice-consul at Tetuan and fluent in Moorish Arabic, made two missions to Mulai Hassan's court. In a three months' stay at Marrakesh in 1887, he had success in some minor matters. In 1888 he proposed mixed native tribunals as an alternative for protection for all native protégés except those officially employed. Of major importance to Great Britain was Sir William's second mission, begun in December, 1890, to secure payment of many British claims and reparation for the Cape Juby "massacre." Founded in 1880 as an adventursome enterprise by a British merchant, McKenzie, the North-West Africa Company at Cape Juby in the Sus had been attacked in 1888 by the Sultan's orders. The manager was killed and two other persons were injured. Since trade had been disappointing, the adventurers agreed to sell out. The strong intervention of the British minister, reinforced by the menacing presence of British ironclads,[172] compelled the Sultan to pay £50,000 to the company and £5,000 to the family of the murdered manager. The British Government acknowledged the sovereignty of the Sultan to the Draa and Cape Bojador, and the Moors agreed never to part with any portion of that district without the consent of Great Britain. Tarfaia was to be opened to commerce under the regular customs system. The Sultan raised some difficulties over minor details of the settlement. The strain of the controversy caused the death of the British minister.[173] On the whole, the Sultan had won the greater advantage in the transaction.

Meanwhile, a prophetic article on future British policy had appeared in the London Times of August 22, 1888 under the title "Great Britain's Policy in Africa, by an African explorer." The author, Sir Harry Johnston, was a man of prestige and influence, and his views thus publicized could not fail to win adherents in high places. His plan was that Great Britain should resign any ambitions in North Africa and use this region as a means to win friends for her legitimate objective to obtain Egypt as a vessel state and the regions south of that, including the Sudan, as a protected area under a chartered company or British residents at the courts of native rulers. A natural division of North Africa would assign Tripoli and Barca to Italy; Tunisia, Algeria, and part of eastern Morocco to France; and the major part of Morocco to Spain. This thesis of Johnston was to become, with modification on Morocco, virtually Lord Salisbury's African policy.[174]

One last serious attempt was made to uphold the British Monroe Doctrine. Arriving as minister at Tangier in November, 1891, Sir Charles Euan-Smith headed another mission to Mulai Hassan's capital. The British envoy came to propose a new commercial treaty designed to end the seclusion and misrule which remained the foundation of the

Moroccan government. Euan-Smith was instructed by Salisbury to avoid any menace in presenting the document, which was to benefit all the signers of the Madrid Convention and was supported by Germany, Italy, Austria-Hungary, and to some degree by Spain, but was covertly opposed by France. After four weeks of negotiations, the Sultan accepted all the articles of the proposed treaty except the three vitally important ones--amendment of the customs tariff of 1856, permission for sea transportation of goods between Moroccan ports without duty, and recognition of the unrestricted right of foreigners to purchase land and other immovable property and to build or rebuild thereon without hindrance. The British minister rejected both the offer of a large bribe to accept the truncated treaty and a new draft prepared by the Moors and submitted unofficially. The Sultan's rejection of the British request for a vice consul in Fez was probably due to his fear that the wealthy Moroccans there would buy protection from such an official and would thus cause the loss of the principal imperial revenues. The French minister, having frustrated the British aims, was disappointed in turn, for he had to return from his mission with little except less than twenty-five percent of the French claims settled--and even these were nullified by the Moroccan way of drawing up the concessions. No blame attached to Euan-Smith for his failure, yet after his leave at home it was learned at Tangier early in January, 1893, that Sir Joseph West Ridgeway was appointed as special envoy to the Sultan.[175]

While Great Britain had been slipping from her once dominant position in the Sherifian Empire, the United States had very emphatically renounced further African adventures. In 1890 the official American hostility to the slave trade, which was still flourishing in Morocco, led to participation of the United States in the Brussels Conference. In its resolution advising the ratification of the General Act for Repression of the African Slave Trade the Senate made very clear its attitude in regard to all African political questions:

> Resolved: ... that the United States of America, having neither possessions nor protectorates in Africa, hereby disclaims any interest whatsoever in the possessions or protectorates established or claimed on that Continent

> by the other powers, or any approval of the wisdom, expediency, or lawfulness thereof, and does not join in any expressions in the said General Act which might be construed as such a declaration.[176]

This resolution served notice on Europe that the United States was not inclined to uphold the independence of Morocco as guaranteed in the Madrid Convention.

The indifference of the American public to the enforcement of this act is indicated in contemporary periodicals. Lambert Tree, in "The Treaty of Brussels and Our Duty," The Forum, XII (Jan., 1892), 614-620, says: "This conference, which sat for the greater part of a year and discussed many problems of vital importance to humanity, attracted scarcely any attention on this side of the Atlantic." The author spoke of the large trade in slaves from Morocco to Persia and suggested that the minimum obligation of the United States should be to guard her own flag from abuse by slavers, to prevent the introduction of firearms and ammunition into Africa, and to punish her own citizens guilty of treaty violation. William Sharp, in "Cardinal Lavigerie's Work in North Africa," Atlantic Monthly, LXXIV (Aug., 1894), 214-227, indicted the European nations also for nonobservance of the treaty. "At the moment, there are international jealousies, half-hearted ideals, and chauvinistic temporizings which together militate strongly against the success of this noble war of emancipation." Writing on "Slavery and the Slave Trade in Africa," in Harper's Magazine, LXXXVI, (March, 1893), 613-632, Henry M. Stanley was especially critical of Morocco. The missions of Sir John Drummond Hay and Sir William Kirby Green to the Moroccan Court had been futile. Only concerted action by England, France, Germany, and Spain could succeed in stopping the slave traffic from the Niger basin and the Sudan into the public slave markets of Morocco. "It is surely high time that the 'China of the West' should be made to feel that its present condition is a standing reproach to Europe .... Morocco remains stupidily indifferent and inert, a pitiful example of senility and decay."

From 1890 on there was a steady and substantial advance of Germany on the economic front of Morocco.

The second Moroccan mission to Berlin in 1889 received an elaborate reception, which may have facilitated the conclusion of the German-Moroccan commercial treaty of 1890. Negotiated by Count Christian von Tattenbach,[177] this treaty was the most favorable yet granted by any sultan. It fixed definite import and export duties, permitted the export of products long on the prohibited list, and provided that the treaty should endure until a new one could be ratified by both parties.[178] Thereafter the German treaty was considered a model for others with Morocco. In 1890 the German trade with Morocco was double that of the previous year, and it continued to increase proportionately over that of France and Great Britain during the next decade. This expansion of commerce is attributable largely to the founding of the first direct steamship line between Germany and Morocco in 1890.[179]

In 1890 Mathews returned to his post at Tangier,[180] replacing Stalker on May 1.[181] It undoubtedly gave him great satisfaction to send to the State Department the clipping describing his "brilliant reception" at the pier by Moors, Christians, and Jews, including all the Moorish dignitaries. The Times of Morocco again castigated his predecessor:

> We cannot help sympathizing with the Colonel in the difficult task which lies before him, in repairing mischief wrought by the remarkable Consul who has lately been removed by the United States Government at the request of the Moorish Government. The only honest course for the United States Government to adopt is to compensate the poor victims of their Representative's eccentricities, for the fearful suffering which he has inflicted upon them. Many are in prison now for debts contracted to satisfy his unjust demands. These should be liberated at once. The Colonel may now look down with dignified pity and forgiveness upon those who so mercilessly slandered him; we feel sure that there is no room for vindictiveness in his large and generous heart.
>
> It would not be a little vexing to the Colonel to find the consulate uninhabitable. We understand that the American Government voted $2500 to put the Consulate

> into thorough repair, but Mr. Reed Lewis merely patched it up in a temporary manner, and the roof and floors are now so completely rotted by long exposure to the soaking rains that they are considered past repair, and even dangerous; but this is a small matter compared with others that await investigation.[182]

The other matters were indeed given priority by Mathews. Erasing the trail of Lewis, marked by numerous corrupt and illegal practices, was a task calling for most of his successor's correspondence between May 29, 1890 and March 25, 1891. Accused of numerous extortions at Casablanca, Roffe complained again to Secretary Blaine of Cobb's irregular proceedings there and of his connivance with Mathews. To this accusation Mathews replied with a complete exoneration of Cobb and character testimonials for him,[183] while condemning Roffe's disreputable career as American vice consul. Numerous instances were related of the selling of protection certificates by Lewis, employment of his subordinates for extortion, and sale of his influence to pseudo-Americans. Mathews also reported that many holders of American protection certificates refused to surrender them unless the purchase price was returned to them.[184]

After describing the ruinous condition of the consulate allowed by Lewis, Mathews obtained the requested appropriation from Congress for both repairs and additions, including a new drawing-room, "the most creditable and elegant hall in the Empire." Mathews was disturbed because the United States had no valid title to the property, since it had been granted to John Mullowny. Mullowny's later sale of half of the ground and Carr's sale of another portion, as well as the attempted sale by Lewis of all the property were all illegal. However, with great difficulty Mathews obtained from his friend, the new bashaw of the province, a _moulkia_, in Moroccan law the most perfect title to the property, even against the Sultan. He therefore sent to the State Department the title deed to the building and ground, obtained at a cost of sixty-five dollars.[185] Since Article XI of the Madrid Convention, granting foreigners the right to purchase real estate, was reputed to be generally violated by the Sultan, it is noteworthy that Mathews referred to "the immense amount of real estate owned by

American citizens in and around Tangier." He even quoted his enemy Perdicaris as follows:

> Extra-mural Tangier is virtually a European and not a Moorish town, since the great majority of the owners of both land and buildings are either citizens or protected subjects of some one or other of the foreign powers .... Notwithstanding the fact that there are but few citizens of the United States who own property in the Empire of Morocco, yet we are the possessors of as much, if not more, real estate in and near Tangier than the subjects of any foreign power.[186]

In his reports on American-Moroccan commerce for 1891 and 1892, Mathews reiterated his admonition of two decades--this trade could not flourish without direct steamship communication. Nevertheless, the possibilities of its development were attested by the fact that both exports and imports were increasing. In 1891, American goods valued at $129,050 had been imported into Morocco _via_ England and Gibraltar, and other articles had passed through second or third hands to be listed finally as imports from France, Germany, and Gibraltar. Mathews called attention to the fact that the recent treaties with Germany and France made certain improvements in export and import rates to which the United States was entitled as a most favored nation.[187]

With an apparent mellowing of his habitual attitude of antagonism toward British activities in Morocco, Mathews deplored the bad relations between Sir Charles Euan-Smith and the Sultan and the subsequent failure of the former to obtain a more favorable treaty of commerce. "There is no question," he wrote, "of any understanding which would unnecessarily excite the susceptibilities of other powers."[188]

Of the secret agreements of Germany concerning Morocco, of course, Mathews knew nothing. In the renewal of the Triple Alliance on May 6, 1891, Germany accepted a considerable extension of her commitments in North Africa. Germany and Italy pledged a maintenance of the territorial _status quo_ in Cyrenaica, Tripoli, and Tunisia. But if both should recognize "after a mature examination" and a "formal and previous agreement" that this was impossible, Germany would support Italy in any occupation or other taking of guaranty in these regions in the interest of equilibrium or legitimate compensation. The accession of Great Britain was to be sought with regard to these areas and Morocco in addition. The Spanish-Italian agreement of 1887 was also prolonged by the identical notes of May, 1891. Spain added a reservation that her freedom of action to maintain the security of her Moroccan frontier should not be impaired.[189]

Italy was disappointed at the check put upon her speedy seizure of Tripoli by this treaty. The exclusion of Morocco from the arrangement was intended to prevent Germany's headstrong ally from conflicting there with France, Great Britain, or Spain.[190] An attempt to make Great Britain a co-guarantor of the German pledges in North Africa was frustrated by a protest in Parliament. When Rosebery succeeded Salisbury as foreign secretary in 1892, because of the opposition of Prime Minister Gladstone and Chancellor of the Exchequer Harcourt, Rosebery could only renew the pledges of 1887 and state that the English Cabinet would not regard with indifference the defeat of Italy by France.[191]

The strength of the repaired network of ententes was tested in August, 1890 and January, 1891, when the Italian and German governments tried to push Great Britain forward to protest against France's reported intention to seize the oasis of Tuat and to rectify her frontiers at Tripoli's expense.[192] The visit of Kaiser William II and Baron von Marschall to Windsor in July, 1891, gave an opportunity for a general discussion of the situation. Salisbury admitted apprehension over France's designs in Syria and Morocco. Marschall refused to commit himself, however; he said that Germany had no interest in Morocco and could not risk war on two fronts by opposing Russia at Constantinople.[193] In view of the frankly expressed indifference of the German Government, the failure to spur Salisbury to action through Spain and Italy is not surprising, for British public opinion would not sanction a war over Tuat.[194]

Since France wisely abandoned any further overt advance at this time, the North African ententes passed away from inaction. The net result of the many agreements to check France and Russia was their drawing together in the preliminary entente of 1891, followed by the military alliance of 1892.[195] France then began to rebuild the diplomatic supports which would enable her eventually to have her way in Morocco and in many other parts of the world.[196]

Henceforth the acquisition of Morocco was to be a national project of France. In 1889 the Comite'de l'Afrique Française was organized to put pressure on the government and to carry on unified and continuous propaganda for colonial expansion.[197] Its select membership of seventy included the business, professional, and political leaders of France, who quickly rallied to their support other organizations interested in colonies. Besides exercising great national influence, this unofficial group brought about the formation of avowed colonial groups in the Parliament itself--in the Chamber of Deputies by 1892 and in the Senate by 1898.[198]

When France denounced her commercial treaties in 1892 and inaugurated a policy of high protective tariffs, the opening up of new markets became a vital matter for other countries. Conversely, countries which had been comparatively indifferent to France's obtaining of political control over backward regions now began to oppose her commercial monopoly there.[199] But hereafter France made no more premature military advances. She waited and prepared while Morocco sank into anarchy.

During the last years of Mulai Hassan's reign, there were many predictions that his empire would die with him. Subduing rebellions had been his perennial occupation ever since his accession, but five revolts in 1892 almost broke his hold on the imperial umbrella. Bonsal, an American journalist who accompanied Euan-Smith to Fez, thought that some members of the Sultan's divan, all of the religious notables, and two-thirds of his subjects were hostile to their ruler. With yearly decreasing revenues, the Sultan found the maintenance of his government and army almost impossible. There were rumors that French agents were busy instigating revolts. Mulai Hassan's last expedition in 1893 ended in a terrible retreat over an Atlas mountain pass from Tafilalt to Marrakesh. During his absence, a Spanish punitive expedition proceeded against some raiding tribes near Melilla. The resulting treaty provided for minor frontier rectifications and an indemnity of $4,000,000 from the Moorish treasury.[200] Mathews made the native revolts and the Spanish retaliations important topics in his dispatches.[201]

On December 13, 1893, less than six months before Mulai Hassan's death, Mathews was retired. However, he remained a resident of Tangier until his death on April 17, 1899,[202] thus affording his three successors a basis for charges that his friends continued intriguing for his reinstatement.

The next American representative was J. Judson Barclay, who used every opportunity to remind his superiors that he was the great grandson of Thomas Barclay. He reinforced his authority by having one son as vice-consul and another as consular clerk at Tangier. His first announced project was investigation of the possibly fraudulent sales of parts of the sultan's original grant of the American consulate property. On March 1, 1894, Barclay sent in the commerce report for the last year of Mathews' service, 1893. There had been a general decrease in trade because of poor harvests caused by drouth and locusts, a rise in rates of exchange, and the introduction of depreciated money from Spain. A surprising item was that about three hundred American tourists were visiting Tangier annually.[203]

As Mulai Hassan's days were becoming numbered, there were many speculations as to which European countries would absorb his empire. Some observers thought that the steadily increasing commerce of Germany, together with her apparent lack of ambition for political control, might lead the Moors to accept German tutelage. Others predicted that the country would be divided between France and Spain, with a port reserved for Great Britain.[204]

Many American newspapers and magazines were now cognizant enough of the Moroccan problem to print news and editorials on it.[205] On January 28, 1892, remarking that the assembling of Spanish, French, and British warships at Tangier was "really to get a share of the empire in case it breaks up," the Nation went on to analyze the claims of the various powers:

> The Spaniards say their claim is stronger than any other, inasmuch as they have held Ceuta and other ports for two centuries, have thrashed the Moroccans in one recent war, and have always been considered the heirs of the last Sultan, whoever he might be. The French appear with a claim founded on the recent aggression of a Moroccan tribe on an Algerian tribe, on their having beaten the Moroccan army in the war with Abd el-Kader, and on their having at one time bombarded Mogador and Tangier. Great Britain claims only the port of Tangier, on the strength of having owned Tangier in the seventeenth century, and on the theory that it is the complement of Gibraltar, and ought properly to belong to the Power which holds Gibraltar, inasmuch as if Tangier were in the hands of an enemy, Gibraltar could not be provisioned. She does not care who has the rest of Morocco, but Lord Salisbury gives notice pretty plainly, through the Standard, that England is going to have Tangier, no matter what any one else thinks about it.[206]

The subjects of Mulai Hassan complained that he yielded too much to European diplomats, while the latter insisted that Christians received no favors and little justice, except under the strongest compulsion. Absolutely no progress had been made in removing the evils of protection, which had become a commodity, varying in price with the kind and degree of immunity offered and the influence of the protector.[207] Mulai Hassan's ineffectual defenses had been his resistance to the extension of foreign commerce[208] and his stubborn refusal to permit foreigners to acquire immovable property.[209] The Moroccans remained in the depths of poverty and degradation because of the venality and cruelty of their governing hierarchy.[210]

The last task essayed by Mulai Hassan was to chastise the never subdued Berber tribes of the Riff which had attacked the Spaniards and to exact as large a contribution as possible to the indemnity demanded by Spain. Barclay described the Spanish military mission to Marrakesh to impose terms on the Sultan and Hassan's preparations for the retaliatory expedition against the Riffians. Later Barclay reported the death of Mulai Hassan on June 7, 1894, when he was near Fez en route to the Riff. An article by Walter Burton Harris, for many years correspondent in Morocco for the London Times, gives a graphic account of the gruesome death of the Sultan and the subsequent intrigues and personal violence against potential rivals which secured the acceptance of his successor at Fez on July 21, 1894.[211]

Just a month earlier there had been some evidence that Great Britain was ready to make a deal dividing the domains of the new sultan, Abd al-Aziz, who at sixteen was rather youthful to cope with the astute diplomats of Europe. On June 21, 1894, the German ambassador in Rome, Bernard von Bülow, wrote to the German Chancellor:

> My English colleague, Sir Clare Ford, told me confidentially he was without doubt that France would be ready to divide Morocco with Spain. France wanted the southeast part of Morocco, the territories east of the Moulaya and south of the Atlas, and if she received these she was willing to renounce the northwestern part of Morocco. In a very careful manner, but still not one to be misinterpreted, my English colleague insinuated that if England should receive Tangier, the fate of the rest of Morocco did not concern her.[212]

By the midyear of 1894, there was no pretense among practitioners in international diplomacy that the system of multiple economic imperialism with a "most favored nation" treatment for all countries in a politically independent Morocco was anything but a failure. In fact, there had never been a sincere effort to make it successful. Within the decade after the accession of Abd al-Aziz the European powers would revert to their traditional competitive political imperialism in Morocco and would make diplomatic arrangements to adjust their conflicting ambitions. The world was spared a war, largely because of the intervention of the non-aligned United States. But the experiment of internationalization in Morocco, and in all of Africa, was ended.

Notes

1. For detailed accounts of the personality and reign of Mulai Hassan, see: Terrasse, History of Morocco, 150-151; Barbour, North West Africa, 87; Mellor, Morocco Awakes, 28-31; Meakin, Moorish Empire, 179-192; Walter Burton Harris, Morocco That Was (hereafter cited as W. B. Harris, Morocco That Was), 1-14; Piquet, Le Maroc, 185-186; Henry M. Field, The Barbary Coast (hereafter cited as Field, Barbary Coast), 253-258. In the last named is a portrait of Mulai Hassan.

2. Mathews to Fish, No. 203, April 9, 1876 and No. 219, Dec. 30, 1876; Mathews to Evarts, No. 245, July 28, 1877; No. 292, Aug. 7, 1878 and No. 300, Oct. 20, 1878; C. D., Tangier, XI. Mathews to Blaine, No. 421, April 11, 1881, Ibid., XIII. Mathews to Frelinghuysen, No. 461, March 5, 1882 and No. 522, Jan. 5, 1884, Ibid., XIV. Aubin, Morocco of Today, 281; Sir Harry H. Johnston, A History of the Colonization of Africa by Alien Races, New Edition (hereafter cited as Johnston, Colonization of Africa), 252-253; Meakin, Moorish Empire, 185-186.

3. In his dispatch of December 1, 1885, Mathews made some new claims relating to his mission to Sidi Muhammad's Court in 1871. The Sultan, Mathews said, "had repeatedly expressed the desire of conferring with me about the Country I represented and the desirability of establishing an American protectorate over Morocco." Mathews claimed credit for some large concessions also: "As a result of my visit to the Emperor, I obtained His Majesty's edict allowing Petroleum to be introduced into the towns of the interior of Morocco, where it was considered dangerous to allow its introduction, and the discouragement of cotton planting in the Country for which Moroccan soil is well adapted. The concessions were at the time considered great victories considering the obstacles put by the Moorish functionaries to all innovations."

4. Mathews to Bayard, No. 561, Dec. 1, 1885, C. D., Tangier, XIV and No. 570, April 29, 1886, Ibid., XV. Bayard to Mathews, No. 267, June 10, 1886, D. S., Instructions, Barbary Powers, XVI. Lewis to Porter, No. 29, June 11, 1887, C. D., Tangier, XVI and Lewis to Rives, No. 132, Nov. 15, 1888, Ibid., XVII.

5. Mathews to Fish, No. 110, Sept. 17, 1873; No. 134, May 29, 1874; No. 139, July 9, 1874; No. 142, Aug. 24, 1874; C. D., Tangier, X; No. 172, June 28, 1875 and No. 177, Aug. 16, 1875, Ibid., XI.

6. The chief reforms urged by Hay were placing a light at Mazagan harbor; building of a pier at Tangier and breakwaters at Safi and Dar-al-Baida; erection of more houses and stores for merchants at the ports; permission to export bones; permission to import sulphur, saltpeter, and lead at 10% duty and abolition of the government monopoly on these articles; extension of the term placed on removal of the prohibition to export wheat and barley; inquiry into the punishment of outrages on Jews; immediate settlement of all British claims; permission to lay a cable between Tangier and Gibraltar.

7. Sir John Drummond Hay, 307-308, 313-317, 329.

8. Sir Harry Maclean, the instructor-general of the Moroccan army, formerly a subaltern at Gibraltar, entered the Sultan's service in 1875. "Kaid" Maclean "acted as tout for concession hunters and other grafters who wanted to get the ear of the Sultan. He was the pillar of strength upon whom the British Legation at Tangier depended to keep French officers out of the Moorish army and to block the French proposals to establish a joint Franco-Moorish police control over the tribes that were opposing the French adminstrative organization of the Algerian hinterland and the western Sahara." Harold Nicolson, Portrait of a Diplomatist. Being the Life of Sir Arthur Nicolson, First Lord Carnock, and A Study of the Origins of the Great War (hereafter cited as Nicolson, Portrait of a Diplomatist), 84: Herbert Adams Gibbons,

The New Map of Africa (1900-1916). A History of European Colonial Expansion and Colonial Diplomacy, Fourth Edition (hereafter cited as Gibbons, New Map of Africa), footnote, 364.

9. Sir John Drummond Hay, 323-324; Cruickshank, Morocco at the Parting of the Ways, 44; Piquet, Le Maroc, 186.

10. For an account of the achievements of Adolf von Conring, who headed the first naval mission to Morocco in 1874, explored the Atlantic littoral and selected the site of Agadir for a German colony or naval base, published a book which stimulated German organization and propaganda for commercial and scientific interest in Morocco, and secured for Krupp a concession to build and equip a fort, see Williamson, Germany and Morocco before 1905, 74-78.

11. Mathews to Fish, No. 123, Jan. 27, 1874, C. D., Tangier, X.

12. Stuart, Tangier, 21-25.

13. Stuart, "International Lighthouse at Cape Spartel," 770-776; F. R., 1864, IV, 428-429 and 432-434; Ibid., 1865, III, 350, 351.

14. An eminent Spanish historian places the blame for the corruption of protection upon Great Britain in this oversimplified and inaccurate account: "It was indirectly through English action that the status quo became so precarious as to lose every right to the name. For in 1856 the British Government obtained the right of protection for all persons who placed themselves under her flag in Morocco, a fact which led, of course, to equal concessions to every other nation. Consular agents were thus enabled to put Moroccan subjects or foreigners under their nation's protection. The difficulties produced by this practice and the malpractices into which it degenerated led, however, to an important step. An international conference met in Madrid in 1880 .... If it did not do much to cure the evils of "protection,"

it inaugurated an era perhaps too hastily closed--that during which Moroccan questions were a matter of international concern." Madariaga, Spain, A Modern History, 265.

15. Wendel, "Protégé System in Morocco," 52.

16. Eugene Staley, War and the Private Investor; A Study in the Relations of International Politics and International Private Investment (hereafter cited as Staley, War and the Private Investor), 160-161.

17. Cruickshank, Morocco at the Parting of the Ways, 7-15.

18. Ibid., 15, 17.

19. A minister, a chargé d'affairs, or a consul general was not limited in the number of his protected employees. By the British and Spanish treaties the number of protégés allowed to a consular official was four--an interpreter, a guard, and two domestics.

20. Great Britain, Commons, Sessional Papers, 1880, LXXIX, Accounts and Papers, XL, Paper 2707 (hereafter cited as Paper 2707), 83; Wendel, "Protégé System in Morocco," 52-53; Cruickshank, Morocco at the Parting of the Ways, 19.

21. F. R., 1864-65, Part IV, 410.

22. Cruickshank, Morocco at the Parting of the Ways, 23-25; Flournoy, British Policy Towards Morocco, 245-247.

23. The statistical report of the Alliance Israelite Universelle for 1864-1880 reported 307 unpunished murders of Jews in the city and district of Morocco (Marrakesh); "Morocco," the Jewish Encyclopedia, IX, 25.

24. Meakin, The Moors, 46.

25. "Morocco," in Jewish Encyclopedia, 12 vols., IX, 25.

26. "Paper 2707," 83.

27. Cruickshank, Morocco at the Parting of the Ways, 32-34, 37.

28. Most Moroccans went to Algeria, Portugal, or Italy for naturalization. A few went to the United States, chiefly to New York. Before 1880, only five had gone to Brazil and about twenty to Portugal.

29. Cruickshank, Morocco at the Parting of the Ways, 34-36.

30. Ibid., 39-41.

31. Mathews to Fish, June 27, 1871, C. D., Tangier, IX; Jan. 1, 1872; July 1, 1872; Jan. 1, 1873; July 1, 1873; Jan. 1, 1874 and Jan. 1, 1875, Ibid., X; July 1, 1875; Jan. 1, 1876; July 1, 1876 and Jan. 1, 1877, Ibid., XI. Mathews to Evarts, July 1, 1877; Jan. 1, 1878; July 1, 1878; Jan. 1, 1879; July 1, 1879; and Jan. 1, 1880, Ibid., XII; Jan. 1, 1881, Ibid., XIII.

32. Cruickshank, Morocco at the Parting of the Ways, 42, footnote 30.

33. Fish to Mathews, No. 35, April 11, 1872 and No. 44, Oct. 2, 1872, D. S., Instructions, Barbary Powers, XV. Mathews to Fish, No. 72, June 17, 1872, C. D., Tangier, X.

34. Cruickshank, Morocco at the Parting of the Ways, 45-47.

35. Mathews had other claims besides his innocence to urge in favor of his exoneration: "As I am the only other Sovereign Representative here who speaks the idiomatic Arabic, as well as every other language spoken here, it is perhaps natural that the marked popularity which my unvarying adhesion to truth and justice in my dealings with the natives and my free distribution of food, clothes and medicines, to both natives and the poor Europeans, including many British subjects has secured for me the ill will from which I should long since have suffered had it not

been for the confidence and support invariably accorded to me by the Department .... and which I venture to trust will still be the reward of one who for the last twenty five years of naval, civil, and military service, has never failed to consider above all his Country's service and honor, and who has endeavoured to so govern his actions that nothing in the conduct of its humble Representative here, should detract from the esteem to which the upright and honest are justly entitled"; No. 247, C. D., Tangier, XI.

36. F. W. Seward (Acting Sec. of State), to Mathews, No. 109, June 27, 1877, D. S., Instructions, Barbary Powers, XV; Mathews to Seward, No. 247, July 30, 1877 and No. 254, Oct. 15, 1877, C. D., Tangier, XI.

37. Cruickshank, Morocco at the Parting of the Ways, 48-49.

38. Evarts to Mathews, No. 119, Dec. 7, 1877; No. 123, Feb. 27, 1878; No. 129, May 27, 1878, D. S., Instructions, Barbary Powers, XV. Mathews to Evarts, No. 270, Jan. 25, 1878 and No. 276, April 29, 1878, C. D., Tangier, XI.

39. United States, 46th Congress, 2nd Session, 1879-80, Executive Documents, XXV, Commerical Relations of the United States, 1879, Part I, Serial No. 1926 (hereafter cited as Ser. No. 1926), 248.

40. Spain was negotiating for the surrender to her of the "Santa Cruz-de-Mar Pequeña" promised in the treaty of 1860. In 1878 a mixed commission fixed a choice of site arbitrarily upon a small harbor in Ifni. Spain was persuaded not to force the cession at this time; it was ratified by the Sultan in 1883. Cruickshank, Morocco at the Parting of the Ways, 67; Bernard, Le Maroc, 284, 308.

41. Cruickshank, Morocco at the Parting of the Ways, 50-62.

42. Mathews served as president of the Board of Health and manager of relief measures during the period of greatest distress. He reported: "I am the only

foreign representative who has subscribed sums for the relief of the poor from my private purse, although the least in rank and salary amongst the Diplomatic body of Morocco."

43. Sir John Drummond Hay, 324-327; Cruickshank, Morocco at the Parting of the Ways, 66-73; Ser. No. 1926, 245. Mathews to Evarts, No. 282, June 14, 1878; No. 287, July 5, 1878; No. 293, Aug. 24, 1878; No. 294, Sept. 7, 1878; No. 296, Sept. 30, 1878; No. 300, Oct. 20, 1878; No. 301, Dec. 9, 1878; No. 303, Dec. 27, 1878; C. D., Tangier, XI; No. 312, March 24, 1879 and No. 342, Dec. 7, 1879, Ibid., XII.

44. For a full account of the proceedings of the meetings of 1879, consult Accounts and Papers, XL, "Paper 1707," 1-78.

45. Ibid., 6-8; Cruickshank, Morocco at the Parting of the Ways, 75, 86-90.

46. "Paper 2707," 1-28.

47. Cruickshank, Morocco at the Parting of the Ways, 90-92.

48. Ibid., 96; "Paper 2707," 9-12.

49. "The policy of the Moorish Government is that of isolation. As regards the outer world, their motto is, 'let us alone and we shall leave you alone.' And without doubt it is a sensible policy. They instinctively feel that, as they are so much behind other nations, and are unable to cope with them in arms, independence lies in isolation. When told of European progress and improvements, they reply that these things are suited for others but not for them .... If, like the Japanese, the Moors adopted the policy along with the arts of Europe, they might take their place among the nations as a strong State. But against this course their religion presents an insuperable barrier." Dr. Arthur Leared, A Visit to the Court of Morocco, (hereafter cited as Leared, A Visit to the Court of Morocco), 44-45.

50. Salisbury to Adams _et al_, Oct. 7, 1879; various diplomats to Salisbury, Oct. 10-Dec. 24, 1879; Salisbury to Sackville-West, March 1, 1880; "Paper 2707," 33-37, 39, 45-48, 53-54, 66.

51. Cruickshank, _Morocco at the Parting of the Ways_, 107-108.

52. The delegates most prominent in the proceedings were: Austria-Hungary, Count Ludolf; France, Admiral Jaurès; Germany, Count von Solms-Sonnewalde; Great Britain and Denmark, Sackville West; Italy, Count Greppi; Morocco, Cid Muhammad Bargash; Spain, Antonio Canovas del Castillo; the United States, General Lucius Fairchild.

53. Cruickshank, _Morocco at the Parting of the Ways_, 106-108; "Paper 2707," 36, 87-90.

54. Sackville-West to Salisbury, Feb. 14 and Feb. 19, 1880, _Ibid._, 60, 64-65; Jaurès to Freycinet, (minister of foreign affairs), Feb. 9 and Feb. 23, 1880; France, Ministère des Affaires Étrangères, Commission de Publication des Documents relatifs aux Origines de la Guerre de 1914, _Documents diplomatiques francais (1871-1914)_, I er Série (1871-1900), Tome III (Janvier 1880- Mai 1881) (hereafter cited as _D. D. F._, Sér. 1, III), No. 19, 17-18; No. 28, 27-28.

55. Cruickshank, _Morocco at the Parting of the Ways_, 106.

56. Saint-Vallier to Freycinet No. 95, April 23, 1880, _D. D. F._, Sér. 1, III, 86-86; Note communicated to the German Government from Paris, No. 98, April 26, 1880, _Ibid._, 87-88; Saint Vallier to Freycinet, No. 133, May 24, 1880, _Ibid._, 115-117; Freycinet to Saint-Vallier, No. 134, June 2, 1880, _Ibid._, 124-125; Saint-Vallier to Freycinet, No. 215, July 16, 1880, _Ibid._, 182. See also Hohenlohe to Solms-Sonnenwalde, May 6, 1880, in _Die Grosse Politik der Europäischen Kabinette, 1871-1914, Sammlung der diplomatischen Akten des Auswärtigen Amtes_, (im Auftrage des Auswärtigen Amtes herausgegeben von Johannes Lepsius, Albrecht Mendelssohn- Bartholdy, Friedrich Thimme) (hereafter

cited as G. P., followed by volume number), No. 664, III, 397-398.

57. Freycinet to Jaurès, No. 116, May 11, 1880, D. D. F., Sér. 1, III, 104-107; Cruickshank, Morocco at the Parting of the Ways, 132-138.

58. The Spanish representative had admitted having the largest number of protégés--124 subjects and their families, exclusive of servants, consular agents, and semsars of Spanish traders, while Mathews had confessed to the smallest number. The American list comprised only 39 native protégés, including all consular agents, interpreters, guards, clerks, household servants, and agents of American citizens. Mathews to Evarts, No. 258, Nov. 9, 1877, C. D., Tangier, XI. Hay remarked on the incongruity of American protection of nineteen Jewish agents in Tangier, Meknes, Fez, and Alcassar for an American trade that was almost nil, while Great Britain, with two-thirds of the commerce of Morocco, did not protect a single native at any of these towns. United States, 46th Congress, 3rd Session, Executive Documents, 1880-81, I, Foreign Relations, No. I, Part I, Ser. No. 1951, 894.

59. Hay to Salisbury, Nov. 18, 1878 and March 29, 1880, "Paper 2707," 48-49, 84; Mathews to Evarts, No. 365, May 16, 1880, C. D., Tangier, XII.

60. Evarts to Fairchild, No. 4, March 12, 1880, D. S., Instructions, Spain, XVIII, 441-452.

61. Evarts to Mathews, No. 162, March 13, 1880, D. S., Instructions, Barbary Powers, XVI; Mathews to Fairchild, April 11, 1880, Ser. No. 1951, 799-801.

62. Fairchild to Evarts, No. 577, April 13, 1880, Ibid., 895-896.

63. Mathews to Evarts, No. 361, April 16, 1880, C. D., Tangier, XII; quotation from Cruickshank, Morocco at the Parting of the Ways, 127, footnote 79.

64. Philip Durham Trotter, Our Mission to the Court of Morocco in 1880 under Sir John Drummond Hay (hereafter cited as Trotter, Our Mission to the Court of Morocco), 5-6.

65. Cruickshank, Morocco at the Parting of the Ways, 138-141.

66. The most complete account of the mission to Fez is in Philip Durham Trotter, Our Mission to the Court of Morocco; see especially 182-186 and 206-208. The following interesting incident is related by Trotter: Hay presented to the Sultan Kaid Maclean's suggestions for the improvement of the Moorish army, and the Sultan agreed to adopt them. The most common type of army weapon seen at the inspection was an old United States rifle. Trotter suggested up-to-date Peabody-Martini weapons and ammunition such as the Turks had, to which the commander-in-chief objected, "But suppose Morocco went to war with America?"

67. Hay to Salisbury, Oct. 28, 1879; Dec. 13, 1879; Jan. 24, 1880; Feb. 2, 1880; Feb. 9, 1880; May 13, 1880; "Paper 2707," 40-42, 52-53; 58-61, 93-94. Sir John Drummond Hay, 329-330, 334-335.

68. There is abundant evidence that Mathews was really a good friend of the Jews. He had consistently tried to shield them ever since officially requested to do so by the Secretary of State on March 20, 1878; Cruickshank, Morocco at the Parting of the Ways, 113. Shortly before the convening of the Madrid Conference, the Italian and American representatives at Tangier visited the western ports of Morocco in vessels of war; Mathews to Evarts, No. 366, May 16, 1880, C. D., Tangier, XII. This action was understood as an open declaration in favor of the Jews and of irregular protection. The commander of the American vessel reported his gratification at "showing off our flag where it was almost unknown, and impressing this people with the fact that we can protect it." He had conspicuously displayed his armament to visitors. He asserted that "intelligent persons in all

the ports are unanimous in saying that protection is necessary" and that the Jews worshipped Mathews. Cruickshank, Morocco at the Parting of the Ways, 118.

69. Cruickshank, Morocco at the Parting of the Ways, 113-123.

70. Fairchild to Evarts, No. 27, May 22, 1880, D. S., Despatches, Spain, XCVIII.

71. Detailed accounts of the proceedings are in "Paper 2707," 91-164; D. D. F., Sér. 1, III, 127-129, 136-137, 145, 147-151, 154-156; Ser. No. 1951, 897-929; Cruickshank, Morocco at the Parting of the Ways, 148-170; dispatches from Fairchild to Evarts, Nos. 23-39, May 15, 1880-July 3, 1880, D. S., Diplomatic Despatches, Spain, XCVIII and XCIX.

72. Freycinet to Jaurès, No. 165, June 14, 1880; Freycinet to Montebello, No. 166, June 14, 1880; D. D. F., Ser. 1, III, 145. West to Granville, June 12, 1880, "Paper 2707," 116-117.

73. West to Granville, June 20, 1880, Ibid., 126; Cruickshank, Morocco at the Parting of the Ways, 161; Jaurès to Freycinet, No. 169, June 16, 1880, D. D. F., Sér. 1, III, 147-148.

74. Sackville-West to Granville, June 26, 1880; June 27, 1880; June 28, 1880; July 1, 1880; and July 2, 1880; "Paper 2707," 136, 140, 141, 155, 164. Cruickshank, Morocco at the Parting of the Ways, 168.

75. Hay to Salisbury, Feb. 10, 1880; "Paper 2707," 63-64.

76. The latter provided that Spanish subjects were not obliged to pay taxes, were exempt from military service, personal charges, and forced loans, and were to have their dwellings, warehouses, and property respected. Spanish subjects or protégés, whether Jews, Christians, or Muslims were to enjoy all the rights of this treaty or those granted to the most-favored-nation.

77. Mathews to Evarts, No. 353, Feb. 28, 1880, C. D., Tangier, XII.

78. Fairchild to Evarts, No. 38, June 26, 1880, D. S., Despatches, Spain, XCVIII; Sackville-West to Granville, June 21, 1880; "Paper 2707," 145.

79. Hay pointed out that the Sultan's toleration of non-Muslims, both Christians and Jews, already greatly surpassed that of some governments of Catholic countries for non-Catholics. Hay to Granville, June 24, 1880, Ibid., 138-139.

80. Hay to Salisbury, Oct. 28, 1879, Ibid., 39-42 and March 16, 1880, Ibid., 75-76.

81. Sackville-West to Granville, June 3, 1880, Ibid., 109-110.

82. Karolyi to Granville, May 30, 1880 and Sackville-West to Granville, May 31, 1880, Ibid., 99-100; Sackville-West to Granville, June 27, 1880, Ibid., 136-137.

83. Evarts to Fairchild, No. 578, June 15, 1880 and Aug. 11, 1880, Ser. No. 1951, 897 and 922.

84. President's Message, Dec. 6, 1880, Ibid., xi.

85. The Nation, XXXI (July 8, 1880), 23.

86. Great Britain, Sessional Papers, Commons, Jan. 6-Aug. 27, 1881, XCIX; Accounts and Papers, XLIII, "Paper 3053," (hereafter cited as "Paper 3053"), 9; Mathews to Blaine, No. 423, May 9, 1881, C. D., Tangier, XIII. Treaties and Conventions Concluded between the United States of America and Other Powers, since July 4, 1776, Revised Edition, I, 1220-1227.

87. Jaurès to Freycinet, No. 189, July 1, 1880; D. D. F., Sér. 1, III, 160-161.

88. American Committee for Moroccan Independence, The Case for Morocco, 33.

89. Williamson, Germany and Morocco Before 1905, 141-142. The German interpretation was upheld by Walter Burton Harris in "The Morocco Carisis," Blackwood's Magazine, CLXXVIII (Aug., 1905), 300-301. The French contentions were set forth by Andre Tardieu, in "La Conférence d'Algesiras," in Le Temps, March 27, 1906 and more extensively in his La Conference d'Algesiras, Histoire Diplomatique de la Crise Marocaine, Third Edition (hereafter cited as Tardieu, La Conférence).

90. Fairchild to Evarts, No. 39, July 3, 1880, D. S., Despatches, Spain, XCIX; Sir John Drummond Hay, 323; Hay to Granville, July 2, 1880, "Paper 2707," 165.

91. Sidney Bradshaw Fay, The Origins of the World War, 2 vols. (hereafter cited as Fay, Origins of the World War), I, 97; William Leonard Langer, European Alliances and Alignments, 1871-1890) (hereafter cited as Langer, European Alliances and Alignments), 218-225.

92. Emile Bourgeois, History of Modern France, 1815-1913, 2 vols. (hereafter cited as Bourgeois, History of Modern France), II, 290-291; Harris, Colonization in Africa, 231-234.

93. For the story of British diplomacy in acquiring Egypt, see Wilfrid Scawen Blunt, Secret History of the English Occupation of Egypt.

94. Bourgeois, History of Modern France, 291-293; George Peabody Gooch, History of Modern Europe, 1878-1919 (hereafter cited as Gooch, History of Modern Europe), 73-86; Sir Edward Grey, Twenty-Five Years, 1892-1916, 2 vols. (hereafter cited as Grey, Twenty-Five Years), 16-17; Alfred Francis Pribram, England and the International Policy of the European Great Powers, 1871-1914 (hereafter cited as Pribram, England and the European Great Powers, 30-31.

95. Busch to Hohenlohe, No. 668, July 16, 1881, G. P., III, 401.

96. Pribram, England and the European Great Powers, 21-22, 26, 28; Arthur Rosenberg, The Birth of the German Republic, 1871-1918, 27; Erich Brandenburg, From Bismarck to the World War; A History of the German Foreign Policy, 1870-1914 (hereafter cited as Brandenburg, From Bismarck to the World War), 16-17.

97. Madariage, Spain, 358.

98. Sir John Drummond Hay, 344.

99. Diasdado to the Spanish minister of state, March 14 and June 27, 1883; quoted by Cruickshank, Morocco at the Parting of the Ways, xxv, 67.

100. Brandenburg, From Bismarck to the World War, 10; Bismarck to Keudell, No. 678, April 6, 1884; G. P., III, 410.

101. Hay to Granville, March 24, 1884; quoted by Cruickshank, Morocco at the Parting of the Ways, 180.

102. Mathews to Evarts, No. 390, Sept. 29, 1880; Evarts to Mathews, Oct. 28, 1880, Ser. No. 1951, 805; Cruickshank, Morocco at the Parting of the Ways, 175-177.

103. Bonsal, Morocco As It Is, 318-320.

104. Fairchild to Evarts, Dec. 2, 1880; Fairchild to Blaine, April 20, 1881, F. R., 1881-1882, 1044 and 1055.

105. Mathews to Evarts, No. 401, Dec. 15, 1880; No. 402, Dec. 21, 1880, C. D., Tangier, XII; No. 411, Jan. 14, 1881, Ibid., XIII. Mathews to Blaine, No. 419, April 3, 1881 and No. 420, April 10, 1881, Ibid., XIII. Mathews to Frelinghuysen, No. 538, Dec. 16, 1884, Ibid., XIV.

106. Mathews to Blaine, No. 435, Aug. 6, 1881, Ibid., XIII; Cruickshank, Morocco at the Parting of the Ways, 178-180.

107. *Ibid.*, 180-183.

108. Ferry was premier of France during 1880-1881 and again during 1883-1885.

109. *Sir John Drummond Hay*, 345-346; Cruickshank, *Morocco at the Parting of the Ways*, 184-189.

110. Ferry to des Michels, No. 273, May 20, 1884, *D. D. F.*, Sér. 1, V, 293-294.

111. Fay, *Origins of the World War*, I, 99.

112. Mary Evelyn Townsend, *The Rise and Fall of Germany's Colonial Empire, 1884-1918* (hereafter cited as Townsend, *Rise and Fall of Germany's Colonial Empire*), 64-87.

113. Halford Lancaster Hoskins, *European Imperialism in Africa* (hereafter cited as Hoskins, *European Imperialism in Africa*), 38-40; Percy Evans Lewin, *The Germans and Africa* (hereafter cited as Lewin, *The Germans and Africa*), 67, 218-223.

114. The countries represented were Austria-Hungary, Belgium, Denmark, Germany, France, Great Britain, Italy, The Netherlands, Portugal, Russia, Spain, Sweden-Norway, Turkey, and the United States. With the addition of Russia and Turkey and the subtraction of Morocco, this was the same group as was present at Madrid.

115. Mr. Kasson, the American representative, reported to the State Dept. on Oct. 13, 1884: "The reason alleged for inviting the United States is that Liberia is under their protection." *House Ex. Docs*, No. 247, Ser. No. 2304, 8-9, (hereafter cited as Ser. No. 2304.)

116. Ser. No. 2304, 3-4.

117. United States, 49th Congress, 1st Session, 1885-86, *Senate Executive Documents*, VIII, Serial No. 2341 (hereafter cited as Ser. No. 2341), 23-27.

118. Frelinghuysen to Kasson, Oct. 17, 1884, Ser. No. 2304, 5.

119. Jesse S. Reeves, The International Beginnings of the Congo Free State, Johns Hopkins Studies in Historical and Political Science, XII, 44-49.

120. Townsend, Rise and Fall of Germany's Colonial Empire, 87-88.

121. Congressional Record, 48th Congress, 2nd Session, 1884-85, XVI, Part I, 446, 464, 580; Part II, 1287-1288; Part III, 2571.

122. The idea of Secretary of State Freylinghuysen had been to work for the neutralization of the Congo Basin for the benefit of all nations. This was the precursor of the principle of international mandates. See Bemis, Diplomatic History of the United States, 569-570.

123. James D. Richardson, A Compilation of the Messages and Papers of the Presidents, 11 vols. (hereafter cited as Richardson, Messages and Papers of the Presidents), VII, 4915.

124. "Although a formal protectorate over Liberia is contrary to our traditional policy, the moral right and duty of the United States to assist in all proper ways in the maintenance of its integrity is obvious, and has been consistently announced during half a century." The President's Message, F. R., 1886, VII.

125. Nation, XL (Jan. 8, 1885), 27. Similar comments on the question, "What are Americans doing in that gallery?" are found in Nation, XL (Jan. 1, 1885), 8-9; March 5, 1885, 190; April 2, 1885, 270.

126. Sir John Drummond Hay, 323, 338-352, 356-361; Cruickshank, Morocco at the Parting of the Ways, 192-195.

127. After his retirement, John Drummond Hay was made a Privy Councillor and was frequently consulted on Moroccan affairs. During the seven remaining years of his life, he divided his time between England and Ravensrock; at his Moroccan home he enjoyed his favorite sport of pigsticking and wrote his reminiscences of life in Morocco. He died on November 27, 1893. Sir John Drummond Hay, 363, 365, 396-397.

128. Cruickshank, Morocco at the Parting of the Ways, 195-196.

129. Sir Charles Prestwood Lucas, The Partition and Colonization of Africa, 96; Isaiah Bowman, "A Note on Tangier and the Spanish Zones in Africa," Foreign Affairs, II (March 15, 1924), 503.

130. Meakin, Moorish Empire, 188, 351.

131. Ibid., 518.

132. Johnston, Colonization of Africa, 323.

133. Saint-Vallier to Waddington, No. 362, Nov. 21, 1878, D. D. F., Sér. 1, II, 403-404.

134. Williamson, Germany and Morocco Before 1905, 8-15, 105-106, 142-143.

135. Langer, European Alliances and Alignments, 394-401; Fay, Origins of the World War, I, 86-87; Alfred Francis Pribram, The Secret Treaties of Austria-Hungary, 1879-1914, 2 vols. (hereafter cited as Pribram, Secret Treaties), I, 94, 116-123; II, 50, 54, 57, 77-81; Count Julius Andrássy, Bismarck, Andrássy, and Their Successors, 139-140.

136. Pribram, Secret Treaties, I, 274-281; Raymond James Sontag, European Diplomatic History, 1871-1932 (hereafter cited as Sontag, European Diplomatic History), 42-46.

137. Ibid., 26.

138. Eugene Newton Anderson, The First Moroccan Crisis, 1904-1906 (hereafter cited as Anderson, First Moroccan Crisis), 6.

139. Mathews to Evarts, No. 383, July 30, 1880 and No. 390, Sept. 29, 1880, C. D., Tangier, XII; No. 412, Jan. 29, 1881, Ibid., XIII. Mathews to Blaine, No. 427, June 25, 1881, Ibid. Mathews to Frelinghuysen, No. 467, May 2, 1882; No. 471, June 29, 1882; No. 479, Sept. 28, 1882; No. 495, Jan. 19, 1883, Ibid., and No. 531, Sept. 23, 1884; No. 534, Nov. 2, 1884, Ibid., XIV. Mathews to Bayard, No. 547, April 9, 1885 and No. 554, July 1, 1885, Ibid. Mathews to Porter, No. 573, July 9, 1886 and No. 584, Oct. 9, 1886, Ibid., XV. Annual reports of Mathews in Executive Documents, 1st session, 48th Congress, 1883-84, XXX, Commerical Relations of the United States, II, Serial No. 2210, 23-26 and House Executive Documents, 49th Congress, 2nd Session, 1886-87, XXVII, Commerical Relations of the United States, 1885-86, II, Serial No. 2486, 1544-1558.

140. Mathews to Evarts, No. 410, Jan. 9, 1881; Mathews to Blaine, No. 426, June 14, 1881, C. D., Tangier, XIII. Mathews to Frelinghuysen, No. 460, March 2, 1882; No. 476, Sept. 14, 1882; No. 486, Nov. 8, 1882, Ibid., and No. 507, July 1, 1885, Ibid., XIV. Mathews to Bayard, No. 571, May 20, 1886, Ibid., XV.

141. Mathews to Blaine, No. 425, June 9, 1881, and No. 447, Oct. 25, 1881, C. D., Tangier, XIII. Mathews to Frelinghuysen, No. 457, Jan. 22, 1882; No. 465, April 16, 1882, Ibid.; No. 507, July 1, 1883, No. 522, Jan. 5, 1884, Ibid., XIV. Mathews to Bayard, No. 548, April 10, 1885; No. 554, July 1, 1885, Ibid. Mathews to Bayard, No. 560, Nov. 22, 1885, Ibid.

142. Mathews to Blaine, No. 441, Sept. 21, 1881, C. D., Tangier, XIII. Mathews to Frelinghuysen, No. 514, Oct. 15, 1883, Ibid., XIV. Frelinghuysen to Mathews, Dec. 18, 1883, D. S., Instructions, Barbary Powers, XVI, 123.

143. Mathews to Evarts, No. 407, Jan. 1, 1881, C. D., Tangier, XIII.

144. Cruickshank, Morocco at the Parting of the Ways, 196-197.

145. Perdicaris, a long time resident of Tangier and originally a great friend of Mathews, became prominent in American-Moroccan affairs again in 1904.

146. Mathews to Bayard, No. 565, Jan. 21, 1866, C. D., Tangier, XIV; No. 566, Jan. 30, 1886, Ibid.; No. 567, Feb. 24, 1886 and No. 570, April 29, 1886, Ibid., XV. Porter to Mathews, No. 266, March 25, 1886, D. S., Instructions, Barbary Powers, XVI, 140.

147. The book, privately printed for Perdicaris about 1886, was entitled American Claims and the Protection of Native Subjects in Morocco by a Foreign Resident. Perdicaris also wrote a novel, Mohammed Benani, A Story of Today, which was published anonymously, to expose the abuses of the protégé system. The Times of Morocco of October 8, 1887, gave the real names of the characters in the novel.

148. Wendel, "Protégé System in Morocco," 58.

149. Mathews to Bayard, No. 572, June 24, 1886, with enclosures from the New York World, and the Times of Morocco, C. D. Tangier, XV.

150. Mathews to Porter, No. 580, Sept. 4, 1886; No. 581, Sept. 9, 1886; No. 582, Sept. 18, 1886; No. 585, Dec. 12, 1886; No. 586, Dec. 15, 1886, Ibid. Wendel, "Protégé System in Morocco," 58-59.

151. Cruickshank, Morocco at the Parting of the Ways, 196-198.

152. Mathews had an important supporter who lamented his dismissal; "For many years the United States was ably represented by the late Col. F. A. Mathews, who maintained the prestige of his people rather by

experienced tact than by threats; but when political wire-pullers succeeded in obtaining the post for a party nominee, the Stars and Stripes were dragged in the mire, and the Moors learned to despise the "Great Country." Meakin, "Yesterday and To-Day in Morocco," Forum, XXX (Nov., 1900), 368.

153. Mathews to Porter, No. 587, Jan. 3, 1887; No. 592, Jan. 19, 1887; No. 595, Feb. 1, 1887; No. 596, Feb. 7, 1887; C. D., Tangier, XV. Mathews to Porter, letter, New York, May 11, 1887. Edward C. Wynne, Assistant Historical Adviser, State Department, letter to Luella J. Hall, Dec. 15, 1931.

154. Cruickshank, Morocco at the Parting of the Ways, 199-200.

155. In his dispatch No. 62 to Porter, Sept. 8, 1887, C. D., Tangier, XVI, Lewis complained: "I am looked upon not only as inferior to the Representatives of other nations but of my predecessor as well, who save in his Communications with yourself, always assumed the title of Consul General, so designating himself upon his visiting cards, official papers and Arms over the Consulate." The title of consul general and diplomatic agent, not conferred upon Mathews until December, 1883, apparently had not been inherited by Lewis. A second application for promotion to this rank (Lewis to Porter, No. 74, Oct. 13, 1887, Ibid.) was endorsed by direction of the Secretary of State on Nov. 4, 1887, Ibid.

156. Mathews to Porter, No. 599, March 14, 1887 and Lewis to Porter, No. 6, March 16, 1887, C. D., Tangier, XV. Lewis to Wharton, No. 158, June 28, 1889, Ibid., XVII. Lewis to Porter, No. 21, May 6, 1887; No. 24, May 11, 1887; No. 62, Sept. 8, 1887; No. 74, Oct. 13, 1887; No. 81, Nov. 5, 1887, Ibid., XVI.

157. Lewis to Porter, No. 70, Oct. 6, 1887; No. 75, Oct. 18, 1887; No. 79, Oct. 27, 1887; C. D., Tangier, XVI. Lewis to Rives, No. 86, Dec. 16, 1887, Ibid.

158. Lewis to Porter, No. 48, July 8, 1887 and No. 82, Dec. 5, 1887, Ibid. Lewis to Rives, No. 148, April 27, 1889 and No. 125, Sept. 20, 1888; Lewis to Wharton, No. 177, Sept. 23, 1889, Ibid., XVII. Report of William Reed Lewis, June 30, 1887; United States, 50th Congress, 1st Session, 1887-88, House Executive Documents, XXXI, Commercial Relations of the United States, 1886-1887, Serial No. 2563, 812-813.

159. Lewis to Porter, No. 12, April 6, 1887 and No. 13, April 14, 1887, C. D., Tangier, XV.

160. Lewis to Porter, No. 19, May 2, 1887; No. 20, May 2, 1887; No. 25, May 11, 1887; No. 30, June 11, 1887; No. 37, May 26, 1887; No. 38, June 24, 1887; No. 39, June 24, 1887; No. 42, June 29, 1887; No. 55, July 22, 1887; No. 73, Oct. 10, 1887; C. D., Tangier, XVI. Cobb to Porter, Aug. 16, 1887, Ibid.

161. Lewis to Porter, No. 65, Sept. 13, 1887 and Lewis to Rives, No. 87, Dec. 31, 1887, Ibid.

162. Lewis to Rives, No. 117, July 30, 1888, C. D., Tangier, XVII.

163. Lewis to Rives, No. 87, Dec. 31, 1887, Ibid., XVI. Ion Perdicaris, "Consular Protection in Morocco" (correspondence), Fortnightly Review, XLIX (May 1, 1888), 729-732.

164. Lewis to Rives, No. 87, Dec. 31, 1887, C. D., Tangier, XVI.

165. Lewis to Bayard, Cable, March 12, 1888 and Cable, March 16, 1888; C. D., Tangier, XVI. Lewis to Rives, No. 92, March 13, 1888; No. 93, March 16, 1888; No. 99, April 21, 1888; No. 100, May 5, 1888; No. 104, May 15, 1888; No. 106, June 15, 1888; Ibid. Moore, Digest, V, 398 and VII, 27-28.

166. Lewis to Rives, No. 134, Dec. 4, 1888, C. D., Tangier, XVII.

167. Lewis to Rives, No. 133, Nov. 16, 1888; No. 145, April 10, 1889; Ibid. Lewis to Wharton, No. 149, May 21, 1889 and No. 150, May 22, 1889, Ibid.

168. Lewis to Rives, No. 140, Feb. 26, 1889; No. 141, Feb. 26, 1889; No. 160, July 6, 1889; Ibid. Charges by Joseph Roffe against Lewis, to Blaine, July 10, July 11, and July 14, Ibid. Roffe to Blaine, July 29, 1889; Aug. 7, 1889; Aug. 9, 1889; Aug. 28, 1889; Sept. 1, 1889; Nov. 12, 1889; Nov. 19, 1889; and Dec. 3, 1889, Ibid. Stalker to Wharton, with enclosure from John Cobb, Dec. 4, 1889, Ibid. Lewis to Wharton, No. 168, Aug. 22, 1889, Ibid.

169. Report from Benjamin Folsom to Sec. Blaine on charge of wife-murder against Lewis, Dec. 21, 1889, C. D., Tangier, XVII. Lewis to Blaine, Cables, Dec. 22, 1889 and Dec. 26, 1889, Ibid. Stalker to Wharton, No. 194, Jan. 11, 1890, Ibid. Meakin, "Yesterday and Today in Morocco," 368-369. Meakin, Moorish Empire, 364.

170. Stalker to Wharton, No. 195, Jan. 13, 1890; No. 201, Feb. 26, 1890; No. 199, Feb. 4, 1890; No. 206, April 15, 1890, C. D., Tangier, XVII.

171. Meakin, Moorish Empire, 350-351.

172. In 1880 Mathews had proposed himself as an envoy competent to arrange for procuring "advantages for our flag and commerce" from the wild tribes of this region; Mathews to Evarts, No. 386, Aug. 29, 1880, C. D. Tangier, XII. Lewis commended the British way of enforcing a settlement upon the Sultan: "arbitration was not discussed, for everyone here knows that the arbitration of a year ago resulted in a total loss of the prestige of the Government which accepted it;" Lewis to Rives, No. 142, March 18, 1889, and No. 145, April 10, 1889, Ibid., XVII.

173. Meakin, Moorish Empire, 412-413; Walter Burton Harris, "Two Years of Moorish Politics", Blackwood's Magazine, CLIII (Feb., 1893), 446-448. (hereafter cited as "Two Years of Moorish Politics")

174. Roland Anthony Oliver, Sir Harry Johnston and the Scramble for Africa, 141-142.

175. W. B. Harris, "Two Years of Moorish Politics," 448-457; Meakin, Moorish Empire, 344-346; Piquet, Le Maroc, 182.

176. See Malloy, Treaties, II, 1964-1992 for the text of the treaty. The Senate resolution is on page 1991.

177. Count von Tattenbach served as Germany's representative in Morocco from 1889 to 1896. He was known as an aggressive concession hunter.

178. The text of the treaty is in British and Foreign State Papers, 1889-1890, LXXXII, 968-972.

179. Williamson, Germany and Morocco Before 1905, 107, 109-110, 112-115, 143.

180. In the letter accepting his reappointment, Mathews made a singular statement: "I was born in Africa, at Tangier, Morocco, as an American citizen " (author's italics). He gave these biographical details also: 'In my boyhood I resided at Brooklyn, New York and in the State of California since 1855, excepting the period of the civil war and from 1869 to 1887 which latter period of eighteen years I resided at Tangier, holding the post of United States Consul." Mathews to Wharton, New York, Feb. 21, 1890, C. D., Tangier, XVII. Mathews thanked the State Dept. for its instruction on Aug. 15 appointing him consul general; Mathews to Wharton, No. 1, Sept. 18, 1890, Ibid., XVIII.

181. Mathews to Wharton, No. 5, May 1, 1890, C. D., Tangier, XVII.

182. Mathews to Wharton, No. 6, May 1, 1890, with enclosure of clipping from the Times of Morocco dated April 26, 1890, Ibid.

183. Of Cobb, who appears later in this history, Mathews wrote Wharton in No. 22, Aug. 21, 1890, C. D.,

Tangier, XVIII: "Capt. John Cobb is a native of Clinton, Conn., seventy years of age, and during our Civil War commanded a transport of our navy. About sixteen years ago he settled in Casablanca as a merchant, introducing American manufactures, and put up the first mill in that seaport."

184. Mathews to Wharton, No. 7, May 29, 1890; No. 8, June 6, 1890; No. 14, July 15, 1890; No. 15, July 26, 1890; *C. D., Tangier*, XVII. Mathews to Wharton, No. 19, Aug. 14, 1890; No. 22, Aug. 21, 1890; No. 7, Oct. 28, 1890; No. 8, Oct. 28, 1890; No. 16, Jan. 18, 1891; No. 22, March 25, 1891; *Ibid.*, XVIII. Roffe to Blaine, letter, June 17, 1890, *Ibid.*, XVII. Mathews to Blaine, No. 23, Aug. 29, 1890, *Ibid.*, XVIII.

185. Mathews to Wharton, No. 18, Jan. 23, 1891; No. 31, May 27, 1891; No. 61, Feb. 11, 1892; *Ibid.*

186. Mathews to Wharton, No. 62, Feb. 18, 1892, *Ibid.*

187. Reports of Felix A. Mathews, Nov. 28, 1891, United States, 52nd Congress, 1st Session, 1891-92, *House Miscellaneous Documents*, XLIX, *Consular Reports, XXXIX*, Ser. No. 3007, 170-175 and Nov. 30, 1892, United States, 52nd Congress, 2nd Session, 1892-93, *House Miscellaneous Documents*, XVIII, *Consular Reports*, XL and XLI, 1892-1893, Ser. No. 3127, 401-402.

188. Mathews to Wharton, No. 79, July 17, 1892, *C. D., Tangier*, XVIII; No. 83, Aug. 17, 1892; No. 98, Feb. 2, 1893, *Ibid.*

189. Pribram, *Secret Treaties*, I, 157, 163, 142-145, 146-149, and II, 98-102.

190. Fay, *Origins of the World War*, I, 143-144.

191. James Linus Glanville, *Italy's Relations with England, 1896-1905* (hereafter cited as Glanville, *Italy's Relations with England*), 22-23.

192. Andrássy, <u>Bismarck, Andrássy and Their Successors</u>, 199-200.

193. Brandenburg, <u>From Bismarck to the World War</u>, 38.

194. Lady Gwendolyn Cecil, <u>Life of Robert, Marquis of Salisbury</u>, 4 vols.; (hereafter cited as Cecil, <u>Life of Salisbury</u>), IV, 382-384.

195. Georges Michon, <u>The Franco-Russian Alliance, 1891-1917</u> (hereafter cited as Michon, <u>Franco-Russian Alliance</u>), 33-34, 61.

196. Germany's non-renewal of her reinsurance treaty with Russia has been exaggerated as the cause for the forming of the Franco-Russian entente and alliance; Fay, <u>Origins of the World War</u>, I, 95-96, 119-120.

197. American readers were informed of the changing popular sentiment toward colonies in France by L. Levy-Bruhl, in "French Political Stability and Economic Unrest," in <u>The Forum</u> XIV (January, 1893), 653-659.

198. Anderson, <u>First Moroccan Crisis</u>, 5-6.

199. Girault, <u>Colonial Tariff Policy of France</u>, 152-153; Woolf, <u>Empire and Commerce in Africa</u>, 134, 325.

200. Meakin, <u>Moorish Empire</u>, 191-192; Bonsal, <u>Morocco As It Is</u>, 19-22, 27, 56-57, 61-62, 65; Piquet, <u>Le Maroc</u>, 182; Madariaga, <u>Spain</u>, 337-338, 341.

201. Mathews to Wharton, No. 57, Jan. 14, 1892, <u>C. D., Tangier</u>, XVIII; No. 59, Feb. 1, 1892; No. 83, Aug. 17, 1892, <u>Ibid.</u> Mathews to Josiah Quincy, Ass't. Sec. of State, No. 121, Oct. 15, 1893, <u>Ibid.</u>, XIX, No. 122, Oct. 20, 1893, and No. 125, Nov. 1, 1893, <u>Ibid.</u>

202. Gummeré to Hill, No. 98, April 18, 1899, <u>Ibid.</u>, XXIV.

203. Barclay to Strobel, 3rd Ass't. Sec. of State, letter, Oct. 20, 1893; Barclay to Josiah Quincy, No. 1, Dec. 13, 1893, *C. D., Tangier*, XIX. Barclay to Uhl, Ass't. Sec. of State, Dec. 14, 1893; No. 6, Jan. 1, 1894; March 10, 1894; No. 15, March 12, 1894; No. 17, March 31, 1894; No. 22, April 27, 1894; *Ibid.* Report of Barclay for 1893, *House Documents*, LV, 1st Session, 54th Congress, 1895-96, *Commercial Relations*, 1894-95, I, Serial No. 3422, 261-265.

204. Barclay to Uhl, No. 7, Jan. 2, 1894, *C. D., Tangier*, XIX; No. 10, Jan. 29, 1894; No. 15, March 8, 1894; No. 13, March 8, 1894; No. 20, April 4, 1894; No. 28, June 11, 1894, *Ibid.* Barclay to State Dept., telegram, June 11, 1894, *Ibid.* Stuart, *Tangier*, 40. Dr. John Scott Keltie, *The Partition of Africa*, Second Edition (hereafter cited as Keltie, *Partition of Africa*), 459. Bonsal, *Morocco As It Is*, 30-34.

205. For example, the New York *Weekly Times*, XLI, Jan. 13, 1892, and July 27, 1892, 5. There were frequent mentions of the Moroccan situation in "News of the Week: Foreign," in the *Independent* from 1890 to 1892.

206. *Nation*, LIV (Jan. 28, 1892), 63.

207. Bonsal, *Morocco As It Is*, 44-45, 49; Meakin, *Moorish Empire*, 417-418.

208. It has been estimated that the total trade remained stationary in the decade from 1886 to 1896. N. D. Harris, *Europe and Africa*, 280.

209. Meakin, *Moorish Empire*, 390-391.

210. Another description of the state of Morocco in 1892 is given in Arthur Silva White, *The Development of Africa. A Study in Applied Geography*, Second Edition, 199-200. "France will develop her African possessions .... Very different is the prospect ... in Morocco, which ... lies stagnating in the name of Allah. The magnificent squalor of the towns, the

dumb evidences of a down-trodden people, whose only advantage under political rule is the opportunity to escape it ... cry out for reparation. Christians are despised, and can only live with security ... under the aegis of their political representatives; exports are crippled by a prohibitive tariff; and native industries are paralysed .... The insensate jealousy between the European Powers in Morocco only complicates matters and retards progress. France and Great Britain have participated for the most part in the exterior commerce of Morocco, but Germany is now taking a foremost place."

211. Walter Burton Harris, "The Accession of the New Sultan of Morocco," Blackwood's Magazine, CLVI (Oct., 1894), 467-484.

212. Bülow to the Chancellor, June 21, 1894, G. P., VIII, 331, quoted by Stuart, Tangier, 40.

Chapter VI

Morocco, The Pawn of the Powers

During the decade 1894 to 1904 there was a complete reversal of the status and affiliates of the great powers as arranged by Bismarck in 1887. He thought that he had isolated France while neutralizing Russia and had deprived Great Britain of all support in her colonial ambitions. His status quo policy, however, began to be challenged and undermined as early as 1890, the year of his dismissal from office. By 1894, France, seconded by Russia, resumed the offensive in imperialism. Unable to make alliances with either Germany or the United States, in 1904 Great Britain finally compromised her differences with France in the Mediterranean, thereby maintaining her life-lines to India and the Far East. It was Germany's turn, now, to be headed for diplomatic isolation, while France and Great Britain shared in varying degrees and areas the management of European imperialism. The Anglo-French entente was not a partnership of complete respect and confidence, however.

An outstanding characteristic of the decade was the rapid rise of three parvenus in Weltpolitik--Germany, the United States, and Japan. Germany had entered the game of imperialism in 1884; now she sought to resume an active role in directing world diplomacy, depending upon the uncertain loyalty of her partners in the Triple Alliance. To supplement the support of France, Great Britain won the active backing of the United States without an alliance and of Japan with one.[1] This diplomatic revolution affected not only Morocco and Egypt in Africa, but also China in Asia and the Caribbean area and Central and South America. It involved a complete modernization of the Monroe Doctrine by the United States and the decline and eventual fall of Morocco as an independent country.

The great seer of American imperialism was Alfred Thayer Mahan, who in 1890 publicly declared the new

American ambition: "Americans must now begin to look outward."[2] He advocated a "cordial understanding" with Great Britain. He soon had a large international following.[3] In the United States he inspired a group of influential disciples, notably Theodore Roosevelt, who shared his ambitions for American naval and diplomatic prestige, and Andrew Carnegie, who openly advocated a "reunion" of Great Britain, Canada, and the United States.[4] Early in 1895, Henry Cabot Lodge, another perfervid expansionist, condemned Cleveland's handling of foreign relations as "everywhere a policy of retreat and surrender." The Democratic party, he asserted, had abandoned the only constructive policy ever practiced by its leaders, that of territorial expansion.[5]

By December, however, the administration had redeemed itself by Cleveland's famous message to Congress demanding arbitration of the boundary dispute between Venezuela and British Guiana and announcing Secretary of State Olney's new edition of the Monroe Doctrine. Both Roosevelt and Lodge enthusiastically endorsed Olney's doctrine that the United States was practically sovereign on the American continents and that three thousand miles of intervening ocean made any permanent political union between a European and an American state unnatural and inexpedient.[6] To Olney's reciprocal declaration of American disinterestedness in the moral and material interests peculiar to Europe and aloofness from European wars or preparations for them, they later offered vociferous dissent.

Within a decade Olney's assertion of American isolation from European politics became obsolete. The policy of aggressive commercial expansion initiated by the United States in 1890[7] made inevitable a readjustment of political relationships. After a long interval of quiescence, the two cardinal principles of American foreign policy received new formulation, application, and acceptance, preliminary to still further development during Roosevelt's second term as president. The United States began active cooperation with Europe in the settlement of European controversies in Asia. Through the Open Door the United States entered into foreign entanglements from which the Monroe Doctrine had hitherto shielded her. New alignments among the great European powers resulted in more than one attempt to attract the United States into new political orbits. Inevitably, there were clashes between the United States and her two rivals for ascendant world power, Germany and Japan.

Between 1894 and 1898 an entirely new cast was selected to play the leading roles in the drama of Weltpolitik. In 1894, when Abd al-Aziz took the chief role in the scene known as "the Moroccan problem," Prince von Hohenlohe began to act Germany's part in the main plot. Because of the latter's incompetence to cope with the "Ersatz-government"[8] operating under Baron Friedrich von Holstein since 1890,[9] the conduct of German international relations was entrusted to Count Bernhard von Bülow, who became minister of foreign affairs on June 28, 1897, and chancellor in October, 1908. Admiral von Tirpitz, appointed head of the admiralty on November 27, 1897,[10] was scarcely less powerful in Germany's international affairs, although Holstein continued to direct operations behind the scenes. In 1897, also, three Americans came into influential official positions to direct the course of world events. After April 8, 1897, Theodore Roosevelt did valiant service as assistant secretary of the navy.[11] Appointed ambassador to Great Britain in March, 1897 and promoted to be secretary of state in September, 1898,[12] John Hay found an able ally for promoting Anglo-American friendship in Henry White, who returned in March, 1897 to his post as secretary of the American embassy in London.[13] Russia, too, was under new management. Tsar Nicholas II, ascending the throne in 1894, with his foreign ministers Lobanov and Muraviev, was responsible for the later war with Japan.[14] But the most aggressive part of all was taken by Théophile Delcassé, the first minister of colonies in the French Cabinet (1894) and minister of foreign affairs in five successive French governments from 1898 to 1905. An expansionist of the Ferry school, he set about the task of acquiring Morocco and the Sudan by strengthening the Russian alliance in 1899[15] and conciliating rival imperial powers outside the Triple Alliance.[16]

The British government challenged by Olney in July, 1895, had come into office the preceding month. It was a Conservative-Liberal Unionist coalition, with its two components led by the prime minister, the Marquis of

Salisbury, and by Joseph Chamberlain, the colonial secretary. It avowed a policy of colonial expansion and imperial solidarity,[17] a dangerous one in view of Great Britain's diplomatic isolation. France and Russia were chronically hostile to Britain because of colonial rivalries. A German offer of alliance had been rejected by Great Britain in 1894,[18] and Salisbury's proposal to effect an Anglo-German rapprochement by the partitioning of Turkey was declined by Germany in 1895.[19] The Kaiser's suggestion of an anti-British continental bloc in December, 1895,[20] coincided with Cleveland's threat of war if Great Britain should refuse to abide by the decision of an American boundary commission.[21]

The spark which almost exploded the inflammable diplomatic material was the Kaiser's notorious Krüger telegram, intended to challenge British advance into the Transvaal.[22] In both Great Britain and the United States the public demand grew that two kindred nations should not expiate in blood the blunders of diplomats. An Anglo-American treaty signed on November 12, 1896, provided for arbitration of the boundary dispute, and shortly afterwards the American commission ceased work. The British-Venezuelan treaty of February 2, 1897, did award most of the disputed territory to British Guiana, but the whole incident was a signal diplomatic triumph for the United States. The American Senate refused to accept the general arbitration treaty proposed by Salisbury and recommended by both Cleveland and McKinley. Isolationists and anti-British groups continued a noisy opposition to an "English alliance," but a closer friendship was evident between the two peoples. By its acceptance of the American interpretation of the Monroe Doctrine, the British government had laid the foundation for an entente on world problems.

Spender doubts whether Salisbury ever really understood the American viewpoint. But he had been induced to say that the United States had "the same sort of interest in the Caribbean Sea as we had in the Channel ports of Belgium and the Netherlands." Spender thus describes the development of the dispute:

> The affair left an impression in European Foreign Offices that there was something mysterious and dangerous in the American mentality which had better in future be handled with caution. Europe comforted itself with the reflection that if the United States had this vast sphere of influence all to itself, it would at least leave other nations alone. But here too, there was a rude awakening. Within three years the United States had annexed Hawaii in the teeth of Japanese opposition, made war on Spain, driven her out of Cuba, and annexed the Philippines. American imperialism was now of the same pattern as the British, and the forward school in both countries hailed the American writer, Mahan ... as their leader and prophet. Under the common inspiration, the British and American navies became at this time all but a band of brothers.[23]

In a speech at Birmingham on January 25, 1896, Chamberlain pled openly for an Anglo-American partnership:

> The two nations are allied, and more closely allied in sentiment than any other nations on the face of the earth. While I should look with horror upon anything in the nature of a fratricidal strife, I should look forward with pleasure to the possibility of the Stars and Stripes and the Union Jack floating together in defence of a common cause sanctioned by humanity and justice.[24]

Before estranging herself from Great Britain, Germany had made an enemy of Japan. After winning the Sino-Japanese War in 1895, Japan had been robbed of a large part of the spoils gained from China, for Russia, France, and Germany combined to forbid her annexation of the Liao-tung peninsula. While the United States and Great Britain earned Japan's gratitude by their non-intervention, Germany's conduct was especially resented. Hitherto friendly to Japan, Germany's new policy was to divert Russia's attention to the Far East, where a Russo-German entente might permit both countries to acquire ports in China. Unable either to join or to weaken the Dual Alliance, Germany was excluded even from the loan made to pay China's indemnity to Japan.[25] Impelled by public demand for advance, the Kaiser spurred on the Tsar toward a clash with Japan, whereby he succeeded finally in alienating both Great Britain and Russia.[26]

Kaiser William realized very early in his career that the United States was destined to become a competitor in colonies and commerce scarcely less formidable than Great Britain herself.[27] In 1893 he urged upon the Tsarevitch Nicholas a European economic league to combat the Pan-American ambitions of the United States, which aimed at the total exclusion of European commerce from all of America.[28] The Alldeutscher Verband, which later raised the spectre of Pan-Germanism in the United States, was founded in 1894 to fan the flame of German chauvinism.[29] Again in 1896 the Kaiser tried to win the Tsar over to the project of a continental league against the yellow races and also the United States with her economic hostility manifested in the McKinley Tariff.[30] Count Sergius Witte says that similar proposals were made to him in 1897,[31] and William II thought that his plan of a Franco-German-Russian bloc[32] to curb the Anglo-American menace had been accepted by the Tsar.[33]

The German fear of the United States was a national sentiment at this time. This is evident from speeches made by responsible government officials[34] and from the hostile opinions expressed by manufacturers, landowners, the press, and university professors, as reported by the American ambassador in Germany.[35] Following his famous dictum, "We do not want to put anyone in the shade, but we demand a place for ourselves in the sun," Bülow advocated a cautious policy toward England and Russia in order to secure Pacific bases for the planned "risk" navy. He planned economic penetration into the Far East and Asia Minor. To ensure peace, he would "provoke no one, but at the same time, allow no one to tread on our feet."[36] The tremendous growth of the German population and the unfavorable balance of trade, in spite of Germany's ranking next to Great Britain as an exporting nation, made markets, trade, raw materials, and world politics vital matters.[37]

Meanwhile, Roosevelt was finding his naval position

advantageous for the expression of his belligerent ideas. He was advocating an isthmian canal and the immediate annexation of Hawaii in order to forestall Japan.[38] Nevertheless, he was willing to concede that both English and German imperialistic ambitions were as legitimate as those of the Americans.[39]

In April, 1898, Roosevelt had a chance to begin carrying out his declared intention of driving every European country out of America, starting with Spain.[40] Admiral Dewey and he had bully fights at Manila and San Juan; together they took the Philippines, and ultimately the exploits of the Rough Rider placed him in the president's chair in time to play a stellar role in Weltpolitik.[41]

The Spanish-American War, the first open clash between Germany and the United States in the Pacific, was likewise the second great milestone along the path to Anglo-American amity. The American public and press built up the legend that only Captain Chichester had prevented Germany from attempting the seizure of the Philippines. But documentary evidence proves that Germany was merely waiting watchfully for a chance to pick up some coaling stations, if the United States did not take the islands. Because of her naval weakness and her resolution not to precipitate hostilities, Germany withdrew from the Philippines.[42]

An indirect American gain from the war was the annexation of Hawaii (July 7, 1898), so long coveted by the American imperialists. The war also stimulated all three of the rising powers to the upbuilding of their naval armaments. Being refused a part in the protectorate of the Philippines, Japan felt keenly the need of implementing her diplomacy.[43] Between 1895 and 1904, Japan heavily reinforced her navy, mostly from British shipyards. The law of 1898, founding the German navy, was passed before the war began, but the naval law of 1900 was definitely aimed at providing a navy which "the most formidable navy" could not hope to attack with impunity.[44] However, Bülow explained to the Reichstag that his aim was a continuance of economic and political development by peaceful means.[45] Hitherto always sporadic, after the great increase in appropriations in 1898, the naval program of the United States made steady progress toward placing the United States among the leading naval powers.[46]

Perhaps the most important effect of the Spanish-American war was the martial spirit aroused in the American people. A frenzied chauvinism manifested itself in lofty moral and philosophical concepts characteristically Anglo-Saxon. In poetry and prose, in press and pulpit, the English-speaking peoples glorified the task of carrying the white man's burden. Only a few voices cried feebly from the wilderness of isolation against the evils of imperialism.[47]

The many demonstrations of British support of the United States, including the offer of alliance publicly made by Chamberlain, naturally gave rise to rumors of a secret Anglo-American entente. Hay denied repeatedly that any such document existed, and none has ever been found.[48] In truty, the Anglo-American understanding rested upon a much broader base than any deal between diplomats. In a direct message to the American people, Chamberlain advocated an ultimate alliance in defense of Anglo-Saxon ideals, to follow Washington's plan of "temporary" alliances for emergencies.[49]

In 1898 the frictions of Great Britain with France in Africa and with Russia and Germany in the Far East, as well as a probable Boer war in South Africa, prompted the British government's overtures for alliances, not only with the United States, but with Russia and Germany. When Russia rejected Salisbury's offers, he permitted the group in his Cabinet favoring a German alliance--Chamberlain, Lord Lansdowne, and the Duke of Devonshire--to try its plan. From March to August, 1898, negotiations were carried on by Chamberlain with Count Hatzfeldt, the German ambassador in London.[50] The former proposed an Anglo-German defensive alliance, publicly sanctioned by Parliament, but not precluding secret articles. Bülow and Holstein feared that an open alliance would expose Germany to attack on two fronts; they preferred a colonial agreement instead. Trying to get the Tsar to better England's offers, the Kaiser was amazed to learn of the British previous approach to Russia.[51] Suspicious of

British good faith, the German government decided to postpone consideration of an alliance until necessity might induce the British Cabinet to make a more attractive offer. Salisbury, also, seemed content to drop the matter. The only semblance of an Anglo-German colonial agreement was the secret pact of August 30, 1898, providing for the division of Portugal's African colonies between them, if Portugal should default on her contemplated loans from them.[52] On October 14, 1899, when Salisbury secretly renewed the treaty of 1661, guaranteeing British protection of all Portuguese colonies, the evidence of British perfidy seemed conclusive to Germany.[53]

Offsetting the British failures to reach accords with Russia and Germany in 1898 was a diplomatic triumph culminating in 1904 in an Anglo-French entente. On July 10, 1898, Captain Marchand planted the French flag at Fashoda, claiming a hinterland that would dominate British-controlled Egypt. The entry of Kitchener into Khartum, Delcassé's policy of conciliating Britain, and France's failure to secure diplomatic support led to the withdrawal of the Marchand expedition. By March 21, 1899, Great Britain and France had made a treaty delimiting their respective spheres of influence.[54]

The confused and conflicting diplomatic situation might have been cleared up at the First Hague Conference, in session from May 18 to June 29, 1899, in which twenty-six states were represented. All of the great powers went reluctantly and skeptically. An English publicist called it the "Parliament of Man." The only rulers not represented were the presidents of the South American republics, the King of Abyssinia, the Grand Lama of Tibet, and the Emperor of Morocco. But the inequality of the countries represented was very evident, as was the domination of the world by three groups of powers.[55] So great were the distrust and recrimination among the important powers, that the conference failed to achieve the chief objectives for which Tsar Nicholas had summoned it--limitation of land and naval forces and the adoption of mediation and voluntary arbitration to prevent war.[56]

At the beginning of the Boer War in October, 1899, Great Britain was still searching desperately for allies.

The removal of the friction caused by the unsatisfactory workings of the tripartite protectorate over the Samoan Islands since 1889 offered an opportunity to conciliate both Germany and the United States. The Samoan group was divided between them, with compensation for Great Britain in the Tonga Islands and part of the Solomon group.[57] Apparently Chamberlain hoped that British concession in the Samoan Islands, Germany's first colonizing project, might prove the basis for a wider understanding.[58] The United States and Germany had now settled all pending problems regarding island colonies in the Pacific. Henceforth their conflicts were to be confined to the Far East and to Latin America.

In November, 1899, Chamberlain began to work for an Anglo-American-German understanding to curb Russian advance in China. The visit of William II and Bülow to England gave an opportunity for conversations on the proposal.[59] Chamberlain suggested that Germany could be compensated by a free hand in Turkish concessions, participation of British capital in the Berlin-to-Bagdad railway, and the Atlantic coast of Morocco. Tangier, of course, was to be Great Britain's share of Morocco.[60] Balfour and Lansdowne seemed less willing to make definite commitments. The Kaiser and Bülow, as before, wanted special agreements on any point requiring adjustment and pointed out that the proposed alliance would make France and Russia hostile to Germany. Nevertheless, they left the way open for further discussions.

Encouraged by Bülow, Chamberlain made a speech at Leicester on November 30, 1899, frankly revealing his plan:

> The natural alliance is between ourselves and the great German Empire .... I cannot conceive any point which can arise in the immediate future which would bring ourselves and the Germans into antagonism of interests. On the contrary, I can see many things which must be cause of anxiety to the statesmen of Europe, but in which that understanding of which I have spoken in the case of America might, if extended to Germany, do more, perhaps, than any combination of arms in order to preserve the peace of the world ....

> If the union between England and America is a powerful factor in the cause of peace, a new Triple Alliance between the Teutonic race and the two branches of the Anglo-Saxon race will be a still more potent influence in the future of the world .... An understanding is perhaps better than an alliance, which may stereotype arrangements which cannot be regarded as permanent in view of the changing circumstances from day to day.[61]

This overture by Chamberlain was answered by a storm of Anglo-phobia in the German press and the Reichstag and with little favor in the British press. In the United States there was indifference, for the fervent devotion to Britain in Spanish-American War days was waning, and Irish and German voters were loud in denunciation of the British attack on the Boers.[62] To counter public criticism, Bülow made a Reichstag speech on December 11, promoting naval appropriations and suggesting that Great Britain's predicament might be used to obtain future advantages for Germany. Shortly afterwards, the strife over the seizure of a German vessel charged with carrying contraband to the Boers and the passage of the German naval law of 1900 effectually ended all talk of an alliance.[63]

However, the German government ignored public sympathy for the Boers and remained neutral. Bülow refused to join a proposed continental coalition to intervene for the Boers, and William II declined to receive a Boer deputation under Krüger.[64]

The American government, also, remained neutral and steadfastly refused to intervene.[65] As before, charges were made freely both in America and in Europe that there was a secret Anglo-American understanding, but Hay used every opportunity to deny these allegations.[66] During the Boer War the British and American governments were busy negotiating settlements on questions relating to the isthmian canal, Canada, and China. The friendly attitude of John Hay helped to make these agreements more favorable to the United States.[67]

During 1898 and 1899 the problem of China was the most important one in world diplomacy. Germany had to force recognition of her aid in saving China from Japan by receiving the Harbor of Kiaochow and many valuable concessions for ninety-nine years in Shantung--nominally as a reparation for two murdered missionaries. By the end of 1898, Russia, France, Great Britain, and Japan had staked out their spheres of activity and had been granted auxiliary privileges.[68] By the end of April, 1899, the powers had made treaties among themselves delimiting their prospective spheres of influence. The Yangtse Valley had been alloted to Great Britain, all China north of the Great Wall to Russia, Shantung and the valley of the Hoang-ho to Germany, and the southern provinces near Tonquin to France.[69] Apparently, China was being partitioned into foreign colonies, following the fate of Africa. In both Africa and China the United States was conspicuously absent from the list of colonizing powers. In China, however, the United States found the locale for the launching of her second fundamental principle of foreign policy--the Open Door. It was this policy which served ostensibly to involve the United States in Morocco for many years.

Like the Monroe Doctrine of 1823, the Hay Open Door Doctrine of 1899 was British-inspired. Beginning in March, 1898, Great Britain had made several requests for American cooperation in maintaining the Open Door in China, a policy supported by both countries independently for almost sixty years.[70] At first unaware of any danger of its violation, President McKinley saw no reason for the United States to connect "with European complications." Unsupported, Great Britain herself joined in the schemes of partition of spheres. Naturally favoring the status quo lest her plans for future commercial penetration of China be frustrated, Japan had been temporarily pacified by Russia's acknowledgment of her special interests in Korea. Hay was too busy to act in the Chinese situation until after the acquisition of the Philippines. The influence exerted upon American public opinion by a British propagandist, Sir Charles Beresford, reinforced by arguments made to Hay by W. W. Rockhill, formerly an American diplomat in China,[71] induced Hay to adopt the policy formulated in a memorandum by Rockhill. Rockhill declared in favor of an independent American policy; he regarded England "as great an offender in China as Russia itself."[72]

During September and November of 1899 Hay declared his policy in identical notes addressed to the governments of Great Britain, Germany, Russia, Japan, Italy, and France. He asked each country to adhere to the American policy and to use its influence to obtain the assent of the others. He proposed no interference with any treaty port or vested interest in any sphere of influence. But the Chinese tariff was to be applied in all ports and to be collected by China, and there was to be equality of harbor dues on all vessels and of railroad rates for citizens of all nations.[73] The replies were variable, but evasive without exception. Great Britain and Russia reserved Kowloon and Manchuria, respectively, and the latter's reply was virtually a diplomatic refusal. Each country made its adherence conditional upon that of the others.[74]

Boldly ignoring all reservations, on March 20, 1900 Hay announced that each power had given a "final and definitive" assent. Hay was hailed as the savior of China, and the prestige of American diplomacy, at home and abroad, was at its zenith.[75]

The Boxer Rebellion threatened to undo Hay's work. The foreign legations were besieged from June 11 to mid-August, 1900, before they were rescued by an allied army. There was every prospect that China's punishment would be death by partition. Again Hay met the emergency by his circular note of July 3, 1900. The United States would hold to strict accountability the perpetrators of all wrongs to American citizens, but she also wished

> to protect Chinese territorial and administrative entity, to protect all rights guaranteed to friendly powers by treaty and international law, and to safeguard for the world the principle of equal and impartial trade with all parts of the Chinese Empire.[76]

It was not Hay's declaration, however, but an Anglo-German agreement of October 16, 1900,[77] to which the other powers adhered. The two powers agreed to uphold the Open Door "for all Chinese territory so far as they can exercise influence," to abstain from obtaining territorial advantages for themselves, to direct their policy toward maintaining the territorial integrity of the Chinese

Empire, and to make an understanding to protect their interests if any other power should obtain territory.[78] Later, when Russia's penetration into Manchuria continued, the German government declared that it had never meant to apply the agreement to Manchuria, which was outside the sphere of German interests and influence.[79] British opinion was indignant at Germany's double-dealing.[80] Bülow had been consistent in his policy of steering a middle course between Russia and England, and another attempt at an Anglo-German rapprochement had failed. Hay refused Salisbury's suggestion that the United States be the third signer of the declaration. He wrote Adee that in the "present morbid state of the public mind toward England, that is not to be thought of--and we must look idly on, and her seeking terms with Germany instead of us."[81]

The triumph of the Open Door policy was illusory. Repeatedly Russia sought to make separate and secret arrangements with China for privileges in Manchuria. On February 1, 1901, Hay was obliged to admit to Japan that the United States was not prepared, either singly or with other powers, to make any forcible defense of the territorial integrity of China.[82] All that the United States could do was to send occasional notes of protest to Russia, such as Hay's dispatch of February 1, 1902.[83]

After the Boxer crisis, the peace protocol, signed on September 7, 1901, gave the United States $25,000,000 of the total $333,000,000 indemnity assessed upon China. Within two years the United States had gone far into foreign politics.[84] It was a far cry from making a most favored nation treaty with China to carrying on an armed intervention and collecting an indemnity there--not to mention attempting to impose on the other powers a new American policy--and the American spirit of isolation was reviving.

At intervals during the entire year of 1901 Great Britain continued to attempt an escape from her isolation by a fourth and last effort to arrange an Anglo-German entente. In informal conversation with Eckardstein,[85] in January, 1901, Chamberlain said that Great Britain must choose between the Triple and the Dual Alliance, of which he preferred the former. He suggested that Morocco might form the basis for a bargain. Later, Lord Lansdowne[96] and Eckardstein discussed a defensive alliance for the Far East. The German government proposed that if Germany were to guarantee the whole British Empire, Great Britain should adhere to the Triple Alliance and bring Japan in also. The British counter-proposal of an entente to ensure the *status quo* in regions where both countries had interests did not appeal to Bülow and Holstein, who wanted a broader base of agreement and were still afraid of being pushed into war against Russia. The evidence seems to show that although Chamberlain, Hatzfeldt, and Eckardstein favored a binding agreement, neither the German nor the British responsible officials ever considered an Anglo-German entente very seriously. Public opinion on both sides of the Channel was too much inflamed over the Boer War to make such an arrangement feasible.[87]

In 1902 Japan paid her debt to Great Britain. The treaty, signed on January 30, was ostensibly a guarantee of the integrity of China and Korea. Its real purpose was to provide an ally for either of the signers if attacked by two powers in a war over her special interests in China.[88] Lamsdorff, foreign minister of Russia beginning in February, 1902, tried to revive the Far Eastern Triplice of 1895. He, too, aimed to safeguard the independence and integrity of China, but also to determine the lines of partition when the *status quo* could no longer be maintained. Since Germany was determined to remain neutral, the Tsar had to be content with a Franco-Russian agreement along the same lines.[89]

The Anglo-Japanese Alliance was the first success of Great Britain in escaping from the "splendid isolation" of half a century. It was the first of a series of power combinations arranged under the ostensible auspices of King Edward VII. In 1902 the diplomatic forces were a triangle of opposing interests, but within five years the British leaders had control of two sides. Meanwhile, Japan considered it a privilege to serve Great Britain as valiantly with sword and ship as the United States had already served her with the pen.

The cultivation of friendship with the United States remained a major motive of British statesmen. Great Britain did not evacuate her Caribbean holdings, but she did surrender her control in the area. The second treaty made to supersede the Clayton-Bulwer Treaty of 1850, the Hay-Pauncefote Treaty, was approved by the Senate on December 16, 1901. Thus Great Britain conceded to the United States the sole right to construct, manage, police, and, by implication, to fortify an isthmian canal. By reducing their garrisons in the West Indies and transferring their chief naval forces to other regions,[90] the British actually won another diplomatic triumph, masquerading as a sacrifice:

> The partnership of beneficence involved in the Far East was not so much a distribution of assets as of responsibilities. England got out of the Caribbean, in a sense, and the United States got into the Far East .... The price paid by the United States was certainly commensurate with the advantages gained.[91]

As president, Roosevelt concentrated on the settlement of the Alaskan boundary dispute and clearing the slate of all Anglo-American controversies, excepting the perennial Newfoundland fisheries question. Roosevelt obtained the Alaskan-Canadian boundary that he demanded, not by his threat of being his own surveyor or by his "impartial" arbitrators, but because British amity outweighed any cost, even to Canada.[92]

As the basic cause of German-American friction, the Monroe Doctrine remained prominent from 1897 to 1902. Whether they were actual attempts or merely rumors or suspicions, a series of incidents was generally credited officially in the United States as German encroachments upon the Monroe Doctrine preserves.[93] Roosevelt and Lodge were especially apprehensive about the large German settlement in southern Brazil, which they feared might emulate the Americans in Texas in 1836.[94]

If confirmation of American suspicions of Germany were needed, it came with the Venezuelan incident of 1902-3. Great Britain had invited German cooperation in a naval demonstration against Castro, the dictator of Venezuela, who refused to pay claims for broken contracts and damages to their citizens. Italy later joined in the intervention. As a means of coercion, the three powers were assured that Roosevelt would not object to a temporary occupation of territory. But when they blockaded ports in December, 1902, shelled two forts, and captured Venezuelan gunboats, it appeared that Germany was planning a Kiaochow in South America. Italy withdrew, and Great Britain was regarded as a dupe of Germany; both finally agreed to arbitration. Public opinion in both British and American circles was indignant at Germany, and in Germany there was no desire for an irrevocable breach with the United States. The chief interest of this affair lies in the later claim of Roosevelt that his personal intervention and threat of war were responsible for the Kaiser's capitulation.[95] At the time, Roosevelt declined the Kaiser's invitation to arbitrate in favor of the Hague Tribunal and publicly congratulated His Majesty on his devotion to the cause of arbitration.

An indirect but important result of the Venezuelan imbroglio was the recall of the German ambassador, von Holleben, and his replacement by Roosevelt's close personal friend, Baron Herman Speck von Sternburg.[96] Coming at the President's request, Sternburg entered the inner circle of the White House intimates, to which belonged also M. Jules Jusserand and Sir Cecil Spring-Rice. All of these men were associated henceforth with Roosevelt's further adventures in Weltpolitik. It worked to the great advantage of their respective countries that the British and French representatives exerted great influence upon Roosevelt's political opinions and official acts. On the other hand, Sternburg was swayed and dominated by the masterful personality of the President. Both Jusserand and his predecessor studied the personality and methods of their German colleague, analyzed his relations with the President, and reported their observations to the Quai d'Orsay.[97]

The diplomatic world developing at the opening of the twentieth century cannot be comprehended from doctrines and documents alone. The personalities, prejudices, and purposes of the leaders were equally important. Of the international characters in 1902, none could rank above Theodore Roosevelt and Emperor William II in strenuosity, vitality, and ability to stay in the headlines. "Newcomers on the scene of world-politics," they "shouted through the same loudspeakers to attract attention."[98] Although outwardly Roosevelt appeared to reciprocate the Kaiser's friendliness and often publicized their good-fellowship, abundant evidence is available to prove that mistrust of Germany and her ruler dominated Roosevelt's thinking.

In 1902 began a sustained campaign by both Germany and France to gain American support for their diplomacy through the medium of gifts, social amenities, and cultural contacts. Among the last was an exchange of professorships between Berlin and Columbia universities and reciprocal foundations to study French and American literature. In Paris, American ambassador General Horace Porter, fostered much cordiality between France and the United States.[99] Jusserand ridiculed the German overtures to Roosevelt,[100] but apparently considered the similar French gestures most proper. André Tardieu thought the French program very effective:

> In Franco-American relations, sentiment, which usually occupies so small a place in politics, plays an indisputably important role. It is the most active leaven in cooperations sometimes imposed by circumstances on the two peoples.[101]

As the year 1904 approached, when world events were to whirl Roosevelt into ever-widening circles of Weltpolitik, the three most aggressive world powers all felt confident of American interest and support. Since 1894, the situation of Morocco had steadily deteriorated, and the powers were now aligned to take full advantage of her weakness without the handicap of dissension among their own groups. Such, at least was the opinion of Delcassé, the architect of the new diplomacy; events were to disprove his theory.

The reign of Abd al-Aziz, destined to be the last independent sovereign of Morocco for almost half a century, is divided into two distinct periods. The first was actually the reign of his grand vizier, Ba-Ahmed, selected by the dying Mulai Hassan as the guardian and regent for his heir.[102] After the death of his tyrannical mentor in May, 1900, the still youthful sultan essayed to govern as well as to reign, and thereby came his downfall. In Ba-Ahmed's time, the European diplomats paid at least lip service to the maintenance of the status quo; in the era of Abd ul-Aziz, French diplomacy moved deviously but swiftly with its financial and military adjuncts to end the anachronistic sultanate. Chamberlain's twice-made suggestion of Morocco as the key to European imperialistic adjustment was finally adopted.

Ba-Ahmed had managed to quell the traditional accession insurrections and to collect enough taxes to maintain an army able to uphold the authority of Abd al-Aziz in the shrinking blad-al-maghzen. The Sultan was kept in seclusion, and his grand vizier used the rivalries of the foreign powers as a shield against radical reformation and further undermining of the sovereignty which had almost always been a travesty in Morocco.[103]

American Consul General Barclay sent his government detailed accounts of Ba-Ahmed's problems and achievements in securing the accession of Abd ul-Aziz and in putting down the various tribal revolts from 1894 to 1896.[104] Although the defeated rebels were under "a yoke more cruel and galling than Egyptian bondage," Barclay piously hoped that the coming of American missionaries under the Rev. Mr. Nathan to Tangier and Meknes would cause Morocco to lose her character as a "terra incognita to Americans, now that the edge of the thin wedge of civilization and Christianity has entered this stronghold of Moorish fanaticism."[105] However, although one of the future authorities on Morocco assured American readers in 1896 that "each successive decade sees more important progress than the last,"[106] as yet the interest of the United States was not actively attracted toward Morocco.

No illusions about Morocco's future were entertained by Sir Arthur Nicolson, the British representative in Morocco from 1895 to the end of this period. He personified the boredom of the British Foreign Office with Morocco, and his "great achievement during the nine years that he ruled at Tangier was that he did nothing." He shunned politics, but he did follow up Sir John Hay's endeavors to promote humanitarian reform. He was appalled by the iniquities of the protection system, especially as practiced at this time by the Brazilian consulate, and he was convinced that only the opening of Morocco to modern industrial civilization could save the country. He wrote Kaid Maclean in 1895 that Great Britain should avoid a predominant position at court with its possibly awkward responsibility.[107]

Unwearied by his self-imposed task of regenerating Morocco from within, Kaid Maclean remained the political and social leader of the anti-French group which plagued the French Foreign Office until 1904. Although disowned by Nicolson, Maclean found favor with Queen Victoria and the British Foreign Office.[108] Closely associated with him in influence was Walter Burton Harris, the Tangier correspondent of the London _Times_, who has drawn a vivid picture of Moroccan conditions around 1900 in _Morocco That Was_, published in 1921.

An able opponent of the unofficial British group was the similarly unsponsored German coterie that began at this time to establish a position in the Sultan's service. Chief among them was Herr von Rottenberg, who designed the first German concession in compensation for two murdered Germans--a fort at Rabat manned with Krupp guns. As the Sultan's consulting engineer and a Krupp representative, von Rottenberg lacked only the British flair for politics to rank him with the Maclean circle in influence.[109]

The official German representatives were likewise unaggressive during this period, serving mainly to support Nicolson's _laissez faire_ policy. After the concession-greedy Tattenbach left in 1896, Baron Schenk von Schweinberg was "mild and conciliatory." From 1899 to 1905 Freiherr Friedrich von Mentzingen won the confidence of both the Moroccan government and his consular colleagues by his policy of cooperation.[110] However, there were intervention incidents in 1894, 1895, 1896, and 1897, unimportant in themselves, but significant as the first instances in which the German government took an active interest in the protection of its subjects in Morocco.[111]

In contrast to the European representatives, the

American consuls continued from July, 1894 to July, 1898, either to be corrupt themselves or to try futilely to redeem the records of their predecessors. Three men served during these four years--J. Judson Barclay, David Burke, and Frank Partridge. Barclay's term was the longest, ending on August 20, 1896. The periods served by Burke (August, 1896 to January, 1898) and Partridge (January to July, 1898) were manifestly too short to permit any significant accomplishment.

Barclay reported to Washington the great success of the British and French missions to the new Sultan's court. The British minister, Sir Ernest Satow, met a princely welcome at Fez, exchanged valuable gifts between the Queen and the Sultan, and sold the English company's settlement at Cape Juby to Abd al-Aziz for L 50,000 and the pledge of a free port there. The French minister was entertained as lavishly without bringing gifts and was able to settle French claims and obtain official recognition of a French vice consulate at Fez.[112] Barclay did not succeed in making these highly profitable missions a precedent for one by himself to settle the claims of American citizens and protégés--a task he declared was impossible to perform from Tangier. For two years he urged the State Department to review the claims pending since 1884 and 1888, which had been neglected by Mathews and reportedly sold by Lewis, and to commission him to make a direct settlement. The State Department suspected that some American claims were fraudulent, and eventually decided to postpone their consideration until Burke could take charge.[113] Barclay also accused both Mathews and Lewis of other serious irregularities.[114]

It was protection which afforded Barclay his greatest opportunity for charges against his predecessors. Challenged by the State Department to explain a large increase in protégés and <u>semsars</u> since 1890, Barclay sent a corrected list. No such list, he asserted, had been filed in the consular archives or heretofore sent annually to the Moroccan minister at Tangier as required by treaty. Later Barclay denied charges that he personally had extended protection to slave owners. To withdraw illegal protection cards granted in the past, he asserted, would be "to consign their present holders, especially the helpless and dependent Hebrews, to the tender mercies ... of the most rapacious, vindictive, and cruel despots on earth." Grave accusations against Barclay and his subordinates made to Washington by two Englishmen promoting a bogus cattle syndicate and refused American protection were negated by their flight from Tangier to escape persecution for fraud in the British courts. There were charges of malfeasance against John Cobb and the interpreter Ramon Azogue. Barclay complained of the difficult task of collecting the numerous protection papers of all grades "scattered over the Empire," which had been issued mostly by Mathews, but some even by McMath. From April 24, 1895 to July 24, 1896, the chief topic of Barclay's dispatches was his denial of charges against him which were sent to his superiors.[115]

Although they were not finally acted upon for about a year, the charges which procured Barclay's dismissal were those made by Robert Stalker, for eight years consular clerk and acting consul for a brief time. When deprived of his clerkship by Barclay, Stalker made definite charges to the State Department detailing Barclay's methods of enriching himself. In August, 1895, Stalker denied countercharges against him by Barclay and asked for a commission of inquiry. Stalker made seven specific charges against Barclay as follows: 1. Appointment of Azogue as interpreter in spite of the strong objection of some Americans in Tangier, although Azogue had been a notorious trafficker in the sale of <u>semsar</u> certificates under Lewis. 2. Remodeling the tariff of notarial fees, thereby gaining $1660 a year, largely from <u>semsar</u> and <u>maholat</u> certificates. 3. Secretly appointing his son vice consul general and two consular agents and permitting the former to serve before he got his commission. 4. Requiring Stalker, as clerk, to divide his salary with Barclay's son. 5. Appropriating the "gain of exchange" on his drafts. 6. Receiving gifts, including rich Oriental carpets and a costly silver service from England and many perishable items sold in the market. 7. Pocketing the sale proceeds of the license for export of 6,000 head of cattle.

Learning from a press report of his successor's appointment, in June, 1896, Barclay made three requests for a leave of absence to obtain proof of the falsity of the charges against him. On August 20 he offered his resignation. On the same day he wrote Rockhill a lengthy reply to a letter signed "J. D. McCook," which, he asserted was an assumed name for Felix Mathews and Robert Stalker, collaborators in a foul conspiracy to ruin him. Barclay denied all accusations against himself and Azogue and presented old and new charges against Mathews. As character witnesses for himself, he named Richard Harding Davis, "all the respectable residents of Tangier, of every European nationality, the Minister of the Sultan, the Missionaries, and the diplomatic corps."[117]

David Burke, American consul at Malaga since 1893, arrived at Tangier on August 17, 1896 to replace Barclay. He reported receiving a most courteous reception from Barclay and his son. Burke's brother became vice-consul and clerk.[118] Before coming to Spain, Burke had had a very successful career in the consular service in South America since 1886 and was considered to be of the right character and ability to carry out his instructions to purge the American consulate in Morocco of its long established corruption.[119]

Burke found his new task so arduous that he must perforce neglect the promotion of American-Moroccan commerce. He asked for an increase of salary to "a decent living figure," since he was no longer collecting illegal fees, and the chief clerk in some legations was better paid than he was as consul general. From all evidence available, he concluded that the ex-interpreter Azogue had been the leader in selling protection, _semsar_, and _mohalat_ certificates, and power of attorney papers. He had used also other forms of extortion and graft. Azogue again denied the "calumnies" against him in the "McCook letter", while Burke criticized the State Department for sending him pseudonym-signed letters apparently written by Azogue. The proof of Barclay's complicity in the scandalous practices of the consulate was evident from his retention and defense of Azogue and the destruction of many official records by the latter and Barclay's son. _Al-Maghreb Al-Aksa_ came out boldly with articles and letters citing specific instances of misdoings under Barclay's management and calling for an investigation.[120]

Burke was kept busy examining and cancelling the certificates of all types bought by persons ineligible for protection by treaty provisions, which he found diffused throughout the country. He discharged and replaced many consular agents for selling these documents or for other discreditable acts. Nevertheless, he did not endorse the State Department's suggestion that all consular agencies except the Tangier office be closed. Local agents, he said, were necessary to check the confiscation and theft of property of American protégés and also their imprisonment by Moroccan officials. The protection lists required drastic revision; by the end of 1897 there remained only sixteen protégés, eighteen _semsars,_ and one hundred four _mohalats_. Regarding the abolition of protection alleged to be favored by Great Britain, France, and Spain, Burke dissented. He thought this was a scheme to stifle the increasing trade of Germany, which, if successful, would result eventually in the exclusion of Spain also and an Anglo-French division of Morocco.[121]

The two main sources of Burke's friction with Minister Sid Muhammad Torres were claims for damages to American agents and protégés and support of Moroccan and Jewish naturalized American citizens. Burke made great efforts to secure compensation for assaults and robberies perpetrated on American consular agents, protégés, and _semsars_. Even the highly respected Col. Mathews lost the sale of some property because the holder of his power of attorney was robbed. After many evasions and delays, the appearances of the _U. S. S. Raleigh_ and Burke's cruise in her down the coast[122] inspired a settlement of the chief claims. However, other long standing cases remained unsettled. Unfortunately, Burke's handling of one claim of a wounded _semsar_ caused a misunderstanding leading to his dismissal.[123]

Burke agreed with Sid Muhammad Torres that many of the "naturalized" American citizens were not entitled to that status or to American protection. There were about twenty-five of this class, mostly non-English speaking Jews, naturalized by American courts without meeting legal requirements for residence in the United States and with the sole objective of remaining in Morocco and carrying on nefarious business schemes under American protection. As the State Department was probably aware,

> They are the source and cause of all the trouble and worry of this Consulate as well as of the abuses that have been carried on which have lowered the American name, American character, and American honor in the eyes of the people of other countries .... They are continually presenting claims against Moors and others for robbery of money, cattle, grain, etc., largely because of the custom of this Consulate in granting them semsars and mohalats.[124]

Like all his predecessors, Burke censured the Moroccan misgovernment. Ba-Ahmed's efforts to control crime and abolish piracy and rebellion were never mentioned. When Burke proposed to his diplomatic colleagues the establishment of an international police force in Tangier, his plan was not approved because of the mutual jealousy of the foreign powers.[125] During 1896 and 1897 Burke reported several acts of piracy, pillage, and capture of crews by the Riffs on French, British, Portuguese and Italian vessels. The Riffs obtained their demands for ransom and exchange of prisoners.[126] During his last months in Tangier, Burke described the growing power and success of the Moroccan armies in many parts of the Empire, but their prowess excited only revulsion at the displays of the heads of slain rebels and the general impoverishment, degradation, and barbarity afflicting the masses:

> Misrule, oppression, tyranny, cruelty, and barbarity are everywhere stamped throughout the empire as characteristics of the Moorish officials following the example of their Great Master .... This awful condition of barbarous and brutal administration will go on from bad to worse till some European power tiring of the painful watch it is keeping upon this enslaved people, tiring of the cruelties and atrocities the Sultan is practicing upon his subjects will make a move to end it all by an agreement with other powers to seize and divide. It must come to this and the sooner the better![127]

Having often assured the State Department of his honesty and efficiency in carrying out instructions, Burke was moved to inquire on December 9, 1897, the reason for his recall. He transmitted letters of endorsement from the principal foreign residents and the Americans of Tangier as well as a copy of a long article in Al-Maghreb Al-Aksa telling of a farewell deputation honoring him. Concerning his conduct of the *semsar* claim for which he had summoned a warship, over a year later Burke presented a complete and satisfactory explanation. Acting properly through Sid Muhammad Torres, Burke had settled the case with honesty and humaneness, while preventing the Moroccan officials from getting a share of the indemnity paid. However, the State Department merely marked the incident closed, blaming the misunderstanding upon Burke's earlier ineptness in communicating the facts.[128]

Appointed on October 20, 1897, Frank C. Partridge took over his office officially on January 20, 1898. He commended the excellent condition of the records and archives left by Burke.[129] During his service of exactly six months, Partridge dealt mostly with the traditional problems of consular agents, claims against the Moroccan government, and protection, with some attention to other foreign powers in Morocco.

A significant item in foreign affairs was the repulse by a Moroccan ship and land troops of a British ship attempting to land arms, ammunition, and other goods at Asaka in the Sus. This intrusion by the Globe Venture Syndicate called attention to Mulai Hassan's promise to Sir John Hay in 1887 to open Asaka to commerce. A Moroccan newspaper advocated the fulfillment of this pledge to benefit both foreign traders and the people of the Sus, who were eager to exchange their produce for foreign manufactures.[130]

Partridge continued Burke's program of reform. He made strict rules to prevent abuses of cattle export permits by American officials and protégés. Following his recommendation, the State Department instructed him to close the consular agencies at Larache, Safi, and Rabat. He transferred their work to agents at Casablanca and Mogador and arranged temporary protection for former agency employees.[131] Of much greater difficulty were the persisting problems of claims and protection.

After an intensive investigation of American claims against the Moroccan government and subjects, mostly pending since the time of Burke, Partridge sent the State Department a complete list of claims, his suggestions for principles to apply to future claims, and an analysis of reasons for dropping many unsettled ones. He admitted that both Burke and he had been deceived by Harry Carleton, former consular agent at Larache, and he advised that Carleton's claims be abandoned.[132]

On the list of protected persons on June 30, 1898, Partridge included only twenty-one official employees, of whom eleven would soon be dropped, twenty-five *semsars*, two protégés for signal services, and one hundred eleven *mohalats* for one year. There were also certain guards for the property of Ion Perdicaris, serving by the Department's consent. Partridge reviewed the whole subject of protection; he said that it should never be granted except when clearly in the interest of the United States. Intervention on humanitarian grounds should be left to Great Britain or France, both ambitious in Morocco. Only business agents were entitled to recognition as *semsars*, and those carrying on American-Moroccan commerce should be given preference. Most *mohalats* wrongly considered themselves as protégés, since only the owner's property, but not his agent, was protected. *Mohalat* certificates needed careful supervision and restriction, as did powers of attorney. Both protection and *mohalat* certificates required frequent renewal and should be investigated by oral cross examination. Partridge agreed with Burke that abuses of American citizenship should be abolished. He had begun a permanent registry of every naturalized citizen, protégé, and *mohalat* in Morocco, the completion of which he recommended to his successor.[133]

The repercussions of the Spanish-American War in Tangier caused Partridge some anxiety. Since the Spanish in Tangier numbered about 5,000 and other foreigners less than 500, and a large part of the former was of low character, there was danger of attacks, supported by Spain, against Americans and their affiliates. The Basha of Tangier moved to safeguard American lives and property. It was rumored that an American squadron would operate against Spain from Tangier. The principal Spanish paper in Tangier argued that the European powers represented in Tangier were obligated to maintain Morocco's neutrality. Sid Muhammad Torres found the concept of neutrality, lacking an Arabic word for it, difficult to comprehend, but he favored it.[134] Since the American ships were fully occupied in the West Indies and the Philippines, the idle rumors soon died out.

As early as March 26, 1898, Partridge had sent his resignation to President McKinley. His successor, Samuel René Gummeré, was appointed with his residence listed as Trenton, New Jersey, but he had, in fact, lived in Tangier for over three years. On July 21, 1898, he began his eleven years of service in Morocco.[135] He owed his position, not to political influence, but to his having accompanied his friend Ion Perdicaris to the State Department when the latter protested against irregular protection by the American consulate at Tangier.[136] Like his British and German colleagues, Gummeré was to refrain from intrigues.

Throughout the regime of Ba-Ahmed, however, plots and counterplots were made in European capitals. These schemes involved Morocco as an integral part of the new rivalry in world politics. All of the other European powers were watchful of the attitude and actions of Morocco's traditional guardian. There were several evidences that Great Britain was finding the burden of supporting the new Sultan wearisome. To be sure, by the treaty of March 13, 1895, Great Britain had acknowledged the sovereignty of the Sultan to the Draa and Cape Bojador, providing that no part of this coast be ceded to another power without British consent. This treaty was not officially communicated to France.[137] But rather than to risk isolation by the Far Eastern Triplice, Salisbury seemed resolved to liquidate the liability of Morocco; he had thought of presenting Constantinople to Russia and Morocco to France. Later he refused to renew the Mediterranean Agreements of 1887.[138] The _status quo_ of Morocco was thus placed in jeopardy.

During and after the Spanish-American War the rapprochement of France and Spain aroused fear of their forward policy in Morocco. Rumors of Russian designs upon Ceuta were started by her establishment of a legation in Tangier[139] in 1898.[140] But Spain wanted to postpone the partitioning of Morocco until she had developed enough strength to secure a larger share. Early in 1899 Foreign Minister Silvela asked for and received assurances that the British government would continue to uphold the status quo in Morocco.[141] Nevertheless, the Spanish government communicated to Germany its apprehension regarding British plans to seize Ceuta. To the suggestion that Spain would welcome a secret entente among Germany, France, and Russia to strengthen her resistance to Great Britain, Bülow replied that such an arrangement was unnecessary and impossible and would interfere with other objectives of the German Foreign Office.[142] However, the several attempts to reach an Anglo-German accord also failed--partly because of Salis bury's antipathy toward William II and partly because of the Kaiser's open indifference to the whole Moroccan problem--and Germany did not acquire the Atlantic coast concession tentatively proposed by Chamberlain.[143]

Spared the knowledge of the plans afoot for his country, Ba-Ahmed was pursuing the time-honored methods of governing it. He was persuaded to grant some minor reforms,[144] but from the viewpoint of the foreigners he was decidedly non-cooperative. Burke and Gummeré pointed out in 1896 and 1899 that the United States continued to lose a great potential market because of the absence of direct shipping connections. They asserted, however, that Ba-Ahmed's misgovernment was the chief obstacle to all foreign commerce. His repeated raids upon rebellious tribes caused loss of life and property, impoverished the natives, and made collection of accounts in the interior difficult for foreign merchants. Gummeré said that an improved harvest in 1898 was accounted for partly by the cooperation of the Maghzen with foreign merchants in buying locust eggs "by the hundred-weight."[145]

Ba-Ahmed's prodigious efforts to save Morocco for his master did not discourage speculation in 1899 concerning the time of the long-deferred partition of Morocco. This was a favorite topic not only in European chancelleries but also in printed works on the country. Budgett Meakin declared that an international organization could reform

Morocco effectively from without, if capable advisers were found such as England had in Egypt. The probable division of the country was thus foretold by him:

> All that England would require consists in the neck of land which abuts on the Straits of Gibraltar .... Germany would like a foothold, ... and has vainly endeavoured to secure the proverbial "coaling station," but that is only to obtain a fulcrum for settling with France. Spain, of course, means to have Morocco, as of birthright, in retaliation for the Moorish rule in the peninsula .... But Spain is not to be reckoned with unless as an ally of France .... The day has also passed when Portugal could have a voice in the question, and Italy, notwithstanding a brave show, can play no more important part than that of makeweight.
>
> Austria, Scandinavia, and Russia, although represented at the Moorish court, are not to be considered any more than the Monroe-disregarding United States. Thus with much vain babbling the balance of power is maintained, as in a pacallelogram of forces. France alone is successfully spinning the yarn for the future waft, and tying political meshes wherewith to secure the spoil.[146]

In 1899 it was impossible to justify the term "Monroe-disregarding United States" in relation to Morocco. The attention and action of both the State Department and Gummeré were concentrated upon obtaining the rights given in the American-Moroccan treaty of 1836 and the Madrid Convention. To be sure, through her irresponsible representatives in Tangier, the United States had violated some provisions of the latter. But Gummeré was the third "reform consul" sent by Washington, and he continued working on the problems left unsolved by Burke and Partridge. Less than a month after his arrival, Gummeré denied the report in a New York paper that American agents were inciting the Moors, as allies of the United States, to attack the Spaniards at Ceuta and Melilla. He also warned persons circulating letters and circulars, some of them Americans, that no American agents were authorized to recruit Moors to assist a coming American fleet in the capture of Ceuta.[147] For several years Gummeré was far too busy putting his consular establishment in order in

Tangier and in the agencies, assisting American missionaries, trying to investigate and settle American claims, and striving to regularize protection and uncover naturalization frauds, to interfere in Moroccan international relations.

The consular building in Tangier required the usual repair. Gummeré asked for $100 to furnish a second office room. He requested that his contingent expenses include a telephone and a subscription to a London daily paper.[148] Since the consulate was no longer suitable for anything but offices, he took a residence just outside Tangier. An allowance of $950 was granted to repair the chronically dilapidated consulate. On March 20, 1899, the first typewriting machine arrived.[149] James W. S. Langerman became vice consul general and Hoffman Philip became deputy consul general. With three Moroccan guards, the American consulate assumed a dignified appearance.[150]

Beginning in June, 1899, Gummeré tried vainly for over five years to secure a house for an American missionary in the Moorish quarter at Meknes or at Fez. The Moroccan authorities would offer living quarters only in the Jewish section. The State Department disapproved Gummeré's suggestion that a _mohalat_ or protection certificate for signal service be granted to any house owner renting to a missionary. Gummeré considered residence in interior cities too dangerous because of the fanaticism of the Moors and the disorder of the times.[151]

Commending the work of Burke and Partridge, in 1898 Gummeré began the arduous task of validating every protection, _semsar_, and _mohalat_ certificate to be renewed. The number of persons in each class increased slightly until 1905. The application of the notorious Azogue for _mohalat_ certificates was rejected. Among the fraudulent _mohalat_ certificates cancelled were two issued to the widow of Mathews, who had testified falsely that these were for her agricultural employees.[152] Gummeré notified every person claiming American citizenship by naturalization that anyone desiring a continuance of American protection must either return to the United States to perform the duties of citizenship there or must give more conclusive proof than hitherto of an intention to return.[153]

Gummeré's most serious intra-consulate controversy was with John Cobb. The pioneer American merchant in Morocco, Cabb had served as a consular agent in Casablanca since 1872, except for one year's vacation enforced by Lewis. Although always a firm friend of Mathews, Cobb had been a controversial character under the other consuls, but none of several charges against him had been proved. The correspondence covering his final exposure and dismissal from his post extended from September 20, 1898, to December 12, 1901. The affair of John Cobb, a long story about an unimportant person, perhaps, presents an interesting case history of the manipulation and evasion of treaty provisions by consular agents and of the difficulty of detection of such fraud by the consul general at Tangier. Cobb admitted that he did no export business and imported only about 150 barrels of American petroleum, used mostly for the engine in his grist and saw mills, his only _bona fide_ business in Casablanca. Yet he had a _semsar_ certificate and there were twenty-one _mohalat_ certificates at his disposal--all but three actually used by his interpreter and business partner. Cobb objected vigorously to being dismissed, made serious charges against Gummeré, and had influential political support in the United States, but he finally submitted to expulsion from the consular establishment of the United States.[154]

Gummeré labored also with the perennial problem of unsettled American claims against the Moroccan government. Some cases were intricate and ambiguous because the claimants were consular agents engaged in corrupt practices. Two American consular agents in Larache with John Cobb, had held nearly half of all the _mohalat_ certificates issued by the American consulate by 1898. Gummeré reported being told that the British and the German ministers had forced payments of long standing claims by sending cruisers with ultimatums. In May, 1899, an American admiral on the _Chicago_ obtained payment of two claims. But Gummeré complained later that the Moroccan government ignored five claims presented after careful investigation. He urged that he be sent on a mission to the Sultan to get these claims paid, as Russian, Italian, and Spanish ministers had done recently. Other matters might be handled by this mission, also, such as the status of naturalized American citizens and the frequent arrests and robberies of American mohalats. At this time, when Sultan Abd al-Aziz was beginning his independent reign, an American mission might be especially appropriate and effective.[155]

For nine months the proposed mission was planned. During this interval two incidents manifested contemptuous and unfair treatment of American dependents. The mission was scheduled for mid-March, 1901, with American vessels to convey Gummeré and his party to Mazagan and back to Tangier. Then the Grand Vizier rejected Grummeré's visit--an unprecedented insult, that was not really atoned for by a later ungracious permission to come. Next the State Department reversed its position, delaying the expedition and cancelling instructions previously given for presenting claims. Gummeré had to sell at a loss the outfit that he had purchased for the trip.[156] The archives contain no explanation of this retreat of the State Department and the humiliation of its representative.

Gummeré soon discovered that the death of Ba-Ahmed had not made any improvement in the Moroccan government. Under Abd al-Aziz the sultanate was completely rebuilt on a pattern unprecedented in all the centuries of Moorish rulers. Pledging himself to make Morocco happy, prosperous, and truly independent, he abandoned the tradition of Moorish exclusiveness and turned from native to foreign advisers. He announced that although he could not overtake Europe in civilization, he would follow in her footsteps.[157] He might have become the kind of ruler that Sir John Hay once labored so many years to educate, for he had intelligence as well as good intentions. But, besieged by concession-hunters and salesmen dividing profits with his viziers, he was led into extravangances that emptied his treasury, demoralized his army, and alienated his subjects.[158]

Not even from England,[159] whose king he imitated, whose citizens were his favorite advisers, and to whom his subjects accused him of selling his country, did Abd al-Aziz receive either sympathy or assistance. His fanatical Muslim subjects looked with horror upon the foreign inventions which he imported and misused. To ape King Edward VII, he was persuaded to have his photograph taken and put on sale--a mortal sin for a

Muslim. He purchased at excessive costs a gold kodak, a sea-going yacht, a coronation coach (pulled by his soldiers and ruined in one heavy rain), a crown, and a number of motor cars. Dressed in English uniforms, his soldiers did not dare to attempt the collection of tribute or the enforcement of his orders.[160]

> Motor cars were brought from Tangier in sections and put together inside the palace. The ladies of the harem were presented with bicycles .... Innumerable clocks of all patterns and shapes adorned the palace walls; and overdressed dolls, musical boxes, phonographs, Teddy bears, and mechanical toys helped to wile away the hours .... Tennis courts and polo grounds were laid out; a billiard table was brought up on the back of a camel, and set up in the palace, and alongside it was constructed a bar at which the thirsty might refresh themselves.[161]

Instead of reforming the country, the Sultan's attempted innovations in taxation and finance resulted in rebellions and an orgy of corruption and misgovernment such as even Morocco had seldom seen before.[162] As in similar situations the world over, the monarch who had no other friends was forced eventually to sign away his independence to European capitalists.

In American periodicals the exotic and spectacular personality of Abd al-Aziz received much comment and criticism, both favorable and otherwise. Ion Perdicaris, the self-appointed authority on Morocco, disagreed with the prevailing opinion that prospects for peace were hopeful. Either the French would provoke native uprisings by further advances from Algeria, he said, or European control on the coasts would not prevent extermination of all foreigners, including Jews, throughout the interior. Perdicaris drew a most unflattering picture of Abd al-Aziz.[163] The Washington Post paid considerable attention to the Sultan. There was a very sarcastic editorial on an exchange of gifts between Roosevelt and the Sultan, concerning which accounts varied as to the number of goats sent by the President. In a long article admiration was expressed for the Sultan's fight "to rescue his kingdom from barbarism and protect it when rescued from the ravenous maw of the European powers." An article entitled "Abd al-Aziz a Sport" contained much biographical material. In 1905 a reprint from Blackwood's Magazine informed Americans "how very human is the personality of Morocco's young Sultan." Among the foreign intimates of the Sultan was one American, an artist named Arthur Schneider, who acted as court painter and wrote about his experiences. In Morocco from 1900 to 1905, Schneider saw the Sultan daily from November, 1900 to March, 1902. Returning to New York in 1905, Schneider specialized in painting Moroccan scenes.[164]

After Abd al-Aziz raised the royal umbrella over his own head, Delcassé needed less than four years to complete the spinning of his diplomatic web. To this happy consummation of his plans, the manners and motives of the Sultan made a substantial contribution. Without waiting for Ba-Ahmed's death, France had made her first aggressive moves late in 1899 and early in 1900 by occupying the oases of Tuat, Gourara, and Tidikelt and beginning railroads toward them. To protests made by Italy, Spain, and Germany,[165] Delcassé replied that France would honor all treaties, respect all neighboring frontiers, and maintain the status quo; the oases, however, were her own territory.[166] However, Morocco took the opposite view. Sid Muhammad Torres appealed twice to all foreign governments represented in Morocco[167] to support his master in opposing French aggression and the breaking of the treaty of 1845 in the seizure of territory recognized from time immemorial as belonging to Morocco.[168]

Fashoda was an alarm bell in the diplomatic night, summoning France, not to war, but to bargaining. The Anglo-French convention of June 13, 1899, by which the hinterland of Tripoli was surrendered to French enterprise, was really the first of the series of agreements by which Morocco was bought. The failures of attempts to reach a Franco-German accord in 1899 and in 1900[169] caused Delcassé to turn next to Spain.

"Spain was in the mood of Don Quixote after the last battle .... But Morocco was there to the south; France there to the north; and England in Gibraltar still a mystery."[170] Accordingly, negotiations resulted in the Franco-

Spanish convention of June 29, 1900, whereby Spain gained territory by the definition of the boundaries of Spanish Guinea and Rio de Oro and gave France the right of pre-emption in both colonies.[171]

In 1900 both Bülow and Holstein saw clearly the viewpoint and interests that they were to try, unsuccessfully, to defend five years later. Bülow recognized that Germany had maritime interests in Morocco, which would be furthered particularly by acquiring the southern Atlantic coast. Moreover, either a British annexation of Moroccan territory or an Anglo-French agreement excluding Germany would have incalculable results for Germany's future internal and external policy.[172] Although Holstein urged an approach to France before she was committed elsewhere,[173] and French public opinion was unusually friendly, Bülow waited for a more favorable opportunity. Since Delcassé received no offers, he decided to ignore Germany.[174] Fearful of failure, the German government also decided not to make the official offer of a Moroccan settlement which Chamberlain suggested after a tentative proposal made by Germany in May, 1900.[175]

During 1900 and 1901 Delcassé made other significant gains. A great breach was made in the Triple Alliance by the agreements of December 14, 1900, and June, 1901 with Italy.[176] Delcassé gave the written assurance that France had no aggressive aims regarding Tripoli and Italy recognized France's rights in Morocco as resulting from her proximity. The second agreement was a verbal promise by Italy that the renewed Triple Alliance should contain "nothing hostile" to France, in return for Italian rights in Tripoli being put on a par with those of France in Morocco. Two overtures for an entente with Germany, made by Delcassé in 1901 were rebuffed. An indirect message suggesting that he would allow Germany to take the initiative toward a discussion met with the response that any agreement likely to estrange a third power must be preceded by a mutual guarantee of territorial integrity. In November Bülow refused to meet Delcassé in a secret conference. Thereafter, Bülow waited in vain for evidence that the French government and people were soliciting closer relations with Germany.[177] Delcassé's lack of success with Germany coincided with the latter's third and fourth failure, evident by December of 1901, to reach an accord with Great Britain.

In affairs relating wholly to Morocco, also, Delcassé had reason to consider 1901 a year of achievement. In reprisal for seizure of the oases, the raids of guerrilla bands from Morocco into Algeria were increasing. This situation furnished the argument needed to prove Delcassé's new thesis, now submitted to French public opinion. His contention that Morocco, at least in the east, was merely a geographical and economic prolongation of Algeria was the basis of his claim that France had a special interest in Morocco. By a speech in the French Senate on July 6, 1901, Delcassé proclaimed publicly France's demand for priority in Morocco in order to eliminate the "enclave in our African possessions."[178] The Foreign Office adopted officially the Delcassé theory in December, 1899 in the Bulletin of the Comité de l'Afrique francaise. Delcassé continued the policy prescribed by the Comité and initiated its internal policy of pacific penetration through the agency of the Sultan.[179]

That the inevitable outcome of such an ostensibly self-denying policy would be the subjugation of Morocco's economic and military resources to France was evident not only to the French public but also to the Maghzen.[180] Hoping to obtain aid, Abd al-Aziz sent a mission to Great Britain and to Germany. Accompanying the mission, consisting of War Minister Al Menebhi and Kaid Maclean, was Nicolson, who wished to divest the mission of political significance.[181] When this mission arrived in Berlin, it was given the same advice as in London--to improve the internal conditions in Morocco and not to provoke France to aggression.[182]

Another mission under Ben Sliman was sent to Paris. In the convention of July 20, 1901, the Moroccan envoys failed to obtain a definite delimitation of the Algerian-Moroccan frontier, but they agreed to the joint policing of the boundary zone by France and Morocco. A warning to the Sultan reminded him that France would be either a powerful friend or a formidable enemy and that hereafter he was to sign no international agreement without France's consent. The instructions sent on July 27, 1901, to Saint-René

Taillandier, recently appointed French minister at Tangier, denoted Delcassé's determination to proceed with a virtual protectorate over Morocco.[183] Al Menebhi, fallen from power after his return home, was unable to initiate any of the promised reforms, and thus Morocco lost her last chance to reform herself.[184]

While tribal disorders had given France license to extend both her territory and authority in Morocco, the Maghzen had been trying to make some reforms. In January, 1900, began Ba-Ahmed's effort to obtain enforcement and modification of the Treaty of Madrid. Two matters in question were the non-enforcement of Article XV relating to naturalization of Moroccans abroad and the privileged position of Brazil. Not a party to the convention, Brazil had numerous consuls, consular agents, naturalized citizens, and protected persons of every class in Morocco. In September the Sultan promised to abolish irregular protection by his country. Discussions of limitations on naturalization, _semsars_, and _mohalats_ continued with the diplomatic corps during 1901 without result.[185] In the fall of 1901 the Sultan instituted two fiscal reforms, providing for coastal trade in food stuffs without duty and reorganization of the basic taxation system, the _tertib_. The latter abolished the ancient Koranic taxes and replaced them by a fixed and common tax on Arabic land, fruit trees, and live stock. In future the _kaids_ were to have no function in taxation except to support the Sultan's tax collectors if force were required. This equitable system, long urged upon the Maghzen, set practically the whole population against the Sultan. It affronted the many with fanatical religious convictions; it enraged the hierarchy of officials from kaids to viziers, who lost both wealth and power; it outraged the _Shirfa_ and the Maghzen tribes, hitherto exempt from taxation. Moreover, since the taxable tribes had paid no taxes for two years, the expenditures for a salary system bankrupted the government, destroyed its financial structure, and weakened its military forces to the point of impotence in maintaining order.[186] It took until the end of 1903 to secure the assent of the foreign powers to apply the new taxation equally to all foreigners and protégés, and then with the proviso that this taxation should not be applied until it was in effect for all Moorish subjects.[187] The great increase in major crimes and disorders in

Tangier, reported by Gummeré in May, 1901, was only a portent of widespread revolts to follow.[188]

Because of the impractical frontier arrangements of 1901 and the murder of two French captains on the boundary commission, the French government demanded greater powers. Two treaties, signed on April 20 and May 7, 1902, provided for the collaboration of the French and Moroccan governments in the political, economic, and military control of the border regions of Algeria and Morocco. The accord did not facilitate French pacific penetration of Morocco via Algeria, however, because of the suspicion that it engendered among the other powers and of the situation now prevalent in Morocco.[189]

By 1902 Abd ul-Aziz was confronted by a rebellion which was not put down until 1912 under his successor. Its able leader was Al Rogui (the Pretender), Bu Hamara, posing as the elder brother of the Sultan and rightful heir to the throne. He won wide support from tribes alarmed by European intrigues and believing that Abd al-Aziz had sold his country to foreign infidels.[190] From his base at Taza, which Bu Hamara retained until the end, he failed to conquer Fez after a ten months' siege. He captured Oudja in 1903. He routed not only the imperial cavalry but also regulars trained for twenty years by French and British instructors. He proclaimed himself sultan in eastern Morocco, a title recognized by Spain in order to obtain food for Melilla, and granted mining concessions to Spain, later disavowed by France. Although military aid against him was offered by France, Abd al-Aziz dared not accept it for fear of confirming the charge against himself.[191]

For a time the Sultan was obliged to flee from the enraged population of Fez,[192] where he had moved his capital early in 1902. Throughout the rest of that year and 1903 he sent out many military expeditions, for sporadic revolts in many parts of Morocco reinforced the main one of Bu Hamara. He accepted French instructors for his troops in three towns. He seldom paid his troops, and his unenthusiastic forces suffered many defeats, but Abd al-Aziz kept his throne. However, the price was prohibitive, for in signing the note for 7,500,000 francs for a loan from French bankers, secured by the official intervention of Delcassé in November, 1902,[193] he signed away his sovereignty.[194]

In his international program, Delcassé was less successful during 1902. His one triumph was the secret Franco-Italian agreement of November 1, 1902. Besides giving each other full freedom to develop their respective spheres in Morocco and Tripoli, the two powers bound themselves to strict neutrality in case either was compelled to attack a third power as a result of direct provocation.[195] Exactly a week later, Spain also made a secret pact with France. After the usual declaration of devotion to the *status quo*, the contracting parties proceeded to divide Morocco into their future spheres of interest. Excluding Tangier, the neutralization of which was not to be opposed, northern Morocco with Fez was to be Spain's portion. To France was allotted the ancient realm of Marrakesh.[196] Apprehending British disapproval, the incoming Silvela ministry rejected the treaty,[197] and Spain lost the best deal ever offered her on Morocco.

The Nation commented with prescience on the developing diplomacy of France:

> The Franco-Spanish *entente*, including, as it has been supposed, a secret treaty covering new delimitations in North Africa, has been taken as a sure index of French ambitions in Morocco .... The fact that Russia not long since established an embassy in Tangier ... (when) there are practically no Russians in the Sultanate, (is) a somewhat ostentatious notification that the Franco-Russian alliance was going to have something to say about the partition of Morocco. Possibly, a new Anglo-French treaty of African delimitation may settle the whole question amicably.[198]

For Anglo-French relations during 1902, however, the record was one of continuous friction and frustration. Ambassador Cambon had several discussions with Chamberlain and Lansdowne over the possibility of agreement on various questions, including Morocco. But the Anglo-Japanese treaty published in February obliged France to draw closer to Russia and Germany.[199] In several dispatches from Tangier, Saint-René Taillandier complained that the British group around Maclean was intriguing to secure industrial concessions and loans for Great Britain and that the Sultan was not to be trusted to heed French warnings against this.[200] Nicolson admitted the existence of this "English Ring," of which he strongly disapproved.[201]

On August 6, 1902, Cambon made an official proposal for an accord on Morocco and Siam.[202] As a personal representative of the Sultan, Maclean went to London in September. He sought a loan and a British or Anglo-German guarantee of the integrity of Morocco, the latter to lapse if the Sultan had not reformed Morocco within seven years. His petition was rejected,[203] but in October Cambon's offer was also refused on the ground of unsatisfactory terms.[204] Thus Delcassé ended the year 1902 without coming to terms with three of his chief rivals in Morocco--Great Britain, Germany, and Spain.

In an interview on the last day of 1902, Cambon made an important declaration of French policy to Lansdowne. France, he said, as always, desired above all the maintenance of the *status quo*, but in view of the critical situation in Morocco, his government thought that interested powers should agree in advance upon any necessary intervention. When asked the meaning of "interested powers," Cambon admitted that Germany was the one that France wanted to exclude. Germany had no concern with Morocco, he said, although on one or two occasions she had tried unsuccessfully to gain a foothold there. Great Britain, France, and Spain were the only really interested powers, and it would be desirable for them to anticipate Germany's attempt to assume a conspicuous role. Cambon added that "it seemed to him not inconceivable that the United States might evince an interest in the matter," which Lansdowne thought not very probable.[205] Because of Cambon's unhesitating assurance that Italy was disinterested, Lansdowne had no doubt that France and Italy had arrived at an understanding.[206]

It might be true that French overtures in June and September of 1902 for German support in Siam could be interpreted as hints for an understanding.[207] Yet on July 15 an official memorandum on the Moroccan question mentioned Great Britain and Spain to be won over and Italy and Russia to be counted upon for the French plan. Germany, it was foreseen, would not be satisfied with an international Tangier and commercial liberty in Morocco, which France was prepared to offer.[208]

Although the French government continued during 1903 to press for the exclusion of Germany from the Moroccan settlement,[209] its precaution seemed hardly necessary. Neither Bülow nor Holstein appeared much interested. In January Bülow expressed a vague hope for a Franco-German rapprochement, paid the customary tribute to the status quo in Morocco, and then declared that German interests there were trifling and insignificant.[210] Late in September he tried to discover through Spain whether in the rumored Franco-Spanish division of spheres in Morocco a place had been reserved for Germany.[211] Holstein regarded an Anglo-German alliance as music for the future.[212]

Meanwhile, the French Foreign Office was watching carefully the growth of German commerical interests in Morocco.[213] A long report from Saint-René Taillandier gave detailed information about the German commercial establishments, shipping, and postal system.[214]

Despite the indifference of the German Foreign Office, various organizations were conducting propaganda for the recognition of German interests there, and the press cooperated in the campaign. Theobald Fischer, a leading exponent of Weltpolitik, had won from his travels in Morocco and his many writings on it the reputation of being a world authority on the subject.[215] With a group of eminent disciples he spoke frequently in 1903 before learned societies as an advocate of his thesis that the Atlas foreland must become a colony for the surplus population of Germany.[216]

Cambon's association of the United States with Germany as a power to be excluded from the Moroccan negotiations was probably inspired by the fear that the two new world powers would turn their attention from the Far East to Africa. Certainly the French were observing uneasily the apparent friendship between Roosevelt and William II, which was widely publicized from 1902 on. Others besides Cambon had had the same apprehension. However, an

English writer dismissed summarily the suggestion of American interference:

> France wants as much of Morocco as may be secured without international complications; .. and the success of Bu-Hamara will give her every necessary excuse for stepping in on behalf of her many subjects. British opposition is concerned chiefly with the Mediterranean corner between Tangier and Tetuan. France will not abandon her plans for the anger of Spain. Germany is the political bagman with an opportunist policy and nothing to justify action in the matter on one side or another. Russia is friendly to France; Austria is indifferent; Italy is contented by reason of the understanding about Tripoli; and America has quite enough to do to look after Germany in the Caribbean Sea without troubling about Morocco. A French occupation of Morocco up to the Atlas Mountains might be balanced by the abolition of mixed financial control in Egypt.[217]

An American writer credited the current reports that Italy and France had exchanged concessions in Tripoli and Morocco. Both Germany and Great Britain, he said, favored the status quo; the former might like a strip in the Sus, and the latter might back Spain in return for commercial concessions and either Ceuta or Tangier. Beyond that,

> the interest of the United States in the question is at present purely a commercial one, yet it is not at all outside the realm of possibilities that she may become the arbiter of the fate of the Moorish Empire. This is, however, too remote a contingency for serious consideration at present.[218]

In the spring of 1903 a London paper published an interview with an American, a Mr. J. W. Langermann. It was in itself of small significance, but the sort of thing which irritated the French government and later gave its subject some space in French diplomatic dispatches.[219] Langermann, just returning from Morocco, where he went to invite the Sultan to take part in the St. Louis Exposition, testified to the hatred of the Fez natives for foreigners.

Eulogizing Abd al-Aziz, he said:

> He is as thoroughly a Moor as he ever was, but he wishes to keep pace with other nations in internal progress, especially in building railroads and opening up trade .... If Europe will leave Morocco alone, matters will soon be settled.[220]

Another reason for the deliberate omission of the United States from the "interested powers" might be that between 1899 and 1901 there were some indications of a reviving American interest in Africa in general and in Morocco in particular. Gummeré's reports on commerce for 1900 and 1901 did not warrant much optimism. The small size of the American colony likewise showed American disinterest in Morocco. Also, since Gummeré's chief duty was in reforming the protection abuses by his predecessors, his post remained a minor one.[221] Since the United States made arrangements for protection of her trademarks in Morocco, however, with Great Britain in 1889 and Germany in 1901,[222] apparently the Morocco market was not considered entirely negligible. Indicating more interest in Africa was the adhesion of the United States on February 1, 1901, to the Brussels convention of 1899 for regulation of the importation of spiritous liquors into certain regions of Africa.[223] Finally, in 1900 the United States had sent a note to Great Britain, France, and Germany protesting against the granting of an exclusive mining concession in Liberia to an English syndicate as a violation of the Open Door.[224] This suggested that this American principle was about to be transported to Africa.

However, the United States showed no disposition to interfere, as she had in the Boxer Rebellion, in the widespread revolts threatening Morocco in 1903. On January 29, 1903, Fez was saved from Bu Hamara, but in the meantime, the Riff had risen in revolt. By May the powerful bandit leader, Raisuli, had cut communications between Arzila and Tangier; in another month he was advancing on Tetuan.[225] Kidnapped and taken to Raisuli's stronghold at Zinat, Walter Harris was rescued by Nicolson on July 5.[226] In this successful coup, Raisuli learned the method of extracting his own price from the Sultan through the medium of the foreign representatives, but he remained quiet for a year before repeating his exploit.

During 1903 the task of France was threefold. It comprised nothing less than the simultaneous military, financial, and diplomatic control of Morocco, all to be achieved without the overt disturbance of the fictitious sovereignty of the Sultan or international complications. In a situation of such complexity and gravity, it is not surprising that Delcassé sometimes clashed with the military authorities of Algeria. He was determined to work by appointment to the Maghzen in carrying out the reforms needed, but the Algerian government thought it useless to negotiate "with nothingness."[227] In his instructions to Saint-René Taillandier, Delcassé repeatedly urged the avoidance of interventions or demonstrations tending to change the ostensible _status quo_.[228] King Edward VII approved of this policy,[229] and the French minister at Tangier found all his colleagues there cooperative.[230]

M. Révoil, the governor-general of Algeria and a former minister to Morocco, was dismissed by Premier Combes, supposedly for too active a policy on the Moroccan border.[231] But the ferocious attacks from Tafilalet, "a state of war against an intangible enemy" led to the appointment of General Lyautey to supervise the most dangerous section.[232]

The French forces controlled the Algerian-Moroccan border regions by the end of 1903, but the Moroccan government notified the diplomatic corps in October that it could not be responsible for foreigners traveling near Rabat, Fez, or Marrakesh. The corps refused to release the Maghzen from responsibility.[233] In November Lansdowne told Ambassador Metternich that France, because of her proximity, could not be prevented from becoming the preponderating power in Morocco.[234] Even Walter Harris now admitted the alternatives:

> The intervention of France--the only power who would undertake the task--or a state of anarchy impossible to imagine, in which the young Sultan, who never ceased to desire improvement and reform, would disappear.[235]

By this ineptitude in finance Abd al-Aziz was passing farther under French control. Both natives and foreigners continued striking against the _tertib_. The Maghzen was forced to subsist upon the reserves and the customs.[236] The loan made earlier by French bankers was supplemented by others from British and Spanish banks, purchased by the bankers at 62% and secured by assignment of customs receipts. Proceeds of the three loans proved insufficient to meet current expenses and crush the tribal revolts. The currency was debased, and by the end of 1903 a suspension of the debt service was imminent.[237]

The Maghzen found itself in a truly desperate situation by the spring of 1904. After being refused more loans in France and Great Britain, the Sultan applied unsuccessfully to Germany and to the United States.[238] The State Department considered the Maghzen's proposition very absurd and declined to act as intermediary with American bankers, who would have to be approached directly by some authorized agent of the Sultan. At this time the United States had no inclination to practice dollar diplomacy in Morocco, but in France the Quai d'Orsay was leagued with the financial and industrial leaders in pursuit of their common objectives. The club of impending bankruptcy was a powerful weapon to force Morocco into accepting the diplomatic arrangements that Declassé had almost completed.[239]

Throughout 1903 both European and American journalists had indulged in speculation about rumored agreements. One writer was reluctant to destroy the fading image of Britain as the queen of imperialism in Africa:

> So far as Africa is concerned, England has created a sort of Monroe Doctrine. No other power may colonize except with her permission, and other European nations whose flags now fly in Africa may not alienate their territory or disturb the existing equilibrium without the permission of Great Britain.[240]

Another American view was more realistic. After giving its own version of the plans for Morocco, it quoted the London <u>Standard</u>:

> Morocco is being pawned. For two years no taxes have been collected except at the ports, and the cost of carrying on the war against the Pretender has been

> met by loans .... This generosity on the part of the powers is not disinterested, and, though cloaked with the pretence of maintaining the *status quo*, can have but one effect--to place Morocco at the mercy of the highest bidder.

The article concluded by discussing the beginning of negotiations in September for a commercial treaty between the United States and Abyssinia. This action was interpreted as signifying the intention of the United States not to be excluded from commerce in Africa.[241]

At the time when the United States was refusing a loan to Morocco, the State Department was giving two indications of acceding to French policy. By a convention of March 15, 1904, the United States surrendered her extraterritoriality in Tunisia, thus virtually recognizing the French protectorate there.[242] At the instance of the French activity in Morocco, the State Department instructed Gummeré on February 16, 1904, to work with his French colleague to secure freedom of religion for Moroccan Jews. Gummeré was surprised at this request, for during his residence in Morocco he had found protection as practiced an effective shield against persecution of Jews.[243]

A combination of factors in the world diplomatic situation at last enabled Delcassé to reach a general understanding with Great Britain. To avoid the involvement of the allies of the combatants in the Russo-Japanese War and to place British control of Egypt upon a sound basis, an entente on Morocco and other controversial problems was worked out without further delay. Like the Franco-Italian pact, the Anglo-French agreement of April 8, 1904, had had a long period of evolution. The foundation for the Entente Cordials was laid by Delcassé in his conciliatory handling of the Fashoda crisis of 1898. Another step was taken by Sir Thomas Barclay in his work through French and British chambers of commerce to promote the Anglo-French treaty of arbitration[244] signed on October 14, 1903.[245] Many difficulties were raised on both sides after the initiation of official negotiations in July, 1903. But with the active interest and cooperation of King Edward, President Loubet, and Lord Cromer, Cambon and Lansdowne were able to agree with Delcassé on the settlement earlier rejected by the British Cabinet.[246]

Of the three documents included in the entente,[247] the one of international significance was that concerning Egypt and Morocco.[248] The published part declared France's intention not to alter the political status quo of Morocco, while Great Britain recognized the special interest of France in preserving order and in providing the necessary "administrative, economic, financial, and military reforms" there. The customary and treaty rights of Great Britain were to be preserved, and full commercial liberty[249] was guaranteed for thirty years. Concessions for public works in both Morocco and Egypt were to be granted on such conditions as to maintain intact the authority of their rulers over them. The free passage and non-fortification of the south shore of the Straits of Gibraltar was pledged. A Franco-Spanish compact safeguarding the interests of Spain was to be communicated to the British government. Finally, the two governments promised mutual diplomatic support in obtaining the execution of this declaration.

In return for France's predominating position in Morocco, Great Britain received the relinquishment of France's special rights in Egypt. Here, also, the intention not to change the status quo was affirmed. Great Britain easily obtained the assent of the interested powers to the reforms in the administration of the Egyptian public debt. Only Germany sought a condition for accepting them--a general settlement including Samoa, the Transvaal indemnities, and the Canadian preferential tariff. As a compromise, Great Britain guaranteed to Germany her Egyptian interests in return for Germany's acceptance of the French obligations there.[250] Thereafter, Germany was deprived of a valuable diplomatic weapon, for the Egyptian problem was solved. Although the Anglo-German arbitration treaty was signed on July 12, it was no compensation to Germany for her complete exclusion from the making of the pacts which were to readjust the balance of power in Europe. Bülow had experienced a major defeat, and Delcassé did not forbear from emphasizing it.

To Germany, whose real interest in Morocco both the British and the French diplomats had conceded from the beginning, Delcassé gave no formal notification of the

Anglo-French agreement. To the United States, with none but commercial treaty interests, great courtesy was shown. Henry White was informed about the published clauses of the entente in London several days before its signing. Later Delcassé sent to Washington an official notice concerning it.[251]

The secret articles of the agreement, unpublished until 1911, but suspected from the beginning, anticipated British suzerainty over Egypt and the division of Morocco between France and Spain, "whenever the Sultan ceases to exercise authority over it." On the basis of the published articles, however, any practical diplomat could predict the probable course of events with a small degree of error. Generally the American press took for granted the eventual assimilation of Morocco into the French Empire. It seems improbable that Roosevelt had any doubts about the ultimate objectives of France. Although, as Jusserand informed the Quai d'Orsay, the President boasted that he did not read the newspapers,[252] few of his biographers would agree with the usually astute Pringle when he says (Roosevelt, 390):

> I can find no evidence in Roosevelt's papers that he knew about the secret provisions of the Anglo-French treaty, that he appreciated the "encirclement" that already confronted the German Empire. Certainly he was not aware that France, England, and Spain had quietly agreed to the partition of Morocco.

Jusserand gives a more realistic view of Roosevelt's knowledge of the secret articles:

> I did not know of any secret clauses and the only text had was the one published in the Yellow Book of 1904. I doubt, however, that a knowledge of these articles which simply made more explicit, arrangements the general trend of which was public, would have appreciably altered the dispositions of the President. He was in favour of our having, to the largest extent, our way in Morocco, and our ultimate aim was no secret.[253]

Before the conclusion of the Anglo-French entente, William II had crippled Bülow's hand and had prevented him from dealing freely with the problem to which the Kaiser now, too tardily, gave his attention. By the well-known renunciation at Vigo, Emperor William congratulated King Alfonso on the rumored Franco-Spanish partition of Morocco, declaring that Germany desired no territory there, but merely the protection of her commercial interests--open ports, railway concessions, and the importation of manufactures.[254] Fernando Po, he told Bülow, might be purchased from Spain. To show his sincerity and to encourage the cooperation of all the powers in restoring order in Morocco, the Kaiser refused to permit a naval demonstration in protest against the murder of one German and imprisonment of another. The Foreign Office accepted his decision.[255] Thus committed by his sovereign, Bülow used a Reichstag speech on April 12, 1904, to declare Germany's lack of objection to the Anglo-French agreement. The elimination of friction between France and Britain was really a cause of satisfaction, he said, since Germany had no reason to think that the entente was directed against a third power or that her economic interests in Morocco would be disregarded or injured.[256] Outwardly, Germany accepted the _fait accompli_ with good grace. However, the Pan-German campaign for a share in Morocco[257] began in May.[258]

The spectacular event putting Morocco into the headlines of the American press occurred on May 18, 1904. Doubling his stakes of the previous year, Raisuli kidnapped and held for ransom two foreigners, the "American", Ion Perdicaris[259] and his stepson, Cromwell Varley, a British subject. Gummeré immediately requested the sending of an American warship and warned the Maghzen that it would be held responsible for any harm done. The correspondence of the State Department indicated the importance that it attributed to the affiar.[260] Both the Mediterranean and the South Atlantic squadrons were sent to Tangier, and a British warship also appeared there. At the request of the United States, the French government ordered its minister at Tangier to assist in the negotiations for the release of the captives. Secretary Hay informed the British government[261] that Raisuli's life would be demanded if Perdicaris were murdered.[262]

In general, American press opinion supported the

editorial caption in Harper's Weekly, "We Should Deal with Morocco as We Dealt with Other Barbary Powers."[263] But the Nation, non-conformist as usual, told some bald facts:

> It would be the height of absurdity to land an expedition to hunt up Mr. Perdicaris, and the seizure of a customs house to pay his ransom would be only nearer opera bouffe because less perilous. ... It should not be forgotten that we are demanding of Morocco guarantees that we could not give to the Sultan himself if he were traveling in the United States. If he had the bad luck to be lynched, we should only disclaim responsibility for the act of a sovereign state and pay an indemnity as a matter of comity .... The excuse for the presence of our squadron at Tangier is the anarchy that impends in Morocco. It greatly behooves us not to apply the match to the powder barrel.[264]

A keen insight into the real attitude of France was shown by Budgett Meakin:

> There has occurred the carrying off of two foreign residents of Tangier--one British, one American--by an insurgent chief, in order to bring the Moorish government to terms through fear of foreign complications. This threatens to force the hand of France, by reason of hot-headed and ill-advised action of Washington, where the situation appears to have been quite misunderstood. Treating the case as one of brigandage, the Moorish government has been held responsible, and France has been appealed to as though this new agreement authorized her to police Morocco. France, however, will probably be too wise to interfere.[265]

In the ensuing negotiations, prolonged by increasing demands of the arrogant Raisuli, the French government was embarrassed by the unwelcome task thrust upon it. Saint-René Taillandier thought that the kidnapping might be utilized to persuade Abd al-Aziz to save himself by listening to French advice; however, similar incidents might provoke an international entente prejudicial to French predominance in Morocco. In supporting the overtures of the British agent at Fez, Saint-Aulaire was instructed not to propose any measures, since the representatives of the two interested powers intended to place the entire responsibility upon the Maghzen.[266] The French government had obtained the good offices of the Sherif of Wazan at the beginning,[267] which was probably its one effective service.[268] Saint-René Taillandier was critical of Nicolson's apparent approval of the presence of seven American cruisers at Tangier. Ambassador Porter in Paris assured Delcassé that Gummeré would follow instructions from Washington to work with his French colleague at Tangier in the general Moroccan situation. The American squadron, Porter explained, had been sent to satisfy public opinion at home. Nevertheless, Delcassé saw the necessity for planning French participation if any disembarkment were made by the Americans. Saint-René Taillandier complained that he did not know the instructions of the American admiral or of Gummeré, whose attitude continued to be very reserved.[269]

The Spanish government viewed the presence of the American warships at Tangier with alarm and suspicion, as Jules Cambon reported on several occasions.[270] Cambon pointed out that the recent Anglo-French accord was a guarantee for Spanish rights as well as French. Spain feared both an American intervention and an international one, for which she was ill prepared. On June 6 Cambon reported that the people of Madrid were bitter against France, which was accused by one journal of playing a comedy of accord with the United States, in order that the latter might obtain on the Atlantic the situation that she coveted.[271] Delcassé urged Cambon to warn the Spanish government of the necessity to avoid irritating and arousing the Moors. If the recent accord were published, the Moroccans would turn _en masse_ against the Sultan, who was already accused of delivering his country to foreigners. Then the burden of a military expedition would fall upon France.[272]

With hindsight upon the real attitude of Delcassé, one can imagine his reaction to the plan which Roosevelt communicated to Hay on June 15--if he had known of it:

> I think it would be well to enter into negotiations with England and France, looking to the possibility of an expedition to punish the brigands, if Gummeré's statement

as to the impotence of the Sultan is true.[273]

By June 17 the ransom was agreed upon, but four days later Gummeré cabled Washington urging that if further delays occurred he might be empowered to issue an ultimatum backed by the landing of marines and seizure of custom houses.[274] After consulting Roosevelt, Hay gave rein to his genius for phrase-making--in this case, it was president-making. His ultimatum, "Perdicaris alive or Raisuli dead",[275] was attributed to the President, and it swept off their feet not only the previously apathetic Republican delegates at the Chicago national nominating convention, but also the American public. That Perdicaris and Varley had been released before the magic formula went on the wires was not publicized. Thus was born another treasured American myth of the might of a Rooseveltian slogan, which continues to be cited in derogation of later presidents who do not display equal prowess in verbal mastery of international crises.

A more "concise impropriety" than Roosevelt's war cry was the doubtful citizenship of Perdicaris, for forty years known as an American. From the American minister at Athens the State Department learned that although Perdicaris was the son of a South Carolinian mother and a naturalized Greek father, he had been naturalized as a Greek in Athens to avoid military service under the Confederacy. Ignoring this information, Hay and Roosevelt sent the famous telegram. After questioning Perdicaris, Gummeré sent to Hay a written confession from his friend and a humble apology from himself. However, it was necessary to keep the matter a secret to save American face and to safeguard the Roosevelt candidacy for president. Later the State Department reversed itself, issuing Perdicaris an American passport as early as November, 1905, but this also was never made public. After Dennett first revealed the duplicity of Roosevelt and Hay in 1933, it was long accepted as a fact that Perdicaris was not an American citizen. However, the State Department's final verdict that Perdicaris "never effectually acquired Greek or divested himself of American, citizenship" must be accepted as official.[276]

The diplomatic significance of the Perdicaris episode

was that it was quite generally interpreted as an official acknowledgment of the Anglo-French entente by the United States. The seeking of France's good offices by the United States and the exaggerated estimate of their value by the European public and press implied American recognition of French predominance in Morocco. This interpretation was exploited by the European press, especially the French, to such an extent that Gummeré thought it necessary to correct any misrepresentation of this Franco-American relationship in the State Department.[277] Many American periodicals were profuse in expressions of gratitude for France's assistance and eager to see her interests advanced in Morocco.[278]

Established in an American citizenship which could not be challenged, Perdicaris apparently reveled as an oracle on Morocco. In July after his release he was in Paris urging the French government to use strong measures to restore order. Surprisingly, he advocated the experiment of supporting Raisuli as "the strongest man now available." In interviews and articles he continued until far into 1905 to tell of his former life, his recent adventure, the history of Morocco, and the nature and solution of her problem. Because of his fulsome praise of his late captor as a courteous and cultured gentleman, the Washington *Post* was inspired to a series of satirical articles on "our Perdicaris alive--not nestling in our amourous embrace, to be sure, but alive and likely to make the United States ridiculous again at any moment." The *Post* even insinuated collusion between Perdicaris and Raisuli to bilk the Sultan and sarcastically debunked Hay's popular slogan which had *not* released Raisuli's captives.[279]

The claims arising from the Perdicaris kidnapping were probably paid more promptly than any others ever on the Moroccan docket. In addition to the $70,000 Spanish paid for ransom to Raisuli, raised by levies on towns and districts, Gummeré presented a bill for expenses, totaling $5,571 Spanish, about $4,000 in American money. This compensation went to the consulate general, the two Sherifs of Wazan, who with their retainers had performed the real work of rescue, and Perdicaris. By September 28, 1904, Gummeré forwarded to Washington receipts for the total of the expense accounts.[280]

The Perdicaris affair thus disposed of, Delcassé proceeded with his projects in finance and diplomacy. On June 12, 1904, the entire Moroccan debt was refunded by a loan of 62,500,000 francs by French banks, secured by the customs receipts at eight ports, to be collected by French agents. A French syndicate obtained the option on all future loans, the coinage of money, and the purchase and sale of silver and gold. At Fez, carrying out the mandate of a conference of political, economic, and military leaders held in Paris in October, Saint-René Taillandier prepared the Maghzen for acceptance of a new police force, a state bank, and a program of public works. The Chamber of Deputies made appropriations for humanitarian works in November. In a speech on the tenth of that month, Delcassé reaffirmed his policy of giving economic aid to Morocco in order to develop her resources for France.[281]

The negotiations for the division of Morocco into spheres of influence for France and Spain were not completed until October 3, 1904. With reviving optimism, Bülow hoped that a harbor in West Morocco for Germany might be his reward for arbitrating the settlement. This fancy had vanished by July, and Germany was unable, besides, to get satisfaction for her grievances against Morocco or to finance the Sultan for resistance to France's pacific penetration. Secret articles were suspected in the Anglo-French-Spanish accords. Since the British Cabinet was non-commital, and William II vetoed a naval demonstration, the petitions of German firms in Morocco for support remained unanswered. In October, the offhand announcement made by France concerning her agreement with Spain confirmed Bülow's opinion that a sphinx-like attitude must be maintained until he could build his own diplomatic machine.[282]

With Lansdowne as a frequent mediator,[283] Delcassé drove a good bargain with Spain. Like its predecessor, the accord included a public declaration and secret articles. The former expressed Spain's adherence to the Anglo-French entente on Morocco and Egypt and stated that France and Spain agreed to fix the limits of their respective rights and interests in Morocco. By the secret articles, Spain's sphere of influence was defined as that part of Morocco from the Moulaya River to Larache and the coastal region and hinterland extending from Rio de Oro northward to the Wad Sus. To France was conceded the rest of Morocco. If the status quo were not maintained, the two countries would assume control in their assigned spheres, but for fifteen years Spain was not to take any action in her sphere without the consent of France. Spain also agreed not to alienate any part of her sphere to any other power than France. The international character of Tangier was to be preserved. Even under the existing political status, the building of public works and the exploitation of mines, quarries, and economic enterprises were to be reserved for French and Spanish nationals. In thanking the British and German governments for their aid in negotiations, the Spanish government informed the latter that complete equality and freedom of commerce and trade had been guaranteed.[284]

After July of 1904 France began to make progress in establishing her military and police control over the Maghzen. French officers were accepted as leaders to organize the Sultan's military forces in Tangier, and a French cruiser under his authority curbed a revolt near Larache.[285] Carrying out the Franco-Moroccan agreements of 1901 and 1902, Lyautey set up military outposts protecting the entire Algerian-Moroccan frontier against raids from Bu Hamara's forces. Lyautey was an advocate of "peaceful penetration" or "penetration by organization," and French politicians visiting the border areas expressed amazement at the peaceful harvests and festivals taking place in regions so dangerous a year before.[286] Yet Gummeré thought that strong measures should be taken immediately for the protection of foreign lives and property:

> France from her position, especially under the new Anglo-French agreement, would seem the proper agent, but she has little or no influence with the Court or people, being cordially detested, and if she depends on her so-called "pacific penetration," her efforts will amount to nothing.[287]

All during the latter half of 1904, in fact, Gummeré and the vice consul general, Hoffman Philip, had sent pessimistic forecasts of Morocco's future. Their prophecies confirmed one made in June by the Washington Post to the effect that a country-wide revolution supported by all important classes of the people was being plotted to depose Abd al-Aziz.[288] Gummeré heard that Raisuli's success had stimulated an avaricious lust for ransom among several tribes, and antagonism toward the French customs officials was very bitter. The dismissal from office of the war minister, Sid Al Menebhi, and his disgrace with confiscation of his property were ill omens. In August some mountain tribes asked the diplomatic corps to protect Morocco from French aggression. Kaid Maclean was kidnapped in December, and a second attack, though unsuccessful, was made on Walter Harris. The abolition of coastal trading enhanced the rebellious spirit spreading even among traditionally loyal tribes. Philip quoted Saint-René Taillandier to the effect that the Sultan's refusal to accept the proposed French reforms would be met by the entry of French troops from the Algerian border. Convinced that France's ultimate aim was the annexation of Morocco without international complications, Philip thought there was a general feeling among the foreign representatives, except the British, that too implicit and hasty an acquiescence in the undefined French policy would be inadvisable.[289]

By December of 1904 Saint-René Taillandier was pursuing the French policy vigorously, seeking to impress upon the Maghzen the vital necessity of establishing order on the frontier and in the towns and of creating a state bank. Among the measures that Delcassé directed him to recommend on his forthcoming visit to Fez was the employment of French officers in various garrisons and the establishment of a new police force, with the native Algerian police, officered by Frenchmen, as a nucleus. Aroused by this clear evidence of France's ambitions, the Maghzen announced the dismissal of the Sultan's foreign advisers and employees, including the French military mission. By withdrawing all French citizens from Fez and threatening to break off diplomatic relations and to visit summary punishment upon Morocco,[290] the French government and press induced the Sultan to reconsider his bold action.[291]

The press propaganda inspired by Delcassé had done nothing to convince the Sultan's subjects that he had not sold them out to France. They did not believe that France's policy was one of friendly cooperation. Of the British press, only the Spectator and the Daily Telegraph gave hearty support to the "pacific penetration," which seemed certain to lead to armed invasion.[292]

An able summary of the situation in February, 1905, just as Morocco was about to find a champion in Germany, was presented by Philip. Anarchy still ruled in the northern part, and the plague was again epidemic. The new silver and gold coinage was rapidly depreciating in value. Although many Frenchmen were arriving from France and Algeria to establish banking and other business enterprises,[293]

> at the present time there appears to exist throughout Morocco a strong feeling among the Moors that the assumption by the French government of a leading role in the administrative affairs of this country is undesirable and a thing to be resisted .... That another power engaging in the same task as has been assumed by the French government would experience numerous and similar difficulties cannot be doubted, yet, a special obstacle to peaceful methods arises from the proximity of Algeria .... The actual knowledge of Algeria and its people on the part of the vast majority of the inhabitants of Morocco is extremely limited; they but unite in considering the Algerians a conquered and subdued people with whom they have no sympathy, and they are also united in the wish to avoid a similar fate. This appears to be the basis of a particular lack of sympathy evinced at this period by the natives of Morocco toward the French Nation as among other Christian Powers.[294]

The vagaries of Abd al-Aziz and the villainies of Raisuli had been so extensively advertised in the American press that every new extension of foreign control over Morocco was sure to win approval in the United States. A typical opinion of the Franco-Spanish agreement was:

> It will be better for the rest of the world, including the United States, when France establishes a full protectorate over Morocco, as her interests entitle her to do. We are not anxious for a repetition of the Perdicaris incident.[295]

The last pathetic gesture of Abd al-Aziz to win American help was in vain. Like the rest of his expenditures for foreign trinkets, the large sum spent upon the Moroccan exhibit at the St. Louis Exposition was wasted.[296] American sympathy and interest were not attracted to Morocco, and the exhibit itself received no publicity.[297] The verdict on the Sultan was that according to American standards he was not working for modern progress:

> He has not done a thing for which any of his subjects can be grateful. He has not built a mile of road; he has not dammed a river or bored an artesian well; he has not improved a harbor; he has not erected a lighthouse; he has not founded a school; he has not even placed his costly toys where they might serve the purpose of a museum. He has handed his country over to the French.[298]

The architects of the Entente Cordiale had had three tasks to accomplish during 1904. The first, to reach an agreement among themselves, was completed by October. The second, to receive the assent of their respective nations or their representatives, was finished by the end of the year. The third, to implement their plans by gaining the submission of the Moroccans, was to remain a major problem of international politics for many years to come.

Although the declaration concerning Morocco and Egypt did not require ratification by any parliaments, since it was an "understanding" regarding policy and not a treaty, the debates on the convention involving territorial transfers were concerned largely with the Moroccan agreement. In Great Britain, there was some adverse criticism in the press, the British merchants in Morocco were opposed to the limiting of commercial freedom to thirty years, and a few leaders in the House of Commons protested various features of the entente. In the House of Lords, one dissenting voice was heard--that of Lord Rosebery, who predicted that eventually the Moroccan pact would lead to war. However, by August 15 the King's speech announced the ratification of the treaty in the general settlement.[299] In the French parliament there was some dissatisfaction with the surrender in Egypt and some objection to arrangements on Newfoundland. But there was general approval of the solution of the Moroccan problem. The treaty was ratified by the Chamber of Deputies on November 12 and by the Senate on December 7.[300] In spite of the minority dissenting opinion in both parliaments, there was a chorus of commendation for a great diplomatic achievement. Delcassé could claim that he had not only made a colonial acquisition for France but had also effected a revolution in international relations.

Officially, the United States made no extravagant claims for her diplomatic prowess in Morocco. The general complacency of the American public was well expressed, however, by this editorial opinion:

> At the beginning of the last century, it was an American fleet that exterminated the Barbary Coast pirates and made the Mediterranean a sea where neutral vessels could go in safety. Now, at the beginning of this century, it looks as if, by sending our fleet and by a diplomatic combination with France, we are to be the cause of the extermination of the land robbers of Morocco, and perhaps even of the establishment of a civilized rule under European supervision in the last of the old African States on the Mediterranean.[301]

Neither Secretary Hay nor the American representatives in Tangier sought to enhance the prestige or power of the United States in Morocco. Philip kept the State Department aware of events during that critical period when only the Sultan's reluctant submission to France's demands prevented armed conflict. He reported the continuance of crime, disorder, and revolt, encouraged by the failure of the Maghzen to suppress contraband trade in arms. He advocated making an up-to-date treaty of commerce with the Sultan directly or under French auspices. If France imposed political stability upon Morocco, economic opportunities for Americans might improve, or they might be restricted by secret articles in the Anglo-French and the Franco-Spanish agreements. In either case, an improved treaty was advisable. The "state of anarchical independence" in Morocco continued because of the slow progress of the Franco-Moroccan negotiations for reform and the "change from active oppression to an undecided inertia on the part of the Maghzen." In March, 1905, Philip made an astute forecast of coming events:

> I am creditably informed that the German government has represented to the Sultan ... that Germany has no official knowledge of the French policy in Morocco, and there are many evidences of the intention on the part of that power to pursue a course entirely separate if not somewhat in opposition to that adopted by the French government. I am of the opinion that the German government would not under any circumstances be inclined to extend to Morocco assistance of a more than commercially advantageous nature, involving mutual benefits, yet the Department will be aware what a strong factor this attitude and a similar, though less accentuated, lack of accord with French measures on the part of other Powers, might prove in the event of the Sultan and his advisers wishing to strongly oppose the policy of the French government.[302]

It is difficult to understand the motive of the State Department in upgrading the status of its representative in Morocco just as that country appeared to be downgrading itself from a nominally independent empire to a protectorate. Since 1902, Gummeré had pleaded for promotion to the rank of minister.[303] Of the ten countries represented in Morocco in 1904, nine had given their representatives the grandiose title of minister plenipotentiary and envoy extraordinary. When on leave in the United States in the last part of 1904, Gummeré made a personal application at the State Department for relief from his "intolerable position."[304] This time his request was granted. On March 29, 1905, Hoffman Philip was informed of his appointment as consul general at Tangier, and on May 8, 1905, Gummeré began his career as the first minister of the United States to Morocco.[305] At the time when the international conflict predicted by Lord Rosebery was about to begin, therefore, the United States had the strongest representation in Morocco since their relations began. It remained to be seen how influential an honest, efficient, and equally ranked ministry would be in determining the course of events.

Notes

1. The closing of the diplomatic ring around Germany and her one remaining ally, Austria-Hungary, was not fully completed until 1908.

2. Alfred Thayer Mahan, "The United States Looking Outward," Atlantic Monthly, LXVI (Dec., 1890), 816-824.

3. "His books on The Influence of Sea Power upon History provided an intellectual basis for the world-wide navalism which was just beginning. Mahan's admirers might justly claim for him the credit for formulating theories which led directly to the great American navy, to the construction of the German and Japanese navies, to a great expansion of the British navy, to the naval rivalry between England and Germany, and even to the World War itself." Joseph Ward Swain, Beginning the Twentieth Century. A history of the Generation that Made the War, First Edition (hereafter cited as Swain, Beginning the Twentieth Century), 186-187. The fifteenth edition of Mahan's book was published in 1894.

4. Andrew Carnegie, "A Look Ahead," North American Review, CLVI (June, 1893), 685-710.

5. Henry Cabot Lodge, "Our Blundering Foreign Policy," Forum, XIX (March, 1895), 8-17. Lodge demanded the building of a Nicaraguan canal, annexation of Hawaii, maintenance of American influence in the Samoan Islands, and "from the Rio Grande to the Arctic Ocean one flag and one country"--all sanctioned by the Monroe Doctrine.

6. The United States, 54th Congress, 1st Session, 1895-96, House Documents, I, Document No. 1, Part 1, Foreign Relations, 1895, Ser. No. 3368, 542-562.

7. Bertha Ann Reuter, Anglo-American Relations during the Spanish-American War (hereafter cited as Reuter, Anglo-American Relations), 21-22, 25-27, 29.

8. Johannes Haller, Philip Eulenburg: The Kaiser's Friend, 2 vols., translated from the German by Ethel Colburn Mayne (hereafter cited as Haller, Eulenburg, I, 124. For interesting views of the personnel and policies of the German government from 1890 to 1909, see Ibid., I, 122-127, 139, 186, 320, 333 and II, 8-9, 34, 39-48, 51-52, 55, 72-73, 136-137, 292-302, 305-310.

9. The erratic policies and extraordinary personality of Holstein, so influential in making the diplomatic history of Germany from 1890 to 1906, have attracted the attention of many writers. Some pertinent references are listed here: Sir James Rennell Rodd, Social and Diplomatic Memories, First, Second, and Third Series (hereafter cited as Rodd, Social and Diplomatic Memories), I, 115; III, 117-118; Baron Hermann von Eckardstein, Ten Years at the Court of St. James, 1895-1905 (hereafter cited as Eckardstein, Ten Years at the Court of St. James), 33-34; Prince Bernhard von Bülow, Memoirs of Prince von Bülow, 3 vols. (hereafter cited as Bülow, Memoirs), I, 216, 252; Sir Valentine Chirol, Fifty Years in a Changing World (hereafter cited as Chirol, Fifty Years), 269-270, 301; Brandenburg, From Bismarck to the World War, 23-25; George Peabody Gooch, Studies in Modern History, "Baron von Holstein," 1-116 (hereafter cited as Gooch, "Holstein").

10. Prince Bernhard von Bülow, Imperial Germany, Revised Edition (hereafter cited as Bülow, Imperial Germany), 19. The three leading German diplomats are characterized thus by James Louis Garvin, in The Life of Joseph Chamberlain, 3 vols. (hereafter cited as Garvin, Chamberlain), III, 293: "Bülow, brilliant but shallow and deceptive; Holstein, the complete logician arguing from false premises; Tirpitz, the inflexible sailor, who saw in his work for the future glory of the sea-service the soul of patriotism."

11. Pringle, Roosevelt, 165-180.

12. Tyler Dennett, John Hay: From Poetry to Politics (hereafter cited as Dennett, John Hay), 179, 196.

13. Allan Nevins, Henry White. Thirty Years of American Diplomacy (hereafter cited as Nevins, Henry White), 217.

14. Swain, Beginning the Twentieth Century, 226.

15. Michon, The Franco-Russian Alliance, 101-106.

16. Frederick L. Schuman, War and Diplomacy in the French Republic (hereafter cited as Schuman, War and Diplomacy in the French Republic), 160-161; Anderson, First Moroccan Crisis, 7-10.

17. Garvin, Chamberlain, III, 23, 28.

18. George Peabody Gooch and Harold V. Temperley, editors, British Documents on the Origins of the War, 1898-1914, 11 vols. (hereafter cited as B. D.), I, 324-325.

19. Fay, Origins of the World War, I, 127-128.

20. G. P., XI, Chapter 64, Dec. 30, 1895-Feb. 18, 1896; cited by Townsend, Rise and Fall of Germany's Colonial Empire, 186.

21. For the violent outbursts of American jingoism against Great Britain and Germany in 1894 see Allen Nevins, Grover Cleveland: A Study in Courage (hereafter cited as Nevins, Grover Cleveland), 607-609.

22. Ibid.

23. J. A. Spender, Fifty Years of Europe. A Study in Pre-War Documents (hereafter cited as Spender, Fifty Years of Europe), 224-225.

24. Quoted by James Ford Rhodes, History of the United States from Hayes to McKinley, 1877-1896 (hereafter cited as Rhodes, History of the United States), 450-451.

25. John Holladay Latané, A History of American Foreign Policy, Revised Edition (hereafter cited as Latané,

History of American Foreign Policy), 564-565; Brandenburg, From Bismarck to the World War, 64-71; William Leonard Langer, The Diplomacy of Imperialism, 1890-1902, 2 vols. (hereafter cited as Langer, Diplomacy of Imperialism), I, 167-191.

26. Nicolson, Portrait of a Diplomatist, 63.

27. The subject of German-American relations during this period has received a great deal of study from German scholars. Among important publications are the following: Hermann von Leusser, Ein Jahrzeit deutsch-amerikanischer Politik (1897-1906), Beiheft 13 der Historischen Zeitschift; Ilse Kunz-Lack, Die deutsch-amerikanischen Beziehungen; Alfred Vagts, Deutschland und die Vereinigten Staaten in der Weltpolitik, 2 vols. (hereafter cited as Vagts, Weltpolitik). The last named, a monumental work, gives much space to such economic problems as tariffs, bimetallism, and capital investments, as well as to colonial controversies.

28. Memorandum of Marschall, No. 1526, Jan. 25, 1893, G. P., VII, 243-244; Marschall to the Ambassador in St. Petersburg, No. 1527, Jan. 30, 1893, Ibid., 244; quoted by Spender, Fifty Years, 136-137.

29. Mildred S. Wertheimer, The Pan-German League, 1890-1914 (hereafter cited as Wertheimer, The Pan-German League), 25, 206-208. Miss Wertheimer points out a fact (208-209) entirely unsuspected in the United States--that the League was a constant handicap and source of embarrassment to the German government.

30. Brandenburg, From Bismarck to the World War, 93-94.

31. Count Sergius Witte, The Memoirs of Count Witte (hereafter cited as Witte, Memoirs), 408-410.

32. "The thought of a continental league implying the French renunciation of Alsace-Lorraine was like a will-o-the-wisp .... Security in their European status, inviolability on land, and the prospect of a

colonial policy no longer fettered by consideration of England, all seemed attainable along this path." Brandenburg, From Bismarck to the World War, 143.

33. Letter from William II to Philip Eulenburg, Aug. 20, 1897, quoted in Bülow, Memoirs, I, 160-161.

34. Dennis, Adventures, 284-285.

35. Andrew Dickson White, Autobiography of Andrew Dickson White, 2 vols. (hereafter cited as White, Autobiography), II, 144-146.

36. Bülow, Memoirs, I, 30-31, 52-56, 66-69, 224. Holstein's secretive policy of keeping a "free hand" to maintain a balance between Great Britain and the Dual Alliance and of winning "compensations" by having "two irons in the fire" was the real basis of German diplomacy. Brandenburg, From Bismarck to the World War, 204-207; Nicolson, Portrait of a Diplomatist, 61-62.

37. Williamson, Germany and Morocco before 1905, 52-71; Townsend, Rise and Fall of Germany's Colonial Empire, 175, 178-180.

38. After several speeches extolling "the supreme triumphs of war" and advocating a navy "not merely for defence" his superiors persuaded him to desist. Pringle, Roosevelt, 171-173.

39. Extracts from a letter by Roosevelt to Sir Cecil Spring-Rice, dated Aug. 13, 1897; quoted in Stephen Gwynn, The Letters and Friendships of Sir Cecil Spring-Rice, 2 vols. (hereafter cited as Gwynn, Spring-Rice), 229-231: "As a German, I should be delighted to upset the English in South Africa and to defy the Americans and their Monroe Doctrine in South America. As an Englishman, I should seize the first opportunity to crush the Germany Navy and the German commercial marine out of existence .... As an American I should advocate ... keeping our Navy at a pitch that will enable us to interfere promptly if Germany ventures to touch a foot of American soil."

40. Letter from Roosevelt to F. C. Moore, Dec. 9, 1898, quoted by Madariaga, in Spain, 359-360: "I should myself like to shape our foreign policy with a purpose ultimately of driving off this continent every European power. I would begin with Spain."

41. Pringle, Roosevelt, 178-233.

42. Lester B. Shippee, "Germany and the Spanish-American War," American Historical Review, XXX (July, 1925), 754-777; Bülow, Memoirs, I, 218, 255; Nevins, Henry White, 145, 203.

43. Bemis, Diplomatic History of the United States, 462, 466-467.

44. Fay, Origins of the World War, I, 234-235.

45. Bülow, Memoirs, I, 480.

46. Hector C. Bywater, Sea-Power in the Pacific. A Study of the American-Japanese Naval Problem (hereafter cited as Bywater, Sea-Power in the Pacific), 69-70, 141.

47. Olney had been converted to the religion of "patriotism of race." See his article, "The International Isolation of the United States," in Atlantic Monthly, LXXXI (May, 1898), 577-588.

48. Nevins, Henry White, 135; Dennis, Adventures, 117-118, 122; Reuter, Anglo-American Relations, 150-155, 159-165.

49. Joseph Chamberlain, "Recent Developments of Policy in the United States and Their Relation to an Anglo-American Alliance," Scribner's Magazine, XXIV (Dec., 1898), 674-682.

50. The German records are in G. P., XIV, Chapter 91. The British official documents consist of two dispatches, Lascelles to Balfour, Aug. 23, 1898, B. D., I, 100-101 and Lascelles to Salisbury, Dec. 21, 1898, Ibid., 103-104. For Chamberlain's

part in these negotiations see Garvin, Chamberlain, III, 254-292.

51. Ibid., 285-289; Walter Goetz, Briefe Wilhelms II. an den Zaren, 1894-1914 (hereafter cited as Goetz, Briefe Wilhelms II. an den Zaren), 309-312; Isaac Don Levine, Letters from the Kaiser to the Czar, (hereafter cited as Levine, Letters from the Kaiser to the Czar), No. 15 and No. 16.

52. G. P., XIV, 347-355; B. D., I, 44-73.

53. For secondary accounts of the negotiations of 1898, see; Pribram, England and the European Great Powers, 69-75; Fay, Origins of the World War, I, 128-135; Brandenburg, From Bismarck to the World War, 105-122.

54. Anderson, First Moroccan Crisis, 41-42; Parker Thomas Moon, Imperialism and World Politics (hereafter cited as Moon, Imperialism and World Politics, 150-154.

55. The Franco-Russian Alliance, the Triple Alliance and its satellites, and the Anglo-American group were the three groups meant. The last named, "although not united in formal alliance, nevertheless is an integer more homogeneous in race, religion, language, laws, and constitution than either of the other governing groups." Japan was often combined with the Anglo-American combination. Spain, Mexico, and China stood apart. W. T. Stead, "The Conference at The Hague," Forum, XXVIII (Sept., 1899), 1-12.

56. For brief accounts of the conference see: Willis Fletcher Johnson, America's Foreign Relations, 2 vols. (hereafter cited as Johnson, America's Foreign Relations), II, 358-364; Dennis, Adventures, 472-479; White, Autobiography, 265-321.

57. The treaty of Dec. 12, 1899 also gave Tutuila and several small islands to the United States.

58. The implication that Samoa was being exchanged for German neutrality in the Boer War is very plain. See Lascelles to Salisbury, Oct. 10, 1899, B. D., I, 126-127 and Feb. 16, 1900, Ibid., I, 131.

59. Bülow, Memoirs, I, 368-379; Garvin, Chamberlain, III, 496-513; Sir Sydney Lee, King Edward VII, A Biography, 2 vols. (hereafter cited as Lee, Edward VII), I, 745-747.

60. Memorandum of Bülow, No. 4398, Nov. 24, 1899, G. P., XV, 413-420; Garvin, Chamberlain, III, 502-503.

61. Lee, Edward VII, I, 748-749; Grey, Twenty-Five Years, I, 41, 43.

62. Dennett, John Hay, Chapter XX.

63. Langer, Diplomacy of Imperialism, II, 659-660; Nicolson, Portrait of a Diplomatist, 96-97.

64. Brandenburg, From Bismarck to the World War, 141-144; Monson to Salisbury, Oct. 27, 1899, B. D., I, 234-235.

65. Dennis, Adventures, 127-128.

66. William Roscoe Thsyer, The Life and Letters of John Hay, 2 vols. (hereafter cited as Thsyer, John Hay, II, 234.

67. Dennett, John Hay, 246-247.

68. Stanley K. Hornbeck, Contemporary Politics in the Far East, 222-229.

69. Jeanette Keim, Forty Years of German-American Political Relations (hereafter cited as Keim, Forty Years of German-American Political Relations, 253.

70. Great Britain had always maintained free trade in her colony of Hong Kong and treaty ports since 1842. The American policy was based upon a most favored

nation treaty secured by Caleb Cushing from China in 1844. Dennis, Adventures, 171-173.

71. Lord Charles Beresford, recently returned from China, made speeches to chambers of commerce in all the principal American cities from San Francisco to New York, urging Anglo-American cooperation in China. It is suspected that a strong secret influence behind both Rockhill and Hay was Alfred E. Hippleley, a Britisher formerly in the Chinese customs service, who came to the United States in 1899. Dennett, John Hay, Chapter XXIV.

72. Dennis, Adventures, 170-171, 181-186.

73. For the text of the notes, see F. R., 1899, 132-133.

74. Ibid., 128-142.

75. Dennett, John Hay, 295.

76. F. R., 1901, Appendix, "Affairs in China," 12.

77. For the text, see B. D., II, 15-16.

78. Austria-Hungary, Italy, and Japan accepted all these propositions, the United States the first two. Russia and France expressed general agreement with the first two clauses, but Russia reserved the right to interpret them herself. Hay's inconsistent behavior in asking permission to establish an American naval station in Fukien Province met with the deserved rebuff of Japan's refusal. Bemis, Diplomatic History of the United States, 487-488.

79. Memorandum of Lord Sanderson, dated 1907, B. D., II, 2.

80. Dennis, Adventures, 238.

81. Ibid., 196, 258.

82. Ibid., 241-242.

83. United States, 57th Congress, 2nd Session, 1902-1903, House Documents, I, Ser. No. 4440, 275-276.

84. For a caustic appraisal of the American Open Door policy see Sydney Brooks, "America and the Alliance," Living Age, Seventh Series, XV (May 10, 1902), 321-328. On page 327 Brooks says: "America's policy in China is one of dispatch-writing simply. She favors the 'open door' and will keep it open so far as scribbling can. She would prefer a 'strong, independent and responsible Chinese government' ... and to this end no pen will flow faster than hers. She values--possibly, like most of us, over-values--her stake in the future of China, and she will not spare the ink in its defence."

85. Eckardstein, first secretary of the German embassy in London, represents himself as prime mover in the attempts to make an Anglo-German alliance. His testimony must be used cautiously, as some of it has been shown to be unreliable.

86. Lord Lansdowne became foreign minister in 1900, but Lord Salisbury retained the premiership until 1902.

87. Source materials on these negotiations include the following: G. P., XVI, Chapter 106 and XVII, Chapter 109; B. D., II, Chapter X; Lord P. C. Thomas W. Newton, Lord Lansdowne, A Biography (hereafter cited as Newton, Lansdowne), 198-208; Eckardstein, Ten Years at the Court of St. James, 184-242; Bülow, Memoirs, I, 386-388; Chirol, Fifty Years, 288-299; George Peabody Gooch, Before the War, Studies in Diplomacy: I, The Grouping of the Powers (hereafter cited as Gooch, Before the War), 6-16.

88. Newton, Lansdowne, 219-228; B. D., II, Chapter XI.

89. Brandenburg, From Bismarck to the World War, 184-186.

90. Howard Copeland Hill, Roosevelt and the Caribbean (hereafter cited as Hill, Roosevelt and the Caribbean),

32-33; Dennis, Adventures, 164-165, 160-162; Bemis, Diplomatic History of the United States, 510-511.

91. Tyler Dennett, "The Open Door," in Empire in the East, edited by Joseph Barnes (hereafter cited as Dennett, "The Open Door"), 279-281.

92. Nevins, Henry White, 186-202; Dennis, Adventures, 149-154; Bemis, Diplomatic History of the United States, 426-428.

93. "It would seem that the only truth to be found in the 'German plot' consisted of schemes and efforts, concocted in German naval and colonial circles .... It cannot be ascertained that they were in any case supported by the government. Officially Germany repudiated by word and deed any concrete opposition to the Monroe Doctrine by attempts to annex territory, and deemed it the better part of wisdom not to antagonize the United States." Townsend, Rise and Fall of Germany's Colonial Empire," 206.

94. Townsend, Rise and Fall of Germany's Colonial Empire, 202-205; Stephen Bonsal, "Greater Germany in South America," North American Review, CLXXVI (Jan., 1903), 57-67. Sydney Brooks, in "Some Aspects of the Monroe Doctrine," Living Age, Seventh Series, XIV (Jan. 11, 1902), 63-76 said on page 71 that the American attitude would condemn South America to impotence and anarchy by ruling out Teutonic civilization.

95. Roosevelt's version of the affair, reprinted in Dennis, Adventures, 304-308, is accepted by Newton, Lansdowne, 257-258. Die Grosse Politik contains no evidence, and Roosevelt's story has been discredited by Hill, Roosevelt and the Caribbean, 100-139; Dennis, Adventures, 282-297; and Pringle, Roosevelt, 283-289. Nevins, in Henry White, 215-216, is inclined to agree with Dennis and Pringle that Ambassador Holleben may have received some kind of informal warning, but nothing so drastic as a virtual threat of war. A witness for Roosevelt's veracity, as always, testifies in What Me Befell, The Remi-

niscences of J. J. Jusserand (hereafter cited as Jusserand, What Me Befell), 237-238.

96. Dennis, Adventures, 348-349. On Feb. 19, 1903, five days after the blockade was lifted, Roosevelt was congratulating Sternburg on the good impression made by Germany's concessions. Also, "in the establishment of an independent state by Germans in Brazil Roosevelt saw the best solution of the South American problem;" G. P., XVII, No. 5151, cited by Dennis in Adventures, 296. In his Autobiography, 31, Roosevelt states the basis of his friendship for Sternburg: "He was a capital shot, rider, and walker .... It was he who first talked over with me the raising of a regiment of horse riflemen from among the ranchmen and cowboys of the plains."

97. Some pertinent remarks are worth quoting. "Sternburg has intimate relations with the President. The Emperor thinks he has done marvelously in nominating here a friend of the President, whose wife is an American. Baron von Sternburg, who was First Secretary in Washington before Count Quadt, has left in the diplomatic corps recollections not at all flattering. They say he is inordinately vain and haughty and affects a complete silence towards his colleagues. One thing is certain, that the attitude of Emperor William toward the United States is full of plunges and contradictions, and that the Emperor seems to be very badly informed about America. Is his embassy responsible for this?" Margerie to Delcassé, Jan. 12, 1903, D. D. F., Ser. 2, III, 24-26. "Roosevelt said, ... I know what I want to do, especially in the Venezuelan affair, and the new ambassador will not make any more change in my ideas than Holleben was able to do." Margerie to Delcassé, Jan. 18, 1903, Ibid., 43.

98. Spender, Fifty Years of Europe, 228.

99. Elizabeth Brett White, American Opinion of France, from Lafayette to Poincare (hereafter cited as White, American Opinion of France, 236-238.

100. Jusserand to Delcassé, March 9, 1903, D. D. F., Ser. 2, III, 162-163.

101. André Tardieu, France and the Alliances (hereafter cited as Tardieu, France and the Alliances), 274.

102. Ba-Ahmad prompted every word of the Sultan when he spoke to the people, "like a raven teaching a little canary to sing;" R. L. N. Johnston, "Morocco and the French Intervention," Review of Reviews, XXXI (June, 1905), 693 (hereafter cited as Johnston, "Morocco and the French Intervention").

103. Meakin, Moorish Empire, 192-195.

104. Barclay to Uhl, No. 29, June 15, 1894; No. 32, June 22, 1894; No. 33, June 27, 1894; No. 40, July 10, 1894; No. 47, Aug. 21, 1894; No. 49, Aug. 24, 1894; No. 50, Aug. 27, 1894; No. 51, Aug. 30, 1894; No. 52, Sept. 1, 1894; No. 54, Sept. 5, 1894; No. 55, Sept. 10, 1894; No. 56, Sept. 19, 1894; No. 61, Sept. 19, 1894; No. 63, Oct. 30, 1894; No. 65, Nov. 12, 1894; No. 67, Dec. 5, 1894; C. D., Tangier, XIX. Barclay to Uhl, No. 84, April 12, 1895; No. 90, June 8, 1895; No. 93, June 15, 1895; No. 124, Nov. 19, 1895; No. 139, March 17, 1896; C. D., Tangier, XX.

105. Barclay to Uhl, No. 72, Jan. 28, 1895, Ibid., XIX; No. 128, Dec. 19, 1895 and No. 134, Jan. 24, 1896, Ibid., XX.

106. J. E. Budgett Meakin, "Peeps Into Barbary," Harper's Magazine, XCIII (Aug., 1896), 387-399.

107. Nicolson, Portrait of a Diplomatist, 82, 88, 89, 90.

108. Count Sternburg, The Barbarians of Morocco, 150-151. The author of this book was a champion of "Morocco for the Moors."

109. The Sultan's only steamer was captained by a German who helped to repel an "invasion" of the Sus by a British exploitation company in 1898. The Sultan's

electrician was also a German. Williamson, Germany and Morocco Before 1905, 121-122, 131.

110. Ibid., 108; Hohenwart to Goluchowski, No. 5175, April 22, 1901, communicated to the Foreign Office in Berlain, G. P., XVII, 328-331.

111. Williamson, Germany and Morocco before 1905, 144-145. The intervention of 1895 was reported to the State Department by Barclay: Barclay to Uhl, No. 87, May 1, 1895; No. 88, May 6, 1895; No. 98, July 11, 1895; No. 99, July 15, 1895; No. 101, July 29, 1895; C. D., Tangier, XX.

112. Barclay to Uhl, No. 64, Nov. 5, 1894; No. 83, April 12, 1895; No. 95, June 25, 1895; No. 103, Aug. 20, 1895; C. D., Tangier, XX.

113. Barclay to Uhl, 3 dispatches, July 16, 1894 to Dec. 24, 1894, C. D., Tangier, XIX; 8 dispatches, March 4, 1895 to May 4, 1896, Ibid., XX; Solicitor's Office to Rockhill, July 20, 1896, Ibid.

114. Barclay to Uhl, No. 66, Nov. 28, 1894, Ibid., XIX; No. 80, April 2, 1895, Ibid., XX.

115. Barclay to Uhl, 13 dispatches, April 24, 1895 to March 7, 1896, Ibid. Barclay to W. W. Rockhill (Ass't. Sec. of State), 7 dispatches, March 9, 1895 to June 30, 1896., Ibid.; 2 dispatches, July 8, 1896 and July 24, 1896, Ibid., XXI.

116. Stalker to Olney, June 29, 1895, C. D., Tangier, XX; Stalker to Adee, Aug. 26, 1895, Ibid.

117. Barclay to Cleveland, June 8, 1896; Barclay to Rockhill, June 12, 1896; Barclay to State Department, June 22, 1896; all cables, C. D., Tangier, XX. Barclay to Olney, Aug. 20, 1896, Ibid., XXI; Barclay to Rockhill, Aug. 20, 1896, Ibid.

118. Burke to Rockhill, No. 5, Aug. 25, 1896, Ibid. New York Times, June 3, 1896.

119. Burke to Rockhill, No. 57, Feb. 10, 1897, C. D., Tangier, XXI, with enclosure, "The U. S. Consul-General," from Al-Moghreb Al-Aksa for Jan. 30, 1897, quoting from the Diplomatic and Consular Review of New York for Jan., 1897.

120. Burke to Rockhill, 7 dispatches, from Sept. 4, 1896 to March 3, 1897, C. D., Tangier, XXI; Azogue (Philadelphia) to Olney, Dec. 22, 1896, Ibid.

121. Burke to Rockhill, 13 dispatches, Aug. 28, 1896 to April 12, 1897, C. D., Tangier, XXI; 3 dispatches, May 7, 1897 to May 25, 1897, Ibid., XXII. Burke to Day, 5 dispatches, June 20, 1897 to July 1, 1897, Ibid., XXII. Burke to Cridler (3rd Ass't. Sec. of State), 4 dispatches, Aug. 11, 1897 to Oct. 4, 1897, Ibid.

122. "It is said she (the Raleigh) will shortly depart for the coast ports with consul general Burke on board. The appearance of the Raleigh at the southern ports will be most gratifying to American citizens and all other foreign residents, as a proof that their interests are not to be left at the mercy of Moorish officials .... It is to be hoped that the Moorish government will also show a sincere disposition and do their best to come to just terms without delay." Al-Moghreb Al-Aksa, July 17, 1897.

123. Burke to Rockhill, 2 dispatches, Dec. 7, 1896 and Feb. 2, 1897, C. D. Tangier, XXI; 2 dispatches, May 20, 1897 and May 28, 1897, Ibid., XXII. Burke to Day, 11 dispatches, June 5, 1897 to Dec. 28, 1897, Ibid. Burke to Cridler, No. 101, Sept. 18, 1897, Ibid. Burke, cable to Sherman, June 26, 1897, Ibid. "American Claims on Morocco," New York Times, Feb. 6, 1898, 19.

124. Burke to Rockhill, No. 16, Sept., 1896; No. 54, Feb. 8, 1897; C. D. Tangier, XXI; No. 75, May 8, 1897, Ibid., XXII.

125. Burke to Rockhill, unnumbered: Dec. 17, 1896 and Dec. 28, 1896; No. 49, Jan. 30, 1897; Ibid., XXI.

126. Burke to Rockhill, 3 dispatches, Oct. 15, 1896 to April 23, 1897, Ibid. Burke to Cridler, 7 dispatches, Aug. 21, 1897 to Nov. 1, 1897, Ibid., XXII. Burke to Day, No. 113, Nov. 13, 1897, Ibid.

127. Burke to Day, Sept. 13, 1897; confidential, Jan. 4, 1898; C. D., Tangier, XXII. Burke to Cridler, Sept. 29, 1897, Ibid.

128. Burke to Day, Dec. 9, 1897 and Dec. 10, 1897, C. D., Tangier, XXII. Burke to Cridler, Jan. 6, 1899; Jan. 18, 1899; Jan. 24, 1899; Ibid., XXIV. Burke to Murphy, Jan. 24, 1899 with appended memorandum to Cridler, Ibid.

129. Partridge to Day, Oct. 28, 1897; No. 1, Jan. 20, 1898; No. 11, Feb. 25, 1898; Ibid., XXII.

130. Partridge to Day, No. 9, Feb. 22, 1898, with enclosure of clipping, "Ports Wanted in Soos," from Al-Moghreb Al-Aksa, Jan. 1, 1898; Ibid.

131. Partridge to Day, No. 21, March 17, 1898; C. D., Tangier, XXII. Partridge to John Bassett Moore, No. 51, May 24, 1898; No. 68, July 7, 1898; Ibid., XXIII.

132. Partridge to Day, No. 19, March 12, 1898; No. 24, March 25, 1898; Ibid., XXII. Partridge to Moore, 7 dispatches, from May 11, 1898 to July 14, 1898, Ibid., XXIII.

133. Partridge to Moore, No. 70, July 9, 1898; No. 79, July 14, 1898, Ibid.

134. Partridge to Day, No. 34, April 21, 1898; No. 38, April 27, 1898, Ibid., XXII. Partridge to Moore, 5 dispatches from May 12, 1898 to July 14, 1898; Ibid., XXIII. Partridge to State Dept., cables, July 11, 1898 and July 14, 1898, Ibid.

135. By background and education Gummeré was well fitted for his consular career. A graduate of Princeton, he had practiced law for several years and had

traveled extensively in Europe. He frequently visited the Perdicaris home in Tangier. Walter L. Wright, Jr., "Samuel René Gummeré, Dictionary of American Biography, 20 vols., VIII, 50.

136. Partridge to the President, March 26, 1898; C. D., Tangier, XXII. Gummeré to Cridler, May 19, 1898; Ibid., XXIII. Gummeré to Moore, No. 1, July 21, 1898; Ibid.

137. Lansdowne to Monson, April 6, 1904, B. D., II, 364; Meakin, Moorish Empire, 412-413.

138. Glanville, Italy's Relations with England, 19-21; Pribram, England and the European Great Powers, 56-62.

139. Edwin Maxey, in "Morocco Moriturus," Forum, XXXIX (April-June, 1908), 568, remarked "As for the Russian subjects in Morocco, there was but one--and he a Jew. When we remember the exceeding tenderness of the Russian Government for its Jewish subjects at home, it is not a little surprising that this extreme solicitude for the protection of this lone Jew in Morocco should have excited suspicion in London."

140. Wolff to Salisbury, May 23, 1898, B. D., II, 253; Monson to Salisbury, Aug. 11, 1898, Ibid., 254; Wolff to Salisbury, Aug. 14, 1898, Ibid., 255; Meakin, Moorish Empire, 274-275, 352.

141. Salisbury to Wolff, Jan. 11, 1899, B. D., II, 255; Wolff to Salisbury, March 10, 1899, Ibid., 256; Salisbury to Wolff, June 7, 1899, Ibid., 257.

142. Radowitz to Hohenlohe, No. 4205, April 15, 1899, G. P., XV, 115-119; Bülow to Radowitz, No. 34, No. 4206, April 27, 1899, Ibid., 119-122. Salisbury to Wolff, March 16, 1899, B. D., II, 256.

143. Salisbury to Lascelles, June 7, 1899, B. D., II, 256-257; Bülow, Memoirs, I, 482-485; Fay, Origins of the World War, I, 137.

144. At the instance of the diplomatic corps in Tangier, the Mecca pilgrimage was prohibited in 1897 because of the plague epidemic and prison conditions were improved by greater cleanliness and more food for the prisoners. Meakin, *Moorish Empire,* 195.

145. Report of Consul General Burke for 1896; United States, House of Representatives, 55th Congress, 2nd Session, 1897-98, *House Documents,* LXVI, *Commercial Relations,* 1897, I, Ser. No. 3694, 73-74; Report of Consul General Gummeré, United States, House of Representatives, 56th Congress, 1st Session, 1899-1900, *House Documents,* XCVI, *Commercial Relations,* 1899, I, Ser. No. 3993, 264-266.

146. Meakin, *Moorish Empire,* 432-433.

147. Gummeré to Moore, No. 5, Aug. 16, 1898, *C. D., Tangier,* XXIII.

148. Notation on the cover page of the dispatch: "Telephone allowed paper--no. Dec. 7, 1899." Gummeré to Hill, No. 171, Nov. 16, 1899, *Ibid.*, XXIV.

149. Gummeré to Moore, No. 24, Oct. 29, 1898, *Ibid.* Gummeré to Hill, No. 83, March 20, 1899; No. 171, Nov. 16, 1899; *Ibid.*, XXIV; No. 468, Oct. 24, 1901; No. 473, Nov. 26, 1901; *Ibid.*, XXVI.

150. Gummeré to Hill, No. 154, Sept. 30, 1899; No. 193, Dec. 14, 1899; No. 174, Nov. 21, 1899; *C. D., Tangier,* XXIV. Gummeré to Hill, No. 465, Oct. 17, 1901; No. 464, Oct. 17, 1901; No. 466, Oct. 18, 1901; No. 471, Nov. 21, 1901; No. 472, Nov. 21, 1901; No. 476, Dec. 12, 1901; No. 523, Nov. 25, 1902, *Ibid.*, XXVI.

151. Ludlow Lilly (Consular Clerk) to Hill, No. 117, June 8, 1899; No. 135, July 26, 1899, *C. D., Tangier,* XXIV. Gummeré to Hill, No. 161, Oct. 28, 1899; No. 170, Nov. 16, 1899; *Ibid.* Gummeré to Loomis, March 26, 1904, *Ibid.*, XXVI; July 19, 1904, *Ibid.,* XXVII

152. Gummeré to Moore, 4 dispatches, Aug. 18, 1898 to Oct. 13, 1898, C. D., Tangier, XXIII. Gummeré to Hill, No. 28, Nov. 15, 1898, Ibid., XXIII; 3 dispatches, Jan. 10, 1899 to Jan. 23, 1899, Ibid., XXIV; 4 dispatches, Jan. 31, 1900 to Feb. 23, 1901, Ibid., XXV; 3 dispatches, April 3, 1901 to Jan. 28, 1903, Ibid., XXVI. Gummeré to Loomis, No. 570, Feb. 15, 1904, Ibid., XXVI. Philip to Loomis, No. 554, Aug. 12, 1903, and No. 643, Feb. 9, 1905, Ibid., XXVI. Lilly to Hill, No. 134, July 24, 1899, Ibid., XXIV.

153. Gummeré to Hill, No. 126, July 6, 1899; No. 149, Sept. 28, 1899; No. 166, Nov. 11, 1899; Ibid., XXIV.

154. The extensive correspondence between Gummeré, Cobb, and the State Dept., between Sept. 20, 1898 and May 15, 1901, covers many pages of C. D., Tangier, XXIII, XXIV, XXV and XXVI.

155. The lengthy correspondence on American claims between Gummeré and the State Dept. extends from Oct. 13, 1898 to June 14, 1900; C. D., Tangier, XXIII, XXIV, and XXV.

156. Gummeré to Hill, 19 dispatches, July 7, 1900 to April 8, 1901, C. D., Tangier, XXV and 3 dispatches, April 8, 1901 to May 30, 1901; Ibid., XXVI.

157. "The Present Holder of the Green Parasol," Current Literature, XXXIX (Oct., 1905), 443-445.

158. Among the many interesting accounts of the extraordinary doings of Abd al-Aziz are the following: Ellis Ashmead-Bartlett, The Passing of the Shereefian Empire (hereafter cited as Ashmead-Bartlett, Passing of the Shereefian Empire), 10-14; Aubin, Morocco of Today, 120-139, 171-178; Gibbons, New Map of Africa, 264-266; W. S. Harris, Morocco That Was, 40, 50-51, 84-87; Rom Landau, Moroccan Journal (hereafter cited as Landau, Moroccan Journal), 115.

159. W. G. Fitzgerald, in "Morocco, the Derelict of Diplomacy," Review of Reviews, XXXVI (July, 1907),

66, says that the importation of foreign toys and luxury articles was brought about by the advice of the Sultan's war minister, Al Menebhi, after his return from a mission to London.

160. Poultney Bigelow, "The Mind of Muley Aziz. Being an Attempt to Explain the Situation in Morocco," (hereafter cited as Bigelow, "The Mind of Muley Aziz"), Independent, LVII (July 14, 1904), 75-78.

161. Ashmead-Bartlett, Passing of the Shereefian Empire, 10-11.

162. Ibid., 12-13.

163. Perdicaris made these remarks about Abd al-Aziz: "If the young Sultan is not a fool he is a misguided freak, who will pay with life and throne for his departures. Moors cannot be ruled by conciliatory methods. To them such rule means leave to revolt. But the probability is that the Sultan is a nonentity, his apparent benevolence--bribery born of fear, his release of his brother, the old Commander-in-Chief of the Army--a reckless piece of panic-inspired bravado, which is likely to cost him very dear." "China and Morocco," (From the London Express), New York Times, July 14, 1900, 7.

164. "Did the Sultan Lose a Goat?", Washington Post, Feb. 6, 1904, 6; John H. Thacher, "Young Abdul Aziz a Sport" (from the London Express), Ibid., July 3, 1904, Second Part, 4; "Very Human Is the Personality of Morocco's Young Sultan," (from Blackwood's Magazine), Ibid., Aug. 13, 1905, Fourth Part, 12. Arthur E. Schneider, "With the Sultan of Morocco," with pictures by the author, Century Magazine, LXVI (May, 1903), 3-30; "The Sultan Of Morocco Journeys Toward Fez," Ibid., (June, 1903), 163-176; "Arthur Schneider, An Artist Is Dead," New York Times, Feb. 18, 1942, 48.

165. Bülow to Münster, No. 5156, April 27, 1900, G. P., XVII, 299-301; Münster to Hohenlohe, No. 5157, May 9, 1900, Ibid., 301-302. Both Spain and Russia

suspected that this move meant an Anglo-French agreement. Wolff to Salisbury, June 9, 1900, B. D., II, 258 and Oct. 11, 1900, Ibid., 258. Nicolson considered Morocco doomed and was reluctant to transmit an appeal from the Sultan to Queen Victoria. Nicolson, Portrait of A Diplomatist, 95-96.

166. Anderson, First Moroccan Crisis, 11-12.

167. Meakin evaluated the incident for American readers: "Her (France's) unjustifiable annexation of the oases of Tuat and Figig this spring ... is only the beginning of the end .... She is content to wait till another deal shall afford another opening .... The colors of the map may as well be changed now as any time later." Meakin, "Yesterday and To-Day in Morocco," Forum, XXX (Nov., 1900), 373.

168. Gummeré to Hill, No. 284, June 20, 1900 and No. 315, Aug. 21, 1900; C. D., Tangier, XXV.

169. Eber Malcolm Carroll, French Public Opinion and Foreign Affairs, 1870-1914 (hereafter cited as Carroll, French Public Opinion), 199-200.

170. Madariga, Spain, 342.

171. Ibid., 360; Lucas, Partition and Colonization of Africa, 102-103.

172. Anderson, First Moroccan Crisis, 63-64.

173. Bülow, Memoirs, I, 503.

174. Carroll, French Public Opinion, 201-202, 207.

175. Anderson, First Moroccan Crisis, 64-65.

176. These agreements had been preceded by a period of rapprochement beginning in 1896, including the recognition of the French protectorate in Tunisia and a commercial treaty. This friendly policy toward France was initiated by the Marquis Visconti-Venosta,

foreign minister from 1899 to 1901, an ideal representative (from the French viewpoint) of Italy at the Algeciras Conference. Fay, Origins of the World War, I, 144-145; Glanville, Italy's Relations with England, 80.

177. Anderson, First Moroccan Crisis, 22, 25-26, 13-14, 45-46.

178. Roberts, History of French Colonial Policy, II, 549.

179. The international program included the making of agreements with interested states (Germany was included in the Bulletin), the assurance of the sovereignty of the Sultan and the independence of Morocco, the guarantee of the freedom of the Strait of Gibraltar, the granting of full commercial liberty, and the satisfaction of Spain's territorial claims. Anderson, First Moroccan Crisis, 6-8.

180. Carroll, French Public Opinion, 206-207.

181. Nicolson wrote Maclean that he was always ready to advise and assist the Sultan in the development or improvement of Morocco, but he did not wish to cause the Sultan any embarrassment by placing him in a false position. Nicolson, Portrait of a Diplomatist, 102-105.

182. In London, Al Menebhi had agreed "in principle" to economic improvements relating to roads and bridges, sanitation and engineering, coastal trade, ports and harbors, and construction of a telegraph line from Tangier to Mogador. The text of this agreement was shown to Cambon, the French ambassador in London. There is no evidence to substantiate Eckardstein's assertion that Nicolson tried to promote an Anglo-German political penetration with assigned spheres of influence in Morocco. Nicolson urged merely that the Germans construct the telegraph line. Nicolson, Ibid., 104-105.

183. The Sultan was to be warned against foreign innovations, such as his recent tax reforms, which might

provoke rebellions dangerous for Algeria. The French minister was to promote in all possible ways the commercial, industrial, and philanthropic projects which would support French influence in Morocco. Anderson, First Moroccan Crisis, 11-16; Nicolson, Portrait of a Diplomatist, 105. The French government gave Great Britain assurances that all their measures aimed only at controlling the lawless tribes on the border. Lansdowne to Monson, July 3, 1901, B. D., II, 261.

184. Nicolson, Portrait of a Diplomatist, 106.

185. Gummeré to Hill, No. 213, Jan. 20, 1900; No. 243, March 9, 1900; No. 297, July 12, 1900; No. 322, Sept. 3, 1900; No. 347, Nov. 16, 1900; C. D., Tangier, XXV; No. 417, April 25, 1901, Ibid., XXVI.

186. Gummeré to Hill, No. 458, Oct. 5, 1901, Ibid. Aubin, Morocco of Today, 203-205.

187. Gummeré to Loomis, No. 564, Nov. 25, 1903; No. 565, Dec. 14, 1903; C. D., Tangier, XXVI.

188. Gummeré to Hill, No. 422, May 20, 1901; Ibid.

189. Anderson, First Moroccan Crisis, 16-17.

190. Gummeré correctly attributed the causes of the uprisings to repeal of the tertib and the "Europeanization" of Abd al-Aziz.

191. Gibbons, New Map of Africa, 366-368; Johnston, "Morocco and the French Intervention," 694; Barbour, North West Africa, 88; Aubin, Morocco of Today, 89, 108. Gummeré to Hill, Sept. 13, 1902; No. 518, Oct. 22, 1902; No. 520, Nov. 8, 1902; No. 524, Dec. 29, 1902; C. D., Tangier, XXVI.

192. The Muslims of Fez resented the Sultan's execution of a sherif who had murdered an English missionary.

193. Delcassé wrote to the French minister in Morocco on Nov. 17, 1902: "We have only one interest, that

the Sultan of Morocco bind himself more and more to us. The political results of the loan in our eyes come before any other consideration." No. 487, Nov. 17, 1902, D. D. F., Sér. 2, II, 610.

194. Anderson, First Moroccan Crisis, 18; Aubin, Morocco of Today, 205, 321-340, 352-360; Schuman, War and Diplomacy in the French Republic, 173-174; Tardieu, France and the Alliances, 117. Delcassé to Gouin, No. 506, Nov. 28, 1902, D. D. F., Ser. 2, II, 632. Gummeré to Hill, No. 525, Jan. 5, 1903; No. 526, Jan. 12, 1903; No. 527, Jan. 14, 1903; No. 528, Jan. 16, 1903; No. 532, Feb. 2, 1903; No. 533, Feb. 9, 1903, C. D., Tangier, XXVI. Gummeré to Loomis, No. 541, May 1, 1903; No. 543, May 11, 1903; No. 545, May 28, 1903; No. 548, June 23, 1903; No. 552, July 16, 1903; Ibid.

195. Fay, Origins of the World War, I, 147-148.

196. The text is given in D. D. F., No. 473, Ser. 2, II, 632.

197. Anderson, First Moroccan Crisis, 39; Madariaga, Spain, 370.

198. Nation, LXXVI (Jan. 1, 1903), 3.

199. Anderson, First Moroccan Crisis, 46-47.

200. Saint-René Taillandier to Delcassé, No. 83, Feb. 12, 1902, 92-95; No. 121, March 5, 1902, 141-143; No. 125, March 9, 1902, 146-152; D. D. F., Sér. 2, II.

201. Nicolson, Portrait of a Diplomatist, 106-108.

202. Cambon to Delcassé, No. 369, Aug. 9, 1902, D. D. F., Sér. 2, II, 439-443.

203. Lansdowne to Maclean, Oct. 24, 1902, B. D., II, 272-273; Intelligence Section of the Army Officers to the Minister of Foreign Affairs, No. 429, Oct. 7, 1902, D. D. F., Sér. 2, II, 522-523; Cambon to

Delcassé, No. 456, Oct. 23, 1902, Ibid., 559-561; Lee, King Edward VII, II, 220-221.

204. Anderson, First Moroccan Crisis, 48-49.

205. Cambon's dispatch to Delcassé did not mention the United States, but Cambon went into detail on reasons for excluding Germany. In case of grave disorders in Morocco, he said, the Kaiser would take the initiative of intervention, leaving France to follow. Lansdowne denied knowledge of Germany's alleged attempt to obtain a coaling station near the Algerian frontier.

206. Lansdowne to Monson, Dec. 31, 1902, B. D., II, 274-275; Cambon to Delcassé, No. 552, Dec. 31, 1902, D. D. F., Sér. 2, II, 686-689.

207. Anderson, First Moroccan Crisis, 47, 49-50.

208. Note on the Moroccan question, No. 333, July 15, 1902, D. D. F., Sér. 2, II, 397-400. Germany was expected to claim certain interests in the Sus and compensation for the privileged position of France and Spain in Morocco. During August dispatches from the French chargé d'affaires at Berlin called attention to the rapid development of German commerce in Morocco and to German press articles asserting that Morocco was not a "negligible quantity" for Germany. Prinet to Delcassé, No. 360, Aug. 3, 1902, D. D. F., Sér. 2, II, 431-432; No. 377, Aug. 17, 1902, Ibid., 452-453.

209. Cambon's conversations with Lansdowne, Aug. 5, 1903 and Dec. 9, 1903, B. D., II, 307, 332. In the latter Cambon suggested that the Spanish proposal of 1887 for a European conference on Morocco might be revived.

210. Bihourd to Delcassé, No. 5, Jan. 13, 1903, D. D. F., Sér. 2, III, 30-31.

211. Richthofen to Radowitz, No. 5200, Sept. 24, 1903, G. P., XVII, 354-356.

212. Gooch, "Holstein," 84.

213. Williamson, Germany and Morocco Before 1905, 82-86, 91-97.

214. Saint-René Taillandier to Delcassé, No. 44, Jan. 27, 1903, D. D. F., Ser. 2, III, 56-59. For an account of the German postal system, see Williamson, Germany and Morocco before 1905, 111.

215. American growing interest in Morocco was shown by the fact that a translation of an article by Fischer, published in a German magazine in 1903, was issued as a government document, the Smithsonian Institution Report, 1904, United States, 58th Congress, 3rd Session, 1904-05, House Documents, CVI, No. 333, Part 1, Ser. No. 4885, 355-372. Fischer emphasized the importance of Morocco because of its size, population, climate, resources, and strategic location.

216. Williamson, Germany and Morocco before 1905, 86-91.

217. S. L. Bensusan, "Morocco and the European Powers," Contemporary Review, LXXXIII (Feb., 1903), 175-176.

218. Edwin Maxey, "The Moroccan Question," Arena, XXIX (March 1903), 246-247.

219. Langermann became very obnoxious to the French government. "The approaching return to Morocco of the adventurer, the Austrian-American Langermann is announced .... He had published in the newspapers an interview encouraging Americans to come to Morocco to trade, promising them good profits and assuring them that the Sultan 'is an ardent admirer of President Roosevelt.'" Jusserand to Delcassé, No. 9, Jan. 6, 1905, D. D. F., Ser. 2, VI, 10. "Morocco appears to be known in the American cities chiefly by the propaganda of M. Langermann, and we would be exposed to this American activity, which has never been represented in Morocco except by adventurers of his sort .... The difficulties of our task could only be increased,

personages such as M. Langermann being the natural enemies of reforms fatal to their industry and seeing only by their intrigues, how to perpetuate in the Maghzen a regime of disorder and corruption particularly favorable to their enterprises." Saint-René Taillandier to Delcassé, No. 108, Feb. 19, 1905, Ibid., 146.

220. "Morocco," Current Literature, XXXIV (April, 1903), 403.

221. About $185,081.16 worth of goatskins was sent to the United States during 1900 and part of 1901. There were about ten native American families, mostly missionaries, and about fifty naturalized Americans residing in Morocco, the majority in Tangier. No American vessel came to Tangier during the year 1901. United States, 57th Congress, 1st Session, 1901-1902, Senate Documents, XXIX, No. 411, Consulates and Consular Agencies, Ser. No. 4248, 571-573.

222. Malloy, Treaties, I, 778-780, 559-560.

223. Ibid., II, 1993-1995.

224. Dennis, Adventures, 440-441.

225. Nicolson, Portrait of a Diplomatist, 109.

226. Walter Burton Harris, "Raisuli," Blackwood's Magazine (hereafter cited as W. B. Harris, "Raisuli"), CCIX (Jan., 1921), 28-39. Among the concessions granted to Raisuli by Abd al-Aziz were his promotion to the governorship of the Tangier district, a ransom of $70,000, the release of his friends from prison, and the imprisonment of his enemies.

227. Maurois, Lyautey, 121-123.

228. See, for example, Delcassé to Saint-René Taillandier, No. 34, Jan. 21, 1903, D. D. F., Sér. 2, III, 45-46.

229. Cambon to Delcassé, No. 49, Jan. 29, 1903, D. D. F., Sér. 2, III, 65-68. King Edward said,

"We ought to keep this affair among ourselves; England, France, and Spain, and thus we shall avoid every difficulty .... We should perhaps make a place for Italy." Ibid., 66.

230. Saint-René Taillandier to Delcassé, No. 131, March 10, 1903, Ibid., 169-175. "As for the representatives of Austria-Hungary, the United States, Portugal, Belgium ... they are not and can not be anything but spectators of the task involved in Morocco among France, England, and Spain .... The representatives of these last powers have manifested in general a sufficiently lively curiousity in regard to events, (but) I have detected among them no hostile or jealous disposition or no tendency to combine against the power which has the most vital interests here and which is also in the best situation to make them finally prevail;" Ibid., 175.

231. Oran James Hale, Germany and the Diplomatic Revolution, 1904-6; A Study in European Press Relations, (hereafter cited as Hale, Germany and the Diplomatic Revolution), 122.

232. Maurois, Lyautey, 102-106; Gibbons, New Map of Africa, 363-364.

233. Maxwell Blake to the Sec. of State, Feb. 18, 1913, F. R., 1913, 1013.

234. Brandenburg, From Bismarck to the World War, 199.

235. Walter Burton Harris, "England, France, and Morocco," National Review, (Nov., 1903).

236. Tardieu, La Conférence, 119.

237. Herbert Feis, Europe, the World's Banker, 1870-1914 (hereafter cited as Feis, Europe, the World's Banker, 399.

238. Reporting the Moroccan request for an American loan, Gummeré said: "Moneyed men in those countries are unwilling to make further advances unless

such loans are in some way guaranteed by their respective governments, which guarantee has so far been refused." Gummeré to Loomis, No. 575, March 14, 1904, C. D. Tangier, XXVI.

239. Adee to Hay, April 4, 1904; quoted by Vagts, Weltpolitik, II, 1817.

240. A. Maurice Low, "Foreign Affairs," Forum, XXXIV (Jan. -March, 1903), 345-346.

241. "In Africa: Is France to Take Possession of Morocco?" Current Literature, XXXV (Nov., 1903), 517-518. Since the French were about to take Morocco, and England was seeking paramount influence in Abyssinia, the United States was in danger of seeing the whole African continent permanently closed to her commerce and influence. German newspapers were quoted as saying that the mission to King Menelik demonstrated the "imperialist mood" of the United States and her ambitions abroad.

242. Malloy, Treaties, I, 544-545. The Senate advised ratification on March 24, 1904 and ratifications were exchanged on May 7, 1904.

243. Gummeré to Loomis, March 24, 1904, C. D., Tangier, XXVI.

244. Similar agreements were made later by Great Britain with Germany (July, 1904), and with Sweden, Italy, Spain, and the Netherlands. Lee, King Edward VII, II, 247.

245. Sir Thomas Barclay, Thirty Years: Anglo-French Reminiscences (1876-1906), (hereafter cited as Barclay, Thirty Years), 175-229, 250, 354; Lansdowne to Monson, Oct. 14, 1903, B. D., II, 318.

246. For a detailed account of the negotiations see: Anderson, First Moroccan Crisis, 81-109; Newton, Lansdowne, 268-294; Lansdowne to Munson, July 2, 1903, B. D., II, 292-293.

247. The only one requiring submission to the British and French parliaments was the convention settling the Newfoundland dispute, modifying the boundaries of certain French and British colonies in Africa, and ceding the Iles de Los to France. The other declaration related to Siam, Madagascar, and the New Hebrides. The three documents together cleared up all current controversies.

248. The text is in B. D., II, 385-395.

249. France made a clear distinction between commercial and economic liberty. The former term she applied to trading operations, the latter to the operation of concessions. The American conception of the Open Door, as popularly understood and as maintained officially in Morocco after the treaty of Algeciras, included both. However, the French followed the precedent established in China, where the Open Door policy had no retroactive effect in abolishing spheres of interest or concessions granted previously. France showed in her treaty with Spain (October, 1904) that her promise of commercial liberty did not restrict her from claiming future exclusive economic concessions.

250. Anderson, First Moroccan Crisis, 147-151.

251. Nevins, Henry White, 240; Vagts, Weltpolitik, II, 1821; Question and answer in the House of Commons, April 6, 1905, B. D., III, 64-65; Lascelles to Lansdowne, March 23, 1905, Ibid., 61; Fay, Origins of the World War, I, 178-179; Lee, King Edward VII, II, 250-251.

252. Jusserand to Delcassé, No. 49, Jan. 25, 1905, D. D. F., Sér. 2, VI, 61.

253. Jusserand, What Me Befell, 311.

254. Wilhelm II to Bülow, No. 5208, March 16, 1904, G. P., XVII, 363; Bülow to Metternich, No. 6569, Ibid., XX, 268-269.

255. Tschirschky to Bülow, No. 6513, April 3, 1904, Ibid., 190-201; Mühlberg to Mentzingen, No. 6520, May 21, 1904, Ibid., 206-207, quoted by Williamson, Germany and Morocco before 1905, 146.

256. Barclay, Thirty Years, 258.

257. Heinrich Class in Marokko Verloren? (Munich, 1904) demanded the entire Atlantic coast of Morocco to use for her surplus population, coaling and naval stations, raw materials, and markets. American public opinion on the aims of Germany was based largely upon the writings of the Pan-German League and related societies.

258. Wertheimer, Pan-German League, 169-171.

259. Sketches of the life of Perdicaris appeared in Harper's Weekly, XLVIII (June 4, 1904), 853; in "Treat with Brigands," Washington Post, May 21, 1904, 1, and in "The Brigandage Case of Tangier," Ibid., 6. A highly interesting and authentic account of the Perdicaris affair is that by Barbara W. Tuchman, in "'Perdicaris Alive or Raisuli Dead,'" in American Heritage, X (Aug., 1959), 18-21, 98-101.

260. The correspondence is published in part in F. R., 1904, 307-308, 338, 496-504.

261. Gummeré to Hay, May 19, 1904; May 30, 1904; June 8, 1904; F. R., 1904, 496-498. Hay to Porter, May 28, 1904; Porter to Hay, May 30, 1904; Hay to Choate, May 31, 1904; Ibid., 307-308, 338.

262. Gummeré cabled the State Department that the absolutely impotent Moorish government could not be held responsible for punishment of Raisuli, who must be warned and severely punished by the countries concerned if he harmed the prisoners. Dept. of State, Archives, Diplomatic Dispatches, Morocco (hereafter cited as D. D., Morocco), I, June 15, 1904.

263. Harper's Weekly, XLVIII (June 18, 1904), 928-929.

After boasting that "we can quickly place in Moorish waters a fleet strong enough to bombard or occupy not only Tangier, but every seaport in Morocco," the editor outlined the history of the American-Barbary conflict from 1803 to 1815.

264. Editorial, Nation, LXXVIII (June 9, 1904), 443.

265. Budgett Meakin, "The Fate of Morocco," Westminster Review, CLXII (July, 1904), 9-16.

266. Saint-René Taillandier to Delcassé, No. 167, May 23, 1904, 185-186; No. 177, May 30, 1904, 195; No. 186, June 2, 1904, 205-206; D. D. F., Sér. 2, V.

267. Delcassé to Saint-René Taillandier, No. 181, May 31, 1904, Ibid., 200.

268. Gummeré deprecated articles in French and English journals praising French activity and confirmed the limitation of their services to instructions to Saint-Aulaire at Fez and to the Sherif of Wazan. Gummeré to Sec. of State, June 16, 1904, C. D., Tangier, XXVII.

269. Saint-René Taillandier to Delcassé, No. 188, June 3, 1904, 207-208; Delcassé to Saint-René Taillandier, No. 194, June 6, 1904, 215-216 and No. 202, June 9, 1904, 234; Saint-René Taillandier to Delcassé, No. 203, June 9, 1904, 235; D. D. F., Sér. 2, V.

270. Jules Cambon (French ambassador to Spain) to Delcassé, No. 175, May 29, 1904, D. D. F., Sér. 2, V, 194. "It is feared that the tendency which the United States has shown at times to get into Mediterranean questions may be an element of perturbation, and at this time may go contrary to the ideas and influence of which France has made herself the promoter."

271. Cambon to Delcassé, No. 183, June 1, 1904, 202-203 and No. 197, June 6, 1904, 217-219, Ibid.

272. "But nothing is more contrary to our often expressed views than a military expedition. It is by pacific

means, by financial support, by an administrative organization, by public works, by material prosperity that we wish to implant our influence in Morocco." Delcassé to J. Cambon, No. 185, June 1, 1904, 203-204; D. D. F., Sér. 2, V, 204.

273. Dennis, Adventures, 444-445. Gummeré's warning to the State Department was: "The country is fast drifting into a state of complete anarchy, the Sultan and his advisers are weak or worse, the governors corrupt, and very shortly neither life nor property will be safe." Gummeré to Loomis, No. 587, May 23, 1904, C. D., Tangier, XXVII.

274. Gummeré, cable to Sec. of State, June 21, 1904, Diplomatic Dispatches, Morocco (hereafter cited as D. D., Morocco), I.

275. The honor of inventing this pithy phrase has been claimed for E. M. Hood, a member of the Washington staff of the Associated Press assigned to the State Department. Dudley Haddock, "Better Brief," Time, LXXXI (March 8, 1963), 15-16.

276. Gummeré to Loomis, Confidential, July 22, 1904, with enclosure of letter from Perdicaris to Gummeré, July 18, 1904, C. D., Tangier, XXVII; Elihu Root to Gummeré, No. 18, Nov. 8, 1905, D. S., Instructions, Barbary Powers, XVI; Harold E. Davis, "Documents: The Citizenship of Ion Perdicaris," Journal of Modern History, XIII (Dec., 1941), 517-526; Dennett, John Hay, 401-402.

277. Hale, Germany and the Diplomatic Revolution, 89; Vagts, Weltpolitik, II, 1822.

278. For examples of recognition of French diplomatic ascendancy in Morocco by American periodicals see the following: "Germany and Morocco," Outlook, LXXIX (April 8, 1905), 866-867; "The Kidnapping in Morocco," and "We Ask France's Good Offices," Review of Reviews, XXX (July, 1904), 23-24; "France Given Credit," Washington Post, June 26, 1904, Part 1, 2. In "Our Successful Diplomacy," and

"Perdicaris Released," Review of Reviews, XXX (Aug., 1904), 146-147, we learn that "France had tendered to Secretary Hay the Grand Cross of the Legion of Honor for services rendered to the cause of international peace and amity." Referring to Hay's deference to the Anglo-French agreement, he was said to have made the "French Government see readily how usefully its African ambitions might be promoted if it should accept this American recognition and at the same time earn it by securing the release of Perdicaris."

279. "Morocco," Independent, LVII (July 21, 1904), 122; Ion H. Perdicaris, "In Raisuli's Hands, The Story of My Captivity and Deliverance May 18 to June 26, 1904," Leslie's Monthly Magazine, LVIII (Sept., 1904), 510-522; "The Perdicaris Episode," Review of Reviews, XXX (Oct., 1904), 495-496; Ion Perdicaris, "The Disintegration of Morocco, Its Immediate Causes and Probable Results," International Quarterly, XI (July, 1905), 177-196; "The Disintegration of Morocco," (Ion Perdicaris in International Quarterly), Review of Reviews, XXXII (Aug., 1905), 217-218; "Praise for Captor," Washington Post, June 13, 1904, 1; "Perdicaris Tells His Story," Ibid., June 27, 1904, 1; "An Unfinished Incident," editorial, July 10, 1904, Ibid., Editorial Section, 4; "Make Raisuli Ruler," Ibid., July 17, 1904, 3; "Resurrection of a Joke," editorial, Ibid., Sept. 7, 1904, 6; "Perdicaris Testifies," editorial, Ibid., Oct. 7, 1904, 6; "Would Have Raisouli Rule, Ibid., Dec. 30, 1904, 5.

280. Gummeré to Loomis, No. 598, July 6, 1904; No. 599, July 7, 1904; Aug. 9, 1904; No. 613, Sept. 6, 1904; No. 617, Sept. 28, 1904; C. D., Tangier, XXVII.

281. Roberts, History of French Colonial Policy, II, 550-551; Hale, Germany and the Diplomatic Revolution, 86; Feis, Europe, The World's Banker, 402-404; Tardieu, La Conférence, 5; Schuman, War and Diplomacy in the French Republic, 175.

282. Anderson, First Moroccan Crisis, 152-158; Hale, Germany and the Diplomatic Revolution, 94-96.

283. B. D., III, 30-52.

284. A detailed account of the negotiations is given in Anderson, First Moroccan Crisis, 118-125.

285. Bertie to Grey, Dec. 15, 1905, B. D., III, 152; Tardieu, La Conférence, 5.

286. Maurois, Lyautey, 131-141, 149-150; Monson to Lansdowne, Oct. 7, 1904, B. D., III, 54-55.

287. Gummeré to Loomis, Sept. 6, 1904, C. D., Tangier, XXVII.

288. "Revolution in Morocco," Washington Post, June 13, 1904, 1.

289. Gummeré to Loomis, 6 dispatches, from July 7, 1904 to Aug. 18, 1904; C. D., Tangier, XXVII. Philip to Loomis, 8 dispatches, from Oct. 19, 1904 to Dec. 28, 1904; Ibid. Vagts, Weltpolitik, II, 1835.

290. Monson commented on a Temps article, which suggested that compliance with French demands might be obtained by the seizure of the eight ports open to commerce. Monson to Lansdowne, Dec. 26, 1904, B. D., III, 55.

291. Hale, Germany and the Diplomatic Revolution, 90-92; Tardieu, La Conférence, 6; Monson to Lansdowne, Dec. 26, 1904, B. D., III, 55.

292. Hale, Germany and the Diplomatic Revolution, 87, 92-93.

293. Report of Acting Consul General Hoffman Philip, Feb. 4, 1905; United States, Dept. of Commerce and Labor, Bureau of Manufactures, Commercial Relations of the United States with Foreign Countries during the Year 1904, 802-805.

294. Philip to Loomis, No. 646, Feb. 13, 1905; C. D., Tangier, XXVII.

295. "Spain and France and Morocco," Review of Reviews, XXX (Nov., 1904), 533.

296. It was James W. Langerman, that bête noire of the Quai d'Orsay, who bore a personal letter and gifts from Roosevelt to the Sultan inviting this exhibit, and who was later in charge of it at St. Louis. Earlier, when appointed as "honorary vice consul general" without salary, at Tangier, he had been a trial to Gummeré. Perhaps his plans for promoting increased trade between the United States and Morocco, especially for establishing a "plant for sardine fishing and curing at Tangier," had made the French consider him a "dangerous adventurer." Gummeré to Loomis, No. 521, Nov. 17, 1902; No. 524, Nov. 28, 1902; No. 550, July 2, 1903; C. D., Tangier, XXVI; Philip to Loomis, No. 555, Aug. 15, 1903; No. 558, Aug. 28, 1903, Ibid.

297. "The Sultan, when he spent a good round sum in giving an exhibit at the St. Louis Exposition, seemingly attempted to interest the United States in Morocco, knowing that if commerce could be established between the two countries, it would strengthen the independence of his empire." Arthur Schneider, "The Truth About Morocco." Harper's Weekly, L (Feb. 10, 1906), 189.

298. Bigelow, "The Mind of Muley Aziz," 78.

299. Lee, King Edward VII, II, 251-253; Robert Offley Ashburton, Marquis of Crewe-Milnes, Lord Rosebery, 2 vols. (hereafter cited as Crewe-Milnes, Lord Rosebery), II, 581-582. The Parliamentary debates are recorded in Hansard's Parliamentary Debates, Fourth Series, CXXXIII, CXXXV, CXXXVII, CXXXVIII, CXXXIX, and CXL, 1904.

300. Lee, King Edward VII, II, 253-254; Monson to Lansdowne, Nov. 9, 1904; Nov. 11, 1904; Nov. 13, 1904; Dec. 7, 1904; Dec. 8, 1904; B. D., III, 11-13, 16-17. Anderson, First Moroccan Crisis, 9-10.

301. "Mr. Hay's Opportunity in Morocco," World's Work, VIII (July, 1904), 495.

302. Philip to Loomis, 10 dispatches, from Dec. 24, 1904 to March 15, 1905; C. D., Tangier, XXVII.

303. An editorial, "Why Not a Minister for Morocco?" in the Washington Post, Dec. 5, 1904, 6, made great sport of Gummeré's ambition, while indicating also the low esteem in which Morocco was held by some of the leading American newspapers.

304. Gummeré to Hill, No. 483, Jan. 13, 1902, C. D., Tangier, XXVI. Gummeré to Loomis, No. 613, Sept. 8, 1904; Oct. 26, 1904; Nov. 25, 1904, Ibid., XXVII.

305. Philip to Loomis, April 17, 1905, Ibid. Wright, "Samuel Rene Gummeré" in Dictionary of American Biography, VIII, 50.

Chapter VII

A Partnership in Peacemaking

By the end of 1904, when Theodore Roosevelt had received the electors' mandate to become president in his own name, he had already won the reputation of being unduly strenuous and adventuresome in foreign affairs. However, his friendly critics asserted that his acts had been fundamentally safe and sane:

> There has never been any foundation for the campaign charge that Mr. Roosevelt was inclined to entangle the United States in foreign complications. The despatch of warships to San Domingo, to Tangiers, to Beirut, and to Smyrna was a legitimate means to exerting pressure upon delinquent and refractory States which had paid no heed to the diplomatic presentation of demands .... Unquestionably, Mr. Roosevelt has had more than one pretext for involving us in international imbroglios. He has availed himself of none of them.[1]

It is immaterial whether Roosevelt's inauguration eve remark referred to American senators or to foreign heads of state. He was quoted thus: "Tomorrow I shall come into office in my own right. Then watch out for me!"[2] Exactly a year after his election, Henry Adams paid him a well deserved compliment:

> You have established a record as the best herder of Emperors since Napoleon. I need your views about the relative docility of Kings, Presidents of South American Republics, Railway Presidents, and Senators.[3]

Among the achievements of 1905, the apex of his career in diplomacy, Roosevelt could count the preservation of the Open Door in China and the successful mediation to end the Russo-Japanese War. More gratifying to his ambition, perhaps, was the temporarily secret repudiation of Monroe's outdated pledge to remain aloof from European quarrels. In the course of making peace in China and keeping it in Morocco, Roosevelt had become the silent member of the Anglo-Japanese Alliance and an active, if unacknowledged, colleague of the Anglo-French entente. However, he had not performed such phenomenal feats single-handed. Accepting the proffered assistance of one whom he was describing meanwhile as being "so jumpy, so little capable of continuity of action, and, therefore, so little capable of being loyal to his friends or steadfastly hostile to an enemy,"[4] Roosevelt had played for several months the role of a partner in peacemaking with William II.

The President's choice of diplomatic agents was likewise extraordinary. He despised and distrusted the "clever, vain, but lying" Count Cassini; therefore he negotiated with Russia through the American ambassador, George von Lengerke Meyer, and his intimate friend, Cecil Spring-Rice, Secretary of the British embassy--both then in St. Petersburg. The latter, with Henry White in London, carried the important messages to the British government which Roosevelt would not entrust to the accredited American and British ambassadors, Whitelaw Reid and Sir Mortimer Durand.[5] John Hay, who went abroad in March, 1905, in a last vain quest for restored health, was already relaxing his grasp on the State Department in 1904. Through Sternburg and Jusserand, his intimate friends, Roosevelt carried on most confidential relations with Germany and France.[6]

With an "effective propaganda" and the "most practicable and farsighted methods," Jusserand "did not wait to be taught anything by the Germans."[7] He was analyzing the characteristics of both the President and the Kaiser in order to turn their supposed friendship to the service of France:

> The personality of Mr. Roosevelt, already so striking, is becoming still more so--his desire for action, his admiration for force and power, and for the people who know how to scorn life. He means to act for himself and in his own way; for the things that he has at heart, he will neither compromise nor retreat before whatever it may be .... The President seems to me to see in his ministers men of experience and judgment, made to inform him, but not at all to direct him. He has,

> I think, fully decided to be, in reality, his own ministry .... On two occasions, the President importuned me, when I have affairs of importance to relate, to address myself directly to him. We may eventually have in this some great advantage for ourselves. Sometimes, if one has the good fortune to make a remark which strikes him, the thought impresses itself upon his memory and works there with efficiency ....
>
> He made this remark: "What I love in France is that with all her literature and fine arts, when she ought to strike, she is always prepared." ... He said at an official dinner at his own table, where was present at some distance from him, Count Cassini, "The Russians lie; they have lied to me here through their ambassador; they have lied to my ambassador in St. Petersburg; and they have lied also in Peking." (Allusion to the promise not kept and never pardoned of an evacuation of Manchuria on October 8, 1903. And the English promises about Egypt?) .... The President said to me one day, "When I think of the future, I can foresee the possibility of war with Germany, with England, with Russia, with Japan; I can see none at all with France." This remark may be a prophecy, and it is agreeable to me to stop in citing it. P. S. I recommend urgently that a strictly confidential character be kept regarding all the observations contained in this report.[8]

Early in 1904 Jusserand had reported on the influence exerted in the United States by the German vote, societies, and professors in American universities. Of Sternburg and his propaganda Jusserand was adversely critical,[9] and on the Kaiser's policy he made some shrewd observations:

> In regard to the United States, ... the policy of Emperor William ... is, in ordinary times, ... to lavish attentions (occasionally touching and delicate), compliments, eulogies, small gifts .... After this the bellicose acts of the German navy in the waters of Haiti and Venezuela, and the immense displeasure, which, to the surprise of Berlin, they cause here .... Gifts and compliments ... will never blind the Americans to their real interests .... The impulsive President .... has many points in common with the impulsive Em-

> peror .... Mr. Roosevelt is not without sincere sympathy for France, but he knows it poorly. I shall apply myself ... to inform him better ....[10]

Unknown to the American press and public, during 1904 the President had been pondering much but acting not at all in regard to the Far Eastern conflict. Ever since 1897 he had recognized the vital importance of American relations with the Orient. At first he considered Japan the dangerous foe, liable to seize the Hawaiian and Philippine Islands. Later the conduct of Russia regarding Manchuria caused him to hope for the strengthening of Japan as a counterweight to Russian hegemony in China. Since Japan was "playing our game," the President rejoiced over her initial victories.[11] As the war went on, he became convinced that to safeguard American interests in the Pacific it must be his mission to prevent any European intervention excluding the United States from the peace settlement. Furthermore, it appeared that the opportunity for American leadership was at hand. For personal and national prestige, Roosevelt was prepared to assume the initiative, but he realized that he must have powerful support. In his determination to direct the settlement of the Russo-Japanese War in a way to favor the interests and prestige of the United States, he was led also into participation in the Moroccan controversy, which, in itself, he considered of no real concern to his country.

Although the President made tentative proposals of cooperation in the Far East to France, Great Britain, and Germany, his only action[12] was taken at the instigation of the last named. Hoping that a war-weakened Russia would turn to Germany, William II spurred the Tsar on to a Holy War against the Yellow Peril. Since he was anxious to forestall an Anglo-French intervention,[13] and had held out to the Tsar the prospect of securing Korea and Manchuria,[14] the Kaiser planned a German-American action to attain both objectives. Only the first aim was achieved. The Kaiser's proposal was that the American government issue a circular note urging all the other powers to persuade Russia and Japan to respect the "neutrality of China outside the sphere of military operations." By omitting the qualifying phrase and adding "administrative entity," Hay avoided conceding Manchuria as a future Russia sphere. All of the powers assented without reservation, except Russia, which excluded Manchuria.[15] Thus France and Great Britain were formally committed to the continued support of the integrity of China.

Through Jusserand, Roosevelt expressed his willingness to collaborate with France in the restoration of peace, while Hay thanked France for her services in the rescue of Perdicaris.[16] In October, 1904, Jusserand commented upon the persistent propaganda of the American press, "accustomed to see in the President of the United States the natural arbiter of nations."[17] The American Senate repulsed two gestures of amity made by France, when it refused to allow Hay to accept the Grand Cross of the Legion of Honor[18] and when it amended a number of proposed arbitration treaties, including one with France, so much that the President decided not to ratify them.[19] Thereafter Roosevelt resolved to avoid treaties whenever possible and entered fully upon a policy of personal diplomacy.

In an "extraordinary conversation" with Roosevelt in October, Sir Valentine Chirol found him obsessed by two conflicting apprehensions. The President feared that Japan would be robbed by European interference and that a world war would probably result from such an intervention. "We are the only people who might talk peace without doing mischief," he said, giving many reasons why peace in the Far East was of the utmost importance to the United States. On the other hand, Roosevelt argued that continuance of the war would save Japan from the danger of becoming so intoxicated with victory that she would raise awkward questions of racial equality and reciprocity of treatment in the United States. The President wanted to know whether the British would back him when the time came to make peace or whether they would support Japan in excessive demands upon Russia.[20] This interview reveals the problem of Anglo-American relations in the situation created by the Russo-Japanese War and also shows Roosevelt's determination to lead in any settlement of the conflict.

In August, 1904, Roosevelt proposed a peace plan in cooperation with Germany. He suggested a Japanese protectorate for Korea and an internationally guaranteed neutralization of Manchuria, under a Chinese viceroy to be named by Germany. The Kaiser was not to be seduced, however, by Bülow's flattering remarks about Roosevelt's friendship for him.[21] He declared his desire to work with the United States in upholding the Open Door, but Russia was not yet defeated. If Russia should fail, William thought that Manchuria should revert to China, although Korea might go to Japan under a guarantee of the Open Door.[22] Thus the matter rested, although Sternburg made encouraging reports of Roosevelt's poor opinion of the British government; the President was quoted (in English):

> England has not a man I can deal with. I do not think much of Balfour and less of Lansdowne. Chamberlain is quite unreliable and might jump into the Yangtze valley at any moment. And how am I to deal with this creature of an ambassador? If I had Spring-Rice here, things might be different. With France I am in a similar position. The only man I understand and who understands me is the Kaiser.[23]

Since April of 1904, King Edward VII had been working to improve Anglo-Russian relations, and during his visit to the Kaiser at Kiel in June he had spoken of offering mediation in the War. The Kaiser therefore found it expedient to warn the Tsar against "Uncle Bertie's" machinations, and Russia rejected all British overtures,[24] as well as one from Roosevelt in November.[25] The position of peacemaker was still open--but Roosevelt had still to find a powerful partner.

Fortunately for the President, the Kaiser also was now in search of a colleague to help him out of the diplomatic morass of the past year--a period of conflicting counsels and disasters.[26] After the Entente Cordiale, lacking confidence in two-timing Italy and self-divided Austria-Hungary, Germany had faced the possibility of the coalition of the Dual and Anglo-Japanese alliances to exclude her from China as well as Morocco. Rejecting Holstein's advice to smash the Entente by force, if necessary, Bülow had waited in vain for Delcassé to give Germany a formal notification of the Moroccan settlement or to offer guarantees and compensations. The Kaiser had failed likewise in his scheme to form a Continental League. The draft treaty for a Russo-German alliance of mutual aid against attack by another European power had actually been accepted by the

Tsar on October 30, 1904. But in spite of Germany's benevolent neutrality and her coaling of the Russian fleet, after Delcassé's mediation had averted war with Great Britain over the Dogger Bank incident, the Tsar had insisted upon consulting France, which was expected to join this alliance, before concluding the treaty. After being made public the abortive treaty had then been abandoned. Its only result had been a nation-wide hysteria of fear and hate in Germany and Great Britain, provoked by the press of both countries.[27] The scattered German fleet had been called home,[28] and the staff of the London embassy, summoned to Berlin for a conference, urged an alliance with Russia as the only escape from isolation.[29]

However, Bülow saw another path opening up for German diplomacy. Recalling Roosevelt's overtures[30] of the previous August, he was ready to support a defensive alliance between Germany and the United States,[31] and Emperor William agreed that "America and Japan must now be cultivated more."[32]

The actual approach to the President, made on January 5, 1905, through Sternburg, was a warning from William II that the integrity of China was being menaced. The German Foreign Office suggested that the United States[33] ask all the powers having interests in the Far East to pledge that they would not "demand any compensation for themselves in any shape, of territory, or other compensation in China or elsewhere, for any service rendered to the belligerents in the making of peace or for any other reason." Hay replied with an expression of his gratification at Germany's attitude. By January 20, 1905, Great Britain, France, Italy, and Germany had all formally pledged themselves to the "self-denying" circular. Germany's qualification that it was her policy "absolutely to stand by her former declarations" might be interpreted, however, to refer to the Anglo-German Agreement of 1900, leaving her free to support Russian claims in Manchuria. Hay could not understand what the performance meant to the Kaiser.[34]

This initial diplomatic success did not offer much compensation for the continuing loss of prestige suffered by Germany in the early part of 1905. February was a month of disasters. It began with the challenging speech of Mr.

Arthur Lee, first civil lord of the British Admiralty, who admitted that the redistribution of the British fleet was directed against Germany. Bülow's promise to agree to any naval budget recommended by Tirpitz for 1906 afforded no immediate safety. Although suffering a series of defeats climaxed by the battle of Mukden on March 10, Russia still unwilling to conclude the agreement of disinterestedness over the territory of Austria-Hungary which Bülow proposed. Nevertheless, rumors of a Russo-German understanding frightened Japan from sending a representative to Berlin. More galling than any of these humiliations, however, was the dispatching of a French mission to Fez in January, with the evident intention of carrying out Delcassé's plans without consulting Germany.[35] The German Sphinx would have to speak soon, or be silent forever.

Goaded by criticism from Socialists, Pan-Germans, and National Liberals, the imperial diplomats had to turn perforce to a democracy to rescue Germany from the results of their professional skill.[36] The twice manifested readiness of the United States to lead in promoting German policies in the Far East suggested a strong probability of further cooperation. Roosevelt had been expressing to Sternburg his eagerness to bring about an improvement in Anglo-German relations. Moreover, since the United States was recently displaying an unwonted interest in trade opportunities in Morocco, there was a good chance that the American principle of the Open Door might be extended in application from China to Morocco. Since, in his attempts to force upon the Sultan the "reforms" which presaged French monopoly of Morocco, Saint-René Taillandier was falsely representing himself at Fez as a mandatory of the European powers,[37] Roosevelt might be convinced that France was playing in Morocco the role essayed by Russia in China. In the meantime, the Kaiser's campaign to win the personal friendship of the President would continue, and the latter would be kept ready to serve in ending the Far Eastern conflict. Jusserand had much to report on these advances to Roosevelt. Within five weeks he noted the following: an offer to the museum at St. Louis of a bronze bust of William II; an offer to the University of Chicago by the <u>Deutscher Kriegerverein</u> of another bronze bust of the Kaiser and a bust of Frederick II; a plan for the exchange of professors between German and American universities--

"plenty of noise has been made on this subject;" titles of doctor conferred on the Kaiser and Roosevelt by the University of Philadelphia (sic), and several other exceptional courtesies.[38]

One can hardly accept Sternburg's optimistic interpretation of Roosevelt's statement that he had adopted the task of improving Anglo-German relations.[39] In February Sternburg reported that the President favored a rapprochement among Germany, England, and America, especially between the first two, to keep Slavic influence from spreading in Europe.[40] Bülow replied that since Germany had no other obligations besides the Triple Alliance, there would be no obstacle to a defensive grouping of the kind desired by Roosevelt.[41] By April 1 this discussion of an American-engineered entente seems to have ended. The British Ambassador had asserted his government's conviction that Germany was merely waiting for a favorable occasion to wage war on Great Britain.[42] Roosevelt was unable to put an end to the Anglo-German enmity. In this effort he had been greatly handicapped because he was always on the defensive against the British belief that he was the Kaiser's henchman.

Though the President had failed in promoting Anglo-German cooperation, the Wilhelmstrasse trusted that the traditional Anglo-American sponsorship of the Open Door would save Morocco from becoming a French dependency. The new status of the American representatives in Morocco was also conducive to securing German-American support of the Open Door there. The recently appointed consul general, Hoffman Philip, had urged a new commercial treaty with the Sultan and an energetic campaign by American business men to secure commerce and concessions in Morocco. In August of 1905, Philip was very emphatic in warning his government of the trend of French policy:

> If nothing occurred ... to change the policy of the French government, Morocco would ... come so entirely under the political and financial tutelage of France as to be unable to uphold treaty obligations wtthout assistance and ... in respect to commerce the country would of necessity in the future assume like conditions as exist in Algeria and Tunisia.[43]

Bülow, of course, was unaware of Philip's warnings to the State Department, or of Gummeré's equally forceful urgings to his superiors:

> The country, within a short time, will be thrown open to the trade of the world .... Concessions for mining privileges, railways, water works ... will be granted, but ... unless immediate steps be taken to place ourselves in the front rank, ... none of all these will come to our countrymen.[44]

Germany felt able to count upon the backing of Gummeré, who, as the first American of ministerial rank, no longer had to bear the stigma of speaking for the one country not represented by a legation. However, to several warnings from Tangier that France's policy was likely to require enforcement by arms and that it was almost certain that it would be challenged by other countries, the State Department returned the admonition to be neutral in act and attitude.[45]

The promotion of Gummeré imposed upon France the necessity of giving Jusserand a difficult task. Jusserand had informed the Foreign Office of the contemplated conversion of the American consulate to a legation in January 8, 1905. On March 3, 1905, Delcassé sent Jusserand instructions:

> The position which we are destined to take in Morocco will tend in the future to transform the existing legations into simple general consulates. The opposite transformation projected by the United States could not fail to be considered, especially by the Maghzen, as being a policy enfeebling that of the accords of April 8, 1904. This impression would be all the more vivid because the economic relations between Morocco and the United States are insignificant.[46]

If convenient, Jusserand was to make an overture to the President or Secretary Hay to secure the abandonment or postponement of the American plan. When Congress passed the law creating the ministry on March 2, 1905, Jusserand reported to Delcassé on March 7:

> It seemed to me that I could at least formulate some useful suggestions as to the choice of an incumbent and the instructions with which he ought to be provided .... I expressed the hope (to Mr. Hay) that a moderate and reasonable man would be chosen. Recalling how, in the Perdicaris affair, the United States had been pleased with our intervention, I asked that the diplomat in question receive instructions to remain in contact with his French colleague.[47]

During February and March of 1905 the German policy of opposition to France was gradually developing through contact with Roosevelt. On February 4, through Charlemagne Tower, the American ambassador in Berlin, the Kaiser declared that the action of the United States had prevented the partition of China which had been planned after the war. Germany, he added, had already given France her refusal to join in such a plot.[48] In his reply the President expressed faith in England but admitted that the actions of France in China looked suspicious.[49]

The first approach to Roosevelt regarding the Moroccan situation followed on February 25, when Sternburg was instructed to ascertain whether the President would interest himself in any way, either for the Open Door or to prevent the domination of a thoroughfare important for all seafaring peoples. After Sternburg reported for the first time that Roosevelt had indicated distrust of France, Bülow proceeded with assurances of his continued cooperation with the United States. At the present time, the Chancellor pointed out, the two countries had similar aims in China and Morocco. China had been saved temporarily by the declaration of disinterestedness. If Germany and America would advise the Sultan to assemble his notables and reform his country in order to check French aggression there, Morocco also might be preserved. Unsupported by England, France would hardly risk a war over Morocco with a silent Germany at her back. Thus the Moroccan problem also could be solved peacefully and quickly.[50]

For mediation in Morocco Roosevelt was unready and unwilling. He excused himself on the plea of a hostile Congress and disapproving public opinion, but promised to instruct his representative in Morocco to keep in close touch with his German colleague there.[51] Bülow professed satisfaction in a cooperation of the German and American ministers for the handling of economic questions and for mutual support of the Moroccan government, which would make a third power more cautious in pressing its pretensions over Morocco.[52]

Meanwhile, Roosevelt had begun in earnest his overtures to make peace between Russia and Japan. In spite of Russia's severe defeat at Mukden on March 10, the Kaiser thought that peace parleys were still premature,[53] and the President's proposals to Russia were rebuffed.[54] William II's requests that American influence be used to prevent a conspiracy of neutrals to exclude Germany from a congress to arrange peace terms won for him the characterizations of "jumpy creature" and "monomaniac about getting into communication with me every time he drinks three pen'orth of conspiracy against his life and power."[55] Since both the Japanese and British ambassadors denied that any peace conference was being planned,[56] the President's path toward peacemaking appeared to be still unobstructed.

From the Anglo-Japanese side, however, strong undercurrents of opposition prevented Roosevelt from reaching his goal. After the visit of Spring-Rice to Washington in February, the President had expected that the British government would back him in promoting an early peace by exerting pressure on Japan.[57] A personal letter and the gift of a miniature of Hampden from King Edward VII emphasized that monarch's desire not to let Anglo-American friendship go by default.[58] But although Roosevelt continued to deny that he was under the Kaiser's influence,[59] evidently it was only to Hay's restraining influence that Lansdowne was willing to entrust American conduct of Far Eastern affairs.[60] Deploring the retirement of Hay,[61] Spring-Rice gave the cue to the attitude of the British Foreign Office after Roosevelt became his own prime minister for a time. The President was considered too rash and too ignorant of the intricacies of world politics to assume leadership in one of the most delicate situations that British diplomacy had ever faced.[62] Therefore, Roosevelt's advances during February and March to improve Anglo-German relations had been repulsed. On April 3,

Lansdowne wrote that the Japanese were becoming distrustful of Roosevelt;[63] two days later, Delcassé offered himself as mediator. Although on April 18 the Japanese government indicated a preference for Roosevelt's services, and agreed to the Open Door in Manchuria and its restoration to China,[64] thereafter negotiations were stalled while the Japanese and British governments waited for further assurances that the United States would subscribe to Anglo-Japanese policy.[65] Very shortly afterwards, Lansdowne's worst suspicions of Roosevelt seemed confirmed when the latter appeared to be a champion of the Kaiser in his attack upon the Anglo-French Entente in Morocco.

In the gradually developing program of the Wilhelmstrasse, a prominent part was assigned to Roosevelt. After the President's refusal to join Germany in support of the convocation of the notables by the Sultan to consider the reform demands made by France,[66] Bülow continued to encourage the Sultan to maintain his independence. On March 10 the assurance was given that Germany and the United States would uphold the status quo and that in English commercial circles there was a movement to support an independent Morocco with equality of rights for all powers.[67] In his Reichstag speeches of March 15 and 29, the Chancellor gave notice that Germany would defend her economic interests and the Open Door in Morocco.[68] By his inquiry to Kühlmann on March 27 as to the probability of England's acceptance of a conference, if it were advocated by Germany and the United States, Bülow indicated the means by which he intended to achieve his objectives.[69]

On March 31 "that clumsy ride of the Kaiser along the ill-paved streets of an African town echoed on every boulevard in Europe."[70] It was indeed true that "Für diesmal wurde die deutsche Diplomatie wilhelmischer als der Kaiser."[71] ("For this time the German diplomacy became more williamish that the Kaiser.") Despite the Emperor's vehement objections, the will of Bülow had prevailed upon him to stop off from a Mediterranean cruise at Tangier. There, after an unsplendid parade through the town, William made a speech in the presence of the diplomatic corps and Moroccan and other notables. Bülow had insisted that a political pronouncement at Tangier would indict France and prepare Germany's case for presentation to international public opinion.[72] By addressing the Sultan as an independent sovereign, with whom he would deal directly for the protection of German economic interests, and by advising great caution in the introduction of reforms,[73] the Kaiser served formal notice that Germany was not bound by the Anglo-French Entente.[74] A week earlier Bülow had ordered the Foreign Office officials to be silent regarding the terms which Germany might accept.[75]

Gummeré considered the Kaiser's visit to Tangier as certain to strengthen the Moroccans against the unpopular French. He gave a long description of the events of the Kaiser's reception and the elaborate preparations for it. The Kaiser was unable to deliver to Gummeré the message suggested in Bülow's instructions for the Kaiser to the effect that there was a parallel between the preservation of the Open Door in China and in Morocco. William II somewhat exceeded his Chancellor's instructions by being over-emphatic about Germany's interest in Moroccan affairs.[76]

Although France was quite generally supported in the British and American press, her own journals acknowledged the expediency of treating with Germany. Outside of Germany, the legal basis of Germany's policy, Article XVII of the Madrid treaty, was ignored;[77] comment was concentrated upon the Kaiser's latest "political fiasco."[78] Delcassé hastened to send to Washington a denial of the German charge that he had not notified Germany of the Accords of 1904 and a declaration of his government's resolution to respect "commercial liberty" for all countries having treaty relations with Morocco.[79]

Impelled by the Emperor's injudicious statements after the Tangier visit, Bülow decided forthwith upon a positive policy. Denying all territorial ambitions in Morocco, he demanded economic equality for all nations and an international conference like that in Madrid in 1880 to formulate a program of reforms for Morocco.[80] He asked Roosevelt to give his moral support to the maintenance of the _status quo_ in Morocco and to speak calmly and academically in favor of equal rights for all nations there. England's sacrifice of Morocco, opposed by her own political and economic interests, could be explained only as the result of France's support of the British acquisition of the Yangtze valley. If America would remain firm in opposition to the partitioning of China, England would abandon the Yangtze project and give only diplomatic aid to France in Morocco.[81] According to Sternburg, the opinion in political circles was that England's compensation might be found in the prevention of Germany's expansion into Austria-Hungary after the death of Francis Joseph.[82]

After beginning a press propaganda for the conference plan,[83] Bülow sent Tattenbach to Fez to persuade the Sultan to adopt this idea instead of the French reforms.[84] The approbation of the United States[85] and Great Britain was taken for granted, especially after Roosevelt was asked on April 13 to recommend the conference to the British Government.[86] Both Austria-Hungary and Russia disapproved of Germany's proposal,[87] Spain would attend a conference only if France and Great Britain did,[88] and Italy was inclined toward neutrality.[89] Undeterred by the royal and public support of France in Great Britain, and still unanswered by both American and British governments, on April 18 Bülow rejected Delcassé's belated offer to remove misunderstandings. The Chancellor insisted that a conference was the best way to resolve the situation.[90]

During April, while Bülow persisted in his attitude of reserve, adverse criticism in the French press and parliament forced Delcassé to attempt negotiations. Although Premier Rouvier defended Delcassé against a severe attack in the Chamber on April 19, he announced that hereafter he would supervise the latter's work.[91] Delcassé was encouraged, however, by the support of the British government. Lansdowne sent a British envoy to Fez to offset the work of Tattenbach, and he offered to join the French government in strong opposition[92] to any move by Germany to gain a port on the Moroccan coast. Bertie reworded Lansdowne's dispatch so that this promise of British support appeared to refer to the whole Moroccan question instead of to opposition to Germany's obtaining a port. Delcassé was honest in his denial that Germany had asked for a port.[93]

Since Lansdowne's offer was translated by rumor into an offensive and defensive alliance, it led later to increased friction and bitterness between the British and

German governments. Replying to an inquiry from Lascelles, Lansdowne denied that an alliance had been discussed on either side. In an interview with Metternich, the German ambassador, Lansdowne displayed the habitual British forgetfulness of the secret articles:

> So far as I understand the Germany policy ... Germany desired to be regarded as the defender of commercial liberty .... There seemed to me to be no antagonism between the British and the German policy, nor were either of them inconsistent with that which was openly proclaimed in the Anglo-French Declaration or with that which, so far as my information went, France was perfectly content to pursue.[94]

Bülow refused or ignored several conciliatory proposals made directly or indirectly by Rouvier between April 26 and May 1.[95] The last offer was a Franco-German agreement similar to the Anglo-French Entente, including such questions as disputed boundaries in Africa and the Bagdad railway,[96] but leaving the Moroccan problem to be solved by direct negotiations with the other powers.[97] Finally, Bülow rejected the mediation of M. Luzzati, Italian minister of finance, through whom Delcassé offered to give Germany any satisfaction desired if she would settle the Moroccan controversy without wounding French honor. Bülow said later in his Memoirs that the "striking act of appreciation" that Delcassé had in mind for the Kaiser was either the Grand Cross of the Legion of Honor or a visit from President Loubet.[98]

Bülow disregarded the advice of his chief ambassadors, Radolin, Tattenbach, and Monts, all of whom advised a direct settlement with France. He also spurned further unofficial proposals made by Eckardstein and Betzold. Like Roosevelt, Rouvier was inclined to use irregular channels of communication. Betzold was an international financier. Eckardstein says that he and Betzold were authorized to offer Germany the dismissal of Delcassé, a coaling station, and eventually a strip of land on the Atlantic coast of Morocco. Bülow and Holstein preferred waiting for a collective settlement.[99]

To obtain this, Bülow had firmly resolved upon an

international conference. Prevented by the Emperor's declarations at Vigo and Tangier from seeking a share of Moroccan territory, and aware that the majority opinion in Germany was averse to immediate colonial expansion, the Chancellor wanted to preserve the "independence" of Morocco until Germany could secure compensation there or elsewhere.[100] The internationalization of Morocco by a conference of the powers, building upon the Treaty of Madrid, seemed to be a proposition unassailable from the viewpoint of international law or commercial interests. Finally, the summoning of France to account at the instance of Germany would restore that international prestige which the country of Bismarck had once enjoyed.

Bülow's afterthoughts on his motives are of interest. A confidant in Paris told him, he says, that Delcassé was prepared to let war come, for he trusted in King Edward's support and in the quick restoration of peace in the Far East. "I felt that I could prevent matters from coming to a head, cause Delcassé's fall, break the continuity of aggressive French policy, knock the continental dagger out of the hands of Edward VII and the war group in England, and simultaneously ensure peace, preserve German honor, and improve German prestige."[101]

The month of May was fully occupied by the German diplomats in persuading Roosevelt to bring the United States and Great Britain to the conference, in inducing Morocco and other powers to participate, and in eliminating Delcassé from French politics.

Roosevelt found that his influence on the British government was scarcely greater in regard to the Moroccan situation than it had been in improving Anglo-German relations. Acting as secretary of state during the President's hunting trip in Colorado, Taft received from Jusserand the French arguments against a conference.[102] In answering a memorandum presented by Sternburg on April 7, Taft admitted that the Open Door did not concern the United States in Morocco as it did in China. While Holstein and Bülow were expressing confidence that the United States and the liberal English groups would rally to uphold the Open Door,[103] Jusserand was presenting in Washington Delcassé's arguments against any conference invoking "the pretended precedent of 1880."[104] When Jusserand argued that Germany's situation in Morocco differed from that of the powers with which France had negotiated in 1880 and that the Madrid treaty had only a special and limited character, Taft replied that noninterference in Mediterranean controversies was the policy of the American government and the wish of the people of the United States.[105]

To Sternburg's request of April 13 for his intervention with Great Britain in favor of a conference, Roosevelt replied both to Taft and to Sternburg. His communication to Taft emphasized the desirability of improving Anglo-German relations:

> The Kaiser's pipe-dream this week takes the form of Morocco .... I do not feel that as a Government we should interfere in the Morocco matter. We have other fish to fry and we have no real interest in Morocco. I do not care to take sides between France and Germany in the matter ....
>
> I am sincerely anxious to bring about a better state of feeling between England and Germany. Each nation is working itself up to a condition of desperate hatred of the other; each from sheer fear of the other .... Now, in my view this action of Germany in embroiling herself with France over Morocco is proof positive that she has not the slightest intention of attacking England .... I do not wish to suggest anything whatever as to England's attitude in Morocco, but if we can find out that attitude with propriety and inform the Kaiser of it, I shall be glad to do so .... If we find that it will make the English suspicious--that is, will make them think we are acting as decoy ducks for Germany--why, we shall have to drop the business.[106]

Sternburg relayed his reply from the President to the Wilhelmstrasse on April 25. From Taft Sternburg learned that Roosevelt's wish for a harmonious procedure of Germany and Great Britain in Morocco would be communicated to London. These remarks of Roosevelt were not sent on to Bülow:

> Our interests in Morocco are not sufficiently great to make me feel justified in entangling our Government in the matter. You do not have to be told by me that I am already working in the most cordial agreement with the Emperor about China and the Japanese-Russian War, while I have matters of my own in Santo Domingo, Venezuela, and Panama to which I must give attention and from which I do not feel it right to be diverted.[107]

From this point on, a still unanswered question keeps recurring--in his frequent failures to interpret his friend and his monarch correctly to each other, was Sternburg guilty of duplicity or merely of inadequacy? The latter seems the more probable.

Since Metternich had already given the opinion that Lansdowne might be influenced if the United States would declare a favorable attitude toward a conference,[108] Bülow found Sternburg's version of Roosevelt's letter highly satisfactory.[109] He would have found the reply of the British government far less reassuring. Durand reported:

> The President thinks England and Germany are unduly suspicious of each other's intentions, and he wishes, if possible, to help in removing any friction which exists. Mr. Taft says that America does not care a cent about Morocco, and has no desire whatever to take sides between Germany and France .... My impression is that the President wants to know your views about the situation in Morocco, preferably for communication to the German Emperor.[110]

Lansdowne's reply was a decided refusal of Roosevelt's good offices:

> We have not and never have had any idea of attacking Germany, nor do we anticipate that she will be so foolish as to attack us. There is ... no subject of dispute between the two powers, or any reason why their relations should not be of a friendly description. As to Morocco, we are quite unable to understand why any trouble should arise--the Anglo-French Agreement contained nothing detrimental to the interests of other powers ... and the attitude of the French Government

is most forbearing and conciliatory .... Private. Be careful to say nothing which could be interpreted as an invitation to the President to act as mediator between us and Germany.[111]

In order to bring further pressure to bear on Great Britain through Roosevelt, Bülow asked again on May 10 that the President be persuaded that his influence was sufficient to induce Great Britain and France to cease their opposition to the conference. Germany would continue to defend the common interests of the treaty powers in Morocco, unless the lack of support from them should force her to choose between a conflict with France and the examination of conditions that France might propose. Moreover, only the opposition of the United States would prevent the Anglo-French-Russian-Japanese alliance which Delcassé was trying to form.[112]

This quadruple alliance to partition China, Roosevelt said later, "seemed to me mere lunacy," and he was not at all impressed by the German protestations of unselfishness regarding Morocco.[113] However, Sternburg reported that the President had expressed anger over England's attitude on the conference, especially since there was some French opinion favoring it, and had promised to continue his efforts through Whitelaw Reid and Durand, who had just departed for London.[114] A few days later Roosevelt told Sternburg that the British government had given him clearly to understand that it did not wish better relations with Germany. A hint that it could take care of its own affairs made it impossible for the President to do more without exposing himself to discourtesy.[115]

Nevertheless, Bülow persisted in forcing upon Roosevelt the role of mediator. In his dispatches of May 25 and May 30 he stated that from reliable sources he knew that both England and France would be willing to cede to Germany a sphere of interest in Morocco. Furthermore, the Morocco question was not isolated; it might become the starting point for a new grouping of the European powers, including Germany, to settle Far Eastern problems. The other alternative for Germany was to fight a war with France. If Roosevelt would ensure the adoption of the conference plan, Germany could and would continue to uphold the Open

Door and equality of rights for all treaty powers in Morocco.[116]

There was indeed a desperate need for some action to prevent the demise of Bülow's altruistic conference ideal from ridicule. On May 28 the Sultan had finally rejected the French proposed reforms and had given his approval of the conference,[117] for which not another power except Germany had yet declared itself. On the same day, the great Japanese naval victory at Tsushima presaged the end of the Far Eastern conflict. To save German diplomacy from being wrecked on both the Far Eastern and Moroccan problems, Delcassé must go.

Ever since May 8, when Rouvier had said that Delcassé must be retained in office to make peace between Japan and Russia,[118] the Premier had received intimations that no improvement could be expected in Franco-German relations while Delcassé presided over the Foreign Office.[119] These German threats, to which Delcassé attributed his eventual downfall, were only partially responsible for it. His long tenure of office, his secretiveness, his friction with Rouvier, and his defense of the Tsarist barbarities in Russia had all undermined his position. As a climax came the bellicose preparations of early June, in which the British fleet appeared ready to implement the alliance which Delcassé said that Lansdowne had pledged. Since Rouvier and his Cabinet would not risk a war for which the French naval and military authorities declared the country unprepared, Delcassé was compelled to resign his post on June 6.[120]

In France public opinion approved the dismissal of Delcassé almost without dissent.[121] Secretly, the Franco-British naval and military consultations continued, and the acute war scare did not begin to subside in France until June 28.[122] The British government and press regarded the sacrifice of Delcassé as cowardly and insulting to Great Britain, whose support of him was thus flouted.[123] But, as Reid told Roosevelt, the British diplomats were soon converted to confidence in Rouvier; his adroit parrying of Bülow's repeated demands for the conference aroused their respect.[124] John Hay,[125] about to depart for his last trip home, wrote Henry Adams that the Kaiser had taken

Delcassé's scalp out of sheer wantonness.[126] In his joy at being relieved from the incubus of isolation, the Kaiser had been willing to surrender Morocco to the French. The stiffening of French policy after the departure of Delcassé was not due entirely to Rouvier's skill or to his backing by French high finance.[127] In addition, Rouvier received masterly guidance from the quartet of diplomats who had been Delcassé's most faithful disciples--the two Cambons, Barrere, and Jusserand[128]--all strategically placed to carry on Delcassé's policy most effectively. These men soon succeeded in restoring the prestige of the Anglo-French Entente and in bringing Italy and the United States into alignment with it.

While Sternburg was misleading his Foreign Office as to the interest and good will of Roosevelt, Jusserand was conducting a counter-propaganda. On May 8 the President said that the United States would not attend a conference, since almost all the powers were opposed to it. A week later, criticizing the German Emperor with great severity, Roosevelt suggested that France might be willing to influence Russia, while he worked on Japan in order to end the Russo-Japanese War. Mentioning the press reports assigning Mogador to Germany, Jusserand did not neglect to emphasize the menace to the United States of a German port near the entrance to the Mediterranean.[129]

The extreme preoccupation of Rouvier with the Moroccan crisis may have been responsible for his failure to second Roosevelt's peace efforts for the Far East. When, on May 31, Japan requested the President to initiate direct negotiations between the belligerents,[130] it was from the untrustworthy Kaiser that Roosevelt received aid to bring Russia to reason. On June 3 the Kaiser advised the Tsar to employ the mediation of the President, who might be able to bring Japan down to equitable terms.[131] In the message sent to Roosevelt through Tower, the Kaiser offered to support silently any move for peace.[132] Roosevelt did not desire "to squeese out of Japan terms favorable to Russia,"[133] but he did not spurn the Kaiser's offer. After negotiations conducted chiefly by Meyer, the Tsar reluctantly agreed on June 7 to receive from the President a public offer of mediation, which was made on the next day.[134]

During the ensuing month, as Roosevelt became more deeply involved in the Moroccan controversy, he was harassed by the quibbling, double-dealing, false pride, and exorbitant demands which threatened to disrupt the preliminary arrangements for the peace parley.[135] Perhaps Lansdowne still feared that the President's overtures were premature,[136] for his replies to two direct appeals from Roosevelt during June were refusals to exert any pressure to moderate Japan's demands.[137] At the same time the British foreign secretary was showing himself equally opposed to Roosevelt's peace-making proclivities in the Moroccan quarrel.

A circular note issued by Bülow on June 6[138] summoned the other powers to accept the Sultan's invitation to the conference, as Germany had done on the preceding day.[139] The basis of Bülow's argument was that since Article XVII of the Treaty of Madrid granted to all signatory powers most favored nation treatment, no reforms could be introduced into Morocco without the sanction of all powers. One power had the right to prohibit any proposed reform, and none could gain a special position without the consent of the others. Consequently, a conference would be the best means to introduce reforms without infringing, as France was trying to do, upon the political and commercial interests of the other treaty powers.

Since the Russian, Austrian, Italian, Danish, and Portuguese governments postponed their replies until Great Britain and France could answer,[140] the attitude of the last two became decisive. Roosevelt was again pressed into service to convince these recalcitrant opponents of the justice of the German cause. That he undertook this mission was due to his conviction that this action was necessary to save from failure the Russo-Japanese negotiations which he was conducting simultaneously.

Following the Delcassé plan of avoiding a conference by a direct understanding, Rouvier offered on June 9 a general agreement including Morocco, the Bagdad Railway, and the Far East.[141] On the next day he admitted the possibility of a conference, if preceded by a previous understanding concerning the reforms permissible for France.[142] Bülow offered to negotiate a program after the Sultan's invitation had been accepted. Since Radolin's unofficial suggestions for the conference program included international reforms and the Open Door, Rouvier's lack of assent is not surprising.[143]

The British Foreign Office, which had already advised the Sultan[144] and the United States[145] to reject the conference, announced on June 8 a postponement of its decision until after France had been consulted.[146] On the same day Roosevelt declined to have the United States represented, because American public opinion was inclined to favor the civilization of Morocco by a strong foreign power. He did not seem impressed by the suggestion that France was creating a dangerous precedent which might be followed in the Far East. In his reply, Bülow asserted that the President could persuade the English and French governments without arousing public opinion against himself.[147] On June 11 Bülow presented a more potent argument--that France would have to choose between the alliance offered by England and an agreement with Germany, probably including a portion of Morocco. War might be forced upon Germany because she was in honor bound to support the Sultan. If the German sea power were destroyed in a war over Morocco, isolated America would be unable to prevent the partitioning of China by a quadruple alliance.[148]

Now Roosevelt began to regard seriously the German threat of war. Deciding not to approach Great Britain again, he informed Sternburg that he would communicate to France his opinion that she would be the loser in a war, even if allied with Great Britain. Therefore, he advised a conference. Sternburg concluded:

> The President was greatly pleased over the further developments of the peace efforts, especially over the policy of His Majesty the Emperor, and promised me to use his full influence for a peaceful solution of the Morocco question.

Bülow's persistent reliance upon Roosevelt is explained by a study of Sternburg's optimistic, misleading reports, which account largely for the Kaiser's "monomania" for calling upon the President. The "peace efforts" mentioned above are the Russo-Japanese negotiations, begun by the Kaiser on June 3.[149]

According to Jusserand, the President wondered whether a conference would not be a lesser evil for France than a German zone of influence in Morocco, especially since nothing very important could result from a conference. When the French government replied that any propitiating offer to Germany would be outside of Morocco, Roosevelt considered this plan wisdom itself. Rouvier asserted that the offer of a Moroccan zone to Germany was as imaginary as the supposed French ultimatum to the Sultan. This seems to indicate that his offer of a general settlement on June 8, including the Moroccan dispute, would not have satisfied Bülow, if the negotiations had been followed up. Bülow was planning the future acquisition of a Moroccan port.[150]

In France there had been some apprehension that the United States might endorse the German thesis on Article XVII of the Madrid treaty, the most favored nation clause.[151] Lansdowne contended that this provision did not exclude the privileged position of one power.[152] Rouvier had Jusserand present a denial that France aimed at the "Tunisification" of Morocco, since the reform program was designed only to improve order and security and not to give to France control of the internal and external affairs of Morocco.[153] When the United States officially participated in the conference, however, she did so nominally to protect American commercial equality.

In May and June French and British propaganda represented the peaceful solution of the Moroccan problem as an extension of the Monroe Doctrine--an evident appeal to American public opinion. A victorious Germany might not only annex all European possessions in the Americas, but could also threaten China and the Philippines.[154] Thus giving Germany a chance to win a war threatened to destroy the two pillars of American foreign policy--the Monroe Doctrine and the Open Door. When Roosevelt appealed to France to accept the conference, he urged it solely as a peace-preserving measure. To the British government he stated his expectation that it would place no obstacle in the way of a peaceful solution of the conflict.[155]

While Roosevelt urged upon Jusserand the granting of some "satisfaction to the limitless vanity of William II" by concession of a conference in which all the other powers would be sure to oppose any injustice to France,[156] Rouvier was dissatisfied with the unofficial explanations of Germany's aims.[157] Encouraged by promises of British support,[158] he accepted the advice of Paul Cambon not to refuse a conference but to persist in negotiations to make one unnecessary.[159] This decision he made known to the American government on June 23.

Rouvier's dispatch to Jusserand contained also a complaint about Bülow's attitude:[160]

> Prince Radolin fails to make in the name of his Government any proposition save that of a conference .... The Emperor takes steps to inform us in Paris that all the forces of Germany are behind the Sultan of Morocco, and he uses the most menacing language towards us at Washington, at Rome, and at Madrid.
>
> Mr. Roosevelt can avert the danger. Tell him that the exceptional authority which attaches to his counsel ... qualifies him in supreme degree to intervene in favor of the maintenance of peace. The insistence with which the Emperor has appealed to him has left the way open for the President to take the initiative that we expect from his friendship.[161]

Roosevelt needed no further stimulus to action. He immediately wrote Sternburg, congratulating the Emperor on his success in securing the French assent to the conference and intimating that an advance program was the usual custom.[162] Two days later, he hoped that this "genuine triumph for the Emperor's diplomacy" would not be marred by raising questions about minor details.[163] Although indignant at Rouvier's craftiness in inspiring Roosevelt's "little bit previous letter" (the Kaiser's comment on Sternburg's dispatch), Bülow thanked the President for his contribution toward sparing Germany a war.[164] Sternburg's next report was that Roosevelt was prepared to accept and to secure England's adherence to the conference and that he was advocating a program in accordance with Germany's previously declared aims.[165]

Meanwhile, Rouvier was proving to be obdurate.

Strengthened by the support of the French press, by British approval of his note of June 23, and by the Spanish declaration of loyalty to the entente,[166] he definitely refused on July 27 to accept a conference without a previous understanding and the concession of the French right to control police reforms along the Algerian border.[167] Nevertheless, on the same day Roosevelt came forward to supply a diplomatic phrase which would enable Rouvier to yield with dignity.[168]

To meet Jusserand's objection that a conference would not be prudent without a prearranged program, the President suggested offhand a formula to save the ententes on Morocco: "The two governments consent to go to the conference with no program and to discuss there all questions in regard to Morocco, save where either is in honor bound by a previous agreement to another power." To facilitate Germany's acceptance of this provision, he informed Sternburg that he had asked England to drop her scruples against the conference.[169] He also promised to telegraph from the German Museum at Harvard an acknowledgment of the great services rendered by William II and his people to America. The astute Jusserand assured his government not only of Roosevelt's support, but also of the Kaiser's harmlessness.[170]

In finally agreeing to the conference on June 30, Rouvier was probably influenced less by Jusserand's entente with Roosevelt than by the general international situation which he analyzed thus to the British chargé d'affaires:

> France could go into it with the support of England, Spain, and possibly Italy, whereas Germany would be alone; Germany was prepared to admit the preponderance of French interests on the Algerian frontier .... So long as the conference was not accepted, Germany considered that she was entitled to a free hand in Morocco .... She would ask for all sorts of concessions, ports, cables, etc., and were the Sultan to accede to such demands, the situation both for France and England would become far more critical.[171]

For some unknown reason, Sternburg altered the message sent to the President by Bülow in such a way as to cause mortification for Germany during a critical time in the conference.[172] The German Foreign Office staff were so thoroughly convinced of Roosevelt's friendship that a warning of the essential community of interests between the United States and the Anglo-French combination, sent to Holstein by Eckardstein, received no credence.[173]

On June 30 Lansdowne frankly notified the United States of the extent to which Great Britain was pledged to France:

> If the friendly overtures which France has made were to be rejected by Germany, and if Germany were to attack France on account of action taken by her in Morocco which she was clearly entitled to take under the terms of the Anglo-French Declaration and which did not involve any encroachment on the rights of other powers, Lord Lansdowne considers that public opinion in England would become dangerously excited.[174]

By this time, however, the war scare was over, and on July 1 Lansdowne approved of the principles of the agreement which Rouvier wished to make with the German government.[175] In the discussions of the following week Roosevelt had no part, and his compromise formula was greatly expanded. The preliminary accord of July 8 pledged Germany to aim at no goal during the conference that would

> compromise the legitimate interests of France or that would be contrary to the rights of France resulting from treaties or arrangements and harmonizing with the following principles: sovereignty and independence of the Sultan; integrity of his empire; economic liberty without any inequality; utility of police and financial reforms, the introduction of which will be regulated for a short period by way of an international accord; recognition of the situation created for France with reference to Morocco by the contiguity, over a long stretch, of Algeria and the Sherifian empire, by the particular relations which result therefrom between the two neighboring countries, as well as by the special interest which results therefrom for France for order to obtain in the Sherifian Empire.

It was agreed further to recall the French and German missions from Fez when the conference began and to formulate a program for submission to the Sultan.[176] Radolin also gave specific assurances that the Anglo-French and Franco-Spanish agreements of 1904 would not be affected.[177]

Within a few weeks the Sultan received acceptances of his conference invitation from thirteen countries, including the United States on July 31.[178] Lansdowne was particularly anxious for the attendance of Russia and the United States.[179] Germany had won a Pyrrhic victory; to obtain the conference she had recognized in advance both the special interests and the ententes of France relative to Morocco. Roosevelt was elated because both the French and the German governments thanked him for his services.[180]

In the lengthy and generally acrimonious discussions which culminated in the conference program on September 28, 1905, Roosevelt had a very small part. The German Foreign Office asked for his backing in its opposition to the French choice of Rêvoil as their delegate and its selection of Tangier as the conference city.[181] Although reluctant to interfere further, Roosevelt replied, he would communicate with Jusserand, then in Paris.[182] The French refused to accept the German suggestions; Rêvoil was retained, and Algeciras was selected as the site of the conference.[183]

It was fortunate that after July 8 Roosevelt was able to devote his time and energy almost wholly to the Russo-Japanese peacemaking project, for more than ever his dealings with the Tsar, the Kaiser, and the Mikado made him content with democracy, even including the American newspapers. His chief problem was how to persuade Japan to forgo an indemnity and to refrain from claiming excessive influence over Manchuria.[184] Even after the peace conference assembled at Portsmouth on August 10, Witte, the chief Russian delegate, frequently expressed a defeatist attitude concerning the possibility of peace.[185] A failure at this stage would make Roosevelt personally and officially ridiculous. Lansdowne would not lend a helping hand, although Roosevelt continued his attempts through Spring-Rice to convince the British government that he was working for its benefit.[186] Roosevelt's exasperation with the peace envoys[187] was not soothed by the report from Sternburg that Lansdowne and Rouvier were preparing to mediate in order to save the Portsmouth conference from failure.[188]

On August 27, when substantial concessions by Japan failed to move the Tsar, the conference seemed doomed to break up over the question of an indemnity and the cession of Saghalin to Japan, the President's appeal to William II to use his influence with Nicholas[189] helped to obtain the compromise which Japan accepted on August 29. Japan made impressive gains by the treaty of Portsmouth: the northern part of Saghalin, predominance in Korea, and the transference of Russia's former lease of the Liaotung Peninsula to her. Russia was saved from the humiliation of paying an indemnity.

Now there were four messages of congratualtion and gratitude for Roosevelt; the monarchs of Germany, Russia, Japan, and Great Britain lauded his great achievement.[190] Yet many others besides Roosevelt[191] thought that Lansdowne had anticipated the President as a peacemaker. The second Anglo-Japanese Treaty, completed on August 12, 1905, was another link in the chain of encirclement which the Kaiser soon saw forged around Germany.

William II could afford to play the minor role that Roosevelt assigned to him in making peace in the Far East.[192] Apparently he did not share the anxiety of his friend, Philip Eulenburg:

> If President Roosevelt comes still more into the limelight, Europe may soon be having a dose of American policy which will take its breath away. Only a coalition of the older States can help us. But how to gain France?[193]

On his way home from the Portsmouth Conference, Count Witte was entertained by William II, who presented his guest a portrait of himself with a significant inscription, "Portsmouth--Björkö--Rominten. Wilhelm rex." Long known as an advocate of a Continental Alliance, Witte was overjoyed at the secret imparted to him by his host.[194] Meeting at Björkö on July 24, the Tsar and the Kaiser had signed a treaty of alliance, which France was to join later. By the Moroccan agreement of July 8, the Kaiser thought, friction with France had been allayed, and Alsace-Lorraine had been forgiven. The treaty was to go into effect two weeks after the signing of the Peace of Portsmouth.[195]

William II fancied himself as a second Delcassé:

> In time to come may not be impossible that even Japan may feel inclined to join it. This would cool down English self-assertion and impertinence, as she is her ally too. The 24th of July 1905 is a cornerstone in European politics and turns over a new leaf in the history of the world; which will be a chapter of peace and goodwill among the great Powers .... The moment the news of the new "groupment" will have become known in the world, the smaller nations, Holland, Belgium, Denmark, Sweden and Norway will all be attracted to this new great centre of gravity .... They will revolve in the orbit of the great block of Powers (Russia, Germany, France, Austria, Italy).[196]

Thus the Kaiser thought he had surpassed Napoleon, too, by uniting the continent of Europe by the pen instead of the sword. That Roosevelt did not learn of the part assigned to the United States[197] in the Kaiser's latest "pipe-dream" was due to Bülow, who refused consent to send the news.[198]

Unknown to most of the world was the fact that Roosevelt had already ranged himself secretly with the Anglo-Japanese Alliance of 1905. The surrender of both Great Britain and Japan to Roosevelt's leadership at Portsmouth had been largely a result of his previous capitulation to their Far Eastern policy. By the "agreed memorandum," negotiated by Taft and Premier Katsura on July 29, 1905, a good understanding had been achieved by Japan and the United States. President Roosevelt had safeguarded the Philippines by conceding Korea to Japan--with the American Senate none the wiser.[199]

Shortly after the completion of the conference program for Morocco on September 28, through the intervention of Witte, it became apparent that the Björkö Treaty was a major failure of German policy. Bülow and his royal master quarreled because the Kaiser had altered the text to make the alliance applicable only in Europe, and there was a most undignified scene of pleading before Bülow consented to retain his office. Witte and Lamsdorff, the Russian foreign minister, pointed out that the treaty violated the Franco-Russian Alliance. The Kaiser's conflict with Bülow affected him scarcely less than the Tsar's nullification of the treaty after its rejection by France.[200] On October 18 Rouvier declined to consider the offer of a general entente with Germany which he had made when he hoped to avoid the conference.[201] Later Rouvier ventured to ask, as a bid for French goodwill, the pre-convention consent of Germany to a Franco-Spanish police mandate in western Morocco.[202] In his despondency over the nullification of his prized treaty, the Kaiser wrote, "The coalition is here in fact! That King Edward has managed in good shape!"[203]

As late as November 3, Sternburg was assuring the Wilhelmstrasse of Roosevelt's loyalty to Germany. Furthermore, the President had declared that Elihu Root, now Secretary of State, had supported German policy in Morocco from the beginning. Roosevelt admitted that he himself had not fully realized the wisdom of the Kaiser's policy until after the fall of that unspeakable scoundrel, Delcassé, and the Matin revelations.[204] With wearisome repetition Bülow pointed out that England's sacrifices in Morocco would be requited by France elsewhere, probably in Asia, and that an isolated Germany could not defend the other powers against the Delcassé program at the forthcoming conference.[205]

It seems incredible that even Holstein in his back room could have failed to observe the many striking evidences of the Anglo-American-French rapprochement during the second half of 1905. Despite their cooperation in the pursuit of peace, Roosevelt's conviction of the Kaiser's untrustworthiness had never been shaken. The hope of Metternich that Reid would prove to be a friend to Germany in London had been vain.[206] To Durand, Roosevelt gave his opinion that the Kaiser was now more than inconvenient in his ways--he was becoming really dangerous.[207] The President was much gratified over a message sent to him by King Edward in August.[208] On their visits to England

and France, Hay and Lodge served virtually as missions of national good will.

Most spectacular of all the signs of the new entente was the exchange of naval visits. The enthusiastic reception given a British squadron at Brest in July was reciprocated so fully for the French navy at Portsmouth in August that these events were hailed as "a public ratification of the Entente Cordiale."[209] The toast of Admiral Prince Louis of Battenburg, "The King first, but the President nex," given during a cordial reception of a British squadron visiting the United States in November,[210] recalled that the Secretary of the Navy had already publicly endorsed an "Anglo-American navy."[211] The appeal of Carnegie in a French journal for a "Franco-English-American Trinity"[212] was seconded by Lodge, who wrote that "France ought to be with us and England--in our zone and our combination."[213]

From Paris, Lodge kept Roosevelt informed of the gratitude and confidence manifested by the French for his part in resolving the Moroccan crisis. The removal to an American battleship of the body of John Paul Jones, recently discovered in Paris, was the occasion for a great popular and official demonstration of friendship.[214] "Your great work in world politics this summer," Lodge wrote to Roosevelt, "will be, when the history of our time is written, one of your most ... certain titles to a really enduring fame."[215]

The selection of the American delegate to the coming conference was discussed thoroughly by Roosevelt and Lodge. Since a man of international reputation was desired, the latter suggested Joseph H. Choate,[216] who later withdrew his acceptance.[217] In November, Henry White, ambassador to Italy since April,[218] regarded by Roosevelt as "the most useful man in the entire diplomatic service,"[219] was named as the senior delegate. Gummeré was selected as his assistant, and Lewis Einstein was to serve as secretary.[220] White was already informed of Roosevelt's sympathy for France.[221]

The formal official instructions issued by Secretary Root on November 28 to the delegates bore little resemblance to the two "personal and confidential" notes sent to

White on the same day. The former stated the objectives of the United States to be equality of rights in Morocco, an international agreement for an effective police force to maintain order, non-discrimination against foreign states in measures of financial reform and public works, and consideration of guarantees of religious and racial toleration in Morocco. In short, "Fair play is what the United States asks, for Morocco and all the interested nations."

White's confidential instructions[222] were not to oppose the protection of France's legitimate special interests. Referring to the allegation that Gummeré was strongly pro-German, Root continued:

> This if true must not be allowed to throw us over into even apparent antagonism to the Anglo-French entente or to make us a means of breaking that up. It is useful to us as well as agreeable. Keep the American end of the business on an even keel. Keep friendly with all. Help France to get what she ought to have, but don't take her fight on your shoulders. Help limit France where she ought to be limited, but don't take that fight on your shoulders. In the broader and really important part that the Conference is to play in the politics of Europe, keep the peace and make it as difficult as possible for any one to pick a quarrel. You are chosen because you know that broader field and have tact, Gummeré because he knows the narrower field of Morocco.[223]

On the same day that Root was dating these directions, the Kaiser's speech was reviewing his peacemaking record in the Reichstag. He was glad to have been able to "support the President of the United States in his successful endeavors to bring about peace in the Far East." Otherwise, he admitted less success:

> The difficulties which had arisen between ourselves and France on the Morocco question originated solely with an inclination to settle without our cooperation matters in which the German Empire also had interests to protect. Such tendencies, checked at one point, may reappear at another. To my satisfaction, an understanding has been arrived at in the Morocco question by diplo-

> matic means with all consideration for the interests and the honor of both parties .... The peace of the German people is to me a sacred thing, but the signs of the times make it the duty of the nation to strengthen its defences against unrighteous attacks.[224]

On the eve of the conference, William II was in a panic for fear of a conflict:

> We know that England and France will be sure to act together in Morocco. Then that Fisher is burning for a chance of destroying our Fleet and Merchant Service .... Our Naval Chief of Staff was quite right then, in estimating the naval changes begun last November as preparations for war, and not as ordinary reshuffling .... The French are resolved on war, even though it goes against the grain .... They have made a number of preparations and continue to make them .... Most important of all, however, is the fact that England has, in effect, made an offer of armed support to France--Mr. Beit made no secret of this--and that this offer continues as before. Lansdowne therefore lied to Metternich.[225]

Kaiser William's vision of a portentous naval attack on Germany was not entirely a chimera. The Entente Cordiale had made possible an extensive shuffling of the units of the British navy. By abolishing the North Pacific and South Atlantic squadrons and reducing the Mediterranean and Chinese fleets, the Channel and Atlantic fleets had been greatly strengthened. During 1905, Admiral John Fisher had inaugurated a revolution in navies by laying down the first Dreadnought, which made all earlier battleships obsolete. By 1906 a formidable Home Fleet in the North Sea challenged Germany to combat.[226] As early as April 22, 1905, however, Fisher wrote Lansdowne that he could undertake, in event of war with Germany, to "have the German fleet, the Kiel Canal, and Schleswig-Holstein within a fortnight."[227]

The naval strategy had been evident, but the Wilhelmstrasse could only speculate about the diplomatic arrangements accompanying it. In December of 1905 the Liberal party came into power in Great Britain. The new

Cabinet was even less inclined to cooperate with Roosevelt than its predecessor had been. Sir Edward Grey, the foreign secretary, continued to know and care little about Roosevelt's involvement in the approaching Moroccan conference. At first Grey tried to hedge when asked for a pledge of armed assistance to France if there should develop a Franco-German war. Later he authorized a continuation of the military and naval discussions begun under Lansdowne. On January 31, 1906, still refusing a definite commitment, Grey promised to do everything in his power to bring England into any Franco-German conflict, and the French government proceeded with confidence in British aid.[228]

As the memorable year of 1905 drew to a close, the senior partner in peacemaking could look back upon his achievement and endorse the opinion of most of the world that it was good. Proud of his amateur status,[229] he could boast of having accomplished tasks at which experienced diplomats had quailed. He could smile at the occasional carping criticism which revealed both envy and ignorance of his real aims and actions, especially if it came from British sources:

> There was no reason why Roosevelt should have interfered. The interests of America were not imperilled. Russia and Japan are grown-up nations .... There are certain temperaments which find the temptation to interfere in other people's affairs irresistible. On either side of the Atlantic we have an admirable example of the International Busybody. William II is well matched by Theodore I ....
>
> Theodore I is for the moment superior to William II because there are more editors and more photographers in America than in the German Empire .... Mr. Roosevelt, for his own glory, wanted nothing but peace, peace good or bad, peace at any price .... Suppose the hasty terms of peace compel in the future a yet more bloody war, he cannot be impeached .... These considerations are as nothing to those whose delight is to make peace for others.[230]

During 1906 a more complicated and difficult situation confronted Roosevelt in finishing the task of making peace in Morocco. In this second task he was to receive no public plaudits or Nobel prizes, but he trusted that posterity would properly appreciate his services in the cause of world peace.

Notes

1. "World-Politics," North American Review, CLXXIX (Dec., 1904), 949.

2. New York World, March 5, 1905; quoted by Pringle, in Roosevelt, 359.

3. Henry Adams to Theodore Roosevelt, Nov. 6, 1905; quoted by Pringle, in Roosevelt, 387.

4. Theodore Roosevelt to Henry Cabot Lodge, May 15, 1905; Selections from the Correspondence of Theodore Roosevelt and Henry Cabot Lodge, 2 vols. (hereafter cited as Roosevelt-Lodge Correspondence), II, 123.

5. Nevins, Henry White, 224-225; Dennis, Adventures, 347-348. Durand distrusted the friendship of both Roosevelt and Lodge for Great Britain and regretted the retirement of pro-British Hay. Durand's account of his hike with Roosevelt reveals much of the reason for their failure to become friends. Sir Percy Molesworth Sykes, The Right Honourable Sir Mortimer Durand...A Biography (hereafter cited as Sykes, Durand), 274-275.

6. For Japan, Minister Takahira and the journalist Kaneko in Washington performed efficient service. For the general diplomatic situation, see also Tyler Dennett, Roosevelt and the Russo-Japanese War (hereafter cited as Dennett, Roosevelt and the Russo-Japanese War), 22-23, 31-34. Hay returned from Europe on June 15 and died on July 1, 1905; Thayer, John Hay, II, 406-407.

7. Maurice Francis Egan, Ten Years Near the German Frontier, A Retrospect and a Warning (hereafter cited as Egan, Ten Years Near the German Frontier), 66.

8. Jusserand to Delcassé, Jan. 25, 1905, D. D. F., Sér. 2, VI, 61-64.

9. Sternburg, Jusserand remarked, was always ready to make speeches, compliments, and eulogies. He cultivated newspaper men, attended conventions, and accepted doctor's hoods from American colleges. Maximilian Harden also ridiculed Sternburg in Die Zukunft of April 28, 1906 (quoted by Vagts, Weltpolitik, II, 1946): "He appears at the station like the minister of a vassal state at the departure of Roosevelt, who, perhaps as payment for such homage, lends him his horse and with a jovial smile calls him Specky. The possibility of a decent trade treaty he has not brought nearer to us. He does nothing. Must not the reputation of a great power be enormously enhanced when its representative pays honor at the station, is being teasingly called by a pet name, and during the President's absence may mount a nag graciously loaned to him?"

10. Jusserand to Delcassé, March 9, 1904; D. D. F., Sér. 2, IV, 443-446.

11. Pringle, Roosevelt, 373-375; Dennett, Roosevelt and the Russo-Japanese War, 3-4, 27.

12. No documentary evidence has been found to substantiate Roosevelt's assertion, made to Spring-Rice on July 24, 1905, that at the outbreak of the war he had notified Germany and France that he would side with Japan if any coalition were formed to deprive her of the fruits of victory. See Vagts, Weltpolitik, II, 1178-1179 and Dr. Evelene Peters, Roosevelt und der Kaiser. Ein Beitrag zur Geschichte der deutsch-Amerikanischen Beziehungen, 1895-1906 (hereafter cited as Peters, Roosevelt und der Kaiser), Appendix C, 158-160. The latter suggests (p. 113) that Roosevelt made this claim to convince Great

Britain that he had been working in accord with the Anglo-Japanese Alliance in order to persuade her to accede to his wishes and exert pressure on Japan to make peace.

13. Bülow, Memoirs, II, 70-71; Dennett, Roosevelt and the Russo-Japanese War, 66-69.

14. Willy to Nicky, Jan. 3, 1904; Levine, Letters from the Kaiser to the Czar, 100.

15. Dennett, John Hay, 407-409; Thayer, John Hay, II, 372-374. The note was issued on Feb. 10, 1904. Its text is given in F. R., 1904, 2-3, 42.

16. Delcassé to the French ambassadors in London and St. Petersburg, June 21, 1904; D. D. F., Sér. 2, V, 278.

17. Jusserand to Delcassé, Oct. 17, 1904; D. D. F., Sér. 2, V, 453-454. In his dispatch of Oct. 18, Jusserand said that Roosevelt was beginning to be uneasy about Japan's victories but was not turning his sympathy toward Russia. The German Emperor was following his usual policy, which was to search for friends and to preserve peace, in spite of belligerent whims designed to keep his soldiers going. Ibid., 456-457.

18. F. R., 1904, 306-307; Thayer, John Hay, II, 393-394; Mende, Horace Porter, 277.

19. Dennett, John Hay, 435-436.

20. Chirol, Fifty Years, 209-212. Chirol corrected Roosevelt when he referred to the Pacific as "our ocean."

21. "The President is a great admirer of Your Majesty and would like to rule the world hand in hand with Your Majesty, since he feels himself to be in a certain measure the American counterpart of Your Majesty." Bülow to Wilhelm II, No. 6264, Aug. 31, 1904; G. P. XIX, 536.

22. Bülow to Sternburg, No. 6265, Sept. 5, 1904; G. P., XIX, 541.

23. Sternburg to F. O., No. 6266, Sept. 27, 1904, Ibid., 541-542.

24. Lee, King Edward VII, II, 284-295.

25. Thayer, John Hay, II, 384.

26. That what Roosevelt called the "sudden vagaries" of the Kaiser were actually caused by a triple struggle among Bülow, Holstein, and their imperial master for the control of foreign policy was first made clear by Raymond J. Sontag in "German Foreign Policy, 1904-1906," American Historical Review, XXXIII (Jan., 1928), 278-301.

27. Brandenburg, From Bismarck to the World War, 213-217; Sontag, European Diplomatic History, 100-102; Hale, Germany and the Diplomatic Revolution, 56-57.

28. Memorandum of Richtofen, No. 6150, Nov. 30, 1904, G. P., XIX, 356-357.

29. Memorandum of Metternich, No. 6140, Dec. 18, 1904; Ibid., 332-340; Schulenburg to Bülow, No. 6154, Dec. 14, 1904, Ibid., 359-367.

30. Spring-Rice wrote Roosevelt on November 5, 1904, that the Tsar and the Kaiser were plotting and that Germany might use her chance to fall upon England. In his reply of May 25, 1904, Roosevelt said that he could not believe that the Kaiser had any deep laid plot against England. Dennett, Roosevelt and the Russo-Japanese War, 73-75.

31. Bülow to Wilhelm II, No. 6274, Dec. 24, 1904; G. P., XIX, 547-549.

32. Wilhelm II to Bülow, No. 6146, Dec. 28, 1904, Ibid., 346-347.

33. In discussing this matter with Jusserand, Roosevelt said: "Sir Mortimer Durand has little information

and few ideas; it is difficult to deal usefully with him; at London, the ministry is feeble and in disagreement; it is probable that England will do nothing, but there is no calculation of probabilities .... I hope that you know me well enough to be of the opinion that in diplomacy, as in other things, I say exactly what I think without evasion." Jusserand to Delcassé, Jan. 15, 1905, D. D. F., Sér. 2, VI, 37-38.

34. Thayer, John Hay, II, 385-388; Bülow to Bussche-Haddenhausen, No. 6276, Jan. 4, 1905, G. P., XIX, 556-557; Bussche-Haddenhausen, to F. O., No. 6277, Jan. 11, 1905, Ibid., 557; Tower to Richtofen, No. 6278, Jan. 14, 1905, Ibid., 558-559; Bülow to Tower No. 6279, Jan. 18, 1905, Ibid., 559.

35. Anderson, First Moroccan Crisis, 178, 181-183.

36. Vagts, Weltpolitik, II, 1825-1830, 1837-1838; Tardieu, La Conférence, 49-50.

37. Note 3, No. 6557, G. P., XX, 255-256.

38. Jusserand to Delcassé, March 6, 1905, D. D. F., Sér. 2, VI, 172-173.

39. Vagts, Weltpolitik, II, 1832-1833.

40. Sternburg to Bülow, No. 6288, Feb. 10, 1905, G. P., XIX, 570-575.

41. Bülow to Sternburg, No. 6299, March 27, 1905, Ibid., 589-590.

42. Sternburg to the F. O., No. 6300, April 1, 1905, G. P., XX, 590-591. On this very day William II was telling Prince Louis of Battenburg that the world of the future would be divided between two virile races--Teutonic and Slav; the three great Anglo-Saxon races must make common cause and march shoulder to shoulder, although they were rivals in trade. Newton, Lansdowne, 333. The Kaiser was evidently doing his bit here to promote Roosevelt's putative project.

43. Philip to State Department, No. 630, Dec. 24, 1904, _C. D., Tangier,_ XXVII; Philip to Adee, No. 4, Aug. 8, 1905, _Ibid._

44. Gummeré to State Dept., Oct. 26 and Nov. 25, 1904, _Ibid._

45. Vagts, _Weltpolitik,_ II, 1835; Philip's dispatches to the State Dept., Dec. 24, 1904--March 1, 1905.

46. Jusserand to Delcassé, Jan. 6, 1905; _D. D. F.,_ Sér. 2, VI, 10; Saint-René Taillandier to Delcassé, Feb. 19, 1905, _Ibid.,_ 145-147; Delcassé to Jusserand, March 3, 1905, _Ibid.,_ 170-171.

47. Jusserand to Delcassé, March 7, 1905, _Ibid.,_ 176.

48. Tower to the President, Feb. 4, 1905; Dennett, _Roosevelt and the Russo-Japanese War,_ 78-80. The German Foreign Office sometimes sent important communications through Tower, but Roosevelt never did. For repetitions of the charge of a plot see Bülow to Sternburg, No. 6851, March 10, 1925, _G. P.,_ XX, 620-622 and No. 6305, April 14, 1905, _Ibid.,_ XIX, 598-599.

49. Roosevelt to Tower, Feb. 16, 1905; Dennett, _Roosevelt and the Russo-Japanese War,_ 82-83.

50. Bülow to Sternburg, No. 6558, Feb. 25, 1905 and footnote 1, _G. P.,_ XX, 256-258.

51. Sternburg to the F. O., No. 6559, March 9, 1905, _Ibid.,_ 258-259; Bishop, _Theodore Roosevelt,_ I, 468.

52. Bülow to Sternburg, No. 6560, March 11, 1905, _G. P.,_ XX, 259-260. The actual instructions given to Gummeré have been cited.

53. Bülow to Sternburg, No. 6296, _Ibid.,_ XIX, 583-585.

54. Meyer to Roosevelt, March 31, 1905; M. A. DeWolf Howe, _George von Lengerke Meyer: His Life and Public Services_ (hereafter cited as Howe, _Meyer_), 145-146.

55. Roosevelt to Hay, March 30 and April 2, 1905; Bishop, Theodore Roosevelt, I, 377-378.

56. Sternburg to F. O., No. 6298, March 31, 1905, G. P., XIX, 587-589.

57. Dennett, Roosevelt and the Russo-Japanese War, 45.

58. The letter is reproduced in Lee, King Edward VII, II, 430-432. Roosevelt's reply, Ibid., 432-433, echoed the King's wish for friendship between the two great branches of the Anglo-Saxon race. In a personal message sent through Henry White, King Edward remarked that he hoped the President would not allow himself to be persuaded that any other sovereign could be as good a friend to the United States as the British monarch was. Nevins, Henry White, 241.

59. Roosevelt to Spring-Rice, May 13, 1905, in Dennett, Roosevelt and the Russo-Japanese War, 90. Durand to Lansdowne, March 10, 1905, in Gwynn, Spring-Rice, I, 454: "I know Specky thinks I am inclined to fall under the influence of the German Emperor, but he is quite wrong. I like the Emperor very much in a way, but I don't trust him, and am not in the least affected by the ridiculous messages he makes Specky bring me."

60. Spring-Rice to Hay, March 15, 1905, Gwynn, Spring-Rice, 462-463.

61. Spring-Rice to Hay, March 29, 1905, Ibid., 463.

62. Sykes, Durand, 275; Dennett, Roosevelt and the Russo-Japanese War, 87-88.

63. Newton, Lansdowne, 322.

64. Dennett, Roosevelt and the Russo-Japanese War, 176-185.

65. On March 29, 1905, Spring-Rice wrote to Mrs. Roosevelt: "The policy which finds most favour here is to make an alliance with Japan on the basis of an understanding in Northern China. This would give

Japan the needed guarantee for a permanent peace .... The basis of the understanding would be the maintenance of the status quo ... the Open Door and the integrity of China. But America wouldn't make such a treaty .... He (the Kaiser) is going to Morocco to show the French that they must reckon with him. I should think that he would like to head a sort of European coalition against something or other. He is always finding a new something. Once it was the yellow peril. Then it was the American peril. Then it was England." Gwynn, Spring-Rice, I, 467-468.

66. That this program was preliminary to making Morocco a counterpart of Tunisia after thirty years was asserted by the Journal des Debats on March 25; Hale, Germany and the Diplomatic Revolution, 99.

67. Bülow to Kühlmann, No. 6561 and note, March 10, 1905, G. P., XX, 260-261.

68. Anderson, First Moroccan Crisis, 186, 192.

69. Bülow to Kühlmann, No. 6591, March 27, 1905, G. P., XX, 293-294.

70. Maurois, Lyautey, 163.

71. Vagts, Weltpolitik, II, 1838.

72. Bülow to Wilhelm II, No. 6563, March 20, 1905, G. P., XX and No. 6565, Ibid., 264-265; William II to Bülow, No. 6564, March 21 (?), 1905, Ibid., 263.

73. Herbert White to Lansdowne, April 2, 1905, B. D., III, 63.

74. The informal warning of Kühlmann, reported to Bülow on Nov. 9, 1904, in No. 6536, G. P., XX, 232-234, was not reported by the French representative to his government until February; Anderson, First Moroccan Crisis, 196-197. In a dispatch to Lansdowne, Feb. 12, 1905, B. D., III, 59, Nicolson reported warning Cambon that the German government had a

legitimate right to demand some consideration of its interests.

75. Bülow to Richthofen, Mühlberg, and Holstein: No. 6573, March 24, 1905, G. P., XX, 271: "Emulate the Sphinx, who, surrounded by inquisitive tourists, gives nothing away."

76. Gummeré to Hay, No. 7, April 1, 1905, Despatches from Ministers, Morocco (hereafter cited as D. M., Morocco), I. Bülow to William II, No. 6576, G. P., II, 277.

77. Hale, Germany and the Diplomatic Revolution, 104-106; Carroll, French Public Opinion, 208-209; Jusserand to Delcassé, April 3, 1905, D. D. F., Sér. 2, VI, 289-291; Lee, King Edward VII, II, 340.

78. Edward VII to Lansdowne, April 15, 1905; Lee, King Edward VII, II, 340. The visit to Tangier preceded by one day the Kaiser's remark to Prince Louis of Battenberg about the desirability of the Anglo-German American entente which Roosevelt was supposed to be advocating.

79. Delcassé to Jusserand, April 7, 1905, Nos. 251 and 252, D. D. F., Sér. 2, VI, 314-315.

80. Memorandum of Holstein, No. 6597, April 3, 1905, G. P., XX, 297-299.

81. Bülow to Sternburg, No. 6302, April 3, 1905, Ibid., XIX, 592-596; Bishop, Theodore Roosevelt, I, 468.

82. Sternburg to F. O., No. 6304, April 6, 1905, G. P., XIX, 597-598.

83. Anderson, First Moroccan Crisis, 204.

84. Bülow to Tattenbach, No. 6611, April 9, 1905, G. P., XX, 315-316. On April 7 Tattenbach had reported that Gummeré was emphasizing the Open Door, because America saw in Morocco an interesting field for expansion, especially for railroad building and

other public works. Tattenbach to F. O., No. 6610, *Ibid.*, 314. On April 9 Delcassé warned the Sultan against assenting to the conference proposed in the German press. Anderson, *First Moroccan Crisis*, 198.

85. The official instructions to Gummeré on March 31, April 4, and April 20 were to avoid entanglements and to be equally friendly to all his colleagues. Vagts, *Weltpolitik*, II, 842, 1846-1847.

86. Bishop, *Theodore Roosevelt*, I, 469.

87. Anderson, *First Moroccan Crisis*, 206.

88. Radolin to F. O., No. 6619, April 12, 1905, *G. P.*, XX, 326-327; Nicolson to Lansdowne, April 14, 1905, *B. D.*, III, 66.

89. Monts to F. O., No. 6617, April 12, 1905, *G. P.*, XX, 324.

90. Bülow to Tattenbach, No. 6624, April 18, 1905, *Ibid.*, 333-334.

91. Carroll, *French Public Opinion*, 209-213; Schuman, *War and Diplomacy in the French Republic*, 178-179; Anderson, *First Moroccan Crisis*, 200-201; Tardieu, *France and the Alliances*, 181-182.

92. Lee, *King Edward VII*, II, 342; Tattenbach to F. O., No. 6639, April 27, 1905, *G. P.*, XX, 348; Lansdowne to Bertie, April 22, 1905, *B. D.*, III, 72-73; Delcassé to Ambassadors at St. Petersburg, Berlin, London, Vienna, Madrid, Rome, and Washington, April 25, 1905, *D. D. F.*, Sér. 2, VI, 417.

93. Anderson, *First Moroccan Crisis*, 211; Bertie to Lansdowne, April 25, 1905, *B. D.*, III, 74-75.

94. Lascelles to Lansdowne, June 12, 1905, *B. D.*, III, 79-82; Lansdowne to Lascelles, June 16, 1905, *Ibid.*, 82-83.

95. These overtures were probably inspired by press articles predicting war, a panic on the Bourse on

April 27, and the French distrust of the British motives for bellicosity; Anderson, *First Moroccan Crisis,* 217-219. On April 26, Rouvier told Radolin that France's only aim was to prevent anarchy on the Algerian border and admitted that the thirty-year limitation on commercial liberty was invalidated by Morocco's treaties with other powers. Radolin to F. O., No. 6635, April 27, 1905, *G. P.,* XX, 344-345.

96. Radolin to Bülow, No. 6647, April 30, 1905, *G. P.,* XX, 360-361 and No. 6645, May 1, 1905, *Ibid.*, 355-357. Bülow to Radolin, No. 6644, May 1, 1905, *Ibid.*, 353-355.

97. Because he was considered too conciliatory, William II was kept ignorant of many of the Bülow-Holstein maneuvers and was not informed of Rouvier's offer of a general colonial settlement until two years later. Then he declared that "the whole of this stupid Algeciras Conference would never have taken place" if he had known of it at the time. Brandenburg, *From Bismarck to the World War,* 250.

98. Monts to F. O., No. 6648, May 2, 1905, *G. P.,* XX, 362; Bülow to Monts, No. 6649, May 3, 1905, *Ibid.*, 363-364. Bülow, *Memoirs,* II, 133.

99. Memorandum of Holstein, No. 6646, *G. P.,* XX, 357-359; Bülow to F. O., No. 6652, May 5, 1905, *Ibid.*, 368-369.

100. Bülow to Tattenbach, No. 6643, April 30, 1905, *Ibid.*, 352. Bülow exposed his motives to Rouvier; on May 7 he suggested that France herself call the conference, since it could have only negative results in relation to Morocco, but would remove the danger of conflict and would keep the future free for the interested powers. Bülow to Radolin, No. 6650, May 5, 1905, *Ibid.,* 364-367. Rouvier refused; Radolin to F. O., No. 6655, May 7, 1905, *Ibid.,* 371-372.

101. Bülow, *Memoirs,* II, 121-122.

102. Jusserand to Delcassé, April 7, 1905, D. D. F., Sér. 2, VI, 309-310. As usual, Jusserand tactfully reminded the United States of "its aid from us at the time of its own difficulties in Morocco."

103. Bülow to William II, No. 6599, April 4, 1905, G. P., XX, 302-303; Memorandum of Holstein, No. 6601, April 4, 1905, Ibid., 304-305; Bülow to Kühlmann, No. 6604, April 6, 1905, Ibid., 307.

104. Delcassé to Jusserand, April 13, 1905, D. D. F., Sér. 2, VI, 350-351.

105. Jusserand to Delcassé, April 14, 1905, Ibid., 363-364.

106. Roosevelt to Taft, April 20, 1905, Bishop, Theodore Roosevelt, I, 471-473.

107. Sternburg, to F. O., No. 6633, April 25, 1905, G. P., XX, 341-342; Roosevelt to Sternburg, April 20, 1905, Bishop, Theodore Roosevelt, I, 473-474.

108. Metternich to F. O., No. 6845, April 19, 1905, G. P., XX, 608-609.

109. Bülow to Sternburg, No. 6634, April 27, 1905, Ibid., 342-344. If a discussion should arise before Roosevelt's return, Sternburg was to point out that a conference was the only certain, peaceful means of guarding the Open Door against France's treaty-breaking encroachments. Refusal of a conference by England would lay her open to the suspicion of having intended to dispose of her own interests, as well as those of other powers, by the agreement of 1904.

110. Durand to Lansdowne, April 26, 1905, B. D., III, 67-68.

111. Lansdowne suggested that Germany might be trying to secure a port in Morocco. Lansdowne to Durand, April 26, 1905, B. D., III, 67-68. On April 26, Spring-Rice wrote to Mrs. Roosevelt: "The Germans have taken advantage of the Russians being taken up to fall on the French .... I see they are asking your President to join in a Conference which will

bring the French to order. I hope he won't." Gwynn, Spring-Rice, I, 469.

112. Bülow to Sternburg, No. 6851, May 10, 1905, G. P., XX, 620-623.

113. Bishop, Theodore Roosevelt, I, 469-470.

114. Sternburg to F. O., No. 6852, May 13, 1905, G. P., XX, 622-623. On May 15 Roosevelt wrote to Lodge, then in Europe: "It always amuses me to find that the English think that I am under the influence of the Kaiser." On May 24 he wrote: "When you see King Edward, explain my very real pleasure that we are able to work together in the Far East. Also say that I appreciate thoroughly that in the long run the English people are more apt to be friendly to us than any other." Roosevelt-Lodge Correspondence, II, 123-125. Roosevelt was still working hard to gain British cooperation in ending the Russo-Japanese war.

115. Sternburg to F. O., No. 6308, May 19, 1905, G. P., XIX, 603-604.

116. Bülow to Sternburg, No. 6667, May 25, 1905, Ibid., XX, and No. 6668, May 30, 1905, Ibid., 385-388; Bishop, Theodore Roosevelt, I, 470-471.

117. Tattenbach to F. O., No. 6672, May 28, 1905, G. P., XX, 392.

118. Anderson, First Moroccan Crisis, 220-221.

119. Ibid., 221-225.

120. Radolin to Bülow, No. 6685, June 11, 1905, G. P., XX, 407-409; Schuman, War and Diplomacy in the French Republic, 178, 180-182; Anderson, First Moroccan Crisis, 228, 231; W. B. Harris, "Morocco Crisis," (Aug., 1905), 295-297.

121. Anderson, First Moroccan Crisis, 232; Hale, Germany and the Diplomatic Revolution, 131-133.

122. Ibid., 156-159.

123. Newton, Lansdowne, 341-342.

124. Royal Cortissoz, Life of Whitelaw Reid, 2 vols, (hereafter cited as Cortissoz, Reid), II, 326-327.

125. Hay had not been informed of Roosevelt's involvement in the Moroccan imbroglio. On July 11 Roosevelt wrote Lodge: "I became the intermediary between Germany and France when they seemed to have gotten into an impasse .... Even Whitelaw Reid does not know it. I had told Taft but not Hay. I shall tell Root." Roosevelt-Lodge Correspondence, II, 166.

126. John Hay to Henry Adams, June 7, 1905; Thayer, John Hay, II, 404.

127. On June 7 the Kaiser expressed to Gen. Lacroix his "conviction that now everything was in the best of order. He had never attached any value to Morocco, he gladly gave it to the French. This ... greatly increased the difficulties of our negotiations with France up to the conference of Algeciras. Holstein wrote me ... in the autumn of 1905: 'while we were working ... to bring the Morocco Struggle to an end which should satisfy both our economic and our political interests, His Majesty had given things up long ago. The French knew this, but our people did not, and so were without any solution to the riddle of why the French Government was soft and yielding before the return of Gen. Lacroix, but tough and tenacious after it. The French had had the direct acceptance of their Moroccan demand from the Kaiser.'" Bülow, Memoirs, II, 137-139.

128. Hale, Germany and the Diplomatic Revolution, 155-156.

129. Jusserand to Delcassé, May 8, May 15, and May 16, 1905, D. D. F., Sér. 2, VI, 488, 509-513.

130. Dennett, Roosevelt and the Russo-Japanese War, 189.

131. The Kaiser to the Tsar, June 3, 1905, Bishop, Theodore Roosevelt, I, 385. Of Roosevelt, the Kaiser wrote: "Should it meet with your approval, I could easily place myself--privately--en rapport with him, as we are very intimate; also, my ambassador is a friend of his."

132. Tower to Roosevelt, June 4, 1905, Ibid., 384-385; Bülow to Sternburg, No. 6312, June 3, 1905, G. P., XIX, 607.

133. Roosevelt to Lodge, June 5, 1905, Dennett, Roosevelt and the Russo-Japanese War, 191.

134. Ibid., 195-196.

135. Ibid., 197-207.

136. Lansdowne to Harding, April 13, 1905: "I am very apprehensive as to ... ill-advised and premature attempts to bring about peace negotiations .... I suspect Roosevelt has been over-anxious in this direction, and, as usual, there has been a good deal of indiscretion as to his sayings and doings," Newton, Lansdowne, 322.

137. Dennett, Roosevelt and the Russo-Japanese War, 210-211.

138. Bülow to Flotow, No. 6687, June 5, (sent on June 6), G. P., XX, 413-415. The same dispatch was sent to the German ambassadors in all the countries signatories of the Madrid treaty.

139. Bülow to Tattenbach, No. 6686, June 5, 1905, Ibid., 413.

140. Anderson, First Moroccan Crisis, 235-236.

141. Flotow to F. O., No. 6700, June 9, 1905, G. P., XX, 425. The Kaiser, who knew nothing of any definite offers, put a marginal comment, "Gut, alles was wir wollen" on a reported wish of Rouvier for an understanding, quoted in a dispatch from Radolin

to Rouvier, June 11, 1905, No. 6685, Ibid., 407-409.

142. Radolin to F. O., No. 6705, June 11, 1905, Ibid., 430-431.

143. Bülow to Radolin, No. 6706, June 12, 1905, Ibid., 431-432; Radolin to F. O., No. 6710, June 14, 1905, Ibid., 438-439.

144. Lansdowne to Lowther, June 5, 1905, B. D., III, 89.

145. Lansdowne to Durand, June 5, 1905, Ibid., 89-90.

146. Metternich to F. O., No. 6697, June 8, 1905, G. P., XX, 422.

147. Sternburg to F. O., No. 6696, June 8, 1905, Ibid., and Bülow to Sternburg, June 9, 1905, note 2, Ibid., 421-422. Jusserand said that Roosevelt refused to attend a conference because it was unacceptable to France. Jusserand to Rouvier, June 6, 1905, D. D. F., Sér. 2, VI, 596-597.

148. Bülow to Sternburg, No. 6856, June 10, 1905, G. P., XX, 626-628; Bishop, Theodore Roosevelt, I, 476-477.

149. Sternburg to Bülow, No. 6707, June 12, 1905, G. P., XX, 433-434.

150. Bülow to Tattenbach, No. 6718, June 19, 1905, Ibid., 448-451.

151. Bihourd to Delcassé, April 5, 1905, D. D. F., Sér. 2, VI, 302-303. Bihourd called attention to propaganda in the German press, especially in the Lokal Anzeiger of April 5: "One can hardly admit that the United States, which has intervened with such energy for the right of the Open Door in the Far East and more recently in Abyssinia in opposition to the projects of England, France, and Italy would accept an injury to her contract rights which would necessarily result from the recent arrangements between England, France, and Spain."

152. Reid to the State Dept., June 7, 1905; B. D., III, 91.

153. Telegram of Saint-René Taillandier, shown to Roosevelt by Jusserand; cited by Vagts, Weltpolitik, footnote 2, 1857, II; from Roosevelt MSS.

154. Vagts, Weltpolitik, II, 1860-1861.

155. Sternburg, to F. O., No. 6713, June 17, 1905, G. P., XX, 442-443. "As I hear, after the reception of Hay in London ... an exchange of telegrams took place between Mr. Hay and the President, through which the former tried to win the President over to England's position on the Morocco question. That he has not succeeded, I could clearly discover today from the President's remarks."

156. Jusserand, What Me Befell, 318-319; Bishop, Theodore Roosevelt, I, 478.

157. Bülow to Radolin, No. 6711, June 16, 1905, G. P., XX, 439-441; Anderson, First Moroccan Crisis, 242.

158. Lansdowne to Bertie, June 16, 1905, B. D., III, 96-97.

159. Radolin to F. O., No. 6720, June 21, 1905, G. P., XX, 452-453. "The Government of the Republic is deeply impressed by the double consideration that the Conference may be dangerous if it is not preceded by an entente, and useless if it follows one. Nevertheless, the French Government did not refuse the conference. It desires solely to know what are, in the mind of the Imperial Government, the precise points which will be treated at the Conference and the solutions which it will offer there." Anderson, First Moroccan Crisis, 245.

160. Bülow had decided to force Rouvier to abandon his "Delcassé program" and had threatened to support the Sultan against France. Bülow to William II, No. 6723, June 22, 1905, G. P., XX, 455-457; Bülow to Radolin, No. 6726, June 23, 1905, Ibid., 461-463 and No. 6730, June 24, 1905, Ibid., 465-466. Roosevelt does not record his reaction to

Sternburg's plea of June 18 that he help promote a German-Spanish concert in Morocco, because with Spain in charge of reforms in Tangier the Mediterranean would be kept open. Roosevelt MSS, cited by Vagts, Weltpolitik, II, 1859.

161. Bishop, Theodore Roosevelt, I, 478-480.

162. Roosevelt to Sternburg, June 23, 1905, Ibid., 482; Sternburg to F. O., No. 6731, June 24, 1905, G. P., XX, 466-467; Bülow to William II, No. 6732, June 25, 1905, Ibid., 467-469.

163. Sternburg to the F. O., No. 6738, June 25, 1905, Ibid., 473-474; Roosevelt to Sternburg, June 25, 1905, Bishop, Theodore Roosevelt, I, 483-485. "I feel that he (William II) stands as the leader among the sovereigns of to-day who have their faces set toward the future, and that it is ... of the utmost importance for all mankind that his power and leadership for good should be unimpaired." Thus spoke Roosevelt.

164. Bülow to Sternburg, No. 6739, June 26, 1905, G. P., XX, 475-476.

165. Sternburg to F. O., No. 6742, Ibid., 479-480. Sternburg quoted Roosevelt: "Germany can then discuss the program with France, that it requires the integrity of Morocco, the maintenance of her government, the Open Door, equality of rights for all foreigners, refraining from interference in the domestic and foreign affairs of the empire and in army questions. Only in the reform questions I must stay out and leave these to the European powers."

166. Anderson, First Moroccan Crisis, 247.

167. Radolin to F. O., No. 6746, June 27 (sent June 28), 1905, G. P., XX, 485-486.

168. Radolin to F. O., No. 6741, June 26, 1905, Ibid., 479; Radolin to Bülow, No. 6745, June 26, 1905, Ibid., 483-484.

169. Bishop, Theodore Roosevelt, I, 485-486; Sternburg to F. O., No. 6743, June 27, 1905, G. P., XX, 480-481; Jusserand, What Me Befell, 319-320.

170. Roosevelt told Jusserand: "Let not people in France take it amiss if I am found particularly flattering toward the Emperor." On June 30, 1905, Jusserand cabled his government: "You may be assured that the President will support, to the best of his ability, the programme you have adopted .... Moreover, one may wonder whether Emperor William really means to go to extremes .... The risk for the Emperor would ... be considerable, now that he has so managed as to cause everybody to mistrust him and that he has collected enmities throughout Europe." Ibid., 320-321.

171. Lister to Lansdowne, June 28, 1905, B. D., III, 107-108.

172. Bülow to Sternburg, No. 6744, June 27, 1905, G. P., XX, 481-482: "If after acceptance of the conference is received from France and we are negotiating with the French and thereby a diversity of opinions should arise, I shall be ready at all times to recommend to His Majesty the Kaiser the same decisions as President Roosevelt will commend as practical and fair." Sternburg to Roosevelt, June 28, 1905, Bishop, Theodore Roosevelt, I, 477: "The Emperor has requested me to tell you that in case during the conference differences of opinion should arise between France and Germany, he, in every case, will be ready to back up the decision which you should consider to be the most fair and practical." In the original message, Bülow was obviously speaking for himself and was referring to the negotiations for a conference program which were expected to begin soon.

173. Eckardstein to Holstein, June 28, 1905, quoted by Vagts, Weltpolitik, II, 1865.

174. Lansdowne to the State Dept., June 30, 1905, Ibid., 1872.

175. Lansdowne to Bertie, July 1, 1905, B. D., III, 110-111.

176. The text of the agreement of July 8 is given in the following: Tardieu, La Conférence, 482-483; B. D., III, 115-116; Documents Diplomatiques, Affaires du Maroc, 1901-1905, 251-252.

177. Radolin's promise is cited in the Memorandum by Hugh O'Beirne enclosed with the dispatch, Bertie to Gray, Dec. 15, 1905, B. D., III, 155.

178. Smith to Lansdowne, July 31, 1905, Ibid., 124. All of the signatories of the Madrid convention accepted except Norway, recently independent from Sweden. Russia, an adherent to the treaty of 1880, also accepted.

179. Lansdowne to Lister, July 6, 1905, Ibid., 114.

180. Roosevelt, to Lodge, July 11, 1905, Roosevelt-Lodge Correspondence, II, 167: "A still more extraordinary thing is that the Emperor should have sent through Speck a statement that he should instruct his delegate to vote as the United States delegate does on any point where I consider it desirable. This is a point, however, about which I shall be very wary of availing myself." This is the Rooseveltian distortion of Sternburg's garbled version of Bülow's statement of June 27.

181. Sternburg to Roosevelt, from Berlin, July 24, 1905; cited by Vagts, Weltpolitik, II, 1870.

182. Bussche-Haddenhausen to the F. O., No. 6778, July 25, 1905, G. P., XX, 528-529. Roosevelt telegraphed Jusserand on July 26: "For God's sake, do not have the slightest fear of ruffling my feelings. My only desire is to do what you think wisest and safest." Jusserand, What Me Befell, 321.

183. Bussche-Haddenhausen to F. O., No. 6779, July 30, 1905, G. P., XX, 529; Bülow to William II, No. 6786, Aug. 3, 1905, Ibid., 537; Anderson, First Moroccan Crisis, 348, footnote 1.

184. Dennett, Roosevelt and the Russo-Japanese War, 206-207.

185. Ibid., 242.

186. Roosevelt to Spring-Rice, July 24, 1905, Gwynn, Spring-Rice, I, 478-480; Spring-Rice to Lansdowne, Aug. 6, 1905, Ibid., 480-481; Spring-Rice to Mrs. Roosevelt, Aug. 10, 1905, Ibid., 483-485.

187. Roosevelt to Jusserand, Aug. 21, 1905, quoted by Pringle, Roosevelt, 385-386.

188. Bülow to Sternburg, No. 6323, Aug. 17, 1905, G. P., XIX, 617-618; Sternburg to Roosevelt, Aug. 18, 1905, quoted by Dennett, Roosevelt and the Russo-Japanese War, 165.

189. Roosevelt to William II, Aug. 27, 1905, Bishop, Theodore Roosevelt, I, 411; Bussche-Haddenhausen to F. O., No. 6325 and footnotes, received Aug. 23, 1905, G. P., XIX, 619-621.

190. Bishop, Theodore Roosevelt, I, 412-413.

191. Roosevelt to Reid, Sept. 11, 1905, Ibid., 415: "I did not get much assistance from the English government, but I did get indirect assistance, for I learned that they forwarded my note to Durand, and I think that the signing of the Anglo-Japanese Treaty made Japan feel comparatively safe as to the future." Pribram, in England and the European Great Powers, 115, gives Great Britain full credit for persuading Japan to grant Russia reasonable peace terms and makes no mention whatever of any part played by either Roosevelt or William II.

192. "The Kaiser did his level best, but neither he nor I had much effect upon the Czar, although doubtless what he did helped make the Czar cede the south half of Saghalin. The Kaiser behaved very well in this business." Roosevelt to Lodge, Sept. 2, 1905, Roosevelt-Lodge Correspondence, II, 188.

193. Eulenberg to William II, Aug. 8, 1905, Haller, Philip Eulenburg, II, 152.

194. Witte, Memoirs, 422.

195. William II to Bülow, No. 6220, July 23, 1905, G. P., XIX, 458-465 summarizes the story of the making of the treaty and gives the text. See also Fay, Origins of the World War, I, 190.

196. Willy to Nicky, July 27, 1905, Levine, Letters from the Kaiser to the Tsar, 178-179.

197. "The 'Continental Combine' flanked by America, is the sole manner effectively to block the way to the whole world's becoming John Bull's private property." Willy to Nicky, Sept. 26, 1905, Ibid., 193-199.

198. "The Emperor and I have concluded an agreement to lend each other mutual help in case any European power should attack one of us, and France is to be the co-signatory to it .... The triple-alliance ... and the dual-alliance ... instead of glaring at each other for (no) purpose at all ... join hands and the peace of Europe is guaranteed. This is the fruit of our understanding with France about Morocco ... upon which you sent me so kind compliments. I am sure that this grouping of powers ... will be of great use in enabling you to fulfill the great mission of peace which Providence has entrusted to your hands for the good of the world." William II to Roosevelt, No. 6221, July 26, 1905, G. P., XX, 466; Fay, Origins of the World War, I, 191.

199. Tyler Dennett, "President Roosevelt's Secret Pact with Japan," Current History, XXI (Oct., 1924), 15-21.

200. For detailed accounts of the Kaiser's two failures to make secret pacts with the Tsar--The Russo-German Alliance of 1904 and the Björkö Treaty of 1905--see Fay, Origins of the World War, I, 172-177; Gooch, "Holstein," 79-83; Brandenburg, From Bismarck to the World War, 233-243; Witte, Memoirs, 425-429.

201. Radolin to F. O., No. 6836, Oct. 18, 1905, G. P., XX, 596-597.

202. Flotow to Bülow, No. 6901, Nov. 23, 1905, Ibid., XXI, 15-17.

203. William II to Bülow, No. 6255, Nov. 26, 1905, Ibid., XX, 524-525.

204. Sternburg to F. O., No. 6896, Nov. 3, 1905, Ibid., XXI, 9-11.

205. Bülow to Sternburg, No. 6897, Nov. 7, 1905, Ibid., 11-12. On October 3, 1905, Le Matin published an article which created tremendous excitement in Europe. It alleged that at his final Cabinet meeting Delcassé had revealed an offer of the British government to aid in resisting Germany's demands in Morocco, even to the extent of seizing the Kiel Canal and landing 100,000 men in Schleswig-Holstein. Official denials did little to convince the public of the falsity of the article.

206. Vagts, Weltpolitik, II, 1853-1854, footnote 3.

207. Sykes, Durand, 287-288.

208. Lee, King Edward VII, II, 433-434.

209. Ibid., II, 345-346. On August 22 Willy thought that the naval entente called for a warning to Nicky. "The British have prostituted themselves before France and the French sailors in the hopes of gaining them over from you and stopping any 'rapprochement' between you, me, and them ... I hope that sensible people have ... seen that ... Britain only wants to make France her 'catspaw' against us, as she used Japan against you." Levine, Letters from the Kaiser to the Czar, 197.

210. "The Reception of Prince Louis," Independent, LIX (Nov. 9, 1905), 1073-1074.

211. Paul Morton, "An Anglo-American Navy," Independent, LIX, (July 6, 1905), 20-22.

212. "The Spirit of the Foreign Reviews," Review of Reviews, XXXII (Nov., 1905), 633.

213. Lodge to Roosevelt, July 2, 1905, Roosevelt-Lodge Correspondence, II, 162.

214. Lodge to Roosevelt, July 8, 1905, Ibid., 164; Mende, Horace Porter, 305-306.

215. Lodge to Roosevelt, July 25, 1905, Roosevelt-Lodge Correspondence, II, 170.

216. Lodge to Roosevelt, Aug. 14, 1905, Ibid., 172-173.

217. Bishop, Theodore Roosevelt, I, 448.

218. Nevins, Henry White, 243.

219. Roosevelt, Autobiography, 356-357.

220. F. R., 1905, 676. Einstein was the third secretary of the American Embassy in London.

221. Roosevelt to White, Aug. 23, 1905; "I want to keep on good terms with Germany, and if possible to prevent a rupture between Germany and France. But my sympathies have at bottom been with France and I suppose will continue so. Still I shall try to hold an even keel." Nevins, Henry White, 267.

222. For the personal and confidential letters of Root to White, see Philip C. Jessup, Elihu Root, 2 vols. (hereafter cited as Jessup, Root), II, 58-59.

223. Nevins, Henry White, 266-267. Both the British and the French governments were informed through their respective ambassadors in Washington that Root had instructed White not to weaken the Anglo-French entente. Durand to Grey, Jan. 11, 1906, B. D., III, 217; Jusserand, What Me Befell, 322.

224. "Germany's Problems," Review of Reviews, XXXIII (Jan., 1906), 18.

225. Report of an interview with Herr Beit; William II to Bülow, Dec. 30, 1905, Bülow, Memoirs, II, 215-216.

226. H. A. De Weerd, "John Fisher, Creator of the Modern British Navy," Current History, XXVIII (Sept., 1928), 916.

227. Newton, Lansdowne, 334-335.

228. Lee, King Edward VII, II, 441; Sontag, European Diplomatic History, 108.

229. Roosevelt to Root, Sept. 14, 1905: 'I particularly do not want to appear as a professional peace advocate--a kind of sublimated being of the Godkin or Schurz variety." Roosevelt-Lodge Correspondence, II, 201.

230. "Musings Without Method," Blackwood's Magazine, CLXXVIII, (Oct., 1905), 545-547.

Chapter VIII

The United States at Algeciras

Between the signing of the preliminary agreement to hold a conference and the meeting of the delegates at Algeciras, there was a period of great activity in diplomacy, propaganda, and preparation for a possible resort to arms. As the mirage of the diplomatic millenium which the Kaiser beheld from Björkö gradually faded, and as the American adherence to the Anglo-French entente became more evident, both of the principals in the coming conflict were recruiting allies by promises or threats. Thus the issue of the conference was practically predetermined; there remained however, those imponderables which tip the scales of the most carefully calculated balances of power.

The tedious and difficult negotiations resulting in the conference program on September 28, 1905, had been complicated by the activities of Count Tattenbach in Fez. He arranged a concession for the construction of a pier at Tangier by a German firm and a "temporary" loan to the Sultan by a German banking syndicate--the latter secured by some of the Sultan's personal property in land.[1]

Later, when Bülow sent Dr. Rosen to Paris, Rouvier offered to make terms with Germany on the Bagdad and Cameroon railways, in return for the latter's concession of a general mandate to France for the financial and police reforms in the whole of Morocco. The deadlock caused by Bülow's refusal was broken by Witte, who had been denied a loan for Russia until the settlement of the Moroccan dispute. Trusting in Witte's assurance that Rouvier had given his verbal promise not to request a mandate for western Morocco,[2] Radolin and Rosen yielded. The *liberum veto* conceded to Germany as a protection at the *conference*[3] was to prove too dangerous a weapon for her to use.

The conference program was a second triumph for France. Ambassador McCormick at Paris assured the

State Department on September 22:

> M. Rouvier has done, and will continue to do, everything possible to bring about an understanding with Germany .... He may be depended upon to act with caution of a financier, while making no political sacrifices of a humiliating character to France.[4]

Police reform and the suppresion of contraband dealing in arms were to be provided for by international agreement, except in the frontier region, where the regulation would continue to be an exclusive affair between France and Morocco. Extensive financial cooperation was to be given to the Maghzen by the creation of a State Bank, the stabilization of the coinage, and the advancing of funds to pay the police and to construct public works. A study was to be made of ways to improve the collection of customs and to create new revenues. The Maghzen was to agree not to alienate any of the public services for the profit of special interests, and the public works were to be let on contract without regard for nationality. The selection of Algeciras as a site of the conference was a part of the settlement.[5]

To gain further freedom at the conference, Rouvier made a declaration to the German government:

> Aside from the agreement to be signed between the two governments, I am not bound on any point .... The guarantee for Germany lies in the fact that, since the decisions of the conference must be unanimous, her opposition will suffice to prevent the general mandate from being given to us.[6]

The French and Spanish governments had already anticipated the nullification of the provision for freedom of access to concessions upon which the German government had been so insistent. By a secret accord of September 1, they not only reserved future economic concessions for French and Spanish groups and the presidency of the State Bank for a Frenchman, but they also selected their respective ports for police officers. The police were to be natives of Morocco, with Spanish officers at Tetuan and Larache and French officers at Rabat and Casablanca. A Franco-Spanish corps at Tangier was to be commanded by a Frenchman. The zones for the suppression of contraband arms were also delimited. France and Spain promised mutual support at the conference.[7]

With protests and misgivings, Abd al-Aziz accepted the program on October 22.[8] Secretary Root notified both the German and the French governments on November 2 that, as a signer of the Madrid Convention of 1880, the United States was ready to participate in the conference, later dated to begin on January 16.[9] The Sultan's invitations, sent on December 1, were accepted by all the signatory powers of the Madrid treaty.[10]

The violent anti-German diatribes in the French press during October,[11] coincident with the Tsar's first attempts to nullify the Björkö Treaty, revived the German fear of the dreaded Quadruple Alliance.[12] The gratitude and loyalty of Abd al-Aziz[13] did not blind Bülow to the fact that his chief task at Algeciras was to avoid isolation.[14] Being unaware that Rouvier was backing an overture for a secret pre-conference pact, the Chancellor rejected this[15] and turned resolutely to his difficult work of securing allies.

Early in December, the speeches of Bülow and Rouvier before their respective parliaments served as public declarations of policy. Germany claimed to be defending the treaty right of all nations to the Open Door, which was menaced by France's disturbances of the _status quo_.[16] Denying any intention to impair the independence of Morocco or the economic equality of other nations,[17] Rouvier placed the special interest of France in police and financial reforms on a broader basis than ever before.

> The special situation that we occupy in Morocco does not arise from the contiguity of our frontiers .... It consists in the fact that France is the great Moslem Power of Northern Africa ... and that the community of languages and religion and race which draws this population to that of Morocco makes it susceptible to all the excitements that may develop in the neighboring state, either from the absence of a regular government or from the institution of a hostile government.[18]

Bülow foresaw three possible results of the conference--a provisorium of three years, when the matter would be re-examined; a separate agreement with France; or a French police mandate for Western Morocco.[19] Nevertheless, he instructed the German delegates to stand for his publicly declared principles--the Open Door, economic equality, opposition to French monopoly in loans and police control, and an international bank. If the police mandate were divided into areas, Germany was to claim her share, preferably a port with possibilities for later expansion into the interior. Isolation was to be avoided at all costs.[20]

Since Germany had learned about the secret Franco-Spanish pact, Bülow probably did not expect a favorable response to the Kaiser's bid for Spain's support; yet Spanish jealousy for France might be exploited.[21] The expected aid from the ally, Austria-Hungary, was pledged.[22] Although Italy was not tempted by Bülow's tentative offer to support her for a police mandate, she could reasonably be expected to exert a conciliatory influence, especially since she was represented by Marquis Visconti Venosta.[23]

Of the support of the United States, the German government was still confident. A report concerning the professed aims of the German delegates was sent to the President on January 6. It was pointed out also that conflict with France could arise only if she threatened the Open Door, and that a French police mandate for all of Morocco would "make the principle of the Open Door practically and in reality wholly illusory." The German police plan was to place the control outside the frontier regions under several powers jointly or under one of the larger or smaller states.[24]

While Bülow was giving his objectives publicity in the American press,[25] the State Department was receiving from its representatives abroad disquieting reports of Germany's aggressive aims. To the tales of suspicion and dread that White heard in Rome, were added reports sent to him by Root. Meyer wrote from Russia that the French were urging the Tsar to appeal to the Kaiser personally not to force hostilities. Meyre added, "in the event of certain circumstances, the President of the United States of all persons may have an opportunity to exercise moral influence with both France and Germany."[26] McCormick wrote from

Berlin that both Lansdowne and Grey had pledged British support to France; he thought the really dangerous antagonism in Europe was the Anglo-German hostility.[27] Rouvier was bargaining for American backing by suspending the execution of a law safeguarding French investors from practices of American insurance companies, then being accused of shady transactions at home and abroad.[28]

Meanwhile, Anglo-American relations continued good. Even to Durand, Roosevelt did not hesitate to express his loyalty to British policy:

> My business was to convey to him Sir Edward Grey's message to the effect that the views of His Majesty's government as to our relations with America were the same as Lord Lansdowne's. The President ... wanted to be on good terms with all countries, but he regarded England as the one country with which America ought to be on terms of close and confidential friendship.[29]

Grey sent another message through Reid, who visited the United States in December. Grey had recently spoken of good relations with the United States as the fundamental principle of his foreign policy. In a letter to Roosevelt, Reid urged the President to show as great cordiality to King Edward as to the Kaiser; the former, he said, was regarded in Europe as "the greatest mainstay of peace."[30]

German relations with Great Britain were the doubtful and, therefore, the dangerous quantity in the equation which the Wilhelmstrasse was trying to solve. The German government was disappointed in its hope of a more friendly attitude from the new Liberal government with Sir Edward Grey in the Foreign Office.[31] With his well established anti-German bias, Grey combined a firm conviction that both the honor and the interests of Great Britain demanded the upholding of the Anglo-French entente.[32] He was not converted by Metternich's explanations of German policy.[33] On January 3 and 10 he warned the German ambassador that British public opinion[34] might demand intervention if France were attacked.[35] Holstein was equally unsuccessful in trying to get the British government to hint that it might not support a French invasion of Morocco. Grey refused to deprecate any action of France which came within the terms of the Anglo-French declaration.[36] He likewise refused to endorse Bülow's plan for an international police force; Rosen had admitted that German policy on the Moroccan police was founded on the fact that if Morocco became a recruiting field, the whole of France's North African army might be thrown against Germany in the dreaded war of revenge.[37] Holstein was decidedly pessimistic about Germany's prospects:

> Will England ... cover the French flank with her armed hand in the conquest of Morocco? .... That would mean that after receiving compensation for her sacrifice, England joins France in forcing the other treaty states to yield without similar compensation .... If England confines herself to her diplomatic role, ... the conference will end in peace and honor for all parties. (In case of war) America would be the only winning party, and it is further evidence of the lofty viewpoint of President Roosevelt, that nevertheless he has never ceased to strive for an improvement of Anglo-German relations.[38]

Bülow concluded that the whole issue of peace and the Open Door depended upon whether France was counting on armed as well as diplomatic support from Great Britain.[39] The German leaders had some hope because King Edward seemed more friendly and was corresponding again with his nephew.[40]

In his official instructions as delegate to the conference, Nicolson was directed to support his French colleague and to encourage the Spanish delegate to do likewise.[41] Later, private instructions emphasized the British aim to help to secure recognition of France's special position in Morocco, reserving the right to sanction any concessions offered by France.[42] On December 22, Grey publicly affirmed his adhesion to the policy of the Entente Cordiale[43] and informed the French government of his loyalty. It was agreed that the British and the French delegates should act in close cooperation,[44] and King Edward also promised unreserved support for France.[45]

The Anglo-French cooperation included not only the planning of the conference procedure and the instructions to the French delegates,[46] but also diplomatic pressure on other countries and the completion of plans for naval and military action. It was decided to reserve the difficult police question until the last and to support a Franco-Spanish mandate as a practical rather than a political measure.[47]

Having received early assurances of the satisfactory attitude of Austria-Hungary and Belgium,[48] Rouvier welcomed British assistance in influencing Italy and Spain.[49] Italy would not promise to flout her alliance openly,[50] and Grey rather feared Visconti Venosta's mediation.[51] Although Spain declared her adherence to her entente partners, they continued to regard her with suspicion.[52] A tight rein was kept on Russia by the refusal of both the French and the British governments to sanction the loan desperately needed to suppress the revolution until she had delivered her support at Algeciras.[53]

In striking contrast to Germany, which made no preparations for war,[54] the Anglo-French group proceeded to perfect its plans for a possible conflict.[55] The official Anglo-French naval conversations begun the previous summer were continued. Unofficial military conversations, made official by January 17 and extended to include planning with the Belgian general staff, supplemented the work of the British Committee on Imperial Defence.[56] However, Grey declined to give France that definite assurance of British aid that would have transformed the entente into an alliance. He depended upon the uncertainty of the British attitude to restrain both France and Germany.[57]

It was a matter of self-congratulation to Grey and Rouvier that Root had officially promised American support to preserve the Anglo-French entente. Moreover, from their viewpoint, Henry White was a most satisfactory colleague. He had a deep personal attachment to France, and most of his political career had been spent in promoting Anglo-American friendship. Through his present association with Marquis Visconti Venosta at Rome, he might be expected to exert desirable influence upon Italy. Because of his tact, poise, and geniality, he placed himself quickly on terms of cordial intimacy with all the delegates and became an ideal mediator.[58]

The delegates assembled at Algeciras were on the

whole an interesting and important group of diplomats. Besides White, Nicolson, and Venosta, the first delegates were: Germany, Radowitz; Austria-Hungary, Welserheimb; Belgium, Joostens; Spain, Almodovar; France, Révoil; the Netherlands, Testa; Portugal, Tovar; Russia, Cassini; Sweden, Sager; Morocco, Sid Muhammad Torres. The sixty-one Moorish delegates in their flowing robes were supernumeraries at this meeting called by their own sovereign, and played scarcely any part except as subjects of camera studies to illustrate magazine articles. Italy, Portugal, Belgium, the United States, Austria-Hungary, and Russia sent as their second delegates their representatives at Tangier. Great Britain, the Netherlands, and Sweden each sent only one delegate.[59]

There are two interesting characterizations of the delegates. Henry White's descriptions may be summarized thus:

> Nicolson--quiet, with invaluable reserve and shrewdness, firm, tactful; Venosta--venerable, the most commanding personality, desirous of acting as conciliator; Cassini, neither liked nor trusted by White; Révoil--a highly trained lawyer, with a mind that ran too much to formulas, excessively ingenious, subtle, and wordy, saved from worse blunders by Nicolson; Radowitz--aging, feeble, hesitant, dominated by his associates; Tattenbach--bustling, arrogant, dogmatic, ill-tempered, unable to see any but his own viewpoint, profoundly convinced of the untrustworthiness of the French.

In his son's biography of Nicolson is found this description, also summarized:

> Torres--octogenarian, pitiable, indignant; Almodovar--Arabian face, challenging but empty, retreating from difficulty behind the barrier of breeding; Venosta--dominating, experienced, rising above all by the glamour of years; Radowitz--gently arrogant, menacingly gentle, an instinctive and professional diplomatist, a soldier in the twirl of mustache and mind; Tattenbach--sergeant-major in face and voice, cracking rude jokes; Révoil--small man, smiling always, smiling at the brilliance of the epigrams he dared not make, smiling admirably at

> all the smaller powers; Cassini--sociable, insinuating, uncertain; Nicolson--shy, diffident, enragingly honest, stating his case in fluent Oxford French, fact upon fact, moderately, calmly, and with an authoritative certainty; White--conciliatory, ignorant, charming, so full of charm there was room for little else.[60]

The negotiators at Algeciras were greatly handicapped by the inadequate living accommodations. All of the delegates, except Nicolson, who had a house, stayed at the ornate Reina Cristina Hotel. There was no privacy from the numerous newspaper correspondents who swarmed from the other hotel into the delegates' quarters. These correspondents were a real nuisance, hampering the work of the conference:

> Half the newspaper correspondents of Europe seemed there, and the French journalists were especially troublesome, buttonholing delegates, putting their own opinions into the delegates' mouths, bringing out faked interviews, and irritating everybody .... The Reina Cristina ... was the paradise of prying reporters .... A delegate could not pass from room to room without being pursued by a pack of reporters famished for news .... In the evening, the correspondents feverishly roamed the parlors and smoking-room, pouncing with their questions on every hapless delegate. Rumors exploded on every hand, canards were being concocted in every corner.[61]

It was realized from the first that the official meetings in the conference hall would be merely a medium of recording decisions already reached in the numerous private discussions. The official reports of the proceedings, therefore, contain little of the real history of the conference. Although the foreign offices of the Great Powers carried on most of the actual transactions, yet the interplay of personalities at Algeciras and the influence of the press were undoubtedly factors of considerable importance. Beginning at once his role of conciliator, White had "little difficulty in winning the confidence of both sides."[62]

At the opening session on January 16, the Duke of Almodovar as presiding officer stated the objective of the conference to be the introduction of urgent and practical reforms based on the triple principle of sovereignty of the sultan, the integrity of his empire, and the Open Door.[63] Révoil, seconded by Radowitz, made a speech endorsing this objective. He also affirmed his adherence to the principles of adjudication of public works and non-alienation of public services to the profits of special interests.[64] The official American instructions had stressed these points as of particular interest to the United States. Following the speeches, the conference was set into motion. It was decided that as a committee of the whole, the delegates were to reach the unanimous decisions to be drafted by a committee of formulation and finally adopted by the whole body in official sessions. The secret discussions held by small groups of delegates of the leading powers became of paramount importance.[65] They served the double purpose of mediating to prevent a Franco-German conflict and of concealing from the Moroccans the dissensions among their saviors.[66] The America-Italian-Austrian delegates served as intermediaries between the German and Franco-British-Spanish-Russian groups.

As the chronicler of the unofficial and official meetings of the conference in his book La Conférence d'Algesiras, André Tardieu gives a contemporary account of great importance. Although extremely biased and chauvinistic, the book remains of value. Regarded as unofficial spokesman for the Quai d'Orsay, the editor of Le Temps was influential in directing the course of the proceedings. For many years, he was the only writer on the conference who acknowledged that the United States had played a part of any significance. His information presumably came from the French Foreign Office. Describing Tardieu's political journalism, Radolin remarked: "As is commonly said ... Tardieu considers himself the most important man in France."[67]

Between January 16 and February 20, while the secret negotiations on the important questions of the bank and the police were going on, the minor reforms were enacted. Little controversy was aroused over the provisions for the suppression of contraband of arms, the better collection of taxes, the creation of new revenues, the customs duties, the repression of fraud, and the declaration relating to public services and to public works.[68] Venturing to take the initiative in presenting a plan for an elaborate protective tariff system, the Moorish delegation was soon disabused of its mistaken idea that this evidence of modernism would win it a hearing at the conference.[69] The taxation project finally adopted gave foreign consuls the right to retain a percentage of the taxes on foreigners, which they were to collect. White's objection that this was an infringement upon the sultan's sovereignty was not pressed when the Spanish delegate dissented.[70]

While the principal opponents at Algeciras were keeping silent on the major issues,[71] Bülow sent for Roosevelt's consideration his second plan of police organization. Already the American press was showing apprehension concerning Germany's sinister motives; a New York Times editorial hoped that the probable election of M. Fallieres as president would not weaken France's policy at Algeciras:

> We are not of those who believe that the German Emperor desires or intends war. But there is much evidence that he desires prestige and influence and dreads "isolation" or the appearance of being negligible. He is capable of calling Germany sharply and rudely to the attention of those disposed to overlook her claims, and to do so by a course logically suggesting war. That beyond all reasonable doubt, he did do in the matter of Morocco last summer. He accomplished his purpose because France was unready. Apparently she is no longer unready, and it would be a great mistake if she did not take full advantage of her readiness. Her designs and her pretensions in Morocco are not of the noblest, but they are recognized as legitimate according to the "custom of the business" of European expansion; they are, if she maintains the Open Door, harmless to the rest of the world.[72]

But Bülow's offering of three alternatives was indicative of a desire to be reasonable--always within the bounds of his demand for internationalization. The first plan contemplated dividing the mandate for eight ports among the treaty powers, with priority for the Great Powers. The period of the mandate could be limited to prevent any chance of permanent occupation. Uniform regulations on arming and training of the police would prevent a conflict of policies. By the second plan, the police would be entrusted to one or several small powers, preferably to Switzerland, but not to Portugal or Belgium. Again the time of the mandate was to be limited. The third plan placed upon the sultan the obligation to maintain a police force under foreign officers at designated points. The selection of the officers could be made either by the sultan or be limited to certain nationalities, perhaps the smaller powers. Admitting that all of these plans had some defects, the Chancellor offered to consider any other solution suggested by the American government which might give permanent assurance of the Open Door.[73] White and Venosta at the same time delivered the German ideas on the police to the French and British delegates.[74] In Madrid the German ambassador tried to bargain for Spain's support, but without success.[75]

On January 23 Secretary Root replied that the United States could take no part in any police organization, but she was interested in it because of her advocacy of the Open Door. He thought Germany's third plan the best, but would discuss the question with the President.[76] On the other hand, White advised a mandate for Italy and considered the second and third German proposals thoroughly impractical. The Moroccan government, White said, would respect only police backed by a Great Power. "Italy is able to do it; her national vanity will be flattered; and it will serve as well her earnest desire to keep Germany from getting a foot-hold in the Mediterranean, which also accords with the French and British views." Root replied:

> The United States could not under any circumstances participate as a mandatory .... The third German alternative would seem to afford the happiest basis of a compromise, subject, however, to a special provision for policing the Spanish and French frontiers of Morocco.[77]

In view of Great Britain's continued support of France's aim to become predominat in Morocco, Sternburg was again reminded of the supreme importance of having the United States back a police plan that would maintain the Open Door.[78]

White immediately informed the French, British, and Italian delegates of the German proposals. Venosta had heard of this triple plan at Rome, but he thought that Germany's real desires were still being hidden. Tattenbach suggested a Franco-Spanish-Italian mandate, while the German ambassador in Madrid intimated there that Germany would want to be the fourth member of the mandatory group. Meanwhile, White reported that his plan of an Italian mandate seemed welcome to the German delegate. At this point, Révoil confessed himself perplexed at the numerous and contradictory plans emanating from the German side.[79]

On January 26 Bülow definitely gave up any idea of offering the police mandate to Italy. Holstein informed Sternburg that it was feared that Italy might transfer Morocco to France in exchange for Tripoli.[80] The prospect for securing active American support seemed very bright, but Bülow cautioned Radowitz against British mediation. White, he said, might be inducted into the role of mediator by allowing him to arrange any concession which the German delegation might make on minor matters. Bülow continued:

> Very confidentially, ... the Cabinet in Washington, with which we have secret separate negotiations, is still considering its attitude provisionally. According to the earlier reports of the Kaiser's ambassador in Washington, I might take it for granted that the American Government will incline toward that solution which will leave as intact as possible the authority of the Sultan. President Roosevelt expressed himself to this effect last summer. Accordingly, America would probably prefer that the Sultan entrust the police reform to foreigners in his service. In case the Cabinet in Washington declares for this view, we shall then follow. I pray you give no intimation of the foregoing to anyone, especially not to Mr. White. He is naturally under the influence of Visconti Venosta, and would perhaps give the latter a premature wink. But in the interests of Germany, the last-named plan of police reform would be preferred by me to an Italian general mandate.

On the same day, Radowitz reported to Bülow that White showed himself more understanding of the German viewpoint than the Italian delegate did.[81]

On January 24, in an article in Siècle, Lanessan had advocated a solution similar to the third plan already tentatively endorsed by the United States. Accordingly, Sternburg was instructed to ask the President to sponsor this plan, which would be as much in the interests of both peoples as had been the joint action of the American and German governments in obtaining the neutralization of China and the declaration of disinterestedness there by the other powers. "The simultaneous upholding of peace and insuring of the Open Door must call forth general satisfaction not only in America and Germany, but also in the rest of the world."[82] Celebrating the forty-seventh birthday of the Kaiser in the Reichstag on January 27, its president also associated the President with German policy:

> In the course of the past year the Emperor together with the high-minded President of the United States, cooperated to end the terrible war in the Far East. He has also aided in dispelling international difficulties in regard to Morocco. Since Charles V no German Kaiser has visited Africa, and Emperor William, by his visit to Tangier, led the Moroccan question in a direction favorable to Germany.[83]

Following Nicolson's advice, Radowitz and Révoil began direct conversations on January 25. The latter was unable to get any information as to German views on the police, but he agreed that the consideration of the plans for the State Bank should begin.[84] On January 29, Regnault outlined the French plan for the bank to Tattenbach. It was truly, as its author described it, a project that gave expression to "the preponderance of French economic interests in Morocco." As the German delegate was reminded, "The Open Door does not signify that those who are in the house must leave it."[85]

Asserting that France had already received her concession on the police question by Germany's grant of exclusive jurisdiction on the Algerian frontier,[86] Bülow refused to consider the suggestions of White and Venosta that German concessions on the bank might lead to a satisfactory understanding on the police.[87] On February 2 the Chancellor definitely rejected the French scheme for the bank[88] as contrary to the Open Door and equality of all nations, as guaranteed by article XVII of the Madrid Convention. He refused to admit the French claim to preference in making loans. To ensure a really international institution, he proposed the use of the Egyptian mixed codes and the equal division of the capital among the powers. Bülow was especially anxious for the participation of American, Austro-Hungarian, and Dutch banking groups.[89]

In the meantime, Bülow was pushing his third plan, now christened the "Lanessan plan." On January 30 Sternburg was directed to inform Root that the Lanessan proposal had been endorsed by both the Austrian and the Italian governments. Sternburg had already suggested that the President could avoid entanglement if White would sound out the various governments confidentially before making the Lanessan proposal formally.[90] The President and Root might be informed also, very confidentially, that the Tsar had declared himself unreservedly for the German viewpoint, especially on the Open Door. America, therefore, would run no risk in making the proposal.[91] White declared the Lanessan plan the best preliminary proposal and said that, after the Germans had made a financial proposition, he personally was prepared to introduce it--or so Radowitz reported.[92] A further argument for American support was furnished by the German rejection of the French bank plan, which would exclude the United States from participation in Moroccan investments.[93]

During the last week of January, however, the alleged support of Russia for the German cause proved to be a fallacy. On January 22 the Kaiser presented Witte with the chain and cross of the Order of the Red Eagle; on the 27th the Tsar's birthday luncheon toast to his "Brother, more than ally" inspired a reporter's comment, "There is no telling how soon the alliance will be allowed to pass into desuetude." The Tageblatt asserted on the 28th that the German plan to police Morocco by neutral powers, supported by the United States, Austria, and Italy, would not be opposed by Russia. On the same day, however, came the reaction--a Russian financial crisis, marked by inactivity in trading in Russian bonds on the Paris market.[94] France still controlled Russian finance.

The Lanessan article[95] aroused such violent opposition

in the French press that Rêvoil demanded from Radowitz immediate and direct negotiations on the police question. In their interview on February 3 the French delegate declared the Lanessan solution inacceptable, because the sultan did not possess the authority to make such a plan adequate. The French counter-proposal was a Franco-Spanish mandate with international regulations as to its form, extent, and control.[96] Radowitz replied that a Franco-Spanish police would be as objectionable as a French force.[97] Although White, Venosta, and Welsersheimb all volunteered to serve as mediators upon request,[98] there was no disputing the fact that by February 3 the conference had come to a serious deadlock on both of its important problems.

Still waiting for the tardy American reply, Bülow saw no occasion for compromise. On February 3, Tattenbach failed to convince Nicolson that British commerical interests would be better served if the latter urged police concessions on Rêvoil.[99] But Count Goluchowski promised Germany support on both the bank and the police issues "through thick and thin."[100] On February 5 White and Venosta suggested a possible compromise, whereby a third power might be associated as a control body over the French and Spanish officers.[101] Tardieu says that the Italian, American, and Russian delegates praised the French plan to Radowitz. White then rejected the idea of a third power, declared France's devotion to the Open Door sincere, and said he would recommend the Franco-Spanish plan at Washington.[102]

On February 6 Radowitz asked permission of his Foreign Office to propose a compromise of his own.[103] Bülow's reply was that the Austrian, American, Spanish,[104] and Italian governments were all apparently favorable to the Lanessan plan. The personal proposal of White and Venosta was scarcely different from the French plan, and Radowitz's idea was also unsatisfactory. Under the Lanessan plan, an effective control could be developed by giving the supervision of the police to the diplomatic corps in Tangier. In regard to the bank problem, Bülow was confident that the efforts of the German banker Mendelssohn to interest the bankers of The Netherlands, Austria-Hungary, and the United States would have great influence upon their respective governments. "We no longer have to fear isolation."[105]

At the same time, Bülow called Rouvier's attention to Germany's concessions on the frontier police and reminded him that a failure of the conference would mean a reversion to the status of the Madrid Convention.[106]

Acting upon White's advice, Root had decided that it would be inadvisable to accede to Bülow's request for an introduction of the Lanessan plan. White thought that proposals were premature until they had been discussed between the French and German delegates. It would be rash to introduce plans without cooperating in them later.[107] Another inhibitory force had been the anti-German arguments presented by Jusserand and Durand. The former successfully guarded Roosevelt and Root against "the sophistry of the German affirmations;" it was he who

> demonstrated that neither Germany nor anyone else could have 'conceded' anything concerning the Algerian-Moroccan frontier; ... claimed in consequence the right of France to defend in the rest of Morocco the 'special interest' recognized by Germany; and showed that police established by the Sultan would be inefficient, that the international police would be a source of conflicts; that France alone, with her Algerian officers, could efficiently organize this police--limited, however, to cities on the coast and perfectly reconcilable with commerical liberty.[108]

While Bülow was relying upon the mediation of the American and Austrian, and eventually the Italian delegates,[109] White had been reporting to Root the abortive German efforts to gain British and Spanish support.[110] On February 5 White cabled that he believed the failure of the conference certain unless Germany would recede.[111] Consequently, Sternburg's dispatch of February 8 promised nothing more than Root's further examination of the matter and discussion of it with Roosevelt. Rather disconcerting also had been Root's question about England's views.[112] Radowitz failed utterly in his endeavor to follow Bülow's instructions, for White and Venosta refused to submit to Révoil any proposal which did not include French or Franco-Spanish police as a basis. White was certain that France would never accept Bülow's latest proposition;[113] his Italian and Austrian colleagues agreed with him.[114] Sir Donald

Wallace also advised Radowitz to be content with the Franco-Spanish police with specific guarantees for the interests of other nations. "White, whom he sees daily, he recently finds very much inclined toward consideration for the *amour propre* of the French." Wallace was the correspondent of the London *Times.* On the next day Radowitz reported another refusal of White to offer mediation on any plan excluding French officers.[115] At long last Radowitz was beginning to understand White's real attitude.

Still Bülow refused to surrender, although a press battle raged. An interview by Tattenbach, appearing in the German papers on February 10, censured the French conduct of the negotiations and their whole Moroccan policy. Tardieu says that both White and Venosta were greatly incensed at Tattenbach's misrepresentations. By comparing notes the delegates discovered that each had received different versions and promises from the German delegates, but that Révoil, "smiling, conciliatory, mild, and amusing" had told them the truth. On February 8 the French Chamber compelled Jaures to withdraw an interpellation asking whether Rouvier accepted the responsibility for the press campaigns tending to create dangerous complications in the Moroccan affair.[116]

However, Bülow renewed his instructions to Radowitz to hold firm on his third plan, with two alternatives. The third plan, of course, was the third alternative suggested to Roosevelt on January 20, or essentially the Lanessan or Moroccan plan. The alternatives of plan three were choosing the police instructors from some minor power, such as the Netherlands, Switzerland, or Belgium, or permitting the Sultan free selection of them.[117] If the hoped for Austrian, American, Italian mediation should not materialize, Radowitz was to deal directly with Révoil. If the latter should reject both alternatives, he was to be asked to make a second French proposal in harmony with the conference principle of the equality of all nations. Révoil's rejection of all these suggestions would lead Radowitz back to Bülow's first plan, dividing Morocco into sectors, with the police in each under a different power. "This solution would also remove White's objection to the exclusion of French officers, since then France, like every other power prepared for it, would receive a mandate."[118] The official German documents do not support Tattenbach's assertion to White on February 8, to the effect that he had instructions to stand fast for the selection of police officers from several minor powers, each assigned a port by the conference.[119]

At Paris and Rome, likewise, the determination of the Wilhelmstrasse to resist further retreat was emphasized. Holstein directed that Rouvier be warned that the Kaiser would not disavow himself and that a failure of the conference would be less undesirable for Germany than the Tunisification of Morocco.[120] Bülow also complained to the new Italian government about Venosta's support of the French plans.[121]

The German Chancellor's peers were not impressed by his show of firmness. Expressing its full confidence in its delegate, the Italian Cabinet declined to take a positive stand in favor of either antagonist.[122] Since Welsersheimb regarded plan three as certain of rejection, and Goluchowski considered the first plan impracticable and hopeless, the Austrian government advised compromise or dissolution of the conference. Austria-Hungary was too near to civil conflict to support a war over Morocco.[123] Lamsdorff, who had already promised backing for the French police plan,[124] now advised the French government to obtain the cooperation of Great Britain, Italy, and the United States in backing the Russian intervention in Berlin.[125] Révoil advised his government to take no action on Lamsdorff's suggestion. Witte was very anxious for a settlement satisfactory to France--he was still waiting for financial aid.[126] In his message to Bülow, Lamsdorff gave the unreserved approval of himself and the Tsar to the French proposals.[127]

To Grey, Germany's rejection of the Franco-Spanish police mandate seemed capable of only one interpretation--her desire to see the conference fail. Otherwise, he could not explain her neglect to ask for more explicit guarantees for the Open Door, which France was willing to give. He refused to admit to Metternich any danger that from police control France would proceed to develop economic predominance. The French proposals alone seemed adequate to fulfill the two British objectives--order and the Open Door.[128]

Acting on his instructions of the previous day, on February 13 Radowitz consulted his American, Austrian, and Italian colleagues. All three advised a direct approach to Révoil; only the representatives of Germany's allies declared for the principle of organization of the police by the Sultan.[129] In the ensuing discussion with the French delegate, only the limiting of police officers to the smaller states was refused outright, and Révoil agreed to transmit the alternative proposal to his government.[130] The German police project now included a force organized and commanded by foreign officers freely selected by the sultan, paid from funds supplied by the State Bank, stationed in designated ports, and inspected by a superior officer from a secondary power, who was to report to the diplomatic corps at Tangier. The last body was to be charged with control over the workings of the police organization, which was to exist for a trial period of from three to five years.[131] The German plan claimed to reconcile the principles of the sovereignty of the Sultan and the internationalization of the police.

In his recapitulation of the German viewpoint on February 13, Bülow declared that no occasion for futher retreat existed. Still perversely logical, he pointed out that the concentration of either the police or the financial power in French hands would close the Open Door; the principle of sacrificing one's own interests, "merely because they obstruct the way of another Power, might lead to consequences which are so hazardous that we regard the wrecking of the Morocco conference as the lesser evil in comparison therewith."[132] Since both Havas and the English press were emphasizing the probability of American intervention, the Chancellor asked Sternburg to try to secure Root's permission for White to attempt adjustment of the police and the bank questions.[133] Bülow was still misinterpreting Root's long silence as support of Germany.

At Washington, Jusserand and White had been outmaneuvering Sternburg. The Tsar's personal intervention with the Kaiser, pledged by Lamsdorff, was being held in reserve. Early in February Roosevelt agreed to perform a similar service. He would await a favorable occasion and avoid compromising his success by a premature initiative.[134] White was compelled to deny Radowitz's assertion that Root supported the German plan and had instructed the American delegation to do likewise. The Kaiser, White reported to the State Department, was probably not really informed about conditions at Algeciras.[135] Root declared his readiness to send an independent statement directly to the German ruler.[136] On February 11 White cabled his opinion that the conference would fail unless the German government could be induced to accept the French position in principle. Conversations with the Austrian delegate had confirmed his impression that the Kaiser was being kept ignorant of the real situation.[137] Nicolson was informed of White's opinions and proposals to Root.[138]

Since February 11 the American press had presented news, articles, and editorials presaging the failure of the conference.[139] Suddenly, on the 14th, headlines over dispatches from London announced that Roosevelt would end the Moroccan controversy and that White was waiting only for a favorable opportunity to present a plan believed acceptable to both parties.[140] The plan for American intervention was quickly deprecated or denied. On February 15 and 16 the New York Times presented contradictory reports. Its first statement was:

> The Ambassador's basic instructions look to the extension of his good offices wherever they can be prudently offered in order to prevent a failure of the conference. It is believed at the State Department that there is a middle ground between the extreme French and German views ... and it is not doubted that Mr. White will endeavor to bring about a compromise if there is promise of success attending his efforts.

On the next day the Times interpreted the demand of Le Temps for a public discussion as indicative of France's desire to end "the efforts which Ambassador White, the Marquis Visconti Venosta, and other representatives ... are making to obtain a private accord." A London dispatch was also quoted:

> Mr. White informs me that the rumors that the United States will arbitrate the differences between France and Germany are absolutely imaginary .... In the event of a failure to reach an understanding, Mr. White thinks it would be best to terminate the conference rapidly.[141]

The press reports of White's activities rested upon a solid basis of fact. White informed Root on February 13 of the unacceptable proposals made by Radowitz on that day. While he was urging France to admit the principle of police inspection by a third power, preferably Italy, he suggested that the President be ready to exert pressure on William II after the expected rejection of the German plan. Through Root, Roosevelt asked immediately for White's opinion of what would be a fair settlement of the issues.[142] Accordingly, when Révoil requested White to intervene on the basis of certain concessions that he was prepared to make, the latter promised not only to present the French project as an American one, but also to have Roosevelt recommend it as such to the German Emperor.[143] The conclusion of the arrangement between White and Révoil occurred on the same day that Grey considered offering a compromise. Grey's idea was the acceptance of the German proposal of February 13, with the head officer French or selected by the French government. He was uncertain whether to propose this through Nicolson to Révoil or directly to Cambon.[144] Rouvier refused Radolin's request for direct discussions at Paris,[145] and Cambon recommended to Grey either American or Italian mediation. Cambon also had a plan, including a French or one French and one Spanish inspector, reporting to the diplomatic corps. He feared that, because of the recent objections of the American Senate to the sending of delegates to Algeciras, President Roosevelt might be reluctant to assume the responsibility.[146]

After long talks with both Révoil and Radowitz, White drew up a series of suggestions for Roosevelt on the basis of the memorandum received from the former.[147] The propositions conformed to the position maintained by Rouvier, who denied having renounced to Dr. Rosen the claiming of a police mandate.[148] The White-Révoil plan included a Moroccan police in the ports, organized and under the nominal authority of the sultan; French and Spanish higher and non-commissioned officers to instruct, manage, pay, discipline, and assist in control of the rank and file; an annual report by the senior French and Spanish officers to the sultan and to the Italian government, the latter of which should communicate it to the powers; and an international bank, furnishing funds for the police, owned in substantially equal shares by all the powers, with a slight preference for France.

The French concession of Italian surveillance was made only on condition that Germany accept previously the Franco-Spanish police. White believed that a direct communication to the Kaiser would secure Germany's agreement to this plan.[149]

The official reply of the French government was presented to Radowitz on February 16. It accepted in principle police organization by the Sultan, payment by the State Bank, and the short duration of the institution, providing that the officers be French and Spanish.[150] White had already declined to recommend Rouvier's suggestion that delegates of the eight Great Powers meet informally to seek for an acceptable solution.[151] The American, British, and French delegates now agreed that public discussion of the police problem must follow the failure to reach a private agreement. White said that he would ask permission to leave the conference if the police question were dropped without a solution.[152]

On February 17 Count Goluchowski began the drive to secure Germany's acceptance of the French proposal. He urged upon Bülow the possibility of compensation in the bank question and the approval of White and Venosta of the French plan as reasons for yielding.[153] Radowitz also was pressed by Welsersheimb and White to recognize this success for German diplomacy.[154] Nevertheless, Bülow rejected the Franco-Spanish police as incompatible with the principle of internationalization--a much-worn formula--and again requested a French project which would accord with the declared principles of the conference.[155]

The prolongation of the negotiations had thus far served to strengthen the cause of France:

> This long period of waiting had permitted us to dissipate in the minds of third parties the prejudgments which Germany had awakened and sustained there .... In desiring to ... hurry ourselves to a vote, we should have risked the displeasure of those delegates ... who feared above all to have to decide publicly between our adversaries and us .... Marquis Visconti Venosta himself ... avowed that, if they voted, he feared that he would be obliged to abstain ....

> The United States was aiding us actively; we knew this and had already proved it. But the action of Mr. White, all the more efficient because it was less public, could it go so far as taking our part in a meeting? His instructions would not permit us much hope.[156]

But now the French government decided that the time had come to force a decision from the conference. In every capital, the French diplomats successfully refuted the "three sophisms" invoked by Germany.[157] The French press, led by Le Temps, demanded that Rouvier demonstrate to the world that the sympathy and confidence of the other powers reposed not in Germany but in France:

> Undoubtedly the Conference did not desire to make a decision. But ... the absolute clarity of our attitude, invariable as to principles, conciliatory as to means, and ... the variations in the German policy, irreducible in its hostility to France, full of contradictions in its dealings with third parties, had created outside of our delegation an atmosphere of sympathy .... As for England and Russia, we could expect a cooperation active and public. Spain, after a moment of uncertainty, kept her place beside us in the most plain and loyal fashion. Italy did not contest the duties which her engagements imposed upon her. The United States assured us an aid, which, for being discreet, was not the less valuable. The debate in meeting ought to give us at least a moral victory.[158]

Although the smaller powers remained neutral,[159] the inclination of Spain toward further compromise was overcome by Great Britain and France.[160] Lamsdorff expressed his gratification that Great Britain and Russia were working together at Algeciras for the maintenance of peace.[161] He advised the French government, however, that the cooperation of England was not enough; he continued to urge that Italy and the United States join in the diplomatic offensive. He further directed the Russian ambassador to impress upon the Kaiser the terrible responsibility which Germany would assume by wrecking the conference.[162] Grey assured Sazonow of Great Britain's unwavering support of France,[163] just as Witte was addressing a personal plea to William II to be conciliatory to France in consideration of the delicate situation of Russia, torn in her allegiance between friend and ally.[164] It remained for Lamsdorff, however, to utter the most poignant irony. He begged the Kaiser not to injure Russia and antagonize France by scuttling the conference, lest the ideal of Björkö might become unrealizable.[165]

Probably Bülow was prepared for the repetition of Grey's warning that Great Britain would not be able to remain neutral if a war resulted from a breakdown of the conference.[166] On the day of this warning, the King's speech in Parliament included an acknowledgment that the satisfactory conclusion of the Russo-Japanese War had been "due to the initiative of the President of the United States." This, editorialized the New York Times, is "a fact which some European writers, especially in Germany, have been reluctant to admit." Another editorial declared that war would be pure madness for Germany, in view of the attitude of Great Britain.[167]

But Bülow may have been surprised at the content of Roosevelt's long-solicited mediation plan, which arrived on February 19. To the White-Révoil proposition the President had added one of his own:

> That full assurances be given by France and Spain and made obligatory upon all their officers who shall be appointed by the Sultan, for the Open Door, both as to trade, equal treatment and opportunity in competing for public works and concessions.[168]

In order to detour the conference from the imminent deadlock, on February 19 Tattenbach asked that the bank project be considered in the committee of the whole on the next day.[169] Tattenbach confided to White the French demand for 40% of the capital, since White had tried to influence Révoil on the bank issue.[170] When Radowitz refused the French police proposal of February 16, the American, Austria-Hungarian, and Italian delegates agreed in advising him to expect no further concessions from Paris on the police and to bring the bank question before the conference without a previous agreement.[171]

The two bank plans, presented on February 20, proved to be as irreconcilable as the police projects had been. The

French scheme was to divide eleven shares of capital equally among the financial groups of twelve powers--France, Germany, Great Britain, Austria-Hungary, Belgium, Spain, the United States, Italy, Russia, the Netherlands, Portugal, and Sweden. Another four shares were reserved for the French consortium which had made the Moroccan loan in 1904 and which agreed to surrender in exchange its right of preference in making loans to Morocco. The bank was to be directed from a Paris office, under French law codes and judicial system, by a _Conseil d'Administration_ of fifteen members, each chosen from the nationality of the shareholding group.[172] The German plan provided for a central office at Tangier, for the bank was to be supervised by a _Conseil de Surveillance_ composed of the diplomatic corps there. Because of the equal division of the capital among the powers, the use of the Egyptian mixed codes, the mixed consular courts for bank cases, and the equal representation of the nations in the _Conseil de Surveillance_,[173] the French delegates charged that it aimed at a political institution directed against France. Proposed powers of the _Conseil de Surveillance_ also caused grave objection--the reserving of funds for the police and public works independent of the sultan, the fixing of the budget, the advising of the sultan on public works, and the ratifying of statutes passed by the _Conseil d'Administration_.

Since the heated debates in committee on February 22 and 24 led to no results, the discussion was adjourned until March 3.[174] Radowitz's early optimism was disappearing rapidly.[175] Grey, also, considered desperately the future prospect of war which the upholding of the Entente Cordiale might entail for his country. To avoid such a catastrophe, he contemplated even the sacrifice of a port or coaling station in Morocco to Germany.[176]

On February 21 Bülow replied to Root's mediation proposal. While agreeing to the President's other points, the German government was unable to harmonize the idea of the Franco-Spanish police officers with the fundamental principle of the conference. The Chancellor suggested a new basis of mediation upon which he would be gratified to have Roosevelt proceed--the selection of officers by the sultan from at least four nations participating in the proposed State Bank, with the ultimate placing of police control in Tangier and perhaps in another port in French hands.[177] Both Roosevelt and Root declined to undertake any mediation of this sort, for they considered it certain to be rejected by France.[178] Thus by February 24 the conference had reached an impasse on both questions, and Roosevelt had made his first disclosure of his real attitude.

The ten days after the exchange of challenges on the bank were a period of intense and often conflicting activity among the diplomats. Neither France nor Germany desired the conference to break down over the bank question.[179] For France it was of special importance to get back to the police problem; an agreement on the bank might cause Germany to refuse one on the police, and meanwhile the criticisms of Jaurès on the financial bases underlying French foreign policy were embarrassing the government.[180] On February 26 Révoil formally offered Radowitz further economic guarantees to make France's police project acceptable, and plans went forward to place the police question on the conference calendar.[181] Anticipating the limitations of American support, both the British and French governments put heavy pressure on other allies. The British diplomats held Spain in the entente,[182] won Portuguese adherence,[183] and aided France to persuade Italy to vote against her ally.[184] The French regarded the United States with a prudent reserve, while well aware of her favor for them:

> The United States representative is, I know, personally in favor of the French view; but considerations of home politics, such as the relations between the President and the Senate, and the desire of the American public not to take a decided line in differences between European Powers, may force him to maintain silence.
>
> At Algeciras everyone knew that Mr. White had plainly taken part in our favor during the private conferences .... A vote in meeting was an imprudence. Neither Mr. Roosevelt nor Mr. Root was, by nature, a partisan of abstention .... But the situation was stronger than their desires.[185]

The British pressure on Austria-Hungary was probably superfluous, for she was aware that Anglo-German relations would continue unfriendly so long as the Anglo-French Entente was under fire.[186] Goluchowski was prolific in expedients, including even the dissolution of the conference.[187] Protesting his loyalty, the Emperor Francis Joseph urged Germany to avoid an isolation unpleasant for both, which might lead to an Anglo-French-Russian grouping. In view of French moderation, he found German obstinancy and evasiveness incomprehensible.[188]

At this time, however, the most persistent pressure on Berlin came from St. Petersburg, stimulated by Grey.[189] The Tsar declared his intention to aid France in every way, diplomatic and personal.[190] Lamsdorff warned Schoen of the serious consequences which might follow the failure of the conference.[191] Reserving the Tsar's intervention for a last resort, Lamsdorff sought a formula which Germany could accept temporarily and with reserves.[192] In their attitude toward American participation, Lamsdorff and Witte disagreed, for whereas the foreign minister suggested the President's intervention,[193] the latter expounded the "American menace" to the Continental Powers.[194] Witte, recently the beneficiary of Roosevelt's peacemaking for his country, said in part (the Kaiser's comments are in parentheses):

> A great political and economic danger threatens the European Powers in the tremendous power and unscrupulous brutality with which America follows her aims .... The immodest Monroe Doctrine, which repulses every interference of European Powers in allegedly exclusive American interests and in no way restrains the Americans from arrogant meddling in European affairs, must be opposed by a strong European alliance. (Jawohl! aber mit England!) .... It is desirable that one call Mr. Roosevelt to account, so that he allows himself to ride an American and not, perchance, a German horse. (Französisches oder Englisches!)

The Kaiser, too, was losing his illusions about Theodore Roosevelt.

On March 1 the Kaiser's reply to Witte's letter arrived. Declaring that Russia ought to advocate moderation to the French government and press, William II nevertheless offered as a new concession the proposition made to Baron Courcel a few days before.[195] The Russo-German friction reached a climax in the publication on March 2 of an article in the semi-official journal, L'Etat Russe, which denounced the German and upheld the French policy.[196]

Holstein, also, had contributed a plan to the German collection. To Baron de Courcel, ex-ambassador to Berlin, had been proposed these terms:[197] the settlement of the Moroccan issues by France and Germany outside of the conference for a four or five year period;[198] French police in one port; officers of various nationalities, including the French and Germans, in equal numbers in seven other ports; a slight advantage to France in the bank.[199] If France would not accept this "last word" of Germany, the latter would prefer to see the disbanding of the conference. Yet, Holstein insisted, there would be no war, since neither France nor Germany wanted one.[200]

As the fateful March 3 approached, the mediation movement so long vainly promoted by the Wilhelmstrasse was under way, but it was not led by the United States. On March 1 Roosevelt wrote Reid, who had had small part in the diplomatic proceedings. However, Reid had inquired about the American attitude concerning Germany's alleged aim to secure an Atlantic port, probably Mogador. Root replied that although the United States wished to help to keep the peace, she did not wish to be charged with meddling and as yet had not considered that any move by her would be practically useful.[201] The President expressed no surprise at the Kaiser's failure to keep his promise of the preceding June and subscribed to the belief that both the military and naval authorities of Germany were preparing to attack England:

> Last June the Kaiser entirely of his own accord and without any need, promised me that if they had the conference and the French and German representatives differed, he would instruct the Germans to follow my directions. As my experience has always been that a promise needlessly entered into is rarely kept, I never expected the Kaiser to keep this one, and he has not.[202]

On March 2, Jusserand cabled the Quai d'Orsay about

the visit to Roosevelt of an unidentified "German whom the Emperor sometimes uses for communications of a more personal character than those which pass through Baron Sternburg." This German refused to admit that any other country could judge of the value of his country's interests in Morocco. He declared that, if the conference failed, Germany was sure of a victory on land and that her success at sea could not be doubted either; "we shall land fifty thousand men in England and this will be enough for us to have that country at our mercy." Since Roosevelt repeats the statement about the "fifty thousand men" in his letter to Reid, this interview is indicated as the source of Roosevelt's conviction that a conference failure would mean war. The unidentified German added that the Emperor, Bülow, and Tirpitz were all convinced of Germany's ability to succeed in a war.[203]

At a Cabinet meeting it was decided that the American delegates at Algeciras should follow the traditional policy of non-interference in the political affairs of another hemisphere. As Root informed White of this decision,

> As neutral onlookers, we felt that our dissociation from all the possibly conflicting interests and our friendship for all participants might enable us to aid towards composing any difference of views among them, and we took such steps as we thought would best tend to realize that hope. As that hope appears to have failed ... we are precluded from going further and sharing in the political considerations from which such differences arise. Faithful to our policy, sanctioned by a century's observance, the U. S. can only remain an onlooker and cannot side with either of the groups.[204]

The American press was predicting war also, and was citing the State Department as authority for the pessimistic view that Germany's obstinacy would lead to conflict.[205] Roosevelt gave assurances to France, however, that "to the very end ... if the circumstances permitted, the American government would maintain with us its efficient cooperation and would remain behind the scenes the useful defender of our propositions."[206]

Faced with the alternative of possible war or certain

retreat, Bülow now took personal direction of the negotiations out of the hands of Holstein.[207] Later Bülow denied that he had ever been dominated by Holstein, yet he charged that Holstein and his henchman, Radolin, had "delayed, evaded, or wrongly executed" his orders to Paris. Gooch says that there is no documentary evidence that Holstein differed from Bülow or was set on violent courses. After the German acceptance of the Austrian compromise on March 12, Holstein took no further part in the affair, and, according to Harden, never mentioned Morocco to Bülow again.[208]

It was Austria-Hungary which now took the lead in presenting a practical compromise. On February 26, Welsersheimb had proposed a plan later modified to provide for police organization in Tangier, Safi, Rabat, and Tetuan by the French; in Mogador, Larache, and Mazagan, by the Spanish; in Casablanca under the command of a Swiss or Dutch official serving also as general inspector. The diplomatic corps at Tangier was to have general control over the police reorganization.[209] Bülow tried first to secure Austrian and Italian mediation for the Courcel plan.[210] Welsersheimb, Visconti Venosta, and White agreed that such a proposition was futile.[211] In his refusal to intervene, Goluchowski strongly endorsed the Welsersheimb project, with the alternative of French and Spanish officers chosen by the sultan.[212] By March 6, when Rouvier declined to consider the Courcel or any other plan for separate negotiations with Germany,[213] Bülow had suffered two public diplomatic defeats which made him eager to accept Austria's aid on her own terms.

Germany lost the first two rounds of her battle on technicalities of procedure. On March 3, after an inconclusive debate of two hours, during which Germany's bank project had been supported only by Austria-Hungary and Morocco,[214] a motion was introduced by Nicolson to return to the police discussion on March 5. Only Austria and Morocco voted with Germany against the proposal. After this meeting, Révoil urged that White and Venosta try to reconcile the bank proposals.[215] A greater humiliation followed when not even Austria defended the German police policy, and the French plan was endorsed publicly by Great Britain, Russia, Spain, and Portugal.[216] The enthusiastic reception of King Edward VII in Paris did not soothe German sensibilities.[217] Since Tattenbach favored the Austrian plan, including the exclusion of French and Spanish officers from Casablanca,[218] Bülow retreated to this point, with the proviso that Germany be given consideration on the bank arrangement.[219] Austro-Italian mediation was then solicited for the new ultimatum.[220]

Roosevelt disregarded his Cabinet's advice, following instead that of Jusserand. The latter reported that the President had addressed "a strong personal communication to the Emperor, based on a sort of promise by the latter about the end of June, to accept in case of deadlock, the former's decision as final. Until French Government hears the result of this intervention it will wisely yield nothing further."[221] When the French Government was weakened by the fall of the Rouvier Cabinet on a minor religious issue, Roosevelt rushed to its rescue.[222] The President returned to his own outdated plan of February 19, urging its acceptance on the ground of the purported pledge of the Kaiser made through Sternburg on June 28, 1905. As a "disinterested spectator," Roosevelt advised Germany to accept this arrangement as a triumph of German diplomacy. If the conference should fail, Root gave warning, "the general opinion of Europe and America would be unfavorable, and Germany would lose that increase of credit and moral power that the making of this arrangement would secure to her."[223] On March 8, however, Root advised White:

> There were some expressions by Germany last summer which affected the President's action regarding the conference and which we think made it appropriate for him to urge a settlement, but he is not claiming the fulfillment of any promise or assuming to decide any question. Correct misunderstanding on this subject ... discreetly and without making any fuss about it.[224]

On March 8, with the favorable reception of the Austrian police plan by the conference,[225] Germany appeared to have passed the crisis. During the first week in March, the Moroccan situation had been reflected in a serious depression on the Berlin Bourse. Reporting on "Rais Uli on the Warpath," the New York Times had recalled the

Perdicaris episode and cited the bandit's latest exploits as evidence of the need for an efficient police force.[226] Accords were reached on all propositions in the bank organization, except the capital, in the meetings of March 8 and 10.[227] Regarding the Austro-German proposal as a great concession, the British government recommended at Algeciras, Paris, and London that France accept it.[228]

However, Rouvier had not finished bargaining. Apparently misled by a conciliatory message from Bülow, transmitted through the Prince of Monaco,[229] Rouvier thought that Germany would accept the control of the Franco-Spanish police by an officer of a smaller power. Accordingly, the French government proposed "modifications" of the Austrian proposal which would effectually dispose of any real internationalization of the police. Casablanca was to be included in the Franco-Spanish regime; the French and Spanish governments were to decide on the distribution of the other ports between their instructors; the inspector-general, from a neutral state, was to have no executive power but was merely to report to the sultan. Rouvier preferred a Swiss or Dane as inspector to one from the Netherlands.[230] When Venosta, White, and Nicolson interceded at Révoil's request, they found Radowitz firm in demanding an instructor-inspector at one port and in refusing to make further concessions on the police in return for French compromises on the bank.[231] Révoil was equally decisive in his rejection of any yielding by his government; a port under a third power, he said,

> would introduce the wedge of internationalization .... The Germans had internationalized the finances, and they now intended to introduce the principle throughout Morocco. France would leave the conference having yielded everything and gained nothing.[232]

In denial of Radowitz's claim that all his colleagues, even the English, now considered France's attitude unjustifiable,[233] Rouvier asserted that France was not isolated and that her friends had been won over by the idea that Germany's concessions were final.[234] At the conference session of March 11, there was disagreement about the censors and capital of the bank,[235] and on the next day Révoil formally rejected the Austrian police plan in regard to

Casablanca, but agreed to an inspector without command, preferably a Swiss, in Tangier.[236]

By March 12 Germany seemed assured of at least a moral victory. Although Révoil had pointed out that the acceptance of the Austrian proposal might weaken the Anglo-French Entente in France,[237] and Grey urged Germany not to regard Casablanca as so vital a point as to prevent agreement,[238] the latter regarded the breakdown of the conference as the responsibility of France.[239]

In his endeavor to ensure success, Bülow conducted a diplomatic and press campaign which brought failure instead. An exaggerated report of proceedings at Algeciras, published in the Lokalanzeiger of March 12, placed France in complete isolation, with Italy, Russia, the United States, and even Great Britain openly taking Germany's side. Simultaneously, the German ambassadors to Austria, Great Britain, Russia, Italy, France, and the United States were informed of the situation and were asked to obtain the intervention of the governments to which they were accredited in order to bring France to reason.[240] The Russian, Italian, and Austrian governments promised to advise France to accept the Austrian proposal, and Grey, while continuing to uphold the Entente, expressed his appreciation of Germany's concessions.[241]

Next the situation was complicated by a change of the French government, formed on March 14 with M. Sarrien as premier and M. Bourgeois as foreign minister. The new Cabinet resolved to challenge boldly the adverse opinions of its erstwhile friends. Supported by the French press, which upheld Rouvier's instructions to Révoil, Bourgeois renewed them and announced that no more concessions would be made on the police. Only on the bank might Germany hope to receive some slight favors.[242] At first only Clemenceau combated the Cabinet's loss of faith in British assistance. But although the British government regretted the French obstinacy, it loyally renewed its pledges of support,[243] and the exchange of confidences continued between the Entente representatives.[244] Before March 17, France had recovered her lost ground. The Austrian government was already preparing a new compromise acceptable to France,[245] and Roosevelt had intervened again in favor of France.[246]

On March 12 the Kaiser had made his only direct communication to the President[247] in reply to the latter's appeal of March 7. Declaring his readiness to consider any advice offered by Roosevelt, William II recommended to the former the Austro-Hungarian plan, which would supplement the American proposal by greater guarantees against French monopoly. In his additional directions, Bülow reprimanded Sternburg for exceeding the instructions of the preceding June, but urged him to use his full influence to secure the President's adherence to the plan now endorsed at Algeciras by all the delegates, including the British and the American. Obviously, Bülow's threat to disavow Sternburg's pledge to Roosevelt could not be carried out.[248]

But Roosevelt denounced the Austrian plan as "absurd" because it would create French, Spanish, and Dutch or Swiss spheres of influence. He would endorse only the placing of French and Spanish officers in the same ports.[249] In two letters to White, Root set forth the American objections:

> Austrian proposal to distribute ports among French, Spanish, Dutch or Swiss appears to us a long step towards partition of Morocco or creation of separate spheres of influence quite inconsistent with continuance of open door, and we disapprove of it on our own account.
>
> The nations to whom these spheres are assigned may be expected in the ordinary course of events to enter into complete control.[250]

A somewhat different version of Roosevelt's attitude is given in his own words:

> We became convinced that Austria was a mere cat's-paw for Germany, and that Germany was aiming in effect at the partition of Morocco, which was the very reverse of what she was claiming to desire. She first endeavored to secure a port for herself, and then a separate port, nominally for Holland or Switzerland,

> which we were convinced would, with the adjacent Hinterland, become in effect German. The French said that they would not yield on these points, and, as you know, it looked as if the conference would come to nothing .... Our view was that the interests of France and Spain were far greater than those of other nations.[251]

It was vain for Bülow to argue that all plans previously proposed, including the French one, were based upon the division of the ports, and that the Austrian scheme had at least the merit of reserving one neutral port as a symbol of internationalism.[252] Moreover, Roosevelt was blind to any danger of the monopolization of Morocco's resources by French banking interests.[253] Although admitting that he was beginning to think that Germany did not really want a war with France, the President had many reasons for not allowing the world to regard him as a "busybody." Sternburg had the difficult task of reporting Roosevelt's frank comments on German policy:

> The President remarked that ... the opinion is continually gaining ground that by her policy of obstruction Germany is aiming to humiliate France. This appears also ... in the speeches of His Majesty the Emperor .... The senators are incessantly pressing him to refrain from interference at Algeciras and to call his delegation back as soon as possible .... Austria and Russia have already worked upon him to give Germany the advice to moderate her demands .... The Austrian proposal is regarded here as inspired by Germany, and they think that behind it Germany is working for a sphere of influence and a port on the Mediterranean .... Only the sensational and badly informed papers, mostly in the West, criticize the speeches of His Majesty the Emperor and make them chiefly responsible for the friction at Algeciras. The French Ambassador here expresses himself about them with special severity, and he also assails the character of Count von Tattenbach. Since the former has a very strong position with the President and in leading circles, I do not doubt that his expressions fall upon fruitful ground.[254]

The official American reply was an emphatic repudiation of the Austrian proposal:

> From our point of view, all the reasons which existed against leaving to France the control of all the ports exists against leaving to France the control of some, to Spain the control of some, and to Switzerland, either in its own interest or in the interests of any other powers, the control of one .... If we had sufficient interest in Morocco to make it worth our while, we should seriously object, on our own account, to the adoption of any such arrangement.[255]

While both Roosevelt and Root disclaimed any intention of offering any proposal conflicting with that of Austria, they hoped that it would be rejected by the powers because of its dangerous tendency toward partition. Root designated Germany's conduct as petty and unworthy of a great nation.[256] Knowing in advance of the President's note,[257] Révoil was emboldened to reject the Austrian proposal regarding Casablanca and the distribution of ports by the conference.[258] Bülow emphasized the sincerity of his denial that Germany contemplated war to gain special interests in Morocco by accepting Roosevelt's suggestion of French and Spanish officers in equal numbers in all eight ports, with a general inspector from another nation. Bishop omits these pertinent comments by Bülow in his telegram to Sternburg for Roosevelt:

> The Kaiser has never thought of a war on account of Morocco, which would not be understood by the German people either .... In view of the various great political successes of the German-American cooperation during the last two years--localization of the war, maintenance of international order, and finally restoration of peace--it seems to me that the maintenance of the former confidence between Berlin and Washington, the undelayed removal of all misunderstanding, is more important than the whole Morocco affair.[259]

In a highly exalted mood, the President conveyed to his former peacemaking-partner, in terms which Sternburg confessed did not "seem to coincide with the facts," his usual flattering message:

> Convey to His Majesty the Emperor my most sincere congratulations on this epoch-making political success

in Algeciras. The policy of His Majesty in the Morocco question has been a masterly one from beginning to end. The Emperor has put through at the conference all that he wanted to put through, and the world must give him deep thanks for the result.

Apparently, Sternburg was learning the Rooseveltian technique:

The President wishes to proclaim to the world in a plainer way how highly America values the unselfish and exemplary policy of His Majesty in Morocco .... I advised the sending of a deputation of the New York _Kriegerbund_ to Washington, in order to transmit to the President the congratulations of the German soldiers _à propos_ of the repeated and successful cooperations of the President and the German Emperor in the Morocco question.

The carrying out of this ludicrous performance was described in the _New York Times_ of April 13.[260]

Among all the interested powers, Roosevelt's "belated brain-wave" provoked resentment. Nicolson judged that the new plan was likely to lead to friction and confusion,[261] while Grey feared that too many peace-makers were at work and that the unworkable American proposal had introduced an unfortunate complication.[262] Spain objected to French officers and police in Tetuan because the Spanish zone from Ceuta eastward would thus be broken.[263] "Without being able to accuse anyone," France found herself in a trap; as Tardieu puts it:

With the American system, there remained nothing of the spirit which had presided at the elaboration of the Franco-Spanish accords, nothing even of the terms of these agreements .... The juxtaposition in all the ports of officers of the two nationalities would be a permanent cause of conflicts and of rivalries, which would render sterile the work of the conference .... To refuse this combination would be a bad thing .... We would risk offending President Roosevelt, whose active cooperation had so usefully served us.[264]

Although Bülow had accepted Roosevelt's latest idea, he readily agreed to the suggestion from Austria, which was preparing a new compromise, that Roosevelt should be informed of the hostile attitude of the other powers, a communication from Szögyeny-Marich to Tschirschky suggested that Roosevelt's plan be ignored. Bülow's comment was: "I fully agree. We should see to it, though, that Roosevelt does not think that we have crossed him in his precious plan." To this Tschirschky added: "I have sent to Sternburg Telegram No. 135, in which Radowitz reports that Nicolson, France, and also Spain are offering opposition to the American proposal."[265]

An unfortunate slip of Germany enabled France to recover her balance. Supported by Le Temps, which published the strongly pro-French instructions to the British and the Russian delegates, and by a vote of confidence in the Chamber,[266] the new Cabinet was strengthened further by renewed assurances of support from Great Britain and Russia.[267] Bülow's fatal error had been to yield on the vital matter of Casablanca without fixing the condition of the mixed police in all the ports.[268] White informed Root about the real attitude of France and Spain:

> The mixing of French and Spanish in all the ports is objectionable to both as likely to create friction between their respective officers in the same place .... France's real objection would be based on emphasis given to the internationalization of Morocco, though she would not probably say so .... I have become pretty well convinced, though French and Spanish delegates will neither admit nor frankly deny it, that the secret agreement between France and Spain, concluded shortly after the English-French agreements in 1904, provided for the assignment of certain ports to France, others to Spain, but there is no reason why the action of the conference should be affected thereby.[269]

Probably as a result of White's information, Roosevelt announced that he would permit Austria to bring his proposal before the conference.[270] Root instructed White:

> If new Austrian proposal embodies views of my note of 17th, support it. We think it better to be made by

> Austria than by us. If joint responsibility for all ports in Morocco is imposed on France and Spain, of course in executing the mandate they can arrange details of officers between themselves to meet practical requirements of administration, and it would be folly for either France or Spain to stand on any point about that now.[271]

But the Austrian representatives were mapping out a new project that left out of account Roosevelt's ideas, and Goluchowski was trying to secure French concessions on the bank in exchange for the abandonment of the Casablanca scheme by Germany.[272]

The President had now decided to solicit the influence of the British government in persuading France to accept the solution to which he claimed he had obtained Germany's assent. Root presented the American case thus:

> We have been in active correspondence with German Emperor during past month based upon certain assurances he had given the President that he would do what the President thought fair. We have been urging him to come to an arrangement for a mandate for police control to France and Spain jointly with an Inspector General of another country to receive, verify, and transmit to all the powers reports showing how the agency was being executed. The German Emperor has now assented to a settlement embodying this principle which the President has said he considered fair. We understand from White and also from Jusserand that France is ready to accept it .... We hope for England's strong influence in that direction. We are satisfied that no further concession will be made by Germany. Indeed we would be bound to approve a refusal by Germany to go further because this is what we have been urging on the ground that it is fair. This saves all that is of importance that France really cares for. We think the only thing to fear is that after so long a struggle, French diplomats may be weary and give undue importance to trifling matters. Against this especially we urge England's influence.[273]

Grey readily acceded to the French request for support of Jusserand in Washington in opposition to the Rooseveltian scheme. The French had the idea that the Kaiser had communicated with Roosevelt independently of Sternburg, and that his envoy had persuaded the President to propose French and Spanish instructors for all eight ports.[274] Although Grey was gratified at the assent given by the German Emperor, he could not agree to any proposal unacceptable to the French and Spanish governments.[275] He trusted that the influence of the President, which had been so beneficially exercised, would be able to arrange satisfactorily a plan to let France and Spain decide their own police distribution. Furthermore, Durand was instructed to support Jusserand in any action which he might wish to take.[276]

Considering the actual reaction of the French government to Roosevelt's untimely and unwelcome interference, Jusserand's account of the episode is extraordinary:

> An Austrian proposal, which was a German one in disguise, concerning the police, was recommended by the Kaiser .... Asked to make us yield, Mr. Roosevelt caused an official answer to be sent, beginning: 'we do not consider the Austrian proposal to be acceptable.' He reminded the Kaiser of his having promised him in case the conference met and there were difficulties, to abide by his judgment, and he offered him his choice: a possibility that the correspondence exchanged be published, or compliments to him and his people for their success, such as it was. The Kaiser chose the latter .... We had no reason to regret having acted in accordance with the President's advice, since the conference safeguarded our special interests .... The part played by America, disinterested, claiming no advantage or compensation in this important intervention in European affairs, had been decisive.[277]

After consultation with Root, Roosevelt informed Sternburg that he would protest emphatically against the opposition of England, France, and Spain to his plan. He was especially critical of Nicolson's attitude. Durand reported:

> My impression after seeing the French Ambassador and the Secretary of State is that the United States Government considers us as opposed to Germany and possibly inclined to push France too far. Neither the President

> nor the Secretary of State have discussed the Morocco Conference with me, and I have asked no questions till yesterday, but I know that the President used to think us unduly suspicious of Germany if not unduly hostile.

Jusserand did not wish Durand to use any pressure at that time.[278]

However, the President's instructions to White, communicated to both the British and the German governments, constituted an abandonment of the principle for which he had practically issued an ultimatum two days before. The distribution of ports, which Roosevelt had declared to be tending toward partition when arranged by the Austrian plan, now became "a matter of detail" to be settled by the two mandatory powers--which had been their original demand:

> We care nothing whether the actual administrative exigencies necessitate in some ports, as they doubtless will in Tangier, for instance, the employment of both French and Spanish officers, whilst at other ports either French or Spanish officers may be employed, or at one time French and at another time Spanish, provided that both countries accept a joint responsibility. All this distribution of officers can and should be settled as a matter of detail between the two mandatory powers ... provided that it is understood that the mandate is joint and not several and the responsibility is universal and not local or distributive. The inspector who on behalf of all the powers inquires into the execution of the mandate will be wholly unaffected ... by any consideration as to which particular power at any particular time happens to have its officers at a particular port.[279]

By his interference, the President had helped greatly to destroy the one vestige of internationalization in the Casablanca region. White wrote Root after the conference, "There is no doubt that the eighth port was saved to the French and Spanish superintendence entirely through the President's action and your admirable note of March the 17th."[280] Roosevelt had retreated promptly from his position when his own scheme was opposed by the entente-partners.[281] A rare admission of the importance of American influence in the official documents is White's statement: "We have reason to believe that this expression of our Government's opinion affected the situation very materially."[282]

It is significant that during the several crises when he had feared war, Roosevelt had never once suggested the Hague Tribunal as a peace agency. He declined to follow the suggestion of Carl Schurz, presented through Oscar Straus (a member of the Court), that the powers be persuaded to refer the controversy to the Tribunal. Germany, of course, was blamed by Roosevelt:

> Modern Germany is alert, aggressive, military, and industrial. It thinks it is a match for England and France combined in war, and would probably be less reluctant to fight both these Powers together than they would be together to fight it. It despises the Hague Conference and the whole Hague idea. It respects the United States only insofar as it believes that our navy is efficient and that if sufficiently wronged or insulted we would fight. Now I like and respect Germany ... but I would be a fool if I were blind to the fact that Germany will not stay with us if we betray weakness. As for this particular case, ... I have been using my very best efforts for peace.[283]

On March 23 Welsersheimb had received from Rêvoil the concession of limiting the French bank shares to three in exchange for Germany's surrender of the neutral police at Casablanca. The remaining questions seemed unsolvable by private negotiation. The German government demanded that the diplomatic corps at Tangier receive the inspector's reports and exercise general supervision over the police, but the entente group wanted no intervention from that body. The French refused the authority over the bank censors by the various governments and the diplomatic corps at Tangier, which was asked by Germany. Bülow's yielding did not yet emulate Roosevelt's in permitting France and Spain to settle with the sultan the division of the ports.[284] Consequently, when the new Austrian proposal embodying the German demands was presented to the conference on March 26, the French delegates held firmly against any concession.[285]

This last deadlock was not difficult to break. At a

private conference held on the evening of March 26, the French, British, Spanish, Russian, Italian, and American delegates worked out the formula on inspection which was accepted on the next day by the German delegates.[286] Since White acted as messenger between the German and the French delegates, the American press had an opportunity to rejoice that his "sagacious intervention" had "saved the day."[287] By agreeing that the inspector should report simultaneously to both the sultan and the diplomatic corps at Tangier, and giving the latter authority to order inquiries concerning the execution of the police mandate in safeguarding foreign interests, France had won a substantial victory.[288] A further safeguard for French interests was the acceptance of Nicolson's proposal that the inspector be Swiss instead of Dutch.[289]

On the anniversary of the Kaiser's fateful landing at Tangier, a settlement was reached on the remaining controversial issues. After foiling Spain's efforts to secure a better bargain, France conceded that the police officers should be Spanish in Tetuan and Larache and Franco-Spanish in Casablanca and Tangier, thus reserving four ports for herself.[290] This arrangement was endorsed by the conference, which also decreed that the police, to function for five years, should be inspected annually by a Swiss officer living at Tangier. The minor details of bank censors, customs, suppression of contraband, and public works were passed in great haste.[291] Root directed that White should not introduce a proposal to have disputes over the interpretation of the final act referred for decision to the Hague Tribunal. The reason given was that this provision would probably be unacceptable to France.[292]

There remained for the Anglo-Saxon colleagues the traditional task of leavening the political mass of the conference with moral motives. Despite the objection of the Moorish delegate that the question was not on the agenda, the other delegates adopted Nicolson's suggestion that the conference go on record against slavery and in favor of better prisons in Morocco.[293] White's crusade for the Jews was considered unwise by both Nicolson and Révoil; it was likely to inspire the introduction of other extraneous matters. Furthermore, extensive investigations by Einstein, corroborated by Gummeré,[294] led White to conclude that the charges in Schiff's memorandum were obsolete, and the Moroccan

Jews themselves regarded intervention at the conference as unjustified and prejudicial to their welfare. Having Root's permission not to introduce the subject at all, White decided to present a motion commending the Sultan's attitude and requesting him to make his wishes for Jewish welfare known to his officials. The innocuous voeu was passed unanimously by the delegates and was endorsed also by the Moorish delegation.[295]

The defeat of Germany could not be camouflaged by Bülow's claim of victory, made to the Associated Press[296] and to the Reichstag, where he collapsed after an attack by Bebel, the Socialist leader.[297] Another casualty of the conflict was Holstein, whose resignation was accepted on April 5.[298]

Again the Kaiser's peace policy had triumphed. Bülow gives testimony to supplement the evidence of the documents in Die Grosse Politik that Germany's surrender was not due to the moral pressure exerted by Roosevelt:

> Never, neither before nor during the Algeciras Conference, had I any intention of allowing a war to break out over Morocco .... William II entirely agreed with me in this. Nevertheless, he increased the difficulties of my task by imprudent speech and action or even, at any crisis in our foreign policy, by too frankly showing his fear of war .... The Emperor did not wish to run the risk of the Conference ending in a stalemate. At the beginning of April we had a long talk ... during which he expressed his firm conviction that, unless we made further concessions at Algeciras, there would be a war, and our chances, for various technical and military reasons, were "at the moment" as unfavorable as they could be. He would not, he said, and could not risk such a war! He said that I must not abandon him now, but preserve him from war, "without dishonoring him"--from a war for which neither the German Princes, the Reichstag, nor our people were in the mood.[299]

From France Roosevelt received more credit for his services than from Germany. Bourgeois declared the activity of the American President to be one more evidence of "the unique place which the United States has attained, and of the great and benign role which 'our sister Republic' would continue to play, with a Chief Magistrate who commanded the respect and confidence of the world at large." Despite the semi-secrecy concerning his role at Algeciras, his deeds would "single him out as the arbitrator to whom all can turn when discussions threaten to bring on war in any part of the globe."[300] Roosevelt modestly gave Jusserand the chief credit:

> In my judgment we owe it to you more than to any other man that the year which has closed has not seen a war between France and Germany, which, had it begun, would probably have extended to take in a considerable portion of the world.[301]

It was rather disconcerting, however, to receive no commendation from London, and to be obliged to call the attention of His Majesty's Government to the value of the contributions to peace made from Washington. To King Edward VII Roosevelt wrote on April 25, 1906:

> I think the outcome of the Morocco business was satisfactory, don't you? White speaks in the highest terms of your man Nicholson (sic); between ourselves, he grew to feel that neither the German nor the French representative at Algeciras was really straightforward .... I had some amusing experiences in the course of the negotiations.[302]

Reid was directed to show to the King and to Grey the long letter in which Roosevelt gave his version and selected documents concerning his part in the Morocco affair, which was published later in Bishop, Theodore Roosevelt, I, 467-505. In June the President was assuring Durand that America had really saved from German clutches the "port opposite Gibraltar" which England "did not seem to mind" her having.[303]

The Moroccan delegates were not deceived by the eulogies of the General Act delivered by the Duke of Almodovar in his closing address to the delegates,[304] and they would not have endorsed White's declaration that every principle of international interest had been sustained.[305] Nevertheless, although they realized that the French control imposed by the conference would make the Maghzen even more impotent and futile, the Sultan reluctantly accepted the program of reforms on June 18.[306] Within a month after the signing of the Act, Root had given official notice that the United States government would not maintain even the minimum of interest in the internationalization of Morocco which would be involved in accepting for its citizens the one share in the State Bank allotted by the conference.[307]

In rendering an account of his mission, White expressed the hope that he had carried out the spirit as well as the letter of his instructions.[308] Roosevelt assured him that he had added to the reputation of his country and had filled to perfection a difficult and trying position. In the President's letter appears also his one expression of irritation over France's rejection of his final mediation:

> I may add that Jusserand, who is a trump, toward the end became very much disgusted with what he evidently regarded as a certain furtiveness and lack of frankness in the French and German diplomats. Until the Conference met I felt that France was behaving better than Germany, but toward the end it seemed to me that neither one was straightforward.[309]

Later in the summer, the President explained frankly to White his policy of "building a bridge of gold" for the retreat of the Kaiser:

> My course with him during the last five years has been uniform. I admire him, respect him, and like him. I think him a big man, and on the whole, a good man; but I think his international and indeed his personal attitude one of intense egoism .... Where I have forced him to give way I have been sedulously anxious to build a bridge of gold for him, and to give him the satisfaction of feeling that his dignity and reputation in the face of the world were safe .... Where I have had to take part of the kernel from him, I have been anxious that he should have all the shell possible, and have that shell painted any way he wished.[310]

Of the many interpretations of Roosevelt's motives and actions in the Algeciras Conference, perhaps none is more interesting than the one made by the French chronicler of the conference, which reveals also his intense chauvinism:

> Mr. Roosevelt had no obligations to us. Did the sympathy which he was going to show for us find its basic origin in the small relish that he had for William II? .... One can hardly deny that it was at first the lofty sentiment which he had concerning the grandeur of his country, concerning his duty as the chief of state, his anxiety to work for the peace of the world, his spirit of justice and equity. In the Moroccan affair he made his policy without concern for opposition. He made it discreetly, because that discretion was the condition of success .... And when he believed that we were right, he said so flatly to Germany. These vigorous and active natures are often carried on to overreach the aim by a certain disdain for contingencies. Mr. Roosevelt made mistakes sometimes. He arrived at mistaken conclusions during the course of the conference, in so much as the Moroccan question escaped him in its details .... It was by the rightness and wisdom of our propositions, pointed out by an ambassador who was his personal friend, that we influenced his disposition.
>
> Mr. Roosevelt supported us ... because he thought that the equilibrium of forces, necessary for the repose of the world, was not menaced by us, but by Germany. The procedures of the German diplomacy during the conference, its openly published pretension to speak in the name of Europe, appeared to Washington as a danger, a danger political and economic together. The day when the idea, dear to William II, took the form of creating, by persuasion or by force, the United States of Europe, the United States of America knew herself to be in peril .... The imperialistic and dominating appearance of the German policy, during the affair in Morocco, irritated the government of the Union ... to do all that its formidable neutrality could behind the scenes to bar the route for German enterprises. Moreover, what we wished to accomplish in Morocco recalled to it, in plenty of ways, what it had realized in Cuba.[311]

Notes

1. Anderson, First Moroccan Crisis, 264-270; Memorandum by Hugh O'Beirne, enclosure with Bertie to Grey, Dec. 15, 1905, B. D., III, 156-157; Hale, Germany and the Diplomatic Revolution, 181-188.

2. Rouvier later denied making the promise. Witte's story is in his Memoirs, 416-418. Somewhat less modest and truthful than his diplomatic colleagues, Witte afterwards spoke of Algeciras as "an assembly which owed its existence to my initiative;" Ibid., 428.

3. Radolin to F. O., No. 6820, Sept. 23, 1905, G. P., XX, 582-583 and No. 6821, Sept. 24, 1905, Ibid., 583-584.

4. McCormick to State Dept., Sept. 22, 1905, cited by Vagts, Weltpolitik, II, 1869, footnote 1.

5. Lansdowne to Bertie, Sept. 30, 1905, B. D., III, 142-144, gives the text of this main and a supplementary agreement, which provided a compromise on the Tattenbach concessions generally favorable to Germany.

6. Radolin to F. O., Sept. 26, 1905, No. 6828, G. P., XX, 589. The British government advised that any subject not on the agenda should be ruled out of order; Gorst to Bertie, Dec. 13, 1905, B. D., III, 149. The American government disregarded this suggestion by including the Jewish problem in its instructions to White.

7. For the text, see Cambon to Lansdowne, Sept. 6, 1905, B. D., III, 137. Lansdowne approved the understanding; Lansdowne to Cambon, Sept. 9, 1905, Ibid., 138.

8. Lowther to Lansdowne, Oct. 22 and Oct. 24, 1905, Ibid., 144-146.

9. F. R., 1905, 675-676, 683-684.

10. Anderson, First Moroccan Crisis, 274.

11. These were inspired by Bülow's attempts at conciliation by interviews in Paris papers, followed by Le Matin's revelations of Oct. 7. Hale, Germany and the Diplomatic Revolution, 195-197; Carroll, French Public Opinion, 218-219.

12. Bülow to Sternburg, No. 6341, Oct. 29, 1905, G. P., XIX, 641-642. Sternburg reported Roosevelt's disbelief in this possibility on Nov. 24; Ibid., note 2.

13. Tattenbach to Bülow, No. 6898, Nov. 4, 1905, Ibid., XXI, 12-14.

14. Memorandum by Bülow, No. 6900, Nov. 23, 1905, Ibid., 14-15.

15. Memorandum by Mühlberg, No. 6906, Nov. 30, 1905, Ibid., 20-22.

16. The text of Bülow's speech is given in Tardieu, La Conférence, 490-494.

17. The facile glibness with which both the British and the French diplomats denied the whole intent and purpose of their secret accords, both publicly to the world at large and privately to the American government, arouses the reluctant admiration of the student of this period. The existence of these hidden pacts, minimized by later apologists, is a factor of great importance in analyzing the diplomacy in relation to the American public, which quite generally gave its confidence to the Anglo-French statements and denied it to the German protestations. The German ulterior motives, of course, were not shared with other countries.

18. Roberts, History of French Colonial Policy, II, 551-552. The German charges and French denials were further elaborated in a Livre jaune and a Weissbuch; Anderson, First Moroccan Crisis, 313-314. A précis of the White Book is given in Lascelles to Grey, Jan. 10, 1906, B. D., III, 215-217. The exchanges of propaganda did not increase good feeling.

19. Memorandum of Mühlberg, No. 6914, Dec. 25, 1905, G. P., XXI, 28-29.

20. Bülow to Radowitz, No. 6922, Jan. 3, 1906, Ibid., 38-45.

21. Cartwright to Grey, Jan. 22, 1906, B. D., III, 233; minute by William II on dispatch, Stumm to Bülow, No. 7024, Feb. 20, 1906, G. P., XXI, 191.

22. Bülow to Wedel, Dec. 22, 1905, Ibid., 27, note 1.

23. Bülow to Monts, No. 6925, Jan. 5, 1906, Ibid., 53-54.

24. By one of the "larger states" Bülow had Italy in mind at this time. Bülow to Sternburg, No. 6926, Jan. 6, 1906, Ibid., 54-55.

25. An authorized interview appearing in the New York Herald on Jan 12, 1906, quoted Bülow: "Neither His Majesty the Kaiser nor anybody else in Germany dreams of exercising the slightest pressure upon France at the expense of the French national dignity at the Conference, where there should be neither vainqueurs nor vaincus. Germany stands for equality of opportunity in the trade of Morocco, the Open Door for all nations alike." Sidney Whitman, Things I Remember, 173-174.

26. Meyer to the State Dept., Jan. 9, 1906; cited by Nevins, Henry White, 265.

27. McCormick to Root, Dec. 15, 1905; Ibid., 265.

28. "Rouvier states that he has taken that course in recognition of the friendly attitude of our government toward France, and as a mark of sympathy and of high deference for our President." Vignaud to Root, Jan. 2, 1906; cited by Vagts, Weltpolitik, I, 234.

29. Sykes, Durand, 299.

30. Cortissoz, Reid, 319-320, 347.

31. Bülow, *Memoirs*, II, 229; Bülow to William II, No. 6882, Dec. 3, 1905, *G. P.*, XX, 679-681.

32. Grey, *Twenty-Five Years*, I, 9-11, 36-37, 41-46, 48-52.

33. Grey to Whitehead, Dec. 20, 1905, *B. D.*, III, 160-161; Metternich to Bülow, No. 6886, Dec. 20, 1905, *G. P.*, XX, 685-690.

34. In reporting the British viewpoint to Sternburg on Jan. 24, 1906, Bülow said: "The more important it is for us, that America interest herself in the formation of a police organization in Morocco which will certainly establish there the Open Door and equality for all nations." No. 6959, Jan. 24, 1906, *Ibid.*, XXI, 105.

35. Grey to Lascelles, Jan. 9, 1906, *B. D.*, III, 209-211; Metternich to F. O., No. 6933, Jan. 10, 1906, *G. P.*, XXI, 64.

36. Lascelles to Grey, Jan. 13, 1906, *B. D.*, III, 222-224; Grey to Lascelles, Jan. 15, 1906, *Ibid.*, 225.

37. Lascelles to Grey, Jan. 11, 1906, *B. D.*, III, 217-219; Lowther to Lansdowne, Dec. 14, 1905, *Ibid.*, 147-149.

38. Memorandum by Holstein, No. 6953, *G. P.*, XXI, 96-97.

39. Bülow to Radowitz, No. 6950, Jan. 17, 1906, *Ibid.*, 94.

40. Lee, *King Edward VII*, II, 524-527.

41. Grey to Nicolson, Dec. 14, 1905, *B. D.*, III, 151. Incidentally, Nicolson was to sanction no arrangement which might impair the rights and privileges secured to Great Britain by the Anglo-French Declaration.

42. Grey to Nicolson, Dec. 20 and 21, 1905, *Ibid.*, 161-162. Grey said: "I should prefer the mixed police force in each port to assigning a port to each Power or to a minor Power; but it is not for us to suggest any concessions."

43. Gooch, History of Modern Europe, 363.

44. Bertie to Grey, Dec. 22, 1905, B. D., III, 163-164.

45. Lee, King Edward VII, II, 326.

46. Geoffrey to British F. O., Jan. 12, 1906, B. D., III, 220-222; Grey to Bertie, Jan. 15, 1906, Ibid., 225; F. O. Memorandum to Cambon, Jan. 15, 1906, Ibid., 226.

47. Grey to Bertie, Jan. 10, 1906, Ibid., 213-214; Bertie to Grey, Jan. 16, 1906, Ibid., 226-227. The "non-political" police theory was that of the second Russian delegate; Nicolson to Grey, Jan. 2, 1906, Ibid., 205-206.

48. Bertie to Grey, Dec. 22, 1905, Ibid., 165.

49. Bertie to Grey, Jan. 16, 1906, with enclosure, Ibid., 227.

50. Grey to Egerton, Dec. 27, 1905, Ibid., 166; Egerton to Grey, Dec. 27, 1905, and Jan. 9, 1906, Ibid., 166-167, 212-213.

51. Grey to Bertie, Jan. 15, 1906, Ibid., 225.

52. Nicolson to Grey, Dec. 22 and Dec. 27, 1905, Jan. 5 and Jan. 9, 1906, Ibid., 163, 167, 209, 212; Bertie to Grey, Dec. 22, 1905, Ibid., 165; Grey to Bertie, Jan. 15, 1906, Ibid., 178.

53. Spring-Rice to Grey, Jan. 2, 1906, B. D., III, 204; Grey to Bertie, Jan. 15, 1906, Ibid., 178; Witte, Memoirs, 296-300.

54. Bülow to Moltke, No. 6943, Jan. 24, 1906, G. P., XXI, 77-78. Bülow expressed confidence that France would accept the German demands rather than resort to war.

55. Declaring the French fear of war so ludicrous as to border on insanity, the Kaiser made no effort to

conceal his own terror of the Anglo-French preparations. William II to Bülow, No. 6887, Dec. 29, 1905, Ibid., XX, 690-696.

56. Viscount Haldane, "Haldane Memoirs Tell of War Fears in 1906," New York Times, Jan. 20, 1909, 6xx; Fay, Origins of the World War, I, 193-210; Anderson, First Moroccan Crisis, 339-343.

57. Ibid., 337-338, 343, 347.

58. Tardieu, La Conférence, 89-90; Nevins, Henry White, 264, 269.

59. Lowther to Grey, Dec. 29, 1905, B. D., III, 204.

60. Nevins, Henry White, 269-270; Nicolson, Portrait of A Diplomatist, 126-127.

61. Nevins, Henry White, 268, 270.

62. Ibid., 269.

63. In La Conférence, 103, Tardieu says that this was intended as a direct challenge to the Germans' charges and was approved as such by White and Venosta. However, Radowitz was glad to second Révoil's speech of approval. Radowitz to F. O., No. 6949, Jan. 16, 1906, G. P., XXI, 92-93.

64. Tardieu, La Conférence, 106.

65. Nicolson to Grey, Jan. 17, 1906, B. D., III, 227; White to State Dept., Jan. 25, 1906, F. R., 1906, 1470-1471, 1478-1479; Tardieu, La Conférence, 105-106.

66. Al Torres was not lacking in intelligence. In an interview with Budgett Meakin on January 17, he asked why the powers did not hold a conference on Russia. New York Times, Jan. 18, 1906, 4.

67. Radolin to F. O., No. 7124, March 25, 1906, G. P., XXI, 315.

68. Tardieu, La Conférence, 108, 111-113, 119-120, 125-128, 129, 131-132.

69. Ibid., 114, 119, 120-121, 128, 130; New York Times, Jan. 28, 1906, 4.

70. Ibid., Feb. 2, 1906, 4; F. R., 1906, Part 2, 1478-1479; Tardieu, La Conférence, 122, 124, 128.

71. "Both the Germans and French, while apparently most conciliatory, are very guarded in showing their hand, which tends to delay." White to Root, Jan. 20, 1906; cited by Vagts, Weltpolitik, II, 1887, footnote 1.

72. New York Times, Jan. 16, 1906, 10.

73. Bülow to Sternburg, No. 6956, Jan. 20, 1906, G. P., XXI, 99-101.

74. Nicolson and Révoil were informed that Germany would in no case agree to a French-Spanish mandate but would reciprocate French concessions on the police by concessions on the bank. Révoil wanted definite proposals on both and said that France must get the guarantees of a third party, such as the United States, for any arrangement that Germany might promise. Nicolson to Grey, Jan. 21, 1906, B. D., III, 231.

75. The German ambassador hinted that if Germany were unable to secure the policing of the west coast ports for herself she would favor giving it to Spain. The Spanish government promised loyalty to its engagements with France. Cartwright to Grey, Jan. 22 and 26, 1906, Ibid., 233, 236.

76. Sternburg, to F. O., No. 6958, Jan. 23, 1906, G. P., XXI, 102-103.

77. White to Root, Jan. 26, 1906, D. S., Special Agents, L; Vagts, Weltpolitik, II, 1887-1888, footnote 3.

78. Bülow to Sternburg, No. 6959, Jan. 24, 1906, G. P., XXI, 103-105.

79. Nicolson to Grey, Jan. 25, 26, and 27, 1906, B. D., III, 235, 238-239, 239-240.

80. Holstein to Sternburg, telegram, Jan. 26, 1906, G. P., XXI, 113.

81. Bülow to Radowitz, No. 6965, Jan. 26, 1906, G. P., XXI, 114-115; Radowitz to Bülow, No. 6967, Jan. 26, 1906, Ibid., 121-122.

82. Bülow to Sternburg, No. 6968, Jan. 27, 1906, Ibid., 123-125.

83. New York Times, Jan. 28, 1906, 4.

84. Nicolson to Grey, two dispatches on Jan. 26, 1906, B. D., III, 236, 237-238. Révoil complained that "Berlin appears to be using different language at Washington, at Madrid, and at Algeciras" and that Radowitz and Tattenbach contradicted each other. Nicolson advised the French to lay their cards on the table.

85. Anderson, First Moroccan Crisis, 352. The French position was impeccable, if the precedent of China, which Germany was always citing, were to be followed. Yet this proposal was undoubtedly a violation of the spirit of the agreement to which France had repeatedly pledged herself.

86. Bülow to Radowitz, No. 6973, Jan. 30, 1906, G. P., XXI, 128.

87. Radowitz to F. O., No. 6975, Jan. 31, 1906, Ibid., 130-131.

88. The bank was to be under the French judicial system. Its capital was to be divided thus: to France, 27%; to Spain, 23%; to Great Britain, 20%; to Germany, 20%; to Italy, 10%. The administrative council of ten members, chosen according to nationality by the shareholders, was to name the directors. The preferential right to make loans to Morocco, already held by the French banks, might possibly be relin-

quished in return for an increase in France's share in the capital. Radowitz to F. O., No. 6974, Jan. 29, 1906, G. P., XXI, 128-130; Tardieu, La Conférence, 141-142.

89. Bülow to Radowitz, No. 6977, G. P., XXI, 132-134.

90. Sternburg to F. O., No. 6971, Jan. 29, 1906, Ibid., 126-127.

91. Bülow to Sternburg, No. 6972, Jan. 30, 1906, Ibid., 127.

92. Radowitz to F. O., No. 6978, Jan. 31, 1906, Ibid., 135.

93. Bülow to Sternburg, No. 6976, Feb. 1, 1906, Ibid., 131-132.

94. New York Times, Jan. 23, 1906, 1; Jan. 28, 1906, 2; Jan. 29, 1906, 1, 11.

95. "All the delegates received this (the Lanessan) article in an envelope"; Tardieu, La Conférence, 147. White and Venosta also warned Radowitz that the discussion on the police could be delayed no longer. Radowitz to F. O., No. 6979, Feb. 2, 1906, G. P., XXI, 135-136.

96. Radowitz to F. O., No. 6980, Feb. 3, 1906, Ibid., 136-137; Tardieu, La Conférence, 148-152. Tattenbach said that Germany would never accept either a French or a Franco-Spanish police; no police at all might be better, since they might aggravate rather than ameliorate the situation. Nicolson to Grey, Feb. 4, 1906, B. D., III, 242.

97. White confessed to Root that the German opinion about a French police force was all too "sound from point of view of maintaining genuine 'open door.'" White to Root, private and confidential telegram, Jan. 26, 1906; cited by Vagts, Weltpolitik, II, 1888.

98. Radowitz to F. O., No. 6980, Feb. 3, 1906, G. P., XXI, 137.

99. Nicolson to Grey, Feb. 4, 1906, B. D., III, 241; Tardieu, La Conférence, 147-148. Nicolson thought that the Germans would not regret the breakdown of the Conference, which would give them a free hand at Fez. He informed the American and Italian delegates of his talk with Tattenbach. Nicolson to Grey, Feb. 5, 1906, Ibid., 243-244.

100. Wedel to F. O., No. 6983, Feb. 5, 1906, G. P., XXI, 140.

101. Radowitz to F. O., No. 6984, Feb. 5, 1906, Ibid., 140-141.

102. Tardieu, La Conférence, 152-153; Nicolson to Grey, Feb. 6, 1906, B. D., III, 241.

103. Radowitz to F. O., No. 6985, Feb. 6, 1906, G. P., XXI, 141-142.

104. Undersecretary Ojeda apparently endorsed the plan.

105. Bülow to Radowitz, No. 6987, Feb. 7, 1906, G. P., XXI, 143-146.

106. Bülow to Radolin, No. 6988, Feb. 7, 1906, Ibid., 146-147.

107. White to Root, cipher telegram, Jan. 30, 1906, D. S., Special Agents, L, 50.

108. Tardieu, La Conférence, 161.

109. Bülow to Radowitz, No. 6987, Feb. 7, 1906, G. P., XXI, 145.

110. White to Root, Feb. 5 and 6, 1906; D. S., Special Agents, L. France's bank proposal, White said, gave Germany "as a sop" a capital share over twice as large as her trade percentage. "France evidently hopes few other countries will wish to participate. I assume we shall not." White to Root, Feb. 1, 1906; Ibid., 90-91.

111. "France claims that her interests ... are too great to confide the police to another Power; that to turn out her officers and instructors, for sometime past in Morocco, would be compromising to her national dignity, and to question good faith of guarantees she is willing to give regarding open door, etc., is inadmissible imputation upon her honor." White to Root, Feb. 5, 1906; D. S., Special Agents, L.

112. Sternburg to F. O., No. 6989, Feb. 8, 1906, G. P., XXI, 147-148. Root did not want to undertake any step not certain of a decisive result. Sternburg thought that his exposition of the bank question to several influential financiers in New York would result in effectual pressure upon the State Department.

113. Tardieu speaks of it as an "eighth variant"--requiring the Sultan to choose his instructors from the nationals of three secondary powers. On February 7 Bülow had urged as one of the advantages of the Lanessan plan that "it gives the least ground for jealousy among the Powers, especially if ... the Sultan is limited to drawing the personnel from the smaller powers, the Swiss, Dutch, Belgians, Swedes, Norwegians, Danes, and Portuguese." Tardieu, La Conférence, 172; Bülow to Radowitz, No. 6987, Feb. 7, 1906, G. P., XXI, 144.

114. Radowitz to F. O., No. 6990, Feb. 9, 1906, Ibid., 148-149.

115. Radowitz to F. O., No. 6992, Feb. 9, 1906 and No. 6996, Feb. 10, 1906, Ibid., 151 and 158.

116. Tardieu, La Conférence, 165, 168-171; Nicolson, Portrait of A Diplomatist, 134-136; Carroll, French Public Opinion, 219.

117. Bülow to Radowitz, No. 6991, Feb. 9, 1906, G. P., XXI and No. 6997, Feb. 12, 1906, Ibid., 149-151, 155-156.

118. Bülow to Radowitz, No. 6991, Feb. 9, 1906, Ibid., 150.

119. Nevins, _Henry White_, 271.

120. Holstein to Radolin, No. 6994, Feb. 10, 1906, _G. P._, XXI, 152-153.

121. Bülow to Monts, No. 6995, Feb. 10, 1906, _Ibid._, 154. On Feb. 8 a new Italian government had taken office under Baron Sonnino.

122. Monts to F. O., No. 7002, Feb. 13, 1906, _Ibid._, 161-162; Bülow to Monts, No. 7003, Feb. 14, 1906, _Ibid._, 162; Monts to Bülow, No. 7008, Feb. 13, 1906, _Ibid._, 168-169.

123. Wedel to F. O., No. 6999, Feb. 12, 1906, _Ibid._, 157-159 and No. 7007, Feb. 14, 1906, _Ibid._, 166-167.

124. On Feb. 3 and Feb. 9 Lamsdorff had agreed to send diplomatic communications to Berlin. Tardieu, _La Conférence_, 159-160.

125. Nicolson to Grey, Feb. 13, 1906, _B. D._, III, 249-250.

126. Nicolson to Grey, Feb. 14, 1906, _Ibid._, 253; Spring-Rice to Grey, Feb. 13, 1906, _Ibid._, 253.

127. Schoen to F. O., No. 6998, Feb. 12, 1906, _G. P._, XXI, 156-157.

128. Grey to Nicolson, Feb. 12, 1906, _B. D._, III, 248-249 and Feb. 13, 1906, _Ibid._, 251-252; Grey to Lascelles, Feb. 14, 1906, _Ibid._, 254-255 and Feb. 19, 1906, _Ibid._, 263; Grey to Bertie, Feb. 13, 1906, _Ibid._, 250-251.

129. Nicolson had argued to White that a police force nominally directed by the Sultan but under officers from neutral powers would lack unity and efficiency of execution. Moreover, only non-commissioned officers from Algeria or the Spanish garrisons in Africa would be capable of serving as links between European officers and native troops. Nicolson, _Portrait of a Diplomatist_, 135.

130. White and Venosta helped to persuade Révoil to receive the German proposal in order "to keep the way open for further negotiation." Tardieu, La Conférence, 177.

131. Radowitz to F. O., No. 7004, Feb. 13, 1906, G. P., XXI, 162-163; Tardieu, La Conférence, 174-177.

132. Bülow to the German ambassadors in Rome, Vienna, London and Washington, No. 7000, Feb. 13, 1906, G. P., XXI, 159-160.

133. Bülow to Sternburg, No. 7005, Feb. 14, 1906, Ibid., 163-164. "Mr. Root's idea that it might be left to the sultan to carry out the police reform himself, yet under international control, after a first abrupt refusal, seems to be taken up again now by France."

134. Tardieu, La Conférence, 161-162.

135. White to Root, Feb. 9, 1906; cited by Vagts, Weltpolitik, II, 1892 and footnote 3.

136. Root to White, Feb. 10, 1906, Ibid., 1892.

137. White to Root, Feb. 11, 1906, D. S., Special Agents, L, 111-112.

138. Nicolson to Grey, Feb. 11, 1906, B. D., III, 246-247.

139. "Failure of Moroccan Conference Expected," New York Times, Feb. 11, 1906, 4, gave the German viewpoint. "Pessimism at Algeciras," Ibid., Feb. 12, 1906, 5, warned Germany of her loss of moral prestige if a conference called to secure economic equality should end in her attempt to establish exclusive predominance in Morocco. "Policing Morocco," Ibid., Feb. 13, 1906, 6, gave the editorial opinion that if Germany became responsible for the failure of the conference, her aims could not be peaceful.

140. "Roosevelt to End Moroccan Dispute," New York Times, Feb. 14, 1906, 1.

141. *New York Times*, Feb. 15, 1906, 2 and Feb. 16, 1906, 6.

142. Nevins, *Henry White*, 273.

143. Tardieu, *La Conférence*, 179-180. The entente was established on February 14 and 15.

144. Grey to Nicolson, Feb. 15, 1906, *B. D.*, III, 258.

145. Grey to Bertie, Feb. 15, 1906, *Ibid.*, 256; Tardieu, *La Conférence*, 200-201.

146. Grey to Bertie, Feb. 15, 1906, *B. D.*, III, 256.

147. Nevins, *Henry White*, 273; Tardieu, *La Conférence*, 180. Of course, Radowitz was ignorant of White's entente with Révoil.

148. Nicolson to Grey, Feb. 16, 1906, *B. D.*, III, 259; Radolin to F. O., No. 7010, Feb. 15, 1906, *G. P.*, XXI, 171-172. The mandate, Rouvier insisted, was neither exclusive nor general, since it associated Spain with France and was confined to the chief ports.

149. Nevins, *Henry White*, 273-274; Tardieu, *La Conférence*, 180-181.

150. Radowitz to F. O., No. 7011, Feb. 16, 1906, *G. P.*, XXI, 172; Nicolson to Grey, Feb. 15, 1906, *B. D.*, III, 257; Tardieu, *La Conférence*, 181.

151. Nicolson to Grey, Feb. 16, 1906, *B. D.*, III, 260. The eight powers were France, Germany, Great Britain, Spain, Russia, Italy, Austria-Hungary, and the United States.

152. Nicolson to Grey, Feb. 16, 1906, *Ibid.*, III, 259.

153. Wedel to F. O., No. 7014, Feb. 18, 1906, *G. P.*, XXI, 175-176. On Goluchowski's alleged desire to gain personal prestige as mediator, see Tardieu, *La Conférence*, 202-203.

154. Radowitz to F. O., No. 7012, Feb. 17, 1906, G. P., XXI, 173.

155. Bülow to Radowitz, No. 7013, Feb. 18, 1906, Ibid., 174; Tardieu, La Conférence, 187; Grey to Lascelles, Feb. 19, 1906, B. D., III, 263-264.

156. Tardieu, La Conférence, 190-192.

157. The "sophisms" designated by Tardieu were the "pretended promise made to Dr. Rosen not to demand for France the police mandate," the voluntary misrepresentation which they put upon the character and extent of this mandate, the misrepresentation in the Wolff dispatch of the attitude of the French delegates at Algeciras and the imputation to France of responsibilities which she could not accept. Ibid., 202.

158. Ibid., 217-218.

159. Ibid., 257.

160. Ibid., 188-190, 200, 207-208, 254, 256; Stumm to Bülow, No. 7024, Feb. 20, 1906, G. P., XXI, 189-191; Grey to Egerton and Cartwright, Feb. 19, 1906, B. D., III, 262; Cartwright to Grey, Feb. 21, 1906, Ibid., 268-269.

161. Spring-Rice to Grey, Feb. 19, 1906, Ibid., 245-246.

162. Tardieu, La Conférence, 197-198, 205. Schoen's arguments made no impression upon Lamsdorff.

163. Grey to Spring-Rice, Feb. 20, 1906, B. D., III, 264-265.

164. Tardieu, La Conférence, 246-247; Schoen to F. O., No. 7025, Feb. 20, 1906, G. P., XXI, 192; Eulenburg to William II, No. 7027, Feb. 22, 1906, Ibid., 194 and Anlage; Witte to Eulenburg, Feb. 20, 1906, Ibid., 195-197.

165. Schoen to F. O., No. 7017, Feb. 19, 1906, Ibid., 178-179.

166. Grey to Lascelles, Feb. 19, 1906, B. D., III, 263-264; Metternich to F. O., No. 7018, Feb. 19, 1906, G. P., XXI, 179-181.

167. New York Times, Feb. 20, 1906, 8 and Feb. 21, 1906, 8.

168. Sternburg to Bülow, No. 7019, Feb. 19, 1906, G. P., XXI, 181-183; Root to Sternburg, Feb. 19, 1906, Bishop, Theodore Roosevelt, I, 489-491; Tardieu, La Conférence, 249.

169. Conversations on the bank had been carried on between Regnault, Tattenbach, and their advisers since Jan. 26. Ibid., 183-187.

170. Radowitz to F. O., No. 7015, Feb. 19, 1906, G. P., XXI, 176-177.

171. Radowitz to F. O., No. 7016, Feb. 19, 1906, Ibid., 177-178. All precautions were being taken at the conference "to throw responsibility of probable rupture on proper shoulders," i. e., Germany's because of her refusal to accept the latest police proposal and her sudden change to the bank problem. Nicolson to Grey, Feb. 21, 1906, B. D., III, 268.

172. Tardieu, La Conférence, 225.

173. Bülow to Radowitz, No. 6966, Jan. 27, 1906, G. P., XXI, 115-119.

174. Tardieu, La Conférence, 227-233.

175. Radowitz to F. O., No. 7032, Feb. 21, 1906, G. P., XXI, 204-205: "In the bank question the representatives of Austria, Italy, America, Holland, and Morocco are more or less frankly on our side." Radowitz to F. O., No. 7035, Feb. 22, 1906, Ibid., 205: "America and Russia, as well as the smaller states, took no part in the discussions, and Marquis Visconti Venosta only to suggest that the disputed points be referred to the editing committee."

176. Memorandum by Grey, Feb. 20, 1906, B. D., III, 266-268.

177. Bülow to Sternburg, No. 7020, Feb. 21, 1906, G. P., XXI, 183-184; Sternburg to Roosevelt, Feb. 22, 1906, Bishop, Theodore Roosevelt, I, 491-493.

178. Sternburg to F. O., No. 7038, Feb. 23, 1906, G. P., XXI, 213. Germany's tariff concessions to the United States were announced that same day; "Reichstag Sanctions the Concession to Us," New York Times, Feb. 23, 1906, 5.

179. White to Root, March 5, 1906; cited by Vagts, Weltpolitik, II, 1895, footnote 6.

180. Tardieu, La Conférence, 260-263; "Jaurès Attacks Rouvier," New York Times, Feb. 24, 1906, 4.

181. Tardieu, La Conférence, 266-267, 270-271, 276: "White promised his cooperation with pleasure, since the vote did not have a character ostensibly political" (276).

182. Cartwright to Grey, Feb. 22, 1906, B. D., III, 270-271 and Feb. 24, 1906, Ibid., 273; Nicolson to Grey, Feb. 23, 1906, Ibid., 271; Grey to Cartwright, Feb. 23, 1906, Ibid., 271.

183. Nicolson to Grey, Feb. 26, 1906, Ibid., 276.

184. Tardieu, La Conférence, 205-206, 253, 254; Nicolson, Portrait of a Diplomatist, 135.

185. Tardieu, La Conférence, 251, 275.

186. Grey to Goschen, Feb. 26, 1906, B. D., III, 276-277.

187. Goschen to Grey, Feb. 24, 1906, Ibid., 273; Tardieu, La Conférence, 258-259.

188. Ibid., 257-258; memorandum of Bülow, No. 7039, Feb. 24, 1906, G. P., XXI, 213-214.

189. Spring-Rice to Grey, Feb. 22, 1906, B. D., III, 269; Grey to Spring-Rice, Feb. 22, 1906, Ibid., 270.

190. Spring-Rice to Grey, Feb. 24, 1906, Ibid., 271; Tardieu, La Conférence, 248. The Tsar considered the German policy contrary to the Kaiser's assurances at Björkö as well as the agreements of July 8 and Sept. 28.

191. Spring-Rice to Grey, Feb. 24, 1906, B. D., III, 274; Schoen to F. O., Feb. 23, 1906, No. 7037, G. P., XXI, 212-213. The downfall of Rouvier, war in Morocco, a general European war, and more revolutions were the specters conjured up by Lamsdorff.

192. Spring-Rice to Grey, Feb. 28, 1906, B. D., III, 278.

193. Spring-Rice to Grey, Feb. 24, 1906, Ibid., 272. Crowe's minute on this dispatch is "The United States will not interfere."

194. Schoen to Bülow, No. 7029, Feb. 24, 1906, G. P., XXI, 198-201.

195. Tardieu, La Conférence, 247-248.

196. Ibid., 249; Schoen to F. O., No. 7052, March 3, 1906, G. P., XXI, 234-235.

197. Memorandum of Holstein, Feb. 22, 1906, Nos. 7034 and 7035, Ibid., 206-209; Bülow to Radolin, No. 7036, Feb. 22, 1906, Ibid., 208-211. Tardieu, La Conférence, 243-245 and Grey to Bertie, Feb. 28, 1906, B. D., III, 278, credit Bülow with the scheme. Holstein and Bülow talked with Courcel on Feb. 20-22, during the latter's visit to Berlin. See also Gooch, "Holstein," 93-95.

198. Germany and France could then make a permanent arrangement, giving Morocco to France in return for German compensation elsewhere.

199. The similarities of this plan to the one proposed to Roosevelt on Feb. 21 should be noted.

200. Lascelles to Grey, March 1, 1906, B. D., III, 280.

201. Cortissoz, Reid, II, 328-329.

202. Roosevelt to Reid, March 1, 1906, Ibid., 329-330.

203. Jusserand to F. O., March 2, 1906; What Me Befell, 323-324.

204. Root to White, March 2, 1906; cited by Vagts, Weltpolitik, II, 1895-1896, footnote 8.

205. "War Over Morocco Feared by America," New York Times, March 2, 1906, 1-2; "Can It Be War?" (editorial), Ibid., March 3, 1906, 8. Rouvier, also apprehensive, was considering a purely Moorish police for two years, until Russia was stronger. Bertie to Grey, March 2, 1906, B. D., III, 281-282.

206. Tardieu, La Conférence, 251-252.

207. Editor's note to No. 7143, G. P., XXI, 338-339.

208. Bülow, Memoirs, I, 572 and II, 125-126; Gooch, "Holstein," 95.

209. Radowitz to F. O., No. 7045, Feb. 26, 1906, G. P., XXI, 223-224.

210. Bülow to Radowitz, No. 7046, Feb. 28, 1906, Ibid., 224-225.

211. Radowitz to F. O., No. 7053, March 3, 1906, Ibid., 235-236.

212. Wedel to F. O., No. 7049, March 1, 1906, Ibid., 228-230 and No. 7056, March 4, 1906, Ibid., 238-239.

213. Radolin to F. O., No. 7067, March 6, 1906, Ibid., 250-251. King Edward VII, visiting in Paris, included among his dinner guests Rouvier and Courcel. The latter admitted that there was no official offer from Berlin, but spoke of the necessity for compromise. Bertie to Grey, March 5, 1906, B. D., III, 284.

214. Radowitz to F. O., No. 7051, March 3, 1906, G. P., XXI, 233-234. The British-French-Spanish-Russian combination was evident for the first time. White and Venosta took no definite stand.

215. Nicolson, Portrait of A Diplomatist, 139-140; Nicolson to Grey, March 3, 1906, B. D., III, 282-284; Nevins, Henry White, 275; Radowitz to F. O., No. 7072, March 7, 1906, G. P., XXI, 258.

216. Tardieu, La Conférence, 283-291; Nicolson to Grey, March 7, 1906, B. D., III, 285-286; Radowitz to F. O., No. 7062, March 5, 1906, G. P., XXI, 244-245.

217. "Enthusiasm in Paris for the British King," New York Times, March 5, 1906, 1; Lee, King Edward VII, II, 510.

218. Radowitz to F. O., No. 7060, March 5, 1906, G. P., XXI, 241-243.

219. Bülow to Radowitz, No. 7063, March 6, 1906, Ibid., 245-246.

220. Bülow to Wedel and Monts, No. 7065, March 6, 1906, Ibid., 248-249.

221. White to Root, March 7, 1906, D. S., Special Agents, L, 188-189.

222. Tardieu, La Conférence, 298.

223. Root to Sternburg, March 7, 1906, Bishop, Theodore Roosevelt, I, 493-495; Sternburg to F. O., No. 7074, March 7, 1906, G. P., XXI, 259-261.

224. Vagts, Weltpolitik, II, 1897, footnote 2.

225. Both the French and the Austrian projects were presented; Radowitz endorsed the latter. Nicolson to Grey, March 9, 1906, B. D., III, 289-291; Tardieu, La Conférence, 296-297, 301-307; 379-381. Venosta refused to cooperate with Welsersheimb; Wedel to F. O., No. 7083, March 9, 1906, G. P., XXI, 269.

226. New York Times, March 5, 1906, 11; March 7, 1906, 1; March 6, 1906, 4.

227. Tardieu, La Conférence, 300-301.

228. Nicolson to Grey, March 9, 1906; B. D., III, 288-289 and March 10, 1906, Ibid., 294-295, Grey to Nicolson, March 10, 1906, Ibid., 292 and March 12, 1906, Ibid., 300; Grey to Bertie, March 9, 1906, Ibid., 289.

229. Radolin to F. O., No. 7080, March 8, 1906, G. P., XXI, 265-266.

230. Bertie to Grey, March 10, 1906, B. D., III, 292.

231. Nicolson to Grey, March 10, 1906, Ibid., 293; Tardieu, La Conférence, 312.

232. Nicolson to Grey, March 11, 1906, B. D., III, 295-297, 298.

233. Radowitz to F. O., No. 7089, March 11, 1906, G. P., XXI, 272-273.

234. Bertie to Grey, March 11, 1906, B. D., III, 296-297.

235. Tardieu, La Conférence, 312-313; Radowitz to F. O., No. 7089, March 11, 1906, G. P., XXI, 272-273.

236. Radowitz to F. O., No. 7094, March 12, 1906, Ibid., 279. This amendment, formulated by Révoil and Almodovar, was approved by Rouvier. Nicolson to Grey, March 11, 1906, B. D., III, 296; Hardinge to Nicolson, March 15, 1906, Ibid., 305.

237. Nicolson to Grey, March 12, 1906, Ibid., 298-299. In minutes on this dispatch, Eyre Crowe said: "If we are anxious to make a last effort, I can only suggest our endeavouring to put the French case as strongly as possible before President Roosevelt and asking him whether he could make a communication at Berlin. Such a move would however come more properly from the French Government themselves. Perhaps France and Great Britain could approach the President together?"

238. Grey to Lascelles and Bertie, March 13, 1906, Ibid., 302.

239. Cambon was informed of Grey's opinion; Grey to Nicolson, March 12, 1906, Ibid., 300. Nicolson held the same views; Nicolson to Grey, March 13, 1906, Ibid., 300-301.

240. Tardieu, La Conférence, 316-318; Instructions of Bülow, No. 7091, March 12, 1906, G. P., XXI, 274-275.

241. Schoen to F. O., No. 7095, March 13, 1906, Ibid., 279-280; Monts to F. O., No. 7097, March 13, 1906, Ibid., 280-281; Wedel to F. O., No. 7099, March 13, 1906, Ibid., 281-282; Metternich to F. O., No. 7100, March 13, 1906, Ibid., 282-284.

242. Tardieu, La Conférence, 321, 328, 326-329, 337-342.

243. Grey, Twenty-Five Years, I, 102, 108-109; Grey to Bertie, March 14, 1906, B. D., III, 303 and March 15, 1906, Ibid., 304-305; Grey to Nicolson, Lascelles, and Bertie, March 14, 1906, Ibid., 304; Hardinge to Nicolson, March 15, 1906, Ibid., 305; Bertie to Grey, March 15, 1906, Ibid., 306, March 16, 1906, Ibid., 307 and March 17, 1906, Ibid., 309-310; Tardieu, La Conférence, 329-330.

244. Nicolson to Grey, March 14, 1906, B. D., III, 303; Hardinge to Nicolson, March 15, 1906, Ibid., 305.

245. Bertie to Grey, March 16, 1906, Ibid., 307-308; Grey to Bertie, March 17, 1906, Ibid., 308-309; Radolin to F. O., No. 7104, March 14, 1906, G. P., XXI, 291-292 and No. 7107, March 15, 1906, Ibid., 295-297; Tardieu, La Conférence, 342-345. On March 17 Radolin made his last attempt to get France to accept the Austrian project in its original form, Ibid., 344.

246. "Upon the double dialog between Washington and Berlin and between Vienna and Paris depended, as everyone knew, the success of the conference;" Ibid., 347.

"British delegate ... tells me confidentially that his Government agrees with him in thinking France cannot with propriety hold out. French delegate who made no concession ... hopes to hear the President has obtained better terms from the Emperor;" White to Root, March 10, 1906; D. S., Special Agents, L, 193.

247. Die Grosse Politik disproves the alleged "three telegrams of William II, dated the 13th, the 15th, and the 17th of March;" Tardieu, La Conférence, 335.

248. Sternburg to Roosevelt, March 13, 1906, Bishop, Theodore Roosevelt, I, 495-497; Bülow to Sternburg, No. 7093, March 12, 1906, G. P., XXI, 276-278.

249. Sternburg to F. O., No. 7102, March 14, 1906, G. P., XXI, 285-286.

250. Root to White, March 13, 1906, cited by Vagts, Weltpolitik, II, 1899; March 17, 1906, cited by Nevins, Henry White, 277.

251. Bishop, Theodore Roosevelt, I, 489.

252. Bülow to Sternburg, No. 7106, March 16, 1906, G. P., XXI, 293-295.

253. Sternburg to Roosevelt, Bishop, Theodore Roosevelt, I, 497.

254. Sternburg to F. O., No. 7112, March 17, 1906, G. P., XXI, 300-307.

255. Root to Sternburg, March 17, 1906, Bishop, Theodore Roosevelt, I, 497-499; Sternburg to F. O., No. 7115, March 18, 1906, G. P., XXI, 305-306.

256. Sternburg to F. O., No. 7113, March 18, 1906, Ibid., 302-303.

257. Rêvoil informed White that Jusserand "was aware of contents of your note of 17th before its despatch and thanked you for it." White to Root, March 23, 1906,

D. S., Special Agents, L, 207. Nicolson knew the main thesis of the note on the 17th and had its full text two days later. Nicolson to Grey, March 17 and 19, 1906, B. D., III, 308, 310-312, 313-314.

258. Nicolson to Grey, March 18, 1906, Ibid., 311.

259. Bishop, Theodore Roosevelt, I, 499-500; Bülow to Sternburg, No. 7118, March 19, 1906, G. P., XXI, 309-310. White showed Nicolson the whole telegram; Nicolson to Grey, March 21, 1906, B. D., III, 315.

260. Sternburg to F. O., No. 7121, March 21, 1906, G. P., XXI, 311-312, "Roosevelt on Result of Morocco Conference," New York Times, April 13, 1906, 10.

261. Nicolson to Grey, March 19, 1906, B. D., III, 313.

262. Grey to Goschen, March 21, 1906, Ibid., 315; Grey to Bunsen, March 21, 1906, Ibid., 316.

263. Ibid.; Bunsen to Grey, March 27, 1906, Ibid., 325-326.

264. Tardieu, La Conférence, 385-386.

265. Szögyeny-Marin to Tschirschky, No. 7127, March 23, 1906, G. P., XXI, 321-322.

266. Anderson, First Moroccan Crisis, 387, 391, 388.

267. Tardieu, La Conférence, 331-333; Spring-Rice to Grey, March 21, 1906, B. D., III, 316-317; Nicolson to Grey, March 21, 1906, Ibid., 315.

268. Tardieu, La Conférence, 387-388.

269. White to Root, March 20, 1906, D. S., Special Agents, L, 201-203.

270. Sternburg, to F. O., No. 7126, March 22, 1906, G. P., XXI, 221.

271. Root to White, March 21, 1906, cited by Vagts, Weltpolitik, II, 1903, footnote 3.

272. Tardieu, La Conférence, 354-355; Nicolson to Grey, March 21 and 23, 1906, B. D., III, 314-315, 318-320; Grey to Goschen, March 23, 1906, Ibid., 318-319.

273. Root to Carter, March 22, 1906, cited by Vagts, Weltpolitik, II, 1903.

274. Bertie to Grey, March 22, 1906, B. D., III, 317-318.

275. The opposition of France was expressed in Le Temps on March 22 and 23; Tardieu, La Conférence, 387; and in New York Times, March 23, 1906, 4.

276. Carter to Root, March 22, 1906, cited by Vagts, Weltpolitik, II, 1903; Grey to Durand, March 22 and 23, 1906, B. D., III, 317.

277. Jusserand, What Me Befell, 324-325.

278. Durand to Grey, March 24, 1906, B. D., III, 321.

279. Durand to Grey, March 24, 1906, Ibid., 320-321; Sternburg to F. O., No. 7130, March 24, 1906, G. P., XXI, 324.

280. Vagts, Weltpolitik, II, 1901.

281. In an even authentic American accounts, the Kaiser's surrender to Roosevelt receives so much empahsis that it is possible to overlook the latter's capitulation to Great Britain and France. See, for example, Nevins, Henry White, 276-278.

282. F. R., 1906, II, 486.

283. Oscar S. Straus, Under Four Administrations, 192.

284. Bülow to Radowitz, No. 7129, March 24, 1906, G. P., XXI, 322-323; Radowitz to F. O., No. 7131, March 25, 1906, Ibid., 324-326; Tardieu, La Conférence, 388-389.

285. Nicolson to Grey, March 26, 1906, B. D., III, 321 and March 27, 1906, Ibid., 322-324; F. R., 1906,

Part 2, 1486; Tardieu, La Conférence, 367-371.

286. Nicolson to Grey, March 27, 1906, B. D., III, 324-325; Radowitz to F. O., No. 7134, March 27, 1906, G. P., XXI, 328; Radowitz to Bülow, No. 7137, March 28, 1906, Ibid., 330-331; F. R., 1906, Part 2, 1487-1488. The formula was prepared in advance by Révoil and Bourgeois, according to Tardieu, La Conférence, 371-372.

287. "American Plan Leads to Morocco Agreement," New York Times, March 28, 1906, 4: "The successful action of the American delegates has made certain the speedy end of the labors of the conference." "Morocco Conference Ends With Agreement," Ibid., April 1, 1906, 4: "Leading delegates say that the agreement was in no small measure due to the efficacy of the mediation on the part of the United States through its chief representative."

288. "We had, in a word, reduced to the minimum an inevitable evil. Was this paying too much for the closing of Morocco to the German police, the definite defeat of internationalization, the practical recognition of our special interests?" Tardieu, La Conférence, 376.

289. Ibid., 374-376; Nicolson to Grey, March 28, 1906, B. D., III, 326-327.

290. Tardieu, La Conférence, 378-385, 390-395.

291. Radowitz to F. O., No. 7138, March 31, 1906, G. P., XXI, 331-332; Nicolson to Grey, April 1, 1906, B. D., III, 328; Grey to Nicolson, April 2, 1906, Ibid., 329; F. R., 1906, Part 2, 1489; Tardieu, La Conférence, 396-403.

292. White to Root, March 29 and April 1, 1906; Root to White, March 29, 1906; cited by Vagts, Weltpolitik, II, 1905.

293. Nicolson to Grey, B. D., III, April 3, 1906, 330; F. R., 1906, Part 2, 1490; Tardieu, La Conférence, 404.

294. In striking contrast to the French and German second delegates, Gummeré played a thoroughly obscure role at the conference and is almost entirely ignored in the reports.

295. F. R., 1906, Part 2, 1471-1476, 1487, 1494.

296. "We Won, Says Bülow," New York Times, April 5, 1906, 6. Bülow's assessment of Roosevelt's influence is of interest: "The European Powers have been aware that President Roosevelt was ready to assist in any proper manner in the effort for an agreement. The American Government's advice and attitude were helpful, especially during the latter stages of the conference. Mr. White was a conciliatory force."

297. "Bülow Collapses in Reichstag," New York Times, April 6, 1906, 7.

298. Lascelles to Grey, April 5, 1906, B. D., III, 333-334. For Holstein's later denial that he was responsible for Germany's foreign policy, see Lascelles to Grey, Oct. 23, 1907, Ibid., 332-333.

299. Bülow, Memoirs, II, 227, 230.

300. McCormick to Root, April 4, 1906, cited by Dennis, Adventures, 507.

301. Bishop, Theodore Roosevelt, I, 503.

302. Roosevelt to Edward VII, April 25, 1906, Bishop, Theodore Roosevelt, II, 257-258.

303. Roosevelt to Reid, Ibid., I, 467-505; Sykes, Durand, 301.

304. Almodovar said that the unanimity of the powers was a guarantee of the maintenance of the Sultan's sovereignty, the integrity of his territory, and the economic liberty without any inequality of all the states. Tardieu, La Conférence, 417.

305. White said that the recognition of France's special financial interests would not militate against the Open Door in commerce, competition for the execution of public works, or the future development of the great mineral wealth of Morocco: F. R., 1906, II, 1495.

306. Lowther to Grey, April 22, 1906, B. D., III, 338; Rosen to Bülow, May 17, 1906, No. 7276, G. P., XXI, 601.

307. Root to Collier, May 4, 1906, F. R., 1906, Part 2, 1494-1495.

308. White to Root, April 14, 1906, Nevins, Henry White, 281.

309. Roosevelt to White, April 30, 1906, Ibid., 280.

310. Roosevelt to White, Aug. 14, 1906, Bishop, Theodore Roosevelt, II, 270-271.

311. Tardieu, La Conférence, 82, 461-462.

Chapter IX

The Modernization of the Monroe Doctrine (1898-1907)

During the Spanish-American War, under the aegis of McKinley, but with the blessing and active assistance of Roosevelt, the United States had begun to transform the Monroe Doctrine. In this war she had intervened to free a rebellious colony of a European country in Asia, while in the Caribbean she had broken Monroe's promise that "with the existing colonies and dependencies of any European Power (in America) we ... shall not interfere." Thus one of the two pledges of the Monroe Doctrine had been repudiated.

As president, Roosevelt continued the metamorphosis of the cardinal American foreign policy. While enforcing strictly the two prohibitions upon Europe, against further colonization of America and oppression or control of any independent American country, he broke the other American pledge of non-interference in European affairs, now extended to cover conflicts in Africa and Asia as well as in Europe itself. However, in updating the American foreign policy of 1823 to prepare the United States for graduation into world power status, he continued to invoke the traditions of Monroeism on suitable occasions. Remarkably, he succeeded in completing all the diplomatic projects that he initiated, in spite of determined opposition from the American press and the Senate and much adverse criticism from European publicists and governments. He became adept at making secret ententes and executive agreements to supplement or to substitute for open convenants openly arrived at. Withal, in playing what he sincerely believed to be the predestined role of himself and of his country, he received greater honor and acclaim than any other American statesmen as the keeper of the peace of the world.

Theodore Roosevelt was interested in both the theoretical and the pragmatic aspects of American foreign policy.

On October 11, 1901, he wrote to Sternburg, then a consul in India, proposing a doctrinal formula applicable to both the Americas and to China and designed to serve United States interests. He regarded the Monroe Doctrine as equivalent to the Open Door in both areas. Qualifying the prohibitions of the Monroe Doctrine, he would reserve to any foreign state the right to "intervene with transitory intervention ... when there was a row with some State in South America," but he admitted that the Monroe Doctrine would work in China only "if the Chinese could be forced to behave themselves--not permitted to do anything atrocious, but not partitioned."[1]

Shortly thereafter, the problem of European countries' collection of loans from Caribbean countries became serious. Too many grab-and-run dictators either left their homelands in bankruptcy or stayed to defy their creditors. The President then abandoned his theory of "transitory intervention" by European states as a proper remedy. In the case of the armed intervention of Germany and Great Britain to collect debts due from Venezuela in 1902-1903, he demanded that Germany accept arbitration instead of "temporary" occupation of a port to enforce payment of Castro's debts. He succeeded in this shift of principle.

Even before the Venezuelan episode, however, a similar situation in Santo Domingo had afforded a practical approach to solution of the international debt problem. In 1901, when Santo Domingo repudiated a receivership granted voluntarily to an American company in 1892, the United States government intervened. On January 31, 1903, representatives of the United States and Santo Domingo signed a protocol providing for settlement of the American company's claims and a board of arbitration to arrange the payments. When the Dominican government became delinquent in payments, the provision for an American agent to take over a customs house was put into effect on October 21, 1904. At Hay's suggestion, a protocol was signed by President Morales on February 4, 1905, turning all customs houses over to the United States, whose agent was to allow the Dominican government 45 percent of the receipts and to use the remainder to liquidate equitably the total debt of Santo Domingo.[2] To this agreement the Senate refused consent, although the President sent a special message on March 6, appealing for immediate action. Considering the situation critical and danger of foreign intervention imminent, Roosevelt proceeded to carry on the arrangement as an executive agreement. A modus vivendi accepted by Santo Domingo enabled Secretary of War Taft to nominate as revenue collectors Americans who served as Dominican officials.[3]

Meanwhile, the German government was urging Roosevelt to take a stand in favor of the Open Door in Morocco and to back up Germany in strengthening the opposition of Abd al-Aziz to French reforms in his country. On March 5, 1905, the President gave the attitude of the Senate as his chief reason for declining to interfere in Morocco:

> In my foreign policy I am going up against enormous difficulties in Congress, because they take foreign affairs so seriously there. My policy in the Far East they understand at last, and on all sides they approve of my accord with Germany there. Two years ago this would have been absolutely unthinkable. But my policy in the Caribbean Sea and in the Southern Hemisphere is as yet entirely incomprehensible to the people here, and Congress gives me the greatest difficulty of all in carrying this out. If I were to let myself in for Morocco also, a country which is entirely unknown here, I would lay myself open to the most serious attacks .... Should I sanction a convening of the notables and excite the expectations of the Sultan, I should be obliged to commit myself to further steps. But on principle I undertake no step in foreign politics if I am not sure that with determination I shall be able eventually to achieve my aim.[4]

Later Roosevelt decided to ignore for the time being the obstructive tactics of the Senate,[5] and during its recess he entered actively into the negotiations leading to the Algeciras Conference. The appointment of Henry White and Samuel Gummeré as representatives to the conference and their instructions by the State Department were not mentioned to the Senate.

In his annual message of December 5, 1905, the President made no mention whatever of the approaching conference.[6] But although the Moroccan problem might be postponed by silence, the fight already begun on Santo Domingo had to be carried on openly.[7] In the message, therefore, Roosevelt devoted considerable space to his Dominican policy. After relating the history of his negotiations, he defended his action in placing the customs under American control as a necessary corollary of the Monroe Doctrine:

> On the one hand, this country would certainly decline to go to war to prevent a foreign government from collecting a just debt; on the other hand, it is very inadvisable to permit any foreign power to take possession, even temporarily, of the customs-houses of an American republic in order to enforce the payment of its obligations, for such temporary occupation might turn into a permanent occupation. The only escape from these alternatives may at any time be that we must ourselves undertake to bring about some arrangement by which so much as possible of a just obligation shall be paid .... For the United States to take such a position offers the only possible way of insuring us against a clash with some foreign power.

Thus was promulgated the doctrine generally known as the Roosevelt Corollary to the Monroe Doctrine. It was simply that to avoid a forcible intervention of a foreign power for debt collection or for any purpose, which was liable to develop into a permanent occupation of territory, the United States herself must exercise the authority of an international police to prevent wrong-doing by other American republics.[8] It was a radical doctrine, sure to be challenged at home and abroad, and Roosevelt had good reason to expect a double attack on his Dominican policy and Moroccan involvement in the Algeciras Conference.

The feud between the President and the Senate was based on their contest for predominance in the unbalance maintained by the check system of the American government. Before the accession of Roosevelt the Senate held the reins of power.[9] At the outset of Roosevelt's presidency, it was predicted that Congress would be the "malignant influence in his horoscope" and that any trouble that he might have would be caused by the Senate.[10] In domestic legislation the President had set a pace on unbroken paths which he made it difficult for Congress to follow. His foreign policy, however, proved to be even more unacceptable for the Senate in its role of protector of the Constitution and guardian of the traditional Monroe Doctrine. Moreover, the Senate was determined to preserve its prerogative of treaty-rejection, a function that aroused the wrath of Hay, who affirmed that "a treaty entering the Senate is like a bull going into the arena; no one can say just how or when the final blow will fall--but one thing is certain--it will never leave the arena alive."[11] The succession of Elihu Root to the post of Secretary of State was undoubtedly a large factor in Roosevelt's eventual victory over the Senate in his two most hotly contested foreign policies. There resulted his two amendments to the Monroe Doctrine, occasioned specifically by the situations in Santo Domingo and in Morocco, which formed precedents for later presidents to follow. When Root assumed his new position, he at once established friendly and intimate relations with the Senate Committee on Foreign Relations, a policy that paid dividends in treaties accepted.[12]

While awaiting the inevitable renewal of the controversey with the Senate over his Dominican policy, the President was subjected to critical questioning from his other _bête noire,_ the American press, frequently citing the European press. Since the Perdicaris affair, Morocco had become a topic of prime interest to Americans, and from the Kaiser's visit to Tangier until the end of 1906, the discussion of Moroccan affairs was frequent. American journalists provided not only a record of Moroccan events, but also extensive speculations about the policies of Great Britain, Germany, France, and Spain regarding Morocco and the relationships of these countries to each other and to the United States. However, the chief focus of American commentators was upon Roosevelt's apparent desertion of traditional foreign policy by becoming involved in European quarrels. A thorough survey of countrywide writings would require volumes, but the trend of press opinion is indicated from representative articles.

The attitude of the American press was mostly favorable to France, except for the German-language newspapers.[13] There was general approval of the system of ententes by which Great Britain, France, Spain, and Italy had secured their "interests and rights" in Morocco. When French victory appeared imminent, the _New York Times_ gave the verdict that France would have "ultimately the control of the whole southwestern littoral of the Mediterranean--a consummation distinctly in the interest of civilization."[14] American readers saw few such indictments of Europeans' conduct toward Morocco as the following one, supposedly made by a Moorish alim:

> What do you want of us, you Christians? ... Have we invaded your land? Did we beg you to come and reside on our soil? Have we not continuously discouraged your so doing? You say our country is "disturbed, that the government is weak, and so on. Is that your affair or ours? ... What have you done that we should love you? You have taught many of us, a nation of water drinkers, to be drunkards. You have also smuggled into our country magazine rifles by the thousand, and sold them at one hundred percent profit, to our rebels, causing the very mischief you complain about. You have first duped and then betrayed our Sultan. Now you say you will help us to govern. We decline your help. We are told, in the writing of Allah, "Oh, true believers, take not the Jews or Christians for your friends," and again, "Oh true believers, take not the unbelievers for your protectors." You would help our Sultan to repress rebellion; and we are to allow you to slaughter our erring brethren? Never! When we have declined your pacific intervention, what then? You will use force. So be it. We also shall fight, for our land, our families, our dead saints, and our living faith. With this difference, we trust in our God; you have none.[15]

The British attitude toward Germany caused much perceptive comment. In the simultaneous reorganization of the British and German fleets, the concentration of the main British fleet in the North Sea, it was explained in a British periodical, was merely a preventive measure to avoid possible hostilities. The cordial fraternization of the British Channel fleet with a German squadron in the Baltic Sea was described in October, 1905.[16] Later the American press took note of several meetings in London of people seeking to promote Anglo-German friendship and of two letters of similar aim in the London Standard, one signed by Germans eminent in science, art, and literature and the other by a group of equally prominent Englishmen. But on the eve of the Algeciras Conference there was a disturbing account of a challenge to Bülow by both the Socialist Bebel and the London Times, bidding him translate into deeds the friendship for Britain which he had been proclaiming.[17]

The anxiety of Roosevelt and European statesmen regarding the danger of war in 1905 was shared by American journalists, who devoted much more space in their articles to war than they did to peace prospects. The dismissal of Delcassé was credited with averting war in June, 1905.[18] An English political writer was quoted as saying that two conditions aggravated the danger of conflict--the restless virulence of the French, German, and British newspapers, all equally guilty, and the bitterness of Anglo-German commercial competition. These causes of friction could be obviated by mutual concessions.[19] Of special interest was the article in the Paris Matin of October 7, 1905, supposed to be inspired by Delcassé and purporting to give the secret history of the June crisis. Both the French and the British Cabinets denied the charge that Great Britain had promised and planned in detail her aid to France if the latter were attacked, or that the British fleet would seize the Kiel Canal and would land 100,000 British troops in Schleswig-Holstein to cooperate with an equal number of French soldiers there. French writers denied that France could have planned a war for which she was unprepared.[20] Another article gave the inside story of the enforced resignation of the too bellicose Delcassé.[21]

For over a year, from March, 1905 to April, 1906, numerous articles appeared in the American press on German-American relations, with strong emphasis on the alleged friendship of Roosevelt and William II and their exchange of gifts and courtesies and on the Emperor's aims and ambitions regarding Morocco. The writers did not have access to the private comments of the two men on each other, and they were invariably pictured as firm friends, whose amity drew their nations closer together--so close, indeed, that a German writer ventured to suggest that a combined German-American navy would surpass the British one and would enable the two countries to establish a "Pax Teutonica" in the world.[22]

Of great interest to American readers was the

German-American intellectual entente established in 1905. In the first commencement address at Clark University, the President praised the recent Schiller anniversary celebration in Germany and paid tribute to German contributions to the United States in blood, scholarship, and idealism.[23] Several articles commended the exchange of university students, with full accreditation of American students in Germany, the exchange of professors, and the Germanic Museum at Harvard. Especially gratifying to American pride was the lecture tour in the United States by Dr. Ludwig Fulda, an eminent poet and dramatist, who conceded that "America is no longer a country of crass commercialism, but has developed a fine appreciation of ideal values and an immense thirst for culture."[24]

American journalists could view complacently a German-American intellectual rapprochement, but their attitude was generally unfavorable toward a possible diplomatic-economic entente. The Kaiser was blamed for the expression "administrative entity" in Hay's Open Door pronouncement, and he was accused of insinuating himself into Hay's Open Door movement in China and Morocco for political motives.[25] His descent upon Tangier and quarrel with Delcassé "over an obscure point of diplomatic etiquette" were considered as wantonly unfriendly to France. Yet an occasional voice was heard asserting that Germany occupied "an unassailable position, both in law and logic," in refusing to be bound by or to recognize the ententes threatening her economic rights in Morocco after thirty years; however, her methods of protest were doomed to failure.[26]

An extreme diatribe against William II in a Washington Post editorial read thus:

> William is the predominant, if not the pre-eminent war lord of his time, and much of his speech is of battle .... He has the most powerful army in the world, and his navy is second to but one, possibly two, other navies. He loves to exploit both and hold them in menace over trembling Europe .... Just now the Emperor is taking a hand in North African affairs .... Is it merely a periodical bullying of France? .... The statesmen of Europe are in a fever of anxiety regarding

> the aims of the German Emperor .... The menace is not in the Moroccan situation, but in the fact that Germany is free to deal with France as she sees fit, without fear of Russia .... What will Emperor William do? What is his ultimate purpose? .... If she is able to enter into favorable arrangements with Germany, Great Britain may be depended upon to leave France in the lurch .... Emperor William's aims all tend in the same direction--the forthcoming advent of Germany as an aggressor, probably against France, possibly against Holland and Denmark, for the purposes of widening the boundaries of Germany and furnishing an outlet for her energies in colonial expansion.[27]

A review of a French article gave Americans much to think about concerning the magnitude and menace of German expansion of population and commerce since 1870 in Europe, Asia, Africa, and the Americas.[28] Other adverse criticism in the American press was directed toward Germany's backing of the Sultan's call for an international conference and her advance of a loan to the Maghzen after July 8.[29] A news dispatch quoted Bebel as naming the German Empire as the world's most reactionary state, while he incited merriment in the Reichstag by recalling the Kaiser's notorious telegram to the Tsar, "The Admiral of the Atlantic greets the Admiral of the Pacific." An editorial expressed hope that, although he was reported to have antimilitarist support, the probable election of M. Fallières as president of France would not weaken France at Algeciras.[30].

For an affair that Roosevelt later labelled as too secret to be shared with any but a small group of his contemporaries--and with posterity--his diplomatic dalliance with William II regarding the Moroccan problem received an extraordinary amount of publicity. From early April in 1905 till the end of the Algeciras Conference a year later, both American and European journalists recorded events and speculated on motives of this German-American collaboration, sometimes with an approximation to facts. The frequent visits of Sternburg and Jusserand to Roosevelt, to Taft, and to Root made real secrecy impossible, and there were doubtless leaks to reporters also.

It was the Journal des Débats which wondered whether President Roosevelt meant to interest himself "characteristically" in the Morocco imbroglio.[31] A negative view was that Sternburg's effort to enlist the President in Germany's fight for the Open Door in Morocco had failed, since, as France claimed, all countries except Austria had refused to rally to the Kaiser's cause.[32] The London Times was quoted as saying that William II's personal note bidding for Roosevelt's aid was virtually a threat that if American support in Morocco were withheld, Germany would close the Open Door in Kiaochau and the vast hinterland and would do her best to hinder development of American trade. An English writer declared a conference useless because all the entente-countries and also the United States were satisfied with the Open Door guaranteed in Morocco.[33] The American interest in Morocco was assumed, an American periodical explained, on the basis of recent efforts of the United States to release Perdicaris from captivity. From another American source came a well-reasoned argument, alleged to have been presented to Taft for the Kaiser, showing that the probable closing of the Open Door in Morocco, followed by the final loss of her independence, might form a precedent for a similar future for China; the United States, therefore, was requested to join Germany in having these Moroccan ententes submitted to an international congress. To this "ingenious but sophistical presentation" of the Kaiser's plan, however, Taft was believed to have replied that the small American trade with Morocco gave no motive for the renunciation of the traditional avoidance of European entanglements by the United States. Accepting the German argument of the incompatibility of the Anglo-French entente with the most favored nation clause of the Madrid Convention, another American periodical pointed out that the much greater prospective American commercial interests in China warranted American intervention to protect the Open Door there; there was no warrant to abandon traditional American policy in Morocco.[34]

Together with some shrewd guesses, much misinformation continued to unenlighten the American public. From Washington came the news that the secret cause of Delcassé's resignation was his refusal to accept the desire of the French Cabinet to comply with the German Emperor's demand that the Moroccan dispute be arbitrated by Roosevelt.[35] Another rumor was that the continental powers were supporting Russia in her demand for a world conference to end the war with Japan, and that to exert pressure upon the United States to support this plan against the wishes of Great Britain and Japan, Roosevelt was being thwarted in Venezuela, Morocco, and China. Germany was credited with being the leader in exerting this pressure, said a London paper, but the United States would not enlist on his side, for

> clever as he is, the Kaiser has never understood America, and he is probably now quite unaware that the suspicion and dislike with which Americans have watched German diplomacy at work in Manila Bay, in South America, and in Washington itself, have not in any way been averted by Prince Henry's visit and the gift of a statue of Frederick the Great.[36]

As the Algeciras Conference date approached, the leading question remained--what was the United States going to do there? One answer was that American delegates were likely to take important parts in the two most controversial issues, the international control of the police and the Open Door, and in these both France and Germany were claiming their support. A third topic, adopted by the United States at the urging of Jacob H. Schiff of New York, was the protection of the Moroccan Jews, which might be difficult to introduce, since it was not on the Franco-German agenda. Another answer was rejected as "a fantastic explanation from Washington, that our historic bombardments of the Barbary pirates entitle us to a place in the conference." European diplomats would presumably attribute Roosevelt's sending of envoys "to his ardent desire to sustain freedom of trade--abroad."[37]

Even more than the malign influence of William II upon Roosevelt the American press viewed the danger of foreign entanglements for the United States, with the consequent abandonment of that part of the Monroe Doctrine relating to European political conflicts. During April, 1905, for example, the Washington _Post_ devoted much editorial space to this matter. Having captured the foreign trade of Abyssinia, the _Post_ said, the United States was in a position to compete with Germany for the commerce of Morocco. The elevation of Gummeré to ministerial rank and the recent presentation of two costly rifles by the President to two native chiefs indicated the inflexible purpose of the American government to cultivate friendly relations with the influential brigands of Morocco. The Kaiser's Open Door policy was too belated an effort to check American influence there. Three days later the Post called for "hands off Morocco!":

> We do not need the deserts of Morocco as an outlet for our superfluous constructive energy, nor do we need the people of Morocco in order to add another color to the kaleidoscopic variety of our population .... There is abundance of room on this hemisphere for altruism and its shadow, annexation, without carrying the game into Africa .... The "Open Door" declaration of a gigantic government like Germany, in dealing with impotent, decayed states like Morocco, means only that Germany demands an equal share in the eventual absorption of the victim .... It does not make a particle of difference to us whether Germany or France shall take Morocco .... In either case our trade with Morocco will be increased .... Morocco under Mulai Abdul-Aziz, with Raisouli as a wicked partner, deserves the fate that awaits her.

In a later issue, the Post commended the Anglo-French alliance as an instrument for peace. It was to be hoped that Taft would continue to refuse to back Emperor William in Morocco; "It is none of our affair." Finally, the Post urged that the United States reaffirm the Senate resolution of 1892 with which that body had accepted the general act for the suppression of the African slave trade and thus maintain the "solid principle of non-interference in trans-Atlantic affairs which is embedded in the traditions of American diplomacy."[38]

The ever-wise Ion Perdicaris presented a contrary opinion, though, in a London paper:

> Would not the American flag at Tangier be a lesser evil, from the Anglo-European point of view, than any international conflict, or than the condition of present native anarchy? ... If the authorities at Washington were at this present moment consulted, they would naturally and inevitably reply that the friendship either

> of France or of any other European Power is infinitely more important to the commercial advantage of the United States than would be the possession of the whole of Morocco, even were that country first swept clean of all its present inhabitants, whose chief merit seems to consist in their eminent adaptability to guerrilla warfare. Yet is it not just possible that were America at some future day very much pressed, or, on the other hand, very indignant over some outrage to her flag or to her interest, she might be amiable enough to take on a corner of the African Continent, just to see how it felt?[39]

In June and July of 1905 the Washington Post returned to its campaign against entangling alliances, still expecting that the State Department would decline to meddle in African questions. "Our unfortunate possession of the Philippine Islands" compelled political participation in Far Eastern affairs, but this should not be extended to Europe. The United States had troubles enough as premier nation on this side of the Atlantic. In England Roosevelt was being hailed as "the world's umpire," and the latest report was that he had brought about the meeting between the Tsar and the Kaiser.[40] But patriotic American citizens, though duly glad of diplomatic triumphs, found no mention of that "world umpire" business in the Constitution, and in Washington's Farewell Address they found earnest warnings against it. The editor mildly suggested that "the administration withdraw for a season from foreign complications and give attention to the numerous problems that confront it at home."[41]

Many collaborators assisted the Post in directing the President back to the path laid out by Monroe, but a large number also endorsed his detouring from it. A magazine of the latter group pointed out that the American people were now ready to follow their president out of isolation:

> We have now a great American public caring about the concerns of mankind from Norway and Sweden to Morocco, and from Tibet to Venezuela .... Our government and our diplomacy have changed in such regards until at length Washington has become a center of activity and influence in the affairs of nations.

A similar view of American status was held by a prominent

weekly periodical, which listed only four great powers left on earth--Japan, Germany, Great Britain, and the United States:

> And if there be left anywhere a moral influence that can stay the arm of the strong and say to the seemingly omnipotent, thus far shalt thou go and no further, must we not look for it on this side of the Atlantic and recognize its source in Washington? It was an American Secretary of State who rescued China's territorial integrity. May it not be reserved for an American President in this, their hour of imminent danger, to safeguard the independence of many a weak European state?[42]

Early in January, 1906, the New York Times set forth a pro-administration--and pro-French--position in informing its readers about the imminent conference. It explained that the instructions of the American delegates, still undisclosed officially, had two objectives--the maintenance of the Open Door in Morocco and the exercise of good offices to prevent the development of friction that might jeopardize the world's peace. With the political future of Morocco the United States had no concern, and the American government had no intention of entering any entangling alliance involving force to carry out any agreement. The conference at Algeciras might be as important as the one at Portsmouth, for it might ultimately deal with matters involving the peace of Europe. The settlement of the Moroccan question concerned the wide world, including the United States, for

> if we go back far enough, the United States is responsible for this situation, since it was her lot nearly a century ago to clear the seas of the "Barbary pirates" and compel the savage chiefs of North African bordering on the Mediterranean to enter into pacts of peace with herself, and as a consequence, with others, and it is by virtue of this record that her representatives will sit around the green table in the City Hall of Algeciras with those of the Governments of Europe.[43]

However, the immediate cause of the conference was Germany's determination to escape her pretended "isolation."

It was natural and reasonable that France, mistress of such extensive territories in Northwest Africa, should affirm the special interests resulting from the long common boundary which compelled her to become the guardian of the integrity and independence of Morocco and to establish order, peace, and stability there. A detailed history was then given of the Moroccan situation since the Entente Cordiale. At the conference there would be a struggle between France and Germany as to who should carry out the basic principles already agreed upon for a settlement. Meanwhile, the attitude of the American government and people must be one of absolute impartiality.[44]

A writer in the Edinburgh Review expressed opinions on American imperialism representative of contemporary British opinion. This "international upheaval," he said, had been proclaimed aloud many times by President Roosevelt, who "succeeded in embodying in his own strenuous and thoroughly American personality the new-born desire of his country to take its place once for all among the expansive forces that are to play the imperial part in the world's destiny. The Monroe Doctrine, as interpreted by Roosevelt and other American statesmen, would have made Monroe turn in his grave." Europeans were justified in their resentment, for

> if it be right that the United States should claim exclusive jurisdiction in the Western Hemisphere, is it tolerable that they should also take part in the affairs of Europe? ... The danger of President Roosevelt's undue activity in all parts of the world seems to us to lie in the fear that he may arouse a resentment that only slumbers in many European Chancelleries, partly provoked by American commercial competition and partly by a too reckless temperament claiming a right to be heard on all and every question of international importance .... After all, as Mr. Roosevelt is well aware, the Monroe Doctrine[45] is not accepted by any civilized people as part of the law of nations.[46]

It is noteworthy that American aversion to entangling alliances for intervention in Morocco was not confined to the President's suspected partnership with the German Kaiser. Equally obnoxious to Monroe adherents was the widely bruited Anglo-French-American entente based on this occasion. However, there was much support both at home and abroad for this new combination of powers and many ingenious arguments were advanced by its advocates. An Italian writer suggested that the Anglo-French diplomatic understanding would prove an insurmountable barrier both to Germany's predominance in the Mediterranean and to her colonial expansion everywhere if the United States were to join the entente. French and British writers and speakers said that the imposing ceremony on the return of the body of John Paul Jones from Paris to the United States indicated the probability of an American-French entente that would develop into a triple understanding including Great Britain.[47]

In their pleas for understanding, members of both French and British parliaments stressed the motive of attainment of universal peace. M. Jules Delafosse, a Conservative deputy, advocated a larger combination than the Russo-Franco-German alliance against England into which the Moroccan affair was trumped up to force France. Instead of this, "An Anglo-Franco-Russian alliance, which, in all probability, Italy, and possibly the United States, might be willing to join" would possess the mastery of the world, making disturbance of the peace impossible. The English foreign policy, declared Sir Charles W. Dilke, M. P., was based on maintenance of the status quo in the Far East and friendship with France and the United States. Dilke deprecated any Anglo-German conflict and spoke of current negotiations for a British arrangement with Russia, made with Japan's support. Japan had accepted the disappointing Portsmouth peace because of the renewal of the Anglo-Japanese Treaty.[48]

Three members of the American press may be cited who made tentative endorsements of the proposed triple entente. Speaking of the discussion in London, Paris, and New York newspapers of American adhesion to the Entente Cordiale, Harper's Weekly pointed out that nobody proposed a formal alliance, but merely a friendly recognition of common interests that might lead to cooperation. With their combined naval and financial resources and consequent moral influence, these three countries could enforce peace. Only her sincere and proved desire for universal peace would induce the United States to enter such a grouping. If the purpose of such an entente were pacific, progressive, and beneficent, and not inflicting of loss or injury upon Germany or any other country, no diplomatic notes would be necessary to secure American sympathy and moral support.[49] The Washington Post was rather cynical about the proposition. It printed an interview with Henry Cabot Lodge in which the senator admitted that a future entente was very close and would probably be an alliance in everything but name. With editorial tongue in cheek, the Post advocated wholesale peace alliances in a merger which American business genius should be able to form.[50] However, the Algeciras Conference came and went with only a "friendly recognition of common interests" for the occasion. By May, 1906, the North American Review evidently regarded the Anglo-French-American entente a closed issue. This denouement was attributed to the continued opposition of millions of American citizens, not only German-Americans, but also of those "native Americans" with too vivid memories of 1776 and 1812. Still more influential, perhaps, was the replacement of the Anglophile John Hay by the unbiased Elihu Root, who, "faithful to the traditions of the Republic" desired "friendship with all foreign powers, but entangling alliances with none."[51]

The year 1906 was a time of difficult and complicated problems for both Root and Roosevelt. At home the press and the Senate intensified their attacks simultaneously on Roosevelt's innovations on the Monroe Doctrine in Morocco, Santo Domingo, and Venezuela. The Algeciras delegates had to be directed in their delicate task of combining overt neutrality with covert favoring of Great Britain and France. Roosevelt had to continue friendly negotiations with the Wilhelmstrasse while keeping both Sternburg and Jusserand satisfied. Finally, toward the end of the year, came the last round of the battle with the Senate to secure its consent to the Act of Algeciras.

In Senator Eugene Hale of Maine, floor leader of the Republicans, Roosevelt had as chairman of the Committee on Naval Affairs a consistent opponent of war and of preparations and propaganda for it.[52] Besides Hale, most of the Democrats and many of the Republicans distrusted the President's adventursome inclinations and alleged leanings toward dictatorship. As a body the Senate was determined to maintain its ascendancy in the conduct of foreign affairs. To accomplish this aim it had to challenge successfully the Roosevelt Corollary to the Monroe Doctrine announced in the President's message of December, 1905.

Immediately after the Christmas recess, Senator Tillman of South Carolina opened the attack on Roosevelt's foreign policy[53] by introducing a resolution of inquiry concerning the status of affairs in Santo Domingo. Under objection from Senator Spooner of Wisconsin, the matter went over until the following Monday.[54]

On January 8 Senator Bacon of Georgia, a member of the Foreign Relations Committee, initiated the discussion of the Moroccan situation. He introduced a resolution calling upon the President, if it were not incompatible with the public interest, to lay before the Senate the documents relative to the invitation given to the United States to participate in the conference at Algeciras, the reply of the United States, any agreements concerning the objects of the conference, and all instructions given to the American delegates, whose names were requested also. The resolution also pointed out that the European situation was so grave as to endanger peace and that the only legitimate concern of the United States with Moroccan affairs was based upon the very limited commerce between the two countries and was in no way connected with the controversy over the political future of Morocco. The President was requested also to inform the Senate whether the American delegates were limited to participation in commercial discussions or whether they had authority to assist in the deliberations relative to the political affairs of Morocco and "to the respective rights and powers of any one or more of said foreign governments relative thereto."[55]

This detailed inquiry on Moroccan involvements was accompanied on the same day[56] by an attack made by Senator Rayner on Roosevelt's Dominican policy.[57] Senators of both parties were determined to have an accounting, since their steward had left them to get their information from the press. Undoubtedly the President now realized more keenly than ever the necessity of concealing the extent of his entanglement in the Moroccan quarrel. On motion of Lodge, who throughout the debates was the chief champion of Roosevelt, Bacon's resolution went over.[58]

After tracing the descent of the Monroe Doctrine from its author to Olney, Rayner declined to admit Roosevelt's Santo Domingo policy into the lineage. Indirectly, he also made some pertinent references to the Moroccan situation by way of repudiating the commandment that the United States must become a World Power:

> If we mean by becoming a world power that we are to take part in all the conflicts between other nations, that whenever a country is to be stolen we shall have an equal opportunity to participate in the plunder, that whenever the territory of a defenceless people is to be partitioned that we are to have a share of the booty, that whenever a national felony or deed of violence is to be committed that we are to have a hand in the pillage, that we are to have equal rights with all the other robbers who have heretofore purloined the fairest portions of the earth, that wherever a helpless state is unable to protect itself and other governments are ready to prey upon it that we must speed our battle ships to the feast and manouvre as a world power for an allotment of its possessions and a dividend of its liberties.[59]

On January 8 Lodge secured the passage of a motion that the Bacon resolution should be discussed behind closed doors.[60] In executive session Bacon and Spooner each took three hours, mainly to discuss whether the debate should be public or secret. The speeches were reported and commented upon in the press.[61] Because of her participation in former treaties with Morocco, Spooner asserted, the United States would have given offence by a refusal to attend this conference. A widely quoted statement by him that the American delegates were instructed merely to listen and debate but not to vote on any question was believed to be officially inspired. The Senate finally decided that the resolution should not be debated in open session.

The Bacon resolution was announced on January 10 as the last business on the calendar, but on motion the Senate went into executive session for ten minutes and then adjourned. On January 11 Bacon carried on a prolonged discussion with several administration supporters in the effort to have his resolution brought before the Senate for public consideration. After further discussion in secret session, the vice-president decided that the resolution had been placed on the calendar and could be taken up only upon motion or by unanimous consent.[62]

Having been brought to public attention by the Senate controversy, the question of American aims at Algeciras would not down. An insight into the real motives of Roosevelt was given in an admission that the principal object of the American delegates would be to harmonize divergent and hostile interests--always, however, under instructions from Washington. In an interview of January 10, when about to leave Rome for Algeciras, Henry White provided ammunition for those fighting foreign entanglements:

> America is again about to make a powerful contribution to the peace of the world. It is a noble mission for this young people, who desire to attain a place in the history of this century, which is to mark the triumph of civilization and the abolition of war.[63]

At his second attempt Bacon succeeded in obtaining an open debate, lasting the entire afternoon of January 15. He now introduced a new resolution:

> Resolved by the Senate that interference with or participation in any controversy between European governments relating to European international questions is a violation of the well-settled, well-defined policy of this government, which has been recognized and observed for more than a century past.[64]

After a caustic criticism of Secretary Root, reported to have shown all official correspondence on the conference to a reporter of the Washington Post, Bacon began his argument. American presence at Algeciras was likely to establish a precedent for future entanglements in every international dispute. Reviewing the history of the traditional American policy of non-interference in European political controversies, he cited the declarations of this doctrine by Washington and Monroe and the reservations of the United States to the Hague Convention. The great question of the Algeciras Conference was whether France should monopolize or should share with other European powers the political control over Morocco; this fact made the meeting exclusively one relating to European politics. As an outcome of the conference, war would be less disastrous for the United States than peace, for the former would be a valuable warning for the future, while the latter would entail exertion of American good offices in every European quarrel. By usage and popular sanction the principles of the Monroe Doctrine and Washington's Farewell Address had become as binding upon the government as any written parts of the Constitution. Furthermore, the Senate repudiated the assertion that commercial interests or the protection of her citizens in Morocco justified interference by the United States. American policy for Europe had always been to avoid entanglements in political issues, regardless of any commercial interests which might be involved. The United States had never recognized any exception for intervention on the possibility of preventing a European war. Otherwise, this country would have been called into every political conference, for all such assemblies pertain to peace or war. Concluding his argument, Bacon said:

> It is an absolute unconditional policy ... that even though we may accomplish good, even though we may secure peace and avert war, nevertheless we shall refrain from entanglements in these conventions, because our highest and first duty is to guard the interests of our own country.[65]

Heckled by Spooner, Bacon replied by examples of international conferences which the United States might properly attend. He considered the Hague Conference justifiable, especially in view of American reservations to the convention. The Madrid Conference of 1880 also had been an "eminently proper one" because it related, not to political control of Morocco, but solely to the rights and privileges of foreigners in Morocco and the commercial rights of the participating nations. In general, participation in any such purely commercial conference was permissible.[66]

When Senator McCumber of North Dakota suggested that there was no evidence that the American delegates would go beyond the sphere conceded by Bacon as legitimate, Spooner mentioned the probability of their withdrawal from the conference after the commercial interests of their country had been provided for. But Bacon made the apt rejoinder that the published contentions of France and Germany had made clear the purely political nature of the conference, and, in fact, any change in the commercial regulations of 1880 had been specifically excluded from the conference agenda. Since the Open Door policy of the United States was thus guaranteed, the one argument for American participation was absolutely without foundation. Moreover, the concentration of European armies on the frontiers and the assembling near Gibraltar of the fleets of all nations, including that of the United States, gave indisputable evidence of the imminent danger of war, into which the United States might be drawn.[67]

The American fleet did appear to be in a state of readiness for any eventuality. The Americanc delegates made a truly Rooseveltian approach to a peace mission. White came from Naples to Algeciras on the *Galveston*, and Gummeré and Einstein traveled with a Portuguese and a Belgian delegate from Tangier on the French cruiser *Galilee*. Their arrival was marked by an exchange of salutes with the land batteries. Most of the delegates came by train from Madrid. Other naval and diplomatic aspects of the delegates' reception were suggestive of the "Big Stick." On January 16, Rear Admiral Sir Edward Chichester, British naval commander, gave a luncheon in honor of the American Rear Admiral Sigsbee, at which the former "recalled the brotherhood of the British and American navies at Manila at the time of the Spanish-American War." The American cruiser squadron, consisting of the armored cruiser *Brooklyn* and the protected cruisers *Galveston*, *Tacoma*, and *Chattanooga*, sailed from Gibraltar on January 18 for Tangier, whence it proceeded on January 20 for Algiers. The town of Gibraltar was another center of activity. American bluejackets were conspicuous on the streets, where they fraternized with the British sailors.[68]

Called to action by the mention of war, Senator Hale received close attention from a profoundly silent Senate. He was glad that this problem was being debated openly, for it was the duty of the Senate to guard the country against being committed to a war policy by its executive. For proof that the makers of the Constitution had intended to give the

Senate the right to discuss treaties before their presentation by the President, he referred to the Madison papers. He regretted that the President and the Secretary of State had sent delegates to a "simon-pure outright political conference," but thought that they would hesitate to do likewise again. He felt positive that they represented the "conservative instinct" which would keep the United States out of trouble; the danger did not come from them, but from the "still ascending prominence of the war sentiment in the country." In proof of his last statement, Hale cited the discussions in the conservative Washington Post, which devoted considerable space to the consideration of complications likely to result from the presence of the American fleet at Gibraltar.[69] In the coming conference, Hale asserted, commerce would never have "an ounce of consideration," and it would have been much better for the United States to keep out of it.[70]

Continuing his indictment, Bacon considered it extremely unfortunate--as he believed every senator did--that the President in his most elaborate message had not mentioned the Moroccan situation, especially since the European governments interested had published everything relating to their connection therewith. He quoted from a Post article the statement that the American delegates had been asked to enter the conference on the same footing and with the same powers as the European delegates. He agreed with Hale on all except one point--he did not feel that there was no cause for apprehension. If it were true, as the press reported, that the United States was expected to exercise great influence, it might be that the deciding vote of this country would determine a policy instigating Germany to declare war. Moreover, the United States could not help to formulate the decrees of the conference and then refuse to assist in enforcement of them. Even if, as suggested by some European papers, the American delegates contributed counsel instead of votes, the moral obligation of the United States would be as great as if her vote had been cast.[71]

Again taking a less pessimistic view,[72] Hale did not doubt that if the situation feared by his colleague should develop, the President and the Secretary of State would summon the American delegates to withdraw from the conference. This would involve no pussillanimity, for the United States had entered to confer not on war, but on commerce.[73]

Bacon cleverly pursued Hale's last argument to its logical conclusion:

> As the senator says, we have no business there; it is a mere matter of tinsel, as far as that goes, a mere parade, so that we may hereafter be classed with the great war powers, a mere sending of delegates to co-operate with delegates from European powers as a matter of pompous show and display, with the simple understanding that they are there merely as a matter of ornament and not to accomplish anything, not to attend to anything; but that if it reaches a point where their participation will determine the result, they will be telegraphed to withdraw.[74]

Conceding that no harm would come to the United States under a good and wise president and secretary of state, Bacon still questioned the wisdom of establishing a precedent under which officials of a different character might act in the future to embroil their people in war for their own advantage. In such a situation, Hale would rely upon the right of Congress to arrest and prevent such a calamity, but the traditional American abstinence from foreign entanglements had never been "qualified or conditioned by the character of our officials or their purposes."[75]

Senator Newlands of Nevada then asked Bacon to differentiate between the action of the President in regard to Morocco and that of John Hay in inviting the great powers to accede to the agreement to guarantee the integrity of China by confining the war to Manchuria. The latter case was as much of a political complication as was the Algeciras Conference, and the United States did not act in China to protect commercial interests. Bacon could see no analogy in the two cases, for regarding China there had been no conference, no delegation of powers to anybody. But, Newlands replied, there was interference in an Asiatic political complication. If the United States had no business in European politics, she could hardly have any in Asiatic affairs, but in the latter she had gone a considerable distance in intervention. Admitting this fact, Bacon insisted that that experience should warn Americans not to proceed still further. However, Hay had called no conference; he had merely sent a note to Russia and Japan asking them to confine their warfare to territory where it legitimately belonged.

Finally reaching a conclusion, Bacon asserted that his opposition to the sending of delegates was an act neither of partisanship nor of personal or official disrespect for the President. He recognized Roosevelt's great service for humanity in making peace between Japan and Russia, and he did not think that his interposition of good offices to stop the shedding of blood contravened the great American principle. But the Doctrine would be gone if the United States were to take part in every European conference called to avoid war. Although he believed the President to be a patriotic man, he was also a strong-willed and impulsive one, and it was the special duty of the Senate to endeavor in a respectful way to guard the institutions and policies of the country. For instance, probably the fact that the President was not a lawyer accounted for his marking "approved" and having printed in a volume entitled <u>Treaties in Force</u> a treaty with Cuba never submitted to the Senate.[76] From the Algeciras Conference no harm was likely to come except in the matter of precedent, for the discussion of the issue in the press and in the Senate would awaken the whole country to safeguard its principles. It should be known, however, that the United States would take part in no future conferences involving questions of peace and war. After this prolonged debate, Senator Bacon's resolution was referred to the Committee on Foreign Relations.[77]

In returning on January 17 to his resolution concerning the administration's policy in Santo Domingo, Tillman berated the Senate for permitting the President to abuse his power:

> The President has used the press, or it has been used by those who are his friends, to create the impression throughout the United States that the Senate today is obstructing him in all of his pet schemes for public welfare, and the country stands watching us to see how far we dare go in the maintenance of our constitutional rights and prerogatives.[78]

The administration was now using the press as an agency to publicize its objectives at Algeciras. Root had come to the defense of his chief. In a dispatch from Washington, dated January 16, he gave the official version of the instructions to the American delegates. He stated that American participation in the conference was based exclusively upon the American treaty rights in Morocco, a rearrangement of which was now proposed by the Sultan. As for the aims of the United States:

> The Government desires not only that the door shall be opened to the world's trade, but that it shall be utilized in a way that shall prove beneficial alike to Morocco and the treaty powers. The American delegates will favor the betterment of religious and class conditions in Morocco, all of which are regarded as important factors in the effective policing of the interior and in paving the way to intercourse between Morocco and the outside world. The treatment of the Jews in Morocco is the subject of a special supplementary letter on instructions .... The delegates are instructed heartily to support plans for the prevention of private monopoly of the public services. Secretary Root's letter to the delegates is calculated to impress the powers with the impartial benevolences and unbaised friendship cherished by the Washington government toward all concerned.

A further reassurance given was that the delegates would be instructed by cable on every point and that any treaty made must be approved by the State Department and the Senate before final ratification.[79]

Two days later the views of Root were amplified at a hearing before a House committee dealing with emergency funds for the diplomatic service. In reply to questions, he made the following successive statements:

> We have no political interest in the Morocco Conference at all .... The ostensible object of the conference is entirely commercial. The political aspect of the conference arises solely from the fact that there are strained relations between Germany and France, and it is supposed that a casus belli may be found there. They (the delegates) have nothing to do with political

> questions, simply trade questions. They are there with just the same interest that the representatives of any other country have, in seeing that the doors of Morocco are not closed to our trade. It is the same thing that we have been doing in China .... (Is there any danger of foreign countries receiving the impression that we are there for the purpose of participating in political questions?) No, no more than our having delegates to the Geneva Red Cross convention or the Hague Conference .... This is one of the recognized ways of looking after one's commercial interests. It is likely that political questions will arise .... The conference relates to provisions for securing peace and order in Morocco--questions of policing--arrangements which will secure the protection of ... the lives and property of the citizens of all countries .... The question of policing Morocco is a question of accomplishing something that each country would have to accomplish for itself unless some arrangement were made. Then the questions of trade restrictions constitute the rest of the subject matter. (Questions of trade, then, are incidential to the main question ... of peace and order and policing in Morocco?) That has a great bearing upon it, but there is also directly the trade question. The program for consideration is very narrow, and nobody would pay any particular attention to it if it were not for the fact that Germany and France have appeared to be on the verge of having a row and it is supposed they might find something or other there to pick a quarrel about .... (If they do, our agents are not bound to participate in it?) They are specifically instructed not to.[80]

The Senate, however, was not fully satisfied with Root's explanations,[81] and debate on Morocco was reopened on January 23 by Spooner, an administration supporter. Speaking of both Moroccan and Dominican affairs, he questioned the advisability of debating treaties or other foreign relations in open session. It was not that the Senate wished to withhold information from it own people, but that current foreign affairs could not be discussed frankly in the hearing of other nations. Analyzing the treaty-making power the senator asserted the validity of certain fundamental principles--the exclusive right of the executive to negotiate and to pocket treaties, before or after their approval by the

Senate; the limitation of the Senate's power to approval of treaties presented to it by the president; the purely advisory character of Senate resolutions on foreign policy; and the supreme authority of the president over all foreign relations. To substantiate these propositions, he quoted at length from eminent authorities on the Constitution.[82]

Passing from general principles to the specific instance of the Algeciras Conference, Spooner asserted that the sending of delegates did not violate the precept of Washington and was not only constitutional but demanded by the situation. Neither the Declaration of Independence nor the Constitution aimed to create a baby or hermit nation, and the latter had established a treaty-making body with full power to make alliances or to exercise a suzerainty over a protectorate. Although an adherent to Washington's doctrine, Spooner demanded the free exercise of the President's constitutional powers to protect the liberty and property of American citizens and to safeguard the commercial interests of the United States. As the country grew in power and wealth, there probably would arise many occasions when the executive would deem it wise to send representatives to foreign conferences, not to entangle Americans, but to preserve their interests and to prevent war. And in the present situation,

> It is not beyond a reasonable belief that Ambassador White ... and his associates may at the right time under instructions from the President, without in any wise jeopardizing our international status, in some way contribute to the peaceful issue of this conference.

Further justification for American participation at Algeciras was found by Spooner in the American-Moroccan treaties of 1787, 1836, and 1880. The attendance of the United States was necessary, also because two of the larger powers had refused to take part unless all signers of the Madrid Treaty were present. The United States would undoubtedly send delegates to any international conference over Manchuria. Washington warned against permanent alliances only; he advocated "temporary alliances for extraordinary emergencies." Furthermore, Washington's exhortation against the encroachment of one branch of government upon the sphere of another bade the Senate "Hands off!" in foreign relations. The President who had hit upon the psychological moment[83] for a successful intervention between Russia and Japan could safely be trusted to direct the acts of the delegates at Algeciras.[84]

Lodge took up the cudgels for the administration on January 24. He agreed with Spooner that American treaty relations with Morocco made it the right and the duty of the United States to protect her citizens and commerce by attending the conference. According to press reports, the United States had declined to join the German Emperor in the preceding June when he protested against the Anglo-French agreement as a violation of the Open Door. Later the President accepted the invitation to send delegates to the conference--a method selected to avoid war. No one had any right to assume that their instructions would violate either the Constitution or the traditional American policies. Lodge endorsed Spooner's views on the presidential and senatorial prerogatives and on Washington's advice. The Farewell Address did not prohibit treaties on commerical, humanitarian, territorial, or peace questions.

Spooner's tentative suggestion of the peace-making motive of the United States at Algeciras was accepted and emphasized by Lodge. An American presence there was justified not only because of participation in previous international pacts on Morocco, but also because of the possibility that the United States might use her good offices to preserve peace. The mediation of the President between Japan and Russia demonstrated the moral influence of the United States for peace. Roosevelt, least of all men, would want to entangle the United States in alliances leading to war. Undoubtedly the attendance of Americans at the conference would lead to both advancement of American commerce and to the infinitely more important peace of the world.[85]

Lodge discussed also Roosevelt's policy on Santo Domingo.[86] In the financial guardianship of that island by the United States he saw the logical development of the Monroe Doctrine. There was no other practical policy to prevent temporary occupation by European powers, inevitably leading to permanent control, as in Egypt, or to avoid eventual annexation by the United States in self-defense. The United States could not tolerate a European power so near the Panama Canal.[87]

On January 25 Senator Money of Mississippi took up the argument for the opposition. He reviewed the connections previously made between the Santo Domingo guardianship,[88] the Monroe Doctrine, and the Algeciras Conference. He reiterated Bacon's charges that the last pertained wholly to European politics. Complimenting Bacon on his correct prognosis in foreseeing the acute crisis reported in the morning papers, he showed Hale to be mistaken in his prediction that the American delegates would be withdrawn. The presence of the United States at Algeciras as a World Power made the President's interpretation of the Monroe Doctrine rather one-sided. The questioning of the wisdom of sending the delegates was legitimate because the Senate had the right to participate in the negotiation of a treaty. Since the situation at Algeciras indicated the imminence of a Franco-German war, and the President did not withdraw the American delegates, there was danger that business interests would suffer, whichever way the representatives of the United States might vote. In fact, no speaker had demonstrated how either the commerical or the political interests of the United States would be advanced by the conference.[89]

Bacon's resolution of January 8, requesting the President to furnish information about the Algeciras Conference, was the next business on the calendar for January 30. Because of the objection of Senator Aldrich the resolution again went over.[90]

A new recruit for the administration forces entered the fray on January 31, when Senator Patterson, a Democrat from Colorado, spoke at length upon the Algeciras and Santo Domingo situations. Deserting his party on these issues,[91] he declared that the President deserved Democratic support because of his espousal of the rights of the common people and his conciliatory attitude toward ex-Confederates. The claim that the United States should take part only in European controversies dealing with the rights of American citizens and commerce fully justified the presence of Americans at Algeciras. There was nothing but commerce involved in this dispute--it was primarily a struggle between France and Germany for the commerce of Morocco. If successful, France would dominate Moroccan markets; if the Open Door policy won, the United States would have an equal chance in competition for Moroccan trade. If the conference should result in an European war, the United States had merely to withdraw and let it go on. No reason could be advanced for not extending American interference in behalf of the Open Door from China and Manchuria to Morocco. Patterson's interpretation of the Monroe Doctrine led him to support also the entire policy of the President in Santo Domingo.[92] It began to appear that Roosevelt's "Monroe Doctrine" was becoming a matter of party politics. Fearing that Patterson's vote would ensure the passage of the Santo Domingo treaty, a party caucus tried to bind all Democrats to vote against it. Patterson introduced a resolution condemning the caucus action as unconstitutional.[93]

On February 5 Bacon's resolution of January 8 and Tillman's resolution on Santo Domingo again went over on objection by Lodge.[94] Nevertheless, Bacon resumed the debate on the Algeciras Conference on the next day. Again he challenged the contention of Spooner that the Senate had no power to consider a treaty before its submission in completed form by the president. On the contrary, the propriety of advice from the Senate at all stages of the negotiations was upheld by constitutional history and precedent. If such powers were withheld from the Senate, the president might conduct foreign relations through his delegates sent to European political conferences without ever submitting any treaty to the Senate. Such a procedure would render the Senate impotent to safeguard traditional American policies. While presenting these propositions, Bacon was frequently heckled by senators Spooner, Beveridge, and Foraker, who contested his opinions at every point.[95]

Objecting to Spooner's earlier assertion of presidential supremacy in foreign affairs, Bacon insisted that the executive shares the powers of declaring war and peace and making treaties with Congress and that he has no control over commerce, shipping, immigration, or intercommunication of any kind. Congress, therefore, is supreme in conducting foreign relations. But "the executive has encroached continuously upon the legislative branch, and it has never been more pronounced in its encroachment than it is today."

Finally arriving at the Algeciras Conference after a criticism of the President's attempts to dictate legislation to Congress and of his high-handed actions in regard to Santo

Domingo, Venezuela, and Colombia, Bacon contrasted the attitude that his resolution was an intrusion upon executive prerogative with a contrary view taken by John Quincy Adams at the time of the Panama Congress. The treaty of 1880, he pointed out, dealt exclusively with the protection of the Moors by foreign legations, the rights of brokers, and the commercial equality of all nations. But the present conference[96] had no connection with the former treaty said to be its basis, for it was occasioned by the animosity of Germany and France, which might involve all Europe in war.[97]

In his reply Spooner said that he had not denied the right to introduce the Bacon resolution, but had questioned the propriety of discussing it publicly. He believed that it had been the President's duty to send delegates because of the Madrid Treaty of 1880 and because of the refusal of Italy and Austria to attend unless the United States did so. This conference would set no precedent for future participation in European conferences to avoid war, because the United States was interested solely in the proposed revision in some items of the treaty of 1880. The conference program, which he had seen, was confined almost entirely to matters covered in that treaty. To this assurance Bacon replied that his original purpose had been to allay public anxiety by securing from the President just such information in regard to the delegates' instructions. But he was sorry to see by press accounts[98] that apparently the instructions as Spooner stated were not being carried out by the American delegates.[99]

Before concluding their debate with a prolonged and verbose disputation[100] over the division of power in treaty-making, Bacon and Spooner again stated their positions in regard to American participation in political conferences. The former opposed attending conventions essentially political in which the pretended commercial interests were mere shams to disguise the real purposes. The latter thought that the United States should attend any conference involving American interests and should use her influence to prevent war between nations friendly to her, with but one limitation, that she should not involve herself in any war.[101]

No further debate on the Algeciras Conference was carried on in open sessions of the Senate. Bacon's resolution of January 8 was on the calendar for April 13, but on motion of Senator Gallinger it went to the calendar again.[102] A truce was made also in the battle over the Santo Domingo treaty, while the Foreign Relations Committee worked to formulate a plan more acceptable than the one originally proposed by the President.[103] The movement later stigmatized by Roosevelt as "muck-raking" was at full tide, and an epidemic of Congress-baiting broke out, mostly directed against the upper house. Although the Senate still had some champions in the press, the chorus of popular approval for Roosevelt drowned out its criticism of his foreign policy. The series on "The Treason of the Senate" by David Graham Philips began about this time. More conservative journals, however, continued to be wary of Roosevelt's foreign policy. The Boston Herald regarded the Senate as a useful check upon the "Hurry" recommendations of an "impetuous and impatient President who too often applies to grave matters of diplomacy or statesmanship the 'hair trigger' practice that he uses in hunting 'big game.'" The New York Journal of Commerce saw the tendency toward centralization as a uniform element of danger in the President's foreign policy.[104]

Before being eclipsed by public disfavor, however, the Senate had placed on record before the country the essential arguments of the administration supporters and opponents in its ranks. The repeated efforts of the former to convince the President's critics that the sole aim of the United States at Algeciras was to protect her commercial interests were in vain. Several of Roosevelt's intimates frankly avowed his real purpose and stated his second amendment to the Monroe Doctrine--namely, that the United States should participate in European political controversies if such cooperation were desirable to prevent war. Thus from being an isolated onlooker in world politics the United States was advanced by Roosevelt's policy to the position of umpire and arbiter in international quarrels. Much of the resistance offered to Roosevelt's action in the Moroccan problem was caused by resentment at his evident intention to manage the matter secretly and to permit the Senate only the signing of the treaty after it had become a fait accompli. In the case of Santo Domingo the President had proceeded with the implementation of his first corollary to the Monroe Doctrine in spite of the refusal of senatorial approval. This unprecedented action naturally made the Senate apprehensive regarding his possible course in Morocco.

During and after the senatorial debates, the State Department was negotiating in two types of foreign relations usually regarded as fields for Congressional action or advice. Roosevelt and Root acted with circumspection, however, to keep these problems out of the Congressional arena. Since these affairs were an impending tariff war with Germany and a threatened war between France and Venezuela, it was a task of the greatest importance to keep these complications from involving the situation of the United States at Algeciras. In both cases the United States occupied the point of vantage, for the attitude of both France and Germany was strongly conditioned by the desire of each to secure American support on Morocco.

That it was hopeless to induce the Congress to reduce the Dingley tariff, long a source of commercial strife with Germany, or to enter into the reciprocity treaties which Germany was concluding with other countries, Roosevelt well knew. On November 29, 1905, the German government gave notice that it would terminate on March 1, 1906, the commerical agreement of July 10, 1900.[105] A counter-proposal to increase the Dingley rates by 25% on products of any country discriminating against American goods was made in the House of Representatives.[106] Although some warnings appeared in the American press that a tariff war would inflict serious injury upon American agriculture,[107] there was little prospect that Congress would relent and make a reciprocal agreement with Germany.[108] As the Algeciras Conference proceeded, reports indicated that the Berlin Bourse was depressed both by unfavorable news from the conference and by anxiety regarding a possible tariff war with the United States. It was reported that the Reichstag preferred a fight to the finish, but the Foreign Office favored concessions to obtain American backing on Morocco.[109] Despite the determined opposition of the German agrarians, the Reichstag finally granted to the United States until June 30, 1907, the same rates that were in effect with countries having reciprocity agreements with Germany.[110] By way of compromise, the State Department worked out modifications of consular regulations affording somewhat better terms and procedures for German exporters.[111]

Although Bülow disclaimed the buying of political friendship by the sacrifice of Germany's economic interests,[112] the Kölnische Volkszeitung quoted him otherwise:

> We wish to avoid a splendid isolation. We want President Roosevelt's republic as a rearguard whenever Great Britain and France unite for an assault upon us. Hence the interchange of professors arranged through the German Emperor between American universities and German universities. Hence, also, the amiability of the Emperor to the United States. Hence, as well, our compliance with the wish of the United States Government that the provisional tariff be extended until next year.

Other German newspapers expressed dissatisfaction with Bülow's diplomacy. The Kreuz Zeitung thought that the nation which defeated the French at Sedan need not have been wiped out by a tariff war with America. A Berlin paper declared that the Reichstag had yielded less to Roosevelt than to a chancellor who had not the knowledge essential for dealing with a democratic government. By vote of the official press, however, the Chancellor had won a great victory.[113] In this connection, American readers had a chance to read some very unflattering comments on Bülow.[114]

If Emperor William sought to use tariff concessions as one means of detaching the United States from the Anglo-French entente,[115] he must have hailed Venezuela as an ally in that project. The unpleasantness between France and Venezuela came to the notice of the American public shortly after January 10, 1906, when official relations were broken off.[116] A technical state of war ensued when the expulsion of the French envoy from Venezuela was followed by the dismissal of the Venezuelan chargé d'affaires from Paris.[117] The diplomatic rupture had been occasioned by the conduct of Dictator Castro, who not only refused to make any payments on an award to French creditors, fixed by an umpire appointed by Roosevelt, but also annulled the concession of the French Cable Company and refused to recognize the French chargé.[118] Preparations for the dispatch of a French squadron to Venezuela were announced,[119] but suddenly they were halted. Coupled with charges in the British and French press that Germany was instigating Castro to embroil France with the United States over the Monroe Doctrine came the assertion that the French and American governments were working in accord and that the punishment of Castro would be postponed until after the Morocco conference.[120]

The evident Franco-American cooperation in Venezuela caused adverse comment from various points of view at home and abroad. An American paper generally suspicious of Germany assailed the President for "chameleon-like Monroeism:"

> France, it seems, has a free hand to do we know not what regarding Venezuela, and nobody thinks that American interests are endangered. But as regards Santo Domingo, it was urgently necessary that we should do something in such haste that the Senate's advice and consent could not be waited for, lest perchance Germany should get a foothold on Samana Bay or some other power should do something else. Now, what is the distinction between Venezuela and Santo Domingo? ... It cannot be maintained that it (the Monroe Doctrine) should mean one thing to one nation and another to another nation. Whether it be a doctrine or a dogma .... it ought not to mean different things at the same moment at the will of any individual.[121]

Looking at a different aspect of the matter, the London Outlook severely criticized Roosevelt for claiming the right to supervise French action in Venezuela while sitting at a round table to decide on a purely European problem:

> This is a conjunction of activities which appears to set in a new light some of the traditions of American foreign policy. Demanding equality in the Old Warld, she (America) enforces monopoly in the New. Intervening in Morocco, she padlocks Venezuela and warns all who approach the barriers that admission can be obtained only with her approval. That is an attitude of the one-sidedness which we firmly believe in the end must prove quite untenable.[122]

Another objection to Roosevelt's corollary was pointed out by one of his critics in the capital. It was improbable, the editor said, that the Kaiser would accept Castro's rumored offer of exclusive navigation of the Orinoco and control of the customs houses along its banks, which would meet with a prompt reaction from the United States. The chief danger did not lie in the attempt of any European power to get a foothold in Latin America, but in the tendency of the

President, through a mistaken fear of European aggression, to entangle the United States in protection of any American republics which did not pay their debts:

> We believe the true "corollary" of the Monroe Doctrine to be that foreigners dabbling in South American republics should do so at their own risk, subject to the laws of the country and the caprices of the rulers. The United States should not only refuse to collect by force the "claims" of its own adventurers, but it should refuse to permit European Governments to use force. Such a policy should be made part of the Monroe Doctrine. It would not only keep European powers out of South America, but it would keep the United States out, which is just as important.[123]

But some kind words were said for France and her foreign policy:

> The moderation and justice of the French contention at the Algeciras Conference have been gradually but surely appealing to the good sense of the rest of the world .... In the rupture with Venezuela, also, the eminently calm and fair attitude maintained by the French Foreign Office has prevented any possible opposition to even the sternest of measures against President Castro.[124]

After the silencing of the Senate, the debate[125] which it initiated was continued in the press. Senator Bacon went to the country in an article in the North American Review, in which he reiterated his arguments presented to the Senate.[126] Now a carping critic of the "Busy Showman" and a supporter of Hale and Bacon, Harper's Weekly presented as a full-page front cover one of the best cartoons on Roosevelt's activities.[127] This magazine was particularly fearful that the United States would be inveigled either into war or into furnishing a contingent for an international constabulary.[128] It also was very indignant at the presumption of the London Statist, which advocated that the United States assume full responsibility for policing Morocco in order to preserve the peace of the world. This absurd notion, the editor said, showed how hard it is for Englishmen, even when exceptionally well informed, to understand this country.[129]

There were some Englishmen, however, who considered themselves fully competent to comprehend the United States, and one of them had a pen debate with Senator Lodge. The latter undertook to write an "authoritative article"[130] answering all the questions of the political layman regarding American relations with the Moroccan problem. Reviewing the several treaties which were the "reason and precedent for American action," he declared that the United States could not rightfully be excluded from the present conference, even if it involved military and political differences threatening war. The American people probably never would depart from Washington's policy of rejecting entangling alliances, but this policy had never been held to exclude agreements affecting commerce or "international conventions entered into for the improvement of conditions in war, or for the promotion of the world's peace."

Lodge emphasized that the Monroe Doctrine did not prohibit the new mission of the United States as a peacemaker:

> The fact that we do not permit Europe to interfere in affairs which solely concern the American continents is no reason why we should not make with the Powers of Europe such agreements as have been described, affecting the trade or commerce or peace of the world.

In Morocco the influence of the United States had been used hitherto in conformity with the policy pursued by President Roosevelt toward Russia and Japan. At Algeciras it would be used again to prevent war between two great Powers, both friends of the United States. Acting according to the language and spirit of the Hague Convention, the United States would not hesitate to use her moral influence to prevent wars, either between European Powers or in any portion of the civilized globe.

A significant reply to Lodge's exposition was made two weeks later by the English publicist, Sydney Brooks.[131] At Algeciras, he said, the question of commerce was wholly subsidiary. "The outstanding and only weighty fact" was that the United States was "sitting and voting at a round-table conference that is predominantly, if not exclusively, an European question." A forceful attack was made upon the Rooseveltian version of the Monroe Doctrine. European opinion could not reconcile America's activity at Algeciras with her limitation of France's action against Castro. The man in the street had always thought:

> A free hand in the new world was to be purchased by non-interference in the old .... If the fiat of the United States is, indeed, as Mr. Olney once declared it to be, law throughout the Americans, it is so only on the well-understood condition that Washington rules itself out from the complications of European politics .... It is a principle that cannot be departed from without disturbance to the whole scheme of Europe's relationship with North and South America.

Moreover, "the instructions to the American delegates were considered in England to outline a policy wholly irreconcilable with the principle of non-interference," [132] and

> It was with more than a little surprise and disappointment that Englishmen learned of America's commitment to the German--that is to say, the "international" solution of the problem. It seemed to them that the American representatives were entering the conference not to reconcile and harmonize, but to take sides; and the side they appeared to favor was not the French and English but the German side. This struck Englishmen as the more remarkable because neither commercially nor politically is Morocco an American interest, nor, it is safe to prophesy, will the United States assume the slightest responsibility for carrying out the recommendations of the conference.

Brooks also showed resentment over the President's Dominican policy:

> It is true that Mr. Roosevelt wishes the United States to exercise a certain supervision over republics whose cause he advocates, and even looks forward apparently to a time when this country will receive something like an international mandate to act at once as the policeman and official liquidator or receiver of the vast southern continent. But the Senate does not seem to relish his policy, and many details of great intricacy and embar-

rassment would have to be adjusted before Europe could assent to it.

As the Algeciras Conference continued, the American press found the many reports of German truculence, rumors of imminent conflict, and indications of serious involvements of Henry White justification for frequent criticisms of Roosevelt's flouting of the Monroe Doctrine. To support France's thesis it was pointed out that "France virtually enunciates in a modified form the principle of the Monroe Doctrine in Northwest Africa."[133]

A clever satire via doggerel verse expressed the mood of many Americans regarding the whole Algeciras affair. In "To Algeciras"[134] the author devoted a stanza to each of the leading contenders--Germany, Britain, and France--bidding each to abjure her pride for peace and concluding with a stanza reminding the world that the United States, also, could be as chauvinistic as any power on appropriate occasions:

> Breathe it gently, Algeciras,
> --- Sus Minerva, oh, inspire us! ---
> That we quarrel with no nation
> And that tho' not now desirous
> For a fight, Oh Algeciras!
> We can easily lick creation---
>   When desirous,
>   Algeciras.

While many newspapers conceded "but slender interest in Morocco," which did not comport with the current protest against European meddling in the Western Hemisphere, others backed the President in his work for peace and the Open Door.[135] One editor took a high moral position:

> In our early history we did the policing of Morocco alone; now we simply unite with other nations ... in deciding how this policing shall be further done. We do it for the sake of peace .... We must take our share in helping and maintaining peace, at some risk, with some entanglements, if we are to maintain the principles of Christian love, international as well as personal, and the dictates of decency, the <u>noblesse</u>

oblige of our position as a first class power.[136]

The disinterestedness and unselfishness of the United States were often emphasized:

> Our influence with the other powers does not come from absence of all interests. Those we have are definite, important, and lasting. But they are not selfish. They do not conflict with other legitimate interests. They do not encroach on the rights of others.[137]

One enthusiastic writer-to-the-editor rejoiced over the Open Door in Morocco, where, with her century of experience in the Far West of America, the United States could develop the Far West of Africa.[138] A German cartoon pictured Teddy riding his Monroe Doctrine horse all around the table at Algeciras without breaking a dish,[139] but an American periodical presented much evidence from European newspapers that "America's presence at Algeciras was resented." An American editor reiterated the familiar argument that it was logically absurd for a nation in world politics from Algeciras to Peking to "deny the commercial and quasi-colonial interests of Italy and Germany in South America."[140]

Nevertheless, Roosevelt and his delegates emerged triumphant from their peace-making mission at Algeciras. When the conference had completed its once apparently impossible task, the General Act was signed by all the delegates. But carefully designed to soothe the Senate's sensibilities was the characteristic reservation of the United States:

> The Government of the United States of America, having no political interest in Morocco and no desire or purpose having animated it to take part in this conference other than to secure for all peoples the widest equality of trade and privilege with Morocco and to facilitate the institution of reforms in that country tending to insure complete cordiality of intercourse without and stability of administration within for the common good, declares that, in acquiescing in the regulations and declarations of the conference, in becoming a signatory of the General Act and to the Additional Protocol, subject to ratification according to constitutional procedure, and in accepting

> the application of these regulations and declarations to American citizens and interests in Morocco, it does so without assuming obligations or responsibility for the enforcement thereof.[141]

In describing his role at Algeciras, Henry White expressed to Roosevelt ideas used later in persuading the Senate to accept the result of his efforts:

> I hope ... that the critics in the Senate of your policy ... must now admit that it is possible for us to take an important part in a European assemblage of this kind, and fully to assert our right to equality of rights commercial and economic, with any other nation, in a country such as Morocco, and yet in no wise to take sides in any of the political questions at issue between certain of the nations gathered there.[142]

Root's official letter of congratulation contains this estimate of the value of White's services:

> I wish to express to you the high approval with which the President and the Department of State regard your performance .... Your task was exceedingly delicate and difficult, and it was admirably performed .... You have avoided any results which might have been distasteful to the United States and have contributed materially to the settlement of a controversy which threatened the peace of Europe.[143]

When the General Act of Algeciras was sent to the Senate for advice and consent on May 25, 1906, Root pointed out that ratifications had to be deposited in Madrid not later than December 31, 1906, and the Senate was asked to act on it before adjournment.[144] A news item of June 24 reported that ratifications might be held up by the continued hostility of Senator Bacon to the treaty. The Senate made no concession except to set the date of December 12 for considering the treaty in executive session.[145]

During the several months when the Act of Algeciras was being weighed on the Senate's scales, the American and European press also found it a topic of enduring interest. There was a consensus that the conference had brought victory to France and a humiliating defeat to Germany, which signified Europe's refusal to recognize an overlord. There was much hesitancy in hailing a victory for peace, for there were few affirmations of belief in improved Franco-German relations and many predictions of a bitter aftermath in Morocco. At the beginning of 1907 there was the disturbing news that, with ratification of the Algeciras convention still incomplete, France and Spain had already been forced to begin their joint task of suppressing the increasing disorder, during which Raisuli was enforcing his own orders in Tangier.[146]

Of special interest to journalists were the role of Roosevelt in the whole proceedings and the still puzzling problem of his real relationship with Germany. Some writers considered him to have been a dupe of William II, acting as a front to put forward German-sponsored conference proposals. Most opinions coincided with the official American claim to disinterestedness and neutrality, and Henry White received much praise for his contributions to harmony and his influence in securing the acceptance of the compromise plan on the police leading to a final agreement.[149]

The debacle of German diplomacy at Algeciras caused a searching of conscience among the politically conscious leaders and classes of Germany. A large share of blame attached to the Emperor himself, but the Pan-Germans and other chauvinistic groups were rebuked also. Because of Roosevelt's public attentions to William II, the United States was still regarded as the friend most likely to aid Germany in redressing the balance of power in Europe. The German press and Ambassador Sternburg were assigned the task of consolidating this partnership.[148] Sternburg needed no prodding to make public pronouncements of friendship for Roosevelt or to propagandize for Germany.[149] Americans had been alerted to expect the downfall of Bülow after Germany's defeat. The Chancellor was fairly well known, for he had often received the opprobrium usually given to the Kaiser. It was undoubtedly a great surprise, therefore, that Germany's mysterious diplomat who resigned on April 17, 1906, had been the real power in the Wilhelmstrasse ever since Bismarck--and his name was Holstein, not Bülow.[150] His departure was one indication that the German Foreign Office intended to alter its course in international politics. However, what was alleged to have been Holstein's guiding principle was not to be abandoned, for "he always kept in close touch with American affairs, and it was his belief that it was America's destiny profoundly to influence Europe." The real cause of Bülow's collapse while speaking in the Reichstag was revealed as the strain of a prolonged struggle with Holstein for control of German foreign policy.[150]

Germany's need for a reorientation in foreign affairs was indeed desperate. Throughout the rest of 1906 after the conference, American periodicals commented on the approaching disintegration of the Triple Alliance, including many citations on the subject from the European press.[151] Anglo-German relations were worsening in spite of British proposals to discuss limitation of armaments in preparation for the Second Hague Conference. Germany countered the new Dreadnaught program of Great Britain by the third naval law of 1906. Haldane gave up his efforts for an Anglo-German rapprochement which had included a proposed intervention by Roosevelt to secure the Kaiser's adherence.[152]

Meanwhile, German-American relations remained outwardly amicable. The exchange of pleasantries continued. Three paintings by an American artist of President Roosevelt, Dr. Nicholas Butler, and Professor John W. Burgess were hung in the Roosevelt Room at the University of Berlin.[153] More significant was a declaration by Burgess in his first address as Roosevelt Professor at the University of Berlin that the American high protective tariff and the Monroe Doctrine "are almost obsolete, and the reconstruction of European States and their constitutions and the acceptance of the United States itself of its position as a world power have made them appear nearly senseless." Burgess also advocated a strong Teutonic tide of emigration to South America. The American press generally rejected him as an official spokesman for the United States.[154] On September 3, 1906, Roosevelt reviewed more than one-third of the American fleet in Long Island Sound to celebrate its attainment of third rank among the world's navies.[155] In Roosevelt's plans for the future, the fleet was important, for in the fall of 1906 he was suspicious of both Japan and Germany. All along the Pacific coast the Japanese were in conflict over American and Canadian policy on immigration and on separate schools for the Japanese. Admiral Dewey thought that the United States needed a stronger fleet than the Japanese in the Pacific and one superior to the German fleet in the Atlantic. Directing his attention to The Netherlands, Roosevelt now felt that she was in danger and prepared to occupy the Dutch colonies in the Caribbean.[156] But in his speech to the Reichstag on November 13, Bülow expressed gratification at the reserved and impartial attitude of the United States at Algeciras and esteem for the harmonizer of antagonisms, Henry White, who had promoted the success of the conference.[157]

In his annual message, delivered to Congress on December 4, 1906,[158] the President made only a brief reference to the Act of Algeciras, basing his request for the Senate's consent to it upon such grounds as to allow that body practically no choice:[159]

> The Algeciras Convention, which was signed by the United States as well as by most of the powers of Europe, supersedes the previous convention of 1880, which was also signed by the United States and a majority of the European Powers. This treaty confers upon us equal commercial rights with all European countries and does not entail a single obligation of any kind upon us, and I earnestly hope it may be speedily ratified. To refuse to ratify it would merely mean that we have forfeited our commercial rights in Morocco and would not achieve another object of any kind. In the event of such refusal, we would be left for the first time in a hundred and twenty years without any commercial treaty with Morocco; and this at a time when we are everywhere seeking new markets and outlets for our trade.

As Senator Bacon had once charitably conceded, the President was no lawyer, and hence he had probably overlooked the clause in the Algeciras Act which negated his argument: "All treaties, conventions and arrangements of the Signatory Powers with Morocco remain in force."[160] No other than the commerical argument was safe to give to the Senate, however.[161] The opposition in the Senate still refused to ignore the implications of foreign entanglement contained in the General Act. On December 5 the Committee on Foreign Relations unanimously reported the treaty favorably, but Bacon declared that he would rally the Democratic vote against it unless an acceptable reservation were adopted. As a sub-committee to draft such a reservation, Senators Spooner, Bacon, and Lodge were appointed.[162]

Without the aid of Henry White, however, the treaty might have been rejected. By special arrangement of the administration, he was given leave in the United States during the last two months of 1906 to exert his influence upon Bacon and other irreconcilables. As a recognition of his great services throughout the Moroccan affair, he was rewarded by being promoted to the embassy in Paris.[163]

The final debate on the Act of Algeciras on December 12, 1906, was held in executive session. It was reported in news articles that Senators Cullom, Lodge, and Spooner had spoken in favor of the administration's policy, that Bacon had delivered a lengthy address against taking part in similar conferences, and that the senators Morgan and Foraker had endorsed the acceptance of the treaty[164] with the attached reservation:

> Resolved, That the Senate ... understands that the participation of the United States in the Algeciras Conference and in the formation and adoption of the General Act and Protocol which resulted therefrom was with the sole purpose of preserving and increasing its commerce in Morocco, the protection as to life, liberty, and property of its citizens residing or traveling therein, and of aiding by its friendly offices and efforts in removing friction and controversy which seemed to menace the peace between Powers signatory with the United States to the treaty of 1880, all of which are on terms of amity with this Government, and without purpose to depart from the traditional American foreign policy which forbids participation by the United States in the settlement of political questions which are entirely European in scope.[165]

The fine hand of Lodge is easily discernible in the phrasing of the resolution. It does seem extraordinary, however, that after the protracted debates the upholders of the Monroe tradition should have been able to overlook the contradiction in "removing friction and controversy which seemed to meance the peace" and in denying departure from the "traditional American foreign policy which forbids participation in the settlement of political questions which are entirely European in scope." Undoubtedly time had worked for the President, and both press and Senate were weary and willing to liquidate the whole affair as quickly as possible. The Senate therefore gave the desired consent on December 12, and two days later the President formally ratified the General Act of Algeciras.[166]

Roosevelt had to wait only until February 25, 1907, for the capitulation of the Senate on his Santo Domingo treaty. Thus, two years before the end of his own term, he had triumphed completely over the Senate. Not only had he maintained the prerogative of the executive in treaty-making, but also had he won senatorial support in promulgating to the world two amendments to the Monroe Doctrine. One sanctioned financial guardianship of the Caribbean countries by the United States, in order to safeguard the independence of these countries. The other permitted the United States to participate in European political controversies if such intervention should seem desirable to preserve world peace.

The truce among the Great Powers, signed at Algeciras and ratified by the leading rivals before the end of 1906, was not to prove to be a prolog to peace in Morocco. In January, 1907, some American periodicals were reporting simultaneously the ratification of the Act of Algeciras[167] and the dispatch of battle fleets to the Moroccan coast. In order to implement the terms of the new international agreement, to keep order at Tangier, and to protect foreigners, the foreign ministers of Great Britain and Germany approved military measures by the recently appointed guardians of Morocco.[168] The American Senate had reason to congratulate itself that it had freed the United States from responsibility for maintaining the independence and integrity of Morocco.

Notes

1. Roosevelt to Sternburg, Oct. 11, 1901, Theodore Roosevelt Manuscripts (hereafter cited as T R MMS) cited by Howard E. Beale, Theodore Roosevelt and the Rise of America to World Power (hereafter cited as Beale, Theodore Roosevelt), 190-191.

2. "In London on July 9, in conversation with American Naval officers, at the King's dinner at Buckingham Palace, members of the British Cabinet are said to have expressed a desire for such an extension of the Monroe Doctrine as would imply United States control over the financial obligations of the central and South American States." "International Affairs, South American Relations," Current Literature, XXXV (Sept., 1903), 258.

3. Graham H. Stuart, Latin America and the United States (hereafter cited as Stuart, Latin America and the United States), 219-222; Dana Gardner Monro, The United States and the Caribbean Area, 102-109.

4. Sternburg to F. O., No. 6559, March 9, 1905, G. P., XX, 258-259.

5. In March, 1905, Roosevelt wrote scathing criticisms of the Senate to Sir George Trevelyan and to J. B. Bishop. To the latter he said in part: "The Senate is wholly incompetent to take such a part (the lead in foreign affairs). Creatures like Bacon, Morgan, et cetera, backed by the Yahoo among the Democratic Senators, are wholly indifferent to national honor or national welfare .... The Senate ought to feel that its action on the treaty-making power should be like that of the President's veto ... it should be rarely used." Roosevelt to Trevelyan, March 9, 1905, President's Personal Letter Book, XXIV, 309-310; Roosevelt to Bishop, March 23, 1905, Ibid., 434-435.

6. The text is in Richardson, Messages and Papers of the Presidents, XVI, 7353-7403. The quotation of the Roosevelt Corollary is from page 7376.

7. An able defense of Roosevelt's policy was made by John Bassett Moore in "Santo Domingo and the United States," Review of Reviews, XXXI (March, 1905), 293-298.

8. Some pertinent criticism is found in "The Roosevelt Doctrine and European Interests," in Living Age, 7th Series, XXIX (Dec. 2, 1905), 565-567: "While we hear repeatedly from President Roosevelt of 'international police power,' we do not hear anything of the tribunal by which the action of that police force is to be set in motion .... The United States are to combine the judicial and the executive functions in ... the Western Hemisphere, except, of course, those portions ... under the sovereignty of European countries .... The future course of affairs ... would be likely to be smoother if there were evolved some international method of deciding ... the occasions for the exercise of United States police control."

9. William Everett, in "The United States Senate," Atlantic Monthly, XCVII (Feb., 1906), 157-166 said that for years the Senate had held the President and the House by the throat and kept them strangled until its terms were accepted.

10. A. Maurice Low, "Theodore Roosevelt," Forum, XXXII (Nov., 1901), 265. The author adds: "The Senate has gradually enlarged its powers until it has come to regard itself as a council of state as well as a legislative body ... and seeks to control the actions of the Executive."

11. Thayer, John Hay, II, 393.

12. Ibid., 270-272; Jessup, Elihu Root, I, 452-453.

13. White, American Opinion of France, 260-261; Tardieu, La Conférence, 100, 252.

14. Editorials in the New York Times, Feb. 25, 1906, 8; Feb. 27, 1906, 8; March 12, 1906, 8.

15. Johnston, "Morocco and the French Intervention," Review of Reviews, XXXI (June, 1905), 691.

16. "The British and German Fleets," Fortnightly Review, LXXXIII (Jan., 1905), 15-26; "British Imperial Policies," Review of Reviews, XXXII (Oct., 1905), 407.

17. "For Anglo-German Accord," New York Times, Dec. 2, 1905, 4; "Attempts to Reconcile Germany and England," Literary Digest, XXXII (Jan. 6, 1906), 22; "Cementing Anglo-German Friendship," Ibid., (Feb. 3, 1906), 167-168; "The Chancellor Challenged," Ibid., (Jan. 13, 1906), 62.

18. "Delcassé and German 'Weltpolitik,' " Review of Reviews, XXXII, (Aug., 1905), 216-217.

19. "As To War between England and Germany," Literary Digest, XXXI (Sept. 9, 1905), 353-354.

20. "England, France, and Germany," Independent, LIX (Oct. 19, 1905), 895-896; "Germany's Threats and France's Unreadiness," Literary Digest, XXXI (Nov. 11, 1905), 710.

21. A. Maurice Low, "Foreign Affairs," Forum, XXXVII (Jan., 1906), 313-332.

22. William C. Dreher, "Recent Events in Germany," Atlantic Monthly, XCV (March, 1905), 394; "The Drawing Together of Germany and the U. S. A.," Grenzboten, XIV (May, 1905), 453 ff., cited by Vagts, Weltpolitik, II, 1853, footnote 2.

23. "An Educational Entente," Nation, LXXX (March 9, 1905), 186; Ibid., (April 27, 1905), 323; "The President at Clark," Outlook, LXXX (July 1, 1905), 560.

24. "The German-American University Exchange," Harper's Weekly, XLIX (Nov. 25, 1905), 1694; "An International Professorship," Outlook, LXXX (Dec. 2, 1905), 799-800; "A German Account of the Beginnings of University Reciprocity," Literary Digest, XXXII (Jan. 6, 1906), 10; "Ludwig Fulda in America," Ibid., XXXII (March 10, 1906), 363-364.

25. "The Week," *Nation,* LXXX (April 13, 1905), 279-280.

26. "World-Politics," *North American Review,* CLXXX (May, 1905), 794; Sydney Brooks, "The Aims of Germany," *Harper's Weekly,* XLIX (May 6, 1905), 649-650.

27. Editorials: "Emperor Eilliam Ponders," Washington *Post,* May 8, 1905, 6; "Emperor William's Ambition," *Ibid.,* June 18, 1905, editorial section, 4.

28. "The Significance of German Expansion," *Review of Reviews,* XXXII (July, 1905), 115-117.

29. "The Week," *Nation,* LXXX (June 8, 1905), 449; "The New Fermant in Morocco," *Literary Digest,* XXXI (Sept. 16, 1905), 392.

30. "Bebel Cites Russia as Warning to Kaiser," *New York Times,* Dec. 8, 1905, 1; "Versailles and Algeciras," *Ibid.,* Jan. 16, 1906, 10.

31. "French Suspicion of German Policy in Morocco," *Literary Digest,* XXX (April 15, 1905), 554-555.

32. "The Moroccan Situation," *Independent,* LVIII (April 13, 1905), 807; "The Moroccan Difficulty," *Ibid.,* (April 20, 1905), 866.

33. The London *Times* quoted in *Literary Digest,* XXX (April 29, 1905), 636; Francis Charmes, "Germany and the Question of Morocco," *Fortnightly Review,* LXXXIII (May, 1905), 957.

34. "Germany and Morocco," *Review of Reviews,* XXXI (May, 1905), 530-531; "World-Politics," *North American Review,* CLXXX (May, 1905), 795-796; "Comment," *Harper's Weekly,* XLIX (July 1, 1905), 929.

35. "How M. Delcassé Was Affronted," Washington *Post,* May 10, 1905, 6.

36. "European Scheme to Exert Pressure Upon the United States," *Literary Digest,* XXX (May 29, 1905), 754.

37. "America's Share in the Conference," New York Daily Tribune, Jan. 10, 1906, 3; "The Conference of Algeciras," Independent, LX (Jan. 11, 1906), 66-67; "The Morocco Conference," Nation, LXXXII (Jan. 11, 1906), 30-31.

38. "Not to Be Outwitted by the Kaiser," Washington Post, April 5, 1905, 6; "Hands Off Morocco," Ibid., April 8, 1905, 6; 'England and France," Ibid., April 11, 1905, 6; "Our Policy in Morocco," Ibid., April 28, 1905, 6.

39. "French Suspicion of German Policy in Morocco," Literary Digest," XXX (April 15, 1905), 555.

40. Evidently the Björkö meeting is meant, at which the two monarchs signed the treaty never put into effect. Roosevelt's complete innocence of this accusation has been made clear.

41. 'Entangling Alliances," Washington Post, June 30, 1905, 6; "The World's Umpire," editorial, Ibid., July 27, 1905, 6.

42. "America's Influence and Concern," Review of Reviews, XXXII (July, 1905), 3; Harper's Weekly, XLIX (July 22, 1905), 10140.

43. In an editorial on the following day, January 7, 1906, 6, entitled "The United States at Algeciras," the Times repudiated this thesis of the "semi-offical statement sent out from Washington," declaring it to be unauthentic. "The Government's view is that America has, by virtue of her ancient interest in Morocco, rights even superior to those of any European state in deciding the critical questions which will come before the conference. The statement goes on to give as the basis of the remarkable assumption the fact that the United States wiped out the piracy of the Barbary States and made with them the treaty which is the foundation of all subsequent agreements with other nations .... This ... notion ... is entirely impertinent and fanciful .... The historic incident referred to in the Washington dispatch ... has no

more relation to the policy we should now frame than Perry's victory on Lake Erie."

44. Editorials: "America as Peacemaker," New York Times, Jan. 6, 1906, 4; "The Conference at Algeciras," Ibid., 8.

45. The author was referring, of course, to American "claims to reserve one vast enclave of the civilized globe for her own."

46. "A British View of American Foreign Policy," Literary Digest, XXXII (March 3, 1906), 329-330.

47. "Failure of the Kaiser's Policy Predicted," Ibid., XXXI (July 8, 1905), 57-58; "French and British Comment on the Return of John Paul Jones." Ibid., (July 29, 1905), 153.

48. "The Spirit of the Foreign Reviews," Review of Reviews, XXXII (Oct., 1905), 504; Sir Charles W. Dilke, "Present English Foreign Policy." Independent, LIX (Dec. 28, 1905), 1511-1513.

49. "Great Britain, France, and the United States," Harper's Weekly, XLIX (Aug. 19, 1905), 1184-1185.

50. "Hints at An Entente," Washington Post, Aug. 14, 1905), 1; "Wholesale Peace Alliances," Ibid., Aug. 10, 1905), 6.

51. "World-Politics," North American Review, CLXXXII (May, 1906), 796-797.

52. Hale had opposed the Spanish-American War and the Philippine phase of it and had thwarted the President as much as possible in his program of naval expansion. "Hale, Senate Leader, A Warrior for Peace." New York Times, Jan. 8, 1906, 9.

53. Roosevelt's antipathy toward the Senate was so great that at this time he did not refrain from expressing it even to Durand. Early in 1906 Roosevelt was very confidential with Durand, who was on an official

visit. "The President speaks freely about the ignorance and wrong-headedness of Congress regarding the Monroe Doctrine and other matters. He said that when he awoke at night and the recollection of their doings came over him, he had to force himself to think of bears and other more agreeable subjects than Congress or he would never get to sleep again." Sykes, Durand, 289, 299.

54. Congressional Record, 59th Congress, 1st Session, Dec. 4, 1905-Jan. 12, 1906, XL, Part 1 (hereafter cited as Congressional Record, XL, Part 1), 683.

55. Ibid., 792; "Senators Are Anxious About Morocco Policy," New York Times, Jan. 9, 1906, 5.

56. Senators of both parties had determined to redefine the Monroe Doctrine in its original terms and to challenge President Roosevelt in their debates with their dissent from his interpretations. "To Define Monroe Doctrine," New York Times, Jan. 3, 1906, 1.

57. "Rayner Denounces Roosevelt's Policy," New York Times, Jan. 9, 1906, 8.

58. Congressional Record, XL, Part 1, 792.

59. Ibid., 792-799.

60. Ibid., 851.

61. New York Daily Tribune, Jan. 11, 1906, 8; "American Envoys Not to Vote at Algeciras," New York Times, Jan. 10, 1906, 4; "The United States and Morocco," Ibid., Jan. 11, 1906, 8.

62. Congressional Record, XL, Part 1, 909-910, 946-948.

63. "Open Minds at Algeciras," New York Times, Jan. 11, 1906, 7.

64. Congressional Record, XL, Part 1, 1069; New York Times, Jan. 16, 1906, 1.

65. Congressional Record, XL, Part 1, 1069-1074.

66. Ibid., 1074-1075.

67. Ibid., 1075-1076.

68. New York Times, Jan. 16, 1906, 2; "Envoys at Algeciras Are Anxious to Agree; Ibid., Jan. 17, 1906, 4;"Moroccan Conference Solves One Problem," Ibid., Jan. 19, 1906, 5; "Fear at Algeciras That Trouble Is Near," Ibid., Jan. 21, 1906, 4; "The Moroccan Conference," Outlook, LXXXII (Jan. 20, 1906), 103-104.

69. American periodicals differed on the propriety of the attendance of the American fleet at Algeciras. One said that the plan to send the fleet there had long antedated the selection of Algeciras as the conference site, and that our government would use its full influence to promote a peaceful settlement. "The Situation Abroad," Outlook, LXXXII (Jan. 13, 1906), 65 and "The Future of Morocco," Ibid., (Jan. 20, 1906), 104. Another considered it the legitimate business of the State Department to safeguard the Open Door in Morocco--"the principal question really underlying the frictions that brought about the Algeciras Conference." "Tariffs and Diplomacy," Review of Reviews, XXXIII (Feb., 1906), 137.

70. "Hale Warns President of Peril in Morocco," New York Times, Jan. 16, 1906, 1; Congressional Record, XL, Part 1, 1076-1077.

71. Ibid., 1077-1078.

72. Hale's remarks excited wide discussion. The Nation, LXXII (Jan. 18, 1906), 43 gave a judicial analysis of the reorganization program, calling for an economic upbuilding of Morocco comparable to Lord Cromer's work in Egypt. What nation was to do the work of rehabilitation? 'If we really have any business in settling the national affairs of Morocco, we must be prepared next to go to work in Crete and Macedonia .... Our trade relations with Morocco are so slight as not to call for a separate item in the monthly and yearly summary of our foreign commerce."

73. Congressional Record, XL, Part 1, 1078-1079.

74. In "World-Politics," North American Review, CLXXXII (Feb., 1906), 316, 320, it was noted that opposition to going to Algeciras was found in both parties in the Senate. Hale's "Tranquilizing declaration" was questioned, because the exemption of the commercial provisions of 1880 from the program could give the American delegates no commercial function at the conference. An editorial on "The Algeciras Conference" in the New York Times, Jan. 17, 1906, 10, gave assurance that White and Gummeré would take part only to safeguard the Open Door and most favored nation principles of the Madrid Convention. Senators Spooner and Lodge were commended for upholding the President's prerogatives in sending delegates and in carrying on all the necessary negotiations for a new treaty. Nevertheless, Hale's warning was not superfluous; it would give notice to European powers that the United States was an impartial onlooker so far as their political differences were concerned.

75. Congressional Record, XL, Part 1, 1079.

76. "Secret Treaty With Cuba," New York Times, Jan. 17, 1906, 1.

77. Congressional Record, XL, Part 1, 1079-1081.

78. Ibid., Part 2, 1173-1179.

79. "Our Delegates Not Free," New York Times, Jan. 17, 1906, 4.

80. "Root Explains Our Attitude," New York Times, Jan. 19, 1906, 5; "Mr. Root on Morocco," New York Daily Tribune, Jan. 19, 1906, 3.

81. Neither was the Nation. In "The Week," LXXXII (Jan. 25, 1906), 63-64, it said that Root with a "curious mixture of frankness and casuistry" had given an "almost excessive emphasis to the fact that the American delegates may treat Algeciras as an

agreeable winter resort, and free their minds from undue preoccupation with the sessions in the Ayuntamiento." On the other hand, the Outlook endorsed the policy of the State Department and gave historical reasons for the cooperation of Americans in exerting a beneficial influence at the conference. "America at Algeciras" and "American Influence," Outlook, LXXXII (Jan. 27, 1906), 144-145.

82. Congressional Record, XL, Part 2, 1418-1420.

83. The Nation, LXXXII (Feb. 1, 1906), 85, ridiculed Spooner's idea of the delegates' withdrawal at the psychological moment. "How are our diplomats to learn how to get out of bad boxes unless first they get in? How may they practice the modest and useful art of self-effacement unless first they have obtruded themselves? Such an argument takes us back to those early Christians who, to demonstrate their faith, voluntarily exposed themselves to the direst temptations .... If you are to recall your delegates at the instant when the peace of the world wavers in the balance, you must first send them. This explains all."

84. Congressional Record, XL, Part 2, 1421-1423; "The United States at Algeciras," Outlook, LXXXII (Feb. 3, 1906), 244-245 fully endorsed Spooner's views.

85. Congressional Record, XL, Part 2, 1421-1422.

86. The discussion on Santo Domingo was part of a lengthy debate on the respective powers of the President and the Senate in treaty-making, with Lodge as the presidential champion. In this connection, the Nation, LXXXII (Feb. 1, 1906), 85 recalled that in an article in the January, 1902, number of Scribner's Magazine Lodge had been an equally staunch exponent of the Senate's power of treaty-making. Lodge's personal defense of the President against charges of usurpation was emphasized in "Roosevelt No Usurper, Cries Lodge in Senate," New York Times, Jan. 25, 1906, 4.

87. Congressional Record, XL, Part 2, 1470-1480.

88. Senator Money gave a lengthy history of the Monroe Doctrine and its connection with the President's handling of the Santo Domingo problem. Senator Heyburn of Idaho advocated the annexation of Santo Domingo to guard the Panama Canal. Money objected to this plan. Congressional Record, XL, Part 2, 1530-1539; "Urges Annexation Cure for Dominican Ills," New York Times, Jan. 26, 1906, 8.

89. Congressional Record, XL, Part 2, 1529-1530.

90. Ibid., 1755.

91. The defection of Patterson to the ranks of the "White House Democrats" created great consternation among the regulars. The charge was made that this defecting group all had terms expiring on March 3, 1907 and were angling for executive patronage and other recognition in order to convince their legislatures of the desirability of their reelection. "The Week," Nation, LXXXII (Feb. 8, 1906), 107.

92. Congressional Record, XL, Part 2, 1801-1806.

93. "New Defection Scares Democrats in Senate," New York Times, Feb. 1, 1906, 1; "Senate Democrats Are Demoralized," Ibid., Feb. 2, 1906, 6; "Loyal Democrats Bitter," Ibid., Feb. 3, 1906, 1; "Democratic Senators Bound Against Treaty," Ibid., Feb. 4, 1906, 1; "Patterson Says Caucus Violates State Rights," Ibid., Feb. 6, 1906, 4; "A Review of the World," Current Literature, XL (March, 1906), 233-234.

94. Congressional Record, XL, Part 3, 2055-2056.

95. Ibid., 2125-2131.

96. The Review of Reviews said editorially, in "America and the Morocco Conference," XXXIII (Feb. 1906), 135: "Its (the conference's) purposes were such that representatives of the United States could be present without embarrassment or without violation of our fixed policy as respects aloofness from European affairs .... Our delegates may be able to aid in the

promotion of harmony. A war between France and Germany over Morocco, or over any other bone of contention, would cause a stupendous disturbance of our business interests. We are justified, therefore, if we proceed with due discretion, in helping to harmonize the Moroccan situation."

97. Congressional Record, XL, Part 2, 2131-2138.

98. At this time, and often later, such headlines as this in the New York Times, Jan. 24, 1906, 4 were not calculated to furnish proof of the administration's sincerity in promising abstention from political adventures: "Americans Take Lead in Efforts for Peace." An even more disturbing caption, "White Busy at Algeciras. American Trying Hard to Settle the Franco-German Dispute," was in the same paper, Feb. 15, 1906, 2.

99. Congressional Record, XL, Part 2, 2138-2148.

100. Senator Spooner said that introduction of the Bacon resolution in open session showed the intention to bring the President to book before the people of the United States. He also declared that the President was "uncontrolled and uncontrollable and not answerable to us or to the other house." "Senators Show Temper Over President's Acts; Bacon and Spooner engage in Lively Tilt in Debate," New York Times, (Feb. 7, 1906), 4.

101. Congressional Record, XL, Part 2, 2141-2148.

102. Ibid., Part 6, 5183.

103. Beginning work on Feb. 8, the committee aimed to set up a "friendly receivership" similar to the British one in Egypt. Roosevelt's temporary executive agreement operated for twenty-eight months, until on Feb. 25, 1907, the Senate approved a new treaty with the substance of the unratified protocol. Thus Roosevelt's first corollary to the Monroe Doctrine was accepted. "Committee Takes Up Treaty," New York Times, Feb. 8, 1906, 2; "Santo Domingo," Ibid., March 2, 1906, 8; Bailey, A Diplomatic History of

the American People, First Edition, 559.

104. "A Review of the World," Current Literature, XL (March, 1906), 231-233.

105. F. R., 1906, Part 1, 640. For the subject of the tariff controversy see Ibid., 640-648; Wolf von Schierbrand, "Our Tariff Differences with Germany," Review of Reviews, XXXII (Aug., 1905), 205-207; Vagts, Weltpolitik, I, 1-205.

106. "Will Raise Tariff to Fight Germany," New York Times, (Jan. 13, 1906), 1.

107. "Tariffs and Diplomacy," Review of Reviews, XXXII (Feb., 1905), 137. It was suggested that the failure of the United States to agree to reciprocity would turn Germany toward Argentina for foodstuffs and toward Europe for supplies. "A Way Out," New York Times, (Feb. 9, 1906), 8.

108. "Doubtless our irreconcilable stand-patters will only discern German weakness in Germany's anxiety, and will harden their hearts against any relaxation of the 'best and bravest' tariff at the assault of a timorous foe." "The World's Finances," New York Times, (Jan. 25, 1906), 8.

109. "Morocco Depresses Berlin," New York Times, Jan. 29, 1906, 11; "The Impending Tariff War," Ibid., Feb. 3, 1906, 8; "Germans Fear Tariff War," Ibid., Feb. 4, 1906, 4; "Reichstag May Forbid Concession to America," Ibid., Feb. 16, 1906, 6; "Germany Expects Aid From Us at Algeciras," Ibid., Feb. 17, 1906, 4.

110. "German Agrarians Angry," Ibid., Feb. 18, 1906, 4; "Reichstag Sanctions the Concession to Us," Ibid., Feb. 23, 1906, 5; "Our Tariff Relations with Germany," Review of Reviews, XXXIII (March, 1906), 273-274.

111. "Germany Expects Aid From Us At Algeciras," New York Times, (Feb. 17, 1906), 4.

112. "Reichstag Sanctions the Concession to Us," Ibid., (Feb. 23, 1906), 5.

113. "Why Germany Is Courting American Favor," Current Literature, XL (April, 1906), 362-363.

114. "The prince is believed to be now high in favor with the Washington government .... Bülow will, therefore, continue indefinitely as Imperial Chancellor, to resolve all debate in the Reichstag, be its subject what it may, into a series of quotations from the poets--tariff wars, Polish unrest, Monroe Doctrine, what you will. He has transformed Germany into a land of government by classical allusion in a sense far more literal than indulged in when France was termed a despotism tempered by epigrams. Nor did the prince drag Schiller, Goethe, Homer, or Shakespeare in by the neck and heels when he discussed the tariff. He caused them to rise as gracefully from a commercial treaty as did Venus from the sea." Ibid., 363.

115. "Comment," Harper's Weekly, L (March 3, 1906), 289.

116. F. R., 1906, Part 2, 1443.

117. "France and Venezuela," Review of Reviews, XXXII (Feb., 1906), 138.

118. "France and Venezuela," Outlook, LXXXII (Jan. 20, 1906), 104-105 and Ibid., (Jan. 27, 1906), 145.

119. On December 15, 1905, Jusserand had given to Roosevelt and Root the promise of France that if force had to be used against Venezuela, as seemed probable, there would be no permanent occupation of Venezuelan territory and any seizure of customs houses would be of as short duration as possible. Dennis, Adventures, 300-301; Jessup, Root, I, 495-496.

120. "Free Hand for France in Punishing Castro," New York Times, Jan. 22, 1906, 1; "France Takes Her Time in Venezuelan Affair," Ibid., Jan. 24, 1906, 4; "Not to Punish Castro Yet," Ibid., Jan. 25, 1906, 5;

"To Attend to Castro Later, Ibid., Feb. 10, 1906, 5; "What Will France Do to Venezuela?" Current Literature, XL (March, 1906), 249-250; "The Franco-Venezuelan Dispute," Review of Reviews, XXXIII (March, 1906), 266-267.

121. "Chameleon-Like Monroeism," New York Times, Jan. 25, 1906, 8.

122. London Outlook, quoted in "London View of the President," Ibid., Jan. 27, 1906, 1.

123. "Would Violate the Monroe Doctrine," Washington Post, Aug. 25, 1905, 6.

124. "France in Her Foreign Relations," Review of Reviews, XXXIII (March, 1906), 271.

125. "The Spooner-Bacon debate is the classic discussion of the respective powers, duties, and responsibilities of the President and the Senate in foreign relations." Wriston, Executive Agents, 308.

126. Augustus O. Bacon, "The Treaty-Making Power of the President and the Senate," North American Review, CLXXXII (April, 1906), 502-512.

127. The President, in formal dress with a Big Stick on his right shoulder, leads a caravan of elephants into Morocco via Algeciras. The elephants carry big guns manned by sailors and wear eagle helmets. The "Busy Showman" introduced his "latest Foreign Exhibit, criticized by the side-show men at the other end of Pennsylvania Avenue as being without precedent. But precedents did not concern him, and no so-called entanglements were to be anticipated as the result of this only Original Grand Exhibition. It was his business to give a good and varied show. Harper's Weekly, L (Feb. 3, 1906), 143.

128. "The United States and the Morocco Conference," Ibid., L (Jan. 27, 1906), 112.

129. "Comment," Ibid., (Feb. 24, 1906), 252.

130. Henry Cabot Lodge, "The Monroe Doctrine and Morocco," Ibid., (March 10, 1906), 332-352.

131. Sydney Brooks, "The United States at Algeciras, from an English Standpoint," Ibid., (March 24, 1906), 402-403.

132. Brooks cited the movement for improvement in treatment of the Jews, "which but for the initiative of Mr. Roosevelt would certainly not have been discussed," and the advocacy of the international system of police, prejudgment "on an issue on which it was known that the success or failure of the conference would depend."

133. "Belgium and Italy Puzzled at Algeciras," New York Times, (Jan. 25, 1906), 5.

134. I. H. G., "To Algeciras," New York Times, Jan. 25, 1906, 8.

135. "Our Slender Interest in Morocco," Literary Digest, XXXII (Jan. 27, 1906), 112-113; "The European Situation," New York Times, Jan. 31, 1906, 10.

136. "Our Foreign Entanglements," Independent, LX (Feb. 15, 1906), 405-406.

137. "The United States and Morocco," New York Times, Feb. 16, 1906, 8.

138. Paul E. Mairesse, "Africa and the Open Door," Ibid., Feb. 19, 1906, 8.

139. "America at the Moroccan Conference" (Cartoon from the Berlin Kladderdatsch), Current Literature, XL (April, 1906), 367.

140. "America's Presence at Morocco Resented," Ibid., (March, 1906), 246-248; "The Week," Nation, LXXXIII (Nov. 8, 1906), 383.

141. Malloy, Treaties, II, 2182-2183. Root authorized the signing of the Act of Algeciras on April 5, 1906, with the reservation; F. R., 1906, Part 2, 1491-1492.

142. White to Roosevelt, quoted in Nevins, Henry White, 281.

143. Root to White, June 2, 1906, F. R., 1906, Part 2, 1495.

144. In letters which he wrote to Senator Cullom, chairman of the Foreign Relations Committee, and to Senator Hale, the President used only one argument. Failure to ratify the Act of Algeciras, Roosevelt warned, would leave the United States without any treaty with Morocco for the first time since 1786. Root used the same allegation later when ratification was obtained. It is hard to believe that the proponents of this idea could have deceived either themselves or the senators by this false statement. Roosevelt to Cullom, June 28, 1906, Roosevelt Papers, XXXV, 23; Roosevelt to Hale, June 27, 1906, Ibid., 45-46.

145. Harper's Weekly, L (Dec. 8, 1906), 1735; Opposition of Bacon, New York Daily Tribune, June 25, 1906, 1.

146. "The Net Outcome at Algeciras," New York Times, March 28, 1906, 8; "Algeciras Will Have a Bitter Aftermath," Ibid., March 30, 1906, 6; "A Victory for France," Ibid., April 1, 1906, 4; "Algeciras and After," Ibid., April 1, 1906, 10; "France's Gain in Prestige," Review of Reviews, XXXIII (May, 1906), 533; E. J. Dillon, "Europe Refuses to Recognize an Overlord," Contemporary Review, LXXXIX (May, 1906), 723-735; "Africa," Independent, LXII (Jan. 3, 1907), 7-8.

147. E. J. Dillon, "Brutus in the Service of Tarquin," Contemporary Review, LXXXIX (May, 1906), 729-730; "Jusserand Sees President; London Outlook Says Moroccan Agreement Will Be due to America," New York Times, March 24, 1906, 4; "Only England Gains by Morocco Dispute," Ibid., March 25, 1906, 4; "Adopt Our Moroccan Plan," Ibid., March 26, 1906, 1; "Moors Are Obstructive," Ibid., March 29, 1906, 1; "Row Lasted Just a Year," Ibid., April 1, 1906, 4; Salvatore Cortesi, "From Portsmouth to Algeciras," Independent, LX (May 17, 1906), 1150-1152;

"The Conference at Algeciras, Ibid., (March 29, 1906), 705-706; Maxey, "Moriturus," Forum, XXXIX (April, 1908), 571; "Results of the Morocco Conference," Current Literature, XL (May, 1906), 481-482; "World-Politics," North American Review, CLXXXII (May, 1906), 796-797; "French Prospertiy," Review of Reviews, XXXIV (Aug., 1906), 135; William C. Dreher, "The Year in Germany," Atlantic Monthly, XCVIII (Nov., 1906), 665; "The Algeciras Conference," American Journal of International Law, " I (Jan., 1907), 140.

148. "World-Politics," North American Review, CLXXXII (June, 1906), 941-947; "How Germany Likes the Result at Algeciras," Literary Digest, XXXII (April 28, 1906), 655-656.

149. Several examples of his activities may be cited. In a commencement address at the University of Illinois he compared Roosevelt to one of the greatest emperors of ancient China; "Commencement Notes," Outlook, LXXXIII (June 23, 1906), 400. He defended German policy at Algeciras; "Baron von Sternburg on Morocco," Ibid., LXXXII (March 17, 1906), 585. To charges such as "Germany as Our Future Rival in This Hemisphere," in Literary Digest, XXXII (April 21, 1906), 619, he made an effective answer in his article, "Phantom Peril of German Emigration and South American Settlements," in North American Review, CLXXXII (May, 1906), 641-650.

150. "Expects Bülow's Downfall," New York Times, March 27, 1906, 5; "Germany's Mysterious Diplomatist Resigns," Ibid., April 18, 1906, 4; "Von Bülow's Prospects of Retirement," Literary Digest, XXXII (April 14, 1906), 576; "Real Cause of von Bülow's Collapse," Ibid., (May 5, 1906), 693.

151. "Germany's Fear of Isolation," Literary Digest, XXXII (April 7, 1906), 527; "Death Agonies of the Triple Alliance," Ibid., (April 14, 1906), 575-576; "Emperor' William's Telegrams, Ibid., (June 30, 1906), 979; "A Lop-Sided Triple Alliance," Ibid., XXXIII (July 7, 1906), 23-24; "The Kaiser's Problematic

Telegram," Ibid., (Nov. 3, 1906), 628-629; "Vitality of Triple Alliance," Review of Reviews, XXXIV (July, 1906), 22; "Why Italy Should Remain in the Triple Alliance--A German Plea," Ibid., (Dec., 1906), 742-744.

152. Fay, Origins of the World War, I, 237-240; Sontag, "German Foreign Policy, 1904-1906," 298-300; Lee, King Edward VII, II, 331, 528-531; Nevins, Henry White, 249-251.

153. "Recent Events in Germany," Review of Reviews, XXXIV (July, 1906), 24-25; "Three American Portraits for Berlin," Ibid., 40-42.

154. "A Roosevelt Professor's Repudiation of the Monroe Doctrine," Literary Digest, XXXIII (Nov. 10, 1906), 664-665.

155. Harper's Weekly, L (Sept. 8, 1906), 1325

156. Jusserand, What Me Befell, 308-309.

157. "Chancellor von Bülow and the German Empire," Independent, LXXI (Nov. 22, 1906), 1196-1197; "Germany's Foreign Relations," Outlook, LXXXIV (Nov. 24, 1906), 689-690.

158. Richardson, Messages and Papers, X, 7442-7443.

159. In a letter to William Laffan, editor and owner of the New York Sun, in reply to an article in the Sun on December 3, 1906, Elihu Root was more truthful. He admitted that "The situation in Europe a year ago was that there was imminent danger of a war between Germany and France over a row about Morocco. The European diplomatists found that they could get out of the difficulty through having a revision of the existing treaty with Morocco .... The United States was a party to the existing treaty relative to Morocco .... Our consent, accordingly, had to be asked to the revision of the treaty. We had no concern in the row between France and Germany, we had no concern in the subject-matter of the row .... but we could not

afford to refuse our assent to having something done which would not inflict any injury on us and would save the peace of Europe." Archives Numerical File, National Archives, Washington, D. C., XLIII, 295/18A. (hereafter cited as A. N. F.)

160. International Conference of Algeciras, General Act of the Algeciras Conference at Algeciras and an Additional Protocol, Chapter VII, Article 123, 43-44.

161. "It is the commercial, and not the political, features of the treaty to which our Federal Senate makes the United States a party." "World-Politics," North American Review, CLXXXIII (Dec., 1906), 1320.

162. New York Daily Tribune, Dec. 6, 1906, 2.

163. Nevins, Henry White, 255.

164. New York Daily Tribune, Dec. 13, 1906, 3.

165. Malloy, Treaties, II, 2183.

166. Surprisingly, Roosevelt's argument for the acceptance of the treaty was not refuted by the press. "The Senate's refusal to ratify the Algeciras Convention would have rendered it necessary for us forthwith to negotiate a separate treaty, and, meanwhile, our citizens who happened to be within the Shereefian dominions would have found themselves without protection," said Harper's Weekly, L (Dec. 29, 1906), 1883, following the administration line.

167. In "Africa in the World's Thought," Review of Reviews, XXXV (Jan., 1907), 27, it was reported that the Act of Algeciras had been accepted by the French Parliament on Dec. 6, by the German Reichstag on Dec. 10, and by the American Senate on Dec. 12.

168. "Moroccan Affairs," Outlook, LXXXV (Jan. 5, 1907), 6-7.

Chapter X

The Aftermath of Algeciras
(1906 - 1912)

As had been prophesied, the aftermath of Algeciras was indeed bitter, especially for Germany and Morocco. During the six years following the international agreement supposed to solve the Moroccan problem, the anti-German diplomats were intensely active in extending their agreements to prevent Germany from again becoming a menace to the peace of the world. First foretold by Bülow in a Reichstag speech on November 15, 1906, the "encirclement" of Germany was completed during this short span of years.[1] In Morocco, France's "peaceful penetration" was converted into a war on Morocco, which Roosevelt and his successor Taft decided was no concern of the United States. Roosevelt failed in his design to keep the door open in China for American commerce, but he learned how to make a secret entente as skillfully as any of his European colleagues.

During 1906 and 1907, the Anglo-French entente expanded. Signed on October 20, 1906, the Anglo-French Convention on the New Hebrides really concluded the Entente Cordiale and removed the last source of friction on colonial questions.[2] Following this, the Anglo-French-Italian Agreement Regarding Abyssinia on December 13, 1906, guaranteed the integrity of Abyssinia and maintenance of the *status quo*, with concerted action if this became impossible--a diplomatic formula denoting danger for any backward country. Since the three countries involved were assigned spheres of economic interest,[3] another large area of Africa was closed to German enterprise, and Germany's already unfaithful ally, Italy, was tempted farther away from her allegiance. More far-reaching in scope was the pact of Cartagena, made on May 16, 1907. In this Great Britain, France, and Spain[4] pledged themselves to maintain the *status quo* in the Mediterranean and in that part of the Atlantic Ocean washing the shores of Europe and Africa.[5] This pact was aimed specifically against Germany's alleged ambition to acquire the Balearic Isles and the Canaries. Since the Anglo-Portuguese Alliance guaranteeing Portugal's African colonies had been renewed in 1903, henceforth any forward move by Germany in the Mediterranean or Atlantic coastal regions was bound to be opposed by Great Britain, France, Italy, Spain, and Portugal. King Edward VII received full blame for these machinations against the Kaiser;[6] William II wrote Bülow, "My reinsurance with Theodore Roosevelt, who fears the Japanese, would be not out of place and worthy of consideration."[7]

The year 1907 was regarded by "peace men" in various countries as a propitious time to supplement by international action the several understandings initiated by the Anglo-French Entente. Originally proposed by President Roosevelt, postponed by the Russo-Japanese War, and then handed over to the sponsorship of Tsar Nicholas, the Second Hague Conference[8] was in session from July 15 to October 18. To the Russian program of improvement of the arbitration court and more exact definition of martial law on land and water, Great Britain and the United States wanted to add the discussion of general disarmament. Although Russia, Italy, and France all opposed the last proposal, these countries left Germany and Austria-Hungary to bear the odium of wrecking the proposals of limitation of armament and compulsory arbitration.[9] Emperor William was convinced that these plans, like all the "ententes," were aimed directly against Germany; Roosevelt held American peace men like Carnegie and Schurz at a distance and considered the American navy far more potent an instrument of peace than any international treaty would ever be. There were minor gains in the improvement of machinery for voluntary arbitration, and conventions on the rules of war, the rights and obligations of neutrals, and regulation of action to collect debts.[10]

The chief importance of the conference decisions to the United States was that the Latin American states were represented and that the assembly adopted the Drago Doctrine as a principle of international law. The doctrine of Dr. Drago, Foreign Minister of Argentina, was sponsored by the American delegate and accepted in a modified form:

> The contracting parties agree not to have recourse to armed force for the recovery of contract debts claimed

> from the government of one country by the government of another country as being due to its nationals.
>
> This undertaking is, however, not applicable when the debtor state refuses or neglects to reply to an offer of arbitration, or, after accepting the offer, prevents any "compris" from being agreed on, or, after the arbitration, fails to submit to the award.[11]

By accepting the Drago Doctrine, Roosevelt substantially modified his first corollary to the Monroe Doctrine, for he agreed to international sanction of non-collection of delinquent debts by force, and he made a bid for Latin American cooperation in American tutelage of her southern neighbors. Still he might claim the triumph of this one of his major international policies.

In the Far Eastern situation, however, complete failure threatened both Roosevelt and William II in 1907. Japan and Russia, who had been depended upon to checkmate each other and thus maintain peace in Asia and the Open Door in Manchuria, were entering into friendly treaty relationships at the expense of Manchuria.[12] Soon interlocking treaties linked the Great Powers together in Asia as they had in Europe and Africa--and Germany and the United States were excluded from all these arrangements.

By the Franco-Japanese agreement, dated June 10, 1907, Japan secured the backing of France. This pact was reminiscent of the Act of Algeciras--it guaranteed the independence and integrity of China and equality of treatment for all nations there. It also pledged the mutual support of the contracting parties in assuring peace and security and in maintaining the respective positions and the territorial rights of both on the Asiatic continent.[13] By the Russo-Japanese agreement of July 30, with terms similar to those of the Franco-Japanese treaty,[14] the erstwhile enemies really closed the Russo-Japanese War and completed the series of agreements of the great sea powers--except the United States and Germany--concerned with China and the entire Pacific coast of Asia. There would be no war in the Far East, at least before 1915, when the Anglo-Japanese treaty was due to expire, unless it were a German-Japanese war.[15] The grand climax of the agreements was reached, however, in the Anglo-Russian entente of August 31, 1907. This divided Persia into three spheres of influence, Russian, British, and neutral, placed Afghanistan under British protection for foreign affairs, and recognized the suzerainty of China over Tibet.[16]

Foretold since late 1905,[17] the Anglo-Russian entente convinced German diplomats that their situation was desperate. Great Britain had settled all disputes with the other powers, and the Anglo-French-Russian-Japanese quadruple entente was able to block German progress in industry and commerce, the building of the Bagdad railway, and colonial expansion everywhere. As a counterweight to this formidable opposition, all that Germany had to offer[18] was the renewal of the Triple Alliance in July, 1907, for six years, made although both Germany and Austria had grave doubts of the loyalty of Italy.[19]

President Roosevelt was also in a dilemma. The Japanese were incensed over the California movement against the rapidly increasing Japanese immigration there after the Russo-Japanese War and the segregation of Orientals in a San Francisco school, decreed in October, 1906. The persistent militarism of Japan awakened the apprehension of all countries bordering on the Pacific, and the jingoistic press found a fertile field in which to sow suspicion of Japan's aims. Supported by the Far Eastern ententes, Japan proceeded to set up an economic hegemony in southern Manchuria, in complete disregard of the promised Open Door. To combat this grave danger to his Far Eastern policy, Roosevelt risked no more encounters with either American public opinion or with Senate oratory. He chose instead to make a secret entente, carrying on for many months simultaneously two sets of negotiations. Despite his experience at Algeciras, William II again trusted Theodore Roosevelt as an ally.

As early as July 4, 1907, Count von Rex, the German minister in Peking, suggested an agreement among Germany, the United States, and Russia, in cooperation with China, to check Japan.[20] Russia soon joined the German adversaries, but Rex continued to be a prime mover for a German-American-Chinese entente.[21]

The negotiations with China proceeded very slowly; both the Kaiser and Roosevelt were much annoyed by the procrastination of the Dowager Empress and her failure to support the Chinese hierarchs, Yuan Shih-Kai and Tang Shao-Yi, who favored the American-German proposals. However, on August 5, 1908, Rex reported that Tang Shao-Yi had been appointed an envoy to Washington, ostensibly to give thanks to the United States for a partial return of the Boxer indemnity, but really to negotiate with the United States and Germany for an understanding.[22] Tang was much disturbed to learn in Honolulu that the Empress Dowager and the Emperor of China had both died suddenly; the new regent would dismiss Yuan Shih-Kai if Tang's mission failed.[23]

Upon his arrival in Washington, Tang discovered that neither he nor William II had made due allowance in their calculations for the diplomacy of Japan or of the duplicity of Roosevelt. While encouraging German overtures, the President had put into effect his favorite dictum, "Speak softly, but carry a big stick," a maxim found workable in dealing with Japan. Perhaps it was Japan that spoke gently; she received Roosevelt's Big Stick, the American fleet on its voyage around the world, with every evidence to prove that the United States was, as Marquis Matsukata said, "our very best friends on earth."[24] Baron Takahira, the Japanese ambassador in Washington, had already talked so amicably to Secretary Root that the two of them signed a general arbitration treaty on May 5, 1908. As a special courtesy, Tang was allowed to read before its signing the Root-Takahira Agreement of November 30, 1908.[25] This pledged the United States and Japan to the maintenance of the existing _status quo_ and to the defence of the principle of equal opportunity for commerce and industry in China, to mutual respect for each other's territorial possessions in the Pacific, to the support of the independence and integrity of China, and to an understanding of measures to be taken if any event should threaten the _status quo_ or the principle of equal opportunity.[26]

The critical phrase was the "maintenance of the existing _status quo_," for all the world knew that Japan had gone far in establishing an exclusive sphere of influence, both commercial and political, in Manchuria. The Chinese were no longer impressed by declarations of the Open Door; they had been squeezed too often in portals said to be ajar. The agreement had the effect in China which Japan desired. On January 2, 1909, Yuan was dismissed from office and Tang was recalled to China.[27]

On the same day Count von Bernstorff, Sternburg's successor, reported to the Wilhelmstrasse the reasons that Roosevelt gave him for finally rejecting the German-American-Chinese entente:

> By this China would probably have been seduced into a policy inimical to Japan. A Sino-Japanese conflict would have found China entirely unprepared, and neither Germany nor America would have been ready in such a case to protect China against Japan .... If it ever has to come to an American-Japanese war, this must happen for purely American interests .... The foregoing line of thought--so far as it concerns America--he has unfolded also very frankly to Tang Shao-Yi ... for entire frankness is the only correct policy. Lies have short legs. "One is always found out."[28]

Roosevelt's logic is unassailable--but why did it take him so long to be honest with China and with Germany? A cynic might argue that frankness so belated had lost most of its pristine virtue. It seems probable that he never had any real intention of joining Germany, but that he considered it expedient to await the results of his independent Japanese policy, while keeping the Kaiser in an amiable and expectant mood. This view is indicated by a letter from Roosevelt to Taft, dated December 22, 1910. Because the United States was neither willing nor able to defend Manchuria by war against Japan, Roosevelt explained, he surrendered Manchuria to Japanese influence in exchange for Japan's acquiescence in the American immigration policy.[29] Thus the Kaiser's third attempt to break the iron ring of encirclement ended as disastrously as had his previous efforts at Björkö and at Algeciras.

Although William II had lost prestige and power at home and abroad by the Daily Telegraph incident, in early 1909 Germany won two successes in diplomacy--the Moroccan treaty of February 9, 1909, with France and the diplomatic victory of Austria-Hungary in the Bosnian crisis. Bülow drew up draft treaties to settle the one great remaining problem--the Anglo-German alienation--but these reached the discussion stage only.[30] On July 14, 1909, Prince Bülow resigned after a parliamentary defeat on a finance bill. His real reason for leaving his post, however, was opposition to the uncompromising naval expansion policy of Tirpitz and William II and his weakened position with the Kaiser after the Daily Telegraph episode.[31]

When Theodore Roosevelt left office on March 4, 1909, he could feel proud of his reputation for success in foreign affairs. He had twice saved the peace of the world, and in so doing had demonstrated that interference in foreign affairs need entail no "entangling alliances." By his secret ententes with Japan, in 1905 and 1908, he had made sacrifices of Chinese territory and sovereignty to save the diplomatic facade of the Open Door. He had worked out a practical method of preventing European intervention in that part of Latin America prone to financial delinquency. He had circumvented the American press and the Senate where a treaty had to be openly considered, and he had successfully used the secret entente where a treaty could not be risked. The failure of the German-American-Chinese entente remained almost unknown for many years,[32] and he managed to remain friends, outwardly, with his partner in planning it. It was a notable record of achievement.

Against the elaborate backdrop of the entangling alliances of the Great Powers concerning Europe, Africa, and Asia--and to some extent the Americas--the Moroccan problem stood out unsolved. Within six years after its conclusion, the Act of Algeciras ceased to be a serious impediment to the achievement of French ambitions in Morocco. Only one country--the United States, seconded for several years by Great Britain--continued thereafter to invoke the Act and her previous treaties in a futile effort to maintain the pretence of Moroccan independence. Only one country--Germany--continued to strive for a better bargain for herself, either in Morocco or as compensation elsewhere.

That the sovereignty of the sultan and the independence of his domain would be mere fiction under the Act of Algeciras was well understood by Abd al-Aziz. The Moroccan delegates had been ignored in the negotiations producing the document. However, the Sultan knew also that he had no alternative but acquiescence in the decisions of the Great Powers. Malmusi, the Italian delegate, presented the ultimatum to Abd al-Aziz on June 5, 1906; by June 18 he had received assurance of the Sultan's adhesion to the Act without reserve. A note verbale from the Grand Vizier on June 27, recording his observations and desires, received no consideration. By the end of 1906, the Act of Algeciras had been ratified by all the signatory powers and was a part of international law.[33]

Soon the State Bank was organized, omitting only the United States, which renounced her right to subscribe a share of the capital. Each subscribing group was represented by one man on the organizing committee, eleven for the powers and two for the French consortium. At two sessions held in May-June and November of 1906, rules and statutes were drawn up, and the bank was prepared for its first important function--furnishing funds for the establishment of the police, which had become a most urgent duty.[34]

The Act of Algeciras did prolong peace in Europe, but to Morocco it brought anarchy, assassination, and widespread rebellion. The Moroccan masses regarded the Sultan's signature as either a voluntary surrender of his country to the infidel or an inevitable result of his years of misgovernment, waste, and corruption. Rebellions preceding the conference increased in strength. Bu Hamara had remained triumphant since 1903 in his stronghold in eastern Morocco; Raisuli continued to rule the Fahs district near Tangier. Walter Harris has described the scene in Fez in 1906. He found an acute famine in the city, caused by the cornering of every necessity of life by a few court favorites who invested their profits in building new palaces. While numerous tribal defections erupted throughout the country, Abd al-Aziz, an isolated recluse in his palace, wandered aimlessly about talking of his plans for reform. Indeed, he sent a representative to Tangier to negotiate practical measures of reform with the ministers of all the powers, ignoring the special position of France.[35]

In addition to embroilments of Moroccans with each other, there were many incidents during 1906 involving foreigners. In April, a tribe under Raisuli murdered two Arabs at the gates of Tangier. In May occurred the assassination of a Frenchman, M. Charbonnier, at Tangier, anti-foreign demonstrations and uprisings at Marrakesh, Tafilelt, and Mogador, and the arbitrary arrest of a domestic at the Russian legation. Several Europeans were injured in August in a battle between the Andjeras and guards of Raisuli at Tangier, and a Spaniard was murdered. The occupation of Mogador by the Berber chief Anflous and of Casablanca by a sorcerer in September was accompanied by the murder at Al Kser of a French protégé and assaults near Marrakesh on a Frenchman and a German.

Following an attack on Arzila and the arrest of a German at Rabat, the French and Spanish governments sent cruisers to Tangier on October 28. After October, there was a series of aggravating incidents at and near Tangier by Raisuli's forces against European protégés, Algerians, and natives. Protests of the Diplomatic Corps to the Sultan on September 22, November 1, and November 23 were totally ineffectual. A note sent to all the other signatory powers in December made no objection to the Franco-Spanish action to safeguard the goods and lives of Europeans in Tangier. An envoy from the Franco-Spanish squadron persuaded Abd al-Aziz to discharge Raisuli from his position and to order his minister of war to attack the brigand's forces. Raisuli's headquarters at Zinat was destroyed, but he escaped to fight again. Early in 1907, mission accomplished, the French and Spanish ships were withdrawn. With the approval of the other powers, the French premier, Pichon, took measures to establish the police without delay.[36]

The portentous events of 1906 were reported to Washington by the American representatives, emphasizing the arrogance and aggressiveness of Raisuli, his attempt to extend his legal control over Fahs into Tangier, the attack on Arzila, and the expulsion of Raisuli.[37] In the midst of the turmoil of the last months of 1906, however, Gummeré was making his first mission to the Sultan at Fez, although this journey had been authorized on June 9.[38] Gummeré sent detailed accounts of his trip from September 15 to September 27, and of his most elaborate reception, "the greatest display and welcome ever given to a foreign minister." In a private audience, Gummeré presented the silver vase purchased for Abd al-Aziz in England,[39] and the Sultan expressed his hope for the support of the United States in his reform measures.[40] Gummeré discussed with the Grand Vizier, Ben Sliman, all the points at issue between their countries and received assurances that all American grievances would be redressed. Gummeré and his party began their return journey to Tangier on December 28; they had been delayed not only by preparations for Ramadan and the concurrent visit of the German mission to Fez, but by the illness of several members of the American group.[41] Gummeré arrived at Tangier convinced that the "first American mission to the Shereefian Court" had been an "almost unprecedented success."[42]

In a letter sent to President Roosevelt by the Sultan, the latter made this significant remark:

> We also confidently hope that your good offices and those of your great nation will be vouchsafed to this Moroccan Empire in accordance with the traditional pure love which has always existed between your most exalted nation and our ancestors and our Shereefian Empire and thus shall the existing state of affairs be improved and the Empire of Morocco shall realize its fondest hopes.[43]

That Abd al-Aziz was looking across the Atlantic for aid was indicated not only by this letter but also by a proposition made to Gummeré by the Sultan at the private farewell audience. To show his appreciation of the first American mission to Fez, the Sultan wished to send a return mission to Washington, as he had done to the capitals of England, France, Germany, Spain, and Russia. The Grand Vizier also expressed a great desire for such a mission. Secretary Root finally decided that it would be highly inexpedient to encourage any special mission from Morocco, and Gummeré was unable to convince the State Department of the desirability of granting the Sultan's request.[44]

During 1907, the decadence of Morocco accelerated. In January, Abd al-Aziz appealed for another loan to pay for an army against Raisuli, Bu Hamara, and a new pretender to the throne, his halfbrother, Mulai Hafid, governor of Marrakesh.[45] A pro-French sheik, Ben Mansour, was assassinated in Tangier in February. After a Frenchman, Dr. Mauchamp, in charge of a dispensary for poor natives, was murdered by a mob in Marrakesh, and the British consular agency there was attacked, the French acted. Their forces in Oran, under General Louis Lyautey, occupied the Udja district on the Algerian frontier. Abd al-Aziz issued an edict calling upon the people to remain quiet, but he protested to Europe against the seizure of Udja as a violation of all treaties. The rebellion begun by Hafid at Marrakesh on May 5 and the Franco-Spanish control established over the customs to protect the Sultan's creditors precipitated civil war in Morocco by the middle of 1907.[46]

The conflict reached a climax in the bombardment of Casablanca on July 31. This affair originated in the murder by natives of Italian and French workmen who were quarrying and transporting stone for the construction of the port; the short railway used for this ran through or close by a Muslim cemetery. A French warship arriving on the scene landed an armed force to protect the Europeans. While the native quarters were under fire from the warship, wild tribes from the interior invaded and pillaged the town. It was a scene of horror and atrocities, with widespread looting and murder. The French force protected the consulates and all but nine of the Christians escaped with their lives. The full force of the attack fell upon the Moors, and especially the Jews, many of whose poor dwellings were burned.[47]

The French government promptly sent its version of the incident to Washington, as it did to the other capitals of the signatory powers. It gave assurance that any measures it might undertake would be strictly in conformity with the Act of Algeciras and that the immediate one would be organization of the police for Casablanca.[48]

During all of 1907 Gummeré and Philip kept the State Department well informed of events in Morocco and commented upon the significance of the various moves of France. There were also dispatches from the American representative in Spain relating Spain's reluctance to join France in punitive measures because of her desire to appear friendly and conciliatory to the Moroccans; however, Spain did cooperate with her entente partner. There were several letters from Mulai Hafid, soliciting European and American support. Among the important items found in these reports was the news that all Americans in Casablanca had their property destroyed, except the American ex-consular agent, Captain Cobb, and that there was a disposition at first to omit the United States and other minor claimants from the commission appointed to determine the "Casablanca Claims" for indemnity.[49]

The uprising at Casablanca was, however, only one of several serious problems confronting the French. Early in July Raisuli again took the offensive, kidnapping and holding for ransom Kaid Maclean, who had visited him, at the Sultan's command, to discuss peace terms. The Sultan sent several <u>mahallas</u> against the bandit, but all dispersed without capturing him. For seven months Maclean remained a captive, and he was eventually released only on payment of 20,000 pounds and the granting of certain privileges to Raisuli.

The challenge to French power at Casablanca had to be met decisively, and it was a task of many months. For over a year, the Casablanca region had been agitated by a sorcerer, who led horsemen overrunning the village for several days before the uprising and preached a holy war. The Pasha of Casablanca had remained impotent and inert. At first the French forces merely defended themselves against attack, but a passive defense was useless, especially in view of the progress made by Mulai Hafid at Marrakesh, where he was proclaimed sultan on August 25. Beginning on August 29, a steady advance was made by the French troops under General Drude, and more successfully under General d'Amade after January, 1908. The whole region of the Chaouia was subdued and twelve tribes were pacified by May 16, 1908.

Meanwhile, the situation near the Moroccan-Algerian border required attention. In September, Abd al-Aziz announced his intention to go to Rabat, where he would rally the loyal troops and make plans for an aggressive campaign against the pretender in cooperation with the French. He had now given up hope of German aid against the French. On September 23, the Sultan arrived in Rabat, and after several weeks of conference with generals Lyautey and Regnault, at the end of October he received the first advance of French money for his campaign. It was not sufficient to relieve him from embarrassment. A convention was also signed to organize a police force on the Moroccan-Algerian boundary. In November, the French were attacked near Udja by the powerful tribe of Beni Snassen. The district of Unja, like the Oran, was then placed under the jurisdiction of General Lyautey. He organized a punitive expedition into the mountains of the Beni Snassen, established French authority there, and assured the maintenance of order by the surrender of the Beni Snassen on the first of January, 1908.[50]

The year 1908 was one of anarchy and confused loyalties and purposes. Abd al-Aziz and Mulai Hafid were contending for the sultanate, while Bu Hamara remained an independent usurper in the Riff and Raisuli was supreme in the vicinity of Tangier. The Riff tribes were menacing Spain on the Mediterranean coast, and France had to fight to maintain her footholds in the Chaouia and Udja. Both Mulai Hafid and Abd al-Aziz asked France for aid. But after encouraging Abd al-Aziz by the talks at Rabat to expect support, France decided on "neutrality" and non-intervention. The rivals set out for each other's capitals--Fez and Marrakesh--but took circuitous routes to avoid a confrontation. An advance of General d'Amade toward Marrakesh could have quelled Mulai Hafid's rebellion, but no move was made. Most ironical of all, the French finally adopted the German policy of recognizing Mulai Hafid.[51]

On January 11, 1908, it was learned that Mulai Hafid had been proclaimed sultan at Fez and that his uncle as viceroy was awaiting his arrival there. With his opposition to the Act of Algeciras, the protégé system, and all Christians in Morocco, and his tendency to foster conspiracies of his partisans on Algerian borders, it was logical that France should work actively to eliminate him. But interpellations in the Chamber of Deputies in late January confirmed the policy of non-intervention, and throughout February and March Pichon's denunciations of Mulai Hafid did not activate the French army to challenge Hafid's encroachment on the Chaouia on his way to Fez. This encouraged him to appeal to Europe for recognition as a belligerent. In the middle of June one of Abd al-Aziz's mahallas deserted to his rival, now at Fez. When marching tardily toward Marrakesh on August 17, the Sultan's army was routed, and Abd al-Aziz barely escaped to take refuge behind French bayonets at Casablanca. His defeat turned the coast towns against him. On August 28,

1908, Mulai Hafid was proclaimed Sultan at Tangier, followed by the other coast towns and ending with Mogador on September 9.

Mulai Hafid thought the time opportune to appeal to Germany for recognition. William II welcomed the new monarch. On September 2, the German Foreign Office announced its intention to recognize Hafid officially and urged other countries to do likewise. Dr. Vassel, sent to Fez, was soon in disfavor because Mulai Hafid saw that Germany did not plan to support him in thwarting the policy of France and Spain in Morocco. The French agent, an Arabic Muslim, then gained the confidence of Mulai Hafid.[52]

Now France considered a change of policy. In accord with Spain, Pichon proposed to obtain from Mulai Hafid, in advance, a pledge to safeguard European interests in general and to respect the Algeciras Act in particular. This proposition was acceptable to Mulai Hafid, for he could not act as sultan unless backed by European money. On September 12 he sent a letter to the Diplomatic Corps promising to respect the Algeciras pact and all international treaties involving Morocco and welcoming the cooperation of all the powers in conducting the contemplated reforms. On the same day France and Spain sent a note to the other signatory powers recommending joint recognition providing that Mulai Hafid would agree to the specified terms. He was asked to confirm the Act of Algeciras and all executive measures already adopted, to recognize all other existing treaties of Morocco, to accept the work of the Casablanca Indemnity Commission, to assume responsibility for all debts of his predecessor up to the time of his abdication, and to disavow officially the holy war proclaimed against all Europeans. He was requested also to treat his brother Abd al-Aziz honorably and to settle promptly and individually with those states which had special interests in or claims against Morocco. On December 5, Hafid officially accepted these terms, and on December 17 the powers announced their recognition of him as Sultan.[53] As for Abd al-Aziz, he had already abdicated in November, 1908, after which he retired to Tangier to live the life of a country gentleman. He was permitted to retain the private property left him by his father, and on December 10, 1908, he took up residence in a house assigned him and began living on a pension of $35,000 a year.[54]

Crowded as the calendar of 1908 was with the incidents of the conflict for the throne, the American dispatches from Morocco in that year gave much space to the associated topics of Spanish opinion and policy on Moroccan affairs, letters from Mulai Hafid to the powers, and the recognition of Mulai Hafid. Other matters discussed were the beginning sessions of the International Commission of Indemnities for Casablanca, Lyautey's work in extending French military and civil power, and the new Franco-German crisis of 1908 over the Casablanca deserters' affair. Items of great interest to Gummeré and Philip were the progress of the French military operations from Casablanca, the turbulence of the tribes, the promises of reform made by Mulai Hafid, the death of Sid al Hadj Muhammad Ben Arby Torres, Germany's anxiety about observance of the Algeciras Act by France, the defeat of Abd al-Aziz, and general economic conditions.[55]

Concerning Spain, the American representative in Madrid quoted press articles and Spanish officials to the effect that Spain would continue to aid France in upholding and implementing the Act of Algeciras and would claim her rights under her treaties with Morocco. The seizure of Mar Chica, an inlet near Melilla, was necessary to prevent arms smuggling into Morocco. The Sultan was asked repeatedly to maintain order in the Riff. A brawl between French and Spanish troops at Casablanca was not indicative of a rift in Franco-Spanish relations, but rather of the popular dislike for armed intervention in Moroccan affairs. Spanish sentiment generally was not averse to acceptance of Mulai Hafid, with proper guarantees, and the Spanish people, jealous of France in Morocco, were not sorry to see the defeat of France's original candidate for the sultanate.[56]

Filed in the State Department Archives are an unsigned letter, purporting to be from the inhabitants of Fez, and five letters from Mulai Hafid, all translated from the Arabic. The first gave reasons for deposing Abd al-Aziz and begged the intervention of the United States to prevent the interference of France in the internal affairs of Morocco; when the Moroccans had decided for themselves which sultan to accept, France could then negotiate with him.[57] One of Hafid's letters was sent to the American consul at Safi, then briefly in the Pretender's hands, one to Henry White at Paris, and the rest to Gummeré at Tangier. All had the same complaint--the injustice of tolerating the occupation of Morocco by France to compel the natives to recognize a deposed sultan. In the last letter Mulai Hafid claimed the submission of the whole empire to himself, promised to adhere to the Algeciras Act, and asked the mediation of the powers to end the anarchy and strife. The State Department approved the notations that none of these letters had been answered.[58]

The indifference of the United States to the political status of the sultanate did not extend to the matter of the Casablanca claims. Abd al-Aziz had set May 31, 1908, as the date for the meeting at Casablanca of the international commission which was to assess the damages due to foreigners for the destruction of their property during the bombardment and looting of Casablanca. Other debts of Morocco previously submitted but unpaid were to be included in a general settlement. Hoffman Philip represented the claims of American citizens,[59] assisted by Mandeville C. Jacobus. The Americans reported difficulties due to a lack of proper procedure, insufficient recording, and nationalistic rivalry among the commissioners. Philip admitted honestly that American claims were hard to prove, partly because the legality of American citizenship or official employment was often doubtful.[60]

While Mulai Hafid was reaching his goal in 1908, General Lyautey was achieving great success in extending French power. In May, 1908, he won a victory near Bu Denib, and another followed in August. By the end of the year he had established two strongholds, one at Udja and the other at Bu Anana and Bu Denib, with a first line of posts. A commission sent to Fez in December secured an agreement concerning the Algerian-Moroccan boundary and opened negotiations with the new sultan in regard to Casablanca indemnities and reforms provided by the Act of Algeciras. A light mobile police force patrolled between the two strong points and kept order. A real buffer state now protected the Algerian frontier, and the German Foreign Office claimed this as evidence of France's design to annex all or a large part of Morocco. But by the end of the year France had reduced her forces in Udja from 7,000 to 3,500 and in the Chaouia from 15,000 to 8,000. As military action was gradually reduced, Lyautey raised to a maximum the political, commercial, and humanitarian functions of his subordinates in the pacified areas.[61]

Considering the disinterest manifested by the United States in the contest for the office of sultan, it is amazing how large a part of the archives for 1908 consist of dispatches on the recognition of Mulai Hafid. Gummeré and Philip reported the successive proclamations of Mulai Hafid and described in detail the crushing defeat of Abd al-Aziz in August, which Philip interpreted as evidence of the "desire of the Morrish people as a whole to escape from French control." When the Maghzen recognized Mulai Hafid in August, Philip declared that "it is impossible for me to point out any result of the energetic French policy pursued in Morocco during the past two years which could be considered of real benefit to ourselves or to any of the powers interested," and he hoped that the French government would not exert undue influence to thwart the evident will of the Moors.[62]

The United States received with reserve the initial proposal of Germany and the later proposal of France that Mulai Hafid be recognized. Philip agreed with the French proposal that definite guarantees be exacted from Hafid before his recognition. To the Spanish government, which independently asked about the American attitude, Alvey Adee, in charge of these negotiations, replied that the reservation under which the United States became a party to the Act of Algeciras appeared to be an obstacle to any influential initiative of the United States. While awaiting the promised joint Franco-Spanish note to the powers, the American attitude would be one of observation and expectancy. Adee made a similar reply to Esme Howard of the British Embassy. On September 14, Philip, who had noted possible difficulties over private loans made to Abd al-Aziz, reported a letter from the new sultan agreeing to the carrying out of all treaties with the powers and requesting their cooperation and assistance in applying reforms. Adee's opinion of the final Franco-Spanish proposition was that it was "a decidedly selfish proposition, looking not only to the perpetuation of the mandate to France and Spain, but to its virtual extension in the interest of France." He suggested the possibility of some Anglo-American-Italian compromise conditions. Reporting on the publication of an alleged copy of the Franco-Spanish demands in a French newspaper in Tangier, Philip confessed to his conviction that France was determined to achieve political domination over Morocco incompatible with the full and equal rights of other powers. Since the German accord with France and

Spain announced on September 25, however, the State Department decided to indicate its assent to the recognition of Mulai Hafid, on condition that "the interests of the United States and their citizens in Morocco shall rest on equal footing with those of other nations." Copies of a memorandum to this effect were sent to all signatory powers on October 9, 1908. On November 19, 1908, the collective note of the powers was delivered to Mulai Hafid by the dean of the Diplomatic Corps at Tangier. The governments signatory to the Act of Algeciras signified their satisfaction with the reply of Mulai Hafid to their collective note on December 17, 1908, with their decision to recognize him as the lawful sovereign of Morocco. By her assent on December 18, the United States was actually the first country to recognize Mulai Hafid. The visit of American battleships to Tangier at this time was "especially happy," Gummeré wrote.[63]

While the recognition of the new ruler was being thus lengthily considered, there occurred the Casablanca deserters affair, often called the "second Morocco crisis." On September 25, 1908, during negotiations concerning the terms of the abdication of Abd al-Aziz, the German consul at Casablanca tried to help six deserters from the French Foreign Legion--three of them Germans--to escape on a German ship. French soldiers seized the deserters and a French officer threatened the German consul with a pistol. The French accused the German consul with exceeding his powers in giving protection to persons under French military jurisdiction; the Germans charged the French military authorities with infringing upon the inviolability of consuls. The minor incident became a matter of national prestige. After the Daily Telegraph interview appeared on October 28, Bülow exaggerated the affair to divert attention from this domestic crisis. The negotiations seemingly came to an impasse, and the press, as usual, talked of war. But the other countries backed France, and the Kaiser told Bülow that the wretched Moroccan affair must be concluded, quickly and definitely; there was nothing to be made of it--the country would be French, anyway. Both France and Germany wanted the quarrel settled because of the Bosnian crisis. On November 10, the controversy was submitted to the Hague Court, which decided that both parties had been partly wrong. The verdict, rendered on May 22, 1909, resolved this difficulty, but did not make friends of the perennial enemies.[64]

The disorders accompanying Mulai Hafid's contest for the throne had been disastrous to both native and foreign interests. Projects for public works, such as port improvements conceded to German firms at Larache and Tangier, were discontinued. The Casablanca indemnity claims remained unsettled; commerce in the interior was almost destroyed; the fields of agricultural associates were often pillaged. The international situation stayed close to armed conflict. Both France and Germany realized that their diplomatic stalemate must be broken if either was to gain from the settlement of the dispute over the ruler. Accordingly, they decided to experiment with an economic partnership.[65]

In official negotiation for just a month, the Franco-German pact of 1909[60] was signed on February 9, 1909. The unprecedented speed in making such an agreement was partly due to Germany's desire to propitiate Great Britain and France for opposing them in the Bosnian crisis. The two governments expressed "a mutual desire to facilitate the Act of Algeciras." Still professing regard for the independence and integrity of Morocco, France promised equality of economic opportunity to Germans there; professing only economic aims, Germany recognized France's special political interests in preserving peace and order and promised not to interfere with these interests. The concluding declaration that they would not pursue or encourage any measure of a kind which created in their favor or in the favor of any power whatsoever an economic privilege was contradicted by one that they would endeavor to associate their nationals in enterprises which they were authorized to undertake. The latter provision implied an economic condominium contrary to the Open Door, and it was clearly in violation of the Act of Algeciras. France was strengthened in her negotiations to obtain the cooperation of Mulai Hafid in financial, police, and frontier reorganization, but Spain was displeased because she was not consulted and sent a large army contingent into Morocco. It was pleasant for Germany to envision an economic condominium. The natives of Morocco, Gummeré reported, viewed this accord as the ultimate betrayal of their cause, since they could no longer count on German interference, and Mulai Hafid became even more unpopular than Abd al-Aziz had ever been.[67]

At the beginning of his reign, due debts and claims

assessed against Mulai Hafid's government totalled 150,000,000 francs, while he had at his disposal revenues of only 9,000,000 francs. He was not receiving certain taxes provided for by the Act of Algeciras. The customs revenues did increase from 6,000,000 francs in 1907 to 13,000,000 francs in 1910, for commerce continued in the coastal regions during the post-Algeciras revolutions. The addition of the French and Spanish claims for support of their armies of occupation, even though payable in annual installments at low interest, made a burden of debt for Morocco intolerable even when she was aided by new loans.[68] Without adequate funds the Sultan could not support an army, and a constantly diminishing army meant no tax-collecting, no public works, and no law or order. Accepted originally at Fez on condition that the city be exempted from all taxation, Mulai Hafid kept this promise only a few weeks. Then he extorted legal and illegal taxes with great gusto and immediately lost all popularity. The tribes would not obey his edicts. French armies were in position to expand their occupation, and the French would not withdraw their troops, as he demanded, until he consented to a definite plan for enforcing the Act of Algeciras and the Franco-Spanish note and consented to pay the Franco-Spanish military expenses. He practiced horrible cruelties and extortions on the populace, aided by his Grand Vizier, Al Glaoui. Soon he was constrained to abandon his originally sincere anti-French position, for there was no help but from France.[69]

Nevertheless, Mulai Hafid did make some gains during 1909 in disposing of his rivals for power. In January, Raisuli was placated by one of the bargains for which he was famous. In June the death of the Sultan's elder brother, Muhammad, probably by poisoning, removed a likely pretender to the throne, and in August Bu Hamara was defeated and captured. The last dispatches of Gummeré were concerned with the disposal of the Raisuli problem and the revolts of Bu Hamara and others near Fez. Raisuli, Gummeré reported, had gone to Fez some months before demanding the governorship of the district around Tangier which he formerly held after his release of Perdicaris. Yielding to blackmail, to obtain the release of Sir Harry Maclean the British government had granted Raisuli protection and £20,000, to be repaid to the British by the Sultan. It was reported that $50,000 had been paid to Raisuli by the Sultan to renounce his British protection, in return for which he agreed to accept appointment as governor of a district from Arzila on the Atlantic to the vicinity of Tetuan, on the Mediterranean, but not including Fahs, which remained under the governor of Tangier. The widespread sale of offices and the assessment of the costs of missions on the districts visited were causing great resentment among the natives. Also reported were revolts of tribes near Fez, increased by the advance of Bu Hamara, the unsuccessful revolt led by Sherif Al Kittany, the head of a powerful religious sect, the sacking of Meknes, and the siege of Fez by rebellious neighboring tribes.[70]

Gummeré was not at Tangier, however, to report the fall of Bu Hamara. He had served eleven years in Morocco, as consul general from 1898 to March 8, 1905, and as minister from then until he left Tangier on June 8, 1909.[71] He was succeeded by H. Percival Dodge, who remained until July 10, 1910.[72] The State Department now reverted to its former policy of granting only short tenure to its representatives in Morocco.

One of Dodge's first tasks was to arrange for a Moroccan mission to attend the Hudson-Fulton celebration in New York. The suggestion came from Mulai Hafid. The eleven members of the party sailed from Gibraltar on September 19 for New York. The Sultan declared his purpose in sending them was to show his high regard for the American people and government. Sid Guebbass, the Moroccan foreign minister, said that Mulai Hafid realized that of all the nations the United States alone had no political aspirations in Morocco, but that the relations between the two governments were only those of pure friendship, which he desired to increase. The plans of the Moroccan delegation included, besides attendance at the New York celebration, the presentation of formal letters of courtesy to the President and Secretary of State from the Sultan and Grand Vizier. Dodge informed Guebbass that presents were not customary in the United States. The Sultan understood perfectly that the affair was a state and not a national project and that the Moroccans would be paid their expenses only while in New York.[73]

The subsequent visit of the mission to Washington was treated with scant courtesy, as befitted the bored indifference with which the Taft administration viewed Moroccan affairs.

The members of the mission were the Sultan's first secretary, a Fez notable, three attachés, an interpreter, a physician, and four servants--"of as high a rank as those recently sent to Madrid." None, except the interpreter, had ever left Morocco before. When asked whether it would be desirable to send a private car for the Moroccans from New York to Washington, Adee replied: "No. The trouble is we would have to entertain them while in Washington and send them back in a private car." Adee later wrote Dodge that the two leading delegates called at the Department of State on October 4 and presented their letters. "In the absence of the President on his southern tour, and also the absence from the city of Mr. Knox, the delegates were received by me. The Department would be glad to have you assure the Sultan of this Government's appreciation of the manifestation of friendship for the United States."[74]

Rebuffed by the United States, Mulai Hafid continued to haggle with the French over the delayed implementation of the Act of Algeciras, while his envoys sought a new loan in Paris. From Dodge's dispatches came much information about the Sultan's triumph over Bu Hamara. In June the Old Pretender was menacing Fez and other powerful tribes favored new claimants to the throne. However, Hafid's most serious problem was his rupture with Al Glaoui and other great kaids near Marrakesh and Safi. The Spanish government had decided upon an energetic policy in its presidios to protect them from neighboring tribes entirely beyond control by the Sultan. In August Bu Hamara was captured and taken to Fez in an iron cage for public exhibition. The Diplomatic Corps sent a collective note to the Sultan protesting against the barbarous tortures inflicted upon the Pretender and his captured soldiers. This appeal was ineffective; the tortures continued, and Bu Hamara was finally shot after Hafid's lions had refused to eat him alive. Mulai Hafid's prestige rose among the tribes all over Morocco as a result of his elimination of Bu Hamara. Dodge referred to the noticeable tendency of the French and their press in Morocco to exaggerate disorders and the necessity for foreign intervention.[75]

While Mulai Hafid was negotiating with France for another loan, Spain thought the time opportune to carry into effect her secret agreement of 1904 for a sphere of interest in northern Morocco. She was jealous of France's success in occupying the Chaouia and eager to stake out her own claims. A pretext for intervention was easily found; near Melilla two large mining concessions granted to Europeans required protection from Riff tribesmen, who menaced a railroad from the mines to Melilla. Thus a campaign, unpopular in Spain, was begun with an ill-equipped army. Reinforcements bringing General Marina's army up to 40,000 men enabled him to occupy towns and plains near Melilla, but the home government stopped the advance. Consequently, the mountains dominating the plain and the hills to the west remained under Riffian control. There was an uprising in Spain because of the terrible costs of this operation in men and money for a small return.[76] Her first encounter with the Riffs was a portent of terribe battles that Spain would have in the future.[77]

In their dispatches, Dodge and others traced the development of the Spanish-Riffian war from July 13, 1909, to the end of the year. Dodge cited the Moroccan argument that Spain had no legal right to the mines, since Bu Hamara had no right to cede them. However, he pointed out, no sultan had had any authority in the Riff for many years until Bu Hamara's usurpation of power there. The riots and other disorders in Barcelona and Catuluna by anarchists and other opponents of the Moroccan policy were described. On September 27, the American government declined, as did the other powers, to take action to support the Sultan in his denunciation of Spain for her infringement of the Algeciras Act. The Spanish government continued to try to allay anxiety as to its intentions. Robertson, temporarily American chargé at Tangier, reported the arrival of four Moroccan delegates at Melilla on October 20, but thought Spain would continue fighting to secure a sufficient indemnity for her expenses and to add additional points for future defense of her territory. During the ensuing peace talks, there was considerable friction between the French and the Spanish, but in December, 1909, the leading *kaids* of the Riff were induced to make their submission.[78]

On August 14, 1909, the Sultan's representative in Paris received from the French government its definite plan for implementation of Mulai Hafid's promises made when recognized by the powers. Thus far, he had evaded his pledges, and, by controlling the customs houses, he planned to avoid a loan. The French now agreed to evacuate the areas occupied by them provided that the Sultan made satisfactory arrangements for creation of the frontier police and settlement of frontier questions, for liquidation of the Moroccan debt, and for the military expenses of France in Morocco. This agreement was supplemented and somewhat modified in subsequent notes in December. Since Mulai Hafid continued to procrastinate, the French consul gave him an ultimatum on February 18, 1910, allowing him forty-eight hours to accept the proposed Franco-Moroccan accord. The Sultan raged but gave his adhesion on February 21, and on March 4 his representative signed a formal treaty.[79]

The accord signed by Mulai Hafid provided for the evacuation of the Chaouia and Udja as soon as the Moroccan government could place in these regions its own forces to be organized and trained under a French military mission. The Sultan was to nominate a Sherifian High Commissioner to cooperate with a French High Commissioner in adjusting Algerian frontier problems, but France was to retain certain border districts to protect Algeria. The French government offered to aid the Moroccan government in securing funds to pay the national debt and to insure an annual income sufficient for the Sultan to organize a well-equipped and reliable army and police, to maintain an efficient administration, and to put his affairs on a stable basis. France offered to postpone for five years the payment of her own indemnity for military expenses in the Chaouia and in Udja.[80]

Secured by the French government from the same group of bankers as the loan of 1904, the loan of 1910 was then made to Mulai Hafid. According to the German government, the German banks were unwilling to make any loans. The loan was for 107,000,000 francs, with five percent interest. Bonds were sold to the bankers at 89 and to the public at 97. The former creditors' control of customs was changed into a general debt control, which included the control of collection. To pay this new loan, new revenues were added--the remainder of the customs, the net product of the tobacco taxes, a tax on landed property in the ports, an urban tax, and others. An increase of two percent in customs was reserved for public works under a plan formulated in collaboration with the powers and controlled by a special international committee. The French government had high hopes for its new plans. The State Bank had stabilized the currency, a firmer control would increase revenues, the public works plan would stimulate economic activity, and the loan would ensure reorganization of the army with resultant peace and order. Since the Spanish government negotiated a similar agreement concerning the finances and administration of their sphere of influence in the Riff and Ceuta regions, approved by Mulai Hafid on December 23, it appeared that Morocco was well reorganized on modern principles by the end of 1910.[81]

The actual results of the Franco-Spanish-Moroccan accords in 1910 were the opposite of those anticipated. On March 24, 1911, Jaures said in the Chamber of Deputies that the loan took away from the Sultan all financial autonomy, all military strength, and all moral authority. In 1910 his expenditures exceeded his revenues by a little over 3,000,000 francs. Out of a total revenue of 24,000,000 francs, 16,500,000 francs were required to pay the debt service and cost of war payments. Mulai Hafid renewed resistance to the French after the loan; but Frenchmen headed the public works, the army training, and the police. He could not borrow money elsewhere, for all his securities were already pledged. It was impossible to levy new taxes; the powers opposed the taxation of their subjects and growing numbers of protégés, and the tribes revolted against being pillaged by the tax collectors. By the spring of 1911 many tribes joined the rebellion, and Hafid became notorious for oppression and cruelty. Another pretender, his half-brother Mulai Al Kebir, arose to challenge his authority. The protégé system remained a "state within a state," and it contributed greatly to the undermining of the Sultan's power and the reduction of his financial resources.[82]

Furthermore, the Casablanca Claims Commission, which Mulai Hafid had reactivated in March, 1909, had added to the burden of Morocco's debts. American claims were minor compared to those of European nations, but all were receiving favorable consideration during 1909--even those of "Americans" whose citizenship was very doubtful.[83] The old Moorish custom of making the sultan pay for the unlawful acts of "subjects" whom he could not claim to control was being maintained.

During his last six months of office, Dodge continued his analysis of the political situation. He said that the news of the forthcoming loan inspired the merchants of Morocco to anticipate prosperity to succeed the depression of the two preceding years. He warned that the apparent submission of the Riffian tribes was merely a prelude to renewed attacks on the Spanish. Another item of interest to Americans was the announcement of the appointment as minister of justice, Sid Al Arby ben Muhammad Zenhashi, one of the recent delegates to the Hudson-Fulton Celebration. That Morocco would be subjected to French control was evident from the agreement in March, 1910. The supremacy of Al Glaoui's influence was noted, as well as the Sultan's custom of appointing kaids from the districts near Marrakesh. Although of mining concession fame, the Mannesman brothers were reported to be farming and cattle raising on a large scale in the Shawia, entirely with German stock, implements, and foremen. Dodge thought that the attempt to build a road from Ceuta to Tetuan was really a Spanish plan to acquire Tetuan. Spaniards, possibly subsidized by their government, had secured a number of contracts for small public works in Tangier. Late in May the Sultan was said to be acting in a way directly contrary to his previous agreements, especially in matters affecting the French, while he alienated leading Berbers by financial exactions. However, while practicing barbarous cruelties toward a recently arrested official and his wives, Mulai Hafid deigned to inform the Diplomatic Corps that he had "the express intention not to exceed the limit of humaneness which is counselled by the Mohammedan religion and which is observed by the civilized governments ... seeing that ... the circumstances ... are no longer of the times and that oblivion of them is necessary." In a final communication, Dodge reported the return of Sid Al Hadj Muhammad Al Mokri after fourteen months in Paris, where he negotiated and signed the loan and other agreements. Recipient of the Legion of Honor insignia in Paris, Al Mokri was the "man of the Hour,"[84] and several foreign representatives were soliciting his favor for their projects. The Sultan was declaring his intention to execute all his agreements, if given time. His brutal tortures continued; it was said that he indulged in periodical opium debauches, when his officials had great difficulty in restraining his homicidal mania. The draft of the mining law was now approved by a commission of British, French, German, and Spanish delegates at Paris. Great dissatisfaction was felt at the lack of system in the adjudication of public works.[85]

Dodge's successor was Fred W. Carpenter, who arrived in Tangier on July 26, 1910. Since the departure of Dodge on July 10 to take a position in the State Department, the Tangier post was in charge of the Secretary of Legation, Cyrus F. Wicker.[86] Wicker's chief contribution to the dispatches concerned the illicit exactions levied upon foreign commerce in the vicinity of Mogador by Kaids Anfloos and Guiloli. By extorting three times the Moroccan customs on trade between Mogador and the interior, these _kaids,_ defying the Sultan, had practically ruined Mogador as a trading center. The trade in goatskins, the principal and most valuable export from Morocco to the United States, had suffered severely. In August George E. Holt[87] reported further on this topic. The _kaids,_ he said, had established a systematic scheme of highway robbery; they levied toll on every load of merchandise entering or leaving Mogador, often equalling 25 percent of the value of the goods. This system of blackmail had existed for five years and had almost bankrupted the city, once an export outlet for all southern Morocco. The impotent Sultan could stop this disobedience of his law only with European aid.[88]

Until the end of 1910, Carpenter and Holt maintained an interest in Kaids Anfloos and Guiloli. In August, Carpenter reported that they had practically stopped all the commerce of Mogador and that they gave no heed to the protests of the Diplomatic Corps. A month later he said that they were barring the roads to the Sus provinces from the French and German mining prospectors, regardless of the incensed French police at Mogador. Holt saw in the appointment of a British commercial attaché the promise of renewed British interest in Moroccan trade. This hope was reinforced by the recent six weeks' visit to southern Morocco by the British minister, Reginald Lister. It was rumored that Kaid Anfloos had agreed to give up his racket. Holt hoped that the revival of British commercial interests would operate in American favor by keeping French interests in check. He had often been assured that Mulai Hafid would welcome any kind of American interests in Morocco; his interest in American affairs had been highly stimulated by the reports of the embassy that he had sent to the Hudson-Fulton Celebration.

In December, however, Carpenter reported that the exactions of Anfloos and other kaids had increased, and it was a "known fact" that Anfloos had collected over one million dollars. For this privilege he was alleged to have paid $1,000 per month to one minister at Fez, $500 to another, and $200 to a third. An appeal was sent to Sid Muhammad Al Mokri, then in Paris.[89]

During the fall of 1910, American representatives in Spain and in Morocco were much interested in the Spanish-Moroccan negotiations taking place in Madrid between the Spanish foreign Minister and his Moroccan counterpart. Señor Prieto and other Spanish authorities vehemently denied French press reports concerning exorbitant indemnities that Spain was supposed to be asking for her military expenses in the Riffian war of 1909. Other powers were much concerned lest the implacable attitude of Spain might lead to a renewal of war in Morocco and to revolt in Spain, still affected by the revolution in Portugal. But the negotiations were concluded satisfactorily on November 15 and a convention was signed by Al Mokri and Prieto on November 18. The Spanish press rejoiced over this convention as a rebuke to France, whose press throughout the proceedings had violently attacked the Spanish government's attitude and had greatly exaggerated its pretensions. The success of the parleys was due largely to the moderating representations of the British and French governments. A distinguished Spanish official described the accord as "a diplomatic codification of all the difficulties which tended to strain the relations between Spain and Morocco." Sir Maurice de Bunsen, British ambassador to Spain, expressed surprise that anyone so ill-tempered as Señor Prieto could achieve such satisfactory results.[90]

The Spanish-Moroccan accord was analyzed in detail by Carpenter. It followed much the same terms as the recent French loan agreement, but it provided for only 1250 police to be created for the Riff, while for the Shawia 1500 police were planned. Spanish and Moroccan high commissioners would be nominated for that part of the Riff occupied by Spanish troops, near Alhucemas and Peñon de Velez de la Gomera; here native police would be established, to be instructed by Spanish officers paid from revenues derived from customs collected at Melilla, market dues, and other imposts, and collected by Spanish officials. Evacuation of

Moroccan territory actually occupied by Spanish military forces would take place when the police force was strong enough and deemed capable of insuring order, freedom of business, and collection of taxes. The Maghzen would not fortify strategic positions to dominate and place in subordination the city of Ceuta. A kaid would be appointed to govern the frontier region, chosen by agreement between the Maghzen and the Spanish government; the police in this region would be taught by Spanish officers and customs houses would be established here whenever Spain should ask for them. Morocco acknowledged the obligation to pay an indemnity of 65,000,000 pesetas Spanish currency (about $12,037,000 American currency), to compensate for the military and naval expenses borne by Spain. This sum was to be paid in seventy-five annual payments of 2,545,000 pesetas each, guaranteed by 55 percent of the portions accruing to the Maghzen from mining rights in the Riff. Finally, Santa Cruz de Mar Pequeña, on the Atlantic coast some 250 miles south of Mogador, was ceded to Spain and a Moroccan commissioner would be appointed who would leave Mogador on May 1, 1911, to meet a Spanish commissioner appointed to take possession of the site.[91]

Carpenter said that this agreement made Spain and France still more competitive in Morocco. Mulai Hafid would find still greater difficulty in maintaining order in his empire, in view of the increased necessity to raise more internal revenue and the dissatisfaction inevitable among a people already subject to so many unjust levies from the *kaids*, who had paid the Sultan large sums of money for their offices. The new agreement deprived the Sultan not only of the customs from Melilla and Ceuta, but also from customs houses to be set up along the coast and the internal taxes from mining in the Riff. However, there were several grounds for hope of a better situation for the Sultan henceforth. In addition to having established peace on a firm basis with France and Spain, his brother, the latest pretender, was a prisoner in the Sultan's palace in Fez, and the exactions of the *kaids* on the commerce of Mogador had largely ceased. However, the Sultan found that some tribes were refusing to accept Raisuli as governor. A delegate to the Madrid meeting told Carpenter that he counted on the assistance of the Diplomatic Corps to carry out the reforms pledged in Morocco; he would value especially any support that the United States could give by her friendly offices.[92]

During 1910 there had been some progress in ameliorating international tensions and in strengthening the internal weaknesses of Morocco. In the next two years there was a renewal of international strife, leading to different agreements, and the Sherifian Empire ceased to be an independent, integrated state. France and Spain greatly expanded their occupation and military activities, and Germany, following "watchful waiting" by a small gunboat outside a closed port, obtained a treaty granting her "compensation" for abandoning the struggle for her rights in Morocco. Under a puppet sultan, Morocco accepted the status of a protectorate divided between her two most aggressive European neighbors.

The year 1911 began with several tribes near Fez in revolt because of heavy taxation and the brutal tyranny of the Grand Vizier Al Glaoui. On January 14 Marchand and several companions were slain by Zaer tribesmen near Rabat, and it seemed unwise to let this outrage go unpunished. Soon the revolt had spread to several more tribes. Early in March the discontent at Fez was brought to a head by Col. Mangin's public execution of two Moroccan soldiers caught deserting. Alarming reports were circulating through the French that the lives of Europeans in Fez were in danger. Carpenter wrote that the revolt started when the Sultan asked the tribes for money to defray the expenses of his trip out of Fez. He was said to be seeking to increase his private fortune as rapidly as possible. Throughout March, Carpenter's dispatches continued to emphasize the gravity of the revolts around Fez. The revolting tribes had an intense hatred for Al Glaoui, and there was even talk of summoning Abd al-Aziz back to the throne, but he was content in his pensioned idleness.[93]

When the revolt spread to Rabat, on April 5 Cambon informed the Wilhelmstrasse that probably France would be obliged to occupy that city, to send a punitive expedition to the Shawia district, and to dispatch a military force to rescue the Europeans in Fez. This action would be taken only under extreme necessity and would aim to preserve the sovereignty of the Sultan in the spirit of the Act of Algeciras. Kiderlen replied that occupying Rabat would look like another step in scrapping the Act of Algeciras. He hoped that Moroccan affairs could be satisfactorily arranged bewteen France and Germany--a hint for German compensation understood by Cambon. Later Cambon reiterated France's pledge to respect the Act of Algeciras and to withdraw her troops as soon as order was restored. Kiderlen pointed out that it was difficult to withdraw in cases like Fez and that if French troops remained there, Morocco could no longer be considered independent. Then Germany would have her liberty of action restored. William II favored allowing the French to send troops to Fez, for this would cost money and tie up many soldiers; if the Algeciras convention appeared to be violated, Germany should allow some other country to protest.[94]

Harassed on all sides by opposing counsels, but trusting the reports of her own envoys in Morocco, France was at last constrained to order the march on Fez. The London Times predicted on April 21 possible complications with Germany and Spain. But Billy, the French representative, reported on April 25 that Berber tribes had pillaged Meknes and proclaimed as sultan there Mulai Zain, a brother of Mulai Hafid. At Fez the Sultan was surrounded by rebellious tribes. Therefore, France ordered General Moinier to start the native mahalla of the Chaouia towards Fez and to move a French company to Bu-Regrer, ready to advance to Fez if necessary. Cruppi informed the European chancelleries of this on April 25. The replies were cautious and reserved. Spain besieged the French and British foreign offices with protests and threats of action; she argued that the French move should give her freedom of action in her northern zone.[95]

In a memorandum dated May 3, 1911, Kiderlen outlined his program in opposition to France. Three years of events had shown, he asserted, that the independence of Morocco could not be maintained under the Algeciras plan against native rebellion and imperialistic pressures of France and Spain. Therefore, after France had occupied Fez for a while, Germany would ask the expected date of withdrawal. If the French did not adhere to the time limit, Germany would announce the annulment of the Algeciras Act and demand compensation. Germany was as much justified as France in taking measures to protect the lives and property of her subjects. Agadir was said to be the best harbor in south Morocco--let Germany occupy it as a pledge until France offered adequate compensation from her colonial possessions. Thus the Morocco crisis could be given a turn which would wipe out Germany's previous failures and have a good effect on the coming Reichstag elections.[96]

Arriving at Fez on May 21, General Moinier found that all Europeans were safe, as German observers had always declared them to be. He stationed his forces to command the capital, but did not enter it with foreign troops. He secured the Sultan's agreement to make reforms and to dismiss Al Glaoui. Some hostility remained among the tribes, and Moinier invaded Meknes to subdue the disorders instigated by the pretender there. In addition to military activities, during May and June France carried on diplomatic maneuvers also to convince the powers that her primary aim was to preserve the Act of Algeciras. At first Germany adopted a sphinx-like attitude.[97]

The French government was as determined as the German one that the Algeciras Act must go--naturally, with all the advantages possible for France. Joseph Caillaux, premier in June, 1911, declared: "Our problem was nothing less than to regain all the ground lost since 1905, and to repair the consequences of the serious diplomatic check which we had suffered." Just as France was preparing to occupy Rabat, Delcassé entered the French Cabinet again with the naval portfolio. As the Germans suspected, he was as implacable an enemy of theirs as ever. Caillaux, a shrewd trader, opened secret negotiations with the German Foreign Office and the Deutsche Bank, leading them to infer that he was willing to concede "compensation" in the Congo or elsewhere, in order to secure a final settlement of the Moroccan question. These secret dealings were carried on outside the purview of the officially appointed negotiators and later caused the political downfall of Caillaux.[98]

Neither Germany nor France was satisfied with the results of the accord of 1909. France had found Germany prone to waving the flag of the Act of Algeciras at her every effort to proceed toward political domination of Morocco; Germany had discovered France to be reluctant to share any benefits of the economic development of Morocco or neighboring French colonies. The two countries could not co-exist profitably in the same colonial situation. After the accord, drawn in vague and general terms, the period of cooperation had been brief; all attempts to "associate their nations" had proved unsuccessful. The mining concessions from Mulai Hafid claimed by the Mannesman brothers conflicted with the claims of the international, but French-controlled Union des Mines Marocaine. A French-German consortium for Cameroon-Congo trade was finally up. The Germans failed to participate in the railways, finances, and public works, and Great Britain also registered objections to her exclusion from the last. The French monopolized loans to Morocco, culminating in the loan of 1910. As for the "economic equality" of the other signatories of the Act of Algeciras, it was of course non-existent, except in very minor matters. Germany was aggrieved that her loyalty to the accord had cost her a port, which Mulai Hafid had offered her in December, 1909. France showed no inclination to admit German securities to the Bourse. It was evident that Franco-German cooperation was inconsistent with the steadily growing political control of France in Morocco, and both were contradictory to the basic principles of the Algeciras Act. To Germany it seemed necessary to scrap both the Algeciras Act and the accord of 1909 and make a new bargain while Germany still had some political resources to offer. Only an addition to her colonial empire elsewhere in Africa, if she could not obtain the southern part of Morocco, seemed a fair exchange for her withdrawal from Morocco.[99]

France soon discovered that she had a second rival challenging her extension of occupation in Morocco. The Spanish prime minister, Señor Canalejes, had given France an early warning that Spain would counter a march to Fez with seizure of points in her prospective sphere of influence. Spain feared that failure to assert her claims in the northern zone would forfeit her right to secure the territory promised her in the secret pact of 1904, which could easily be forgotten in the new political situation being created by French arms. A fortnight after the French military expedition had occupied Fez, Spanish forces landed at Larache; the next day they occupied Alcazar. Spain excused her acts as a rightful reprisal for two assassinated protégés. Later Spain invaded Tetuan. France denounced Spain's efforts to seize her zone as dangerous, because "they amounted to a real partition of Morocco and could give Germany an excuse to announce the annulment of the Algeciras Act." British attempts to restrain Spain resulted only in keeping the Spaniards out of Tetuan until the French were settled in Fez. The Spaniards continued to insist that French action had brought into operation the second contingency provided for in the entente of 1904. Thus, in defiance of public opinion, the Spanish government yielded to the military forces and pushed forward its colonial ambitions in Morocco.[100] The Spaniards apparently thought that the Jibala would be more easily conquered than the Riff. Colonel Sylvestre, the Spanish commander, was a man with strong desire for personal glory. At once he came into conflict with Raisuli, who regarded this part of Morocco as his own family estate and soon regretted his assistance to the Spanish at their landing. From this time on, Spain was doomed to a tragedy of indecision--her leaders could never decide the better approach into Morocco, whether into the Riff or into the Jibala, with only sea communications between Ceuta and Melilla. Long years of war lay ahead.[101]

From April 20 until June 16 the State Department was kept informed of Spanish doings in Morocco through the Spanish Minister at Washington. At first there was talk of establishing merely police posts near Ceuta; later the occupation of Alcazar was called "purely an operation of police," "no less justified than that of France at Fez and Meknes and no more threatening to the integrity of the Moroccan Empire." Carpenter reported on adverse French comment on Spain's proceedings and sympathized with the latter's desire to protect her prestige and claims in Morocco. He forwarded also the apologia of the Spanish minister at Tangier to the Diplomatic Corps and the protest of Al Guebbass to the same body. Interesting enclosures in dispatches from Carpenter were articles from the French press in Tangier and Paris, setting forth the illegality of the Spanish invasions of Larache and Alcazar, and an official protest from Al Mokri to the Diplomatic Corps at Tangier.[102]

Respecting each other's talents since they had worked together in the Casablanca affair and the accord of 1909, Jules Cambon and Kiderlen-Waechter were sparring to find some solution to their economic and political problems. Each was trying to avoid making the first proposal, but the latter's program of May 3 awaited only the Kaiser's consent to be put into operation. In a conversation on June 20, Cambon stated a definite principle to which France maintained adherence--she would consider no settlement that involved the partition of Morocco. The Caillaux Cabinet was completed on June 28, but the premier's opponents accused him of opening non-official negotiations with Kiderlen prior to June 20. In the ensuing discussions, de Selves, the French foreign minister, was almost ignored. Caillaux personally took a large part in the proceedings, often secretly and unofficially. On a visit to England, the Kaiser was received with such marked courtesy and friendliness that he was convinced that Kiderlen's program would not be opposed by Great Britain and therefore would not lead to war. On June 26 Kiderlen understood the message "Ships granted" from the imperial yacht.[103]

By July 1 the German government thought the opportune time had arrived to take advantage of the Spanish threat to destroy the Algeciras fiction. On that day official notes informed the signatory powers of a *fait accompli*--the German gunboat *Panther* had taken up a vigil at Agadir to protect German nationals endangered in that region. The news fell upon Paris like a bomb--it was as threatening a gesture as the Kaiser's visit to Tangier. The alleged motive was fatuous. Agadir was a closed port, and there were no Germans legally there, although Mogador, to the north, was a center of German trade and influence. The reason for the selection of Agadir for a demonstration is unknown, but probably Kiderlen hoped at first to secure southern Morocco as a compensation--this was the Pan-German dream--and he chose Agadir as the best harbor in Morocco. There was a general understanding among diplomats, however, that Germany had signified a desire for negotiations in a characteristic manner. Schön's statement to Selves on July 1 was that the Algeciras Act was too much violated to survive and that a return to the *status quo* was impossible. Germany wanted to eliminate the Moroccan problem permanently from international politics. The press of Germany and France showed surprise and uncertainty; in other countries, there was little attention at first to the incident.[104]

Originally, Caillaux was unfavorable to negotiating with Germany without the cooperation of Great Britain and Russia. Germany refused to consider another conference.

Caillaux, also, lost all interest in the conference idea after Grey suggested that a conference should provide for a complete return to the status quo ante by evacuation of all ports held in Morocco by France, Spain, and Germany. Since Russia was evidently reluctant to support France vigorously,[105] Caillaux decided upon separate negotiations with Germany. Consequently, the focus of the ensuing negotiations was shifted from the former attempts to implement the Franco-German accord of 1909 to the broader base of securing "compensation" sufficient for Germany's complete withdrawal from Morocco.[106]

After some preliminary skirmishing between Cambon and Kiderlen, the negotiations proceeded in Berlin from July 15 to November 4, 1911, when an accord was reached. For many weeks before the *Panther's* appearance, the British had feared that Germany's objective was a naval base on the Atlantic coast. On July 4, Grey warned the German government that Great Britain would not recognize any new arrangement obtained without consulting her. On July 15 Kiderlen offered a startling compromise--Germany would exchange for the whole of the French Congo her colony of Togoland. Indignantly, Cambon declared this a wholly unacceptable proposition. Receiving no reply to his communication of July 4, and alarmed further by Germany's demand of July 15, Grey decided it was time to give Germany a public warning. This was done in the famous Mansion Hall speech of Lloyd George on July 21, in which he referred unofficially and incidentally to the Morocco dispute in a talk on national finance. But his remarks had been approved in advance by Asquith, Grey and Churchill, and his meaning was clear:

> But if a situation were to be forced upon us in which peace could only be preserved by the surrender of the great and beneficent position Britain has won by centuries of heroism and achievement, by allowing Britain to be treated, where her interests were vitally affected, as if she were of no account in the Cabinet of nations, then I say emphatically that peace at that price would be a humiliation intolerable for a great country like ours to endure.

The day before this speech, a secret, unofficial conference had been held between the British and French chiefs of staff, seeking preparations for possible war with Germany. A later speech by Asquith reinforced the Mansion House declaration. There was no doubt that Great Britain would support France to the extent of making war with her. This evident fact, as well as a financial depression in Germany, which on September 9 almost caused a panic on the Berlin Bourse, forced Germany to assume a conciliatory attitude.[107]

William II was another factor in Germany's new attitude. From the beginning he had opposed the martial maneuver of sending the Panther. After the effect of this action was apparent, he pressed Kiderlen to a peaceful settlement in the face of almost unanimous German public opinion. In fact, the Kaiser's urgent demand for a pacific settlement of the crisis was so strong that in order not to prolong the negotiations Kiderlen felt obliged to reject Caillaux's revival of Rouvier's offer to liquidate all colonial questions in dispute.[108]

Even the French government was sobered by Britain's attitude and worked more diligently toward an accord. In August Caillaux placed the negotiations under his ministry's control, and he continued to use secret agents to supplement the official French representative. Yet altogether the people of Europe had to endure four months of suspense and threat of war. The increase of nationalist sentiment was stimulated to strengthen the government's policy in both countries, but it often delayed the settlement. Final agreements were reached on the two problems of German exodus from Morocco and her compensation for this between October 15 and November 4, 1911. At the request of Caillaux, the Panther sailed away from Agadir at the end of November. Another great crisis had ended without war.[109]

While the Franco-German negotiations were proceeding and the Spanish advance into Morocco went on, the United States government received abundant news and comments on on these topics. The German government gave the United States prompt notice of the sending of the Panther. Al-Maghreb Al-Aksa printed an alleged secret treaty between France and the Sultan, made about April 10.[110] Carpenter and others occasionally enclosed clippings from newspapers; from Le Temps, giving the French viewpoint on the affair; from the London Times, endorsing Asquith's speech; from the Novae Vremia, reproving Germany for disregarding the Act of Algeciras and the accord of 1909; and from Al-Maghreb Al-Aksa and the Daily Chronicle, revealing an English sentiment not favorable to France. An interesting item sent by the American chargé at Berlin ascribed Germany's dramatic descent upon Agadir to a desire to test whether the death of King Edward VII had weakened the Triple Entente.[111]

Like his predecessors, Carpenter was critical of the French attitude towards the rights of other countries in Morocco. He said that the United States must insist upon her rights, even in trivial matters, or else the Moroccans would think that American interest was decreasing; they already suspected this, because the American list of protéges and semsars was being cut down, whereas other legations were increasing theirs. The German and Spanish challenges to France were likely to improve the lot of the other signatories. The French were trying to prevent sales of real estate near towns to others than their own countrymen. Only the British, German, and French legations could count on having their desires respected. As Morocco developed industrially, Carpenter hoped, the Americans would become interested in securing their share of the business. He thought that the United States should send a cruiser to Morocco as soon as the political situation became more settled. The Minister of the Netherlands had recently stated that in case of any future international conferences, he thought that the United States, Austria-Hungary, The Netherlands, and Belgium should stand together strongly to protect the Open Door. Carpenter also passed on the news that Austria-Hungary felt not only her prestige but also her trade menaced because France, Germany, and Great Britain were negotiating to settle the Moroccan dispute among themselves. The recent installation of the wireless between Tangier, Rabat, and Fez was bringing Morocco into close touch with the outside world.[112]

Commenting later on the French role in Morocco, Carpenter stated that if France obtained more freedom there, he hoped the other signatory powers would secure very definite business guarantees from her. Of French interference with the legitimate rights of other traders, there were accumulating evidences. The French officials were vigorously suppressing the smuggling of goods from Spanish ports. The

United States had a special interest in the Agadir region, by reason of the fact that she ranked second to Great Britain in the goatskin export trade from there. Carpenter also advised careful consideration before doing away with protection certificates. In two enclosures, one from Le Temps and the other from the London Truth, Carpenter presented further opinion from Europe. In the first, the French advocated an equitable and mutual understanding with Germany, followed by international adherence, rather than an immediate international discussion. The second article, "The Moor Under the Harrow," was one of those rare presentations of the Moorish viewpoint to be found chiefly in British journals.[113]

As late as September there had been speculations about the possibility of war terminating the Franco-German discussions. In a Moscow periodical, Russoye Slovo, there was a detailed explanation of the war in which the rival system of alliances and ententes then in force could drag all of Europe, including neutrals, into a world war; it was an uncanny prophecy of 1914. The Dutch, also, were showing apprehension for their own safety. In late September and October, however, there were several dispatches foretelling the imminence of a peaceful outcome of the quarrel.[114]

Until finished with Germany, France postponed the inevitable confrontation with Spain.[115] Soon after her occupation of Larache and Alcazar, Spain began wooing the favor of the United States. The State Department early declared that it would treat the occupation of Fez and of Alcazar and Larache on the same basis, following the terms of the Senate resolution regarding the Algeciras Act:

> Our only ... interest ... would be to see that our citizens and their property are adequately protected, it being of course understood that our interests, rights, and privileges in Morocco under the Algeciras Convention and other treaties would remain undisturbed.

On July 17 the State Department declined to express any views regarding the Germans at Agadir and the Spaniards at Larache.

On September 1 Spain informed the United States that no answer had been received regarding her request for a

Maghzen representative to be at Mogador on September 3 to surrender Ifni. Wicker's dispatch of September 13, 1911, reported conflicts between Riffians and small bodies of Spanish surveyors and explorers and an attack on Spanish military outposts. Wicker enclosed a clipping from Le Temps containing a history of the Spanish interest in Ifni, which Spain was to occupy according to her treaty with Morocco, signed on November 17, 1910. The French were much opposed to the Spanish attempt to occupy Ifni at a time when France was preoccupied with difficult negotiations with Germany.

Late in September, Wicker reported disturbances of the natives near Sefrou and in the Eastern Riff and an attack on Spanish outposts by several thousand Riffians. There had been heavy losses. Meanwhile, two Spanish gunboats patrolled the coast west from Melilla, bombarding and destroying native villages. In a conversation with Sir Maurice de Bunsen, Gustave Schille of the American legation in Madrid learned that both Spain and Great Britain were only awaiting a Franco-German peace pact to adjust their positions in Morocco. It was expected that Spain would insist on her rights in a Spanish sphere of influence as provided in the secret agreement of 1904. On the other hand, France would probably claim that her recent agreement with Germany had materially altered conditions since 1904. Great Britain would have to intervene if France tried to claim compensation from Spain to carry out the 1904 agreement. Since she would prefer a weaker power as her immediate neighbor, Great Britain would help Spain. Wicker concluded by reports that Moroccans were disinterested in the Italo-Turkish war, but conflict in the Riff went on, with heavy losses for the advancing Spanish. At the end of October news from the Riff was that Spanish operations near Melilla were at a standstill because of heavy rains.[116]

Definitely abrogating the Franco-German Accord of 1909, the agreement of November 4, 1911, also nullified a large part of the Act of Algeciras and provided for the future drastic revision of the Madrid Treaty of 1880. Morocco was to become a protectorate of France, for France was granted complete freedom to introduce such administrative, judicial, economic, financial, and military reforms as deemed essential for good government--all with the Sultan's consent, of course. Moreover, France was to control the diplomatic and consular services of the Empire and to represent the Sultan in his foreign affairs. To avoid ambiguity regarding the protectorate, in an accompanying note it was stated that "in the event of the French Government deeming it necessary to assume the protectorate of Morocco, the Imperial Government would place no obstacle in the way." Remnants of the Algeciras Act remained in several economic provisions. The rights of the signatory powers to equality of economic treatment in customs and taxes were protected, and opportunities to obtain concessions for public works and highways were guaranteed in vague phrases. The constitution of the State Bank remained intact. France promised to levy no export taxes on minerals or tax on mineral production, and mineral enterprises were to be permitted to build connections to main lines and ports. Although the construction and management of new railways were to be under French control, other powers could participate on an equitable basis in the letting of contracts. For this liberal grant of powers to France the compensation of Germany was 100, 000 square miles of the French Congo, giving Germany two very desirable river outlets to the Congo for the export of Cameroon products. As a sop to French public opinion, Germany in turn conceded to France a small tract of valueless Cameroon territory. To supersede the Madrid treaty, consular jurisdiction was to be eliminated as soon as a new judicial system could be established; in the interim, all civil suits were to be settled by arbitration under French supervision. After agreement with the other powers, a revision of lists and regulations of the status of protégés were to be made.[117]

Supplementary to the main agreement were several explanatory documents. Two notes concerned the delimitation of the new frontier and the terms of the lease of certain lands to France in Equatorial Africa. Four explanatory letters provided for arbitration of all future disagreements over various articles of the treaty. In another letter, Germany urged the building of the Tangier-Fez railway before any other and demanded a fixed share in its construction.[118]

Only the agreement to exchange territory required confirmation by the French parliament, but the two instruments were considered together. There was a spirited debate of about three weeks. Unfavorable public opinion was strengthened when the series of secret pacts on Morocco was published by French newspapers: Le Matin, on November 8, the French-Spanish entente of October , 1904; Figaro, on November 10, the Franco-Spanish entente of 1902, blocked by Great Britain; La Petite Republique, on November 10, confirmation of the existence of secret articles in the Entente Cordiale; Le Temps, on November 11, the entire Entente Cordiale; Le Temps, on November 12, the Franco-Spanish Treaty of 1905; and Le Echo de Paris, on December 11, the exchange of secret letters in the Franco-German Accord of 1909. By the disclosure of these secrets, it was revealed for the first time that France was bound to share Morocco with Spain. In the Chamber of Deputies, where ratification was regarded as a disagreeable necessity, the agreement was ratified on December 20 by a vote of 393 to 36, with 150 abstentions. A Senate commission of twenty-six members, including Bourgeois, Pichon, Clemenceau, and Poincaré, investigated the charges of secret unofficial parleys of Caillaux with influential Germans. Caillaux ably defended the agreement, but made the mistake of denying the press disclosures that he had carried on private negotiations. De Selves begged not to reply when asked to confirm Caillaux's denial, and resigned. On January 11 the Caillaux ministry fell,[119] and Poincaré formed a new cabinet with himself as foreign minister. After a favorable report from the commission, on February 10 the Senate also accepted the accord by a vote of 212 to 42.[120]

In Germany the reception of the new accord was generally hostile, or, at best, unenthusiastic. It embittered relations with both France and Great Britain. Bethmann-Hollweg and Kiderlen had to defend the agreement in the face of the resignation of the colonial secretary and the chief of the colonial office. The German press bitterly attacked Great Britain, and threats of war were made. Fretting ever since the Act of Algeciras, the Pan-German League now "choked with rage;" Kiderlen was accused of promising southern Morocco to them and then palming off on them swamp and desert. Many business men and industrialists protested to the government, and the entire press supported the colonialists. Even the Social Democrats ridiculed the "Strong government" for its "spineless" handling of the affair. The Reichstag demanded the right to sanction any future exchange of colonial territory and secured a favorable report on this. But, as in France, prudence prevailed, and the Bundestag ratified the accord. Mulai Hafid had given his assent to the arrangement on November 9.[121]

The French government found that its chief problem was getting the Moroccan convention ratified by the signers of the Act of Algeciras. Many of them did sign the new pact before the legislatures of the principal powers had done so. However, a number of reservations, objections, and attempted bargainings for advantages complicated the diplomatic proceedings. While agreeing to adhere to the accord as early as November 14, 1911, Great Britain asked for and received France's assurance that the economic clauses extended to all the powers and that the pact contained no derogation of Articles 4 and 7 of the Anglo-French Entente of 1904; in addition, the French government was trusted to concur in adequate arrangements to place Tangier under international control.[122] Great Britain also gave close attention to the Franco-Spanish negotiations to ensure Spain her share of Morocco.

France's ally, Russia, sought to exchange for her adhesion the support of France in the Straits question and in achieving Russian ambitions in Manchuria, Mongolia, and Chinese Turkestan. Nevertheless, without such definite assurances, Russia adhered on November 13, 1911.[123]

The allies of France having been satisfied, it remained to obtain the assent of Germany's partners. Until December 29, 1911, Austria-Hungary delayed her adhesion, while her foreign minister, Aerenthal, tried in vain to blackmail France for a loan of a milliard francs and made the pretext that his parliament must ratify the convention. The Quai d'Orsay refused his demand even before Russia raised objections to the loan, which she feared might be used against her.[124] Although much preoccupied with the Tripolitan war, begun on September 29, 1911, Italy carried on an extensive correspondence before agreeing to the accord and caused delay by referring the matter to her parliament. She was using the opportunity to collect the note for Tripoli given to her by France in 1900. The French ambassador in London feared that with Tripoli in hand Italy might cede to Germany a coaling station on the Mediterranean.[125] Incidentally, by the Treaty of Lausanne of October 10, 1912,

Italy antedated Spain over a month in the acquisition of their spheres in North Africa.

Two of the minor powers raised difficulties over the accord. The Belgian government was highly irritated because a clause of the Congo convention pledged France to consult all the powers signatory to the Treaty of Berlin before exercising her right of preemption to the Belgian Congo, in case Belgium decided to sell it. There was anxiety also over division of the islands in the rivers between Germany and Belgium. Finally Belgium agreed to submit the matter to her parliament after the French parliament had adopted the treaty.[126] Fearful of offending Spain, who had asked her to wait until the conclusion of the Franco-Spanish agreement on Morocco, and apprehensive lest the Congo settlement might presage future menace to the Portuguese African colonies, Portugal caused some delay. British pressure was applied successfully to Portugal.[127]

Of all the signatory powers to the Act of Algeciras, the most reluctant to sign the Franco-German convention of 1911 were Spain, France's quasi-partner in Morocco, and the United States, the archneutral in European political affairs.

After about fourteen months of negotiations, France and Spain reached an agreement over their mutual rights and responsibilities in Morocco. As early as November 6, 1911, Spain declined to adhere to the recent Franco-German arrangement before she "had obtained the necessary guarantees for her interests and rights as fixed in the special accord of October 3, 1904." Mulai Hafid received a similar notification.[128] To Spain's comfort and gain, Sir Maurice Bunsen, British ambassador in Madrid, assisted Señor Garcia Prieto, Spanish foreign minister, and Geoffray, the French ambassador, in the negotiations. France began with the premise that, having made all the sacrifices and done all the work in connection with the German convention, she should receive compensation from Spain. Her extreme demands were that she receive Ifni and, except for the Tangier area, the entire Atlantic coast of Morocco from Cape Spartel to Ceuta. But Great Britain would not allow France opposite Gibraltar. Spain feared having to pay both Germany and France--the former possibly by the absorption of Spanish Guinea into

Cameroon. Spain refused to accept any modification of her zone of 1904 until assured that her agreement with France was the total of her obligations. Besides the delimitation of zonal boundaries, other outstanding problems were supervision of the customs, regulation of railway construction, especially of the Tangier-Fez line, the advisory power over the sultan and many administrative regulations. The lines of boundary demarcation fixed in the 1904 pact were found to be geographically unsatisfactory and impossible for policing.[129]

Signed at Madrid on November 27, 1912, the Franco-Spanish treaty was approved by the Cortes on December 17 by a vote of 216 to 22. Reduced in area for the third time in twelve years, the Spanish zone was finally limited to 18,300 square miles, while France obtained 460,000 square miles. Receiving her zone from France, Spain had only a sub-protectorate, not transferable to a third country without French and Moroccan consent. Spain retained Ifni, Larache, and Alcazar and received from France an area north of her Rio de Oro in exchange for a portion of the Riff ceded to France. The fiction was maintained that the sultan retained political and religious authority over all Morocco, and customs unity in the two zones helped to promote this idea. In the Spanish Zone the sultan's sovereignty was to be exercised by a Khalifa appointed by him from two persons selected by Spain. Like France, Spain was granted full authority to establish the essential administrative, economic, financial, judicial, and military reforms in her zone. Spain controlled customs in her zone, but had to pay annually about $100,000 toward the interest and amortization of the Moroccan debt. The Tangier-Fez railway was to be built by a single company, in whose capital stock France was to own 56%, Spain, 36%, and other countries, if they wished, 8%. As in the agreement with Germany, the lists of protéges were to be revised, with the ultimate objective of modifying or abolishing the Treaty of Madrid, and extraterritoriality was to be eliminated when a judicial system was organized. There were two provisions furthering British interests; no fortifications were allowed between Melilla and the heights of the right bank of the Sebou, and it was stipulated that "the city of Tangier and its environs constitute a special zone which will be granted a system of government to be determined later."[130]

Eight months before France and Spain had settled their account, Mulai Hafid had been compelled to accept the French protectorate over his empire. In March of 1912 two men credited with large responsibility for this returned after over a year in Paris. They were M. Regnault, French minister to Morocco, and Hadj Muhammad Al Mokri, foreign minister of Morocco. They came to arrange for Mulai Hafid the formal treaty for the French protectorate, since his approval of the Franco-German Accord of November, 1911, was not considered sufficient. They were also to reconstruct public administration to curb the power of the _kaids_, to collect all the legal taxes, and to send out expeditions to rebellious districts.[131]

Although Mulai Hafid had threatened abdication several times rather than to introduce France into his empire, he had now been driven by French interference and by the increasing anarchy in Morocco to request French assistance. When the large mission under Regnault reached Fez, the streets were empty except for a small section where the local authorities had summoned all available prostitutes to make a "spontaneous demonstration" of welcome from the city's women. Under strong protest, the Sultan signed the protection treaty on March 30, 1912. All classes of the population regarded his action as a betrayal of both Morocco and of Islam.[132]

The provisions of the protectorate treaty gave France many powers and responsibilities. France was pledged to protect the person, prestige, and throne of the sultan and to guarantee the free exercise of the Muslim religion and preservation of its institutions. The reorganized Maghzen was to introduce administrative, judicial, educational, economic, financial, and military reforms, promulgated in the name and with the consent of the sultan. After consultation with him, the French were to undertake such military occupation and police supervision as was necessary. However, the real ruler of the country would be the French Resident or Commissioner General, who was to approve all the sultan's decrees, act as intermediary between the ruler and foreign powers, and handle all affairs of foreigners in Morocco. The sultan could conclude no international act or make no public or private loan or concession without the approval of France. The diplomatic and consular agents of France were to protect Moroccan subjects and represent their interests abroad. Committed by treaties and promises to the Moroccan government and by public declarations of leading officials, France was bound to a policy of justice, equity, and political integrity. Finally, the French government promised to stop all reported abuses in the sale and occupation of land by foreigners, to protect the rights and customs of the natives, to encourage the loyal cooperation of the Moroccan people, and to employ Moroccan chiefs and leaders whenever possible in administration of local affairs. The city of Tangier was to keep its special character to determine its later municipal government.[133]

The crowning infamy of the protectorate treaty precipitated an uprising in Fez on April 17-18, which resulted in the massacre of many French officers and civilians under circumstances of great horror and cruelty. The rebellion was put down after hard fighting, but by the time that General Moinier arrived with a relief column, the city was besieged by the hill tribes. To quell this major conflict, the French government appointed General Lyautey. Arriving at Fez on May 24, 1912, Lyautey managed to subdue the hill tribes and save the city from looting. He then set about reconciling the notables of Fez and securing their cooperation. However, Mulai Hafid had wearied of his impossible situation and was fearful for his life. The last weeks of his reign were spent wrangling with the French authorities and changing his mind about abdicating almost daily. He moved to Rabat, from where he departed on August 31 for a visit to France. He had finally exchanged his abdication document[134] for a check for ₺ 40,000 from the French. To succeed him, his half-brother, Mulai Youssef, had been selected and kept in waiting for some time.[135]

By the end of 1912, the Moroccan problem, perennial controversy of European politics, appeared to have been "permanently" solved. Moreover, other questions concerning European imperialism in Africa had been answered also. Great Britain was satisfied with control over Egypt and a future guarantee that Tangier would later be internationalized. France held sway over all the Maghreb, except for the small share of Morocco granted to Spain. Italy had wrested from Turkey the provinces of Tripoli and Barca. Thus all of North Africa had been brought under European influence and power. At only a slight loss of her African territory, Germany had been removed from too close a proximity to the Mediterranean to an enlarged Congo. In all Africa, only Liberia and Ethiopia remained "independent" nations, and thus the "Dark Continent" was relieved from imperialistic strivings and territorial changes until the Versailles Treaty in 1919. By a series of international ententes and treaties the best diplomatic brains of Europe had been able to preserve the status quo of 1912 for less than seven years.

Still protesting complete disinterestedness in the political aspects of the Moroccan settlements, however, the United States continued to hold back from surrendering her economic rights. In his efforts to bring the United States into line with the other signatory powers of the Act of Algeciras, Jusserand found the Taft administration much more intractable than that of his friend Roosevelt.

The State Department had stated its basic principles regarding the changes proposed by the French protectorate some time before the conclusion of the Franco-German agreement of 1911. The American position was as follows:

> The Department is interested in seeing that in the pending Moroccan settlement among the European powers the interests of the United States in the Mediterranean be not ignored or treated disadvantageously. The interests of this country there have been coexistent with its existence as a nation. They also have been conserved and maintained from the beginning in a spirit of accord and friendly cooperation with France ....
>
> After the establishment of independence one of the first treaties of peace and friendship negotiated by the United States was with the Government of Morocco in 1786. It was provided ... that the commerce of the United States should be on the same footing as the commerce with most favored nations ....
>
> The historical rights which the United States asserted and established in this part of the Mediterranean have in no way been impaired by the lapse of time, nor is the present commerce necessarily the measure of prospective trade and the commercial relations which it is

> desirable to safeguard. This government could not accept or consent to any settlement by the European powers among themselves which would have the effect of abrogating or impairing the commercial interests of the United States.[136]

Jusserand began his campaign to secure American adhesion promptly on November 3, 1911. The Franco-German arrangement, he explained, was an "undertaking of pacification and progress contemplated by the Act of Algeciras," aimed at maintaining order and the normal development, on a footing of perfect equality, of the economic interests of the powers concerned." Since "the freedom of trade provided by the treaties ... shall ... be firmly maintained," and "the Government of the United States seeks nothing more in Morocco than the development of the economic interests of its citizens," "my Government fondly cherises the hope that" the treaty "will gain the Federal Government's sanction .... as soon as possible." Acting Secretary of State Adee replied that since the adherence of the United States seemed to imply the modification of certain existing treaty rights, it could be given only with the advice and consent of the Senate.[137]

After a disappointing interview with the third assistant secretary of state, Jusserand tried to get a favorable recommendation from the President and the State Department for consent by the Senate. It was called to the attention of Secretary Knox that the Franco-German agreement disregarded all interests of Spain and that of the three principles upon which the Algeciras Act was based, only economic liberty without any inequality was even partially safeguarded. He was advised to wait until all other powers had adhered, when American adhesion in a treaty with France could be made to preserve existing American treaty rights under the treaties of 1836 and 1880. Later Knox told Jusserand that the Spanish protest to the agreement was embarrassing to the United States and that Department opinion was not favorable to American adhesion.[138]

Transmitting to the State Department the texts of the explanatory notes accompanying the Franco-German accord, Jusserand again urged that the French reforms would respect and develop American economic interests. He asked for the assurance that Knox would take the necessary steps to secure Senate approval. The governments of Russia, England, Italy, Sweden, and Morocco had already signified their acceptance of the treaty. In reply, Knox pointed out that the American government must refrain from expressing any opinion on any political parts of the treaty. Adhesion to the articles relating to commercial rights and the administration of justice would require a treaty made with the advice and consent of the Senate. At the proper time the State Department would feel inclined to undertake negotiations to make a treaty appropriate for modifying existing extraterritorial rights and the rights of American protégés, provided that the commercial and other advantages secured to the United States under the existing treaties were preserved.[139] On December 15 Jusserand interviewed Root,[140] who said that there was no reason whatever for postponing Senate action on the adhesion. Jusserand at once informed Knox of Root's opinion. Later Jusserand confessed to his chief his disappointment over the negative results he had achieved from seemingly favorable conferences with Knox, Root, and Lodge, and the endless quibblings of Hale, the third assistant secretary. He had discovered that the real objection of the State Department was the establishment of the French protectorate, specifically mentioned in the explanatory letters.[141]

Carpenter brought up another point for consideration. He urged that the French be advised that before the United States would acquiesce in the Franco-German accord the Moroccan authorities would have to settle pending or possible American claims and cease petty and annoying discriminations against American nationals and trade. From the Belgian legation in Washington came an inquiry concerning the probable suppression of diplomatic representation in Morocco and its replacement by consular agents--did the American government expect this to be immediate after the ratification of the accord, or did it expect further negotiations? Huntington Wilson, assistant secretary of state, replied that probably American representatives would remain until the United States had made a new treaty with France to protect her commercial interests and future trade opportunities.[142]

On January 27, 1912, Jusserand informed Knox that the time was arriving for the promised negotiation of a Franco-American treaty regulating the questions concerning the capitulations, etc. The French Senate expected to ratify the accord soon, and after that France would immediately begin to establish the protectorate. Knox replied that he was entirely ready and would give instructions to have the documents prepared. Jusserand recalled that in the case of Tunisia in 1904, he and John Hay had signed a most simple text which the Senate had then ratified without difficulty.[143] But the days of Roosevelt and Hay, and also of Root, were past, and the impatient Jusserand could no longer influence the American government. For many years a new Franco-American commercial treaty remained a source of contention, but it was never attained.

Notes

1. Brandenburg, From Bismarck to the World War, 260.

2. "Anglo-French Convention Respecting the New Hebrides," American Journal of International Law, I (April, 1907), 482-483.

3. "Anglo-French-Italian Agreement Regarding Abyssinia," Ibid., 484-485.

4. "This agreement ... amounts to a second Triple Alliance, an alliance of Great Britain, France, and Spain .... In view of this new "triplice" and the lukewarmness of Italy toward her neighbors in the Dreibund, the subject of speculation is "What will be the German Kaiser's next move?" "The New Triple Alliance," Review of Reviews, XXXVI (July, 1907), 21.

5. Grey to de Villa Urrutia, No. 39, May 16, 1907; de Villa Urrutia to Grey, No. 40, May 16, 1907; Pichon to Leon y Castillo. No. 41, May 16, 1907, and Leon y Castillo to Pichon, May 16, 1907; B. D., VII, 32-34.

6. Lee, King Edward VII, II, 543-544; William II to Bülow, No. 7203, Jan. 17, 1907, G. P., XXI, 465.

7. Ibid.

8. "Program of the Hague Conference," Independent, LX (May 3, 1906), 1053-1054.

9. Brandenburg, From Bismarck to the World War, 275-277; Fay, Origins of the World War, I, 233-234.

10. For a detailed discussion of Roosevelt and the Second Hague Conference, see Beale, Theodore Roosevelt and the Rise of America to World Power, 337-352.

11. Latané, History of American Foreign Policy, 495-497; Bemis, Diplomatic History of the United States, 524-525.

12. Fay, Origins of the World War, I, 218-219.

13. F. R., 1907, I, Part 1, 754-755.

14. Thomas Millard, America and the Far Eastern Question, 280.

15. Review of Reviews, XXXVI (Sept., 1907), 278.

16. Fay, Origins of the World War, I, 220; Langer, Encyclopedia of World History, 755.

17. "Proposed Alliance of England and Russia," Literary Digest, XXXI (Nov. 4, 1905), 662; A. Maurice Low, "Foreign Affairs," Forum, XXXVII (April, 1906), 471; "Anglo-Russian Entente Regarded as Certain," New York Times, April 14, 1906, 4; "The New Triple Alliance," Literary Digest, XXXII (June 23, 1906), 949.

18. Too little and too late (April 23, 1908) were the Baltic Sea Convention and the North Sea Convention. The first was signed at St. Petersburg by Germany, Sweden, Denmark, and Russia; the second was signed at Berlin by Germany, Great Britain, Denmark, France, The Netherlands, and Sweden. They provided mutual guarantees for the *status quo* on the shores of the two seas and for consultation if the *status quo* were threatened. Suggested by the Pact of Cartagena, these treaties were designed to give

to the world in general and to Great Britain in particular proof of Germany's pacific intentions in these regions. They were welcomed by the smaller states. A French ambassador said that the latter was the first important political agreement with Germany since the Franco-Prussian War. Freiherr Wilhelm von Schoen, The Memoirs of an Ambassador, 64, 66.

19. Brandenburg, From Bismarck to the World War, 264.

20. Rex to Bülow, No. 8547, July 4, 1907, G. P., XXV, Part 1, 67-69.

21. For a detailed account, see Luella J. Hall, "The Abortive German-American-Chinese Entente of 1907-8," Journal of Modern History, I (June, 1929), 219-235.

22. Rex to Schön, Aug., 1908, G. P., XXV, 98.

23. Herbert Croly, Willard Straight (hereafter cited as Croly, Willard Straight), 273.

24. Review of Reviews, XXXVIII (Nov., 1908), 539-540.

25. Croly, Willard Straight, 274.

26. Westel W. Willoughby, Foreign Rights and Interests in China, 174-175.

27. Croly, Willard Straight, 275, 278; Millard, America and the Far Eastern Question, 368-369.

28. Bernstorff to F. O., Jan. 2, 1909, G. P., XXV, 97.

29. Dennett, Roosevelt and the Russo-Japanese War, 320-321.

30. Fay, Origins of the World War, I, 256-257; Townsend, Rise and Fall of Germany's Colonial Empire, 339.

31. Langer, Encyclopedia of World History, 757.

32. Dr. John W. Burgess, the "Roosevelt Professor" at the University of Berlin, seems to have had an uncanny insight, or intuition, regarding the behind-the-scenes diplomacy of this time. In an address in the spring of 1908, he set forth the German idea of world politics. In the Asiatic world, he said, "We find that the interests of Germany and the United States are in entire harmony, viz. : to redeem China and Central Asia, neither through the sway of Japan nor England, nor Russia, over them, nor by the division of them among the three, but by holding the doors of commerce wide open to all nations and giving the natives a fair chance to work out their own civilization under these great transforming influences." _Review of Reviews_, XXXVII (March, 1908), 372-373.

33. Tardieu, _La Conférence_, 425-426.

34. _Ibid._, 426-430.

35. Ashmead-Bartlett, _The Passing of the Shereefian Empire_, 16-17; Gibbons, _New Map of Africa_, 380; Harris, _Morocco That Was_, 104-113; Gummeré to Root, No. 130, Oct. 3, 1906, _A. N. F._, XLIII, 295/6.

36. Tardieu, _La Conférence_, 430-435; Harris, _Europe and Africa_, 291; Gummeré to Sec. of State, Sept. 7, 1906, _A. N. F._, CXXV, 880 and Sept. 8, 1906, _Ibid._, 880/1; W. B. Harris, "Raisuli," _Blackwood's Magazine_, CCIX (Jan., 1921), 39-45.

37. _A. N. F._, CCXXIII: Philip to Root, No. 133, Oct. 22, 1906, 2151/1; No. 134, Oct. 26, 1906, 2151/2; No. 137, Nov. 2, 1906, 2151/3; No. 142, Nov. 23, 1906, 2151/4; No. 147, Dec. 3, 1906, 2151/5. Gummeré to Root, _Ibid._, No. 153, Dec. 13, 1906, 2151/7; No. 157, Dec. 18, 1906, 2151/8; Dec. 29, 1906, 2151/12.

38. Robert Bacon, Acting Sec. of State, to Gummeré, No. 39, June 9, 1906, D. S., _Instructions, Barbary Powers_, XVI, 181.

39. Alvey A. Adee, Second Assistant Secretary of State, deliberately eliminated most of his comments from diplomatic dispatches. However, a few remain, often initialed "A". This was his comment on Gummeré's gift: 'Did you see the photo of the remarkable Bacchanalian Cup presented to a tee-total Mohammedan? What would the W. C. T. U. say if they saw that cup?" A to Bacon, No. 131, appended memo, Oct. 23, 1906, A. N. F., XV, 41/30.

40. The Moroccan representative in Fez, Hadj Muhammad Al Mokri, was angling for American support also. "Hadj Mohammed Al Morki laid much stress upon the fact that the Sultan appreciated highly the friendly and disinterested attitude of the American Government towards Morocco and that His Shereefian Majesty in his great desire to see the reforms, for the good of his country, put into effect, looked forward to the good will and support of the United States." Philip to Root, No. 132, Oct. 6, 1906, A. N. F., XLIII, 295/7.

41. Adee to Sec. of State, Nov. 17, 1906, A. N. F., XV, 41/38, appended memo: "The Algeciras Conference appears not to have settled all the intestinal troubles of Morocco."

42. Gummeré to Root, No. 150, Dec. 10, 1906, A. N. F., XV, 41/52.

43. Translation of letter from Abd al-Aziz to Theodore Roosevelt, enclosure with No. 151, Dec. 12, 1906, A. N. F., XV, 41/53. See same source for general accounts of the mission. Philip to Root, No. 127, Sept. 16, 1906, 41/25; Gummeré to Root, Aug. 21, 1906, 41/9; Gummeré to Root, No. 1, Sept. 29, 1906, with enclosures, Gummeré to Abd al-Aziz and Sultan's reply, 41/27-29; No. 2, Oct. 1, 1906, 41/31; No. 4, Oct. 15, 1906, 41/33; No. 7, Oct. 25, 1906, 41/37; No. 10, Nov. 7, 1906, 41/42; No. 11, Nov. 15, 1906, 41/44; No. 15, Nov. 25, 1906, 41/48; No. 16, Nov. 25, 1906, 41/49; No. 152, Dec. 12, 1906, 41/54-58.

44. A. N. F., CCCXXVI: Bacon to Gummeré, No. 155, Dec. 14, 1906, 3517; and Jan. 21, 1907, 3517/1. Root to Gummeré, Jan. 17, 1907, 3517 and Jan. 29, 1907, 3517/1. Gummeré to Root, Jan. 18, 1907, 3517/1; Jan. 18, 1907, 3517/3 and Feb. 12, 1907, 3517/4.

45. Three times before his overthrow, the French government persuaded French banks to grant Abd al-Aziz advances. The State Bank had already loaned him almost all of its capital. Feis, Europe, The World's Banker, 407-408.

46. Gibbons, New Map of Africa, 380-381; Tardieu La Conférence, 542-544; Maurois, Lyautey, 167; Harris, Europe and Africa, 291.

47. Harris, Morocco That Was, 116-118; Tardieu, La Conférence, 546-547.

48. French chargé to Acting Sec. of State, Aug. 7, 1907, F. R., 1907, Part 2, 890-891.

49. Dispatches from Tangier are from Jan. 7, 1907 to Dec. 30, 1907, and are found in A. N. F., CCXXIII and CCXXIV, cases 2151 to 2151/105. Dispatches from Spain are: Collier to Root, No. 382, Aug. 6, 1907, 2151/42 and No. 385, Aug. 9, 1907, 2151/45; Buckler to Root, No. 431, Nov. 20, 1907, 2151/92 and Dec. 6, 1907, 2151/95.

50. W. B. Harris, France, Spain, and the Rif, 94; F. R., 1907, Part 2, 876-879; Tardieu, La Conférence, 546-549, 551-553, 584.

51. Gibbons, New Map of Africa, 381-382; Harris, Europe and Africa, 293-294.

52. Ibid., 294-295; Tardieu, La Conférence, 554-557.

53. "A new reign commenced, burdened by the same difficulties, both local and international, as had weighed upon the preceding one." Tardieu, La Conférence, 559.

54. *Ibid.*, 557-559; Harris, *Europe and Africa*, 297-298.

55. *A. N. F.*, CCXXIV, 1906-1910: No. 307, Jan. 6, 1908, 2151/107; No. 309, Jan. 17, 1908, 2151/111; No. 315, Jan. 27, 1908, 2151/118; No. 332, March 11, 1908, 2151/133; No. 357, June 4, 1908, 2151/157; No. 378, Sept. 13, 1908, 2151/220; Telegram, Sept. 16, 1908, 2151/216; No. 379, Sept. 14, 1908, 2151/222; No. 389, Oct. 7, 1908, 2151/237.

56. *A. N. F.*, CCXXIV, 1906-1910: No. 459, 2151/108; No. 470, Jan. 28, 1908, 2151/116-117; No. 480, Feb. 17, 1908, 2151/122; No. 487, Feb. 28, 1908, 2151/126-127; No. 496, March 11, 1908, 2151/132; No. 552, May 25, 1908, 2151/150; No. 516, March 28, 1908, 2151/137; No. 593, Aug. 30, 1908, 2151/210.

57. "The United States being one of the greatest nations of the world, renowned for her justice, her prominent position in the world, emanating from her equity, moderate policy, her opposition to every arbitrary act and to all unjust wars, it is not compatible with her dignity nor to be believed on her part that she will show indifference, but we confidently hope that she will undertake the matter with the illustrious French Nation." *A. N. F.*, CCXXIV, 1906-1910, No. 333, March 14, 1908, 2151/134-135.

58. *A. N. F.*, CCXXIV, 1906-1910; No. 328, Feb. 19, 1908, 2151/123-124; No. 333, March 14, 1908, 2151/134-135; No. 106, March 3, 1908, 2151/130-131; No. 348, May 12, 1908, 2151/143-144; No. 330, May 20, 1908, 2151/200-201; Aug. 3, 1908, 2151/188-189.

59. The commission consisted of three Moroccans, and one member each selected by France, Great Britain, Germany, Spain, Portugal, and Italy. The representatives of other powers were to sit on the commission only when claims of their own nationals were to be decided. Gummeré to Root, May 16, 1908, 2151/147-149, *A. N. F.*, CCXXIV 1906-1910.

60. Gummeré to Root, May 16, 1908, 2151/147-149; Philip to Root, Aug. 15, 1908, 2151/194; Jacobus to Henry White, Aug. 18, 1908, 2151/195-197; Philip to Root, Oct. 30, 1908, 2151/247-250, A. N. F., CCXXIV, 1906-1910.

61. Harris, Europe and Africa, 297-298; Maurois, Lyautey, 181-183; Tardieu, La Conférence, 584-587.

62. A. N. F., CCXXIV, 1906-1910; Philip to Root, No. 308, Jan. 13, 1908, 2151/112; No. 310, Jan. 20, 1908, 2151/113; Telegram, Aug. 23, 1908, 2151/190; No. 371, Aug. 24, 1908, 2151/205; No. 372, Aug. 29, 1908, 2151/208-209. Gummeré to Root, No. 354, May 27, 1908, 2151/151; No. 361, June 12, 1908, 2151/161; June 15, 1908, 2151/164; June 18, 1908, 2151/166; No. 368, July 15, 1908, 2151/184.

63. There are a very extensive correspondence and a number of memoranda, too much for individual citation, between Root and Adee and between the State Department and Gummeré and Philip, as well as the French and Spanish representatives in Washington, Esme Howard, and Hatzfeldt. The documents are filed in A. N. F., CCXXIV, 1906-1910, are dated from Sept. 2, 1908 to Jan. 15, 1909, and are numbered between 2151/198 and 2151/315.

64. Fay, Origins of the World War, I, 246-248; Carroll, French Public Opinion, 226-230; Ima Christine Barlow, The Agadir Crisis (hereafter cited as Barlow, Agadir Crisis), 62-67. The last reference is the most complete account of the period covered in the chapter--but it tells the story without mention of the United States.

65. Ibid., 67-69, 75-76.

66. For the text of the declaration see Feis, Europe, the World's Banker, 415.

67. Fay, Origins of the World War, I, 248-249, 252; Stuart, Tangier, 50; Barlow, Agadir Crisis, 70-80. A. N. F., MXVII, 1906-1910: White to Sec. of

State, Feb. 10, 1909, 17883/1; Feb. 11, 1909, 17883/2; Gummeré to Bacon, No. 418, Feb. 10, 1909, 17883/3. Collier to Bacon, No. 708, Feb. 12, 1909, 17883/4 and Collier to Knox, No. 760, May 15, 1909, 17883/9.

68. Feis, Europe, The World's Banker, 408-409.

69. Harris, Morocco That Was, 121, 297-302; Mellor, Morocco Awakes, 36; Harris, Europe and Africa, 299-300.

70. A. N. F., CCXXV, 1906-1910; Gummeré to Knox, No. 426, March 11, 1909, 2151/325; March 26, 1909, 2151/327; April 1, 1909, 2151/329; April 22, 1909, 2151/330; April 30, 1909, 2151/334; No. 438, May 11, 1909, 2151/437.

71. On Sept. 23, 1908, because of the length and quality of his services in Morocco, because Hay had promised him such a promotion several years before, and because of his health, Gummeré requested promotion, preferably to Bern. The State Department had assured him of a promotion the previous December. But when Gummeré offered the customary resignation at the change of administration, it was accepted with no mention of another position. After his retirement, Gummeré lived in Washington, England, where he died on May 28, 1920. During World War I he worked actively among the wounded in both England and France. Gummeré to Root, letter, Sept. 23, 1908, A. N. F., DXXXVII, 6873/14; Knox to Gummeré, telegram, April 21, 1909, Ibid., 6873/14A. Walter L. Wright, Jr., "Samuel René Gummeré," Dictionary of American Biography, VIII, 50.

72. Dodge to Knox, A. N. F., CCXXV, 1906-1910, July 10, 1910, 123D66.

73. Dodge to Knox, No. 73, Sept. 16, 1909, Ibid., MXII, 17706/328-331.

74. Adee to Dodge, No. 18, Oct. 7, 1909, Ibid.

75. A. N. F., CCXXV, 1906-1910: Dodge to Knox, June 24, 1909, 2151/349; No. 8, June 24, 1909, 2151/350; Aug. 26, 1909, 2151/354; Aug. 27, 1909, 2151/356; No. 67, Sept. 9, 1909, 2151/360-362; No. 75, Sept. 18, 1909, 2151/363-364; No. 68, Sept. 9, 1909, 2151/359; No. 82, Sept. 29, 1909, 2151/365-367; Harris, Morocco That Was, 114.

76. "Small wonder! In a few months, Spain had more men engaged and lost more killed and wounded than France had during the whole period from landing at Casablanca until all Morocco was, six years later, under French control." Gibbons, New Map of Africa, 386.

77. Harris, France, Spain, and the Rif, 55-57; Mellor, Morocco Awakes, 37-38.

78. Harris, Europe and Africa, 300. A. N. F., 1906-1910, MLXXXVIII, Dodge to Knox, No. 17, July 13, 1909, 20453/14; No. 27, July 23, 1909, 20453/15-16; No. 26, Aug. 7, 1909, 20453/17; No. 45, Aug. 18, 1909, 20453/18; Sept. 23, 1909, 20453/20; No. 80, Sept. 24, 1909, 20453/6-9; No. 87, Oct. 9, 1909, 20453/31. Ibid., Ide (San Sebastian) to Knox, No. 29, July 30, 1909, 20453/4; No. 46, Aug. 28, 1909, 20453/19; No. 58, Sept. 14, 1909, 20453/21-22; No. 59, Sept. 15, 1909, 20453/23-24; No. 104, Nov. 29, 1909, 20453/37. Ibid., Robertson to Knox, No. 98, Oct. 20, 1909, 20453/32. Ibid., Hill (Barcelona) to Knox, Nov. 6, 1909, 20453/33-35. A. N. F., CCXV: Adee to Dodge, Sept. 27, 1909, 2151/369.

79. Harris, Europe and Africa, 301; Feis, Europe: The World's Banker, 409-410. A. N. F., CCXXV, 1906-1910: Dodge to Knox, No. 170, Feb. 1, 1910, 2151/373. Ibid., CCCCLIII, Wilson to American legation, Tangier, Feb. 21, 1910, 5444/3A; Dodge to Knox, No. 179, Feb. 11, 1910, 5444/7; Feb. 21, 1910, 5444/4; Feb. 22, 1910, 5444/5; No. 196, Feb. 23, 1910, 5444/8; Feb. 23, 1910, 5444/6; No. 205, March 7, 1910, 5444/9; No. 216, March 16, 1910, 5444/10.

80. Harris, Europe and Africa, 301-302.

81. Ibid., 302; Feis, Europe, The World's Banker, 410-411.

82. Ibid., 411-412; Knight, Morocco As a French Economic Venture, 28; Barbour, North-West Africa; 90; Gibbons, New Map of Africa, 384-385; Barlow, Agadir Crisis, 21.

83. A. N. F., CCV, 1906-1910: Gummeré to Knox, No. 423, March 10, 1909, 2151/323; Dodge to Knox, April 19, 1909, 2151/346-347; Adee to Knox, July 23, 1909; Philip to Knox, April 12, 1909, 2151/331 and April 16, 1909, 2151/335-341; Dodge to Knox, No. 260, April 29, 1910, 2151/381 and No. 263, May 6, 1910, 2151/383.

84. Al Mokri was appointed vizier of foreign affairs in July. He continued as vizier of public works and vizier of the treasury, the latter until the work of the Financial Embassy, which had made the recent loan, could be completed. Carpenter to Sec. of State, No. 5, Aug. 1, 1910, A. N. F., CCXXV, 2151/390.

85. Dept. of State, Division of Information, Series C, No. 7, Morocco No. 2, "Political Conditions in Morocco,": Dodge to Knox, No. 154, Jan. 10, 1910; Ibid., Series B., No. 4, Morocco No. 3, Dodge to Knox, No. 262, April 30, 1910 and No. 254, May 6, 1910. A. N. F., CCCCLIII: Dodge to Knox, No. 228, March 29, 1910, 5444/11 and No. 257, April 29, 1910, 5444/13. Ibid., CCXV: Dodge to Knox, No. 275, May 27, 1910, 2151/384; No. 280, June 4, 1910 and enclosure, 2151/385; No. 294, June 25, 1910, 2151/386.

86. Carpenter to Knox, A. N. F., 123 C 22, July 27, 1910.

87. George E. Holt was vice and deputy consul general from Nov. 9, 1907 to Jan. 8, 1912. Hoffman Philip, deputy consul general from Nov. 6, 1901, was appointed vice and deputy consul general on Nov. 18, 1902. Philip then served as secretary of legation and consul general from March 8, 1905 to April 19, 1909.

Edward C. Wynne, Assistant Historical Adviser, Dept. of State, letter to Luella J. Hall, Jan. 7, 1932; H A 116.3/2039.

88. A. N. F.: Wicker to Knox, No. 319, July 23, 1910, 611.8115; Holt to Knox, No. 132, Aug. 1, 1910, 611.8115 and No. 142, Aug. 12, 1910, 611.8115/2 with enclosure.

89. A. N. F.: Carpenter to Knox: No. 24, Aug. 22, 1910, 881.00/391; No. 31, Sept. 19, 1910, 881.00/392; No. 47, Dec. 8, 1910, 881.00/393. Holt to Knox, No. 183, Nov. 25, 1910, Ibid., 611, 8115/3.

90. Turner (Madrid) to Knox, No. 268, Oct. 23, 1910, 752.81; Ide (Madrid), to Knox, No. 285, Nov. 19, 1910, 752.81/3 and No. 286, Nov. 23, 1910, 752.81/5; Ibid.

91. Meakin says of this somewhat mythical place on the Sus coast: "Known as Santa Cruz de Mar Pequeña, a claim which she forced the Moors to recognize after the war of 1860, although her own authorities have never yet been able to agree as to its whereabouts. It appears to have been somewhere on the extreme frontier of the Morocco of those days, .. but since to have been lost sight of, as it was destroyed by the Moors in 1524." He also says that a fruitless attempt was again made by a commission in 1877 to determine the exact site. Quoted in Carpenter to Knox, No. 43, Nov. 22, 1910, A. N. F., 752.81/4.

92. Carpenter to Knox, No. 43, Nov. 22, 1910, 752.81/4 and No. 45, Nov. 28, 1910, 752.81/6; A. N. F.

93. Fay, Origins of the World War, I, 278; Harris, Europe and Africa, 303; Carroll, French Public Opinion, 235. A. N. F.: Carpenter to Knox, No. 73, Feb. 17, 1911, 751.81/15; No. 79, March 1, 1911, 751.81/16; No. 82, March 8, 1911, 881.00/396; No. 88, March 17, 1911, 881.00/397; No. 95, March 29, 1911, 751.81/18; No. 100, n. d., 881.00 /398.

94. Fay, Origins of the World War, I, 278-279; Brandenburg, From Bismarck to the World War, 370-371.

95. Barlow, Agadir Crisis, 188-193. A. N. F.: Carpenter to Knox, No. 106, May 1, 1911, 881.00/405; No. 111, May 17, 1911, 881.00/410; No. 118, June 5, 1911, 881.00/412.

96. Fay, Origins of the World War, I, 281-282; Brandenburg, From Bismarck to the World War, 371.

97. Barlow, Agadir Crisis, 199-202. A. N. F.: Carpenter to Knox, No. 116, June 5, 1911, 881.00/413; No. 128, June 29, 1911, 881.00/420.

98. Harris, Europe and Africa, 306; Fay, Origins of the World War, I, 280-281.

99. Brandenburg, From Bismarck to the World War, 343, 370; Carroll, French Public Opinion, 234-235; Staley, War and the Private Investor, 482-484; Fay, Origins of the World War, I, 277-278; Feis, Europe, The World's Banker, 416-418; Nicolson, Portrait of A Diplomatist, 200; Barlow, Agadir Crisis, 84-152.

100. "In a conversation with Sir Maurice de Bunsen ... he said that the Spanish government was pursuing its old, unwise policy of attempting to acquire colonial possessions which it could not govern, and that it was filled with dreams of largely extending its sphere of influence in Africa, and was making sure of the disturbed conditions of affairs there as an excuse for pushing itself further into the interior, and that it watched very jealously every movement that France made in that direction, with a view to a like movement on the part of Spain, so that the latter country might get as large a share of the territory to be subjugated as France would get." Ide to Knox (from Madrid), No. 369, April 20, 1911, A. N. F., 752.81/7.

101. Barlow, Agadir Crisis, 202-206; Fay, Origins of the World War, I, 283; Madariaga, Spain, A Modern History, 303; Mellor, Morocco Awakes, 38-39.

102. A. N. F. : C. P. A., note verbale, April 20, 1911, 881.00/432; memoranda from the Third Assistant Secretary, May 8, 1911, 881.00/403; May 11, 1911, 881.00/404; May 23, 1911, 881.00/406; June 5, 1911, 881.00/411; June 16, 1911, 881.00/414. Carpenter to State Dept., No. 121, June 16, 1911, 881.00/416; No. 122, June 19, 1911, 881.00/418; No. 129, June 29, 1911, 881.00/421.

103. Barlow, Agadir Crisis, 209-228; Carroll, French Public Opinion, 240.

104. Barlow, Agadir Crisis, 231-237; Fay, Origins of the World War, I, 284-285.

105. After lengthy negotiations and many misunderstandings, Germany and Russia achieved an entente on Aug. 19, 1911, whereby Germany renounced interest in Persia in exchange for Russia's pledge to place no more obstacles against Germany's building of the Bagdad railway. Fay, Origins of the World War, I, 275-276.

106. Carroll, French Public Opinion, 242.

107. Ibid., 244-245; Brandenburg, From Bismarck to the World War, 374-381; Fay, Origins of the World War, I, 286-292; Harris, Europe and Africa, 307.

108. Townsend, Rise and Fall of Germany's Colonial Empire, 322-324.

109. Carroll, French Public Opinion, 245-246; Harris, Europe and Africa, 309; Brandenburg, From Bismarck to the World War, 382-383; Barlow, Agadir Crisis, 363-375.

110. A. N. F. : Imperial German Embassy, aide memoire, July 1, 1911, 881.00/417; Carpenter to Knox, July 1, 1911, 881.00/415; No. 145, July 8, 1911, 881.00/429.

111. A. N. F. : Carpenter to Knox, No. 147, July 11, 1911, 881.00/423; No. 148, July 12, 1911, 881.00/424; No. 152, July 22, 1911, 881.00/418. Wheeler (St.

Petersburg) to Knox, No. 634, July 12, 1911, 881.00/425. Laughlin (Berlin) to Knox, No. 1001, July 13, 1911, 881.00/426.

112. *Ibid.*, Carpenter to Knox, No. 149, July 14, 1911, 881.00/427; No. 154, July 25, 1911, 881.00/435; No. 155, July 28, 1911, 881.00/155.

113. *Ibid.*, Carpenter to Knox, No. 167, Aug. 14, 1911, 881.00/441.

114. *A. N. F.* : Snodgrass (consul general, Moscow) to Knox, Sept. 1, 1911, 881.00/448. Beaupre (The Netherlands), to Knox, Sept. 8, 1911, 881.00/445 and No. 563, Sept. 15, 1911, 881.00/451. Bacon (Paris) to Knox, Sept. 22, 1911, 881.00/449 and Oct. 26, 1911, 881.00/456. Wicker to Knox, No. 186, Oct. 30, 1911, 881.00/465.

115. Quotation from enclosure from *Le Matin* of Oct. 25, 1911, in dispatch of Wicker, Oct. 30, 1911, *A. N. F.*, 881.00/465; "the Franco-German accord regarding Morocco establishes our protectorate over *all* Morocco .... The negotiations can take place on one footing: the evacuation of Alcazar and Larache which Spain has occupied contrary to the provision of the Franco-Spanish treaty of 1904."

116. *A. N. F.* : J. R. C., State Dept. memorandum, 881.00/434; H. W., Dept. of State, memorandum, July 17, 1911, 881.00/437; Legation of Spain, memorandum, Sept. 1, 1911, 881.00/450. Wicker to Knox, No. 175, Sept. 13, 1911, 881.00/453; No. 178, Sept. 28, 1911, 881.00/454; No. 184, Oct. 17, 1911, 881.00/458; No. 187, Oct. 30, 1911, 881.00/464. Scholle (Madrid) to Knox, No. 459, Oct. 3, 1911, 881.00/455.

117. Feis, *Europe, The World's Banker*, 420-421; Stuart, *Tangier*, 52; Fay, *Origins of the World War*, I, 290; Harris, *Europe and Africa*, 309-310.

118. *Ibid.*, 309-312.

119. On January 19, 1912, Carpenter reported to the State Department that the adhesion of the United States, Belgium, The Netherlands, Portugal, and Spain was not yet announced. From the *Daily Telegraph* he cited the comment that the German Government's action at Agadir "was not quite the sudden inexplicable bolt from the blue which we in this country believed it to be, but that it was rather an angry reminder to France that compensation elsewhere had already been distinctly suggested .... It is now fairly clear that the crisis of last summer was really brought to a head by a financial, rather than a political arrangement." He enclosed also an editorial and an article from the London *Times*, suggesting that the Caillaux revelations might cause the other powers to ask France for future guaranties when accepting the Franco-German accord, especially as to the right to purchase land in Morocco. There were constant complaints about difficulties placed in the way of other nationals than French who desired to purchase lands. No. 227, *A. N. F.*, 881.00/488.

120. Schuman, *War and Diplomacy in the French Republic*, 185-186; Carroll, *French Public Opinion*, 248-250; Harris, *Europe and Africa*, 313-314.

121. *Ibid.*, 312-315; Nicolson, *Portrait of a Diplomatist*, 254; Townsend, *Rise and Fall of the German Colonial Empire*, 326-328. Berkheim (Berlin) to de Selves, No. 120, Nov. 15, 1911, *D. D. F.*, Sér. 3, I, 106; Mulai Hafid to de Selves, No. 27, Nov. 6, 1911 and No. 79, Nov. 9, 1911, *Ibid.*, 37 and 76.

122. Grey to Daeschner, No. 128, Annexes I and II, Nov. 14, 1911, *D. D. F.*, Sér, 3, I, 113-114; de Selves to Daeschner, No. 137, Nov. 16, 1911, *Ibid.*, 123.

123. Michon, *Franco-Russian Alliance*, 199-200; Isvolsky to de Selves, No. 18, Nov. 4, 1911, *D. D. F.*, Sér. 3, I, 14-15; No. 52, Nov. 7, 1911, *Ibid.*, 55; Neratoff to de Panafieu, No. 130, Nov. 13, 1911, *Ibid.*, 118.

124. Bernadotte Schmitt, "French Documents on the War," Journal of Modern History, I (Dec., 1929), 638; Crozier (Vienna) to de Selves, No. 152, Nov. 19, 1911, D. D. F., Sér. 3, I, 133-136 and No. 153, Nov. 19, 1911, Ibid., 136; Saint Aulaire to de Selves, No. 371, Dec. 20, 1911, 373-375 and No. 434, Jan. 4, 1912, Ibid., 441-443.

125. Avant-Propos, Ibid.; Schmitt, "French Documents on the War," Journal of Modern History, I (Dec., 1929), 638, 640.

126. Ibid., 638; Klobukowski to de Selves, No. 87, Nov. 10, 1911. D. D. F., Sér. 3, I, 82-83 and No. 295, Dec. 5, 1911, Ibid., 281-282.

127. Schmitt, "French Documents on the War," Journal of Modern History, I (Dec., 1929), 638; Saint-René Taillandier to de Selves, No. 176, Nov. 21, 1911, D. D. F., Sér. 3, I, 166-168; Cambon to de Selves, No. 288, Dec. 4, 1911, Ibid., 272; Saint-René Taillandier to de Selves, No. 334, Dec. 11, 1911, Ibid., 326.

128. Geoffray to de Selves, No. 35, Nov. 6, 1911, Ibid., 43-44; Billy to de Selves, No. 86, Nov. 10, 1911, Ibid., 80-81.

129. Barlow, Agadir Crisis, 376-378; Stuart, Tangier, 53; Harris, Europe and Africa, 316.

130. Ibid., 317; Knight, Morocco as A French Economic Venture, 31-32; Madariaga, Spain, A Modern History, 305; Stuart, Tangier, 53.

131. Carpenter to Knox, No. 232, March 7, 1902, A. N. F., 881.00/493 and No. 234, March 16, 1912, 881.00/495.

132. Landau, Moroccan Drama, 82; Stuart, Tangier, 53-54.

133. Ibid., 78; Harris, Europe and Africa, 320-322.

134. "The night before the signing of his official abdication

Mulai Hafid destroyed the sacred emblems of the Sultanate of Morocco .... He burnt the crimson parasol which on occasions of state had been borne over his head. The palaquin he hewed in pieces and consigned also to the flames, together with the two cases in which certain holy books were carried. The family jewels he took with him. From Rabat, Mulai Hafid proceeded to France, where ... he made a protracted tour .... He returned to Tangier, where his immediate family and retainers--in all about 160 persons--had meanwhile arrived. The old Kasbah was placed at H. M.'s disposal, and there he took up his residence. Almost immediately after his arrival at Tangier began the discussion of the terms of his abdication, for only its more general lines had been settled at Rabat, and in a very short time the ex-Sultan's relations with the French were seriously embroiled. Mulai Hafid did not apparently regret having abdicated .... What he did regret was that he had not made better terms for himself, and he still hoped to be able to extort more money and more properties." W. B. Harris, Morocco That Was, 124-125.

135. Mellor, Morocco Awakes, 43-46; W. B. Harris, Morocco That Was, 123-124; A. N. F., Carptenter to Knox, No. 249, April 22, 1912, 881.00/501; No. 256, May 17, 1912, 881.00/506; No. 276, June 21, 1912, 881.00/512; No. 293, Aug. 15, 1912, 881.00/Y92.

136. Adee to Bacon (Paris), No. 285, Oct. 9, 1911, Ibid., 611.8131/2A.

137. Jusserand to Sec. of State, Nov. 3, 1911, F. R., 1911, 621-622; Adee to Jusserand, Nov. 8, 1911, Ibid., 622.

138. Jusserand to de Selves, No. 60, Nov. 8, 1911, D. D. F., Sér. 3, I, 59-60; No. 81, received Nov. 10, 1911, Ibid., 77; Nov. 21, 1911, Ibid., 165-166. Hale to Knox, memorandum, Nov. 15, 1911.

139. The American Embassy in Paris received a similar answer for transmission to the French government.

Knox to American Embassy, Paris, Dec. 16, 1911, A. N. F., 881.00/476.

140. A note appended to Jusserand's letter on this visit, stamped "Secretary of State," Dec. 20, 1911, reads: "Dear Mr. Anderson: Please take this matter up so we may come to some final decision. Jusserand is making my life miserable. P. K."

141. A. N. F. : Jusserand to Knox, letter, Dec. 6, 1911, 881.00/532; Knox to Jusserand, Dec. 15, 1911, 881.00/532; Jusserand to Knox, letter, Dec. 8, 1911, 881.00/477. Jusserand to de Selves, No. 353, Dec. 16, 1911, D. D. F., Sér. 3, I, 348-350.

142. A. N. F.: Carpenter to Knox, No. 216, Dec. 26, 1911, 881.00/484; Belgian Legation to State Dept., memorandum, Feb. 21, 1911, Ibid., Wilson to Hale, Feb. 21, 1912, 881.00/491.

143. Jusserand to Poincaré, No. 537, Jan. 27, 1912, D. D. F., Sér. 3, I, 557.

Chapter XI

The Era of Lyautey
(1912 - 1925)

On May 12, 1912, General Louis Hubert Gonzalve Lyautey arrived in Tangier. By a presidential decree of April 28 he had been promoted from a General of Division in Algeria to be the first French Resident General of Morocco,[1] with attributes and powers fixed by a later decree.[2] After marching on Fez with a strong force, his first task was to drive the invading Berbers from the city. By June 1 the rebels were totally defeated by Col. Gourad at a nearby town, and another French force was preparing to attack Taza. These military events were the final arguments to persuade Mulai Hafid of the wisdom of abdicating, which he did on August 12. Ranking high in initiative, ability, and experience, Lyautey thus demonstrated at the outset the qualities that would make him the dominant personage among French colonial administrators of his time.[3] He became Lyautey of Morocco, and for thirteen years he ruled his fief as absolutely as any medieval baron--the Quai d'Orsay notwithstanding.

The choice of the new Sultan favored Lyautey's success. Mulai Youssef, the half-brother designated as his heir by the abdicating sultan, was accepted by the ulema of Fez, the sherifs of Wazan, and the chief cities. From the French viewpoint he was an ideal ruler, for his religious temperament and love of pageantry directed his ambitions toward these interests and away from politics and government. The populace loved his frequent displays of pomp and ceremony. The immediate job of Lyautey was to make the Sultan militarily secure. This was done by clearing Fez of insurrection and sending a large force to expel Al Hiba from Marrakesh. The latter feat was accomplished by the aid of the Great Kaids of the Atlas, especially Al Thami Glaoui, who thereafter became one of the props of French power. After this, Lyautey directed a systematic plan of military advance in all directions, and on May 12, 1914, the French troops from east and west made a junction at Taza, thus opening a corridor for railway and motor transport all across the country.[4]

During 1912 the dispatches from Carpenter and Maxwell Blake[5] gave graphic descriptions of Lyautey's difficulties in his adventures against Al Hiba and the Atlas rebels. In July, with the Franco-Spanish protectorate agreement still months in the future, the French Senate was discussing the abolition of protection and French officials were acting as though the forthcoming regime were a fait accompli. Carpenter criticized the Germans for their illegal seizure of land in the Tangier zone and mentioned that Raisuli had been chastised by the Spaniards. Blake was critical of the unseemly haste of the French in substituting their authority for that of the Maghzen before they had received the mandate of the powers to do so. Morocco was under a French military dictatorship, with only Tangier possessing a vestige of Moorish or foreign government. Not only natives, but Europeans as well, suffered spoliation and aggression from French subjects, often "committed with the incredible connivance of French functionaries." Thus at the very beginning of the French protectorate the American representatives in Morocco became hostile critics of the French tactics.

Lyautey had long range projects also that occupied all of his term of office. The "spirit of Lyautey" has been thus described by one of his friendly admirers:

> The exercise of the protectorate ... was ... in the hands of one ... who understood, loved, and admired this country and its people and made it his aim to turn it into a modern nation while fully preserving its characteristics and traditions. On the one hand he demonstrated a brilliant flair for publicity in launching Morocco as a new country and promoting capital investment in it, and on the other he demonstrated a conservative zeal for the preservation of its state and religious institutions, its towns, its antiquities, and its natural wealth. The opening up and exploitation of the Moroccan phosphate mines, which gave the country its first big industry, and their nationalization for the benefit of the Moroccan state, which was thereby put

> on a sound financial footing, bore witness to a far more vigilant concern for the country's interests than had been shown by any sovereign ruler in the Middle East at that time. The "spirit of Lyautey" ... was a strange mixture of extreme modernism and the colonizing spirit of the *ancien regime*, which regarded colonization, not as a business and not just as a matter of prestige, but as a mission ....
>
> French suzerainty over the Sherifate as Lyautey conceived it had a glamourous quality of chivalry and feudal loyalty, which fitted in well with the character of Morocco, but badly ... with the spirit of the plebeian money-seekers who were irresistibly attracted by the North African "California" which was now opened up.[7]

To maintain a nominally "independent" Maghzen, Lyautey set up a Sultan who was really supreme as a religious and social leader, but who docilely signed all political and economic decrees or *dahirs* presented to him by the Resident General. The ancient Maghzen remained, but largely as a shadow government, for French "advisers" were gradually trained to direct every official of the Moorish hierarchy. The Moroccan officials of all ranks were accorded the highest honors and respect by their French monitors, in return for which they gave obedience. Two exceptions may be noted to this general plan; in the town the municipal councils retained a large measure of self-determination, and in the southern part of the country the Great Kaids were practically autonomous feudal lords in collaboration with their French protectors. A notable achievement of Lyautey's administration was the reduction of the corruption and venality so dominant in Moorish political life for many centuries.[8]

The continuous expansion of Moroccan territory by the conquest and control of the *blad-es-siba* was an important element of Lyautey's policy, and for this he had his own system. Tribe after tribe was subdued through a combination of military force, conciliation, and subsequent economic organization, with the ultimate objective of converting today's enemies into friends. By 1914 he had under control twice the territory that he had conquered by 1912. Even during World War I, when German incitement of the natives to rebellion was very active, Lyautey not only held the territory already gained, but also added an additional 20,000 square miles of land. To keep the peace by military insurance, he developed and began operating an elaborate system of transportation and communication. The prodigious task of integrating so many hitherto independent regions was a slow one, however, and Lyautey did not complete it. It was not until 1934 that Morocco might be said to be a consolidated state, with actual boundaries corresponding to the map.[9]

Lyautey's entire work was motivated by his idea of what a protectorate should be:

> The conception of a protectorate is that of a country retaining its institutions, governing itself with its own agencies, administering itself, under the simple control of a European power, which, replacing it in foreign representation, takes over the adminstration of its army and its finances, and directs its economic development. What dominates and characterizes this conception is the idea of control as opposed to that of direct administration.[10]

To Lyautey, the Sultan's sovereignty was not a sham, but a shield to protect himself from the interference of the French parliament. He did not intend to degrade Morocco to colonial status. By gradual evolution he aimed to modernize the antiquated Moroccan government rather than to replace it by a French administration. He wished to be Morocco's representative in France as much as France's representative in Morocco--and in both roles he was "as omnipotent in his African empire as any human being can be," but his despotism was always enlightened.[11]

Lyautey's sole concessions to self government were the regional chambers of agriculture and of commerce and industry. They were appointive and French from 1913 to 1919, and elective for the French and appointive for natives after 1919. However, these bodies were consultative only, having no power but to give the Residency information or advice, when asked, and to pass resolutions. The national Governmental Council met annually to be consulted about the budget already drafted by the Residency. Lyautey granted that some European private enterprise was essential to furnish experiments and models for improving the native society.

But he fought fearlessly against the wrecking of his realm by the Paris government. He reiterated that Morocco was an "autonomous state," and that those who wanted centralization of government were "bureaucrats," "immutable mandarins," "guardians of the sacrosanct administrative verity," "adversaries of all initiative," or "the enemy," He was an opponent of large scale French immigration, and up to his retirement in 1925, only 1.4 million acres were nominally Europeanized, much of it not farmed. These earlier French settlers invested their own capital and bought directly from native owners. They displaced few Moroccans, though they bought the land cheaply from the natives who did not realize its potential value.[12] In his zeal for a scientific reorganization of the country, Lyautey called upon the highest French authorities in finance, land tenure, Muhammadan law, education, and politics to work out plans for regenerating Morocco.[13]

In addition to the military subjugation of dissidents, the modernization of agriculture and industry, the development of an elaborate Franco-Moroccan structure of government safe from Paris, the cultivation of sympathetic and cordial social relations between the French and Moroccan peoples, and the education of a native élite to raise their people to independent status as an ally of France, Lyautey undertook other scarcely less formidable tasks. These were chiefly in the field of foreign relations. Despite the Congo concession to their government, the Germans as individuals refused to consider Morocco closed to their economic activities, especially in the Spanish Zone. In the two wars of Lyautey's experience, they found both the Spanish Zone and the Tangier area ideal environments for intrigues with the Spanish and native conspirators, both directed against the French protectorate. There was much controversy over the eventual type of government for Tangier. Several countries were exasperated over the persistent disregard of the Open Door and the economic equality promised by France in Morocco; the United States continued to demand the right of keeping her capitulatory system. In fact, the American government was inconsiderate enough of France's aims in Morocco to insist on retaining for herself the Act of Algeciras. Furthermore, Lyautey played a big part in saving Morocco for France and in bringing France to victory in World War I. Although he was not in office long enough to defeat

Abd al Krim, Lyautey did help to establish the Franco-Spanish collaboration which resulted in French victory.

American-French relations were really irritating, considering their amicability during the time of Roosevelt, of whom Taft was no passive imitator. Since President Taft had publicly spoken of the agreement of November 4, 1911, as removing the Moroccan question from international concern,[14] France had expected his administration's ready acquiescence in that pact. Also, Jusserand had pointed out to Knox a simple and easy way for the surrender of the capitulatory rights of the United States. However, in the tradition of her Open Door policy and in an endeavor to see whether the deeds of the French government would carry out the promises of Jusserand, the United States maintained an attitude of watchful waiting. The Franco-Moroccan treaty of March 30, 1912, gave a final sanction to the French Protectorate. When sending the text of this treaty to Knox on January 8, 1913, Jusserand requested the adherence of the United States. The reply on January 22 was similar to that given when refusing adherence to the Franco-German treaty of 1911. Knox declined to express any opinion on such parts of the treaty as might be deemed of a political nature. The State Department, he said, was of the opinion that the Franco-Moroccan treaty was not sufficiently detailed in its provisions to permit its being submitted to the treaty-making power of the United States. But if France would give assurance that American interests and rights in Morocco, as safeguarded by existing treaties, would continue to receive the same consideration in the future as in the past, the Government of the United States, on such an understanding would be inclined to view favorably the reforms which the French Protectorate contemplated introducing into Morocco.[15]

During 1913 the American representatives were observing carefully the various devices of the French to secure a privileged position for their nationals. New regulations on land tenure appeared to be "a familiar reassertion ... that preference for her subjects will not be voluntarily abandoned by France in Morocco." As Blake put it:

> The land scandals associated with French policy since the inauguration of France's unrecognized protectorate excite the gravest official suspicions concerning her

> future intentions .... France formerly attacked the evasive policy of the Moorish Government in preventing land acquisitions by foreigners .... French and Moorish jurists now emit certain theories that all land within the Sherifian Empire belongs to the Moorish community, but that the Sultan (read the French Resident General) is fully empowered to dispose of it within the limits defined by the Shera. This theory is probably designed to justify the extensive category of the inalienable lands.

Concerning a dahir imposing military servitude on land within a radius of 250 meters around towns and fortified quarters, Blake said:

> The confiscatory provisions of this proposed regulation are in obvious conflict with treaty rights under extraterritoriality .... The Department cannot but have observed the great anxiety of France, under cover of Sherifian commands, to bring into operation, before the recognition of her Protectorate by the powers, a variety of the most anomalous regulations, such as the arbitrary measures attached to the proposed procedure of land transfers; the tenure of habous property; the attempted restrictions to the right of travel; and now this utterly absurd decree respecting military servitude.

The Department of State backed Blake's protests to the French government, as it did also his action in the next year declining to acknowledge formally a dahir communicated by a minor French official which contravened an article of the Madrid Convention respecting appeals on decisions on land ownership.[16]

During 1913 also the entire Diplomatic Corps was watching intently the progress of Lyautey's efforts to gain control over the serious rebellion in south Morocco. On December 21, 1912, the Sultan's minister for foreign affairs in Tangier drew attention of the Corps to the existing insecurity in various parts of the Empire and requested them to notify their nationals in these regions of the dangers there. The warning undoubtedly emanated from the French headquarters at Rabat. The other powers interpreted it as an attempt to shift France's responsibility for order to the sham Maghzen. In their reply of April 30, the Diplomatic Corps reserved the right to determine, in each particular instance, the extent of the responsibility of the Maghzen.[17]

Blake regretted the large loss of life caused by the immature plans and preparations of the French previous to the actual legal attainment of their protectorate. In their anxiety to realize their political pretensions, he thought, both France and Spain made military matters of incidental rather than primary importance. In July the French Zone was reported quiet after a near disaster and heavy casualties for a French army. In October, however, pacification was reported to be proceeding slowly, with a large part of the Sus in a "state of anti-Protectorate ferment and trade routes north to Mogador at the mercy of holy warriors." To offset this adverse appraisal of Lyautey's campaign, the French Embassy in Washington presented to the Secretary of State a summary by Lyautey of the administrative work done during the past year under his direction. The Residency was planning also for the early creation of French courts in Morocco, which would permit negotiations with the powers signatory to the Act of Algeciras to do away with capitulations.[18]

Communications from the French government regarding the desired American adherence to the French protectorate agreement were frequent during 1913 and until the outbreak of World War I in August, 1914. Many were notifications from Jusserand and others of the adhesion of other powers, designed to make the United States follow suit.[19] Blake informed the State Department that the consensus of opinion in the Diplomatic Corps was that France was beginning efforts to have the other missions suppressed. However, it was not believed that any of the powers would recognize the protectorate until the outstanding difficulties relating to the Tangier government were satisfactorily disposed of; in this prediction Blake proved to be mistaken. Yielding to Jusserand's repeated requests, however, on July 9, 1913, Secretary of State Bryan informed the French government that the post of minister to Morocco was vacant[20] and would remain so; hereafter the United States would have only a consular official in Morocco.[21] On September 30, 1913, Blake reported that all powers except Great Britain, Portugal, and the United States had recognized the French Protectorate, but only three legations had been converted into diplomatic agencies and consulates general; all others were under chargés. Great Britain continued to inform France that she would not recognize the protectorate or apply to her nationals the various measures promulgated by the French Resident General until the international formula for Tangier had been definitely accepted. The original draft for a Tangier convention, unofficially published, had aroused such intense opposition from the French press in both Tangier and Paris that it was now being restudied. There was no doubt, Blake concluded, that France would use every weapon to secure for Tangier a regime international in name but permitting under various disguises the preponderance of French influence.[22]

To obtain a definite opinion concerning recognition, John Bassett Moore, councellor of the State Department, addressed an inquiry to the American representatives at Vienna, Brussels, Berlin, London, Rome, the Hague, Lisbon, St. Petersburg, and Madrid, asking for the conditions of recognition, if granted. The replies, received between January 16 and March 10, 1914, stated that all powers except Great Britain and the United States had now accepted the French protectorate. Germany still kept her minister in Morocco. Franco-German relations were based on the treaty of November 4, 1911, although there were some commercial questions remaining unanswered. Great Britain had made her recognition dependent upon the conclusion of an international agreement on the future government of Tangier. All of the other recognitions had been given without conditions or reservations.[23] However, Russia had not renounced her capitulations in the French Zone until February 10, 1914.[24]

Meanwhile, as the French government continued to press the United States for recognition of her zone, Spain was asking for acknowledgment of her status as a protector state. On April 17, 1913, the Spanish minister informed Bryan of the exchange of ratifications of the Franco-Spanish Treaty on April 2. He next introduced Mulai Mehdi Ben Ismael Ben Muhammad as the newly appointed Khalifa and General Don Felipe Alfau as the first High Commissioner of the Spanish Zone. Blake criticized the doubtful propriety of such an announcement before the formal recognition of the Spanish Protectorate, although it was less irregular than the announcement of the abdication of Mulai Hafid by the French agency at Tangier. Although none of the required formalities had as yet been complied with regarding either French or Spanish occupation in Morocco, yet the Moorish government had passed out of existence. Theoretically, the treaty relations of the powers with Morocco should continue until the protectorates were recognized. Practically, however, all the power of the Sultan's minister for foreign affairs had been completely absorbed by the French and Spanish officers in their zones, and he had been "reduced to a discredited and impotent functionary whose sole privilege it is to receive the complaints of the neutral powers without the faculty of offering redress." Blake also objected because a note received from Al Guebbas named him as "Representative of the French Resident General, General Lyautey, who is the Vizier for Foreign Affairs" of the Sultan. A new rupture in Franco-Spanish relations was approaching because Spain would not concede that France was the sole intermediary between the Sultan and the powers in all affairs; she would agree only to French control over matters affecting all Morocco. In May the French minister gave notice that Moorish subjects in the United States were hereafter under the protection of the Spanish consular establishment in this country.[25]

Some good advice on the Moroccan problem was given to Bryan by his subordinates in the State Department. A memorandum of March 13, 1913, by the Third Assistant Secretary, Chandler Hale, gave an opinion on the proper reply to Jusserand's request of March 8 for American adhesion to the Franco-Moroccan treaty of March 30, 1912. Hale asserted that only on condition of France's giving the United States an official written statement of willingness to assume all the obligations of existing American-Moroccan treaties could the United States comply with the request of France. Without such a safeguard, there would be no appeal to secure American treaty rights. The abrogation of existing treaties with Morocco could be done only by the United States Senate.[26]

In a lengthy communication of March 15, 1913, Blake discussed the argument between France and Spain over their respective powers in Morocco. The point at issue was whether the Anglo-French agreement of 1904 and the Franco-German agreement of November, 1911, authorized the territorial partition of Morocco or only a political division of power within the respective French and Spanish zones. France upheld the former view, which was unacceptable to Germany and Great Britain. The eventual decision was that despite the triangular administration of France, Spain, and international Tangier, all directing Moroccan functionaries, the integral sovereignty of the Sultan would remain in theory. The advantage was that goods paying customs at any point of entry would have free and unrestricted circulation throughout all parts of Morocco. Under cover of a military regime, Blake warned, France would find it more convenient to restrict other European enterprises which tended to usurp the privileges she wanted to reserve for her own nationals. Blake continued:

> French diplomacy ... is in a state of constant antagonism with international obligations and with the stipulations of various existing treaties .... There is a noteworthy silence in the French press and in the official utterances of French functionaries as to the obligations France is under to respect the rights of European nations in Morocco ....
>
> She (France) has repeatedly failed to observe the conventional formalities expected of her and has consistently striven to set aside certain economic and other restrictions under which she is bound by the limitations of her Protectorate as well as by the provisions of treaties between the Powers and the Maghzen.[27]

Another instance of France's insidious extension of her powers was an announcement sent to the State Department by the French ambassador in Washington on August 29, 1913. The trying losses sustained by the French army in recent engagements constrained the authorities to put an end to the smuggling of arms and munitions into the French zone. Accordingly, Lyautey had decided to declare martial law against contraband of arms. Infractions of the law would be tried by military courts.[28] Another change in treaty provisions was reported by Blake. It was a decree changing the regulations regarding the agency of appeal by foreigners and protégés from judgments in real estate cases. This communication was also irregular because the United States had not yet recognized the protectorate.[28]

The indefatigable Jusserand persisted in urging American recognition of the new French courts as a test of friendship for France. Asking for the opinion of the United States about the advisability of submitting to the new judicial organization, the Cuban chargé in Washington was told that the matter was being considered, but that it seemed proper to have outstanding questions with the Moroccan government settled as a part of the recognition of the French protectorate. However, Blake advised waiting for the action of other powers. As a substitute for the existing consular tribunals, France had nothing to offer except a recently established court of French jurists at Rabat, to which appeals from French consular courts were made. Moreover, could the powers without formal conventions renounce their treaties in the French Zone and continue to apply them in the Spanish Zone and in Tangier? Yet Spain with her unsolved military problems was in no position to set up an adequate judicial system.[29]

For over five months before the beginning of World War I, the United States made earnest efforts to settle all causes of dispute with France, while holding fast to her basic principle of safeguarding her treaty rights in Morocco. An extensive and comprehensive summary was prepared by J. B. Moore, then acting secretary of state, to inform the French government of American desires. It was a reply to the French Embassy's notes of August 29, September 14, and October 7, 1913 and January 7, 1914. These notes referred to Lyautey's declaration of martial law, the designation of a delegate to assist in revising the American protégé lists, the placing of American citizens under the French judicial system, and finally the urgent request that the new French courts be recognized at the earliest possible date. Moore's answers to these requests became the official statement of the American position.[30]

Concerning the revision of the lists of American protégés, Moore quoted the provisions of the American-Moroccan Treaty of 1836 and the Madrid Convention of 1880; in neither could he find any warrant for the French contention that the Moroccan government had any right to decide who might become American protégés. That right rested with the American government exclusively. On the French Protectorate, the United States had already expressed itself favorably to the reforms contemplated in the Franco-German Treaty of 1912, providing that the American rights and interests, commercial and otherwise, be preserved as guaranteed by existing treaties. French infractions of these rights were then cited. Quoting the Convention of Madrid and the Act of Algeciras, Moore pointed out that recent regulations gravely threatened the right of Americans to hold land in Morocco. Trade discriminations as practiced by the French authorities included the imposition of customs arbitrarily and withun uniformity, unreasonable export duties or surcharges, and denial of free and open competition in bidding for construction of public works or furnishing of supplies. Examples of these discriminations were given, including the Vacuum Oil Company. The American government desired equal opportunity for its commercial interests "not only to maintain the present standing in Morocco but also to share in the country's commercial development." The United States desired that the awards of the Commission of 1910 be fully paid to the American claimants and that assurance be given that awards under consideration by the present commission be paid within a reasonable time. Mention was made of the case of Jacob Benatuil, an American citizen, for some years in litigation for a strip of land arbitrarily taken for a highway; this case should be settled. There were other matters requiring discussion, but the case mentioned represented the maintenance of American commercial interests in Morocco and the protection of the liberty and property of American citizens and protéges. On these matters the United States desired a definite understanding and settlement preliminary to the recognition of the French Protectorate. In conclusion, Moore called attention to the favorable situation of American missionaries in Morocco and expressed the hope that their privileges would be safeguarded and every facility be granted them to carry on their work.

Blake continued to counsel caution in the surrender of American capitulatory rights. All of the principal signers of the Algeciras Act had received some definite compensation for renouncing their capitulations. The United States was the only great power which had neither received nor expected compensations in exchange for acquiescence in the establishment of the protectorate. It would be inopportune for the United States to surrender any treaty right until satisfied that the regimes substituted by France and Spain had been demonstrated in practice to be acceptable alternatives. Great Britain was refusing formal recognition until the prospective Tangier regime had been accepted by all the signers of the

Algeciras Act. Only then would she discuss revision of her treaties or renunciation of the capitulations on condition of a simultaneous action by France for Egypt. Although Blake endorsed Moore's statement of the American position, he mentioned other cases to consider, the most important being that of Driss Al-Kittany. This American protégé had had several thousand acres of land included by Mulai Hafid shortly before his abdication in a large tract sold to a Spanish subject in the Spanish Zone.[31]

A master of strategy, Jusserand again called at the State Department to repeat his request that the United States accept the jurisdiction of French tribunals in Morocco; the Foreign Office had informed him that the American claims had now been cleared up, except the Vacuum Oil Claim. The Foreign Office would like to know the nature of this claim. Jusserand would prefer an exchange of notes instead of a treaty for the acceptance of French jurisdiction. William Phillips, the third assistant secretary, who conferred with Jusserand, asked Lansing, new secretary of state, whether anything could be done to satisfy Jusserand before the conditions fixed by Moore's note had been met. He also explained the claims of the Vacuum Oil Company; the amount in question was about $1,000, asked for the loss of goods and cash stolen from the company's store during the revolt in Meknes in April, 1911. For Lansing's information, the Counsellor of the State Department sent him a précis of Moore's note of February 13 and mentioned that this note had been neither acknowledged nor answered by the French government.[32]

On April 22 Jusserand did answer Moore's note of February 13. He began by speaking of the high value which France would attach to the acceptance of the French proposal for relinquishment of American consular courts and other extraterritorial privileges in the French Zone. He enclosed the draft of a declaration which fitted the situation to be cleared up. He repeated his assurances that "the Government of the Republic is quite ready to settle in the most friendly spirit the questions of interest to the United States in Morocco that may still be pending."[33] He then proceeded to demolish Moore's list of American grievances. The protégés were of no practical importance to the powers that agreed to recognize the new French courts. All that had been done regarding alien rights of land ownership was to take a "few urgent measures having relation to strategy or prompted by the necessity of checking speculation in land intended for public use." The complaint of the Vacuum Oil Company about customs discrimination had not been brought to the notice of the French government, which recalled "that the treaties in force guarantee equal fiscal treatment to all the Powers." In view of its firm intention to settle in a friendly way the few questions still unsettled, the French government hoped that the United States government would coincide in the views he had just submitted.[34]

However, the Residency evidently considered Moore's list of pending and unsettled cases as worthy of attention. On April 28, 1914, Blake informed the Secretary of State that the French diplomatic agent in Tangier desired a list. He again urged the withholding of recognition of the protectorate until after the satisfaction of these claims. Lansing informed Jusserand that a memorandum was being prepared. On May 14, 1914, Blake transmitted the list of cases, fourteen in all. In presenting it, Blake stated to the Residency that he had not been informed of his government's recognition of the French Zone, to which he had been asked to confine the cases. Later Blake added two supplemental complaints from the Vacuum Oil Company.[35]

To encourage home resistance, Blake reported a recent speech of Zimmerman in the Reichstag, denying that negotiations were proceeding for the suppression of German capitulations. Zimmerman also complained about the French violations of Algeciras Act provisions for public adjudication of public works. As usual, the French had a pretext to justify themselves--the Algeciras Act applied to works ordered by the protectorate government, and not by municipalities, they said.[36]

According to Jusserand's note of June 10, 1914, he had forwarded the State Department notes of February 13 and April 30 to his government, which had promptly taken steps to settle the claims. An agent of the Vacuum Oil Company had informed Lyautey that he had no complaint on customs. Again Jusserand laid stress upon the importance of the earliest possible granting of his request by the American government. Russia, Spain, and Norway had already renounced their extraterritorial rights by signing a declaration like that enclosed in his note to the State Department. Reinforcing this plea was another note which added to the list of countries accepting the French tribunals the names of Luxemburg, Servia, Greece, Montenegro, Sweden, Switzerland, Portugal, and Denmark; Italy and Austria-Hungary were about to act likewise.[37]

Two notes from the French Embassy added weight to Jusserand's arguments. It was admitted that discontinuance of the consular courts would end protection and would also return all former protégés to native status. To prevent any injury to ex-protégés, France would take them under the jurisdiction of the French courts in Morocco as long as they lived. Copies of the law codes in force in the French Protectorate were enclosed to show that the guarantees extended to all foreigners ought to expedite adhesion to the new system by the few countries still outside it. The second note summarized the Residency's reply to Moore's letter of February 13. Excepting in the cases of the Vacuum Oil Company and Benatuil, the State Department had formulated but did not specify any but demands of a purely general character. The protectorate government would respect to the fullest extent the principle of economic equality for all foreigners. It appeared that the United States was questioning the very principle of the Protectorate's regulatory powers. It was never the intention to abolish protection, but merely to stop improper use of it through a joint revision of the lists --which was hardly in accord with the other note. The question of land purchase appeared to have been incompletely studied by the Washington government. In bringing forward the principle that some land is public domain and inalienable, the Resident General was merely availing himself of the power to issue regulations granted by the Franco-German treaty. The Protectorate government was ready to give full consideration to customs grievances when specified. Learning that the customs complaint of the Vacuum Oil Company was at Safi and not at Casablanca, Lyautey was now having the matter investigated. American claims against the Maghzen would be examined as would be all the claims of all foreigners, and claims passed upon by the Commission of 1910 would be paid in full. The Benatuil dispute lay within the Tangier Zone. As for Blake's fourteen claims recently presented, seven were at once stricken out, for five belonged in Tangier and two in Alcazar and Larache. The other seven cases were merely routine judicial ones not of a sort to afford the United States ground for further postponing the relinquishment of her extraterritorial jurisdiction. The Resident General was now having these cases investigated. In conclusion, there was the usual reminder of the high value that the French government would place upon the early accession of the United States to the request first made on August 29, 1913.[38]

But the State Department was now convinced of the need for caution and further study of French diplomacy. Again turning to Blake for advice, it asked him to compare each condition that the Department had stated to be necessary for recognition of the French Protectorate with the statements in the French reply and to furnish it with his views as to what steps to take next. The State Department did not demur to the French government's position that it could answer only for cases in its own zone. Blake's reply was dated November 5, 1914; he had assumed that the war would suspend all negotiations with the United States as it had on the Tangier government. As the promised settlement of the American claims had not been made in three months, there was no reason to delay his reply longer.

Apparently there was a wide discrepancy in the exchange of views. The State Department seemed to be considering a simple recognition of the French Protectorate, but the French chargé had repeatedly stated that the discussions concerned the acceptance of the jurisdiction of the French courts in Morocco by the United States. This confusion had to first be cleared up. It would seem that the formal recognition of the protectorate must come first. An act of recognition implied no abatement of treaty rights. Great Britain was postponing her recognition until after the international status of Tangier was settled, and the United States was conditioning hers upon the prior settlement of all claims against the government to be superseded. Recognition of the protectorate was entirely separate from the suppression of the capitulatory regime. Only Great Britain and the United States had not recognized the protectorate; only Russia, Spain, Portugal, Luxemburg, and some Scandinavian states had surrendered their extraterritoriality. Italy was still seeking for compensations. Before the outbreak of war, both Germany and Austria-Hungary had recognized the French Protectorate but had refused to give up their extraterritoriality until the French tribunals had offered a sufficient guarantee for the rights of their subjects. The American note had not even mentioned the surrender of capitulary rights. The Department had no alternative but to question the regulating powers of a protectorate administration attempting to promulgate legislation affecting the vested interests of American subjects, not only before its power to do so had been officially recognized by the American government, but also when the legislation appeared to be contrary to treaty provisions. The French government was well aware that protection would be nullified by the abolition of the consular tribunals. Until the last few weeks, it had been impossible to obtain transfers of property purchased and sold by American citizens in the Tangier Zone more than two years ago, because the Moorish authorities contended that the new land regulations interdicted the transfer. Recently two transfers had been completed. Locally, every effort had been directed toward the retroactive application of the land regulations to American holders of Haboo properties. Unless strict insistence was maintained upon the fulfillment of treaty provisions, the determined aim of the French to undermine foreign rights in Morocco would be reached as rapidly as possible. As for bids on public works, the Department could ask for nothing else than a strict observance of the Act of Algeciras. If France were really sincere, a few hours' parley could settle all American complaints. The Department might consider it inexpedient at present to consent to any substitute for the form of government provided for in American treaties. In no event must France expect more than the formal recognition of the protectorate, after all American claims had been settled. The American Legation at Tangier, replaced by an agency and consulate general could then discuss all reforms contemplated by France and Spain. It could then accept and apply to its nationals all decrees and any laws not incompatible with existing treaties. Finally, when the Department had observed the satisfactory workings of the French and Spanish judicial systems, it would be in a position to examine benevolently the question of the suppression of American consular courts in Morocco.[39]

The guns of August echoed over a Morocco only partially prepared militarily or economically to maintain herself as a political entity. That it remained a French protectorate was one of the authentic miracles of World War I. The capture of Taza on June 10, 1914, opened up direct communication between eastern and western Morocco, for this town commanded the one pass through the Atlas Mountains. It enabled the transfer of troops to Agadir, from which a campaign was planned to subjugate the federation of the Great Kaids, who had never submitted to any sultan. It also created the possibility of using the Oran-Fez trade route, whereby the French could bypass the Open Door through the Atlantic ports of Morocco. On July 26 General Gourad set off to conquer the few remaining hill tribes near Taza, when suddenly the world conflict intervened--a rude interruption of the French imperial program in Morocco. However, in a little over two years, in addition to his impressive work in military "pacification," Lyautey had achieved a rapid centralization of officialdom at Rabat, from which he sought to persuade the other powers to renounce their special treaty privileges and to eliminate all foreign interests in Morocco.[40]

On July 27, 1914, Lyautey received a message from the French minister of foreign affairs stating that war was probable and instructing him to reduce the occupation to the chief coastal ports and, if possible, to retain also Kenifra and the Meknes-Fez-Udja railway. He was to send to France every available soldier. Lyautey's decision was to save Morocco for France. He not only sent all the fighting troops asked for, but he also extended the boundaries of his command and held it with "territorials" sent from France. He trained new native troops to send regularly to France and to supplement his own forces. From France he received industrial experts to take charge of the economic front which he was planning. He himself by personal example set up an impregnable psychological front, inspiring in the natives an air of nonchalance toward the war. No counter-propaganda was necessary--the increase of prosperity brought by the war promoted a sense of security and material well-being. At last Lyautey was freed from the obstructions to his program from the French parliament, so harassing that during the summer of 1913 he had seriously considered resignation. While the war lasted, his power in Morocco was greater than any king. He was the only one of his group of colonial administrators who achieved anything like its ideal of a free hand with responsibility. He suffered only one brief interruption from his work in Morocco. With General Gourad relieving him as resident general, he became minister of war in France on December 13, 1916. However, he was without real power in Paris, and he resigned on March 14, 1917. By May 29, 1917, he was back at work in Casablanca.[41]

The economic development begun before the war was accelerated as a war measure. Lyautey designed it to create a demand for labor and to impress the natives by the rapid expansion of markets and commercial facilites. Chosen by him as the principal port, Casablanca grew from a small fishing village to be the commercial capital of the country. Harbor improvements were extensive and the European section was a model of city planning. Many outposts of expansion developed into real towns.[42]

Of great value for the morale of the natives were the fairs held in Casablanca, Fez, and Rabat in 1915, 1916, and 1917 to exhibit the industrial and artistic products of France and other parts of Europe, together with the native arts and crafts. The pageant-loving Moroccans flocked to see the exhibits, and a great impetus was given to the development of the exhibitions and schools of native art industries which Lyautey was building at the time.[43]

Transportation was the basic necessity for any sort of development. In 1911-1912 the movement and supplying of troops had revolutionized the primitive transport facilities. Wheeled traffic was introduced to replace the overworked camels, who were inadequate to carry certain indivisible loads. In many places at once narrow-gauge railways were begun to make vital connections. The sixty-mile line from Casablanca to Rabat was completed in three months. Trails were converted into dirt roads with the necessary bridges for wheeled vehicles. Automobiles were soon running even on poor roads. By the end of 1919, there were 1400 miles of national roads and 1600 miles of secondary roads, and although they were hard to keep in repair, there was much truck and motorbus traffic on them. Since the Franco-German treaty required the building of the Tangier-Fez line before any other commercial railways, the building of the latter was delayed. The chief cities of the Atlantic coast were soon connected by narrowgauge military railroads, which were open to commerce also in March, 1916. In 1917 the railway system totalled about five hundred miles.[44]

Throughout the war, all types of public works were constructed--not only roads and railways, but bridges, harbors, water power and irrigation systems, telegraph and telephone lines, public buildings, infirmaries, and schools. This was a policy of prestige; the natives had to be convinced that France was able, even in wartime, to care for their welfare. The Resident General was now successful in obtaining almost all the French financing that he asked for.[45]

Since finance had long been one of the major problems of Morocco, it may seem extraordinary that she could afford such large expenditures during wartime. As an indigent state, Morocco had been living on loans since 1904. These loans were not money advanced by the French government, but were guaranteed sums it had authorized Morocco to borrow from capitalists. From the occupation of Casablanca in 1907 to the end of 1913, the French parliament appropriated about $95,000,000 for "additional expenses" of the army in Morocco. This was supposed to be about forty percent of the total expenses, the other sixty percent being regular grants sufficient for the troops in French barracks. Not until after the French intervention in 1911 was there any surplus to invest in economic development. Specifically authorized by the Act of Algeciras was the revenue from a two and one half percent ad valorem additional import tax. Added to this were loans of 242,000,000 francs guaranteed by France in 1914-1916 and 110,000,000 francs from surpluses of 1915-1920 inclusive. In 1916 Morocco began to assume local police and military expenses formerly borne by France. After order was restored, expenditures of the Moroccan government rose from 16,000,000 francs (about $3,000,000) in 1913-1914 to 31,000,000 francs in 1914-1915 and from 84,000,000 francs in 1918.

In 1918 Blake commented on the very liberal policy in allocating to Morocco the sums required for execution of public works projected before the war. These expenditures, he said, were actuated by political considerations "to reduce discontent and intrigue by absorbing, as far as possible, the energies and activities of native labor." He noted also that the last Moroccan loan, authorized on February 24, 1918, was for 205,000,000 francs, to be devoted to the building of public works.[47]

The general military occupation caused a great increase in commerce. Imports rose from about 50,000,000 francs in 1910 to 181,000,000 francs in 1913; exports lagged far behind. An enormous import balance has been characteristic of French Morocco. Much of this excess of imports represented equipment, both public and private, financed by French investors. A minor part of the capital was brought to Morocco by private owners. Military expenditures stimulated economic life greatly and presented no problem of later repayment. From 177,000,000 francs in 1912, Morocco's trade increased to 707,000,000 francs in 1919.[48]

Fulfilling his promise to extend the boundaries of the _blad al maghzen_, Lyautey proceeded relentlessly but always diplomatically to use his depleted forces to the best advantage. His mobile guards patrolled constantly to protect subdued tribes and to forestall revolts. He acted on the principle that today's enemy may be tomorrow's ally. During Lyautey's absence in France, General Lamothe crossed the Atlas, occupied Agadir and Tiznit, and proclaimed the Sultan's authority in the Sus. After his return, the garrisons at Meknes, Debdu, and Bu Deneb joined hands over the intervening spaces. At the end of 1917, France held securely about 90,000 square miles. There remained unconquered an isolated region just south of Taza, a strip along the Spanish Zone, and the main block of the south central mountains. In 1920 Lyautey drew up plans to complete the conquest in three years. This proved to be impossible. In July, 1922, about one third of the country was still unsubdued, and Parliament was forced to retrench and cut down the French forces drastically in 1923 and 1924. The flexibility of Lyautey's policy allowed him to adopt the Great Kaid policy. The great feudal chiefs were bribed to accept French overlordship over one fourth of Morocco southward from Marrakesh and entirely in the Sus. Here the cohorts of the Glaoui, the Goundafui, and the M'Tougi princes kept order and quelled revolts, enabling the diminished French forces to maintain peace elsewhere and Lyautey to send Moroccan divisions to the French front. As a reward, the chiefs were permitted to maintain a benighted and brutal feudal system in their domains.[49]

By practically stripping the pacified coastal regions of troops, Lyautey accomplished wonders with his improvised army. French reservists were sent over to serve as his main military and industrial army. These were supplemented by detachments of Berbers, black riflemen from Senegal and the Sudan, Algerians, and the French Foreign Legion. The last group, composed chiefly of Germans, but containing many other Europeans and even Americans, was famous for its reckless bravery. Of the 163,000 Negro troops who fought in World War I, 30,000 fought in the Somme. However, they were most effective fighting in the Moroccan contingents against the Berbers of the Atlas regions.[50]

Of the numerous wartime problems of Lyautey, none was more serious than the Germans. Before the war, they had determined to compel France to observe her treaty with them in respect to the commercial equality of all countries in Morocco. While Germany kept her capitulations there, a number of her merchants watched to see that France did not "Tunisify" Morocco gradually. At the outbreak of the war, all Germans were either arrested or expelled from the French Zone to the "neutral" Tangier and Spanish Zones. From Tangier, Tetuan, and Larache, the Germans carried on an impassioned campaign against the French. Among the hostile tribes and in the Spanish Zone the call to a Holy War was sounded. Money was poured into these regions to purchase adherents to Germany's cause, and Turkish agents flooded the dissident areas with anti-French literature. Spying became a common occupation. The Spanish authorities were benevolent toward the German agents, and Raisuli, still the paid agent of the German consul, laughed at both Germans and Spanish. One of the greatest necessities was to keep open the Fez-Taza-Ujda railway and road. Repeatedly the Germans tried to cut this line. From the Spanish Zone, many raids were made by Riffs in German pay and also by a rebel renegade in charge of Riffian and Arab tribesmen. Occasionally the telegraph wires were cut. It was feared also that the rebels of the "<u>tache de Taza</u>" might join those from across the Spanish line. By establishing posts to the north of the railroad, the number of raids was decreased. In spite of much insidious propaganda, the French Moroccans remained loyal; Lyautey's deeds spoke louder than the Germans' words. Yet it was a great temptation to Morocco, emerging from chaos, to decide against the continuance of a foreign and religiously alien domination and for a possible restoration of their country's independence and integrity and a sovereign sultan of their own nationality and religion.[51]

Concerning the German propaganda, there are two interesting reports from American agents. In 1916, Hoffman Philip, now stationed at Constantinople, enclosed a report from a former French official describing the propaganda being carried on in Germany to persuade Muslim sharpshooters taken prisoner in Belgium and northern France to go to Constantinople. There some were allowed full liberty at the price of near starvation; the majority joined the Turkish army and some had already left for Asia Minor.[52] Blake described German propaganda in Morocco. Spies were extensively employed, and Spain was the base for the propaganda, directed by German and Austrian consuls in the Spanish Zone. Recently rumors had been disseminated of enormous loss of life in the sinking of American transports and of the total absence of American soldiers on the European front. Promises were made by Germany to restore the independence of Morocco under the rule of Raisuli. While the natives were perhaps incapable of appreciating the issues or the motives for American entry into the war, they believed that the war would have been lost but for American intervention.[53] Later reports from Blake during 1918 confirmed these news items and opinions, emphasizing the Spanish hatred for the French because of Tangier and the growing popularity of the American army in Europe. Lyautey was praised for his "clever coordination" in carrying on pacification with constantly depleted forces.[54]

As the representative of the chief neutral power in Morocco, on August 14, 1914, Blake had been assigned the protection of German and Austrian nationals and their property in the French Zone.[55] A very extensive correspondence ensued during 1914 and 1915 between the American, French, German, and Austrian representatives concerning the disposition of the prisoners, which included all Germans and Austrians in the French Zone, except those who escaped before they could be taken into custody. They were accused of espionage, possession of contraband weapons, correspondence with Moroccan rebels, incitement of revolts, and similar offenses. Blake tried to offer impartial service for the Germans, who were first interned at Oran and later taken to Casablanca for court martial. Regarding several he expressed the opinion that the evidence against them was insufficient or untrustworthy; some were charged with offenses prior to the protectorate. There were some summary executions, but Blake's influence probably secured a reduction of some long prison terms. Two of those executed, Blake thought, "represented, in the eyes of the natives, German influence and German policy, and it was considered that the public execution of these two prominent and formerly influential German merchants would convince the Moors of the futility of looking henceforth for any support from Germany. However, Blake refused to judge whether public opinion was warranted in considering the condemned merely as political victims.[56] The French government refused to exchange any of their German prisoners for Frenchmen accused of similar offenses in Germany.[57] As an instance of Blake's loyalty to the Allied cause, after the United States entered the war, may be cited the fact that he suggested hydroplane stations at Tangier, the Azores, and the coast of Portugal for aerial scouting to guard against submarine attacks in the Atlantic approaches to the Mediterranean.[58]

The loyalty of the masses in French Morocco was demonstrated not only by their refusal to be enticed by Germany, but also by their postive contributions to the economy of their country. Immigration from France was practically stationary during the war. It was the few French colonials and the majority of the natives who produced most of the cereals, eggs, vegetables, and hides exported to Europe at good prices.[59] In some ways the war improved conditions in Morocco. The capital there was augmented by exports but also by military appropriations and loans. Many Moroccans were serving for pay in France, in the armed forces and in industry, and their remittances home made life easier there. Lyautey shrewdly kept sugar plentiful at moderate prices, and the farmers had no way of knowing that France was not paying them full world market prices for their products.[60]

The war was still young when an American columnist proposed a solution for such causes of international strife as existed in backward countries like Persia and Morocco. He said that an international protectorate would deprive competitive imperialism of its excuse and its stimulus to war.[61] Throughout the war, however, Lyautey never forgot that his aim was to abolish international control, limited as it was, over Morocco. There are numerous dispatches from Blake in the files of the National Archives relating violations of the Act of Algeciras or former treaties by the Resident General. The complaints were varied. They included the appeal of a case to the French Court of Appeals instead of to the Sultan's minister for foreign affairs at Tangier, a decree of the Residency prohibiting export of certain goods, numerous calls for bids for public works put out by the Residency instead of the Committee of Public Adjudications and Contracts, and abrupt withdrawal of the power of the Diplomatic Corps over maritime sanitary matters.[62] All were in violation of treaty rights still claimed by the United States. The big cause of Franco-American friction, however, was the refusal of the United States to accept the French Protectorate or to surrender her extraterritoriality. On November 4, 1914, Jusserand returned to his unfinished task.

Reiterating his request for American surrender of capitulations, the ambassador disposed of the claims submitted by Blake in summary fashion; they were settled, to be settled by habou law, or were minor matters being investigated for settlement. Blake pointed out that Lyautey had inquired about the claim of the Vacuum Oil Company at Casablanca, where the loyal sub-agent was incompetent to answer for company affairs in all French Morocco. In late December Blake reported that Great Britain had proclaimed a protectorate over Egypt and would recognize the French Protectorate in exchange for recognition of her Egyptian protectorate. It was reported that a rapid agreement had been made about internationalization of Tangier, but the suppression of British capitulations had been reserved for future discussion. Blake saw no reason to depart from the position on American capitulations that he had consistently advocated.[63] But the United States was now threatened with a new isolation in defiance of French policy on Morocco.

The next dispute was over two wartime regulations by the Resident General. The first was a "sultanic" decree, or dahir, that goods imported into Tunisia and Morocco must have certificates of origin and the visa of a French consul. Putney of the Division of Near Eastern Affairs advised reminding the French officials that the United States was maintaining her stand that her demands already presented must be met before she would agree to any innovations or surrender any rights in Morocco. Lansing informed Jusserand to this effect. In reply, Jusserand quoted Briand as saying that the requirement of certificates of origin was intended to prevent Germany from exporting to Morocco her own goods which had been fictitiously nationalized in a neighboring country. This measure was unlikely to apply to American goods.[64] The second case was the decision of the Resident General that the dahir of August 10, 1915, relating to military requisitions should be of the competency of the military courts and that it would be applied to everyone, even to a "ressortissant" of a power still retaining capitulatory rights in French Morocco. This application to American nationals was protested to the French Minister for Foreign Affairs, Aristide Briand. He replied that the Resident's order was a military regulation necessitated by the state of siege declared in August, 1914 and was not a permanent change of judicial regime. Moreover, Lyautey's action had helped to keep good order by placing certain cases under the military authorities.[65] France was taking every possible advantage of her military situation, as Blake had predicted.

During 1916 the recognition-capitulations battle continued. On February 12, 1916, Jusserand suggested that American compliance with French wishes re Morocco would be much appreciated in return for France's past conformity with American policy in Haiti. He understood that all important American claims had been satisfied. Again Blake was asked to state his views on American conditions. If the State Department did not choose to demand first the full satisfaction of claims pending against the old Moorish regime, only two of which had been definitely settled since July 16, 1914, Blake had other suggestions. Before recognition of the French regime, the United States should obtain explicit guarantees from the French and Spanish governments for equality of economic treatment, preservation of the Open Door, and reaffirmation of the Act of Algeciras provisions on customs and adjudication of contracts for public works. Recognition would in no wise alter any previous American treaties or the most favored nation clause. Following recognition of the protectorate, the abrogation of capitulations would be reserved for future consideration and would depend upon satisfactory settlement of all claims in the French and Spanish zones. In the latter the settlement of the Kittany claim was important; arbitration by three impartial members of the Diplomatic Corps might be substituted for the treaty provision on appeal.[66]

Responding to Lansing's inquiry as to which countries had recognized conditionally and which unconditionally the French and Spanish protectorates,[67] Blake replied that Belgium, The Netherlands, and Portugal had given an unreserved acceptance of them. Great Britain was making conditions on Tangier and France's recognition of the Egyptian protectorate. The question of Italy's surrender of capitulations was reserved and conditions were imposed, such as the right to establish Italian schools in the French Zone. As from March 20, 1916, Italy had withdrawn her capitulations in the French Zone, but she was still negotiating about the Spanish Zone. Italy refused verbal agreement with France and required the publication of the concessions granted by France. Mr. White, the British diplomatic agent, said that a British reservation was that no taxes were to be levied on British subjects without their government's consent. Little attention was being paid to the Spanish Zone, where there was tribal unrest and hopeless administrative chaos.[68]

Apparently, in the latter part of 1916 Jusserand was nearing his goal. On July 1, 1916, Lansing sent him a communication detailing the conditions under which he was prepared, out of friendship for France, to recognize the French Protectorate. The government of France was asked to guarantee six conditions. The vested rights of American citizens and protégés in property would be respected and confirmed, and existing treaty rights respecting the purchase and sale of land would be preserved. Equality of opportunity would be accorded to American commercial interests, including equal treatment on import and export duties and equal chance to share in construction of public works and furnishing of governmental supplies. The United States and her citizens should possess the rights of the most favored nation within the French Zone, and, so far as France was concerned, within the international zone of Tangier. The American claims against the government of Morocco would be adjusted within a reasonable time, including the awards of the Claims Commission of 1910 and of the present Claims Commission as well as subsequent claims. The American rights in the Spanish Zone or in the Tangier Zone would not, in any way, insofar as France was concerned, be prejudiced or adversely affected by either recognition of the French Zone or the surrender of capitulary rights. If a mixed court of justice should be created in Tangier to exercise judicial powers formerly held by consular officers under the capitulations, the United States should have the right to appoint an American as a member of such a court or courts, without prejudice to American rights in Tangier. A Franco-American treaty would be the most practical way to divest American consuls of their judicial powers and Lansing would be pleased to enter into negotiations for the surrender of capitulatory rights when the guarantees mentioned were assured to the United States.[69]

Countering Lansing's proposals, on July 21, 1916, Jusserand sent him a declaration signed by all the powers signatory to the Act of Algeciras (except the United States) and by the South American republics.[70] It provided for the abrogation of capitulations only, and was desired for the sake of uniformity. Jusserand suggested that a modiciation of the last paragraph might be necessary to include the necessary ratification by "the President of the United States." As usual, Blake was called upon for comments and suggestions. He pointed out that this declaration was simply for the abolition of capitulations, and if signed before recognition of the protectorate, the Moroccan government would not become a party to it. He felt that French tribunals would not be competent to pass upon the present subject of controversy, and this reservation as well as all other guarantees ought to be confirmed by separate communications.[71]

On July 26, 1916, Jusserand apparently sought another formula to evade those vexing conditions upon which the State Department was so insistent. He told Polk, the acting secretary of State, that the United States "should not require the French Government to definitely state exactly what they would do, as he felt that a general statement would be sufficient and we could rely on his Government to do their part." Later he wrote Lansing that his government would have no objection to having the abrogation of capitulations be effected by a treaty instead of a declaration. He suggested a form similar to that used for Tunisia in 1904, which, however, was in no sense a treaty. On October 3, 1916, Jusserand had still another idea. His government was disposed, he reported, to accompany an exchange of notes with a convention relative to the abrogation of capitulations and to the recognition of the French Protectorate. The notes would contain four stipulations decidedly altering the demands last made by Lansing.[72] Lansing assured Jusserand that the views of the American government would be presented as soon as there was opportunity to consider them.[73] Thus the matter rested at the end of 1916.

During the next year some definite progress appeared to be made by France. On January 2, 1917, Lansing answered Jusserand's communications of July 31, August 26, and October 3, 1916. He had decided that because of the Senate's busyness at that time, a treaty concerning capitulation was not feasible. Therefore, the best procedure would be to act separately on recognition of the Protectorate and on capitulatory rights, as all the European powers had done. Lansing was prepared to recognize formally the French Protectorate and to recommend that the item of salary for the minister in Morocco be changed in the pending appropriation bill in Congress to one for a diplomatic agent. The question of capitulatory and other American rights in Morocco could then be considered in due time. Jusserand replied with appropriate emphasis on friendship, but earnestly requested an immediate decision on the capitulations so that the Senate could act on the treaty as soon as possible. As he admitted, "recognition of our Protectorate will have its effects only when this question is settled." Lansing's formal note of recognition,[74] dated January 15, 1917, read as follows; "The Government of the United States ... has concluded to recognize, and hereby formally recognizes, the establishment of the French Protectorate over the French Zone of the Sherifian Empire." This note was sent after a lengthy written review of the Moroccan situation had won President Wilson's approval of it.[75]

The question of the recognition of the French Protectorate was still <u>not</u> answered, however. On January 19 Jusserand objected to Lansing's formula, saying "In reality the Protectorate established by France in Morocco, with the assent of its ruler, covers the whole of that country as evidenced by ... the treaty of March, 1912 .... Every power, Spain included, has recognized that our Protectorate was coextensive with the total area of Morocco .... Kindly cause this involuntary error to be amended." Lansing tried again, formally recognizing "the Protectorate of France over Morocco." Then the Spanish ambassador in Washington stated that his country could not agree to American recognition of the French Protectorate over the whole of Morocco unless the Spanish Zone were clearly set forth. Thereupon Lansing inquired at Madrid, London, and Tangier regarding the expression used by the other powers when granting recognition. Page, American ambassador in London, reported that the British recognition consisted of adherence to the Franco-Moroccan treaty of March 30, 1912, and Blake cited similar action by Russia, Belgium, The Netherlands, and Italy. Blake pointed out that this treaty defined Spain's special rights and privileges and guaranteed the special government for Tangier. However, Spain went on to inform the United States that according to the Franco-Spanish Convention of 1912, there were two protecting governments over Morocco. Moreover, the Spanish government was exercising its protectorate under conditions prohibiting any intervention by either France or the Sultan. Therefore, the United States should recognize both protectorates at the same time, stating in both recognitions that in practice there existed two zones of protection, entirely independent of each other.[76]

As always, Blake kept a close watch on British action concerning capitulations. He sent to the State Department an article republished from The African World, a British publication. This told of the incorporation of the British Merchants' Morocco Association to promote and protect British interests by seeing that Moroccan treaties were respected and that British rights were not bartered away. The British Chamber of Commerce at Tangier had recently been formed for similar purposes. France's aspiration to establish commercial exclusivism was indicated not only by the flood of innovations from the Residency and the arbitrary applications of these regulations, but also by public utterances of the Resident General. At a banquet at Casablanca on April 2, 1916, Lyautey said:

> They (existing tariffs) are imposed upon us by international acts from which we shall be able to liberate ourselves only after the war, but ... at Paris ... and here ... consideration without respite is being given to the regime which will allow us later on to develop industry, agriculture, and commerce in new conditions of

> liberty .... Certainly, we will refrain from all exclusivism .... But at least ... we Frenchmen, who have brought here our blood, our efforts, and our capital, should have the right to benefit here of ... priority which ... I shall always be the first to vindicate.

The British community in December, 1916, addressed a memorial to the Foreign Secretary. All the questionable "reforms" dealt with were reported to the State Department by Blake. Sooner or later the United States would have to give serious consideration to preserving the Open Door. Neither Great Britain nor Italy would envisage the closing of Morocco to the enterprise of their nationals.[77]

Not until October 20, 1917, did the State Department try to satisfy both "protectors" of Morocco. Then a note was issued recognizing the French Protectorate over Morocco, subject to the informal note of January 2, 1917, and subject also to the special rights and privileges of Spain in Morocco.[78]

Reporting the confidential information that negotiations were under way for a reciprocal suppression of capitulations by Great Britain in Morocco and by France in Egypt, Blake thought that in such an event the French government would undoubtedly urge American renunciation of capitulations also. Again he warned that such actions should be conditional upon the settlement of all outstanding matters between the United States and French Morocco. A few days later he sent a detailed report to the Residency concerning the claims of two Americans and the estate of Captain John Cobb, all dated in 1917, but of many years standing. Apparently Lyautey was at last impressed by American insistence on settlement of claims, for on February 28, 1918, Blake notified the State Department that a _proces verbal_ had been drawn up defining the method of disposing of all still unsettled claims. By March 9 he was able to report that Al Khazan of the Tangier agency had traveled around to investigate the claims, accompanied by a representative of the Residency, that there were no serious difficulties, and that agreement had been reached in all cases.[79] This was a real triumph for Blake. There now seemed to be no reason for further delay in American renunciation of capitulations.

During the last year of the war, however, there was

a new turn of events. On April 14, 1918, Jusserand conveyed Briand's message that "the special rights and privileges of Spain in Morocco" were exclusively those given her by the Franco-Spanish convention of November 27, 1912. He hoped that the Secretary of State would sign with him the declaration submitted in his note of July 31, 1916. The willingness of the French government to settle American claims had been demonstrated. On April 25 Jusserand wrote of the final settlement of the last American claim in Morocco. Again he asked for the signing of the declaration; there was no longer any cause for the United States to maintain extraterritoriality in a country where her interests were small and her citizens and protégés were few.[80]

Another plea for advice went to Blake, with a particular inquiry about the present and prospective status of Tangier. British consular jurisdiction would be surrendered, Blake thought, when an understanding was reached concerning Morocco and Egypt. Her agent said that Great Britain proposed to negotiate a new treaty ultimately to safeguard equal commercial and economic opportunity in Morocco. So far, France had not attempted to enforce any edicts in Tangier, but since the war began France had claimed that the administration of the city was provisionally under the Sultan. As usual France and Spain were rivals for prestige in Tangier. Blake saw no objection to withdrawal of American capitulations in Tangier, but this action must in no wise affect American privileges in Tangier or Spanish Morocco. It was not an opportune time, however, to make a treaty until the future of all parts of Morocco could be foreseen. Amerian judicial privileges might be withdrawn from the French Protectorate, leaving arrangements for the other parts to a future date. The Division of Near Eastern Affairs suggested that France might be informed that it would be too difficult at present to get Senate action on a treaty dealing only with one aspect of the Morocco problem. It might be best for the State Department to suspend extraterritorial rights in French Morocco temporarily. Then, after the fixing of the status of Tangier, the settlement of all American-Spanish disputes, and the decision of the respective rights and authority of France and Spain in Morocco, by a single treaty the United States might answer the whole Moroccan question. As the exclusive agent of the Sultan, France could settle by treaty all matters in dispute. However,

Jusserand should be told again that the United States expected a share in the control of Tangier. The Solicitor's Office added the comment that the guarantee of Franco-American treaties by the proposed declaration would be worth little if the rumor were true that France intended to renounce all her commercial treaties soon. The same office gave the opinion that if extraterritoriality could be suspended temporarily, it could be indefinitely; Congress had made such suspensions before. All pending matters, not merely claims, should be taken care of before further concessions by the United States.[81]

Before Jusserand could dispatch another plea, the Armistice intervened. On November 14, 1918, he wrote Lansing for a reply to his two unanswered notes of April. He tried to dispel any apprehension about the aboliton of capitulations. It appeared that by adhesion to the agreements of November 4, 1911, and March 30, 1912 the United States had virtually bound herself to close her consular courts in Morocco. To ensure commercial equality in Morocco, he invoked the guarantees of the most favored nation clause, the Algeciras convention, and the treaty of November 4, 1911. As before, he reminded the United States of the good will that France had given her in several countries over which American control had been exercised for a number of years.[82]

Shortly thereafter, Blake informed the State Department of a revised Moroccan policy which France might present to the coming peace conference. New elements entered the confused Moroccan situation. The United States was preparing to refund the 1912 loan to Liberia, thus ousting Great Britain and France from financial control of that country. France replied orally that she would not release the United States in Liberia unless her request regarding Morocco were granted. In a review of State Department policy since July 1, 1916, the Solicitor's Office suggested that the urgency of France might be due to her desire to have the matter settled before the peace conference. The French were probably much more desirous of having the United States out of Morocco than the Americans were of getting France out of Liberia. The best policy would be to negotiate a treaty surrendering capitulatory rights and obtaining for the United States equal commercial opportunity and protection of vested interests in Morocco.[83]

Now that the great war was over, all the world statesmen were preoccupied with the grand design of building a new international order. But the treaty of peace was being planned by architects who proposed to advance the objectives of their own countries. In regard to Morocco, France, Spain, and Great Britain particularly considered the treaty of peace as a welcome opportunity to correct the errors of the past. Undoubtedly, Blake warned the American Peace Mission at Paris, these three countries had definite plans for revision of the status of that country. The United States must take a positive stand, probably with the support of Great Britain, Italy, and the smaller neutral powers, to maintain the Open Door policy.[84] In a second more comprehensive memorandum containing a history of the Moroccan problem since 1904, Blake suggested a compromise solution to resolve conflicting national ambitions in Morocco.[85]

At a meeting of the Bureau of the Conference on February 18, 1919, Clemenceau first gave notice that France desired to abolish some stipulations of the Act of Algeciras. Speaking for France at a later meeting of the Bureau, M. de Peretti exposed her full demands. They were the abolition of the Act of Algeciras, the Franco-German Agreements of February 2, 1909, and November 4, 1911, and all treaties and agreements between Germany and Morocco. France would keep the Open Door in Morocco, but Tangier must be annexed to the French Zone. In a long and impassioned speech, Peretti denounced Germany for her decade of harassment of France and her obstruction to the spread of civilization. Spain also received her share of castigation for her conduct during the war.[86]

Again, on February 25, 1919, Blake came to the rescue of the Algeciras Act. The first two principles of the Act had already been repudiated--the Sultan was no longer sovereign and the integrity of the empire was gone--but the policy of the Open Door was still theoretically intact. It was felt that the guarantees of full economic liberty and non-discriminatory taxation should be safeguarded. Also, other correlative rights given by the Algeciras Act should be maintained for all foreigners alike, such as the right to own real property, the freedom of coastwise traffic, freedom to develop the mineral resources, prohibition of unfair expropriation of real estate, and international participation in contracts for public works.[87]

At a meeting of the Conference of Foreign Ministers on March 28, 1919, after discussion of a longer resolution, the following one was adopted:

> The Supreme Council of the Allies, after hearing the statement made by the French Government of its claims against Germany regarding Morocco, considers that in the Peace Treaty all servitudes of an international character to which that country was subjected as a result of German intervention should be cancelled.
>
> Consequently, the Supreme Council, taking note of the declarations of the French Government regarding the maintenance of the Open Door in Morocco, that is to say, economic, commercial, and industrial equality for all the Allied Nations, in consideration of their surrender of all servitudes of an international character, entrusts a commission, on which Belgium, France, the United States, Great Britain, Italy, and Portugal, allied powers signatories of the Algeciras Convention shall be represented, with the task of examining the provisions it will be necessary to introduce to that end and in the Treaty of Peace, in accordance with the proposal of the French Government.

The commission so designated met three times from March 31 to April 5 under the chairmanship of the French member. It also drew up accompanying clauses to be inserted in the Treaty of Peace with Austria-Hungary. The Commission's report did not modify the treaties between France or Morocco with the Allied or neutral powers; it referred entirely to penalties assessed upon Germany and Austria-Hungary.[88] The report was adopted, but it was subsequently discussed and criticized in the Conference of the Foreign Ministers, in which Lansing took a prominent part.

The punishment of Germany was detailed in Articles 141 to 146 of the Treaty of Versailles; similar but less drastic provisions were contained in the treaties of Saint-Germain and Trianon for Austria and Hungary. France lost her main objective regarding the Act of Algeciras. The Act was not abrogated, but its benefits were denied to Germany, Austria, and Hungary. Article 141 of the Versailles Treaty states: "All treaties, accords, arrangements or contracts made by her (Germany) with the Shereefian Empire are considered abrogated as of August 3, 1914." The further provision that Germany agreed not to "intervene in any way in the negotiations which may take place between France and the other powers relative to Morocco" presaged that general settlement of the Moroccan problem to France's benefit which Lyautey had promised in 1916, but which did not take place. The regime of the capitulations with its benefits was denied to Germany in Article 142. Article 143 withdrew German protection from native protégés, and gave to the Sherifian government the regulation of the conditions of German nationals in the Empire. The later articles provided that German state property become the property of the Maghzen and that private property of German citizens was to be sold and the proceeds credited to Germany's reparations account. Losing all treaty rights to equal treatment, the German trade and citizens in Morocco were put under special restrictions.[89] In her treaty of peace with Germany, the United States assumed no obligations with respect to the Versailles treaty provisions and several other areas.[90]

An interesting but inconsequential incident of the war was that ex-Sultan Hafid addressed to President Wilson a letter dated July 7, 1920. The President did not officially receive it. It was a lengthy account of his alleged mistreatment by the French government. The gist of his complaint and appeal was as follows:

> I, who have been sovereign of a state and belong to a dynasty that has reigned for five centuries in Morocco, am now obliged to live poorly in Spain, forced, against all right and justice, to be separated from my family, and without being able to dispose of pecuniary resources that belong to me. I am writing to you, being persuaded that you, guided by your upright and just sentiments, your proved love of mankind and your principles of liberty and equality for all men, will do for me what your equanimity, rectitude, and justice dictate, and by your mediation obtain for me, instead of the persecutions that I am unjustly being made the object of, fairness and justice, returning me my liberty, my family, and my

property, to which I have the right.[91]

After the peace conference, Lyautey was free to continue his interrupted work of making Morocco a model protectorate. However, he found that he received little gratitude for saving Morocco for France. The "colonialist lobby," agitating against him for years, became more aggressive.[92] On October 18, 1920, Blake reported on Lyautey's post-war situation:

> General Lyautey ... has returned to this country, resuming the functions of supreme dictator with, if anything, an enhancement of his dictatorial powers. The intrigue against his security ... carried on at the French Foreign Office and elsewhere for some years, has collapsed as a result of bold personal propaganda on the part of the General and his host of political admirers in France. It is rumored that the oak leaves of a Marshal of France, in official recognition of his services in Morocco, will shortly be conferred upon him .... In spite of the undeniable success which has attended his rule in Morocco, ... corruption is widespread in most of the civil departments, and the course of justice is not infrequently deviated from.

A December dispatch repeated the item about Lyautey's coveting of the rank of marshal and further criticized his administration:

> The French Zone of Morocco is an empire under the sole control of one man, General Lyautey, surrounded by a coterie of his own selection, which, with the General's advancing age and fatigue of personal administration, is gradually absorbing the actual exercises of his powers.[93]

Nevertheless, the General had confronted and confounded his opponents in 1920, leaving himself almost five more years of power, challenged though it continued to be. While continuing his major task of pacification, he enlarged his civil administration. Public works, including schools and hospitals, kept their priority in the budget. Agricultural colonization was encouraged, and the spread of peace and order made agriculture more secure. But there was a serious imbalance in the economy, and from about April 1, 1920, until well into 1924 Morocco suffered a severe economic depression.

Foreign relations continued to weigh heavily upon Lyautey's time and patience. Unfortunately, he had not abolished the Act of Algeciras or other impediments to the French monopoly of domestic trade and foreign commerce, but his administrators learned to circumvent these treaties to a large extent. Although the United States had reluctantly recognized the French Protectorate in October, 1917, she stubbornly refused to surrender her capitulatory privileges, and she complained continually about French infringements of the Algeciras Act and her other treaties. In the retention of capitulations, the United States had only one companion, Great Britain, but the French regarded the British attitude of more significance and labored to change it. The German problem had been eliminated, supposedly, by the Versailles treaty, but the Americans interfered in the application of its principles. The Tangier problem was "solved" in 1923, but Franco-Spanish relations remained precarious, until finally France was forced into an alliance with Spain against the Riffians. It was a strenuous five years for Lyautey.

By 1921 Lyautey had completed his wartime project of subjugating the most rebellious tribes in the Middle Atlas south of Meknes. He maintained his strategy, a "combination of guns, diplomacy, and lavish subsidies," and he was aided greatly by peasant satisfaction with the peace he enforced. His final effort was to establish a bridge between the French forces in the north and in the south and to conquer the still dissident tribes of the Middle and High Atlas. Although initiating this final phase, Lyautey did not see its completion in 1934, for he left Morocco in 1925. By the Riffian War of 1924-1926, the consolidation of French forces in the north was much delayed. Nevertheless, it was Lyautey's basic strategy which in the end brought about the absorption of the _blad es siba_ into the _blad al Maghzen._ In only thirteen years Lyautey had achieved more than what native sultans had tried vainly to accomplish for almost as many centuries. Furthermore, the war benefitted Morocco financially because of the heavy military expenditures there.[94]

As usual, American dispatches informed Washington of events, such as the important Riffian War, including the French capture of Wazan and some successful campaigns of the Spanish forces. Surplus armaments from the World War were of great assistance to the French forces. An interesting item related to Pasha Glaoui of Marrakesh. A richly subsidized minion of the French for several years, his cruelty had alienated his subjects, and in 1924 the French were steadily shearing away his authority and favoring the natives as much as possible.[95]

Undoubtedly, Blake and other American representatives were correct in naming the French Protectorate a dictatorship. Lyautey did rule despotically with the aid of an elaborate machine of civilian and military officials, and there was nothing of the Sultan in the numerous dahirs issued except his signature. Yet Lyautey did hope for freer government when peace was fully achieved, and he did lay some foundations for future representative bodies in creating the councils. These councils of agriculture and commerce, at first of Europeans only, were later granted to the Moroccans also. Although they had no right except to be consulted, they afforded some training of a political character. Envisioning a broader field of cooperation were the North African Conferences. The first of these, in 1923 and 1924, were attended by Lyautey and his colleagues of Algeria and Tunisia with their civil and military advisers. Among the subjects on the agenda were sanitation, health institutions, fisheries, travel, native affairs, meteorology, communications, customs, tariffs, and tourism.[96]

Unlike his successors, Lyautey saw the danger of the French administration for the future entente of France and Morocco. In a prophetic warning to the French government in 1920, he laid down the lines for the future development of the protectorate--the formation of a Moroccan élite, their ever-increasing association with the French administration, and their training to manage their own affairs. He spoke like a later Moroccan nationalist:

> It would be a grave illusion to believe that the Moroccans will accept this exclusion from public affairs .... They are neither a barbarous nor a dull-witted people. They are curious about world events and well informed

> .... A young generation is growing up which wants to live and to act and has a taste for education and public affairs. As our state offers them so few and inferior openings, they will seek their way elsewhere, with European groups all of which are ready to accept them and use them against France, ... and in the end they will all join together and make their demands .... We can be certain that all around us and without our knowledge ideas are seething, secret meetings and conversations are taking place about world events and the position of Islam, and that one day all these will break out and take shape, unless we concern ourselves with these and straight away assume the leadership of this movement ourselves.[97]

Since the World War, as before it, Lyautey gave public works first call upon the available finances. To him material prosperity was the foundation of success. Better communication meant commerce and importation of modern machinery to bring Morocco up to the European economic level. Several of the important trunk lines of railroad were built in the 1920's--all broad gauge lines. In 1921 the railroads from east and west met in Fez. Two other lines were completed in 1923 and 1924. An intercity automobile line was established with a heavy government subsidy. The building of the Casablanca city and harbor was Lyautey's outstanding accomplishment. Marrakesh, well supplied with good transportation, became a tourists' Mecca. By government charter, a plan of electrification was started in July, 1923.[98]

Education and health needs of the population were not neglected either. Beginning in 1913, the French devised three categories of schools for the natives--schools for the sons of notables, urban schools, and rural schools. The curricula varied much as in European schools, each catering to social class needs and including both Arabic and French studies. There were two native colleges, at Rabat and at Fez, and Jewish schools, both antedating the Protectorate. French and Spanish private schools served the children of these nationalities.[99]

Before the Protectorate the great mass of Moroccans had no medical attention and no health advisers except Negro slaves or ex-slaves using magico-religious rites. Only the imperial court and the notables could summon European doctors. Lyautey planned to make medicine a major factor in his work of modernization. One doctor, he often declared, was worth several battalions to him. In addition to attending the soldiers, army doctors were expected to give consultations in the villages and markets, to deal with epidemics, and to vaccinate the villagers. Later civilian doctors came into pacified areas. All these medical services were given free in hospitals and dispensaries. They paid large dividends in winning over the natives.[100]

It has been charged that Lyautey developed public works and built up cities and harbors too fast, before there was a productive hinterland to support the railroads and mercantile establishments of the towns. Since ninety percent of the population was rural, and since the country dwellers had suffered for centuries from plague, drouth, and locusts and had besides only the most primitive tools and little education in agriculture, some critics contended that Lyautey should have devoted his efforts and money first to them. This judgment may have come primarily from the colonial lobby, who wanted large scale immigration of French settlers to help convert Morocco from a protectorate into a colony. The criticism seems unjust. Lyautey worked first and foremost in the towns and adjacent areas which first came into firm occupation by France. The large dissident areas had to wait for assistance and uplift in agriculture until they were pacified. The evidence shows that Lyautey tried to introduce the most progressive economic institutions known in France into the rural districts. It is true that he favored only a gradual introduction of Europeans and that he disfavored their crowding the natives off their land.

The problem of land titles was very difficult to solve. With four types of land--privately owned, <u>maghzen</u> lands, <u>habous</u> (mosque) lands, and tribal lands, that available to colonists was scarce. Titles to such property were in a state of chaos and Lyautey set about having them investigated individually and then registered according to the Torrens system. Disregarding the special commission provided in the Act of Algeciras to determine land ownership, he had the work done by members of his staff. For new settlers, <u>maghzen</u> lands were sold and tribal tracts were either leased or made available through expropriation by the government. Reclaimed areas and former German real estate also furnished some acreage. At first the United States objected to this bypassing of the Algeciras Act, but later the French method was accepted. In June, 1924, Russell reported that since 1913 the area of land released for colonization amounted to 178,750 acres.[101]

In 1917 the movement to speed up European colonization was begun with offerings of small, medium, and large farms purchased on credit. From then until 1920 a number of farms were sold. Nevertheless, an American dispatch of 1923 said that the local press referred to Morocco as the colony without colonists. Of the 35,000 Europeans then living in Morocco, the majority lived in the coast cities, and it was estimated that not more than 1,000 families lived on and tilled the soil. Little or no attention had been paid to the colonist; he lacked adequate irrigation and found the tertib tax hard to pay out of capital funds when his crops failed. In the exploitation of Morocco's resources, agriculture and colonization had been left to the last. Now that railways were ready to use, the next step must be to create tonnage--an essential hitherto overlooked.[102]

Another American consular report described measures to help the farming population. On January 15, 1919, a dahir established an agricultural credit system similar to that of France, which advanced over $100,000 to farmers and cooperatives during its first year. During 1920, the protectorate government advanced, without interest, more than $100,000 to the thirty-nine farmers' organizations created in the last few years. Much was expected from the study of cooperative agriculture by the various chambers of commerce, industry, and agriculture.[103] Another consul remarked, however, that government aid went to the Europeans, not to the Moroccans, who were the large majority. The protectorate government showed in every way its desire to make Morocco French, but the French type of colonist was a most unfortunate one. Practically no skilled farmers came from France, and the amateurs were often "ne'er-do-wells." Most of them either failed at farming or bought land on speculation. During 1919 and 1920 there was a tremendous land boom, and prices of land went up like a sky rocket. Banks caught the speculative fever and lost money on land loans, and the government prevented a real disaster by stopping wholesale foreclosures. The majority of these land speculators left Morocco, and land values fell to less than one-fifth of the boom years. The years 1919 and 1920 saw the greatest exodus of foreigners in the modern history of Morocco. Since 1920 no statistics were published, for the government did not want the world to know that emigration was exceeding immigration. Many vacant stores and factories in the cities gave mute evidence of the departures during the economic depression.[104]

Every report on economic conditions received from Morocco during the period 1920-1924 emphasized the gravity of the depression there. A judicious explanation of the causes of this situation was made in a consular dispatch to Washington dated in April, 1923:

> A wide propaganda regarding the commercial resources of Morocco, carried on principally upon the continent of Europe, had given rise to an exaggerated estimation of the true situation and created many false ideas as to the potential economic value of Morocco. The effects of laying out new cities on elaborate plans, improving harbors all along the Atlantic seaboard, building roads, railways, subsidizing an interurban automobile service, setting up a complete governmental machinery housed in many public buildings of pleasing appearance, have been to casue an influx of immigrants, create an unusual local demand, and give rise to a wild speculation .... Harbors were inadequate to accommodate arriving ships bearing passengers ... Importations mounted, values of all kinds rose, money changed hands freely, and Casablanca, the principal port of entry, became suddenly a modern city.
>
> This speculation reached its summit in 1920 .... and at the present time business is at a standstill, building has ceased, except the finishing of these edifices started lately, values have receded and caused immense losses, more people are leaving the country than arriving, there is an excuse of housing, bank statements are still very favorable since they have not written off their losses and are carrying paper credits .... The tourist and visitor is inspired with enthusiasm by regarding the

> accomplishments of the French Protectorate authorities in the short period since Morocco has been in their hands .... They hear of the immense resources of the country and go away with pleasing impressions and add to the already misconceived world notion of Morocco.[105]

Some other immediate causes of the depression were noted in other American dispatches. One was the depreciation and fluctuation of the franc in relation to the pound sterling. Other monetary difficulties arose from the efforts to establish a Moroccan franc and abolish the silver Hassani, the traditional currency of Morocco. Poor crops for three years and the hoof and mouth disease in cattle greatly decreased exports, as well as the consumers' ability to buy imported goods. Foreign trade was heavily handicapped by the inadequate loading and discharging facilities of the Atlantic coast ports, even of Casablanca. A heavy depreciation in the prices of sugar and cotton goods caused great loss to importers. In 1921 the French government chose an inopportune time to suggest that the Sherifian budget be so administered as to pay for public works and social and economic improvements. The _tertib_ tax was reducing the buying power of the farmers. The phosphate monopoly, created on January 27, 1920, was still operating at a loss.

American visitors to Morocco were probably no more gullible than those of other countries.[106] The first three mentioned in the following paragraphs were there at the height of the boom, and certainly they had no reason to look behind the facade of prosperity. Lt. Col. Thomas F. Van Natta, military attaché to Ambassador Willard at Madrid, visited Morocco with his chief on June 3 to 28, 1919. They were escorted and entertained by two aides of Lyautey and were much impressed by visits to several towns. Van Natta concluded his dispatch, which was forwarded to Washington, thus:

> The country is peaceful and prosperous. Natives appear friendly and on excellent terms with the French. This is not one of the least of General Lyautey's accomplishments.[107] Remarkable work has been done, and we have been given an opportunity to see it all.[108]

The third visitor, Edith Wharton, wrote a book, _In_

Morocco, published in 1920, which showed her great fascination with the exotic land and appreciation for its leader. Invited to make a tour of Algeria and Morocco by the Committee of France-America, four Americans and their wives had another guided tour in 1923. One of them was William Milligan Sloane, whose book, Greater France in Africa, expressed an intense admiration and respect for Lyautey and his land.[109] Another member of the party was former Attorney General Wickersham, whose presence was due, it was rumored, to the Protectorate's desire for an American loan.[110] One more prominent American visitor may be cited--Dr. David P. Barrows, president of the University of California, who also was inspired to write a book, Berbers and Blacks, Impressions of Morocco, Timbuktu and the Western Sudan. An extract from a letter of his in January, 1924, sent to the State Department by its recipient, repeats the general approbation of the French:

> The French are credited with undue reserve as to their colonial affairs and intentions, but I have found nothing but frankness in their reports, which are excellent, give everything. They have spent a lot of money here. The public debt is over a billion francs ... and taxation is heavy .... Their political and military achievement appears admirable--a combination of tact and force, with high standards of justice and consideration.[111]

In both France and Morocco there was a vigorous campaign during 1923 to conceal the true state of Morocco by skillful propaganda. The State Department remained well informed of the true situation by its consuls, one of whom wrote:

> There is a wide campaign in France for the dissemination of information regarding the industrial, economic, and colonizing possibilities of Morocco. Besides the principal office of the French Protectorate in Paris, the various Chambers of Commerce have been supplied with literature and information. Lectures and cinematographic pictures are offered on numerous occasions describing this little known country. Newspapers and occasionally trade reviews contain articles regarding the possibilities in Morocco. In Morocco itself, school books relate the traditional and unselfish friendship of

France for Morocco and the solicitude the former always exercised for the latter on all occasions of aggression by other powers; a solicitude to preserve the unity and integrity of the Moroccan Empire. It is explained that the Protectorate is the logical culmination of this solicitude. Public documents, paintings, and photographs visualize in detail the various phases of the traditional and unbroken course of this friendship.[112]

Thus the protectorate lived on through inflation and depression in an apparent prosperity. Blake had reported as early as December, 1919, that the constant rise in the cost of imported commodities and manufactures and the instability of exchange due to the sudden collapse of the franc in October made life increasingly difficult. He also complained of the lack of housing accommodations for the continual additions to the European population.[113] This was at the peak of the boom. However, the French statistics continued year after year to show a regular surplus of receipts over expenditures, although Morocco had a huge yearly adverse trade balance. There were four explanations of this economic paradox. First, large military expenditures from France's budget helped Morocco. Second, a heavy capital movement generated budget receipts at the Morocco end. Third, the protectorate monopolized the phosphate mining, which eventually became very profitable. Fourth, the surpluses were largely spurious, a combination of political and accounting tricks to get more money than the French Parliament would have given if the true figures had been recorded in the regular budget.[114] And these were the frank reports that Dr. Barrows had said "gave everything."

Throughout the Lyautey regime, there were numerous references in American dispatches to Washington to his evident intention and acts to close the Open Door as quickly as possible to any but Frenchmen. In his communication of October, 1920, Blake said:

> Past tendencies develop progressively in the direction of converting the Sherifian Empire into a preserve to be closed to all but French exploitation and enterprise. Many of the ordinances promulgated in Morocco in the form of Sherifian _dahirs_ are novel and experimental, and perhaps at times are designed and disguised as tests

> probing to what extent they will be allowed to pass unchallenged. These principles of government are undoubtedly being laid down with the full sanction of Paris .... To circumvent the mineral rights accorded by treaties to all alike ... the Moroccan State ... has stepped forward to confer upon itself a monopoly for the exploitation of the very extensive phosphate beds recently discovered.[115]

In an earlier dispatch, Blake had enclosed a speech in the Chamber of Deputies during discussions of the Moroccan budget. The speaker was especially concerned about British opinion:

> It was necessary that the government, in the negotiations with Britain, which were about to open, should consider the question of the Open Door in Morocco, which could not be indefinitely maintained.[116]

Undoubtedly, the French Parliament fully endorsed Lyautey's policy of monopolizing the trade and commerce of Morocco. Yet Lyautey was implementing this bold policy not only to exclude other nations, but also to eliminate the Parliament itself from interference with his plans. He used the dogma of the sovereignty of the Sultan to make his own will sovereign over the natives, foreigners, and his own government:

> A protectorate maintains a facade of native sovereignty and authority, not only to handle the native population but also to deal with international problems. Lyautey used the sultan's theoretical sovereignty to escape the interference of the French Parliament. He ... used it to circumvent the treaty prescription of economic equality. Thus enterprises like railways, phospahte extraction, coal mining, and oil prospecting have been organized by the Moroccan "State" to keep them strictly in French hands. Not merely in the expropriation and disposal of agricultural land but also in the giving of state aid to settlers, the fiction of Moroccan sovereignty has enabled a French Protectorate to avoid either denouncing or living up to France's agreement concerning "economic freedom with no inequality whatsoever."[117]

The promulgation of the decree of February 27, 1920,

making phosphate mining a quasi-public monopoly, directly violated the Act of Algeciras providing for an international commission to adjudicate claims under the Moroccan Mining Code of 1914. Phosphate became a "budgetary manna," and the monopoly plan was extended to other minerals.[118] This bold treaty evasion worked so well that the Residency was encouraged to make other attempts to break through the treaty provision for the Open Door.

In the State Department archives there is a tremendous number of dispatches reporting violations of the Act of Algeciras and other treaties of the United States. On one pretext or another, redress was usually denied. The American consuls reported that American _semsars_ were harassed in order to drive them from their jobs and that Americans were given no opportunity to bid on public works contracts. They protested against customs discriminations on American goods, such as farm implements and typewriters. Among other controversies was one regarding the treatment of American missionaries. The Gospel Missionary Union complained that ten of their converts had been imprisoned because they were leaving Islam. After nine months of correspondence, Lyautey made it clear that they had been arrested not for religious reasons, but because they refused to pay taxes and were inciting rebellion in their tribe. No missionaries were allowed to attempt conversion of Muslims to Christianity, and the missionaries had to be content with the release of their converts from custody.[119]

Perhaps the greatest objection was made by the United States in 1924 when informed of a plan proposed by the French director of customs. His scheme contemplated the scrapping of the customs provided by the Act of Algeciras for a new schedule of duties regarded as more favorable to French interests; it revealed the "subtle processes of attrition by means of which it is sought to impair the position secured to foreign powers by treaties." Fortunately, this customs revision aroused so much active opposition from the chambers of commerce and consuls in Morocco that it was abandoned.[120]

The French authorities showered the American consuls with _dahirs_ for the compliance of their _ressortissants_. The American government maintained that a _dahir_ was not effective without its approval; if approved, it was with the reservation that enforcement be under consular jurisdiction.[121] Much correspondence with the State Department was devoted to the acceptance or rejection of these *dahirs*. A great deal of it was on matters trivial in themselves, but the American government was determined to refuse obedience to any regulation violating its treaty rights. Altogether, the State Department accepted five special taxes besides those named in the Act of Algeciras.[122]

Regarding the restrictions upon Germans and their trade, the Americans were drawn into a benevolent interference, not through sympathy for the Germans, but because of the apprehension that their own rights might be adversely affected. All *dahirs* relating to German-Moroccan commercial relations or to German licenses to be in Morocco were to be applied by the court of the Pasha of Tangier, and this court also had authority to judge whether any former German subject had become naturalized in order to be free from restrictions. The State Department asked that any case involving naturalization in the United States be referred to it, as it was notorious that in the past many citizenships had been conferred illegally in American courts. Another *dahir* found objectionable was one requiring a certificate of origin to prevent any German goods from escaping the surtax. All these *dahirs* were made applicable to Tangier, although Great Britain, France, and Spain had agreed that pending the new regime for Tangier the *status quo* would remain undisturbed there.

As usual, Blake was alert to the possibility that these regulations affecting Germany might be interpreted in a way to injure American interests. After extended correspondence, the State Department reached a decision in December, 1924. The United States neither accepted nor rejected these *dahirs*, but made the reservation to make formal objection if they were found in practice to deprive American nationals of most favored nation status. However, the Residency was informed that by treaty provisions American nationals could not be asked to pay more than the 12-1/2 percent ad valorem duty on goods imported by them into Morocco from any source, without the sanction of their government. None of the other powers had made any objection to the *dahirs*, and Great Britain even made them applicable to her subjects in the French Zone by royal regulation. All powers represented in Tangier had given passive acquiescence to the French regulations.[123]

Russell reported that only in special cases had entry and sojourn of Germans in Morocco been licensed, but any infraction of this requirement was severely punished. No serious steps were taken to prevent importation of Austrian goods. Only one shipment of known German goods was brought into Morocco in 1922. This consignment, of enamelled goods, sold at prices far below those of any competitor, in spite of special duties assessed. No more import permits were issued thereafter.[124]

Since November 14, 1918, the question of relinquishing the American capitulations in French Morocco had been in abeyance. Considering the matter about a year later, the Solicitor's Office concluded that it would be advisable to decide it for the whole of Morocco at one time. In the following June, the Division of Far Eastern Affairs suggested the possibility that the Moroccan problem might be coordinated with the Open Doors question in French China.[125] At the beginning of 1921, the French revived the issue, which remained a vexing dispute until the end of French control of Morocco in 1956.

On January 6, 1921, Jusserand returned to his familiar task. Since all matters in question had been settled since February 14, 1918, he said that his government would appreciate receiving assurance that the United States no longer objected to relinquishing her extraterritorial rights in Morocco. The American government would not make any sacrifice of consequence, considering its few nationals in Morocco and their unimportant interests. The opinion was that the desired change would be not only a mark of friendship for France, but would also prevent such incidents as that of the Swede recently selling forged certificates of American protection at Tangier. The Solicitor's Office examined former requests of Jusserand and found no evidence that Secretary Bryan had ever promised Jusserand a renunciation of capitulations merely for the settlement of monetary claims. Moore's note of February 13, 1914, had listed not less than five requirements, and later a note of Secretary Lansing had enumerated no less than six. Also, Jusserand's allegation that the United States had virtually abandoned capitulations by signing the Franco-German agreement of February 4, 1911, and the Protectorate Treaty of March 30, 1912, was not a fact; the United States had never adhered to either treaty. The reply of Secretary of State Hughes to Jusserand was that he would be informed as soon as a decision[126] was reached by the State Department.[127]

In addition to Blake, Leyton, the American consul at Casablanca, was requested to give advice on the Moroccan situation. The Division of Western European Affairs and the Solicitor also furnished opinions. The former cited Blake's previously stated view that it would be practical to await a general solution of the Moroccan problem by a treaty with all interested powers. Meanwhile, it seemed opportune to press for settlement of the case of an American semsar court-martialed by French military authorities and to protest against the making of phosphates a state monopoly. The Solicitor's contribution was a comprehensive list of all the rights claimed by the United States by her treaties and international agreements with Morocco. Supplementing this was a list of the numerous violations of these rights by the French authorities. In Blake's analysis there was a brief history of past negotiations. He recalled that all the powers surrendering capitulatory rights had received compensations. The American government was free to revert to its original position requiring a simultaneous action for all three zones. However, should the United States be willing to make a treaty for the French Zone alone, the conditions previously set forth by Lansing should form the basis of negotiations. To these should be added the principle of the Open Door as detailed in the Act of Algeciras. It might be well to add a provision that the French government would not restrict the destination of the exports of any of the resources of Morocco and to question its right to discard the Mining Code sanctioned by the Act of Algeciras. Also, American protégés and semsars should be granted the lifetime privilege of being under French court jurisdiction. Blake emphasized again that France's constant preoccupation with the abrogation of capitulations was caused by "the general desire to remove every vestige of constraint ... in the pursuit of her ultimate aim to completely assimilate" her protectorate to the regime of a French colony.[128]

In 1924 the controversy on capitulations was resumed

again. Consul Rand reported on an investigation carried on in Casablanca, Rabat, Marrakesh, and Fez. From interviews with American citizens and protégés, he had direct evidence of the antagonism of the French authorities to American extraterritorial rights and their methods in continuous efforts to nullify them. He cited several cases of semsar persecution designed to cause them to cease working for American firms. In response to protests from the American agency, the Residency had manifested a most intransigent attitude. Since Blake's communication of September 15, 1921, the Tangier problem had been settled among Great Britain, France, and Spain, and it was expected that British capitulatory rights would soon be surrendered. The contemplated abandonment of these rights gave great concern to British firms in both England and Morocco carrying on business in the latter. The United States had no interests to balance the relinquishment of treaty rights in Morocco. French maneuvers against American semsars aimed to render American capitulatory rights worthless. Again Lansing's note was recommended as the basis for a Franco-American treaty. Such a treaty should not be considered until full satisfaction had been obtained for the wrongful imprisonment of an American semsar, even if that were the only case in dispute. Two months after the foregoing dispatch, Rand reported that the British Chamber of Commerce in Tangier had received assurances that there was no time limit in the documents upon which the British government was basing its Open Door privileges in Morocco. While an early surrender of capitulations was not planned by the British government, if it did come, British interests would be fully safeguarded by commercial treaties.[129]

Corroborative of the views of Blake and Rand were those of Russell, who stated that he would not trust even an iron-clad treaty with France guaranteeing the Open Door in Morocco, if American capitulatory rights were renounced. The French attitude had been made clear over several years by their treatment of American semsars and their long list of illegal dahirs. In the future, American markets in Morocco were sure to develop,[130] and it was likely, too, that Moroccan control of their own affairs would grow; then the country with capitulatory rights would have an advantage. French efforts to colonize Morocco had been largely a failure, and their building up of the country had resulted in depression and stagnation. Trade conditions were still very poor, and speculation had ruined or crippled many banks and business houses. France alone had not the wealth to develop Morocco, but she was straining every nerve to keep it for her sole exploitation. Later Russell wrote of the inexplicable perversity of the Residency, which should be cultivating the confidence and willing collaboration of the Americans and the British, but instead was carrying on a policy of discrimination, interference, delay, and innumerable petty but exasperating annoyances, with occasionally more serious ones.[131]

But Rand was becoming discouraged. Most American _semsars_ were employed by the Singer Sewing Machine Company, and his experience with this firm invalidated the practical value of protection. He thought it might be advantageous to offer France the surrender of capitulatory rights in exchange for a commercial treaty giving economic and trade equality and most favored nation status. In this treaty, based on Lansing's outline, he would include all the other provisions suggested by Blake and others, and the presettlement of pending causes of disputes must be effected. He thought it would be an advantage to get this ideal treaty before the British surrendered their capitulations.[132]

During 1925 the State Department was still discussing the proper procedure to end the disagreeable relations with France. The Solicitor's Office recalled that during the war a draft treaty had been drawn up by which the United States relinquished all capitulatory rights. It also contained the renunciation of the right of invoking in French Morocco the American treaty of 1836 and the Madrid Convention of 1880. This treaty had never been offered to France; it was followed by a new theory that the renunciation should be made in all three zones at once. However, this one general treaty was to be preceded by recognition of several American rights. By a Congressional act, the rights might be suspended indefinitely, but the surrender of capitulations could be done only by a Senate-approved treaty. At this time the outstanding questions appeared to be the rights of _semsars_; the rights of Americans by the Treaty of 1836, the Madrid Convention, and the Algeciras Act; the protection of American commercial interests by duties imposed alike upon all American goods, whoever the importer; and equal economic opportunities for Americans in Morocco. There were two ways to secure these rights--either by a new treaty suppressing previous ones, or by a temporary suspension of American capitulatory rights upon the condition that American interests would be respected. The treaty made by France with each power giving up its capitulatory rights did not appear satisfactory to the United States. If capitulatory rights were abrogated and the United States relied simply upon the new treaty, she would have no protection of her rights except diplomatic representatives. It would appear that a suspension of capitulatory rights would be preferable to a treaty, because there would be the resumption of these rights as a possibility if the French did not respect American rights in general.[133]

The Solicitor's Office also evaluated Rand's pessimistic dispatch of November 28, 1924. Its comment was that all importers of American goods were on an equality in duties, so there was no need to require them to be Americans. Even if the British did heed the French behest to surrender their capitulations, the United States could maintain its own independent position, based on treaties. It did not seem propitious to take the initiative in proposing discussions with France. A memorandum to the State Department in July, 1925, from Consul Murphy reported a talk with an Englishman representing the Vacuum Oil Company in Morocco. He believed that the British Foreign Office had changed its mind about giving up capitulations and said that in his business *semsars* were invaluable. If not protected, successful *semsars* were exploited and robbed, especially by the Great Kaids in the south.[134]

At that point Franco-American relations reached another impasse. The Resident General was far too busy and troubled to devote much attention to those annoying Americans with their curious faith in obsolete treaties. All France was preoccupied with a greater problem, and Marshal Lyautey, who had been desperately ill,[135] was engaged in one of the most dangerous tasks of his life, for the French Protectorate had been pulled into the maelstrom of the Riffian War against the Spanish.

Under the leadership of Abd al Krim,[136] one of the most prominent characters in Moroccan history, the Riffian

War had its inception in 1921. The Spaniards were engaged in guerrilla warfare with the Riffians throughout most of that year, and they suffered a major defeat in Anual. Abd al Krim had won a victory over the Spanish General Silvestre, and he went on to be so successful in warfare that he became renowned as a liberator and a religious and patriotic hero.[137] In the fall of 1924, the Spanish situation became so desperate that the Spanish dictator, General Primo de Rivera, withdrew all the garrisons to the coast. Even Sheshuan was abandoned. This strategy relieved Abd al Krim of Spanish pressure and encouraged him to move southward against the French. There was another reason for Abd al Krim's advance. After World War I the French had moved northward to occupy the "no-man's-land," a broad strip of land on the Franco-Spanish border never conquered by France, Spain, or the Sultan. Into the Spanish portion Abd al Krim had invaded, and by the end of 1923 he was in full control, collecting taxes and calling upon the tribes to supply soldiers for him. In the spring of 1924 the French likewise advanced into their section of the border area, occupying the hills on the north bank of the Wergha River without resistance. At that time Abd al Krim refused assistance to the border tribes who were disturbed by the French approach. A year later he attacked the French for two good reasons: the French challenged his authority over the border tribes; they cut Abd al Krim's army off from its principal granary in the Wergha valley.[138]

Apparently Abd al Krim was in a strong position. Besides the Riffian and border tribes, the Jibala, whose erstwhile leader (Raisuli) was his prisoner, also supported him. These tribes held the Spanish forces in check, leaving Abd al Krim free to move his army to the French front. While waiting for the Riffian advance, the French set up and strongly fortified their line. The French also carried on a very active political campaign among the Beni Zerual, one of their subject tribes, although occupying an enclave in the Spanish Zone. Their principal agent was the influential Sherif of the Derkawa sect, located in Amjat at the tribe's center. Knowing Abd al Krim's hostility to religious sects, the Sherif was defending himself and his holy city, Amjat, and with French aid in arms and money he hoped to save both. While the French were building up their military and political fronts, Abd al Krim was also busy. He connected his capital, Ajdir, by telephone to the French front and to Sheshuan, with branch lines to Dar Rei near Tetuan and to the Beni Mauar near Tangier. He redistributed his troops, installed military posts and seats of government at various spots not far from the French front. He organized the tribes that had recently joined him. From all these centers his agents carried on an effective propaganda.[139]

In February, French reinforcements went to the front. On April 13, 1925, Abd al Krim launched an attack on the Dekawa Sherif at Amjat and on two other towns. Amjat was pillaged and burned, and the Riffians and the Jibala advanced to the French lines, passing through them in places. Many French posts were surrounded and some tribes behind the lines rose. Only twenty miles away, Fez was in grave danger, and the attitude of many hitherto loyal tribes toward France was in doubt. Four battalions of Algerian tribes arrived. The mobility of the Riffians was astonishing--they seemed to be everywhere, inciting rebellion and burning the villages and crops of any who refused to join them. Lyautey arrived in Fez on May 2 and drew up with General de Chambrun a plan of campaign against Abd al Krim. At last the French began to understand why the Spaniards had seemed to be incompetent and disorganized.[140]

The Riffian successes brought severe censure upon Lyautey, and his longtime enemies at the Quai d'Orsay and in the Ministry of War accused him of deliberately refusing to aid the Spaniards. Toward the end of 1924, Lyautey had asked Paris for more troops, but they had been sent very reluctantly and in smaller numbers than asked for. Moreover, he could not cross the Spanish border with them for diplomatic reasons. By the middle of May, 1925, the situation looked so serious that Lyautey suggested to the French government an agreement with Spain to launch a joint offensive. A French emissary to the Riffian leader reported upon Krim's military and political strength. At first inclined to advocate Spain's acceptance of an independent Riff under Abd al Krim's rule, Lyautey soon realized that this solution would be a precedent for the independence of French Morocco.

Meanwhile, Herriot had been succeeded as premier by Paul Painlevé, who was also minister of war. Painlevé came in person to Morocco to investigate the situation and to see Lyautey. After the premier's return to Paris there was a series of intrigues to replace Lyautey as military commander. Lyautey himself urged the government to send Weygand, Gourad, or Guillaumat to serve under him. In July came the surprising news that Marshal Pétain, the "Victor of Verdum," was coming to Morocco as Inspector General of the French Armies to draw up strategic plans. Lyautey trusted Pétain, who acted however as an inquisitor searching out Lyautey's faults and failures. Having worked out a plan of campaign to the last detail, Lyautey had hoped to see it tested with a friendly colleague. But on August 18 he received Painlevé's order putting Pétain in general command of the military services in Morocco--"a disgrace hardly disguised," as Lyautey said. For a short time Lyautey remained as resident general. On September 9 the armies of France and Spain joined in a large scale offensive, and before long it was evident that Abd al Krim had made a fatal error in attacking the French. On September 24, 1925, Lyautey sent in his resignation.[141] The era of Lyautey was ended.

According to his intimates, Lyautey left Morocco with disillusionment and bitterness. He remained in France until his death in 1934, always interested above all in Morocco. About his dismissal he resented most that it had been brought about finally by high army officials. It is well known that there was much sympathy for Abd al Krim outside of France, but in France herself the Chamber of Deputies had some members who openly voiced encouragement for him, and the Communists carried on an active anti-war campaign and advocated withdrawal from Morocco.[142]

Diplomatic dispatches from Europe and Morocco commented on every facet of the Riffian War, even on rumors later discredited. There was much adverse criticism about Rivera's withdrawal policy, said to be a shirking of duty by the Spanish, who had bound themselves by treaty to be responsible for their zone. Lyautey was quoted as denying France's alleged ambition to become heir to the Spanish Zone; the Riff was not worth anything, but it would cost an enormous price to subdue it. Italy and Great Britain were said to be interested in the future of Spanish Morocco, but there was a repudiation of any international conference over it. The initial attack on the French and subsequent hostilities were well described. There were efforts to blame the Germans and the Pan-Islamic government for the rebellion of the Riffs. The opposition of the communists to the war was admitted.

In April, 1925, Consul Murphy visited the Riff and brought back favorable accounts of Abd al Krim's organization and progressive methods, as well as of the great administrative ability of his two brothers, one the leader of the army. In an American military attaché's report, it was remarked that the mobility of the Riffian troops afforded them a successful substitute for anti-aircraft guns, gas masks, defensive artillery, and fortifications, which they lacked. Aside from what he obtained from the retreating Spaniards, considerable supplies reached Abd al Krim from the coast, brought there by contraband runners, using Spain mostly as a base. Communist agents were active in France and North Africa spreading the idea that this was a war of liberation.

Finally the long over-due Franco-Spanish conference at Madrid was announced. The visit of Painlevé to the Sultan was interpreted as a renewed pledge of France's defense of his "sovereignty." From the press one learned that some were demanding compensation for France's burdens and sacrifices in reestablishing the sovereignty of the Sultan in the Riff. France expected charges of imperialism from the British and the Americans. In July the fall of Wazan was announced, together with the almost impassable state of the Fez-Taza route. It was reported also that the Kaids Glaoui and Goundafui were stirring up the Marrakesh area against the French, while the Riffs were constantly attacking near Meknes and Fez. Inevitably, Lyautey was taxed with incapacity.

Later in July, the Communists urged peace negotiations, while opposition to the war continued in the Chamber of Deputies and among the people. Small handbills were posted on Paris streets, reading "Self-determination for the Riff," "Down with French aggression!" On July 16, Blake reported secret parleys of the French and the Spanish with Abd al Krim, seeking a peace at almost any price. Still later Russell wrote of a still menacing situation in the south, where the Pasha of Marrakesh, "more than suspected" of subsidizing Abd al Krim, had refused to raise a harka for the French; but the consul thought the time for a successful rebellion of French Morocco was now passed. In August Russell told of the completed reorganization of the French army and the acceptance of a plan of campaign by Lyautey. The central idea of the plan was "disarming the Riff but not occupying a territory full of ambuscades."

The conclusion of this long series of dispatches, dated August 20, 1925, was news of the failure of peace negotiations with Abd al Krim. A new military campaign costly in men and money was the purport of this news. With "absolute and unconditional independence of the Riff" as a starting point, Abd al Krim made negotiations impossible; France and Spain were prepared to offer only "an autonomy most ample and liberal" under the nominal sovereignty of the Sultan. In the press Painlevé and Rivera predicted that early autumn would see the problem solved. At long last the French and the Spanish were prepared to collaborate.[143]

At the time of Lyautey's resignation, there were many evaluations of his career and of his service for France and for Morocco. Of special interest are the estimates of him and his work made by Americans. The enthusiastic approval of his achievements by eminent American visitors during the boom years has already been cited. Sloane gave special attention to Lyautey's good treatment of the natives, especially to his emphasis upon the education of the rising generation. Barrows was critical of the economic aspects of the Protectorate:

> The French have expended money on Morocco faster than the investment warranted; ... foreign traders and settlers have been encouraged to come in, in numbers disproportionate to existing opportunities; and in their solicitude to make government impressive, to preserve the beauties of Moorish architecture, to protect antiquities, and to make solid and substantial their improvements of ports and their development of communications, they have outstripped the commercial development of the land.[144]

Of more value for the historian are the opinions of those who knew Lyautey best--the American representatives in Morocco, who dealt with him often, and frequently in opposition. Bradford, the consul in Casablanca, said of him in 1923:

> Marshal Lyautey is now sixty-nine years old. His sentiments as expressed are strongly monarchic. He believes that all wars are horrible and every effort should be made to avoid them, excepting colonial wars, which he believes are great civilizing influences .... As a military administrator, his treatment of the native population in Morocco has been sympathetic and conducted understandingly .... The military penetration has ... been accomplished with the minimum of bloodshed. He loves praise and publicity. He is lavish in expenditure and entourage, but with the development of civil control and a large administrative organization in Morocco, and with declining years, his prodigious activity and energy show signs of decline, and the active direction of the Protectorate has been practically surrendered into the hands of M. de Sorbier de Pougnadoresse, secretary general of the Protectorate.

When Rand reported the departure of de Pugnadoresse in January, 1925, he spoke of him as "this influence (that) has been responsible for unnecessary difficulties in the relations between the French Residency General and this Diplomatic Agency." His successor was more conciliatory. When Russell reported the approaching resignation of Lyautey in August, 1925, he also commented upon the character of the Marshal's entourage:

> In the thirteen years that have elapsed since the present government was established, a regular "court" has grown up at Rabat, full of intrigues and underground workings, frequented by officeholders and hangerson of a most bureaucratic form of government, in which some most astounding examples of the power of bribery and corruption have flourished. This entourage of the Marshal has set an example that has unfortunately been followed in too many instances by minor officials to the detriment of good government and justice.[145]

As expected, it was Blake who made the most comprehensive analysis of the personality of Marshal Lyautey. In a dispatch of January 28, 1926, he declared that "the fall of the adventurous, daring, and vehement Marshal Lyautey, senile but still ebullient, whose conceit had hitherto eminently qualified him to face undaunted all obstacles, constitutes an event too important to be passed over in silence." He continued:

> Love of power and pettiness were his outstanding frailties, and ... his occasional exhibition of magnanimity was always more akin to an impulse than to an inspiration. Belief in his own endowments led to growing excesses and indiscretions .... Notwithstanding a harshness of form and a demonstrative, if not a bullying manner, Lyautey loved the Court more than the Camp .... He preferred society to soldiering, although parade in any form was always pleasing to him .... This weakness for social show and ceremony (was) one of the direct causes of his downfall. His army in Morocco was full of picked flatterers and aristocratic parasites. The Cabinet at Rabat was likewise recruited ....
>
> He was entrusted with the initiation and direction of a French Islamic policy seeking the creation of an alliance between France and the entire Mohammedan world .... His was the dream of founding a United North African Empire, under a single religious and political head, the Sultan of Morocco (with himself in control), and this explains his connivance with the native movement against Spain in her zone, his desire to eliminate that power from Morocco, his maneuvering for the mastery of Tangier .... He was awakened from his vain dreams, with his prestige and power shattered at the hand of a rebel chieftain from the Riff mountains ....
>
> He has been an extraordinary figure in the life of this country. It would be foolish ... to question his passion, his assiduity, or his vast and restless energy ... always accepting the fullest responsibility .... But in spite of his various virtues or reputed vices ... he has been ambulatory, extravagant, flamboyant, and always cocksure of his own hallucinations .... The Riff revolt was the only real problem that he encountered

> throughout his entire administration of Morocco, and the one, almost at the touch of which he crumbled into dust .... He conquered the peasant inhabitants of the plains .... He respected the glories of the faithful and paid ... tribute to the legends and shrines of Mohammedan saints, and ... in most of the minor forms of native contact, he was both shrewd and successful. He built roads in Morocco, adding to its material prosperity, ... but here ... his talents end .... Marshal Lyautey worked to make of Morocco a personal preserve, a place in which his presence was indispensable, rather than to create for France a strong and independent political planet, and consequently his claim to fame, as an administrator, is bound to suffer with the lapse of time.[146]

In striking contrast to this rather extreme and even antagonistic view is the appraisement of Lyautey by a friend of Morocco and the Moroccans:

> This outstanding man ... came to Morocco when it was enfeebled and in a state verging on chaos. His aim, broadly speaking, was to help the natives to help themselves, to infuse them with the determination and the abilities to regain their full sovereignty and independence and with an enlightened and universally respected Sultan. The immensity of his task might easily have defeated a lesser man, for side by side with the social and political rehabilitation of the Moors he had to ensure their ever-increasing physical well-being. He had to introduce them to countless aspects of modern thought and practice without disparaging the best of their old modes. In 1925 when the reactionaries in France were alarmed at the accumulating evidence of his human liberality, he was recalled, to Morocco's inestimable loss. But the foundation which he had embedded seemed sufficiently strong to support any edifice that his successors might erect upon them.[147]

Notes

1. A. N. F.: Herrick (Paris) to State Dept., April 30, 1912, 881.00/503 and No. 36, June 13, 1912, 881.00/511; Carpenter to State Dept., No. 256, May 17, 1912, 881.00/506.

2. From the decree dated June 11, 1912; "The Resident Commissioner General is invested with all the powers of the Republic in the Cherifian Empire. He is the sole intermediary between the Sultan and the Representatives of foreign powers. He shall approve and promulgate, in the name of the Government of the Republic, the decrees issued by His Cherifian Majesty. He shall direct all the administrative services; he shall have command in chief of the land forces and the disposition of the naval forces." Herrick (Paris) to the State Dept., No. 36, June 13, 1912, A. N. F., 881.00/511.

3. Lyautey had won great fame during his period of command on the Algero-Moroccan frontier and his special mission to the tribes after the bombardment of Casablanca. Walter Burton Harris, "Morocco in War-Time," Contemporary Review, CXII (Sept., 1917), 273.

4. William Milligan Sloane, Greater France in Africa (hereafter cited as Sloane, Greater France in Africa), 139-142; Mellor, Morocco Awakes, 46-47; Maurois, Lyautey, 226-234, 214-215; W. B. Harris, France, Spain, and the Rif, 178-182.

5. Maxwell Blake was "brilliantly successful because of his wide background and experience as much as because of his innate ability;" Stuart, Tangier, 189. He served as consul general from Dec. 14, 1910 to April 10, 1922, and from July 1, 1924 to May 14, 1925, and as diplomatic agent and consul general from May 14, 1925 until June 19, 1940.

6. A. N. F.: Carpenter to State Dept., No. 286, July 19, 1912, 881.00/513 and No. 298, Aug. 26, 1912, 881.00/518; Blake to State Dept., No. 305, Sept. 14, 1912, 881.00/519; No. 311, Oct. 10, 1912, 881.00/522;

No. 316, Oct. 31, 1912, 881.00/524.

7. Herbert Lüthy, France Against Herself; A Perceptive Study Of France's Past, Her Politics, and Her Unending Crises, translated by Eric Mosbacher (hereafter cited as Lüthy, France Against Herself), 255-256.

8. W. B. Harris, France, Spain, and the Rif, 187-190; David Prescott Barrows, Berbers and Blacks, Impressions of Morocco, Timbuktu and the Western Sudan (hereafter cited as Barrows, Berbers and Blacks), 45-47, 63-65; Sloane, Greater France in Africa, 146-149.

9. N. D. Harris, Europe and Africa, 325; Hahn, North Africa, 61; Barbour, North West Africa, 92.

10. Sloane, Greater France in Africa, 142.

11. Barbour, North West Africa, 92; Maurois, Lyautey, 216.

12. Knight, Morocco as A French Economic Venture, 127-128, 56-59.

13. N. D. Harris, Europe and Africa, 322.

14. In his annual message to Congress on December 7, 1911, Taft observed: "The Moroccan question, which for some months was the cause of great anxiety, happily appears to have reached a stage at which it need no longer be regarded with concern." F. R., 1911, xix.

15. Jusserand to Knox, Jan. 8, 1913, F. R., 1914, 905 and Knox to Jusserand, Jan. 22, 1913, Ibid., 905-906.

16. A. N. F.: Blake to Sec. of State, No. 351, Jan. 6, 1913, 881.52/9 and No. 366, Feb. 20, 1913, 881.52/10; Adee to Blake, March 24, 1913; Blake to Sec. of State, No. 367, Feb. 24, 1913, 881.52/11; Adee to Blake, No. 118, April 12, 1913, Ibid.; Blake to Sec. of State, No. 425, Jan. 22, 1914, 881.52/13; J. B. Moore to Blake, No. 134, Feb. 27, 1914, Ibid.

17. A. N. F.: Blake to Sec. of State, No. 363, Feb. 18, 1913, 881.111; No. 370, March 4, 1913, 881.111/1; No. 401, June 30, 1913, 881.111/2; F. R., 1913, 1011-1016.

18. A. N. F.: Blake to Bryan, No. 407, July 19, 1913, 881.00/549 and No. 414, Oct. 8, 1915, 881.00/553; E. de Perette de la Rocca to Sec. of State, Sept. 16, 1913, 881.00/552. F. R., 1914, 906-907.

19. A. N. F.: Jusserand to Sec. of State, undated, 881.00/493-1/2; Blake to Sec. of State, No. 355, Jan. 24, 1913, 881.00/533; No. 375, March 14, 1913, 881.00/538; No. 412, Sept. 30, 1913, 881.00/554.

20. Maxwell Blake continued as consul general after the departure of Carpenter at the end of 1912. In all respects he assumed the duties and responsibilities of a minister also.

21. A. N. F.: Blake to Sec. of State, No. 361, Feb. 17, 1913, 881.00/535; Bryan to Jusserand, No. 1190, July 9, 1913, 881.00/556A.

22. Ibid., Blake to Sec. of State, No. 412, Sept. 30, 1913, 881.00/554.

23. A. N. F.: Moore to American Ambassadors, Jan. 16, 1914, 881.00/554 and to Caffery (Stockholm), Jan. 16, 1914, 881.00/7180. Wilson (St. Petersburg), to State Dept., No. 683, Jan. 30, 1914, 881.00/559 and No. 695, Feb. 19, 1914, 881.00/570. Van Dyke (The Hague) to State Dept., Feb. 3, 1914, 881.00/558. Caffery to State Dept., No. 363, Feb. 1, 1914, 881.00/363. Willard (Madrid), to State Dept., 41, Feb. 2, 1914, 881.00/562. Gerard (Berlin) to State Dept., No. 76, Feb. 3, 1914, 881.00/566; Birch (Lisbon), to State Dept., No. 6, Feb. 4, 1914, 881.00/565. Page (London), to State Dept., No. 239, Feb. 5, 1914, 881.00/564. Page (Rome) to State Dept., No. 60, Feb. 9, 1914, 881.00/567. Dearing (Brussels) to State Dept., Feb. 10, 1914, 881.00/569. Penfield (Vienna) to State Dept., No. 75, Feb. 13, 1914, 881.00/571. Blake to State Dept., No. 434, March 10, 1914, 881.00/575.

24. Ibid., Blake to State Dept., No. 428, Feb. 10, 1914, 881.00/568.

25. Ibid., Blake to State Dept., April 17, 1913, 881.00/539; April 28, 1913, 881.00/541; No. 389, May 5, 1913, 881.00/543; No. 393, May 14, 1913, 881.00/545. Riaño to State Dept., May 22, 1913, 881.00/544.

26. Ibid., C. Hale to Bryan, memorandum, March 3, 1913, 881.00/536.

27. Ibid., Blake to State Dept., No. 376, March 15, 1913, 881.00/537.

28. Ibid., De la Rocca to Bryan, Aug. 29, 1913, 881.113/21; Blake to State Dept., No. 425, Jan. 22, 1914, 881.00/557.

29. Ibid., Jusserand to Bryan, Jan. 7, 1714, 881.041/1; Cuban Chargé to Moore, Feb. 3, 1914, 881.00/560; Moore to de la Vega, Feb. 4, 1914, 881.00/560; Blake to State Dept., No. 428, Feb. 10, 1914, 881.00/568.

30. Ibid., Moore to Jusserand, Feb. 13, 1914, 881.00/574 A.

31. Ibid., Blake to State Dept., No. 435, March 13, 1914, 881.00/574.

32. Ibid., Phillips to Lansing, memorandum, April 20, 1914, 881.00/574; L H W to Lansing, memorandum, April 21, 1914, 881.00/574.

33. Pencilled notation in the margin of the document, made by someone in the State Dept. : "All right, but let's settle them."

34. A. N. F.: Jusserand to Sec. of State, with enclosed declaration, April 22, 1914, 881.00/576.

35. Ibid., Blake to Sec. of State, telegram, April 28, 1914, 881.00/578; Bryan to Blake, telegram, April 29, 1914, 881.00/5788. Lansing to Jusserand, No. 1315, April 30, 1914, 881.00/578; Lansing to Blake, No. 136,

April 30, 1914, 881.00/578; Blake to State Dept., No. 443, May 14, 1914, 881.00/579 and No. 448, May 25, 1914, 881.00/581.

36. Ibid., Blake to State Dept., No. 446, May 21, 1914, 881.00/580; Gerard (Berlin) to State Dept., No. 184, July 7, 1914, 881.00/584.

37. Ibid., Jusserand to Sec. of State, June 10, 1914, 881.00/582 and June 23, 1914, 881.00/593.

38. Ibid., Clausse to Bryan, July 16, 1914, 881.00/585 and July 16, 1914, 881.00/586.

39. Ibid., Phillips to Blake, No. 140, July 24, 1914, 881.00/586; Blake to State Dept., No. 458, Nov. 5, 1914, 881.00/590.

40. Ibid., Blake to State Dept., No. 450, June 10, 1914, 881.00/583; Maurois, Lyautey, 235-236.

41. Ibid., 241-247, 252-257, 285, 289, 312-313; Knight, Morocco as a French Economic Venture, 38-39.

42. Barrows, Berbers and Blacks, 44-45; Maurois, Lyautey, 315-317.

43. Edith Wharton, In Morocco (cited hereafter as Wharton In Morocco), 220-221.

44. N. D. Harris, Europe and Africa, 327-328; Knight, Morocco as a French Economic Venture, 36-37.

45. N. D. Harris, Europe and Africa, 329; W. B. Harris, "Morocco in War-Time," 277.

46. N. D. Harris, Europe and Africa, 329, 331; Knight, Morocco as a French Economic Venture, 35-36.

47. Blake to Sec. of State, No. 34, April 1, 1918, "Quarterly Information Series", No. 1, A. N. F., 881.00/668.

48. Knight, Morocco as a French Economic Venture, 37-38; Maurois, Lyautey, 314.

49. Mellor, *Morocco Awakes*, 48, 54; W. B. Harris, "Morocco in War-Time," 274; Sloane, *Greater France in Africa*, 36-37, 149-150; N. D. Harris, *Europe and Africa*, 324-325.

50. Knight, *Morocco as a French Economic Venture*, 39-40; Barrows, *Berbers and Blacks*, 53-55, 182.

51. Knight, *Morocco as a French Economic Venture*, 38-39; W. B. Harris, "Morocco in War-Time," 270, 272-275, 277-279; W. B. Harris, *France, Spain, and the Rif*, 196.

52. Philip to State Dept., No. 1150, April 1, 1916, *A. N. F.*, 763.72/2597.

53. *Ibid.*, Blake to State Dept., April 1, 1918, "Quarterly Information Series," No. 1., 881.00/668.

54. *Ibid.*, Blake to State Dept., June 30, 1918, 881.00/652 and Oct. 1, 1918, 881.00/658, "Quarterly Information Series, No. 2 and No. 3.

55. *Ibid.*, Gassett to State Dept., No. 716, Aug. 17, 1914, 881.00/587.

56. *Ibid.*, Blake to Sec. of State, No. 469, Feb. 27, 1915, 381.62/75.

57. The correspondence is found in *A. N. F.*, 381.62 to 381.62/127.

58. *Ibid.*, Blake to Sec. of State, telegram, July 5, 1917, 763.72/5705.

59. During the war and immediately thereafter, Morocco made notable contributions to the food supply of France. From 1915 to 1919 inclusive she shipped there the following items: 18,460,929 bushels of barley, 3,376,818 bushels of wheat, 3,401,699 bushels of beans, 2,957,247 bushels of corn, 1,146,402 bushels of chickpeas, 1,091,109 bushels of sorghum, 27,504 short tons of eggs, and 75,987 hogs. Evans (vice consul in charge), to Sec. of State, April 14, 1921, *A. N. F.*, 881.61/881.

60. Knight, Morocco as a French Economic Venture, 40.

61. Walter Lippman, The Stakes of Diplomacy, 169-170.

62. A. N. F.: Blake to Sec. of State, No. 473, March 20, 1915, 881.52/15; No. 472, March 17, 1915, 611.819; No. 478, April 13, 1915, 611.819/1; No. 151, May 17, 1916, 611.819/2; No. 482, May 11, 1915, 881.15/4; No. 493, July 26, 1915, 881.15/5; No. 510, Jan. 4, 1916, 881.15/7; No. 514, Jan. 13, 1916, 881.15/8; No. 515, Jan. 18, 1916, 881.15/9; No. 522, March 1, 1916, 881.15/10; No. 523, March 6, 1916, 881.15/11; No. 527, March 20, 1916, 881.15/12; No. 529, April 3, 1916, 881.15/13; No. 519, Feb. 22, 1916, 881.124/35.

63. Ibid., Jusserand to Sec. of State, Nov. 4, 1914, 881.00/588; Blake to State Dept., No. 459, Nov. 5, 1914, 881.00/591 and telegram, Dec. 20, 1914, 881.00/592.

64. Ibid., A P, Dept. of State, memorandum, Dec. 8, 1915, 881.00/622; C H, Dept. of State, memorandum, Dec. 4, 1915, 881.00/622; Lansing to Jusserand, No. 1640, Jan. 18, 1916, 881.00/622; Jusserand to Sec. of State, April 17, 1916, 881.00/623.

65. Ibid., Blake to Dept. of State, No. 506, Dec. 8, 1915, 881.00/608; Polk to Sharp (Paris), No. 793, Dec. 29, 1915, 881.00/608; Sharp to State Dept., No. 1989, Feb. 11, 1916, 881.00/612.

66. Ibid., Phillips to Putney, memorandum, Feb. 12, 1916; State Dept. to Blake, telegram, Feb. 14, 1916, 881.00/611; Blake to Sec. of State, telegram, Feb. 18, 1916, 881.00/610.

67. Shih Shun Liu, in Extra-Territoriality, Its Rise and Its Decline, 167-168, gives the following list by years: 1914--Russia, Spain, Norway, Greece, Sweden, and Switzerland; 1915--Denmark, Bolivia, Japan, and Belgium; 1916--Italy, Portugal, The Netherlands, and Costa Rica.

68. A. N. F.: Lansing to Blake, telegram, March 23, 1916, 881.00/614A; Blake to Sec. of State, telegram, March 26, 1916, 881.00/615; Lansing to Blake, telegram, April 4, 1916, 881.00/615; Blake to Lansing, No. 530, April 8, 1916, 881.00/618.

69. Ibid., Lansing to Jusserand, July 1, 1916, 881.00/623; Sec. of State to Polk, memorandum, July 3, 1916, 881.00/642.

70. The text of the declaration reads as follows: The undersigned, duly authorized by their governments, make the following joint declaration: Taking into consideration the guarantees of judicial equality offered to aliens by the French Tribunals of the Protectorate, the Government of the United States of America relinquishes its claim to all the rights and privileges growing out of the Capitulation regime for its consuls, the persons subject to its jurisdiction and its establishment within the French Zone of the Sherifian Empire. The treaties and conventions of every description in force between France and the United States extend as of right, unless otherwise specifically provided, to the French Zone of the Sherifian Empire. The present declaration will go into effect within-----days from the date of its signature. Done in duplicate, at Washington, this----------

71. A. N. F.: Jusserand to Polk, July 31, 1916, 881.00/624; Polk to Blake, telegram, Aug. 3, 1916, 881.00/624; Blake to Sec. of State, telegram, Aug. 8, 1916, 881.00/626.

72. The stipulations read as follows: 1st. Such American claim as may still be pending in Morocco would be settled in the shortest possible time and in a most conciliatory spirit; 2nd. Insofar as it may lie in our power the rights of American citizens in the Spanish and Tangier zones shall not be affected by the relinquishment of the capitulations vouchsafed to us in our zone; 3d. Nothing will be omitted to secure in the French Zone of Morocco the same equal rights with French citizens in Morocco as are enjoyed by American citizens in France; 4th. In the event of a

Mixed Court being created in Tangier, the French Government would take into benevolent consideration the ground upon which the American Government might base a request that one of the judges be of American nationality.

73. A. N. F.: Office of the Counselor to Putney, Aug. 17, 1916, 881.00/630; Jusserand to Sec. of State, Aug. 26, 1916, 881.00/628 and Oct. 3, 1916, 881.00/631; Lansing to Jusserand, Oct. 12, 1916, 881.00/631.

74. The recognition of a government or the refusal to recognize one is an executive prerogative, not requiring any action by the Senate.

75. A. N. F.: Lansing to Jusserand, No. 1631, Jan. 2, 1917, 881.00/631; Jusserand to Lansing, Jan. 8, 1917, 881.00/634; Lansing to Jusserand, Jan. 15, 1917, 881.00/634; Lansing to Wilson, Jan. 15, 1917, 881.00/634.

76. Ibid., Jusserand to Lansing, Jan. 19, 1917, 881.00/633; Copy of Lansing to Jusserand, No. 1977, to Herrick (Paris), Feb. 7, 1923, 881.00/633; Lansing to American Embassy, Madrid, telegram, Sept. 1, 1917, 881.00/630; Lansing to Page (London), telegram, Oct. 5, 1917, 881.00/635; Lansing to Blake, telegram, Oct. 5, 1917, 881.00/635; Page to Lansing, telegram, Oct. 9, 1917, 881.00/640; Blake to Lansing, telegram, Oct. 11, 1917, 881.00/642; Ministry of State, Madrid to Spanish Embassy of the United States, memorandum, Nov. 21, 1917, 881.00/644.

77. Ibid., Blake to Sec. of State, No. 5, Aug. 22, 1917, 881.00/639.

78. Ibid., Office of the Solicitor, L W H to Phillips, memorandum, Nov. 30, 1918, 881.00/672.

79. Ibid., Blake to Sec. of State, telegram, Dec. 4, 1917, 881.00/643; No. 24, Jan. 17, 1918, 381.11/13; telegram, Feb. 28, 1918, 881.00/646; No. 31, March 9, 1918, 481.11/97.

80. Ibid., Jusserand to Lansing, April 14, 1918, 881.00/648 and April 25, 1918, 881.00/649.

81. Ibid., Lansing to Blake, telegram, May 14, 1918, 881.00/648; Blake to Sec. of State, May 17, 1918, 881.00/650; A P, Division of Near Eastern Affairs, to Phillips, May 23, 1918, 881.00/650; Office of the Solicitor, J A M to Woolsey, memorandum, June 28, 1918, 881.00/651; L H W to Phillips, memorandum, June 18, 1918, 881.00/695.

82. Ibid., Jusserand to Lansing, Nov. 14, 1918, 881.00/655.

83. Ibid., Blake to Lansing, telegram, Nov. 21, 1918, 881.00/656; Ass't. Sec. of State to Woolsey, Nov. 27, 1918, 881.00/693; L H W, Office of the Solicitor, memorandum, Nov. 30, 1918, 881.00/672.

84. Ibid., Blake to Sec. of State, No. 57, Nov. 21, 1918, 881.00/660; transmitted to the Mission of the United States to the Conference to Negotiate Peace, on Dec. 26, 1918 by Frank K. Polk, Acting Sec. of State, and filed as 185.1152/2.

85. Ibid., Blake to State Dept., memorandum, Jan. 17, 1919, 881.00/716; also filed as Blake to American Mission to Negotiate Peace, Jan. 17, 1919, 185.1155/4.

86. Ibid., Minutes of a Meeting of the Bureau of the Conference, held on Feb. 18, 1919, American Commission to Negotiate Peace (1918-1919), CCCXII, 185.1155/8; Minutes of a Meeting of the Bureau of the Conference held on Feb. 25, 1919, Ibid., 185.1155/6; Brief of Statement by M. de Peretti Respecting the Moroccan Question, Ibid., CCCLIV, 185.214/1.

87. Blake to Sec. of State, No. 65, Feb. 25, 1919, A. N. F., 881.00/664; Blake to Ammission, Paris, telegram for Mr. Beer, Feb. 26, 1919, American Commission to Negotiate Peace, CCCXII, 185.1155/7.

88. Notes on a meeting of the Big Five Foreign Ministers, March 28, 1919, Ibid., R G 256, 180.03201/2;

Minutes of a Meeting of the Conference of Foreign Ministers, March 28, 1919, Ibid., 185.1155/15. Report by the Committee for the Examination of the Provisions to be Inserted in the Preliminaries of Peace with Regard to Morocco, April 5, 1919, Ibid., CXLVIII, 181.22302/1.

89. Stuart, Tangier, 70; N. D. Harris, Europe and Africa, 335; Knight, Morocco as a French Economic Venture, 44-45.

90. "Congress passed a joint resolution on July 2, 1921, declaring that hostilities had ceased, and reserving to the United States the rights and privileges of the victorious Powers. In this manner America claimed the fruits without shouldering the responsibilities. Late in August, 1921, nearly three years after the Armistice, separate treaties were signed with Germany, Austria, and Hungary and were promptly approved by the Senate." Bailey, Diplomatic History, 681-682.

91. A. N. F., Willard (Madrid) to Sec. of State, No. 1954, July 9, 1920, 881.00/688.

92. The activities and aims of this powerful group are fully described in the chapter entitled "Lobby and Settlers," in Landau, Moroccan Drama, 239-246.

93. A. N. F.: Blake to Sec. of State, "Quarterly Information Series," No. 9, Oct. 18, 1920, 881.00/700 and No. 10, Dec. 31, 1920, 881.00/703.

94. Landau, Moroccan Drama, 101-103; Knight, Morocco as a French Economic Venture, 42.

95. A. N. F.: "Quarterly Information Series," Blake to Sec. of State, No. 6, Dec. 31, 1919, 881.00/677; No. 9, Oct. 18, 1920, 881.00/700; No. 10, Dec. 31, 1920, 881.00/703; No. 11, Aug. 15, 1921, 881.00/751. Rand to Sec. of State, No. 19, April 30, 1924, 881.00/921. Denning to Sec. of State, No. 15, Nov. 20, 1922, 881.00/789; Russell to Sec. of State, No. 22, June 2, 1924, 881.00/939.

96. N. D. Harris, *Europe and Africa*, 333-334, 336-338, *A. N. F.*: Dow (Algiers) to Sec. of State, No. 83, Feb. 27, 1923, 881.00/799; Elkington to Dept. of State, Report from Casablanca, April 5, 1926, 881.00/1215.

97. Hahn, *North Africa*, 63; Barbour, *North West Africa*, 93.

98. Landau, *Moroccan Drama*, 106-108; N. D. Harris, *Europe and Africa*, 328-329; *A. N. F.*, Bradford to Sec. of State, April 9, 1923, 881.00/804.

99. Evans to Sec. of State, report, June 14, 1921, *Ibid.*, 681.42.

100. Barbour, *North West Africa*, 112-113.

101. *A. N. F.*: Blake to Sec. of State, No. 73, April 26, 1919, 481.11/99; Russell to Sec. of State, reports, May 27, 1924, 881.52/21 and June 25, 1924, 881.52 /22.

102. *Ibid.*, Evans to Sec. of State, report, April 14, 1921, 881.61; Bradford to Sec. of State, report, April 9, 1923, 881.00/804.

103. *Ibid.*, Evans to Sec. of State, report, April 14, 1921, 881.61.

104. *Ibid.*, Russell to Sec. of State, reports, June 25, 1924, 881.52/22 and June 18, 1924, 881.55.

105. *Ibid.*, Bradford to Sec. of State, report, April 9, 1923, 881.00/804. Between 1920 and 1924 there were numerous dispatches on the depression from Blake, Denning, Bradford, Nutting (London), and Rand.

106. "There is a well-oiled machinery in Morocco for the reception of distinguished visitors, who are shown the country from the French standpoint and only those things which redound to their credit." Bradford to Sec. of State, April 9, 1923, *Ibid.*, 881.00/804.

107. "A subsidized press publishes a stream of articles laudatory of French achievements in Morocco, while censorship prevents any criticism of Lyautey or his regime." Brandford to Sec. of State, July 27, 1923, Ibid., 881.50/2.

108. Ibid., Willard (Madrid) to Sec. of State, No. 1564, July 12, 1919, 881.00/669.

109. Sloane, Greater France in Africa, v-vi, 10-12.

110. "It is rumored that the Protectorate is seeking a loan from American sources, as French financial circles are reported as being chary of pouring further millions into Morocco. It is generally believed that the recent visit of a party of Americans headed by former Attorney General Wickersham was arranged by the Protectorate authorities in the hope of negotiating a loan .... They were shown the imposing public works in different parts of Morocco, but no opportunity was given for independent investigation of the country .... The party returned to Paris with glowing accounts of flourishing state of Morocco, accounts which appeared in both the French and American press." A. N. F., 881.50/2.

111. C. Van H. Engert to J. Butler Wright (Third Ass't. Sec. of State), copy of a letter from Dr. David P. Barrows, Havana, Jan. 2, 1924, A. N. F., 881.00/885.

112. Ibid., Bradford to Sec. of State, April 9, 1923, 881.00/804.

113. Ibid., Blake to Sec. of State, "Quarterly Information Series," No. 6, Dec. 31, 1919, 881.00/677.

114. Knight, Morocco as a French Economic Venture, 47-48.

115. A. N. F.: Blake to Sec. of State, "Quarterly Information Series," No. 9, Oct. 18, 1920.

116. Ibid., Blake to Sec. of State, No. 154, Aug. 5, 1920, 881.00/697.

117. Knight, Morocco as a French Economic Venture, 34.

118. N. D. Harris, Europe and Africa, 330-331; Knight, Morocco as a French Economic Venture, 51-53. A. N. F.: Blake to Sec. of State, report, Jan. 31, 1922, 881.63/2; Bradford to Sec. of State, April 9, 1923, 881.00/804.

119. A. N. F.: Bartholomaeus to Sec. of State, letter, Aug. 14, 1922, 381.116/1; Denning to Sec. of State, telegram, Aug. 26, 1933, 381.116/3 and No. 58. Nov. 6, 1922, 381.81/127; Mayer to Castle, letter, Feb. 16, 1923, 381.116/13; Denning to Sec. of State, No. 120, March 29, 1923, 381.116/13 and "Quarterly Information Series," No. 17, May 7, 1923, 881.00 /806; Division of Western European Affairs, memorandum, May 14, 1923, 381.116/16.

120. Ibid., Russell to Sec. of State, No. 16, May 15, 1924, 681.51r 3/5; Rand to Sec. of State, No. 249, May 26, 1924, 881.00/930; Russell to Sec. of State, No. 38, Aug. 4, 1924, 881.00/956.

121. Ibid., F M A, Office of the Solicitor, memorandum, Nov. 9, 1922, 881.111/7.

122. Ibid., Blake to Sec. of State, No. 135, June 10, 1920, 681.11247/1; Russell to Sec. of State, No. 153, May 16, 1925, 881.044. During the interval of almost five years between these two dispatches, there were fourteen important communications regarding dahirs involving several American consuls besides Blake.

123. A. N. F.: Blake to Sec. of State, No. 205, March 21, 1921, 681.11213/-- and No. 23, Sept. 21, 1925, 681.11212/6; Grew to Rand, No. 321, Dec. 24, 1924, 681.11212/5.

124. Ibid., Russell to Sec. of State, report No. 10, Sept. 18, 1924, 681.6212/--.

125. Ibid., Office of the Solicitor, memorandum, Nov. 13, 1919, 881.00/674; MacM, Division of Far Eastern

Affairs, memorandum, June 18, 1920, 881.00/699.

126. The Secretary of State evidently was not to be hurried; his decision was dated September 15, 1921. It seems strange that an experienced diplomat like Jusserand continued to urge trivial and untrue reasons for American surrender of capitulatory rights.

127. A. N. F.: Jusserand to Acting Sec. of State, Norman Davis, Jan. 6, 1921, 881.00/702; Office of the Solicitor to Western European Division, memorandum, March 8, 1921, 881.00/702; Hughes to Jusserand, April 8, 1921, 881.00/702.

128. Ibid., Carr to Layton, April 8, 1921, 881.00/718 and Carr to Blake, April 8, 1921, 881.00/718 B; Office of the Solicitor, memorandum, Aug. 22, 1921, 711.81/2; Blake to Sec. of State, No. 242, Sept. 15, 1921, 881.00/738.

129. Ibid., Rand to Sec. of State, No. 229, March 20, 1924, 881.00/911 and May 21, 1924, 881.00/923.

130. Russell said: "Even now American firms have a practical monopoly in this market in such items as mineral oils and by-products, sewing machines, windmills, tractors and other large agricultural machinery and implements, and small autos, and also sell considerable quantities of flour, sugar, and industrial machinery." Russell to Sec. of State, No. 25, June 26, 1924, Ibid., 881.00/946.

131. Ibid., Russell to Sec. of State, No. 25, June 26, 1924, 881.00/946 and No. 81, Nov. 18, 1924, 881.00/1002.

132. Ibid., Rand to Sec. of State, No. 321, Nov. 28, 1924, 881.00/1004.

133. Ibid., Office of the Solicitor, memorandum, March 3, 1925, 881.00/1042.

134. Ibid., Turlington, Office of the Solicitor, to Hackworth, memorandum, March 28, 1925, 881.00/1043; G H H, Office of the Solicitor, to Castle, April 6,

1925, 881.00/1044; Murphy to Sec. of State, memorandum, July 27, 1925, 881.00/1112.

135. W. B. Harris, France, Spain, and the Rif, 200.

136. The father of Abd al Krim was an influential and highly respected chieftain. Abd al Krim attended and studied law at the Karaouine in Fez and later became a Cadi near Melilla. He also edited the Melilla newspaper. His anti-French attitude caused protests from the French authorities. Probably on account of this he was imprisoned at the end of the war by the Spanish authorities. Thereafter he vowed implacable enmity to the Spaniards and all foreign influence in Morocco. After his escape from prison in 1921, he launched his military campaign. Landau, Moroccan Drama, 122: Barbour, North West Africa, 149.

137. Ibid., 91-92.

138. W. B. Harris, France, Spain, and the Rif, 198-200, 204.

139. Ibid., 202-203, 205-210.

140. Ibid., 211-215.

141. Landau, Moroccan Drama, 124-127.

142. Ibid., 128-129; W. B. Harris, France, Spain, and the Rif, 217, 224-225.

143. The dispatches and State Dept. memoranda from which the foregoing excerpts were culled are too numerous for individual citation. They are dated from July 28, 1924 to August 20, 1925. All are filed in A. N. F., 881.00/ category, and their numbers range from 881.00/948 to 881.00/1143.

144. Sloane, Greater France in Africa, 155; Barrows, Berbers and Blacks, 69-70.

145. A. N. F. : Bradford to Sec. of State, April 9, 1925, 881.00/804; Rand to Sec. of State, "Quarterly Information Series," No. 21, March 31, 1925, 881.00/1034; Russell to Sec. of State, No. 191, Aug. 10, 1925, 881.00/1141.

146. Ibid., Blake to Sec. of State, No. 54, Jan. 28, 1926, 881.00/1199.

147. Rom Landau, The Sultan of Morocco, 15.

Chapter XII

International Tangier and Spanish Morocco (1912 - 1939)

During his short regime, Lyautey had laid a remarkably strong foundation for the French Protectorate. For the lesser parts of Morocco, also--Tangier and the Spanish Protectorate--the period of Lyautey and his successors was replete with significant incidents and movements. The "internationalization" of Tangier created new problems; the Riffian War was concluded satisfactorily; internal occupation and development of the Spanish Zone were finally progressing; and Spanish Morocco became the incubator of the Spanish Civil War, concluded just in time to form a prelude for the Second World War. Refusing to be drawn into the concurrent European complications, the United States continued to stand firm in the maintenance of her treaty rights, as she had done in French Morocco, and to demand the Open Door and equality of economic opportunity in all parts of the Sherifian Empire.

Tangier and Spanish Morocco were closely associated. Appealing to history, of course Spain wanted all of Morocco, and it was adding insult to injury that an enclave was cut out of her narrow strip of coast at the behest of the country holding her precious Gibraltar. Since the Spaniards formed a large majority of the population of polyglot Tangier and the Spanish language and money were the most popular there, the city seemed a natural part of Spanish territory. If Spain could not have Tangier as part of her zone, at least she thought it only just that she should be the dominating power there in any international organization. On the contrary, France was working after the Algeciras Act to become dominant over not only her allotted zone but also over the two other sections of Morocco. The neutrality of Tangier was an international embarrassment during World War I (and later World War II), the Riffian War, and the Spanish Civil War because the city was too convenient a base for spies, saboteurs, inciters of rebellion, and purveyors of illicit armament. However, Great Britain would have none but a second-rate power occupying the northern coast of Morocco and only an internationally controlled city dominating the entrance to the Mediterranean. Thus arose the Problem of Tangier, which plagued European politics during the first half of the twentieth century.

It is convenient to begin the history of the two divisions of northern Morocco with the year 1912. After many months of acrimonious negotiations, on November 27, 1912, the Franco-Spanish treaty was signed organizing the Spanish Protectorate. The treaty provided also that there were to be no fortifications between Melilla and the heights dominating the right bank of the Sebou and that "the city of Tangier and its environs constitute a special zone which would be granted a system of government to be determined later."[1] Thus in theory the Spanish and the international zones got on the map simultaneously.

However, the city of Tangier had a long evolution toward a recognized international status. It began late in the 18th century when the Sultan of Morocco permitted the representatives of foreign powers to reside in Tangier and to carry on business with his representative there. This edict made the city the diplomatic capital of Morocco. The system of capitulations greatly enhanced the power and prestige of the consular body throughout the whole country, especially since this regime was supposedly regularized by the Madrid Convention of 1880. Additional duties had been given to the foreign representatives in 1840 when the Sultan placed them in control of maritime sanitary affairs and public health in all Moroccan ports open to commerce. In 1867 the administration and upkeep of the Cape Spartel lighthouse came under consular jurisdiction. By the Act of Algeciras the representatives of the signatory powers became associated with the Maghzen in the administration of public works, customs, taxation, and other matters. About the year 1892, known as the Hygiene Commission, they formed an embryonic municipal council, which was recognized about 1908 when the Sultan assigned a delegate to it and some Maghzen property for its budget.[2]

Several treaties regarding the division of Morocco into zones from 1902 to 1912 had recognized the special position of Tangier. The draft Franco-Spanish treaty of 1902, never ratified, contemplated the eventual neutralization of Tangier. Article 9 of the Franco-Spanish Secret Convention of October 3, 1904, stipulated that "the city of Tangier shall preserve the special character which it derives from the presence of the Diplomatic Corps and from its municipal and sanitary institutions." The Franco-German Treaty of 1911, giving Germany's permission for a French Protectorate, omitted any reference to Tangier, but Sir Edward Grey's note of November 14, 1911, reminded the French government of its obligation to make agreements placing the city "ultimately under international supervision." The Franco-Moroccan Treaty of March 30, 1912, provided that the city of Tangier should conserve the special character which it had been recognized to have and which should determine its municipal organization. British influence was probably strong in securing for Spain the extent of her zone in the Franco-Spanish agreement of November 27, 1912. The treaty defined the boundaries of the Tangier Zone and provided that "the city of Tangier and its outskirts shall be endowed with a special regime which shall be determined subsequently."[3]

Following the last named treaty, negotiations began in March, 1913, to carry out the Tangier provision. By the end of June a conference of French, British, and Spanish delegates meeting in Madrid had completed an international statute. The French government objected to some powers conceded to Spain, and publication of the document inspired a violent campaign of the French and French Moroccan press against it. Negotiations were resumed through diplomatic channels which produced a revised draft dated November 5, 1914. Now Spain declined to accept the treaty on the ground that in wartime it was unfair to make any arrangement without Germany and Austria-Hungary.[4] Undoubtedly, her motive was to wait for a possibly better bargain for herself as a result of the war.

Meanwhile, since 1909 Spain had been carrying on guerrilla war to effect an occupation of the region promised to her in the secret treaty of October 3, 1904. The Franco-Spanish Treaty of November 27, 1912, gave Spain a legal right to claim her protectorate, but with a third reduction in area, for which the Spanish held the British government responsible.[5] The treaty gave Spain the duty to assist the Maghzen in the introduction of all administrative, economic, financial, judicial, and military reforms and all regulations needed to obtain such reforms. The Sultan retained complete civil and religious authority, but could intervene in the zone's affairs only through the Khalifa chosen from two candidates presented by the Spanish government. The Spanish Protectorate was, therefore, practically autonomous, especially since the Spanish-nominated Khalifa was under the Spanish High Commissioner. Furthermore, Spain had only a sub-protectorate, since the diplomatic relations of the Sultan with foreign governments were reserved for France.[6] Raisuli had hoped to become the first Khalifa, since he was at this time the only Spanish ally among the native leaders. Since his past record condemned him, the Spanish chose Mulai al Mehdi, a cousin of the Sultan and only fourteen years old. The Khalifa lived in a palace more gorgeous than the Sultan's at Rabat, surrounded by elegantly dressed courtiers, and he was wholly subservient to his Spanish masters.[7] During 1916 the Spanish proceeded to organize the civil and military structure of the Spanish Zone.[8]

Throughout World War I, Tangier continued to be governed under the Algeciras Act and largely by the Diplomatic Corps. But France asserted authority over the Moroccan officials on the ground that she had control over all Morocco, with no qualification of her power as in the Spanish Zone. The French used every opportunity to tighten their hold on the Tangier Zone. They assumed control over provisioning, policing of the natives, travel permits for the interior, permits for movement of merchandise and traders' stocks, even granting a concession for the water supply to a French company. They expelled Germans and Austrians, putting the German legation archives under the American minister, and confiscating their property. German protégés reverted to Moroccan nationality. Although conceding that Tangier was legally under the sultan's jurisdiction, Spain protested against the treatment of the Germans. The international administration was very unsatisfactory, even in matters of long experience; the Diplomatic Corps showed itself most ineffective in dealing with rudimentary public health measures and the influenza epidemic of 1918. The various police services were most undependable, and justice in the capitulatory courts was irregular and uncertain.[9]

Very inadequately and hopelessly, Spain was struggling

to expand her zone of occupation, but even with an army of nearly 80,000 troops made little effort to gain footholds outside the towns. Many German agents tried to rouse the natives against France and sold them arms. As the real dictator of the zone, Raisuli governed both natives and Spaniards. He collected and kept revenues from all the tribes, besides receiving money from Spain for the pay of his Moroccan troops.[10] Among the natives the Germans had little difficulty in winning over some other persons of position, including Abdel Malek el-Meheddin[11] and the Abd al Krim family, father and sons. Many natives were also employed in smuggling arms and in spreading anti-French propaganda. These German activities gave the natives opportunity for profitable employment and distracted them from observing the slow advance of the Spaniards into the Riff. The disloyalty of the Spanish toward the Allies has been severely criticized, yet the neutral attitude of the Spanish government seems impeccable. There is no doubt that some subordinate officials in Spanish Morocco did take full advantage of the opportunity to aid the Germans.[12]

It appears unquestionable, also, that the Spanish government saw hope in a peace settlement whereby a chastened if not beaten France might be induced to surrender Tangier to Spain. An incident in the first part of 1915 suggests that Spain did not intend to await the end of the war to assert her claim to Tangier. Blake from Tangier and Willard from Madrid reported rumors of the intended landing of Spanish troops at Tangier, which both regarded as an act of incredible folly. The reports were given credit because of Spain's mobilization of her fleet at Algeciras, the speeches of many leaders demanding the cession of Tangier, and the return of the Spanish Chargé from Madrid to Tangier with the title of envoy extraordinary, which made him the head of the Diplomatic Corps. The energetic press campaign was another evidence of Spanish intentions. However, the expected invasion of Tangier did not occur; both France and Great Britain labored successfully to convince Spain of the inopportuneness of such a venture, and the Spanish government countermanded the landing of troops.[13] However, Spain's passionate propaganda for the acquisition of Tangier continued unabated, sometimes taking very extreme forms.[14]

Neither Spain nor France was the gainer at the Versailles peace Conference. France had been very confident that she would be able to add Tangier to her zone. She might have done better than that--the rumor current at the conference was that the Spanish government had made an offer to sell the entire Spanish Zone to France.[15] In a report prepared for the Commission for the Study of Colonial Questions Presented by the War, France had a perfect brief for her case. The report declared that the Tangier Zone had remained under the sovereignty of the Sultan, and France might lawfully exercise her protectorate over it. France's economic interests were great; she had almost one-half of the general commerce, three-fourths of the immovable property, and most of the banks. Strategically, since Spain had her peninsula, and Great Britain had Gibraltar, France should have Tangier. Many articles from the European press were cited to show that international public opinion favored French control. It was even asserted that liberal elements in Spain wanted to be rid of Morocco.[16] On February 25, 1919, the director of the North African section in the French Foreign Office presented to the Council of Ten a written demand for the incorporation of Tangier into the French Protectorate. Nevertheless, the Tangier Zone remained an entity, and France got no benefit from the Versailles Treaty except the elimination of Germany from Morocco. The French government insisted that the clauses regarding Germans and their property extended to all of Morocco, by dahirs issued from 1920 to 1922, and proceeded to apply them to Tangier.[17]

While the war was progressing, the United States began with Spain the same sort of wearisome negotiations as had characterized her relations with France over American claims, recognition of the Spanish Protectorate, and the surrender of American capitulations in Spanish Morocco. As the years went on, the results were, if possible, even more frustrating.

On September 20, 1914, the Spanish Ministry of State addressed American Ambassador Joseph Willard in Madrid asking the American government to place its subjects in the Spanish Zone immediately under the regime of the Spanish courts there, thus renouncing the jurisdiction of its consular agent. From the Spanish Embassy at Washington came to the State Department on the following February 6 a repetition of this invitation, with the news that France had already accepted the Spanish judicial jurisdiction, while Italy and Norway had accepted it in principle. Following the advice of the Division of Near Eastern Affairs, the State Department replied to the Spanish Embassy on February 19, 1915. Before the United States could agree to surrender any capitulary rights in Morocco, she would want to see the settlement of certain American claims now pending against Spanish Morocco, satisfactory guarantees for the proper protection in the future of legitimate commercial interests, and establishment of a satisfactory form of government for the international zone. Furthermore, consent to the new regime in the Spanish Zone could not be given before the United States was ready to agree to the new regime in the French Zone and the new government for the international zone of Tangier. In addition, Ambassador Willard was informed, the United States expected to have a member on any international court set up in Tangier.[18]

The next move came from the Spanish Ambassador, who called at the State Department on January 24, 1917, to request that negotiations be opened for the recognition of the Spanish Protectorate in Morocco. Now that the United States had already recognized the French Protectorate, naturally one would expect that she would wish to recognize the Spanish one in the same way. Five days later the Assistant Secretary of State, Phillips, explained to the Spanish Ambassador the wording of the original American recognition and told of Jusserand's request that it be changed to cover all of Morocco. Phillips asked for a clarification of the situation. On February 9, 1917, Blake urged that prior to any move to recognize the Spanish Zone the claim of Sid Driss El-Kittany,[19] an American protégé for signal services, be settled. Throughout 1915 and 1916 this claim had been the topic of extensive correspondence between Blake and the State Department. Repeated efforts had failed to effect a settlement. The dispute now hinged upon the question of to whom to appeal in case of an adverse initial verdict. The Spanish insisted upon the Spanish High Commissioner, although the Spanish government was a defendant in the suit. Blake advocated the Sultan's minister of foreign affairs at Tangier, as provided by the Madrid Convention. Since the United States had not recognized the Spanish Protectorate, she must follow the provisions of her treaties. Better still would be local arbitration by the Spanish diplomatic agent and the American chargé at Tangier.[20]

By July 16, 1917, the Spanish government had taken a new direction, its ambassador calling at the State Department to ask now that the American government renounce the regime for capitulations, just as France, Belgium, Russia, Italy, Switzerland, Denmark, and Sweden had done. The Division of Near Eastern Affairs advised that it had already been decided that the abolition of capitulations could be effected only by a treaty ratified by the Senate. However, on July 25, 1917, the Spanish ambassador again asked for American renunciation of capitulations, since the courts of justice had been in operation about three years and offered ample safeguards for Europeans. He expressed his government's high gratification at such a renunciation which would "recognize the said Spanish Zone as has already been done by the nations above cited." In his reply of August 20, 1917, Secretary Lansing again informed Don Juan Riaño that the United States Constitution required Senate approval of any surrender of capitulatory rights. In turn, the Spanish government replied that it could not agree to the American recognition of the French Protectorate unless at the same time the Spanish Zone were clearly set forth.[21] Presumably, the revised formula for the recognition of the French Protectorate was satisfactory to Spain; it provided for recognition of the French Protectorate subject to the informal note of January 2, 1917, and subject to the special rights and privileges of Spain in Morocco.

The two decades between the first and second world wars were a period of many events and much turbulence for both Spanish Morocco and Tangier. Throughout the whole time Spain was striving for prestige and power--and for Tangier. She wanted her protectorate to be recognized as that of France had been. The internationalization of Tangier was followed by revisions of the original agreement and the rise of Mussolini's Italy demanding and receiving the status that Spain had been refused. Unfortunately, Tangier's version of international government did not foster peace or prosperity, and the city suffered a severe economic decline. Spain's military occupation of her zone, continuing since 1909, culminated in the Riffian War, which threatened both the Spanish and French Protectorates. Chronically plagued by various dissident groups, Spain suffered several insurrections, followed by a military dictatorship and a republic and ending in one of the most terrible civil wars in history.

Meanwhile, independent and aloof above all this international turmoil, the United States remained firm in all parts of Morocco, often circumvented by her "protectors," but continuing to insist on the Open Door and equality of economic opportunity guaranteed by her treaties with Morocco and refusing to be bound by pacts made without her since the Act of Algeciras.

The ambition of Spain to achieve American recognition of her zone and renunciation of capitulations there was not attained. Instead, from 1920 to 1939 there continued to be a series of futile communications and broken agreements on claims which resulted in American refusal to accede to Spanish wishes. For the sake of continuity the story will be completed before consideration of the other happenings of the period.

On August 13, 1920, Ambassador Riaño answered Lansing's note of almost three years previously. The Ministry of State, he said, had no objection to adopting the procedure suggested by Mr. Lansing. Therefore, his government desired that the United States prepare

> "a declaration or agreement in which could be embodied the clause relating to approval by the North American Senate, under which declaration or agreement, the United States would relinquish the capitulations system in the Spanish influence zone in Morocco, recognizing said zone of influence, as has been done by the other nations mentioned to Your Excellency."[22]

Both Jusserand and Riaño seemed singularly obtuse about the meaning of Senate consent to an American treaty.

During 1921, the State Department paid some attention to the problem of the Spanish Zone. A memorandum of the Division of Western European Affairs[23] dated May 18, 1921, advised the preservation of the status quo until after a satisfactory agreement on the Tangier problem, although all countries except the United States and Great Britain had now recognized the Spanish Zone. Blake's suggestion was quoted; it was that recognition be extended with American retention of capitulary rights, providing that three pending claims were satisfied in advance. In his own dispatch of September 15,

1921, Blake reported that his diplomatic agency was preparing a list of outstanding claims which should be liquidated as a preliminary requirement for recognition of the Spanish Zone. However, before the surrender of extraterritorial rights, Spanish authority should be securely established throughout the zone and a proper judicial regime should be put into operation. Regarding Tangier, when France, Great Britain, and Spain reached an understanding, their joint scheme would probably be submitted to the approval of the other powers signatory to the Act of Algeciras--excluding the Teutonic powers, of course.[24]

On March 2, 1923, Riaño ventured to remind the new Secretary of State, Charles Evans Hughes, that his note of August 13, 1920, was still unanswered. The Division of Western European Affairs advised that the procedure followed for the French Protectorate be used again, that is, a recognition which reserved the question of renuniciation of capitulations for future negotiation. For the present it might be wiser to secure a settlement of American claims; then, if the pending commercial treaty with Spain were satisfactorily concluded, the United States could recognize the Spanish Zone immediately. Omitting mention of any commercial treaty, Hughes gave this answer to Riaño on March 19, 1923. In May the Spanish High Commissioner tried to make applicable to American ressortisants a ten percent consumption tax without even notifying the American Agency. The American Diplomatic Agent later assented to the suggestion of the Spanish official that the matter be taken up directly between the two governments, since their agents were not officially on speaking terms because of the non-recognition of the zone by the American government. Discussing the taxation situation, on July 27, 1923, the Solicitor gave the opinion that the President, in his recent consent to taxation, had the power to pass upon what foreign authorities were in control of particular areas and to make appropriate arrangements with them which would not curtail the practical operation of commercial benefits acquired under prior treaties. The dispute over the American adhesion to the dahir creating the consumption tax was reported settled on December 8, 1922, by the agreement that the United States would accept the tax when all other countries had done so. This case illustrates the great difficulty which the American agent in Tangier had for years in communicating with the non-recognized Spanish Zone officials.[25]

During 1924 the question of levying taxes upon American nationals continued in controversy. On March 20 Rand gave his opinion on the general judicial situation. In the Spanish Zone, he remarked, there was not even a semblance of an attempt to reform the administration of justice--which was not surprising, considering that the Riffian War was at its height at this time. It was impossible to think of any substitution for American jurisdiction, even if all outstanding American claims had been disposed of. In the Tangier Zone, the proposed International Court, from which American judges had been excluded, had yet to evolve "from a complicated and burdensome project to the stage of practical application." Riaño, in a note of September 30, 1924, invoked Article I of the Franco-Spanish Convention of 1912 to justify any measure of taxation which the Spanish government thought necessary. However, the Solicitor of the State Department contended, the new taxation proposed far exceeded that allowed in the Act of Algeciras and had no parallels in the French Zone. The stamp tax decree contained at least one provision discriminating in favor of Spanish products. It was suggested that Blake be consulted regarding the acceptability of the proposed taxes. In Blake's opinion, it was unwise to give any further recognition to the Spanish authorities until conditions were more normal, as otherwise the United States would ultimately arrive, by piecemeal concessions, at a position in which there was no inducement for Spain to meet the American requirements for formal recognition of her zone. The United States had already departed from this policy by agreeing to the consumption taxes on certain articles, but the Spanish officials had been conciliatory in refunding taxes illegally levied prior to the Department's acquiescence. The stamp tax was particularly objectionable.[26]

During 1927 there was further discussion. Inquiring about the decision regarding taxation, the Spanish ambassador was told on May 20 that this was a part of the question of recognition, which in turn depended on settlement of American claims. On July 26 the Spanish government, now with a new ambassador, Alejandro Padilla y Bell, informed the Secretary of State that it was ready to study the claims. However, the State Department wanted the claims examined not in Madrid, but in Tangier, and by the local American and Spanish diplomatic agents. By Blake this timing was considered most opportune, as the Spanish Zone was completely pacified and ready for economic development.[27]

In 1928 the American and Spanish governments agreed to submit the claims question to Blake and the Spanish consul general at Tangier, Antonio Pia, who were to prepare a joint report.[28] This report was completed on July 12, 1928, and the State Department informed the Spanish government on November 22 that it was prepared to use it as a basis for settlement of the American claims.[29]

On September 4, 1929, Pia now promoted to the office of vice secretary general in Madrid, repudiated his own report. Some claims were disallowed, and the others were to be paid after the relinquishment of her capitulatory rights by the United States. After a conference with Jordana in May, Blake had reduced the claims by 125,000 pesetas. It seemed that the rejection of the El Kittany claim, after being accepted by both Pia and Jordana, was incredible, but the Spanish government denied all responsibility for the usurpation of this property in 1912. The new Spanish proposal was rejected in November. Blake's opinion was that no settlement of claims would ever be made by the Spanish government unless vigorous pressure were put upon Primo de Rivera.[30]

Between 1930 and 1936 voluminous correspondence was exchanged between the American and Spanish governments on the same problems of unpaid claims and recognition of the Spanish Zone. The State Department maintained the view that the surrender of capitulary rights should be done integrally for all three zones in one treaty with the consent of the Senate. Meanwhile, the American government refused to apply the <u>dahirs</u> on taxation to its nationals in Spanish Morocco.

Probably in retaliation, the officials of the Spanish Zone imposed more restrictions upon American trade. When it came into power, the Spanish Republican government made no move toward settling the dispute. The American claims kept mounting because of illegally levied taxation. Communication between the American diplomatic Agency and the Spanish authorities at Tetuan remained almost impossible, since Blake's protests, made through the Spanish minister in Tangier, were not answered. The only satisfaction obtained by the American Agency at Tangier came through the intervention of British consular officials who secured the release of some American nationals and protégés from illegal detention by the Spanish.

For a time it appeared that Claude Bowers, American ambassador at Madrid, might be able to break the impasse, and Blake went to Madrid to assist him. At the first Foreign Office interview, Blake thought that Señor Castano epitomized the Spanish attitude in her dealings with the United States:

> His remarks obviously showed that the Spanish government entertained no anxiety to secure ... the advantage of American recognition of their protectorate in Morocco. They felt that they were entitled to follow the example of the authorities in the French Zone by doing much as they liked in their own zone regarding the stipulations of the Moroccan treaties, which they look upon as outworn restrictions upon their "civilizing" mission in Morocco ... Spain was reaping no profit from the occupation of her zone, her irksome engagements there were purely in the interest of the balance of international influences in the Mediterranean, and ... the Spanish government felt that it was justly entitled to the amplest moral and material assistance from the powers claiming interests in Morocco. With or without American recognition, they felt they were justified in freely pursuing their own policies.

Evidently Blake was right in thinking that the Spanish desire for recognition and freedom from capitulations had reversed itself to indifference in early 1935. There were desultory exchanges until July, 1939, but the Second World War opened without any agreement on the long disputed problems.[31]

After the first World War, in addition to this conflict with the United States on the diplomatic front, Spain was engaged on two other fronts--against the natives of her zone, which resulted in the Riffian War, and against France for possession of Tangier. If the first contest was a drawn battle, the second was saved from failure only by the aid of Spain's arch-rival, and the third was a failure.

For Marshal Lyautey, when he resigned in September, 1925, the Riffian War was unfinished business and the nearest approach to a defeat in his long career of successes. For the Spanish leaders it was the climax of several years of warfare to occupy their zone. The prologue to the war began in 1919, when General Berenguer arrived in Tetuan and reversed the wartime policy of his government to pamper Raisuli and to buy his favor. A series of small engagements near Tangier resulted in heavy losses for the Spanish. Then a limited success for the Spanish was followed by promulgation of a <u>dahir</u> by the Khalifa, removing Raisuli from office, confiscating his property, and declaring him an outlaw. Thereupon Raisuli declared war on the Spaniards. Brigandage, aggressions on travelers, attacks on the Spanish posts, and an ambush of a Spanish garrison threw the whole Jibala region into anarchy. Berenguer occupied Sheshuan on October 20, 1920, but there were many more battles and losses for the Spanish before Raisuli submitted on September 28, 1922, ending the war in the western part of the zone.[32]

Meanwhile, before the war against Raisuli was finished, another more serious conflict engulfed the eastern part of the Spanish Zone, and a more formidable antagonist of Spain emerged there. Early in 1920, Abd al Krim the elder with a body of his Beni Uriaghel tribesmen joined a band of Riffi guerrillas to oppose the further advance of the Spanish. Escaping from a Spanish prison in the spring of 1920, his elder son Mohand joined his father and a brother already arrived from Madrid. When the father died, the elder son, known to history as Abd al Krim, was elected Kaid of his tribe. From Melilla the army of General Sylvestre was busily consolidating its position and advancing rapidly southward. In the Melilla district were 20,000 Spanish and 4,000 native troops to oppose the small band of Riffians who attacked them. But the Spanish troops were untrained, undisciplined, and very inefficient. The lines of communication with the base were poorly guarded, and the army posts had no intercommunication and were inadequately manned and ill-supplied --a situation often found in Spanish armies. Moreover, in Sylvestre the army had a leader of flamboyance and recklessness.[33]

On July 21, 1921, came the great disaster--the fall of Anual. The furious attack of the Riffs resulted in the evacuation of the post, the retirement of the garrison, and the death of General Sylvestre and his staff, either by suicide or by enemy assault. The Spanish army fled in a panic from all its posts, abandoning artillery, transport, stores of arms, and ammunition. They were joined in their flight to Melilla by peasants and colonists. In three days twelve years of work and sacrifice by the Spaniards had been wiped out, and the entire Riff was lost. All this had been accomplished by about 2,000 to 3,000 tribesmen, armed with contraband weapons, and without a machine to make even a rifle or a cartridge. Organized propaganda was now disseminated by Spain, especially in Great Britain, to minimize this "incident of colonial warfare."[34]

For the next five years the Spanish were to be preoccupied with implacable and incessant warfare against the Riffs. Debates in the Cortes and a parliamentary inquiry revealed the real causes of the disaster--the corruption of the administration, the immorality of the officers, and the sufferings of the troops. The whole nation was aroused to action. General Berenguer and many others were court martialed and punished, but there was a general conviction that the civilian government was fundamentally at fault. A new ministry was formed on August 8 under Señor Maura, which sent another army of 70,000 men to begin again the conquest of the Riff. In October, 1921, the advance began, and in a year and a half the lost ground had been regained, but at a terrible cost. In 1923 the finance minister admitted that the last two years of war in Morocco had cost over ₤43,000,000.[35]

The several changes in the office of High Commissioner of Spanish Morocco did not bring success to Spanish arms. In the summer of 1922 Berenguer was succeeded by General Burguete. It was the latter who secured the temporary submission of Raisuli. Very soon, however, adherents of Abd al Krim were infiltrating into the western region and agitating it again. A successful advance of the Spanish front in the Riff was suspended under opposition pressure on the government. In December, 1922, the appointment of a civilian high commissioner, Señor Silvela, did not improve the military situation, again becoming dangerous in the west.[36]

A further step toward governmental reform was the installation of a military dictatorship in September, 1923, under Primo de Rivera. He attained office with no weapon but an old-fashioned pronunciamento and with the willing assent of King Alfonso XIII. With his cabinet of military officers, his was "the only Spanish Government of the century to give the country any rest from political murders, strikes, and sterile political intrigue."[37] In one of his first public speeches he denounced the methods of his predecessors as "the most expensive, the most protracted, the most useless and the most unworthy." His main objective was winning the Riffian War, and to this end he introduced many improvements in the service.[38] However, he discovered his task to be a prodigious one, too great for his unaided power.

De Rivera appointed still another High Commissioner, General Aizouru. The latter was responsible for confirming the peace agreement with Raisuli. However, Raisuli was no longer a menace. His leading role in the rebellion against the Spanish had been taken by Abd al Krim, who had elected himself President of the Republic of the Riff. His domain included, besides the Riff, the Gomara tribal area and Lau, very close to Tetuan.[39]

During 1922 and 1923 Blake received one official communication and Post Wheeler, American chargé in London, received two from the government of the Riff Republic. All were written in the ornate and florid Arabic style, and in that language. The first one, dated January 4, 1922, recited a long list of grievances which had impelled the Riffs to rebel. Over his own signature, Mohamed Ben Abd-El-Krim El-Kihittabi appealed to the civilized world for help. He declared that his country was open to modern civilization (so long as it did not contradict the Muslim religion), to commerce, and to schools. The Riffs had treated military prisoners kindly, in spite of the dum dum bullets, asphyxiating gases, close artillery fire, and bombs from airplanes used against the natives. The two other missives, both addressed to Wheeler and from different London addresses, were dated September 6, 1922 and August 21, 1923. The first, signed Muhammed Abdul Karim, was an appeal to the civilized world to help free the Riff from their miscalled "Protectors," who were really brutal oppressors. The third letter was sent by "L. A. Gardiner, Minister Plenipotentiary for the Government of the Riff." It was a declaration of independence, proclaiming that the Riff, never under any control before 1906, had regained its complete independence on June 10, 1920, from the Spanish and since then had sought vainly to make peace with them. The declaration was signed by the four ministers of the Republic. It ended with an invitation to all countries to send their diplomatic representatives to the Riff.[40]

By 1924 the situation all over the zone was recognized as serious. In May Abd al Krim launched simultaneous attacks in the east and on the Wadi Lau west of Tetuan. He was driven back, but continued the attack in July. Spain was losing faith in her dictator, who now had to make a crucial decision. His plan was one of semi-abandonment of the zone. He would establish and fall back on a line against which the Riffs would be exhausted, and meantime he would build up the protectorate in areas under his control. In view of the danger of an overwhelming enemy advance once the retreat was begun, de Rivera came in person to Morocco in October 1924 and took over both command of the army and the high commissionership. The withdrawal was a success; the rebel lines were unable to penetrate the well-defended Rivera line. Beyond it, however, Abd al Krim occupied Sheshaun and in January, 1925, he attacked Raisuli in Tazerut. The old bandit preferred to be taken prisoner by his own people, and he died obscurely among them three months later.[41]

The Spanish wars with the natives had been well reported in American dispatches since 1909, but especially ably since 1921. Some interesting comments are contained in them. In January, 1923, it was said that "the Moorish insurgents were sustained from the beginning by regular deliveries of arms, ammunition, food, and probably money from the French Zone." The commercial depression in all three zones of Morocco was noted in a dispatch of April 30, 1924. On September 3, 1924, Russell at Casablanca spoke of the well armed Moors:

> Where do these munitions come from? The Mediterranean coast of Spain is so closely blocked by the Spanish fleet that the amount that may be smuggled is small. Supplies could come only from the French Zone, from Algeria, or from Tangier.

At the last of October, 1924, Abd al Krim was circulating among the inhabitants of the Riff and Jibala a proclamation stating the terms on which the Spaniards could secure peace from their conquerors. A dispatch of May 18, 1925, quoted de Rivera as saying in a speech in Seville:

> It must not be concealed that neither now, nor ever, can we have any economic future in Africa, and that it would consequently be senseless to spend there the gold of the country and the blood of our children. We must therefore confine ourselves ... to fulfill strictly the obligations issuing from the international treaties, and to guard the coasts, because of their importance.[42]

During 1924 and 1925, Abd al Krim was encouraged and emboldened by support or sympathy from other countries. Great Britain remained strictly neutral and refused to intervene--an attitude declared in the House of Commons as early as August 8, 1922. In June and July of 1925, she took no part in the Franco-Spanish conversations, refused to participate in blockading the coast or to accept surveillance of her ships beyond the three-mile limit, and declined to land troops to defend Tangier. The United States also stayed officially neutral, but the State Department planned to prevent the shipping of airplanes to the Riffs. Like the British, the American government would not recognize the right of either France or Spain to interfere with its vessels outside the three-mile limit, or within that limit except as provided by the Act of Algeciras. However, the Emergency Foreign Policy Conference urged in November that the American government tender its friendly offices as mediator in an effort to end the war.[43]

In the State Department files in Washington are several documents revealing the intense interest taken by the Comintern in the Riffian War. Thousands of gold rubles were appropriated for agitation against colonial powers, with France and Spain the prime targets. No money was given to aid the Riffs directly, but great sums were allotted to French and Spanish Communists to arouse the Moroccans against their colonial overlords. Abd al Krim was mentioned as one "whom we assisted in negotiating with Raisuli." A large sum was given to the French Communist Party for "the organization of propaganda against the war in Morocco." Russell noted the prevalence of articles in the French Communist press and the eventual prohibition of the importation of such material into French Morocco. In Algeria subversive literature was circulated until the police arrested the distributors. In a speech in the Chamber of Deputies on June 23, 1925, Painlevé presented a bitter indictment of the Communist activities in appealing to the soldiers and workers in Morocco and in congratulating Abd al Krim on his victory over Spain. Painlevé's speech to the Chamber won an overwhelming vote of support.[44]

The impact of the Riff rebellion upon the Pan-Islam movement was frequently discussed. A conference of several leaders in Berlin during November, 1925, was reported to have made one of its objectives the prevention of the conclusion of peace and the breaking down of all unofficial negotiations. In a discussion of "A Moslem League of Nations" in the _Journal de Genève_, Abd al Krim was named as the future leader of this league.[45]

Of great significance was the interest which the Riffs and their leader aroused in the United States. Two American correspondents were especially proficient in making the Riffian situation well known there--Paul Scott Mowrer, who wrote a series of articles for the Chicago _Daily News_, and Vincent Sheean, who wrote both press accounts[46] and a book, _An American Among the Riffi._ Sheean was very sympathetic to the Riffians and expressed great admiration for their chief, whom he visited at his headquarters. In an interview with Primo de Rivera in Madrid on February 9, 1925, Sheean even acted as an intermediary for Abd al Krim, who was eager for peace negotiations with the Spanish and wanted to know their peace terms. Rivera replied that twice since October he had sent a peace envoy to Abd al Krim, but the Moor's demand for munitions, airplanes, and submarines had caused the breaking off of negotiations. Spain would never tolerate a warrior state in the heart of the Protectorate, where guerrilla leaders rose and fell in cycles of ten or twelve years. Spain, also desiring peace, must impose as a _sine qua non_ complete disarmament and Abd al Krim's recognition of the present Sultan.[47]

An American volunteer organization to aid the Riffians was the American Friends of the Riff, which established the Americas' Commission for the Riff. On February 6, 1926, this group sent to the Secretary of State four enclosures to keep on file and to inform him of their aims. With Herbert Myrick as leader, it started organizing at Springfield, Massachusetts. The commission's aim was ambitious; it was the association of the nations of North and South America to secure justice and "autonomy for an unconquerable people." The American Commission hoped to join a similar British group, whose secretary, Captain Gordon Canning, had returned from Morocco as the accredited representative of Abd al Krim. With a somewhat bizarre version of their history, an eulogistic description was given of the characteristics of the Berbers. France was praised for the work in her zone, but Spain was condemned for her graft, inefficiency, and exploitation. Shortly before Myrick's communication, Captain Canning and his committee had been exposed as having possible German connections and a personal interest in Moroccan mines. Canning had been trying to negotiate for Abd al Krim for about eighteen months, but Premier Briand refused to see him. He was also accused of attempting to use Tangier as his base of operations.[48]

Another unofficial American connection with the Riffian War should be recorded. On August 10 and 11 the much-heralded American aviators arrived to join the French forces against the Riffs. The French officials and press attempted to impress upon the Moroccans that the aviators had the sanction of the United States Government, without actually saying so. They were enlisted as volunteers into the Sherifian Air Guard. Comments in the Moroccan press suggested that the aviators' enlistment was another evidence of American interest in the Riff; there had been much unfavorable criticism of an alleged sale of mining and other concessions by the Mannesmann brothers to an Anglo-American financial group. Blake was disturbed at Painlevé's speech to the aviators before they left Paris, welcoming them to the fight of Western civilization against the Islamic culture. Furthermore, he thought that the aerial bombing of undefended centers of population, which these aviators did, was prohibited by international agreement. To a protest from the Women's International League for Peace and Freedom, the State Department made the reply that its diplomatic agent in Morocco had been asked to call attention to the fact that the laws of the United States made unlawful the enlistment, in the United States or in countries where she enjoyed extraterritorial privileges, of American citizens for service in foreign armed forces. Nevertheless, the fourteen men continued to serve until they were disbanded and returned to France on November 5. On their departure they received from Marshal Pétain a collective citation for "executing daily difficult and distant liaison, reconnoitering, and bombing expeditions carrying out in six weeks more than three hundred fifty war missions and dropping more than forty tons of projectiles."[49]

While these small gestures of aid or sympathy might have encouraged Abd al Krim, they did not seriously affect the main business of the war in its last year. As previously related, Abd al Krim might have been inspired by the withdrawal of the Spaniards to the Rivera line, but more probably his lack of food impelled him to attack the French who had occupied the Wergha Valley. His whirlwind assault along the Wergha River brought some of his forces within twenty kilometers of Fez. The whole interior of French Morocco was in danger. To meet this new challenge, Marshal Lyautey was removed and succeeded as commander-in-chief of the French army by Marshal Pétain. The latter set up his own plans of defense. Brought together by the common peril, Spain and France now decided to cooperate. A conference was held in Madrid in June and July, 1925, to formulate military and political means of ending the war. Public opinion inimical to colonialism was strong in many countries, even in France itself, and both French and Spanish representatives thought it necessary to offer a "guarantee of administrative, economic, and political autonomy for the Riff and Jibala tribes." However, the initiative was passed to Abd al Krim. Through his failure to make a public approach, he may have lost more favorable terms of surrender.[50]

On August 10, 1925, Primo de Rivera announced that an envoy claiming to be from Abd al Krim declared that the chieftian would negotiate only after the recognition of the independence of the Riff. It was understood that the secret terms then offered to Abd al Krim were recognition of the "religious sovereignty" of the Sultan and acknowledgment by Spain and France of the administrative autonomy of the Riff and organization of an adequate Riff police force under French officers. Instead of agreeing on peace terms, Pétain and Rivera then proceeded to prepare plans for simultaneous action against Abd al Krim. While the French advanced to the limits of their zone, the Spanish were to occupy Alhucemas Bay, capture Ajdir to open communication between this town and Melilla by land, and to advance from Alcazar to Sheshuan. Then the two armies were to meet in the Spanish Zone.

By September 8, 1925, the Spanish troops had succeeded in landing at Alhucemas. Abd al Krim's diversionary attack in Gomara could not halt the Franco-Spanish action in the Melilla region, and by the end of September Ajdir was captured. Victory was now apparently in sight for France and Spain. A new Khalifa, Mulai Hassan Ben al-Mehdi, son of a former Khalifa, was installed in Tetuan with magnificent ceremony, and Rivera returned to Spain, leaving General Sanjurjo as high commissioner. On September 24 occurred the resignation of Marshal Lyautey as resident general--General Pétain had displaced him as military commander some time before this. His critics of the Parliamentary Left were very voluble in their comments on Lyautey; his advance into the Wergha Valley had precipitated the whole French involvement in the war, he had been ambitious to add the Spanish Zone to the French possessions, and personally he was obnoxious--self-opinionated, superannuated, and unable to take criticism, opposition, or contradiction. His friends, of course, had the opposite view of Lyautey, but at this time his enemies had the last word.[51]

During the ensuing rainy season there was an opportunity for the French and Spanish to build up their economic and political fronts preparatory to a spring offensive. Abd al Krim had increasing difficulties because of the blockade and the reported defection of important tribes. In January 1926, Blake thought that Abd al Krim made a bad mistake in placing any dependence upon either Gordon Canning or Vincent Sheean as his peace envoys.[52] He thought concentration of peace maneuvers should be made on Spain, since France had now reoccupied practically all territory wrested from her by the Riffians' initial advance.[53]

In April Abd al Krim sent delegates to Ujda to sue for peace. Many diplomats thought that this meeting was a bluff on the part of all three parties and predicted its failure. The negotiators haggled over the terms offered--autonomy of the Riff, removal of Abd al Krim, disarmament of the Riff, sovereignty of the sultan. The negotiations lasted from April 18 to May 7 and ended in failure. On May 8 hostilities were resumed. The French held their entire line with a terrific bombardment by artillery and planes and took Tarfuist, but the Spanish bore the brunt of the heavy fighting, moving southward from Melilla and Ajdir. On May 27, 1926,

Abd al Krim surrendered to the French north of Tarfuist. There were rumors that he had been beaten by dissidence in his own forces and also he was accused of selling mining rights and keeping the proceeds. It was even said that he had accepted a large French subsidy to surrender.[54]

A controversy now arose concerning the custody of the defeated rebel. France had him; Blake charged that she had bought him. His choice of France as his captor was dictated by a secret plan of M. Steeg, the successor of Lyautey, Blake asserts, whereby Steeg first purchased the good will of Abd al Krim's leading adherents and then offered him safety and a comfortable living abroad in return for correspondence exchanged with agents of European powers. Rivera demanded the person of Abd al Krim in order to try him by court martial, and when refused this, he even threatened to call an international conference to deal with Moroccan matters. Dispatches from other sources confirmed this general view and spoke of Spain's chagrin at being hoodwinked. Because of his brutal treatment of Spanish prisoners, the Spanish government wanted Abd al Krim to be punished as a common criminal. From June 14 to July 10 Franco-Spanish conversations in Paris considered measures to terminate the war. Suggestions of another international conference over Morocco in the British and Italian press gradually subsided, but the interest of these two countries and also Germany in the talks was noted in the European press. In the French Chamber of Deputies Premier Painlevé absolutely rejected the idea of a conference in June. An accord was finally reached providing for Spain's occupation of her zone, the right of pursuit by each party into the territory of the other, and a mixed commission to delineate the frontier more thoroughly, following the principle of the line of 1912. However, Abd al Krim remained a guest of the French at Fez.[55]

On August 27, 1926, accompanied by his family, his brother and uncle and their families, and several Moroccan servants, Abd al Krim was brought from Fez to Casablanca and embarked upon a steamer for Marseilles, enroute to exile in the island of Reunion in the Indian Ocean. Since the natives never saw him as a captive, rumors continued to be credited that he was at large. His party reached their destination at Saint Denis on Reunion on October 10, 1926. There he leased the Chateau Morange at an annual rental of

20,000 francs and settled down[56] with a French pension to enjoy a peaceful life.[57]

Although the leader was eliminated, the Riffian War was not yet finished. There remained a number of dissident areas which had to be pacified by arms or diplomacy. On August 25, 1926, Shashuan was reoccupied without a fight. By the end of 1926, 30,000 rifles, 135 cannon, eight mortars and 199 machine guns had been confiscated in the Spanish Zone. Most of these had originally been captured from the French or Spanish soldiers after their defeats. It had required about 250,000 men with every kind of modern weapons to subdue the Riffians. Very few prisoners were recovered and not any officers; they had died under the harsh treatment given them. It was necessary to carry on mopping up operations into 1927; there were a number of battles in the mountains that spring. By July 10, however, General Sanjurjo announced that peace existed throughout the Spanish Zone. In December the Madrid press published the statement of Premier Painlevé and M. Poincaré in a Chamber of Deputies debate. Both said that the military agreement made by General Pétain and General Primo de Rivera had ceased to be effective. Poincaré added that France and Spain were abiding by the treaty of 1912 regarding their respective zones and that the said treaty was to be considered in effect for other nations as well.[58]

In 1926 there were two interesting incidents related to the Riffian War. The first was Sultan Youssef's visit to France in early July, which Blake described as an occasion for "public courtesies, whitewashing and propaganda." Ostensibly, the Sultan came with a large retinue of Moroccan notables to consecrate the newly completed mosque in Paris--a project of Lyautey's. His visit was also meant to commemorate the end of the war and probably to testify that it had not been an aggressive, vindictive war to satisfy colonial ambitions. Of course, anything to encourage French commerce was also highly desirable.[59] The second event was the making of the Pact of Madrid--a Spanish-Italian treaty of perpetual neutrality announced on August 7. In the French and British press it was interpreted as directed against their countries' interests. Blake pronounced it a "further evidence that the real dimensions of the Moroccan problem continue to be, as in the past, a political variant, condemned, as it seems, by predestination, to a state of perpetual flexibility!'[60] Both opinions proved to be correct.

Throughout the Riffian War, and after it, the Tangier problem was the occasion of a fiercely fought diplomatic war between France and Spain, with Great Britain as a neutral friendly to the latter for British reasons. Disappointed that she did not receive Tangier by the Treaty of Versailles, France nevertheless tried to profit by contrasting her World War record with that of Spain. France contended that since all restrictions on her liberty of action in Morocco had been due to Germany's presence there, the effects of these servitudes should now disappear, since the Treaty of Versailles had abolished all Germany's former treaty rights. Moreover, she tried to repudiate her engagement regarding Tangier in the secret treaty of 1904, while Great Britain continued to insist on the French promise of internationalization of the city. Immediately after the war, the Spanish proceeded to expel the Germans who had used her zone as a base of anti-Allied activity, thereby strengthening her claim to the addition of Tangier to her zone. In December, 1919, Blake viewed the Tangier question as the outstanding problem in Morocco; he reported that "every form of propaganda, public, private, and political, is in full activity in both the French and Spanish communities of the town towards a determination of the award in their favor." Six months later he reported that negotiations on Tangier had again been deferred, while France was entrenching herself more securely in the Tangier sector.[61]

During 1920, the French colonial press asserted that since Tangier was under the Sultan, it was therefore under the French Protectorate. On the contrary, the Spanish papers emphasized the immemorial economic, political, historical, and geographic rights of Spain in Tangier. For the United States, Blake pointed out her interest in Tangier and declared an international or condominium regime the only conceivable solution. He thought that Lord Curzon might support France in this question, but the naval advisers of the British government were unanimously opposed to the establishment of France at Tangier.[62]

For over a year in 1921-1922 there was an interesting attempt to bring the United States in as a fourth partner in setting up the proposed international regime in Tangier. It was started by Vice Admiral A. P. Niblack, who wrote two letters to expound his views. He thought that the United States should participate with France, Spain, and Great Britain in the internationalizing and financing of Tangier to ensure an American base for coal and oil for the merchant marine and a free port of entry for American goods. Reviewing the treaty history of Morocco since 1902, he concluded that every European power got something valuable, but the United States got only a scrap of paper, the Act of Algeciras, which was, however, sufficient authorization for his proposal. In his second letter the Vice Admiral said 'We should ... propose to France, Spain, England, and Italy that we get together and internationalize Tangier." In March, 1922, Cyrus Woods, American ambassador at Madrid, wrote protesting that Spanish papers had never mentioned the United States in connection with reports of the forthcoming conference. The Office of Naval Intelligence reported to the State Department a quotation from the Niblick letter. In commenting on the dispatch from the Embassy at Madrid, the Division of Far Eastern Affairs thought it inadvisable for the United States to participate in any conference with the three other powers because it would be almost impossible to divorce the political from the economic phases. It would be better to arrange informally for Great Britain to safeguard American potential commercial interests in Tangier and Morocco as a whole. Apparently the matter was dropped after an interpellation in the House of Commons on June 22, 1922, was answered for the Foreign Office by saying that to revise the tripartite agreement between France, Spain, and Great Britain, it was proposed to limit the conference to these three countries.[63]

Among a number of schemes used successfully by France to obtain control of the vital resources on Tangier since the Armistice, none was so sensational as the Sherifian Dahir of June 2, 1921. This granted to a so-called international company, "La Société Internationale pour le Developpement de Tanger," a concession for the exclusive rights to construct, operate, and administer the harbor of Tangier. The society had been formed originally in 1913 by French, Spanish, British, and other financiers, with the French holding 30 percent of the stock. As revived in 1921, the company had eliminated the German members, and the French now controlled 53 percent of the stock. The British were incensed at the French attempt to force such a flagrant implementation of their theory of the Sultan's sovereignty over Tangier,[64] and they were joined in their protest by the entire Diplomatic Corps--except the French representative--at Tangier. Blake thought that American capital should be included in any international company to develop the Tangier harbor.[65]

From August 15, 1921 to February 20, 1923, there was a great deal of correspondence to and from the State Department concerning this concession. This included many lengthy dispatches from Blake and his successor Denning at Tangier and several from Herrick at Madrid, besides several State Department dispatches and memoranda, searching and researching American-Moroccan treaties.[66] The American government objected to the breaking of the Algeciras Act when the Sultan's representative ignored the prerogative of the Diplomatic Corps by himself setting the date for the adjudication of contracts before the concession was even approved. Three times the French Embassy at Washington tried to persuade the United States not to support a probable objection to the concession by Great Britain and Spain, offering as a bribe the position of observer on the council of the Société to an American and finally a share in the capital stock. The Secretary of State pointed out that the French government would have actual control over the port until 1999; furthermore, he thought it premature to make any port concession until the political control of Tangier had been decided upon. To uphold the Act of Algeciras, the United States could not insist upon the protection of the treaty and at the same time make a separate deal with France.[67] On July 21, 1922, Secretary Hughes was assured that Great Britain intended to stand firm in her stand taken in the Briand-Curzon conversations[68] at Cannes on January 9, 1922.[69]

It was encouraging to the State Department to have Great Britain declare on August 2, 1922, practically the same policy as that of Hughes. The question was one, His Britannic Majesty's Government said in its protest to France, the consideration of which should be preceded by an agreement on the future administration of Tangier; the present proposal had been made in entire disregard of the authority of the diplomatic body, as recognized in the Act of Algeciras. In view of French predominance in the Société Internationale, it was necessary to secure equal opportunity to participate in the work for the nationals of the countries chiefly concerned. Moreover, viewing this latest concession in conjunction with the general policy of France within recent years, it indicated a desire of the French government to place Tangier on the same footing as the French Protectorate. In three dispatches Denning corroborated the British idea of French intentions and urged defense of an international Tangier, opening a field for future American commercial activity. Denning charged also that the disorganization of the Diplomatic Corps because of the French refusal to recognize the doyen, the Spanish minister, was deliberately contrived. To urge action on Tangier, Rear Admiral A. P. Niblack sent a third letter directly to William Phillips, Under Secretary of State. He said that the State Department should take the position that meddling in Tangier was meddling in African, not in European affairs, and should demand financial and political participation in the internationalization of Tangier under the Act of Algeciras.[70]

The ingenuity of the French in treaty misinterpretation was illustrated further in a note from the Sultan's representative at Tangier replying to the American official note of protest of June 23, 1922. This reply stated that the Franco-German Treaty of 1911 "entirely relieved the Sherifian government of the obligation to have recourse to adjudication for the granting of concessions." By adhering to the French Protectorate Treaty of 1912, which implied recognition of the foregoing treaty, the note asserted, the United States had accepted the 1911 principles. The French had paid no attention to the reiterated denial of American acceptance of the Protectorate Treaty of 1912. The State Department could not reconcile the actions of the Sherifian government with Poincaré's assurance that the Open Door remained in force in Morocco. On November 3, 1922, a "last word" message from the French Foreign Office repeated the above argument and added that it was strange that no previous American objections had been made, although two concessions had been made during the eleven years that the Franco-German Treaty had been in operation. As for the French preponderance in Société, that came from the request of the Moroccan government that France receive the former German and Austrian shares. The note then repeated the invitation for participation of American capital in the company and for an American member of the council of the organization. A final plea was that the United States would give the same consideration to this case as France had invariably shown in the different territories of the American continent and the Western Coast of Africa every time a special American political interest was involved.[71]

Just six days after the above note, word was received from Herrick and Denning that the port adjudication had been postponed temporarily. The British Agency was informed that Poincaré agreed to postponement until after the Lausanne conference because of the personal plea of Lord Curzon. A month later Poincaré said in a letter to the president of the Comité Franco-Tanger that the French government sought to settle as soon as possible the financial difficulties causing the postponement of the port project. However, Denning believed that the American protest of October 6 and the reply of the United States to the French answer had had a demoralizing effect upon the French point of view. He thought the American threat of concerted action with Great Britain and Spain really played a decisive part in the French retreat. On the other hand, Fred Mayer, secretary of the American Agency at Tangier, was convinced that there was a genuine financial problem because the financiers backing the Société were not prepared to proceed in face of the opposition of three powers.[72]

Still the French premier seemed unable to distinguish between the act of recognition of the French Protectorate and the adhesion to the Franco-Moroccan Treaty of 1912, and French officials in the Foreign Office continued to be unimpressed by evidence that the United States had protested against former violations of the Act of Algeciras. A final reminder was that the French government had been careful to concede to American interests in Liberia and now expected reciprocal treatment in Tangier.[73]

At length an agreement was reached to hold a conference in London among France, Spain, and Great Britain to draft a government plan for Tangier. The delegates met on June 29, 1923; after the second meeting the conference was adjourned until August 21. Each country had held firm in its former position, except that Great Britain now suggested that the League of Nations be given the right on intervention in international matters. Suddenly, early in July, Spain adhered to the British principle. When the experts reconvened the British proposed another postponement until September 28. Meanwhile, the French drew up their plan to protect the sovereignty of the Sultan in Tangier.[74]

Italy now broke into the Tangier arena. Reminding the French chargé of the Panther incident was the landing of a detachment of Carabineri from the Italian destroyer at Tangier on August 30. The pretext for their visit was the violent seizure of Italian subjects under arrest by their own consular agents and their maltreatment by the Spanish military police.[75] This gesture was followed by the Italian demand to participate in the conference in London. Disregarding her pledges to France in 1900 and 1902 giving France full liberty in Morocco in exchange for the Italian free hand in Tripoli, Italy now advanced her theory of the Tangier situation. Since Tangier was outside the French Protectorate, Mussolini asserted, the Italian pledge did not apply to Tangier; furthermore, as a leading Mediterranean power, Italy should be consulted about Tangier, which was a Mediterranean and not a Moroccan problem. On the contrary, France argued that in 1900 and 1902 there had been only one Morocco, and the agreements covered the whole of it. The London conference, moreover, was merely a continuance of those of 1912, in which Italy had not taken part. Lord Curzon also declined an invitation to Italy on similar grounds.[76]

On the day when the experts resumed their work, September 28, 1923, Italy was given some support. The London Times of that date contained an article by Walter B. Harris advocating a new proposal by France. France would accept internationalization of the local government of Tangier, including its port, railroads, tribunals, and police, but with the Sultan wanted to continue control over the Islamic institutions, the Sultan's authority over the Muslims, and the administration of Muslim civil law in the native tribunals. The zone so internationalized, Harris said, should be under France in peacetime and under the League of Nations in wartime, to ensure its neutrality. In a Times editorial of the next day, it was suggested that two other powers should take part in the conference--the United States because of her important commerce with Tangier and Italy because Tangier was a Mediterranean affair. The Times supported the British position.[77]

Delayed for three days by the alleged insistence of Mussolini on being invited, the conference began work on October 25, 1923, in Paris. Twice during the negotiations the United States gave warning to the three conferring powers that, although she claimed no political interest in Morocco, as a signatory of the Act of Algeciras she was interested in the maintenance of the Open Door and trusted that the conference would not violate this principle. Facile as ever in such promises, the French government stated that the Open Door would be maintained and all foreign interests in Tangier would be protected. The text of the treaty when complete would be submitted for approval by all signatories of the Act of Algeciras in good standing. The concluding hope expressed by France was for the adhesion of the United States to the Tangier convention and the suppression of American capitulations in the French Zone.[78]

In its friendly reply to Italy, the French government regretted having received her request only after the conference had already begun its deliberations, too late for an affirmative reply. Again it was mentioned that the meetings were the outcome of conversations of the experts in London and of negotiations begun in 1912, in neither of which Italy had participated.[79]

Without the presence of press representatives, the meetings of the conference were secret. Some information did leak out, however, and received comment in American diplomatic dispatches. On November 27, 1923, a fairly complete summary of the proposed statute was published in the London *Times*. The convention was not signed until December 18, 1923, but the Spanish delegates, as instructed by their government, signed only *ad referendum*. Before the signing of the three conference powers, the signers of the Act of Algeciras, except Germany, Austria-Hungary, and Russia, were given the terms of the Tangier Statute, and the United States government had informally indicated that some of the provisions were not satisfactory to it.[80]

Primo de Rivera asked for time to examine the document, since press opinion seemed to be divided. One Spanish paper went to the extreme of saying that if Spain could not have Tangier, the whole of the Spanish Zone should be internationalized, except Ceuta and Melilla. Early in January,

1924, The Directorate notified the other powers that it could not ratify the Tangier convention unless some changes were made. On January 21 Rivera himself talked of internationalizing the whole of the Spanish Zone.[81] Eventually Poincaré offered Spain eight concessions which Spain accepted in writing, thus adhering to the convention. On May 14, 1924, Great Britain, France, and Spain deposited their ratifications in Paris.[82]

It had been hoped to put the Statute into effect by July 1, 1924, and the six other powers eligible to sign it were pressed to do so by that date. But since they had not helped to make the Statute, they felt no hurry about signing it. Portugal had no responsible government to take action, and the Netherlands had to call her Parliament to do so. Sweden had not had any diplomatic representative in Tangier for many years, but she signed the document on December 5, 1924. However, she affixed two reservations to her signature; her adhesion meant only a suspension of her capitulary rights for the term of the convention, which was twelve years, and if she sent a consular officer to Tangier, she wanted to participate in the Committee of Control. Although there were only twenty Belgians in Tangier, Belgium asked for a Belgian judge and two police officers. But Belgium was satisfied with two subordinate military officers and signed the Statute on December 6, 1924. The Netherlands followed on October 5, 1925, but Portugal did not adhere until January 28, 1926, and the other powers were not notified of this action until May 18, 1926. Italy now had her revenge for not being invited to the diplomatic party--she not only refused to agree to the Statute, but also declared her intention of not recognizing the international regime. The United States did not sign the convention. After several postponements, the Statute was declared to be in force on June 1, 1925, but without three powers: Italy, Portugal, and the United States.[83]

The constitution of the internationalized Tangier Zone was an elaborate document consisting of three parts. They were "A Convention Regarding the Organization of the Statute of the Tangier Zone," with fifty-six articles and an annex of fourteen articles regulating the police force; "A Draft Sherifian Dahir Organizing the Administration of the Tangier Zone," consisting of fifty-seven articles, and "A Draft Dahir Concerning Organization of an International Jurisdiction at

Tangier," with twenty-two articles. The boundaries were those fixed by the Franco-Spanish Convention of 1912; included were the city and the port of Tangier and surrounding territory of about 140 square miles. Among the chief general provisions were the permanent neutrality of the zone, with no military establishments; control over diplomatic affairs by the French Resident General; maintenance of existing treaties, with economic equality from such treaties preserved even if the treaties were abrogated or modified; making of future international agreements only by consent of the legislative assembly; abrogation of capitulations and protection after establishment of the Mixed Court; maintenance of postoffice and cable stations owned by certain powers; and establishment of the Moroccan franc and the Spanish peseta as legal moneys, without prohibition of the native _hassani_. Diplomatic agencies were to be replaced by consulates, and all existing commissions and committees were abolished. The official languages were French, Spanish, and Arabic, and laws were to be written in all three languages. If none of the signatory powers demanded revision six months before expiration, the life of the statute, originally for twelve years, would be automatically renewed for one or more equal periods.

In a sense, the government was bifurcated, being based on the two principles of sovereignty of the sultan and internationalism. For the former, the sultan's representative was the _mendoub_, who administered the natives with the aid of a Moroccan staff appointed by the sultan. He presided over the international legislative assembly and promulgated the laws passed by it, but had no vote. It was his duty to see that the natives had freedom of religion and to maintain the Muslim and Jewish festivals and ceremonials. In the international Legislative Assembly, in addition to the 17 European and American representatives[84] provided for, there were six Muslims nominated by the _mendoub_ and three Jews nominated by the _mendoub_ from nine names submitted by the Jewish community. Acting as a Committee of Control were the consuls of the powers signatory to the Act of Algeciras; their function was to ensure observance of economic equality among all nations and to see that provisions of the Statute were carried out. An administrator executed decisions of the Assembly and directed the international administration. For the first six years, he was to be French. A Spanish assistant administrator was in charge of health regulations and a British assistant headed financial services. A French engineer for state public works had a Spanish counterpart for municipal public works. To supersede the former consular jurisdictions, the Mixed Court, with French, Spanish, and British judges was created. The native police force was under a Belgian officer with French and Spanish subordinates. There was no doubt that France was the predominant power in the so-called "international administration."[85]

Official American criticism of the Statute of Tangier had begun even before the exchange of ratifications among its three authors. The Division of Western European Affairs took particular exception to the granting of only one American representative in the legislative assembly, whereas Italy had two. Since 1918 the United States had maintained fourth place in the trade of Tangier, as compared with tenth place in 1913, and also fourth place in the total Moroccan trade.[86] The Division also objected to the abolition of semsars, who were much needed for the distribution of petroleum products in the interior.[87] Rand made a lengthy critique of the new regime. The secrecy of its making had removed the Statute entirely from consideration by the Diplomatic Corps at Tangier. There was no provision for modification of the numerical representation of the powers in the Assembly. In wartime, neutrality of the zone was threatened by permitting the passage of French and Spanish troops through the Tangier Zone to their own zones. The Tangier Port concession had been transferred to the Tangier Zone government, which had the right to take over the concession in case of forfeiture or to expropriate it at its expiration. With the competence of the consular body limited to the Tangier zone, there was no longer any agency to deal with the head of Morocco as a whole; this was the "final demolition of the vestiges remaining of the undivided political entity of the Sherifian Empire which is the proclaimed principle in the Act of Algecira." The mendoub and all his staff brought jurisdiction over all the natives under the French Residency General at Rabat; responsibility to authorities outside the Tangier Zone made his alleged autonomy a fiction. The Mixed Court had a committee of experts working to adjust the Napoleonic Code as used in Tunisia to the Tangier situation. With separate courts for natives and foreigners, there were sure to be injustices, especially in serious criminal and civil cases involving the two groups. Extraterritorial jurisdiction was not eliminated;

it was merely monopolized for all foreigners by the British, French, and Spanish judges.[88]

Following the deposit of the ratifications of the Tangier Statute at Paris by the three governments, on May 29, 1924, their embassies in Washington delivered similar and simultaneous messages asking for the adherence of the United States. On June 4, Ambassador Jusserand called on Secretary Hughes to urge American adherence. He said that the Statue was made to American specifications; it recognized the Open Door, was a practical plan of administration, and assured freedom of economic opportunity. There would be no trouble about American interests in Tangier; there were only two American companies there, and, he thought, only two _semsars._ There was no reason to fear that interests of American protégés would not be safeguarded. As for the judicial system, it was surely as good as offered by Turkey, where the United States had recently given up capitulations. Regarding representation in the Legislative Assembly, the French would be glad to have more Americans there, but representation had to be in some proportion to the interests concerned. The British ambassador, Sir Esme Howard, called on the Secretary of State on the next day. Admitting that the agreement was unsatisfactory, the British envoy said that it was the only alternative to dangerous riots giving the French an opportunity to march in and occupy the zone. He hoped that the United States would adhere, because her refusal to do so would influence other countries negatively.[89]

During June Secretary Hughes received much sage advice from Rand in Tangier and the Division of Western European Affairs in Washington, pointing out the inadequacies of the Statute and the capability of the proposed regime for the injury of American and the enhancement of French interests in Tangier.[90] On July 3 Consul General Skinner at London forwarded an article from the London _Times_ entitled "America and Tangier." This contribution by Walter B. Harris ridiculed the American representation at Tangier, especially the supposedly naïve diplomatic agent, Father Denning, and reported that Washington could not understand Britain's _volte face_ on the Tangier question. The same article was transmitted by Rand, together with his denunciation of Harris as one with "a universal reputation as a dangerously indiscreet, unscrupulous, and unreliable journalist, as a known creature of the French authorities and as a declared opponent of Spain in Morocco."[91]

In his reply to the invitation to join the Tangier regime, made to the sponsoring powers on July 11, Hughes was very forthright and direct, as was also Acting Secretary Grew in his interview with the press on the same day. This government would not care to assume the responsibility of participation in the zone administration with so small a representation as to have no appreciable part in formulating policy or conducting affairs. Since the Tangier Zone was not to be an independent political entity, but a municipality, and its administration would not be accountable to any one power, with no central authority responsible, difficulty might be experienced in obtaining proper recognition of rights. However, to cooperate with any honest effort to improve conditions in Tangier, after having had an opportunity to examine the regulations and codes referred to in the Statute, the United States would consider the possibility of suspending its extraterritorial rights to the extent that such rights appeared to be safeguarded, on five conditions. The conditions were as follows: (1) that the provisions concerning the observance of economic equality be explained with greater particularity to ensure with no uncertainty the principle of the Open Door;[92] (2) that the signatories to the Statute should assume full responsibility for any acts or omissions of the administrative authorities which would ordinarily give rise to a right of international reclamation; (3) that the United States be permitted to name from the American consulate in Tangier an associate judge to sit in any case involving an American citizen; (4) that the provisions regarding semsars were not intended to affect the existing rights in other parts of Morocco; and (5) that no future international agreement concluded by His Sherifian Majesty with other powers should abridge the rights of American citizens in Tangier without the consent of the United States.[93]

Meanwhile the Tangier port concession had again come into controversy. On May 22 an American consul remarked that the chief interest of the United States was not in port construction, but in the allotment of space for coal and oil storage and in port management. The Solicitor of the State Department gave the opinion that the port concession was granted in violation of the rights of the United States under the Act of Algeciras, which also made all port dues subject to control by the Diplomatic Corps. Putting this control under the Port Commission, as provided in the Statute, would deprive the United States of all voice in obtaining economic equality in the working of the port. Moreover, granting an exclusive port concession to a company controlled by one country was a violation of the Open Door principle. To Rand's notice that the date for bids for port construction would be decided on June 24, Hughes replied that Rand should maintain the American government's objection to the adjudication as a violation of the Act of Algeciras. On July 10 the French chargé called at the State Department to inquire the reasons for Rand's objections. He said that bids would remain open for 150 days--enough time for American bidders to compete. Also, the French government was examining the request of the Atlantic Oil Company to establish reserves in Tangier, and he believed that it would be granted. He was, in effect, objecting to the short period which had been allowed for bidding on the Panama Canal, feeling that French firms never had a chance to compete. The chargé then expressed the hope that the American government would soon surrender its capitulatory rights in the French Zone and would adhere to the Statute of Tangier. The Undersecretary of State replied that the American attitude on adjudication was being reserved until a reply was received to the note on the Tangier Statute.[94]

A reply was received to Hughes's note from the British government on October 10, 1924, and a similar one from the French government on October 31, evidently written in collaboration. The conditions demanded in the Hughes note were answered in order: (1) The American version of the Open Door was accepted fully; (2) Diplomatic matters were the responsibility of the French Resident General, as provided in the Protectorate Treaty of 1912; (3) Since judges could not hold any other public office, members of the American consulate would be ineligible to sit on the court, but an American citizen acting as an auxiliary member of the consulate staff might be acceptable; (4) Concerning semsars, no change was contemplated in the existing rights of protégés in other sections of Morocco; (5) No future treaties would be made restricting the rights of American citizens without the consent of their government.[95]

Not fully satisfied, the State Department sent another note of inquiry on December 20, 1924, asking for further explanation concerning the responsibility of the French government in diplomatic matters, the American representation on the court, and the abolition of the Diplomatic Corps. The Department was probably inspired to take this action by the Solicitor and the Division of Western European Affairs. The latter considered the Statute a temporary one, probably anticipating the withdrawal of Spain from her zone, in view of her recent reverses in the Riffian War. When the final date set for the beginning of the Statute arrived on June 1, 1925, both the British and the Spanish governments were informed that without receipt of satisfactory assurances on the questions in the December note, the United States would not adhere to the Statute. On July 8, 1925, a representative of the Italian Embassy calling at the State Department discussed American reasons for non-adherence and expressed his opinion that the new regime would not work satisfactorily and that eventually a new conference on Tangier would include Italy.[96]

With premature action reminiscent of the French Zone, the government of the Tangier Zone was organized far in advance of the announced beginning date. The mendoub, Sid El-Hadj Muhammad Buasherin, arrived in Tangier on December 1, 1924. All delegates to the Legislative Assembly had been chosen before March 31, 1925. The code of laws was promulgated by a dahir of January 15, 1925; the first meeting of the Committee on Control was on January 27; and the Legislative Assembly met on February 16--despite the non-adhering absentees, who were counted as present. Early in February the Port Concession Company enforced new excessive lighterage and harbor dues supposed to be levied by a Port Commission not yet chosen. On June 4 the three dominant powers attempted to abolish the Sanitary Council. A Sherifian dahir was presented withdrawing all powers delegated to that body by the Maghzen since 1840.[97] Supported by the American representative, the Italian diplomatic agent, who was president, refused absolutely to recognize the legality of the decree.[98]

Among the townspeople the Statute was very unpopular. A revision of the economic clauses was demanded by a petition signed by 800 nationals representing commerce and industry, and the new harbor dues were protested by closing most of the business places for a day. With the refusal of the American and Italian governments to let their nationals pay new taxes or the higher port dues, there was no economic equality. The intense psychological and economic distress of the populace was reflected in many items from the Spanish and Moroccan press and in the London Times (by Walter Harris, by this time an opponent of the Statute).[99] One of the most pertinent is this extract from "The Statute of Tangier" in El Sol of June 9, 1925:

> And here we are, with the perspective of a port unconstructed but with tariffs which make all commerce impossible, with a railway whose construction runs parallel to that of the port, of an Administration which has the name of Tangerine but the procedure of importation; with a land tariff which is a halter around the neck of the people of Tangier, and imposts which neither the Italians, the Americans, nor the Port will ever pay. In short, a Statute of whose benefits the People of Tangier dreamed and which have proved beneficial only to the subjects of those nations which have not adhered to the Convention.[100]

In Blake's lengthy and hostile criticism of the Statute after three months of operation, he emphasized three main defects. They were the utterly inadequate financial support provided for Tangier, the difficulties and restraints imposed upon private trade, and the chaotic condition of the judicial system. The Statute was international neither in origin nor in purpose; it seemed designed to destroy Tangier as a city and as a port,[101] as shown by the provision that the Tangier customs officials could levy duties and taxes only on goods destined exclusively for consumption in the zone.[102]

On the first anniversary of the international regime, "a reasoned disappointment had succeeded an unreasoning hope." Unfavorable criticism by the British and Spanish was reinforced by local and unofficial French dissatisfaction. The Echo de Tanger, an independent French weekly, gave a balance sheet for the first year. As debits were listed, new taxes, heavier obligations, an abnormal increase in the cost of living and rent, a numerically imposing corps of functionaries, the future necessity to pay for a gendarmerie, the customs cordon erected by the Spanish, the continuance of gambling at no profit to the city, increased moral delinquency, and a long list of other unhappy conditions. On the credit side were only the improved condition of the streets, a municipal dispensary, a somewhat cleaner city, and a better court system. The recent removal of the Spanish customs cordon brought only slight encouragement, the writer of the article added. An American consular report in August, 1926, mentioned a successful European demonstration against press censorship and a serious threat of native demonstrations against the mendoub for the use of torture in the native courts. "Symptoms of hysteria were apparent even in official quarters."[103]

Although Italy was the most persistent and vociferous opponent of the Tangier regime in 1926,[104] the Spanish took the initiative in bringing the matter to an issue. For Spain the longing for Tangier was of several centuries' duration; now the impact of taxation fell most heavily upon her nationals there. France had a major role in the new government, and Spain had suffered from the use of Tangier as a hostile base in the Riffian War. As early as June-July, 1925, conference on Franco-Spanish cooperation in the Riffian War, France and Great Britain had opposed Spanish efforts to abolish the Statute just beginning operation. Temporarily, Spain was mollified by strengthening the neutrality of Tangier by retaining the Franco-Spanish directed police and by a tripartite naval patrol of the zone. Soon Spain used nuisance measures to secure revision of the Statute--her tariff wall around Tangier[105] and the violation of treaties concerning Italian and American citizens and protégés. Next followed a vigorous campaign of propaganda in the Spanish press to incorporate the Tangier Zone into the Spanish Zone. De Rivera gave two interviews, one declaring that "Any other policy is uncertain, temporary, and dangerous." On August 18, 1926, when the Spanish-Italian treaty of friendship and arbitration was announced, it did not require de Rivera's hint to let the world know that new diplomatic alliances were being formed to resettle the Tangier argument.[106]

At the September, 1926, meeting of the League of Nations at Geneva came Spain's next trial of strength. Having been regularly reelected to a temporary seat on the League Council, Spain now decided to try for a permanent seat there and thus forestall Germany's intention to enter the League with a permanent Council seat. Spain's proposal to the American, British, French, and Italian governments was that she be allowed annexation of Tangier to her zone. She would give definite pledges of its non-fortification, freedom and equality of commerce, and maintenance of order. If this were impossible, she asked for a mandate over Tangier of from thirteen to fifteen years under the League of Nations, as a trial period, preliminary to cession. She also called for a conference of all powers still under the Act of Algeciras on September 1 at Geneva. In case of refusal, Spain threatened to resign from the League of Nations. The American government did not comment on the proposed transfer of Tangier, but thought it might be expedient to participate in the conference, where by indirect support it might make a friend of Spain.[107]

To France and Great Britain the idea of submitting the Tangier Question to the Algeciras signatory powers was repugnant. They saw no logical connection of Tangier with the League of Nations and they insisted that any reopening of the question should be by the three powers which had formulated the Statute. Naturally, Italy favored the Spanish proposal and was willing to attend a general conference. However, Spain was humiliated by another failure in Moroccan affairs and had to save face by withdrawing from the League of Nations as a protest. Spanish-Italian bonds were strengthened. Renewed Spanish press propaganda demanded that if a tripartite reconsideration of the Tangier problem should fail, an international conference should work out a definite solution. Late in November of 1926 the Al-Moghreb Al-Aksa and Tangier Gazette reported that Mussolini had agreed to the procedure of modifying the Statute without a conference. After "conversations" between Spain and France had produced an agreement, it was to be turned over to Great Britain and Italy for their approval. No other country would need to be consulted.[108] However, Spain accepted the idea of these preliminary conferences with the plan of an eventual submission of the whole problem to the signatories of the Algericas conference--excepting of course, Germany, Austria, and Russia. In January and February Spain was still holding to her demand for abolition of the Statute and incorporation of Tangier into her zone.[109]

From February 7 to August 11, 1927, the Franco-Spanish conference dragged on, vainly trying to effect a compromise. Spain presented a number of proposals making her virtually the protector of Tangier. In return, she did offer to assume many responsibilities, including the expenses of the Cape Spartel Lighthouse and the deficits of the city. She complained bitterly that during the Riffian War there had been no opposition but hers to the use of Tangier as a base for Abd al Krim's activities.[110] France was firm in her refusal to accept any of Spain's demands, and when Spain later turned for support to Great Britain, there was another impasse. However, as Blake remarked during the conference, "The repulse of Spanish diplomacy ... does not make a dead issue of the Tangier question .... The Tangier question ... will be reconsidered, because it deals with a set of conditions that must ultimately be reconstituted."[111]

Again Spain met her formidable opponent, but this time the burden of negotiations was borne by the Spanish ambassador in Paris and the Quai d'Orsay. Spain's ambitious program of revision had undergone downward revision, and a settlement was reached on February 21, 1928, although not published until March 3. The principal changes were but three: a revision of the Statute and the penal code to secure more effective repression of contraband in arms and political disturbances, a Spanish officer to act as inspector general of police, and the dissolution of the military tabors and their replacement by a gendarmie under a Spanish officer. Thus Spain was given full control of the police. A further agreement was to invite the British and Italian governments to send representatives to a conference in Paris to consider the adherence of Italy to the Statute. Thereafter, the results of this conference would be laid before other interested governments for their approval.[112]

As early as July, 1926, Italy had replied to a British inquiry concerning her claims regarding adhesion to the Tangier Statute, which she made as a great Mediterranean power entitled to full equality in the settlement of Mediterranean questions.[113] Her demands were neither modest nor indefinite. She asked for nine points of parity: a military or naval attaché at Tangier; participation of the Italian navy in policing Tangier waters; one of Italy's two representatives in the Assembly to serve as vice-president; an Italian judge and an Italian clerk on the Mixed Court; judicial codes to conform to Italian law; Italian participation in public works, the port enterprise, and international organizations; security of the customs regime as affecting Italian interests; Italian consuls general who were members of the Italian diplomatic corps; the right of Italy to be consulted in any future changes in the Tangier government.[114]

After the failure of the half year's Franco-Spanish discussion in 1927, Mussolini thought it an opportune time to draw attention to his continued interest in Tangier by one of his theatrical stunts. On the fifth anniversary of the Fascist march on Rome, a new Italian school and dispensary in the former palace of Mulai Hafid were to be dedicated. The King's cousin, the Prince of Udine, came for the occasion with a squadron of three warships. To make sure that no one misunderstood the significance of the event, the Prince detailed Walter Harris to make Italy's position clear in the London Times. The American press also took great interest in this affair. The signing of a treaty between France and Yugoslavia on November 11, 1927, provoked intense bitterness in Italy, although it was in no sense an answer to the naval visit, and had in fact been intended to include Italy as a third party.[115] After several conciliatory gestures of Great Britain and France toward Italy, however, the four countries were ready to take part in the Conference of Paris which was provided for in the published Franco-Spanish accord on March 3, 1928.[116]

The conference of the Big Four at Paris lasted about four months--from March 20, 1928 to July 19, 1928. Great Britain failed to get adopted her first resolution that the revised Statute should be in force for only twelve years. On April 5 it was announced that the Franco-Spanish agreement had been accepted after modification.[117] Because of Great Britain's objection to a military police force of five hundred, the number was reduced to four hundred at first, with a later reduction to two hundred, any surplus over two hundred being paid for by France and Spain equally. A Spanish officer with the title of inspector general of security headed a Mixed Bureau of Intelligence. The gendarmie was under a Spanish officer, and to replace the Belgian formerly commanding, a Belgian judge succeeded to a judgeship formerly held by an English judge. Italy obtained all of her demands except two unimportant ones. She now had these rights and privileges: the right of the Italian naval force to patrol in Tangier territorial waters with the three other navies; the assurance of a fair participation of Italian capital and labor in the construction and administration of the Port of Tangier; the replacement of the Italian diplomatic agency in Tangier by a consulate general with a diplomatic service officer of the rank and title of consul general; the making effective of the Paris Convention of December 18, 1923, for Italian subjects and interests in the Tangier Zone within six months after the adhesion of Italy to the convention. Her list of important officers was a long one: an officer at the consulate general to see that neutrality regulations were strictly enforced; three members in the Legislative Assembly, one a vice-president; an assistant administrator as director of judicial services; and a magistrate and a clerk secretary in the Mixed Court. Italy was now on a par with Great Britain in the administration and far in advance of Spain,[118] who had done so much fighting for small rewards.[119]

The revised Statute was signed by representatives of its four makers on July 25, 1928, and it was ratified by these countries by September 14, 1928. This was enough ratification to put it into effect, but it was thought expedient to get as adherents as many of the Act of Algeciras signers as possible. Belgium adhered on July 25, 1928, Sweden on October 19, 1928, Portugal on January 15, 1929, and the Netherlands on June 12, 1929. Only the United States, whose wishes had been ignored, remained as a non-conformist--she never did adhere to this convention.[120]

On March 16, 1928, although uninvited to the conference, the United States instructed its ambassadors in London, Paris, Madrid, and Rome to present a memorandum on American views. Recalling a similar action prior to the conference of 1923, the memorandum continued:

> This government took occasion to remind the conferring Powers of its position as a party to the Act of Algeciras and it stated that while it had no political interest in Morocco it had a fundamental interest in the maintenance of the Open Door and in the protection of the life, liberty, and property of its citizens in Morocco. It further indicated that it presumed that nothing would be done by the conferring powers to interfere with the principle of the Open Door or with the rights and interests of the United States.

> The views of the United States regarding Tangier which were further set forth in its correspondence ... regarding the possibility of its adherence to the Statute of Tangier remain unaltered. The Government of the United States would accordingly advise the Powers now about to confer that it makes full reservation of its position on any decisions taken by the Conference which may in any way effect or touch upon its rights and interests in Morocco and in Tangier.[121]

In its reply to this note, the French Foreign Office gave its usual soothing assurances that the new proposals would in no way affect the existing situation in regard to international trade rights and invited the United States to send an observer. The final protocol presented to the United States was accompanied by a note stating that the new agreement was based upon respect for existing treaties and upon the maintenance of economic equality between nations.[122]

"The existing situation," however, was decidedly not desirable for American trade. The State Department files from 1924 through 1939 contain numerous notifications of new taxes which American traders or consumers were asked to pay. In 1928 and 1929 financial conditions were so desperate in Tangier that the British government asked the United States to aid with taxes from its nationals. However, the United States declined to accept the "Padlock Law," whereby the Tangier Administration, after notifying the Legislative Assembly and posting new schedules in the custom house, could levy increased consumption taxes on imports. The United States did accept conditionally four increased consumption taxes, and later other taxes were requested and were granted with reservations.[123]

During 1928 and 1929 Blake kept the State Department informed of the steadily worsening of conditions in Morocco, both economic and political. France thought that at the 1928 conference on Tangier she had made progress toward eventual extinction of the Act of Algeciras. Spain found her control of the police illusory, for the mendoub had his own police force to control the natives. Once declared banned, the Diplomatic Corps was being restored by the four leading powers. The Statute of 1923, as revised, was inadequate either for local government or for international cooperation. The Department of Justice was conducted in a most deplorable fashion. Both the British and the Spanish Chambers of Commerce protested the increased budget caused by the necessity to pay a larger number of functionaries to serve the political interests of the Four Powers. To augment the resources of Tangier, the French authorities advocated a patent tax and a gambling concession. At a public speech before local chambers of commerce with Marseilles members as guests, the French consul general at Tangier created consternation by asserting that Tangier was under the Sultan, like any other foreign city, and by predicting the possible collapse of the administration.[124] During 1929 and for several years thereafter, of course, Tangier suffered from the world-wide economic depression.

Almost incredible was the new orientation of French foreign policy that took place in the latter part of 1929--her rapprochement with Spain. It was inaugurated by the visit of General Jordana, then high commissioner of the Spanish Zone, from November 20 to 29, to several northern cities of the French Zone from Fez to Rabat. The visit was one of elaborate ceremonial parades, and fervid declarations of enhanced Franco-Spanish collaboration. The French Resident General spared no effort to make Jordana's visit the greatest reception yet accorded any visitor. The press made many comments on the outstanding significance of this cordiality to a rival and opponent of many years. France, the journalists declared, was in search of an ally to replace Great Britain, who at the recent Hague Conference, under the new Socialist-Labor government, had shown herself independent of France. The tendency of the British Labor party to grant much independence to her Muslim dependencies in the Near East was thought to endanger France's control of her Muslim colonies and protectorates. Moreover, the protection of the British navy was no longer assured to France. With the collapse of the Entente Cordiale and the disappearance from power of Sir Austen Chamberlain, France was reduced to courting the friendship of a power which she had systematically snubbed and disdained since the time of Napoleon. A close liaison between the French and Spanish administrations in Morocco was bound to make many difficulties of the Spanish Zone disappear and to improve Spanish status in Tangier.[125]

However, momentous changes were soon to occur in

Spain. Probably discouraged by his lack of success in diplomacy and his ill health, General Primo de Rivera resigned on January 28, 1930. He died on March 16. He had failed to obtain a vote of confidence from the garrisons--his only supporters. The King was the next to leave office, after restoring the constitution on February 8, 1931, and seeing an overwhelming victory for the Republicans on April 12. Alfonso XIII left Spain without abdicating, but was declared guilty of high treason and was forbidden to return. On April 14, 1931, began the provisional government of the Second Spanish Republic, which was to have a turbulent and disastrous career.[126]

After the end of the Riffian war, the organization of the Spanish Zone had been the chief preoccupation of the authorities. Imitating Lyautey's methods, they sought to build up the religious and social institutions of the people. Officials similar to the French _controleurs civile_ established many reforms. With the aid of the Spanish-commanded Moroccan constabulary, they disarmed the tribes. Land tenure was reformed and the collection of taxes was systematized. Health conditions were improved and education was begun. The Public Works Department drew up plans for the first roads to be constructed. New official and private buildings enlarged Tetuan, and urban centers began to develop near the military camps of Alhucemas and Puerto Capaz. In June, 1930, France and Spain signed an agreement to operate telephonic and telegraphic services.[127] The Spanish were beginning in 1927 the development in their zone that Lyautey had begun in 1912 in the French Zone. However, they had no military problem still to solve, as Lyautey had had.

During the period of the Spanish Republic at peace (1931-1936), the Spanish Zone mirrored the confusion and unrest in Spain itself and was ruled no more liberally than under the monarchy or dictatorship. The native nationalist movement, emerging also in French Morocco, received no more toleration than in the latter. Beginning with General Jordana, who fled from violence at the start of the Republic, there were seven high commissioners during the next five years.[128] A workers' demonstration and a Foreign Legion disturbance were suppressed, as was also a small rebellion of the Derkawa confraternity. An attempt to replace the military by civil service personnel resulted in some unfortunate appointments. There was much less violence and disorder than in Spain itself, however.[129]

Along with renewed discussion of the possibility of Spain's withdrawal from her zone, there was much apprehension that the French Zone would be incited to rebellion by Bolshevist and German agitators operating from the Spanish Zone. Italy, too, seemed to be planting agents there. Instead of withdrawing, however, the Spanish premier decided to retrench on the expenses for military and civil personnel in Spanish Morocco. According to Blake's opinion, Spanish native policy was more conciliatory than the French, for the Spanish had not confiscated communal lands for Spanish settlers and there was no attempt to stimulate Arab-Berber antagonism.[130]

One colonial advance was made by the Spanish Republic in 1934. By the initiative of Señor Rico Avello, high commissioner at Tetuan, Colonel Capaz raised the Spanish flag in Ifni on April 7. On April 29 it was placed with the Spanish Sahara and the Rio de Oro under the High Commissioner of Spanish Morocco.[131] At long last Spain had occupied the Santa Cruz de Mar Pequeña ceded to her by Morocco after the Hispano-Moroccan War of 1860 and defined in the Franco-Spanish Convention of November 27, 1912.[132]

During the transitional year between dictatorship and republic, (1930-1931), the American representative was vigorously fighting the actions of the Tangier administration in violation of the Act of Algeciras. The specific contracts illegally granted were the Tangier Port Concession, the electric light concession, many tar and cement contracts, and the Tangier Motor Bus Concession. The French Resident General, as usual, backed the Committee of Control, and American protests were unavailing.[133]

From 1930 to 1936 Blake sent many lengthy dispatches to Washington, describing the economic difficulties of the Tangier Zone, which he had foreseen and predicted from the beginning. A statement of grievances drawn up in March, 1931 for the Committee for the Defense of the Economic Interests of Tangier for transmission to the various countries administering Tangier gave a good summary:

> The people of Tangier compalin of being treated, not only without any consideration, but with excessive severity. There has been imposed upon it an administrative regime so onerous that all the past economies of the town have been entirely absorbed. It has been detached from the Moroccan Empire to be isolated in a zone of 375 square kilometers which produce nothing. It has been prevented from exploiting the excellent conditions of its climate and of its seashore, and finally it has been denied the rights of citizenship which are enjoyed by all peoples of the civilized world .... The working class is without work and suffering from hunger; commerce is paralyzed and ruined.[134]

On April 25, 1932, delegates of chambers of commerce and other representative organizations presented to the mendoub and the administration demands for economic reforms. They wanted charges for the customs administration shared by the two other zones and relief from the annual payments on the upkeep of the gendarmerie and the annual charge on the Tangier-Fez railroad. In the London Times of August 5, 1932, Walter Harris published a severe condemnation of the Tangier experiment. The people of the zone were very unhappy at being disfranchised and made a peaceful demonstration in the spring of 1932 large enough to seriously disturb the Committee of Control. Early in 1934 the Tangier branch of the International Federation of League of Nations Societies, formed in 1932, drew up a petition to the International Federation for a revision of the administration of Tangier under League auspices. Both the French and the Italian branches of the International Federation opposed the submission of the Tangier problem to the League of Nations.[135]

Above all other sources of friction, however, was the everactive Franco-Spanish contest for control of the Tangier Zone. In 1931 the newly formed Spanish Republic claimed the city for a time. In 1933 began the usual Spanish campaign for a revision of the Statute to bring in new industries and more capital and to provide an equitable administration of the customs. To forestall a conference at the time for expiration of the Statute in 1936, the French government initiated negotiations with Spain which led to an agreement on November 13, 1935. Again Spain failed to reach her objective of attaining predominance in Tangier, but she made substantial gains in power. Spain was to furnish the chief administrator for the next twelve years (1936-1948) and an assistant director in the customs administration, while the assistant administrator was to be French; French and Spanish delegates were to vote for each other. For the Legislative Assembly, the Spanish consulate general would nominate two of the native Muslim members and one Jewish member. A Spanish Roman Catholic bishop was to be maintained in Tangier. Control of the Spanish commander was extended over the local gendarmerie previously under the actually independent assistant French officers. Spain was unable to wrest from France the key position the latter held in control of the natives.[136]

Foreshadowing the Spanish Civil War, in May and June of 1936 the extremist character of political movements in Spain had repercussions in Morocco. In the Spanish Zone workers demonstrated to demand action to better the lot of Spanish laborers. In Tangier Spanish workmen presented their demands to the Administrator and held a mass meeting. The French authorities were worried over possible effects on the Moors in all three zones. If an extremist Spaniard were elected administrator, Tangier might be thrown open to agitators from Spain or the Spanish Zone, and there was danger of Communist backing of the Moroccan nationalists. Accordingly, at a closed session of the Legislative Assembly on May 7, the proposal of a British representative to prolong the terms of the present administrator and his associates for six months was adopted. The Assembly vote showed that the French were voting against the Spanish. The Spanish in Tangier reacted violently, sending three members of the Assembly to Madrid with a petition calling upon the Spanish government ot withdraw from the Tangier Statute and revert to the capitulary regime and threatening a boycott of the Tangier organization. On the verge of financial bankruptcy, Tangier must have a reform of judicial and police organizations if it were to survive. Means were sought to overcome the Franco-Spanish agreement to have a Spanish administrator.[137]

By July 17, 1936, many groups of Spaniards besides its original opponents were disillusioned with the Spanish Republic and wished for its overthrow. Decisive action came, however, from Spanish Morocco, the cradle of the revolt, which developed into almost three years of savage civil war and ended with a million persons and one "republic" dead. Of the nine men who plotted the death of the republic, there finally emerged as the all-powerful leader General Francisco Franco, who, flying from his post as military governor of the Canary Islands, took command in Spanish Morocco. Ceuta and Melilla had fallen into rebel hands two days before his arrival. Both the Spanish Protectorate and several large cities in Spain were taken over rapidly as centers of rebellion. But the military coup failed in its original purpose of seizing power immediately. In the bitter struggle that followed, both Nazi Germany and Fascist Italy, supporting the Nationalists, and Soviet Russia, backing the Republic, used Spain as a proving ground for the new weapons they used later in World War II. In a very real sense, however, the revolt was a product of the Spanish Zone. The army rebelled because the Republican administration was reducing the armed forces, and to forestall trouble had exiled many leading generals to obscure posts. Morocco had been the training area for Spanish armies from 1909 to 1927, and the army officers saw there their only opportunity for experience and advancement in rank. Moreover, in spite of the indispensable aid of Germany and Italy, neither Fascist leader would have backed the rebels unless Franco's hard core army of the Spanish Foreign Legion and the Moroccan regulares had proved their ability to win with some foreign aid. Throughout the war, Morocco remained a reservoir for more troops.[138]

When the Spanish Civil War began, France, Great Britain, Italy, and Portugal sent warships into Tangier harbor, and the British and French governments warned the Spanish government to keep out of the harbor. The Spanish insurgents under Franco had already promised to respect the neutrality of Tangier. When eight Spanish war vessels entered Tangier for refueling, Blake advised the Vacuum Oil Company not to furnish any oil pending instructions from Washington. In the interest of international cooperation, the State Department would not support any American firm breaking neutrality rules. The ships departed after being refueled from a Spanish auxiliary ship. Franco protested vehemently to the mendoub because another Spanish warship came into the harbor. On July 28, 1936, the Committee of Control created to aid it a committee of commanders of the war vessels sent in by the neutral powers. Finally, on August 6, Franco sent an ultimatum to the Comittee of Control demanding the departure of all Loyalist ships and recognition of passports issued by his authority. By a majority vote, the Committee of Control, the administration, and the committee of admirals granted both requests of the insurgent leader. Further measures to preserve neutrality were taken when the Committee of Control and the Assembly forbade the unofficial display of national colors and the Assembly voted to close the frontiers to prevent the possible passage of volunteers.[139]

A dispatch from Madrid pointed out three factors responsible for Franco's failure to obtain an early victory. They were the loyalty to the legitimate government of the Civil and Assault Guards at Madrid and Barcelona, the loyalty of a large part of the navy and air force, and the extraordinary enthusiasm of the masses of the people in supporting the government, in which many women were very active. In his comprehensive analyses of the general situation, Blake showed that the position of Tangier could become critical. An anarcho-communist triumph in Spain would endanger Tangier; on the other hand, if Franco threatened Tangier, then France, Italy, and Great Britain would be obliged to intervene. The Jews in Tangier and in the Spanish Zone openly favored the Spanish legitimate government, but the Muslims appeared undivided in their sympathy and admiration for the insurgents. Franco's call for recruits to the Moroccan "*regulares*" met with a good response.[140] These conditions, described early in the war, continued to exist throughout its duration.

The use of the term "Nationalist" as applied to both Moroccans and Spaniards at this time undoubtedly gave the former a false sense of kinship for the insurgent movement. Shortly before the uprising, two emissaries of Moroccan nationalism in the Spanish Zone went to Madrid to secure a promise of independence from the republican Popular Front Government. They were warmly received, but with words, not with action. But the insurgent Nationalist Spanish leaders were soon promising to "offer Morocco the most resplendent roses when the blossoms of peace unfold." Many Moroccans thought that the insurgents were taking the only possible course to escape submission to Communist rule. From the beginning, the Spanish Nationalists claimed that their policy was based on two principles: that Morocco was one and indivisible and that the purpose of the protectorate was to restore the country's historic personality. An allowance of greater freedom of the press, the promotion of schools, the introduction of Egyptian teachers, and the granting of two high government posts to Moroccans, all combined to satisfy the Moroccan elite of the Spanish Zone. The result was the complete tranquillity of this zone throughout the Spanish Civil War.[141] The Sultan, that is, the French Resident General, condemned the enlistment of Moroccans in Franco's army. The Spanish insurgents counteracted this by having the Khalifa make a state progress in reportedly anti-Franco districts, where he made pro-Franco declarations. He met demonstrations of loyalty everywhere he went.[142]

Vehement asserter that he was of his interest in the Mediterranean balance of power, Mussolini should now have been upholding the neutrality of Tangier for which he was a sponsor. Instead, Italy and Germany supplied many airplanes and tanks, with skilled operators, from the very beginning of the war. The French government gave some aid to the Loyalists, and in the last phase of the war the Soviet government shared in the Spanish government as well as in its armaments. Claude Bowers, American ambassador to Spain, had a clear perspective of the struggle as early as October, 1936. Everything, he wrote, favored the rebels, with their vast advantage in planes, tanks, and heavy artillery poured in by Italy, Germany, and Portugal, while "neutral" Europe had combined in refusing to sell war material to the Madrid government. While the Spanish premier, Largo Caballero brought some order and discipline into Madrid, his recent appointment of a Socialist, a Communist, a Syndicalist, and an Anarchist as war commissioners indicated a dangerous dependence upon extremists. Spain had become an international battleground; she was no longer fighting a civil war. Franco's forces were mostly foreign mercenaries--the cosmopolitan Foreign Legion, the Moroccans, the Germans and the Italians.[143] "The people of Spain, who are neither fascistic nor communistic, are merely brushed aside and their territory converted into a battleground of foreign isms." In December, Bowers commented that the Non-Intervention Agreement had served only the rebel cause.[144]

True to tradition, Germany evoked a war scare on January 7, 1937. The French government heard that 8,000

Germans were preparing to land in Spanish Morocco to construct barracks and gun emplacements at Ceuta and Melilla. Premier Blum protested, and the German ambassador in Paris was reminded that the Franco-Spanish Treaty of 1912 forbade fortification of this area. The Germans denied having troops in Morocco. French, British, and German warships converged at strategic points in the Mediterranean, and French troops gathered along the Franco-Spanish Border in Morocco. Then the French press entered the fray. When the French and British officers and reporters inspected Morocco, at the invitation of Col. Juan Beigbeder, they found only a few hundred German mining technicians and Nazi "volunteer" aviators at Melilla, to which the treaty did not apply. On January 11, Hitler formally declared to the French ambassador in Berlin that he had no intention of interfering with the territorial integrity of Spain or the Spanish possessions.[145] The pseudocrisis was over.

The desperation of the Spanish Loyalists after the tide of war started to rise in Franco's favor is shown by a glimpse behind the scenes at Geneva. There, at a meeting of the Council of the League of Nations in early February of 1937, the British and French delegates received a communication from the Spanish Foreign Minister. It contained an offer from Spain to surrender her rights to the Spanish Zone, together with other vaguely hinted territory, in favor of France and Great Britain in return for the active intervention of these powers against Germany and Italy. The note was published in the German, Italian, and French press. Both the British and the French governments rejected the offer as being an open violation of international treaties.[146]

At frequent intervals during the war, reports came to the State Department of difficult conditions in Tangier. On October 20, 1936, there was listed the almost total loss of the grain crop, the loss of the tourist trade due to the outbreak of the war, the rise in crime, the greatly increased cost of living, and the devaluations of the florin and the franc. Tangier was fortunate, however, to have retained the French administrator, a man of ability and tact, who was able to curb the officiousness of the Italian head of the Committee of Control.[147] A different sort of problem arose during 1937, when most of the Spanish officials in the Tangier administration espoused the Nationalist cause. Spain made no contribution to its collaboration dues for 1936 and 1937, adding to the deficit in the Tangier budget.[148] When the end of the war was in sight, it became necessary to effect a reconciliation between the Nationalist and Loyalist factions in the Spanish population of Tangier. The Spaniards, about 12,000, were the largest European group in the city and were mostly Loyalist in sympathy. Blake was asked to serve as adviser at a meeting between the former foes, which succeeded in making a transfer of authority without disorder.[149]

Early in the evening of March 31, 1939, an aide reported to General Franco that the Nationalist troops had occupied their final objectives. "Very good," he replied without looking up from his desk, "Many thanks." Thus ended a war more ferocious than most civil wars. About 600,000 people had lost their lives, and the official cost of the war was 3,000 million pounds in 1938 money. Many other kinds of losses were incalculable. Fascism had won a notable victory, and Franco was destined to remain in power many years after the death of his collaborators, Mussolini and Hitler.

Throughout the war, the United States had been considered the most truly neutral of any of the great nations. During the Abyssinian crisis of May, 1935, Congress passed a Neutrality Act making it illegal for any American citizen to sell or transport arms to belligerents after the President had proclaimed a state of war. This law did not apply to civil war, but the American government acted as if it did. There were many influential Americans who sympathized with the Spanish Republic, including President and Mrs. Roosevelt and Claude Bowers. But Secretary of State Hull insisted upon impartiality and the enforcement of the Neutrality Act, which cut off American aid from the Spanish Loyalists. However, American public opinion became fiercely partisan. Torrents of propaganda flowed from the Nationalist and Loyalist headquarters in New York City. The American press war was even more violent than that waged by the newspapers of France and Great Britain.[150] Many idealistic young Americans who served, as they thought, the cause of democracy by fighting in the Abraham Lincoln Battalion, found themselves later tarred with the Communist brush.

The Diplomatic Agent in Tangier, Maxwell Blake, had continued to advise the State Department on its Moroccan policy. At the end of 1938 he felt that he had given good counsel in advocating the non-adherence of the United States to the Tangier Statute:

> Our present extra-statutory vantage ground ... enables us to take our position objectively and independently on all matters in which we are concerned ... and without incurring the odium of political bias against some particular nationalistic pretension. Our present independent position ... implies no tendency to provide a privileged position for American ressortissants, since the Department's assent is invariably given to their subjection to all local laws, regulations, and taxation which do not involve discrimination or otherwise violate important treaty principles. It is also undesirable to subject Americans to the cumbersome, corrupt, and politics-ridden Mixed Tribunal.[151]

Notes

1. Stuart, _Tangier_, 53.

2. Blake to Sec. of State, No. 65, Feb. 25, 1919, _A. N. F._, 881.00/664.

3. Blake to Sec. of State, No. 1405, Dec. 6, 1938, _Ibid._, 881.01/50.

4. _Ibid._

5. Madariaga, _Spain, A Modern History_, 305.

6. Divison of Near Eastern Affairs, memorandum, Nov. 10, 1937, _A. N. F._, 881.014/14.

7. Landau, _Moroccan Drama_, 167.

8. Barbour, _North West Africa_, 163-165.

9. Blake to Sec. of State, No. 1405, Dec. 6, 1938, _A. N. F._, 881.01/50; Stuart, _Tangier_, 66-68.

10. The courtship of Raisuli by the Spanish officials in Morocco was defended by a spokesman for the Conservative party in February, 1919. He declared that the policy of conciliation pursued by Generals Marina and Jordana had been productive of good results for the years 1916 and 1917. Willard (Madrid) to Sec. of State, No. 1474, Feb. 26, 1919, A. N. F., 881.00/663. In May, 1915, becoming involved in the murder of a Spanish emissary to Raisuli, Generals Sylvestre and Marina were both recalled. General Jordana found negotiating with the irate Raisuli a lengthy and difficult task. Finally, shortly before the Armistice, an agreement was reached whereby the Spanish government recognized Raisuli as a powerful and semi-independent chieftain of the Jibala. Mellor, Morocco Awakes, 57.

11. Abdel Malek, grandson of Abdel Kader, became a secret German agent in Tangier, then fled from threatened exposure into the Spanish zone. With German money he bought immunity from capture and from the Spanish zone waged a Holy War on the French. In 1917 he was considered a serious menace. In 1925 he took command of a large native force for the Spanish despite the French demand for his surrender. He was killed in battle just as he was about to be pardoned by Marshal Lyautey on condition of his leaving Morocco permanently. W. B. Harris, France, Spain, and the Rif, 61-64.

12. Landau, Moroccan Drama, 165; W. B. Harris, "Morocco in Wartime," 270-271; W. B. Harris, France, Spain, and the Rif, 59-60, 64-65, 101, 106-107.

13. A. N. F.: Blake to Sec. of State, telegram, Feb. 11, 1915, 881.00/594; No. 468, Feb. 15, 1915, 881.00/596; No. 480, April 24, 1915, 881.00/598 and No. 9, Sept. 10, 1917, 881.00/642. Willard (Madrid) to Sec. of State, No. 227, March 5, 1915, 881.00/597 and No. 255, May 14, 1915, 881.00/599.

14. "Writing in 1917, Gonzáles-Blanco expends a great deal of effort in order to show that the British and Yankee peril should be met by Pan-Hispanism. He urges the

denunciation and abrogation of the treaty of Algeciras with the aim of recovering the Strait of Gibraltar, and the consolidation of the Iberian Peninsula by a federation with Portugal, in order to render the holding of that Strait by another nation perilous in the future. When the geographical integrity of Spain is thus restored, the Hispanic-American states may be invited to enter what is destined to be the great 'Iberian United States.'" Pan-Iberianism might ally itself with Germany in order that Iberismo and Germanismo might wrest from the Anglo-Saxons the palm of victory in the fight for the direction of humanity. James Fred Rippy, Latin America in World Politics, An Outline Survey, 211, reviewing Edmundo Gonzáles-Blanco, Iberismo y Germanismo. Espana ante el Conflicto Europeo, Valencia, Editorial Cervantes, 1917.

15. Morocco was much too expensive a luxury for a poor country like Spain to keep. The American Consul General at Barcelona reported that 'It is estimated that the close of 1915 will show a total expenditure by the Spanish Government in Morocco of some $35,000,000, which will bring up the total amount of expenses for this country since 1908 to over $300,000,000." Hurst to Sec. of State, Nov. 27, 1915, A. N. F., 881.00/609.

16. Spain considered it grossly unfair that a committee of the five great powers should consider the Moroccan question in which she had such a vital interest without allowing her representation similar to that of the other interested powers. She had not expected this kind of penalty for being neutral during the war. She asked the American commissioners at the Peace Conference to support her petition to be present at meetings on Morocco and to obtain also the support of the British, Italian, and Japanese delegates. Willard (Madrid) to American Commission, telegram, Feb. 27, 1919, Ibid., 852.00/38 and telegram, March 1, 1919, Ibid., 852.00/40; Spanish Embassy at Washington, Pro-memoria for the Sec. of State, March 3, 1919, 881.00/662, Ibid.; Polk to American Mission, Telegram, March 4, 1919, 185.1155/11, Ibid.

17. Stuart, Tangier, 69-70.

18. A. N. F.: De Lema, Ministry of State, Madrid, to State Dept., No. 147, Sept. 20, 1914, 881.00/589; Spanish Embassy to State Dept., Feb. 6, 1915, 881.00/595; Putney to Phillips, Division of Near Eastern Affairs, Feb. 8, 1915, 881.00/595; Dept. of State to Spanish Embassy, Feb. 19, 1915, 881.00/595; Lansing to Willard (Madrid), No. 84, 881.00/595.

19. The claim dated back to August, 1912, when El Kittany bought about 2,000 acres of land near Alcazar Kebir. In March, 1912, previous to his abdication, Mulai Hafid sold all Maghzen properties in the Spanish Zone to an agent of the Spanish government, who proceeded to annex El Kittany's non-adjacent land. Blake to Phillips, memorandum, Feb. 9, 1917, A. N. F., 481.11/114 A.

20. A. N. F.: Blake to Sec. of State, No. 485, June 10, 1915, 481.11/82 and No. 487, June 25, 1915, 481.11 /83; Osborne, Acting Sec. of State to Blake, No. 153, Aug. 10, 1915, 481.11/82; Blake to Sec. of State, No. 499, Oct. 4, 1915, 481.11/85; Osborne to Blake, No. 156, Nov. 23, 1915, 481.11/85; Blake to Sec. of State, telegram, Dec. 18, 1915, 418.11/87; Lansing to Blake, No. 161, Jan. 13, 1916, 481.11/87; Adee to Blake, telegram, Feb. 14, 1916, 481.11/87A; Blake to Dept. of State, telegram, Feb. 18, 1916, 481.11/88 and No. 531, April 14, 1916, 481.11/89; Adee to Blake, No. 164, June 8, 1916, 281.11/89; Blake to Sec. of State, No. 541, Sept. 2, 1916, 481.11/95; W P to Putney, Jan. 24, 1917, 881.00/638; Phillips to Wollsey, Jan. 29, 1917, 881.00/720.

21. A. N. F.: Phillips to Putney, July 16, 1917 and Putney to Phillips, July 16, 1917, 881.00/694; Riaño to Sec. of State, July 25, 1917, 881.00/638; Lansing to Riaño, No. 600, Aug. 20, 1917, 881.00/658; Phillips to Putney, Aug. 30, 1917, 881.00/719.

22. Riaño to Sec. of State Colby, Aug. 13, 1920, Ibid., 881.00/691.

23. In this memorandum a new reason was given for American interest in the Moroccan problem. "Morocco's value and political importance to Mediterranean powers is out of all proportion to any economic interest it might have for the United States, but American rights there should be jealously guarded because of their obvious influence in European questions."

24. Division of Western European Affairs, memorandum, May 18, 1921, Ibid., 881.00/7181/2; Blake to Sec. of State, No. 242, Sept. 15, 1921, Ibid., 881.00/738.

25. A. N. F.: Riaño to Hughes, March 2, 1923, 881.00/797 1/2; Division of Western European Affairs, memorandum, March 17, 1923, 881.00/798; Hughes to Riaño, March 19, 1923, 881.00/797 1/2; Denning to Sec. of State, Information Series, No. 17, May 7, 1923, 881.00/806; The Solicitor, memorandum, July 27, 1923, 881.00/837; Denning to Sec. of State, Information Series, No. 18 (prepared by Rand, Aug. 30, 1923), Dec. 8, 1923, 881.00/881.

26. Rand to Sec. of State, No. 229, March 20, 1924, 711.813/3; The Solicitor, memorandum, Nov. 6, 1924, 881.512/47; Blake to Sec. of State, No. 25, Sept. 22, 881.512/49; Ibid.

27. A. N. F.: Division of Western European Affairs, memorandum, May 20, 1927, 881.512/55 1/4; Amaedo to Kellogg, July 26, 1927, 452.11/198; Castle, State Dept., memorandum, Oct. 28, 1927, 881.00/1410; W R C, State Dept., to Hackworth, Oct. 28, 1927, 881.00/1410; Kellogg to Padilla y Bell, Nov. 7, 1927, 452.11/198; Blake to Sec. of State, No. 238, Nov. 15, 1927, 881.00/1361.

28. Padilla to Sec. of State Kellogg, Feb. 11, 1928; Kellogg to Padilla, Feb. 25, 1928; Kellogg to Blake, Feb. 25, 1928; F R, 1928, III, 346-348.

29. "Joint Report on Settlement of American Claims in the Spanish Zone of Morocco," July 12, 1928, Ibid., 353-357; Kellogg to Hammond (Madrid), Nov. 22, 1928, Ibid., 366-367.

30. A. N. F.: Blake to Sec. of State, No. 433, Sept. 4, 1929, 452.11/233; Cotton to Whitehouse, No. 637, Nov. 6, 1929, 452.11/236; Blake to Sec. of State, telegram, Dec. 3, 1929, 452.11/237.

31. Among the large number of documents between 1930 and 1939 relating to recognition of Spanish Morocco, the following are especially pertinent: A. N. F.: Blake to Sec. of State, No. 1007, Dec. 27, 1934, 681.003/124; Bowers (Madrid) to Sec. of State, telegram, Jan. 14, 1935, 681.003/131; Blake to Sec. of State, No. 1016, Jan. 23, 1935, 681.003/148; Blake to Sec. of State, No. 1019, Feb. 6, 1935, 681.003/154.

32. W. B. Harris, France, Spain, and the Rif, 107-114.

33. Ibid., 67-69.

34. Ibid., 70-72, 74.

35. Ibid., 74-77; Landau, Moroccan Drama, 165.

36. Barbour, North West Africa, 150.

37. Hugh Thomas, The Spanish Civil War (hereafter cited as Thomas, Spanish Civil War, 110.

38. Landau, Moroccan Drama, 165.

39. Barbour, North West Africa, 150-151.

40. A. N. F.: Blake to Sec. of State, Quarterly Information Series, No. 13, Jan. 4, 1922, 881.00/759; Wheeler (London) to Sec. of State, No. 1664, Sept. 6, 1922, 881.00/784 and No. 2821, Aug. 31, 1923, 881.00/839.

41. Barbour, North West Africa, 151.

42. A. N. F.: Woods (Madrid) to Sec. of State, No. 449, Jan. 16, 1923, 881.00/795; Rand to Sec. of State, Quarterly Information Series, No. 19, April 30, 1924, 881.00/921; Russell to Sec. of State, No. 53, Sept. 3, 1924, 881.00/964; Ferrin (Consul at Madrid) to Carter, Jan. 5, 1925, 881.00/1013; Murphy to Sec. of State, May 18, 1925, 881.00/1058.

43. Wheeler (London) to Sec. of State, No. 1579, Aug. 8, 1922, 881.00/780; Houghton (London) to Sec. of State, telegram, June 4, 1925, 881.00/1055 and telegram, July 14, 1925, 881.00/1097; Riaño to Hughes, Feb. 11, 1925, 881.348/--; Hughes to Riaño, Feb. 20, 1925, 881.348/--; Moore (Madrid) to Sec. of State, No. 630, July 3, 1925, 881.00/1110 and Kellogg to American Embassy, San Sebastian, telegram, July 31, 1925; Ibid.; Kellogg to Daescher (French ambassador to the United States), Aug. 1, 1925, 881.00/1084; Statement of Emergency Foreign Policy Conference, received Nov. 9, 1925, 881.00/1167; A. N. F.

44. White (Riga) to Sec. of State, No. 2513, Nov. 19, 1924, 881.008/--; Coleman (Riga) to Sec. of State, No. 2711, March 17, 1925, 881.00/1029; No. 2745, April 1, 1925, 881.00B/2; and No. 3016, July 8, 1925, 881.00B /5. Russell to Sec. of State, No. 163, June 1, 1925, 881.00B/3. Haskell (Algiers) to Sec. of State, No. 51, June 19, 1925, 881.00/1085. Whitehouse (Paris) to Sec. of State, No. 5322, June 24, 1925, 881.00/1086; A. N. F.

45. Ibid.: Herrick (Paris) to Sec. of State, No. 5773, Nov. 27, 1925, 881.00/1185; Allen (Constantinople), to Sec. of State, No. 6246, with enclosure of translation of "A Moslem League of Nations," May 18, 1926, 867.404/165.

46. An interesting article is his "Abd El-Krim and the War in Africa," in the Atlantic Monthly, CXXXVI (August, 1925), 251-263. Sheean thought that there should be another international conference to abolish the immoral treaties of 1902 to 1912 and to grant the Riff independence.

47. A. N. F.: Herrick (Paris) to Sec. of State, telegram June 10, 1925, 881.00/1060; Martin (Madrid) to Sec. of State, American Foreign Service Report, No. 87, Feb. 10, 1925, 881.00/1023.

48. Ibid.: Myrick (Springfield, Mass.), with enclosures, Feb. 6, 1926, 881.00/1196; Blake to Carter, with enclosures, Jan. 30, 1926, 881.00/1200 and Feb. 2, 1926, 881.00/1200; Martin (Madrid) to Sec. of State, No. 822, Feb. 1, 1926, 852.00/1588.

49. *Ibid.*: Russell to Sec. of State, No. 196, Aug. 12, 1925, 881.00/1142 and No. 203, Aug. 24, 1925, 881.00/1147; Blake to Castle, Sept. 16, 1925, 881.00/1155; Blake to Sec. of State, No. 26, Sept. 24, 1925, 881.00/1153; Blake to Castle, Sept. 25, 881.00/1165; Hannah C. Hull to Kellogg, Oct. 15, 1925, 881.00/1154; Grew to Hannah C. Hull, Nov. 7, 1925, 881.00/1162; Herrick (Paris) to Sec. of State, No. 5701, Nov. 10, 1925, 881.00/1179; Blake to Carter, Nov. 25, 1925, 881.00/1191.

50. *Ibid.*: Blake to Sec. of State, No. 4, July 16, 1925, 881.00/1115; Barbour, *North West Africa*, 151-152.

51. *A. N. F.*: Whitehouse (Paris) to Sec. of State, No. 5597, Oct. 9, 1925, 881.00/1156; Barbour, *North West Africa*, 152.

52. "Neither Gordon Canning in Paris (whose expenses were borne by a German steel group, and whose motives are consequently likewise suspect by France), nor Mr. Sheean, as the agent of a syndicated and spectacular press (whose animosity to Spain has been publicly declared), can be accepted by good faith by either side, as appropriate mediums for the opening of peace negotiations. In addition to the disqualifications indicated, and imputable to their haphazard, jejune, and meddlesome enterprises, it is obvious that the path of both these novices in Morocco is beset with diplomatic and psychological difficulties inevitably leading them into a labyrinth from which, it is credibly suggested, that neither possesses sufficient ingenuity to effect a successful escape." Blake to Sec. of State, No. 54, Jan. 28, 1926, *A. N. F.*, 881.00/1199.

53. *Ibid.*

54. *Ibid.*: Herrick to Sec. of State, No. 6279, April 23, 1926, 881.00/1213; No. 6249, April 30, 1926, 881.00/1214 and No. 6325, May 14, 1926, 881.00/1218. Russell to Sec. of State, No. 256, June 1, 1926, 881.00/1237.

55. Ibid.: Ferrin (Madrid) to Carter, June 1, 1926, 881.00/1231; Herrick to Kellogg, June 4, 1926, 881.00/1232; Blake to Sec. of State, No. 105, June 5, 1926, 881.00/1234; Hammond (Madrid) to Sec. of State, No. 74, June 7, 1926, 881.00/1238; Russell to Sec. of State, No. 258, June 17, 1926, 881.00/1250; Herrick to Sec. of State, No. 6418, June 17, 1926, 881.00/1243; Herrick to Sec. of State, No. 6426, June 18, 1926, 881.00/1244; and No. 6497, July 15, 1926, 881.00/1253.

56. Abd al Krim did not serve his life sentence of exile in Reunion. In 1947 the French decided to transfer him to house arrest in France, but he jumped ship at the Suez Canal and was granted asylum in Egypt. He died at the age of 81 on February 6, 1963, and was given a hero's funeral in Cairo. He had planned a return to Morocco in May. His career was romanticized in "The Desert Song." New York Times, CXII (Feb. 7, 1963), 1, 7.

57. A. N. F.: Russell to Sec. of State, No. 271, Aug. 31, 1926, 881.00/1307; Thompson (Tananariva, Madagascar), No. 1080, Oct. 18, 1926, 881.00/1317.

58. Barbour, North West Africa, 152-153; A. N. F., Blair (Madrid) to Sec. of State, No. 682, Dec. 12, 1927, 852.00/1733.

59. Ibid.: Blake to Sec. of State, No. 109, June 8, 1926, 751.81/19; Russell to Sec. of State, July 8, 1926, 751.81/20.

60. Ibid.: Sterling (London) to Sec. of State, No. 1279, Aug. 19, 1926, 841.00/963; Blake to Sec. of State, No. 130, Aug. 25, 1926, 881.00/1302.

61. Ibid.: Blake to Sec. of State, Q I S, No. 6, Dec. 31, 1919, 881.00/677; Q I S, No. 8, June 30, 1920, 881.00/692; No. 1405, Dec. 6, 1938, 881.01/50.

62. Ibid.: Blake to Sec. of State, Q I S, No. 7, March 31, 1920, 881.00/682; Q I S, No. 9, Oct. 18, 1920, 881.00/700; Q I S, No. 10, Dec. 31, 1920, 881.00 /703.

63. Ibid.: Navy Dept. to Sec. of State, with enclosure of letter from Vice Admiral Niblick, March 2, 1921, 881.00/705; Niblick to Fletcher, Nov. 12, 1921, 881.00/764; Woods (Madrid) to Sec. of State, No. 146, March 6, 1922, 881.00/763; Office of Naval Intelligence, memorandum for State Dept., March 8, 1922, 881.00/761; Division of Far Eastern Affairs to Castle, April 6, 1922, 881.00/765 1/2; American Consul General (London) to Sec. of State, No. 13,311, June 26, 1922, 881.00/723.

64. Blake accused Walter B. Harris, the London *Times* correspondent in Morocco, of being the most enthusiastic and active coadjuter of the French at Rabat in putting over this plan. When Harris went to London to raise 1,000,000 francs, approximately the British share in the company, his mission was a failure, as British bankers and financiers refused to consider a scheme lacking the sanction of the British government. Blake to Sec. of State, No. 234, August 15, 1921, A. N. F.: 881.00/731.

65. Ibid.: Blake to Sec. of State, No. 234, Q I S, No. 11, Aug. 15, 1921, 881.00/731.

66. The number of documents is too great to make individual citations, but they are summarized in the text.

67. A. N. F.: Hughes, memorandum of interview with French ambassador, July 10, 1922, 881.156/31.

68. In these conversations Curzon had rejected the proposal of the French ambassador in London. The French plan was to abolish the Diplomatic Corps and to set up a municipal government for Tangier to be elected by the residents, including both Muslims and Jews. All legislative and administrative matters, however, would be dealt with by the Sherifian state--that is, by the authorities of the French Protectorate. Great Britain wanted a real international government based on the Statute of 1913. Briand said that France was ready for an international system and agreed to London as a conference site. Unfortunately, the conciliatory Briand was soon replaced by the tough-minded

Poincaré, and the controversy was resumed. Blake to Sec. of State, No. 274, Feb. 3, 1922, A. N. F., 881.00/760.

69. Harvey (London) to Sec. of State, telegram, July 21, 1922, 881.156/29, Ibid.

70. Ibid.: aide memoire for Castle by Peterson of British Embassy, Aug. 2, 1922, 881.156/32; Denning to Sec. of State, Aug. 14, 1922, 881.156/39; No. 27, Aug. 17, 1922, 881.156/38; Q I S, No. 14, Aug. 19, 1922, 881.00/782. Niblick (Charleston, S.C.) to Phillips, Aug. 16, 1922, 881.00/929, APN-81 8/16.

71. Ibid.: Phillips to Whitehouse (Paris), No. 432, Sept. 21, 1922, 881.156/36; Herrick (Paris) to Sec. of State, telegram, Nov. 3, 1922, 881.156/46 and Nov. 3, 1922, No. 2524, 881.156/52.

72. Ibid.: Herrick (Paris) to Sec. of State, telegram, Nov. 9, 1922, 881.156/50; Denning to Sec. of State, telegram, Nov. 9, 1922, 881.156/51; No. 62, Nov. 15, 1922, 881.156/56; No. 69, Dec. 9, 1922, 881.156/60; No. 74, Dec. 20, 1922, 881.156/62 and Q I S, No. 16, Feb. 20, 1923, 881.00/800. Division of Western European Affairs, memorandum for Sec. of State, Dec. 21, 1922, 881.156/59.

73. Ibid.: Herrick (Paris) to Sec. of State, No. 2553, Nov. 11, 1922, 881.156/54 and No. 2571, Nov. 16, 1922, 881.156/55.

74. Stuart, Tangier, 77-78.

75. A. N. F.: Rand to Sec. of State, telegram, Aug. 25, 1923, 881.00/838 and No. 166, Aug. 31, 1923, 881.00/841.

76. Stuart, Tangier, 78.

77. Ibid., 78-79.

78. F. R., 1923, II, 723 and 580; Dept. of State, Press Release, Oct. 23, 1923.

79. Stuart, Tangier, 79-80.

80. Ibid., 80.

81. A. N. F.: Johnson (Madrid) to Sec. of State, No. 184, Dec. 29, 1923, 881.00/887; No. 206, Jan. 12, 1924, 881.00/892; telegram, Jan. 21, 1924, 881.00/889; No. 219, Jan. 21, 1924, 881.00/894. Kellogg (London) to Sec. of State, telegram, Jan. 15, 1924, 881.00/886.

82. Stuart, Tangier, 81-82.

83. Ibid., 82-83, 88.

84. The allocation of seats was as follows: French, 4; Spanish, 4; British, 3; Italian, 2; American, 1; Belgian, 1; Dutch, 1; Portuguese, 1. Since the French controlled half of the 26 votes, it was usually not difficult for them to add a vote or two for a majority on questions in which they were interested.

85. Stuart, Tangier, 85-87.

86. In 1922, the United States had five percent of the total trade of Tangier and Italy had three percent; the same ratio continued for the first half of 1923.

87. A. N. F.: Division of Western European Affairs, J T M to Castle, memorandum, Jan. 29, 1924, 881.00/1121.

88. Ibid.: Rand to Sec. of State, Q I S, No. 19, April 30, 1924, 881.00/921.

89. Ibid.: Sec. of State, memorandum of interview with Jusserand, June 4, 1924, 881.00/918; Sec. of State, memorandum of interview with Howard, June 5, 1924, 881.00/916.

90. Ibid.: Rand to Sec. of State, No. 252, June 7, 1924, 881.00/937; Marriner, Division of Western European Affairs, memorandum on policy for Grew, June 12, 1924, 881.00/1127.

91. Ibid.: Skinner (London) to Sec. of State, No. 17,470, July 3, 1924, with clipping from London Times, 881.00/942; Rand to Sec. of State, No. 285, Aug. 7, 1924, 881.00/952.

92. The practices detailed to be avoided in the future were all those which had caused so much friction with the French since 1912.

93. A. N. F.: Hughes to French Embassy (similar notes to British and Spanish Embassies), July 11, 1924, 881.00/918; press interview, July 11, 1924, received from M. J. McDermott, Chief, Division of Current Information, May 24, 1928.

94. Ibid.: Murphy to Sec. of State, report, May 22, 1924, 881.156/67; F M A, Solicitor, memorandum, May 26, 1924, 881.156/82; Rand to Sec. of State, telegram, June 20, 1924, 881.156/70; Hughes to Amlegation, Tangier, telegram, June 24, 1924, 881.156/70; Under-Sec. of State, conversation with Laboulaye, July 10, 1924, 881.156/74.

95. F R, 1924, II, 463-468; Stuart, Tangier, 84.

96. Ibid., 84--85. A. N. F.: Solicitor, memorandum, Nov. 28, 1924, 881.00/916; Division of Western European Affairs to Grew, Dec. 1, 1924, 881.00 /1102; Grew to Riaño, June 18, 1925, 881.00/1052; Kellogg to Chilton, June 18, 1925, 881.00/1048; Division of Western European Affairs to Grew, July 8, 1925, 881.00/1105.

97. From that time on, the only active members of the Sanitary Council, the representatives of the United States and Italy, alternated in the presidency for quarterly periods. In January, 1929, when Italy adhered to the Statute, the American Legation received the archives, funds, and effects, and the American representative carried on alone. Stuart, Tangier, 25-26.

98. A. N. F.: Rand to Sec. of State, Q I S, No. 21, March 31, 1925, 881.00/1034; Stuart, Tangier, 88.

99. Ibid., 88-89. A. N. F.: Blake to Carter, Feb. 2, 1926, 881.00/1200. Ferrin (Madrid) to Sec. of State, No. 103, June 10, 1925, 881.00/1076; No. 109, June 22, 1925, 881.00/1090; No. 111, June 25, 1925, 881.00/1091. Blake to Sec. of State, No. 1, July 6, 1925, 881.00/1106; No. 93, April 26, 1926, 881.00 /1217; No. 118, July 7, 1926, 881.00/1252.

100. Ibid., Ferrin to Sec. of State, No. 103, June 10, 1925, 881.00/1076.

101. Every piece of merchandise interchanged between the Tangier and Spanish zones had to pay import and export duties twice, by action of the Spanish authorities. Blake to Sec. of State, No. 106, June 5, 1926, Ibid., 881.00/1236.

102. Ibid., Blake to Sec. of State, No. 16, Sept. 4, 1925, 881.00/1148.

103. Ibid., Frost to Sec. of State, political report, July 30, 1926, 881.00/1266 and Aug. 20, 1926, 881.00/1295.

104. A significant demonstration of Fascism in Tangier was arranged by the Italian diplomatic agent under the authority of his government. The occasion was the blessing of the flags of the Fascisti units in Morocco, coinciding with the visit of several hundred members of the Italian Navy League and attended by many foreigners as guests. The ceremony was held in the legation garden and was very dignified and impressive. Frost (vice consul) to Sec. of State, political report, July 12, 1926, Ibid., 881.00/1258.

105. Spain later withdrew this customs wall for the price of 25 percent of the sums collected at Tangier. Stuart, Tangier, 91.

106. A. N. F.: Reed (San Sebastian) to Sec. of State, No. 100, July 6, 1926, 881.00/1251; Whitehouse to Sec. of State, telegram, Aug. 17, 1926, 881.00/1262; Houghton (London) to Sec. of State, telegram, Aug. 19, 1926, 881.00/1265; Hammond (Madrid) to Sec. of State, weekly report, Aug. 23, 1926, 852.00/1642. Stuart, Tangier, 91-93.

107. Ibid., 93; F R, 1926, II, 726 ff. A. N. F.: Kellogg to American Embassy, San Sebastian, telegram, Aug. 25, 1926, 881.00/1263; Division of Western European Affairs, memorandum, Aug. 26, 1926, 881.00/1310; Grew to American Embassy, San Sebastian, telegram, Aug. 31, 1926, 881.00/1275.

108. Ibid.: Blake to Sec. of State, No. 146, Dec. 2, 1926, 881.00/1321; Stuart, Tangier, 93-94.

109. A. N. F.: White (Madrid), to Sec. of State, No. 257, Jan. 15, 1927, 881.00/1327 and No. 284, Feb. 14, 1927, 881.00/1330.

110. The London Times of March 3, 1926, admitted that Tangier served as a safe haven for distributors of subversive correspondence and propaganda and for journalists championing Abd al Krim. It denied that Tangier had been a source of contraband of war. Sterling (London chargé) to Sec. of State, No. 859, March 11, 1926, Ibid., 881.00/1204.

111. Ibid., Blake to Sec. of State, No. 201, June 15, 1927, 881.00/1344; Stuart, Tangier, 94-96.

112. Ibid., 96.

113. As quoted by the London Times of March 19, 1928, the Rome Tribune referred frankly to the need for a comprehensive agreement of the Great Powers on general Mediterranean policy. "Tangier is regarded as a minor question. The ulterior, and far more important, objective is the creation of a united front which will enable the interested Powers to set up, for example, a barrier against the violent economic pressure of the United States in the Mediterranean and also to check the constant attempts of the Arabs to revolt." Skinner (Athens) to Sec. of State, No. 554, April 20, 1928, A. N. F., 868.51/1101.

114. Stuart, Tangier, 97.

115. Ibid., 98; Edwin L. James, "Italians at Tangier Arouse Frenchmen, Draw Berlin's Fire," New York Times,

Oct. 30, 1927; James T. Gerould, "France's Efforts to Prop Up the Versailles Treaty," Current History, XXVII (Dec., 1927), 407; Eloise Ellery, "The Roman Question and Fascism," Current History, XXVII (Dec., 1927), 436; Othon G. Guerlac, "Briand Steers Europe Toward Peace," Current History, XXVII (Jan., 1928), 593-594.

116. Stuart, Tangier, 98-99.

117. Blake said that Spain's one important gain from the preliminary agreement, control of the police, now appeared to be merely nominal. It had to be shared with French officers and was entirely subjected to the authority and direction of the French administrator. Blake to Sec. of State, No. 297, May 3, 1928, A. N. F., 881.00/1407.

118. On March 22, 1928, Primo de Rivera announced that Spain's resignation from the League of Nations had been cancelled. Henry G. Doyle, "Pre-Election Political Issues in France," Current History, XXVIII (May, 1928), 306.

119. Stuart, Tangier, 99-101.

120. Ibid., 101, 104.

121. F R, 1928, II, 371-372.

122. Stuart, Tangier, 103-104.

123. F R, 1929, II, 505-520. Only a few of the numerous documents can be cited here. Among them are, in A. N. F.: Blake to Sec. of State, No. 17, Sept. 5, 1925, 881.512/48; No. 343, Dec. 4, 1928, 881.512 /63; and No. 360, Jan. 25, 1929, 881.512/72. Howard to Kellogg, No. 573, Dec. 7, 1928; Claudel to Kellogg, note verbale, Jan. 3, 1929, 881.512/68 and State Dept. memorandum, Feb. 27, 1929; Castle to Howard, Feb. 27, 1929, 881.512/60; Cotton to Blake, No. 573, Jan. 8, 1930, 881.512/77.

124. Ibid.: Blake to Sec. of State, No. 314, July 21, 1928,

881.00/1418; No. 337, Nov. 15, 1928, 881.00/1432; No. 1405, Dec. 6, 1928, 881.00/50; No. 362, Jan. 29, 1929, 881.124/40; No. 388, April 26, 1929, 881.00 /1442; No. 448, Nov. 8, 1929, 881.00/1452.

125. Ibid., Blake to Sec. of State, No. 455, Dec. 9, 1929, 881.00/1455.

126. Langer, Encyclopedia of World History, 981-982.

127. Barbour, North West Africa, 153-154.

128. They were Generals Jordana and Sanjurjo, and Señors Lopez Ferrer, Moles, Rico Avello, Moles, and Alvarez Buylla. Ibid., 154-156.

129. Ibid., 154-157.

130. A. N. F.: Blake to Sec. of State, No. 608, May 12, 1931, 881.00/1491; No. 614, June 2, 1931, 881.00 /1492; No. 619, June 11, 1931, 881.00/1494; No. 641, Aug. 14, 1931, 881.00/1502; No. 685, Jan. 12, 1932, 881.00/1523; No. 728, May 4, 1932, 881.00/1537. Dawson (Paris) to Sec. of State, No. WD962, Nov. 7, 1931, 852.00/1877; Bigelow to Sec. of State, No. 699, Feb. 20, 1932, 881.00/1529; Laughlin (Madrid) to Sec. of State, No. 657, April 2, 1932, 881.51/41.

131. None of these territories was considered a part of the Spanish Protectorate; they were all colonial possessions of Spain, like Ceuta and Melilla.

132. A. N. F.: Bowers to Sec. of State, No. 335, April 11, 1934, 881.00/1563; Schoellkopf (Madrid), No. 483, Sept. 1, 1934, 881.00/31; Blake to Murray, Dec. 8, 1937, 781.003/81.

133. The protests of Blake are too numerous for citation. Two documents containing summations are in A. N. F.: D F B to Culbertson, Dec. 13, 1930 and Blake to Sec. of State, No. 640, Aug. 11, 1931, 881.154/5.

134. Ibid.: Blake to Sec. of State, No. 598, March 27, 1931, 881.00/1486.

135. Stuart, _Tangier,_ 105. _A. N. F._: Blake to Sec. of State, No. 728, May 4, 1932, 881.00/1537; No. 760, Aug. 10, 1932, 881.00/1541. Gilbert (Geneva) to Sec. of State, No. 1093, Nov. 20, 1934, 881.00/1572; Division of Western European Affairs, memorandum, Dec. 8, 1934, 881.00/1572; Gilbert to Sec. of State, No. 1152, Jan. 17, 1935, 881.00/1576.

136. Blake to Sec. of State, No. 1117, Dec. 4, 1935, _Ibid._, 881.01/36; Stuart, _Tangier,_ 105-106.

137. _A. N. F._: Doolittle to Sec. of State, No. 1156, May 2, 1936, 881.00/1599; No. 1158, May 9, 1936, 881.00/1601; No. 1159, May 12, 1936, 881.00/1159; Blake to Sec. of State, No. 1171, June 17, 1936, 881.5045/3.

138. Richard Scott Mowrer, "Spain's Nine Men," _New Leader_, XLI (Aug. 4-11, 1958), 17-18; Thomas, _Spanish Civil War,_ 58-59; 486-487; E. Allison Peers, _The Spanish Tragedy, 1930-1937: Dictatorship, Republic, Chaos, Rebellion, War,_ Sixth Edition (hereafter cited as Peers, _Spanish Tragedy_), 211-212; Doolittle to Sec. of State, report, Aug. 5, 1936, _A. N. F._, 852.00/2729.

139. Stuart, _Tangier,_ 106-107. _A. N. F._: Blake to Sec. of State, telegram, July 19, 1936, 881.00/1610; telegram, July 20, 1936, 881.00/1611; telegram, July 21, 1936, 852.00/2190; telegram, Aug. 7, 1936, 852.00/2462; No. 1187, Aug. 7, 1936, 852.00/2736. Hull to American legation, Tangier, July 22, 1936, 852.00/2190; Wilson (Paris) to Sec. of State, telegram, Aug. 7, 1936, 852.00/2463.

140. _Ibid._: Wendelin (Madrid) to Sec. of State, No. x-5, Aug. 12, 1936, 852.00/2980; Blake to Sec. of State, No. 1190, Aug. 21, 1936, 881.00/1620.

141. Barbour, _North West Africa,_ 157-159.

142. Blake to Sec. of State, No. 1202, Sept. 18, 1936, _A. N. F._, 881.001/40.

143. On January 8, 1937, Bowers reported to Washington that the Italians had withdrawn from the Balearic Isles and had sent large forces to Spain, where the Germans also were rushing reinforcements to France. This resulted in a great increase in bombing operations. Franco's Foreign Legion and Moroccan troops had been largely wiped out by this time. Bowers to Sec. of State, No. 1246, Jan. 6, 1937, Ibid., 852.00/4428.

144. Bowers to Sec. of State, No. 1226, Oct. 21, 1936, 852.00/3644 and No. 1240, Dec. 10, 1936, Ibid., 852.00/4179.

145. Thomas, Spanish Civil War, 340; "French Hear 8,000 Germans Will Reach Morocco Today," New York Times, Jan. 10, 1937, 1, 28; Albion Ross, "Germany Heeding Morocco Warning," Ibid., Jan. 17, 1937, 4 E.

146. Blake to Sec. of State, No. 1267, March 24, 1937, A. N. F., 881.00/1661.

147. Ibid., Doolittle to Sec. of State, report, Oct. 20, 1936, 881.51/61; Blake to Sec. of State, No. 232, with enclosure, Dec. 19, 1936, 852.00/4323.

148. Doolittle to Sec. of State, report, Oct. 30, 1937, Ibid., 881.51/64.

149. Blake to Murray, letter, March 2, 1939, Ibid., 702.5281/2.

150. Thomas, Spanish Civil War, 233.

151. Blake to Sec. of State, No. 1405, Dec. 6, 1938, A. N. F., 881.01/50.

Chapter XIII

French Morocco After Lyautey (1925 - 1939)

Marshal Lyautey had spent thirteen years of his career in establishing French dominium over Morocco. During the next period of equal length, French Morocco had five "protectors", of whom the last three were in office during 1936. This rapid turnover of resident generals reflected the turbulence and uncertainty of French politics, which in turn was symptomatic of the world-wide conflict of ideologies finally terminating in the Second World War. The five successors of Lyautey were Theodore Steeg (1926-1929), Lucien Saint (1929-1933), Henri Ponsot (1933-1936), Marcel Peyrouton (May-October, 1936), and General Auguste Noguès (October, 1936-June 5, 1943). Already at his retirement Lyautey was becoming a legend, and his theory of governing through a Franco-Moroccan entente was honored in speech, but not in action, by his successors.

After the parliamentary "abdication" of 1891, only a few senators and deputies were among the "fifty people interested in colonies," and even this interested group was directed by the administrators and the industrial group working with them. At this time the decentralizing group of colonial administrators, of whom Lyautey was one of the most eminent, made their great achievements. Following the first world war, a sentiment of gratitude to the subject peoples who had fought loyally for France led to a movement to improve their lot. The parliamentarians had no idea that the contemplated extension of suffrage and other privileges to the natives would undermine the whole colonial system. With the triumph of the Left in the 1924 elections in France, most of the supporters of the administrators overseas went out of power. The new colonial bloc made few reforms, except to cut military expenses in Morocco, which almost led to disaster in the Riffian War and was a factor in the dismissal of Lyautey. There was also a revolt in Syria and serious unrest in Indo-China, all aggravated by a barrage of anti-imperialist propaganda by Communists in the French Parliament. A swing toward imperial centralization was the natural reaction. The Parliament resolved to study the colonial situation at first hand and sent its members on mission to govern some of the most important possessions. Deputy Varenne went to Indo-China, Senator Violette to Algeria, and Senator Steeg to Morocco. The French Parliament was no longer indifferent to its empire.[1]

In some departments Lyautey's successors continued his work. They completed his task of pacification and unification, which had never been accomplished under the independent sultanate. All of them, whatever their merits or failings, contributed to the upbuilding of a modern administration and economic system, but all insisted upon treating Morocco simply as an economic entity, forgetting that ninety percent of the population cherished certain spiritual concepts and had ideas and ambitions of its own.[2]

Theodore Steeg was an eminent man in France--he had been premier and governor general of Algeria. It was rumored that he had accepted the post in Morocco as a stepping stone to the presidency of France. He was rated as a liberal, too, but his governmental system was less acceptable to the natives than Lyautey's benevolent autocracy. While Lyautey thought of himself as a "protector," Steeg treated Morocco as a colony. Beginning his administration by a change of personnel, Steeg replaced Lyautey's assistants, who were trained in and for Moroccan conditions, with new officials unacquainted with the country. Instead of making direct contacts with the natives, Steeg studied Moroccan problems through office files. He maintained personal contact only with the Sultan, and that was practically limited to a "Sign here!" command on dahirs. His examples was followed by the entire French officialdom, and soon "under the juridical fiction of a protectorate, the Residency practiced the methods of direct administration." Senior public servants and even minor officials came flocking from France, with an ever increasing burden on the budget of Morocco. Lyautey had begun preparing the natives for future work in the government; Steeg made no move to train a native civil service. There was no school for the education of native administrators and lower officials. Although taxes on natives paid over ninety percent of the Moroccan budget, this large army of French functionaries was paid from local taxes and not by subsidies from France.[3]

An early estimate of Steeg's personality and policy was made by Blake, which also reveals his well known bias against Lyautey:

> Senator Steeg (is) a man of modesty but of medium measure, undistinguished in appearance, but rumored to be competent, steady and self-possessed, and esteemed by those who know him for the impeccable rectitude of his principles. As an administrator, M. Steeg gave evidence of his talents in Algeria, and as a reformer, he has already proved in Morocco that the old Lyautey Regime, once so deeply embedded in the life of this country, is dead and is to be swept away, with all its ostentation and egotism.
>
> There is little doubt, in view of his past associations in North Africa, that M. Steeg will steadily pursue a policy of political and economic union between Morocco and Algeria, with the ultimate goal of the practical annexation of Morocco by France, should France be able to raise the hypothecations of international treaties, in regard to international liberty of trade and economic development in the Sherifian Empire.[4]

Early in 1926 there were two interesting dispatches to the Secretary of State, both from American officials, yet presenting very different views of the Moroccan situation. On March 24 Blake wrote of a petition presented to Steeg personally, signed by twelve leading men of Fez. It had been kept secret and unmentioned by the press. This public disclosure of the petitioners for redress of fourteen grievances called for constructive measures by the French to win native support for a new policy, Blake said. The other, a personal letter dated April 23, was an account of a holiday trip by motor in Morocco, written by Ambassador Herrick stationed in Paris. His opinion was that the order, progress, and steady material development visible on every hand were accompanied by wide contentment of the native Moroccan. All the French officials, he thought, from the top to the bottom, seemed to be carrying out with a sort of fanatical piety Marshal Lyautey's three cardinal principles ... generosity, sympathy, and religious tolerance.[5] Of course, the change in personnel was just beginning at this time, and Herrick's tour was French-conducted.

Steeg's first big task was aiding in the conclusion of the Riffian War. Since the French army was now under separate control, Steeg's responsibility was less than Lyautey's had been. However, Steeg was credited with being responsible for the peace negotiations at Udja on April 18. It was reported that Briand, Painlevé, and Pétain had all been convinced of the necessity for a spring campaign, but Steeg threatened to resign unless negotiations for peace were undertaken. The failure of the Udja parleys was followed by a victorious French offensive, and on May 26 Abd al Krim addressed to Steeg a request for further negotiations. Krim's letter was unanswered, because the French were convinced of his imminent collapse. The debacle came on May 27, and the pitifully few prisoners still alive were released by the Riffians. The French press, excepting _L'Humanité_, was elated and bestowed much praise upon Steeg, General Boichut (leader of the army), Painlevé, and Pétain, according to the political persuasion of each paper. Even after the last letter from Abd al Krim, _L'Humanité_ had held forth the prospect of continued Riffian resistance, but it now contented itself with eulogizing the defeated enemy. The French authorities proceeded with pacification in a conciliatory spirit, and the Riffian tribesmen were welcomed back to allegiance to the Sultan and his protectors with open arms. Steeg received the submitting tribesmen with tact and skill, but in a manner to inspire them with respect for French authority.[6]

Commenting on native discontent, Blake expressed doubt that Steeg was "capable of including in his policy of prayer, piety, and compromise the sufficient element of firmness indispensable in dealing successfully with an eastern population." He recalled that Lyautey had once admitted to him that French rule would continue only as long as force was applied. In a recent conversation, General de Chsmbrun, one of Lyautey's few lingering friends and favorites in Morocco, had confided that Lyautey had stipulated a time limit of thirty years as the maximum period of French rule in Morocco. Blake pointed out several smouldering causes of native unrest. One was the demonetization of native silver currency a few years before; "where the profits vanished which grew out of this usurious transaction has never been declared .... It created greater antagonism ... than any other decree of the French Administration since its inception." In turn, Steeg had committeed a blunder equally serious--his policy of planting French colonists upon the communal tribal lands and diverting the waters of streams from the cities and villages for the irrigation of these settlements, which the natives feared was the first move in finally depriving them of their lands. The country was honeycombed with favoritism and nepotism, and the bitter strife among the 60,000 French functionaries in Morocco was carried on in the open, even to a scandalous degree in the press itself.[7]

From his Algerian experience, Steeg was convinced that foreign rule in an overseas territory could be founded securely only upon European colonization of the land. Lyautey had yielded reluctantly to the settlement of only 1,000 Europeans in Morocco. In Steeg's administration the number of French landholders trebled. Lyautey had preferred the wealthier group of colonists who brought sufficient capital, took up large tracts, and maintained French prestige without public aid or supervision. On the contrary, Steeg sought for large numbers of small-scale farmers, for example, war veterans, who had to have public aid. These French immigrants could be settled on land only at the expense of the tribes who already owned it and its necessary water supply. Land was therefore either expropriated from the natives or purchased from them at prices set by the Residency officials. Deprived of their land, the native ex-farmers were forced to migrate to the cities, chiefly to Casablanca, where they became the proletariat, a class previously unknown in Morocco. Many of the small colonists displacing them failed at farming, and they had to be helped from budgetary funds provided chiefly by the Moroccan taxpayers.[8]

During 1926 consular reports from Russell at Casablanca discussed several causes of Moroccan dissatisfaction. In July, 1926, the rising cost of living and the paralysis of the import trade were attributed to the depreciation of the Moroccan franc, declining with the French franc. Steeg's announcement of a new policy was criticized adversely on October 12, 1926, by Russell who declared that Steeg's plan to establish a consultative body to represent consumers, workers, members of professions, and functionaries was valueless because the majority of Moroccans would have no voice in government and must continue to bear the heavy budget, which contained little for education and material improvement of the natives. "The policy of water must dominate all others," said Steeg, but the loan needed made immediate water development impossible. Steeg hoped that the natives would form groups around European farms in order to learn modern farming methods, but Russell had heard that French colons around Meknes had forced neighboring natives to become virtual peons. The Udja-Fez railroad would be completed after the Casablanca-Marrakesh line. The Hassani currency would not be restored and the French franc would not be abandoned. In Paris, Steeg as resident general was given control over the French military commander.[9]

In his 1927 reports, Russell was scarcely more optimistic. The third agricultural exposition at Casablanca was far inferior to the earlier ones and lacked the enthusiastic support of the first two. Bad crops and business depression were largely responsible for this situation. American exhibits of oil, automobile, and harvesting machinery companies were few, but excellent in location and presentation. A June dispatch told of an increasing lack of coherence and of central authority in the Protectorate administration during the last twenty-one months. This refusal to accept responsibility had been evident for several months in a total disregard of American treaty rights. The blame for this condition Russell placed on the vacillating policy of the Resident general. Steeg had not curbed the "Red" propaganda among the Europeans in the French Protectorate. In the Sus, still largely unpacified, the French had been able with a few troops to plant outposts all through the area and to control the tribes directly, making the Kaids mere figureheads. However, starvation was rampant throughout the Sus. A certain amount of restricted trade was now being allowed through the port of Agadir.[10]

By a change in the sultanate in November, 1927, Steeg's problem of government was made easier. For some months before this the French government had been troubled by the necessity of finding a successor to Mulai Youssef who would be wholly devoted to its interests but still not too obviously a figurehead. It was reported that the former Sultan Abd el Aziz had been approached several times but had declined the honor unless he could have a free hand and some real authority. Russell described the Sultan's eldest son as a "fat nonentity," and the second son as intelligent but leading a highly flamboyant life; neither of these was respected by the Moroccans. The third son was reputed to be sober and studious, but intelligence and cleverness were qualities not commendable in a sultan under a French Protectorate. It was expected that no change would be made in the Residency until the question of the succession to the throne was satisfactorily answered.

There could be no doubt that Steeg desired to resign. His disqualifications for his position were many:

> In addition to his vacillating policy, his refusal or inability to see things as they are, and his refusal either to shoulder responsibility or to delegate it to those who would be willing to do so ... which things have caused an increasing lack of coherence and of central authority in the government of French Morocco, he is a disappointed man--disappointed inasmuch as he has been unable to carry out his program for the Protectorate, a program that he aided in putting through in Algeria when Governor General of that colony.

His program had been an ambitious one of public works--railroads, roads, bridges, ports, and power and irrigation projects. To accomplish this by 1935, without further borrowing, Steeg outlined a radical cutting down of French functionaries and a sharp reduction in governmental expenses. Instead of accepting this, the French Parliament and Protectorate government greatly increased the number of functionaries and raised the salaries of most of them. This led to heavier taxation, which, coinciding with a series of bad crop years in southern Morocco, had brought the natives to the verge of ruin and forced the remission of taxes there wholly or partially. Steeg was said to have attempted in vain to obtain further loans in France, because the banks and great industrial companies already had a stranglehold on practically all the natural resources of the French Zone.[11]

On November 18, 1927, Blake was officially informed of the death of Sultan Mulai Youssef on the previous day at Fez. Blake thought it likely that either his first or his second son would succeed him. Instead, Mulai Muhammad, the third son, was named by the Council of Notables of Fez on November 18 and officially entered Rabat on November 21, 1927. At the formal reception to all the official dignataries in the place, Steeg emphasized the loyalty and friendship of his father for the French Protectorate government, inferentially notifying the new ruler of what was expected of him.

Perhaps the selection of Mulai Muhammad in preference to his older brothers was the most momentous event of Steeg's administration, for it was destined eventually to have the most unfortunate consequences for France. At the time of his accession he was only eighteen years old, but he was reputed to be unusually proficient in both Koranic learning and in the French language. Returning from a tour of France, on August 24, 1928, the Sultan went ashore from the Marechal Lyautey in Tangier Bay. His Majesty held a ceremonial reception on board for the foreign representatives and local officials. Blake attended when assured that as Dean of the Diplomatic Corps (now two members, the American and the Italian) he would be received ahead of all other officials. The Sultan's visit to Tangier was a token of his authority over the International Zone. At this time Blake was not at all impressed by the monarch's appearance.[12]

During Steeg's administration were held the third, fourth, and fifth North African Conferences in the years 1926, 1927, and 1928. The third conference, held in Tunis from March 22 to March 24, was attended by a representative of French West Africa also. The president, Lucien Saint, resident general of Tunisia, listed a number of problems, mostly affecting native welfare. They were public safety, epidemics, conditions of laborers, communications, financial difficulties, agricultural problems, sea and air navigation, and the raising of social and moral standards among the natives. Steeg remarked on the improbability that the three parts of French North Africa would ever be united. He also gave assurances that the Riff rebellion was ending in a way satisfactory to France. David Williamson, American vice consul at Algiers, believed nevertheless that the unification of North Africa was the ultimate objective of these conferences.[13] The Fourth conference, beginning May 7, 1927, added a delegate from the Sudan. The topic of the unification of North Africa was most prominent.[14] For the present, increase of communication facilities was emphasized; later would follow economic unity, and eventually political unity, to be established gradually, perhaps within thirty years.[15] The fifth conference, held at Rabat beginning July 4, 1928, dealt with finance, agriculture, commerce, colonization, tourism, public works, post offices, telegraph, and political and administrative matters. Railroads in the north and a trans-Saharan railway were the chief topics discussed. Standardization of administration and of laws in the three countries was also on the agenda. Standardization of customs had to be reserved for Morocco because of treaty restrictions. Another report said that the general aim of the resolutions was to unify the North African possessions by the removal of causes of friction in order to form them into an economic and homogeneous whole. Blake pointed out that the unification of Tunisia, Algeria, and Morocco under a French colonial regime had undoubtedly been the ultimate purpose of these conferences and that France was using every scheme to free herself from the customs regime in Morocco.[16]

The Franco-German Convention of August, 1927, abrogated the greater part of the restrictions placed on German trade in French Morocco by the Treaty of Versailles.[17] German goods were placed again on an equality basis in customs, and German ships might call and trade freely at Moroccan ports. Still prohibited without special permission was the residence of Germans in French Morocco. German firms could not establish branch offices there, and agencies of German firms could not be handled by German nationals.[18] The French Protectorate government kept close watch on subversive propaganda entering the country. In an article entitled "The Assault upon French Morocco," Le Temps said that eighty-eight publications had been prohibited there, including ones printed in French, Spanish, English, German, Greek, Polish, Russian, Bulgarian, Urdu, Annamite, and sundry dialects such as Corsican and Alsatian, although the majority were in the various Arabic idioms of Tunisia, Algeria, and Egypt. Some came from Muslims in Brazil and in Argentina, and even from San Francisco.[19] The Germans were now only one source of the subversive material which was a danger to the French dependencies.

The nadir in the political status of Morocco probably came in connection with Secretary of State Kellogg's Peace Pact abolishing war. When Ambassador Herrick asked the French Foreign Office to invite Morocco to adhere to the treaty, the French expressed real consternation and the hope that the United States would not insist on this step. They protested that the French Protectorate established by the treaty of 1912 conferred upon France the diplomatic representation of Morocco. Furthermore, the Sherifian Empire was not represented at the drafting and signing of the treaties of Versailles and Saint Germain, in which provisions pertaining to Morocco were included. To admit Morocco to a place in signing the Peace Pact would give her status as an independent state.[20] An American writer considered this action of France to be the final degradation of Morocco. It denied the Moroccans any standing in international law. Even the League of Nations could not take up Moroccan claims or rights. There was no forum in which to examine administration, no international pledge to administer Morocco by high standards, or to develop a constitution for the people, or to prepare them for eventual self-government.[21]

At the close of October, 1928, occurred the long-expected hostile reaction of the tribes to Steeg's colonization policy. The occasion was the kidnapping of a Spaniard near Kasbah Tadla. The Vigie Marocaine, usually a pro-Residency paper, pointed out that the impotence of the troops of occupation was caused by the ultrapacificist influences at the Residency General. As a result of this, the colonial settlements and the friendly natives bordering on the unsubmitted regions had been subjected to repeated outrages and lived in conditions of chronically precarious security. Vice consul Henrotin reported that from all sides demands were made for a strong hand again. Public opinion agreed that the ransoming of a nephew of Steeg in 1927, at a high cost, had had a deplorable effect upon the dissident tribes, especially since no punitive expedition had been made since that time. Henrotin observed further that the outrages which were of daily occurrence among the native employees of the Protectorate were not mere acts of bandits, but were retaliatory for oppressive measures and spoliation by Protectorate officials and French colonists. Blake reported that there was ample evidence that the outbreak of brigandage, kidnapping, and homicidal attacks in certain regions in the interior of Morocco was in reprisal for the wholesale stealing of tribal lands, either by the Protectorate government or by individuals supported by them. A call was made for colonization territories, and the Domain Department was told to "Scoop in energetically," which they did in all directions, whether the land belonged to the Maghzen or not. There was not a single tribe that did not complain of lands filched from them by the Maghzen. An article from a Nice journal was entitled "M. Steeg is losing Morocco." The spoliations, reported by Blake for years, had been slurred over by general denials until the reprisals came.[22]

On January 2, 1929, Steeg found an easy way out. Taking advantage of a new law limiting to six months, without prolongation, the missions confided to members of Parliament, he telegraphed his resignation to Briand. Pierre Mas, a leading newspaper publisher in Morocco, stated that Steeg was lucky to get out before he had any "Riff War" in the Atlas, anti-Atlas, and Tafilalt and that in spite of his reputation for personal honesty, his politics would not allow him to interfere with groups of dishonest persons of his political persuasion. Additional outrages had recently occurred. Steeg had sent commendatory letters for himself to Poincaré from the Sultan, his party men, and La Presse Marocaine, probably in hope of a high office in France. His preoccupation with French politics had marked his mission to Morocco with weakness, vacillation, and confusion. Concerning the successor of Steeg, Blake remarked that M. Lucien Saint, during eight years as resident general in Tunisia, appeared to have handled with success a series of difficult and delicate situations.[23]

Arriving in Casablanca on February 22, 1929, Lucien Saint was received with sympathy and hope. Since he was both a friend and an admirer of Lyautey, there was hope that he might revive the Marshal's policies and return to promotion of protectorate rather than colonial status for Morocco. But Saint did not become the good friend of the natives. Only the district officials, forced by their duties to do so, came into close contact with them. On the whole Saint's policy came to resemble Steeg's rather closely.[24]

After an interview with Saint, Blake analyzed his personality and probable policy. In Tunisia Saint had left a reputation for order and industry and had exhibited unsurpassed faculties of sympathy and intuition in dealing with native questions. He had also handled successfully several situations bordering on revolution. He impressed one as a practical and professional administrator with a cautious sense of proportion and with patient concentration. He was in close touch with the French colonial party in the Chamber and would therefore devote himself to their policies. Saint realized that his most urgent problem was reestablishment of security in the unsubmitted tribes of central Morocco, and since his arrival he had been absorbed in this problem. Another larger project was the pacification of Tafilalet and the district near Colomb-

Bechar. The situation on the Sahara frontiers of Algeria and Morocco had always been serious; in 1927 and 1928 there had been ninety-three clashes between the tribesmen and the Algerian military police, with many casualties in the French forces. Unfortunately, Saint had already shown a disposition to challenge international rights. He was contemplating making the petroleum deposits a French monopoly, prohibiting the entry into French Morocco of foreign wheat and flour, imposing a consumption tax corresponding to the drop in world prices of wheat and flour, and an increase in customs. All of these measures were, of course, inimical to the American-Moroccan treaties. Therefore, there could be no relaxation of the American agency in its vigilance to protect American treaty rights in the Sherifian Empire.[25]

The agricultural situation was another of Saint's chief problems. Its importance to France was signified by the visit in October, 1929, of a Parliamentary consultative committee, a delegation of twelve members of the "Commission des Colonies, de l'Algerie, et des pays de Protectorate de la Chambre." The places visited paid their expenses. They visited the chief cities of Morocco and several tourist centers and discussed agricultural matters with local authorities. Phosphates were recognized as the only readily available wealth. The matter of complementary production for France and Morocco was a vexing one; wheat was the only product permitted to Morocco, since the French farmers demanded vines and fruit culture for themselves. Also strong, the colonial party was demanding a foreign market for Moroccan surplus crops. To protect the wheat market, a dahir of June 6, 1929, attempted to prohibit the importation of foreign wheat and its products into French Morocco, which was a flagrant violation of the Act of Algeciras. The French government was then persuaded to admit a certain part of Moroccan wheat to France duty free. In 1929 excellent wheat harvests in both Morocco and France made some solution of the problem imperative. Part of Saint's policy was to make the economies of Morocco and France harmoniously interdependent.[26]

Likewise important was the continuance of the study and planning of Morocco's relations with her African neighbors. Saint took part in two North African conferences, the sixth at Algiers in 1930 and the seventh at Tunis in 1931.

The Algiers Conference was notable, not only for including the representatives of French West Africa and of French Equitorial Africa, but also for marking the centenary of France's invasion of Algeria. The problems discussed were chiefly economic and administrative, but little publicity was given to the discussions except for the resolutions passed. One interesting resolution was to send a mission to California to study the modern processes of irrigation and of fruit raising and marketing.[27] The seventh conference likewise included all five colonial divisions of French Africa. The inaugural speech of the presiding officer emphasized the agenda items of sanitary liaisons, the fight against prevailing diseases, suppression of infant mortality, augmentation of labor, development of ports and public works,[28] the locust pest, and the development of the Sahara. As the reporter of the conference pointed out, the resolutions adopted included several possibly damaging to interests of the United States. The resolutions mentioned were for protection of North African cereals in the French and local markets, organization of production and standardization of fruit and early vegetables and their sale in European markets, a customs union of Tunisia with France and Algeria, and regulation of importation of phonograph records and filming of motion pictures.[29]

Because he came into power in 1929, the year of the beginning of the world-wide economic depression, Saint was unfortunate. In February the annual report of the British Merchants' Morocco Association had announced that Morocco was making rapid progress in all sections.[30] There was a great scare over an invasion of locusts in the two last months of the year, but the Protectorate government took extensive precautions against the spread of the pest.[31] For the year as a whole, American consul Henrotin at Casablanca reported that the native trade had been depressed during the whole period, but the European trade suffered a general recession only during the second half of the year. The latter was due to the deflation in the price of cereals and the poor yield of the 1928-1929 crop raised by European colonists. Much anxiety was felt in banking circles as to prospects for 1930.[32] During 1930 and 1931 Morocco continued, with the rest of the world, to suffer from the anticipated depression. Some enterprises failed, others were able to survive, but the French government was obliged to take over large shares in enterprises of national importance. Among young countries,

Morocco suffered particularly, because under the Act of Algeciras she must apply the same tariff to all countries importing to her but was unable to retaliate for dumping by other countries.[33]

In spite of this severe setback, however, the Protectorate government remained sanguine and planned new economic developments. On January 9, 1930, at a banquet in Paris given him by politicians and financiers, Saint announced the forthcoming opening of the port of Agadir.[34] This had been closed since 1765 to favor the building up of Mogador, but had resulted in the economic ruin of a large part of the Sus. Even at the expense of its treaty obligations, Saint intimated, the French government would keep international enterprise out of this region to be developed. The French had two urgent tasks to undertake in the Sus--the final pacification of the tribes and relief measures for the population, suffering from several years of drouth and a typhus epidemic.[35]

In his report of June 11, 1930, American consul Buhrman outlined an ambitious plan for development of all parts of Morocco, which would require a large loan, to be amortized by income from the phosphate mines. Part of this loan, contemplated in late 1929, had been delayed by the depression. It was unlikely that these developments would offer any opportunities for American engineers or contractors, as it was almost certain that all contracts would be given to French firms. Buhrman mentioned also the plight of the French colonists, who would need relief from the government.[36] In December, 1931, Buhrman told of the negotiations for an equipment loan of 1,600 to 1,800 million francs for port, irrigation, water supply, and railway projects. In October of 1932 he notified the State Department of a _dahir_ to prohibit the influx of the unemployed from Europe. There had been a surplus of labor in French Morocco since 1929.[37]

The statistics of American-Moroccan trade for 1928-1929 and from 1924 to 1929 indicated a steady growth of imports and exports. The table for the longer period was especially encouraging. As usual since the conclusion of the first treaty with Morocco, American consuls were always optimistic about the future. They placed their chief hope at this time on trade in automobiles, petroleum, agricultural machinery, and office equipment.[38] In 1932, twenty-one members of the American Chamber of Commerce in France accepted Saint's invitation to tour through Morocco from April 19 to April 30. They visited various cities, the water power development, the electric light plant, and industrial and agricultural projects. The Sultan conferred on three leading members the Order of Alaouite. Presumably the tour was intended to counteract the unfavorable effect produced upon the Chamber by quota discriminations against American products in France. The Moroccan authorities gave the impression that they would welcome American participation in the development of Morocco. On the contrary, Buhrman was convinced that the French would view with keen disfavor any effort of American business to aid in Morocco's upbuilding.[39]

Saint has been charged with responsibility for the so-called "Berber Dahir." This was a sultanic decree signed and promulgated on May 16, 1930, giving "a legal status to the jurisdiction based upon Berber tribal customs in regions where this regime existed before the French occupation of Morocco." This measure provoked widespread resentment in the Arabized section of the population. Pledged to "respect the exercise of the Mussulman religion and its religious institutions," France was assumed to undertake the obligation to impose the Koranic jurisprudence upon the Berber tribes as soon as they were brought under subjection to the Sherifian government. According to the popular view, the _dahir_ legalizing the profane Berber law was merely an attempt by the French to alienate the Arabs from the Berbers; it was the ancient "divide and rule" stratagem. Public meetings were held to protest in all important cities of the French Zone. The French tried to shift responsibility for the _dahir_ to the Sultan and left repressive measures to the native authorities. Also, they attempted to blame the Moroccan protests upon the intrigues of Great Britain and Italy; one paper included Germany and Russia with these two.[40]

Agitation against the "Berber _Dahir_" did not die down. Propaganda circulars were posted and distributed widely, and their authors, if found, were arrested and deported as Communists. The circulars, well written in scholarly Arabic, were printed, probably, in the Spanish Zone, Egypt, or Algeria. Blake sent the State Department the translation of a communication to him, unacknowledged, making an appeal to the President of the United States from the "Maroc Mussulman." This document contained a long list of the misdeeds of "imperialistic France," of the demands of "Islamic Morocco," and of the reasons why the "stripling French Sultan" was not acceptable to the people. The dahir of May 16, 1930, it was asserted, had separated one people and their territory into two parts. "Imperialistic France" was now intensifying its propaganda to convert the Berbers to Christianity. All the powers who had made the Act of Algeciras were asked to revise it to make it truly international. The document concluded with the notation that copies of it had been sent to all these powers.[41]

That the Berber Dahir was deliberately designed to promote a division among the Moroccans was shown by its being followed shortly by special Berber schools. The teachers in these schools were regarded as agents and collaborators of the French officials. A number of French writers admitted frankly that the French purpose was to gain a control over the Berbers which would make them utilizable against the Arabs. Both Berbers and Arabs understood the French aim and resented it bitterly.[42]

The suppression of the agitation by brutal means continued. The Sultan was influenced to regard opposition to the dahir as antidynastic and anti-religious. Learned jurists of Morocco, however, addressed the Sultan and censured him for the marked decline in Muslim teaching and practice during his reign and for the neglect of Muslim schools. As a result, Sultan Muhammad repaired the mosques and schools of Salé and issued a dahir making study of the Koran compulsory before students could study French.[43]

With astonishing speed and strength opposition to the Berber Dahir spread over the whole Muslim World. Muslims were advised to protest to the League of Nations, to the great powers, and to the French government, and, if necessary to secure redress, to boycott French commerce. Committees for the defense of Moroccan Muslims were established in Cairo, in Berlin, even in Java. Protests and petitions flooded national and international organizations. The police in Morocco kept the local riots in check, and French authorities dismissed them as "hooliganism of irresponsible elements." But the eventual result of the dahir was that it made nationalism the cause of the masses and led, in not much more than a quarter of a century, to the independence of Morocco.[44]

It has been said that Saint's good intention of reintroducing the native policy of Lyautey was frustrated because he was too much preoccupied with the military problem which he inherited from Steeg.[45] After Steeg's military inertia, the situation was indeed critical. On June 8, 1929, Saint met his first serious reverse when a French garrison out reconnoitering in the Great Atlas was ambushed with heavy casualties. Saint had not agreed with Lyautey's idea that "he did not recognize the Atlas as part of Morocco," but he believed that the conquest of the Atlas was his legitimate task. Because of Socialist opposition in Parliament, however, Saint found it difficult to obtain enough credits for the necessary campaign. In October of 1929 occurred the third occasion of the year when dissident parties from the Tafilalet inflicted severe losses on the French forces. This happened while a French parliamentary delegation was touring the "pacified" region. Recent declarations of Saint concerning the economic development of the Protectorate made pacification of the Tafilalet a prime necessity. Nevertheless, a sub-commission of inquiry sent to Morocco by the French Army Commission found both the Resident General and his military officials opposed to a big offensive. They asserted that banditism could be controlled by fixed posts of occupation with mobile native and Legion forces, assisted by aviators. At a recent conference of Saint with the Spanish high commissioner it had been alleged that the insecurity in this region was caused by the many Riffian rebels who had joined the bandits of the south after the Riff War.[46]

Not until January 26, 1932, were the French military forces able to make formal entry into a pacified Tafilalet. The occupation of Tafilalet was important because it had long been not only the granary but also the principal haven of rebellious bands operating in Algeria and in pacified regions of Morocco. It was also the last center of the slave traffic into Morocco and Algeria. Since Lyautey had failed to subdue Tafilalet in 1917, it had remained under a despotic chieftain, practically independent.[47]

On a tour of inspection in May, 1932, Blake noted the optimism and activity among the Europeans. Reasons for their confidence were abundant rains in February and March, the complete pacification of the tribes of the Tadla district in the Middle Atlas, and the occupation of Tafilalet province, which established complete security on the Algerian-Moroccan frontier. Also, French uneasiness over the uncertain loyalty of Al Glaoui was now dispelled. His loan of 50,000,000 francs on his real properties, mostly in Casablanca and other cities, was well secured in French hands. Saint was now immensely popular, for he had succeeded in obtaining in Paris a loan of 1,535,676,000 francs voted by the Chamber of Deputies on March 24, 1932. The loan was to be devoted principally to the economic development of the Protectorate, including the ports of Casablanca and Agadir, roads, railroads to the phosphate mines, an irrigation system, waterways, and forestry. Saint's promotion of public works was designed to relieve the economic crisis. A month later, Blake's picture of the pacification process was less optimistic. A French blockade had been set up to encircle unsubmitted Berber tribes in the Atlas Mountains. After the annihilation of an entire column in the Tafilalet, Saint was reported to be demanding more adequate forces and equipment. All available forces had been sent to the Tafilalet.[48]

Saint had to leave unattained his chief objective--the final pacification of French Morocco. In January, 1933, he was elected to the French Senate, limiting his further stay in Morocco to six months. In spite of the expectation that he might be granted an extension of time, he failed to gain the support of the French government for a full and immediate program of the economic assimilation of France and Morocco, as desired by him and the Colonial Office. In French Morocco his brief period of popularity was soon over because of his inability to avert the economic crisis. On July 14, 1933, the Moroccan press reported the appointment of Henri Ponsot to succeed him.[49]

Henri Ponsot was a man of great intelligence and diplomatic skill. By his diplomatic training he was less equipped for the work of an executive. His new position called for forcefulness and ability to impose his views on the French colons in Morocco and their allies, his own bureaucracy and the colonial lobby in Paris. By now the colons were well organized and tried to make the Resident General their tool. Ponsot was between two strong opposing groups--the French settlers, strengthened by Steeg and not chastened by Saint, and the emergent natives demanding their rights. Eventually he failed to gain the confidence of the Moroccans because he was unable to prevent the further advance of "direct administration." Since sixty-five percent of the country's budget was absorbed by the French officials, he tried to reduce their numbers and to cut their high salaries. But as a political bloc, supported by the colonists and their French friends, he found the administration too powerful for one man to subdue.[50]

About a year after Ponsot's arrival, Blake wrote a lengthy and important dispatch about the new resident general and his views. On a recent tour of Morocco, Blake's own favorable impressions of Ponsot had been confirmed by information from many sources. By his understanding and sense of justice, Ponsot had gained the gratitude of the natives, but he was very unpopular with the bureaucracy. With a total absence of pose, he was quiet, sagacious, and possessed of a slow but supple intelligence, and he tried to gain his objectives by compromise. His special equipment seemed to be industry, thoroughness, and an aptitude for cautious strategy. He was resolutely trying to retrieve the mistakes left him as a heritage. Cordially distrusting the bureaucracy over which he presided, he in turn was feared and disliked by his subordinates.[51]

Blake had called on Ponsot to obtain adjustment of various claims arising from the arbitrary confiscation of property of American ressortissants; some cases decided under Lyautey had not yet been settled. The two men then discussed the general Moroccan situation. As Blake pointed out, the very existence of the claims he was presenting tended to invalidate any argument for withdrawal of the capitulations. He spoke of the legislative impracticability of dealing piecemeal with any partial abrogation of the Moroccan treaties and of the chaotic conditions in the Spanish Zone, which emphasized the necessity of maintaining the safeguards afforded by the capitulations. Ponsot then dealt with his economic problem in Morocco. By the Act of Algeciras, Morocco was open to the commerce of the world, but it was claimed that she had not the right to demand similar access to foreign markets. The trade of Morocco with the world must in future rely upon a basis of reciprocity. Ponsot had recently been obliged to sanction a dahir prohibiting the importation of babouches into Morocco, or otherwise that native industry would have been ruined by Japan's importations. Blake said that Moroccan produce was admitted into the United States on as favorable terms as similar products of any other country, and there was a good market there for certain Moroccan exports. Ponsot denied the intention of closing the Moroccan markets to any signatory of the Act of Algeciras. One of the difficulties of his task was to reverse a current of opinion which advocated an integration of the Moroccan and French economies. Morocco's economic existence depended upon the position that she could make for herself on an international plane, and it was important that her economic interests not be shackled to those of France.

To Blake it seemed obvious that the economic difficulties of French Morocco were inherent in the vast expenditures undertaken in the interest of French national, strategic, and political aims, in the promotion of monopolies of influential French financial groups, and in the unbalanced and overambitious equipment of the French protectorate. Every effort would be made to avoid the summoning of an open international conference on Morocco. Therefore, Ponsot had been authorized to explore the possibilities of the revision of the treaties with individual signatories of the Act of Algeciras. It was evident that a far-reaching policy for modifying existing international rights in Morocco was being pursued by both the French and Sherifian governments.[52]

In the completion of pacification Ponsot succeeded very quickly. After twenty years of effort, the conquest of all Morocco was effected. The subjugation of Tafilalet province and of the regions south of the Grand Atlas was completed in December, 1933. A brilliant campaign of one month, to the beginning of April, 1934, extended French domination over the vast deserts of the Anti-Atlas down to the river Draa, adding about 200,000 people and an area of about 10,000 square miles to the Sultan's domains. Another result of the French military operations was the precipitate occupation of Ifni by the Spanish. The Moroccans at length realized that they were vanquished.[53] But they were not conciliated. Their major grievances remained unalleviated.

However, during 1935 and 1936 several American consular dispatches gave Ponsot credit for a more liberal native policy and for a number of minor reforms to implement it. He seemed to be trying to create an image of the Sultan as the powerful intermediary between France and his subjects. Ponsot worked to bring about a cessation of harsh methods of the military authorities, to support the civil authorities, and to suppress spies and informers. Removal of undesirable officials from office won native approval. Moroccans were granted the right to open private schools and to have benevolent associations and clubs--privileges formerly denied. A better reception was given to petitions for reforms made by political organizations, and the press put on a campaign urging cessation of abuses suffered by the natives. Anti-malarial missions were sent out to prevent epidemics of this disease. Without publicity, a number of natives imprisoned because of disturbances were pardoned or released. A strike of mountaineer students at Karouyine University at Fez was treated as amusing and not as cause for punsihment. In collecting all taxes, more humane and considerate methods were employed. Ponsot promised permission for a group of influential natives to open an agricultural bank to loan money cheaply to natives. Still the native opinion was that more effort was expended in lecture and in press propaganda than in practical benefits. Largely untouched, they complained, were their serious problems--the excessive taxation to support unnecessary functionaries, the archaic native courts, the limiting of opportunity for higher education for Muslims, and the French policy of favoring quotas, contingents, and preferential tariffs.[54]

An analysis of colonization in French Morocco as it was just before Ponsot took office contrasted the independent and the official colonists. The 2,068 of the former class were small farmers, had sufficient capital, and had devoted themselves to constructive and profitable agriculture. They had been mostly unsuccessful. On the contrary, the 1,625 of the latter class were subsidized by the government and came after Lyautey's regime. They had been generally unsuccessful because they were improperly selected as farmers, they lacked capital, and they suffered from the unfavorable climatic conditions. However, France did not measure the success of her colonization in terms of the prosperity of the individual colonist, but in terms of their usefulness in furthering her political aims. The colonists contributed not only to making France politically dominant in Morocco, but also to exercising a stranglehold upon the trade of the country. When necessary for the colonists' welfare, France had not hesitated to break treaties.

The antagonism of native and colonist interests was evident. It was to the interest of the colonists to take the land from the natives and to reduce them to common labor and soldiery for their living. Furthermore, the native saw the increase of Christian churches in Morocco and feared that his own religion was threatened. Paying at least eighty-five percent of the taxes, the natives finally became aware that most of the money was being spent for the benefit of France and her colonists. This was the basic problem of Ponsot's regime.[55] As a patriotic public servant, his first duty was to uphold the interests of his country and of its colonists.

On his periodic tour through Morocco in May, 1935, Blake detected an undercurrent of uneasiness and discontent among both the European and native populations. The French were alarmed at the organization of Moroccans' parties to secure their rights. Even more disturbing to the Protectorate authorities was the disillusionment of the foreign population. The French community now realized that the economic crisis which they were experiencing was not primarily a reflex of world conditions, but was caused by maladministration, lavish and injudicious public expenditure, enormously overstaffed and overpaid administration, costly and overambitious colonization, and uneconomic exploitation of certain enterprises. Bitter disappointment and antagonism appeared to be general and was openly expressed against Ponsot.[56]

During Ponsot's regime a number of prospecting companies combined and with government aid continued searching for oil in commercial quantities. Considerable opposition was expressed by the French <u>colons</u> at this use of government funds. <u>Dahirs</u> had been promulgated in 1934 permitting the control of all petroleum territory by the combined prospecting companies. Unfortunately for Ponsot, the several finds of oil proved to be of too small a quantity to give the United States a competitor in supplying Morocco with petroleum and its by-products.[57] The economic situation was not improved,[58] either, by the discovery of a valuable source of increased income for Morocco.

In March, 1936, Blake gave a fair and sympathetic departure notice for Ponsot, who, he said, had been opposed almost from the beginning by industrial, commercial, and political circles. When he issued decrees on taxation and other subjects without the customary previous consultation with the Government Council, Ponsot had an open breach with the French colony. Although he tried to retain his office, the French government was unable to resist the demand for his removal. The Moroccan press barely mentioned his transfer, although it published reports of the sumpathetic farewells given Marcel Peyrouton, who came from Tunisia to succeed him. Blake summed up Ponsot's career in this way:

> M. Ponsot tried to improve the economic situation inherited from his predecessors, but his economic schemes were not only impotent to straighten out confusion, but even threatened, by undermining the long existing liberal regime of Morocco as established by treaties, to impair the economic potentialities of Morocco, by bringing the economy within the narrow regime of French colonial exclusiveness. He honestly worked for the best interests of France in Morocco and made resolute efforts to improve the situation of the natives.[59]

American consul George Hopper of Casablanca said that the departure of Ponsot was welcomed by most French business men as bringing to an end the bitter controversies existing for six months prior to the change. The press voiced high hopes for the future of Morocco under the able leadership of Peyrouton because of his success as a colonial administrator, especially in Tunisia. Both the French and the Moroccans believed that the new resident general would have the full support of the Quai d'Orsay.[60]

Marcel Peyrouton's regime in Rabat was too brief for him to have much influence on the course of events. Ponsot left Morocco in January, 1936, Peyrouton arrived in May, and he was in turn replaced by General Noguès after being in office only four months. During this short period Peyrouton was the storm center of an economic crisis as well as of a political struggle between the French factions which had extended their battle area from the homeland to French Morocco. Peyrouton was opposed by the Popular Front adherents and championed by the Rightist groups, prominently by the Croix de Feu. He was known as a friend of the Moroccans, but was considered a foe of the Jews, who had joined with the lower class Spanish, Portuguese, and Italians in pseudo-Leftist organizations.

At this time occurred the first strikes and sit-ins in which both natives and foreign workmen cooperated. The natives, however, were usually driven out of the buildings by the police, leaving the foreign workers in possession. The police also dispersed the opposing groups in their attempts to stage parades and counterparades in Casablanca. The foreign business men, including the Casablanca Chamber of Commerce, wanted to give Peyrouton a longer period to prove his abilites, and Sultan Muhammad also approved of the measures that he had initiated to reform conditions for the natives. Meanwhile, Peyrouton tried to show moderation in his treatment of the strikers.[61]

Even Blake approved of Peyrouton's policies. Peyrouton, he said, showed courage and energy in pursuing his program. He was simplifying administration and centralizing control in himself. He promulgated dahirs to prevent abuses by European employers of native labor. Among the specific projects that he began were public works for about 100,000,000 francs for relief of unemployment, suppression of usury, progressive demolition of native slums, building homes for lower class natives, and measures to facilitate their return to the land. Hopper commended Peyrouton's bold conceptions and adroit actions, which seemed to have placed the natives on an equality with the European settlers; he even admitted natives to the Government Council and to commissions to investigate projects of legislation. In announcing his recall in September, Blake gave Peyrouton high praise:

> From the Moroccan standpoint it is unfortunate that this interesting and picturesque personality, whose characteristics have created such a strong appeal to both Europeans and natives--second in the line of popular esteem only to Lyautey himself--is to pass from the Moroccan scene after having, during the brief period of his office, aroused such wide expectations and held such promise for the rescue of the country from the administrative, economic, and political decline into which it has been slowly sinking for the last few years.[62]

The choice of General Auguste Noguès as a successor to Peyrouton seemed most appropriate to Blake, who thought that no one but a high army official could meet the situation. Noguès was highly recommended because of his military and administrative experience in North Africa. As a former officer under Lyautey, he was well acquainted with Moroccan problems, and he had also served under Saint as director of political affairs. The Civil War in Spain also made it desirable to have a military man as resident general of French Morocco. Arriving at Casablanca on October 6, 1936, Noguès was met by a large assembly. The next day he visited the Sultan, with whom he became very friendly. Press comment was almost entirely complimentary, and there was general approval of the appointment of Noguès to be both resident general and military commander, as Lyautey had been. As a professional soldier, however, he soon displayed lack of diplomatic skill together with the conviction that force was the language best understood by the natives, who were prone to consider discussions of reform as a sign of weakness on the part of the French.[63]

In the month of his arrival, Noguès also had to face a problem inherited from his predecessors. He had publicly proclaimed that he would enforce the reforms initiated by Peyrouton and in general would follow Lyautey's policies. But the Moroccans were now pursuing nationalism aggressively, even adopting a militant approach to achieve it. After a number of mass meetings in October, the nationalists presented demands for increased educational facilities for natives, reform of the native courts, and freedom of press and assembly. In reply, Noguès imprisoned most of their leaders. By the middle of December he relented somewhat. He released some of the prisoners and on December 24 issued a decree permitting the establishment of trade unions, but restricting them to Europeans, who were less than two percent of the total population. On January 19, 1937, he authorized the publication of three dailies--*L'Atlas*, *El Maghreb*, and *El Amal*--and of the weekly *El Ouidad*, but all were placed under French censorship. A final step was the proscription of the nationalist party on March 18, 1937, which drove the movement underground and made martyrdom an honorable estate.[64]

In August, 1937, another incident further alienated the Resident General from the natives. At the behest of four

French settlers farming near Meknes, French officials diverted to their farms some of the water from a river supplying Meknes and its vicinity. Nationalist propaganda spread the rumor that the French aimed to dry out native agriculture in the area. Many petitions poured into Rabat, and a French plan to increase the native water supply came too late. On September 1 there was a large demonstration outside the French administrative offices. The arrest of the five ringleaders and their sentencing to three months' imprisonment instigated riots in which many were killed and wounded, followed by more arrests and demonstrations. Finally, Noguès in person quelled the riot by giving definite assurances about the water supply, but he failed to discipline the officials who had started the trouble. This aroused further suspicion that the Resident General aimed to oppress the natives, and protest meetings and arrests spread all over the country. The foremost nationalist leader, Allal al Fassi, was exiled by Noguès. A superficial and uncertain peace was restored by the end of 1937, but there was no spirit of cooperation with their leader displayed by the Moroccans. Both Blake and Hopper reported evidence that the dissident movement was inspired by the extremist left wing of the French Popular Front. American consul Doolittle pictured the situation of the natives proletariat as the cause of these violent demonstrations:

> One crop failure has generally been sufficient to cause the forced sale of all the belongings of thousands of fellahs now to be found in misery in slums of Casablanca, Meknes, or other cities. Many of these slums are constructed of discarded packing boxes, metal strips from oil tins or asphalt drums, or even tents of gunny sacking, and French authorities have started efforts to clean them up. The possibility of this is doubted, however, since there is no known type of construction rentable for nothing a year.[65]

Adding to the economic difficulties of the French Protectorate was the terrible drouth which existed in the Moroccan deserts during 1937. Once fierce fighters of the Sahara, the Tuaregs had been pacified and induced to become sedentary near Ifni in March, 1934. In April, 1937, they were dying of starvation, and the few who made their way northward were too many for Agadir and Marrakesh to handle. In

July it was reported that 1,500,000 starving tribesmen of the Moroccan deserts had received another appropriation of 10,000,000 francs from the Protectorate authorities. Hundreds of oases had been burned out by the drouth, and thousands of cattle had died. French colonial civil servants had agreed to contribute up to six percent of their salaries to provide food. The government was obliged to send troops to bar the way of 20,000 refugees on their way to Marrakesh.[66]

During 1937 and 1938, American representatives sent to Washington a number of reports on projected reforms for French Morocco. The alleged prosperity of the natives of the Spanish Zone, together with the large scale enlistment of natives from both the Spanish and French zones in Franco's army was causing the Residency to consider appeasing the Moroccans by satisfying some of their demands. Noguès repealed the tax in rural markets, but heavily increased the taxes on sugar, tea, and other articles. He had promised to revise the whole system of taxation, and this remodelling, with abolition of thirty to forty percent of the functionaries was intended to permit a considerable reduction of taxes. The French appeared to be trying to discover some formula to appease the natives without creating any appreciable change in their material or moral status. The existing condition of the native population benefitted all French political and financial groups, and the French as a whole; any amelioration of this condition would be strenuously opposed by all selfish groups in France. In Morocco, the religious authority of the Sultan had always been used to check native demands for reform, which, when submitted to the Ulema by the Sultan, had always been denounced as contrary to Koranic law. The Haut Comité Mediterranean, sitting in Paris under Premier Blum, was considering the future policy of France in North Africa. It was believed that "the emancipation of natives in North Africa will be a deliberately lengthy process, extending over an extremely long period and terminating most probably in their complete francization." Blake considered the position of Noguès precarious; it was reported that he was commanded from Paris to conform with the Popular Front social and political policies, although he personally wanted to shield the natives from the baneful French politics and to govern by the precepts of Lyautey.[67]

Investigations by successive residents general had long

indicated that the basic cause of native discontent was the corruption of the Maghzen and the more immediate cause was the assignment of large tracts of land to French colonists and the usurpation of irrigation resources in their favor. Corruption of the Maghzen meant that native public offices had been sold overtly, that litigants were plundered in the courts, and that native administrators had enriched themselves through extortion and injustice. The French Protectorate was pledged by treaty to safeguard the Muslim religion and to reform the Sherifian Maghzen. Only the first promise had been partially fulfilled. Now, in October, 1937, the reform of the Maghzen was coming to be considered vital, and it was reported that the continuance of Noguès in office was dependent upon his willingness to effect the reforms and to dismiss from office some high Moroccan nobles as well as French officials. The contemplated reforms included the dismissal of many vizirs, reformation of the native courts, suppression of the extortionate methods of assessing and collecting taxes from natives, reforms in the spending of Habous revenues, and reorganization of the native agricultural institutions. Reform measures were actually begun by a dahir of November 5, 1937, instituting the "career principle" with fixed salaries for the kadis, native Koranic judges. In a speech to war veterans at Meknes, however, a high French official warned Moroccan nationalists not to raise the question of the very existence of the Protectorate:

> We have decided to oppose an unbreakable defence to the attempts of fanatics, who would throw the country back again into chaos in seeking to remove the rule under which Morocco has experienced a marvelous rebirth.[68]

During 1938 American consul Herbert S. Goold announced a number of reforms either begun by dahirs or contemplated. These included concentration camps for the support and training of destitute natives, extension of agricultural loans, construction of irrigation projects, the increase in value and quantity of agricultural property exempt from judicial seizure, and admission of Moroccans to government posts. Native workers were angered, however, by a decree promulgated by Noguès on June 24, 1938, forbidding a Moroccan to join a labor union. This dahir, however, increased the minimum wage from twenty-five to fifty percent as compared with the one of two years earlier and fixed the age for apprenticeship of native labor at eighteen years. This was the first real protective legislation for Moroccan workmen.[69]

During 1937 and 1938 the Moroccans were seething with the alien doctrines of fascism and communism and the traditional one of Pan-Islam. These ideologies were introduced by foreign propaganda and propagandists, by their own small student élite studying in France and returning home to agitate, and by the French and other Europeans in Morocco. Pan-Islamism originated in Egypt, but was now actively propagated in Tunisia and Algeria also, where nationalism was in advance of Moroccan development. With such diverse and antagonistic doctrines as sources of discontent, the movement known as Moroccan Nationalism had a number of versions and leaders. Noguès did not succeed in isolating French Morocco from these foreign influences, and Franco's Spanish fascist nationalism was especially hard to exclude, since Spanish Morocco was the base from which the Spanish Civil War was being fought.

In the American press were many news items, editorials, and special articles on the Moroccan situation.[70] An editorial in the New York Times of November 7, 1937, entitled "Unrest in French Morocco," mentioned the appointment of Albert Sarraut as coordinator of French North Africa as an important step in restoring French prestige there. The editorial made an able analysis of the causes of Moroccan disorder, pointing out that France needed more than obedience from her African soldiers--she needed loyalty:

> The basis of discontent in Morocco is both economic and political. An elaborate French regime, imposed upon a poor and economically undeveloped people, though it brought them some material benefits, greatly increased their taxes. More serious was the dislocation of the economic life of the country, caused first by the artificial emphasis on cultivation for the foreign market, and subsequently by the virtual collapse of that market for Moroccan wheat, wine and oil. The consequent impoverishment of the producers, elimination of the small agriculturists, growth in the numbers of the unemployed, and increased cost of living for both country and urban dwellers provided fertile soil for nationalist agitation. Sons of Moroccan notables, educated in Paris, returning

home to enforced idleness, became active in political work. They found encouragement in the writings and speeches of many of the French Left opposition leaders. Nationalist activities, suppressed by previous Cabinets, were tolerated and sometimes condoned by the Radicals and Socialists in the Popular Front. The Moroccans were quick to press their advantage.

So also were diverse foreign influences ready to make capital of the situation. General Franco, having made large promises to the Moors in Spanish Morocco, was not reluctant to see that territory used as a base for anti-French propaganda among the Moors across the southern border. Advocates of Pan-Islam appealed to Moroccans to throw off the yoke of French imperialism .... Communist, Nazi, and Fascist voices made their varied appeals to the Moroccan masses. 'Night after night,' the Moroccan ether 'is full of incitements--in the vernacular--to insurrection and disorder.'

While striving to ameliorate the distressing economic conditions and to repress the nationalist agitation there, Noguès was actively engaged in defending French Morocco from possible involvement in the Spanish Civil War. In power at the outbreak of the war, Peyrouton initiated reforms long studied and judged necessary by many French commissions, and not new measures promulgated by the Blum cabinet. But Peyrouton feared the effects of a communist government,[71] also apprehended in Spanish Morocco before Franco seized control there. However, Noguès carried out the policy of the Popular Front, which had the main objective of maintaining the "sovereignty" of the Sultan in all of Morocco.

The French forces, augmented early in 1937, were concentrated along the border between the two zones all the way from Casablanca to east of Fez, with headquarters at Meknes. They were well supplied with mobile artillery, airplanes, and light tanks, as well as with all horses and mules available. This military mobilization was designed to prevent the exodus of the French Moroccans into the Spanish Zone to join Franco's army, to keep out foreign propagandists, and to overawe the militant nationalists. The French set up embargoes of petroleum products, autos, and food for the Spanish Zone, which, however, injured chiefly the French and native farmers of northern Morocco. After the signing of the non-intervention pact, vessels of the Madrid government were never denied the use of Casablanca harbor, which served as a base for supplies from the Atlantic ports to the Spanish Mediterranean ports. When the insurgent Junta de Burgos promised to consider favorably colonization of the Spanish Zone by Italians and Germans for the development of mining and public works, the French government was alarmed and angry. The French press conducted a vigorous campaign against this proposal, reiterating a well-worn argument that Spain was bound by treaty not to change the status of her zone without the consent of France and the Sultan of Morocco. It was rumored that France and Great Britain would not recognize Franco unless he agreed not to change the juridical status of Spanish Morocco. Every effort was made to ridicule Franco's regime. Hopper doubted that France had any right to object to any commercial bargain made by Spain for her zone.[72]

In January, 1937, occurred the war scare caused by the reports to the French government that Germany was about to land troops in Spanish Morocco with the aim of occupying the country. The German general staff denied the presence in Morocco of any Germans except an aviation crew of three hundred, which was about a fifth of the aviators that Italy had had there for some time. Blake did not support the sensational press rumors about German troops, and he pointed out that Germany had been purchasing seventy-five percent of the output of the Riff mines for many years, although there were no Germans operating or directing the mines. There was much diplomatic haggling over the charge, also, although President Lebrun of France told the American ambassador, Bullitt, that the French press had made a mountain out of a molehill in a most distasteful manner. Finally, on January 12, the matter ended when Havas published this announcement:

> At yesterday's diplomatic reception in Berlin, Hitler assured the French Ambassador that Germany did not and never had any intention of infringing upon the integrity of Spain or Spanish possessions. The French Ambassador gave assurance that France was firmly determined to respect the integrity of Spain and the statute of Spanish Morocco within the framework of existing treaties.

Nevertheless, the French Protectorate continued to build up its military forces and supplemented the civil governments at Fez, Meknes, and Marrakesh by military regimes. On February 20, 1937, the Residency promulgated a dahir prohibiting military service of French Moroccans in Spain, following decrees of non-intervention by the French government.[73]

Claude Bowers, American ambassador to Spain, was a liberal and a democrat, and he did not hesitate to inform the State Department of his views concerning the real issue of the Spanish conflict. He rejected the "stupid or deceptive propaganda of the press ... that this is a rebellion of noble Spaniards to save their country from communism." Franco was working for a military dictatorship, while Azaña was striving to preserve the democratic republic. However, various groups on each side were trying to convert the rebellion into a revolution for their own ends. At this time (March, 1937) the Russian Communists had failed after months of effort to subordinate Spanish Syndicalism to communism. The Syndicalists had now promised to postpone their revolution until the Nationalist revolution was defeated. On Franco's side, the military regulars, the Carlists, and the Fascists were so antagonistic that Franco dared not attempt to combine them in one fighting force, and the Moroccans, of course, were alien to all the others. Unless Franco could use his Foreign Legion, the Moroccans, the Italians, and the Germans with the Spanish fascists, it seemed impossible that the fascists could impose their form of government upon the Carlists, the monarchists, the nobility, and the industrialists. The prime interest of the Fascists was to force a fascist revolution upon Spain.[74]

The insurgent Burgos Junta accused the French Protectorate authorities of trying to create disturbances in the Spanish Zone to furnish a pretext for French intervention. The French action was charged with violating the Franco-Spanish treaty in which both countries were to preserve peace in Morocco. The protesting note took the position that the Act of Algeciras was still the fundamental basis of public law in Morocco. Consequently, the Spanish Nationalist government requested the powers signatory to the Act, including the United States, to appoint an international commission to investigate its charges. It was suggested also that the Non-Intervention Committee in London might take steps to end the

French plots. This proposal originated in a speech by Azaña in January, in which he intimated that the Spanish Republic might give up the Spanish Zone. This possession, he said, had cost Spain many sacrifices and had created a base used successively by dictators and rebels against the established government in Spain. The Spanish insurgents construed Azaña's words as an offer to surrender the Spanish Zone to France. The Burgos note was a retaliation for the exploded French newspaper campaign charging Nationalist Spain with the plan to deliver Spanish Morocco to Germany. The Franco-Moroccan press published a disclaimer.[75]

On March 18, 1937, nine days after the insurgents' note, the Loyalist government of Spain presented another note to the British and French governments. The Spanish Republic now offered to these two states an active collaboration in its future international policy. Moreover, it would now modify its position in North Africa in favor of these two powers only. It would sacrifice Spanish Morocco on one condition--that the Franco-British collaboration stop further Italian-German intervention and that all foreign troops be withdrawn immediately from Spain. Thus the legitimate government of Spain would be able to suppress its own rebellion and save the lives of its people. The reply of France, printed in Le Temps of April 13, 1937, though couched in classic diplomatese, was not hard to understand.[76] The French government noted with satisfaction the Spanish proposal of complete suspension of foreign intervention in Spain, a principle long supported by the French representative in the London Committee to hasten the end of the Civil War. The possibility of a political arrangement regarding the situation of Spain in Northern Africa could be usefully examined only when order was reestablished in Spain. Any solution of the problem could be reached only in conformity with the accords which for a number of years had bound France and Spain in a friendly collaboration.[77]

In the latter part of 1937, American consuls commented at length on the social and political unrest pervading French Morocco. The "Berber Dahir" was blamed for a demonstration dispersed by the army at Khemisset on October 27; water rights caused the Meknes demonstrations; and the Nationalist movement inspired the simultaneous sympathetic uprisings all over the country. Efforts at suppression and the banishment of Allal al Fassi cowed rather than pacified the natives. Although French declarations made much of the role of foreign agitators--Spanish, Italian, and Russian--Blake considered the foreign factors but reflex influences. The primary responsibility, he thought, lay on the French Popular Front. Another disturbing influence was a large section of the native Jews, acting under "the infatuation of new and exotic idioms." Goold reported that Noguès, on a trip to Paris, had conferred with Sarraut and had been severely criticized by Premier Blum for his harsh measures against the Nationalist demonstrators. Accordingly, Noguès had directed many cases to be dismissed. Some relief for the native situation seemed imminent. The press on November 29, 1937, reported the issue of a loan of 300,000,000 francs to the Moroccan government, with repayment in 1988 at the latest.[78]

On December 28, 1937, Noguès made a speech to the Government Council introducing the budget and outlining his plans for reform. It was a comprehensive survey of the whole economic and social situation of French Morocco. It contained one section of particular interest to the United States:

> 1937 will be a date in the history of the Protectorate by virtue of the abolition of the capitulatory regime brought about by an important diplomatic agreement between France and Great Britain .... This convention is .... of a nature to facilitate our negotiations with the United States with a view to the abolition of the capitulatory regime of which they are now the sole beneficiaries.
>
> The friendly spirit which has characterized the Franco-British conversations ... permits us to pursue the revision of the Anglo-Moroccan treaty of 1856 with its tariff clause of ten percent, the abolition of which appears essential in order to allow Morocco to establish her own tariff.
>
> It is necessary that the principle of economic equality provided for by the Act of Algeciras should be completed by the principle of reciprocity which will permit us to market our products.
>
> The suppression of the capitulations is the commencement of the removal of international mortgages which have hindered the development of the country.[79]

Goold had a number of interesting comments on the Moroccan budget for 1938, among them the following:

> The Government anticipates increased customs revenue without resort to changes in duties. Changes probably depend upon the outcome of the French-American negotiations for the relinquishment of the capitulations and for the conclusion of a new commercial convention, following the recent Anglo-French commercial arrangement .... The prospect for the abolition of the present nominal twelve and a half percent system, under the Act of Algeciras, still is uncertain.
>
> Military necessities, political demands, and the need for ameliorating the widespread native distress that produced the bloody riots of last fall have forced France, not only to forego various possible collections from Morocco, but also to make special advances to its protégé. Patently, a great part of all expenditures in Morocco, whether protectorate or metropolitan, contribute substantially to the military power of France.[80]

As a part of his speech to the Government Council early in July, 1938, Noguès gave a glowing account of the reforms being carried out under his direction. Among them were the successful campaign against the typhus epidemic, the building of new hospitals and dispensaries and homes for aged Muslims, the proposed abolition of "bidonvilles," famine relief, the expansion of irrigation, the registration of land titles, education in agriculture, extension of markets, production of minerals, extension of roads and railways, minimum wages for workers (six francs per day), preparatory measures for admission of Moroccans to government employment, establishment of new Muslim schools, improvement of Radio-Maroc programs, and classification of Kadis in the reorganization of native courts. In December Blake commended the "energetic amelioration" of the new policy of Noguès. He approved of the measures regarding the famine districts of the south, for which the Protectorate government had now supplied free seed grain and money allowances to enable the people to live pending the harvest. In both southern and northern Morocco, military recruitment had been systematically organized, and native troops now totalled about 100,000 men. Eventually the French considered it possible to enlist for military service from 650,000 to 1,000,000 Moroccans. So long as the French were on the winning side, Blake thought, the Moroccan troops might be relied upon.[81]

Two annual reports of American consuls on French Morocco during 1938 offer additional information about conditions there. Stanton reported that the standard of living, except for the uppermost two percent, was still extremely low, even primitive, in the rural areas. However, there was a general improvement in 1938 over the previous year. Agricultural production was good, livestock conditions were better, and mineral export had advanced in value. Industrial production had increased materially, while foreign trade was well advanced in value. The typhus epidemic was almost stamped out, and there was great satisfaction over the avoidance of war the previous fall. There were some repercussions from the Spanish Civil War, but other foreign relations were good. Again mention was made of the business men's optimism because of the Anglo-French agreement of July 18, 1938, and the expected completion of the current negotiations between France and the United States for the relinquishment of American capitulatory rights in French Morocco and for a concurrent Franco-American commercial convention. On his annual tour of the country, Blake noted the contentment and cheerful activity of the natives as being due to freeing of Noguès from the hampering influences of extremist left wing politicians in France and the abundant crops in all parts of Morocco. Noguès had banned the interference of French political parties in native affairs, and the "clamorous leaders of the largely artificial Moroccan Nationalist Party had been imprisoned or sequestrated." Listing the numerous reforms initiated by Noguès, Blake quoted the resident general as being desirous of reviving and extending Lyautey's conciliatory and paternal administration of native affairs. However, the Moroccans were still apprehensive over their heavy and often inequitable taxation, and the Europeans in Morocco were affected by the tension and nervousness in Europe leading to preparatory mobilization.[82]

Looking forward to a successful year, Noguès gave his budget speech for 1939 to the Government Council. The budget provided the following percentages: thirty for debt, forty for personnel, five for administration, and twenty-five for supplies, including public works. For the first time in many years it did not include a substantial subsidy from the French government, which desired the Protectorate to become self-supporting. Noguès initiated a Five-Year Plan of economic recovery as the first stage of a century program of agricultural reorganization to develop natural resources for a population of about 25,000,000. This program was based on a large number of hydraulic works designed to increase the water supply seven fold, to be built at a total cost of about $130,000,000. Again Noguès referred to the Anglo-French Commercial Convention of July 18, 1938, and foresaw the time when Morocco would recover its tariff liberty upon the conclusion of the pending negotiations. He did not name the United States. Stanton's report also emphasized, among other measures to secure the loyalty of the natives, the efforts of the Protectorate government to provide increased educational facilities for Moroccan youth, especially in secondary schools. Noguès also announced his intention to create a native budget commission similar to the French one in the Government Council.[83]

In the spring of 1939 the international situation in Europe continued to appear favorable for peace. Since they had not taken full advantage of their opportunities in the Spanish Civil War, Hitler and Mussolini seemed appeasable for the time being. For practical purposes the Spanish conflict was over on February 27, 1939, when Great Britain and France recognized Franco as the master of Spain. President Azaña resigned the next day. Not until March 28 occurred the final surrender of Madrid and Valencia, but the recognition of the Franco government by the United States on April 1 spelled the doom of the Spanish Republic. Shortly after February 27, Noguès and the Spanish High Commissioner met in the French Zone. They discussed military dispositions on the frontier and the resumption of normal traffic and trade relations between the two zones. Noguès favored a conciliatory policy to dispel the apprehensions in the Spanish Zone regarding France and to neutralize Spanish sympathies for Germany and Italy. There were reports that all Italian and German "volunteers" would leave Spain before the end of May and that Franco did not consider himself bound to the Rome-Berlin Axis in the event of aggression.[84]

Ever since Lyautey's successors had come into power, however, they had continued the economic-diplomatic war on the Algeciras Act that Lyautey had begun. In 1939 that conflict appeared to be ending in a complete French victory, in spite of the determined defense put up by Blake and the Consuls under him for American rights and interests. However, the United States was saved from surrender in Morocco by another world war.

From two statements of State Department policy in 1929 and 1931, it is evident that American policy toward Morocco had never changed since its inception in 1836. By the most favored nation status granted her originally, the United States was entitled to all privileges granted to other nations in later treaties, including the British-Moroccan Treaty of 1856 and the Spanish-Moroccan Treaty of 1861, and all nations were granted most favored nation status by the Madrid Convention of 1880. The United States stressed the declared aims of the Act of Algeciras, "the introduction of reforms based upon the triple principle of the Sovereignty of His Majesty, the Sultan, the integrity of his domains, and economic liberty without any inequality." Although the United States denied political interest in Morocco, she could and did point out that France had been violating all these principles since she obtained her protectorate in 1912, but the principle which the United States upheld was the Open Door, or "economic liberty without any inequality." To protect her economic rights, the United States was impelled to maintain her capitulatory privileges. Neither France nor Spain had been willing to pay American claims or give any guarantees of future consideration of American rights. In regard to Tangier, the United States had not been invited either to form or to revise the Statute, in which American interests had been disregarded.[85]

In the State Department archives are to be found innumerable dispatches from Blake and other consuls reporting on _dahirs_ levying taxes or making all sorts of regulations and asking for the American government's permission to apply them to American nationals. The State Department gave its assent in a large proportion of cases. More serious in effect, perhaps, were the many petty annoyances and interferences with the work of American _semsars_, discriminations against American merchandise, often under customs officials, and efforts to shut out American goods, such as wheat and flour, autos and auto parts, and exclusion of American firms from bidding on public works. Other countries, notably Great

Britain, Belgium, and the Netherlands, had similar treatment. But the United States was often singled out for special harassment because her trade was growing and because she was the most recalcitrant country in clinging to her treaty rights and insisting on an economic policy that the French declared to be outdated. As a grand finale to many years of insidious undermining of the Algeciras Act, in 1934 and 1936 the French launched an overt frontal attack determined to extirpate every trace of that document which they had failed to have eliminated by the Treaty of Versailles.

French politicians and publicists used the French and Moroccan press effectively to create the popular opinion that Morocco's unfavorable balance of trade was caused by the Open Door policy of the Algeciras Act. The resulting popular belief supported the Protectorate policy of using decrees and manipulations of customs regulations to defeat the Act and to increase French trade. This propaganda ignored the fact that the Moroccan balance of trade was unfavorable with every country, as was to be expected for an agricultural country with but slight industrial development. At this period Morocco's unfavorable balance was due partly to the world surplus of agricultural products and largely to the unwise policy of encouraging grain production to benefit French _colons_ who were subsidized by the French government. Instead of exporting, as formerly, both livestock and garden produce, Morocco in 1933 imported cattle and had barely enough orchard products for domestic needs. To relieve the situation, France was not interested in negotiating agreements with other countries to provide outlets for Moroccan products which did not include the surrender of capitulations by them and the abrogation of all treaty rights in Morocco. France was especially determined not to strengthen, or even to tolerate, the Open Door policy in Morocco. The United States was the largest supplier of agricultural implements and one of the largest suppliers of petroleum products, radios, typewriters, and autos. Increasing exports of Moroccan wine to the United States would strengthen the Open Door policy.[86] Thus Blake had analyzed the economy of Morocco in 1933.

Ponsot, indeed, had seen the need of diversifying agricultural production. However, he still placed the major blame for the Moroccan depression upon the American Open Door policy. In November of 1933, he announced a new policy to replace it:

> The customs regime, born of the Conference of Algeciras and of the anterior treaties, does not respond to the actual conditions of the country .... This system is unjust and superannuated. It is justifiable only in regard to a country without industry, without economic activity, such as Morocco was indeed thirty years ago .... It is logical that the Powers should admit the right of Morocco to defend itself .... Morocco does not protest against the principle of equal chance for all its suppliers, but this condition cannot be maintained without the admission of the principle of reciprocity, which would permit the country to balance its trade.

In an interview with Blake, Ponsot reaffirmed his new policy of "Economic equality of rights for the powers, and equality of rights for Morocco." To the State Department Blake analyzed the Moroccan crisis as being due to

> the overambitious schemes of the Protectorate government, lavish expenditures on embellishments of facade, huge subsidies for the artificial creation of colonial agricultural enterprises, the upkeep of supernumerary functionaries, and the engagement of the State, in derogation of treaty stipulations, in phosphate and mining enterprises on uneconomic bases.

Blake would have been willing to recommend a doubling of the tariff rates, if all the Algeciras signatories agreed, but he doubted that this would satisfy France, who was really aiming at a complete monopilization of the Moroccan economy.[87]

Before the pronouncement of Ponsot's economic doctrine, the American officials in Morocco had become very despondent over the continuation of Lyautey's policy of promoting French economic progress at American expense. The denial of American participation in public works was illustrated by the French neglect to inform Americans of a project to build a pipeline to supply water to Casablanca and by the letting of a contract to complete and operate the port of Safi. As Consul Russell put it, "These large tenders for public works have always been camouflaged or arranged in such a way ast to prevent American companies from participating under treaty rights."[88]

There was also an exchange of notes over Saint's admission that the proceeds of the special tax of two and a half percent provided for public works by the Act of Algeciras would henceforth be incorporated with the general budget. The British government also inquired concerning this seeming misuse of funds. Saint's reply was that the actual outlay on public works by the Protectorate government far exceeded the proceeds of the special tax allotted.[89] Concerning the point of adhering to treaty provisions, Saint appeared to be unconcerned.

Among the more notorious attempts of the Protectorate authorities to injure American trade were the attacks on auto sales in 1927 and 1929. The Atalaya Company, for several years doing a good business in American autos in Casablanca, first alerted the consul there to the situation. A consortium of firms selling French autos and accessories was trying to obtain agencies for American autos in order to kill their sales by non-promotion. The consulate reported that General Motors was about to be taken over by the French company, C. T. M. Either General Motors was being hoodwinked by its Paris representatives, or it was adopting a suicidial policy in French Morocco. The Atalaya Company was being pressured to sell out to the C. T. M. or to lose its contract with General Motors through a scheme of the company's Paris office. Informed by the State Department of this nefarious plot in its Paris office, the American general European agent of General Motors at London took measures to strengthen his company by putting an American manager in charge of the Moroccan territory.[90] Several other American auto companies had to contend with various schemes of their French agents to undermine their business.[91]

In 1929 the Protectorate government drafted a plan to tax automotive vehicles according to their cylinder capacity, which was much larger in American cars. A new auto trade paper, published in Casablanca, contained scurrilous jibes at the United States and pilloried French functionaries who drove American cars. Russell thought that this paper was supported by the Residency after two French auto companies ceased backing it. This automobile campaign was used as a cover for the most bitter and chauvinistic attacks on the United States and the alleged ultimate aim of its policies, such as the "conquest of Morocco." The State Department had its ambassador in Paris protest to the French government against the proposed discriminatory tax on American autos. In the French Foreign Office's most polite reply of September 19, 1929, it was stated that no dahir of the nature mentioned had been or was about to be issued; "there could be no question of issuing a dahir which would tend to create discriminations contrary to the regime of economic equality established by existing treaties."[92]

Other outstanding causes of controversy were the prohibition of the importation of foreign wheat and flour, increase of oil companies under French control to compete with American firms in a restricted market, discrimination against American merchandise by French command, and threat of quotas and discrimnatory customs evaluation of American goods. The French were especially obdurate regarding the prohibition of wheat and flour importation, so obviously a violation of the Open Door, but from June to December of 1929 the Residency advanced the argument of necessity to justify it. The new oil refineries were established by French capital mainly, but one was Spanish. Buhrman was reliably informed that the Protectorate authorities were directed from Paris not to purchase any but French merchandise if it were obtainable. This command was issued at the behest of powerful French banking and political groups, which were, "for all intents and purposes, the French government." Whenever small French firms obtained government contracts, they labelled the American goods used with their own trademark, concealing their origin. A Belgian chamber of commerce report in March, 1933, complained of the policy of the Residency as a preferential regime for French importers, protection by the government, and prohibition or limitation of imports to replace a customs regime impartial to all nations. In June, 1934, Buhrman wrote that businessmen in Casablanca importing and distributing American products were anxious lest quotas be imposed on it, particularly on autos. These merchants were trying to secure the entry of Moroccan wines into American markets to forestall the setting up of quotas on American goods. The French government would not hesitate, it was thought, to establish quotas or any other measures needed to give French goods a preferential treatment, regardless of any treaty provisions. The customs authorities were assessing imported goods on their wholesale value in the country of destination, instead of in the country of origin, which enabled them to collect higher duty. The United States had a special problem in her Moroccan trade, because most of the dealers selling American goods were not Americans.[93]

The apprehensions of Americans and other non-French importers of goods into Morocco were well founded, for it was during 1934 and 1935 that France mounted a vigorous offensive to overthrow the customs provision of the Act of Algeciras by raising the customs and introducing quotas. France aimed to make bilateral treaties which would enable her to control the economy of Morocco and to adjust it to her own advantage. Ponsot's program of November, 1933, was to be put into effect; Morocco was to be rescued from her subservience to the Open Door theory and other countries were to be allowed quotas of imports which would be proportioned to the amounts of exports sent them by Morocco. This was Ponsot's principle of reciprocity. The Moroccan trade statistics for 1932 for the first time revealed a new factor in Morocco's international commerce that furnished the French with a concrete argument for their reciprocity policy. In that year Japan's import trade, non-existent before 1928, was rapidly increasing, while she bought hardly anything from Morocco. Japan was dumping upon Morocco goods cheap enough to undersell the British, French, Italian, and Spanish producers. Prices fixed to suit the native purses were giving Japan almost a monopoly in cotton piece goods, cotton and rayon and rayon piece goods, cotton knitted goods, canvas rubber-soled shoes, canned salmon, electric light bulbs, enamel ware, haberdashery, bicycles, and other goods. For the first four months of 1934 Japan ranked second in imports to Morocco.[94] The Japanese freight rates on regularly scheduled ships were lower than freight rates from the United States. Japanese merchants employed many active salesmen, and they were beginning to import Moroccan wines. In January, 1938, the opening of the Nippon Trade Agency in Casablanca and the arrival of a Japanese consul were announced.[95]

In December, 1934, the United States government instructed its ambassador at Paris to point out informally to the Foreign Office that it regarded the quota system as inherently discriminatory and that such a system would not only destroy the principle of commercial equality but would erect new trade barriers at the time when nations were striving to encourage the fullest volume of mutually profitable trade.

Later the French proposed to the United States a five-point program: a quota system applied equally to all countries on the basis of their trade during certain years, new tariff rates to replace those in vogue since 1906, a committee to hear tariff disputes, equalization of the so-called port taxes, and application of the new system to the whole of Morocco. Then the State Department learned that Great Britain exchanged notes with France in January 1935, sanctioning the proposed system if agreed to by the Tangier authorities, and also that Italy had accepted the French proposal, with reservations, but that The Netherlands was opposed to it on principle. On April 6, 1935, the United States formally advised the French Foreign Ministry that it could not usefully negotiate on the French proposals, and it protested against the proposed establishment of the new customs regime.[96] As was customary, the French government could see no validity in the arguments of the United States.

Throughout 1935 and 1936 there was an insistent demand from France for the abrogation of the Algeciras Act. The Protectorate authorities presented the propaganda that the deficits in the Moroccan budgets for 1933, 1934, and 1935 were caused by the economic restrictions of the Act. In December, 1934, when it was reported that Great Britain had assented to quotas based upon reciprocity and to raising of customs dues, the Moroccan public, especially the natives, became alarmed that this would mean the elimination of Japanese importations, highly prized for their cheapness. The French industrialists in Morocco wanted no increase in the cost of living to make the sale of their products more difficult, but wanted customs to be a barrier to importations injurious to Morocco. Articulate opinion in Morocco was, therefore, adverse to the French proposals for change in customs regulations in order to balance the budget.[97] In January, 1936, the Algiers Chamber of Commerce expressed a desire to have the Act of Algeciras abrogated. The unification of the French African possessions was much discussed in private conversations in Algeria, although the press was silent; the great obstacle to this plan was Morocco, and the necessary prelude to its realization was the abolition of the Act of Algeciras.[98]

Inevitably, the position of the United States in Morocco remained largely influenced by that of her one colleague there,

Great Britain. On April 27, 1936, the United States replied to an aide memoire of the British Embassy of the previous September, requesting the American view of the proposed changes in the commercial regime of French Morocco. The reply was that the United States government remained steadfast in its position that the doors of Morocco should be kept open on a basis of commercial equality for all nations, including France. A system of quotas would run counter to that position and also to the trade program of the United States, which aimed at lowering the barriers hampering international trade and at liberating it from the many extraordinary restrictions placed upon it in recent years. However, the government of the United States had already stated its willingness to acquiesce in reasonable increases in existing customs rates on goods imported into Morocco. The American government was not convinced that quotas on certain items would increase the revenues of the Sherifian government or would contribute to the best economic interests of the Moroccan people. As evidence of its sincere desire to cooperate with the British and the Protectorate governments, the government of the United States was prepared to participate in a frank discussion of the problems involved between representatives of all the interested powers.[99]

Temporarily, the question of higher tariffs and quotas was shelved by the French, probably as much because of Moroccan opposition as of American objection. Early in 1937, however, the French Foreign Office returned to the long neglected topic of American capitulations.[100] In March Blake commented on the recent Anglo-Egyptian treaty which provided for the suppression of capitulations in Egypt and which presaged a mutual renunciation of French capitulations in Egypt and of British capitulations in Morocco. Later American consular reports wrote of persistent rumors of Franco-British negotiations on the surrender of British capitulations in Morocco and of the consequent anxiety of both British and American merchants concerning the harmful effects of this move to themselves. On July 30, Blake quoted a statement from a recent memorandum by the French Foreign Office to the American Embassy in Paris, pointing out that the American-Moroccan Treaty, concluded for a duration of fifty years, was now subject to denunciation, upon twelve months' advance notice. This fact, Blake suggested, might diminish the value of American capitulatory rights to the vanishing point.[101]

On July 29, 1937, the long-expected Anglo-French treaty renouncing British capitulations in Morocco was signed in London, to enter into effect on January 1, 1938. Again the United States was invited by France to abandon its splendid isolation _re_ capitulations, preferably by an exchange of letters rather than by a special convention similar to the Anglo-French agreement.

Assessing the situation caused by the defection of Great Britain, Blake reiterated that the suppression of capitulations would entail the loss of a considerable measure of practical protection of American general, economic, and commercial rights in Morocco. As compensation for their surrender, the United States should obtain first a settlement of outstanding claims (one antedating the limited recognition of the protectorate in 1917), and second the largest possible confirmation and safeguarding of American economic rights now existing under treaties with Morocco. Eventually it would be necessary to make a new treaty for the second objective. Ambassador Bullitt in Paris agreed with Blake's observations and asserted that negotiations for the surrender of American capitulatory rights were now unavoidable.[102]

Early in 1938 the Anglo-French commercial treaty on Morocco was being negotiated. Asserting its right to negotiate any change in Moroccan customs, the Belgian government inquired about the attitude of the United States on this matter.[103] Blake thought that whatever side won the Spanish Civil War, France would arrogate to herself the benefit of any arrangement regarding trade in the Spanish Zone. The United States could not rely on customs provisions of the Spanish-Moroccan treaty of 1861, but could effectively maintain other rights provided there. Article 17 of the Madrid Convention of 1880 would guarantee the United States most favored nation status even if the French should abrogate the American-Moroccan treaty of 1836. Moreover, the Act of Algeciras was intended to guarantee the maintenance of the ten percent ad valorem import duties for all signers. Upon the Act of Algeciras, therefore, the United States could take a firm stand against the revision of Moroccan customs without her consent. In an historical analysis of the whole series of Moroccan treaties with foreign powers since the twelfth century, Blake demonstrated that the ten percent rate was based on Koranic law.[104] In his opinion, the American position against bilateral modification of the customs rates was based on both Koranic custom and international treaties of many centuries' duration.

However, France and Great Britain were not deterred by Blake's legalistic arguments. On July 18, 1938, the conclusion of the Anglo-French Commercial Treaty was announced. This document accorded for seven years the French Zone customs autonomy and abrogated the Anglo-Moroccan Treaty of Commerce of 1856. France also repeated her willingness to introduce the quota system into Moroccan commerce on certain articles. British pressure for such quotas, coming chiefly from Manchester, had been met by the informal agreement of December, 1934. Failure to put these quotas into effect, the French alleged, had been due to objections of the United States. The British decline in the cotton goods trade was really alarming. In 1925 Great Britain had had about two-thirds of this trade, but by 1936, though entering the market only in 1932, Japan had taken nearly eighty-five percent, leaving Great Britain only about six percent. American representatives denied sole responsibility for blocking the quota system; this was opposed also by the Netherlands, Belgium, Italy, and Portugal. The opposition of the United States was based on the broad principle that Morocco was almost the world's last free market of any consequence, and a quota system would be devised to exclude all but French trade. The Japanese trade in cotton goods had increased primarily because of the poverty of the Moroccans, who could afford nothing better than the cheapest goods available.[105]

Among the press comments in Morocco on the treaty may be quoted this excerpt from La Voix Nationale of September 1, 1938:

> We are witnessing, undoubtedly, the first blow of the axe ... at the juridical edifice of the Act of Algeciras. There suddenly bobs up again that unforgettable quarrel between the partisans and adversaries of the famous Act. But not for long! The French Government has pronounced, in beginning adroitly, without noise, the dethronement of the international compromise of 1907 ....
>
> In initialling the treaty of July 18, 1938 the protecting

> nation has just taken a vast diplomatic action .... France will seek--on a give-and-take basis--and will successively obtain from all powers signatory to the Act of Algeciras, protocols of disinterestedness until the moment comes when she will find herself alone before a disarmed Morocco, vainly arguing from a yellow and scratched parchment, destined for the dust bin of scraps of paper.[106]

While the State Department continued to receive other analyses and comments on the meaning and possibilities of the new Anglo-French agreement, it was making the best of a bad situation by negotiating with France for a new commercial treaty. Following Blake's often expressed formula, it began by trying to effect a settlement of American claims against Morocco. Beginning in October, 1937, Secretary Hull proposed a settlement to the French chargé, and in June and August of the following year, it informed the French government that Blake was authorized to deal with their representatives on this matter. On September 9, 1938, Noguès informed Blake that since negotiations had now begun in Washington on American capitulations, the examination of claims had been transferred to the Minister of Foreign Affairs in Paris. Until April 10, 1939, the Protectorates authorities had made no move for a settlement conference. More than ever, Blake was convinced that the United States should insist upon a settlement of claims prior to serious negotiations for a new treaty. If the American capitulations were abrogated in the French Zone, the recognition of the Spanish Zone and abrogation of American capitulations there could then follow.[107]

Meanwhile, without the desired settlement of claims, negotiations were proceeding. The Counselor of the Danish Legation was informed of February 28, 1939, that the State Department had submitted to the French ambassador the drafts of three proposed treaties relative to French Morocco. A proposed capitulations convention followed in general the provisions of the Anglo-French convention of July 29, 1937. A draft treaty of establishment, commerce and navigation was based on the standard measures of such American treaties, as well as on the Anglo-French commercial treaty of July 18, 1938. The third treaty was one concerning naturalization and military obligations.[108] Undoubtedly, by thus seizing the initiative, the State Department hoped for a more favorable settlement. However, it had not yet had experience of direct dealings with French negotiators. Perhaps the United States overvalued her goodwill in assenting, in her treaty draft, to the principle of quotas, although she still considered the Open Door the only appropriate policy for Morocco.[109]

Nevertheless, the American government proceeded cautiously in making the new arrangements. A State Department memorandum of January 26, 1939, gave the opinion that if the French government should intimate its intention to abrogate all or part of the treaty of 1836, the United States could repudiate its recognition of the French Protectorate and consider the French as usurpers in French Morocco.[110] At the Department's request, Blake furnished a memorandum on the violations of treaties and discriminations against American nationals in the French Zone in recent years,[111] to be used as arguments against the French negotiators.[112]

On May 19, 1939, the State Department was informed by the American Embassy in Paris that Leon Marchal, a member of the Residency's staff in charge of treaty negotiations for the Moroccan government, was sailing for the United States on June 3 to carry on negotiations already started by the Division of Near Eastern Affairs and the French ambassador in Washington. Marchal was most conciliatory in his views that full agreement was possible on all important issues, but he indicated that all necessary provisions could be included in one treaty instead of three.[113]

Prospects seemed dim for the success of the desired treaty. On May 23 Noguès said that American claims could be dealt with only provisionally, since they must be subordinated to the general accord being discussed by France and the United States. This customary evasiveness of French diplomacy was familiar to Blake. He at once denied that the claims settlement must await the treaty conclusion, since the two matters were independent and the claims long antedated the treaty negotiations. On June 22, 1939, Blake appointed Consul Doolittle and Interpreter Al Khazan, experienced technicial expert on claims, as his representatives in dealing with the claims question at Rabat.[114]

Between June 13 and July 11, seventeen meetings were held in Washington to discuss the proposed American-French agreements on commerce and capitulations. Participating were Leon Marchal and two representatives of the State Department, J. Rives Childs and Harry R. Turkel. In the concluding meeting Marchal stated that the French government did not desire to reaffirm the principle of economic liberty without any inequality in any new treaty. Since the capitulations convention dealt only with that specific subject, the French government would make no commitments on other matters, such as other American rights in Morocco. Although the French did not intend to violate the principle of economic equality, they would neither reaffirm nor reinterpret a principle so distasteful to them, which had been extorted from them under the menace of war. On July 11 Marchal made the suggestion that the negotiations be suspended for some weeks in order to reopen them on a more extended basis, to include not only the renunciation of American capitulary rights in French Morocco, but also the abrogation of all American rights under the Act of Algeciras, including the principle of economic liberty without any inequality. In return the draft treaties on capitulations and commerce would be merged into one treaty for a thirty year term. In such an instrument the United States would obtain definitive and concrete undertakings in respect to matters of particular interest to her in French Morocco.

The Act of Algeciras had changed the original provision for economic equality for thirty years (in the Anglo-French Entente of 1904) into a permanent obligation. Many changes had occurred since that time, and equally great changes must be anticipated during the coming thirty years. France wanted a wholly new treaty flexible enough to permit future developments. In general, the United States might obtain a most favored nation treatment with other nations, except the French. The customs treatment of a specified list of American goods might be equal to that accorded similar French goods, and special safeguards might be fixed for quotas and monopolies affecting American products. Since the United States was the last nation to renounce its capitulatory rights, it would be quite fitting for her to be the first to surrender the other rights enjoyed under the Act of Algeciras. Two courses were open to France--one, the denunciation of the Act of Algeciras; the other, the abrogation of that Act through bilateral accords with the signatories. The final meeting on July 11 was attended also by the French ambassador and the American representatives Murray and Alling.

Every assurance was given of American satisfaction with the French proposals to be made, and it was agreed that Marchal would return about September 15 to resume negotiations.[115] The American capitulation to French diplomacy seemed complete.

In Morocco, American efforts to secure a settlement of their claims were stalled. On August 4, 1939, Blake reported that the Protectorate authorities continued to associate the claims settlement with the treaty negotiations in Washington and were trying to restrict their proposals to a partial solution by eliminating the case of the American protégé Al Yacoubi,[116] the largest pecuniary claim. In reply, the State Department could only cite a contrary view from the Paris Embassy's telegram of June 3, 1939. This quoted Coursier as stating that the French Foreign Office "does not entertain the idea that settlement of the claims can be made contingent upon the conclusion of new treaties" and that a settlement of the claims regardless of the outcome of the Washington negotiations was an unassailable proposition. The State Department wanted all claims settled and could delay ratification of any treaty which might be made until the claims were fully met.[117]

However, Fate, as personified by Adolph Hitler, intervened and prevented the conclusion of the treaty so persistently sought by France. On September 1, Hitler invaded Poland, and two days later Great Britain and France had declared war on Germany. Nearing the end of his long and outstanding career in Morocco, Blake reflected with some optimism that his policy on Morocco might still prevail:

> Since the war in Europe seems to have been inevitable, it is fortunate, perhaps, that when it did break out, it came just in time to interrupt our treaty negotiations regarding Morocco. When at the end of the war they may be eventually renewed, we may then find the French in a more rational state of mind. There is no doubt that, but for the war, our negotiations would have been carried through under the influence of the French exclusivist trade aims in Morocco. It seems now that even in Morocco administrative circles, where the dream was entertained of the Sherifian Empire as a closed preserve for French trade, there is an awakening to the ruinous consequences of artificial trade barriers. There is talk

in these circles to the effect that, even after the termination of a victorious war, the open door policy for trade would probably be maintained in French Morocco ... However, French interests in Morocco are largely dominated by influential private financial groups, and we must still be cautious, and, at this time, give away nothing which may prejudice our efforts to set American trade in Morocco, as it is to be governed by the revised treaties, on a fair and rational basis.[118]

Notes

1. Knight, Morocco as a French Economic Venture, 59-61.

2. Landau, Moroccan Drama, 140-141.

3. Ibid., 133-134.

4. Blake to Sec. of State, No. 54, Jan. 28, 1926, A. N. F., 881.00/1199.

5. Blake to Sec. of State, No. 82, March 24, 1926, Ibid., 881.00/1208; Herrick (Paris) to Kellogg, letter, April 23, 1926, Ibid., 881.00/1218 1/2.

6. Whitehouse (Paris) to Sec. of State, April 16, 1926, Ibid., 881.00/1211; Herrick (Paris) to Sec. of State, No. 6388, June 4, 1926, Ibid., 881.00/1230.

7. Blake to Sec. of State, No. 96, May 5, 1926, Ibid., 881.00/1216.

8. Knight, Morocco as a French Economic Venture, 61-62; Landau, Moroccan Drama, 134-135.

9. Russell to Sec. of State, No. 266, July 26, 1926, A. N. F., 881.5151/-- and No. 278, Oct. 12, 1926, Ibid., 881.00/1314.

10. Russell to Sec. of State, No. 327, April 11, 1927, 881.607/3; No. 344, June 15, 1927, 881.00/1; No. 385, Oct. 10, 1927, 881.00/1353; Ibid.

11. Russell to Sec. of State, No. 370, Aug. 31, 1927, Ibid., 881.00/2.

12. A. N. F., Blake to Sec. of State, telegram, Nov. 18, 1927, 881.00/3; Russell to Sec. of State, No. 404, Nov. 23, 1927, 881.001/6. Blake to Sec. of State, No. 248, Dec. 13, 1927, 881.001/7 and No. 322, Aug. 30, 1928, 881.461/4.

13. Elkington to Dept. of State, report, April 5, 1926, Ibid., 881.00/1215; Williamson (Algiers) to Dept. of State, No. 27, April 10, 1926, Ibid., 881.00/1210.

14. George Tait, American vice consul at Algiers, said that the proceedings were secret and only partially reported in the press. His opinion of future plans for unification was based on informal talks with French officials, private citizens, representatives of foreign governments, and press representatives. Tait to Dept. of State, No. 35, May 9, 1927, A. N. F., 881.00/1335.

15. Tait (Algiers), to Dept. of State, No. 35, May 9, 1927, Ibid., 881.00/1335.

16. A. N. F., Blake to Sec. of State, No. 313, with enclosure from vice consul Henrotin (Casablanca), July 19, 1928, 881.00/1417; English (Algiers) to Sec. of State, report No. 56, Aug. 10, 1928, 881.00/1422; Blake to Sec. of State, No. 318, Aug. 9, 1928, 881.00/1423.

17. Under the next Resident General, Lucien Saint, the prohibition of German residence in French Morocco was practically removed. By a dahir of March 15, 1933, German nationals were permitted to enter the French Zone if they held passports visaed for Morocco by a French diplomatic, consular, or prefectorial authority. The visas were valid for six months from date of entry and might be extended. Crews of German vessels were allowed to go ashore without passports. German citizens were allowed to plead, without special authorization, before the courts in the French Zone. German commercial firms engaged in business in Morocco

could be represented by resident agents of their own nationality; they might also conclude contracts or leases and acquire real property where they resided for the use of their business. The above decrees did not apply to the Tangier Zone, where the Germans were still under the restrictions of the Treaty of Versailles. Blake to Sec. of State, No. 837, April 28, 1933, Ibid., 881.111/21.

18. Henrotin to Sec. of State, report, Sept. 28, 1927, Ibid., 651.6231/226.

19. Herrick (Paris) to Sec. of State, No. 8335, Feb. 18, 1928, Ibid., 851.00 P. R./7.

20. Herrick to Sec. of State, telegram, Aug. 18, 1928, Ibid., 711.8112/Anti--War/1; Kemp (Danzig) to Sec. of State, No. 862, Jan. 28, 1929, Ibid., 711.8112 Anti-War/2.

21. Luther Harris Evans, "Some Aspects of French Imperialism in Morocco Since the World War," Annals of the American Academy of Political and Social Science, CLXII (July, 1932), 227.

22. A. N. F., Blake to Sec. of State, No. 333, Oct. 31, 1928, 881.00/1429; No. 336, Nov. 9, 1928, 881.00/1431; No. 340, Nov. 23, 1928, 881.00/1436; No. 344, Dec. 6, 1928, 881.00/1437.

23. Blake to Sec. of State, No. 354, Jan. 12, 1929, Ibid., 881.001/12.

24. Blake to Sec. of State, No. 372, March 5, 1929, Ibid., 881.001/13; Landau, Moroccan Drama, 135-136.

25. Blake to Sec. of State, No. 397, May 29, 1929, A. N. F., 881.001/14.

26. Blake to Sec. of State, No. 443, Oct. 22, 1929, Ibid., 881.00/1451.

27. Blake to Sec. of State, No. 529, Aug. 7, 1930, Ibid., 881.00/1469; Heizer (Algiers) to Sec. of State, No. 57, Sept. 25, 1930, Ibid., 881.00/1472.

28. The policy of linking France's three North African domains by air and rail was going steadily forward in 1934. Within the preceding year the last section of railway in Morocco which connected the whole of North Africa from Gabes, Tunisia to Casablanca was completed. The plan to connect all the North African coast by mail and passenger air service was under way. Walker (Tunis) to Sec. of State, No. 80, Sept. 1, 1934, Ibid., 851s.00/75.

29. Smith (Tunis) to Sec. of State, report, June 14, 1931, Ibid., 881.00/1495.

30. "Morocco Making Rapid Progress in All Sections," Christian Science Monitor, Feb. 28, 1929.

31. Russell to Sec. of State, No. 580, Nov. 22, 1929, A. N. F., 881.612/7 and No. 586, Dec. 10, 1929, Ibid., 881.612/8.

32. Henrotin to Sec. of State, No. 41, March 4, 1930, Ibid., 881.156/87.

33. Elizabeth Monroe, The Mediterranean in Power Politics, 107-108.

34. France made an unusual gesture of comity to the United States in 1931. The French Ministry for Foreign Affairs informed the American Embassy at Paris that the Municipal Commission of Rabat had decided to give the name George Washington to an open space near the city of Rabat. His name would also be given to one of the arteries in the city of Agadir. Edge (Paris) to Sec. of State, No. 1860, Oct. 15, 1931, A. N. F., 811.415 Washington Bi-Centenary/840.

35. Blake to Sec. of State, No. 470, Jan. 22, 1930, Ibid., 881.00/1453; Buhrman to Sec. of State, report, May 15, 1930, Ibid., 881.156/88.

36. Buhrman to Sec. of State, No. 48, June 11, 1930, Ibid., 881.50/11.

37. Buhrman to Sec. of State, Dec. 30, 1931, Ibid., 881.51/40 and Oct. 25, 1932, Ibid., $\frac{800.504/36.}{283h}$

38. Henrotin to Sec. of State, No. 41, March 4, 1930, *Ibid.*, 881.156/87; Bigelow to Culbertson, Division of Western European Affairs, Dec. 13, 1930, *Ibid.*, unindexed letter following 881.154.

39. Buhrman to Sec. of State, No. 193, May 19, 1932, *Ibid.*, 611.8131/18.

40. Blake to Sec. of State, No. 540, Sept. 18, 1930, *Ibid.*, 881.00/1470.

41. Blake to Sec. of State, No. 595, March 16, 1931, *Ibid.*, 881.00/1483.

42. Landau, *Moroccan Drama,* 143, 145.

43. Blake to Sec. of State, No. 758, Aug. 8, 1832, *A. N. F.*, 881.00/1540.

44. Landau, *Moroccan Drama,* 146-147.

45. *Ibid.*, 136.

46. Blake to Sec. of State, No. 414, June 26, 1929, *A. N. F.*, 881.00/1447; Blake to Sec. of State, No. 454, Dec. 7, 1929, *Ibid.*, 881.00/1454.

47. Buhrman to Sec. of State, report, Feb. 17, 1932, *Ibid.*, 881.00/1531; Bigelow to Sec. of State, No. 704, Feb. 25, 1932, *Ibid.*, 881.00/1530.

48. Blake to Sec. of State, No. 728, May 4, 1932, *Ibid.*, 881.00/1537 and No. 744, June 30, 1932, *Ibid.*, 881.00/1539.

49. Blake to Sec. of State, No. 859, July 14, 1933, *Ibid.*, 881.001/22.

50. Landau, *Moroccan Drama,* 137.

51. Blake to Sec. of State, No. 958, Section II, July 12, 1934, *A. N. F.*, 881.00/1567.

52. *Ibid.*

53. Blake to Sec. of State, No. 958, Section I, July 12, 1934, _Ibid._, 881.00/1567; Hopper to Sec. of State, No. 114, April 30, 1936, _Ibid._, 881.00/1603.

54. _A. N. F._, Hopper to Sec. of State, report, July 13, 1935, 881.00/1590; No. 93, Dec. 28, 1935, 881.00 /1595; No. 102, Jan. 20, 1936, 881.00/1597; No. 142, Oct. 20, 1936, 881.00/1631.

55. Buhrman to Sec. of State, report, May 29, 1933, _Ibid._, 881.52/27.

56. Blake to Sec. of State, No. 1064, June 4, 1935, _Ibid._, 881.00/1588.

57. _A. N. F._, Buhrman to Sec. of State, No. 337, May 31, 1934, 881.6363/13. Hopper to Sec. of State, No. 34, Feb. 20, 1935, 881.6363/23; No. 50, May 14, 1935, 881.6363/26; No. 75, Oct. 21, 1935, 881.6363/31. Goold to Sec. of State, No. 8, Nov. 24, 1937, 881.6363/34.

58. Although extolling Tangier as a place of residence, a retired British admiral admitted the bad economic conditions in Morocco. "Morocco is suffering from the universal depression and is dead as far as business is concerned. Travel is also very light, especially in the interior, where the big modern hotels located in the new European towns built outside the walls of the old cities of Fez and Meknes are empty except for the officers of the French Foreign Legion who are quartered there. At Fez, which depends upon its carpet, leather, and native jewelry industries, there is virtually nothing being exported and the workmen are idle." T. Walter Williams, "Retired Admiral Extols Morocco," _New York Times_, Oct. 27, 1935, 36L.

59. Hopper to Sec. of State, No. 87, Dec. 12, 1935, _A. N. F._, 881.00/1594; Blake to Sec. of State, No. 1143, March 20, 1936, _Ibid._, 881.001/34.

60. Hopper to Sec. of State, No. 113, May 1, 1936, _Ibid._, 881.00/1600.

61. A. N. F., Blake to Sec. of State, No. 1171, June 17, 1936, 881.5045/3; No. 1172, June 25, 1936, 881.00/1608; No. 1203, Sept. 25, 1936, 881.00/1626. Hopper to Sec. of State, No. 118, June 18, 1936, 881.5045/4.

62. Blake to Sec. of State, No. 1176, July 10, 1936, 881.00/1612 and No. 1202, Sept. 18, 1936, Ibid., 881.001/40. Hopper to Sec. of State, No. 142, Oct. 20, 1936, Ibid., 881.00/1631.

63. Blake to Sec. of State, No. 1202, Sept. 18, 1936, Ibid., 881.001/40; Hopper to Sec. of State, No. 139, Oct. 14, 1936, Ibid., 881.001/43. Landau, Moroccan Drama, 139.

64. Ibid., 138-139; Hopper to Sec. of State, No. 142, Oct. 20, 1936, A. N. F., 881.00/1631.

65. Ibid., Blake to Sec. of State, No. 1166, June 3, 1936, 881.00/1606; No. 1225, Dec. 3, 1936, 881.00/1640; No. 1273, April 22, 1937, 881.00/1670. Doolittle to Sec. of State, report, Dec. 4, 1936, 881.00/1639. Landau, Moroccan Drama, 139-140.

66. Jean Perrigault, "Starvation Stalks the Blue Men," New York Times, April 3, 1937, 1; "Famine Strikes Moroccan Tribes Due to Drouth," San Francisco News, July 5, 1937, 4.

67. A. N. F., Hopper to Sec. of State, No. 157, Jan. 8, 1937, 881.00/1644 and No. 167, March 12, 1937, 881.00/1658; Blake to Sec. of State, No. 1273, April 22, 1937, 881.00/1670.

68. Stanton to Sec. of State, No. 201, Oct. 22, 1937, Ibid., 881.00/1679; Goold to Sec. of State, No. 5, Nov. 17, 1937, 881.041/6 and No. 28, Feb. 15, 1938, Ibid., 881.01/47.

69. Goold to Sec. of State, No. 47, April 14, 1938, 881.00/1690; No. 79, Sept. 20, 1938, 881.504/12; No. 93, Oct. 12, 1938, 881.504/13, Ibid.

70. Some random examples are: "Moroccan Revolt Halted by French," New York Times, Oct. 24, 1937, 30; "Moroccans Restless," San Francisco News, Oct. 30, 1937, 2; "French Army Acts," Ibid., Nov. 4, 1937, 2; "France Prepares for Arab Uprising," Seattle Daily Times, Dec. 24, 1937, 7; Sisley Huddleston, "French Face Vast Movement for Independence in Africa," Christian Science Monitor, Nov. 11, 1937, 5; Dr. René Kraus, "The Coming Moroccan Revolt," Ken, I (April 7, 1938), 19-21, 53-55.

71. An interesting interview with Marcel Peyrouton was described in a letter from Alexander W. Weddell, American ambassador to Argentina, where Peyrouton had recently been exiled as French ambassador. He said that he had been dismissed from Morocco because he favored a policy of strict neutrality in the Spanish Civil War. He denied having any violent hatred of the Germans, which most Frenchmen had, but he did consider them un peuple diabolique in interfering with France and her possessions. This meddling had taken the form of promoting anti-Semitism in North Africa. He spoke earnestly of his belief in democratic institutions and of democracy as the hope of the world today, remarking that Hitlerism had been born of a defeat, that Stalinism was the outcome of centuries of misgovernment, and that Fascism followed on the heels of a decay or breakdown of democratic institutions. He considered these three forms of government identical in essentials, notwithstanding their antecedents, and their leaders were attempting to impose their views on the rest of the world. Weddell (Buenos Aires) to Sec. of State, letter, Jan. 13, 1937, A. N. F., 852.00 /4476 1/2.

72. Hopper to Sec. of State, No. 138, Oct. 9, 1936, Ibid., 852.00/3564 and No. 151, Nov. 24, 1936, Ibid., 852.00/4064.

73. Ibid., Bullitt (Paris) to Sec. of State, telegram, Jan. 9, 1937, 852.00/4305; Dodd (Berlin) to Sec. of State, telegram, Jan. 11, 1937, 852.00/4320; Blake to Sec. of State, telegram, Jan. 11, 1937, 852.00 /4325; Bingham (London) to Sec. of State, Jan. 11, 1937, 852.00/4326; Bullitt to Sec. of State, telegram,

Jan. 11, 1937, 852.00/4328; Blake to Sec. of State, No. 1243, Jan. 12, 1937, 852.00/4551; Dodd to Sec. of State, telegram, Jan. 12, 1937, 852.00/4335; Hopper to Sec. of State, No. 165, Feb. 25, 1937, 881.00/1653.

74. Bowers (Madrid) to Sec. of State, No. 1263, March 8, 1937, Ibid., 852.00/4976.

75. Caldwell (Lisbon) to Sec. of State, telegram, March 10, 1937, 881.00/1652 and No. 1218, March 11, 1937, Ibid., 881.00/1656; Blake to Sec. of State, No. 1264, March 12, 1937, Ibid., 881.00/1657.

76. That incorrigible cynic, Maxwell Blake, had some pertinent remarks to make about the Spanish notes. "No doubt the French have been seeking a pretext for occupation of the Spanish Zone and have concentrated along the border an adequate army to accomplish this with speed and success. This military scheme is counterbalanced by weighty political considerations. First, the Spanish Moors are 'sympathetic to a man' with Franco. Secondly, it is believed that Great Britain has prevented France from carrying out her coup. Great Britain's opposition was manifest at the exploded German scare, which had been carefully worked up by the French in the international press, at the cost, it is said, of millions of francs .... The suggestion is also current here (in the French Zone) that French encouragement prompted Azaña's speech on Spain's relinquishment of her rights in Morocco and the note of February 9, 1937, by which Spanish Foreign Minister Alvarez del Vayo proposed cession of Spain's Moroccan rights and other territorial adjustments in favor of France and Great Britain in return for assistance to the Valencia Government. French intervention now seems ended by the replies of the French and British governments to this note." Blake to Sec. of State, No. 1273, April 22, 1937, Ibid., 881.00/1670.

77. Kirk (Rome) to Sec. of State, No. 277, March 19, 1937, Ibid., 852.00/5060; Wilson (Paris) to Sec. of State, April 13, 1937, Ibid., 852.00/5193.

78. Blake to Sec. of State, No. 1328, Nov. 12, 1937, 881.00/1681; Goold to Sec. of State, No. 9, Nov. 26, 1937, Ibid., 881.00/1686; Wilson (Paris) to Sec. of State, No. 1300, Dec. 2, 1937, Ibid., 881.51/66.

79. Goold to Sec. of State, Dec. 29, 1937, Ibid., 881.51/68.

80. Goold to Sec. of State, No. 35, March 4, 1938, Ibid., 881.51/69.

81. Goold to Murray, letter, July 20, 1938, Ibid., 881.00/1693; Blake to Sec. of State, No. 1414, Dec. 23, 1938, Ibid., 881.00/1703.

82. Stanton to Sec. of State, annual report, Feb. 18, 1939, Ibid., 881.00/1705; Blake to Sec. of State, No. 1450, April 27, 1939, Ibid., 881.00/1713.

83. Stanton to Sec. of State, No. 126, Jan. 18, 1939, Ibid., 881.51/70 and No. 127, Jan. 21, 1939, Ibid., 881.51/71.

84. Blake to Sec. of State, No. 1450, April 27, 1939, Ibid., 881.00/1713.

85. Anderson (solicitor), Dept. of State memorandum, Oct. 14, 1929, Ibid., 711.81/3; Dept. of State, Division of Western European Affairs, divisional policy memorandum, Aug. 11, 1931, Ibid., 711.80/1.

86. Buhrman to Sec. of State, No. 269, May 4, 1933, Ibid., 681.1111/8.

87. Blake to Sec. of State, No. 889, Nov. 9, 1933, Ibid., 681.003/51 and No. 897, Nov. 29, 1933, Ibid., 681.003/52.

88. A. N. F., Russell to Sec. of State, No. 442, April 29, 1928, 881.151/1; Kellogg to Amlegation, Tangier, telegram, May 29, 1928, 881.151/1; Blake to Sec. of State, No. 307, June 22, 1928, 881.151/2; No. 317, Aug. 1, 1928, 881.151/3; No. 838, May 1, 1933, 881.156/97. Phillips to Blake, No. 252, July 27, 1933, 881.156/97.

89. Castle to Blake, No. 695, June 23, 1932, Ibid., 881.512/105. Blake to Sec. of State, No. 787, Nov. 24, 1932, 881.51/48 and No. 791, Dec. 15, 1932, Ibid., 881.51/49.

90. In 1933 Buhrman reported that the American automobile trade in French Morocco was again precarious. A substantial monopoly in sales of American car was held by one French group at Casablanca, which also had the agencies for French and Italian autos. Buhrman to Sec. of State, No. 283, June 7, 1933, A. N. F., 681.1117/4.

91. A. N. F., Russell to Sec. of State, No. 308, Feb. 8, 1927, 681.1112/1; No. 326, April 9, 1927, 681.1112/3; No. 330, April 26, 1927, 681.1112/4; No. 338, May 19, 1927, 681.1112/5; No. 367, Aug. 26, 1927, 681.1112/8; No. 371, Sept. 1, 1927, 681.1112/9; No. 388, Oct. 12, 1927, 681.1112/12 and No. 406, Dec. 2, 1927, 681.1112/13. Lee F. Warren (General Motors representative), letter, June 21, 1927, 681.1112/7.

92. A. N. F., Blake to Sec. of State, No. 412, June 24, 1929, 881.512/Motor Cars/1; No. 421, July 25, 1929, 881.512/Motor Cars/9. Russell to Sec. of State, No. 552, Aug. 20, 1929, 681.1112/15; Stimson to Amembassy, Paris, telegram, Sept. 5, 1929, 881.512/Motor Cars/12; Armour (Paris) to Sec. of State, No. 9849, Sept. 19, 1929, 881.512/Motor Cars/14.

93. A. N. F., Russell to Sec. of State, telegram, June 9, 1929, 611.8131/15; Edge (Paris) to Sec. of State, No. 35, Dec. 24, 1929, 741.812/3. Blake to Sec. of State, No. 571, Dec. 10, 1930, 881.512/95. Buhrman to Sec. of State, No. 185, May 11, 1932, 881.02/1; No. 315, Feb. 24, 1934, 681.003/57; No. 345, June 29, 1934, 681.116/45. Hopper to Sec. of State, No. 17, Nov. 16, 1934, 681.113/18.

94. Statistics of trade for the first four months of 1934 revealed the position of the leading countries in the foreign commerce of Morocco as follows:

		Values in Francs	
		Imports from:	Exports to:
1.	France	208,059,649	83,767,312
2.	Japan	31,588,572	958
3.	Belgium	24,347,747	3,355,989
4.	United States	22,613,794	1,472,197
5.	China	21,239,353	2,940
6.	Great Britain	20,275,997	5,183,541
7.	Roumania	18,914,115	15,270
8.	Italy	16,720,754	9,945,656

Of the twenty-eight countries listed separately, the only countries which consumed more Moroccan products than they exported to Morocco were Spain, Algeria, Denmark, French West Africa, the Canary Islands, and Norway. Buhrman to Sec. of State, No. 343, June 22, 1934, A. N. F., 681.9417/7.

95. Henrotin to Sec. of State, report, Feb. 27, 1934, 681.9417/6; Buhrman to Sec. of State, No. 343, June 22, 1934, 681.9417/7; Goold to Sec. of State, No. 17, Jan. 14, 1938, 681.9415/1; Ibid.

96. Dept. of State to Danish Legation, aide memoire, May 7, 1935, Ibid., 681.003/184; Marriner (Paris) to Sec. of State, No. 1767, April 8, 1935, Ibid., 681.003/178.

97. Hopper to Sec. of State, report, Feb. 5, 1935, Ibid., 681.003/157.

98. Ives (Algiers) to Sec. of State, No. 173, Jan. 16, 1936, Ibid., 681.51R3/6.

99. Dept. of State to British Embassy, aide memoire, April 27, 1936, Ibid., 681.003/205.

100. Bullitt (Paris) to Sec. of State, telegram, Jan. 8, 1937, Ibid., 881.00/1641.

101. Blake to Sec. of State, No. 1263, March 4, 1937, Ibid., 741.83/216; Hopper to Sec. of State, No. 178, May 26, 1937, Ibid., 881.00/1672; Blake to Sec. of State,

No. 1298, July 30, 1937, Ibid., 781.003/32.

102. A. N. F., Blake to Murray, letter, Sept. 1, 1937, 781.003/50; Blake to Sec. of State, No. 1325, Nov. 1, 1937, 781.003/52; Bullitt (Paris) to Sec. of State, No. 1219, Nov. 6, 1937, 781.003/53.

103. Belgian Embassy to Sec. of State, note, Feb. 7, 1938, Ibid., 781.003/86.

104. Blake to Murray; letter, Feb. 17, 1938, 781.003/94 1/2; letter, March 5, 1938, 781.003/110, Ibid.

105. Tait (Manchester) to Sec. of State, No. 161, Aug. 11, 1938, 641.8131/20; Doolittle to Murray, letter, Aug. 23, 1938, 641.8131/21; Dept. of State, Division of Near Eastern Affairs, memorandum, Aug. 24, 1938, 781.003/150 1/2; Ibid.

106. Goold to Sec. of State, No. 72 with translated enclosures, Sept. 1, 1938, Ibid., 641.5131/125.

107. Blake to Murray, letter, April 10, 1939, Ibid., 481.11/134.

108. State Dept., memorandum of conversation between Eichoff and Childs, Feb. 28, 1939, Ibid., 781.003/186.

109. Dept. of State, Division of Near Eastern Affairs, memorandum, Dec. 10, 1938, Ibid., 781.003/185.

110. Dept. of State, Division of Near Eastern Affairs, memorandum, Jan. 26, 1939, Ibid., 781.003/197.

111. Moore to Blake, No. 1017, Jan. 31, 1939, Ibid., 781.003/179A; Blake to Sec. of State, No. 1437, March 17, 1939, Ibid., 781.003/191.

112. Blake's charges are familiar to the readers of this narrative. He listed many specific instances of discrimination against American ressortissants in violation of the Act of Algeciras concerning the letting of public contracts and concessions. To these were added discriminations in the application of gate taxes,

dock dues, and railroad rates. There were also restrictions on liberty of trade and industry and violations of customs valuations. Blake to Sec. of State, No. 1437, March 17, 1939, A. N. F., 781.003/191.

113. Wilson (Paris) to Sec. of State, No. 4375, May 19, 1939, Ibid., 781.003/217.

114. Blake to Sec. of State, No. 1458, June 3, 1939, Ibid., 481.11/135 and No. 1465, June 22, 1939, Ibid., 481.11/141.

115. Minutes of negotiations held in the Dept. of State with M. Léon Marchal for drafting of American-French Capitulations Convention and Commercial Treaty concerning French Morocco, June 13-July 11, 1939, Ibid., Case Number 781.003/258.

116. The claim of Al Yacoubi concerned the confiscation by the municipality of Meknes of water rights, which had been confirmed to him by vizirial decree and given publicity in the Bulletin Officiel of the Protectorate. The State Department had instructed Blake on Nov. 19, 1937, that he should demand that property confiscated by the French authorities should be returned to its owners or the regulations for the expropriation of private property should be applied. Blake to Sec. of State, No. 1477, Aug. 4, 1939, Ibid., 481.11/145.

117. Blake to Sec. of State, No. 1477, Aug. 4, 1939; Murray to Blake, letter, Aug. 24, 1939, Ibid., 481.11/145.

118. Blake to Murray, letter, Dec. 21, 1939, Ibid., 881.00/1740.

Chapter XIV

Morocco in World War II

Throughout the year 1938 and until the end of August, 1939, American consular dispatches commented at length on preparations for war being made in French Morocco. The Atlantic ports were to be fortified, especially Casablanca; there were plans for a submarine base at Port Lyautey and a seaplane base at Agadir. Other problems studied were improvement of the Algerian-Moroccan railway, expansion of the highways, troop recruitment, food supply, and transportation. Exports of produce were forbidden or required to be licensed, and stocks of minerals were collected. The number of French troops was increased. Air raid defense drills were practiced in the towns. Espionage was banned, and the possible occupation of the Spanish and Tangier zones was considered by France. It was thought that the natives would be loyal, since they had enjoyed two years of comparative prosperity. To Noguès the Sultan promised the loyalty and friendship of his subjects. By the end of April, 1939, French Morocco was practically on a war footing, and preparations for conflict went steadily on. On July 29, Noguès made a most optimistic report to the Government Council on the state of the protectorate, but economic and military preparations continued during August.[1]

American periodicals had many articles on the war situation.[2] Before the Spanish Civil War ended on March 28, 1939, and the German and Italian forces were withdrawn from Spain in May and June, the emphasis had been on the danger of the expansion of that war to France and French North Africa; William C. Bullitt, American ambassador to France, had warned the State Department of this possibility on April 18.[3] From April until the end of August, apprehension of a general European war was strong, with France almost surrounded by the three Fascist powers, all of them in excellent locations to attack her African empire. Meanwhile, Mussolini's strident scream, "Tunis, Corsica, Nice!" echoed over the Mediterranean to herald the debut of another candidate for world power. The New Republic took what comfort was possible by recording the Franco-British military alliance and by presenting a detailed analysis of the probable outcome of the imminent war, concluding that "the balance of victory seems inclined toward the Allies."[4]

Ever since the rise of Hitler in 1933, President Franklin D. Roosevelt had been cognizant of the threat of world war and had been considering the role of the United States. Rebuffed by the other democracies and by American public opinion in his summons to a quarantine of the aggressors in 1937, he had tried other means of preventing the conflict. He contrived methods of skirting the neutrality laws to furnish supplies to Great Britain. During 1938 and 1939, he made determined efforts, encouraged by Bullitt, to arrange with Edouard Daladier and Jean Monnet for the production of American planes for France. Unfortunately, the planes could not be delivered in time to protect France in 1939, but they did speed the liberation of France in 1944.[5]

The long-threatened war began on September 1, 1939, with the German invasion of Poland, followed by her rapid subjugation. On September 3, Great Britain and France reacted by declaring war on Germany. On the twenty-eighth of the month Germany and Soviet Russia arranged the division of Poland between them. Then ensued the period of the "phony war," while Germany worked mightily for a swift and certain triumph, and Russia apparently struggled to defeat little Finland in a war lasting from November 30, 1939, until March 22, 1940. The respite was too short, however, and evidently not too well utilized, to enable Great Britain and France to get ready for the coming Nazi onslaught.

During the "phony war" French Morocco, like Europe, was almost quiescent. According to precedent, the United States maintained that her treaty rights were unaffected by the emergency war measures decreed. Secretary Hull reminded the French protectorate authorities that the United States would not approve of the application to American nationals of legislation which might be regarded as direct governmental assistance to any belligerent, since neutrality of the United States had been declared by the President. However, Blake was instructed to cooperate in aid to Moroccans that did not prejudice the neutrality of the United States or the maintenance of American treaty rights.[6]

After a most ruthless mobilization of manpower, French Morocco reorganized quickly, for Premier Reynaud of France realized that for a successful war economic production was as necessary as fighting. Recruiting of troops was stimulated among the natives by subsidies to the men and their families which seemed generous. There was some covert sympathy for Germany in the coastal cities and in central Morocco, but elsewhere almost the entire native population professed genuine support of France. The Residency appreciated the Sultan's adhesion to France and issued orders to treat the natives kindly and to give them all possible favors. Communists were reported routed from the country. Following Lyautey's policy, Noguès had decided to withdraw troops from the south and to entrust that region to Hadj Thami Glaoui and other neighboring great kaids. The Southern Atlantic Naval Command was established at Casablanca. Crops were excellent, and prospects continued good. However, there was a serious economic problem--the scarcity of shipping. Marchal stated that the French government was seriously considering setting up war industries in Morocco, controlled by the state.[7] The fatal weakness of North Africa in manufactures became evident very soon:

> In 1940, when the question arose whether the war which had been lost in the motherland should be continued from North Africa, the hitherto unobserved fact came to notice, and weighed heavily in the scales, that after a hundred years of French colonization, North Africa was totally lacking in the essential facilities necessary to repair a rifle or a pair of boots, to manufacture a shell, or to replace the buttons of a uniform.[8]

When the Nazi war machine thundered across northern and western Europe in the spring of 1940, France and Great Britain discovered many more serious deficiencies in their equipment, both material and moral. On April 9, Denmark and Norway were invaded, and despite desperate attempts by British and French forces to rescue them, they passed under the Nazi yoke for the duration of the war. A month and a day later, the Netherlands, Belgium, and Luxemburg were attacked and likewise vanquished, although King Leopold did not withdraw the Belgian armies from the fight until May 28.

Hitler reached his great objective on May 14 when the Reichswehr overwhelmed the French Fifth Army at Sedan. Both the Maginot Line and the French Army had failed to deflect the motorized troops of Hitler. From Paris Bullitt notified the President that only a miracle could save that city. The Nazi hordes continued to advance.[9]

Summoned to an emergency session, Congress heard an address by President Roosevelt on May 16, exhorting the American people to recast their thinking about defense. Roosevelt asked Congress for a mechanized army and 50,000 aircraft to be provided annually. He also advocated the acquisition of bases from which aggressors could be prevented from establishing their bases in territory of vital interest to Americans. Throughout his discourse ran the theme of keeping war at a distance--the line of defense now rested somewhere in the Atlantic. The Blitzkrieg had exposed a frightened France, made helpless by national fatigue, internal strife, corruption, industrial weaknesses and obsolete military thinking.[10]

On June 13, three days after Italy had declared war on Great Britain and France, Paris was occupied by the German army. Three days more, and Premier Reynaud, receiving sympathy but not promise of immediate material aid from the United States, had been succeeded by General Philipe Pétain. Still reeling from the Dunkirk disaster, the British could offer France no aid except joint Anglo-French citizenship. On June 22, France succumbed to the cabal of defeatists surrounding Pétain, and the Franco-German armistice was signed. The small group of patriotic leaders who went to Morocco to try to establish a French government in North Africa as a base for continuing the war were thwarted by Noguès and went back to France.[11]

For France and Great Britain, June, 1940, had been a month of degradation and humiliation. But for both countries July was a time of greater trial and disaster. On July 22, Lord Halifax broadcasted the British rejection of Hitler's peace offer; this defiance was followed by the aerial "Battle of Britain," lasting until November, when the Royal Air Force saved the country. France sank deeper into the slough of defeat. The Vichy government severed relations with Great Britain after the naval battle at Oran on July 5.

The breaking of the Anglo-French alliance made easier the official conversion of Vichy France into a Fascist state on July 10. Marshal Pétain, soon to be known as "the Marshal," aged eighty-four, the "Chief of the Executive Power," was ably assisted by Pierre Laval, who called for loyal collaboration with Germany and Italy. By a vote of 395 to three in the Chamber of Deputies and 225 to one in the Senate, the French Parliament handed over their powers to Pétain, until a new constitution ratified by the people should be put into operation. Pétain abolished the presidency, and Parliament was adjourned until "further notice"--which never came. Pétain then entrenched himself as dictator by a series of Constitutional Acts. In domestic affairs, his "National Revolution" aped the Third Reich in a total revision of French society.[12] Hitler had cause to congratulate himself on the moderation of his armistice terms. He had occupied only Paris and the northern part of France, needing an "independent" French government in Vichy to neutralize and control (without fighting) the fleet, North Africa, and France's scattered colonies. As long as Germany had to fight not only Great Britain, but probably also Russia and the United States, it seemed necessary that France be kept under the illusion that she possessed some independence and could hope for honorable peace terms when Germany was victorious.[13]

The reaction of the American government to Hitler's progress in Europe was prompt and vigorous. The German-French armistice was followed by the passage of a National Defense Tax Bill raising $994,300,000 a year and the increase of the debt limit from forty-five to forty-nine billion dollars. On September 16, Congress enacted the Training and Service Act under which drafting of the armed forces began at the close of December. Another potential enemy of the United States then became active; on September 22, 1940, Japan began the occupation of French Indo-China, and five days later she joined Germany and Italy in the Three-Power Pact, commonly called "the Axis." During the rest of 1940 Nazi progress continued. In October, Rumania passed under German control and Italy attacked Greece; in November, Hungary and Rumania endorsed the Three-Power Pact. There was but one item of good fortune for Great Britain--after a plot to overthrow his superior, Laval was removed from the vice premiership by Pétain on December 14.[14]

After the fall of France, the United States gradually adopted what was known as the Vichy policy. Bullitt was instrumental in establishing this controversial policy after Sedan; it was he who obtained the solemn pledges of Reynaud, Daladier, and Lebrun (all three shortly out of office), and also Pétain and Darlan that the French fleet would never be surrendered to Germany. Bullitt was also responsible for the safe transfer of $241,000,000 of French gold to New York.[15] Fully aware of the nature of the Vichy government, Bullitt was nevertheless confident that maintenance of American relations with it would help Pétain to resist German demands to surrender the fleet and naval bases; it might even prevent the French from making war on Great Britain. Furthermore, the morale of the French people might be strengthened by this gesture of American support. At its inception, the Vichy policy was one of expediency, "a day-to-day attempt to purchase for the Atlantic powers that invaluable time" during which "the fleet could be kept immobilized."[16]

To continue the Vichy policy for almost two years was difficult in view of the British policy of lending sympathy and aid to Charles de Gaulle and of general disapproval of it by both American and British public opinion. Even within the State Department and in other American agencies, many believed the whole policy a mistake.[17] Robert Murphy insists that the policy was no "gamble," as William Langer called it; there was no alternative before 1943, he says.[18]

Basically, the American Vichy policy was another adaptation of the Monroe Doctrine. On June 15, 1940, Hitler declared to a Hearst correspondent his disinterest in the American colonies of France and The Netherlands, but he warned that his policy was also "Europe for the Europeans." Three days later Hull warned Germany and Italy that, in accordance with traditional policy, the United States would recognize no transfer of sovereignty in this hemisphere from one European state to another. This warning was based on similar Senate and House resolutions. The Pan-American Conference in Havana on July 27 strengthened the position of the United States by planning for a joint trusteeship of European colonies in the Western Hemisphere.[19]

However, during August, 1940, when Great Britain's survival was still doubtful, Roosevelt's idea of protective and preventive bases carried American concern across the Atlantic, seeking there defensive points to guard America from attack. On August 27, Adolph Berle, in charge of African affairs in the State Department, suggested to Hull, "Why not try to protect our South Atlantic flank and assist the British by holding the French African colonies out of the Axis orbit?" Since this viewpoint coincided with Roosevelt's already lively interest in keeping out of Germany's hands such important ports as Casablanca and Dakar, from which Germam submarines and airplanes might menace South America, it furnished the foundation for the American North African policy. As Berle said in an address in February, 1942:

> There was assigned to Mr. Hull the task of holding, in time of peace, not merely the American hemisphere, but also all that was left of France and of French Africa; to hold at bay the Japanese ambition and to provide uninterrupted supply lines for Great Britain.[20]

In the last month of 1940, one of Germany's enemies told the United States how to combat Hitler. In his first interview granted to an American correspondent (John MacVane of the NBC Broadcasting Company) de Gaulle anticipated later American plans. He foresaw a quick German victory in the Balkans, followed by a clash with Russia which would cause Germany to lose the war eventually. His advice to the United States was also prophetic:

> You Americans will come into the war before it is over. If you and the British strike now at French North Africa, you will establish your bases for the eventual attack on Europe .... Land in North Africa. You will find little resistance there. Then you will be in a position to stab at the Germans anywhere. You can pick and choose your points at which you will invade the Continent, and Germany will be helpless to protect them all.

At this time the President had the major problem of securing the support of American public opinion. In a fireside chat in late December, he proclaimed the United States the "great arsenal of democracy" and bore down heavily on the "defeatists" and "appeasers" who were clamoring for a negotiated peace. Isolationist circles in the United States were stirring up opposition to the lend-lease proposal, and expansion of the country's war industry was very slow.[21]

Almost two years were to elapse before the United States was ready to take de Gaulle's advice.

While Roosevelt was experiencing frustration in his efforts to incite the American public to action in the second half of 1940, Hitler was having difficulties in his efforts to wreak destruction upon the Continent. He had failed to bomb Great Britain into submission, and he had lost the opportunity to deal her a mortal blow in the Mediterranean. Balked by the shifty Franco, who refused to pay his debt by joining the Axis and permitting or joining an invasion of North Africa,[22] by the ineptitude of Mussolini in Egypt and Albania, and by the senility of Pétain, Hitler had refused to follow the advice of Grand Admiral Raeder to gain control of the Mediterranean areas during the Winter. After that, Raeder pointed out, an advance from Suez to Turkey would put Russia at Germany's mercy. Raeder could not convince Hitler of the danger of a British-Gaullist invasion of North Africa. But Hitler never did appreciate any strategy which involved the employment of the navy--except submarines--and from this time until finally beaten by Stalin his chief target was Russia,[23] with the eventual result predicted by de Gaulle.

The year 1941 saw a greatly increased activity of all parties in the war. The Axis continued a military and political advance, reinforced by Bulgaria in November, while Russia became alienated from Germany and was invaded by Hitler on June 22. In the United States, military and political preparedness received popular support and went forward rapidly. With Great Britain, the United States now served not only as an arsenal, but as an ally, with whom public proclamation of war aims was made, which received the endorsement of Hitler's victims. Finally, Japan's attack on American islands in the Pacific caused the United States to declare war on Japan, who was supported at once by Germany and Italy. This was the year also when many Allied and Axis agencies were plotting at cross purposes to gain control of French North Africa.

Among the notable achievements in the preparedness program of the United States during 1941 were passage of the Lend-Lease Act, Roosevelt's proclamation of an unlimited state of national emergency and prolongation of military service for eighteen months, and extension of the draft to men from twenty to forty-four years of age. Congress appropriated a total of $13,620,577,005 for defense and lend-lease aid and extended a $1,000,000,000 lend-lease credit to Russia.[24]

These moves of the no longer "America First" United States were instigated by Hitler's renewed advances. On March 31, General Erwin Rommel began the land drive that brought the African coast from Tunisia almost to Alexandria under Axis control. During April the Germans almost completed the conquest of the Balkans and Greece, making British communication with Egypt difficult, and the Russo-Japanese neutrality treaty was menacing to the British. Although Great Britain again valiantly beat off a bombing attack in May and June, American officials feared two possible German invasions--from Bizerte to Dakar, and thence to South America, and from Spain into Morocco. In May, as the American leaders suspected, there was indeed grave danger of the first of these plans being implemented. Although Laval bears the title of appeaser-in-chief to Hitler, as a matter of fact, Admiral Jean François Darlan, his successor as premier, was far more yielding than Laval to German blandishments.[25] Darlan conferred with Hitler and received promises of German concessions to France in return for French collaboration against Great Britain. By the secret accord of May 28, 1941, Darlan agreed to support a rebellion in Iraq against the British, threatening the Suez Canal; to grant the Axis use of Bizerte in Tunisia and the railway thence to Gabes; and to allow Germany to use Dakar as a base for submarines, planes, and warships. This plot to turn North Africa over to Germany was foiled by dissension within the Vichy organization. The American ambassador to Vichy, Admiral Leahy, threatened an immediate break with the United States. From the French proconsuls in Africa, General Weygand in Algeria, Admiral Esteva in Tunisia, and General Boisson in West Africa, came heavy pressure on Pétain to reject this agreement and promises to resist by arms a German landing in North Africa. On June 6, Pétain yielded to these protests, and Hitler lost a second opportunity to add North and West Africa to his conquests.[26]

There was a reason for Hitler's acceptance of this rebuff. He had decided to postpone smashing Britain until his Continental victory had been assured. On June 22 he invaded the vast domains of his Poland-partitioning partner on a 2,000 mile front. Already his final defeat was in sight, especially if the United States should enter the war. It was a definite gain for the Axis, however, when on June 23 Vichy announced that Japan had been granted control over French Indo-China. The release of Nazi pressure on the West enabled the British to force the Governor of Syria to turn over that French protectorate to de Gaulle and to stop Rommel before he could reach Egypt. Roosevelt still resisted the demands of most of the American press that he break relations with Vichy and recognize de Gaulle as head of the French government in exile.[27]

Undoubtedly Hitler's greatest error in military strategy was the invasion of Russia, leaving Great Britain unconquered and French North Africa unoccupied. Less than a month later, on July 13, 1941, Great Britain and Russia concluded a mutual aid treaty. In August the Atlantic Charter, a statement of peace aims, was issued by Roosevelt and Churchill. It served as a declaration of alliance between their countries, which was reaffirmed shortly by Churchill's promise to aid the United States if war came with Japan. Soon afterwards Churchill and Stalin set up a government in Iran friendly to themselves. Internationally, the Atlantic Charter proved to be a most potent propaganda tool. On September 24, fifteen governments (nine of them in exile) endorsed its principles, and in January of the next year, twenty-six nations, including the Big Three, signed the declaration of the United Nations, pledging support of the Atlantic Charter and cooperation for world peace after the war was over.[28]

While military and political events were forcing the United States and Russia into active alliance with Great Britain, French North Africa was becoming a maelstrom of plots and counterplots in which both the Allies and the Axis were involved. It was an extraordinary situation that, from the fall of France until the virtual end of the war in 1945, when de Gaulle celebrated his full triumph in being accepted as the head of the French government, Roosevelt and Churchill were able to follow divergent ways toward solving the problem of France, yet remained efficient collaborators in winning the war. While Churchill continued to champion the cause of de Gaulle and to give him financial and moral support after Britain's break with France on July 5, 1940, Roosevelt was equally determined in his support of any French leader who might be able to supersede de Gaulle--whether it be Giraud, Darlan, or Giraud again. Admiral Leahy, sent to Vichy as American ambassador to influence Pétain and to keep French bases and navy out of German hands, worked also with Robert Murphy, Roosevelt's personal representative, and General Weygand in Algiers to prepare French North Africa for an American occupation.

Throughout the war, the American representatives in Morocco varied greatly in number and titles and shifted in headquarters. The pre-war holdover was Maxwell Blake, always located at Tangier. Blake first served as consul general from December 14, 1910, to May 14, 1925. On the last date he was promoted to be diplomatic agent and consul general, a title which he held until his retirement in July, 1940. Blake's successor, with the same rank, was John Campbell White. He served only briefly in this position, from July 19, 1940, for the office of diplomatic agent was reported vacant from January 1, 1941, until May 2, 1945. White also served at Tangier. Continuing in Tangier was J. Rives Childs, the first secretary and consul, with a second secretary and sometimes a third secretary and one or more vice consuls, from December 23, 1940 to March 30, 1944. Then Childs was made counselor of legation and consul general, a position which he retained until May 2, 1945. The war was concluded during the term of Paul H. Alling, diplomatic agent and consul general with the rank of minister from May 2, 1945 to July 10, 1947, located at Tangier. Alling was succeeded by Edwin A. Plitt on July 10, 1947, with the same title and also residing at Tangier. Beginning in 1941, the headquarters of the American establishment changed to Casablanca, where Consul General H. Earle Russell had consuls, Murphy's "vice consuls", and a number of military, naval, and air attachés on his staff. Some of the attachés were also at Tangier, under J. Rives Childs. Russell ranked as consul general from February 19, 1941, until Childs again resumed that title on March 30, 1944, and his office was always at Casablanca. The United States was represented at Rabat by a consul general, a consul, and a vice consul from May 22, 1943, until after the end of the war.

The customary peacetime business of the American establishment went on, and in addition there were the innumerable wartime activities to carry on. As the only country still maintaining protection, the United States found this system a subject for frequent consular discussions.[29] Attrition of the Algeciras Act continued; in July, 1939, Belgium had been approached to make a treaty with France similar to the Anglo-French treaty of 1938. There were instances of discrimination against American goods sold in Morocco and in favor of Germany and German-occupied countries and of an export tax on Moroccan products.[30] Several reports during 1940 and 1941 described the difficulties of carrying on American commerce with French Morocco because of the French restrictive measures and the British blockade. Four reports on economic conditions, sent by Russell to the State Department between July 15 and November 18, 1941, remarked that direct American trade was almost non-existent and that there was a serious threat of inflation menacing Moroccan economy.[31] Under war conditions, there were serious epidemics of bubonic plague, typhus, typhoid, and smallpox; for the treatment of the first, the United States Public Health Service sent advice.[32] Resuming their plea for the surrender of American capitulatory rights in French Morocco, the French authorities were told that first there must be a commercial treaty safeguarding American interests, and the State Department again made a summary historical survey of its attitude on the matter.[33]

The diligence and intelligence of the regular consular staff in studying and reporting on every phase of the war affecting Morocco are attested by the voluminous reports made to the State Department. Most of these reports bore the signatures of Herbert S. Goold at Casablanca, John Campbell White at Tangier, H. Earle Russell, at Casablanca, and J. Rives Childs at Tangier. Since Murphy's "vice consuls" reported to their superiors in rank at Tangier or Casablanca, their dispatches were often sent on to Washington. Of the two other American agencies gathering information, the three groups of attachés reported to the War Department, but the O S S (Office of Strategic Services), in Morocco since October, 1941, reported to the regular consular head officers. The consular "establishment" was not altogether favorable to the vice consuls, and there was considerable friction between it and the O S S. An interesting comment on the O S S was made by Childs:

> We have had very effective cooperation from the O S S representatives here ... and none of the difficulties which I believe have marred the relations of O S S representatives with certain other missions .... As in the past, we shall forward to the Department only such O S S reports as we think merit attention .... O S S reports include rumors and hearsay .... I have informed the O S S representative here that he should not submit to the Department any recommendations on policy .... There is a greater possibility for inaccuracy in O S S reports, as we are careful not to send the Department any information which we have not checked in advance, or ... we state the fact with full reservations. The political reporting would be rated by me as of almost negligible importance, the economic reporting as of greater value, and the reporting of technical military data as of the greatest value. We have found the agents helpful in running down specific inquiries and in doing jobs indiscreet for Legation staff to undertake.[34]

Since Robert Murphy reported to the State Department, but had been told by the President himself, "If you learn anything in Africa of special interest, send it to me; don't bother going through State Department channels,"[35] and since the State Department not only had two schools of thought on North Africa questions, but also was frequently at odds with the Treasury Department on them, it can be seen that the situation was sometimes chaotic.[36] Furthermore, although instructed to cooperate closely with British intelligence, Murphy often found its aims and methods divergent from his, and so worked independently as much possible.[37]

However, all American agencies took great interest in the discovery and evaluation of Axis propaganda and in disseminating American counter-propaganda. Sent into Morocco to enforce the armistice provisions and to prevent any organization of resistance, the Italian and German Armistice Commissions were closely watched. However, the German group[38] succeeded in sending to Germany many items useful for the war. There were many German, Italian, and Spanish intelligence and police agents, including the Gestapo, not connected with the commissions. Noguès warned Moroccans and local Europeans not to associate with the commissioners and punished some who did so.[39] There were other organizations dangerous to the Allied cause, such as the S O L (Service d'Ordre Legionnaire), with a Casablanca chapter of about 400 men devoted to Vichy and armed and trained to resist any invasion. Later, S O L was reinforced by the Parti Populaire Français (P P F), founded by Jacques Doriot.[40] Even among the native Moroccans there developed an intricate network of espionage, probably not operating through semsars, but gathering information through the native guards, messengers, and house servants of foreign consular establishments.[41]

The large volume of correspondence sent to Washington by the American consuls indicates the high value placed by them on the American counterpropaganda. During 1940, Radio Berlin broadcasts in Arabic were considered very extensive and popular, but toward the end of the year, there began to be great interest in French broadcasts from Boston and New York, which refuted "the lying propaganda of certain foreign nations."[42] In 1941 it was difficult to get coverage of speeches of prominent Americans, such as Hull and Knox, and those accounts published were filtered through Vichy or Berlin. The French Moroccan newspapers also suppressed news of American war preparations and economic resources. To supplement British broadcasts in answer to Franco's support of Germany, the American consuls endorsed a defense issue of Life and illustrated pamphlets demonstrating the extent of the American production of armaments. Many anti-American articles appeared in the Spanish and Spanish Moroccan press, and both the French and Spanish press in Morocco gave much prominence to the speeches of ex-Col. Lindberg and ex-President Hoover. Efforts to publicize American economic aid to French Morocco proved to be futile. In November a dahir prohibited listening to broadcasts from Allied countries, which did not apply to American nationals. Although the French Residency objected to the distribution of informative pamphlets by the vice consuls after December 8, the State Department shipped over hundreds of copies of speeches by Roosevelt and Hull for distribution in the Tangier Zone.[43]

Despite the difficulty of securing adequate publicity for the President's speeches in May and September of 1941, Childs believed his distribution of the September speeches in French and Spanish had a favorable reaction except from Fascist extremists. The French Moroccan press gave prominence to Roosevelt's Navy Day speech in October, and copies of this speech were widely disseminated. However, the Spanish censor in Tangier deleted parts of this speech from the British Tangier Gazette.[44] Although the Roosevelt-Churchill declaration of the Atlantic Charter received the expected derogatory treatment by both the French and the Spanish press in Morocco, minor officials of the French Residency said that it had made an excellent impression.[45] Russell reported that the entry of the United States into the war had had a most favorable reaction. As expected, many minor officials of the French Residency now became more cordial toward the Americans. The average Frenchmen felt that he could let his natural pro-ally sympathy develop, while the natives followed the balance of power like a weather vane. "The popularity of the United States and of its cause is greatly increased."[46]

It was during 1941 that Roosevelt put into operation his rather nebulous plans of 1940 regarding North Africa. The pioneer investigator of this land, so little known to Americans, was an obscure American naval attaché to France, Commander Roscoe Hillenkoetter. In the summer of 1940 he made a rapid survey of North and West Africa. Finding there about 125,000 combat-trained French soldiers on active duty with 200,000 others in reserve, he reported to Washington that if France were to fight again anywhere, he thought that North Africa would be the place. Reaching the President, this report so impressed him that he summoned from Vichy the American Counselor of Embassy there--Robert Murphy. Roosevelt directed Murphy to secure permission[47] for another more careful study of the area. According to Robert Sherwood, the President's speech writer and later head of the Overseas Branch of the O W I, by August of 1940 the President had already decided upon an Allied invasion of North Africa to prevent probable attacks of the Nazis on numerous parts of the Atlantic seaboard. When Murphy made his inspection tour of North and West Africa in December, 1940, he was convinced that the French forces there could defend these dependencies if supplied by the United States with military equipment, petroleum, and consumer goods to satisfy native wants. Thereupon Roosevelt launched his personal policy for North Africa, which he maintained stubbornly in spite of much hostile criticism and obstruction, until finally in November, 1942, the first major confrontation of American and German forces took place in North Africa.[48]

Meanwhile, during 1941 before the United States was an active participant in the war, a very complicated diplomatic game was being played for the possession of French North Africa. After the armistice, which General Maxime Weygand, named commander-in-chief of the French forces too late to save France,[49] had advised as a military necessity,[50] Weygand was appointed proconsul of North and West Africa. There the task assigned him by Pétain was to hold these French territories, neutral and demobilized, out of the war. Weygand's reputation as an anti-German patriot encouraged Roosevelt to believe that his help might be obtained in bringing the French African regions over to the side of the Allies. To implement his designs, the President relied on two key diplomats: Admiral William Leahy, his ambassador in Vichy, and Robert Murphy, the President's personal representative, who worked with Leahy and later under General Eisenhower. While Leahy worked to prevent Pétain from handling the French empire or fleet over to Nazi control, Murphy labored with Weygand to lay the foundation for a political or military takeover of North Africa (and West Africa, if possible) by the United States. As previously explained, Murphy had his "vice consuls", the O S S and the O W I assisting him in his underground work against the many Axis organizations aiming to subvert North Africa.[51] Meanwhile, although a consistent opponent of General de Gaulle ever since his failure to take Dakar in September, 1940, Roosevelt was collaborating closely with war supplies and in ideology with Churchill, who was the chief friend and sponsor of de Gaulle. American consuls testified that throughout 1940 and 1941 there was a great deal of British propaganda in French Morocco favoring de Gaulle and that there were numerous imprisonments of alleged Gaullist sympathizers.[52]

Arriving at Vichy on January 5, 1941, Admiral Leahy did not disguise the fact that he was anti-Axis in sympathy. Although outspoken and frank in his dealings with Pétain, Leahy succeeded in establishing very cordial relations with the French head of state. Pétain was impressed by Leahy's store of information, gathered by a large staff, and also by his blunt honesty. Many American liberals, however, opposed both Leahy's mission and the sending of food to France by the American Red Cross. The French government not only withheld American credit for feeding France, but also aroused American resentment over Darlan's attempted collaboration with Germany, which Leahy helped to thwart. Another triumph of American diplomacy was Vichy's declaration of neutrality after Pearl Harbor.[53] However, Leahy was so exasperated at Vichy's aid to Rommel in Africa in February, 1942, that he threatened to resign.[54] But the restoration of Laval to the premiership gave such clear evidence of further Vichy surrender to the Germans that on April 15, 1942, all American residents in unoccupied France were called home and Leahy was summoned to Washington "for consultation." To the French people Roosevelt announced his policy in a fireside chat on April 28, 1942:

> We are now concerned lest those who have recently come to power may seek to force the brave French people to submission to Nazi despotism. The United Nations will take measures, if necessary, to prevent the use of French territory in any part of the world for military purposes by the Axis powers. The good people of France will readily understand that such action is essential for the United Nations to prevent assistance to the armies or navies or air forces of Germany, Italy, and Japan .... We know how the French people really feel. We know that a deep-seated determination to obstruct every step in the Axis plan extends from Occupied France through Vichy France to the people of their colonies in every ocean and on every continent.[55]

Already during 1941 there was much speculation in the press that North Africa was one part of the French empire that the United States would try to save from becoming a French military base for further expansion. American periodicals carried many discussions of the trans-Saharan railway being built under Nazi supervision from Oran to terminate ultimately at Dakar.[56] Since the "slave battalions" constructing the road were composed of thousands of German, Austrian, Czech, Polish, and Spanish refugees who had chosen to enlist in the Foreign Legion instead of being imprisoned in concentration camps in North Africa, the project was particularly obnoxious to the Allies. The Acting Resident General at Rabat protested against an article in Life of November 17, 1941, which charged that this railroad was being built to "favor an eventual attack of a foreign power against the American continent." The Germans abandoned the work unfinished after the Allied landings in North Africa.[57]

In his North African assignment, Robert Murphy was occupied much longer than Leahy had been at Vichy. When Weygand arrived in Algeria in the summer of 1940, he found that the economy of that country, as well as of Morocco and Tunisia, was disrupted by the British blockade, which had been imposed on both the French Empire and the Axis countries. The Moroccans were clamoring for tea and sugar, cheap cottons, and, more importantly, for tractor fuel, parts for their farm machinery, fertilizers, nails, wire, binder twine, bags, and lubricating oil. Also in demand were kerosene, coal, condensed milk for infants, and tobacco. Murphy discussed there needs with Pétain in Vichy. American business men wanted olive oil, cork, and other Moroccan products. When Murphy reached Algiers on December 18, Weygand was receptive to negotiations for economic aid for North Africa.[58]

The first problem was to make some agreement with the British government allowing American shipments to enter North Africa. There was opposition both in London and in Washington to breaching the blockade, but Roosevelt, Hull, and Berle were insistent. After several weeks of discussion, the British Ministry of Economic Warfare sent David Eccles to Washington, who made the desired agreement. On February 7, 1941, the British government expressed willingness to grant navicerts to ships bringing American goods to North Africa, providing that the United States would send an adequate crew of control officers to ensure that the goods did not reach the Axis. On February 26, Murphy and Weygand signed an agreement to that effect,[59] which was accepted by both American and Vichy governments.[60]

Although the Murphy-Weygand agreement had been intended to permit reciprocal American-Moroccan trade, it fell short of attaining that goal. American merchants wanted cork, tartar, and especially olive oil. However, Noguès refused Weygand's request that olive oil be exported to the United States. This action might have been caused by the intense jealousy of Noguès toward Weygand or by the fear that the accommodation of American desires might involve them both in Vichy displeasure. Darlan violated the agreement by shipping North African supplies to Rommel, and American supplies were very inadequate to supply Moroccan demands.[61] Cobalt, manganese and other ores were exported to "France," while the Allies could obtain no minerals from Morocco.[62] Still the agreement remained nominally in force as an evidence of American good will, and it enabled the "vice consuls" of Murphy to continue operating.

Without the cooperation of Weygand and his associates, American infiltration of North Africa would have been impossible. Weygand was devoted to Pétain and to the Marshal's type of French Fascist state, but he was patriotic enough to welcome aid from foreign states to restore the independence of France. He believed that no country except the United States could help France in 1941; he opposed any premature military invasion, but approved the economic approach arranged with Murphy. Meanwhile, Weygand kept up French morale in Africa and held his unarmed army together and in good spirits, while he collected and secreted as many supplies as possible for D-day. He was continually harassed by radio reports from London, which he attributed to de Gaulle, that he was preparing for independent action. Weygand was very bitter about de Gaulle's propaganda, which, he said, misrepresented the armistice terms and instigated disloyalty toward the Marshal's regime before it could prove itself.[63]

From June, 1941, when the American vice consul arrived in North Africa, until his recall from there in November, 1941, Weygand cooperated with the Americans. He clashed repeatedly with the German and Italian armistice commissions, and he opposed the Nazi-inspired measures favored by Vichy to relax his vigilant watch over North Africa. It was said that the German army actually favored American economic aid to North Africa, because it helped to keep this region quiet while Germany was using all her strength in the renewed effort to conquer Russia. Thus North Africa was isolated from the war at the cost of three tankers of oil products and six cargoes of other merchandise until Weygand's removal caused a suspension of the economic accord by the State Department.[64]

The dismissal of Weygand was not difficult to foresee. In May he refused collaboration with Darlan's proposed partnership with Hitler, in which Vichy had agreed to an infiltration of North African ports by German "experts," a sharing of Weygand's viceroyalty with the Nazis, and a campaign against the Free French in Equitorial Africa based upon North Africa.[65] Returning from Vichy in May, Weygand had gone so far as to discuss with a pro-American subordinate the possibility of a concrete detailed plan capable of being applied "from the moment that zero hour is reached."[66] He left as his legacy to the Americans the dissemination of his viewpoint among many civil and military commanders and their subordinates,[67] an inheritance that Darlan later dissipated by installing Vichy appointees throughout North Africa. The Nazis succeeded in ousting Weygand because of his unconcealed enmity toward them, the articles in the Allied press making him their hero, and the jealous hatred of Darlan for him.[68]

With Leahy and Weygand removed from the scene of diplomatic warfare, the completion of the project of taking over North Africa was left to Murphy and his group of vice consuls and the other American secret agents. Early in June, 1941, the vice consuls began to arrive. They were an odd assortment of individuals for the job--"recruited by the Army and Navy, but chaperoned by the State Department" as ostensible supervisors of the execution of the Murphy-Weygand agreement. But Kenneth Pendar, the most prominent of the group,[69] was informed by the military attaché that they were really glorified spies. He told Pendar what the army and navy expected from them--military maps and intelligence about the ports, the beaches, the ship movements, the size of armed units, the condition of roads, and the location of bridges, tunnels, and roads. The vice consuls were instructed to establish a secret communication and courier system and to organize the local patriots into underground resistance groups.[70] As director of their political activities, Murphy had control over their liaisons with the local French and Moroccans. With Weygand's secret permission, the vice consuls used their own codes and employed secret couriers with locked pouches, which made them most effective intelligence agents. The Germans avowed no fear of this timid, parochial, and amateur group; their secret report described them as a "perfect picture of the mixture of races and characteristics in that wild conglomeration called the United States of America .... Totally lacking in method, organization and discipline." This estimate proved to be somewhat of an exaggeration, although none of the vice consuls had any knowledge of Arabic or of conditions in Muslim countries, and only one had had any experience with shipping.[71]

From the beginning, Murphy's coterie of assistants, originally twelve, of whom half had dropped by October 1, 1941, found themselves in a difficult and dangerous environment. They escaped personal violence or theft, but were enmeshed in "a spider's web of espionage and counter-espionage." They learned to expect tapped wires and to talk always in an elaborate code, liberally ornamented with nicknames and American slang. Unfortunately some talked too much and to the wrong persons. Two men were sent to Oran, and the same number to Algiers and to Tunis; the others remained in Morocco. Murphy gave special assignments to each, and Pendar was delighted to receive the task he most desired--getting acquainted with the Moroccans and learning how to make them friends of America.[72] The German armistice commission watched the vice consuls closely, as did the Vichy secret police, and they were unwelcome at the American consulate in Casablanca. To Murphy, Pendar gives credit for unfailing tact and patience in building up an efficient group of assistants. Their economic work the vice consuls performed most capably, when the accord was in effect, but there were many interruptions in its operation, due largely to false rumors of impending German invasions of North Africa. At this time de Gaulle was making rapid progress in bringing West Africa and island colonies of France under the Cross of Lorraine, but in North Africa he was generally hated as a British stooge.[73] The Americans were more preoccupied with the German menace than with de Gaulle. Often Noguès was unfriendly and unwilling to remember the special position of Americans in Morocco. And until the Vichy axe fell in November, 1941, the precarious position of Weygand was a matter of great concern to his American collaborators.[74]

Nevertheless, Murphy did not despair of the success of the American plan even without Weygand. He had grown to trust many of the close associates of Weygand, and with Leahy's support was able to persuade the State Department that they would be as cooperative as their ex-leader had been. But the Murphy-Weygand accord was continued not so much because of Murphy's arguments as because of the attack on

Pearl Harbor. The December meeting of Churchill and Roosevelt in Washington was concerned almost wholly with French North Africa. Both leaders wanted their first expeditionary force to go to this area as soon as possible. And so the accord was revived, and more goods were sent forthwith to French North Africa. Again after Laval's return as premier in April, 1942, the agreement was resumed to prevent a blackout of the whole region. As before, every small shipment incited in Washington inter-agency arguments,[75] reductions, and delays until the actual November, 1942 invasion.[76]

A pertinent comment on the French in Morocco, whom the Americans were laboring to convert to the Allied cause, is given by Pendar:

> The men with whom we worked regularly ... were the French officials, army and civilian, the permanent population in Morocco. Like most colonels and military men, they were conservative, intensely nationalistic, intensely parochial. People back home wondered audibly why we didn't find de Gaullists or "liberals" with whom to work. We worked, like everyone else, with what we had, and what we had were people who were French and patriotic to their fingertips, but politically the equivalent of any group of stockbrokers in an exclusive Long Island club.
>
> ... North Africa was passionately loyal to Marshal Pétain .... The truth about Pétain had not percolated through to North Africa .... The French with whom we had to work ... were not only pro-Vichy; they were definitely anti-British. (There) was a parallel feeling against de Gaulle whom they considered a British puppet .... Back in America, I had taken it for granted that all anti-Nazi Frenchmen must be pro-de Gaulle. In Morocco, I found the men who could most help us in any military action, men of the highest character and devoted patriotism, were more anti-de Gaulle than they were anti-British ....
>
> This, then, was the political atmosphere of the French world in Morocco; anti-British, anti-de Gaullist, mystically believing in the old Marshal at Vichy, and yet, incredibly as it seemed to our American eyes, patriotic, anti-Nazi and largely willing and even anxious to co-

> operate with us as we began to build an American underground in North Africa .... In the meantime, as we made French contacts, we also made Arab ones.[77]

In this unfavorable milieu Murphy and his diminished group resolutely proceeded with the original plan of gaining political control over French North Africa, preparing the way for an ultimate military takeover. This task occupied most of the year 1942. In his assignment of cultivating the cooperative friendship of the natives, Pendar found that British propaganda from Tangier was disliked by them. He had to proceed cautiously, for Auer wanted him expelled for distributing anti-German tracts in French and Arabic--a charge that he denied. Childs also advised discretion to avoid antagonizing Noguès.[78] Pendar reported that up to March, 1942, German propaganda had been mostly ineffective, because based on so many broken promises and accompanied by the requisitioning of food needed in Morocco for use in Germany and Italy. Now a new and perhaps dangerous type of propaganda was about to begin, conducted by cosmopolitan and learned Muslims and appealing to religious and economic interests.[79]

During 1942 Russell reported extensively on unfavorable conditions causing native distress and unrest. The various epidemics then prevalent in French Morocco were caused by food shortages reducing the natives to semi-starvation, by a scarcity of clothing, and by high unemployment. Severe penalties were imposed for protests or criticisms of the current situation and crimes against Europeans. The Moroccans were either apathetically resigned or sullenly resentful in their complaints to trusted Europeans. Axis propaganda from the Spanish Zone or from the armistice commissions' agents was directed partly against the Sultan, whose replacement by the Khalifa of the Spanish Zone was advocated. In Fez there was much friction between the French and the natives. The Nationalists were looking anxiously around for some power to displace France as a protector. In Marrakesh, the populace was reported to be in general pro-British or pro-American, and considerably anti-French, in accordance with the known sentiments of their pasha, Al Glaoui. French requisitions of cattle and wool in the southern districts made them very unpopular. In the Sus, the natives fought off the militia sent to seize their sheep. In the south, German propaganda was unsuccessful as it produced neither food nor clothing. Wartime support of craft guilds in Marrakesh was certainly only temporary, in view of the French policy of having all manufactured goods imported from France.[80]

The work of recruiting reliable French collaborators for the American enterprise was even more difficult than attracting the Moroccans. Since the departure of Weygand, under Premier Darlan there had been a systematic weeding out of French officials suspected of being pro-American. General Alphonse Juin, appointed head of the military establishment of North Africa, had taken office under a pledge not to fight the Germans again. The dismissal of Monick, secretary general of the Residency, as well as lesser officials at Rabat, made Noguès more cautious than ever of showing friendship for Americans. After Laval's return to power in April, 1943, French officials practically broke off social relations with the Americans. Even in Tangier, the entire staff of the French Consulate General was discharged for being over-friendly with their American consular colleagues.[81]

An article in an American newspaper thus summed up the Vichy control over French Morocco on September 12, 1942:

> During Weygand's rule, the German armistice commission ... already controlled the economic life and interfered increasingly with the French administration there. German commissioners efficiently supervised public services, especially land and air transportation .... Yet, General Weygand and ... General Noguès were opposed to German interference and succeeded in stabilizing French rule over the natives.
>
> Today, however, French military command and civil service have been thoroughly purged and hundreds of officers and colonial administrators suspected of anti-German or pro-Allied feelings have been dismissed and returned to France .... (Juin) and many other high-ranking officers of his staff are ardent collaborationists and they faithfully follow Vichy's lead. New Vichy officials have taken over, who willingly bow to German wishes.
>
> For all practical purposes, French North Africa is on the way to become a Franco-German condominium ....

> Fighting French propagandists ... have been unable to persuade the natives of North Africa that General de Gaulle is fighting not only to liberate France but to protect the colonial peoples against Nazi domination. United States entry into the war, however, has not failed to impress the population of North Africa .... The Arab is realistic enough to understand that America's production power may change the outcome of the war .... American shipments of food and clothing .... which have been recently resumed, contribute to remind the natives of American wealth and of her good will toward the North Africans.[82]

It was the prime responsibility of Murphy to seek out, to evaluate, and to select the Frenchmen who could and would assist him in converting North Africa to pro-American feeling and action. This was a most difficult task. For eleven months after Pearl Harbor, offers of help were made to him --some sensible, others wildly impractical and by Frenchmen of extraordinarily mixed motives. Supporters of a revived monarchy under the Comte de Paris, advocates of a reformed republic like the Gaullists and others, and even defenders of the Pétain-Laval type of authoritarianism, all sought American aid to defeat Germany and Italy and to liberate France. From these many offers of aid, Murphy finally selected the "Group of Five," with whom he worked for almost a year, and who "patiently endured Washington's in-again, out-again, hesitations." Through this group, Murphy came into contact with the resistance underground in Algeria, Morocco, and Tunisia and even with a small underground Gaullist group in Algiers, headed by René Capitant, editor of the clandestine Combat. The other groups, however, lacked confidence in the Gaullists. It was Murphy's aim to obtain the support of the officers of the French navy, army, and air force, who were at that time predominantly hostile to de Gaulle. De Gaulle's popular support was impossible to estimate, because it was forced to be underground in the prevailing Vichy atmosphere. Murphy has given a graphic picture of the difficulties of dealing with these Frenchmen and of his disappointment in failing to secure the cooperation of Noguès and Michelier, the latter in command of the navy defending the entire coast of North Africa.[83]

The Five chosen by Murphy were a strange assortment of persons, reactionary, the Americans knew, but apparently sincere in their declared aim of establishing in French North Africa a provisional government operating independently of France. They hoped to find a suitable military leader, a task occupying the early spring of 1942.[84] After several months, events proved that the majority of them were Vichyites, not of the "legitimate" group, but the representatives of the Big Business establishment aiming to maintain a Franco-German economic monopoly in Europe. As such, their selection by Murphy and support by the American government won more severe castigation than the earlier Vichy policy had done.

Predominant among the Five was Jacques Lemaigre-Dubreuil, an aggressive business man of powerful personality, referred to as "Robinson Crusoe," who had moved to Algiers shortly after the fall of France. He claimed a false police record in Nazi hands showing him to be a pro-Nazi collaborator long before the war, which enabled him and his agents to travel freely all over France and in both West and North Africa. Murphy, who had known Lemaigre-Dubreuil since his Vichy days, regarded him as "a sincere and patriotic Frenchman who was doublecrossing the Germans and his Vichy connections so as to prepare the way for France's revival." By his marriage he had gained control of Le Seur and Company, the largest cooking oil concern in France; it was a business favored by the Germans as it utilized the olive oil of North Africa and the peanut oil of West Africa. Traveling between his factories in Dakar, Dunkirk, Casablanca, and Algiers, he had an excellent opportunity to bring Murphy information about relations between French industrialists and the Germans.[85] Apparently, Murphy did not know about Lemaigre-Dubreuil's pre-war record, which was extremely reactionary. He had been head of the Taxpayers League, always employing obstructionism, and with his brother-in-law organized the department stores to fight labor laws aiding their employees. With a controlling interest in Le Jour, he made it the Chicago Tribune of France. A fixer, a negotiator, an intriguer, rather than a banker, he nevertheless became a regent of the Bank of France as representative of the notorious "two hundred families." This regency tied him to the other Frenchmen who served Germany by delivering French economy to the Reich, in which the Banque Worms was the leader.[86] A more unlikely ally of the Americans could scarcely be imagined. His motives revealed themselves as the North African drama was being played.

As his chief lieutenant in organizing the subversive movement, Lemaigre-Dubreuil had his man "Friday," Jean Rigault. Nominally he was the business agent of Lemaigre-Dubreuil's oil company; actually, he worked only for the Murphy conspiracy. He had once been a Cagoulard. Pendar testifies that Rigault "served our interests loyally, risked his life for us, worked harder than anyone I have ever known for the cause, and after the landings, urged Giraud toward a democratic, liberal policy which the General unfortunately adopted too late." Jacques de Saint Hardouin was a career diplomat, ranking as counselor of embassy in the French Foreign Service. Since he repudiated Laval and Vichy, he was on leave of absence from the Foreign Service. His value to the conspiracy was that he could spend a great deal of time with Murphy without arousing suspicion. The fourth member of the group, Henri d'Astier de la Vigerie, known as "Uncle Charlie," was an important leader in the local youth movement in Algiers--the _Chantier de la Jaunessee_. A fanatical royalist and a devout Catholic, he had an almost hypnotic effect on young people, both Catholic and Jewish. He was largely responsible for plotting in Oran. His assistant and shadow, the Abbé Cordier, was younger; he was an equally fervent royalist and a Jesuit priest. "Both men," Pendar confesses, "were dangerous; both had a very odd reputation of political and even bloody intrigue back of them; both, used by the de Gaullists after the landings, turned against their former American friends." Finally, there was Col. A. S. van Ecke, "a great, brusque redheaded Dutchman of fifty ... known as "Robin Hood," for twenty years a member of the Foreign Legion. As the head of Pétain's youth movement in North Africa, van Ecke had an eager and willing army of youth to dispatch travel free about the country--an incomparable asset to the conspiracy, which had to operate in a vast area with one rail line, a scarcity of gasoline and strictly controlled air travel.[87]

These were "the Five." Lemaigre-Dubreuil personally attended to all contacts with France, "Saint Hardouin stuck close to Murphy, van Ecke issued false passes, d'Astier set about spreading the plot and recruiting adherents, and Rigault kept the conspirators' archives, which, for safety, he consigned to ... the Abbé Louis Pierre Marie Cordier, ... who, for extra safety, hid them in the Convent of the Sisters of Notre Dame d'Afrique."[88]

As long as Weygand was in charge of all North Africa, Murphy had hoped to enlist a number of French officers to aid the Allies. Weygand declined to head a revolutionary movement,[89] even when solicited by Roosevelt to command six or eight French divisions in North Africa equipped by the United States. In the spring of 1942 many French officers of various ranks in all parts of the region either promised to help or else offered only passive complicity. Among outstanding recruits was Brigadier General Emile Marie Béthouart, commander of the Casablanca Division. Another was Lt. Col. Louis G. M. Jousse, in the Algiers Headquarters, recommended by the Gaullist Achiary to Lemaigre-Debreuil. With Rigault, Jousse drew up a detailed plan of equipment needed by six divisions and 300 fighter planes.[90] But by April it was evident that only a massive invasion force to forestall the Germans from entering French Morocco had any chance of success.

Exasperated by the delays of the American government, on May 1 the Five informed Murphy that after sixteen months of clandestine planning with no definite response, they would be obliged to ask the British for help on May 20; if Murphy wished to continue work with them, he must promise to deal with their group alone. As a result, Roosevelt sent a messenger, Col. Solborg of the O S S, who made a formal promise that the United States would carry out the North African operation. All that the United States was waiting for, said Solborg, was a suitable military leader to command the resistance movement.[91]

Murphy had already been convinced by Lemaigre-Dubreuil that de Gaulle was not the leader they were seeking. All the high army officiers in North Africa were violently against him, and he had lost standing with the French because of his association with the British. Some leader must be chosen of undoubted prestige who had popular support. Lemaigre-Dubreuil was audacious enough to approach Edouard Herriot, the great democratic leader of the Radical Socialist party, pro-American, anti-German, and an opponent of the Vichy collaboration policy. But Herriot apparently did not wish to supplant de Gaulle, and he knew the record of those inviting him and suspected their motives. He refused the invitation on nineteen different occasions. Finally the choice was shifted to someone less suspicious of Lemaigre-Debreuil's motives.[92]

Lemaigre-Dubreuil then decided upon General Henri Honoré Giraud. In urging Murphy to accept Giraud, the Five cited many advantages he could offer. On April 17, 1942, he had escaped from the Königstein fortress,[93] which made him a national hero. He was undoubtedly sincerely anti-German; he had escaped from the Germans in World War I also, and at Königstein he had refused collaboration with them. He knew North Africa well, for he had seen years of military service there. Not being associated with the Vichy regime, he had not been tainted by British policy.[94] Murphy cites all these reasons for approving Giraud as leader, and still another:

> The American purpose in working first with Weygand and then, after he was cashiered by Vichy, hitting almost in desperation in Giraud, was that we needed a well-known military leader who would be satisfied to fight the war and postpone political decisions for post-war France.[95]

In other words, Giraud was acceptable because he was non-political; one of the chief objections to de Gaulle by both Roosevelt and the State Department was that he seemed to aspire to political as well as military control over France.

Probably his supporters did not know that although not openly "associated" with the Vichy regime, Giraud wrote Pétain a letter shortly after his escape (May 4, 1942) which was definitely a pledge of loyalty to the Marshal:

> You, as well as the Chief of Government (Laval), were kind enough to explain to me the policy towards Germany which you intend to follow. I am in complete agreement with you. I give you my word of honor as an officer that I shall do nothing which can, in any sense, disturb your relationship with the German government, or interfere with the task which you have put into the hands of Admiral Darlan and Premier Laval to carry out .... My past is a guarantee of my loyalty.

A second document shows the identity of Pétain and Giraud's political views. It was a 17,000-word analysis of the causes for the defeat of France, in which he duplicated one after another Pétain's reactionary and totalitarian opinions. Although Giraud might be an enemy of the Germans, he admired Hitler's principles and was happy to see the Nazi system applied to France, which Pétain was trying to do.[96]

Later, at the time of the invasion, the American press tried to make Giraud a glamorous figure.[97] His independence from Vichy was untrue, and his supposed military brilliance was equally fictitious. To his military credit nothing could be cited except the escapes from the Germans and being second in command under Lyautey in the Riff Campaign. He was anti-German, but he was also anti-British and anti-Russian, and he disliked the Americans. As Root sums up his character:

> Giraud was an excellent choice for Lemaigre-Dubreuil and his friends. A politically naïve general with reactionary ideas, Giraud could easily be manoeuvred in the direction they preferred. His chief task was to keep out de Gaulle and the republic, both dangerous to themselves .... He would not be wooed away from them by his new allies, the Americans and British, because he disliked them also. It was his role to divert their power, which the collaborationists had feared would be exerted for the reestablishment of democracy.

But Murphy was profoundly innocent of the real aims of Lemaigre-Dubreuil, and, although he became disillusioned later, he does not discuss in his book what time revealed as the real nature of the conspiracy of his chief collaborator. However, Pertinax (Andre Geraud) realized the true situation at the time:

> All Frenchmen opposed to Germany who at the same time want to save the Vichy Regime and prevent the restoration of the republic will flock to General Giraud, while former republicans take their stand by General de Gaulle.[98]

Lemaigre-Dubreuil reported to Murphy that Giraud was planning an American invasion of France, and several meetings were necessary to persuade him to participate in a North African campaign. He agreed finally on condition that the operation be entirely American and accompanied by a simultaneous landing in France. Also, he stipulated that he or another French officer be placed in over-all command of both French and American troops fighting on French soil. The matter of command was still unsettled at invasion time, and

General Eisenhower had the difficult task of convincing Giraud of American prerogatives in this affiar.[99]

While Murphy was conducting these secret and supposedly exclusive negotiations with the Five, he was also dickering surrepitiously with Darlan, at the latter's initiative. A five-star admiral and the founder of France's modern navy, Darlan was rated by Leahy as a "complete opportunist." Perhaps it was this characteristic that caused him to weigh the chances of the United States winning the war and to reinsure himself of being on the winner's side in any event.[100] After being deposed by Laval in April, 1942, he emphasized his own superior power as head of all naval, army, and air forces of France; again he pledged the departing Leahy that the French fleet would not be used against the United States. Then Darlan transferred his overtures to Murphy through his agent in Algiers, Admiral Fenard. On May 6, 1942, Fenard approached Murphy to propose that henceforth the United States should consider French Africa as a separate unit which could and would resume hostilities against the Axis "but only when the Americans are able to provide the material which will make such action effective." Darlan feared that any abortive raid similar to that on Dakar would precipitate the German occupation of North Africa. Throughout the next six months before the Allied invasion, Fenard kept in close touch with Murphy, as did also Darlan's naval officer son, Alain Darlan. Darlan proposed that French soldiers and sailors should be included in the Allied plans for Africa and for France.[101]

From Washington came no response whatever to Murphy's reports on Darlan's overtures. Only when serious planning started for the African expedition was the "Darlan problem" considered in London and Washington. Murphy thinks it was first discussed by Eisenhower's Anglo-American staff during his visit to London in September. The planners of the expedition needed all the help they could get--and both Roosevelt and Churchill wanted those French warships under Darlan's control. For the nineteen months preceding the invasion, Murphy and Darlan had neither correspondence nor personal meetings. When the night of the Allied landing arrived, therefore, the probable reaction of Darlan was still doubtful. No firm understanding had been reached with him, for two reasons. First, none of the Allies really trusted the Anglophobe admiral. Secondly, a definite agreement had been made to include Giraud in the landing, and it seemed difficult to persuade both him and Darlan to accept a joint enterprise on such short notice.[102]

Soon after negotiations began with him, Giraud named as his representative in Algiers General Charles Emmanuel Mast. The first general to join the Allied project, Mast was the deputy commander of the XIX Army Corps in Algeria. When Murphy returned from Washington on October 16, he had on his hands Mast, representing Giraud, and Fenard, representing Darlan. Both made new overtures to him, which Murphy reported only to the White House and to Eisenhower, as directed by the President. Acting for Roosevelt, Leahy authorized Murphy to make any arrangement that might facilitate military operations. Eisenhower devised a formula to induce Darlan and Giraud to share the top French command between them. Churchill was especially eager to obtain Darlan's--and his fleet's--participation. None of the American war planners had any idea that the "Darlan deal" would be disfavored either in Washington or London.[103]

In June, 1942, Churchill and Roosevelt had conferred again in Washington. Ever more insistently Stalin was demanding that a "second front" be opened by the Allies to relieve the Nazi pressure on Russia. In 1941, the decision to "beat Germany first" had been made, but Churchill maintained firmly that the Allies could not be ready for a cross-Channel operation until some uncertain date in 1943. General Douglas MacArthur's proposal that the second front be established under him in the Pacific against Japan was rejected. Opposed to the launching of a North African front in 1942 were MacArthur, King, Marshall, and Stimson. But Roosevelt and Churchill agreed that an invasion of North Africa was the only feasible action. On July 24, 1942, the Combined Chiefs of Staff in London voted tentatively for Torch, the occupation of Morocco and Algeria. Roosevelt and Churchill promptly made the decision definite, and on July 26, Marshall informed Eisenhower that he had been selected to be Commander in Chief of the Allied Expeditionary Force for North Africa. It was Churchill's job to break the news to Stalin of this nominal "second front" aimed primarily at stopping Rommel from reaching Egypt.[104]

The planning went on actively in Washington, in London,

and in Algiers. Murphy returned to Washington on August 31 to discuss plans and problems with the President and the chief and military leaders. He found Marshall and Stimson very skeptical of Torch; the former heavily discounted the plan on which Murphy had been working for almost two years in getting aid from French collaborators. Again Roosevelt declared his unwavering wartime policy toward the French: to refrain from the recognition of any one person or group as the government of France and to let the liberated French population choose their own government freely. Then Murphy traveled incognito to London where he gave Eisenhower and his planning staff much information and advice about the political factors of the situation. He found that

> the General disliked almost everything about the campaign; its diversion from the central campaign in Europe; its obvious military risks in a vast, untried territory; its dependence on local forces who were doubtful at best and perhaps treacherous; its bewildering complexities involving deadly quarrels among French factions, and Spanish, Italian, Arab, Berber, German, and Russian politics.

It was agreed that absolute secrecy must be maintained about the exact date, with the French collaborating leaders to receive only four days' notice.

Back in Washington, Murphy tried vainly to get the Board of Economic Warfare to release ships with supplies in time to reach North Africa by the date of invasion. He was made a "personal representative of the President" prior to the invasion and thereafter became the "Operating Executive Head of the Civil Affairs Section and Adviser for Civil Affairs under General Eisenhower." He also formulated for the President the rationale[105] under which the American troops would enter North Africa.[106]

Eisenhower has given a detailed account of the intricate planning in London for Torch. It involved all aspects, not only of the North African situation, but also of the entire world war. To General Mark Clark, first his chief of staff and later his deputy, Eisenhower gives the chief credit for the effective coordination of details in this first Allied plan for amphibious attack in the Mediterranean. That de Gaulle was excluded from the invasion landing, Eisenhower affirms, was because all reports from American consuls and other officials testified that his presence would incite determined opposition from the French officers and garrisons.[107]

Since the western part of the three-pronged amphibious operation was wholly American in ships and ground forces, detailed planning for that was done in the United States. This task introduced into the war one of its best (or worst) known generals--swaggering, swearing, pistol-toting, "war-intoxicated man," General George S. Patton. He had been training the nucleus of an American Panzer army at the Desert Training Center at Indio, California, from March 27 to July 30, 1942, when he was called to Washington to see Marshall. With only perfunctory plans, Marshall offered Patton the position of the first American general to lead American troops in action. Presenting great objections to the Torch plan, because he preferred a direct attack on France, Patton refused the assignment. Later he reconsidered and worked on plans for Torch in Washington from August 3 to 10, when Marshall sent him to London to investigate the deadlock in planning there. Converted to enthusiasm for Torch, within ten days Patton became the decisive influence in winning over Eisenhower and his staff to advocacy of the plan. When back in Washington, Patton continued planning for the Western Task Force. The 40,000 officers and men were to be shipped on thirty-six transports, cargo vessels, and tankers, escorted by sixty-eight warships, from Norfolk to French Morocco. An initial severe conflict between Patton and Admiral Henry K. Hewitt was converted into a harmonious relationship. The American navy arrived "on the dot," "probably the most remarkable feat ever accomplished by any navy at any time in the history of war." Patton's planning was impressionistic and fragmentary, which caused the Moroccan landing to be the most difficult of all. Patton's task force were to land at Safi, at Fedala, and at Mehedia and to converge on Casablanca. The men were assembled and trained by October 20.[108]

To the Center Naval Task Force, about 39,000 American ground troops, was assigned the taking of Oran. The Eastern Naval Task Force, about 23,000 British and 10,000 American soldiers, was to capture Algiers. Both were escorted and covered by the British Royal Navy and consisted of troops mounted in the United Kingdom. All expeditions were threatened by the Nazi U-boats on sea and while unloading and all were endangered by high surf at the landing places. One of the most astounding things about the whole operation was the secrecy with which it was surrounded.[109] To be sure, the evidence is plentiful that the Germans knew that such an invasion was planned, but they thought that it was coming in the spring of 1943, or that it was aimed at Dakar.[110]

De Gaulle declares that "the conspiracy of silence was futile, for information flowed in from America, from England, from France."[111] As early as August 27 he announced to his London Delegation the forthcoming incursion of the American troops into North Africa.[112] The American chargé at Vichy reported that Laval had discussed with the Nazis in Paris a Franco-German pact to defend French Africa against the Anglo-Saxons, who, the Paris papers asserted, were about to assault it.[113] However, by the end of the summer of 1942, Hitler seemed to be once more in the ascendant. German U-boats were sinking Anglo-American shipping faster than it could be replaced. Although Nazi forces in the West had been stripped of most of their troops, tanks, and planes to finish off Russia, their coastal fortifications on the Atlantic were strong enough to discourage any cross-Channel invasion. By September, 1942, Hitler's conquests looked staggering on the map. The Mediterranean had become an Axis lake, with Germany and Italy holding most of the northern shore from Spain to Turkey and the southern shore from Tunisia to within sixty miles of the Nile. German troops had reached the Volga just north of Stalingrad on August 23--on the same day that Rommel launched his offensive at Al Alamein to break through at the Nile.[114] Surely, nobody but a pair of visionaries like Roosevelt and Churchill would have had the temerity to risk sending their men and ships into such a maelstrom.

The high echelon planning of Torch in Washington and London was gradually extended to the politico-military field of North Africa, where Murphy continued its direction under Eisenhower, with Lemaigre-Dubreuil as master of ceremonies. The latter claimed later that he had advocated starting the invasion with Giraud commanding the Americans and then persuading de Gaulle to cooperate with Giraud. This subsequently became the basis of the Anglo-American policy. The plan to give Giraud command of French forces in North Africa to receive the American forces without opposition was approved by Laval, who also was secretly plotting with Lemaigre-

Dubreuil.[115] Just after Mast was selected as Giraud's representative in North Africa, Vichy appointed Mast head of the Algiers Division. Immediately Mast obtained Col. Jousse as his subordinate commander. Thus the conspirators got access to the secret reports, letterheads, and official seals, as well as all the military data to check with Murphy's laboriously collected materials. Then they knew all about every gun in North Africa and had a communication network available for instant use.[116]

There remained the problem of persuading Giraud to abandon his plan of an invasion of France and to concentrate on French Africa. After Murphy's talks with the Five on October 15, 18, and 19, an official accord was drafted in the form of letters exchanged between Murphy and Giraud. The French forces were to aid the American landings. In return, the United States government was pledged by Murphy, in the President's name, to the principle of restoration of France to full sovereignty and territorial integrity, both metropolitan and colonial, as of 1939. Also, the United States would enter North Africa only at French request, on a day selected by France, and would treat France as an ally, leaving untouched the internal administration of the areas temporarily occupied by her troops. Furthermore, the United States would arm France's new army.[117] This pact was of course, tailored to the pattern of Laval and Lemaigre-Dubreuil and was not one which Giraud could afford to reject.

To secure for himself the great power which the accord promised, Lemaigre-Dubreuil had to arrange a conference between the forces of Eisenhower and Mast. This meeting took place in an isolated farmhouse near Cherchell, about seventy-five miles west of Algiers. The Americans who attended, under General Clark, were General Lyman Lemnitzer and Captain (later admiral) Jerauld Wright and two other officers, who came in a submarine from Gibraltar. Mast and his French group represented Giraud; Murphy was attended by Knight, a vice consul, Rigault, d'Astier, Jousse, and Aboulker. Because of the secrecy imposed about the time of the landing, the meeting failed to achieve definite decisions. The Mast group thought that they had months to prepare for D-day, which was really only sixteen days away. Giraud's demand for over-all command of both American and French forces was evasively passed over. The status of Darlan was left undetermined, for Mast rejected the Giraud-Darlan formula devised by Eisenhower, and declared that the Allies did not need Darlan, because Giraud could easily secure the support of all branches of the French armed services. Mast made no objection to the inclusion of British forces in the Mediterranean for later service eastward into Tunisia. He presented a detailed study of airfields, arsenals, batteries, and other key points and a plan of invasion surprisingly almost identical with the American one. It was decided to neutralize all unfriendly senior officers by arresting them on invasion night. The meeting ended on October 23. There were some comic interludes, such as the police raid, when the French officers fled to the woods, Clark and his companions hid in the cellar, and Murphy and Knight put on a faked poker party with their host. All ended well, but Clark and his friends had a perilous return on the submarine. Later some French officers expressed bitterness over the lack of confidence shown them by the Americans and the consequent inefficiency imposed upon them in the landing operations.[118] However, Mast had an opportunity to vindicate himself and the Gaullist group to which he belonged in the American press.[119]

With the invading forces approaching rapidly, Murphy was left to cope with the problems of "legitimate" Darlan vs. "dissident" Giraud support and of securing the backing of General Juin, reported to be pro-American, but unfortunately released from a German prisoner camp on parole. On October 22, during the Cherchell meeting, Darlan started an inspection tour of West and North Africa--ostensibly to ascertain that all defenses were adequate to ward off an American attack. Accompanied by much official Vichy propaganda, the trip took him to Rabat and Casablanca, where he reviewed French and Moroccan troops and delivered a message from Pétain to the Sultan. On October 28, Darlan conferred with Juin and other generals on the defense of the empire. On the next day, after reviewing the Algiers Division under Mast, Darlan had a conference with Juin at which Murphy's October 13 agreement with Major Dorange[120] was discussed. After visiting his son Alain, ill with polio in an Algiers hospital, Darlan left Algiers on October 30. Returning to Vichy, Darlan made a speech pointing out the possibility of an allied attack on Dakar, upon which an elaborate feint had been made. Then he went home and burned many secret and private papers.[121] His conduct was truly an enigma--but hardly more double-dealing than that of Murphy.

Within the two weeks left before the landings, Murphy not only had to alert his partisans all over North Africa, but he also had to placate Giraud and Mast, without letting anyone know until November 4, the date of D-day. On October 27, Lemaigre-Dubreuil brought back from France a disturbing letter from Giraud, who wanted a written agreement that he would be placed in charge of the "International Command" within forty-eight hours after the expedition's arrival. He also wanted an Allied invasion of France very soon after the African operation began. On October 28 Eisenhower gave Murphy permission to inform Mast that the expedition would arrive "early in November." Mast was angered over American lack of confidence in the French allies, but he finally agreed to continue cooperation. On November 1 a letter from Giraud declared the impossibility of his leaving France before November 20. To Roosevelt Murphy then sent a message imploring a delay of the expedition for two weeks--an impossible arrangement, with the large American and British fleets already under way. In reply to Murphy, Leahy urged him to do his utmost to obtain the cooperation of the French officials. Accordingly, Lemaigre-Dubreuil flew again to France bearing Murphy's assurances to Giraud couched in ambiguous phrases. Murphy's final letter to Giraud emphasized that the United States would treat France as an ally and would put the military command of the region under the French "as soon as possible." Murphy said nothing about the British troops in the expedition or the Americans' decision not to make simultaneous landings in France. After "an avalanche of reproaches" for Lemaigre-Dubreuil, Giraud finally consented to come to Algiers a day or two before the invasion date to be there when the Americans arrived.[122]

The Vichyite part of the conspiracy also impinged upon events of the pre-landing week. A new actor now appeared upon the scene. He was General Jean Marie Bergeret, Inspector General of Air Defense. Reputed to be thoroughly anti-Allied, French historians assert that throughout the war he was secretly in touch with British intelligence.[123] In the Pétain trial it was testified that as early as October 30 Bergeret had informed Pétain that the allied invasion was set for November. Murphy saw Juin on November 2 and confirmed the agreement of October 13 about the Allied landings, but he did not reveal the date. On the next day Darlan sent Col. Chretien, head of the counterespionage branch of the French

Intelligence Service in Algeria to see Murphy. At their meeting at Guyotville on November 3 or 4, Murphy again "encouraged the Admiral's offer." At this time, says Admiral Docteur, a captain on Darlan's staff in Vichy informed Bergeret of a coded telegram from Lemaigre-Dubreuil, who had returned to Algiers, saying "Date advanced. Landings imminent." But that was the very day that Murphy decided that he must tell Lemaigre-Dubreuil and Mast that the landings were scheduled for the night of November 7-8. Bergeret immediately went with the news to Pétain, urging him to go to North Africa in order to dictate their course of action to the military leaders there. The Marshal refused to go; he would not "abandon forty million Frenchmen." That the Marshal had pre-knowledge of the landings is confirmed by Alain Darlan, who says that his father informed Pétain of "all the important events and facts of which he learned during the months before the landings."[124]

Earlier accounts of the curious coincidences of this period asserted that Darlan returned to Algiers on November 5 solely to visit his sick son. Ample evidence shows that he came secretly on a plane furnished by Laval and, finding his son improved, announced that he would stay until the tenth. On November 6 Bergeret informed Darlan that the landing was imminent. Admiral Fenard, who had summoned Darlan to Algiers, also knew that the convoys gathering at Gibraltar were destined for North Africa.[125] Laval was on the ground to assure that any change in the North African regime would be under his control and direction, and not managed by some non-official industrialist. There was, of course, the alluring possibility that by a successful takeover in North Africa Darlan could triumph over his hated rival, Laval--all in the name of the revered Marshal.

Meanwhile, Murphy and Mast worked frantically to use the three days before the landings to prepare their civilian and military forces to cooperate with the expected Americans and British. Remarkably, Giraud with a party of three escaped again--this time from a seaside villa in southern France, in spite of the surveillance of the local police and a special Gestapo dragnet. In transferring from the submarine sent to meet them, Giraud narrowly escaped drowning while moving into a plane. He insisted on going to Gibraltar first before proceeding to Algiers, where he was overdue, to get

Eisenhower's assurance that he would command the entire Allied forces.[126] Then, as Eisenhower tells it, "November 7 brought me one of my most distressing interviews of the war." Until past midnight he tried in vain to persuade Giraud to accept command of only those French who voluntarily joined him. On the next day Giraud agreed to accept this French command, but returned to his previous demand for an immediate attack on southern France; he could see no need for North Africa as a base for invasion of Europe. Finally, Giraud agreed to a compromise; the supreme command would go to the French as soon as they had the largest number of units, newly equipped, in the field, and the field would be North Africa. Four days late, on November 9, Giraud and two companions were flown to Algiers to meet the complicated problem of the anti-American resistance there. Landing at the airport in the afternoon, Giraud found no one to meet him, but was rescued by Murphy,[127] who was in search of Clark. He was sent in a car to the headquarters of the Five, where there was no one but Lemaigre-Dubreuil's private secretary to greet him. Darlan was now in practical control of the situation.[128]

In the absence of the American-selected leader, the three prongs of Torch had hit their targets. During the morning of November 7, the conspirators in the know had been thrilled by the announcement broadcast over the French program of the B B C: "Allo, Robert, Franklin arrive"--the signal of the invasion. During the night and the early morning of the next day, encouraging reports came to Eisenhower's headquarters. Because of the extensive preparations of Mast and his soldiers and the large contingents trained by Murphy and the Five, the landings met almost no opposition at Algiers, and the city was taken with no bloodshed. At Oran there was strong resistance from the French forces in that area, especially the navy. But by November 10 all fighting had ceased at Oran with an Anglo-American victory. Concerning the triple landings in Morocco, aimed to converge on Casablanca, Eisenhower was much worried because he received no reports either from Patton or Hewitt. On November 10 Darlan was induced to send a general cease-fire order. This stopped a general American assault prepared for Casablanca; at the other places fighting had stopped before the order was issued. From November 9 to 13 came the launching of the political offensive in North Africa, in which General Clark took the responsibility of finding a leader whom the North African French would follow. Since the French officers repudiated Giraud and would obey only their "legitimate" Vichy leader, the "Darlan Deal" was finally concluded on November 13. Thus runs Eisenhower's brief summary of the invasion.[129]

Murphy explains why "no campaign of World War II depended upon so many intangible factors." There was the grave danger that Spain, Germany, or Italy might intervene. The four days' notice allowed was far too brief to enable the pro-American French to prepare properly for assistance to the Americans. Giraud arrived after the event. Because British submarines failed to deliver equipment promised for the French underground fighters, most of them were able to obtain only a weird collection of inadequate weapons. An excessive number of major mishaps disturbed the military and political plans during the critical twenty-four hours before the landing in Algiers. No notice was given Murphy of the cancellation of a planned expedition to Tunisia in the first wave. Most serious of all problems, of course, was the conflict over the leadership of North Africa, centered in Algiers, the political capital.[130]

On the night of the expected landing, when Murphy was assured that Algiers was ready for a shotless capture, he had Juin wakened at his residence and informed him that half a million men were about to land along the coasts. Startled and shocked, Juin inquired whether the convoys seen the day before were going to North Africa, instead of to Malta. Murphy said that the United States was not attacking the French, but was coming to liberate France at the request of Giraud. Reminded of his frequently expressed pro-Allied sentiments, Juin said that Darlan was his superior and must be consulted. In response to a phone call, Darlan arrived quickly with Fenard. At first Darlan wrathfully accused the Americans of having the same genius as the British for making massive blunders; if the Americans had waited a few weeks they could have received effective French cooperation in a simultaneous military operation in France. Now France was endangered by a premature unilateral attack. Unyielding to Murphy's arguments, Darlan finally admitted that he would cooperate if Pétain approved. A message deliverd by Pendar to the admiralty was not acknowledged, but Vichy was informed that Darlan and Juin were American prisoners. While waiting for the arrival of the American troops, Murphy prolonged his talk with Darlan and Juin as long as possible. Learning the story of the arrangement with Giraud, Darlan passed judgment thus: "Giraud is not your man. Politically he is a child. He is just a good divisional commander, nothing more."[131]

At 6:30 A. M., Juin and Darlan were released by fifty Gardes Mobiles. There was no sign of the Americans, and the French army had been alerted. Murphy was held in Fenard's custody until midafternoon. Then Darlan released him to establish contact with Major General Charles W. Ryder, the commanding general of the Eastern Task Force, whose troops were now approaching Algiers. Murphy took Ryder to French headquarters where they met about fifty French officers headed by Darlan and Juin. After a short discussion, both parties signed a preliminary cease-fire which permitted orders to be given to stop the shooting in the Algiers area. On the night of November 8, many did not "suspect how deceptive was this outward appearance of spectacular success ... and how unsettled the relationships were between disputing French factions." Having initiated the "Darlan deal," Murphy was compelled to continue making independent decisions until five o'clock on the afternoon of November 9, when Clark flew into Algiers.[132]

Clark's arrival brought about a conference between him and Ryder and Darlan with their staffs. Clark tried to bluff Darlan with the claim that 150,000 Allied troops had already landed (there were only about 3,400 troops on shore near Algiers), but Darlan and Juin were skeptical. The conference was then postponed until the next day. On the table the Americans had left an envelope containing the harsher of the terms of two armistices. Darlan asked all present what was to be done. The consensus was that the French could no longer resist, and it would be better to accept the more lenient terms. Darlan cabled Pétain the terms of the milder armistice and added by a secret channel that his general officers agreed with him that it was acceptable. The Marshal cabled secretly that he was "in intimate agreement with Darlan" but could not answer officially before Laval's discussion with the Nazis. Darlan now considered himself free to deal with the Americans as he saw fit. He had one problem remaining--Giraud.[133]

Confronting Murphy in his office, Achiary, Jousse, and

Brunel angrily complained that he had no right to deal with a traitor like Darlan, especially since he had worked for almost two years with the "real Resistance." Murphy said he was sorry, but "I have my orders." At Dar Mahieddine, headquarters of the Five, the conspirators assailed Giraud for arriving too late for the landings. Giraud replied meekly that he had come to fight the Germans; if his superior, Darlan, was in charge, he could do nothing about it. Vainly the Five tried to convince him that France would never stand so good a chance with the Allies under Darlan as she could with Giraud, who had the support of the Americans. Giraud would think about it. At this point Van Ecke arrived from downtown Algiers to report that everywhere the opposition was winning; the heads of the Resistance were to be disciplined for breaking their oath to Pétain; many young rebels were in jail. Before midnight, Dorange accosted Giraud at Dar Mahieddine, demanding that he choose between asserting his authority and submitting to the alleged "legality" of Darlan. Worn out with fatigue, Giraud said that any position would suit him, if it led to resumption of fighting against the Nazis, and that he would be happy to resign governmental duties and devote himself to military affairs; Juin, he was confident, would accept a command from him. In an early morning meeting with Juin, Giraud accepted the title of commander in chief of the French forces, which Juin conferred upon him. But Dorange still had the task of persuading Darlan to accept Giraud--which, Darlan declared at four A. M., was still too early.[134]

On November 10, Clark succeeded in obtaining a general cease-fire order for North Africa from Darlan. But Darlan still hesitated; in Morocco, he thought, Noguès continued to fight, in Oran, General Boisseau held out against the Americans encircling the city,[135] and the Germans were rushing troops into Tunisia. Darlan asserted his necessity to hear from Pétain and stalled until Clark threatened to bring in Giraud to sign for the French. When Juin interjected that Giraud had no power and no one would follow him, Clark said it would be necessary to take Darlan under his "protection." Thereupon, Juin pled for five minutes; after eight minutes of heated argument, the French officers by themselves persuaded Darlan to give way. He then issued orders to the chiefs of the French armed forces to cease hostilities and observe neutrality. Furthermore, Darlan stated his price for compliance: "In the name of the Marshal, I assume authority in North

Africa. The present military chiefs retain their commands, and the political structure and administration remain intact. No changes may be effected until further orders from me." Thus easily did Darlan place himself in command of North Africa. Clark insisted that the problem of Giraud be postponed until after the cease-fire had been implemented.[136]

Although Darlan eventually agreed to add "and her Allies" to the order ending resistance to "the forces of America," he continued to be obstructive. That same afternoon of the 10th, he showed Clark a radiogram from Pétain dismissing him as commander-in-chief of all French forces and appointing Noguès as his successor. It would be necessary, he said, to withdraw the order he had given in the morning. Clark's reply was to make Darlan a prisoner under guard. Giraud now stepped boldly forward and demanded to be declared commander-in-chief of all French forces at once. Clark persuaded him to wait till the next day, while Clark tried to get Darlan to order the fleet to leave Toulon and sail to North Africa and to order the French forces in Tunisia not to resist the Allies. Darlan yielded to argument and sent some ambiguous orders to that effect.[137]

The German seizure of formerly unoccupied France gave Darlan a chance to strengthen his position. Another secret message from Pétain disavowed the dismissal of Darlan, saying that it had been sent under German duress. To Vichy Darlan replied that since Germany had broken the armistice and ended Pétain's independence, he would be faithful to the Marshal's inner thoughts and do his best for France. Juin then came to the rescue; he resurrected an old army rule that no French soldier could take orders from a chief in enemy hands. However, two French generals refused to march into Tunisia at Juin's "illegal" orders, permitting the Germans to consolidate the Tunisian bridgehead. Enraged, Clark threatened to arrest every general and admiral in Africa. Seizing the opportunity, Lemaigre-Dubreuil was able to send Giraud in full uniform to place a wreath on the tomb of the Unknown Soldier--an exercise appropriate for November 11. Giraud then issued a new proclamation, taking over North Africa in the name of Pétain to lead it against the Axis. But Clark had decided to support Darlan. Now Noguès returned his mandate to Darlan, and at the suggestion of Noguès, Giraud was assigned the task of recruiting volunteers to fight with Juin's regular army. On the following day, Juin, who had acted as a conciliator throughout the quarrel, got Noguès to agree that Giraud was worthy of a higher position. Noguès made three conditions; that de Gaulle not set foot in North Africa, that Giraud place himself under Darlan's orders, and that he hold his command in the name of the Marshal. The fighting generals yielded to Clark's ultimatum, and he assigned their positions; Darlan, chief of political affairs; Giraud, commander-in-chief of the armed forces; Noguès, governor of Morocco; Yves Chatel, governor of Algeria.[138] This appeared to be a final and equitable arrangement of a vexing problem;[139] it proved to be but the beginning of many vicissitudes for Giraud.

Although he had threatened arrest for all officers who refused cooperation with American plans, Clark allowed them to keep their powers unimpaired. At his first press conference in Algiers, Clark explained that he dealt with Darlan because he had discovered that he alone had effective power, but Clark's main desire was to unite both Darlan and Giraud factions. Clark cabled Eisenhower that he hoped that he had conciliated all parties under Darlan's general leadership. Eisenhower endorsed the compact for the American government. "Undesirables could be removed afterwards," Clark suggested, but this was not done.[140]

Meanwhile, although he was acutely resentful at his omission from the operation in North Africa, de Gaulle was doing his best to promote the peaceful surrender of the French to the Anglo-American forces. On the eve of the invasion he radioed this message from London:

> French leaders, soldiers, sailors, airmen, civil servants, French colonists, arise! Help out allies, join them unconditionally! The France that fights adjures you. Don't worry about names or formulas. Only one thing counts--salvation of our country.

Justifiably proud of the large part played by the Gaullists in the landing at Algiers and appreciative of the role of the Five in liaison work, de Gaulle regretted that the messages of Roosevelt had not ensured the success of the plans of Leahy, Murphy, and Clark. He prepared to send a mission to North Africa. On November 11 he addressed a great rally of the French of Great Britain. In his speech he claimed the right to lead in the reunification of the French people and denounced the so-called parallel enterprises that were dividing France's war effort.[141]

Beginning on November 7, Roosevelt had taken the lead in international propaganda by issuing a series of proclamations and appeals, in which Eisenhower also joined. To Pétain the President expressed his sympathy for the sufferings inflicted upon France and offered the continuing friendship of the United States in France's present resolution to prevent Germany and Italy from invasion and occupation of French North Africa, which

> would constitute for the United States and all of the American republics the gravest kind of menace to their security--just as it would sound the death knell of the French Empire .... The ultimate and greater aim is the liberation of France and its Empire from the Axis yoke. In so doing we provide automatically for the security of the Americas.

In his appeal to the French people, "my friends," Roosevelt stressed the historic Franco-American friendship. He said the Americans came solely to defeat and rout their enemies, and he appealed for France's help. Eisenhower issued proclamations to the French armed forces and to the people of North Africa. Roosevelt's special messages to the leaders of Spain and Portugal stated the same aims as in the message to Pétain and assured these rulers that they had nothing to fear from the United States. In a general public statement of war aims, the President was more explicit:

> This combined Allied force, under American command, in conjunction with the British campaign in Egypt, is designed to prevent an occupation by the Axis armies of any part of Northern or Western Africa and to deny to the aggressor nations a starting point from which to launch an attack against the Atlantic coast of the Americas. In addition, it provides an effective second-front assistance to our heroic allies in Russia.

On November 11, speaking in Rabat, Eisenhower saluted the memory of Marshal Lyautey with "the solemn assurance that his achievement--the North African Empire--shall remain French." Finally, the President thanked the Sultan of Morocco for his cooperation with the American forces[142] and declared that American victory would inaugurate a period of peace and prosperity for Morocco.[143]

From both Franco of Spain and Carmona of Portugal Roosevelt received replies indicating friendship and desire for peace. The reaction from Pétain was a severance of diplomatic relations with the United States and a sharply worded rejection of Roosevelt's statement of American motives and plea for cooperation.[144]

Secretary Hull utilized the occasion to claim credit for the North African invasion, although the plans had been made only by Roosevelt and Murphy, and much of the correspondence on them had not been seen by Hull until weeks after the events. Murphy has made this situation very plain:

> The State Department, which I still formally represented, did not receive my most significant reports until some time afterward .... The State Department asked me on March 10, 1943--four months after the invasion--to forward my last-minute correspondence with Giraud .... Roosevelt's decision to draft me for work under his personal direction, and his determination not to confide in Secretary Hull ... had one unfortunate consequence .... On November 8, before Hull really knew what was happening, the Secretary called a press conference and claimed a large measure of credit for the State Department .... For years he had been unfairly criticized for his "Vichy Policy," which in fact was Roosevelt's personal policy .... Now, when our relations with the Vichy government seemed to be paying off, Hull was disposed to exult at the discomfiture of his journalistic and other critics.[145]

As expected, from Hitler came the strongest reaction. Preoccupied with his war on Russia, he had from the beginning disregarded all warnings and advice from his staff concerning the importance of North Africa. Recently he had paid some attention to supporting Rommel at Al Alemain. The first news of the Anglo-American landings caused Hitler to instruct the Gestapo to bring Weygand and Giraud to Vichy and put them under surveillance and to direct Marshal von Rundstadt to seize unoccupied France. The occupation met only a feeble protest from Pétain. Then the Italians occupied Corsica and German planes flew in troops to seize Tunisia before Eisenhower's forces could arrive. On November 27 came the German attempt to take over the French fleet at Toulon, which resulted in the scuttling of most of the vessels by their crews. Hitler poured into Tunisia nearly a quarter of a million Germans and Italians, setting up a major obstacle for Eisenhower in his progress eastward.[146]

In the masterly fashion befitting a graduate of the Vichy school of politics, Darlan assumed his new role with the title of High Commissioner. His realm was virtually an independent country. After a farewell to Pétain, he had his secret radio destroyed. A public proclamation announced that Noguès had returned to him the powers received from Pétain. French North Africa continued to be a Vichy state; as many key positions as possible were given to Vichyites, and the S O L and P P F were reorganized. In Morocco they were formed into shock troops like the Nazi S A. Everywhere in Algiers smaller portraits of Darlan appeared beside those of Pétain. Gaullists were thrown into jail, and the very name of de Gaulle was taboo. Political news was controlled by 400 censors and the police state laws of Vichy. But Darlan needed to ingratiate himself with the Americans. He planned to do this by two clever actions: obtaining the adhesion of West Africa to the Allies' cause through Bergeret's efforts and incorporating the Five into his organization. On November 15 Darlan proposed his merger. He said that he had known about and had protected the clandestine conspiracy of the Five for a long time. A dinner celebrated Darlan's new cabinet: Saint-Hardouin, foreign minister; Rigault, minister of the interior and information; and Henri d'Astier de la Vigerie, chief of police for North Africa. Bergeret was Darlan's deputy. Preferring anonymity, as always, Lemaigre-Dubreuil had himself put in charge of a mission to the United States. There he planned to make deals, not only with business and financial leaders, but with Roosevelt and Hull. Still secret was the name of Darlan's director general for economics, Alfred Pose. But on November 17 Roosevelt had publicly announced Darlan to be a "temporary expedient" and had virtually apologized for his appointment.[147] Incidentally, on that same date Laval was appointed successor to Pétain and given power to make laws and issue decrees. The Marshal, too, had become expendable.

While the bitter ten-day political war was being fought in Algiers, the war in Morocco had been a military-naval conflict. Noguès had escaped the responsibility of Algeria craved by Darlan and returned to Rabat to resume his busy life there and to maintain the Vichy ideals in Morocco. He had already done his valiant best, before his visit to Algiers, to resist the Western Task Force under Patton and Hewitt.

On November 2, Rigault had begun the impossible task of preparing all military posts in Morocco for the D-day scheduled for the 8th. With General Béthouart, commander of the Casablanca Division, he worked out a plan to help the Allies land. The conspirators would neutralize Noguès and his commanders of the army and air forces so that Béthouart's orders to the French to aid the Americans would be obeyed. Resistance forces would cut off the Casablanca naval base from the rear. Unfortunately, Béthouart's plan that the landings be made at Rabat, Salé, Mazagan, and Safi, where his forces could help them, was ignored. On the evening of the seventh, Béthouart informed both Noguès and Michelier that the Americans were coming in force. The two men conferred and decided that the threat was merely a hoax; the most to be feared was a commando raid with possibly a Gaullist uprising. When the scheduled two A. M. landings had not occurred at five A. M., Béthouart himself lost faith in the announced coming, called his battalion back to its barracks, and surrendered to Noguès. The Casablanca commander likewise abandoned Béthouart. Thus the plan for a safe unopposed landing was ruined. Everywhere in Morocco the subordinate commanders were under orders to resist any invaders that might appear.[148]

On the absolutely dark night of November 7, one of the largest armadas ever assembled reached the Atlantic shore of Morocco. It divided into three sections, which, shortly before midnight, took their positions before Safi, Fedala, and the mouth of the Sebou river[149] near Port Lyautey. The 4,500 mile voyage had been miraculously successful. Warships of every type zigzaged constantly, feinting now toward England, then far southward toward Dakar. They passed unscathed through three separate screens of Nazi submarines, each of over two dozen submarines. In "submarine alley" between the Azores and the Canaries, about forty submarines waited for the ships, but the American destroyers dropped enough depth bombs to save every American vessel. Patton came with the intention of disregarding Marshall's directive not to attack the French forces unless they attacked first. It was Patton's own inefficiency, however, that forced a serious delay in his three-pronged attack.[150]

Landing at Safi at about 4:45 A. M., November 8--the first Americans ashore--were 6,500 troops under General Ernest N. Harmon. Overcoming French resistance, the Americans soon occupied the harbor, the railroad station, the postoffice, and the highways entering the city from the south. By nine A. M. of the tenth Harmon headed his tanks northward to Casablanca, one hundred forty miles away. At Port Lyautey the delay in landing caused the failure of Béthouart's arrangements, and the Americans had to fight four days against the French troops reinforced by mechanized cavalry. Attempting to take a letter containing Roosevelt's message to the French commander at Port Lyautey, Colonel Delmas F. Craw became the first American killed in the war.[151]

Meanwhile, the main American attack on Casablanca went forward from the landing beaches near Fedala.[152] Had Béthouart's advice to land at Rabat been followed, even after he capitulated to Noguès, the latter could have judged the expedition's size and power and would probably have decided to surrender without fighting. The landing was delayed several hours, many of the landing craft were swamped, and a number of soldiers were drowned. Patton himself spent eighteen hours on a beach helping to unload the supply boats. Without aerial reconnaisance and signal communications, Patton could not communicate with Eisenhower. The Americans initiated a bombing attack on the French submarines in the harbor and on the _Jean Bart_, immobilized at its mooring. Receiving information that Algiers was still resisting, Noguès did likewise. A fierce naval battle occurred on the 8th, and by nightfall Michelier informed Vichy that all ships of the second squadron were either sunk or unable to function. About 1,000 French sailors were casualties. Michelier lined up the survivors into battalions to oppose the Americans on their way from Fedala. By official defenders of the "Darlan deal," much credit has been given to Darlan for stopping hostilities by his cease-fire order. As has been indicated, the firing had ceased in Algeria and Oran _before_ his order. That the surrender of Noguès at Casablanca was not influenced by Darlan was admitted by Noguès in an interview published in the Chicago Daily News on February 9, 1943. In this he said that he had decided to quit fighting on Monday (Darlan's order reached Casablanca on Wednesday morning), after notifying Vichy and securing the approval of the local German armistice commissioner. He did not mention Darlan. On the 10th, the Jean Bart was sunk by American fire. Patton had now decided to take Casablanca by a combined assault of all his forces. But a message from Juin got through just in time on the morning of November 11 for Michelier to surrender before Patton began his attack. Thus Casablanca was saved from destruction.[153]

Later in the day, Patton, Hewitt, Noguès, and Michelier met for a polite conference, at which Noguès refused to accept the armistice terms offered. Noguès had his way about Béthouart and five of his subordinates; they were imprisoned and charged with rebellion. Luckily for them, Eisenhower intervened and secured their release; on November 17, Béthouart and Magnan were flown to Algiers. As for the situation imposed upon Morocco by Noguès, it was similar to the regime set up in Algeria by Darlan:

> For an undue length of time pro-American French remained in custody, while those hostile to the Allies before the landings, followers of Pierre Laval, remained in positions of trust and power. The Frenchmen of authoritarian sympathies, some of them members of fascistic societies like the Service d'Ordre Legionnaire des Anciens Combattants and the Parti Populaire Français and others in less formal associations seemed prepared even to assist an Axis counter invasion. They propagandized against the Allies.[154] Frenchmen of pro-Allied views, whether Giraudist or Gaullist, were the object of their surveillance and open hostility. Specific denunciations of these anti-American individuals to American civilian officials were of little or no avail, for their hands were tied by military control. The position which General Patton took was that 'the anti-Darlan-Noguès group does not have the personnel nor is it in a position to control Morocco if given that mission.' ... Noguès was suspected of maintaining ties with Vichy and perhaps thus with the Germans even after November 15 .... General Patton became in effect a defender of General Noguès as

an indispensable agent who could keep the native population in hand while the French in Morocco were in general kept friendly and neutral.[155]

For three months after November 15, 1942, "General Patton's letters read like the travelogues of a starry-eyed tourist rather than a conquering hero and commanding general of an army that still had most of the war ahead of it." On November 16 Patton began his grand tour of Morocco. He paid several visits to Noguès and the Sultan at Rabat; the former always received him with splendid pageants. Among the parades and reviews were participation in a festival of sheep and a boar hunt. Apparently he was reviving the role of a Moorish pasha of the 16th century. While his troops bivouaced in a cork forest between Casablanca and Rabat, Patton moved his office into the ultramodern Shell building in Casablanca. With a huge Packard equipped with a special horn announcing his arrival, he traveled everywhere. He resided in an elegant villa in an exclusive suburb of Casablanca. Craving military action all his life, he now sank into a lethargy of luxury. However, his headquarters staff worked hard to clear up the rubbish of battle, to open the ports, and to train his troops for integration with the French forces into the Allied war machine. Yet it seemed highly incongruous that Patton's headquarters became a gay social center while desperate fighting was going on in Stalingrad, Tripoli, Tunisia, and on the Atlantic.[156]

The Morocco radio became an instrument of Vichyite operators to broadcast pro-Axis propaganda, and Noguès himself discussed with Hitler's agents in France measures to oust the Americans from Morocco. Twice Churchill voiced to Roosevelt his alarm and disapproval at conditions in Patton's domain and in Algeria. Pendar, who had worked so many months to liberate Morocco from Vichy, now regarded Patton's fraternization with the Vichyites as a betrayal of American trust. Apparently, Patton was both dazed and fascinated by the pomp, ceremony, and imperial glitter which Noguès displayed for his seduction.[157]

However, Patton rightly valued the "correct" behavior of Noguès. He was keeping his bargain to cooperate with the Allies for military purposes. He kept public order. For the supplies pouring into the ports, he supplied native labor for handling, and he guarded the shipment of these supplies to the battle front over hundreds of miles of narrow-gauge railways and rough roads. Above all, he relieved Patton of interference in "French politics," and he managed the "Jewish problem" adroitly.[158]

On March 5, 1943, came Patton's great opportunity to give up the position in Morocco for which he was so unsuited and to get back into combat. He had already been asked to prepare for the invasion of Sicily, named by code "Husky." Now he was directed to reorganize and help to lead the army fighting in Tunisia, which was in danger of disintegration. The conquest of Tunisia brought together the trio who eventually won the war in Europe--Eisenhower the coordinator, Bradley the thinker, and Patton the fighter. The Tunisian campaign did not end until May 13, 1943. It was a valuable exercise in Anglo-American cooperation in battle, and it taught the inexperienced Americans how to fight Germans.[159]

From the beginning, the attitude of the Muslims in North Africa and elsewhere toward the Anglo-American occupation had been important, although only their leaders were articulate. The natives of North Africa refrained from revolts, which might indicate either approval or apathy, or possibly efficient suppression. Hitherto a good friend of Noguès, after the Allied landings Muhammad V dissociated himself from the Resident General and made common cause with the Americans. A large number of Moroccan troops were placed under Allied commanders. On November 25 the President received an answer to his letter of the 7th, saying that the Americans had been received as friends as soon as Morocco had discharged her debt of honor to France. Congratulatory messages were received also from the political heads of Trans-Jordan, Iraq, Syria, and Lebanon. Loyalty of Muslims to the Allied cause was pledged by members of the Permanent Council of War Economy, representing Algerians, Moroccans, Tunisians, and French West Africans. Leaders representing most states of the Arab-speaking world asked that Anglo-American aid be given, not to separate North Africa from France, but to guarantee the natives greater economic, educational, and cultural advantages. This could be done, they said, within the framework of the Atlantic Charter.[160]

While Patton had been enjoying the life of a proconsul

in Morocco, the political intrigues continued in Algiers. Darlan suffered a loss of prestige because of the scuttling of his fleet in Toulon. Vichy revoked his French citizenship and castigated him as a hoarder of rationed food. On November 30, in an attempt to strengthen his position he formed an Imperial Council to rule all French Africa by decree. Its members were Noguès, Boisson, Chatel, Bergeret, and Giraud. He had not consulted the Allies about this move, which was repudiated in the British Parliament. Eisenhower also received a message telling of Hull's wish for all civil matters in North Africa to be put under the State Department as soon as the military situation permitted. Just then Eisenhower received a heavy blow; the attack headed by the British General Anderson aimed at driving the Germans from Tunisia by Christmas was smashed.[161]

Just as Darlan was facing a storm of opposition from Great Britain and Eisenhower was debating with whom to replace him, de Gaulle was extending his influence. Shortly after the American landings, fighting France extended her authority over all the French colonies in the Indian Ocean. A French corps under General Leclerc, brought across the Sahara from Chad, conquered Fezzan and entered the combat on the Mediterranean coast. De Gaulle annexed Fezzan on January 13, 1943. Learning of virulent criticism of Darlan by Vichyites, Gaullists, and the Five's adherents, de Gaulle determined to send a mission to Algiers. Washington and London had "invoked a thousand pretexts" to prevent the earlier mission proposed. Early in December, Eisenhower granted permission for General François d'Astier de la Vigerie[162] to go to Algiers. General d'Astier arrived in Algiers on December 20, 1942. He found there a bitter conflict smothered by the police machinery. Humiliated by his whole career in North Africa, Giraud was willing to cooperate in military matters with de Gaulle. The Count of Paris offered to arbitrate any dispute over the union of French forces. Boldly, Lemaigre-Dubreuil offered to make de Gaulle minister of war in a provisional government under himself as premier. It was surprising that for a time Darlan favored offering de Gaulle the vice-presidency of the Imperial Council. Henri d'Astier, however, proposed the Count of Paris, not as a monarch, but as a mediator. Encouraged by Murphy, de Gaulle's envoy obtained an interview with Darlan, who insisted that he himself was the only possible rallying point for French union. Darlan then reproached the envoy for stirring up trouble and demanded that he leave Algiers. D'Astier returned to London on December 24--the day that Darlan involuntarily abandoned his position.[163]

To get rid of Darlan "legally," the plotters tried to revive a law of 1872, which granted to the General Councils of the departments of France the powers of the government if France were incapable of governing herself. So Henri d'Astier met with the three elected heads of the Algerian departments and asked their assistance to restore constitutional government. The three councilors wrote Darlan a letter, charging that since Pétain was now a German prisoner and Algeria was liberated, Pétain's delegation of authority to Darlan was therefore void. They suggested that Darlan should vacate his office. Similar letters to Darlan and to Roosevelt were unanswered. A coup was then planned for December 18, supported by "certain military figures," the councilors would call on Darlan personally and eject him by force if he refused to resign. Then they would summon the Count of Paris to take his place. Rebuffed earlier by Pétain and Laval, the Count now said that he would take the lead, not as a candidate for the throne, but as a conciliator, on two conditions--that there be no bloodshed and that the Allies approve of his action. On December 10, under the pseudonym of M. Robin, the Count was told that Giraud, Noguès, Boisson and Bergeret would choose him as head in North Africa if Darlan should disappear. Then came a sudden end to the plot. Eisenhower refused to consider any political change that might endanger his efforts to mount a major attack in Tunisia. That same day the American government gave Darlan further support by announcing that his army would receive its arms and supplies through Lend-Lease as a military arrangement. The Count of Paris then retired quietly from the contest, but Henri d'Astier continued to plot for him. On December 20 a new conspiracy was formed. Excluded from it were Bergeret, Rigault, and Lemaigre-Dubreuil.[164]

Darlan had refused François d'Astier permission to travel all over French Africa to talk with Gaullists. But d'Astier's hotel room in Algiers became a meeting place for all opponents of Darlan, and he decided to form a secret Gaullist triumvirate in Algeria to promote the Gaullist movement. The trio was to be composed of his brother Henri, René

Capitant, and Louis Joxe. He gave his brother Henri $38,000 in cash, presumably for Gaullist propaganda. How Henri d'Astier could sponsor Gaullist and royalist plots simultaneously is not clear. On December 23, after a luncheon for several Allied leaders, Darlan told Murphy of "four plots to assassinate me" and asked what the Americans would do if one of them succeeded. He also showed Murphy a list of possible successors to himself, on which were the names of de Gaulle, Giraud, Flandin, Reynaud, and Herriot.[165]

On the next day, Darlan's premonition was fulfilled; he was shot when entering his office at the High Commissariat and died before evening. Bearing a false identity card and a passport for Spanish Morocco, the assassin was identified as Fernand Bonnier de la Chapelle, a youth of twenty. Clark and Murphy urgently summoned Eisenhower and Giraud from the front.[166] The Americans could not afford to allow the election of Darlan's successor to take place without their guidance and approval.

The contest for succession to Darlan was in full force on Christmas Day. The Count of Paris, lunching with Bergeret, asked the latter's support of his candidacy before the Imperial Council; he wished to hold the position of High Commissioner only until victory, when he would return his power to the French people. Bergeret agreed to report the demarche to the Council, but called Boisson, Noguès, and Giraud to a conference. Learning that Bergeret's preference was for Noguès, Murphy said that American public opinion would never stand for him. Murphy then recommended Giraud, who was endorsed also by Saint-Hardouin. Then Giraud arrived from Tunisia; in a hurry to return to the battle front, he had no desire to become High Commissioner. However, he yielded to the persuasions of Clark and Eisenhower. Bergeret decided to support Giraud also, and Murphy, who had encouraged the Count of Paris, asked instructions from Washington. The President, too, favored Giraud. As Eisenhower says in his Crusade in Europe, "In our inner councils we doubted Giraud's ability to establish himself firmly in the chief position--but no one else was both acceptable and immediately available." Meanwhile, acting under a secret decree of December 2, the Imperial Council had selected Noguès to act in the emergency. He made it clear that he did not want the position permanently. The Count of Paris was still naïve enough to think that he had a chance. On December 26, going to Giraud to plead for the assassin, the Prince was informed that the murderer had been executed and received from Giraud a bluff denial of his ambition to act as "conciliator." At the noon meeting of the Imperial Council, the Prince was not even mentioned, and Giraud was elected unanimously, for he voted for himself. His title was "civil and military commander-in-chief."[167]

At the court martial on the night of December 25, the young assassin was proved to have been a member of the *Chantiers de la Jeunesse* and to be now in the *Corps Franc*. Bonnier repeatedly insisted that he had acted without accomplices "to bring justice to a traitor who stood in the way of the union of France." His defense lawyer asserted that the inquest had been too hasty, but the military judges contended that Bonnier's confession and capture in the act obliged them to rapid action. After a short deliberation, the tribunal condemned him to military degradation and death by shooting at the next dawn. Both Noguès and Giraud refused the plea of Henri d'Astier for a stay of execution. In vain the Abbé Cordier endeavored to get support for the youth. In his last few minutes, Bonnier wrote a note to the Abbé pleading for immediate intervention. At exactly 7:45 A. M. he received the fatal volley of shots. As one reporter wrote, the War Council, "octogenarian reactionaries," would soon try to "bury the Admiral, bury the boy, and bury the story."[168]

But the story would not stay buried. Police investigations uncovered some startling evidence that the murder had involved several persons, in spite of the confession reported by two police officers who had guarded Bonnier the last night of his life, in which he had claimed sole responsibility. A wild rumor developed that another greater plot to gain power for someone called for the assassination of Giraud, Murphy, Chatel, and others. Giraud was "truly amazed" at the list of suspects shown to him, for everyone on the list had worked in the *coup* of November 7 to put him in power. Bergeret could not trust Rigault or d'Astier to arrest the suspects, so he impressed the *Gardes Mobiles* into service to "arrest certain German spies." In all, fifteen lawyers, jurists, professors, doctors, police chiefs and industrialists were arrested as Axis spies. They were the leading Gaullists, arrested by Bergeret, with Giraud's approval. Esquer charges that Bergeret, "in accord with Rigault, Chatel, and the financiers, devised the whole scheme of an imaginary plot to murder Giraud and Murphy." Later when Reneé Gosset asked Rigault whey he had attacked the Gaullists, he replied, "Because they bothered me. They agitated too much. They bothered even the Americans." Behind Rigault stood Lemaigre-Dubreuil.[169]

On December 28, in Washington, Hull had a visitor, Lemaigre-Dubreuil. The Secretary expressed his gratification at the election of Giraud to power. Two days later Lemaigre-Dubreuil wrote Leahy requesting that the Darlan-Clark accord be given up in favor of the Murphy-Giraud agreement as the basis of Franco-American relations. Also, he asked that Giraud's government be permitted to accredit diplomatic representatives abroad. What Lemaigre-Dubreuil wanted was the complete elimination of de Gaulle from power.[170] Further discussions at the State Department determined the conditions under which Giraud, besides being the military leader of the French, would also represent and defend abroad French interests, of which he was to become trustee. Thus the Murphy-Giraud agreement was restored to its original validity. In the meantime, Churchill in London was preparing for the support of de Gaulle's Free French committee, trusting that a union of Giraud with de Gaulle would enable the latter's superior political ability to triumph over Giraud's political naïveté. Rigault could find no better way to defend Giraud's position than to damn the principal supporters of de Gaulle in Algiers as plotters of assassination.[171]

In chains, the alleged plotters were sent to a concentration camp 200 miles into the Sahara. From there their probable destination was 3,000 miles away across the desert to a prison camp in Mauretania. From this fate they were saved by American newsmen and members of the Psychological Warfare Branch.[172] At a press conference Giraud refused to name the prisoners, intimating that some were Axis agents. The affair was purely an internal affair for the French, he said. At a second conference Rigault said that the arrests were merely to clear up Darlan's murder and to make sure that no more were planned. Rigault then suggested that the reporters should not reveal the truth that the men arrested had Gaullist connections, as this would make a union of Frenchmen more difficult. The whole affair was censored from the North African press.[173]

The clearing up of the Darlan murder came not from the arrests but from a police commissioner, Garidacci, who told the prefect of Algiers that the four policemen arrested were entirely innocent. The Abbé Cordier and Henri d'Astier de la Vigerie were both implicated. A search of d'Astier's house in Algiers revealed the $38,000 brought by François from London and the dummy front page of a newspaper announcing a coup d'état. A large photograph of the Count of Paris was flanked on either side by pictures of Giraud and de Gaulle. The headline space was vacant--apparently to announce the departure of Darlan. Under a three-column headline was the proclamation of the assumption of power by the Count of Paris. Through the work of three security men arriving from France on January 3, by January 9 a formal report could be drawn up for the Civil Tribunal of Algiers. Signed by the Gaullist Achiary, the report began by accusing the Abbé Cordier and Henri d'Astier de la Vigerie of being the direct instigators of the murder of Darlan. They had had the Admiral assassinated on behalf of the Count of Paris. To this charge Achiary added much personal testimony. Achiary had not reported earlier because he still regarded d'Astier as a comrade with faith in the final victory of the Allies and as a chief of resistance against the Germans; also, d'Astier was the chief of police and was probably acting for the government.[174]

When Murphy learned of the arrest of Cordier and d'Astier at six A. M. on January 10, he was horrified. Later Alfred Pose was charged with leadership in the plot and two other men were indicted for minor parts in it. The Abbé Cordier claimed innocence, saying merely that he had heard Bonnier's confession on the morning of the crime in an isolated street; he then took shelter behind the privilege of sacerdotal secrecy. On January 11, Commissioner Garidacci was arrested and confessed to having acted in a "flagrantly criminal" manner. He admitted that he had withheld Bonnier's original confession and had revealed instead a second one in which the boy insisted that he had acted alone. The true confession ran thus:

> I affirm having killed Admiral Darlan ... after having told the Abbé Cordier that I would do so in the form of a confession. It was M. Cordier who gave me the plan of offices at the Commissariat and of the office of the

> Admiral; it was through him that I was able to obtain the pistol and shells which I used to execute the mission I had assigned myself which was to dispose of the Admiral ....[175]

Further investigation showed that Bonnier was a member of the Corps Franc, a group of young men, mostly veterans of the coup of November 7, and volunteers under General Monsabert, but officially recognized by Giraud's order of November 25. Ever since Darlan had stolen their victory of November 7, they had resolved that he must go. On December 19 they decided that the time had come. When two young men selected by lot refused the job, Bonnier volunteered to do it. The details of the task were all arranged for him by the main conspirators, and the Abbé Cordier gave him absolution before the crime. Garidacci himself had persuaded Bonnier to make the second confession. At first Giraud had demanded light on the affair; later he felt required "to let silence grow heavy" on it.[176]

During the inquest a rumor had spread through Algiers that the assassination had been planned by the Allied Secret Services and that two British intelligence agents involved in it had been identified. Eisenhower threatened to resign if any British connection with the deed could be established. But the military investigators ended their work with the confession of Garidacci. The American reaction was to strengthen support of Giraud. At a Cabinet meeting on January 7, Roosevelt confirmed Eisenhower as chief over North African Affairs with Murphy as civil affairs adviser under him. Then Churchill increased his influence by getting Roosevelt's consent to having Harold Macmillan as his personal representative at Eisenhower's headquarters. On January 11 a broadcast from Algiers first informed the world about the royalist plot and the principals in the conspiracy.[177] Still to many the murder of Admiral Darlan remains a mystery.[178]

President Roosevelt denounced the assassination as "first degree murder," and Secretary Hull condemned it as "an odious and cowardly act." In his memoirs Murphy, who consistently supports the "Darlan deal," said of its abrupt ending:

> Many commentators in the United States and England wrote

> that Darlan's death was a fortunate break for the Anglo-Americans, relieving us of the intolerable burdens of the "Darlan deal." That never was my feeling. President Roosevelt knew he could have Darlan's resignation instantly if he requested it. Clark and I ... agreed that Darlan had contributed as much as any Frenchman to the success of a highly speculative military and diplomatic venture.

However, it is almost certain that the majority opinion of the informed public in both Great Britain and the United States was expressed by Freda Kirschwey, editor of the Nation:

> The assassination of Darlan was a free gift to the United States. Everyone felt this, no matter what he said publicly .... What the unknown Frenchman gave America was a second chance.[179]

For the ultimate benefit of de Gaulle's France, Darlan left an important legacy--the new American-equipped French army. As early as the beginning of May, 1943, the American press reported the progress being made in the rearmament program. Murphy thus summarizes the achievements under the Clark-Darlan agreement:

> The United States fully equipped and trained eight French divisions in North Africa, partially outfitted and trained three more in France, supplied equipment for nineteen air squadrons, and also extensively re-equipped the French navy .... The United States supplied the French with fourteen hundred aircraft, thirty thousand machine guns, three thousand artillery guns, five thousand tanks and selfpropelled weapons, and fifty-one million rounds of ammunition. Whatever Darlan's apparent failing during his Vichy period, he proved during his last weeks that he was a French patriot.[180]

Early in 1943, just as Roosevelt and Churchill were preparing to meet at Casablanca to make plans for further military advance from Tunisia and to try to solve the de Gaulle-Giraud problem, another controversial Vichyite character was introduced into Algiers. On January 12, it was announced from Washington that Marcel Peyrouton was leaving his position as French ambassador in Argentina to assume an important post in Algeria. Later it was learned that he was to replace Chatel as governor of Algeria and member of the Imperial Council. Darlan had asked for him. Giraud renewed the request, Murphy got Eisenhower's endorsement for him, and Hull overruled the objections of Sumner Welles to him. Thus "one of the most dangerous of Vichyites, determinedly anti-democratic and anti-allied ... the choice of Lemaigre-Dubreuil," with no virtue credited to him except being anti-naval, was a fitting replacement for Darlan. The State Department emphasized his experience in North African administration; he had been briefly secretary to the governor general of Algeria in 1930; twice, in 1933 and 1934, resident general in Tunisia; resident general of Morocco from March to September, 1936; and finally, resident general of Tunisia from June 3, 1940 to July 8, 1940.[181] Naturally, the American announcement did not mention Peyrouton's career as Pétain's first minister of the interior, when he was notorious as the originator of the first anti-Semitic drives, organized the Vichy police system, and threw numerous anti-Vichy Frenchmen into jail. British public opinion was aghast at his appointment. An American journal spoke of him as

> A Martin Dies with a policeman's club. His speciality was repressive measures, his philosophy Red-baiting, his pride toughness. Whoever thought of calling him back was a fool or worse.[182]

Conceived orignally as the first of the Big Three Conferences with Stalin, the meeting at Casablanca assembled without the too-busy Russian leader. For four days before Roosevelt's arrival on January 14, the Anglo-American Combined Chiefs of Staff discussed the next target in the war. To the great relief of the British, who still dreaded a cross-channel invasion as premature, the military leaders decided on "Husky," the invasion of Sicily. Neither the State Department nor the British Foreign Service was represented. Thus the Combined Chiefs of Staff substituted the British Mediterranean strategy for the previous American plan. But it was Roosevelt who coined the phrase at Anfa, "Unconditional Surrender," "that was to spell the immediate defeat of Lemaigre-Dubreuil (and the forces behind him), the eventual defeat of Giraud, and the triumph of de Gaulle."[183]

Misinterpreting "Casablanca" as "White House," in a

Spanish spy report, a German intelligence official probably saved the villas of Roosevelt and Churchill and the hotel of the military leaders from bombing. The site of the conferences was really at Anfa, a suburb of Casablanca, which was protected by barbed wire fences, anti-aircraft batteries, and patrols of Patton's troops. The President's son, Elliott, attended his father and later wrote a book valuable for both descriptions of persons and events and for the revelation of his father's inmost thoughts. Harry Hopkins was also an interested observer. An early caller was Murphy, "eager," says Elliott, "to fill Father in on Giraud, how competent he would be as an administrator, how ideal a choice for the Americans to back." Elliott began to understand why Murphy was "on the pan"--his governing concern seemed to be to ensure that any future government in France would be dominated by the same men who had been among the principal appeasers in the pre-war years.[184]

Urgently summoned by Churchill to meet Giraud at Casablanca, de Gaulle resented the peremptory invitation, and at first refused to come. Later, when so advised by his London Staff, he at long last decided to confront his rival, even at the instance of intermediaries. On January 22 he arrived, and that evening he had his first interview with Roosevelt--"for some thirty minutes, he and Father talked, Father being charming, de Gaulle non-committal." After de Gaulle's departure, Roosevelt discussed the problem of de Gaulle with Churchill, Hopkins, and Murphy. Roosevelt found a simple solution:

> These two: equal rank, equal responsibility in setting up the Provisional Assembly. When that's done, French democracy is reborn. When that Provisional Assembly starts to act, French democracy takes its first steps. Presently French democracy will be in a position to decide for itself what is to become of Giraud, or of de Gaulle. It will no longer be our affair.[185]

Talking with Elliott later, the President referred again to the problem of colonialism as a breeder of past and future wars:

> When we've won the war, I will work with all my might and main to see to it that the United States is not wheed-

> led into the position of accepting any plan that will further France's imperialistic ambitions, or that will aid or abet the British Empire in its imperialistic ambitions.[186]

Roosevelt's suggested compromise of a two-leader provisional government would, of course, favor the politically clever de Gaulle. Therefore, Murphy presented another plan --a triumvirate, consisting of Giraud, de Gaulle, and a third party, who could not yet be named. De Gaulle promptly rejected the Count of Paris. It is probable that Murphy was about to name Lemaigre-Dubreuil, wholly objectionable to de Gaulle. At this point the Giraud cause was saved by Hull, from Washington, who suggested on January 16 that Lemaigre-Dubreuil return promptly to Casablanca. Here the latter drew up a memorandum providing that the Giraud-Murphy accord should be the basis of future Franco-American relations, with Allied recognition of Giraud as the trustee for all French interests. Giraud insisted on presenting this document to the President without the presence of his mentor. To the amazement of Lemaigre-Dubreuil, Roosevelt not only initialed the memorandum but added a clause fixing the dollar-franc rate of exchange at 1 to 50. But Churchill still had the last word, after the President had returned to the United States.

To influence public opinion, the entire Anglo-American press corps was flown to Anfa to testify to the reconciliation of de Gaulle and Giraud by photographing them shaking hands. Later, when the two rivals tried to formulate their own communique, Giraud rejected the statement of their goal as "the triumph of democratic liberties," de Gaulle accepted "human liberties" instead. Challenged for his policy, Giraud would answer nothing but "I want to make war." Thereupon, de Gaulle charged him with being in full accord with the "regime of dictatorship and oppression actually reigning at Vichy," and Giraud did not deny his allegiance to the Marshal. At Algiers, Rigault tried to suppress the news of the supposed coming together of Giraud and de Gaulle, but he finally had to permit pictures of de Gaulle to appear in the papers. What was actually happening was:

> A desperate stand by the anti-British, anti-Gaullist group to rally round Giraud and consolidate his position on the basis of Lemaigre-Dubreuil's memorandum, and so smother the Gaullists that de Gaulle would not have the

necessary popular support in North Africa with which to impinge on Giraud's dictatorship.[187]

A highlight of the Anfa conference was the dinner party which Roosevelt gave for Sultan Muhammad V on the evening of January 22. The others present were the Sultan's Grand Vizir and Chief of Protocol, Hopkins, Churchill, Noguès,[188] Elliott Roosevelt, and the Sultan's son, Mulai Hassan. Especially gratifying to Muhammad V was his unwonted recognition as a ruler of importance. It was a Muslim meal, without alcohol, which might have caused Churchill's glum silence. But it is more likely that the lively conversation of Roosevelt and the Sultan, in French, and their evident pleasure in the interchange, was provocative of Churchill's displeasure. Their topic was the wealth of natural resources in Morocco and the possibility of their development for the raising of health and educational standards for the Moroccans. The Sultan, Roosevelt asserted, should not allow other countries to obtain concessions to drain off Morocco's resources. Roosevelt suggested that the needed Moroccan engineers and scientists could be educated in American universities; American firms might carry out resource development plans on a percentage basis. As they left the table, the Sultan exclaimed with a glowing face, "A new future for my country!" Both Noguès and de Gaulle (who heard of the dinner conversation later) might consider Roosevelt's proposals decidedly subversive. Later on, the Sultan received two friendly letters from Roosevelt, which encouraged his hopes for postwar support--a hope made vain by Roosevelt's early death.[189]

After the Anfa meetings, the Allies opposed de Gaulle's wish to go to Libya, and on January 26 he returned to London on a British plane. On February 9 he told a press conference what had really happened at Anfa. On March 3 the British government informed him that he would not be furnished the means to go to the Middle East. Meanwhile, both American and British newspapers and commentators became more critical of de Gaulle's "deplorable pride" and "frustrated ambitions." Most critics accused de Gaulle of planning a dictatorship for liberated France, while Giraud was extolled as the "bulwark of democracy."

In North Africa, however, the furor touched off by the coming of Peyrouton continued to grow. On February 4

Giraud announced the abolition of the Imperial Council, consisting of Peyrouton, Bergeret, Noguès, and Boisson. It was replaced by a War Committee--with identical membership. In a broadcast on the same day de Gaulle challenged the Vichyites of Algiers by declaring:

> The French nation is determined to gain its freedom by blood and arms, helped by Allies whom it has helped in the past, whom it is still helping. It is determined to recover in due course all the liberties of which it was deprived either by the enemy or by an odious usurpatory regime. It intends to rebuild its house free from the pillars of cunning privilege and artificial power built on its misery by the high priests of disasters.[190]

During the first week in February, in a secret visit to Algiers, Churchill put de Gaulle back on the main road to his goal. Churchill told Murphy that an item in the Anfa memorandum written by Lemaigre-Dubreuil and initiated by Roosevelt was evidently drawn up in a hurry and would have to be changed; he referred to the item about the trustee for French interests. Since there were two French chiefs, the item would have to refer to both or neither. Could not the amendment be made while Churchill was in Algiers? An interesting scene took place between Murphy, Lemaigre-Dubreuil, and Col. Julius Holmes. Holmes accused the Frenchman of lying when he had agreed to retire from politics and rejoin his family; instead, he had injected himself into the Anfa conference. When appealed to, Murphy did not support his former comrade in conspiracy, but suggested that he go to London to work for a union with the Free French. The next day Murphy supported Churchill's proposal and obtained Giraud's ready acceptance. When Lemaigre-Dubreuil explained to Giraud that "this wipes out all I painfully achieved in Washington and all you obtained at Anfa," Giraud wrote Murphy to recall his assent. By the 19th Roosevelt's retraction of the Anfa agreement was confirmed by Murphy.[191]

During February, Gaullism grew rapidly in numbers and influence, both in France and in French Africa. In France, undoubtedly inspired by the compulsory labor service to furnish manpower for Germany, instituted on February 16, many groups of resistants joined de Gaulle. His envoys traveled throughout France to organize and coordinate these groups, the National Council of the Resistance was formed, and a French general worked with Allied leaders to organize the secret army to assist Allied landings when they were made in France. In French Africa new members embraced Gaullism from combat groups and Leclerc's army; sailors in particular rallied to de Gaulle. Gaullist envoys found access and success in Niger, Dahomey, Togo, Guinea, the Ivory Coast, and Upper Volta. Many notables joined de Gaulle's central office in London.[192]

On February 21, Jean Rigault was dismissed from his post as secretary for information and propaganda. Soon the Combat appeared on the streets, but it was several months before freedom of the press was obtained. From London, General Georges Catroux came to Algiers to explore a way for union of the two factions. On February 23, the National Committee wrote a memorandum addressed to Giraud defining the requisites for union. It was suggested that Giraud and de Gaulle be dual presidents of a new committee, directing and signing jointly all decisions. To effect this compromise, de Gaulle insisted on the previous abolition of all Vichy-inspired legislation, repudiation of the Armistice, and the dismissal of all personnel implicated in the surrender of June 22, 1940. As an adviser for Giraud, Jean Monnet left Washington in February for Algiers to give Giraud the benefit of his economic and administrative talents and his American connections. To meet the demands of the National Committee, Monnet pressed upon Giraud many democratic manifestations during March. Among them were a speech condemning Vichy and paying homage to the Republic, an offer to receive de Gaulle to give effect to the union, and a series of ordinances rescinding Vichy legislation in some areas. Support of Giraud's new principles was declared by Churchill and Hull and also by Noguès and Boisson. However, Bergeret and Lemaigre-Dubreuil resigned their positions. From the American and British press and radio rose a chorus of approval for Giraud, to whom, they said, the Gaullists could no longer offer any reasonable objection.[193]

Nevertheless, further obstacles lay in de Gaulle's path. Macmillan and Archbishop Spellman warned de Gaulle not to refuse Giraud's proffered entente. Churchill, also, intervened to say that an understanding must be reached before de Gaulle went to Africa. Eden and Winant, the latter just back from

Washington, urged upon de Gaulle the advantages he would gain if he subordinated Fighting France to Giraud. Even some of de Gaulle's intimate London colleagues thought that for the sake of unity de Gaulle should grant Giraud political preponderance and military command. On April 10, Giraud's answer to the February 23 memorandum professed high principles, but placed a "Council of Overseas Territories," with administrative but no political power, under the interallied command. France would no longer exist as a state and could not reestablish her sovereignty until after the war's end. The National Committee, now united behind de Gaulle, reiterated conditions necessary for cooperation with him.[194] The successful Tunisian campaign, where the Allied army fought with units of the Fighting French, the May Day parades, the adhesion of Col. Van Ecke and his troops, the popular demonstrations everywhere in favor of de Gaulle, all combined to show that de Gaulle, and he alone, was the choice of the French people in North Africa. When the National Council of the Resistance in Paris declared for de Gaulle on May 15 and asked for a meeting in Algiers to form a provisional government under de Gaulle with Giraud as military chief, the unity of the French people in favor of de Gaulle's political leadership was no longer in question.[195]

With only Giraud to greet him, de Gaulle landed at the Algiers airport on June 1. But the silence of the press did not conceal his arrival. That very evening de Gaulle demanded the immediate removal of Noguès, Boisson, and Peyrouton, which Giraud refused in a fury. On the following day an underground coup to arrest de Gaulle and his chief followers was foiled because the leaders dared not call upon either the troops or the police. Winston Burdett of C B S declared that this was the last desperate stand by Lemaigre-Dubreuil and Rigault. On June 3 Giraud announced the dismissal of Noguès, Bergeret, Peyrouton, and Mendigal. In their place a French Committee of National Liberation was formed as a provisional government for France and her empire, with Louis Joxe as secretary general. Lemaigre-Dubreuil resigned as Giraud's adviser and Jean Rigault was ordered deported to Morocco.[196]

All of the dominant Vichyites in the French African government, except Giraud, were now ousted from power--Noguès, whom Eisenhower had long wished to dispossess of

Morocco, among the last. Many articles in the American press had found him hostile to democracy. It was surprising, therefore, that in a March interview he, too, gave evidence of conversion to the new politics now affected by Giraud:

> The government which I envisage for Metropolitan France after the war is modeled as far as possible on that of the United States--a republic as before the German occupation but strengthened in its framework to give greater stability and avoid overfrequent changes of administration which weaken the national fabric in every respect .... France could never be a Fascist state .... None other than a republican type of government is possible or desirable in France.[197]

The apparent conversion of Noguès was too late, however, to save him from expulsion and exile.[198] His later career is of interest. On June 13, 1954, he returned to Paris from Portugal, where he had been an exile since 1943, to give himself up as a prisoner. In 1947 a high French court had sentenced him *in absentia* to twenty years of hard labor as a Nazi collaborator.[199]

With the creation of the French Committee of National Liberation, known as the C F L N, de Gaulle began his painful duel to overcome the "absurd duality" at its head. Giraud violently objected to the idea that he, as military chief, should be subordinated to the "government," on which body he had only minority support. He could count on Eisenhower's help and also that of certain members of the O S S. Trying to build up an independent following, Giraud organized his own intelligence service to promote a separate resistance movement in occupied France; there he planned to assume power with Pétain at the top. From Algiers, unknown to the rest of the C F L N, Giraud had an O S S agent dropped into France to find out the possibility of his return as Pétain's head of the French forces. Another man, later proved to be a Communist, by Giraud's orders contacted several military groups in the Midi; he gave them coded signals to be broadcast from Algiers to indicate the time and place of Allied landings. Though the Anglo-American governments tried to keep Giraud under the control of Eisenhower, de Gaulle refused to permit this.[200]

By August of 1943, de Gaulle had reconstituted the French state. All the overseas empire had been united under him, except Indo-China, still in the hands of the Japanese; the C F L N was functioning as a cabinet under his presidency; all the scattered units of the French fleet, from Alexandria to the Antilles, had been assembled to fight Germany; the separate diplomatic, economic, and military missions of Vichy and Fighting France were now united in the United States and Great Britain. Following the lead of several other countries, on August 26, 1943, the C F L N was officially recognized by the United States, Great Britain, and Soviet Russia--each with a different formula. Recognition by the United States was the most restricted; the Committee was accepted only as administering the overseas territories which acknowledged its authority.[201] The new Consultative Assembly convened early in November. In October the National Committee of Liberation adopted a decree to have only one president--de Gaulle--and Giraud, unwittingly, signed it. On November 9, 1943, just a year after the Anglo-American landings, the changes in the composition of the Committee were made. However, Giraud persisted in trying to make the army his independent instrument and to carry on his activities in France. In April, 1944, the government stripped him of his function as commander in chief and appointed him inspector general of the army. Giraud refused the office and retired[202] to a villa near Mostagnem.[203]

Another principal of the great American adventure in North Africa had preceded Giraud in departing from the scene --Robert Murhpy. In July of 1943, Murphy says, "de Gaulle's committee had every appurtenance of a full-fledged government, and all of us in Algiers accepted the inevitable." However, still refusing to recognize such a government, Roosevelt was finally persuaded by Churchill to assign an American ambassador to work with the committee. Feeling that his mission in North Africa was completed, Murphy was happy to be appointed to work with Macmillan at the Allied Force Headquarters on the Advisory Council for Italian and Balkan Affairs.[204] During his last year in North Africa, and at later dates, several articles have appeared in American periodicals, notably in the Saturday Evening Post, giving the official version of the North African story. In none of these accounts is there mention of the intrigues of Lemaigre-Dubreuil and his associates or of the great conspiracy at the foundation of their activities.[205]

The Gaullists were early aware of this incredible conspiracy, which led to "a monstrous civil war between those who yearned to revive the moribund republic and those who wished only to see it buried." Peter Tompkins summarizes the Franco-German war thus:

> To counter Vichy's powerful lobbies in London and Washington, the Gaullist publicists constantly hammered home their message: that the Vichy regime was not the mere result of an honorable and inevitable defeat of the French army in the field at the hands of overwhelmingly superior German forces; that such a defeat had instead been plotted by certain of the vanquished in collusion with the victors, so as to dispose once and for all of the Third Republic, replacing it with an authoritarian state; that when these Frenchmen realized the Allies might defeat the Germans, they quickly tried to salvage their position by endearing themselves to the Allies through the offer of helping them into Africa and Europe. To support their theme the Gaullists adduced a great deal of evidence--plus the gospel that only with de Gaulle could the record be straightened.[206]

According to a detailed study by Geoffrey de Cherney of many hitherto secret reports, the foundation of the Franco-German organization which Lemaigre-Dubreuil represented was the Synarchie, known in France as the _Mouvement Synarchique d'Empire_, or M S E.[207] This was defined as an international organization, "born after the Versailles Treaty, financed and directed by certain groups of high international banking circles" with the purpose "to overturn the parliamentary regimes wherever they existed, on the ground that they were too hard to handle by virtue of the number of individuals that had to be controlled." Branches of the organization were in Germany, Italy, Spain, Portugal, the Argentine, Mexico, and the United States, as well as France. The Synarchists aimed to create, without revolution, an economic system analogous to that of the Russian Bolsheviks, but dominated by the bourgeoisie selected from among the _ancien cadre._ During the 1920's the M S E placed their secret adherents in the permanent civil service, the inspectors of finance, and the high ranks of the army and navy. By controlling policy through Cabinet ministers, their plan was first to discredit, then to immobilize, democratic government--a task extremely well performed in France. Outside the Cabinet were such officers as those in the Council of State, the Audit Office, the army, the navy, and the Ministry of Finance, which could perpetuate themselves by selecting and training their own members.[208]

The existence in France of a number of Rightist "leagues" and political parties during the 1920's and 1930's which were likewise anti-parliament[209] aided the M S E by both intellectual and physical reinforcement. Two attempts by the M S E and other extreme Rightist groups to seize power failed--first, the *coup* of February 6, 1934, when they could not unite the two chambers into a National Assembly in Versailles, and second, the collapse of the 1937 plan to seize power by a *Cagoule* insurrection. It was then realized that the only way to destroy the republic was by losing a rigged war against the Nazis. French cabinet members, generals, and admirals by June, 1940, became members of a giant conspiracy, accepting German victory as the necessary prelude to their achieving power and prosperity in a fascist world. A short war was planned, after which their leader, Pétain, was to secure terms of surrender favorable to an authoritarian France. At his trial, it was proved that Pétain was involved in such a scheme long before the fall of France. The law of August 16, 1940, succeeding the Bank Reform Law of July 6, putting all financial transactions into their hands, allowed the Synarchists to control every industrial enterprise in France. Suppression of all civil liberties and concentration camps established by Pucheu prevented all opposition. Defeated in war, the men of Vichy were victors in a larger enterprise, the complete subjection of France to Germany. This grand design involved:

> The fusion of the heavy industries of the two countries, the exploitation of the colonial empire by mixed French-German corporations, a preferential French tariff for German products, cooperation between the banks and the industries of the two countries, so close it would force the eviction of all American and British banks, a military alliance, and, finally, for the French, the re-orientation of education to make this vassalage acceptable.[210]

As harbingers of the future fraternal Franco-German economic collaboration, German agents followed the army everywhere to gain control of French property, the transfer of which was compulsory. These purchases cost the Germans nothing; the funds came from the German charges for the costs of occupation, for which the French paid about 300 million francs a day. "Gradually all of France became German property: factories, mines, communications, insurance companies, public services, and everything of importance .... The French had to become willing junior partners in a Franco-German heavy-industry combine which would dominate all of Europe, even if ... their own country had to be defeated in battle."[211]

Leading in the work of looting France was the Paris banking firm of Worms and Company, interested in other banks, such as the Bank of Indo-China, the Banque Nationale de Crédit, and the Banque de Paris et des Pays-Bas, and owning shares in coal, shipping, and other foreign enterprises, especially railroads. This bank, says Root, "appeared in the financing of all pre-war activities hostile to the Third Republic, notably the Cagoulard plot, and ... it was the center of the transfer of France's businesses to German ownership." When the Vichy government was formed, practically the entire board of the Worms bank appeared as Pétain's ministers. And it was Lemaigre-Dubreuil who was elected a member of the board of the Worms Bank. Another interesting member of the Worms Bank board, who became Pétain's minister of the interior and organized the Franco-German steel cartel, was Pierre Pucheu. He was smuggled by Giraud via Spain and Portugal to Algiers. Another significant fact is that the interlocking directorate of the Vichy government and Worms Bank was suspected, because of abundant evidence, of being also members of the _Mouvement Synarchique d'Empire_.[212]

When the conspirators were threatened with a British victory and the triumph of de Gaulle, a substitute had to be found for both Pétain and de Gaulle, strong enough to support the Synarchie in their positions and to enlist a popular following to keep himself in power. Weygand was the first choice, because of his past business connections and his good standing with Americans--but he refused on account of his age. Then Lemaigre-Dubreuil came forward as the ideal liaison man to build up collaborationist ties with the Americans. Shortly after Pearl Harbor, he made contact with the Americans, who wanted Herriot, but he, who had previously refused Lemaigre-

Dubreuil's invitation, now refused the bid of the Americans. Almost in desperation, Lemaigre-Dubreuil now produced Giraud, sold him to the Americans, and upheld him during the long struggle against de Gaulle. As an interloper, Darlan temporarily shelved Giraud. It seems evident that the Synarchists might have preferred Darlan from the beginning, but his open alliance with Hitler in May, 1941, precluded offering him to the Americans. Rejected by the French underground, Darlan kept in touch with Leahy and later with Murphy. Both Darlan and Giraud planned an "anti-Hitler officers'" coup in Germany to forestall the Führer's suicidal onslaught on Russia. Darlan was conspiring with Admiral Canaris through Deloncle, former head of the Cagoule, later head of a brigade of French anti-Bolshevik volunteers in the Reichswehr. Canaris tried to reach Allied agents through Deloncle to negotiate a compromise peace, but Deloncle was shot by the Gestapo. As is well known, all of the German officers' attempts to eliminate Hitler also failed.[213] In the end, it was Roosevelt's policy of "unconditional surrender" that prevailed, and it was Churchill's "puppet" who triumphed to carry out that policy. The Synarchists had no opportunity to exchange territorial or other concessions for keeping their economic empire intact.

The Synarchie began to operate in North Africa before the American landings there. At his trial for treason in Algiers in March, 1944, Pucheau testified that he warned Darlan of the prospective invasion. Darlan then went to Algiers, where Flandin joined him, and Pucheu came along later. They came, as Paul Winkler reported in the Nation, to carry out "an important mission entrusted to them by certain French financial circles which, in full agreement with German industrial groups, plan a joint control of the European economy." The mission, in which Lemaigre-Dubreuil was also important, was a massive transfer of capital from France to French North Africa, especially by the two largest Franco-African companies--a chemical company owned mainly by the I. G. Farbenindustrie and the Trans-Africa Company[214] under majority control of the Deutsche Bank and several German industrial firms. Other French industries with much German capital also transferred large sums to North Africa. Root estimates that in the three weeks before the landings about nine billion francs from France were deposited in the French banks in North Africa. Then these Franco-German enterprises tried to cash in their francs, bought at 150 per dollar on the open market, for 50 per dollar at the rate granted by Roosevelt at Anfa. Thus they could triple their money. But there were not enough dollars in North Africa available for the exchange. So the North African representative of the Worms Bank induced three American banks to loan fifty million dollars to the Giraud government. All the Americans had to do was to exchange the money--not to hand it over. This clever scheme was wrecked by the United States Treasury Department, in an instance when it would not cooperate with the State Department. Thus American banks were prevented at this time from becoming involved in the success of the Synarchie plan.[215]

At least a part of the American press was alerted to the Synarchie scheme. Heinz Pol told of a crisis in Germany as early as January 10, 1942, when Hitler fired several high army officers and assumed the supreme command of the army himself. One cause of the crisis, he said, was that

> a steadily growing circle of important German industrialists and business men has seriously begun to ponder the possibility of liquidating the Nazi Party, and even Hitler, in order to obtain a compromise peace. They are prepared to make territorial and political concessions in return for substantial freedom of action to German industry and commerce in Europe .... In recent months crucial industries in France, Belgium, the Netherlands, Luxembourg, and the Danubian and Balkan countries have been combined into great iron, coal, steel, and dye trusts, under German corporate control .... The recently formed French Trans-Africa Company ... bids fair to assume economic control of the French colonial empire.

Another article, dated May 10, 1943, told of the halting of the franc exchange by the United States Treasury. It concluded:

> The reasons why important financial and industrial groups in France helped to stage the "liberation of North Africa" are obvious. These men had played the German card as long as they believed Hitler would win and that they would be allowed to share in Germany's exploitation of conquered Europe. When, however, the Nazis failed to crush Russia, they began to feel uneasy. When the United States entered the war, they eventually decided it was

time to turn their coats.[216]

The most urgent tasks of de Gaulle were the purging and punishing of the traitors of Vichy. On September, 1943, the National Committee of Liberation unanimously resolved to assure as soon as possible the operation of justice for Marshal Pétain and the members of his pseudo-government. Most of those in key positions with responsibility for the surrender or collaboration would be tried in France by the High Court. However, one of Pétain's ministers, Pierre Pucheu, former minister of the interior, was in Algiers and was arrested on August 14. He was tried promptly and convicted of having furnished the Nazis a list of men whom he wanted executed; these men were said to be Communists, and this group was now an important part of the resistance and was clamoring for revenge.[217] De Gaulle records that he died bravely. A number of the North African Vichyites were also punished for their deeds. Admiral Michelier was retired from the navy and forbidden to live near any port; Admiral Derrien died in prison. Bergeret was arrested, charged with arbitrary sequestration, and finally was jailed in a cell near Flandin and Boisson.[218] Charged with treason, Peyrouton spent five years in jail. In October the Gaullist Provisional Assembly passed a law aimed to punish those who had had financial relations or clandestine commerce with the Germans. About to be arrested under this law, Lemaigre-Dubreuil escaped with Rigault to Spanish Morocco and then to Spain. After France was liberated, the two men returned but were arrested on the charge of having "negotiated with a foreign power." Through the intervention of Murphy, the case against both of the accused was dropped.[219] On July 12, 1955, Lemaigre-Dubreuil was shot to death on the doorstep of his Casablanca home. He had just acquired the controlling interest of the <u>Maroc Presse</u>. The verdict was that he had been the "victim of counter-terrorists." Working with a friend, Rigault became the author of a two-volume work on his North African adventures. By 1955 he was back with Flandin editing a financial paper.[220]

In striking contrast to the fate of the Darlanites was the reward given to his enemies. On the anniversary of his execution, a group of about fifty eminent personages, most of them officials under de Gaulle, met at the grave of Fernand Bonnier de la Chapelle. They paid him homage by laying a wreath on his tomb and observing a minute of silence. Among those present was Secretary of the Interior Emmanuel d'Astier de la Vigerie. Afterwards Bonnier's crime was erased from the record. An Algerian Court of Appeals annulled his sentence, citing as one reason that "documents found after the liberation of France ... showed conclusively that Admiral Darlan had been acting against the interests of France and that Bonnier's act had been accomplished in the interests of the liberation of France." Since Bonnier had committed no crime, neither had his accomplices. In September, 1943, Giraud pronounced a non-suit in favor of Henri d'Astier, Cordier, and Garidacci, who were released from custody. D'Astier received the *Croix de Guerre* with palms from Giraud and the Medal of the Resistance from de Gaulle. Cordier's award was only the *Croix de Guerre*. Garadacci was fired from his police job. Of the twelve accused of conspiracy against Murphy and Giraud, seven were given responsible government positions, including Capitant, a minister in de Gaulle's cabient, and Louis Joxe, ambassador to Moscow.[221]

The apparent triumph of de Gaulle over his rival was only partial:

> The elimination of Giraud towards the end of 1943 ... did not mean the elimination of Giraudism; on the contrary, de Gaulle had, willy-nilly, to inherit all the Giraudist elements who became a sort of infectious Trojan horse in the midst of the Free French .... Giraud had the support of high finance, of big business, of the North African *colons*, of all the upper ranks of the army and administration .... These people began to "convert" many of the Free French surrounding de Gaulle to their own way of thinking .... Long before the Liberation, many of these "exiles" found themselves in their "natural" milieu again--a process which was ... precipitated by the tendency of the Resistance in France itself to come under the spell of the Communists.[222]

In each of the three North African countries there was a different political development after Giraud's fall. In Morocco, where many resistance groups developed, there was an intense rivalry between a federation of the more extreme Leftist groups and one of the more moderate Gaullist groups; yet on the whole the government and *colons* remained the most pro-Vichyite of the three. Algeria was the most pro-Communist, and Tunisia formed parties more like those of pre-war France. A large number of American consular dispatches, mostly signed by Russell in Casablanca, and dated from September 20, 1943, to November 2, 1944, gave detailed accounts of the conflict between the Moroccan groups.[223] Since Communist propaganda was advised and directed from the party in Algeria, the Residency of Morocco opposed it as out of place in the Protectorate, particularly as the Communists supported the native Nationalists' demand for immediate independence and worked actively among the Moroccans.[224]

Succeeding the notorious Noguès, Gabriel Puaux served as resident general of Morocco until March, 1946. As secretary general in Tunisia from 1919 till 1922 and as high commissioner in Syria and Lebanon at the beginning of the war, he had earned the reputation of being thoroughly reactionary. Without pretension of being a Gaullist, he nevertheless appeared to have the approval and support of de Gaulle for his work in Morocco. As a proconsul in the Roman manner, he tried to strengthen French authority by arresting the militant nationalists and by depriving the Sultan of all real power; perhaps this policy appealed to de Gaulle, determined to hold on to all the pre-war French Empire. Communication between Moroccans and American consuls was restricted as much as possible, while American military authorities fraternized with ex-Vichyites rather than their true friends. Puaux made frequent declarations of policy, promising reforms, such as the elimination of Vichyites from positions of power, the release of Gaullist or pro-American prisoners, the solution of economic problems, the abolition of the black market, the punishment of collaborators, and the establishment of schools. He was the subject of repeated press attacks. However, as Catroux wrote in his book, Dans la Bataille de la Méditerrannée, "in Morocco nothing really concrete was done, on the political plane, to modify the former (Vichy) Protectorate regime."[225]

According to the testimony of American consuls, after the passing of Giraud there continued to be much anti-American feeling in French Morocco. Russell advised that the United States recognize that the French had full freedom to solve their own problems; the American delay in giving de Gaulle complete recognition enhanced the inferiority complex of the French. After the arrival of de Gaulle in Algiers, there was much suspicion of Anglo-American motives and "harping criticism of our military, economic, financial, and political performance." Consul Chapin added:

> We know that de Gaullist elements in North Africa for months have carried on a subtle campaign against Americans, casting suspicion on American motives, for example, the whispering campaign that the United States intended to keep Morocco and American troops would never leave here. When our troops left Morocco, the same circles commenced stories that the Americans were buying up railways and public utilities and intended to dominate the economic life of French Africa.[226]

Although the consular dispatches do not mention the deeper roots of Gaullist resentment against the United States, there is no doubt that it proceeded from the Vichy policy as a whole and also Murphy's involvements with Lemaigre-Dubreuil and Darlan. The American official conduct relating to Morocco had often been contrary to the declared democratic aims of the United States.

While French Morocco had been the battleground of French and German and Russian ideologies and their proponents, and had suffered not too gladly the intervention of two powers who wanted to be her friends and allies, the two other sections of Morocco had pursued a separate course of action. Although many of his subjects became expert in the wartime occupation of spying for Germany and Vichy France, Franco had refused to enter the war against or for Germany. To Spain the war apparently offered an excellent opportunity to achieve her ambition to add the Tangier enclave to her zone and finally to attain her "natural boundaries."[227]

As the only signatory of the original Statue of 1923 who was neutral in the war, Spain assumed the duty of protecting Tangier's statutory neutrality against a possible intervention by Italy. Col. Beigbeder, Franco's minister of foreign affairs, in notifying France of the intention to extend the Spanish protectorate over Tangier, promised that this action would be temporary and would not be prejudicial to the permanent international regime. Under the Khalifa of the Spanish Zone, the occupying forces entered Tangier on June 14, 1940. The Spanish High Commissioner notified the interested powers and the Tangier Committee of Control of Spain's action, and it was stipulated that the existing administrative organization would be maintained.

Perhaps Col. Beigbeder would have kept his pledge, but he was replaced on October 17, 1940, by Serraño Suñer, the pro-Nazi son-in-law of Franco. Shortly thereafter the head of the occupation forces, Col. Antonio Yuste, became governor general of Tangier and delegate of the Spanish High Commissioner. At once he abolished both the Committee of Control and the Legislative Assembly and extended the Spanish Zone over Tangier. Within two years the international administration was destroyed--administrators, Port Commission, and gendarmerie--and the Cape Spartel lighthouse was annexed. Then followed the replacement of the Moroccan officials by others from Spanish Morocco. In March, 1942, the Sherifian postal, telephone, and telegraph service (all except the British post office) were put under the Khalifa. A decree of February 6, 1941, subordinated the Tangier economy to the Spanish Directorate. All currencies still circulated, but payments of customs duties and taxes were required in pesetas.

The powers whose treaties were thus broken protested frequently, particularly France. The British government finally worked out a modus operandi which guaranteed the protection of many of its rights. Only the Mixed Court remained of the international establishment. Still disclaiming political interest in Tangier, the United States notified Spain that American treaty rights of the Open Door and the neutrality of the Tangier Zone were still binding.

In March 1941 Germany reestablished a consulate general in Tangier, and from this center spying was conducted in North Africa and the Straits area, and Axis propaganda was disseminated all over Morocco. Although both the United States and Great Britain made many protests against these German activities, no attention was paid to them until February, 1944, when the United States suspended all oil shipments to Spain. Then Spain reluctantly suppressed the German consulate and expelled the Nazi espionage and sabotage agents from both Spanish Morocco and Tangier.

The Spanish government claimed that Tangier had benefitted by its occupation, but American and British authorities did not agree. Since the Anglo-American successes in the war in North Africa during 1943 and 1944 presaged an Allied victory, Spain gradually prepared to withdraw. Upon the basis of American and British studies of the Tangier problem, a State-War-Navy Coordinating Committee prepared a memorandum for the State Department recommending that as soon as the war ended, the interested parties should ask Spain to withdraw from Tangier and the United States should join with the other interested powers to establish an interim administration, pending the future status of the zone to be decided by the proposed world organization.

When Germany surrendered on May 8, 1945, Spain had already begun her exodus. Representatives of Great Britain, France, and the United States agreed to meet in Paris to decide upon the reorganization of the Tangier regime. The settlement of the Tangier status, like that of the rest of Morocco, was an important item on the postwar agenda. The United States was no longer withdrawn from any phase of the Moroccan problem. Morocco was entering a new era; before and during World War II, the irresistible independence movement had developed so far that soon after the middle of the century it carried Morocco to nationhood.

Notes

1. A. N. F.: Goold to Sec. of State, No. 31, Feb. 28, 1938, 881.20/8; Doolittle to Sec. of State, No. 1386, Sept. 10, 1938, 881.00/1696; Goold to Sec. of State, No. 78, Sept. 16, 1938, 881.044/11; Doolittle to Sec. of State, telegram, Sept. 29, 1938, 740.00/478; Chapman (Gibraltar) to Sec. of State, report, Oct. 12, 1938, 849A.00/6; Stanton to Sec. of State, No. 137, Feb. 10, 1939, 881.345/1; Goold to Murray, April 3, 1939, 881.00/1710; Blake to Sec. of State, telegram, April 21, 1939, 740.00/1060 and No. 1450, April 27, 1939, 881.00/1713; Goold to Sec. of State, No. 171, May 19, 1939, 881.20/17; No. 185, June 15, 1939, 881.00/1717; No. 197, July 1, 1939, 881.00/1718 and No. 221, Aug. 28, 1939, 881.20/19. Blake to Sec. of State, telegram, Aug. 28, 1939, 760c.62/1134; telegram, Aug. 29, 1939, 760c.62/1164 and telegram, Aug. 31, 1939, 881.014/22.

2. A few examples are: J. Salwyn Schapiro, "The French War Machine," Events, III (Feb., 1938), 132-136; R. Ernest Dupuy, "Jaunty Fighters Keep The Tricolor in Africa," New York Times, Jan. 22, 1939, "New York Times Magazine," 6, 21; "Paris Courts Arabian Chieftains With French Food and Friendship," Life, VI (March 27, 1939), 18; P. J. Philip, "France Strong in Africa," New York Times, May 27, 1939, E5.

3. Bullitt (Paris) to Sec. of State, telegram, April 18, 1939, A. N. F.: 740.00/945.

4. "The Franco-British Alliance," New Republic, XCV (May 11, 1938), 4; George Fielding Eliot, "If War Breaks Out Tomorrow," Ibid., XCIX (May 24, 1939), 63-66.

5. John McVicker Haight, Jr., "Roosevelt as Friend of France," Foreign Affairs, XLIV (April, 1966), 518-526).

6. Blake to Sec. of State, No. 1500, Oct. 25, 1939, A. N. F., 881.5151/9; Hull to Blake, Dec. 4, 1939, F R, 1939, IV, 693.

7. A. N. F.: Goold to Sec. of State, No. 245, Oct. 26, 1939, 881.00/1737; No. 254, Nov. 17, 1939, 881.00 /1738; No. 257, Nov. 20, 1939, 68.111/13; No. 272, Jan. 9, 1940, 8/51.34581/5; No. 273, Jan. 9, 1940, 881.00/1741; report, Feb. 14, 1940, 881.00/17421/2; No. 297, March 15, 1940, 881.00/1743; No. 298, March 15, 1940, 881.50/22. Blake to Murray, letter, Dec. 21, 1939, 881.00/1740.

8. Herbert Luethy, France Against Herself: A Perceptive Study of France's Past, Her Politics, and Her Unending Crises (hereafter cited as Luethy, France Against Herself), 79.

9. Forrest Davis and Ernest K. Lindley, How War Came, an American White Paper; From the Fall of France to Pearl Harbor (hereafter cited as Davis and Lindley, How War Came), 44.

10. Ibid., 44-46.

11. For the important events and personalities involved in the collapse of France see the following: Davis and Lindley, How War Came, 60-61, 65, 67-72, 74-78; Charles de Gaulle, The War Memoirs of General de Gaulle, Vol. I, The Call to Honor (hereafter cited as de Gaulle, Call to Honor), 79-80; Waverley Root, The Secret History of the War, 3 vols. (hereafter cited as Root, Secret History), II, 424; William L. Shirer, The Rise and Fall of the Third Reich: A History of Nazi Germany (hereafter cited as Shirer, Rise and Fall of the Third Reich), 756-757.

12. Floyd A. Cave and Associates, editors, The Origins and Consequences of World War II, 584-585; Davis and Lindley, How War Came, 79; "France Goes Fascist," New Republic, CIII (July 15, 1940), 70-71.

13. Leon Marchal, Vichy, Two Years of Deception, 24-25, 52; Shirer, Rise and Fall of the Third Reich, 740-745.

14. Langer, Encyclopedia of World History, 1136.

15. Gold was also held to French account in Canada, London, and elsewhere, and a quarter of a billion dollars was sequestrated in the harbor of Martinique. This last shipment was also bound for New York at Bullitt's urging, but the armistice caused a change of destination. Davis and Lindley, How War Came, 57.

16. Ibid., 56-57, 79-82.

17. Kenneth Pendar, Adventures in Diplomacy: Our French Dilemma (hereafter cited as Pendar, Adventures in Diplomacy), 5-8.

18. Robert D. Murphy, Diplomat Among Warriors (hereafter cited as Murphy, Diplomat Among Warriors), 64-65.

19. Davis and Lindley, How War Came, 131-134, 136-137.

20. Ibid., 124, 138-141.

21. John MacVane, Journey into War: War and Diplomacy in

North Africa (hereafter cited as MacVane, Journey Into War), 33; Davis and Lindley, How War Came, 170-171.

22. Franco's price for joining the Axis in the war was rather excessive, considering his already acquired debt to Germany and Italy. On August 8, 1940, his territorial demands were: Gibraltar, French Morocco, part of Algeria, and enlargement of Rio de Oro and the colonies near the Gulf of Guinea. In a talk with Hitler at Hendaye on October 23, 1940, Franco was unimpressed by Hitler's boast that England was already defeated and refused to alter his demands. He had also required that Germany supply Spain liberally with arms, gasoline, and foodstuffs. Shirer, Rise and Fall of the Third Reich, 814; Neal Stanford, "How Franco Aided Axis Exposed in Nazi Files," Christian Science Monitor, XXXVIII (March 6, 1946), 1, 4.

23. Shirer, Rise and Fall of the Third Reich, 812-822.

24. Langer, Encyclopedia of World History, 1136-1138.

25. "All the records that have come to light tend to confirm the impression that, of the three Vichy periods--Laval's July-December, 1940, Darlan's February 1941-April 1942, and Laval's April 1942-August 1944--it was during this middle 'Darlan period" that the Head of the French Government hankered most for the least excusable kind of collaboration with Germany." Alexander Werth, France, 1940-1945 (hereafter cited as Werth, France), 80.

26. Samuel Eliot Morison, History of the United States Naval Operations in World War II: Vol. II, Operations in North African Waters, October 1942-June, 1943 (hereafter cited as Morison, Operations in North African Waters), 7-8.

27. Ibid., 8-9.

28. Langer, Encyclopedia of World History, 1137; Cave, Origins and Consequences of World War II, 730.

29. A. N. F.: White to Sec. of State, No. 97, Jan. 2, 1941,

381.81/286; Childs to Sec. of State, No. 178, April 25, 1941, 381.11/86 and No. 346, Sept. 13, 1941, 381.11 /90; Stanton to Sec. of State, No. 472, May 17, 1941, 178.1/25; Russell to Sec. of State, No. 21, June 16, 1941, 178.1/26; Wilkes to Sec. of State, report, Oct. 17, 1941, 381.81/297.

30. A. N. F.: Joseph E. Davies (Brussels) to Sec. of State, No. 526, Nov. 21, 1939, 781.003/287; Blake to Murray, letter, Jan. 15, 1940, 681.116/61; White to Sec. of State, No. 7, Aug. 12, 1940, 681.116/65 and No. 24, Sept. 10, 1940, 681.116/66; Childs to Sec. of State, No. 207, May 29, 1941, 681.006/79; No. 229, June 25, 1941, 681.62212/1; No. 371, Oct. 3, 1941, 681.62212/3; No. 380, Oct. 8, 1941, 600.817/8 and No. 397, Oct. 16, 1941, 600.817/9.

31. A. N. F.: Goold to Childs, Jan. 12, 1940, 681.00/7; Goold to Sec. of State, No. 281, Jan. 22, 1940, 681.116/60; Moore to Blake, No. 1066, March 20, 1940, 681.116/60; Goold to Sec. of State, No. 306, March 29, 1940, 681.116/63; No. 307, March 29, 1940, 681.116/64; No. 299, March 18, 1940, 681.116/62; No. 372, Oct. 29, 1940, 740. 00112 European War 1930/1919; telegram, Jan. 4, 1941, 740.00112 European War 1939/2033. Russell to State Dept., annual report, July 15, 1941, 160/1992; No. 177, Oct. 10, 1941, 681.00/10; No. 181, Oct. 13, 1941, 681.00/11; No. 184, Oct. 15, 1941, 681.00/12; No. 265, Nov. 18, 1941, 681.00/13.

32. A. N. F.: Goold to Sec. of State, telegram, May 11, 1940, 158.811/42; telegram, May 23, 1940, 158.811 /43; telegram, Aug. 29, 1940, 158.811/44; No. 380, Nov. 14, 1940, 158.811/44; No. 404, Jan. 3, 1941, 158.811/46; No. 420, Feb. 4, 1941, 158.811/47. Stanton to Sec. of State, No. 461, April 29, 1941, 158.811/48. Russell to Sec. of State, telegram, June 23, 1941, 158.811/49; No. 50, airmail, July 5, 1941; telegram, Aug. 4, 1941, 158.811/51; No. 104, Aug. 26, 1941, 158.811/52; No. 109, Sept. 2, 1941, 158.811 /55. Executive Assistant of Federal Security Agency to Sec. of State, letter, Washington, Oct. 21, 1941, 158.811/54. Russell to Sec. of State, No. 250,

Nov. 10, 1941, 158.811/55, telegram, Dec. 31, 1941, 158.815/3; telegram, Dec. 3, 1941, 158.819/43.

33. A. N. F.: to Sec. of State, telegram, Sept. 9, 1939, 781.003/279. Blake to Sec. of State, telegram, Sept. 13, 1939, 781.003/281. Goold to Murray, letter, Jan. 19, 1940, 651.003/855. Goold to Sec. of State, No. 285, Feb. 7, 1940, 781.003/289; No. 292, Feb. 24, 1940, 781.003/290. Murray to Goold, No. 285, March 11, 1940, 781.003/289.

34. Childs to Alling, letter, May 13, 1943, Ibid., 881.00 /2584.

35. Murphy, Diplomat Among Warriors, 70; Peter Tompkins, The Murder of Admiral Darlan; A Study in Conspiracy (hereafter cited as Tompkins, Murder of Admiral Darlan), 18.

36. Morison, Operations in North African Waters, 11.

37. Murphy, Diplomat Among Warriors, 79-80.

38. Theodor Auer, appointed consul general in Casablanca, headed the German Armistice Commission. His group failed to forewarn Berlin of the exact time of the American invasion of Morocco. As punishment, Auer was dismissed from office by Ribbentrop; eventually he was captured by the Russians in Berlin. Ibid., 78-79.

39. A. N. F.: Stanton to Sec. of State, telegram, Dec. 29, 1940, 740.0011 European War 1939/7317. Gould to Sec. of State, telegram, Jan. 3, 1941, 740.0011 European War 1939/7412. Stanton to Sec. of State, telegram, March 1, 1941, 740.0011 European War 1939 /8732 and telegram, March 2, 1941, 740.0011 European War 1939/8727. Childs to Sec. of State, telegram, April 24, 1941, 740.0011 European War 1939/10280. Stanton to Sec. of State, telegram, May 7, 1941, 881.00/2008. Childs to Sec. of State, telegram, May 15, 1941, 740.0011 European War 1939/11006 and No. 245, July 7, 1941, 881.00/2031.

40. Russell to Sec. of State, No. 732, Aug. 31, 1942, Ibid., 881.00/2331.

41. Shillock to Sec. of State, No. 355, Sept. 18, 1941, A. N. F., 800.20281/2.

42. A. N. F.: Goold to Sec. of State, No. 290, Feb. 17, 1940, 881.00N/1 and No. 291, Feb. 24, 1940, 881.00N/2. White to Sec. of State, No. 22, Sept. 9, 1940, 881.00/1764. Goold to Sec. of State, No. 367, Oct. 21, 1940, 881.00/1783. Stanton to Sec. of State, report, Dec. 23, 1940, 811.76 Radio Manufacturers' Association, /325.

43. A. N. F.: Childs to Sec. of State, telegram, April 28, 1941, 740.0011 European War 1939/10414 and telegram, May 18, 1941, 740.0011 European War 1939/11074. Stanton to Sec. of State, telegram, May 19, 1941, 740.0011 European War 1939/11066. Childs to Sec. of State, telegram, June 9, 1941, 740.0011 European War 1939/11829; No. 284, July 30, 1941, 841.20202528/1; telegram, Aug. 6, 1941, 740.0011 European War 1939/13730; No. 324, Sept. 1, 1941, 740.0011 European War 1939/14907; telegram, Aug. 14, 1941, 849A.761; No. 331, Sept. 4, 1941, 841.202528/3; No. 341, Sept. 11, 1941, 740.0011 European War 1939/15544. Shillock to Sec. of State, No. 352, Sept. 15, 1941, 881.9111/5. Childs to Sec. of State, No. 369, Oct. 2, 1941, 881.9111/6; telegram, Oct. 21, 1941, 811.20 Why We Arm/ 97. Wilkes to Sec. of State, Oct. 29, 1941, 811.91281/7 and Oct. 29, 1941, 881.911/7. Russell to Sec. of State, No. 234, Nov. 7, 1941, 881.00/2068 and telegram, Nov. 10, 1941, 881.761/1. Childs to Sec. of State, No. 438, Nov. 10, 1941, 881.761/2; No. 454, Nov. 25, 1941, 702.2381/2; No. 469, Dec. 6, 1941, 841.20281/5; No. 473, Dec. 9, 1941, 740.0011 European War 1939/17896; No. 513, Dec. 22, 1941, 740.0011 European War 1939/18482; No. 502, Dec. 17, 1941, 811.001 Roosevelt Public Papers, /37.

44. A. N. F.: all citations from 740.0011 European War 1939: Childs to Sec. of State, telegram, May 16, 1941, 10990; telegram, May 17, 1941, 11064; telegram, May 29, 1941, 11476; No. 246, July 7, 1941, 13362; No. 304, Sept. 3, 1941, 14645. Shillock to Sec. of State, No. 353, Sept. 16, 1941, 15506. Childs to Sec.

of State, No. 388, Oct. 14, 1941, 16328; telegram, Oct. 30, 1941, 16255; No. 433, Nov. 7, 1941, 17241; No. 434, Nov. 7, 1941, 17232.

45. Ibid., Childs to Sec. of State, telegram, Aug. 15, 1941, 13997; telegram, Aug. 16, 1941, 14045; telegram, Aug. 29, 1941, 14543.

46. Ibid., Russell to Sec. of State, No. 317, Dec. 20, 1941, 18456.

47. Murphy was delayed in Vichy almost a month after his return from the study of government documents on Africa in Washington--a pitifully small collection. By a coup d'etat organized by Peyrouton, Laval was deposed as premier. Then Murphy received not only permission to visit Africa but much assistance from French officials there. He first met General Weygand on this tour, which occupied only about three weeks. Murphy, Diplomat Among Warriors, 70-73, 79-81.

48. Tompkins, Murder of Admiral Darlan, 17-18; Murhpy, Diplomat Among Warriors, 66-70.

49. Weygand says: "Africa would have been powerless to offer effective opposition .... The armistice thus preserved for France a territory, a government, men, her overseas possessions, her ships and armed forces. It placed in her hands a text enabling her to fight against oppression and violence .... It offered a respite while awaiting the moment for resuming the struggle." General Maxime Weygand, Recalled to Service; The Memoirs of General Maxime Weygand (hereafter cited as Weygand, Recalled to Service), 217, 219.

50. Weygand has given a detailed story of the military situation impelling his advice to accept a reasonable armistice and his views concerning the advantages of an armistice over a capitulation. Ibid., 157-205, 210-221.

51. During World War II "North Africa" included Algeria, a department of France, and the two French "protector-

ates" of Morocco and Tunisia. There was a constant tendency of the French government at this time to combine the three under one official and to issue uniform regulations for all. The American State Department, of course, was not especially amenable to these practices. There were many events, personalities, and movements, however, that were distinctly Moroccan. Since the political capital of the region was Algiers, this city became the headquarters for the Americans as well as the French.

52. A. N. F.: White to Sec. of State, No. 20, Sept. 9, 1940, 881.00/1760; No. 23, Sept. 10, 1940, 851.01/136. Russell to Sec. of State, No. 33, June 25, 1941, 881.20/28; No. 59, July 12, 1941, 881.20/29; No. 60, July 14, 1941, 881.00/2034; No. 94, Aug. 11, 1941, 851.01/284. Childs to Sec. of State, No. 265, July 18, 1941, 851.01/260 and No. 305, Aug. 15, 1941, 851.01/280. A. N. F.: 740.0011 European War 1939: White to Sec. of State telegram, Sept. 14, 1940, 5519; Goold to Sec. of State, telegram, Sept. 28, 1940, 5774; No. 366, Oct. 21, 1940, 6825; telegram, Nov. 29, 1940, 6954. Stanton to Sec. of State, telegram, Dec. 17, 1940, 7354; telegram, Dec. 29, 1940, 7317. Russell to Sec. of State, No. 37, June 28, 1941, 13153; No. 145, Sept. 19, 1941, 15573. Childs to Sec. of State, No. 238, July 5, 1941, 13152.

53. Davis and Lindley, How War Came, 143-144, 180, 193-197, 313.

54. Robert E. Sherwood, Roosevelt and Hopkins (hereafter cited as Sherwood, Roosevelt and Hopkins), 499-500.

55. Ibid., 538, 548-549.

56. Typical articles are: "Trans-Saharan Line Provided," Christian Science Monitor, March 26, 1941, 4; "Nazis Force Vichy to Cross Sahara With Railway Linking Mediterranean Ports with French Dakar," Ibid., July 17, 1941, 4; Heinz Pol, "Vichy's Slave Battalions," Nation, CLII (May 3, 1941), 527-529; "The Government of Pétain Has Beaten Its Own Record," Ibid., (June 28, 1941), 739; "The Nation Has More Than Once Printed

Stories," Ibid., CLIII (Aug. 2, 1941), 82; Rudolf Selke, "Trans-Saharan Inferno," Free World, II (Feb., 1942), 57-62.

57. Childs to Sec. of State, telegram, Dec. 24, 1941, A. N. F., 880.77/11; "U. S. Aid Sought for Sahara Railroad," Christian Science Monitor, May 16, 1949, 2.

58. Doolittle to Sec. of State, No. 13, Aug. 20, 1940, A. N. F., 740.00112 European War 1939/1731; Davis and Lindley, How War Came, 147-148.

59. The provisions of the Murphy-Weygand agreement were as follows. No war materials were to enter North Africa, and no goods could be re-exported in any form or under any subterfuge. All American imports were for current consumption only. The United States Treasury would set up a special account in the Franco-American Banking Corporation of New York, through which blocked francs in the French government account could be "unfrozen" to meet any adverse money balance against North Africa. In case the balance was against the United States account, dollar exchange could not be used to meet it. All cargoes were to be shipped on French vessels tied up in American ports, and after each voyage the ships were to return to the United States. Control officers, attached to American consulates, were to be granted free access to harbor installations, railway and truck stations, warehouses, and oil-storage plants. Ibid., 189-190.

60. Ibid., 149-150; Morison, Operations in North African Waters, 5.

61. Pendar, Adventure in Diplomacy, 67-68.

62. Wilkes to Villard, letter, Nov. 14, 1941, A. N. F., 811.20 Defense (M)/5161.

63. Murphy, Diplomat Among Warriors, 73-74; Weygand, Recalled to Service, 254-255, 229-230.

64. Davis and Lindley, How War Came, 191-192.

65. Ibid., 235-236.

66. Childs to Sec. of State, telegram, May 15, 1941, A. N. F., 740.0011 European War 1939/10967.

67. Davis and Lindley, How War Came, 310.

68. Tompkins, Murder of Admiral Darlan, footnote, 27.

69. Learning of the proposed group from a navy friend, Kenneth Pendar left his position at the Harvard Library to join it. He had worked in France from 1937 to 1940. (The one common talent of the vice consuls was their acquaintance with France or her language.) Pendar won his primacy in the vice consular band partly because he alone wrote a book about his experiences. He enjoyed also the special trust of Murphy, who took him as his special assistant to Algiers when intrigues at the Casablanca consulate forced him out of service there. Pendar, Adventure in Diplomacy, 1-3.

70. Ladislas Farago, Patton, Ordeal and Triumph (hereafter cited as Farago, Patton), Dell Paperback edition, No. 6853, 218.

71. Murphy, Diplomat Among Warriors, 89-91.

72. "The Atlantic Charter struck the chord of idealism in the Arab mind. The Arabs also admired our apparently boundless power. Fortunately for my work with the Arabs, I was able to live in the sort of quasi-oriental splendor they enjoy and respect. When I went to live in Marrakesh, the winter of 1941-42, I was lent one of the show-places in the world, a magnificent and famous villa called La Saadia. It was one of the very few American properties in Morocco and belonged to the estate of a rich American. His widow very kindly allowed me to live there during her absence." Pendar, Adventure in Diplomacy, 42-43.

73. "The most fantastic plot we ran across in North Africa was the attempt of Churchill in the spring of 1941 to have the Comte de Paris issue a manifesto and rally the French to the royalist standard with British backing .... The British invited him to Lisbon in March, 1941 .... A French agent had gone to London before-

hand to establish a basis for negotiations with the Prime Minister. Luckily, the Comte de Paris discussed the project with a Frenchman who had a basic knowledge of the situation and realized the danger of the plan. He persuaded the Comte to return to Morocco and abandon the undertaking .... It proved something we already suspected; that the British were not wholly convinced that de Gaulle, who was not informed of this episode, would prove to be the best possible leader for France." _Ibid.,_ 46-47.

74. _Ibid._, 9-14, 17-19, 19-22, 37-42, 47-55; Murphy, _Diplomat Among Warriors,_ 82-95.

75. The Board of Economic Warfare, supported by the State Department Economic Adviser, Herbert Feis, often impeded the Murphy program.

76. Murphy, _Diplomat Among Warriors,_ 95-97.

77. Pendar, _Adventure in Diplomacy_, 32-36.

78. Murphy (Algiers) to Shaw, letter, March 23, 1942, _A. N. F._, 881.00/2141; Childs to Sec. of State, telegram, May 11, 1942, _Ibid._, 881.00/2150.

79. Cole (Algiers) to Sec. of State, telegram, Jan. 24, 1942, _Ibid._, 881.00/2091; Murphy to Shaw, letter, March 23, 1942, _Ibid._, 881.00/2141.

80. _A. N. F._: Russell to Sec. of State, No. 436, March 18, 1942, 881.50/43; No. 514, April 28, 1942, 881.00 /2174; No. 560, May 26, 1942, 881.00/2173; No. 588, June 13, 1942, 881.00/2182; No. 668, July 20, 1942, 881.00/2209.

81. Childs to Sec. of State, No. 941, Aug. 4, 1942, _Ibid._, 881.00/2317.

82. Egon Kaskeline, "In Africa: Hitler Rewrites 'Beau Geste'," _Christian Science Monitor_, Sept. 12, 1942, "Magazine Section," 3, 15.

83. Murphy, _Diplomat Among Warriors,_ 109-112.

84. Tompkins, *Murder of Admiral Darlan,* 29.

85. *Ibid.*, 25-26; Pendar, *Adventure in Diplomacy,* 85-86; Murphy, *Diplomat Among Warriors,* 116-117.

86. Root, *Secret History of the War,* II, 428-429.

87. Pendar, *Adventure in Diplomacy*, 86-87; Tompkins, *Murder of Admiral Darlan,* 28-29.

88. *Ibid.*, 29.

89. Six months after Weygand's dismissal, S. Pinkney Tuck, Counselor of the American Embassy in Vichy, reported to Washington some news purporting to be from Weygand, then under strict surveillance in Cannes, which Tuck thought had "the ring of authenticity." Weygand advised that the Allies should land in continental France, preferably in the occupied portion, rather than in North Africa. Since his departure, Weygand said, morale had so deteriorated in North Africa that an American landing would meet with general apathy if not direct hostility. But practically the whole French army in metropolitan France would desert the tottering government of Vichy and support an American force landed in France. Sherwood, *Roosevelt and Hopkins,* 550.

90. Tompkins, *Murder of Admiral Darlan,* 26-27, 29-30, 31.

91. *Ibid.*, 32-34.

92. Root, *Secret History of the War,* II, 432-433.

93. There are many stories extant concerning the agents and events of Giraud's escape. One author concludes: "the circumstantial evidence seems fairly strong in support of the belief that it was Lemaigre-Debreuil and his (German) friends who got Giraud out of Konigstein." *Ibid.*, 444-446.

94. *Ibid.*, 433; Tompkins, *Murder of Admiral Darlan,* 34-35.

95. Murphy, *Diplomat Among Warriors,* 115-116.

96. Root, Secret History of the War, II, 433-435.

97. Lemaigre-Dubreuil once gave a facetious reply to an inquiry concerning his reason for selecting Giraud as the French Leader: "I chose him from his photograph. Giraud is the typical type of French general ... just as they cast them in Hollywood. He was bound to be agreeable to the Americans!" Tompkins, Murder of Admiral Darlan, 37.

98. Root, Secret History of the War, II, 439-441.

99. Murphy, Diplomat Among Warriors, 117.

100. "If, in November, 1942, Darlan went over to the Americans, it was a class reflex on his part, combined with anglophobia and russophobia. The tide of war having, by this time, turned against Germany, he thought that he could not only assure with American help the perpetuation of the Vichy regime, but also checkmate, all at once, the British, their protégé de Gaulle, and also the Resistance, which, to Darlan, looked like a monster born from the unholy union of Gaullism and Communism." Werth, France, 1940-1945, 80.

101. Murphy, Diplomat Among Warriors, 113-114; Tompkins, Murder of Admiral Darlan, 56-60.

102. Murphy, Diplomat Among Warriors, 115.

103. Ibid., 117-118.

104. Samuel Eliot Morison, The Two-Ocean War: A Short History of the United States Navy in the Second World War (hereafter cited as Morison, Two-Ocean War), 220-221; William L. Langer, Our Vichy Gamble (hereafter cited as Langer, Our Vichy Gamble), 285-290; Sherwood, Roosevelt and Hopkins, 590-630; Dwight David Eisenhower, Crusade in Europe (hereafter cited as Eisenhower, Crusade in Europe), 71-73.

105. The text of the rationale read as follows: Information having been received from a reliable source that the Germans and Italians are planning an intervention in

French North Africa, the United States contemplates sending at an early date a sufficient number of American troops to land in that area with the purpose of preventing occupation by the Axis, and of preserving the French sovereignty in Algeria, and the French administration in Morocco and Tunisia. No change in the existing French civil administration is contemplated by the United States. Any resistance to the American landing will of course be put down by force of arms. The American forces will hope for and will welcome French assistance.

The American forces will provide equipment as rapidly as possible for those French troops who join in denying access to French North Africa to our common enemies .... The American government will guarantee salaries and allowances, death benefits and pensions of those French and other military, naval and civilian officials who join with the American expeditionary forces. The proposed expedition will be American, under American command, and it will not include any of the forces of General de Gaulle. Murphy, Diplomat Among Warriors, 106-107.

106. Ibid., 99-108.

107. Eisenhower, Crusade in Europe, 76-94.

108. Farago, Patton, 166-191.

109. Morison, Two-Ocean War, 222-224.

110. Donald Q. Coster, first one of Murphy's vice consuls and later in the O S S, started a plan to deceive Auer which succeeded. At the time of the invasion there was a heavy concentration of submarines and planes to prevent the expected landing at Dakar. Donald Q. Coster, "We Were Expecting You at Dakar," in Secrets and Spies, Behind-the-Scenes Stories of World War II, 230-235. A movement of troops and munitions from Casablanca to Dakar is mentioned in Childs to Sec. of State, No. 1093, Oct. 27, 1942, A. N. F., 881.00 /2366.

111. In extenuation of the American official policy of keeping de Gaulle uninformed and uninvited to join the invasion in 1942, Pendar has this to say:

> We had a declared policy of helping anyone who was willing to oppose the Nazis .... even before we were in the war. We had already given de Gaulle and his forces Land-Lease by re-transfer from Great Britain under an agreement of November, 1941. But in North Africa ... de Gaulle's unpopularity was enough by itself to make it impossible to use him. But there were also other reasons ... that made the government resolve, by 1942, to use some reserve with the de Gaullist group. De Gaulle's attitude toward the United States at the time of the St. Pierre and Miquelon episode, his anti-American broadcasts from Brazzaville, his lack of cooperation with us in New Caledonia in the Pacific, in fact the increasingly anti-American tone de Gaulle began to use generally caused trouble within the de Gaullist mission itself in Washington that spring of 1942, just as the State Department was making its plans for North Africa .... Episodes like these left the administration convinced ... that de Gaulle and his followers could not be used in any operation as delicate as the North African landings." Pendar, Adventure in Diplomacy, 87-88.

112. De Gaulle, Complete War Memoirs, 330-331.

113. Tuck to Sec. of State, telegram, Oct. 11, 1942, A. N. F., 881.00/2352

114. Shirer, Rise and Fall of the Third Reich, 913-914.

115. The extent of Vichyite plotting with Lemaigre-Dubreuil or independently in the supposedly anti-Vichyite plans of Murphy is extraordinary. In his book, Alger et ses complots, Marcel Aboulker maintains that Lemaigre-Dubreuil really preferred a "legal" dissidence under Pétain, which he had often proposed to Laval, and that he turned to "illegal" action only when he had lost all hope of getting legal action from Vichy. Gabriel Esquer, in his book, The 8th of November, says that both Laval and Lemaigre-Dubreuil hoped for a nego-

tiated peace with Germany; to make France strong in such a settlement, she would need a large army with modern equipment. Laval thought that he could obtain the needed equipment from the Germans; Lemaigre-Dubreuil insisted that only the Allies would furnish it. Laval authorized Lemaigre-Dubreuil to explore the proposition with the Americans. Tompkins, Murder of Admiral Darlan, 38.

116. Ibid., 35-37.

117. Ibid., 42.

118. Ibid., 42-54, 60-61; Murphy, Diplomat Among Warriors, 118-120; Frederick C. Painton, "Secret Mission to North Africa," Secrets and Spies: Behind-the-Scenes Stories of World War II, 217-225.

119. General Mast's story concluded: "Although in Morocco and at Oran our plans, for various fortuitous reasons, miscarried, in Algiers they succeeded perfectly. The groups of resistance which I had organized there, and which were composed exclusively of civilians, the majority of them partisans of General de Gaulle, took over the city before dawn; they made virtual prisoners of all pro-Vichy leaders, including Darlan; and they saw to it that the Anglo-American forces were able to occupy the place almost without firing a shot." Michael K. Clark, "The Plot that Took Algiers," Nation, CLVII (July 3, 1943), 13-14.

120. A journalist friend of Dorange states that the Murphy-Dorange conversations of October 13 resulted in a pro memoria as follows: The government of the United States wishes to deal only with the French government or with any person either officially or secretly delegated by it. The United States does not wish to make any gesture of hostility toward French territory, and will intervene only at French request, and under conditions fixed by France. Were the French to appeal for aid, the United States would be ready to bring, not only war material, but the aid of her armed forces. René Richard and Alain de Serigny, L'Enigme d'Alger, cited by Tompkins, Murder of Admiral Darlan, 59.

121. Ibid., 61-63; Arno Dosch-Fleurot, 'Dakar 'Ready' Darlan Tells Colonies," Christian Science Monitor, Nov. 2, 1942, 1, 6.

122. Murphy, Diplomat Among Warriors, 120-122.

123. It appears that Churchill also essayed to play a double game with de Gaulle and Pétain. As early as July 25, 1940, Churchill, while publicly arranging a military agreement with de Gaulle, decided on a secret arrangement with Pétain. As he wrote to Eden, "I want to promote a kind of collusive conspiracy in the Vichy government whereby certain members of that government, perhaps with the consent of those who remain, will levant to North Africa in order to make a better bargain for France from the North African shore and from a position of independence." Tompkins, Murder of Admiral Darlan, 63.

124. The French authorities cited are Jules T. Docteur, Darlan, amiral de la flotte, le grande enigme de la guerre and Alain Darlan, L'Amiral Darlan parle. Tompkins, Murder of Admiral Darlan, 63-64.

125. Ibid., 64-66.

126. Ibid., 56, 66-67.

127. Before Giraud's arrival, and while Darlan was still negotiating about surrender to the Americans, Murphy had sent a message to Eisenhower saying that the presence of Darlan had rendered obsolete their agreement with Giraud. Ibid., 115.

128. Ibid., 111-113, 115-116; Eisenhower, Crusade in Europe, 99-103, 186.

129. Ibid., 103-109.

130. Murphy, Diplomat Among Warriors, 124-127.

131. Ibid., 127-131.

132. Ibid., 131-134.

133. Tompkins, Murder of Admiral Darlan, 114-115.

134. Ibid., 116-119.

135. Root declares that at this time fighting had ebbed at Algiers and Oran and Noguès had decided some time before on surrender at Casablanca; Secret History of the War, II, 474. Thus Darlan does not deserve the credit usually given him, that he saved American lives by his cease-fire order. In all North Africa, it was really Anglo-American military and naval might, not orders from any French officer, that ended hostilities.

136. Tompkins, Murder of Admiral Darlan, 119-122.

137. The Admiral at Toulon refused to accept Darlan's "suggestions," and he scuttled the fleet soon afterwards when the Germans attempted to capture it. Darlan's orders to Tunisia to cease fighting the Americans were revoked, without consulting the Americans, by Darlan's subordinates. Soon after this, too late for Darlan to intervene, Vichy ordered General Barré, commander in Tunisia, not to resist the Germans. Clark threatened both Darlan and Juin with arrest and said that he would set up an American occupation government, a threat not carried out. Root, Secret History of the War, II, 476.

138. Ibid., 474-476; Tompkins, Murder of Admiral Darlan, 122-128, 130.

139. Murphy dropped out of the picture during these arrangements, putting Clark in the foreground. Mme. Reneé Gosset, in Le Coup d'Alger, says that it was really Murphy who set aside Eisenhower's agreement to make Giraud the civil and military head in North Africa, putting Darlan in the head position instead, but leaving to Eisenhower the responsibility for the new plan. Root, Secret History of the War, II, 475-476.

140. Ibid., 476-477; Eisenhower, Crusade in Europe, 104-114.

141. De Gaulle, Complete War Memoirs, 351-355; Alden Hatch, The De Gaulle Nobody Knows: An Intimate Bi-

ography of Charles de Gaulle, first edition (hereafter cited as Hatch, The De Gaulle Nobody Knows), 125-128.

142. The President was slightly amiss in his history in saying "Our traditional friendship dates from the time of George Washington ... to whom your noble predecessor gave, as a mark of personal affection, the building which houses the American Legation in Tangier." The administration of Washington ended in 1797, and the presentation of the consular building was in 1821, during the administration of Monroe.

143. Cornwell B. Rogers, editor, "American War Documents: Roosevelt to Pétain and Roosevelt to the French People," Current History, III (Jan., 1943), 440-442; "Appeals and Proclamation to French People," New York Times, Nov. 8, 1942, 8; "Spanish and Portuguese Reassured on New Front," Christian Science Monitor, Nov. 9, 1942, 5; "President's Statement," New York Times, Nov. 8, 1942, 1; "Eisenhower Pledges Free French Empire," Christian Science Monitor, Nov. 12, 1942, 3; "Greeting Sent Sultan of Morocco," Ibid., Nov. 24, 1942, 5.

144. "Franco Reply to Roosevelt 'Satisfactory,'" Christian Science Monitor, Nov. 14, 1942, 5; "Added Assurance Given from Spain," New York Times, Nov. 15, 1942, 12; "Addition to Franco's Reply Says Spain Seeks Only Peace," Christian Science Monitor, Nov. 17, 1942, 3; "Pétain Rejects Roosevelt's Statement," Ibid., Nov. 9, 1942, 1, 4;"Pétain Intends Africa Defense," Ibid., Nov. 9, 1942, 5; "Vichy-Washington Severance After Long French Meeting," Ibid., Nov. 9, 1942, 5; Joseph G. Harrison, "Vichy-U. S. Break: All Trade Banned," Ibid., Nov. 10, 1942, 1, 4.

145. Murphy, Diplomat Among Warriors, 122-123.

146. Shirer, Rise and Fall of the Third Reich, 920-925.

147. Tompkins, Murder of Admiral Darlan, 131-135.

148. Ibid., 147-154.

149. In "12 Desperate Miles," Saturday Evening Post, (Aug. 28, 1943), 14-15, 53-55, Bertram B. Fowler has given a fascinating account of one of the most spectacular exploits of the war. He tells of the dangerous journey, first across the Atlantic Ocean, and then up the shallow, winding and treacherous Sebou river to deposit a store of ammunition and fuel essential for the air force attacking Port Lyautey. The ship was the Contessa, "a war-battered old tub," nearing the end of her usefulness.

150. Tompkins, Murder of Admiral Darlan, 154-155; Robert Wallace, in collaboration with Parker Morell, "Africa, We Took It and Liked It," Saturday Evening Post, (January 16, 1943), 20.

151. Tompkins, Murder of Admiral Darlan, 155-157.

152. The American Army was very proud of capturing some of the members of the German Armistice Commission staying at the Hotel Miramar. They were sent to the United States as prisoners of war. The Americans heard much about their luxurious living and the great stores of food, minerals, wool, and other goods that the Germans had shipped to Germany. Sergeant Richard N. Ryan received the Army Silver Star for guarding the documents they left behind when they fled. "Morocco Germans on Their Way Here," New York Times, Nov. 29, 1947, 5; "New Yorker Is Decorated," Ibid., Dec. 6, 1942, 67; "Germans Thrived in Morocco," Christian Science Monitor, Dec. 1, 1942, 4.

153. Tompkins, Murder of Admiral Darlan, 157-169; Farago, Patton, 169-171.

154. Childs asked the State Department for copies of certain French publications for the use of the chief of the Press Bureau at Rabat to counteract the anti-Allied propaganda. "The confused opinions, the doubts and uncertainties still prevailing in all too many French minds, would find clarification in these reasoned analyses of the causes of the downfall of France." Childs later reported Axis propaganda in Arabic, circulated in Tangier and Spanish Morocco. He also objected to

German posters and propaganda material displayed in the Tangier market. Childs to the Sec. of State, No. 1214, Jan. 5, 1943, A. N. F., 881.00/2404 and No. 1271, Feb. 6, 1943, Ibid., 881.00/2460.

155. Tompkins, Murder of Admiral Darlan, 169-171.

156. Farago, Patton, 215-218.

157. Ibid., 223-225.

158. Murphy, Diplomat Among Warriors, 152.

159. Farago, Patton, 231-236, 239; Morison, Two-Ocean War, 237.

160. Landau, Sultan of Morocco, 26; " 'Sincere Friendship' of Morocco Pledged U. S.," Christian Science Monitor, Nov. 27, 1942, 3; "Tyranny Ousted," Ibid., Nov. 24, 1942, 5; Joseph G. Harrison, "Moslems in North Africa Ask Anglo-American Aid, Ibid., June 3, 5; "Arab Chief Hails A. E. F.," New York Times, Nov. 15, 1942, 12; "Africa Step Hailed by Arabian Leader," Ibid., Nov. 22, 1942, 38; "Moslems Pledge Loyalty to Allies," Ibid., March 7, 1943, 32.

161. Tompkins, Murder of Admiral Darlan, 138-139.

162. There were three brothers involved in the politics of this period, all nephews of Cardinal d'Astier de la Vigerie. Henri, the Gaullist in North Africa, was one of the original Five of Murphy's conspiracy. François, the eldest, had been a general officer in the Air Force, had been working with de Gaulle in London since 1940, and was deputy commander of the Free French forces; he was de Gaulle's envoy to Algiers. Emmanuel, a journalist and author, had sold his possessions in France to finance an underground movement with leftist leanings. Ibid., footnote, 179.

163. Ibid., 173-174, 179-184; de Gaulle, Complete War Memoirs, 365, 372-378.

164. Tompkins, Murder of Admiral Darlan, 174-179.

165. Ibid., 181, 183-185; Murphy, Diplomat Among Warriors, 142-143.

166. Tompkins, Murder of Admiral Darlan, 185-190.

167. Ibid., 191-194; de Gaulle, Complete War Memoirs, 383.

168. Tompkins, Murder of Admiral Darlan, 195-197.

169. Ibid., 199-207.

170. On December 29, the day when the orders to arrest were given, Giraud refused to discuss with de Gaulle the establishment of a central provisional government in Algiers to unify all French forces. Giraud repeated this refusal three times in ten days. Tompkins, Murder of Admiral Darlan, 206; De Gaulle, Complete War Memoirs, 383-386.

171. Tompkins, Murder of Admiral Darlan, 207-208.

172. The part played by Tompkins in this rescue is revealed thus: "For the sake of historical clarity let me add that it was in a secret code over a private radio link I had established between Algiers and New York that early in the morning of the 30th I advised the Deputy Director of Psychological Warfare of the secret arrest; my message, promptly relayed via Sherwood and Hopkins to F. D. R.'s desk, brought back a sizzler from Marshall to Eisenhower: 'Tompkins says ....' The Cat was out of the bag." Ibid., 209, footnote.

173. Ibid., 208-210.

174. Ibid., 210-214.

175. Ibid., 215-217.

176. Ibid., 217-225.

177. "Amazingly, even twenty years after the fact, Murphy was to write in his memoirs: The motive for the assassination of Darlan still remains a mystery .... Whoever influenced young de la Chapelle to commit the

murder, supplying him with the pistol and apparently assuring him that he would be a national hero and would be fully protected from harm, never has been identified.' " Tompkins, Murder of Admiral Darlan, footnote, 228; Murphy, Diplomat Among Warriors, 143.

178. Tompkins, Murder of Admiral Darlan, 225-228; Murphy, Diplomat Among Warriors, 163-164.

179. Ibid., 143; "F. R. Assails Killing of Admiral Darlan," San Francisco News, Dec. 25, 1942, 1; Bertram D. Hulen, "Hull Hails Darlan for Aid to Allies," New York Times, Dec. 27, 1942, 5; Freda Kirchway, "Darlan--and After," Nation, CLVI (Jan. 2, 1943), 3-4.

180. "U. S. Training Frenchmen," New York Times, May 9, 1943, 33; Murphy, Diplomat Among Warriors, 141.

181. Waverly Root goes so far as to claim that Peyrouton was the Vichy agent for the retention of North Africa. He says that Peyrouton performed this service when resident general of Tunisia. On June 9 the surrender of France and the birth of the Vichy government occurred; on that date also Peyrouton set out for Tunisia, from which vantage point he succeeded in obtaining the allegiance to the Vichy government of North Africa and Syria. Root, Secret History of the War, II, 424-425.

182. Murphy, Diplomat Among Warriors, 71, 158-160; Eisenhower, Crusade in Europe, 131; Root, Secret History of the War, III, 159-165; Mallory Browne, "Peyrouton," Christian Science Monitor, Jan. 21, 1943, 1-2; "The North African Mess," New Republic, CVIII (Jan. 25, 1943), 102.

183. Murphy, Diplomat Among Warriors, 162-163, 166-168; Morison, Two-Ocean War, 238-239; Tompkins, Murder of Admiral Darlan, 262.

184. Ibid., 229-230; Elliott Roosevelt, As He Saw It (hereafter cited as Roosevelt, As He Saw It), 79-80, 85.

185. Ibid., 89-92; Tompkins, Murder of Admiral Darlan, 230-233.

186. Roosevelt, As He Saw It, 112-116; de Gaulle, Complete War Memoirs, 387-388; Murphy, Diplomat Among Warriors, 171-177.

187. Tompkins, Murder of Admiral Darlan, 234-239; Roosevelt, As He Saw It, 119-120.

188. During the Casablanca conference, Noguès and all his chief officials received the Anglo-American correspondents in the beautiful resident general's palace. Noguès claimed that he had fooled the German Armistice Commission--he had been "able to hide some armaments from them." The trouble was that he had used them against the Americans. Noguès seemed very intelligent, but he did a very stupid thing. Talking with several of his officials, he said in the hearing of Merrill Mueller, who spoke French: "These Americans are easy to handle. I can make them do anything I want." MacVane, War and Diplomacy in North Africa, 142.

189. Roosevelt, As He Saw It, 109-112; Landau, Moroccan Drama, 211-213; Murphy, Diplomat Among Warriors, 172-173.

190. De Gaulle, Complete War Memoirs, 399-400; Tompkins, Murder of Admiral Darlan, 240-241.

191. Ibid., 263-265.

192. De Gaulle, Complete War Memoirs, 400-406.

193. Ibid., 407-409; Tompkins, Murder of Admiral Darlan, 265-266.

194. The conditions demanded by de Gaulle were the formation of an effective power exercising its authority over all territories that were or would be liberated, particularly that of metropolitan France, and having under its command all French forces without exception; the subordination to this power of all residents general and governors general, and above all, of the commander-in-chief; the removal of the men who had taken a personal responsibility in the capitulation and in the

collaboration with the enemy. In order to constitute the governmental organ, it was indispensable that the president and several members of the National Committee be able to go to North Africa without any conditions being imposed upon them. De Gaulle, Complete War Memoirs, 413.

195. Ibid., 409-417.

196. Ibid., 419-425; Tompkins, Murder of Admiral Darlan, 266-267.

197. Egon Kaskeline, "Noguès Found Hostile to Democracy," Christian Science Monitor, Feb. 18, 1943, 5; R. Maillard Stead, Ibid., "Noguès' French Plan: U. S. Type Republic," March 15, 1943, 1, 4.

198. From November 5, 1943 to March 18, 1954, there was much correspondence about the request of General and Mme. Noguès to return to Tangier to get property stored there (probably jewels and private papers) with the Spanish Mendoub after the landings. Childs to Legation, telegram, Nov. 5, 1943, A. N. F., 881.00 /2696; Hayes (Madrid) to Sec. of State, telegram, Dec. 7, 1943, Ibid., 881.00/2698; Childs to Sec. of State, No. 1875, Dec. 28, 1943, Ibid., 881.00/2731; Elbrick to Sec. of State, No. 2012, March 18, 1944, Ibid., 881.00/2834.

199. "Vichy General Returns From Exile, Gives Up," San Francisco Chronicle, June 14, 1954, 9.

200. Tompkins, Murder of Admiral Darlan, 267-268, 269-270; de Gaulle, Complete War Memoirs, 425-428, 430-438.

201. On October 23, 1944, Washington, London, and Moscow officially recognized the Provisional Government of the French Republic. De Gaulle is caustic in claiming that Roosevelt gave this full acknowledgement because of the coming election in which he sought a fourth term, knowing that the voters were impatient "with his unjustifiable attitude toward their ally France." Ibid., 717.

202. At his home Giraud narrowly escaped assassination by a bullet in his jaw. The identity of his assailant was never discovered. He died shortly after the liberation of France and was buried in the Invalides next to Foch's grave. Tompkins, Murder of Admiral Darlan, 270.

203. De Gaulle, Complete War Memoirs, 447, 451, 441, 457-458, 467-470, 492-494.

204. Murphy, Diplomat Among Warriors, 184-185.

205. Demaree Bess, "Our Secret Diplomatic Triumph in Africa," Saturday Evening Post, (Dec. 26, 1942), 20-21, 81-82; "We Had to Play the Game," Ibid., (May 22, 1943), 17, 105-106; "The Backstage Story of Our African Adventure," Ibid., (July 3, 1943), 14-15, 51-53; Ibid., (July 10, 1943), 18, 87-88, 90; and Ibid., (July 17, 1943), 20, 81-82, 84. Julius C. Holmes, "Eisenhower's African Gamble," Collier's, CXVII (Jan. 12, 1946), 14-15, 33-34. Robert Murphy, "Diplomat Among Warriors," Saturday Evening Post, CCXXXVII (Feb. 22, 1964), 32-34, 37-38, 41, 46, 48, 52-53.

206. Tompkins, Murder of Admiral Darlan, 241.

207. There are many references to the Synarchie in Root, The Secret History of the War, 3 volumes. Other accounts are given in Werth, France, 1940-1954, 82-86 and in MacVane, Journey into War, 21-23.

208. Geoffrey de Charnay, Synarchie, quoted by Tompkins, Murder of Admiral Darlan, 248-249.

209. The Action Française, originally a newspaper, became an intellectual movement, but had its political association, the Camelots du Roi. Other important Rightist organizations were the Croix de Feu, reorganized as the Parti Social Français; the Parti Populaire Français; and the Cagoule, a secret political association, armed and connected with many high army officers, which apparently planned a coup d'état with the help of the army. Paul Farmer, Vichy: Political Dilemma, 31-34, 44-45, 50-53.

210. Tompkins, Murder of Admiral Darlan, 249-250.

211. Ibid., 251-252.

212. Ibid., 252-254.

213. Ibid., 255-257.

214. "The Trans-Africa Company, in which both Lemaigre-Dubreuil and Charles Bedaux had a large hand, was based on plans for a railway from the Mediterranean all the way across the Sahara to Dakar and Nigeria to open up West Africa and develop it as a jumping-off base for operations in South America, and eventually the United States. A pet project of the Synarchists, it was revived by Darlan and Pucheu, who underwrote it with a huge government bond issue." Ibid., footnote, 259.

215. Ibid., 258-261; Root, Secret History of the War, III, 194-195.

216. Heinz Pol, "Hitler's Restless Reich," Nation, CLIV (Jan. 10, 1942), 30-32; Egon Kaskeline, "French Profits Tied to Invasion," Christian Science Monitor, May 10, 1943, 2.

217. Reporting to the Secretary of State about the feeling in Casablanca regarding the Pucheu execution, Russell said: "I do not believe that I have ever noted in French Morocco more unanimity of opinion than in this case among French people. The feeling is almost universally one of regret and uncertainty as to future political conditions .... Even the Communists express no satisfaction." Russell to Sec. of State, No. 1334, March 27, 1944, A. N. F., 881.00/2846.

218. Russell transmitted the January 18 issue of the leftist paper Libération, calling attention to an article criticizing the reported action of the American and British representatives who intervened with the C F L N on behalf of Boisson, Peyrouton, and Flandin. The United States was particularly blamed because she was believed to be more interested in their safety than Great

Britain was. Russell to Sec. of State, No. 1258, Jan. 19, 1944, A. N. F., 881.00/2774.

219. "In May, 1945 ... Murphy succeeded in persuading the French Provisional Government to quash the indictments against Jacques Lamaigre-Dubreuil and Jean Rigaud (sic.), the leaders in the attempt to link British and American influence with the economic collaborationists of Vichy in North Africa." Root, Secret History of the War, III, 53.

220. De Gaulle, Complete War Memoirs, 454, 505-507; Tompkins, Murder of Admiral Darlan, 268, 272.

221. Ibid., 270-271.

222. Werth, France, 1940-1954, 212-213

223. American consular dispatches to Sec. of State, mostly from Russell in Casablanca, Sept. 20, 1943--Nov. 2, 1944, A. N. F., No. 1111, 881.00/2643 to No. 1627, 881.00/11-244.

224. Cole (Rabat) to Sec. of State, airgram, April 10, 1944, A. N. F., 881.00/2848.

225. Landau, Moroccan Drama, 213-214, 251; Georges Catroux, Dans la bataille de la Méditerrenée: Egypte, Levant, Afrique du Nord, 1940-1944, cited by Landau, Moroccan Drama, 214. Among the many American consular dispatches commenting upon the regime of Puaux are the following, all from A. N. F.: Cole to Sec. of State, No. 164, June 7, 1944, 881.00/2895; Childs to Sec. of State, No. 1602, Aug. 2, 1943, 881.00/2619; Russell to Sec. of State, No. 1109, Sept. 18, 1943, 881.00/2644 and No. 1122, Sept. 29, 1943, 881.00/2656; Mayer to Sec. of State, No. 51, Oct. 28, 1943, 881.00/2682 and No. 101, Jan. 26, 1944, 881.00/2783; Russell to Sec. of State, No. 1383, May 9, 1944, 881.00/2873; Childs to Sec. of State, airgram, Aug. 15, 1944, 881.00/8-1544; Pasquet to Sec. of State, No. 203, Sept. 12, 1944, 881.00/9-1244; Russell to Sec. of State, No. 1627, Nov. 2, 1944, 881.00/11-244; Pasquet to Sec. of State, No. 233, Dec. 4, 1944,

881.00/12-244 and No. 239, Dec. 27, 1944, 881.00/12-2744.

226. A. N. F.: Russell to Sec. of State, No. 1190, Nov. 24, 1943, 881.00/1701; Mayer to Sec. of State, No. 71, Dec. 6, 1943, 881.00/2703; Chapin (Algiers) to Sec. of State, telegram, June 4, 1944, 851.01/3912.

227. The following account of Tangier during World War II is based upon that in Stuart, Tangier, 143-150.

Chapter XV

The Winning of Independence

Since the founding of Morocco under the Idrissid dynasty (788-1061), three movements have dominated her history --territorial expansion and contraction, development of national unity, and the struggle for independence from foreign control. Perhaps one should include a fourth motif--the all-prevading influence of Islam. The Morocco of today is but a small remnant of the areas at various times included in her realm--the Iberian peninsula, all of the Maghreb to the western border of Egypt, and the Negro kingdoms of Gao and Timbuktu. The problem of national unity has been caused chiefly by the difficulty of integrating into one people Arab, Berber, and Jew, but also by the persistence of tribalism and by the antagonism of city and country dwellers which have hindered national patriotism. The warfare against foreign domination has been waged mainly against western Europe, but also at an early critical period against the Turkish Empire expanding from Algeria. Since 1415, when the Portuguese captured Ceuta, Morocco has been harassed by a succession of invasions by European powers in rivalry to occupy parts of her territory. Her fight for independence has been lengthy, and it has been conducted in the fields of diplomacy, economics, and religion, as well as by terrorism and guerrilla combat. There has never been a general "war" for independence as the term is usually used.

It was not until near the middle of the nineteenth century, however, that there was "the first dawn of modern Moroccan awakening." After the decisive defeat of the Moroccan army by French forces in the Battle of Isly in 1844, the Moroccan Sultan agreed to cease supporting Abd al-Kader's fight for Algeria. There followed an outpouring of literature demanding modernization of the army and economic regeneration and development. Sultan Abd er-Rahman began these reforms by establishing an artillery school, a printing press, and the sugar industry. By his successor, Mulai Hassan (1873-1894), the work of reformation was greatly extended. This ruler modernized the Maghzen, the army and the navy and started the armaments industry in Fez. He sent student missions to Europe and imported foreign technical experts to Morocco. He encouraged local industry and investment of capital. By the Conference of Madrid in 1880 with its resultant treaty, he aimed to eliminate the evils of protection and to place all foreign countries on an equal footing in his domains. Hoping to abolish consular jurisdiction gradually, he began to set up civil courts under pashas and kaids. Slavery was officially abolished and Jews were granted full citizenship. He associated himself with Turkey in Pan-Islamism and championed religious reforms within Morocco which later led into the independence movement. He promoted a cultural and religious revival which contributed to the same cause. The three basic principles of his policy were refusal to accord any foreign power a privileged position in Morocco, creation of a modern progressive state guaranteeing all citizens equal rights and obligations, and preservation of the independence of Morocco.[1] Thus it is evident that substantial foundations had been laid for progress towards nationalism and independence before the reign of Abd al-Aziz.

Unfortunately, Hassan did not choose his successor wisely. His minor son, Abd al-Aziz, under guardianship until 1900, was well intentioned and intelligent, but totally incompetent to deal with the aggressive foreign powers determined to use Morocco as a pawn in their diplomatic deals. France made bargains with Great Britain and Spain whereby, by secret treaties presaging the eventual collapse of the Moroccan Empire, it was divided into three parts. By his childish misunderstanding and misuse of European inventions, Abd al-Aziz made his attempts at "modernization" of Morocco pathetic failures, and by his extreme extravagance and taxation "reform" he alienated all his subjects. The *blad es siba* expanded rapidly; *roguis* threatened the rightful *sultan*; the country was plunged into insurrection, anarchy, and near bankruptcy. Apprehending the French scheme to take over the country, Germany interfered to prevent French financial reforms and finally succeeded in obtaining the Algeciras Conference in 1906, which put Morocco under international guardianship of the signatories of the Act of Algeciras ratified by that assembly. By this Act, France dominated the police and financial reforms, but the document cynically guaranteed the sovereignty of the sultan, the independence and integrity of Morocco, and "economic liberty without inequality" for all foreign nations in Morocco. As a result of "selling his country to the infidel," Abd al-Aziz was deposed by his brother, Mulai Hafid, who had risen in rebellion and was elected the new ruler.

Sultan Hafid proved to be as disappointing as his brother had been. He took office under conditions imposed by his supporters, the leading personages of Fez. He had promised to work for the restoration of Morocco's territorial integrity, the abrogation of the Act of Algeciras, the expulsion of France from Moroccan territories under occupation, the cancellation of foreign privileges, the exclusion of foreigners from the government, and the making of no contracts with powers on commercial or civil matters without prior consultation with the people.

A small group of intellectuals formed a secret society which published a constitution for Morocco in their paper. Other groups sprang up, including "the reformer, the superstitious man, the traitor, and the patriot," who worked with the intellectuals for nationalism and a constitutional government. At first opposed by France, Mulai Hafid was later supported by her against his brother and adopted policies negating his pledges. The advance of the French army on Fez led to the imposition of the Protectorate on March 30, 1912,[2] and later to the establishment of the Spanish Zone.

The reaction to the proclamation of the Protectorate was the rebellion of the royal army at Fez, followed by sporadic outbursts throughout the country. These military events helped to persuade Mulai Hafid to abdicate on August 12, 1912. As his successor, his half-brother Mulai Youssef proved to be a docile collaborator with the first French resident general, Lyautey, who took the full responsibility for the "pacification" of French Morocco. Because of his military genius, his organizational work in civil government, his alliance with the Great Kaids of the South (especially Thami al Glaoui), his economic development, and his skillful use of his medical forces, Lyautey was able to fight successfully not only in Morocco but also to send troops to Europe for World War I and to aid Spain in the Riff War. However, the final subjugation of the South was not accomplished until nine years after Lyautey's departure from Morocco.

In her zone Spain was militarily engaged from 1909 until the end of the Riff War in 1926. By some neutral historians the war has been depreciated as the over-ambitious project of a self-seeking Riffian craving power; naturally this is the view taken by most French and Spanish writers. In the story of the winning of Morocco's independence, however, the Riffian War has an outstanding position. Abd al Krim resented its being called a rebellion; it was, he said, 'nothing less than a war of liberation against the foreigner." Although he took the title of Sultan of the Riff, he declared later that he maintained his loyalty to the Alouite dynasty. He did succeed in mobilizing and activating the moral and spiritual forces of the anarchic Riffian tribesmen in the cause of national liberty and independence. It is notable also that in 1921 the broadly based National Assembly set up a provisional government. This body drew up a constitution which, as befitted wartime, centralized power in the president, Abd al Krim. As future objectives the Riff leaders named independence and a constitutional government--which became the program of all later national groups in Morocco. From the Riffian War, Morocco received also a national hero, Abd al Krim, whose exploits against two great military powers inspired other leaders for independence.[3]

During the period of intense military struggle, from 1912 to 1934, as the grip of the foreign occupation tightened, the nationalist leaders made greater efforts to prepare the people of Morocco for the spiritual and moral battle which was to succeed the armed conflict. As early as during World War I a Moroccan sheikh went to Constantinople to join the Islamic Congress and obtained the support of the Caliphate and the Party of Union and Progress. He then participated in a mission to the Scandinavian countries to gain support for Moroccan independence; his speeches were distributed to the world press. After the war he was welcomed to Egypt. On three occasions Lyautey was forced by popular clamor to withdraw his measures infringing on Moroccan liberties. Throughout the Riffian War[4] a huge quantity of written propaganda was widely distributed in Morocco. North African workers in France staged many demonstrations for the Riffs. The capitulation of Abd al Krim was followed by a flood of eulogistic literature by the press, the poets, and the nationalist leaders.[5]

The fierce and sustained resistance by the natives

against the official policy of colonization and land settlement instituted by Resident General Steeg between 1926 and 1929 was part of Moroccan warfare against the French. This policy was the largest single factor in undermining the faith of the Moroccans in the efficiency of pacific resistance. Civil resistance led to terrorism, which took the form of harassment, abduction, and murder of French colonists and officials. Even the mild-tempered Sultan Youssef was moved to appeal for Steeg's removal; during a six months' waiting period, the ruler passed away. Then Steeg was removed from his post.[6] It was under the next Sultan Muhammad V that the long fight for independence was eventually successful.

It was during these spontaneous uprisings that a concerted movement for religious reform and cultural revival was begun, which was to develop into the "Kutlah al-Amal al-Warani" (or bloc for national action), progenitor of the later independence movement.

Religious reform, known as the Salafiyah movement, was introduced into Morocco from Egypt. The French opposed this movement, because it was aimed against their stooges, the sheikhs of the religious fraternities. The reform succeeded largely because espoused by Mulai Youssef, who used his greatest efforts against imposters, charlatans, and superstitions. The Salafiyah movement reinforced the nationalist creed, for it advocated not only rejection of superstition, but also general enlightenment, thorough reforms, and abandonment of static and anachronistic modes of living. To revive the greatness of their forefathers, Muslims must accept Islamic solidarity, which implies individual freedom of belief and the national right of self-determination. Freedom of belief means freedom of association through such organizations as associations, parties, and trade unions. The Arabic language must be that of the Muslim world, and Islamic jurisprudence should be based on the Shariah law, subject, however, to constant review and interpretation. Such legislation and review are the tasks of a popularly elected assembly, operating under a constitution based on popular sovereignty, as exercised through competent and elected representatives. Independence of the state is essential for individual freedom of choice and its responsibilities. However, the Salafiyah rejects the idea of a secular state; the Islamic state is to be a guardian of the ethics and mores of the people. Thus the logic of the religious creed leads directly to the program of the political group with which it was associated.

The Salafiyah movement made a tremendous appeal to Moroccan youth in colleges of Morocco, France, and Egypt,[7] who formed associations and exchanged vacation visits. A number of "reform" schools were established in various parts of the country to serve as rallying points for local activities. Frequently the French authorities closed these educational centers or imprisoned their staffs, provoking vigorous public protests.[8]

In the Berber Edict of May 16, 1930, the French culminated their policy of repression. This aimed at breaking down the cohesion of the Moroccan populace and furthering the process of assimilation into the French state. The alienation of the Berbers was to be effected by suppressing the Arabic culture among them and introducing a new civilization under French auspices. The tribal organizations, whose traditional powers had been limited to defense, management of local affairs, and representation before the Sultan's court, were to be transformed into courts of law. Certain pre-Islamic Berbers' customs which had survived were made rules of law. In Berber areas criminal jurisdiction was given to the French courts. Thus the Berber majority of the people was removed from the sultan's religious and secular authority, as exercised in the Shariah and Maghzen judiciaries. Moreover, the edict closed Koranic schools and mosques and forbade Islamic divines to instruct the Berbers in religion. As the ultimate goal of the French program, the Arabs foresaw the proselytism of the Berbers in Catholic schools; many French writers had openly advocated education of the youth as the primary method of winning the Berbers away from Islam.[9]

The Moroccan youth put on a widespread campaign to educate the public about the real significance of this policy of assimilation and proselytism. Assemblages of crowds in mosques, street demonstrations, and protests to the authorities were answered by arrests and jailing of the leaders, including even protest delegations from the Berbers. The French head of native affairs in Fez issued a statement reassuring the people about the Islamism of the Berbers.[10] But the edict remained on the books, a potent threat for the future.

Opposition to the Berber Decree was difficult because under Moroccan rule there had never been any concept of civil rights--freedom of speech, press, or assembly. Two periods of rebellion (1907-1914 and 1920-1939) and two world wars enabled the French authorities to follow the Moroccan tradition of tyranny. Organized into the National Action Bloc, the nationalists challenged the Berber Decree by informing the public in France and elsewhere and preparing the Moroccans for the coming struggle.

In addition to thousands of pamphlets posted on walls or distributed over the country, propaganda was carried on by national songs and slogans taught to the masses and with dissertations dealing with the Berbers and their valuable contributions to Islam. A campaign was launched to boycott French goods and to substitute Moroccan manufactures for them, which met with considerable success. Spread to the Berber areas, the campaign inspired even the shepherds to prepare for the defense of Islam. Beginning in 1932, the Kutlah established several French-language magazines and Arabic newspapers, some in the Spanish Zone. On twenty-four occasions attempts to ban the lectures of al-Fassi failed, despite persistent efforts of the French Residency. However, al-Fassi was expelled from the Spanish Zone and thereby gained the opportunity for seven months of intensive activity in Paris before returning to his lecturing at Karawiyin University. At this time there was a close cooperation between several extremists of the Socialist Party in Paris and some French-educated Moroccan intellectuals, such as Muhammad Hassan al Ouazzani, Ahmed Balafrej, Muhammad Lyazadi and Mekki Naciri, who called themselves "Young Moroccans." They published the newspaper Maghreb for almost two years. Student groups in Paris and Morocco worked also for the nationalist cause, as did the Muslim Boy Scouts. According to al-Fassi, this movement was partly responsible for the removal of Lucien Saint and his replacement by Ponsot as resident general of Morocco. It helped to coordinate Tunisia's Destour movement, the Etoile Nord Africaine of Algeria, and the National Action Bloc of Morocco.[11]

In 1930 the American representatives in Morocco had different opinions on the significance of the nationalist movement, as shown by answers to a State Department inquiry concerning a closer association reported between Arabs in the

Middle East and those in North Africa. Blake considered the "amorphous aspirations toward Moroccan nationalism" to be "entirely unconnected with any Pan-Islamic agitation .... With the overthrow of Abdelkrim, this fleeting show of unity and enthusiasm rapidly subsided into a traditional inert and fatalistic resignation." There was but little prospect, Blake concluded, of any successful resistance to the iron rule of France. On the contrary, Buhrman thought that Morocco was passing through a definite stage of political evolution expressing itself in disorganized nationalism and a desire to emulate the movement toward national expression in other Arabic countries. He added, "A well defined young Moorish movement, almost without leadership, undoubtedly influenced by Pan-Islamic propaganda, (has) its motivating cause rather in the emulation of other Arabic communities which have succeeded in greater national expression."[12]

By 1934, Blake's view seemed the more plausible. French control over her two protectorates was apparently firmly established, for in 1934 military occupation of Morocco was completed. Morocco was a full generation behind Tunisia in political evolution, however; Tunisia had been conscious of nationalistic ambitions on the eve of World War I. The Moroccan nationalists had to fight a double battle--against France and against Arab-Berber division. Moreover, they were greatly handicapped by disunity caused by the three zones. Religious traditionalism was far more firmly fixed in Morocco than it was in Tunisia. But from 1934 on the two protectorates were to march together toward their goal of independence, although that aim was not yet admitted by either. Three events of 1934 mark the new nationalist movement. In Tunisia it was the founding of a dynamic new party, the Neo-Destour, under the leadership of Habib Bourguiba. In Morocco, a visit by Muhammad V to Fez on May 8, 1934, inspired a nationalist demonstration and initiated the movement leading to independence within twenty-five years.[13] In that same year also a group of young Moroccan intellectuals in Paris, with the help of certain left-wing French politicians, promulgated a "Plan for Moroccan Reforms." It was a moderate and modest program, demanding a strict adherence to the Protectorate treaty, a dimunition of French power, admission of Moroccans to all administrative offices, the formation of a native national assembly, and the acceptance of Arabic as the official language of Morocco. The reform program also included economic and social reforms, such as the Open Door policy, protection of native industries from foreign competition, nationalization of public resources and utilities, and improvement of public health.[14]

The reform plan was assigned to appropriate committees of the Residency and won high commendation. However, it remained "largely ink on paper .... The French had no intention of voluntarily pulling out of Morocco." In 1935 and 1936 there was a prolonged conflict over demands of the French consultative councils, never recognized by the Sultan, for being accepted as representatives bodies in domestic legislation. The _Kutlah_ opposed their pretensions, as foreigners in the country, to represent it. When the controversy increased to a dangerous intensity, the French government relieved Ponsot of his post as resident general and postponed settlement of the issue. As appeasment for the French _colons_, Peyrouton was appointed as resident general; his suppression of the _Destour_ movement in Tunisia had won the approval of the French _colons_ there.[15]

Peyrouton's brief occupation of the Residency, from May to October of 1936, did not permit the solution of any problems. Before his arrival, the colonial press had publicized his threat to suppress the _Kutlah_, as he had the _Destour_, and his declaration of a policy of force and violence toward the natives. Thereupon, Señor Moles, high commissioner of the Spanish Zone, told the press that he had the same policy as Peyrouton. The latter immediately made a large loan in the Moroccan budget for colonists' credits and 6,000,000 francs for a number of leading kaids. A delegation from the _Kutlah_ presented its demands to Peyrouton in May--the first meeting between a resident general and Moroccan representatives. For three hours Peyrouton harangued his visitors, sparing no foul language in disparaging the leaders of the _Destour_ and of the Popular Front, just installed in office under Premier Blum. To secure the Resident's removal, the nationalists typed a verbatim record of the meeting and distributed copies to the press, the deputies, and the leaders of the Popular Front. For good measure, they published the text of a cable from Peyrouton to the manager of the government bank in Tetuan, instructing the latter to pay 500,000 francs to the Spanish Falange. The nationalists used other opportunities to depreciate the new resident general, and the

Popular Front government soon removed him and appointed in his place General Noguès, who was to serve until June 5, 1943.[16]

Likewise, because of the outbreak of the Spanish Civil War in July, 1936, High Commissioner Moles failed to execute his threat of ruining the nationalist movement. The leaders, Naciri and Abdel-khalek Torres, went to Spain and offered to help the Loyalists in exchange for the independence of their zone. They were rebuffed, so they turned to Franco, who was using the Spanish Zone as a base for his armies and supplies. A bargain was made; Franco made a vague promise of stronger reforms in return for the enlistment of Moroccans in his forces and a laissez faire attitude toward his policies. Open cooperation between nationalists in the two zones was impossible, but some contacts continued. The Spanish Zone nationalists now called themselves the Party of National Reforms, or Reformist Party, which was led by Torres. Soon, supplied with funds by Moles, Naciri formed a second organization, the Party of Moroccan Unity.[17] Like the French, the Spaniards practiced the proverb of "divide and conquer."

In the fall of 1936 began the split in the French Moroccan nationalist movement. At a congress held in Rabat on October 25, al-Fassi emerged as leader; he was planning a series of meetings under his presidency while al Ouazzini was in Paris. However, a second congress scheduled for November 14 was forbidden by the Sultan, "advised" by Noguès. Protest rallies gave an excuse to arrest al-Fassi, Lyazadi, and al Ouazzani. Many popular demonstrations and arrests followed. Until the end of the year repression continued. Then Noguès adopted a conciliatory policy, freed the prisoners, and again permitted meetings and the publication of newspapers. A second party cleavage took place in January, 1937, after the granting of freedom of the press. Al-Fassi's group started two papers in Rabat, the Arabic weekly El Atlas and L'Action Populaire, labelled as the official organ of the Party of Moroccan Action. Al Ouazzini and his followers revived his old paper L'Action du People as "the weekly of National Moroccan Action." Both men agreed on fundamental aims--basic reforms and civil liberties under the Protectorate, but they were separated by personal rivalry and disagreement on organization. Al-Fassi, whose policy eventually prevailed, favored a centralized body under himself, while al Ouazzani wanted an individualistic system of lossely organized clubs largely autonomous. The final break came after a decree of March 17, 1937, forbidding party meetings; both groups then had to reorganize as "movements," not yet legally proscribed. Al-Fassi and Lyazadi named their group "The Moroccan Movement for the Plan of Reforms." Later they became the "National Party for the Plan of Reforms."[18] Al Ouazzani then organized his following into the "Popular Movement." There was no overt opposition between the two movements, but there was little real cooperation.[19]

The year 1937 was a disastrous one economically for Morocco. After several years of inadequate rainfall, the crops failed completely in the south. Despite relief measures afforded by the French authorities, a large number of rural Berbers died of starvation, and thousands of others fled to Marrakesh, Casablanca, Fez, and Meknes. The economic situation not only aided the nationalists, but it also encouraged propaganda from Pan-Islamic and Communist sources. American consular dispatches reported at length on the political and economic situation, describing the sufferings of the natives and their consequent rioting and demonstrations.[20]

Toleration of the movements was short-lived. On September 1 and 2, 1937, a climax was reached. The people of Meknes demonstrated against the taking of some water from the city to benefit <u>colon</u> farms. This resulted in police firing on mobs, violent denunciations of the French by nationalist papers, and sympathetic demonstrations in other cities. The punishment of the Moroccans was severe. The nationalist papers were suppressed, agitators were arrested, and the National Party was prohibited, al-Fassi, Lyazidi, and two other leaders were arrested. On November 3 al-Fassi was exiled to Libreville, Gabon, where he spent the next nine years under arrest, while al Ouazzani was sent to forced residence in the Sahara. From this time until World War II began, nationalism existed underground without its well known leaders.[21] It appeared that Noguès had subjugated the nationalists.

Because of the foreign support received, the nationalists had been much encouraged during 1937. Both the Tangier and the Spanish zones staged demonstrations of sympathy. Since October 29, 1937, Tetuan had held massive demonstrations to support independence, a unified Morocco under one monarch, and the arrested leaders. Under the leadership of Torres and Naciri there had been a general strike and public meetings. Protests were sent to the French authorities and press. The press in the Spanish Zone gave full coverage to events and editorial support to the nationalists. The Muslim world generally, including Algeria and Tunisia, supported the Moroccans. A broadcasting battle engaged the French against the Italians, the Germans, and the Arab countries. The secretary general of the National Party carried on a propaganda campaign in France and Switzerland. In Fez the publicity and organization of the nationalists continued under the party youth. In 1938, the release of al-Yazidi furnished a party leader of discretion and foresight.[22] The optimism of Noguès proved to be very much premature. In realization of this fact, the French government set up a committee to coordinate the North African administration for reforms in all three countries. The committee agreed upon a program to end practically all the abuses complained of by the nationalists. Furthermore, Noguès set about founding new schools and hospitals, helping the refugees, and making a general restoration of the _medersas_.[23] But this beginning of reforms was impotent to stem the tide of nationalism.

In the Spanish Zone, during 1938, the National Reform Party submitted to the Khalifah, to the Spanish authorities, and to the people a plan of reforms similar to those demanded by the _Kutlah_ in 1933. In conspiracy against the Khalifah, who was acting to secure rights for the natives, the Spanish people agitated to deprive him of his powers and to return to the former policy of repression. In 1938 Franco replaced Beigbeder by General Asensio, who accepted the Nationalist demands on condition of their gradual implementation. Instead, the new high commissioner increased his control over the Khalifah and the national movement. As a consequence,

> Morocco remained until the declaration of World War II under a system of arbitrary and oppressive government .... The ministers of the right as well as those of the extreme left in the Third Republic were in collusion on the maintenance of things as they were. Naturally this convinced the Moroccan nationalists that it was futile to seek cooperation with a regime which had withheld its hand from them and had flouted even the provisions of the 1912 agreement.[24]

However, when the second world war broke out, the Nationalists decided to demonstrate good will to France, and they sent a delegation to the Resident General to pledge their allegiance to Sidi Muhammad in his desire not to hinder the war effort or to risk winning French victory. To the Sultan, the war was an opportunity for Morocco to attain status as a belligerent state, fighting against Hitler's racialism and totalitarianism, so that after the war Morocco might achieve nationhood. After the Allied landing in November, 1943, the Sultan refused the request of Noguès that he leave Rabat, and he welcomed the Allies whom Noguès tried so hard to repulse. The Armistice of 1940 had cost France a great loss of prestige in Morocco, but still, in spite of the pro-Vichy regime that followed, the Sultan had faith in the ultimate victory of the Allies. The Nationalists unanimously refused collaboration with the Nazis. Through Ahmed Balafrej, who personally investigated German promises to Morocco, and other agents in Europe, the Nationalists were completely disillusioned with German propaganda. On the other hand, loyalty to France was not encouraged by Noguès, whose policy "consisted entirely of repression, martial law, and wild accusations against the innocent." The Protectorate's repressive actions continued after the Allied landings, as if in defiance of the opinion of the large number of Americans and Europeans who witnessed the wretchedness of the Moroccans, perhaps to demonstrate the will to continue its tyranny and to cause the Moroccans to give up hope of foreign assistance. This ungrateful attitude of the French led the National Party to resolve to abandon the policy of gradual reform and to adopt one of "unequivocal and expeditious independence."[25]

After 1940, a new situation arose in the Spanish Zone because of its extension to include the International Zone of Tangier. The Fascists in Spain demanded the occupation of the French Zone also. Franco did not venture so far, but he allowed the Germans to carry on military training in the Spanish Zone and to occupy a number of Moroccan ports. The Sultan's Khalifah was expelled to Tangier and his palace was given to the German Embassy. In both Tangier and in French Morocco the Nationalists were strongly opposed to Franco's tactics. Until it appeared that Germany was losing the war, the Nationalist leaders in the Spanish Zone had pro-Axis leanings.[26]

It was the promulgation of the Atlantic Charter on August 14, 1941, that created a profound faith of the Moroccans in the Allies. Of special promise were the articles giving to all peoples the right to choose their own government, which was regarded as good American doctrine. Moroccan intelligentsia then recalled that Morocco had had friendly relations with the United States since Washington's time, that Theodore Roosevelt had helped to preserve Morocco's independence, and that Americans were always sympathetic to down-trodden people,[27] such as the Chinese, the Ethiopians, and the Riffians. During 1941, also, there had been strong hope that, as a declared exponent of a democratic republic, de Gaulle would join the United States after the war in rewarding Morocco with independence. De Gaulle, building up his control over French colonies in Africa, contacted al-Fassi in Gabon, hoping that the latter might initiate nationalist activities against Vichy. Nothing came of the negotiations, because al-Fassi insisted that "General de Gaulle comprehend the aspiration of the Moroccan people" to independence before he would give his cooperation to de Gaulle. However, de Gaulle would not violate his declared principle of saving all France's empire for her; and even if he had decided to make an exception of Morocco, he would never have yielded to the Allied request that he send al-Fassi back to Morocco with his endorsement of her independence. The Americans thus became the Nationalists' last hope of assistance.[28]

The Sultan's faith in Roosevelt's coming aid reached its high point at the dinner party given by the latter in Anfa on January 22, 1943. The President remarked about Morocco's "sovereign government" and suggested an economic policy to build up the country's independence after the war. Later, it is said, he sent the Sultan two letters promising to "act personally at the end of the war to hasten the coming of Morocco's independence." This was not official American policy, but both the Sultan and the Nationalists accepted it as such. The chief importance of Roosevelt's remarks is that they emboldened the Sultan to assert himself against Vichy, as he did in his refusal to enforce the Nuremburg anti-Jewish laws. Hereafter, the Sultan thought of independence as an attainable goal, and he assisted the Nationalists actively, and in turn they were encouraged to increase their demands. This new confidence caused Balafrej to slip into Rabat in January, 1943, and to spend the next ten months rallying former members and directors of the National Party, enrolling new members, and even winning over many partisans of al Ouazzini. By December of 1943 he had founded the Istiqlal, the "independence" party whose title was its program. For himself, Balafrej took the office of secretary-general; al-Fassi later became the president.[29]

Al-Fassi is undoubtedly correct in saying that many influences besides Roosevelt's encouragement led to the founding of the Istiqlal Party. The weakening of France by the war, the Atlantic Charter, the Allied landings in North Africa, and the declaration of independence of Syria and Lebanon--all these played a part. But the refusal of the French government to cooperate in vital reforms led also to the new resolution to abandon gradualism in reform and to try for a final solution of the conflict. A general conference at which all kinds of opinion had representatives was held at Rabat on January 11, 1944, where the Istiqlal party was launched. It comprised a large number of intellectual, official, and religious bodies. On the Party's birthday it presented a charter to Sidi Muhammad and to representatives of France and of the Allies. It demanded the independence and complete unity of all the Moroccan zones and the establishment of a democratic government. Furthermore, by her participation in the war, Morocco had earned a place at the peace table and future membership in the United Nations. For the first time, the Sultan was named "King" as a harbinger of the future "constitutional and democratic monarchy."[30]

At first the Istiqlal manifesto caused no commotion. Lyazidi discussed it with American Vice Consul Dumont at Rabat on January 11. Lyazidi said that, in order not to impede the war effort, only peaceful methods would be used in the liberation movement, but independence could not wait for peace, when a victorious France would never release Morocco. He made it clear that the interposition of the Allies was considered essential for success; "it would be criminal to start a movement of liberation without the sympathy of the United States and Great Britain." American consul Mayer reported that he had told several Moroccans that the United States could not favor any political movement tending to detract from the war effort. Copies of the declaration were sent also to Russell at Casablanca and to an American O S S official. At Tangier, Childs was informed of the document by Mulai Larbi, a Sherifian functionary. In talking with the Resident General, Childs denied any American complicity in the pronouncement, and he told the State Department that he considered the movement ill-timed and dangerous.[31]

Soon there was a strong adverse reaction from the colons, apprehensive of danger for themselves and for France. On January 18 Balafrej pledged the Sultan that his party would safeguard French lives and property. In a public speech the next day he asserted that the Istiqlal would never try to reach its goal by force. But fears of the Istiqlal increased, for it appeared that the Sultan and several pashas and kaids were aligned with it. Then the Commissioner of Foreign Affairs at Algiers came to Rabat to inform Muhammad V that Morocco's aid to France during the war was merely repayment for France's services to Morocco for many years; Morocco deserved no "reward."[32]

The Protectorate authorities were also becoming afraid of the growing numbers and influence of the Istiqlal, although they still refused to admit publicly that the Nationalists included were more than an insignificant minority of the populace. The Istiqlal now had enrolled the majority of the bourgeoisie and the intellectuals, but they had not yet reached the new proletariat in the cities and the masses of the rural population. An increasingly violent opposition met the Nationalists from those groups who derived power from the Protectorate, such as the prominent families in control of certain tribes in the provinces and the heads of religious confraternities. To support the enemies of Istiqlal, the Residency decided to kill the new party before it had really begun to act. Declaring that the Istiqlal was threatening the successful outcome of the war because of its past and present contacts with the Axis leaders, Puaux had Balafrej, Lyazidi (a new leader), and others arrested on a charge of collaboration with the enemy. After some protest demonstrations, followed by mass arrests,[33] Balafrej was exiled to Corsica. Lyazidi and some others were soon released, but Bouabid and other militants were imprisoned until 1946. In November Puaux proposed a program of minor reforms, but the Istiqlal refused to accept trifling reforms instead of independence, and nothing was done. Again the Istiqlal was convinced that appeals to Paris were futile and that their only hope of aid lay in foreign countries and international organizations.[34]

One of the chief recipients of pleas for aid was the United States. From the time of the Anfa Conference, through 1943 and 1944, there was much correspondence and many contacts between American representatives and spokesmen for the Sultan. In February, 1943, Vice Consul Bagby learned from a Moroccan named Hadjoui that the Sultan was much gratified by his reception by Roosevelt and was certain that things the President had told him augured well for Morocco. Although feeling strengthened by the liaison established with the American consulate, Muhammad V was disappointed that the initiative seemed to come all from his side. Hadjoui thought the Noguès desired a reconciliation with the Nationalists in order to prevent their falling under American influence. (From November 8, 1943, till the end of their Protectorate, the French remained suspicious of American motives and ambitions in Morocco.) Although the Americans could not carry out their promises to bring justice to all parts of the world, Hadjoui thought that they might, "while continuing to recognize French rights in this area, take certain measures which would assist the Moroccans in their struggle for liberty. Such measures might be verbal encouragement of the Sultan, ... the liberation of the press in matters unconnected with war, and, above all, the establisment of an American college in Morocco .... to hasten the evolution of the Arabs towards self government." Childs approved of the suggestion for an American college, of which he had heard frequently from both Moroccans and British.[35]

Accompanying a copy of the Istiqlal manifesto sent to Roosevelt was an appeal to him signed by five leaders of the Istiqlal. Professing faith only in God and in the President, the Moroccans asked the latter's aid to rescue them from the serfdom that they had endured for thirty years. They beseeched the President, the inspirer of the Atlantic Charter and the Four Freedoms, to help them recover the greatness of their glorious past under the guidance of their beloved sovereign.[36]

In June, 1943, Robert Murphy attended the ceremonious visit of Muhammad V to Udja, where the Sultan was a guest of General Clark and the American military forces. French officials and Moroccan notables manifested mutual cordiality and good will, as well as enthusiasm for the American forces. Regarding a talk with the Sultan, Murphy reported:

> The Sultan dwelt at length on the value which he and his people attached to liberty. He repeatedly expressed the desire to cooperate actively and enthusiastically with the American authorities in the war effort and, of course, added many references to the hope of the Moroccan population for the support of the United States in the future. The Sultan has also sent me word ... that he desires to speak to me confidentially as soon as may be convenient. There is no doubt in my mind that, as a result of the friendly treatment given by the American military authorities to the Moroccan Arabs, we may count on their friendship .... There is also little doubt of their growing hope that the United States may intervene in their behalf to relieve them from the French Protectorate .... It is a situation which calls for considerable tact to avoid a campaign ... of the Arabs for our support in obtaining a political adjustment at some future date. I do not believe that the Cherifian authorities hope for such an adjustment prior to the termination of hostilities, but it is apparent that they are constructing a plan looking to that ultimate result. I have been careful to avoid several suggestions emanating from Rabat for a "confidential" discussion with the Sultan.[37]

In August, 1943, Childs denied a charge by the Spanish High Commissioner that Americans were subsidizing an organizer of the Moroccan Unity Party, whose program was the independence of both zones under the Sultan. It was alleged also that the Americans had promised liberty to Abd al Krim and to Allal al-Fassi. Childs defined the American policy as being to refrain in both zones from coming between the protecting power and the Moroccans.[38]

On December 1, 1943, Stettinius instructed Russell and Meyer that, in view of the Atlantic Charter and the Four Freedoms, the State Department would like full reports on all political and social developments affecting the welfare of the Moroccans. In reply, Russell said that a certain resentment against any protecting power was natural, but even the very small fraction of educated Moors who were Nationalists had no unanimity of opinion that at present absolute independence was possible. Otherwise, there was a variance of opinion regarding the preferred protecting powers; some even favored Germany, and others Great Britain, the United States, or two or more powers. Russell could see no change in the last two and a half years in the French attitude that could cause friction and complaint. Advising Edmund C. Wilson, American representative to the French Committee of National Liberation at Algiers, Murray admitted that there was no well-defined policy on American relations with the indigenous inhabitants of North Africa. However, the directive of December 1 would serve as a foundation to formulate the American policy.[39]

In view of al Glaoui's later enmity toward Sultan Muhammad, the attitude of the Marrakesh chief toward his sovereign in 1943 is of interest. At his interview with C. B. Elbrick, American chargé at Tangier, al Glaoui discussed the future status of Morocco. He looked forward to the elimination of protectorates and a unified Morocco. He castigated Spain for the failure in her zone, and thought that the French had treated the people of their zone but little better, especially in their refusal to grant educational facilities and in keeping the populace in penury. He and all other Nationalists hoped that the United States would aid them to restore the Moroccan state according to the Atlantic Charter. He desired "political, social, and economic aid." Present at this interview, Mulai Larbi[40] stated his belief that the United States would have a great interest in Morocco because of air communications with Europe and Africa and hemispherical defense. As an intermediate step, after the war, Morocco should be placed under an inter-Allied mandate, with the United States in the principal role. With experts and technicians from the Allied powers to build up the country, Morocco could be ready after several years for full sovereignty and independence.[41]

With many calls and communications, during 1944 Mulai Larbi pursued his career of unofficial liaison man between the Sultan and the American consulate. On January 26 he called to explain Muhammad's views on nationalism. He said that the Sultan realized that this was no time for political agitation, but the Moroccans had been much alarmed by the proposal in the Consultative Assembly in Algiers that after the war Morocco should be united with Algeria and Tunisia to form a unified whole in the French Empire. In view of Morocco's international status, Childs replied, this was inconceivable. Larbi said that the Sultan and other realists did not expect independence at this time; the most they sought was an international mandate, including France. The Sultan wished merely moderate reforms for workers and public instruction, introduced now and progressively, with greater opportunity for Moroccans in public service after the war. Larbi paid tribute to the French civil controllers in the south for their concern for native interests. In the north, the Moroccans had been forced to sell their land for paltry sums. On February 12, Childs forwarded a lengthy memorandum prepared by Larbi in which were detailed all the grievances and wrongs suffered by the Moroccans under the Protectorate. The Sultan, he concluded, now desired an official relationship with the Allies to assure his liberty of action in a maximum prosecution of the war with their advice and control, with a view to proving worthy of national liberation. In the future, Morocco demanded the right to participate in all international discussions regarding herself. The Sultan hoped for an international mandate definitely excluding Spain, but admitting France if she would renounce all colonial ambitions. Tangier might remain international, with a representative of the Sultan. In all branches of administration, including the courts, American and British functionaries would be participants. Childs thought it a feasible idea to have an international mandate, but not one placing France in an inferior position. The Americans and British might well be associated with administration of education, scientific agriculture, health, and hygiene, but France should have the primary responsibility for security and native affairs.[42]

In late April, 1934, there was a brief lull in French-Moroccan antagonism. General Catroux, Governor General of Algeria and Commissar for Muslim Affairs in the French Committee of National Liberation, came to Morocco on a tour of "appeasement." The conversation between Catroux and Muhammad V was "in part prepared and agreed to in advance with intervention of the Residency officials" and was reported with exceptional accuracy by the Echo dc Maroc. The general theme of the Sultan's remarks is indicated by these excerpts:

> Whether under Marshal Pétain, General Giraud, or General de Gaulle, the Moroccans know only one thing: France, to whom they bring eternal gratitude for what she has done for them .... The events of January are but a surface impulse, regretted by all ... Those responsible for them do not represent the people on any grounds. They are young hotheads, foolish and ignorant .... It is not the moment for the Moroccans to think of

> rapid evolution, for at present there is a more imperious duty, the liberation of France .... The question of reforms will be examined afterwards.[43]

Apparently at this time the Sultan had three views on independence--one for the Nationalists, one for the French, and the third for the Americans.

From June to August of 1944, Larbi continued his efforts to obtain American assistance. On June 17 Childs sent the State Department a lengthy memorandum by Larbi, which the latter had sent to Murphy also. Childs said that Larbi had espoused the cause of the Istiqlal in frequent talks with legation staff. In the opinion of the American consul, the Lebanese crisis had been the spark, "fanned by German propaganda funds," which had set off the sudden demand for independence in January. Naturally, Larbi blamed the resulting disorders entirely on the French, ignoring the part played by the Sultan and some of his high officials in the nationalist agitation. In his memorandum Larbi spoke of the Moroccans' disappointment that the American landings had brought no amelioration of their situation and that de Gaulle and his Algiers Committee were interested only in problems of France in Morocco. It was the planning of the Algiers Assembly to combine Morocco into a federation of French colonies that had precipitated the January declaration of independence. Also, the Sultan had suggested that it would be wise to give advance notice of Morocco's intention to claim independence at the postwar peace conference. He also consulted Puaux on the advisability of a general mobilization in Morocco to aid directly in the war, but had been repulsed insolently by the Resident General, and there was also a military plot to remove the Sultan. The arrest of Balafrej, followed by the general strike and many casualties, was brought about by the military plotters, and Fez had become the martyr city. Larbi concluded: "The Moroccans are wondering whether the Allies have armed the French to weaken us or to fight against the Germans .... Our prisoners have neither the British, nor the Americans, nor the Germans with them."[44]

On July 13 Larbi called on Childs to state that Sidi Muhammad was dissatisfied with the Moroccan situation and feared a recurrence of the January troubles in Rabat and Fez. Childs interpreted this concern as being due to the reported success of de Gaulle's mission to Washington. Perhaps the Sultan feared that he would no longer be able to play off the French against the British and Americans. Again Childs reminded Larbi that the paramount consideration was the winning of the war against Germany. On June 27, Childs had written that Larbi had presented two memorials addressed to the Sultan by Torres and Naciri, pledging the full devotion of the Moroccans in the Spanish Zone to Muhammad V and their complete support of the independence party. In a memorandum of July 29, Larbi gave a full account of German relations with the Moroccans, in the course of which he testified that although the Germans had temporarily seduced the Moroccans in the Spanish Zone, it was thanks to Balafrej that they had been totally rejected in the French Zone. The injustice of Balafrej's arrest on charges of working with the enemy was therefore made clear. At a meeting in Rabat on August 23, Larbi informed Childs that he would soon make two communications to the American and British governments, one an outline of the Istiqlal plan for the future status of Morocco, the other an outline of the Sultan's desires. In La Dépêche Marocains of September 10, 1944, there was an announcement that Larbi had accepted the post of Delegate of Education in the Sherifian government. This was probably the work of Puaux, who had wanted for some time to get Larbi out of Tangier and away from such ready access to the American consulate there.[45]

American consul Cole, at Rabat in July, was as anxious as Childs to be neutral in the French-Moroccan conflict. Cole reported the visit of Abdellatif Sbihi, a moderate Nationalist and former editor and publisher of La Voix Nationale, which he had stopped in protest after the January disturbance. Sbihi agreed with al Glaoui that nothing short of an American university in Morocco would be satisfactory for the education of the youth there. Sbihi praised the Sultan for his desire to advance the education and freedom of women. The main purpose of the visit, however, was to inform the consulate that Sbihi and his friends desired to form an American-Moroccan society for cultural exchange and friendly social relations. Cole asked the advice of the State Department concerning this, apprehending an unfavorable reaction from the Residency. Hull replied that at present no official encouragement should be given to the project, but Sbihi should not be discouraged if the group desired to take the risks involved.[46] A 'Roosevelt Society" was formed by Sbihi about this time.[17]

Throughout January and for several months afterwards there were many dispatches concerning the January rift between France and Morocco sent to the State Department by Russell, Mayer, Cole, and Childs.[48] Secretary Hull approved the cautious attitude of Cole:

> This is not the moment to argue the question of political independence, but ... broad changes in the concept of colonial or protectorate administration may be anticipated after the war .... An open dispute with the French at present could only harm Morocco and work to the advantage of Axis agents and propaganda.[49]

In this extraordinary war when even close friends like Great Britain and the United States were often working at cross purposes and when the identity of France and her status as friend or foe was in question, another anomaly was the relation of Russia to her "allies." The expansionist ambitions and infiltrating tendencies of the Communists were a matter of grave concern to the Americans in Morocco. The Communists in French Morocco, directed by those in Algeria, had encouraged the Nationalists in their independence drive. Challenged by the National Front, the Communist Party admitted their encouragement of Arab aspirations for a free Morocco, but, they said, when they discovered that the Nationalist leaders were interested, not in Communism, but in working for themselves and in the interest of imperialism, they had broken off relations with the Nationalists. (The Communist party in Morocco had been admitted as a unit of the otherwise non-political National Front.) Cole alleged that Communist support to the Nationalists was continuing:

> It is ironical that the French Communist party, which claims a super-patriotism almost to the exclusion of all other Frenchmen, should permit a subsidiary organization such as the Moroccan Communist party to indulge in a French Protectorate in native propaganda clearly subversive of France, and which, moreover, is tainted with at least the suspicion of being in part influenced by Axis agents.

However, the Secretariat of the Moroccan Communist Party criticized the Residency by urging a general amnesty for those imprisoned after the January outbreak, because "it is clear that the systematic refusal to satisfy the primary economic rights of the People of Morocco and the absence of any democratic liberty were among the causes of these events and served as a starting point for the fascist Hitlerian provocation." (The underlining is Cole's.)[50]

When President Truman proclaimed the end of the war on May 8, 1945, the nationalist cause was not very propitious. The Moroccan Communist party tainted all nationalism and gave the French good grounds for opposing the Nationalists. Nevertheless, Muhammad V continued to be recognized as a leader for independence. When he visited Marrakesh in February, 1945, there were nationalist slogans on walls everywhere demanding the ending of the Protectorate. Large crowds hailed "the King," and they understood him when he said, "Everything that saddens you, saddens me; everything you hope for, I hope for too." The Istiqlal was reviving, also; under Lyazidi the central committee was enlarged and a systematic recruitment drive was organized. However, a great disappointment was caused by the failure of Morocco to be admitted to the United Nations, in response to Lyazidi's petition for membership in March, 1945. When the peace treaty was finally completed, there was no recognition of Morocco as an independent nation.[51] The year 1945 was one of great suffering and despair for the Moroccan masses, for the drouths of 1944 and 1945 brought famine and death to unknown numbers.[52] An American veteran wrote of still another cause for the Moroccans' despondency--the loss of faith in the United States:

> Most Moslems were friendly with the American soldiers, when we would let them. In the spring of 1945, however, their attitude toward us took a sharp turn. They seemed shocked and angry that following V-E Day the American troops began to leave North Africa. They asked us why, after having to fight our way into Africa against the Vichy forces, we were returning their country back to the French. The French treatment of the native population varied little as between Vichyites and prewar colonial administration. Following demonstrations and subsequent bloodshed in Algiers on May Day, 1945, the American troops were subject to a hostile attitude on the part of the Moslem population .... The change of feeling upon seeing the American Army depart was obvious and intense. The North African Arabs do not feel that we were their

> "liberators" as we tried so hard to convince them that we were. They only know that we were the "liberators" of their hated enemies, liberating the French so that they could continue to misuse the Arab.[53]

During 1945, however, there were two bits of evidence that the cause of Moroccan nationalism could enlist support in foreign countries. Coincident with the birth of the United Nations was that of the Arab League, far more congenial to the Nationalists. In October, 1945, the secretary of the Arab League demanded for both Morocco and Tunisia "the right to attach themselves to the Arab League" and "freedom to express their own views on ... their future status." In Paris a group of fourteen of the most distinguished professors, several of them Orientalists, made to the French government proposals for improvement of Franco-Moroccan relations. Asserting that the Protectorate "no longer meets the deeply felt aspirations of the Moroccan people, which looks for political emancipation in accordance with the principles proclaimed by the United Nations," the signatories requested a number of reforms, particularly such elementary rights as freedom of the press, freedom of assembly, and freedom to set up native trade unions.[54]

In 1946 the situation of the nationalists became more promising. Puaux was replaced by Erik Laboone as resident general on March 30. The Istiqlal was revitalized by the return to Morocco of several of their first rank leaders; al-Fassi came back from his nine-year exile in Gabon on June 10, Balafrej returned from his exile in Corsica shortly afterwards, and al Ouazzani left his prison in the Atlas. Providing competition for the Istiqlal and thereby pleasing the French <u>colons</u>, al Ouazzani organized his small group into the Democratic Party of Independence (P D I). Thereafter, the French had to deal with a suspicious and resentful Istiqlal, which even a liberal like Labonne found difficult.[55]

A career diplomat, Labonne had previously served as secretary general in the Residency at Rabat and brought to his task not only knowledge of Morocco, but liberality and imagination. He began by freeing the political prisoners and bringing home the exiled leaders of the Nationalists. On July 22 he proposed to the Council of Government an elaborate program of reform--decent housing for all workers, founding of schools, development of fallow lands, trade unions, and places on political and administrative bodies for the Moroccans. Even discussion of these reforms in the Council was refused by the _colons._ Both the _colons_ and the Istiqlal opposed Labonne's plan to defend state enterprises against undermining by private enterprise. The Sultan's refusal to sign the proposed _dahirs_ for once pleased both the _colons_ and the Istiqlal. Nothing but a fundamental change in the structure of the government could satisfy the Istiqlal; they no longer talked of "reforms."[56]

To remind the world that he was by treaty sovereign of a united country, Muhammad V decided to travel through the Spanish Zone and to make a formal visit to Tangier, which no monarch had visited since 1889. Surprisingly, the Quai d'Orsay permitted the journey. The Spanish authorities at Tetuan made futile objections, while the Spanish nationalists were very much pleased.[57] It was a triumphal tour in both zones. Because of a serious riot with heavy casualties in Casablanca on April 7, 1947, the Sultan altered his speech at Tangier, thereby creating a sensation. Departing from the text censored by the Residency, Muhammad V publicly praised the Arab League for its work in unifying Arabs. He also insinuated that France's position in Morocco was only temporary; even more subversive was his omission of the usual praise of French achievements in Morocco. He went further; on April 12 he told foreign correspondents at a press conference:

> It goes without saying that Morocco, being a country attached by solid bonds to the Arab countries in the East, desires to strengthen those bonds even more resolutely, especially since the Arab League has now become an important factor in world affairs.

For this bold and unequivocal statement the Sultan was criticized even by some moderate nationalists, but al-Fassi and most of his party rejoiced.[58]

Allied with certain French army circles, the _colons_ of Morocco attacked Labonne to the extent of virtual insurrection and blackmail against the French Foreign Ministry. Being an honorable man too proud to search for a scapegoat, Labonne assumed full responsibility for the Sultan's speech, resigned, and left Morocco within a month of Muhammad's return home.

On May 14, 1947, the new resident general, Alphonse Juin, assumed office. He was to dominate the Moroccan scene for many years, even after his term of office was over. As a strong believer in the superiority of the French people and civilization, he announced at the beginning his intention to keep Morocco within the French orbit: "I shall permit nobody to indulge in demagogic agitation .... Morocco, which France has united, must be a Western country and turn away from Eastern alliances." Thus he rejected the Sultan's recent declaration of loyalty to Arab leadership. Moreover, he decided not to make the Istiqlal a martyr; he permitted even publication of Nationalist papers, with censorship, and allowed open party meetings.[59]

Prevented from establishing Labonne's economic program by opposition from both the colons and the Sultan, Juin concentrated on his political program. His aim was to cement more firmly the Franco-Moroccan governmental bond through amalgamation of the Maghzen with their French administrative counterparts. Six new members were appointed to the Maghzen, and by having only joint meetings of the French and Moroccan members, he made sure that the Sultan could never take any independent action. By proposing that new members of the Council of Government be elected instead of appointed, he hoped to increase the popularity of the P D I. Juin's new principle of government was co-sovereignty, but it was a rule in which France was definitely dominant. The Sultan signed the dahirs concerning the Council, but he balked at Juin's proposal of new municipal councils with equal French and Moroccan membership. He declined to sign away not only his own local authority but also the sovereignty of Morocco. Through its Council membership of fifteen out of twenty-one members, its representation on many vizieral reform committees, and the Sultan's refusal to sign dozens of dahirs, all seeking to extend the scope of co-sovereignty, the Istiqlal was able to obstruct political changes for three years.[60]

Although the Istiqlal continued recruitment at home, in 1947 its base of propaganda shifted to Cairo, where two nationalist leaders of the first rank soon appeared. Escaping from police surveillance in Tangier, al-Fassi appeared in Cairo on May 25. After spending twenty years in Reunion, Abd al Krim was on his way to further detention at Marseilles when he left the ship at Port Said. He was granted royal sanctuary by King Farouk. While al-Fassi directed propaganda from the Maghreb office, Abd al Krim advocated a direct fight and open negotiations with the French. He also declared his loyalty to Muhammad V and to his fight for independence. The young nationalist propagandists in Cairo alerted all the Middle East to the precarious situation of Morocco and formed a useful liaison between the Moroccans and the Arab League.[61]

In a speech delivered at the Academy of Colonial Sciences in Paris on November 18, 1949, Juin exposed his policy of co-sovereignty in Morocco. Becoming weary of the impasse, the Moroccan members boycotted the Government Council in July, 1950. This "meaningless gesture" bothered the new cabinet of Pleven; some action seemed necessary to win the friendship of the Sultan. The French president, Vincent Auriol, extended an invitation to visit Paris, not only to Muhammad V, but to his family, cabinet, and court. Serving notice of his intention to discuss the political problems of his country, the Sultan arrived with his party on October 11, 1950. Despite the ceremonial reception, the Legion of Honor conferred on Prince Mulai Hassan, numerous receptions, and magnificent presents exchanged, the Sultan was not deterred from the main purpose of his visit. Muhammad sent two formal notes to Auriol and discussed his demands with Auriol, Pleven, and Schuman. The French reply to the first note promised a lessening of press censorship, establishment of trade unions, and improved legal practices, but ignored the Sultan's demand for recognition of Sherifian sovereignty. To the second note stating clearly that only proposals for abolishing the protectorate could be considered, there was no reply. Leaving for home on November 5, without any token of success in his mission, Muhammed had nevertheless won the greatest approbation of his subjects. At Casablanca and Rabat he was greeted enthusiastically by thousands, even by Berbers from the Atlas. The Quai d'Orsay announced a committee to study the Moroccan problem, but it was never appointed. The *colons* denounced even the mild reforms offered by France and railed against the Sultan's "megalomania" and "medieval despotism." Juin met the Sultan's challenge by resolving upon the employment of force; this resulted in the "crisis of 1951."[62]

At a session of the Government Council in December, 1950, two Istiqlal members made violent speeches denouncing

French economic policy as designed to further colon interests alone. When Juin, who presided over Council meetings, ordered one of them to leave the room, all the Istiqlal members went. Going immediately to the palace, they were received by the Sultan. Juin then decided to enlist Thami al Glaoui against the Sultan. Al Glaoui had but recently returned from Paris, where he had accompanied the Sultan. On December 21, at an interview with Muhammad, the Pasha of Marrakesh shouted at his sovereign, "You are not the Sultan of Morocco; you are the Sultan of the Istiqlal!" Being ordered never to return to the palace unless summoned, al Glaoui, erstwhile nationalist as Larbi believed, became an implacable and formidable enemy of Muhammed V. In alliance with Juin, al Glaoui planned his campaign against the Sultan, contacting neighboring kaids to carry it out.[63] The modernizing program to which al Glaoui objected had three principal features: universal education, emancipation of Moroccan women, and national Moroccan labor syndicates.[64]

The opening of Juin's campaign to bend or break Muhammad V came on January 26, 1951. About to depart for Washington with the French Premier in order to discuss American air bases in Morocco, Juin delivered an ultimatum at the imperial palace. Either the Sultan would disavow the Istiqlal, or he must abdicate. Juin would depose him if necessary. Being above parties, the Sultan replied, he could not denounce any particular one. Apparently, in Washington Juin was advised officially to conciliate the Sultan; if so, the advice only made him more resolute. On February 12 he enlarged his demands on Muhammad; the latter must now eliminate from his entourage all nationalists, nominate a large number of French candidates for the offices of pashas and kaids, and punish all opponents of al Glaoui. The Sultan conceded the dismissal of all national officials at his court and in the Maghzen; but, advised by his viziers and some leading members of the ulema, he asserted that in neither Muslim law nor in the treaty of 1912 had he any power to outlaw the Istiqlal. To Juin's next demand that the Grand Vizier publish a denunciation of the Istiqlal as atheists and expel them from Islam, the Maghzen gave a firm refusal. Muslims could think of no more sacrilegious act than to condem fellow Muslims on religious grounds at the command of Christians. Next, Juin summoned the entire Maghzen to the Residency, where he abused and threatened them with a descent of Berber tribes upon the cities, unless they would condemn the Istiqlal. The Sultan's cabled plea to Auriol to arbitrate the dispute was answered by the advice that he compromise.

Meanwhile, the cooperation of al Glaoui and Juin had been effective. Tribal leaders and all ranks of officials had been obliged to sign petitions against the Sultan and the Istiqlal which al Glaoui had circulated for several weeks. The French controleurs civile assembled all tribal horsemen and sent them towards Fez and Rabat. The horsemen had been mobilized under various pretexts, but Juin called their gatherings "a spontaneous uprising." At Rabat, the Sultan's palace and Hassan's villa were "protected" by armed troops with guns and tanks "against the Berber revolt." Already Juin had dismissed the Sultan's personal Imperial Cabinet and removed the rector of the Karaouine University--all Nationalists. Now Juin gave the Sultan a second choice--to accept Juin's demands or to renounce the throne. Since his viziers saw no alternative to surrender, that evening, February 25, 1951, the Sultan signed Juin's document, but he declared that he had done this to avoid bloodshed and that he did not consider anything signed under duress to have legal value.

Juin's triumph over both the Sultan and the Istiqlal appeared to be complete. The Nationalists were out of office or arrested, and the Sultan had capitulated. But Juin's treatment of the ruler had achieved within a few days "what the Nationalists had failed to accomplish in as many years." Soon realizing that they had been duped, the Berber tribesmen reacted by giving Muhammed V a loyalty he had never won from them before. The Nationalists actually gained in strength. On April 10 the three minor political parties united with the Istiqlal, pledged to refuse any proposal but independence, to have no connection with the Communists, and to work with the Arab League. At every event of the 1951 crisis, the other Arab countries had reacted violently, and the American press had a full coverage on the affair. Most gratifying of all results to the Moroccans, perhaps, was the decision of the French government on August 28, 1951, to remove Juin from office.[65] On September 14 Juin said farewell to the Sultan in a formal speech which must have sounded very ironical.[66]

The arrival of the next resident general, General Augustin Guillaume, produced no alleviation of the Moroccan situation. As a veteran of Lyautey's campaigns, Guillaume knew every part of Morocco; he spoke both Berber and Arabic and was genuinely interested in the country. Despite his announcement that he would welcome foreign journalists, he soon showed that he would tolerate no adverse criticism of French policy from them, and he threatened "fanatics" of Nationalist views until the Quai d'Orsay temporarily put a curb on his public utterances. He was under the sway of Juin and his henchmen left behind in high offices in Morocco. Soon Guillaume replaced Juin as the chief guardian of the colonists.[67]

Guillaume's duties were increased by the Moroccans' decision to use the forum of the United Nations to appeal for world support in their pursuit of independence. Before 1951, there had been friendly feelings, but little cooperation between Morocco and Tunisia in their separate campaigns for independence. Beginning in that year, however, their mutual failure to progress toward their goal led to the conviction that only united action could achieve freedom for each, and from 1952 to 1955 the two countries worked together to develop world opinion in their favor. In 1953 they were joined by Algeria in the Cairo Pledge, in which Nationalists of the three countries swore never to make any agreements with France that might be harmful to any of them.[68]

While the Arabian, and later the Arabian-Asian, Muslim bloc was sponsoring the cause of Morocco and Tunisia in the United Nations, the Sultan continued his pressure on the French government to grant Morocco's demands. In his speech from the throne on November 18, 1951, the Sultan expressed hope that new negotiations with France might lead to "a convention that would guarantee Morocco its full sovereignty," placing her relations with France "on new foundations." Receiving no reply, on March 20, 1952, he asked Guillaume to forward a note to Auriol. The note proposed that France should agree to discuss the status of the Protectorate, after ending the "state of siege;" the Sultan should be empowered to form a government of persons competent to negotiate with France; and, lastly, the negotiations should deal with a revision of Franco-Moroccan relations on the basis of the Sultan's note of October 1950. The Nationalists soon added a clarification of these proposals: France's legal rights and interests could be guaranteed in a new convention, aimed to assure the continuance of Franco-Moroccan relations within a framework giving satisfactory scope to Moroccan aspirations. The aim of both the Sultan and the Istiqlal was a constitutional monarchy with real powers of self-government, but with a continuation of Franco-Moroccan cooperation.

After six months, a reply from Paris contained only "reforms," most of them a reaffirmation of co-sovereignty. Stressing the magnitude of French achievements in Morocco, the Quai d'Orsay proposed the establishment of administrative djemas elected in rural districts and of Franco-Moroccan commissions in the cities and in rural areas, and a speedy presentation of proposals regulating the administration of justice. Finally, the French note submitted that "the administration in Morocco has a mixed character, that is, Franco-Moroccan under control of the French administration." In his reply of October 3, Muhammad stressed the inadmissible character of the French proposals; co-sovereignty, of course, was the very principle over which he had fought Juin, and which he asserted was a violation of the Treaty of 1912. The Sultan's position had been adopted on August 27 by the International Court of Justice at the Hague, which had reaffirmed the sovereignty and independent status of Morocco.[69]

Guillaume, a writer as well as an administrator and a soldier, was fully aware of the importance of obtaining American support for France against Morocco. In an American periodical he found an appropriate medium to appeal to the American political elite. Some of his pertinent remarks were as follows:

> A word which the French think cannot be used about their overseas activities is "colonialism," because the term implies racial domination and commercial exploitation, denied, they believe, by the work they have accomplished .... Strategically, North Africa protects the southern flank of Western Europe just as Great Britain protects the northern flank .... The development of Morocco and provision for its security are then essential elements in Western defense. They can be achieved only by a combination of industrial progress, agricultural modernization, social organization, and political stability. The *sine qua non* for each of these is Franco-Moroccan unity.[70]

In December of 1952 there was a disastrous chain of events for Morocco. On the 6th occurred the murder of Ferhat Hashed, one of the most highly esteemed Nationalists of Tunisia and a labor leader associated with American trade unionists. The Tunisians were convinced that his assassin was French, and there was great anger in the Muslim world. A sympathy strike in Casablanca resulted, on December 7-8, in clashes between the police and the natives. The French public at first accepted the official report of a few casualties. Later thirteen French professors at Casablanca denounced the official version of the riot, claiming that the death list was grossly understated and that the police instigated the affair. Colonialist and non-colonialist newspapers battled over the numbers of French or Moroccans killed, and the American press had many accounts uncomplimentary to the French. Special correspondents for both right-wing and non-political French papers agreed that official reports of the origin and events of the affair were unworthy of credence. Many groups in France, such as the Circle of Catholic Intellectuals and the Association France-Maghreb demanded the truth about the unfortunate happening, but Guillaume declared that he would never accept an official commission of inquiry. As punishment for the disturbance, hundreds of Nationalists were imprisoned, and it was twenty-two months before the fifty-one members of the Istiqlal charged with instigation of the riot were discharged for lack of evidence. Many pro-nationalist Frenchmen were also arrested and exiled to France, but anti-nationalist journalists and editors received no punishment for false rumors or incitements to murder. However, Moroccan hopes centered on New York, where the U N Assembly was debating the Moroccan question for the first time.[71]

The Moroccan imbroglio reached its climax during 1953. During the summer the Sultan was virtually in custody, imprisoned in his palace, his person and throne were in peril, and many of his supporters were imprisoned or exiled. His loyal son, Prince Mulai Hassan, helped by bringing his French friends to talk with his father. Muhammad V had now finally formulated his philosophy of resistance; his aim was not only to prevent the further degeneration of his country into a colony, but also to revise the Protectorate treaty to enable Morocco to progress eventually to a completely independent state. In an official communique published on June 17, 1953, he again tried to reassure France:

> Our intention has always been to permit the country to conduct its own affairs democratically ... safeguarding the interests of France and of French people in Morocco. To achieve this aim, we have tried to reach common understanding with the French government, so that an overall plan, in keeping with modern ideas, might be prepared.

In August the Sultan made his last appeal to Auriol, protesting against the unrestricted activity of his opposition,[72] who moved about freely, organizing demonstrations and plotting to overthrow him and to get France to violate her treaties. No reply was received from Paris.[73] By this time, the desperate war to recover Indo-China for the Empire had led the French to adopt a "tough policy" regarding North Africa, and to resolve to hang on to the latter if Indo-China must be abandoned.[74]

Awaiting the expected disaster, Moroccan crowds marched day after day in the *medina* at Rabat, chanting the *Latif*, a prayer for divine mercy used only in times of great danger. The Sultan refused to summon his supporters to a civil war. Early in August Guillaume and the French government each made feints at restricting al Glaoui, who declared that "the Sultan would continue to be unfit to be Morocco's spiritual and temporal leader." Some journalists in Paris condemned the French policy as designed to serve the interests of a few wealthy persons. Finally, on August 13, Guillaume gave his ultimatum: the Sultan must sign all the decrees which for years he had refused to sign, including a delegation of his powers to a Franco-Moroccan Committee. Few Frenchmen knew that Guillaume's proposed "reforms" would have deprived the Sultan and the Maghzen of their last vestiges of power and would have granted the French in Morocco privileges to which as foreigners they had no right. After six months of training the Berber tribesmen, al Glaoui was at last ready to execute his coup. France was busy combatting a general strike; even Foreign Minister Bidault, often before sympathetic to Morocco, now saw the Moroccan situation as "a fight of the Cross against the Crescent."[75]

Al Glaoui and al Kittani selected as their puppet sultan Arafa al Alaoui, an uncle of Muhammad V, but a stupid and hitherto completely obscure individual. He was a very wealthy man and, incidentially, a son-in-law of al Glaoui. On August 15 the conspirators had Mulai Arafa elected Imam, leaving only his secular powers for Sidi Muhammad. Such a separation of the secular and religious functions of the sultanate was unprecedented and invalid in Muslim law.[76]

There remained to be accomplished the deposition of the "secular" ruler. On August 20, Guillaume entered the palace with the chief of the Security Services to find the Sultan in his siesta pajamas. Muhammad refused the abdication that Guillaume demanded. The Sultan was arrested and rushed with his two sons to an armored car which drove them to a military camp where they were held incommunicado under guard. Still in siesta clothing, the three Alouites were sent off in a plane towards Corsica.[77]

On the same day occurred the "March on Rabat and Fez,"--the occupation of these cities by mixed French troops and Moroccan tribesmen. In all their accounts of the events of August 15-20, the French emphasized the "purely native" character of the conflict "between the Moroccans and the Sultan," in which the French "took absolutely no part." Negating the French claim of non-participation was a photograph in the London _Observer_ of August 30 showing the beginning of the march--it was headed by two jeeps, in each of which were French officers. Most of the tribesmen thought that they were going to celebrate a big holiday in the city. It was French officers who arrested the royal family and sent them off. A _colons'_ paper, moreover, thanked Guillaume for his adroit management of the whole affair. Finally, Premier Laniel claimed credit on June 24, 1955, for the French government's successful handling of the Sultan's deposition.[78]

On the evening of August 20 the _ulema_ of Fez were summoned by French police to a meeting on the next day. The only two members who refused to sign the _beia_ for the new Sultan were punished--one by arrest, the other by a beating; the others signed in the presence of Berber tribesmen armed with knobbly sticks. The election party consisted of "some of the oldest and most feudal-minded men Morocco could produce." There was no popular rejoicing over the new ruler in Rabat. Accompanied by the Grand Vizier, al Glaoui, and al Kittani, he rode between columns of Berber tribesmen who held back silent crowds. During Arafa's first ceremonial visit to a mosque, he barely escaped assassination by a native. The colonialist press was jubilant over the dawn of a new era of general happiness, but French magazines joined in unfavorable criticism, many of them blaming Juin. In general, French public opinion showed sadness rather than gladness--it was too conscious of its seven years' war in Indo-China, and it wanted no repetition of that. Mitterand resigned from the Cabinet in protest, and others spoke in Parliament against the Sultan's deposition.[79]

Throughout 1953 American newspapers and magazines gave the Moroccan conflict a prominent place. There was a division of opinion between those who accepted the French version of persons and events[80] and those who saw the Sultan's side of the picture. That even a usually well-informed paper might be misled by some pro-French propaganda is shown by the following excerpts from an editorial:

> [The Istiqlal,] the French say, was resented by the Berbers ... since independence might mean for them a harsher rule by the Arabs of coastal cities than government by France ....
>
> French officialdom, headed by Resident-General Augustin Guillaume, has preserved order, while a sharp clash between Arabs and Berbers, the two major elements in the population, resolved itself ....
>
> The presence of strategic American air bases in Morocco now adds influence to that of French and Jewish colonists who would probably suffer if the Nationalists succeeded in an autocratic state along Mohammedan lines ....[81]

Mulai Arafa lost no time in finishing the task assigned to him. During the month of "perfect peace," before the stunned populace came back to normal life, he signed everything that anyone placed before him, not excepting a restaurant menu, it is said. By his ready use of his signature, he gave the French direct administration which the *colons* had so long demanded. His executive powers were given to an Inner Council; his legislative powers he presented to a Council of Viziers and Directors consisting of fourteen Moroccans and sixteen Frenchmen. Municipal elections were decreed to form councils in which Frenchmen and Moroccans would be equally represented. All of these governmental bodies were so constituted as to be under French control. Many minor adherents of Arafa got jobs or promotions and many had Legion of Honor decorations to display. But some of the really large rewards expected were not bestowed by the French. For example, al Glaoui remained the true power behind the throne (he, too, stayed under French control), but his sons were not made viziers or pashas. The French were too astute to risk a Maghzen or regional administration under al Glaoui's domination.[82]

Then came the wakening of the people. The great majority of them felt that the humiliating removal of their spiritual leader, the embodiment of the nation, had wronged them all personally. Thus developed a devotion to the "true" sultan which took many bizarre forms. People refused to enter mosques, where they would hear prayers in the name of Mulai Arafa. A moon cult was popular--thousands believed that they saw a real image of Muhammad V in his white djellabah in the shadows of the moon. Folk songs cried out for his return. Soon the wounded religious susceptibilities were transformed into violence, first against the Moroccan collaborators with the French, and then against the French in Morocco.[83]

Encouraged by the sympathy of the Muslim World as well as by many French liberals, the lower echelon leaders of the Istiqlal came forward to launch a campaign of violence in the autumn of 1953. The revolters had new recruits now from the industrial proletariat who in 1952-53 had grown rapidly in the cities, especially Casablanca. Labelled as "terrorism" by the press, the Moroccans regarded their guerrilla warfare as a national war of liberation. Since the strategy of the insurrection consisted perforce of sabotage, boycott of French goods, assault, and murder, many undesirable elements were attracted--adventurers, desperados, hotheads, and criminals--to swell the ranks of the patriots. After the assault on Moroccan "traitors," the campaign attacked French persons and property. For a second time Mulai Arafa narrowly escaped assassination by a bomb, and many prominent Moroccans and French were murdered. For two years after the deposition of Muhammad V, a real civil war was waged between the French and the Moroccans.[84] From the cities the reign of terror spread to the rural regions, where sabotage was particularly menacing. The French authorities, both in France and in Morocco, reacted vigorously with counter-terrorism[85] against French thought to be friendly to the revolt as well as against the Moroccans, and their methods consisted of sending more troops from France and imposing sterner repressive police measures. Since the Istiqlal movement was originally represented as tiny and later as dead after the clean-up of December, 1952, the French declared the revolt to be the work of gangsters and a few Istiqlal criminals. The French seemed utterly unable to realize that the magic of "the Sultan in the Moon" was the force underlying the national upheaval.[86]

For a brief time a hope existed that the French authorities might become aware of reality and act accordingly. On June 18, 1954, the rightwing Cabinet of Laniel was succeeded by that of Pierre Mendès-France, a progressive known for anti-colonialist views. Relieved of his office in May, 1954, Guillaume was replaced by Francis Lacoste, a professional diplomat of wide experience in important capitals and in the United Nations. He served only until June 16, 1955; Mendès-France had already retired in February. As Juin's chief adviser for two years, Lacoste had gained the confidence of many liberal Moroccans and Frenchmen rather than of his chief. This new leadership should have improved the rapidly deteriorating situation. However, after granting autonomy to Tunisia. Mendès-France found Morocco a dilemma; he could not decide between al Glaoui and his supporters, to whom Muhammad V was anathema, and those Moroccans who demanded the Sultan's return as a _sine qua non_ to peace. The Secretary of the Istiqlal laid down three preliminary conditions: the return of Sidi Muhammad, the trial of all Moroccans detained in prison for alleged acts of terrorism, and abolition of all laws passed since August 20, 1953. The Secretary promised Istiqlal support of any agreement made by Muhammad and declared that the legitimate French interests would be safeguarded by the Sultan, all native political parties, and all the ulema.[87]

During the spring and summer of 1954, the French authorities were said to be seeking a replacement for the unpopular Mulai Arafa, too afraid of assassins to appear in public. Prince Abdallah was suggested, as was also a temporary Regency Council representing the various Moroccan factions. Meanwhile, Lacoste followed the old precedent set by residents general: he presented a detailed program of reforms for immediate adoption on September 20. Political changes were to be discussed later by a special Franco-Moroccan council. The Lacoste reforms were all good. They included the raising of the natives' standard of living, a wider distribution of labor, further development of small scale local industries, higher minimum wages for rural workers, lowering of the prices of certain products essential for farming, permission to form trade unions, and enlarged employment of Moroccans in administration. Lacoste also speeded up the trials of the Istiqlal leaders imprisoned for alleged instigation of the riots of December, 1952; all were acquitted for lack of evidence. But the dynastic question was postponed for future settlement, and so the impasse continued.[88]

By the autumn of 1954 the Moroccan revolt had ceased to be a French problem; it had become an important factor in Islamic and Western relations. This came about as a result of the Algerian revolt for independence in November, 1954. The Algerian nationalist movement, supported by both Algerians and most Algerian workmen and students in France, had been underground for many years. Though often disbanded by the authorities, it always emerged again stronger and more popular. Egypt's championship of North African nationalism became more militant in 1954. "The Voice of the Arabs" made daily broadcasts from Cairo, urging deeds of violence and resort to arms. Still the French government's <u>immobilisme</u> continued.[89]

There was a new French government early in 1955, for Edgar Faure succeeded Mendès-France on February 2, 1955. There was also an increase in French counter-terrorism, but the murder of Lemaigre-Dubreuil in June "as no other incident had done ... shocked France into a sense of urgency." Finally the French began to realize that the counter-terrorists were enjoying the indulgence and often the cooperation of the French police. Moreover, they employed professional killers imported from France and were supported by <u>colon</u> organizations. Although Moroccan terrorists were sometimes arrested and convicted, no counter-terrorist murderer was ever molested. As a scapegoat, the resident general was always expendable; now the French Cabinet decided on June 16, 1955, to recall Lacoste. He had failed because of the lack of a feasible policy at the Quai d'Orsay and the power of the <u>colons</u>, but he was accused of inability or unwillingness to bring French terrorists to justice.[90]

In July, 1955, resolved to end the increasing violence

and anarchy, Faure appointed as resident general Gilbert Grandval, formerly French High Commissioner to the Saar. As usual, Grandval formulated a program of reforms, adding the advice that Mulai Arafa's abdication and replacement by a representative regency council might solve the dynastic problem. Granval's brief period in office--till late August--was marked by harassment from the colons' leaders, who refused to cooperate with him. He was attacked for his amnesties to political prisoners and for his Jewish ancestry. On two occasions he narrowly escaped lynching. During July, "Grandval to the Gallows!" echoed in the city streets. On July 29 the Arab-Asian bloc again asked the United Nations to take action on the Moroccan situation. Requested to form a government on a broadly based coalition, Mulai Arafa refused, offering instead a government of his own followers. The Quai d'Orsay declined this offer and decided on a consultation with Moroccan leaders, including Istiqlalists.[91]

The events of July apparently confirmed the Nationalist charge--expressed, however, by the French Schuman himself--that the true rulers of Morocco were neither the French government nor the resident general, but a coalition of colons, lobbyists, big business, and the local police. But the events of August showed that there was a force capable of terrifying even this formidable alliance. Spurred on by Radio Cairo and Radio Damascus, on August 20 tens of thousands of Berber tribesmen revolted in Algeria and in the Moroccan countryside. The unofficial death toll for the two countries was 800 within two days, but another outbreak in Marrakesh brought the total to 1,000. The most notorious episode was the descent of the Berbers upon the little town of Oued Zem, near the Middle Atlas, in which every French man, woman, and child was massacred. A new feature of the August risings was the participation of women, who marched in the front ranks of the demonstrators in most of the affairs. Feminine violence was displayed in both town and country and among both Arabs and Berbers. It was a tribute to their emancipator, now the women's national hero and martyr. The most fierce outbursts occurred, significantly, where the Istiqlal organization had lost control, and where the people were leaderless and desperate--at Oued Zem, at Khenifra, and in the phosphate mines of Khouribga. Shortly before these revolts, a number of kaids had telegraphed Faure their condemnation of al Glaoui. A much alarmed American State Department urgently requested

France to end this situation, so dangerous for American air bases and for the prestige of the West in North Africa.[92]

The conferences regarding the throne were ineffectual. The Nationalist delegates insisted upon immediate removal of Arafa, the return of Muhammad V, formation of a representative throne council, and a Moroccan government approved by Muhammad V. These conditions were unacceptable to Faure, or to Bidault and Juin[93] in his cabinet. Renewed pressure from Washington, now worried about the use of American military equipment against North Africans, and from French liberal groups, caused Faure's proposal of a compromise: removal of Arafa to please the Nationalists and dismissal of Grandval to satisfy the colons. Arafa refused to abdicate, but Grandval resigned; to take his place General Boyer de Latour was summoned from Tunisia, arriving at Rabat on August 31. This was another triumph for the "Morocco lobby," which had already deposed Sultan Muhammad and had turned out Mendès-France from the premiership.[94]

De Latour tried to persuade Arafa to resign in favor of a new plan to have the Maghzen select a three-man regency or throne council which would ask a prominent Moroccan to form a government representing all political tendencies. The Nationalists would not accept such a plan unless the legitimate sultan, recalled from exile, would agree to it. Bolstered up by the chairman of the French Assembly's Defense Commission, who urged him to hold his throne, Arafa asserted that only God could release him from his responsibilities. On October 1, however, Faure overcame the combined opposition of the lobbyists, the colons, and the generals, including de Latour. He secured Mulai Arafa's departure on a plane for his future residence at the former home of his uncle, Abd al-Aziz, in Tangier. But Faure was not strong enough to obtain the type of throne council contemplated, and Arafa merely left his throne "in charge" of an obscure cousin, a son of Mulai Hafid, instead of abdicating. The Istiqlal repudiated the throne council selected and also the man, backed by the Quai d'Orsay, chosen to head a "representative Moroccan government." Meanwhile, sent to interview Muhammad V in his exile abode in Madagascar, General Catroux announced another plan accepted by the deposed ruler. It was an uncomplicated, simple plan, one that gave the Nationalists everything that they had been asking for: the creation of a free, sovereign state, permanently allied with France through conditions to be defined in an act of independence. On September 12, 1955, Faure announced the surprising decision to grant Morocco "independence within interdependence." Still Faure had to fight strong opposition to such a drastic reversal of plans to subdue Morocco, but he emerged finally a victor over the reactionary forces in France and Morocco.[95]

The yielding of the French government was caused by several influences. One was military necessity. Battle-weary veterans of the disastrous war in Indo-China, supposedly returning to civilian life, were sent instead to war in North Africa.[96] France had not the military strength to battle all of North Africa. Her leaders finally decided that she should save Algeria as an integral part of France and give up trying to make colonies of Morocco and Tunisia. Morocco had degenerated into virtually a new *blad es-siba*, no longer fighting against the sultan, as in former days, but for the restoration of their legitimate ruler. In the Middle Atlas and near the Riff the Berber guerrilla war defied the largest French army ever assembled in Morocco. For many years French relations with her protectorate had been based on myths, which were by 1955 fully discredited; "the myths of the dichotomy of Arab and Berber, the unpopularity of Muhammad V, the unrepresentative character of the Istiqlal, and the general weakness ness of nationalism." Another factor in France's surrender was the pressure of world opinion--in the United Nations, in the Arab League, in Asia, in Europe, in the United States, and in France itself. A third potent influence was that of France's arch-rival in Morocco--Spain, which, according to custom, sought to take advantage of France's distress there.[97]

The denouement of the long struggle was sudden and dramatic, with al Glaoui appearing first on the stage. On October 26 the Pasha appeared with his son before the throne council that nobody approved of. He announced that he did not recognize this council, but that he wished to submit to "the will of the Moroccan people" and to welcome Muhammad back to his rightful throne. His act, whatever his motives, broke the impasse created by the devious French plans for choosing the next sultan. Muhammad was promptly brought back from his two-year exile in Madagascar to Nice and then to Paris, where he was received with elaborate ceremony. Sherif al-Kittani declared in his favor, and all over France and Morocco thousands hastened to jump on his bandwagon. Arafa sent his abdication from Tangier, and al Glaoui proclaimed his immense joy at the Sultan's return. At Sidi Muhammad's Paris headquarters, the old Pasha prostrated himself at the feet of his former enemy, begging forgiveness and receiving assurance that he would be judged by his future conduct alone. Muslim and Jewish leaders expressed their happiness over the settlement of the problem. The Throne Council resigned. With Foreign Minister Pinay, the Sultan negotiated for establishment of the new status of Morocco. So swift had been the course of events, that among them the advent of a new resident general was scarcely noticed. André Dubois, formerly chief of the Paris police, became on November 9, 1955, France's fourth governor of Morocco within a year. Finally, on November 16, Sultan Muhammad was received by his subjects in scenes of fanatical rejoicing. On the 18th, Fete of the Throne Day, he was officially reinstated as Sultan of Morocco.[98]

Knowing so well the need of foreign capital, Muhammad began his reign by a conciliatory policy toward France and by opening the door to the United States. In a special audience to Julius Holmes, American minister in Rabat, he affirmed a common policy toward communism. Reviewing the long history of American-Moroccan relations since the first treaty, he reaffirmed that the Treaty of 1836 granting Americans special privileges would continue to be honored. A few days later he conferred with five American businessmen of Casablanca, promising protection for their investments and asking for more American capital and the assistance of American technical know-how in Morocco.[99]

The demand of the Istiqlal for complete unification of Morocco after the Sultan's return brings into review the Spanish policy since 1951. There had never been any real friendship or cooperation between the leaders of the French and the Spanish zones. In December 1951, Guillaume had visited his colleague, the high commissioner of the Spanish Zone. Their communique stressed the identity of future French and Spanish aims in Morocco and condemned "fanatical Arab nationalism." Most space was devoted, however, to the Americans, whose diplomatic representatives were accused of financing Moroccan Nationalists and inciting them to extremes and thereby endangering "the evolution and security not merely of Morocco but of the entire Western world."[100]

In 1952, being still a pariah among Western states because of her war record and her totalitarian regime, Spain made a determined effort to form an entente with the Arab states.[101] The mission of Foreign Minister Artajo to the Middle East brought about several cultural and economic agreements. Franco's unwillingness to promise autonomy for Spanish Morocco prevented Artajo from making the hoped-for Mediterranean pact. As long as there remained a Moroccan problem, however, Franco found it of advantage to use his possession there as a bargaining point with both Arab and non-Arab governments.[102]

After the Artajo mission and during 1953, Franco continued close contacts with Arab leaders. The deposition of Muhammad V gave him independence in Moroccan affairs. Only Guillaume's speedy sending of the Sultan to Corsica, the French claimed, had prevented the sheltering of Muhammad in the Spanish Zone. Franco declared that France's unilateral action in this coup and failure to inform Spain in advance of it destroyed any unity of policy between the two countries. In the Spanish Zone, the Khalifah at Tetuan continued to represent Muhammad V, mosques there offered prayers in his name, and Nationalists from the French Zone had asylum there. On January 21, 1954, a great meeting of Moroccans, mostly Berbers, occurred at Tetuan. A petition signed by 430 influential Moroccans repudiated utterly the deposing of the legitimate sovereign. It announced non-recognition of Mulai Ben Arafa and requested temporary separation of the Spanish Zone from the French Zone under the full sovereignty of its Khalifah. Throughout the Middle East the Spanish action at Tetuan was acclaimed. The Arab League called upon its eight member nations to support Spain's stand on Morocco, and Arab newspapers named Franco a "true friend of the Muslims." On February 13 Franco announced that Spain would not recognize Arafa as Sultan. Secret radio stations in the Spanish Zone began broadcasting to the French Zone, giving instructions to terrorists. The Residency had Arafa protest to Paris.[103]

The French government was seriously embarrassed by the Tetuan demonstration, which informed the world of the true story of Muhammad's expulsion. It protested to Madrid, and Arafa was informed that steps would be taken to protect his authority in the Spanish Zone--which was obviously impossible. Many Moroccans considered themselves betrayed by the Western powers, and they showed a new willingness to ally themselves with Communists; this was strongly disapproved by their leaders in exile. Now Franco emerged as the sole defender of the Moroccans, although past history did not furnish much ground for confidence in his promises. In August, 1954, the Spanish High Commissioner announced that he would soon submit to his government a "project for increasing the participation of Moroccans in the administration." Spain's new policy, he asserted, would continue until the Moroccans were prepared to rule their own destinies. At the end of 1954 very cordial relations existed between the Spanish and the Moroccans in Tetuan, and Nationalist refugees from the French Zone received great hospitality and practical help. Three Nationalists were actually made members of the ministry of the administration. Supported by Franco, General Valiño was said to be responsible for setting a good example for the French Zone in the treatment of Nationalists.[104] There was much smuggling of arms from the Spanish Zone to the terrorists in the French Zone.

Throughout 1955, the crucial year of French Morocco's struggle for independence, Franco maintained his role of patron of Moroccan nationalism. His aims and activities were duly chronicled in the American press. At this time Spain was slowly making her way into membership in the United Nations. Henry Cabot Lodge was credited with aiding her to obtain an observer there. As a conciliatory gesture, the French government withdrew its financial subsidy to the Spanish Republican Government in exile. The chairman of a Gaullist Party committee protested the broadcasts of Radio Cairo, Radio Budapest, and Radio Tetuan, which had resulted in "the most bloody anarchy in North Africa." General Valiño denied that the Riffian guerrillas were receiving any aid from Spanish Moroccans. However, by late November there was "a turnabout in Morocco." Franco dropped his Muslim mask on November 30,[105] when he made this statement to five Anglo-Saxon journalists:

> France commits a grave error in trying to introduce democratic measures in Morocco. Morocco's main problem lies in the lack of unity of its people, divided as they are between urban, labor, and an undisciplined rural

> population. It would be dangerous to assume that the Moroccans are capable of imposing order and peace in their country at this time. The Moroccan working class is subject to the influence of terrorists, and the Moroccan peasant understands nothing but force.

At a meeting in Rabat, however, the Istiqlal formulated demands on December 2 for the termination of foreign intervention in all Morocco, and the secretary general declared that the party's program had been accepted by the Sultan.[106] Thus Franco and the Istiqlal parted company.

From the end of World War II until she achieved her independence, Morocco had been a multiple problem for France. There had been the long and bloody struggle to colonize Morocco and Tunisia, ending instead in their becoming independent. There had been the persistent problem of communism, both in France and in Morocco. There had been the constant vigilance necessary to prevent Morocco from becoming involved in international relations with Spain, or the Arab states, or the United Nations in such a way as to threaten France's hegemony over her. But most persistent and incomprehensible, perhaps, was France's conviction that the United States sought to replace her as the dominating colonial power in Morocco. Probably an objective review of the many interests of the United States in Morocco after V-E Day would indicate that France had some plausible reasons for her unfounded suspicion of the United States--or might have had, in the preceding century.

The oldest grievance of France against the United States, of course, was the latter's maintenance of extraterritoriality and refusal to give up the rights claimed through the Treaty of 1836 and the Act of Algeciras. The attempt of France to force the negotiation of a new treaty of commerce had failed. During World War II, de Gaulle was not the only French leader who felt sure of Franklin D. Roosevelt's intent to control the future destiny of Morocco, perhaps of France herself.

In view of the active part that she had taken in "freeing" Morocco in World War II, the United States was in no mood to be ignored as she had been in 1923. That she expected to play a large role in the formation of the permanent government of Tangier was indicated by the drafting by the State Department of Professor Graham H. Stuart of Stanford University to prepare a constitution for the city. Dr. Stuart left Stanford University on December 7, 1945, and traveled by air to Tangier, stopping enroute at Washington. He spent about four months on his project. In his article, "The Future of Tangier," appearing in the July, 1954, issue of Foreign Affairs, he expressed optimism regarding the future of the city's government. If the interested powers could agree to respect a truly international constitution, he asserted, the weaknesses and petty jealousies prevalent under the original constitution could be eliminated.[107] Events proved, however, that "internationalism" was as distant from the goal of the powers as it ever had been in Morocco.

After World War II, Spain had to fight to regain her place on the governing board of Tangier. She had to surrender her usurped control of the International Zone. By a temporary arrangement, set up by France, Great Britain, the United States and the U. S. S. R., Spain was allowed to participate in Tangier government, but she lost all of her former administrative posts. When the six months' period prescribed for the establishment of a permanent government passed without change, Spain began pressing for action. For the next several years she took advantage of her zone's location to make herself a nuisance. From the riot of March 30, 1952, in Tangier, requiring the aid of French and Spanish troops to suppress it, came the argument that Spain should be reinstated in her former position in the Tangier government. On May 23, 1952, Spain demanded a return to the Statute of 1923, and Italy asked for her former position in judicial affairs also. To exert extra pressure, Spain posed as a champion of Arab freedom and permitted the return of Torres to Tetuan after an absence of four years in Tangier. Finally the new Tangier government was established by a protocol of November 10, 1952, practically restoring Spain to her former standing in the 1923 Statute. One important provision of the agreement was that the administrator must be from a power little interested in the zone, such as Belgium, The Netherlands, Portugal, or Sweden. Another provision gave the United States more recognition; powers having at least three members in the Assembly were allotted one vice-president each. Thus the United States and Italy could take turns with Great Britain, France, and Spain in presiding over the Legislative Assembly in the absence of the Mendoub. By this convention, with later adhesions, the Mixed Court became one of international jurisdiction on July 22, 1953; in this the United States had one judge. The power of the United States in the Tangier government was still small, but American participation in making the statutes and in being represented in the government personnel showed an increased interest of the United States in Tangier affairs.[108]

The enlarging American stake in Tangier was manifested also in several other ways. There was a great increase in American exports to Tangier. The French Resident objected to the building of wireless stations by the R C A and McKay systems in 1946 and of a government-financed overseas transmitter powerful enough to bring the Voice of America to every country in Europe, North Africa, Asia Minor, Russia, India, and Iran. The United States, of course, had never recognized the Treaty of Fez, by which France claimed a right to radio monopoly. The French feared also that constant advertising of the virtues of the United States over the radio would diminish their own prestige. Another objection to the radio network and transmitter station was that the purchase of large tracts of land for them had set off a sky-rocketing speculative land boom. In 1952 the Soviet Union was reported to be so alarmed at the growing influence of the American land ownership and radio broadcasting in Tangier that it was about to establish a bank there to enable Soviet funds to be transmitted directly to the Moroccan nationalists.[109]

Equally repugnant to the French, undoubtedly, were the American cultural investments in Tangier--the library and the school. Under the auspices of the United States Information Service, the library employed three Americans and six local residents in 1955 and was well patronized. Both its book collections and its films were in English, Spanish, French, and Arabic. The weekly newspapers of Tangier used more English, French, Italian, and Spanish plates, features, and news from the U S I S than did the Spanish and French daily papers. The American School began on October 1, 1950, under the temporary tutelage of Mrs. Alexander Davit, wife of the American commercial attaché, who was succeeded the next year by Miss Elizabeth Cooper of California, employed by the State Department. It was financed locally the first year by American and Muslim bankers and business men. The next year the State Department added a contribution of money and books. All over Morocco the American School won enthusiastic acclaim. A magazine article written in May, 1953, was headed, 'Why They Love Us in Tangier; Here's a warm story of some plain Americans who, acting on their own, gave U. S. prestige a bigger boost than a dozen government programs. It all started with a small school." From the beginning the school was open to all nationalities, races, and religions. Of the library and school Rom Landau says:

> With its Library and its School, the two most highly esteemed and most efficiently run institutions of their kind in the Free City, the small American community can claim to have contributed more to the cultural life of Tangier than any other national group.[110]

An earlier benevolent contribution of the United States to all of Morocco was in the economic field. The French probably regarded it as a part of the American economic invasion, for it did stimulate a market for American agricultural machinery and supplies. This contribution was made by Thomas D. Campbell, head of the Campbell Farming Corporation of Hardin, Montana, reputed to be the largest individual wheat grower in the world. During World War I the United States Army planned to send him to North Africa to increase wheat production there, but decided to use his services in the United States. As a brigadier general in the Air Force during World War II, he made a study of possible wheat production in North Africa, which was supplemented by a further study in 1948. The French government sent a commission representing Algeria, Morocco, and Tunisia, headed by Madam Caillaux, to Montana in 1948, and they carried back all the information that Campbell could give on dry farming. Paul Hoffman accepted Campbell's recommendations to send certain machinery, and the governments of North Africa adopted his methods of moisture conservation for use on demonstration farms. Later Campbell was awarded the third highest rank in the French Legion of Honor.[111]

Honors were not awarded, however, to American journalists for their analyses of French policy. Although there were many papers which printed French versions of events, two leading papers of the United States featured articles by experienced correspondents notable for insight into the complexities of the Moroccan problem. From the Sultan's visit to

Tangier in 1947 to his deposition from his throne and his later restoration, the significance of every happening was astutely analyzed.[112] In its influence upon official policy, however, the American press was not potent.

In 1951 and 1952 there was a good chance for the formation of a strong liaison between the United States and Morocco. In the former year many accusations were made by the French that the United States was encouraging the Nationalist movement in North Africa. An American columnist warned:

> Along with most Istiqlal leaders, the Sultan still pins his hopes for Moroccan independence on American "arbitration" of the problem .... Here in Morocco a way must be found, soon, to convince native leaders that the free world, under American leadership, stands for freedom, not imperialism.

In October, 1951, a French Foreign Office spokesmen charged:

> The United States has lent encouragement to Nationalist movements in colonial and semi-colonial nations of the Middle East and North Africa. The U. S. view is that that is the way to win over the Nationalists before the Russians do.

Talking to the American Club in Paris on November 15, 1951, Juin asserted that American policy falsely encouraged the extreme elements in Morocco:

> Our policy has met reverses on the part of Americans. North Africa, figures the State Department, is a strategic area of the highest interest to the United States. In case of conflict, therefore, order must reign there. There are nationalist currents which can produce major disorders, so it is necessary for us to take the hands of the local chieftains and give them at once whatever they ask, say the Americans.[113]

Since 1949 the United States had apparently been supporting the sovereignty of the Sultan in international affairs. Morocco demanded that she be made a member of N A T O in her own right, not under the signature of France; she also claimed the right to participate in all agreements affecting her destiny. Although concerned at being excluded from the Atlantic Pact, because France was not permitted to sign for her and would not allow her to sign as an independent state, Morocco gave the United States credit for adhering to the Algeciras Act and insisting on Morocco's status as a sovereign state. Since North Africa was to play an important role in the Western military defense plan, however, Morocco was partially reconciled to being omitted from N A T O. Morocco hoped that interest in her industrial development by the United States might open the way to rid herself of French and Spanish rule.[114]

The American Marshall Plan, or European Recovery Plan, might have served in part to fulfill Morocco's hope of independent industrial development. Instead, a letter to Senator Tom Connally, Chairman of the Foreign Relations Committee, charged that E R P funds were being used to strengthen French colonialism in North Africa and to suppress independence movements in that area.[115] The complaint was made by the Committee for the Freedom of North Africa, of which Abd al Krim was president. In condoning the French misuse of E R P money, the United States was accused of violating the "sacred principles of international law" and of putting expediency above morality. The committee's letter continued:

> In practice, American dollars, exclusively distributed to French settlers and businessmen, were used to further the dislocation of the national economies of Tunisia, Algeria, and Morocco for the benefit of their French masters, French trusts, and monopolies .... When the State Department agreed on December 31, 1949, to waive for an indefinite period treaty rights which the United States acquired as a result of a pact of friendship and commerce with the Sultan of Morocco in 1836, it violated both the juridical status of Morocco and the sovereign rights of the Sultan.[116]

Another article said that the total investment of $250,000,000 in North Africa during the postwar years had been used in large scale development projects, such as petroleum, many kinds of machinery, especially tractors and agricultural machinery, rubber, and textiles. The large projects were irrigation systems, the soil conservation plantings (the needs of Campbell's agricultural program were seen here), electric and water power projects, and mining. In "We're Invading North Africa Again," Demaree Bess wrote of the economic partnership of France and the United States:

> Funds appropriated for the European Recovery Program have been used in this region, thus confirming our acknowledgment that African development is essential to the recovery of France .... Africa now has been fitted into America's new economic plans, just as Africa was fitted into our military plans during World War II .... North Africa, then, has now reverted completely to French rule, and today, its three districts are being administered once more like colonies, despite French efforts to conceal this fact, even from themselves .... The wretched poverty of the African majority here, contrasted to the relative prosperity of the French minority, is all too evident.

This American viewpoint is a confirmation of the charges made by Abd al Krim--E R P funds did not bring greater prosperity to the Moroccan masses.[117]

Another grievance of the Sultan's government was the establishment of American airbases in Morocco by a Franco-American arrangement without consulting Moroccan wishes. In 1946 the Middle Eastern command of the United States was transferred from Cairo back to Casablanca. The plan was to concentrate all American military forces along the Atlantic coast, closing down the bases in northern and equatorial Africa. Only the naval base at Port Lyautey and the air and army bases at Casablanca remained American; all other airports had been turned over to France.[118] In 1951 Morocco figured largely in American defense plans for the Mediterranean area, and an agreement was made with France for construction of originally five airbases, later changed to four, at Nouasseur, Sidi Slimane, Benguerir, and Boulhaut. Construction was by an American company employing American technicians, but both American and local labor. A big scandal arose over the waste of millions of dollars in crash construction of the first base with substandard materials, leading to a Congressional investigation. However, the first base at Sidi Slimane went into operation on December 5, 1951, and work on the fourth base was completed by May, 1955. As usual the French authorities made difficulties for the Americans by such devices as trying to set wage scales for native labor, limiting the number of squadrons to six, refusing permission for a television station, and restricting the number of air base personnel in Morocco.[119]

Despite the disregard of Moroccan interests shown in the E R P and airbase affairs, there was much official sympathy expressed for the North African aspiration for independence. In 1951 four members of Congress toured North Africa. On returning, they declared:

> In past years many Nationalist groups in North Africa have felt that the United States is their best friend. In recent years, however, the United States has found itself in the position of siding more and more often with the colonial powers and against Nationalist groups .... As long as the United States remains the champion of freedom in the world it cannot ignore the natural aspirations for freedom of colonial peoples .... Consideration might well be given by Congress to the inclusion in future foreign aid legislation of a statement giving voice to the general sympathy and understanding of Americans for the aspiration of colonial peoples for freedom.

In April, 1952, President Truman had said in reference to Asia and Africa:

> We want to help the people of these areas ... above all, we want to help them find out and apply the secret of our own success, the secret of the American revolution.

A well known journalist and author goes so far as to assert that the Truman administration was known to be favorable to the Nationalists, but that the Eisenhower administration immediately adopted a "neutral" attitude toward Morocco and Tunisia. By the end of 1952, accordingly, the French government found it expedient to enter upon ruthless repression in North Africa, hoping that the free hand given it by the United States would enable it to intimidate the Moroccans into submission.[120]

Many specialists, scholars and mere American observers who had visited North Africa during and since the war said that supporting outdated colonialism was no way to fight communism--rather, it would only encourage Moscow--and warned that unless Americans gave North Africa help and understanding, they would some day regret it. But during the Korean War of 1952-53 American officials were obsessed with the dangers of a Communist war and dared do nothing to antagonize France, whose aid was essential for defense of the West. When a Nationalist like Balafrej discussed his party's position on communism with high American officials, he found himself rejected and then tried to reassure the American people by public statements of loyalty to the West. The Moroccan Nationalists were suspect because of being backed by the Arab League, known to be the arch-enemy of Israel, which had won her place on the map with American blessing.[121]

The American dilemma of choosing between support of the Moroccans fighting to attain the American ideal of independence and an alliance with France in the struggle against expanding Communism was a complex problem. Ever since the founding of the Protectorate in 1912, the economic war between France and the United States had been waged in Morocco, and two world wars during this period had enabled France to employ the plea of military necessity to attempt evasions of American "treaty rights." Now that peace was restored, the French were using their economic policy of favoring French trade to the detriment of American commerce. But although the State Deprtment, historically always the champion of American treaty rights, now was complaisant to French policy, there was a small but growing and dynamic class of American business men in Morocco and in the United States determined not to permit French violation of their interests. This situation led eventually to elevating the quarrel from the status of diplomatic exchanges to that of settlement by the world's highest tribunal.

In October, 1949, a suit for a permanent injunction against the State Department was brought in the Federal District Court in Washington, D. C., enjoining it "from relinquishing our treaty rights in Morocco." The suit was started by Lt. Col. Robert E. Rodes, Commander of the American Legion Post in Morocco and spokesman for the American Trade Association of Morocco. The Court was asked to determine whether or not United States treaties "may be set aside by simple executive action." The occasion of the suit was the State Department's acceptance of a Moroccan decree embargoing most American products and restricting all others. In effect on January 15, 1949, the decree was lifted on May 23, but it was reinstated on June 10, with a promise that American grievances would be satisfied later. Meanwhile, all American business had been frozen. The State Department, Rodes said, had waived the "most favored nation" provision of the treaty of 1880. To conserve dollar exchange for Morocco, "Thirty-five percent of the 1948 trade controlled by forty independent Americans has been transferred from them to favored French interests."[122]

On December 31, 1949, the State Department "reluctantly" agreed to a compromise to let the French "for an indefinite period" regulate American imports into Morocco, but under the same restrictions as applied to French business. Congress agreed with the administration that the temporary waiving of treaty rights was for the good of Europe's recovery. It was expressly stated that this agreement in no way limited American treaty rights in Morocco. Rodes announced that he would press for further Congressional action,[123] and the Istiqlal objected that the agreement was made by the French Ministry of Foreign Affairs instead of by the Protectorate government.[124]

The next step in the controversy was taken by France. On December 28, 1950, the government explained that after protracted diplomatic negotiations had failed to effect an agreement with Washington, it had decided to appeal to the International Court of Justice for a definition of American treaty rights in Morocco. The passage of the Hickenlooper amendment to the United States foreign aid act was undoubtedly a stimulus to France's action. It provided that after November 1, 1950, credits would be withheld from any country having dependent territories where, in the opinion of the President, United States treaty rights were being violated. This amendment had been adopted at the request of American traders in Morocco, represented by Rodes.[125]

The case of the Rights of Nationals of the United States in Morocco, the first contention of the United States before the World Court, was under consideration from October 28, 1950, until August 27, 1952. The verdict of the court upheld the American claim to "economic liberty without any inequality," based on the Treaty of 1836 and the Act of Algeciras; France, therefore, had no privileged economic position in Morocco. But the American businessmen were not exempted from French currency restrictions, and the pegging of the Moroccan franc to the French franc gave French merchants a virtual monopoly of Moroccan foreign trade. However, on October 2, 1952, the French Resident General announced the rescinding of the decree of December 30, 1948.[126]

Every year from 1951 until after the restoration of Muhammad V in 1955, the Moroccan Nationalists, sometimes associated with their Tunisian counterparts, followed two avenues of approach to their goal. First, they greatly widened the scope of their propaganda to include the United States. Probably their spokesmen, reinforced by the American press, did have some influence on public opinion. However, their arguments did not prevail in their second endeavor, for in their appeals to the United Nations they were greatly disappointed at not receiving the vote or the support of the American delegates.

In the extension of propaganda, a number of "information offices" were established in many cities, such as Jakarta, New Delhi, and Bagdad, but the most important were in the United States. The Tunisians formed a liaison with American labor unions through Ferhat Hached. He had first joined his labor union to the W F T U, but finding that it was dominated by Communists, in June, 1950, he joined the British and Americans in the new International Confederation of Free Trade Unions. In September, 1952, he accepted an invitation of the A F L to address its convention in San Francisco. From that time on there was a close association between American labor unions and Hached's union. The assassination of Hached was regarded as a great loss to international labor as well as to nationalism. Hached paved the way for Ladgham, who received the aid of American labor when he arrived in New York in April, 1952, to establish the "Tunisian Office for National Liberation." Another Tunisian who spoke before the A F L convention at San Francisco in September, 1951, was Habib Bourguiba, leader of the Destour party and a "veteran of seven years in exile and three terms in French and Tunisian military prisons." Bourguiba warned that the very fabric of North Atlantic security was endangered by French insistence on maintaining colonial control in North Africa. He also pledged the support of all North Africans in the Western fight against Communism.[127]

Morocco had more spokesmen in the United States than Tunisia had. In 1951, Dr. Mehdi ben Aboud, a Moroccan physician doing post-graduate work in the United States, opened the "Moroccan Office of Information and Documentation" in New York. Dr. Aboud's work was the production of large numbers of brochures written by Moroccans, by Rom Landau, Pierre Parent and others.[128] He also published a weekly newsletter, and beginning on April 23, 1953, a monthly 8-page pamphlet called Free Morocco, with the semi-monthly Bulletin, which continued into 1955. Before the autumn session of the U N General Assembly in 1952, other Nationalists arrived to aid Dr. Aboud, al Fassi, Balafrej, and Laghzaoui for the Istiqlal and five representatives of the three other Nationalist parties.[129] Muslim groups throughout the United States held frequent meetings, and the Istiqlal had a second headquarters in Washington, D. C. As before, the American periodicals aided in disseminating news about Morocco, with articles often written by Americans. Ahmed Balafrej wrote frequent letters to American papers also.[130]

Since the rejection of her application for membership at the founding of the U N, the question of Morocco had not been discussed in that body until 1951. Then, on October 4, the foreign minister of Egypt asked the Secretary General to place on the agenda a complaint regarding "violation of the principles of the Charter and of the Declaration of Human Rights by France in Morocco." This was done "in order to satisfy the just aspirations of the Moroccan people and to avoid the developments to which this state of tension, dangerous to peace in that region might give rise." Iran, Lebanon, Saudi Arabia, Syria and Yemen joined with Egypt in this request. The meeting of the United Nations was in Paris. Denying that France was accountable to the Assembly, the French representative was supported by the American delegate, Warren Austin, who doubted that a discussion would help the Moroccan people. By a six to four vote in the General Committee, with four abstentions, a Canadian motion was passed to postpone the question. When the matter came up again before the plenary session in November and December, under the leadership of Pakistan, by a vote of 28 to 23, with seven abstentions, the Assembly voted to defer all discussion. Again the American delegate had favored postponement, which was to be the

American policy during the next four presentations of the proposition.

In Tunisia, during most of 1952, there was a repetition of Morocco's experiences, complete with the arrest and imprisonment of leaders, banning of a Neo-Destour Congress, censorship, dissolution of the Destour, demonstrations, protests, and hundreds of casualties. Omission from promised French reforms of Tunisian "sovereignty," rejection of negotiations by Bourguiba, "clean-up" operations in Nationalist centers, and killings and atrocities by French soldiers were followed by Tunisian counter-terrorism. A puppet government and a state of siege finally induced eleven nations of the newly formed Asian-African bloc in the United Nations to ask the Security Council to put the Tunisian question on its agenda. This request was made on April 2, 1952.

After a prolonged debate, the seven affirmative votes needed to place the question on the agenda were not obtained. Six countries had voted yes, but France and Great Britain voted no, and one of the four countries abstaining was the United States. The American delegate declared that intervention by the U N would probably hinder rather than help progress in Tunisia; the projected French reform program, he hoped, offered a basis for negotiations leading to home rule for Tunisia. During the summer, both in Morocco and in Tunisia, the proffered French reforms were unacceptable as usual, and the repressions, terrorism, and counter-terrorism increased in Tunisia. By the autumn of 1952 the Arab nations, strongly backed by the Asian states, especially India, declared that the dispute was an international matter and under the Assembly's jurisdiction. French spokesmen, on the contrary, gave notice that France would permit no foreign power or organization to interfere in "purely domestic French matters." The French government refused to be represented at the debates. Thus France was defying the recent decision of the International Court of Justice, which had ruled on August 27, 1952, that Morocco remained a sovereign state under the Treaty of Fez. This time the United States was one of the majority which placed the resolution on the agenda. However, because the Latin American states changed sides to support the French, the Asian-African resolution was defeated. Finally a mild Latin American resolution was passed which pleased no one, but was an admission that the Assembly was competent to pass on the matter. The head of the American delegation, Philip C. Jessup, explained the American negative vote as "determined by the belief that the Committee could not lawfully concern itself with specific problems which could be solved only in direct negotiations between the parties concerned." That the French had repeatedly refused negotiations seemed not to impress the United Nations delegates.

When the Assembly met in October, 1953, the summary exiling of Muhammad V was regarded by other nations besides those of Africa and Asia as a deliberate defiance of the U N by France. France had not only neglected negotiations; she had committed acts to aggravate the tension. Accordingly, thirteen Asian-African powers presented a resolution recommending that martial law and other exceptional measures should be terminated, political prisoners should be released, and civil liberties should be restored. Also, democratic representative institutions should be established through free elections based upon universal franchise, and complete independence and sovereignty should be established in Morocco within five years. On October 19 this drastic resolution was adopted by the Political Committee, but two weeks later it failed to obtain the required two-thirds majority in the plenary session of the Assembly. The non-participating French delegates worked behind the scenes and secured the support of Latin American delegates, which had almost one-third of the vote. Again the United States voted with the colonialist powers in rejecting the resolution.[131] For Morocco were 32 votes, while 22 were against her; there were five abstentions. Nationalist China and the Soviet countries voted for Morocco.

When fourteen countries asked the Assembly in 1954 for consideration of the Moroccan situation, they presented a very mild resolution. It recommended only that negotiations be carried on "between the true representatives of the Moroccan people and the French Government for the realization of the legitimate aspirations of the Moroccan people in conformity with the purpose and principles of the Charter." Since Mendès-France had now promised Tunisia self government, the expectations of Morocco for a similar boon were considered good. The delegates of Lebanon and the United States suggested that France should be given another opportunity to handle the Moroccan problem. Therefore, the sponsors introduced another resolution, noting that negotiations were said to be pending, and they decided to postpone for the time being further consideration of this item. The substitute resolution was adopted on December 13, 1954.

No Franco-Moroccan negotiations did take place. In a worsening situation, on July 29, 1955, the fourteen Asian-African countries again asked to have the Moroccan question placed on the U N agenda. When time came for the debate, however, the Sultan Muhammad V had been restored to his throne, and the demand for the debate was withdrawn unanimously.[132] Thus Morocco had at length won her "independence" under her legitimate ruler, not by the aid of the United Nations, but through the power of religious fanaticism inspiring her only available methods of civil war--terrorism and guerrilla warfare.

But as Muhammad V apparently knew from the beginning, his restoration was merely the preliminary phase of his war for independence. His exile had changed not only his outward demeanor, but also his characteristics. Even before his return from Paris to Rabat, he knew that the many complex and opposing elements among his subjects could not immediately become reconciled and that he must become the arbiter. On November 12 his first meeting with Resident General André Dubois was marked by reports of continued terrorism, and pamphlets signed by the "Black Crescent" announced that terrorism would continue until Morocco could achieve total independence. The Sultan broadcasted an appeal for his return home in peace, but in Casablanca there were deaths in riots inspired by the fear that the Sultan had become too friendly with the French during his stay in Paris. Even in his own palace courtyard, where the ruler received delegations, several were slain in melees.[133]

During the last days of November, there was a Berber ambush of a French military convoy with 27 casualties, and reports from the Riff area said that some tribes were refusing to pay taxes or obey their chieftains.[134] As on many previous occasions, the French authorities charged that these revolts were Communist-inspired and that the party was infiltrating the extremist wing of the Istiqlal to take it over from its middle class leaders. In a recent manifesto, however, the Communists had declared their willingness to participate in any national government. Allal al-Fassi, moreover, declared on

December 10, 1955, that an independent and sovereign Morocco would join the world-wide struggle of free nations against Soviet Communism. Until Morocco had attained full independence, however, the Army of Liberation would continue guerrilla operations in the Riff and in northeast Morocco.[135]

Of prime importance in achieving peace and harmony was the Sultan's maintenance of his personal and official prestige. The forming of a new government with a democratic and constitutional base had been promised by him and long demanded by the Istiqlal and other nationalistic parties. While still in Paris, Muhammad had dismissed all viziers appointed by Mulai Arafa and had abolished the rest of the Maghzen. On November 27 he asked al Bakkai to become the premier to form Morocco's first representative government. This body was to negotiate with Paris the new pact to replace the Protectorate by an independent Morocco, linked to France by ties of "interdependence." Already, six days after his return, the features of the political map were discernible--the popular hostility against kaids and pashas, the rivalry among political parties, the danger of extremism among the detribalized Moroccan workers in cities and the undisciplined hill tribes. The establishment of a stable government was of utmost urgency for both France and Morocco.[136]

In setting up his Cabinet, Muhammad divided the offices among different parties, thus preventing the hegemony of any one group. Bekkai was premier of a cabinet of fifteen members, of which the Istiqlal received seven posts, the P D I four, and independents the rest. Lyazadi became minister of commerce and industry, but the two Istiqlal leaders were not yet invited into the government. There were four ministers of state without portfolio, of whom two were Istiqlal members. The Cabinet took office on December 7, 1955.

For the next two months both Morocco and France prepared for the talks scheduled to begin in February. This was an unquiet period. Several acts of violence were committed against former adherents of Arafa, there were some serious encounters between French Legionnaires and the Army of Liberation, and there was mounting friction with the authorities of the Spanish Zone. The Istiqlal continued its demands for complete independence and unification of Morocco, which meant the expulsion of Spain from her zone. Extremely reluctant to surrender his Spanish Empire, after several years of posing as a friend of the Moroccans, Franco suddenly revealed his real sentiments. In November and December he announced his opposition to any liberalizing of the government of Tetuan or any introduction of Western-type democracy. Moreover, he demanded that Spain be consulted in all future negotiations on Morocco. On December 19 he had promised the Moroccans in the Spanish Zone a larger share in their government, but in mid-January he vaguely promised that Spain would relinquish her zone. At a conference of the heads of the French and Spanish zones on January 10, there was an agreement for co-operation against the Riff rebels, whom the French had charged the Spanish were aiding. In Spanish Morocco, the rising tide of nationalism worried Franco. On January 21 the Spanish government refused to recognize the independent government formed in Rabat.[137]

After several preparatory meetings, the Franco-Moroccan conference began on February 15 at the Palais de l'Elysee in Paris. The Sultan personally demanded the abrogation of the Protectorate Treaty of 1912 and the granting of Morocco's right to conduct her own foreign affairs and defense. On February 29 the radical nationalist Al Amal threatened that "Moroccan independence will be declared within twenty-four hours with or without France." No menace was necessary; on March 2, Foreign Minister Pineau and Bekkai signed the Declaration of Celle St. Cloud, declaring that the Treaty of 1912 "no longer corresponds to the needs of the modern world and can no longer govern Franco-Moroccan relations." Full independence was granted to Morocco, implying her own diplomacy and army.[138] Definition of the interdependence of the two countries, notably in defense, external relations, economy, culture, and the rights of Frenchmen in Morocco and Moroccans in France were reserved for future arrangement. The Sultan was given control of legislation and of the army, for the creation of which France would lend assistance. Morocco was to remain in the French Union, with a voice in policy-making for that area. Hereafter the resident general would be known as the high commissioner. Nine-tenths of the area of Morocco was now under the rule of Muhammad V.[139]

The Spanish Zone was soon added to the former French one. Nothing was left for Franco except to play his favorite role of being "a better-friend-than-France." Balafrej conferred with Spanish officials, and by March 20 he reported Spain's desire to follow the example of France. Balafrej was soon appointed Morocco's first foreign minister. On April 3, the Sultan with his two sons and a large entourage was greeted in Madrid with great ceremony. Three days later, the protocol for the independence of the Spanish Zone and its ingegration with independent Morocco was signed. Many details of Spanish withdrawal remained for future negotiation, which dragged on till the end of 1957. Not until January, 1958, did Spain agree to withdraw the peseta as the official currency of the northern zone.[140] Spain, of course, kept her ancient presidios and Ifni; their return to Morocco was still a matter of dispute in 1968.

The integration of Tangier with the rest of Morocco was a prolonged and complicated affair. Rumors of coming independence had driven both men and large sums of money out of Tangier to European banks, principally in Switzerland. On July 8, 1956, Muhammad appointed a Moroccan governor, and thereafter Moroccan officials took over the chief functions of government. The formal termination of the international status of the city came on October 20, 1956, when Morocco and representatives of the eight states ruling Tangier reached an accord on a declaration to be referred to their governments. After a century of service, the British postoffice was closed on April 30, 1957. The future status of Tangier was apparently determined by a royal charter granted on August 30, 1957, under which it received a privileged financial position. It became a free money zone, with import and export of goods without licensing, customs equal to other ports, and no income tax. However, the banking community feared a revocation of this bonanza, and the businessmen began developing tourism to replace the money industry. On October 18, 1959, the government recalled Moroccan deposits abroad and announced the repeal of the Charter within six months. The date October 18, 1960, marks the final economic integration of Tangier into Morocco. By royal proclamation, Tangier was appointed to be the summer capital of the country.[141]

When the independence of Morocco was assured, the United States hastened to recognize the new nation. On January 26, 1956, the Department of State announced that it would ask Congressional action to end American extraterritoriality in Morocco. On October 6, 1956, the American ambassador notified Ahmed Balafrej that this action had been completed. Congratulatory messages were sent to the governments of both France and Morocco upon the success of their negotiations. The United States and Morocco exchanged ambassadors[142] promptly, and the United States representative to the Security Council on July 20, 1956, urged approval of admission of Morocco to the United Nations.[143] Less than four months later, on November 13, 1956, the United Nations welcomed nineteen new members, bringing its total membership to seventy-nine. Among the new additions were three North African states--Morocco, Tunisia, and Libya.[144]

By the end of 1956, Morocco had nominal independence, an approach to territorial integrity, international status, and a sovereign free to wcrk out his own power. The interdependence with France, however, remained to be defined. It soon became clear that by interdependence the French meant the exclusion of all economic and military influences except their own. After sixteen months of "independence" the Moroccans still had 143,000 foreign troops on their soil--French, Spanish, and American. The American military spending was a real asset to the country, and it was hoped that the American Air Force would train an air force for Morocco; the Americans were, therefore, welcome. The French claimed that their army was necessary to protect the French in Morocco and to help defend the country; the Moroccans insisted that their own army of 20,000 was sufficient to defend all people in Morocco. Privately the French admitted that their presence was to prevent Morocco from giving assistance to Algeria. The new French Premier publicly announced that economic aid depended upon the continuance of the French army in Morocco. No one --except possibly the Communists--was asking the Spanish army to leave, for their departure might be a signal for a French attempt to reconquer Morocco.[145]

Besides foreign armies, Muhammad V had a host of other problems. The need for economic reforms required the insuguration of a Two-Year and a Five-Year Plan. The former Spanish Zone was backward economically, socially, and politically. Again a _blad es-siba_ was forming, for many tribes refused to pay taxes. The Army of Liberation, composed largely of anti-Istiqlal veterans of guerrilla warfare, refused to disband or to join the national army formed by Mulai Hassan with French funds. The problem of controlling rival political parties and developing a constitutional government was formidable. To build a stable and democratic society out of a majority of illiterate, ignorant, and poverty-stricken people might well be a task of generations. The efforts of Nasser and the Communists to subvert and exploit the Moroccans were grave perils to the integrity of the state. Finally, there was the Algerian War, the last great struggle for independence of Arab people from French rule, which deeply concerned the two nearest Arab neighbors.[146]

Despite these heavy burdens, however, Sultan Muhammad V was to pursue a steady course toward progress for his subjects. He earned their respect, gratitude, and affection. At his untimely death at the age of fifty-one, he left his son, Mulai Hassan, a throne still precarious, but a heritage full of promise and opportunity.

Notes

1. Allal al-Fassi, The Independence Movements in Arab North Africa (hereafter cited as al-Fassi, Independence Movements, 79-83.

2. Ibid., 86-91.

3. The events and significance of the Riffian War are discussed in an interesting and informative manner in Ibid., 92-105.

4. American consul Russell at Casablanca was greatly impressed by the very strong patriotism developing in Morocco to replace the religious fanaticism of fifteen years before. The natives felt, he said, that France was doing everything possible to transform the Protectorate into a colony. Any surplus funds in the annual budget were used for a new building program, thus preventing the reduction of the Moroccan debt to France. Almost nothing had been done in agricultural and trade training of the native youth. The more educated of all classes were taking a great interest in national movements in other Muslim countries. In the Riff situation the French were suffering a great loss of prestige. Russell to Sec. of State, No. 48, Aug. 25, 1924, A. N. F., 881.00/965.

5. Al-Fassi, Independence Movements, 106-109.

6. Ibid., 109-110.

7. The foreign education obtained by favored upper class Moroccans, both in reformed religion and in nationalism, was due to the presence Française in Morocco, which rescued the country from its former isolation. Both Pan-Arabic and westernized groups were formed during the 20's; Allal al-Fassi belonged to the former. Hahn, North Africa, 64-65.

8. Al-Fassi, Independence Movements, 110, 117.

9. Rom Landau gives a comprehensive discussion of the differentiation between the Berbers and the Arabs in their "natural" characteristics, but he denies that these traits constitute a cleavage between them such as the French sought to exploit. Of their religion he says: "The form of Islam embraced by the Berber contains a number of non-Muslim elements, and in spite of this their religious sentiments differ little from those of their Arab brothers .... If we consider some of the religious fraternities so popular with Moroccan Arabs .... we instantly realize that Berber and Arab share an identical religious background. The Sufi beliefs and practices of an Arab fraternity in Fez merely represent a higher and more spiritualized version of the cruder beliefs held by the Berbers." Landau, Moroccan Journey, 55-61, 82-84, 88-89.

10. Al-Fassi, Independence, Movements, 118-125; Hahn, North Africa, 66-67.

11. Ibid., 65-66; 67-69; al-Fassi, Independence Movements, 126-130.

12. Blake to Sec. of State, No. 497, May 6, 1930, A. N. F., 881.00/1463; Buhrman to Sec. of State, Oct. 4, 1930, Ibid., 881.00/1471.

13. In February, 1934, the French government had placed Morocco under the Ministry of Overseas France--a direct threat to Moroccan independence. This provoked violent nationalist editorials in the one nationalist news-

paper, a flood of telegrams to the Quai d'Orsay, and street demonstrations. The Sultan's visit to Fez was an opportunity not to be missed, for the nationalists were seeking one leader of authority and prestige. Sidi Muhammad was deeply impressed by the enthusiastic reception that he received from the crowds on his first real public contact with his people, and conversations with al-Fassi and other leaders informed him of the aims and importance of the nationalist movement. From this time on, the Sultan watched nationalist activities closely, and gradually he developed into the leader sought by the Kutlah. Hahn, North Africa, 69-72.

14. Bernard Newman, Morocco Today (hereafter cited as Newman, Morocco Today), 221; Hahn, North Africa, 71-73; Barbour, North West Africa, 50-51; al-Fassi, Independence Movements, 137-140.

15. Ibid., 141-146.

16. Ibid., 146-149.

17. Hahn, North Africa, 74-75.

18. Al-Fassi gives a detailed account of the activities of the National Party (al-Hizb al-Watani) which Noguès finally permitted to organize under that name. The party worked on behalf of democractic freedoms and in defense of the underprivileged classes. Its most notable achievement was its energetic publicity campaign at home and abroad. The support of the Jews was enlisted, as well as that of both French and Moroccan left-wing parties. Against the kaids, who were henchmen of the French, and against al Glaoui and his cruel extortions of his subjects, some victories were won. The Residency reacted with intensified attacks on nationalists throughout Morocco; by mid-October over 10,000 had been interned. The Atlas and other papers were suppressed. At a Rabat conference held on October 13, 1937, a National Covenant was adopted reciting the outrageous acts of the Residency and condemning them. Al-Fassi, Independence Movements, 166-193.

19. Hahn, North Africa, 74-76.

20. Mellor, Morocco Awakes, 190-198; Stanton to Sec. of State, No. 197, Oct. 11, 1937, A. N. F., 881.00/1677; Goold to Sec. of State, No. 2, Nov. 10, 1937, Ibid., 881.00/1680.

21. Hahn, North Africa, 76-77.

22. Al-Fassi, Independence Movements, 193-195.

23. Mellor, Morocco Awakes, 198-201.

24. Al-Fassi, Independence Movements, 196-198.

25. Ibid., 198-201.

26. Ibid., 201; Hahn, North Africa, 77.

27. In commenting on a Moroccan newspaper article concerning the need of a reform of Moroccan justice, Vice Consul Philip Bagby said: "The Moroccan judicial system is one of the four features of the French administration which are most criticized. The others are the educational system, the lack of free speech, and the economic exploitation for the benefit of France and Frenchmen." Russell to Sec. of State, No. 297, Dec. 1, 1941, A. N. F., 881.044/27.

28. Hahn, North Africa, 77-78; al-Fassi, Independence Movements, 204-212; Landau, Moroccan Drama, 210-211.

29. Hahn, North Africa, 78-81; Newman, Morocco Today, 222-223.

30. Al-Fassi, Independence Movements, 213-215; Hahn, North Africa, 80-82.

31. A. N. F.: Mayer to the State Dept., No. 91, Jan. 11, 1944, 881.00/2751 and telegram, Jan. 12, 1944, 881.00/2737; Russell to Sec. of State, No. 1249, Jan. 12, 1944, 881.00/2763; Childs to Sec. of State, telegram, Jan. 14, 1944, 881.00/2738.

32. Hahn, North Africa, 82; Landau, Moroccan Drama, 214-215.

33. After detailing the terrible punishments inflicted upon the demonstrators, including many students and other youths, al-Fassi concludes: "The events which followed January 11, and the great sacrifices which the people had willingly offered in the cause of independence, clearly attest to the popular strength of the Istiqlal Party. Moreover, the drastic measures resorted to by the Residency against the people had destroyed to a considerable extent the reputation of France ... throughout the Arab world .... All the charges which the French administration had levelled against the Istiqlal leaders went astray and they emerged unscathed. The French themselves were compelled to acknowledge the nobility of purpose that had animated the National Party and later the Istiqlal, whose leaders' sole aim is the liberation of their country .... The movement had attained a degree of diffusion and publicity surpassing by far anything that had preceded it." Al-Fassi, Independence Movements, 233-234.

34. Hahn, North Africa, 82-83; Barbour, North West Africa, 95; Landau, Moroccan Drama, 215-216; Brooks to Sec. of State, No. 1686, Dec. 15, 1944, A. N. F., 881.00/12-1544.

35. Childs to Sec. of State, No. 1298, Feb. 25, 1943, Ibid., 881.00/2474.

36. Mayer to Sec. of State, No. 91, Jan. 11, 1944, Ibid., 881.00/2751, with enclosure of letter from Fez, leaders of Moroccan National Party to President Roosevelt (rough translation; French and Arabic texts also included), June 15, 1943, Ibid., 881.00/2639.

37. Murphy to Sec. of State, airgram, Algiers, June 26, 1943, Ibid., 881.00/2576.

38. Childs to Sec. of State, No. 1645, Aug. 25, 1943, Ibid., 881.00/2623.

39. A. N. F.: Stettinius to Russell and Mayer, Washington, Dec. 1, 1943, 881.00/2724 7C; Russell to Sec. of State, No. 1217, Dec. 17, 1943, 881.00/2708; Murray to Wilson, undated letter, 881.00/2720; Childs to Sec. of State, telegram, Dec. 30, 1943; Villard to Childs, letter, Jan. 28, 1944, 881.00/2722.

40. "Moulay el Larbi ... first came to Tangier some months ago to represent the Sultan in negotiations looking to the settlement of the estate of the late ex-Sultan Abd al-Aziz. Larbi has remained in Tangier except during brief visits to Rabat to confer with the Sultan, and apparently the Sultan proposes to maintain him in Tangier as his unofficial representative, for since the withdrawal of the Mendoub in early 1941 under Spanish pressure, the Sultan has been without any representation in this city." Childs to Sec. of State, No. 1967, Feb. 12, 1944, A. N. F., 881.00/2806. "Mouley Larbi al Aloui .... is a first cousin of the Sultan." Childs to Sec. of State, No. 2367, Sept. 27, 1944, Ibid., 881.00/9-2744.

41. Childs to Sec. of State, No. 1719, Oct. 2, 1943, enclosing memorandum by Chargé Elbrick at Tangier, Ibid., 881.001/83.

42. Childs to Sec. of State, No. 1947, Jan. 31, 1944, Ibid., 881.00/2794 and No. 1967, Feb. 12, 1944, enclosing memorandum of Mulai el Larbi on Moorish aspirations, Ibid., 881.00/2006.

43. Cole to Sec. of State, No. 160, May 22, 1944, Ibid., 881.00/2876.

44. Childs to Sec. of State, No. 2154, June 17, 1944, enclosing memorandum by Mulai el Larbi, Ibid., 881.00/6-1744.

45. A. N. F.: Childs to Sec. of State, No. 2176, June 27, 1944, 881.00/6-2744; airgram, July 18, 1944, 881.00/7-1844; No. 2251, July 29, 1944, 881.00/7-2944; airgram, Aug. 15, 1944, 881.00/8-1544; airgram, Aug. 29, 1944, 881.00/8-2944; No. 2367, Sept. 27, 1944, 881.00/9-2744.

46. Ibid., Cole to Sec. of State, No. 178, July 24, 1944, 881.00/7-2444 and airgram, July 25, 1944, 881.00/7-2544; Hull to American Consul, Rabat, airgram, Aug. 16, 1944.

47. Information furnished by the State Department in 1968.

48. American consular dispatches, Jan. 14, 1944-Nov. 16, 1944, 881.00/2740- 881.00/11-1644, Ibid.

49. Hull to American Consul, Rabat, telegram, Jan. 31, 1944, 881.00/2737, Ibid.

50. Russell to Sec. of State, No. 1277, Feb. 4, 1944, 881.00/2790 and No. 1282, Feb. 11, 1944, 881.00 /2800; Cole to Sec. of State, No. 143, April 13, 1944, 881.00/2849; Ibid.

51. Hahn, North Africa, 83-84, 86; Landau, Moroccan Drama, 249-250.

52. Harry Grayson, 'Dusty Nomads' Land," San Francisco News, June 20, 1945, 11.

53. Jack D. Bock, "French vs. Moslems," (correspondence), Christian Science Monitor, Sept. 30, 1952, 12.

54. Landau, Moroccan Drama, 250-251.

55. Hahn, North Africa, 86-87.

56. Ibid., 86-87; Landau, Moroccan Drama, 251-254.

57. A former assistant administrator and director of finance in the Tangier zone wrote of a press conference at which Si Mekki Neciri, leader of the party of Moroccan Unity, referred emphatically to the sovereignty of the Sultan over all Morocco. The writer remarked that "the studiously moderate terms in which the nationalist views have been stated are expressed in a favorable contrast with more violent moves in other countries." C. Vernon Dicken, "Sultan Expected to Wage Bitter Fight Against Division of Morocco," Christian Science Monitor, Dec. 11, 1946, 6.

58. Landau, Moroccan Drama, 255-256; Hahn, North Africa, 87-89; Landau, Sultan of Morocco, 35-42; C. Vernon Dicken, "North African Pageant: The Sultan in Tangier," Christian Science Monitor, May 6, 1947, 9.

59. Landau, Moroccan Drama, 254, 257; Hahn, North Africa, 89-90; Stuart, Tangier, 157-158.

60. Hahn, North Africa, 90-91; Landau, Moroccan Drama, 261-262.

61. Ibid., 262-265; Hahn, North Africa, 91; al-Fassi, Independence Movements, 298-305.

62. Landau, Moroccan Drama, 266-270; Hahn, North Africa, 91-92.

63. Ibid., 92-93; Landau, Moroccan Drama, 272-274.

64. Arno Dosch-Fleurot, "Feudal Lord Bucks Plans For Reforms in Morocco," Christian Science Monitor, Jan. 29, 1951, 10. Other pertinent articles by the same author are: "France Rejects New Policy of Morocco," Ibid., Feb. 14, 1951, 4 and "France Walks Thin Line Over Sultan of Morocco," Ibid., Feb. 26, 1951, 5.

65. The story of the "crisis of 1951" is based upon these references: Hahn, North Africa, 93-94; Landau, Moroccan Drama, 274-282.

66. The conclusion of Juin's speech was: "I am conscious of having done everything within my power and within the framework of the treaty to give satisfaction to legitimate aspirations of your Majesty's people--particularly in so far as their accession to the management of their own affairs is concerned." Landau, Moroccan Drama, 282.

67. Ibid., 283-284.

68. Hahn, North Africa, 95-97.

69. Landau, Moroccan Drama, 284-286; Stuart, Tangier, 159.

70. General Augustin Guillaume, "The French Accomplishment in Morocco," Foreign Affairs, XXX (July, 1952), 625-636.

71. Landau, Moroccan Drama, 286-291.

72. The opposition to Muhammad V had come to a head under two Moroccan leaders--al Glaoui, chief ally of the Residency, commanding most of the pashas and kaids and their subservient tribesmen, and Sherif Abd al Hadj Kittani, leader of the reactionary religious confraternities. These men were very active in propagandizing and organizing their followers during 1953, traveling freely all over the country while the Sultan was shut up in his palace, "surrounded by armored cars, tanks, and guns pointing toward the palace." Landau, Moroccan Drama, 308.

73. Ibid., 306-309.

74. Werth, France, 1940-1955, 504-506.

75. Hahn, North Africa, 114-116; Landau, Moroccan Drama, 309-313.

76. Ibid., 312-313; "Rabat Greets New Ruler," New York Times, Aug. 23, 1953, 31.

77. Landau, Moroccan Drama, 315-316.

78. Ibid., 314-315; Hahn, North Africa, 116.

79. Landau, Moroccan Drama, 318-321.

80. A favorable news item concerning the new Sultan said that he had introduced one good innovation: "The Sultan said there would be no more kneeling or prostrating before him by his subjects, and that he also was eliminating festivals at which gifts were traditionally offered to the monarch." "Sultan Drops Ceremony," New York Times, Sept. 6, 1953, 28.

81. "New Order in Morocco," editorial, Christian Science Monitor, Aug. 22, 1953, 16.

82. Hahn, North Africa, 117; Werth, France, 1940-1955, 628-629; Landau, Moroccan Drama, 321.

83. Ibid., 323-324; Hahn, North Africa, 117.

84. "The Berbers were faithful Moslems who felt as deeply as the Arabs that a blasphemy had been committed. And at least as much as the Arabs, they were fighters .... Thus soon there were manifestations among the tribesmen demanding the return of 'our beloved Sultan,' raids against French outposts, and eventually, highly organized guerrilla activity." Hahn, North Africa, 123.

85. In June, 1955, French counter-terrorists "assassinated Lemaigre-Dubreuil, owner of Maroc-Presse, an adventurous and legendary figure in the history of French North Africa, who had, however, in the last few years, conducted, both in France and in Morocco, a vigorous campaign for a more humane and liberal policy." Werth, France, 1940-1955, 629-630.

86. Landau, Moroccan Drama, 324-332, 335.

87. Ibid., 359-362.

88. Ibid., 362-364.

89. Ibid., 364-367.

90. Ibid., 367-369.

91. Ibid., 369-371; Werth, France, 1940-1955, 630; Hahn, North Africa, 177-178.

92. Ibid., 178-179; Landau, Moroccan Drama, 371-373.

93. As early as July 3, 1955, however, Juin was reported to have advised Faure that he would not occupy himself further with North African affairs. He also deserted the cause of the colons, so long championed by him: "Marshal Juin disavows all Frenchmen in Morocco who, whatever their opinions, make Moroccan policy in Morocco." "Morocco Die-Hards Criticized by Juin," New York Times, July 3, 1955, 4.

94. Landau, Moroccan Drama, 373-375; Hahn, North Africa,179.

95. Ibid., 179-182; Landau, Moroccan Drama, 375-379.

96. A troop mutiny caused by great inefficiency and disorganization was described by Volney D. Hurd in "NATO examines Effect of French Troop Mutiny," Christian Science Monitor, Sept. 14, 1955, 10. This event caused great perturbation in NATO countries, including France.

97. Landau, Moroccan Drama, 376-377, 379-380.

98. Ibid., 379-383; Werth, France, 1940-1955, 630-631; Hahn, North Africa, 182-183; Joan Thiriet, "Return of Exiled Moroccan Sultan Looms," Christian Science Monitor, Nov. 1, 1955, 1; Henry Giniger, "Ben Youssef Gets French Approval To Rule Morocco," New York Times, Nov. 6, 1955, 1, 4; Volney D. Hurd: "Morocco Throne Rift Ends," Christian Science Monitor, Nov. 2, 1955, 1; "Ben Youssef Stiffens Hold in Two Moves," Ibid., Nov. 4, 1955, 2; "French Recognize Sultan of Morocco," Ibid., Nov. 8, 1955, 2; "Sultan Accepts 'Surrender,'" Ibid., Nov. 10, 1955. 2.

99. Hahn, North Africa, 183-184.

100. Landau, Moroccan Drama, 336.

101. Representative American newspapers were fully aware of Franco's designs. The following are a few of the articles on this subject: Robert C. Doty, "Spain Seeks Role as Champion of Arabs," New York Times, April 13, 1952, 4 E; Richard Mowrer, "Spain Attempts to Hike Role in Mediterranean," Christian Science Monitor, May 6, 1952, 5 and "Franco's Freest People; Moors Belie Iron Rule," Ibid., July 17, 1952, 7.

102. Landau, Moroccan Drama, 170-173.

103. Ibid., 337-339; Richard Mowrer, "France's Policy Vexes Madrid Regime," Christian Science Monitor, Sept. 21, 1953, 11.

104. Landau, Moroccan Drama, 339-343.

105. On November 18, the "day of the Throne," when Muhammad V was officially reseated on his throne, the Spanish Zone celebrated as jubilantly as the French Zone did, and Radio Tetuan predicted reactions against France's stupid policy. Landau, Moroccan Drama, 342.

106. Edmund Stevens, "Spain Weighs Plan For Free Morocco," Christian Science Monitor, Feb. 10, 1955, 7; Mario Rossi, "Spain's Role at U N Credited to Lodge," Ibid., March 7, 1955, 1; Camille M. Cianfarra, "Paris Said to End Spanish Exile Aid," New York Times, May 8, 1955, 19 and "Spain Bars Help to Rebels in Riff," Ibid., Oct. 9, 1955, 6; "French Protest Radio Tetuan," Iberica, III (Sept. 15, 1955, Late News and "Turnabout in Morocco," Ibid., (Dec. 15, 1955), 14.

107. Stanford Alumni Review, I (Dec., 1945), 10.

108. Stuart, Tangier, 161-166.

109. Ibid., 186-187; Arno Dosch-Fleurot, "Tangier Seen Base for U. S. Radiocasts," Christian Science Monitor, July 5, 1947, 3; "U. S. Influence in Tangier Reflected in Land Boom," Ibid., Feb. 9, 1950, 1; "'Voice' Pushes Completion of Tangier Station," Ibid., Aug. 8, 1950, 7; 'Europe Wary of 'Voice' Talks to Africa," Ibid., Feb. 11, 1950, 5; "U. S. Influence in North Africa Seen as New Russian Target," Ibid., March 24, 1952, 4.

110. Stuart, Tangier, 187; Dee and Tom Hardie, "Triumph for Tangier's American Schoolmarm," San Francisco Chronicle, Feb. 17, 1953, 65; Harrison Negley, 'Why They Love Us in Tangier," Collier's, CXXXI (May 16, 1953), 68-73; Board of Directors of the American School of Tangier, The American School in the International City of Tangier, 28 pp.

111. Thomas D. Campbell, "A Land That Could be Europe's Granary," New York Times, Nov. 23, 1947, "New York Times Magazine," 12-13, 64-65, 67; Russell

Porter, "U. S. Wheat Expert to Advise Africans," New York Times, Nov. 14, 1948, 28; "Wheat Yield Rise in Africa Sought," New York Times, Dec. 5, 1948, 34; Mary Hornaday, "Africa: New Granary for Europe? Profile of 'Wheat King,'" Christian Science Monitor, Dec. 13, 1948, 9; Thomas D. Campbell, Albuquerque, N. M., to Luella J. Hall, Feb. 28, 1959.

112. The two newspapers referred to are the New York Times and the Christian Science Monitor. The articles are too numerous for individual citation. Of special note was a series of twenty-five articles in the Christian Science Monitor from February to May, 1955 by Edmund Stevens.

113. William Atwood, "Dateline: Your World," San Francisco Chronicle, July 15, 1951, 13; John Roderick, "French Blame U. S. for Middle East Troubles," Ibid., Oct. 30, 1951; Volney D. Hurd, "Juin Says U. S. Policy Stirs False Hopes in Morocco," Christian Science Monitor, Nov. 17, 1951, 1.

114. Arno Dosch-Fleurot, "Sultan of Morocco Demands Say in Atlantic Pact," Christian Science Monitor, March 15, 1949, 2; "Morocco Voices Concern at Atlantic Pact Exclusion," Ibid., March 31, 1949, 2; "U. S. Rights Color Moroccan Pact Bid," Ibid., April 12, 1949, 4; Egon Kaskeline, "North Africa Seen Vital in Western Defense Setup," Ibid., Dec. 16, 1949, 3.

115. The injustice of using E R P funds against the interests of North African natives was shown by these arguments: "(A) The North African peoples and their leaders never applied for American financial assistance. (B) It was the Sultan of Morocco and not the French who assisted the American forces' landing in Morocco and mobilized Morocco's physical and material forces to fight on the side of the Allies (in exchange for which, incidentally, numerous unfilled promises were made by American authorities during the war). (C) President Roosevelt pledged American support for the independence of Morocco in his interview with the Sultan in Casablanca. (D) Finally, there were only 7,800 Frenchmen fighting in the so-called 'Free French

Forces,' while North Africans numbered 275,000, some 65,000 of whom died on the Allies' battlefields." Homer Metz, "French Accused of Using E R P to Boost African Rule," Christian Science Monitor, March 2, 1950, 2.

116. Homer Metz, "French Accused of Using E R P to Boost African Rule," Ibid., March 2, 1950, 2.

117. Demaree Bess, "We're Invading North Africa Again," Saturday Evening Post, CCXXII (June 18, 1949), 22-23, 132, 134, 136, 138.

118. Arno Dosch-Fleurot, "Yanks Gather at Casablanca from All Corners of Africa," Ibid., June 7, 1946, 1.

119. "Big Air Base Opens in Africa," Ibid., Dec. 5, 1951, 14; Stuart, Tangier, 188-189.

120. Hahn, North Africa, 108-109; Werth, France, 1940-1955, 574.

121. Hahn, North Africa, 109-110.

122. Thomas F. Conroy, "Treaty Procedure Is Subject of Suit," New York Times, Oct. 23, 1949, 1 F.

123. This is an example of editorial criticism: "It is a strange commentary on the strength of American diplomacy that an individual citizen should be forced to put on a one-man campaign to preserve the right of Americans to do business in a country in which this right is guaranteed by treaty .... In continuing its approval of the French decree, the State Department is ignoring repeated criticism in the Senate and is ignoring the evidence of discrimination and anti-American acts, which was presented to the State Department by Mr. Rodes and other businessmen and trade organizations at a public hearing. This hopeless attitude by a nation which is shelling out billions of dollars to promote the revival of trade among nations bodes ill for whatever success is to be expected from Point Four .... If we can't protect the clear treaty rights of a small group of ambitious Americans to do business abroad, what is

likely to happen to the billions we export under the chaperonage of bureaucrats and do-gooders?' Saturday Evening Post, CCXXII (Jan. 28, 1950), 10.

124. Neal Stanford, "Washington Sees Pact Dictated by E C A's Aims," Christian Science Monitor, Jan. 27, 1950, 2; Arno Dosch-Fleurot, "U. S. Traders in French Morocco to Take Import Protest to Congress," Ibid., Jan. 27, 1950, 2.

125. Michael Clark, "France Explains Moroccan Action," New York Times, Oct. 29, 1950, 24; Daniel L. Schorr, "Paris Asks World Court Ruling on U. S. Trading in Morocco," Christian Science Monitor, Nov. 10, 1950, 2.

126. Joseph M. Sweeney, "Treaty Rights of the United States in Morocco," Department of State Bulletin, October 20, 1952, 620-623; "Morocco Lifts Restrictions on Imports," Ibid., 623; Joan Thiriet, "World Court Redefines U. S. Rights in Morocco," Christian Science Monitor, Aug. 29, 1952, 1; Edmund Stevens, "Cartels Branded Exploiters of Morocco," Ibid., Jan. 9, 1953, 2.

127. Hahn, North Africa, 98-99; "Tunisian Nationalist Here Protests French Control," San Francisco Chronicle, Sept. 22, 1951, 8.

128. Hahn, North Africa, 99, 103; Kenneth Campbell, "Moroccan Reports Increase in Unrest," New York Times, Jan. 27, 1952, 26; Rom Landau, "The Sultan Is Impatient," Reporter, VI (March 4, 1952), 11-13. The Reporter article is a brief but comprehensive and convincing exposition of the Moroccan viewpoint.

129. "Guillaume .... detests the Moroccan Nationalists, and thought that anybody who had dealings with them at all was an enemy of France .... American policy perplexed Guillaume mightily. He told me he thought that it was little short of demented of us to spend half a billion dollars on the Moroccan bases on the one hand, and with the other give asylum in New York to nationalist "insurrectionaries." Gunther, Inside Africa, 73.

130. A few of the many American articles may be mentioned: Edward Toledano, "Will Blood Flow Next in Morocco?", Saturday Evening Post, CCXXIV (April 19, 1952), 42-43, 130, 132-133, 135; Theodore Draper, "The Coming Battle for Morocco," Reporter, VII (Oct. 28, 1952), 23-27; William O. Douglas, "The French Are Facing Disaster Again in Morocco," Look, XVIII (Oct. 19, 1954), 33-37. A pamphlet of 16 pages was distributed by the Free Trade Union Committee of the American Federation of Labor. It is a compilation of quotations from American speakers and writers by Marjorie Rodes, entitled "The United States and the French-Moroccan Problem--'The Other Side' ". Both Miss Rodes and Balafrej wrote frequent letters to leading newspapers presenting the Moroccan view.

131. The first public response of the United States government to the deposition of Muhammad V was made on August 22. A State Department official was then authorized to say that the United States "views with deep concern" the removal of Sultan Sidi Mohammed Ben Youssef by France and "earnestly hopes" for the restoration of order. "U. S. Voices Concern at French Action in Ousting Sultan," New York Times, Aug. 23, 1953, 1. However, this comment was retracted later in the day when the French Embassy sought and received assurances that it did not accurately reflect American policy. "U. S. Retracts 'Protest' on Morocco," San Francisco Chronicle, Aug. 23, 1953, 5. The weakness of United States policy was emphasized by C. L. Sulzberger in "French Policy Shifts Seen in Indo-China and Morocco," New York Times, Sept. 6, 1953, 2: "The United States has had a completely paradoxical and meaningless policy in this corner of Africa. Alone among the nations it has maintained a minister accredited to the Sultan although the latter's theoretical domain is divided into three sections .... Alone among the nations, largely as a result of American business interests, the United States has insisted on retaining archaic rights in Morocco."

132. The main sources of information for the Moroccan appeals to the United Nations are: Hahn, North Africa, 99-102 and Landau, Moroccan Drama, 347-358.

133. Volney D. Hurd, "Morocco Sultan Faces Test," Christian Science Monitor, Nov. 11, 1955, 15; "Morocco Sultan Confers with New French Chief," Ibid., Nov. 12, 1955, 10; "World News in Brief: Morocco," Ibid., Nov. 16, 1953, 4; Camille Cianfarra, "Morocco's Foe Slain in Palace Courtyard Melee," New York Times, Nov. 20, 1955, 1, 22.

134. Camille Cianfarra, "Berbers Ambush a French Convoy," New York Times, Nov. 27, 1955, 16; "French Cleanup Drive Runs Into Riff Ambush," Christian Science Monitor, Nov. 28, 1955, 2; "Rebel Chief Names," Ibid., Nov. 29, 1955, 2.

135. Camille Cianfarra, "Moroccan Offers Aid Against Reds," New York Times, Dec. 11, 1955, 12; Egon Kaskeline, "Morocco Revolt Laid to Communists," Christian Science Monitor, Dec. 12, 1955, 2.

136. Camille Cianfarra, "Sultan Dismisses Moroccan Viziers," New York Times, Nov. 13, 1955, 17; "Sultan Looks to Paris Pact: Cabinet Waited," Christian Science Monitor, Nov. 21, 1955, 2; "Si Bekkai Premier-Designate," New York Times, Nov. 27, 1955, 16; Joan Thiriet, "New Dangers Stalk France: Power Conflict Tears Morocco," Christian Science Monitor, Nov. 23, 1955, 1.

137. Hahn, North Africa, 184-185; Richard Mowrer, "Spain Seeks Voice in Moroccan Plans," Christian Science Monitor, Jan. 4, 1956, 4; Joan Thiriet, "Meeting With French: Spain Indicates Shift on Morocco," Ibid., Jan. 12, 1956, 2; "France, Spain to Join Forces Against Rebels," Palo Alto Times, Jan. 11, 1956, 2; "Spain Rejects Bid by Rabat Leaders," New York Times, Jan. 22, 1956, 29.

138. Even while the Sultan was being enthusiastically received at Rabat after his return from Paris with independence in his hands, terrorism continued in rural areas. The French considered this post-independence violence as a test of the justice of American accusations of "colonialism." Their argument ran thus: "If the disorders do not stop, then apologies will be in order. We will then have proved our case--namely

that it has not been basically a question of colonialism or independence, but rather an international conspiracy to dominate and subjugate a poor, illiterate people in the regular Communist manner .... It will stand out at last that the Communists really are trying to build an anti-Western Arab empire running from the Middle East across all North Africa to the Atlantic." Volney D. Hurd, "French Test U. S. in Morocco," Christian Science Monitor, March 7, 1956, 6.

139. Hahn, North Africa, 185-186.

140. Ibid., 186-187, 202.

141. Thomas F. Brady, "Tangier Parley Reaches Accord," New York Times, Oct. 21, 1956, 4; Egon Kaskeline, "Morocco Tie Stirs Tangier to Turmoil," Christian Science Monitor, Oct. 24, 1956, 14; "British Post Office in Tangier Is Closed," New York Times, May 5, 1957, 129; Thomas F. Brady, "Tangier Remains Free Money Zone," Ibid., Aug. 31, 1957, 3; "Tangier Strives for New Future," Ibid., Sept. 22, 1957, 21; "Morocco: Cleaning Up Tangier," Time, LXXIV (Nov. 2, 1959), 20; Thomas F. Brady, "Tangier Braces for Trade Slash," New York Times, April 10, 1960, 15.

142. Cavendish W. Cannon became the first American ambassador to Morocco by confirmation of the Senate on July 21, 1956. On September 5, the newly appointed ambassador of Morocco, Dr. El Mehdi Ben Muhammad Ben Aboud presented his credentials to President Eisenhower. Jones, A Survey of United States Relations with Morocco, 90.

143. Jones, A Survey of United States Relations with Morocco, 89-92.

144. Nora E. Taylor, "U N Welcomes 19 New Members," Christian Science Monitor, Nov. 15, 1956, 7.

145. Stephen O. Hughes, "Morocco Evaluates Triple 'Occupation,'" Christian Science Monitor, July 1, 1957, 4.

146. Charles F. Gallagher, The United States and North Africa: Morocco, Algeria, and Tunisia, 123-126; Hahn, North Africa, 191-196, 201-202.

Glossary

Words not otherwise designated are of Arabic origin, transliterated into the Roman alphabet, often with alternative spellings. Non-Arabic words are designated thus: E, English; F, French; S, Spanish; B, Berber.

Abbasids: Second dynasty of Arab Caliphs succeeding the Prophet (750-1258).

abd: Slave.

abou: Variant of bou, possessor or father of.

Acharites: Orthodox believers in the Koran as identical with the word of God.

adrar (B): Mountain or mountainous mass.

Agadir (B): Fortress; name of a city of Morocco on southern Atlantic coast.

Ahl Kitab: The Peoples of the Book, that is, Christians or Jews.

aid: Feast.

ait (B): Sons of.

al (el): The.

Alaouites: Ruling Moroccan dynasty of Arab descent from the Tafilalet, founded in 1640.

alim: Singular of oulema (or ulema); theologian or professor.

Allah: God.

Almohads: Berber dynasty from the High Atlas, ruling the Moroccan Empire at its greatest extent (1149-1269).

Almoravids: Berber dynasty from the southwestern Sahara, ruling Morocco and part of Spain (1061-1149).

aman: Demand for peace.

amghar (B): Elected chief of a Berber assembly.

amir (or emir): An independent chieftain; a title given to certain descendants of Muhammad.

Anfa: Medieval name of Casablanca; anfa, aniseed.

bab: Gate.

baraka: Supernatural power thought to be in descendants of Muhammad, holy men, sacred words, and certain inanimate objects; power to bestow benediction; the beneficial influence that emanates from all sherifs.

basha: The Arabs' pronunciation of "pasha," as there is no "p" in the Arabic alphabet.

beia (or baia): Oath of allegiance tendered in the name of the Muslim people.

ben: Son of; pl., beni.

Beni Hillal: A tribe, originating in what is now Yemen, which was responsible for the principal infusion of Arabic blood into Morocco.

Beni Merin or Merinids (B): Berber dynasty ruling Morocco (1213-1524) during period of glory before European invasions.

Beni Wattasi: Zeneta Berbers who acted as regents for the last rulers of the Merinid dynasty.

Berbers: Aborigines of Morocco.

bidonville (F): Shantytown made of flattened gasoline tins; found near old established cities.

blad al maghzen: The portion of Morocco recognizing the temporal as well as the religious authority of the sultan.

blad es siba: The regions recognizing only the religious leadership of the sultan; "the country of insolence."

burnous: Hooded woolen cloak.

cadi (or kadi): A Muslim magistrate who tries cases involving Koranic law.

Caid (or Kaid): A tribal chief or governor.

caliph: Successor; temporal and spiritual successor of Muhammad.

Caliphate: The office whose holder is the authoritative head of the Islamic community and guardian of the faith; it is open to any believer whom the faithful consider suitable.

Chaouia: The coastal plain east of Casablanca.

cheik (or sheik, sheikh): Religious chief of a tribal faction.

chorfa (or shorfa): Patrilineal descendants of Muhammad, reputed to possess peculiar religious powers.

Chra (or Sharia): Islamic law derived from the Koran.

colon (F): Colonist.

dahir: Royal decree with the force of law.

dar: Palace.

Destour: Independence movement in Tunisia.

djamaa: Mosque.

djebel: A mountain or range of mountains.

djellabah (or djellaba): A short, hooded wooden cloak with wide sleeves.

djemaa: The tribal or village assembly of the Berbers, composed of all adult males, which decided all matters relating to war and justice.

Djezira al-Maghreb: Island of the West, the Arabic name for Northwest Africa, commonly shortened to the Maghreb.

djinn: Supernatural beings which can take many shapes--human, animal, and inanimate.

dyezya: The special tax paid by the Jews.

Etoile Nord Africaine (F): Independence movement of Algeria.

evolués (F): Moroccans of two cultural worlds--France and Islam.

fantasia: An exhibition of horsemanship and "powder play" similar to the Spanish rodeo.

fellagha (pl., fellaghas): Originally, a bandit; later, a guerrilla fighter.

fellah: A peasant farmer.

Filali Dynasty: Another name for Alouite Dynasty.

fondouk: An inn for man and beast; a large enclosure used for stabling of caravans or livestock.

Frazawi: French, a Frenchman.

gharb: The region of alluvial plains between Rabat and Larache.

goum: Native militia during the Protectorate.

goumier: A native policeman, a light horseman; in Barbary the goumiers form a force of mounted constabulary.

guich: Tribes giving military services instead of paying taxes.

hadji: A pilgrim, distinguished by a green scarf about his turban when he has made the Mecca pilgrimage.

harem: The wives and concubines of a Muslim or the apartments allotted to them.

harka: A military expedition; a band of fighting men, varying in number.

Hegira: Muhammad's flight from hostile Mecca to friendly Medina.

heydia: The traditional custom of presenting gifts to the sultan on the three major Muslim holidays.

al-Hizb al-Watani: The National Party.

Idrisid Dynasty: The first Moroccan dynasty (788-987), which founded the Moroccan state.

Ifriqiya: Africa or Tunisia, the Roman province in former Carthage.

igh: A clan or group of families living close together.

imam: A prayer leader; a descendant of Muhammad who exercises both princely and priestly powers, believed by the Shiite sect to be divinely inspired and able to interpret the Koran--a power that Sunnis deny even to Caliphs.

Islam: The word of Allah revealed to the prophet Muhammad by the angel Gabriel; also the collective countries practicing this religion.

istiqlal: Independence; el Hisb el-Istiqlal: The party of independence, commonly called Istiqlal.

Jihad: The Holy War of Muslims against the infidel.

kasbah: A fortress or castle.

Khalif (or Caliph): A title of the successors of Muhammad, both as temporal and spiritual rulers; later used by the sultans of Morocco.

Khalifah: A representative or viceroy of the Khalif.

Koran: The Muhammadan scriptures, containing the professed revelations of the angel Gabriel.

ksar (pl., ksour): Fortified habitation; Saharan village.

Kutlah al-Amal al-Warani: Bloc for National Action.

lalla: Princess, madam.

Latif: Invocation for divine clemency, intoned only in times of grave danger.

Maghreb (or Moghreb, Maghrib): Land of the setting sun; the North African West, including the area of modern Morocco, Algeria, and Tunisia.

Maghzen (or Makhzen): The central government of Morocco; an Arab organization alien to Berber tradition.

mansour: Victorious; a victor or conqueror.

marabout: Member of a religious brotherhood; a saintly person; a shrine, usually built over a saint's tomb.

medersa: A school, college, or college dormitory.

medina: The native portion of a Moroccan town.

mehalla: A division of the sultan's army recruited from the tribes but having French instructors as officers.

mellah: The segregated section of a town or city reserved for the Jewish population.

mendoub: The representative of the sultan at Tangier.

Merinids: A Berber dynasty ruling the Maghreb (1248-1420).

minaret: Tower of a masque used for the call to prayer.

Moor: A vague term meaning in general people of northwestern Africa and Muslim Spain, but often applied to Moroccans.

moulay (or mulai, mouley, or maulay): Title of nobility often given to a sultan or sherif.

moulkia: The most binding title deed to real estate, unrecoverable even by the sultan.

muezzin: The person who calls the faithful to prayer.

Muslim (or Moslem): A follower of Islam.

Nazrani: A Christian.

nefya: A meeting of tribal leaders to pay homage to the sultan.

Ommayids of Damascus: Second Moslem Dynasty of the Near East (661-750).

Ommayids of Spain: Ruling dynasty of Cordova Caliphate (756-1013).

Ouatassids (or Watassids): Branch of Merinid Dynasty ruling Morocco (1420-1550).

oued: A dry river bed except during seasonal rains; English transliteration, wadi.

oulema (or ulema): A body of theologians or professors; singular, alim.

pasha: A Turkish title of rank, still used in Algeria and Morocco; mayor of a city.

protégé (F): A person wholly or partially under foreign rule during the regime of protection in Morocco.

rahman: Compassionate; Abd er-Rahman, slave of the Compassionate (God).

Reconquista (S): Reconquest of Spain from the Moors.

ribat: Monastic border fortress for spreading Islam in a Holy War.

rogui: An illegitimate pretender to the throne of the sultan.

Saadians: A Sherifian Dynasty from the Draa River region ruling Morocco (1550-1668).

Salafiyah: A movement for religious reform to aid in the struggle for independence.

Sanhadja: The Great Berber Confederation with northern and Saharan branches; enemies of the Zenata.

sherif: A reputed descendant of the Prophet Muhammad.

semsars (or censaux, F): Agents of foreign merchants, both Jews and Moroccans, serving in interior districts of Morocco, often under irregular protection.

sidi: Sir, Majesty; a title often used by sultans.

Souira: A small rampart; the post-independence name of Mogador.

souk: A rural market or the market section of a city.

tabor: A native regiment with French officers.

tertib: A land tax.

Touareg: Muslim Berber nomads from the Libyan desert to Timbuktu; of which the men are veiled, the women unveiled; the only Berbers with a written language.

touat (B): Oases.

vizier (or vizir): A minister of state in the Maghzen.

zaouia: A monastic community of Muslim brotherhoods.

Zenata: A Great Berber confederation, enemies of the Sanhadja.

INDEX